FOURTH EDITION

WRITING MATTERS

A **Handbook** for Writing and Research

Rebecca Moore Howard
Syracuse University

WRITING MATTERS

Published by McGraw Hill LLC, 1325 Avenue of the Americas, New York, NY 10019. Copyright ©2022 by McGraw Hill LLC. All rights reserved. Printed in the United States of America. No part of this publication may be reproduced or distributed in any form or by any means, or stored in a database or retrieval system, without the prior written consent of McGraw Hill LLC, including, but not limited to, in any network or other electronic storage or transmission, or broadcast for distance learning.

Some ancillaries, including electronic and print components, may not be available to customers outside the United States.

This book is printed on acid-free paper.

1 2 3 4 5 6 7 8 9 LCR 24 23 22 21

ISBN 978-1-265-99244-6
MHID 1-265-99244-4

Cover Image: *McGraw Hill*

All credits appearing on page or at the end of the book are considered to be an extension of the copyright page.

The Internet addresses listed in the text were accurate at the time of publication. The inclusion of a website does not indicate an endorsement by the authors or McGraw Hill LLC, and McGraw Hill LLC does not guarantee the accuracy of the information presented at these sites.

mheducation.com/highered

Writing Matters is dedicated
to the memory of my sister, Sandy

Dear Colleagues and Students:

Welcome to *Writing Matters*! I started this project as a way of giving back to the composition community and helping students to develop as writers. Working on this handbook has also been a source of my own development: My life and teaching have been immeasurably enriched by the students and instructors I have met during my travels to discuss *Writing Matters* and my responsibilities-focused approach to writing.

Rebecca Moore Howard is Professor of Writing and Rhetoric at Syracuse University. Her work on the Citation Project is part of a collaborative endeavor to study how students really use resources.

While developing all the editions of *Writing Matters*, I have also been working on the Citation Project, a study of the researched writing that 174 students (from 16 colleges and universities nationwide) produced in their composition classes. Some of the results of that research are available at citationproject.net. There you will see a variety of evidence that students may not be reading their sources carefully and completely and that their research projects suffer accordingly. Drawing on the findings of the Citation Project, *Writing Matters* includes an array of materials that help students think dialogically and rhetorically as they work from sources. These include best practices in concrete techniques, such as marking where the source material ends and the student writer's own voice begins. These materials provide guidance for students as they work to fulfill their **writer's responsibilities to other writers, to their readers, to their topics,** and most especially, **to themselves.**

The result is a teaching and learning framework that unites research, rhetoric, documentation, grammar, and style into a cohesive whole, helping students to find consistency and creativity in rules that might otherwise confound them. Students experience responsible writing not only by citing the work and creativity of other writers accurately but also by treating those writers' ideas fairly. They practice responsible writing by providing reliable information about a topic at a depth that does the topic justice. Most importantly, they embrace responsible writing by taking their writing seriously and approaching writing assignments as opportunities to learn about new topics and to expand their scope as writers.

Students are more likely to write well when they think of themselves as writers rather than as error-makers. By explaining rules in the context of responsibility, I address composition students respectfully as mature and capable fellow participants in the research and writing process.

Sincerely,

Rebecca Moore Howard

Where to Find What You Need in *Writing Matters*

Writing Matters is a reference for all writers and researchers. Whether you are writing a research project for class, giving a multimedia presentation for a meeting, or preparing a résumé for a job interview, you are bound to come across questions about writing and research. *Writing Matters* provides you with answers to your questions.

The Table of Contents. If you know the topic you are looking for, scan the brief contents on the inside front cover. If you are looking for specific information within a general topic (how to evaluate a source for relevance and reliability, for example), go to the detailed table of contents on pages xxv–xxxvii.

The Index. The comprehensive index at the end of *Writing Matters*, on pages I1–I40, includes cross-references to all topics covered in the book. If you are not sure how to use commas in compound sentences, for example, look up *"commas"* or *"compound sentences"* in the index.

Documentation Chapters (18–21). For help and models for citing sources, see the chapters in Part Five on documentation styles: MLA (Ch. 18), APA (Ch. 19), *Chicago* (Ch. 20), and CSE (Ch 21). The menus in the margins of these chapters guide you to specific types of sources.

Grammar Chapters (33–42). For help with correcting grammar errors, see the chapters in Part Eight (33–42) where you will also find examples of grammar challenges, models for how to fix them, and cross-references to pages where concepts are discussed.

Glossaries. If you are unfamiliar with a term or not sure if you are using a particular word (such as *who* or *whom, less* or *fewer, can* or *may*) correctly, see the Glossary of Key Terms on pages G1–G13 or the Glossary of Usage on pages G15–G20.

Chapters for Multilingual Writers (Chapters 43–47). For help with articles, helping verbs, prepositions, and other common problem areas for EFL writers, see pages 757–800.

Quick Reference Menus. See the inside back cover for comprehensive lists of student and professional writing models, self-assessment checklists, EFL and tech tips, Quick Reference boxes, and Writing Responsibly advice.

Connect Composition for Writing Matters. Access a digital, searchable, accessible ebook version of the handbook that you can personalize using tools such as highlighting and annotating; and any practice or homework assignments from your instructor. Also included in Connect Connect Composition for Writing Matters are practice activities, Writing Assignment Plus, Power of Process, and the Adaptive Learning Assignment platform.

Navigation and Learning Features

- **Running heads and section numbers** give the topic covered on that page as well as the number of the chapter and section letter in which the topic is discussed.
- **Main headings** include the chapter number and section letter (for example, 33d), as well as the title of the section.
- **Examples,** many of them with hand corrections, illustrate typical errors and how to correct them.
- **EFL boxes** provide useful tips and helpful information for writers whose first language is not English.

640 33d gram Grammar Matters • Understanding Grammar

3. This spring the twins were excited about the newly arrived pandas.
4. By the time Rennie and the twins finally got to the zoo, the pandas had become accustomed to visitors and were chewing calmly on some bamboo.

33d Adjectives

More about Adjectives, 725–31

Adjectives modify nouns or pronouns with descriptive or limiting information. They answer questions such as *What kind? Which one?* or *How many?*

WHAT KIND?	a warm day
WHICH ONE?	the next speaker
HOW MANY?	seven roses

Adjectives most commonly fall before nouns in a noun phrase and after *linking verbs* as *subject complements.*

- The young musicians played a rousing concert.
- They were enthusiastic.

linking verb A verb that conveys a state of being linking a subject to its complement
subject complement An adjective, pronoun, or noun phrase that follows a linking verb and describes or refers to the sentence subject

Many adjectives change form to express comparison: *young, younger, youngest; enthusiastic, more/less enthusiastic, most/least enthusiastic.*

Possessive, demonstrative, and indefinite pronouns that function as adjectives—as well as the articles *a, an,* and *the*—are known as ***determiners*** because they specify or quantify the nouns they modify. Determiners always precede other adjectives in a noun phrase. Some, like *all* and *both,* also precede any other determiners.

- The new gym is in that building with all those solar panels on the roof.

More about Comparative adjectives, 729–31

The Ordering of Adjectives The ordering of adjectives in noun phrases and the use of articles and other determiners in English can be challenging for multilingual writers. English sentences tend to place adjectives before nouns, while adjective placement in other languages varies, and some languages do not use articles at all. For more on these topics, see pages 786 and 768–74.

3 Organizing and Drafting Your Project

IN THIS CHAPTER
a. Thesis, 35
b. Organization, 39
c. Preparing to draft, 44
d. Drafting, 45
e. Collaboration, 51

Student Models
For Michael Wedd, "Issues with Alternative Energy" (First Draft): Informal (Scratch) Outline, 42; Topic and Sentence Outlines, 43; First Draft of a Researched Essay (MLA style, annotated), Michael Wedd, "Issues with Alternative Energy," 47

GaudiLab/Shutterstock

Before producing a new line of clothing or an automobile, designers sketch the product, planning and arranging the shapes before dressing them in colors and textures. Writers, too, begin with a plan. They take into account the writing situation (purpose, audience, topic, context, and genre), then sketch their ideas in words and arrange them in sentences and paragraphs. Designers and writers alike sometimes erase initial ideas and revise early efforts. Until that first sketch is penned, the finished work is merely an idea.

3a Crafting an Effective Thesis

A *thesis* is a brief statement (one or two sentences) of the central claim you will make. It not only identifies your topic but also gives your audience an indication of the focus and direction of your writing project. Drafting a preliminary thesis statement as early as possible and then testing, revising, and even replacing it as you learn more about your topic and develop your project will help you evaluate, focus, and clarify your ideas.

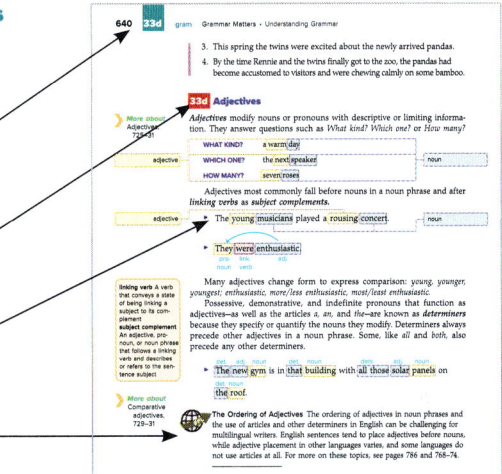

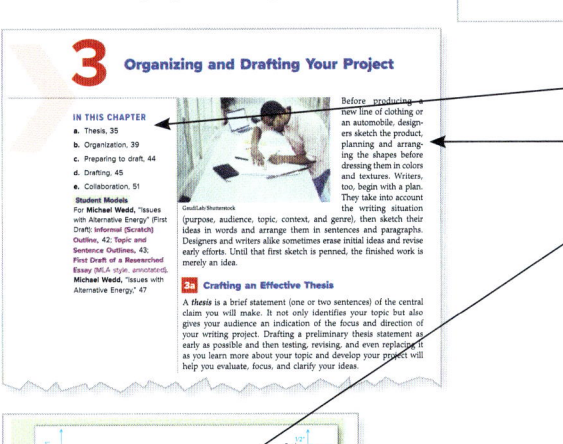

- **Chapter table of contents** identifies the topics covered in the text.
- **Chapter introductions** contextualize concepts explored in the upcoming lesson.
- **Annotations** to writing models point out and critique writers' choices.
- **Tech tips** offer support for using familiar technology to your advantage while avoiding pitfalls.

Beck 1

Isabel Beck
Professor Moore Howard
Writing 205
30 April 2021

Fast Fashion: An Unethical Industry That Harms Garment Workers and the Environment

When I was growing up, the best piece of advice my mother gave me was to take care of my things. If I ever left anything—even the plainest, most replaceable of t-shirts—wrinkled in a ball on the floor of my bedroom, she'd tsk under her breath and hold the fabric to my face to show me the many, many ways I was harming its lifespan. Soon, hanging and folding clothes became second nature to me, as did a curiosity about where they came from. When I was old enough to start shopping for myself, it seemed that no matter how well I cared for some items, they never held up against my "all-time favorites." When I expressed this observation to my mother, she gave me her second-best piece of advice: Quality over quantity, always.

At the time, this practical advice was slightly annoying, but as I grew older, I began to see the wisdom behind it. I eventually stopped buying cheap items for the sake of buying them, and instead started to focus on building a wardrobe full of classic staples that would see me through my early adult life, even if it meant spending more money overall. I believe that if others shopped this way too, they would save money and help garment workers and the environment and its people. Ultimately, they would

9b Media Matters • Designing Accessible Print and Digital Documents

FIGURE 9.2 Analysis of the accessibility of a website design: *The CRAM Foundation.* The creators of the CRAM Foundation's website use contrast, proximity, and alignment to provide an interface that is understandable, perceivable, and operable. Clearly labeled link descriptions on contrasting backgrounds make it easier for persons who are blind

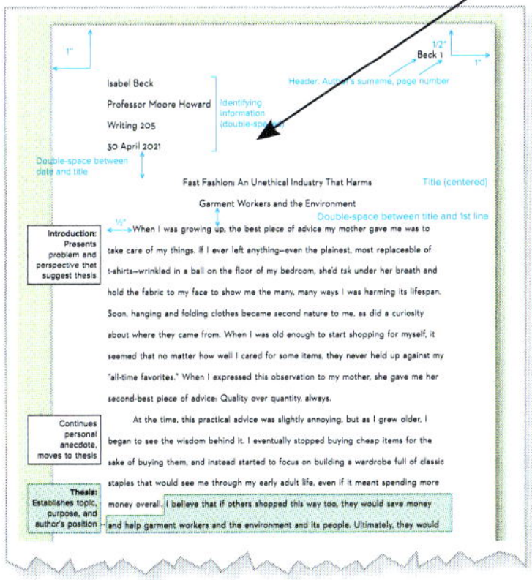

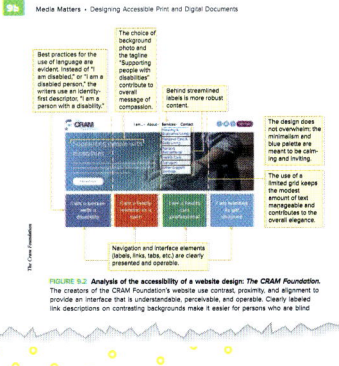

Empowering Students as Writers . . .

Writing Matters offers instructors and students an accessible four-part framework that focuses the rules and conventions of writing through a lens of responsibility, ultimately empowering students to own their ideas and to view their writing as consequential.

Writing Matters helps students see the conventions of writing as a network of **responsibilities . . .**

> **to other writers** by treating information and sources fairly and accurately, and crafting writing that is fresh and original;
>
> **to their audience** by writing clearly, designing accessibly, and providing readers with the information and interpretation they need to make sense of a topic;
>
> **to their topic** by exploring an issue thoroughly and creatively, assessing sources carefully, and providing reliable information at a depth that does the topic justice;
>
> **to themselves** by taking their writing seriously, approaching the process as an opportunity to learn and to expand research and writing skills, and to capably join larger conversations in which their voices can and should be heard.

Features that Support a Writer's Responsibilities

The four-part framework of a writer's responsibilities is supported by features throughout *Writing Matters* and its companion Connect course. Students are guided to consider their responsibilities—to other writers, to the audience, to the topic, and to themselves—throughout the writing process via exercises, toolboxes, checklists, annotated writing models, and more that help students learn to meet their obligations and to produce meaningful writing.

Writing Responsibly tutorials and guidance

Five 2-page citation tutorials, in Chapters 7, 13, 15, and 16, draw from Rebecca Moore Howard's published Citation Project, a research study that used empirical methods to explore the top challenges experienced by composition students when they work with sources. Supporting students in meeting a writer's responsibility to the topic and to other writers, these five tutorials offer best practices for researched composing, and include practical insights, relatable before-and-after examples, and a targeted self-assessment checklist. The example presented here, "Understanding and Representing the Entire Source," encourages students

Writing **Responsibly**

Explaining Your Choice of Sources

Make It Your Own! When college writers share their opinion of their sources, their text is more interesting and convincing. Rather than just quoting from your sources, tell *why* you are quoting them, and your writing will be more persuasive.

In much of your college writing, you select and work with sources: You decide how to use sources to help convey your thesis. Your basic responsibility is to acknowledge those sources, cite them correctly, and provide full publication information about them at the end of your project. When you talk *about* your sources—tell what you think of your source and its information—you invite your audience into your thinking processes and portray yourself as an experienced academic writer.

When college writing instructors involved in the Citation Project studied research projects from US colleges, they noticed how few students talked about their sources. Most of the projects just pulled out information—usually a brief quotation—from sources, as if all the sources were alike. The nature of the sources and the student's thoughts about them remained invisible to the audience. The following example, from a project on sexism and sexual violence, shows the drab result:

First draft

[Student's voice] Hostility toward women can be seen even in the ancient West. [Tom Stevenson observes,] [Quotation] "Livy's underlying message, it would seem, is that Roman men have to regulate public contributions by prominent women, and not accept female advice too easily, without prolonged consideration" (189). [Citation]

The material from the Stevenson source is accurately quoted and cited, and the sentences flow. But the passage provokes questions rather than insights. Who are Stevenson and Livy? Where did this source come from? Why did the writer choose it? Why should the writer's audience respect Stevenson's opinions? What else did the source say? What was the context in which the quotation appeared? These are the kinds of questions readers ask, and answering them will bring your text to life:

Revised draft

[Student's voice] Hostility toward women can be seen even in the ancient West. [Tom Stevenson,] a classics [Citation] [Credentials of author and publisher] scholar at the University of Queensland, writes in the scholarly journal *Classical World* that the Roman historian Livy described women who supported their menfolks' success, which might seem to be a compliment to the women. But notice that the women aren't having their [Summary of the remainder of the source] own successes. Furthermore, all of Livy's women are either described too briefly, or they are to avoid pasting an isolated "killer quote" from the first couple of pages of the source, and to instead read through their sources in order to incorporate insights purposefully and responsibly.

In addition to tutorials, suggestions throughout the text frame writing skills in terms of a writer's responsibilities—to their audience, topic, other writers, and themselves. Contextualized best practices encourage the writer-as-citizen.

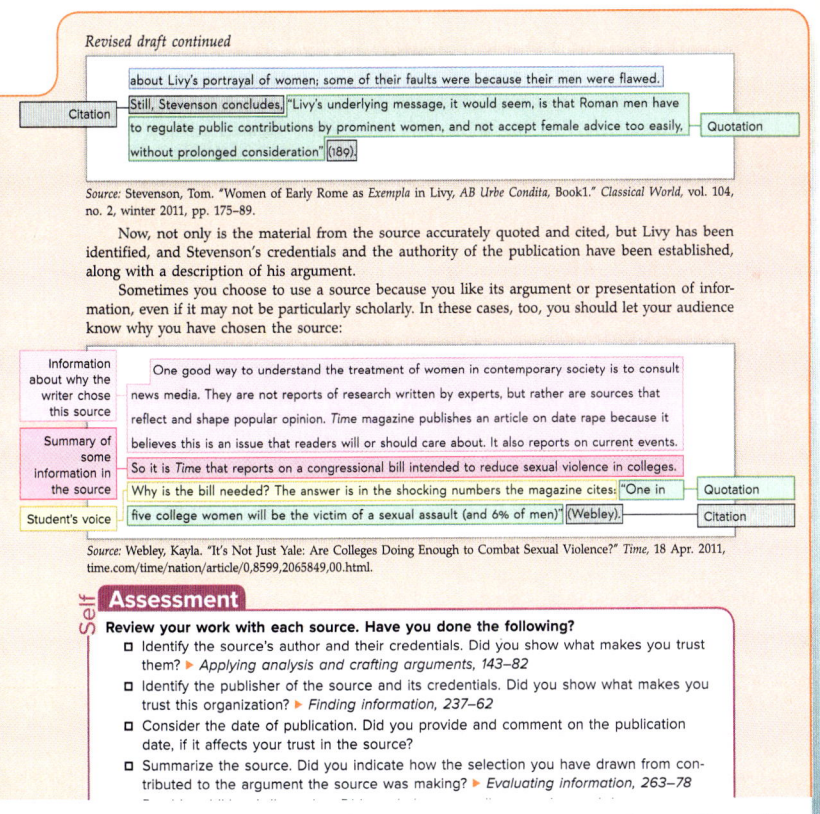

Annotated student and professional models of writing

More than one dozen student projects and professional articles—including literary analyses, reviews, press releases, outlines, and cover letters—are explored in detail, with callouts identifying the unique features of each and analyses of the components of compelling writing. Annotations in the student project in Chapter 22 ("Writing in Literature and the Other Humanities"), for example, call attention to the important elements of a literary analysis, such as the thesis statement, citations, and supporting evidence in a student project, a close reading of Mohsin Hamid's *The Reluctant Fundamentalist*. Student and professional models allow students to see how other writers have met the four writer's responsibilities.

Accessible ebook and online resources

At McGraw Hill Higher Education, our mission is to accelerate learning through intuitive, engaging, efficient, and effective experiences, grounded in research. Assignments in Connect are WCAG compliant and updates to the ebook of

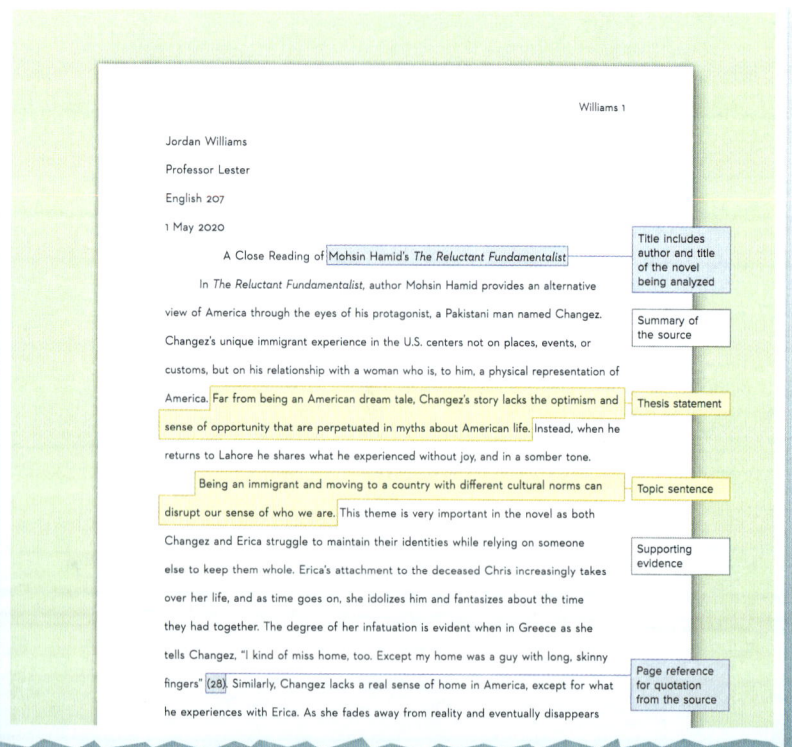

the 4th edition of *Writing Matters* go beyond WCAG compliance to create an improved reading experience for all learners. These enhancements include improved functionality for viewing annotated readings and editing marks. We are committed to creating universally accessible products that unlock the full potential of each learner, including individuals with disabilities.

MLA Style and APA Style citation tutorial

Part Five, *Documentation Matters,* begins with a special four-page reference section modeling citation styles. Pages from books, journals, websites, and databases present the features of popular and academic sources. On the page below, citations for a printed book are shown in both MLA and APA style. All MLA citations follow the current guidelines of the 2021 *MLA Handbook,* 9th Edition. Also updated are

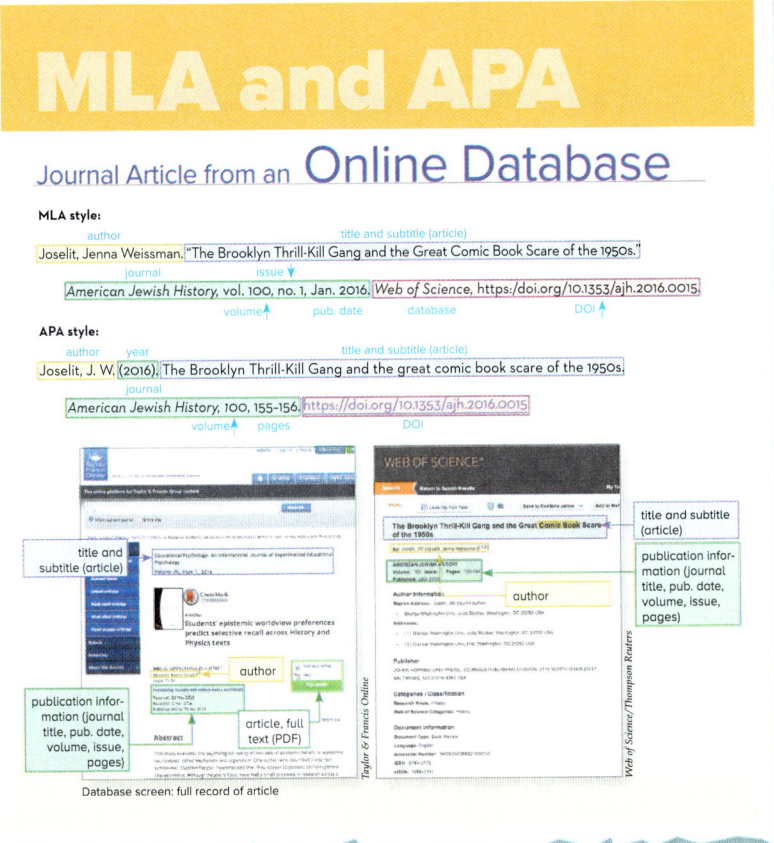

the APA citations, now formatted according to the 2019 *APA Manual*. By providing accurate and complete citations, students meet their responsibility to the audience.

Self-Assessment checklists

Helpful checklists guide students to review their work at every step of the writing process, from drafting to revising to proofreading a piece before publication. In Chapter 17 ("Citing Rhetorically"), this checklist reminds students to emphasize their own insights when working with sources, and to provide contextual information that shows why a source is authoritative, thus guiding students to meet their responsibilities both to themselves by taking their own writing seriously and to the topic by carefully assessing sources.

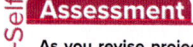

As you revise projects that use sources, review your draft, revising as necessary, to be sure you:

- ☐ Cite your sources. Have you named any from which you are paraphrasing, summarizing, or quoting?
- ☐ Use signal verbs. Have you conveyed the attitude of your source?
- ☐ Use signal phrases and parenthetical references. Have you shown where each source use begins and ends, even when it is unpaginated?
- ☐ Emphasize your own insights. Have you commented on or analyzed the source, rather than just repeating it?

Writing Assignment Plus

McGraw Hill's new Writing Assignment Plus tool delivers a learning experience that improves students' written communication skills and conceptual understanding with every assignment. Assign, monitor, and provide feedback on writing more efficiently and grade assignments within McGraw Hill Connect®. Writing Assignment Plus gives you time-saving tools with just-in-time basic writing and originality checker.

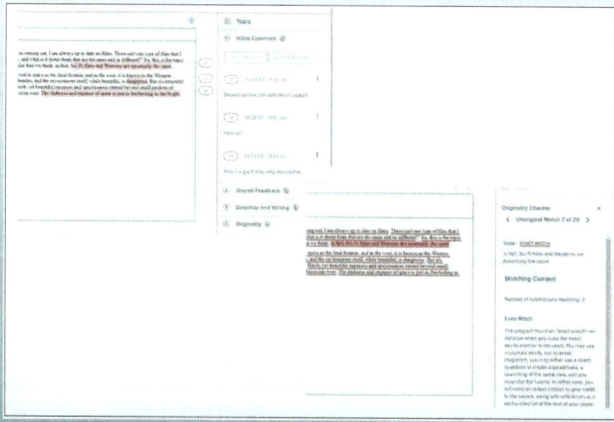

Power of Process

In addition to the readings throughout *Writing Matters*, Power of Process in Connect provides 100 additional readings. Power of Process guides students to engage with texts closely and critically so that they develop awareness of their process decisions, and ultimately begin to make those decisions consciously on their own—a hallmark of strategic, self-regulating readers and writers. Power of Process provides strategies that guide students in learning how to critically read a piece of writing or consider a text as a possible source for incorporation into their own work. After they progress through the strategies, responding to prompts by annotating and highlighting, students are encouraged to reflect on their processes and interaction with the text. Instructors can choose from a bank of carefully chosen readings within Power of Process, readings from *Writing Matters*, or upload their own readings. In keeping with McGraw Hill's commitment to equity, diversity, and inclusion, fifty percent of the readings in Power of Process are by Black, Indigenous, and People of Color (BIPOC) authors.

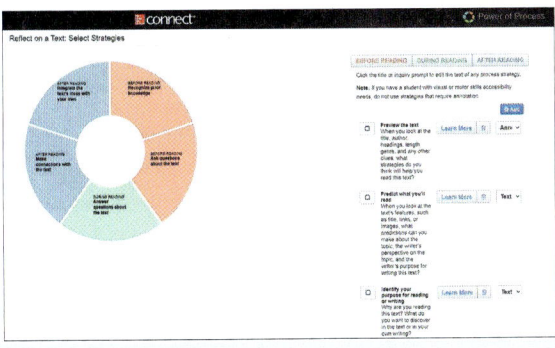

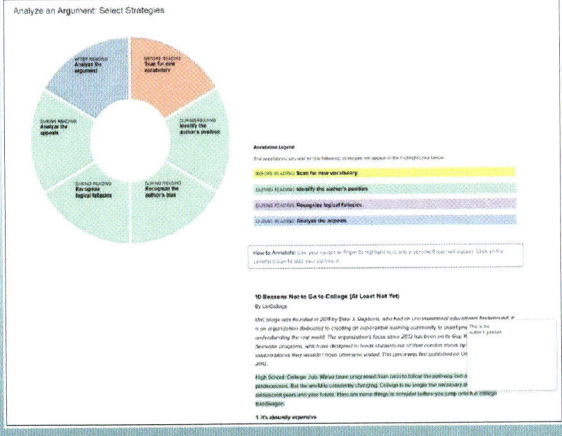

XV

Quick Reference toolboxes

Major concepts are summarized to focus students on the important skills, strategies, and issues to keep in mind when writing. In this reference box from Chapter 14 ("Evaluating Information"), the characteristics of a source are listed, to help students assess the quality and reliability of the texts they discover during the research process and meet their responsibility to the topic.

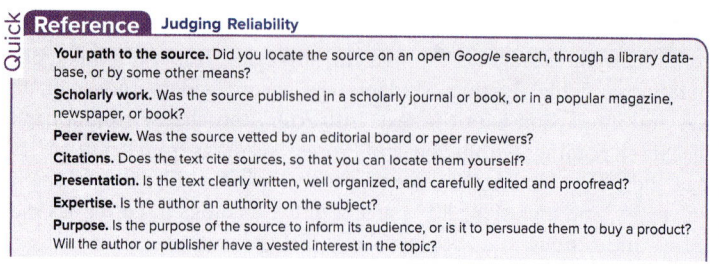

Adaptive Learning Assignment

Found in Connect, the Adaptive Learning Assignment platform provides each student a personalized path to learning concepts instructors assign in their English Composition course. The assignments continually adapt to the individual, identifying knowledge gaps and focusing on areas where remediation is needed. All adaptive content for topics such as the Writing Process, the Research Process, and Grammar—including questions and integrated concept resources—is specifically targeted to, and directly aligned with, the individual learning objectives being assessed in the course.

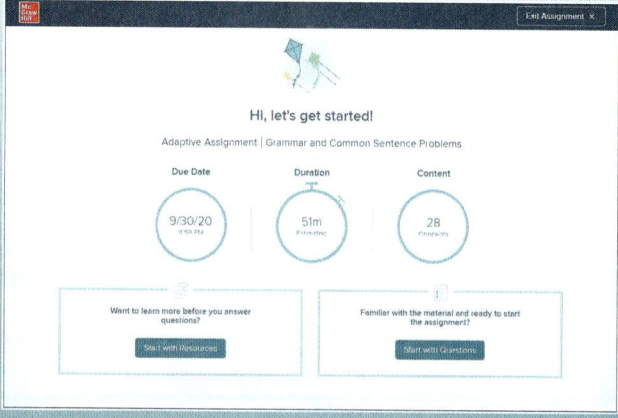

Grammar tutorial

To help students in their responsibility to both themselves and their audience, Part Eight, *Grammar Matters,* begins with a six-page reference section that explores common grammar challenges such as subject–verb agreement, comma splices, and shifting tenses. On the page below, two sentence fragments and four agreement conflicts are modeled, each with edits showing how to correct the problem. Cross-references point students to the chapters that discuss the concept.

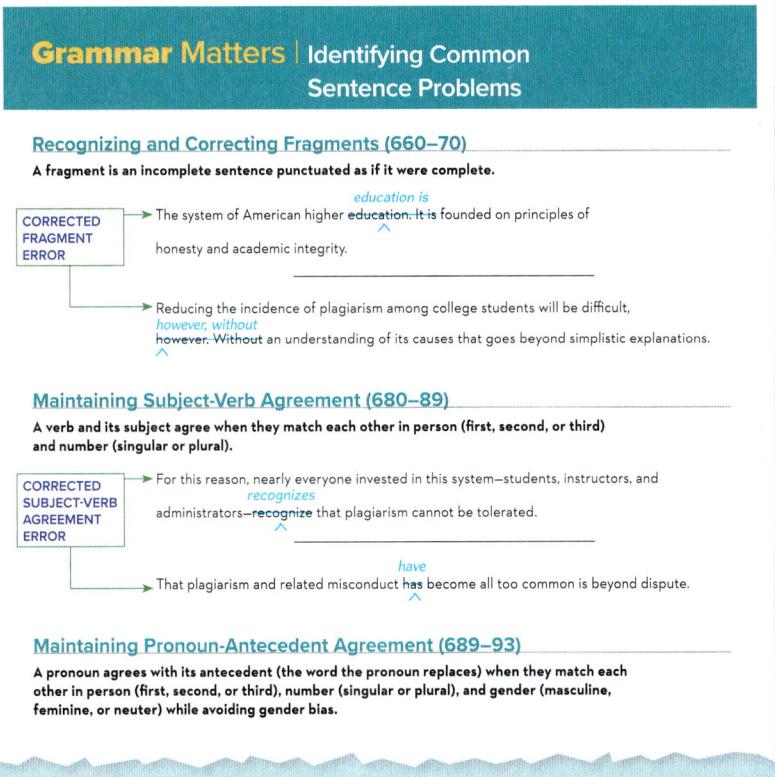

Focused exercises

More than 140 exercises help students explore the most important chapter concepts. Exercises gauge individual students' grasp of key skills, and group projects promote teamwork, peer-to-peer feedback, and collaboration. Many of these exercises help students break the writing process down into smaller parts to focus, for example, on setting a schedule, generating ideas, or conducting a database search. The array of core concepts covered by these exercises strengthen students' development of all four of a writer's responsibilities. Additional exercises can be assigned through Connect.

> **EXERCISE 17.1** Integrating and identifying source material
>
> Read Isabel Beck's essay "Fast Fashion: An Unethical Industry that Harms Garment Workers and the Environment" (pp. 383–96) and note how she integrates her source material. Use one of four different-colored highlighting markers to identify each of the different rhetorical moves she uses:
>
> - Parenthetical references that are the only acknowledgment of the source in the sentence (that is, any sentences that have no signal phrases or other cues; just the parenthetical reference)
> - Signal phrases
> - Phrases that clearly signal her own voice speaking

Make It **Your Own**

Choose a source-based project you have already written or a draft in progress, and working on a printout of your project, use one of four different-colored highlighting markers to identify each of the four different rhetorical moves described in Exercise 17.1.

Work **Together**

When you have completed the highlighting, exchange your work with another student and use that paper's highlighting and what you have learned so far in this chapter to evaluate the ways the student has integrated sources. For any revisions you recommend, be sure to include the page reference in this book where an explanation can be found.

Tech tips

While today's students are tech savvy, *Writing Matters* draws their attention to potential complications that may occur when using even the most familiar technology. Chapter 12 ("Planning a Research Project") advises students to meet their responsibility to themselves by backing up their research to a separate place as a guard against data loss.

> **Tech** **Back Up Your Electronic Research Log**
>
> Do not be a victim of a computer crash: If you keep your research log in electronic form, be sure to back up your files after every session, and store the backup files in a separate place—on a cloud server, for example. If you cannot save your files to a second device, email the files to yourself or print out the new material after each session.

EFL tips

Targeted advice on grammar, usage, and culture provide additional support for students for whom English is a foreign language. This EFL tip in Chapter 26 ("Writing Concisely") clarifies for students that, in the US, there is an expectation for academic writing to be concise. This example helps foreign students to meet their responsibility to the audience.

Modal Verbs English modal verbs have a range of meanings and unusual grammatical characteristics that you may find challenging. For example, they do not change form to indicate number or tense:

▶ In a close election, one or two votes ~~cans~~ make a difference.
                                                                can

Support for *Writing Matters*

Writing Matters includes an array of resources for instructors and students. Under the leadership of Rebecca Moore Howard, experienced instructors created supplements that help instructors and students fulfill their course responsibilities.

Instructor's manual. The instructor's manual includes teaching tips, learning outcomes, and suggestions for additional exercises using Connect Composition and Power of Process. *Instruction Matters* connects each instructor and student resource to the core material and makes the exercises relevant to instructors and students.

Test bank. The *Assessment Matters* test bank includes more than a thousand test items to ensure students grasp the concepts explored in every chapter.

Practice Matters exercises. Corresponding to content presented step-by-step throughout the chapters, the *Practice Matters* collection gauges student comprehension of all aspects of the text.

- Writing Exercises for Students
- Language Exercises for EFL Students
- Grammar Exercises for Students

PowerPoint slides. The *Presentation Matters* PowerPoint deck is designed to give new teachers confidence in the classroom and can be used as a teaching tool by all instructors. The slides emphasize key ideas from *Writing Matters* and help students take useful notes. Instructors can alter the slides to meet their own needs and, because the PowerPoints are WCAG compliant, the deck can be shared with students using screen readers.

LMS and gradebook synching. McGraw Hill offers deep integration for a range of LMS products. Deep integration includes functionality such as single sign-on, automatic grade sync, assignment level linking and calendar integration.

Reporting. Connect Composition generates a number of powerful reports and charts that allow instructors to quickly review the performance of a specific student or an entire section.

Chapter-by-Chapter Changes

Revision Highlights of the Fourth Edition

Writing Matters has been revised to include key updates from the field and to provide new examples and models.

- All content has been reviewed for inclusivity to ensure the text is free from words or images that reflect prejudiced, stereotyped, or discriminatory views of particular people or groups, and free from material that could potentially exclude people from feeling accepted.
- All in-text citations, bibliography notes, and Works Cited pages are updated to reflect the rules of the ninth edition of the *MLA Handbook*, the Modern Language Association's 2021 update on citation formats.
- The text incorporates the use of the singular "they" to follow current MLA and APA guidelines.

Part I: Planning Drafting, Revising, Editing, Proofreading and Formatting (Chs. 1–6)

- Updated Writer's Responsibilities checklists for self-assessment (Part I opener)
- New student model (research paper): Excerpt from Isabel Beck's MLA research paper, "Fast Fashion: An Unethical Industry that Harms Garment Workers and the Environment," to illustrate the parts of a paper and use of figures (Part I opener)
- New student model (article): Megan Ginsie's, *Plagiarism an Issue on Campus, Faculty Says*, from the student paper *The Collegian*, to illustrate a writer's responsibilities (Ch. 1)
- Expanded annotations for: Michael Wedd's paper, *Issues with Alternative Energy* (Ch. 3)
- New student model: Excerpt from Joe Fernandez's paper [title] on René Brooks' article, "Time Blindness," to show a paragraph's topic sentence, evidence, and conclusion (Ch. 3)
- Fresh examples to demonstrate the crafting of paragraphs: thesis, topic sentence, transition, equivalent expressions, and patterns (Ch. 3)
- Updated and new examples for using visuals as evidence in academic writing (Ch. 5)
- Revised examples of titles for academic works (Ch. 6)
- Updated student model: new sources for Michael Wedd's "Rethinking Alternative Energy" (Ch. 6) to bring the content up to date and exemplify the MLA documentation style
- New advice on creating a portfolio and a "personal statement to accompany it (Ch. 6)
- Updated advice for conducting peer review (EFL box, Ch. 6)

Part II: Reasoning Matters (Chs. 7–8)

- New student model (summary): Joe Fernandez's "Summary of René Brooks' 'Time Blindness'" to show how to summarize a text as part of reading comprehension (Ch. 7)
- New professional model (article): Bahar Gholipour's "How Accurate Is the Myers-Briggs Personality Test?" to provide an interesting work for readers to comprehend and write about (Ch. 7)
- New professional model (annotated): René Brooks's "Time Blindness: Timely Advice for Dealing With It" to provide an interesting text and demonstrate close reading and critical annotations (Ch. 7)
- New student model (reading journal): the "Double-Entry Reading Journal" for Bahar Gholipour's article, to illustrate a reader's response and model quoting, summarizing, and paraphrasing. (Ch. 7)
- Updated advice on rhetorical analysis: Revised "Preparing to Write" section includes new coverage of rhetorical superstructure, logic, rhetorical appeals, intertextual analysis, and use of a citation index. (Ch. 7)
- New student model (claims and evidence analysis): an artifact of Joe Fernandez's writing process to show analysis of René Brooks's article (Ch. 7)
- New student model (rhetorical analysis of an image): Aiden Kelley annotates and writes an analysis of a Soviet space poster (Ch. 7)
- New student model (annotated, critical response essay): Joe Fernandez's "A Critical Analysis of René Brooks' article 'Time Blindness'" to show how to present a thesis, make claims, and use evidence (Ch. 7)
- Updated Chapter 8: Applying Analysis and Crafting Arguments: emphasizes exploration and learning as goals for writing arguments

xxi

- Updated section on persuading, exploring, and affirming (Ch. 8)
- Updated material on ethos, pathos, and logos with new examples (Ch. 8)
- Revised content on using rhetorical appeals in Writing Responsibly: Preparing Oral Arguments (Ch. 8)
- New student example (researched argument): Excerpt from Brianna Davids' paper "Inmate Access to Technology: Safer Prisons and More Successful Reentries to Society" to model use of counterevidence as a response to alternative viewpoints (Ch. 8)
- New sections on "Evaluating Alternative Viewpoints" and "Dealing with Hate Speech, Misinformation, Disinformation, and Trolls" (Ch. 8)
- New student model (annotated researched argument, MLA): Brianna Davids' paper "Inmate Access to Technology: Safer Prisons and More Successful Reentries to Society" to illustrate an exploratory argument, which looks at how communications technologies improve lives and reduce recidivism, and models for students concrete ways to draw on sources to examine a complex topic; an extensive works cited page models the use of diverse sources (Ch. 8)
- New student model figure (annotated web page): From Brianna Davids' paper, an annotated version of a web page from a company that produces technologies for prisons (Ch. 8)
- New content, "Using Tone and Style Effectively and Ethically," with contemporary advice on fallacies: projection, subtweeting, and gaslighting (Ch. 8)

Part III: Media Matters (Chs. 9–11)

- New Ch. 9: Designing Accessible Print and Digital Documents: to introduce students to universal, empathy-driven design and the POUR principles for accessible web design; fresh advice for incorporating visuals, using color, and providing alt text
- In Ch. 9: new professional and student models, annotated to highlight choices writers and designers make to create and present accessible content
  - New figures: an analysis of effective webpage design (screen from *Black Lives Matter* site); an analysis of accessible website design (screen from *CRAM Foundation*);
  - New student model: *A Well-Designed Document* (report) to demonstrate the use of headings, contrast, color, white space, visuals, captioning, and alt text
- In Ch. 10: Writing for Multiple Media: new annotated figure (screen from *Poetry Foundation*) to illustrate website organization and navigation tools
- In Ch. 11: Presenting with Multiple Media: new introductory image and new advice on planning presentations that are accessible for all audiences

Part IV: Research Matters (Chs. 12–17)

- Ch. 13: Finding Information: new section, "Searching Rhetorically," to assist student researchers; new advice on searching rhetorically; revised Writing Responsibly box, "Using Wikipedia Responsibly"; new tips for narrowing search results; new annotated figures (screens from Google keyword search and advanced search; screen from a search of EBSCO database); updated information on using Google Scholar; revised Quick Reference box, "Conducting a Boolean Search"
- Ch. 14: Evaluating Information: new introductory image; revised content in "Evaluating for Relevance and Reliability" section; revised Quick Reference box, "Judging Reliability"; new advice on previewing a source in the context of a research question, and then reading and evaluating a potential source (and its sources) more deeply; new advice on evaluating a source in the context of its author; new material on peer review and reliability; new section, "Misinformation, Disinformation, and Fake News" and coverage of evaluating social media to address challenges faced by student researchers; new advice in "Evaluating Visual Sources" section on how to evaluate infographics and memes
- Fully revised Ch. 15: Overcoming Fear of Plagiarizing: Paraphrase, Summary, and Rhetorical Note-Taking: to help students feel confident when they write from sources; new and updated coverage of researching rhetorically, understanding plagiarism (with information on ghostwriting, contract cheating, self-plagiarism, lack of citation, lack of quotation marks, and patchwriting), taking notes rhetorically, citing accurately, paraphrasing elegantly, summarizing eloquently, and quoting strategically, with annotated examples
- Ch. 16: Writing the Research Project: new student model of a research question, hypothesis, and thesis

statement, annotated (introduces new MLA paper in Ch. 18 on ethics of fast fashion); new student model of topic outline, annotated; new student model for analysis, interpretation, and synthesis, annotated; new example for how to include an image in a paper

- Ch. 17: Citing Rhetorically: new advice on thinking of citations not only as "plagiarism insurance" but as a part of a writer's conversation with sources and readers; all examples of parenthetical citations and signal phrases new, annotated;

Part V: Documentation Matters (Chs. 18–21)

- Fully updated Ch. 18: Documenting Sources: MLA Style: all advice and models represent guidelines of latest MLA handbook (9e, 2021); new coverage of citing social media posts including memes and comments; fresh, contemporary examples of parenthetical citations and works-cited list entries; new student research paper on the ethics of fast fashion to exemplify the use of sources, MLA documentation style, and inclusion of figures, annotated

- Fully updated Ch. 19: Documenting Sources: APA Style: all advice and models reflect the latest APA handbook (7e, 2020); student research paper on nature, nurture, and birth order updated, annotated

- Ch. 20: Documenting Sources: Chicago Style: notes and bibliography entries refreshed with new sources

- Fully updated Ch. 21: Documenting Sources: CSE Style: all advice and models reflect the latest CSE handbook (8e, 2014); citations and reference list entries updated; student reference list updated with current sources

Part VI: Genre Matters (Chs. 22–25)

- Ch. 22: Writing in Literature and Other Humanities: new student model: *A Close Reading of Mohsin Hamid's The Reluctant Fundamentalist* (annotated) to demonstrate an interpretive analysis of a work of fiction

- Ch. 23: Writing in the Social Sciences: a new assignment and an updated student model: *A Field Research Report on the Mental Health of College Students: What Support Should Institutions Provide?* (annotated) to illustrate a research report on social science in APA style

- Ch. 25: Professional and Civic Writing: updated section on "Using Business Letter Formats" to align with expectations of the digital age more closely; updated coverage of digital résumés; new example of a report (from the White House) and a press release (from Habitat for Humanity)

Part VII: Style Matters (Chs. 26–32)

- Ch. 30: Choosing Appropriate Language: revised to ensure students are purposeful in their sentence structure and language
  - New introductory example of "Choosing Appropriate Language"
  - Updated "Gender bias" section to show how to avoid it by using the singular *they, them,* or *their*
  - Updated "Cultural labels" section to include "Latinx" as a gender neutral descriptor of individuals of Latin descent

- Ch. 31: Choosing Effective Words: updated introduction to refer to language in context of contemporary protests and civil rights movement

Part VIII: Grammar Matters (Chs. 33–42)

- Ch. 33: Understanding Grammar: updated Quick Reference box, "Pronouns and Their Functions," to include singular *they/their;* sentence examples updated

- Ch. 36: Maintaining Agreement, updated Writing Responsibly box, "Using a Plural Pronoun with a Singular Antecedent" to reflect contemporary context

- Ch. 40: Avoiding confusing shifts: updated "Avoiding Awkward Shifts in Person and Number" section to explain the use of a plural pronoun with a singular antecedent

- Ch. 42: Avoiding Mixed and Incomplete Constructions: updated introductory example to use architecture as metaphor for chapter's focus

Part IX: Language Matters (Chs. 43–47); Part X: Detail Matters (Chs. 48–58)

- Refreshed examples throughout to interest students, reflect contemporary life

- Adjusted design to better distinguish between explanations and examples

Acknowledgments

The creation and evolution of *Writing Matters* has been an exciting and humbling experience. I began in the belief that I knew what I was doing, but I quickly realized that I had embarked on a path not only of sharing what I know but also of learning what I should know. *Writing Matters* lists a single author, Rebecca Moore Howard, but that author is actually the central figure in a collaboration of hundreds of students, teachers, and editors.

I thank the instructors who have provided invaluable insights and suggestions as reviewers and members of the board of advisors. Talking with instructors at all sorts of institutions and learning from them about the teaching of writing has been an unparalleled experience. As a result of this project, I have many new colleagues, people who care deeply about teaching writing and who are experts at doing so. I also thank the many students who have shared their thoughts with us through class tests and design reviews. I particularly thank the students who have shared their writing with me and allowed me to publish some of it in this book. *Writing Matters* has been improved greatly by their contributions.

Manuscript Reviewers

Butler Community College: Andrea McCaffree-Wallace
Delgado Community College: Emily Cosper
East Carolina University: Tracy Morse
Indian River State College: Camila Alvarez
Kennesaw State University: Jeanne Bohannon
Lone Star College-CyFair: Andrea Hollinger
Metropolitan State University of Denver: Jessica Parker
Missouri Western State University: Kay Siebler
Oklahoma City Community College: Michael Franco
Oklahoma City Community College: Candie McKee
Palm Beach State College: Patrick Tierney
Pitt Community College: Anthony Holsten
Pitt Community College: Daniel Stanford
Robert Morris University: Julianne Michalenko
Salish Kootenai College: Christa Umphrey
St. Charles Community College: Byronie Carter
St. Johns River State College: Paul Andrews
St. Johns River State College-Orange Park: Melody Hargraves
St. Johns River State College-Orange Park: Jeannine Morgan
Tri-County Community College: Lee Ann Hodges
University of Arizona: Dev Bose
University of Memphis: William Duffy
University of Mississippi: Alison Hitch
University of Providence: Curt Bobbitt
University of Providence: Aaron Parrett

Personal Acknowledgments

Writing Matters is the result of rich collaboration with a creative, supportive, knowledgeable team who have a deep understanding of both teaching and publishing: Tom Howard, senior lecturer in University Studies at Colgate University, has worked with me from the beginning to the end, and his intelligence and ingenuity are evident everywhere in this project. Patrick Williams and Krista Kennedy, both of Syracuse University, reviewed key chapters in their areas of expertise, helping me update and reframe several of the core chapters. In this edition, Krista Kennedy joined me as a coauthor of "Designing Accessible Print and Digital Documents" (Ch. 9). She, Jeff Ward, and Greg Craybas contributed fresh new images that appear throughout the text.

For previous work on *Writing Matters* that carries forth to this edition, I'd like to thank Amy Rupiper Taggart from North Dakota State University, who drafted "Designing in Context: Academic and Business Documents"; Ted Johnston, formerly of El Paso Community College, and Maggie Sokolik, of University of California, Berkeley, who drafted "Language Matters: Guidance for Multilingual Writers" (Part 9) and EFL Notes. Sandra Jamieson, Drew University, and Bruce R. Thaler drafted many of the exercises; and a number of instructors—David Hooper, of Western Washington University; Tom Howard, of Colgate University; Ann Marie Leshkowich, of College of the Holy Cross; Leslie Yoder, of Southwestern College; and Paul Yoder, of University of Arkansas at Little Rock—kindly contributed sample exercises designed to help students learn the art of analyzing arguments.

In addition, *Writing Matters* has benefited greatly from the efforts of an extended editorial team: Erin Cosyn, portfolio manager, and Cara Labell, lead product developer, were amazing in the guidance and insights they brought to the project. Cheryl Ferguson contributed copyediting so perceptive that it not only corrected errors in the manuscript but also helped me articulate and expand my ideas. Finally, I feel privileged to have worked with Ellen Thibault, an extraordinarily skilled, creative, and supportive editor.

Contents

Part One: Writing Matters
Planning, Drafting, Revising, Editing, Proofreading, and Formatting 1

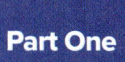

Tutorial Writing Matters Writer's Responsibilities Checklists 2

1 Writing Responsibly, Writing Successfully 7
a. Your Responsibilities to Your Audience 8
b. Your Responsibilities to Your Topic 9
Writing Responsibly Your Responsibilities as a Writer 9
c. Your Responsibilities to Other Writers 9
d. Your Responsibilities to Yourself 11
Writing Responsibly Taking Yourself Seriously as a Writer 12
Student Model Newspaper Article 12

2 Planning Your Project 14
a. Analyzing Your Writing Situation 14
Writing Responsibly Seeing and Showing the Whole Picture 20
b. Analyzing an Assignment 23
c. Generating Ideas, Topics 25
Writing Responsibly Note Taking and Plagiarism 26
d. Narrowing or Broadening a Topic 31
e. Working with Others: Planning a Collaborative Project 32
Student Model Freewrite 27; Brainstorm to Generate Ideas 28; Idea Cluster 29; Journalists' Questions 30; Brainstorm to Narrow a Topic 32

3 Organizing and Drafting Your Project 35
a. Crafting an Effective Thesis 35
b. Organizing Your Ideas 39
c. Preparing to Draft 44
d. Drafting: Explaining and Supporting Your Ideas 45
Writing Responsibly Made-up Evidence 46
e. Writing with Others: Collaborative Projects 51
Student Model Informal (or Scratch) Outline 42; Topic Outline and Sentence Outline 42; First Draft of a Researched Essay 47

4 Crafting and Connecting Paragraphs 52
a. Writing Relevant Paragraphs 53
b. Writing Unified Paragraphs 53
c. Writing Coherent Paragraphs 58
Writing Responsibly Guiding Your Audience 62
d. Developing Paragraphs Using Patterns 64
e. Writing Introductory Paragraphs 68
f. Writing Concluding Paragraphs 70
g. Connecting Paragraphs 73
Professional Model Speech 74

xxv

5 Drafting and Revising Visuals 77

a. Deciding Whether to Illustrate College Writing Projects 77
b. Using Visuals as Evidence 78
Writing Responsibly Exploitative Images 81
c. Deciding Whether to Copy Visuals or to Create Them 82
d. Revising Visuals 82

6 Revising, Editing, Proofreading, and Formatting 86

Revising Globally: Analyzing Your Own Work
a. Gaining Perspective 86
b. Revising Your Draft 87
Writing Responsibly The Big Picture 89
c. Reconsidering Your Title 90

Revising Locally: Editing Words and Sentences
d. Choosing Your Words with Care 91
e. Editing Your Sentences 91
Writing Responsibly Making Your Text Long Enough without Wordiness 92
Revising with Others
f. Revising with Peers 93
g. Revising with a Tutor or an Instructor 95
Proofreading and Formatting
h. Proofreading 96
Writing Responsibly Beware the Spelling Checker! 97
i. Formatting an Academic Text 98
j. Creating and Submitting a Portfolio 106
Student Model Final Draft of a Researched Essay 99; Personal Statement 108

Part Two Reasoning Matters
Reading, Thinking, and Arguing 111

7 Thinking and Reading Critically 112

a. Comprehending 112
Writing Responsibly Engaging with What You Read 112
b. Reflecting 119
c. Preparing to Write 127
Writing Responsibly Drawing Inferences 133
Writing Responsibly Understanding Criticism 133
Professional Model Essay 116; Article (annotated by a student) 121
Student Model Summary of an Article 115; Double-Entry Reading Journal 125; Annotations to an Image: 126; Claims and Evidence Analysis 129; Rhetorical Analysis of an Image 130; Critical Analysis Essay 135

Writing Responsibly Understanding and Representing the Entire Source 141

8 Applying Analysis and Crafting Arguments 143

a. Persuading, Exploring, and Affirming 143
b. Making Claims 146
Writing Responsibly Choosing an Engaging Topic 148
c. Choosing Evidence Rhetorically 150
Writing Responsibly Establishing Yourself as a Responsible Writer 154
Writing Responsibly Preparing Oral Arguments 156
d. Considering Alternative Viewpoints 156
e. Discovering Assumptions and Common Ground 158
Writing Responsibly The Well-Tempered Tone 159
f. Organizing Arguments: Classical, Rogerian, and Toulmin Models 174
g. Avoiding Logical Fallacies 176
Writing Responsibly Visual Claims and Visual Fallacies 177
h. Using Tone and Style Effectively and Ethically 181
Student Model Exploratory Argument 159

Part Three — Media Matters
Designing, Writing, and Presenting 183

9 Designing Accessible Print and Digital Documents 184
  a. Understanding the Four Principles of Design (CRAP) 184
  b. Understanding Universal, Empathy-Driven Design 186
  c. Understanding the Principles of Accessible Design (POUR) 187
  d. Planning Your Design Project 188
  e. Applying Traditional, Universal, and Accessible Design Principles 190
  Writing Responsibly Selecting Fonts with Readers in Mind 192
  Writing Responsibly Establishing a Consistent Font 193
  Student Model A Well-Designed Document 190

10 Writing for Multiple Media 199
  a. Writing and Answering Email 199
  Writing Responsibly Maintaining Confidentiality in Email 201
  Writing Responsibly Making Considerate Attachments 202
  Writing Responsibly Understanding Email and Privacy 203
  b. Creating Websites and Web Pages 203
  Writing Responsibly Checking Accessibility 209
  c. Writing in Social Media 210
  Writing Responsibly Flaming 210

11 Presenting with Multiple Media 212
  a. Identifying Your Purpose, Audience, Context, and Genre 213
  b. Devising a Topic and Thesis 214
  c. Organizing the Presentation 214
  d. Preparing and Rehearsing the Presentation 215
  e. Delivering the Presentation 219
  Writing Responsibly Listening Actively 219
  f. Speaking Responsibly 219

Part Four — Research Matters
Finding, Evaluating, and Citing Sources 221

12 Planning a Research Project 222
  a. Analyzing the Assignment's Purpose, Audience, and Method of Development 222
  b. Setting a Schedule 223
  c. Choosing and Narrowing a Research Topic 224
  d. Drafting Research Questions and Hypotheses 225
  Writing Responsibly Using Printed Sources 227
  e. Choosing Research Sources Strategically 227
  f. Establishing a Research Log 228
  Writing Responsibly Avoiding Accidental Plagiarism 230
  g. Building and Annotating a Working Bibliography 230

13 Finding Information 237
  a. Searching Rhetorically 237
  b. Finding Reference Works 238
  Writing Responsibly Using *Wikipedia* Responsibly 239
  Writing Responsibly Going beyond Reference Sources 241

c. Finding Information on the Web 242
d. Finding Reliable Interactive Media 245
e. Finding Articles in Journals and Other Periodicals Using Databases and Indexes 246
Writing Responsibly Really Reading Real Sources 246
f. Finding Books Using Library Catalogs 251
g. Finding Government Information 254
h. Finding Multimedia Sources 255

> **Writing Responsibly** Choosing and Unpacking Complex Sources 256

i. Conducting and Reporting Field Research 259
Writing Responsibly Conducting Interviews Fairly 259
Writing Responsibly Avoiding Manipulation and Bias in Observations 260
Writing Responsibly Reporting Results Fairly 262

14 Evaluating Information 263

a. Evaluating for Relevance, Reliability, and Diversity 263
Writing Responsibly Keeping an Open, Inquiring Mind 267
Writing Responsibly Online Plagiarism 269
b. Misinformation, Disinformation, and Fake News 270
c. Evaluating Digital Texts: Websites, Blogs, Wikis, Discussion Forums, and Social Media 271
d. Evaluating Visual Sources 274

15 Overcoming Fear of Plagiarizing: Paraphrase, Summary, and Rhetorical Note-Taking 279

a. Researching Rhetorically 280
b. Understanding Plagiarism 280
Writing Responsibly Using Illustrations and Avoiding Plagiarism 284

c. Taking Notes Rhetorically 286
Writing Responsibly Highlighting versus Making Notes 287
d. Citing Accurately 287

> **Writing Responsibly** Blending Voices in Your Text 290

e. Paraphrasing Elegantly 292
f. Summarizing Eloquently 295
g. Quoting Strategically 297
Writing Responsibly Using Quotations Fairly 298

> **Writing Responsibly** Acknowledging Indirect Sources 300

Student Model Summary of a Source 296;
Reading Note: Integrating Borrowed Ideas and Words 299

16 Writing the Research Project 302

a. Drafting a Thesis Statement 303
b. Organizing Your Ideas 304
Writing Responsibly Acknowledging Counterevidence 305
c. Drafting Your Research Project 307
d. Revising, Proofreading, Formatting, and Publishing Your Project 311
Student Model Thesis Statement for "Fast Fashion" by Isabel Beck 304; Outline for "Fast Fashion" by Isabel Beck 306; Supporting Claims from "Fast Fashion" by Isabel Beck 309

17 Citing Rhetorically 312

a. Integrating Source Material Responsibly 313
b. Showing Source Boundaries 314
c. Emphasizing Your Voice 316
d. Providing Context 318
e. Integrating Altered Quotations 322

> **Writing Responsibly** Explaining Your Choice of Sources 326

Part Five Documentation Matters 329

Tutorial Documentation Matters
Documenting a Source: MLA Style and APA Style 330

18 Documenting Sources: MLA Style 334

a. Creating MLA-Style In-Text Citations 335
Writing Responsibly Citing and Documenting Sources 335
Writing Responsibly Using Signal Phrases to Demonstrate Your Relationship with Sources 340
b. Preparing an MLA-Style List of Works Cited 352
Books—Printed and Electronic 352
Periodicals—Printed and Electronic 361
Other Electronic Sources 366
Audio and Visual Sources 370
Miscellaneous Sources—Printed and Electronic 376
c. Using MLA Style for Informational Notes 378
d. Formatting a Paper in MLA Style 379
Writing Responsibly Of Deadlines and Paperclips 382
Student Model Research Project: MLA Style: "Fast Fashion," by Isabel Beck 383

19 Documenting Sources: APA Style 397

a. Creating APA-Style In-Text Citations 397
Writing Responsibly Citing and Documenting Sources 398
b. Preparing an APA-Style Reference List 408
Books—Printed and Electronic 408
Periodicals—Printed and Electronic 415
Other Electronic Sources 419
Audio and Visual Sources 422
Miscellaneous Sources—Printed and Electronic 424
c. Using APA Style for Informational Notes 425
d. Formatting a Paper in APA Style 426
Writing Responsibly Of Deadlines and Paperclips 430
Student Model Research Project: APA Style 430

20 Documenting Sources: *Chicago* Style 439

a. Creating *Chicago*-Style Notes and Bibliography Entries 440
Writing Responsibly Citing and Documenting Sources 441
Books—Printed and Electronic 442
Periodicals—Printed and Electronic 449
Other Electronic Sources 454
Audio and Visual Sources 455
Miscellaneous Sources—Printed and Electronic 457
b. Using *Chicago* Style for Tables and Figures 458
c. Formatting a *Chicago*-Style Research Project 458
Writing Responsibly Of Deadlines and Paperclips 459
Student Model Research Project: *Chicago* Style 459

21 Documenting Sources: CSE Style 470

a. Creating CSE-Style In-Text Citations 470
Writing Responsibly Citing and Documenting Sources 470
b. Preparing a CSE-Style Reference List 472
Books—Printed and Electronic 473
Periodicals—Printed and Electronic 477

xxx Contents

Miscellaneous Sources—Printed and Electronic 480
c. Formatting a CSE-Style Research Project 482

Writing Responsibly Of Deadlines and Paperclips 483
Student Model Research Project: CSE-Style Reference List 483

Part Six: Genre Matters
Writing in and beyond College 485

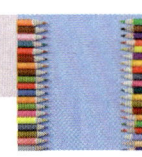

22 Writing in Literature and the Other Humanities 486
a. Adopting the Approach of Literature and the Other Humanities 486
Writing Responsibly Reading with Study Guides 487
b. Using the Resources of Literature and the Other Humanities 489
c. Citing and Documenting Sources—MLA and *Chicago* Style 491
d. Using the Language of Literature and the Other Humanities 491
e. Writing about Fiction 494
f. Writing about Poetry 501
g. Writing about Drama 507
Student Model Textual Analysis 488; Writing about Fiction: Interpretive Analysis 496; Writing about Poetry: Explication 501
Professional Model Writing about Drama: Review of a Play 507

23 Writing in the Sciences and Social Sciences 510
a. Adopting the Approach of the Sciences and Social Sciences 510
b. Using the Research Methods of the Sciences and Social Sciences 511
c. Citing and Documenting Sources—APA and CSE Style 511
Writing Responsibly Presenting Data Accurately 511
d. Using the Language of the Sciences and Social Sciences 512
e. Writing Assignments in the Sciences and Social Sciences 513
Student Model Research Report 516

24 Preparing for and Taking an Essay Exam 530
a. Preparing for an Essay Exam 530
b. Previewing the Exam 532
c. Writing an Effective Answer 533
Writing Responsibly Using Your Computer during an Essay Exam 534
Student Model Effective Essay Exam Response 535

25 Professional and Civic Writing 537
a. Using Business Letter Formats 537
b. Writing Business Letters 540
Writing Responsibly Letters to the Editor 542
c. Writing Business Memos 542
d. Writing Job Application Letters 543
Writing Responsibly Personal Emails and Text Messages at Work 545
e. Writing Résumés 547
Writing Responsibly Representing Yourself 550
f. Writing Reports and Proposals 552
g. Writing Press Releases 554
Student Model Job Application 546; Traditional Résumé 548; Scannable, Optimized Résumé 550
Professional Model Business Letter: Apology 541; Business Memo 543; Report 553; Press Release 554

Part Seven — Style Matters: Writing Engagingly 557

26 Writing Concisely 558

Writing Responsibly Conciseness versus the Too-Short Paper 558
a. Eliminating Wordy Expressions 559
b. Eliminating Ineffective or Unnecessary Repetition 561
c. Avoiding Indirect Constructions 562
d. Consolidating Phrases, Clauses, and Sentences 563

27 Using Coordination and Subordination 565

a. Coordinating Terms, Phrases, and Clauses 566
b. Coordinating Effectively 567
c. Identifying Important Ideas and Supporting Information with Subordination 570
d. Using Coordination and Subordination Together 575

28 Using Parallelism 578

a. Using Parallelism for Paired Items and Items in a Series 579
b. Maintaining Parallelism in Comparisons 581
c. Including Function Words to Maintain Parallelism 581
Writing Responsibly Using Parallelism to Clarify Relationships among Ideas 582
d. Maintaining Parallelism for Items in Lists and Outlines 582
e. Using Parallelism to Create Emphasis 584

29 Engaging Readers with Variety and Emphasis 586

a. Varying Sentence Length and Structure 587
b. Varying Sentence Openings 587
c. Creating Emphasis with Rhythm 590
d. Creating Emphasis with Punctuation 591
e. Using Questions, Commands, and Exclamations 592
f. Using Strategic Repetition 592
g. Creating Emphasis with Emphatic Verbs 593
h. Choosing the Active or Passive Voice 593
Writing Responsibly Voice and Responsibility 594

30 Choosing Appropriate Language 596

a. Using Language in Context 596
Writing Responsibly Avoiding Online Shortcuts 598
Writing Responsibly Euphemisms and Doublespeak 600
b. Avoiding Biased or Hurtful Language 600

31 Choosing Effective Words 604

a. Diction: Finding the Right Word 604
b. Choosing Compelling Words and Figures 606
Writing Responsibly Word Choice and Credibility 607
c. Mastering Idioms 610
d. Avoiding Clichés 610

32 Using the Dictionary and Spelling Correctly 613

a. Choosing a Dictionary 613
Writing Responsibly Choose Accurate Synonyms 615

b. Using a Dictionary 615
c. Avoiding Common Spelling Problems 618
d. Remembering Spelling Rules 620

Writing Responsibly Spelling Errors 620
e. Forming Plurals 623
f. Improving Your Day-to-Day Spelling 625

Part Eight: Grammar Matters
Writing with Clarity 627

Tutorial Grammar Matters Identifying Common Sentence Problems 628
Student Model First Draft with Sentence Problems 630

33 Understanding Grammar 634

Writing Responsibly Why Grammar Matters 635

Parts of Speech
a. Nouns 635
b. Pronouns 637
c. Verbs 639
d. Adjectives 640
e. Adverbs 641
f. Prepositions 642
g. Conjunctions 643
h. Interjections 644

Sentence Structure
i. Subjects 645
j. Predicates 647
k. Verb Types and Sentence Patterns 648
l. Phrases 651
m. Independent and Subordinate Clauses 654
n. Sentence Types 657

34 Avoiding Sentence Fragments 660

a. Recognizing Fragments 660
b. Correcting Fragments 664

Writing Responsibly Sentence Fragments and Context 664

c. Using Intentional Fragments Effectively and Judiciously 669

35 Avoiding Comma Splices and Fused Sentences 671

a. Correctly Joining Independent Clauses 671
b. Identifying Incorrectly Joined Independent Clauses: Comma Splices and Fused Sentences 672

Writing Responsibly Clarifying Boundaries 672

c. Recognizing When Comma Splices and Fused Sentences Tend to Occur 673

Writing Responsibly Is a Comma Splice Ever Acceptable? 674

d. Correcting Comma Splices and Fused Sentences 675

36 Maintaining Agreement 680

Subject-Verb Agreement
a. Understanding How Subjects and Verbs Agree 680

Writing Responsibly Dialect Variation in Subject-Verb Agreement 682

b. Ignoring Words That Intervene between the Subject and the Verb 682
c. Distinguishing Plural from Singular Compound Subjects 683
d. Distinguishing Singular and Plural Indefinite Pronouns 685
e. Understanding Collective Noun Subjects 685
f. Finding Agreement When the Subject Is a Measurement, a Number, or the Word *Number* 686

Contents **xxxiii**

    g. Recognizing Nouns That Are Singular Even Though They End in -s 687
    h. Treating Titles, Words as Words, and Gerund Phrases as Singular 687
    i. Matching a Relative Pronoun (*Who, Which,* or *That*) to Its Antecedent When the Pronoun Is the Subject of a Subordinate Clause 688
    j. Finding Agreement When the Subject Follows the Verb 688
    k. Matching a Linking Verb with Its Subject, Not Its Subject Complement 689

Pronoun-Antecedent Agreement
    l. Matching Pronouns with Indefinite Pronoun and Generic Noun Antecedents 690
    m. Matching Pronouns with Collective Noun Antecedents 692
    n. Matching Pronouns with Compound Antecedents 692

37 Using Verbs 694

Verb Forms
    a. Understanding the Basic Forms of Verbs 694
    b. Using Regular and Irregular Verb Forms Correctly 696
    c. Combining Main Verbs with Helping Verbs to Form Complete Verbs 697
    d. Including -s or -es, -d or -ed Endings When Required 700
    e. Distinguishing *Rise* from *Raise, Sit* from *Set, Lie* from *Lay* 701

Tense
    f. Understanding Which Verb Tense to Use 702
    g. Following Conventions for the Use of the Present Tense 705
    h. Using Tense Sequence to Clarify Time Relationships 706

Mood
    i. Understanding Verb Mood 707
    j. Using the Subjunctive Mood Correctly 708

Writing Responsibly Using the Subjunctive in Formal Writing 708

Voice
    k. Understanding Voice 709
    l. Choosing between the Active and Passive Voice 710

38 Understanding Pronoun Case and Reference 712

Pronoun Case
    a. Using the Subjective Case for Subject Complements 714
    b. *She and I* or *Her and Me*? Keeping Track of Case in Compounds 714
    c. Keeping Track of Pronoun Case in Appositives 716
    d. Deciding between *We* and *Us* before Nouns 716
    e. Using the Objective Case Both before and after an Infinitive 716
    f. Deciding on Pronoun Case with the *–ing* Form of a Verb 717
    g. Clarifying Pronoun Case in Comparisons with *Than* or *As* 717
    h. Using *Who, Whom, Whoever,* and *Whomever* 717

Writing Responsibly Case and Tone 718

Clear Pronoun Reference
    i. Avoiding Ambiguous Reference 720
    j. Avoiding Confusingly Broad Reference with *It, This, That,* and *Which* 720
    k. Avoiding Implied Reference 721
    l. Reserving *You* for Directly Addressing the Reader 721
    m. Avoiding the Indefinite Use of *They* and *It* 721
    n. Designating People with *Who, Whom,* and *Whose,* Not *That* and *Which* 722

39 Using Adjectives and Adverbs 724
a. Differentiating Adjectives and Adverbs 724
b. Using Adjectives, Not Adverbs, as Subject Complements after Linking Verbs 725
c. Choosing *Bad* or *Badly, Good* or *Well* 726
d. Using Negatives Correctly 728
e. Avoiding Long Strings of Nouns Used as Adjectives 728
f. Using Comparative and Superlative Adjectives and Adverbs 729

40 Avoiding Confusing Shifts 732
a. Avoiding Awkward Shifts in Tense 732
b. Avoiding Awkward Shifts in Mood and Voice 733
c. Avoiding Awkward Shifts in Person and Number 735
d. Avoiding Awkward Shifts in Direct and Indirect Quotations and Questions 737

41 Avoiding Misplaced and Dangling Modifiers 740

Misplaced Modifiers
a. Avoiding Confusing or Ambiguous Placement 741
b. Avoiding Disruptive Placement 743
Writing Responsibly Misplaced Modifiers in the Real World 744
Dangling Modifiers
c. Identifying Dangling Modifiers 746
d. Correcting Dangling Modifiers 747

42 Avoiding Mixed and Incomplete Constructions 749

Mixed Constructions
a. Recognizing and Correcting Grammatically Mixed Constructions 749
b. Recognizing and Correcting Mismatched Subjects and Predicates 751
Incomplete Constructions
c. Adding Essential Words to Compound and Other Constructions 753
d. Avoiding Incomplete or Ambiguous Comparisons 754

Part Nine

Language Matters
Guidance for Multilingual Writers 757

43 Understanding English Word Order and Sentence Structure 758
a. Observing Standard Word Order 758
b. Including a Stated Subject 758
c. Managing *There* and *It* Constructions 759
d. Eliminating Redundant Subject and Object Pronouns 760
e. Structuring Sentences with Direct Objects, Indirect Objects, and Object Complements 761
f. Observing Word-Order Patterns in Questions 763
g. Observing Inverted Word Order When Certain Conjunctions or Adverbs Begin a Clause 764

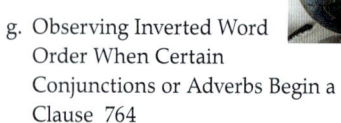

44 Using Nouns and Noun Determiners 767
a. Understanding Different Types of Nouns 767
b. Using Nouns with Articles (*a, an, the*) and Other Determiners 768

Contents **xxxv**

45 Managing English Verbs 776
  a. Using Phrasal Verbs 776
  b. Using Gerunds and Infinitives after Verbs and Prepositions 779
  c. Using Participles as Adjectives 781
  d. Using Helping Verbs for Verb Formation 782

46 Managing Adjectives and Adverbs 786
  a. Placing Adjectives in the Proper Order 786
  b. Choosing the Correct Prepositions with Adjectives 787
  c. Placing Adverbs Correctly 788
  d. Dealing with Confusing Adverbs 790

47 Using Prepositions 793
  a. Recognizing Prepositions 793
  b. The Functions of Prepositions 794
  c. Using Prepositions Correctly 798
  d. Necessary and Unnecessary Prepositions 799

Part Ten — Detail Matters
Punctuation and Mechanics 801

48 Using Commas 802
  Writing Responsibly Commas and Clarity 802
  a. Using Commas in Compound Sentences 802
  b. Using a Comma after Introductory Elements 805
  c. Using Commas to Set Off Conjunctive Adverbs and Most Transitional Phrases 807
  d. Inserting Commas to Set Off Interjections, Contrasting Information, Expressions of Direct Address, Parenthetical and Conversational Expressions, and Tag Questions 807
  e. Using Commas to Separate Items in a Series 808
  f. Using Commas to Separate Coordinate, Not Cumulative, Adjectives 809
  g. Using Commas to Set Off Nonessential Appositives, Phrases, and Clauses 811
  h. Using Commas with Quotations 813
  i. Using Commas with Numbers, Names and Titles, Place Names and Addresses, and Dates 814
  j. Using Commas to Avoid Ambiguity 817
  k. Avoiding Commas between Subjects and Verbs, Verbs and Objects, and Prepositions and Objects 817

49 Using Semicolons 820
  Writing Responsibly Sending a Signal with Semicolons 820
  a. Using a Semicolon to Link Independent Clauses 820
  b. Using a Semicolon before a Conjunctive Adverb or Transitional Phrase Linking Two Independent Clauses 822
  c. Using a Semicolon to Mark a Series with Internal Commas 823
  d. Repairing a Comma Splice 823
  e. Avoiding Overuse 824

50 Using Apostrophes 827
  a. Using Apostrophes to Indicate Possession 827
  Writing Responsibly Contractions in Formal Writing 827
  b. Using Apostrophes in Contractions and Abbreviated Years 831
  c. Moving Away from Using Apostrophes to Form Plurals of Abbreviations, Dates, Numbers, and Words or Letters Used as Words 831

51 Using Quotation Marks 834

a. Setting Off Direct Quotations 834
Writing Responsibly Using Quotations Fairly 835
b. Indicating Titles of Short Works 837
c. Indicating Words Used in a Special Sense 837
d. Misusing Quotation Marks 838
e. Punctuating Quotations 839
f. Altering Quotations with Ellipses and Square Brackets 840
g. Introducing and Identifying Quotations 840

52 Using End Punctuation: Periods, Question Marks, and Exclamation Points 843

a. Using Periods to End Statements and Mild Commands 843
b. Using Question Marks to End Direct (Not Indirect) Questions 844
Writing Responsibly Question Marks and Exclamation Points 844
c. Using Exclamation Points with Strong Commands or to Express Excitement or Surprise 845

53 Using Other Punctuation: Dashes, Parentheses, Brackets, Colons, Ellipses, and Slashes 847

a. Using Dashes 847
b. Using Parentheses 849
Writing Responsibly Em Dashes, Parentheses, or Commas? 850
c. Using Brackets 851
Writing Responsibly Using [sic] 852
d. Using Colons 852
e. Using Ellipses 854

Writing Responsibly Altering Quotations 855
f. Using Slashes 856

54 Capitalizing 858

a. Capitalizing the First Word of a Sentence 858
b. Capitalizing Proper Nouns and Proper Adjectives 860
c. Capitalizing Titles and Subtitles 861
d. Capitalizing the First-Person Pronoun *I* and the Interjection *O* 862
Writing Responsibly Capitalizing in Email, Social Media, and Text Messages 862
e. Capitalizing Abbreviations and Acronyms 863

55 Italics and Underlining 865

a. Italicizing Titles of Longer Works 865
Writing Responsibly Using Italics for Emphasis 867
b. Italicizing for Emphasis 867
c. Italicizing Names of Vehicles 867
d. Italicizing Words, Letters, or Numbers Used as Words 867
e. Italicizing Unfamiliar Non-English Words and Latin Genus and Species 868

56 Using Abbreviations 869

a. Abbreviating Titles before and after Names 871
b. Using Familiar Abbreviations: Acronyms and Initialisms 871
Writing Responsibly Using Online Abbreviations Appropriately 872
c. Using Abbreviations with Specific Years (BC, BCE, AD, CE), Hours (a.m., p.m.), Numbers (no.), Dollars ($) 872

d. Avoiding Abbreviations of Names, Words, Courses, Parts of Books, States and Countries, Days and Months, Holidays, and Units of Measurement in Prose 872
e. Replacing Latin Abbreviations with English Equivalents in Formal Prose 873

57 Using Numbers 874

Writing Responsibly Ethos and Convention 874
a. Spelling Out Numbers When They Can Be Expressed in One or Two Words 874
b. Following Conventions for Dates, Times, Addresses, Specific Amounts of Money and Other Quantitative Information, and Divisions of Literary Works 875

58 Using Hyphens 877

a. Using Hyphens to Form Compounds 877

Writing Responsibly Hyphenating with Readers in Mind 878

b. Using Hyphens to Break Words at the Ends of Lines 879

Glossary of Key Terms G1
Glossary of Usage G15
Index I1
EFL Index EFL1

Part One

Writing Matters

Planning, Drafting, Revising, Editing, Proofreading, and Formatting

1 Writing Responsibly, Writing Successfully 7
2 Planning Your Project 14
3 Organizing and Drafting Your Project 35
4 Crafting and Connecting Paragraphs 52
5 Drafting and Revising Visuals 77
6 Revising, Editing, Proofreading, and Formatting 86

Writing Matters | Writer's Responsibilities Checklists

Self Assessment — To fulfill your responsibility to your AUDIENCE, ask yourself the following questions:

As you research, develop, and write your project, ask yourself the following questions, revising as necessary to improve your work.

- Have you chosen a topic that is appropriate and interesting to your audience?
- Does your title prepare your audience for what follows?
- Does your introductory material indicate what your thesis or claims will be?
- Will your audience find your explanations logical and compelling?
- Have you supplied enough relevant evidence to persuade your audience to accept (or at least to consider) your position?
- Have you explained alternate points of view (counterevidence)?
- Have you provided transitions to connect paragraphs and keep your audience mindful of your thesis?
- Is your project written at an appropriate level for your audience?
- Is your tone appropriate to your rhetorical situation?
- Have you revised, edited, and proofread your project?

Self Assessment — To fulfill your responsibility to your TOPIC, ask yourself the following questions:

As you research, develop, and write your project, ask yourself the following questions, revising as necessary to improve your work.

- Have you explored your topic thoroughly and creatively?
- Have you conducted research (when needed), using the most in-depth and reliable sources available to you?
- Have you provided sufficient evidence to support your thesis?
- Have you used visuals when they are an effective way of presenting supporting evidence or examples?
- Have you assessed your sources carefully and presented evidence from reliable sources?
- Have you represented ideas borrowed from sources accurately and fully?

Writing Matters | Writer's Responsibilities Checklists

Self Assessment — To fulfill your responsibility to OTHER WRITERS, ask yourself the following questions:

As you research, develop, and write your project, ask yourself the following questions, revising as necessary to improve your work.

- Have you given credit to those whose words or ideas you have summarized, paraphrased, or quoted?
- When paraphrasing, have you restated the text in fresh words and sentence structures?
- Have you represented the ideas of other writers accurately and fairly?
- Have you treated other writers respectfully, even when you disagree with them?
- Have you considered alternative viewpoints?
- Have you addressed alternative perspectives that conflict with your own position?

Self Assessment — To fulfill your responsibility to YOURSELF, ask yourself the following questions:

As you research, develop, and write your project, ask yourself the following questions, revising as necessary to improve your work.

- Have you used the project to learn something new and to expand your scope as a writer?
- Have you represented your ideas clearly, and in detail accurately?
- Have you integrated your own ideas or your own synthesis of sources to provide a text that is fresh and interesting?
- Have you used language inclusively, avoiding bias and representing yourself as a respectful human being?
- Have you written in a voice that is true to yourself and in keeping with your rhetorical context (academic, business, public) and genre (college essay, presentation, newsletter)?
- Have you revised, edited, and proofread your project to make sure your presentation reflects the effort you have put into the writing?
- Is your project a good representation of yourself?

Isabel Beck

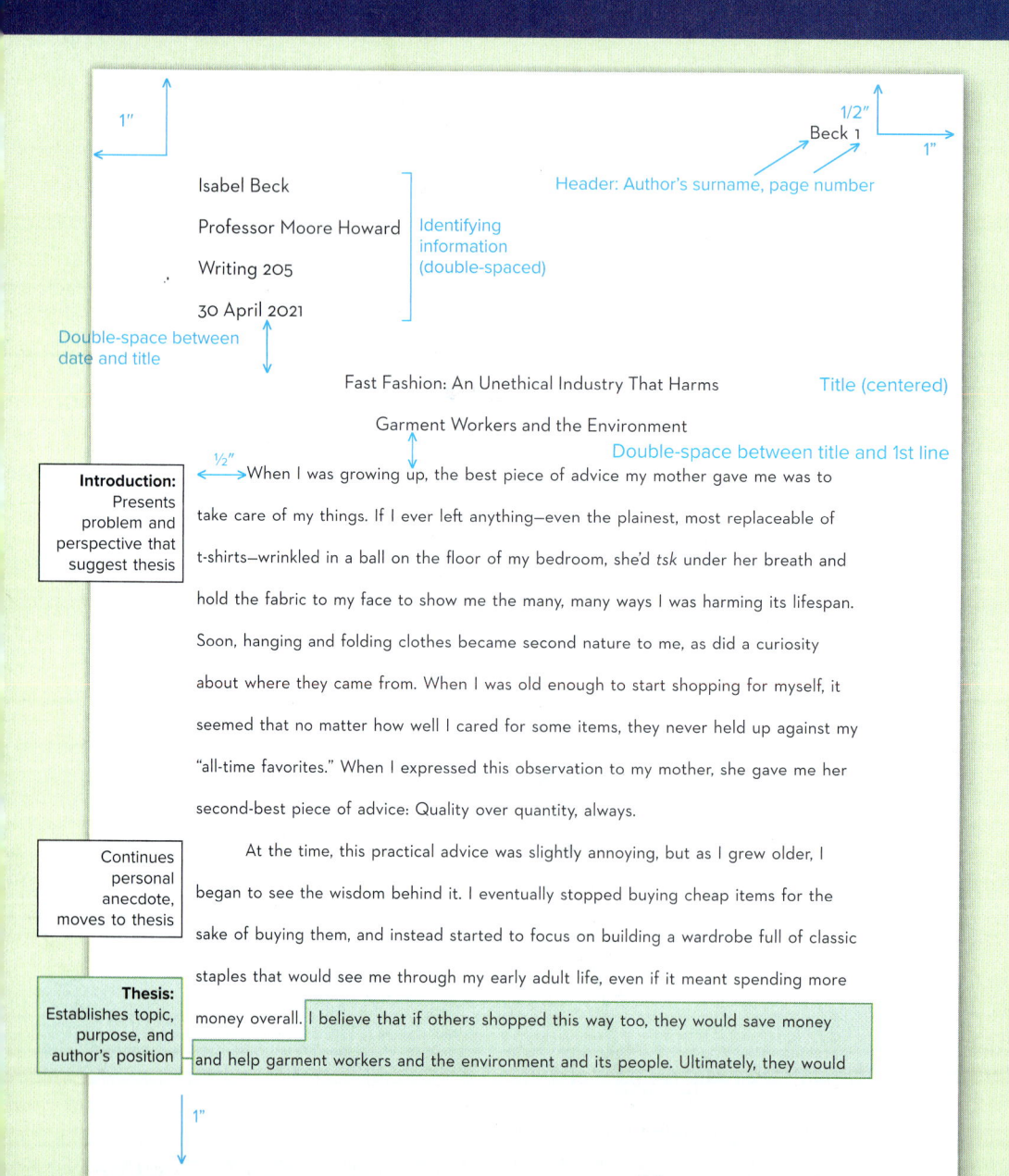

Professor Moore Howard

Writing 205

30 April 2021

Fast Fashion: An Unethical Industry That Harms Garment Workers and the Environment

When I was growing up, the best piece of advice my mother gave me was to take care of my things. If I ever left anything—even the plainest, most replaceable of t-shirts—wrinkled in a ball on the floor of my bedroom, she'd *tsk* under her breath and hold the fabric to my face to show me the many, many ways I was harming its lifespan. Soon, hanging and folding clothes became second nature to me, as did a curiosity about where they came from. When I was old enough to start shopping for myself, it seemed that no matter how well I cared for some items, they never held up against my "all-time favorites." When I expressed this observation to my mother, she gave me her second-best piece of advice: Quality over quantity, always.

At the time, this practical advice was slightly annoying, but as I grew older, I began to see the wisdom behind it. I eventually stopped buying cheap items for the sake of buying them, and instead started to focus on building a wardrobe full of classic staples that would see me through my early adult life, even if it meant spending more money overall. I believe that if others shopped this way too, they would save money and help garment workers and the environment and its people. Ultimately, they would

This project appears in full on pp. 384–96.

Beck 2

see a better return on their investment. In order for better shopping habits to become widespread, however, as consumers, we need to understand the consequences of supporting the fast-fashion industry.

Fast fashion is the opposite of durable and classic. *Good on You*, an app that allows users to search for a fast-fashion retailer and rate it based on how socially responsible it is, defines fast fashion as "cheap, trendy clothing that samples ideas from the catwalk or celebrity culture and turns them into garments in big stores at breakneck speed." Indeed, clothes shopping used to be a relatively biannual affair: something that happened with the changing of the seasons, or out of wardrobe necessity. The existence of fast fashion, however, has turned shopping into something more akin to entertainment than anything else.

As fig. 1 indicates, fast fashion increases the number of fashion seasons from two (spring/summer and fall/winter) to fifty. We're buying sixty percent more clothing

TRADITIONAL: 2 CYCLES PER YEAR

DEC NOV OCT SEP AUG JUL
JUN MAY APR MAR FEB JAN

FAST FASHION: 50 CYCLES PER YEAR

DEC NOV OCT SEP AUG JUL
JUN MAY APR MAR FEB JAN

Fig. 1. Traditional vs. "Fast" Fashion. This graph shows at a glance the differences between the standard two-cycle fashion year and the fast-fashion cycle that breaks down to approximately one cycle per week in a given year. This is not sustainable (Drew and Yehounme).

Sources: True Cost, World Resources Institute

This project appears in full on pp. 384-96.

Beck 3

than we used to. And because fast fashion is cheap and flimsy, we keep such garments for half as long as we would keep better-made clothes (Drew and Yahounme).

The negative effects of the fast fashion industry are far-reaching. First and foremost, it is terrible for the environment. An article from the *Environmental Health Perspectives* journal titled "Waste Couture: [The] Environmental Impact of the Clothing Industry," asserts that "globalization has made it possible to produce clothing at increasingly lower prices, prices so low that many consumers consider this clothing to be disposable . . . some call it 'fast fashion'" (Claudio). But there are consequences; according to Forbes, the fashion industry is responsible for "10% of global carbon emissions and remains the second largest industrial polluter, second only to oil." Making things worse for the industry and environment are fast fashion garments. On average, we wear fast fashion items fewer than five times and keep them for just thirty-five days; these same items produce over four hundred percent more carbon emissions per item per year than do higher-quality garments that are worn fifty times and kept for a full year (Conca).

Annotations:
- In-text citation for article
- Topic sentence supported by summary and quotation
- Signal phrase identifies source
- Topic sentence follows an introductory sentence that provides context
- Parenthetical citation names author

6   This project appears in full on pp. 384–96.

1 Writing Responsibly, Writing Successfully

IN THIS CHAPTER

a. Your responsibilities to your audience, 8

b. Your responsibilities to your topics, 9

c. Your responsibilities to other writers, 9

d. Your responsibilities to yourself, 11

Student Model
Newspaper Article, 12

Megan Ginsie, "Plagiarism an Issue on Campus, Faculty Says"

Krista Kennedy

> *More about*
> Writer's responsibilities checklists, 2–6 (*Writing Matters* tutorial preceding this chapter)

Whether you are studying business, philosophy, science, sociology, rhetoric, technology, literature, or a host of other academic topics, you are likely to be doing a lot of writing in college. The same is true of your workplace, your home, your community: Writing is everywhere. With all the technologies available to us—pen and paper, smartphone, tablet, laptop—everyone can write at just about any time or place. Why, then, does it seem so hard? Why do the projects stack up and sprawl out in a mess so bad that the cat decides to make a bed of them? The problem is especially acute if you think of yourself as a "bad writer" with little self-confidence. It is even more acute if your writing projects seem unfamiliar and unrelated to each other.

The purpose of *Writing Matters* is to help you move your writing forward, regardless of whether you currently think of yourself as an expert writer, an inept writer, or someone in between. Begin that process by considering your goal: successful writing that achieves your purpose.

Successful writing holds out the promise of self-expression, even self-discovery. It is also a valuable asset in the workplace: A report from the National Commission on Writing revealed that

American corporations expect their salaried employees to be able to write clearly, correctly, and logically. Eighty percent of finance, insurance, and real estate employers take writing skills into consideration when hiring.

Whether drafting business emails or making PowerPoint presentations, texting friends or commenting on an Instagram picture, writing in a personal journal or even composing a project for a college course, we write to develop and evaluate beliefs and ideas, to move others, to express ourselves, and to explore possibilities. For all these reasons and more, writing matters.

You can become a more successful writer by taking yourself out of isolation and thinking of yourself as a member of a community—the community in which your writing is produced and received. As a community member, you have responsibilities to your readers, to the topics you address, to the other writers from whom you borrow and to whom you respond, and perhaps especially to yourself as a writer with ideas and ideals to express. These are not simple "duties" or "expectations"; these are ways of connecting yourself and your writing to others. Attending to these responsibilities produces more satisfying, more successful writing.

1a Your Responsibilities to Your Audience

Audience members make a commitment to you by spending their time reading your work. To help them feel that this commitment was worthwhile, you can do the following:

- Choose a topic that your audience will find interesting and about which you have something you want to say.
- Make a claim that will help your audience follow your thoughts.
- Support your claim with thoughtful, logical, even creative evidence drawn from sources that you have evaluated carefully for relevance and reliability.
- Write clearly so that your audience (even if that audience is your composition teacher) does not have to struggle to understand. To write clearly, build a logical structure, use transitional techniques to guide readers, and correct errors of grammar, punctuation, and spelling.
- Write appropriately by using a tone and vocabulary that are right for your rhetorical situation—your topic, audience, context, and genre.
- Write engagingly by varying sentence structures and word choices, avoiding wordiness, and using repetition only for special effect.

More about
Designing accessible print and digital content, ch. 9
Writing business memos, 542
Creating PowerPoints, 216
Writing in literature and other humanities (ch. 22), 486–509
Writing in the sciences and social sciences (ch. 23), 510–29
Reading critically (ch. 7), 112–42
Interpreting visuals, 126, 130–32, 134
Incorporating visuals, 98, 381, 428

More about
Writing Responsibly, tutorial preceding ch. 1
List of Writing Responsibly boxes, following the index
Devising a topic, 25–31
Finding information (ch. 13), 237–62
Using supporting evidence, 45–47
Evaluating sources (ch. 14), 263–78
Organizing, 39–44
Providing transitions, 59–60
Correcting grammar, 627–756 (part 8, Grammar Matters)
Correcting punctuation, 801–82 (part 10, Detail Matters)
Writing with flair, 557–626 (part 7, Style Matters)

1b Your Responsibilities to Your Topic

Examples of writers who did not take seriously their responsibility to their topic are everywhere. Here are three:

1. A six-year-old child who won tickets to a Hannah Montana concert with an essay about her father's Iraq War death; her father had *not* been killed in Iraq. She lost those tickets.
2. Jayson Blair, a *New York Times* reporter who concocted "eyewitness" stories about events in far-away places without leaving his apartment or witnessing them online; he was forced to resign.
3. The president of Raytheon Company, who plagiarized large sections of his book *Swanson's Unwritten Rules of Management* from a book published in 1944; he was fined a million dollars by the company's shareholders.

You treat your topic responsibly when you explore it thoroughly and creatively, rely on trustworthy sources, and offer supporting evidence that is accurate, relevant, and reliable. You show respect for your topic when you provide enough evidence to persuade readers of your claims and when you acknowledge viewpoints that do not support your position. In a college writing project, not fulfilling your responsibilities to your topic might lead to a bad grade. In the workplace, it could have great financial, even life-and-death, consequences: The Merck pharmaceutical company, for example, was accused of suppressing evidence that its drug Vioxx could cause heart attacks and strokes. As a result, Merck faced a host of lawsuits, trials, and out-of-court settlements.

> **More about**
> Avoiding hypothetical evidence, 46
> Avoiding altering images inappropriately, 81–85

> **Writing Responsibly** — Your Responsibilities as a Writer
>
> When you write, you have four areas of responsibility:
>
> 1. To your audience
> 2. To your topic
> 3. To other writers
> 4. To yourself

1c Your Responsibilities to Other Writers

You have important responsibilities to other writers whose work you may be using.

Acknowledge your sources Writing circulates easily today, and vast quantities of it are available online, readily accessible through search engines such as *Bing* and *Google* and databases such as *JSTOR* and *ProQuest*. It may seem natural, then, simply to copy the information you need from a source and paste it into your own text, as you might if you were collecting information

> **More about**
> Using a search engine, 242–44
> Using an online database, 246–51
> Using an electronic library catalog, 251–54

More about
When to quote, paraphrase, or summarize, 292–94
Using quotation marks (ch. 51), 834–42
Formatting block quotations, 339, 346, 380–81, 836–37
Adjusting quotations using brackets and ellipses, 840, 851, 856–57

about a disease you were facing or a concert you hoped to attend. But when you provide readers with information, ideas, language, or images that others have curated or created, you also have a responsibility to *acknowledge* those sources. Such acknowledgment gives credit to those who contributed to your thinking, and it allows your audience to read your sources for themselves. Acknowledging your sources protects you from charges of plagiarism, and it builds your authority and credibility as a writer by establishing that you have reviewed key sources on a topic and have taken other writers' views into consideration.

To acknowledge sources ethically in academic writing, you must do *all* of the following:

1. When quoting, copy accurately and use quotation marks or block indention to signal the beginning and end of the copied passage; when paraphrasing or summarizing, put the ideas fully into your own words and sentences.
2. Include an in-text citation to the source, regardless of whether you are quoting, paraphrasing, or summarizing.
3. Document the source, providing enough information for your readers to locate the source and to identify the type of source you used. This documentation usually appears in a bibliography (often called a list of works cited or a reference list) at the end of college research projects.

More about
Citing and documenting sources, 329–486 (part 5, Documentation Matters)
Avoiding plagiarism and "patchwriting," 286, 312–14

Writing Responsibly around the World Concepts of plagiarism vary from one culture or context to another. Where one may see cooperation, another may see plagiarism. Even if borrowing ideas and language without acknowledgment is a familiar custom for you, writers in the United States (especially in academic contexts) must explicitly acknowledge all ideas and information borrowed from another source.

Obtain copyright clearance While plagiarism is concerned with acknowledging sources of ideas or language, copyright focuses on the right to compensation for the use of writers' words and ideas in a public context. When writers use a substantial portion of another writer's text, they must not only acknowledge the source but may also need to obtain the original author's permission, often in exchange for a fee.

As a student, your use of sources is generally covered under the *fair use* provision of US copyright law, which allows you to include copyrighted material without permission when you are doing your college assignments. What counts as fair use cannot be expressed in percentages or checklists.

> **Quick Reference** — **Your College's Plagiarism Policy**
>
> Most colleges publish their plagiarism policies in their student handbook, which is often available online. **Find your plagiarism policy** by searching the student handbook's table of contents or index. Or search your college's website, using key terms such as *plagiarism, cheating policy, academic honesty,* or *academic integrity*. Before writing a research project, **read your school's plagiarism policy** carefully. If you are unsure what the policy means, talk with your adviser or instructor. In addition to the general policy for your college, **read your course syllabi** carefully to see what specific guidelines your instructors may provide there.

The Center for Social Media at American University provides a "Codes of Best Practices" website that can guide you through your fair use of multiple media. If you copy someone else's text or music files without permission, you are violating copyright. But if you are using parts of a text or a song for educational purposes, and if you are not interfering with the copyright owner's ability to profit from the material, you are making fair use of it and do not need the copyright owner's permission. Because plagiarism and copyright are separate issues, though, you must always acknowledge your source, even when no permission is needed.

Copyright protections also apply to you as a writer: Anything you write is protected by US copyright law—even your college assignments.

Treat other writers fairly Your responsibility to other writers does not end with the need to acknowledge your use of their ideas or language. You must also represent *accurately* and *fairly* what your sources say: Quoting selectively to distort meaning or taking a comment out of context is irresponsible. So is treating other writers with scorn.

> **More about**
> Bias, 600–3
> *Ad hominem*, 180

It is completely acceptable to criticize the ideas of others. In fact, examining ideas under the bright light of careful scrutiny and debate is central to higher education. But, contrary to what can be seen in online chat rooms and social media, treating the people who developed the ideas with derision is not. Avoid *ad hominem* (personal) attacks, and focus your attention on other writers' ideas and their expression of them.

1d Your Responsibilities to Yourself

Your writing is an expression of your identity, and the act of writing is a means of enacting one's sense of self. Writers represent themselves on paper and screen through the words and images (and even sounds) they

> **More about**
> Synthesis, 133
> Common sentence problems (Grammar Matters tutorial preceding ch. 33), 628–33

More about
Style, 557–626 (part 7, Style Matters)
Grammar, 627–756 (part 8, Grammar Matters)
Punctuation and mechanics, 801–82 (part 10, Detail Matters)

create and borrow. Readers draw conclusions about the person who wrote the text, even when they don't know the author. To take responsibility for yourself as a writer, make sure that the writing "avatar," or *persona,* you create is the best representation of yourself it can be. Encourage readers to view you with respect by treating others—not only other writers but also other people and groups—respectfully and without bias. Earn your audience's respect by synthesizing information from sources to produce new and compelling ideas and by using language clearly, correctly, logically, and with flair.

If you graduate from college having learned to be an effective writer, you will have learned something that employers value highly. More importantly, though, you will have fulfilled a key responsibility to yourself.

Writing Responsibly | Taking Yourself Seriously as a Writer

Many students enter writing classes thinking of themselves as "bad writers." This belief can be a self-fulfilling prophecy: Students fail to engage because they already believe they are doomed to fail. Remember that writing is not an inborn talent but a skill to be learned. Instead of thinking of yourself as a bad writer, think of yourself as a writer in progress, someone who has something to say and who is learning how to say it effectively. If you speak or have studied another language, think of yourself as someone who is learning to draw on that experience.

to SELF

EXERCISE 1.1 Assessing the writer's responsibilities

Read "Plagiarism an Issue on Campus, Faculty Says," written by California State University–Fresno student Megan Ginsie for her college newspaper *The Collegian*. To what extent do you agree with Ginsie's argument? What reservations do you have about it? What other writers' responsibilities might a revision of the article take into account?

Student Model Newspaper Article

Plagiarism an Issue on Campus, Faculty Says

By MEGAN GINSIE

"The first time I ever saw it, I found it in one paper. Then I started looking in other papers, and it was horrible. I lost five pounds, because it was personal. I felt like [my students] were cheating on me."

Fresno State communication professor Judith Scott had a problem. In 2006, Scott caught a student plagiarizing. [S]he began to search for others. "[T]hat was when I found out approximately 50 percent of my students were plagiarizing," Scott said.

Ida Jones, a business professor, said she found a similar case of plagiarism that year. Thirty percent of students in her graduate business ethics and law class cheated on their take-home midterm assignment. "I was just shocked," Jones said.

Scott and Jones decided to start a plagiarism and cheating workshop for students and faculty. The workshop aims to help prevent plagiarism on campus, as well as to find more data about why students were cheating. Since [then], Scott said the plagiarism rate in her classes has dropped to about 8 percent. However, that hasn't stopped some students from trying. "[I]f you don't get [taught about plagiarism] in high school, and nobody recognizes it, you just keep doing it," Jones said.

"We did a study a number of years ago, just asking faculty what percentage of students they thought plagiarize, and the faculty said something like 20 percent, and the students said around 80 percent. So, obviously, there's a gap in how the faculty are reading it, or that they aren't reporting it but just letting it slide" [Jones said].

Scott agreed with Jones, but said, "It took [faculty] a while to understand what we were doing and how big of a problem it really was, and once they saw it, we have at least tripled [. . .] the charges on campus."

Quentin Sanford, a finance student, said stress and time-management play a role. "We are trained to pass a test, to achieve a certain grade percentage, and to move forward to the next step," Sanford said. "Because of this, many students fall into plagiarism because of the demand to perform, and lack of engagement. I believe fewer students would violate the honor code if their pursuit was closer aligned to learning rather than passing."

Another consequence for students who plagiarize is the depreciation of a college degree. [. . .] Scott said, "I have a degree from this university . . . and I think it's important that the value stays attached to [it]."

Text Credits

Pg. 4–6 Source: Final Research Report, Isabel's Portfolio; **Pg. 12–13** Megan Ginsie, "Plagiarism an issue on campus, faculty says," *The Collegian*, 2015. Used with permission.

2 Planning Your Project

IN THIS CHAPTER

a. Writing situation, 14

b. Analyzing an assignment, 23

c. Generating ideas, topics, 25

d. Narrowing, broadening a topic, 31

e. Collaboration, 32

Student Models
For **Michael Wedd,** "Issues with Alternative Energy" (First Draft): **Freewrite,** 27; **Brainstorm to Generate Ideas,** 28; **Idea Cluster,** 29; **Journalists' Questions,** 30; **Brainstorm to Narrow a Topic,** 32

Krista Kennedy

Just as a needleworker designs a pattern before beginning a new creation, so, too, does a writer create a plan that takes into account the project's purpose, audience, context, and genre. Just as a needleworker gathers tools such as yarn, crochet hook, and scissors that are needed for completing the design, a writer must select an engaging topic, devise ideas that will resonate with the reader, fulfill the terms of the assignment, and do it all on time.

2a Analyzing Your Writing Situation

A first step in planning a writing project is to consider your *writing situation* (or *rhetorical situation*):

- What is your **purpose**? What might you accomplish with the text?

- Who is your **audience**? Who will be reading the text you produce, and why?

- What **topics** might interest them, and why? What information about the topic might the audience be expected already to know, and what might you need to explain?

- What **tone** is appropriate to your purpose and audience?

- What are the **context** (academic, business, personal) and **genre** (or type) of writing you will produce (research report, résumé, *Facebook* status update)? How will your context and genre affect the way you write this project?

Rhetorical situations are seldom stable; your purpose may shift as you develop your project, for example, or your tone may change as you get to know your audience. Be flexible and keep the needs of that audience in mind at all times. Throughout the writing process—planning, drafting, revising, and editing—you can refine or reconsider your initial decisions.

1. Establish a purpose.

Writers write for a variety of reasons, or *purposes*: to entertain, inform, or persuade an audience; or for the writer's own self-expression or learning.

- **To entertain.** Entertaining your readers (by providing them with an engaging reading experience) is a goal all writers share, but it is unlikely to be your primary purpose in academic or business writing.

- **To express feelings or beliefs.** In *expressive* writing, an experience is often conveyed through *description,* and the language is richly evocative. The purpose of the following paragraph is expressive; the writer's goal is to convey the feelings and experiences of a small would-be ballerina.

> *More about*
> Description, 64

> She stood in the doorframe shivering. She was a tiny girl, about four years old, and her wispy blonde hair was tied back with a pink satin ribbon. Leaning against her mother's leg, she gazed into the unfamiliar room. Other girls her age were twirling and jumping with confidence, laughing at their reflections in the mirrors, spinning on the slippery wooden floors. The girl's mother handed her the ballet shoes, gave her a quick peck on the cheek, and stepped back into the snowstorm. Alone now, the girl retreated to the wall and slid into a dark corner. She bent her knees against her chest and wrapped her arms around her legs. There she sat.
> —Amanda Godfrey, McHenry County College, "Ballet Blues"

In most college courses, an expressive purpose is unlikely to be primary, but it may well play a secondary role, as you draw on your own experiences to illustrate a point.

Writing about Personal Experiences Depending on your life experiences, writing about personal issues and experiences may seem odd in an academic writing course. Instructors at US colleges and universities, however, sometimes assign expressive essays as a way to get their students to write about something they already know. If you are uncomfortable writing on a personal topic, discuss the issue with your instructor.

- **To inform.** An *informative* (or *expository*) text may explain a concept, describe a sequence of events or a process, or analyze a relationship. Scientific, technical, journalistic, and business writing are typically informative. The abstract below, which comes from a psychology research project, is expository because it informs the reader of the results of a psychological study:

  > This study explores the potential influence of stereotypical appearances on male subjects' stated opinions regarding entertainment perceived as "feminine." The findings show that participants were more likely to give a favorable ranking of a "chick flick" in the presence of a counter-stereotypical male than in the presence of a stereotypical male. The discussion focuses on possible explanations for participant behavior, with a theoretical basis in gender role conflict.
  >
  > —Heather DeGroot, James Madison University, "The Power of Wardrobe: Male Stereotype Influences"

> **Student Models**
> Informative projects:
> **Michael Wedd,**
> "Rethinking Alternative Energy" (Final Draft), 100–5
> **Robyn Worthington,**
> "Nature vs. Nurture," 430–38

- **To persuade or argue.** Texts that try to convince readers to adopt beliefs or opinions or to take action have a *persuasive* (or *argumentative*) purpose. Editorials, book and movie reviews, grant proposals, and much academic writing have a persuasive purpose. The paragraph below comes from an editorial. It draws on evidence from studies to support its claim that Head Start is a worthwhile program:

  > Head Start, the federally funded pre-kindergarten program, has been under attack recently as a waste of money, because some say the effects don't last long enough to make a difference later in life. I beg to differ. Studies show that eighth graders who were in Head Start do as well as kids who received education from a private pre-school. Poor children who do not attend Head Start do no better than their parents. To raise our population out of poverty, children must learn at an early age to have confidence, have goals and strive for them, and receive the best education they can. Head Start provides a good start.
  >
  > —Lynn Holmlund, Bentley College, "Going Public: Head Start"

> **More about**
> Analyzing and crafting arguments (ch. 8), 143–82

- **To learn.** As writers struggle to find the words to express a complex thought, they are actually struggling to understand what they are writing about. "How do I know what I think until I see what I say?" the writer E. M. Forster is quoted as saying. Writing a summary of a source involves pushing oneself to understand that

> **More about**
> Summary (ch. 15), 295–97
> Rogerian argument (ch. 8), 175–76

source. Explaining its relationship to another source involves thinking critically about both sources. Many college writing assignments are designed not only to have you practice your writing techniques but also to help you grasp the material you are writing about. The work of psychologist Carl Rogers inspired a method of argument, *Rogerian argument*, whose purpose is not so much to persuade an audience but to explore possible interpretations of and solutions to difficult topics.

EXERCISE 2.1 Analyzing purpose

Read the following passages and determine whether the primary purpose of each passage is expressive, informative, or persuasive:

> Camels do not store water in their humps. They drink furiously, up to twenty-eight gallons in a ten-minute session, then distribute the water evenly throughout their bodies. Afterward, they use the water stingily. They have viscous urine and dry feces. They breathe through their noses, and keep their mouths shut. They do sweat, but only as a last resort, after first allowing their body temperatures to rise 10 degrees Fahrenheit. As they begin to dehydrate, the volume of their blood plasma does not at first diminish. They can survive a water loss of up to one-third of their body weight, then drink up and feel fine. Left alone, unhurried and unburdened, they can live two weeks between drinks.
>
> —William Langewiesche, *Sahara Unveiled*

> Gentlemen, I want you to suppose a case for a moment. Suppose that all the property you were worth was in gold, and you had to put it in the hands of Blondin, the famous rope-walker, to carry across the Niagara Falls on a tight rope. Would you shake the rope while he was passing over it, or keep shouting to him, "Blondin, stop a little more! Go a little faster!"? No. I am sure you would not. You would hold your breath as well as your tongue and keep your hand off until he was safely over. Now the Government is in the same situation. It is carrying an immense weight across a stormy ocean. Untold treasures are in its hands. It is doing the best it can. Don't badger it! Just keep still, and it will get you safely over.
>
> —Abraham Lincoln, "Reply to Critics of His Administration"

> Have you ever had to ask for help, knowing your children will suffer unless you get it? Think about asking for a loan from a relative, if this is the only way you can imagine asking for help. I will tell you how it feels. You find out where the office is that you are supposed to visit. You circle that block four or five times. Thinking of your children, you go in.

> Everybody is very busy. Finally, someone comes out and you tell her that you need help. That never is the person you need to see. You go see another person, and after spilling the whole shame of your poverty all over the desk between you, you find that this isn't the right office after all—you might repeat the whole process, and it never is any easier at the next place.
>
> —Jo Goodwin Parker, "What Is Poverty?"

2. Identify and address your audience.

A text is seldom written for the writer alone. Rather, it is intended for an *audience,* and this fact shapes the text in large and small ways. That is why, for a piece of writing to be effective, the writer must make a careful analysis of the intended reader (or readers) and keep the needs of that audience in mind throughout the writing process.

Before writing, consider the characteristics of your audience, such as age and gender, occupation and interests, educational background, abilities, sexualities and identities, political or cultural affiliations, possible biases and ethnic or religious background. Then, consider the audience's expectations:

- Are your readers already well informed about the topic, or are they reading your text to learn about something new?
- Are your readers eager to learn about your topic, or do they have only a passing interest?
- Do readers hold strong opinions about your topic, or are they likely to be open-minded?

Next, consider what will make your writing most effective for this audience:

- **What information will your audience need in order to understand and appreciate what you are saying?** A general audience will need you to define all specialized terms as you use them, as well as to provide any background information necessary for them to understand the topic. A specialist audience, on the other hand, may be bored by too much explanation, but these readers will still need you to define any terms you are using in an unusual sense and to provide background information about aspects of the topic likely to fall outside of their area of expertise. An instructor, while an expert, may expect you to write for a nonspecialist reader.
- **What kinds of language, examples, or evidence will be most effective?** Someone arguing for the legalization of marijuana in front of

a group of college students might make very different choices than would someone arguing the same position in front of an audience filled with parents or police officers.

One way to write for an audience is to picture a few specific people (representative of your audience) and then to think about what each of them will need in order to understand and appreciate what you are saying.

Writing for a Multilingual Audience If you have a different cultural or linguistic background than your prospective readers—whether you are a native English speaker or not—try to find classmates, peers, instructors, tutors, or advisers who may share experiences with the readers you have in mind. They might be able to help you determine how much background information your readers will need and what kinds of evidence they will find most effective.

The excerpt below shows a writer crafting a text with her audience in mind:

> Dear Governor:
>
> Your effort to improve education has been quite extensive. Throughout these past few years the creation of after-school programs that have offered tutoring for students has been possible because of your involvement. You have also formed the National Teachers Academy in Illinois, which works to improve the quality of teaching in schools. In addition, you secured several hundred million dollars that gave libraries the ability to replace many outdated books. Although you have made some great accomplishments for education, the conditions of our schools still call for much improvement. By striving to implement a voucher system, you could cause a nationwide education reform, and give every child a chance at a quality education. . . .
>
> —Amanda Godfrey, McHenry County College

> **More about**
> Writing letters
> (ch. 25), 537–56

By imagining the governor's reactions, what he might appreciate and what he might resist, Godfrey knows to start her letter by listing the actions he has already taken to improve the state's schools. *Then* Godfrey argues for a new school voucher program.

In much of your college writing, you will have an audience of one—your instructor. To satisfy that audience, begin with a careful analysis of what the instructor hopes you will learn from the assignment. These objectives may be specified in the assignment or in the course syllabus, but sometimes you will simply need to ask. Generally, your instructor will be a specialist reader who wants to be reassured that you have done

> **More about**
> Reading to comprehend, 112–16
> Reading to reflect, 119–26
> Reading to write, 127–35
> Analysis, 127–32
> Synthesis, 133

the reading, understood the issues, and synthesized the information from classroom lectures, discussions, and assigned reading. In addition, most instructors want to see that you can express yourself clearly and correctly in writing. To accomplish these goals, provide the following:

- Important background information
- Definitions of key terms
- Explanations of key concepts
- Analysis of the issues
- Synthesis of evidence from assigned reading and classroom discussion to support claims
- Synthesis of *counterevidence* (opposing or alternative interpretations or opinions) from assigned reading and classroom discussion, to provide a whole picture
- Citations and a list of works cited or references for source-based writing

> **More about**
> Citing and documenting sources, 312–27 (MLA style), 334–96 (APA style), 397–438 (*Chicago* style), 439–69 (CSE style), 470–84

Writing Responsibly — Seeing and Showing the Whole Picture

As a writer, you have a responsibility to look beyond your own experiences and beliefs, beyond your own self-interest. As you explore an issue, give thorough, respectful attention to interpretations that contradict or conflict with yours. Figure out what motivates the supporters of opposing positions. Consider whether your own opinion should be revised. Then, as you write, no matter which position you support in your text, let your audience see all the viewpoints and the reasons for them.

to AUDIENCE

3. Match your tone to your purpose and your audience.

When you speak, your *tone* of voice, gestures, facial expressions, and body language all convey your attitude. Are you patient, annoyed, angry, pleasantly surprised? All of these attitudes are conveyed in a moment by the pitch of your voice or the look on your face. Writers convey their attitude toward their readers and their subject through their tone. In writing, tone is conveyed primarily through **level of diction** (formal or informal) and the ***connotation*** (emotional resonance) of the words you choose. To write at a formal level of diction, use standard American English; avoid regionalisms (such as *y'all*), colloquial language (such as *what up*), and slang (such as *hot* rather than *good* or *exciting*); and write in complete sentences (*Are you coming?* rather than just *Coming?*).

> **More about**
> Developing a thesis, 35–38
> Level of diction, 599
> Connotation and denotation, 604–6

Although most college instructors will expect you to adopt a formal level of diction, the individual decisions you make will vary from one writing situation to another. In some courses, using the first-person pronoun *I* might be perfectly acceptable or even required, but for others (such as economics and sociology) it might be considered too informal.

> **Recognizing Differences in Connotation** A word in your first language might share a literal meaning with a word in another language but have a very different connotation. The word *ambitious* ("eager for success"), for example, can be positive or negative in English; in Spanish, *ambición* is generally negative. If you are not sure how key words are used by your prospective readers, consult a cross-language or bilingual dictionary or check with classmates, a writing tutor, or your instructor.

> More about
> Dictionaries for second-language learners, 614

> More about
> Writing in literature and the other humanities, 485–509
> Writing in the sciences and social sciences, 510–29
> Exploratory arguments, 159–74
> Considering alternative viewpoints, 156–58

Whatever the particular demands of your course, all disciplines expect you to adopt a reasoned tone. In general, opt for connotatively neutral language: Shrill or sarcastic prose will suggest to your audience that your opinions spring from your heart and not your head. This does not mean that emotional topics are off limits or that you may not express your beliefs, but temperance (moderation, self-restraint) is highly valued in academic discourse. Your instructor will expect you to have looked at all sides of an issue carefully before drawing a conclusion and to exhibit respect for those with whom you disagree.

Make It **Your Own**

Draft a paragraph on one of the topics below as if you were writing to knowledgeable adults (perhaps even college professors). Carefully consider your purpose and your audience as you do so. Next, revise the paragraph to address an audience of high school students. Finally, revise it to appeal to a general audience.

1. The importance of participating in local government
2. Restrictions on language, dress, and behavior in public schools
3. Cell phone etiquette
4. Individual participation in recycling projects

Work **Together**

Working in pairs or small groups, compare your paragraphs with those of your classmate(s). Are the purpose and audience clear for each? Discuss the connotations of specific words, assess the

> level of formality of each sample paragraph, and point to words or sentences that make the diction more formal or less formal.
>
> Next, write a paragraph reflecting on this process. Consider the similarities and differences you observed among the paragraphs and the things that surprised you. Make a note of the challenges you faced as you drafted your paragraphs and how you responded to those challenges. List the strategies you plan to use next time you write for a specific audience.

4. Consider context and genre.

> **More about**
> Business writing, 537–56
> Public writing, 537–40, 552–55

As earlier sections on addressing an academic audience have implied, the *context* (or setting) in which your text is to be read will affect all your writing decisions. So, too, will the *genre* (or type) of writing you produce.

The contexts in which you are likely to write, now and in the future, are *academic, business, public,* and *personal.* Like academic writing, business writing generally adopts a formal level of diction and uses words with neutral connotations. Public writing, which ranges from blog posts to press releases and reports, generally maintains a formal level of diction (it is directed to a wide-ranging audience), but its tone may be more impassioned than would be appropriate in an academic or business context. An informal tone is most appropriate in a personal context, but even then, the audience makes a difference: A casual, bantering tone and highly informal level of diction might be appropriate in a text message to a friend, while a warm but slightly more formal tone might be appropriate for an email to a grandparent. Nor is the distinction between public and private communications always clear: A post in a lifestyle blog might be public and widely circulated, but it might also be quite informal. Whenever you write in an unfamiliar context, consulting examples can help you hit the right note.

> **Student Models**
> Editorial (public), 12–13
> Essay (academic), 47–50, 99–105, 135–39, 535–36
> Research project (academic), 383–96, 430–38, 459–69, 516–28
> Essay exam (academic), 535–36
> Memo (business), 543
> Résumés (business), 548, 550

> **Professional Models**
> Article (public), 121–24
> Essay (public), 116–19
> Review (public), 507–9
> Letter (business), 541
> Business report (business), 553
> Press release (public), 554

In literature classes, you may have learned that poetry, drama, fiction, and nonfiction were the four major literary genres, but genre extends beyond literature to include social media posts, presentation software, narratives, and the like. If you are unfamiliar with the genre in which you will be writing, it may be helpful to find several examples of that genre and think about what characteristics they have in common. This handbook contains sample documents in a variety of genres. Your instructor may also be able to provide examples, or you could locate examples in your library or on the internet. Whether you are writing a business email, a scientific report, a grant proposal, or a letter to the editor, the expectations readers have for this type of writing will affect every choice you make.

2b Analyzing an Assignment

Recognizing the purpose of an assignment is crucial to your success in completing it. If you are asked to *argue* for or against the goals of the plain speech movement of the 1920s, for example, and, instead, you *describe* those goals, you will probably not get an A. When analyzing an assignment, look for words that indicate purpose.

The audience for an assignment is, of course, your instructor, and the instructor's goal in assigning the project is to assess your knowledge of the facts, to gauge how well you have synthesized this information with other knowledge, and to assess your ability to express your understanding in writing. Occasionally, your instructor may ask you to imagine another audience—the readership of a particular magazine, for example.

Frequently, an assignment will specify the approach you should take. If you are asked to analyze, your instructor will expect you to break a topic, issue, or text into its component parts and, perhaps, evaluate each one. If your instructor asks you to summarize a reading assignment, you will be expected to write the main idea and key supporting points briefly, in your own words and using your own sentence structures.

Sometimes, an assignment will specify the genre, although the genre may be taken for granted. A biology instructor teaching a laboratory class may assume that you understand that a laboratory report is required. If you are not sure what the genre of the assignment is, or what it requires, ask your instructor.

> **More about**
> Analyzing,
> 127–32, 308–11
> Summarizing,
> 114–15

Quick Reference — Analyzing the Purpose of an Assignment

If the assignment asks you to . . .	The purpose is . . .	The approach is . . .
describe, explain	informative (expository)	to put into words what something looks, sounds, feels, smells, or tastes like; to discuss *how* something functions
assess, evaluate, argue	persuasive	to make a judgment based on evidence or offer an interpretation based on close reading, and to explain *why*
analyze, consider, discuss	informative or persuasive	to break a topic, reading assignment, or issue into its component parts and explain how it works; to reflect critically on the pros and cons of an issue, offer an interpretation based on a close reading, and sometimes explain why you have reached this conclusion

> **More about**
> Time management, 223–24
> Online assignment calendar, 224

Finally, an assignment will usually include a due date. In order to meet that date, you will have to create a realistic schedule. Start by listing the steps in the writing process in reverse order on a sheet of paper or in a new computer file so that you can work back from the due date. Next, list all your other obligations: other assignments, studying for exams, work, rehearsals or team practices, family and social obligations. Then work backward to figure out how much time you can allot to each task. The more obligations you have, the more time you will need to leave between steps. Finally, write the intermediate due dates on a calendar—a date book, the calendar on your computer, or your phone. For each of these due dates, write down not just the name of the project ("English paper") but also the specific action that you need to have taken by that date ("outline English paper"). A schedule for a five-page project that does not require research might look like that shown in Figure 2.1.

SEPTEMBER

Sunday	Monday	Tuesday	Wednesday	Thursday	Friday	Saturday
		19 Track meet	20	21 Comp. assignment distributed	22 Analyze Comp. assignment and writing situation	23 Work Date with Jordan
24 Generate ideas, develop topic, draft thesis for comp. paper	25 Review notes, draft outline for comp. paper	26 Study for Econ quiz	27 Write first draft, make appt. at Writing Center	28 Econ quiz	29 Bring draft to class for peer review	30 Work

OCTOBER

Sunday	Monday	Tuesday	Wednesday	Thursday	Friday	Saturday
1 Lunch with Mom & Dad	2 Bring essay to Writing Center	3 Revise comp. essay →	4	5	6 → Revise comp. essay	7 Work Proofread & edit comp. paper
8 Format & print comp. paper	9 Comp. paper due	10 Study for psych midterm →	11	12	13 → Psych midterm!	14 Work

FIGURE 2.1 A sample calendar
Your calendar will differ depending on the complexity of the assignment, the time you have to complete it, and your other obligations.

EXERCISE 2.2 Analyzing an assignment

Read the following assignments; indicate whether their purpose is informative, persuasive, or both; and underline the words that indicate purpose.

1. Describe two or three medical services available to families in your community, and explain how a family nurse-practitioner could use these services.
2. Evaluate the constitutionality of judicial review, explaining its origins and offering several examples from US Supreme Court decisions.
3. Analyze the impact an increase in the price of higher education in the United States would have on the market for higher education in India.
4. Assess the main arguments of Handlin's *Boston's Immigrants* (1941) in light of the other assigned course reading. Are they still persuasive? Why or why not?

Make It Your Own

For an upcoming writing assignment or one already under way, analyze the assignment and set up a schedule that takes into account all your other obligations.

2c Generating Ideas, Topics

For some writing projects, especially in college or business, your *topic* will often be assigned. When you are required to come up with a topic on your own, ask yourself these questions:

- What topics are appropriate to the assignment?
- What topics will interest, annoy, or intrigue me *and* my audience?
- What topics do I have special access to or knowledge about?

You will be most engaged when you choose a topic that interests you, but your audience will be most engaged when you offer some special knowledge or insight into what you are writing about. You can create that special knowledge by doing research, but you can also create special knowledge by thinking critically about your topic.

Invention techniques, like those outlined below, can help you devise and develop a topic. No single strategy works for everyone, and most writers use several methods. If you have tried some of these before, experiment with the others. Drawing on new techniques may increase your creativity.

> **More about**
> Finding information (ch. 13), 237–62
> Reading and thinking critically (ch. 7), 112–42

Generating Ideas in English or Your First Language If English is not your first language, you might find it helpful to keep a journal, freewrite, or brainstorm in English. If you get stuck, try using words and phrases from your first language. But be careful when returning to your notes to translate not merely your *words* but also your *ideas* into English appropriate for your readers.

1. Keep an idea journal or commonplace book.

In the nineteenth century, the philosopher Ralph Waldo Emerson wrote his essays from ideas he had jotted down in a notebook. In the twenty-first century, writers often use apps or online tools such as *Evernote, Google Docs,* or *OneNote* to store ideas. Whatever medium you use, you may find that keeping an ***idea journal*** or a ***commonplace book*** (or both) is an effective part of the creative process.

> *More about*
> Keeping a reading journal, 124–25
> Keeping a research log, 228–29

Like a diary, an idea journal is something to write in every day. Unlike a diary, it is not a record of your life but rather of your thoughts. A commonplace book records the ideas (quotations, summaries, paraphrases) of others that you might find useful in the future. You can also use your commonplace book to record your reactions to those ideas. As you jot notes in your commonplace book, record your sources and use quotation marks to separate carefully the words of others from your own.

> *More about*
> Avoiding accidental plagiarism, 286, 292–94

Writing Responsibly — Note Taking and Plagiarism

Many people have unintentionally plagiarized sources because of a faulty note-taking system, saying that they did not record the source when taking notes or that they failed to put quotation marks around passages they copied. To avoid finding yourself in such a situation, consider putting all quotations, summaries, and paraphrases in one column of your journal or commonplace book and your own comments and reactions in another. That way, even if you forget to put quotation marks around a quotation or to record a page number, you will not be lulled into believing the words or ideas were your own—and your sources will get proper credit.

to OTHER WRITERS

Make It **Your Own**

Keep an idea journal for one week. Write in it daily about the topics discussed in your classes, and at the end of the week read through your notes. What topics have arisen repeatedly? Which are most engaging? What ideas could be developed into a project?

2. Freewrite.

Have you ever found yourself sitting in front of a blank screen, knowing you had to begin writing but just not being able to get started? Try *freewriting:* writing the first thing that enters your head and then continuing to write nonstop for ten to fifteen minutes (or for a set number of pages). What you write about does not matter; if you draw a blank, just write (or type) the same word over and over again until something comes to you.

To be useful, freewriting must be fast and spontaneous. If you find that you cannot resist correcting and revising, turn the brightness down until your screen is very dim or even black. Here is a sample of freewriting for Michael Wedd's essay:

Student Models
Draft thesis, 36
Revised thesis, 37–38
Outlines, 42–43
Michael Wedd, First draft, "Issues with Alternative Energy," 47–50
Michael Wedd, Final draft, "Rethinking Alternative Energy," 99–105

Student Model Freewrite

> Drawing a blank about what to write about. Maybe should go to the park for a run. Need to figure out schedule for next sem. Can't decide b/w bio and environ science. Oooh, that reminds me I need to find out if I can recycle my old laptop somewhere.

Once the time has elapsed, read through what you wrote. Even among random thoughts you might find a usable idea. Michael Wedd's essay topic—the environmental movement—appears in this freewriting snippet, for example. But the exercise is also beneficial for freeing the mind and exorcising writer's block.

A variation of freewriting is *focused freewriting.* Instead of starting from the first idea to pop into your head, start from something specific: your topic, a quotation, a memory, an image. If you stray from the topic, just keep writing, trying to circle back to it.

3. Brainstorm.

Brainstorming (or *listing*) is writing down everything you can think of on a topic. Brainstorming helps get ideas percolating and provides a record of that percolation. Here is a snippet of brainstorming for Michael Wedd's essay on the environmental movement:

Student Model Brainstorm to Generate Ideas

- Types of alternative energy: solar, wind, hydro.
- Advantages/disadvantages of each.
- Alt energy may benefit consumers; might harm wildlife.
- Who is for it, against it. Their different arguments.
- Where is alt energy movement strongest, weakest? Why?
- Why alternatives to fossil fuels needed.
- History of oil exploration and development of alternatives.

After you have amassed a useful number of items, sort through the material to make connections: Move items around or draw lines to connect related items. Then brainstorm about the idea groups that seem most important, interesting, or challenging.

4. Cluster.

Clustering (or *mapping*) is a visual method for identifying and developing ideas. To create a cluster or idea map, follow these steps:

1. Write your topic in the middle of the page, and draw a circle around it.

2. Write other ideas related to your topic around the central idea bubble, and draw a circle around each of those.

3. Draw connecting lines from the word bubbles to the central topic or to the other word bubbles to show the relationships among the ideas.

When creating a cluster, keep two things in mind:

1. Keep your topic and idea notes brief—if you write more than a word or two, the diagram will quickly become difficult to read.

2. Use a pencil—you will probably make many changes as you work.

The cluster diagram on the next page (Figure 2.2) shows some of Michael Wedd's ideas for his project on alternative energy.

Writing Matters • Generating Ideas, Topics   **2c**   29

Student Model Idea Cluster

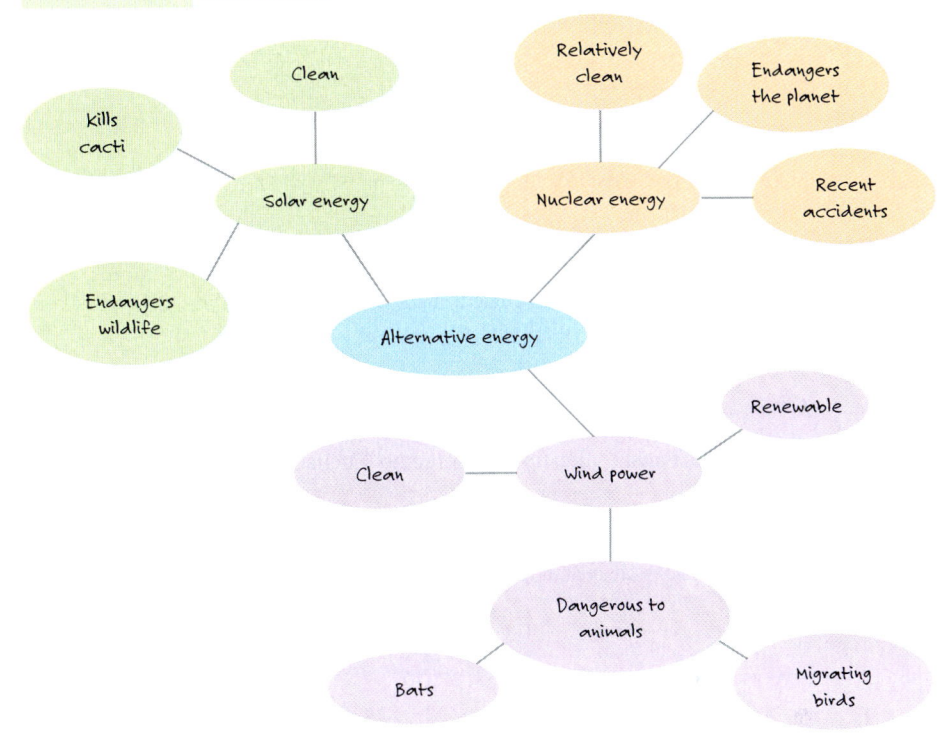

A cluster diagram centered on "Alternative energy" branching to:
- *Solar energy: Clean, Kills cacti, Endangers wildlife*
- *Nuclear energy: Relatively clean, Endangers the planet, Recent accidents*
- *Wind power: Renewable, Clean, Dangerous to animals (Bats, Migrating birds)*

FIGURE 2.2 A sample cluster diagram

> **Tech** Brainstorming with Word Clouds
>
> Your word choices echo the ideas and opinions that resonate most with you. You might process some of your early brainstorming through programs like Wordle to get "word clouds" of your most frequently used words. The visualization of that information may help you figure out what you're emphasizing, which can help lead you to your thesis.

5. Answer the journalists' questions.

The *journalists' questions*—*who, what, where, when, why,* and *how*—not only can help you generate ideas about your topic but also can help you figure out what you need to learn in order to write the paper. When considering a topic, ask yourself questions like these:

- **Who** are the key figures?
- **What** did they accomplish, or what are the issues?
- **Where** and **when** did the main events occur?
- **Why** did they do what they did, or why did these events transpire as they did?
- **How** did it happen?

As a college student, you will also benefit from adding two additional questions to the journalists' list:

- What is the **significance?**
- What are the **consequences?**

The journalists' questions tailored to Michael Wedd's topic are shown in Figure 2.3.

Student Model Journalists' Questions

> Who is affected by the building of wind farms? Who will benefit from their being built?
> What other sources of energy do we have? What impact do they have on the environment? What impact will the wind farms have?
> Where are wind farms being built?
> When will the wind farms go online? When will the courts rule on the challenges to these wind farms?
> Why is there disagreement within the environmental community about whether wind farms should be built?
> How will the issues be resolved? How can animals be protected?

FIGURE 2.3 The journalists' questions

6. Discuss your topics with friends and classmates.

Sometimes just informally chatting about possibilities with friends, family, classmates, tutors, or instructors can help you generate ideas. This can be as casual as a late-night chat with your roommate or texting with a friend ("What do you think about . . . ?"), or it can be as formal as a scheduled brainstorming session with a collaborative writing group. Whatever approach you take, keep the discussion open enough that people feel free to speak their minds but focused enough that your discussion does not drift too far from your topic, and always be ready to record ideas.

7. Use the internet, the library, and classroom tools.

Surfing the internet can provide direction and stimulate ideas when you are faced with a new topic. Start by searching a *subject directory,* a collection of websites organized into groups by topic and arranged hierarchically from most general to most specific to get a sense of the range of related subtopics. Subject directories are useful for narrowing or expanding your topic. For very current topics, searching a news site or locating a specialized blog can also be useful.

> **More about**
> Blogs, 245
> Evaluating online sources, 271–74

The reference sources provided by your college library are another resource for generating ideas. Browse through general encyclopedias and dictionaries to get a sense of how your topic is usually discussed, or turn to specialized dictionaries or encyclopedias to get a more detailed introduction. Some reference sources may be available online through your college library's website.

Finally, because you will often be writing about topics that were introduced in class, you can get ideas often by reading (or rereading) course materials, such as your textbook, class notes, and any handouts your instructor has distributed. Any of these may provide context or help you identify a topic that interests you.

> **More about**
> Reference sources, 238–41

Make It **Your Own**

Use focused freewriting, brainstorming, or clustering to develop one of the ideas that came out of your weeklong experiment with keeping an idea journal (p. 26) or an idea from the reading in one of your classes.

> **More about**
> Note taking, 127–33, 286
> Annotating, 119–24

2d Narrowing or Broadening a Topic

Once you have devised a topic, consider whether you can do justice to it in the assigned length. In most cases, you will need to narrow your topic further; occasionally, you may have to broaden it.

1. Narrow your topic.

To narrow a general topic, use brainstorming or one of the other idea-generating techniques to develop a list of subtopics. Michael Wedd wanted to write about alternative energy, but the topic was so big, he could not cover it in a three- to five-page project; he had to narrow it. Some of his possible subtopics are listed in the brainstorming example below.

Student Model Brainstorm to Narrow a Topic

> The green movement has been around for a while but has been gaining in recognition in recent years.
> Many aspects of the green/environmentalist movement: climate change, preservation, endangered species, alternatives to fossil fuels, etc.
> People can feel very strongly about these issues. Some modify how they eat and what they buy; some join groups like Greenpeace and are willing to be arrested and/or put themselves in danger to fight for change.
> Are there conflicts within the green movement? What might they entail?

2. Broaden your topic.

While you are much more likely to have to narrow your topic, you may occasionally find yourself struggling to come up with something to say about the topic you have selected, in which case your topic may be too narrow. If, for example, you were thinking about exploring whether social workers in your town are pressured to overreport their contact hours with Medicare patients, but you were finding too little research on this topic, you could broaden your topic by expanding the region (from social workers in your town to social workers throughout the country), or you could broaden the type of caregivers you studied by including medical personnel (doctors, nurses, and technicians) and social workers. The idea-generating techniques discussed in *section 2c* can help you broaden, as well as narrow, your topic.

2e Working with Others: Planning a Collaborative Project

In academic and professional contexts, collaborative work is common. Working in a group can be challenging, but there are several steps you can take to make collaborative work more satisfying and less frustrating.

1. Form a cohesive group.

Start group projects by establishing rapport. A few small steps taken at the outset can help:

- Meet face-to-face, at least at the start.
- Start your first meeting by having group members introduce themselves and mention some detail—hometown, favorite book, a special interest or talent—to help everyone get to know one another.
- Make an effort to learn everyone's name.
- Discuss members' skills and challenges. Learn what each member brings to the project: Is there a good proofreader in the group? A good designer? A good researcher? A good organizer? Consider, as well, accessibility issues within the group: Do any members have physical limitations that should be taken into account when assigning duties and schedules?
- Distribute the contact information, such as email addresses and phone numbers (with best times to call), for every group member at the end of the first session.

2. Anticipate pitfalls.

Anyone who has participated in a collaborative project knows that pitfalls abound: One person is consistently late, another lets other team members do all the work, a third dominates the proceedings, and a fourth is resentful but never says a word. Before starting a project, work together to figure out the likely pitfalls and to decide in advance how the group will respond:

- What will you do if someone does not complete assigned work?
- What will you do if someone does assigned work badly?
- How will you want the instructor to grade the completed project, if it is a class assignment?

Once you have developed a list of potential problems and how the group will resolve them, put it in writing, have everybody sign the document, and distribute copies to all members. This written agreement not only will provide a record but also will remind all members of their responsibilities to the group. If something does go wrong, address the problem immediately; do not let it fester.

> **Self Assessment**
>
> To ensure your group is effective, pause regularly to reflect on every member's contribution. Be sure every member participates in the following tasks:
> - ☐ Deciding on a topic
> - ☐ Drafting a thesis statement
> - ☐ Brainstorming ideas
> - ☐ Organizing the project
> - ☐ Assigning tasks

3. Devise a schedule and assign tasks.

> *More about*
> Analyzing the writing situation, 14–22
> Devising a topic, 25–31
> Drafting, 44–47
> Revising globally and locally, 86–93
> Drafting and revising visuals (ch. 5), 77–85
> Proofreading and formatting, 96–98

The writing process for individual projects applies to collaborative projects as well. Some additional steps include the following:

- Select a recorder. That role can be performed by one person or can rotate among group members.
- Brainstorm project ideas, making sure everyone participates.
- List component tasks (such as coordinating the group; researching the topic; drafting, revising, and editing the text; identifying or creating appropriate visuals).
- Establish dates by which each task needs to be completed, and construct a timetable.
- Divide the work among group members, taking into account people's talents, interests, and schedules and the difficulty of each task. Keep in mind that some phases of the project should be done by the entire group. (See the Self-Assessment checklist above.)
- Plan periodic meetings to discuss progress and problems.
- Distribute a schedule of meetings and due dates.

3 Organizing and Drafting Your Project

IN THIS CHAPTER

a. Thesis, 35
b. Organization, 39
c. Preparing to draft, 44
d. Drafting, 45
e. Collaboration, 51

Student Models
For **Michael Wedd,** "Issues with Alternative Energy" (First Draft): **Informal (Scratch) Outline,** 42; **Topic and Sentence Outlines,** 42; **First Draft of a Researched Essay** (MLA style, annotated), **Michael Wedd,** "Issues with Alternative Energy," 47

GaudiLab/Shutterstock

Before producing a new line of clothing or an automobile, designers sketch the product, planning and arranging the shapes before dressing them in colors and textures. Writers, too, begin with a plan. They take into account the writing situation (purpose, audience, topic, context, and genre), then sketch their ideas in words and arrange them in sentences and paragraphs. Designers and writers alike sometimes erase initial ideas and revise early efforts. Until that first sketch is penned, the finished work is merely an idea.

3a Crafting an Effective Thesis

A *thesis* is a brief statement (one or two sentences) of the central claim you will make. It not only identifies your topic but also gives your audience an indication of the focus and direction of your writing project. Drafting a preliminary thesis statement as early as possible and then testing, revising, and even replacing it as you learn more about your topic and develop your project will help you evaluate, focus, and clarify your ideas.

Stating the Main Idea In some contexts and cultures, it is appropriate to imply the main idea rather than state it explicitly. However, readers in the United States, especially in academic and business contexts, will usually expect you to express your main idea clearly and directly, usually at the beginning of your written document or project.

1. Devise a thesis statement.

Before you begin to draft a thesis, review your notes. Do any ideas jump out? If not, return to the idea-generating stage. If so, focus on an aspect of your topic that will engage you and your audience and that is appropriate to your purpose, context, and genre. Next, ask yourself probing questions about your topic and then answer them. Review your answers, looking for ones that identify your topic and make a claim about it. Choose one that will allow you to bring your own insights to the topic, and use that as your preliminary thesis. Here are some sample questions and answers, with the claim highlighted in yellow and the topic underlined:

> **More about**
> Generating ideas, 25–31

Questions	Answers
What drove the ivory-billed woodpecker to near-extinction in the United States?	The direct effects of the two world wars led to the near-extinction of the ivory-billed woodpecker.
What kinds of privacy violations or other social mischief occur with social networking sites like *Snapchat, Instagram,* and *Facebook*?	Social networking sites open new avenues for privacy violations and other social dangers, such as publication of incriminating photographs, stalking, and contact with inappropriate new "friends."
What motivates students to plagiarize, and what can we do to reduce the number of incidents?	Reducing the incidents of plagiarism among college students requires understanding its causes, which include late-night desperation, fear of a bad grade, lack of interest in a course, ignorance of citation requirements, and societal norms.

Student Model
Exploratory argument (researched, MLA style, annotated):
Brianna Davids, "Inmate Access to Technology: Safer Prisons and More Successful Reentries to Society," 159–74.

If you are not sure how to answer your question, use idea-generating techniques to develop possibilities.

> **EXERCISE 3.1 Selecting a topic and developing a preliminary thesis**

Make a list of at least five topics that interest you. Select two of the topics (or two from the following list) and write one or more questions for each. Then answer those questions to create a preliminary thesis.

Optional Topics

1. Trolls on social media
2. Compulsory military service

3. Standardized testing
4. The COVID pandemic

Underline each of your two topics, and circle your claims.

2. Revise a thesis statement.

A well-crafted thesis statement will indicate your topic and make a claim that is appropriate to your purpose and will be expressed in language that will engage the audience. Only rarely does a writer accomplish all of these objectives in the first draft of the thesis. Most writers need to revise the thesis statement repeatedly as they draft.

Purpose: Informative The thesis of an *informative* project makes a *claim of fact*, a claim that can be verified. To be engaging, an informative thesis must make a claim of fact that is not yet widely known to or accepted by the audience, and it must be specific enough that the writer can explore it in depth.

> **More about**
> Claims of fact, 146–47
> Common knowledge, 283–84

DRAFT THESIS
This paper is about conflicts within the environmental movement. — Topic

This draft thesis establishes a topic but does not make a claim of fact, and it is far too general to explore in depth.

REVISION 1—FOR AN INFORMATIVE PROJECT
There are many conflicts within the environmental movement. — Topic

This thesis statement establishes the topic and makes a claim of fact, but the claim is too general. Because the writer has not specified which conflicts she has in mind, she would potentially have to explain all possible conflicts within the environmental movement to satisfy the promise of the thesis.

Self Assessment

When revising a thesis, ask yourself the following questions. If the answer to any question is no, make the revisions necessary to strengthen your thesis.
- ☐ Does your thesis identify your **topic**?
- ☐ Does it indicate your **purpose** (informative or persuasive)?
- ☐ Does it make a **claim** (or assertion) that you can support—a claim of fact (a verifiable issue) for an informative project, or a claim of judgment or value (a belief or opinion that can be supported by credible, unbiased evidence) for a persuasive project?
- ☐ Will it **interest** your readers?

REVISION 2—FOR AN INFORMATIVE PROJECT

[Topic] Among the |conflicts within the environmental movement| is the one between those who want to reduce global warming by replacing fossil fuels with alternatives like wind energy and solar energy, and those who fear that new energy-generating plants will harm local wildlife.

The thesis statement now narrows the claim—makes it specific—so that it focuses solely on one area of conflict within the environmental movement. It will intrigue readers interested in environmental issues and will inform those who know little about the conflicts.

> **More about**
> Claims of value, 147
> Claims of judgment, 148–49

Purpose: Persuasive The thesis of a *persuasive* writing project must make a *claim of value* (a belief about the way the world should be) or *judgment* (an opinion or a provisional decision that is not widely shared). The claim must be one that can be supported with credible, unbiased evidence. The revised informative thesis above clearly specifies a topic and will probably intrigue readers, but it is not appropriate for a persuasive project because it makes a claim of fact, not a claim of value or judgment.

REVISION 3—FOR A PERSUASIVE PROJECT

[Topic] As serious and time-sensitive as the issue of climate change is, |alternative energy| is not a solution if it will be just as harmful to wildlife as conventional energy.

This thesis still specifies the topic, but it now also makes a *claim of judgment* ("alternative energy is not a solution"). Because it is narrow, focusing on just one issue ("alternative energy [that] is . . . harmful to wildlife"), it can be explained in a brief essay. And because it demonstrates the importance of the topic ("As serious and time-sensitive as the issue of climate change is"), it is likely to interest readers.

Because it makes clear that there are multiple legitimate opinions about the issue, it invites readers to engage with the problem.

Your thesis statement should focus on a claim you can support and that will interest your reader. Evaluate whether the evidence you provide for your thesis statement is unbiased and credible, and whether it supports the claim. If not, either find more pertinent evidence or revise your thesis statement so that it is supported by the available evidence. Also consider counterevidence: information or perspectives that contradict your claim, or doubts you have about it. If the counterevidence is more credible than the evidence, consider revising your claim.

EXERCISE 3.2 Revising a thesis statement

Revise the thesis statements you drafted in Exercise 3.1, and explain why you made your revisions.

> ### Make It **Your Own**
>
> For a project that you are currently working on in this or another class, draft and revise your thesis statement so that it makes a claim you can support convincingly.

3b Organizing Your Ideas

Most writing projects will be improved by your attention to organization both *before* and *after* the first draft. Organizing beforehand makes the project easier to draft; reviewing the structure after you have written a draft can show you where your thesis needs more evidence or explanation, whether the project is logically organized, and whether any of the evidence is irrelevant or insufficient.

> **More about**
> Reorganizing a draft, 88–90

1. Review your prewriting and make a list of ideas.

Start organizing by reviewing all the preparatory writing you have done. Then write your preliminary thesis statement at the top of a clean sheet of paper or in a new electronic document. Below the thesis statement, list all the reasons you believe it is true or at least plausible.

> **More about**
> Keeping a journal, 26
> Freewriting, 27
> Brainstorming, 27–28
> Clustering, 28–29
> Journalists' questions, 29–30

2. Arrange your ideas into logical groupings.

Read through your list of reasons for believing your thesis. How are they related? Create a cluster diagram or table to group ideas by topic. Or create a *tree diagram* to arrange ideas from most general to most specific: Write your main idea at the top of the page and let subsequent ideas branch off below it (Figure 3.1).

> **More about**
> Cluster diagrams, 28–29

3. Consider your project's overall shape.

Essays and many other writing projects typically have three basic parts:

- Introduction
- Body
- Conclusion

> **More about**
> Organizing paragraphs, 55–57, 64–68

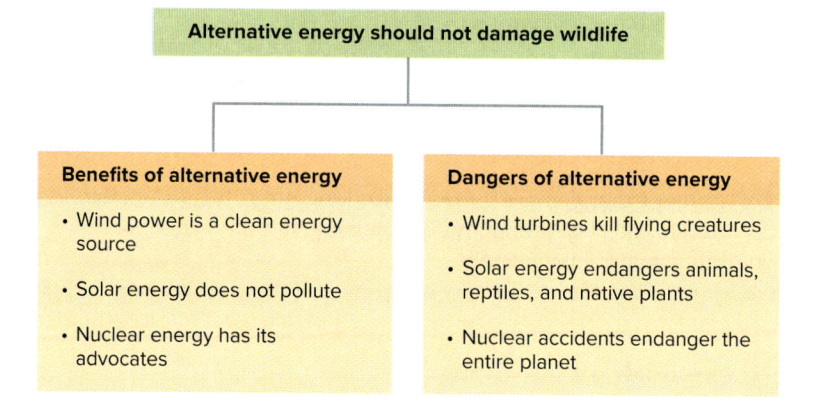

	Alternative energy should not damage wildlife	
Benefits of alternative energy		**Dangers of alternative energy**
• Wind power is a clean energy source		• Wind turbines kill flying creatures
• Solar energy does not pollute		• Solar energy endangers animals, reptiles, and native plants
• Nuclear energy has its advocates		• Nuclear accidents endanger the entire planet

FIGURE 3.1 A sample tree diagram A tree diagram can help you organize your thoughts before begin writing.

In its simplest form, the typical essay becomes a "five-paragraph theme": one paragraph for the introduction, three for the body, and one for the conclusion. Of course, effective writing seldom takes such a tidy form. Instead, it is more likely to unfold in this manner:

> **More about**
> Writing the introduction, 68–70

Introduction The introduction is typically brief (one to three paragraphs, depending on the overall length of the project). Often the thesis statement appears in the introduction, where it can shape readers' expectations of what follows. What goes into the introduction depends on your purpose, audience, context, and genre, but it should entice readers to carry on and should prepare them for what follows.

> **More about**
> Relevance, 53, 263–64
> Unity, 53–58
> Coherence, 58–64
> Development, 64–68
> Evidence, 45–47
> Conclusion, 70–73

Body The body is the longest portion of the project, with its length depending on the complexity of ideas being conveyed and the amount of explanation needed to convince the audience. Each paragraph in the body should typically make one main point, expressed in a topic sentence. The body paragraphs should supply explanations and evidence that support the topic sentence; and each topic sentence should support or develop the thesis. In most types of academic writing, counterevidence is included in the body: Explain why, although it is credible, you find other evidence more convincing.

Conclusion Like the introduction, the conclusion is usually rather brief (one to three paragraphs, depending on the length of the project). Just as the introduction should entice readers, so the conclusion should convince them that they have spent their time well.

4. Choose an organizational strategy.

Once you have collected and organized your notes, choose the order in which to present your ideas that best fits your thesis and supporting materials. One or more of the following basic organizational patterns may provide useful models for you:

Chronological organization   Use *chronological* (or *time*) order to tell a story (narrative) or explain a process (process analysis).

Spatial organization   Organize your project spatially—from left to right, inside to outside, top to bottom—when describing a scene or structure.

Logical organization   This is probably the most common organizational scheme for academic projects: Begin with an introduction that includes a general statement—the thesis—and then proceed to the body, where specific evidence is provided. With an indifferent or skeptical audience, consider reversing this order: Begin with something specific—an interesting anecdote, some dramatic statistics, a provocative illustration—that will gain your audience's interest, attention, or sympathy, and then move on to the general conclusion.

If you are writing for an audience likely to balk when faced with new ideas or ideas that challenge their beliefs, organize your project from *familiar to unfamiliar*. To startle your audience into seeing a familiar issue in a new light, use *unfamiliar-to-familiar order*.

You may choose to organize your body paragraphs in *climactic order*, from least to most exciting. You might even save your thesis until the end.

> **More about**
> Description, 64
> Narration, 64–65
> Exemplification, 64
> Comparison-contrast, 65–66
> Cause-effect, 66–67
> Analysis, 67
> Definition, 67–68

> **EXERCISE 3.3 Reviewing organizational strategies**
> Read the student models on pages 42 and 43. What organizational strategies does each use? What organizational changes would you recommend?

5. Choose an outlining technique that is appropriate for you.

Outlines, whether formal or informal, not only guide you as you draft, but also allow you to experiment with ways of sequencing your supporting paragraphs.

An informal outline   An *informal* (or *scratch*) *outline* is simply a list of the ideas in your project in the order you want to present them. You can jot down your ideas in words, phrases, complete sentences, even pictures—whatever you need to jog your memory about what to put next. Here is a sample scratch outline for Michael Wedd's draft essay on conflicts within the environmental movement.

Student Model Informal (or Scratch) Outline

> Intro
> Green/environmental movement: brief explanation
> Growing importance and awareness in recent years → conflict within the movement about how to handle these issues
> Thesis: A major goal of the green movement is to find fossil fuel alternatives, but some members are concerned that wind, solar, and nuclear power sites will also harm the environment.
>
> Body
> Benefits/importance of alternative energy; types of alternative fuel being proposed: wind, solar, nuclear
> Problems with alternative energy sources: harmful to animals, their habitats, and safety for humans
>
> Conclusion
> Conflicts might be inevitable, but we have to move forward, find creative compromises, use less energy

---

Student Models
Researched essays (MLA style, annotated) by **Michael Wedd:**
First draft, "Issues with Alternative Energy," 47–50
Final draft, "Rethinking Alternative Energy," 99–105

A formal outline (topic or sentence) A *formal outline* uses roman numerals (I, II, III), capital letters (A, B, C), arabic numerals (1, 2, 3), lowercase letters (a, b, c), and indentions of five spaces (or half an inch) to indicate level of generality, with roman numeral headings being most general and lowercase letters most specific. Each level of a formal outline should include at least two entries.

A *topic outline* uses words and phrases to indicate the ideas to be discussed. A *sentence outline* uses complete sentences. Some writers prefer a topic outline because it is easier to construct. Others prefer a sentence outline because it provides a starting point for drafting. Which type of outline you choose depends entirely on your own preferences, the complexity of your project, and your instructor's expectations.

Student Models Topic Outline and Sentence Outline

Compare a section of a topic outline with a section of a sentence outline for a later draft of Michael Wedd's essay:

Thesis

A major goal of the green movement is to find fossil fuel alternatives, but some members are concerned that wind, solar, and nuclear power sites will also harm the environment.

Topic Outline

I. Changing perspectives on alternative energy to include risks as well as benefits

    A. Benefits of alternative fuel

        1. Fewer greenhouse gas emissions/less warming

        2. Sustainable renewable energy sources: the sun, wind, and water

    B. Drawbacks

        1. Bad for environment: scenery, humans

        2. Destruction of animal habitats, extinction

        3. Future problems unknown without tests

Sentence Outline

I. The issue of global warming is urgent and serious, but we ought to consider the costs of alternative energy production that we deploy

    A. There are numerous potential benefits of using alternative fuel sources.

        1. Alternative energy produces fewer carbon dioxide and other greenhouse gas emissions, improving air quality and slowing the rate of global warming.

        2. Renewable energy sources, including the sun, wind, and water, are sustainable; they cannot be depleted and therefore can be used for the foreseeable future.

    B. Although there are many advantages to alternative fuel sources, there are drawbacks as well.

        1. New structures can have negative consequences on their surroundings, ranging from ruining picturesque views to endangering human health.

        2. Animal habitats may be destroyed, leading to extinction of species.

        3. The long-term effects of building new facilities is still largely unknown and could present even greater problems in the future.

> **More about**
> Coherence, 58–64
> Unity, 53–58

6. Check your outline for unity and coherence.

Once you have completed your outline, review it critically for *unity* and *coherence.* Unity is achieved when all the supporting paragraphs are relevant to the thesis and when all the evidence and explanations are relevant to the main idea of the supporting paragraph. Coherence is achieved when the supporting paragraphs, with all their evidence and explanations, are organized logically so that readers can move from idea to idea without having to pause to figure out the relationships among the parts.

3c Preparing to Draft

When the moment comes to combine words and sentences into paragraphs and paragraphs into a draft of your project, set aside some time and find a place where you can concentrate. Begin by reviewing the writing you have done while generating ideas, drafting your thesis, and creating an outline. Even in the best circumstances, you may encounter writer's block, but by using appropriate techniques, you should be able to get past it. If you get stuck, try the strategies outlined in the Quick Reference box on page 45.

1. Get ready: Allocate enough time and find a good place to write.

Ideally, set aside a substantial block of time for writing your first draft. How you define *substantial* depends on how long or complex your project will be: An hour or two might be enough for a three- to five-page essay; a longer project will require more. If you are unable to find an uninterrupted block of time, work in smaller chunks over several days. Do not delay starting just because you have only short bits of time available.

Next, consider what places work best for you: a study carrel in the library or a table at a sidewalk café? Whatever your preference, focus on the task at hand by turning off your phone and closing your internet browser.

2. Start writing.

The writing you have done while analyzing your writing situation and devising your topic, drafting your thesis, and organizing your ideas will provide you with a starting point. Begin by reviewing this material, and then try one of the following methods (or a combination of them):

- **Method 1: Fill in your outline.** Use your outline as scaffolding, filling it in and fleshing it out until it becomes a first draft.
- **Method 2: Start with what you have.** Instead of beginning at the beginning, start writing whatever parts of the project you feel confident about—an interesting example, a descriptive passage in support of one of your ideas, or even just a sentence or a phrase

that captures a relevant thought. Continue writing out-of-order thoughts until you can stitch them together and fill in the gaps.

- **Method 3: Write straight from your brain.** Type your thesis statement at the beginning of your document, and then just start writing. This may produce a brief, general first draft, but it will be one that actually expresses your thoughts. You can fill it out later.

Whatever method you choose, do not worry about the language you use to present your ideas. Just get words on paper. You can smooth out the kinks later, when you revise and edit.

3. Overcome writer's block.

Gene Fowler—a newspaper columnist, novelist, and screenwriter—once said, "Writing is easy: All you do is sit staring at a blank sheet of paper until drops of blood form on your forehead." Fortunately, there are techniques to help you avoid writing trauma.

> **Quick Reference** — Overcoming Writer's Block
>
> - **Take a break.** Doing something else, like taking a walk or doing your laundry, can help.
> - **Write something else.** Just the act of writing can help unblock you.
> - **Write what you can.** You do not have to start at the beginning and keep writing until you get to the conclusion. Instead, write the parts you *can* write, even if you cannot yet string them together.
> - **Start from what you already have.** Use your outline, brainstorming, and other notes to jump-start your writing.
> - **Write a message to yourself.** Write a note to yourself: "What I want to say is . . . ," and then finish the sentence.
> - **Talk, text, or email.** Tell a tutor, an instructor, a classmate, or a friend what your project will be about. Then use your own words as a starting point for writing.
> - **Change your situation.** Switch media—from pencil and paper to laptop, or vice versa—or change the setting in which you are writing.
> - **Avoid perfection.** It is the rare writer who produces a masterpiece on the first try. If you cannot avoid focusing on problems, turn off your computer screen so that you cannot see what you have written until it is time to start revising.

> *More about*
> Finding information (ch. 13), 237–62

3d Drafting: Explaining and Supporting Your Ideas

To draft a thesis statement for your project, you asked yourself a question and wrote a tentative answer. The body of your project will explain *why* you believe that your answer is true and why your audience should agree with you. The topic sentence (or main idea) in each supporting paragraph will form the backbone of your project, and your evidence and counterevidence will be the flesh that covers the skeleton.

Specific evidence is needed to make your writing convincing and interesting. Some kinds of evidence you can draw on include the following:

- Facts and statistics
- Expert opinion
- Examples
- Observations
- Case studies
- Anecdotes
- Passages from the text you are studying

Writing Responsibly: Made-up Evidence

In 2014, two stem cell experts resigned their positions at the Riken Center for Developmental Biology, one of Japan's leading research institutes, following revelations by the journal *Nature* that their lab had falsified data; one of the researchers later committed suicide. A few years earlier, noted anesthesiologist Scott S. Rubin had been fired by Massachusetts' Baystate Medical Center, then sent to prison and ordered to pay $420,000 in restitution, for falsifying data. Such punishments are increasingly common, but, as the Riken incident shows, they are not always a deterrent. Millions of research dollars have been wasted, professional reputations destroyed, and hopes for cures dashed by scientists who faked results in studies on problems as diverse as cancer, AIDS vaccines, obesity, and pain treatment. Commentators have noted that competition is often a factor in such cases. The desire for acclaim became more important than the desire for truth.

The highly competitive academic environment may tempt you, too, to make up "facts" to support a thesis in a project. It is easy to alter data, invent statistics or quotations, or manipulate an image so that it "shows" what you want it to. Resist the temptation: The short-term benefits are not worth it. Not only are you likely to get caught—fabricated evidence often *sounds* fake—but you are also sacrificing the opportunity to learn something about your topic and about the writing process.

to TOPIC

The paragraph below uses facts and examples:

[Topic sentence] The physical demands on competitive cyclists are immense. [Support: Facts/Examples] One day, they will have to ride two hundred kilometres through the mountains; the next day there might be a long, flat sprint lasting seven hours. Because cyclists have such a low percentage of body fat, they are more susceptible to infections than other people. (At the beginning of the Tour, Armstrong's body fat is around four or five percent; this season Shaquille O'Neal, the most powerful player in the N.B.A., boasted that his body-fat level was sixteen percent.)

—Michael Specter, "The Long Ride," *The New Yorker*

This paragraph uses facts and statistics:

> One of the most important, if often unnoticed, features of American life in the late twentieth century was the aging of the American population. After decades of steady growth, the nation's birth rate began to decline in the 1970s and remained low through the 1980s and 1990s. In 1970, there were 18.4 births for every 1,000 people in the population. By 1996, the rate had dropped to 14.8 births. The declining birth rate and a significant rise in life expectancy produced a substantial increase in the proportion of elderly citizens. Almost 13 percent of the population was more than sixty-five years old in 2000, as compared with 8 percent in 1970. The median age in 2000 was 35.3, the highest in the nation's history. In 1970, it was 28.0.
>
> —Alan Brinkley, *American History: A Survey*

Topic sentence: "One of the most important... aging of the American population."

Support: Facts and statistics (remainder of the paragraph)

As you draft, ask yourself: Have I supplied *enough* evidence to persuade my audience? Does the evidence convincingly explain my belief in the thesis?

> **More about**
> Relevance, 53, 263–64

Tech — Protecting Your Work

Because terrible things happen to computer files all the time, it is important to **save early and often,** and to **save your file in multiple locations:** Copy it to a secure location in the cloud, save it on a flash drive, or email a copy to yourself. Remember to date each version of a file so you know which is the most recent and so you have a backup of your research.

EXERCISE 3.4 Analyzing evidence

Analyze the two sample paragraphs in the previous section and list the types of evidence provided. Note whether there is sufficient evidence to support the topic sentence, and explain your response.

Make It Your Own

For a project that you are working on, produce a first draft using one of the drafting methods described in this section.

Student Model First Draft of a Researched Essay

The first draft of Michael Wedd's essay on conflict within the environmental movement, which he has researched and formatted in MLA style, appears on the pages that follow. Note that in this draft he does not worry about polished writing or even perfect grammar and spelling. He knows he can make changes as he revises. For now, his focus is on getting his ideas down in a logical order and on supporting his thesis. Consider what he will need to do as he revises to fulfill his responsibilities to his audience, his topic, other writers, and himself.

> **Student Model**
> Draft thesis, 36
> Revised thesis, 37–38
> Outlines, 41–44
> Final draft of a researched essay (MLA style), **Michael Wedd,** "Rethinking Alternative Energy," 99–105

DRAFT 1

Wedd 1

Michael Wedd

Professor Zheng

English 102

19 Sept. 2021

Issues with Alternative Energy

    The rise of Alternative Energy Industries has been challenging, controversial, and turbulent these days. With the availability of many forms of alternative energy systems globally (wind, solar, nuclearetc.), it is worth pausing for a minute to ask some questions. People are talking at many levels of society about both the costs and the benefits of alternative energy. The problematic relationships between Alternative Energy Industries and the things they claim to be protecting are emerging as a key focus of these debates.

    Environmentalists are conflicted when it comes to alternative energy. Most agree that fossil-fuel-based power plants are damaging the climate and making life harder for many of the worlds species. One of the primary benefits of alternative energy sources is that they are in practically limitless supply. They are producing energy all the time anyways. Obvious benefits aside, the structures needed to produce these forms of alternative energy can have bad affects on their surrounding environments (Pulitzer, Cherry, DW, McCurry). The issue of global warming is urgent and serious and we ought to consider the costs of alternative energy production that we deploy. Alternative energy might be putting the environment in danger. Maybe its time to question the way we as a society use these alternatives.

Annotations:
- First draft, so not concerned with spelling, style, grammar, or title
- Thesis statement makes a claim of fact, appropriate if purpose is informative but not if purpose is persuasive.
- Facts and specifics needed to better support writer's points
- Sources cited even in first draft
- Would "climate change" be a more accurate term than "global warming"?

Wedd 2

Wind energy seems to be a harmless, passive, and effective way of producing energy, but upon closer inspection it also has its drawbacks. Wind turbines are killing birds and other airborne creatures at fast rate. A report by *The American Bird Conservancy* states that "[t]he United States now has 48,000 wind turbines installed from coast to coast, with many more planned. Those turbines killed nearly 600,000 birds in 2012, from Golden Eagles to migratory songbirds" ("Bird Strikes"). These wind turbines reach hundreds of feet into the air and threaten birds. By 2030, "a ten-fold increase in turbines is expected to boost annual bird mortality to 1.4 to 2 million."

Solar energy is another alternative that at first seems benign but is actually putting airborne wildlife in grave danger. At the $2.2 billion-dollar Ivanpah solar facility in the CA desert, which is part of the largest solar energy complex in the world, birds are being burn mid-flight and plummeting to earth like meteorites. A report by the Pulitzer Center states that "[u]nsuspecting birds fly through Ivanpah's airspace, where the superheated air between the heliostats and the towers can reach temperatures as high as 900 degrees Fahrenheit. flesh catches fire as the birds are ignited in midair" (Pulitzer). The way we are generating solar electricity is producing high risks for a number of animals.

The most controversial of these alternative energy sources is the atom. Japan's 2011 Fukushima nuclear meltdown is still recent. Naoto Kan believes that the Japanese gov. isn't taking the dangers of nuclear power seriously enough after the recent meltdown. He was quoted in *Deutche Welle* saying, "Unfortunately, I have the impression that neither the Japanese public nor the experts have learned the right

Wedd 3

lessons from the disaster" (DW). We must carefully consider the dangers of nuclear power before embracing it as the clean energy of the future.

People acknowledge how important it is to check global warming and diversify our energy portfolio, but it is crucial that we also protect the flora and fauna with which we share this planet. It's not enough to be environmentally conscious about the sources from which we draw our energy; we also need to be careful about how we harvest from them. The solution to this will have to include ideas for not only increasing renewable energy production safely but also of reducing global consumption equilaterally.

Margin notes:
- Citation needs revision to follow MLA style.
- Add latest news on Fukushima? Is the site and surrounding land and water still contaminated?
- Conclusion
- Contractions may be too informal for college writing.

Wedd 4

Works Cited

Bird Strikes. American Bird Conservancy.

"The Fall Of Icarus: Ivanpah's Solar Controversy." *Pulitzer Center.*

"Former Japanese PM Naoto kan: 'Fukushima radically changed my Perspective' Asia *DW.COM* 25.02.2015. DW.COM.

Mccurry, Justin. "Japan Restarts First Nuclear Reactor since Fukushima Disaster." The Guardian August 11th, 2015. *The Guardian.*

Margin notes:
- Cites sources even in first draft
- Citations need revision to follow MLA style.

50

> **EXERCISE 3.5 Analyzing a draft**
> Create a topic outline for Michael Wedd's draft above. (Tip: Outlines of the first part of his draft appear on pages 42 and 43.) Based on your outline, how unified is his draft? How cohesive is it? Now consider the evidence he provides: Is there enough? Is it specific enough?

3e Writing with Others: Collaborative Projects

The work of many academic courses is conducted collaboratively, as are many workplace writing projects. Collaboration may mean that each team member is responsible for a separate part of the project, but often projects are *coauthored:* Group members work together to draft a thesis, devise an outline, and even write the text.

Drafting collaboratively can be a challenging process to manage, but it can also be rewarding and creative. The following principles will help keep the experience a happy one:

- If possible, keep groups small; smaller groups can reach the "critical mass" needed for creativity without the many management difficulties (such as finding a time to meet) that larger groups face.
- As with planning, it is important to the drafting process that each member has an opportunity to contribute. Make an effort to restrain overbearing members and to encourage reluctant participants.
- Treat everyone's writing respectfully. Some group members may be more skilled than others, but insightful ideas may be coaxed from initially unimpressive material.
- Whether your group is collaborating over email or courseware such as *Blackboard,* in a chat program such as *GroupMe* or *Slack,* or face to face, make sure everyone has a copy of the latest draft and schedule following each session.

> **More about**
> Planning a collaborative project, 32–34
> Peer response, 93–95

Make It Your Own

Use the material in this chapter to analyze a project you are working on or have recently completed. Identify the thesis statement or main idea; then analyze how well each paragraph supports it. Does the evidence support each paragraph's main point? If so, write a note in the margin explaining how; if not, revise the paragraph. Finally, make a topic outline and use it to check for unity and cohesion.

Text Credits
Pg. 48–50 Courtesy of Michael Wedd.

4 Crafting and Connecting Paragraphs

IN THIS CHAPTER

a. Relevant paragraphs, 53

b. Unified paragraphs, 53

c. Coherent paragraphs, 58

d. Developed paragraphs, 64

e. Introductory paragraphs, 68

f. Concluding paragraphs, 70

g. Connecting paragraphs, 73

Professional Model Speech, John F. Kennedy, "City Upon a Hill" 74

Everett Historical/Shutterstock.com

GagliardiPhotography/Shutterstock

American landscape architect Frederick Law Olmsted created in Manhattan a deceptively natural-looking oasis that appears always to have been there. Olmsted's hills and bridges, paths and ponds were as essential to Central Park as the park itself became to the city of New York.

Similarly, a writing project will be most effective—and a pleasure to read—when each paragraph is essential to the whole. When is a paragraph essential? It is essential when it is relevant, unified, coherent, well developed, interesting, and carefully connected to the paragraphs that come before and after it. A paragraph will be an essential part of the whole when it is all of the following:

- **Relevant.** It should support the main claim of the project (the *thesis*) and, when needed, remind readers of what that thesis is and how this paragraph supports it.
- **Unified.** It should have a clear point (*topic*) and include only the material that explains that point.
- **Coherent.** It should include connections that make clear how the sentences are related to each other.
- **Well developed.** It should supply the information your readers need to be persuaded of your claim.
- **Carefully connected.** It should begin and end so that your readers can see how it relates to the paragraphs that precede and follow it.
- **Interesting.** It should make your readers want to move on to the next paragraph and follow the development of your ideas.

4a Writing Relevant Paragraphs

A *relevant* paragraph not only describes the general topic of your project but also contributes to the reader's understanding of or belief in the main claim of the project (the *thesis*). Compare this paragraph to the essay's thesis:

> Brooks' discussion of the negative consequences experienced by time-blind people is effective. This is especially true because she refers to struggles that she's had, such as being late for meetings and feeling singled out and vulnerable in the workplace, and because she brings in the perspective of a neuropsychologist. She makes a solid case that there are social and professional costs to time blindness. A particularly detrimental consequence of time blindness and frequent tardiness is that neurotypical people "begin to exclude the ADHD person from activities" and say hurtful things that reveal their lack of trust and confidence (Brooks). The author offers further proof that time blindness is a real problem by linking to a video featuring Russell Barkley, who gives an overview of ADHD, time blindness, and an ADHD person's relationship with time. Overall, Brooks has helped me understand the challenges that people with time blindness face and clued me in to what neurotypical people like me can do to better support them.
>
> —from Joe Fernandez, Syracuse University, "A Critical Analysis of René Brooks's Article 'Time Blindness'"

Thesis: Brooks does a great job describing major aspects of time blindness, from what it is and how it feels to ways to manage it. She successfully details her points in a way that is persuasive and informative. My main critique, however, is that the article would be more effective with the addition of a scientific source or two.

Topic Sentence
Example 1
Example 2
Example 3
Example 4
Concluding sentence (also recalls thesis)

Student Model
Joe Fernandez's complete essay, 135–39.

4b Writing Unified Paragraphs

Paragraphs are **unified** when they focus on a single main idea. Unifying a paragraph is easiest when it includes a ***topic sentence***, a single sentence (sometimes two) that clearly states the main idea of the paragraph. That way, you can check each supporting sentence against this main idea and eliminate all those that are not relevant.

1. Focus the paragraph on a central idea and delete irrelevant details.

All the sentences in a supporting paragraph should support or explain the paragraph's main idea or topic, and each supporting paragraph should provide evidence for or develop further your project's main idea.

> Last year I inherited a library—not just the books, but the whole building. I didn't see it as a boon at first; I saw it only as a legal nuisance. In the 1950s, my grandfather, I discovered, had donated the library to the town. Fifty years later, when the townspeople built a new library and decided to sell the old building, they discovered that they couldn't: The deed specified that if they ceased to use the building as a library,

Topic Sentence

Irrelevant: Focus of ¶ is on how writer came to inherit, not writer's or city attorney's reaction or library's location—cut

Relevant: Explains why writer inherited library

> it would revert to the owner or his heirs. When the city attorney found the deed, he called every member of the town council. I was that heir. So now I owned the library in which I had spent so many hours as a girl. The building stands on a shady corner in what was once a quiet town.

When revising, hone your paragraphs until they focus on a single supporting idea: No matter how much you may like a certain sentence, if it does not support the main idea of the paragraph, it must be cut.

EXERCISE 4.1 Unifying a paragraph

Underline the topic sentence or main idea of the sample paragraph below. Then cross through any sentences that do not support that main idea.

> As we consider American dietary habits we also need to think about how people learn about nutrition. How do we know if our favorite foods are good for us? The national shift to convenience food is a problem too, because we don't know what is in it. Few people know that since 1909 Americans doubled the amount of sugar we eat (Amrock 8). Schools teach about the Federal Dietary Recommendations, but they change. First we had a Food Pyramid, and now we have a plate with different sized portions of food types. Carole Davis and Etta Saltos explain that it changes as understanding of nutrition grows (34). How can we trust something that keeps changing? The Food Pyramid said 6–11 servings of grains and only 3–5 of vegetables (www.nal.usda.gov/fnic/Fpyr/pmap.htm), but now portions of grains and vegetables are the same size (choosemyplate.gov). Having fewer vegetables was easier and popular with kids. Some people cut fat or carbohydrates to lose weight. My friends just exercise a lot or count calories. People can also get nutritional information from websites, but not all of them are healthy. The Harvard School of Public Health has an interactive website that clarifies nutritional information ("Knowledge").

EXERCISE 4.2 Writing unified paragraphs

Using the topic sentence and some of the supporting details given below, write a unified paragraph. Be selective: Not all the supporting details provided may be relevant.

> **Topic sentence:** Over the last four decades, the average American has increased the amount of food eaten from 16.4 pounds to 18.2 pounds per week and Americans' obesity rate has doubled.

Possible Supporting Details

1. The government recommends that fruits and vegetables should make up half of what we eat (choosemyplate.gov).

2. The US Department of Agriculture (USDA) compiles food consumption figures.
3. Corn syrup consumption in the US increased by 387% from 1970 to 2005 (Wells and Buzby 17).
4. What we eat is as important as how much we eat.
5. In 2005, 86 pounds of added fats and oils were consumed per person in the United States; we consumed 53 pounds in 1970 (Wells and Buzby 12).
6. In 1970, US consumption of added sugars and sweeteners was 119 pounds per person and by 2005 that number was 142 pounds (Wells and Buzby 17-18).
7. According to Schlosser, half of the US food budget is spent on fast food.
8. The National Health Nutrition Examination Survey (NHANES) tracks obesity.
9. In 2014, NHANES found that 80 million adult Americans (36.5%) were obese.

2. Place the topic sentence appropriately.

Topic sentences can appear at the beginning, middle, or end of a paragraph, but they typically appear at the beginning or end.

Topic sentence at beginning of paragraph   The most common placement for a topic sentence is at the beginning of the paragraph:

> Environmentalists paint a bleak picture of aquaculture. The David Suzuki Foundation, for example, maintains that fish waste contained in the fishery pens kills organisms living in the seabed. Yvon Gesinghaus, a manager of a tribal council in British Columbia, Canada, also notes that the scummy foam from the farms collects on the beaches, smothering the clams that provide the natives with food and money. George K. Iwama, Biksham Gujja, and Andrea Finger-Stich point to the destruction of coastal habitats in Africa and Southeast Asia to make room for shrimp ponds.
> —Adrianne Anderson Speas, Texas Christian University

In the paragraph above, the main idea is spelled out in the first sentence, so readers can easily see the relationship between the main idea and the supporting evidence and explanations that follow.

Topic sentence at end of paragraph   Writers may place the topic sentence at the end of a paragraph to draw a conclusion based on the evidence presented and to enhance dramatic effect.

> When I was a little girl, Walt Disney's *The Little Mermaid* was my favorite movie, and Ariel (the title character) was my favorite character. I watched this movie three times a day, repeating Ariel's lines word for word. I wanted to be like her—cute and little and sweet and lovable, with big eyes and a tiny waist. But when I watched *The Little Mermaid* for the first time in more than seven years, I noticed things I had overlooked as a child. Was Ariel unhealthily thin? Was she more childlike than a full-grown woman should be? Was Ariel too willing to make sacrifices for Prince Charming? **Maybe *The Little Mermaid* wasn't the innocent entertainment I had once thought.**
>
> —Heidi Johnson, North Dakota State University

[**Topic Sentence**: Maybe *The Little Mermaid* wasn't the innocent entertainment I had once thought.]

Holding the topic sentence until the end of the paragraph and starting with dramatic statistics or (as in the example above) a thought-provoking anecdote may stimulate your readers' interest before you draw your conclusion. Remember, though: The relationship between evidence and claim must be clear, or you might leave your readers puzzled.

Topic sentence in middle of paragraph Occasionally writers place the topic sentence somewhere in the middle of the paragraph:

> We live in a world where diversity is at the forefront of the news agenda. #MeToo, Pride, and Black Lives Matter have all made a substantial impact on public consciousness around the world. The publishing industry is also becoming more diverse. Globalization means we are increasingly working with a more diverse range of people—from different countries, in different time zones, with different cultures and ways of life. Social media is bringing us closer to our authors, readers, and customers, who hail from every walk of life. **Since the dissemination and absorption of knowledge should not discriminate, we need to make sure we are including people from all backgrounds within our industry.** The statistics suggest that, at present, this is not the case when it comes to disability.
>
> —Simon Holt, Katy Alexander, Becky Degler,
> "The Problem Solvers You Don't Know About Yet:
> Valuing Disability in the Publishing Industry,"
> *The Scholarly Kitchen*
> Used with permission.

[**Topic Sentence**: Since the dissemination and absorption of knowledge should not discriminate, we need to make sure we are including people from all backgrounds within our industry.]

In cases where the main idea appears in the middle of the paragraph, it acts as a linchpin: In this example, the paragraph begins with examples of diversity and it ends with a sentence indicating that diversity is lacking in the publishing industry. The topic sentence links these two different kinds of support.

3. Decide whether to leave the main idea unstated.

Some paragraphs (especially descriptive and narrative ones) may leave the main idea unstated. The main idea of the paragraph below, for example, is implied by the details and the word choices. The words and phrases that suggest the main idea are highlighted.

> The sound of discreet footsteps echoed in my ears as our choir followed a monk through one of the dark, damp archways into a grand hall furnished with ancient tables and chairs; it had been immaculately preserved by the family that had inhabited the old palace, which now served as a monastery, school, and museum. From the hall we passed into a room filled with religious relics that had belonged to the old prince. In another room, brown music manuscripts in Beethoven's and Haydn's own handwriting lay in crystal cases. In a third, bright tapestries woven from gold thread hung from the shiny stone walls, and sparkling crown jewels bedecked glass cabinets. We passed quickly through room after room filled with rusty (or bloodstained?) torture devices. Just before we reached an open-air walkway, we passed doors that seemed to belong to dwarves: They were entrances to the rooms of children who attended school here.
> —Christina Huey, Georgia Southern University

In this paragraph, the implied main idea—something like "Everything in the monastery seemed strange and remarkable"—comes through without Huey's having to state it explicitly. Write such paragraphs with the explicit thesis statement clearly articulated in your own mind, so that you don't include irrelevant material that might make the paragraph incomprehensible.

EXERCISE 4.3 Identifying the topic sentence

Identify the topic sentence (main idea) in the following paragraphs:

1. Rock music had always been a vehicle to express frustration, rebellion, and obloquy, but as the 1970s proceeded, these themes were often softened to achieve mass acceptance. The notion of rock as mainstream entertainment was gaining ground steadily. David Bowie, for example, who in an earlier era might have been considered too inaccessible a figure for television audiences, turned up as a smiling guest on Cher's variety show in 1975. Rock was becoming a common language, the reference point for a splintered culture. In March 1976, presidential candidate Jimmy Carter told a lecture audience that Bob Dylan, Led Zeppelin, and the Grateful Dead were among the artists who had inspired him to work hard as governor of Georgia, and once he won the election, Carter continued to court rock by inviting numerous musicians to the White House.
   —Ken Tucker, "The Seventies and Beyond," in *Rock of Ages: The Rolling Stone History of Rock & Roll,* p. 520

> 2. We spend so much of our lives hiding and pretending to be someone we're not. It's incredibly liberating to let your appearances reflect who you are, and what you're going through. Imagine looking in the mirror and saying: yep, I look like *me*. I've had some pretty insane haircuts, most recently including long hair with designs shaved into the sides, a curly little pixie, and an awkward mohawk. But even the mohawk (which really didn't look great) represented me well, because I was just coming out of a major breakup. My ex's lifestyle had required that I show up places wearing dresses, heels, and a blow-out, looking pretty and "appropriate." It never felt right to me, and by cutting my hair like a weirdo, I released my old identity and let my true Self show through better. I am odd and wild, creative, boyish, and happy; it's thrilling and liberating to actually express that, instead of hiding it.
> —Jessi Kneeland, "8 Lessons on Unconditional Self-Love (aka: Crazy Hair Don't Care)," *Remodel Fitness*
> Used with permission.

> **Make It Your Own**
>
> Select a paragraph from a recent or current writing project. Underline the topic sentence or main idea; then cross through any sentences that do not support it.

4c   Writing Coherent Paragraphs

A paragraph is *coherent* when readers can understand the relationships among the sentences without having to pause or ponder. Readers are most likely to find a paragraph coherent when all the sentences in the paragraph are relevant, when the paragraph is clearly organized, and when transitional words and phrases link sentences.

1. Organize your paragraphs logically.

There are many ways to organize a paragraph logically. Most paragraphs follow deductive order: They begin with a topic sentence (the most general statement in the paragraph), and the supporting evidence follows:

> I'd known Sam for all of a month before I got him a dog in 2006. Belle, now nine years old, is half Border Collie, a female pup out of our friend Thad's Australian Shepherd. Neither of us had any experience with making a pup into a stock dog. **But one thing I *did* know before my impulsive purchase was the value of an obedient working dog.** After several summers on cattle ranches, I'd seen just how handy it was to send dogs into thickets where cattle shaded up. I'd watched them work a cow that didn't want to stay with the herd until she turned back and joined them. One cowboy with a good dog or two could easily handle several hundred cattle, the same number it might take five people to drive. (Hiring day

> help could set you back around five hundred bucks.) And well-intended but inexperienced cow hands can end up in the wrong place, but a seasoned dog is rarely mistaken about where the cattle need to go.
>
> —Laura Jean Schneider, "Ranch Diaries: One Dog Can Be Worth Three Hands" *High Country News*, September 8, 2015.
> Copyright © 2015 High Country News. Used with permission.

A less common option is to organize the paragraph inductively, so that it begins with the supporting details and concludes with the topic sentence:

> His trademark character Mr. DOB (who appears in the sculpture *DOB in the Strange Forest*) is reminiscent of both Mickey Mouse and Sonic the Hedgehog. But there's something heavier going on here. It's hinted at in the manic eyes of Murakami's characters. It's unleashed fully in the show's centerpiece painting *Tan Tan Bo Puking*, aka *Gero Tan*, where the cartoon character subject is bearing fearsome jagged teeth, and the whole lot is melting. [Supporting evidence] It's like cartoon Dali, sure, but it's also another reminder that Japan experienced the flesh-melting horror of atomic attack. [Topic Sentence]
>
> —Daniel Etherington, "Nasty Cartoons from Japan," bbc.co.uk

A third option is to organize the paragraph by increasing order of emphasis or interest:

> Monotonously the trucks sway, monotonously come the calls, monotonously falls the rain. It falls on our heads [Least emphatic] and on the heads of the dead up the line, on the body of the little recruit with the wound that is so much too big for his hip; it falls on Kemmerich's grave; it falls in our hearts. [Most emphatic]
>
> —Erich Maria Remarque, *All Quiet on the Western Front*

A fourth option is to organize the paragraph by posing a problem or question and then resolving it:

> So why exactly is the protagonist drawn to the dreams of the past? [Question] It may be because those dreams are not the trivialities of modern times. They are not about realizing suddenly that you are standing at your locker naked or unable to get to the airport in time for your flight. Instead, the dreams of the past are dreams of death, of unknown gods, of devouring monsters. [Answer]
>
> —Michael Parr, McHenry Community College, "The Importance of Dreaming in Sylvia Plath's 'Johnny Panic and the Bible of Dreams'"

2. Use transitions within (and between) paragraphs.

In addition to omitting irrelevancies and being well organized, a coherent paragraph provides guideposts that point readers from one sentence to the next. These are *transitional words and phrases.* They alert readers to the significance of what you are saying and point up the relationships among your ideas. The following paragraph uses transitional words and phrases to guide readers through differences between one film and two others:

> Yes, *Black Panther* is another multizillion-dollar installment in the burgeoning Marvel Cinematic Universe, but that is not all that it is. Other superhero movies have dabbled in big ideas—the *Dark Knight* trilogy most notably, and the *X-Men* franchise to a lesser degree. But their commitments to the moral and political questions they contemplated were relatively haphazard and/or peripheral. The arguments *Black Panther* undertakes with itself are central to its architecture, a narrative spine that runs from the first scene to the last.
> —Christopher Orr, "*Black Panther* Is More than a Superhero Movie," *The Atlantic*

[*Emphasis / Comparison / Contrast*]

Make sure you choose the appropriate transition for the situation, and vary your selection to avoid ineffective repetition. (For some sample transitions, see the Quick Reference box on the next page.)

> **More about**
> Avoiding repetition, 561

3. Repeat words, phrases, and sentence structures.

Repetition—especially repetition used for padding—can annoy readers, but repetition used consciously, to knit sentences into a cohesive paragraph or to call attention to an idea, can be an asset. The following paragraph repeats words and phrases (*deer hunting, hunting, deer season*) to emphasize the point made in the final sentence, where the writer uses the word *deer* on its own.

> **More about**
> Developing without padding, 92
> Effective repetition, 592–93

> I don't object to deer hunting: let everyone have his sport, I say. I don't for a moment doubt the value, importance, and dignity of hunting for those who do it. Deer hunting teaches skill, discipline, and patience. More than that, it teaches the moral lesson of seriousness—that certain things must be entered into advisedly, done with care, and done right. That hunting provides an education I am very willing to believe. And yet deer season is for me a sad couple of weeks. Because with all its profound advantages for the hunter, the fact remains that deer season is a little tough on the deer.
> —Castle Freeman, "Surviving Deer Season: A Lesson in Ambiguity," *Atlantic Monthly*, December 1995. Used with permission of the author.

The paragraph above repeats sentence structures ("I don't object," "I don't . . . doubt"; "Deer hunting teaches," "It teaches") but largely relies on the repetition of words (*deer, hunting, season*) for emphasis. The paragraph below uses related concepts (the word *gangster*, the names of gangsters and others from the FBI's Most Wanted list), but it mainly relies on repetition of phrase and sentence structures to lend emphasis.

> When he said he'd been a gangster, they smiled. Sure you were, pops. When he said he'd been Public Enemy Number One—right after John Dillinger, Pretty Boy Floyd, and his old protégé Baby Face Nelson—people turned away and rolled their eyes. When he said he and his confederates had single-handedly "created" J. Edgar Hoover and the modern FBI, well, then he would get bitter and people would get up and move to another

table. He was obviously unstable. How could you believe anyone who claimed he was the only man in history to have met Charles Manson, Al Capone, and Bonnie and Clyde?

—Bryan Burrough, *Public Enemies*

4. Use pronouns, synonyms, and equivalent expressions.

Pronouns (I, you, he, she, it, we, they), synonyms (words that mean the same thing), and equivalent expressions not only help writers avoid having to repeat the same word over and over (unintentional repetition) but also create coherence by establishing links to words and phrases that appeared earlier. The following paragraph, for example, uses several equivalent expressions for the word *perfectionism* as well as the pronoun *it* to refer to this concept:

> Destructive perfectionism is debilitating, draining, joy-sapping. Its focus on product, on task, on over-achievement, and exceeding all expectations can sabotage the creative process. It can lead to paralyzed decision-making, or procrastination (aka "insecure perfectionism"), as any budding self-confidence you might've mustered is shred to a pulp.
> —Margaret R. Rutherford, "Does Perfectionism Kill Creativity or Feed It?" *Psychology Today*

Quick Reference   Sample Transitional Expressions

To add to an idea: *again, also, and, and then, besides, further, furthermore, in addition, incidentally, likewise, moreover, next, still, too*

To indicate cause or effect: *accordingly, as a result, because, consequently, hence, since, then, therefore, thus*

To indicate chronology (time sequence): *after, afterward, as long as, as soon as, at last, before, earlier, finally, first, formerly, immediately, in the first place, in the interval, in the meantime, in the next place, in the last place, later, latter, meanwhile, next, now, often, once, previously, second, shortly, simultaneously, since, sometime later, subsequently, suddenly, then, third, today, tomorrow, until, until now, when, years ago, yesterday*

To conclude: *all in all, finally, in brief, in conclusion, in other words, in short, in sum, in summary, that is, to summarize*

To concede: *certainly, granted, of course*

To compare: *alike, also, in the same way, like, likewise, resembling, similarly*

To contrast: *after all, and yet, although, but, conversely, despite, difference, dissimilar, even so, even though, granted, however, in contrast, in spite of, instead, nevertheless, nonetheless, notwithstanding, on the contrary, on the other hand, otherwise, regardless, still, though, unlike, while this may be true, yet*

To emphasize: *after all, certainly, clearly, even, indeed, in fact, in other words, in truth, it is true, moreover, of course, undoubtedly*

To offer an example: *as an example, for example, for instance, in other words, namely, specifically, that is, thus, to exemplify, to illustrate*

To indicate spatial relationships: *above, adjacent to, against, alongside, around, at a distance from, behind, below, beside, beyond, encircling, far off, farther along, forward, here, in front of, inside, near the back, near the end, nearly, next to, on, over, surrounding, there, through, to the left, to the right, to the north, to the south, up front*

Writing Responsibly — Guiding Your Audience

As a writer, you have a responsibility to guide your audience from point to point, highlighting the relationships among your words, sentences, and paragraphs. Do not leave readers to puzzle out the relationships among your ideas for themselves. Few academic readers in the United States will think that explicit claims and transitions insult their intelligence.

<u>to AUDIENCE</u>

5. Combine techniques.

The example paragraphs in *section 4c* used more than one technique to achieve coherence. When revising your own paragraphs, draw on a variety of techniques to make your paragraphs cohere.

EXERCISE 4.4 Analyzing coherence

For each of the following paragraphs, identify how the paragraph is organized, underline the transitional words and phrases, and circle the words that are repeated or the pronouns or synonyms that replace them.

1. Readers of this novel can attribute multiple meanings to the word *paradise* depending on whose point of view they are looking from. The founders of Ruby consider *paradise* to consist of preserving the history of the Old Fathers and remaining isolated from outsiders, but this view proves faulty and falls apart. On their journey toward seeking comfort, the women of the convent realize that *paradise* means coming to terms with one's past instead of running from it or letting it determine who they are, and this understanding leads them to show compassion and mercy toward those who have harmed them.

   —Sonu Ray, Drew University, "Journey to *Paradise*: Discovering Its Gateway"

2. The group worshipped unharassed until 1667. At that time, the Court acted on the complaints of the orthodox churches of the area against Myles and his followers. In an order from the Plymouth Court dated July 2, 1667, the members were fined five pounds each for "setting up of a public meeting without the knowledge and approbation of the Court to the disturbance of the peace

of the place" (King 30–31). The Court offered them three alternatives: They could discontinue their worship services, leave the town, or petition the Court for an alternate site of worship. Mr. Myles moved his church to New Meadow Neck, just south of Rehoboth, which is today in Barrington, Rhode Island.

—Robyn Worthington, Bristol Community College, "The Covenant between Church and Town in Swansea, Massachusetts"

3. First, use the cork borer to cut two cylinders out of the potato and then slice the cores into pieces 2 cm long. It is a good idea to place the slices in a beaker to prevent them from drying out. There should be two potato cylinders for each treatment. Weigh the two cylinders for each treatment and record the weight in grams: that is your initial weight. Next, blot the cylinders with a paper towel and put each of the sets of cylinders into 100 ml beakers (there should be 5) and place 50 ml of each solution in the beakers.

—Stephanie Warnekros, Johnson County Community College, "Osmosis in Potato Cubes"

EXERCISE 4.5 Unscrambling the "Gettysburg Address"

The sentences below make up the final paragraph of Abraham Lincoln's "Gettysburg Address," but they have been scrambled. Without checking the original, use the clues within the paragraph to restore Lincoln's sentences to their proper order. Then list the coherence techniques that helped you put the paragraph back together again.

1. It is rather for us to be here dedicated to the great task remaining before us—that from these honored dead we take increased devotion to that cause for which they gave the last full measure of devotion—that we here highly resolve that these dead shall not have died in vain—that this nation, under God, shall have a new birth of freedom—and that government of the people, by the people, for the people, shall not perish from the earth.
2. The world will little note, nor long remember, what we say here, but it can never forget what they did here.
3. But, in a larger sense, we cannot dedicate—we cannot consecrate—we cannot hallow—this ground.
4. The brave men, living and dead, who struggled here, have consecrated it, far above our poor power to add or detract.
5. It is for us the living, rather, to be dedicated here to the unfinished work which they who fought here have thus far so nobly advanced.

> **Make It Your Own**
>
> Select a paragraph from a current or recent writing project and assess its coherence. List the techniques you used to weave the sentences together into a paragraph and note what you could do to make it even more coherent.

4d Developing Paragraphs Using Patterns

Using *patterns*—description, narration or process analysis, exemplification, comparison and contrast, cause and effect, analysis, and definition—can help you develop your paragraphs (and your whole project) into a cohesive and unified whole.

Description When describing, include details that appeal to the senses (sight, sound, taste, smell, touch) and organize them spatially (from left to right, top to bottom, near to middle to far) to mimic how we normally take in a scene. Spatially organized paragraphs rely on indications of place or location to guide the audience by the mind's eye (or ear or nose).

> A few moments later French announces, "Bottom contact on sonar." The seafloor rolls out like a soft, beige carpet. Robison points to tiny purple jellies floating just above the floor. Beyond them, lying on the floor itself, are several bumpy sea cucumbers, sea stars with skinny legs, pink anemones, and tube worms, which quickly retract their feathery feeding arms at *Tiburon's* approach. A single rattail fish hangs inches above the bottom, shoving its snout into the sediments in search of a meal.
>
> —Virginia Morell, "OK, There It Is—Our Mystery Mollusk," from "Monterey Menagerie," *National Geographic,* June 2004. Copyright © 2004 by Virginia Morell. Reprinted by permission of the author.

Sensory description
Indications of place or location

Exemplification: Explaining through example Exemplification works by providing examples to make a general point specific:

> While attitudes about food have changed through these last years, fortunately the principles of good cooking have not. The more one knows about it, the less mystery there is, the faster cooking becomes, and the easier it is to be creative and to embrace new trends and ideas—in addition, the more pleasure one has in the kitchen.
>
> —Julia Child, *The Way to Cook*

Example 1
Example 2
Example 3
Example 4
Example 5

Narration and process analysis A paragraph that tells a story or describes a process unrolls over time. Include each step or key moment, and describe it in enough detail that readers can envision it.

The very first trick ever performed by Houdini on the professional stage was a simple but effective illusion known generally as the "Substitution Trunk," though he preferred to call it "Metamorphosis." Houdini and his partner would bring a large trunk onto the stage. It was opened and a sack or bag produced from inside it. Houdini, bound and handcuffed, would get into the sack, which was then sealed or tied around the neck. The trunk was closed over the bag and its occupant. It was locked, strapped, and chained. Then a screen was drawn around it. The partner (after they married, this was always Mrs. Houdini) stepped behind the screen which, next moment, was thrown aside—by Houdini himself. The partner had meanwhile disappeared. A committee of the audience was called onstage to verify that the ties, straps, etc. around the trunk had not been tampered with. These were then laboriously loosened; the trunk was opened and there, inside the securely fastened bag, was—Mrs. Houdini!

—Ruth Brandon, *The Life and Many Deaths of Harry Houdini*

The sequence of events in the Substitution, or Metamorphosis, trick is depicted in Figure 4.1.

Comparison-contrast: Showing similarities and differences A paragraph that is developed using comparison-contrast points out similarities or differences (sometimes both). A comparison-contrast paragraph can proceed by either the ***block method*** or the ***alternating method.*** In the block method, the writer groups all the traits of the first item together before discussing the second item. In the alternating method, the writer proceeds point by point, discussing each common or divergent trait of both items before moving to the next trait. In the block method, readers must remember everything you have said about item A while they read about item B, so the more complex your material, the more your readers are likely to need the alternating method.

FIGURE 4.1 A visual process analysis

Block Method	Alternating Method
A	A
A	B
A	
	A
B	B
B	
B	A
	B

The first paragraph below uses the alternating method; the second uses the block method.

Asante kente cloth is made from strips in a single weave with alternative double-woven panels such that when the strips are sewn together, the effect is similar to a checkerboard. It is noted for its vivid colors and the abstract motifs woven into the strips, unlike Ewe kente, in which the colors are more subdued and the motifs are more lifelike. Like adinkra, the motifs used in Asante kente cloth weaving have specific names; however, the cloth is usually named for the colors and design of the background, which is often striped. As with adinkra, kente is named for historic figures and events and also for Asante values. The design *kyeretwie*, or leopard catcher, for example, symbolizes courage, while *aberewa* ben, or "wise old woman," indicates the respect accorded older women in Asante society.

— Boatema Boateng, "The Copyright Thing Doesn't Work Here: Adinkra and Kente Cloth and Intellectual Property in Ghana"

- colors and motifs
- colors and motifs
- names based on motifs
- names based on cloth
- symbolism
- values

Europeans interpreted the simplicity of Indian dress in two different ways. Some saw the lack of clothing as evidence of "barbarism." André Thevet, a shocked French visitor to Brazil in 1557, voiced this point of view when he attributed nakedness to simple lust. If the Indians could weave hammocks, he sniffed, why not shirts? But other Europeans viewed unashamed nakedness as the Indians' badge of innocence. As remnants of a bygone "golden age," they believed, Indians needed clothing no more than government, laws, regular employment, or other corruptions of civilization.

—James West Davidson et al., *Nation of Nations*, 5th ed.

- "barbarism"
- "innocence"

Cause-and-effect: Reasons and consequences A cause-and-effect paragraph explains why something happened or what its consequences are:

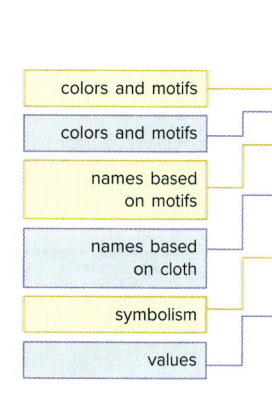

Writing Matters • Developing Paragraphs Using Patterns   **4d**   **67**

> Here is a modest suggestion for what Twitter can do to fix one of the problems that most annoy me and I imagine many other users: the problem of crackpot, abusive tweets. The paradox of Twitter is that the more followers you have (I currently have over 20,000), the more abusive tweets you are likely to get calling you various scatological names or passing along insane conspiracy theories. Some of this is bearable, but after a while you want to take a hot bath and never go back into the cesspool again. I'm not suggesting that these offensive tweets comprise the bulk of what's on Twitter—far from it. I would have stopped using it long ago if that were true. But it's more of a chore than it should be to find the good stuff in your feed among all the abusive attacks that are out there.
> —Boot, Max, "Abusing Anonymity" *Commentary*, February 23, 2016. Copyright © 2016 Commentary, Inc. Used with permission.

Analysis: Dividing a whole into its parts   Analysis divides a single entity into its component parts:

> The central United States is divided into two geographical zones: the Great Plains in the west and the prairie in the east. Though both are more or less flat, the Great Plains—extending south from eastern Montana and western North Dakota to eastern New Mexico and western Texas—are the drier of the two regions and are distinguished by short grasses, while the more populous prairie to the east (surrounding Omaha, St. Louis, and Fort Leavenworth) is tall-grass country. The Great Plains are the "West"; the prairie, the "Midwest."
> —Robert D. Kaplan, *An Empire of Wilderness*

Definition: Explaining the meaning of a word or concept   Like those in a dictionary, a definition explains the meaning of a word or concept by grouping it into a class and then providing the distinguishing characteristics that set it apart from other members of that class:

Term to Be Defined	Class	Distinguishing Characteristics
Argument is	a way to discover truth	by examining all sides of the issue.

Extended definitions (definitions that run to a paragraph or more) analyze in detail what a term does or does not mean. They go beyond a desktop dictionary, often using anecdotes, examples, or reasons for using the word in this particular way:

> The international movement known as theater of the absurd so vividly captured the anguish of modern society that late twentieth-century critics called it "the true theater of our time." Abandoning classical theater from Sophocles and Shakespeare through Ibsen and Miller, absurdist playwrights rejected traditional dramatic structure (in which action

moves from conflict to resolution), along with traditional modes of character development. The absurdist play, which drew stylistic inspiration from dada performance art and surrealist film, usually lacks dramatic progression, direction, and resolution. Its characters undergo little or no change, dialogue contradicts actions, and events follow no logical order. Dramatic action, leavened with gallows humor, may consist of irrational and grotesque situations that remain unresolved at the end of the performance—as is often the case in real life.

—Gloria Fiero, *The Humanistic Tradition*, 5th ed.

Make It **Your Own**

Write two paragraphs. For each, choose one of the patterns of development discussed in this section. Check to make sure that they are unified and that they use appropriate transitions to guide the reader.

Work **Together**

Exchange paragraphs with a classmate and make a note of which patterns you see. Mark any places where the paragraph lacks coherence or needs additional transitions.

4e Writing Introductory Paragraphs

Introductory paragraphs shape readers' attitudes toward the rest of the text. Yet writers often have a hard time producing these paragraphs. Many writers find it helpful to draft the body of the project before tackling the introduction.

> **Avoid Praising the Reader in Your Introduction** In some contexts and cultures, writers win the approval of readers by overtly praising their taste, character, or intelligence, whether the writing is intended to be wholly personal or not. Generally, however, this is considered inappropriate for a college project, and academic and professional writers in the United States avoid referring directly to the reader and occasionally will actually challenge the reader's beliefs.

Whether you write the introduction first or last, it should prepare the audience for what follows. In many cases, this means including the thesis in the introduction. A common placement for the thesis statement is at the end of the introduction—this is the *funnel introduction.*

Regardless of whether you include your thesis in your introduction, hold it until your conclusion, or merely imply your main idea, your introduction should identify and convey your stance toward your topic, establish your purpose, and engage readers to make them want to read on. One or more of the following strategies can help you write an effective introduction:

- Begin with a vivid quotation, a compelling question, or some interesting data.
- Start with an engaging—and relevant—anecdote.
- Offer a surprising but apt definition of a key term.
- Provide background information.
- State a commonly held belief and then challenge it.
- Explain what interesting, conflicting, difficult, or misunderstood territory the project will explore.

(For some opening gambits to avoid, see the Quick Reference box on page 70.)

In the introductory paragraph that follows, the writer uses several effective strategies: She begins with a question that challenges the audience to examine some common assumptions about the topic, she provides background information that her readers may lack, and she concludes with a thesis statement that explains why reading her text should be important to the audience.

> Many people enjoy sitting down to a nice seafood dinner, but how many of those people actually stop to think about where the fish on their plate came from? [Opening question] With many species of wild fish disappearing because of overfishing, increasingly the answer will be a fish farm. But while fish farming can help to supply the demand, it can threaten the environment and cause problems with wild fish. It can also threaten the health of consumers by increasing the risk of disease and increasing the quantity of antibiotics consumed. [Answer that provides background information] In fact, as a careful and conscientious consumer, you would do well to learn the risks involved in buying and eating farm-raised fish before one winds up on your dinner plate. [Thesis]

—Adrianne Anderson Speas, Texas Christian University

Brief essays may require only a one-paragraph introduction, but longer projects often need more. A text of twenty pages may have an introduction that runs several paragraphs, and introductions to books are generally the length of a short chapter. While there are no firm rules about the length of the introduction, it should be in proportion to the project's length.

Quick Reference: Seven Don'ts for Introductions

Avoid common problems that can undermine your introduction's success:

1. **"In my paper I will . . ."** While announcing your topic is acceptable in some academic disciplines (in the sciences, for example), announcing what your project is or will do is usually unnecessary and boring. Also avoid referring to your own text by its title.
2. **"In this paper I hope to . . ."** or **"In this paper I will try to . . ."** These openers share the shortcomings of *"In my paper I will . . ."*; they also state something your instructor already assumes, and they undermine your credibility by emphasizing your lack of confidence.
3. **"I don't know much about this topic, but . . ."** Introductions that apologize for your amateur status undermine your credibility as a writer and give readers an excuse to stop reading.
4. **"I have a lot of expertise in this topic."** Refrain from claiming more prestige or credit than is your due.
5. **"According to *Merriam-Webster's Third Unabridged Dictionary*, . . ."** While starting with a definition can be an effective opening strategy, merely providing readers with a definition they could easily find for themselves is tedious.
6. **"Ever since the beginning of time, . . ."** Start your project at the beginning of your material, not before recorded history.
7. **"The greatest problem facing our society today . . ."** Do not make claims that your project cannot support with concrete evidence.

4f Writing Concluding Paragraphs

As with the introduction, the conclusion is a part of the project that readers are likely to remember. In fact, because it is the last thing the audience will read, it is what they will probably remember best. Thus, it demands a writer's best work.

The shape of the conclusion is often what might be called an *inverted funnel:* While the introduction often starts at a general level and then narrows down to the thesis, a common strategy for the conclusion is to start out specific—with a restatement and development of the thesis (in different words)—and then to broaden out. The restatement of your thesis should add perspectives that you have developed in the body of your project and not be a simple paraphrase of what appeared in your introduction. The final draft of Michael Wedd's project (pp. 99–105) demonstrates the technique:

Thesis in the introduction

> Despite how serious and pressing the issue of global warming is, we must be careful to consider not only the benefits but also the costs of the forms

of alternative energy production that we deploy. If alternative energy ends up putting the environment—and in some cases humanity directly—in jeopardy, then we need to rethink the ways in which we use it.

Thesis in the conclusion

Clearly, environmentally conscious citizens acknowledge how important it is to check global warming and diversify our energy portfolio, but it is crucial that we also protect the flora and fauna with which we share this planet.

In Wedd's introduction, the thesis raises a problem and indicates the possible conflicts. In Wedd's conclusion, the *if* is gone, replaced by *clearly*. The body of Wedd's project has described the conflicts as being very real, so in his conclusion he can state his thesis in much more definite terms.

The purpose of the conclusion is to provide readers with a sense of closure and to make them feel that reading the text was worthwhile. To achieve closure and convey the importance of the project, try one or more of the following strategies:

- Return to the anecdote, question, or quotation with which you began.
- Summarize your findings (especially in long or technical projects).
- Discuss how what you have learned has changed your thinking.
- Suggest a possible solution (or solutions) to the problems raised in the text.
- Indicate additional research that needs to be conducted or what the audience can do to help solve the problem.
- Leave readers with a vivid and pertinent image, quotation, or anecdote.

(For some strategies to avoid when writing your conclusion, see the Quick Reference box on the next page.)

The concluding paragraph below provides an example of an effective conclusion.

> The farmers of nineteenth-century America could afford to do here what they had not dared to do in the Old World: hope. This hope—for greater economic security, for more opportunity for themselves, their children, and their grandchildren—is the optimism and idealism that has carried our country forward and that, indeed, still carries us forward. Although the American dream has evolved across the centuries, it survives today and is a cornerstone of American philosophy. It is what underlies our Constitution and our laws, and it is a testimony to the vision of the farmers who founded this nation.
>
> —Leonard Lin, University of Southern California, "The Middle Class Farmers and the American Philosophy"

Annotations:
- Makes the audience feel time reading was well spent by showing importance of American dream
- Restates thesis (American dream = hope for greater security, opportunity)
- Achieves closure by recurring to introduction with mention of American dream

Quick Reference: Five Don'ts for Conclusions

Avoid common problems that can undermine your conclusion's success:

1. **Don't offer additional support for your thesis in your conclusion.** Such conclusions undermine the feeling of closure and leave readers wanting and expecting more.
2. **Don't end with a generality or a cliché.** Almost nothing will more undermine the readers' sense that they have spent their time well than ending with something trite.
3. **Don't apologize for the shortcomings of your project.** Such an ending will leave readers feeling they have wasted their time. If your project is truly bad, you should have revised your draft, not shared its shortcomings with readers; if it is not, you have nothing to apologize for.
4. **Don't repeat your introduction.** It may be useful to return to the anecdote or statistics with which you began, but merely repeating your introduction or thesis will insult your audience. They do not want to read the same text a second time.
5. **Don't announce what your project has done or shown ("In my paper, I have shown . . .").** In a long or complicated text, a summary can be useful to readers, but your readers will be reminded of what your text has done when they read your summary; there is no need to announce it.

→ EXERCISE 4.6 Writing introductory paragraphs

Revise the following introductory paragraph to make it more effective:

> People aged 50 and older cannot see as well at night as younger people. The small muscles that control the size of the pupil get weaker with age, and with age there may be a loss of rods, which are crucial for night vision. This affects older people's ability to adapt to the dark. This can cause problems when driving at night after the bright headlights of a car pass or just walking from well-lit to dark parts of a home. Older people need to recognize their decreased ability to see at night and to take measures that will help them be safe in the dark, whether driving, walking outdoors, or getting around the home. This paper presents the reasons why night vision is weaker in older people and some methods of compensating for this problem.

→ EXERCISE 4.7 Writing concluding paragraphs

Revise the following concluding paragraph to make it more effective:

> To summarize the point of this essay, the majority of experts acknowledge that every one of the world's seven species of marine turtles is

threatened by extinction. At present humans are causing more turtle deaths than natural forces. A key cause is habitat destruction and alteration. Coastal development is rapidly eliminating access to beaches for female turtles to nest and lay eggs. Another important cause is predation for turtle meat, eggs, hides, and shells. Incidental capture in fisheries increases the loss of turtles. Masking the threat is the slow maturation of turtles, which can hide the effect of overexploitation for many years. We need to greatly expand our knowledge of marine turtle life history patterns and the true conservation status of turtle populations, as well as the level and types of exploitation. With this knowledge we need to formulate and implement effective management and conservation strategies to preserve viable marine turtle populations. If we do not, time will run out for one of the most intriguing creatures on the face of the earth.

Make It **Your Own**

Review the introduction and conclusion of a current or recent writing project. What strategies did you use? Referring to the Quick Reference boxes and the strategies discussed in this chapter, revise your introduction and conclusion.

Work **Together**

Exchange your revised introductions and conclusions and note what strategies your classmate used in the revision. Did they work? What strategies might make these paragraphs more powerful?

Before reviewing your classmate's comments, write a paragraph reflecting on this process. What did you learn about effective introductions and conclusions by reading and evaluating someone else's? Did your classmate use any strategies you might try? Next, review the comments you received and make a note of any revisions that you plan to make.

4g Connecting Paragraphs

Readers need to know not only how sentences connect to one another but also how paragraphs are connected. One way to connect paragraphs is by using one of the patterns of development (*section 4d*) for the project, just as you would do with individual paragraphs. You can also link paragraphs using these transitional devices:

- Providing transitional expressions (and sentences)
- Repeating words and phrases strategically

- Using pronouns and synonyms to refer back to words and ideas
- Creating parallel sentence structures

A final way to create coherence among paragraphs is by referring back to the project's main idea.

The following speech by President-elect John F. Kennedy, delivered on January 9, 1961, to the General Court of the Commonwealth of Massachusetts, uses all of these strategies to create a unified and cohesive text:

Professional Model Speech

City Upon a Hill

BY JOHN F. KENNEDY

I have welcomed this opportunity to address this historic body, and, through you, the people of Massachusetts to whom I am so deeply indebted for a life-time of friendship and trust.

[Words chosen to emphasize the speaker's bond with his audience]

For fourteen years I have placed my confidence in the citizens of Massachusetts—and they have generously responded by placing their confidence in me.

Now, on the Friday after next, I am to assume new and broader responsibilities. But I am not here to bid farewell to Massachusetts.

For forty-three years—whether I was in London, Washington, the South Pacific, or elsewhere—this has been my home; and, God willing, wherever I serve this shall remain my home.

It was here my grandparents were born—it is here I hope my grandchildren will be born.

[Evidence for the claim that follows: Massachusetts is a model for the world]

I speak neither from false provincial pride nor artful political flattery. For no man about to enter high office in this country can ever be unmindful of the contribution this state has made to our national greatness.

Its leaders have shaped our destiny long before the great republic was born. Its principles have guided our footsteps in times of crisis as well as in times of calm. Its democratic institutions—including this historic body—have served as beacon lights for other nations as well as our sister states.

For what Pericles said to the Athenians has long been true of this commonwealth: "We do not imitate—for we are a model to others."

And so it is that I carry with me from this state to that high and lonely office to which I now succeed more than fond memories of firm friendships. The enduring qualities of Massachusetts—the common threads woven by the Pilgrim and the Puritan, the fisherman and the farmer, the Yankee and the immigrant—will not be and could not be forgotten in this nation's executive mansion.

[thesis]

They are an indelible part of my life, my convictions, my view of the past, and my hopes for the future.

Allow me to illustrate: During the last sixty days, I have been at the task of constructing an administration. It has been a long and deliberate process. Some have counseled greater speed. Others have counseled more expedient tests.

But I have been guided by the standard John Winthrop set before his shipmates on the flagship Arabella three hundred and thirty-one years ago, as they, too, faced the task of building a new government on a perilous frontier.

"We must always consider," he said, "that we shall be as a city upon a hill—the eyes of all people are upon us."

Today the eyes of all people are truly upon us—and our governments, in every branch, at every level, national, state and local, must be as a city upon a hill—constructed and inhabited by men aware of their great trust and their great responsibilities.

For we are setting out upon a voyage in 1961 no less hazardous than that undertaken by the Arabella in 1630. We are committing ourselves to tasks of statecraft no less awesome than that of governing the Massachusetts Bay Colony, beset as it was then by terror without and disorder within.

History will not judge our endeavors—and a government cannot be selected—merely on the basis of color or creed or even party affiliation. Neither will competence and loyalty and stature, while essential to the utmost, suffice in times such as these.

For of those to whom much is given, much is required. And when at some future date the high court of history sits in judgment on each one of us—recording whether in our brief span of service we fulfilled our responsibilities to the state—our success or failure, in whatever office we may hold, will be measured by the answers to four questions:

First, were we truly men of courage—with the courage to stand up to one's enemies—and the courage to stand up, when necessary, to one's associates—the courage to resist public pressure, as well as private greed?

Secondly, were we truly men of judgment—with perceptive judgment of the future as well as the past—of our own mistakes as well as the mistakes of others—with enough wisdom to know that we did not know, and enough candor to admit it?

Third, were we truly men of integrity—men who never ran out on either the principles in which they believed or the people who believed in them—men who believed in us—men whom neither financial gain nor political ambition could ever divert from the fulfillment of our sacred trust?

Finally, were we truly men of dedication—with an honor mortgaged to no single individual or group, and compromised by no private obligation or aim, but devoted solely to serving the public good and the national interest.

Courage—judgment—integrity—dedication—these are the historic qualities of the Bay Colony and the Bay State—the qualities which this state has consistently sent to this chamber on Beacon Hill here in Boston and to Capitol Hill back in Washington.

And these are the qualities which, with God's help, this son of Massachusetts hopes will characterize our government's conduct in the four stormy years that lie ahead. Humbly I ask His help in that undertaking—but aware that on earth His will is worked by men. I ask for your help and your prayers, as I embark on this new and solemn journey.

EXERCISE 4.8 Identifying paragraph-building techniques

Review John F. Kennedy's "City Upon a Hill" speech as follows:

1. Check each paragraph for relevance, unity, and coherence. Highlight topic sentences and identify the patterns used to develop paragraphs. (Patterns may be mixed.) Note examples of strategies described in this chapter.
2. Identify and review the introductory and concluding paragraphs. Note the techniques used to begin and end the speech.
3. Identify the methods Kennedy used to weave the paragraphs into a unified and cohesive whole: Circle the repeated words, underline the transitional expressions, and draw a box around the pronouns and synonyms that refer back to earlier passages.

Make It Your Own

Select a current or recent writing project and review it using the three steps described in Exercise 4.8. Write your observations in the margin and note any revisions you might make to develop your ideas more fully. If this is a project you are currently drafting, use this review to help you revise it.

Text Credits

Pg 55, 69: Adrianne Anderson Speas; **Pg 56:** Simon Holt, Katy Alexander, Becky Degler, "The Problem Solvers You Don't Know About Yet: Valuing Disability in the Publishing Industry," The Scholarly Kitchen; **Pg 57:** Jessi Kneeland, "8 Lessons on Unconditional Self-Love (aka: Crazy Hair Don't Care)," Remodel Fitness; **Pg 58–59:** Laura Jean Schneider, "Ranch Diaries: One Dog Can Be Worth Three Hands," High Country News, September 8, 2015. Copyright © 2015 High Country News. Used with permission. **Pg 60:** Castle Freeman, "Surviving Deer Season: A Lesson in Ambiguity," Atlantic Monthly, December 1995. Used with permission of the author. **Pg 64:** Virginia Morell, "OK, There It Is—Our Mystery Mollusk," from "Monterey Menagerie," National Geographic, June 2004. Copyright © 2004 by Virginia Morell. Reprinted by permission of the author; **Pg 67:** Boot, Max, "Abusing Anonymity," Commentary, February 23, 2016. Copyright © 2016 Commentary, Inc. Used with permission. Pg 74–76: Source: John F. Kennedy, "City Upon a Hill" speech delivered to a Joint Convention of the General Court of the Commonwealth of Massachusetts, The State House, Boston, January 9, 1961.

5 Drafting and Revising Visuals

IN THIS CHAPTER

a. Illustrating a college project, 77

b. Visuals as evidence, 78

c. Copying and creating visuals, 82

d. Revising visuals, 82

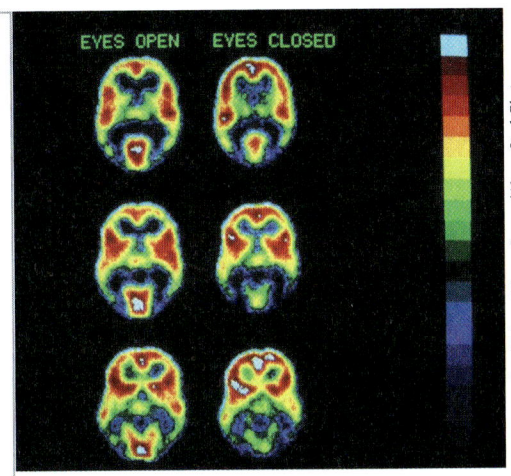

Visuals can bring life to a written text: A Facebook page, a political ad, a website—all would be boring without images. Visuals play a much more important role than mere decoration, however; they also help us understand the world. The colors in these PET scans, for example, inform researchers about the portions of the brain that are activated when a subject's eyes are open (left) or closed (right). Images from the Hubble Space Telescope make the theoretical real: They inform viewers about the universe that surrounds our home planet.

5a Deciding Whether to Illustrate College Writing Projects

In personal writing, visuals are often used to entertain or express the writer's thoughts or feelings. In business and public writing, visuals can make an arguable claim and provide evidence for it. In academic writing, visuals may engage or persuade readers, but their primary role is to aid understanding. A photograph of a painting you are analyzing for an art history course, a graph comparing voter turnout among age groups for a political science project, a video or animation that describes the course of a disease for a biology assignment—all these would be appropriate illustrations in an academic text.

Writing Matters • Drafting and Revising Visuals

> **More about**
> Purpose, 15–17
> Audience, 18–21
> Context and genre, 22

To determine whether a visual is appropriate in a college project, ask yourself these questions:

- **Does this visual reinforce my purpose?** The primary purpose of visuals in academic writing is to inform. They may have a secondary persuasive purpose—evidence should be chosen that the audience will find convincing—but the primary purpose will be informative rather than persuasive.

> **Student Models**
> Visual support, 131, 161, 170, 385, 387, 388, 438, 463

- **Is this visual appropriate to my audience, context, and genre?** To determine whether illustrations are appropriate, look at articles from journals in your field or ask your instructor.

- **Does the "tone" of the visual match that of the text?** While a caricature might be an amusing or pungent feature of a political magazine or poster, it would not be appropriate in most college projects. For an example of the appropriate use of a visual, see the image in the student paper by Isabel Beck on p. 388 and Aidan Kelley on p. 131.

Photographs in Job Applications In Europe and Asia, it is common to include a personal photograph with a job application. In the United States, however, it is generally considered inappropriate for a résumé to include a photograph (or a physical description of the job candidate). In fact, US employers are barred by law from asking applicants personal questions, such as their age, marital status, race, religion, or sexual orientation.

5b Using Visuals as Evidence

In academic writing, visuals are used primarily as evidence. Choose the right type of illustration for the information you wish to convey.

1. Information graphics

Information graphics such as tables, bar graphs, line graphs, and pie charts convey and depict relationships among data.

Tables Tables, such as Table 5.1, organize large amounts of information in rows and columns for easy viewing. The information in a table can be textual, graphic, or numeric, but it is usually numeric. Tables are frequently the best choice for presenting data on more than four variables or data that include decimals.

Bar graphs and pie charts Bar graphs and pie charts allow comparison of data in two or more categories. A bar graph (Figure 5.1) uses bars of different colors and heights (or lengths). A pie chart (Figure 5.2) uses segments of a circle to

Writing Matters • Using Visuals as Evidence   **5b**   79

TABLE 5.1 | **CHILDREN 3 TO 21 YEARS OLD SERVED IN FEDERALLY SUPPORTED PROGRAMS FOR THE DISABLED, BY TYPE OF DISABILITY (2018–19)**

Disability type	2018–19
Autism	11
Developmental delay	7
Emotional disturbance	5
Hearing impairment	1
Intellectual disability	6
Multiple disabilities	2
Other health impairment	15
Orthopedic impairment	1
Specific learning disability	33
Speech or language impairment	19

Source: US Dept. of Educ., Inst. of Educ. Sciences, Natl. Center for Educ. Statistics, *Digest of Education Statistics*, 2020.

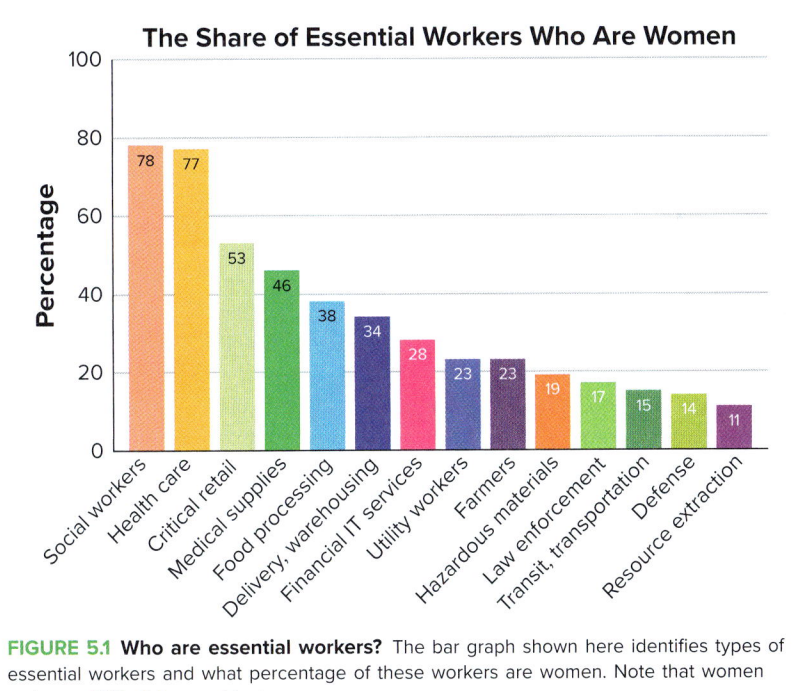

The Share of Essential Workers Who Are Women

Category	Percentage
Social workers	78
Health care	77
Critical retail	53
Medical supplies	46
Food processing	38
Delivery, warehousing	34
Financial IT services	28
Utility workers	23
Farmers	23
Hazardous materials	19
Law enforcement	17
Transit, transportation	15
Defense	14
Resource extraction	11

FIGURE 5.1 Who are essential workers? The bar graph shown here identifies types of essential workers and what percentage of these workers are women. Note that women make up 52% of the workforce.
Source: American Community Survey micro data and *The New York Times*. https://www.nytimes.com/2020/09/24/learning/whats-going-on-in-this-graph-essential-workers.html

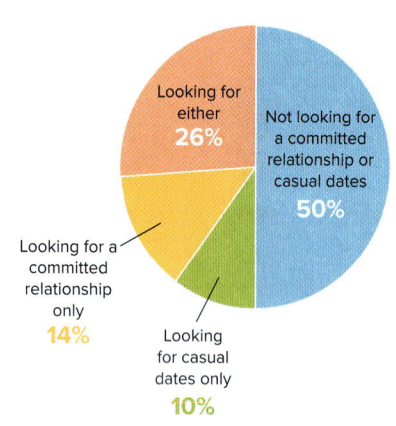

FIGURE 5.2 Americans' view on relationships and dates This pie chart breaks down the views of 4,860 adults who responded to a question in a national survey conducted in October 2019 by the Pew Research Center. Because the information to be conveyed is relatively simple (there are just four different percentages), it can easily be conveyed in a pie chart that totals 100.
Source: Data from Pew Research Center, Oct. 16–28, 2019. pewresearch.org.

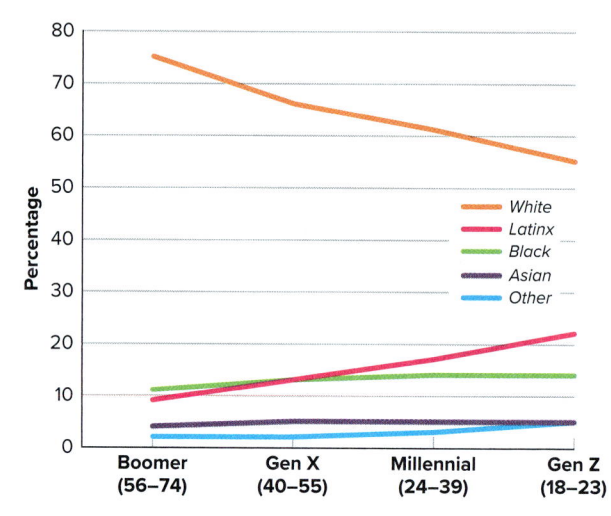

- Not looking for a committed relationship or casual dates: 50%
- Looking for either: 26%
- Looking for a committed relationship only: 14%
- Looking for casual dates only: 10%

FIGURE 5.3 Generation Z voters: One-in-five are Latinx This line graph allows readers to see at a glance the diversity of Gen Z voters (7- to 22-year-olds) in comparison to earlier generations of voters. The Pew Research Center put this data together based on the analysis of the 2020 Current Population and Economic Supplement (IPUMS).
Data from Pew Research Center, 1970, 1987, 2003, 2019. pewresearch.org.

Student Models
Isabel Beck, "Fast Fashion: An Unethical Industry that Harms Garment Workers and the Environment" (research paper, MLA style), 383–96
Brianna Davids, "Inmate Access to Technology: Safer Prisons and More Successful Reentries to Society" (exploratory argument, researched, MLA style), 159–74
Robyn Worthington, "Nature versus Nurture" (research paper, APA style), 430–38

depict portions of a whole. Choose a pie chart when comparing percentages that add up to 100. Both bar graphs and pie charts work best with a small number of categories where the differences among them are clear. Isabel Beck, Brianna Davids, and Robyn Worthington use bar graphs to supply evidence succinctly.

Line graphs Line graphs (such as Figure 5.3) are especially useful in illustrating change over time. The more lines, the more types of data that can be compared (but the more complex the graphic). As with bar graphs and pie charts, line graphs work best when you are comparing only a few variables. Too many variables make it difficult to convey the information clearly.

2. Images

Academic writers use images such as photographs, screenshots, film stills, and architectural renderings as references, as when writing about a work of art or a scene from a movie, and they use them as examples. The photograph in Figure 5.4 would provide an effective example in a project exploring the connections between past and current immigration issues.

FIGURE 5.4 Photographs in history
Photographs are frequently used in history projects to supply visual evidence. This image taken by the photographer Lewis W. Hine was originally titled: "Italian Immigrants at Ellis Island, 1905." Hine's original caption reads: "Lost baggage is the cause of their worried expressions. At the height of immigration the entire first floor of the administration building was used to store baggage."

Everett Collection/Shutterstock

Just as a historian might include an image of an eighteenth-century map to show readers the area explored by the first Europeans in the Pacific Northwest, Isabel Beck's project includes an image of a garment factory disaster to illustrate the dangers that fast fashion poses to workers (page 388).

EXERCISE 5.1 Using visuals as evidence

For one of the thesis statements you revised in Exercise 3.2, describe the type of visuals you might use as support.

Writing Responsibly | EXPLOITATIVE IMAGES

When using images in your academic work, keep in mind that ethical writing cannot include images that might be seen as manipulating the audience emotionally or exploiting people the images depict. As you review your selection of images, think about what is useful for developing your topic; how much respect you are extending to the people depicted; and how those people might feel about your use of the image.

> **More about**
> Placing visuals on the page, 381–82 (MLA), 428–29 (APA)

to TOPIC

5c Deciding Whether to Copy Visuals or to Create Them

Artwork that you create can often be more effective than material derived from others. Some illustrations, however, must come from an outside source, either because the subject is inaccessible (as with a historical photograph) or because the software that would be needed for creating the visual is beyond the writer's expertise.

Whenever you borrow images from an outside source, be sure to identify your source, either in the figure caption (for most illustrations) or in a source note (for tables). While you are not required to obtain permission to use a visual in your college projects, you will need permission if you plan to publish your project, even on the web.

5d Revising Visuals

As you revise your project, reconsider not only your words but your visuals, too. Make sure they are clear and accurate and that they avoid distortion.

1. Avoid visual clutter.

Revise your information graphics so they are clean, simple, and easy to understand. Omit lines around cells in a table; use them only to set off headings or to indicate major divisions (Table 5.2). Leave space between columns, and align numbers to make graphics easier to read. Avoid using special views or shading that could make your visual more difficult to interpret (Figure 5.5).

2. Keep visuals clear and accurate.

Double-check the numbers in tables and figures to make sure totals are accurate and that percentages in a pie chart total 100. (If rounding the numbers

---

Tech — **Consider the Size of Your Document**

Submitting an illustrated document brings with it certain concerns:

- If you will be submitting your project on paper, make sure you have access to a printer of sufficient quality to handle your graphics.
- If you will be submitting your project electronically, think about how large a file your email program—and that of your recipient—can handle. Because image files dramatically increase the size of a document file, you may wish to compress them before sending.
- If you will be delivering your project online, make sure to optimize your graphics for the web so that they load quickly into the reader's browser.

TABLE 5.2 Less is more Instead of enhancing clarity, lines around cells and abbreviations in headings in the table on the left can make the visual more difficult to read.

Johnsville Tigers Batting Statistics

NAME	AB	R	H	SO	BA
Tamika	12	2	5	7	.416
Alyssa	14	0	1	13	.071
Travis	12	5	7	5	.583
Jose	15	3	5	10	.333
Akira	13	6	8	5	.615
Walid	14	7	7	7	.500
Taylor	5	4	1	4	.200
Leslie	11	2	4	7	.363
Chloe	9	3	5	4	.555
Derek	8	7	6	2	.250
Maria	14	4	6	8	.571
Ahmed	12	5	3	9	.250
Carlos	12	4	4	8	.333
Antoine	14	6	5	9	.357
B.J.	5	2	2	3	.400
Sasha	15	7	6	9	.400

NAME	AT BATS	RUNS	HITS	STRIKE OUTS	BATTING AVERAGE
Tamika	12	2	5	7	.416
Alyssa	14	0	1	13	.071
Travis	12	5	7	5	.583
Jose	15	3	5	10	.333
Akira	13	6	8	5	.615
Walid	14	7	7	7	.500
Taylor	5	4	1	4	.200
Leslie	11	2	4	7	.363
Chloe	9	3	5	4	.555
Derek	8	7	6	2	.250
Maria	14	4	6	8	.571
Ahmed	12	5	3	9	.250
Carlos	12	4	4	8	.333
Antoine	14	6	5	9	.357
B.J.	5	2	2	3	.400
Sasha	15	7	6	9	.400

up or down has caused inaccuracy, indicate this in a note.) Label all parts of your tables and figures (columns, rows, vertical and horizontal axes, "slices" of a pie chart) so that readers can understand them without having to read the text. Avoid abbreviations that might be unfamiliar or confusing (Figure 5.5).

3. Avoid distortion.

Make sure the information supplied in visuals is complete. The graph on the left in Figure 5.6 distorts the disparity in number of dog and cat owners by starting the scale at 30,000. Changing the vertical axis in the revised graph on the right more accurately reflects the difference. Cropping photographs to eliminate background or to focus on the main action is acceptable, but cropping to distort information is unethical, as is using image-processing programs to change or distort an image.

4. Do not manipulate.

Advertisements may use photographs that tug on readers' heartstrings or tap insecurities (Figure 5.7). An academic audience, however, will expect images that stir the emotions to be supported by arguments grounded in logic.

> **More about**
> Logical appeals (logos), 150–53
> Emotional appeals (pathos), 154

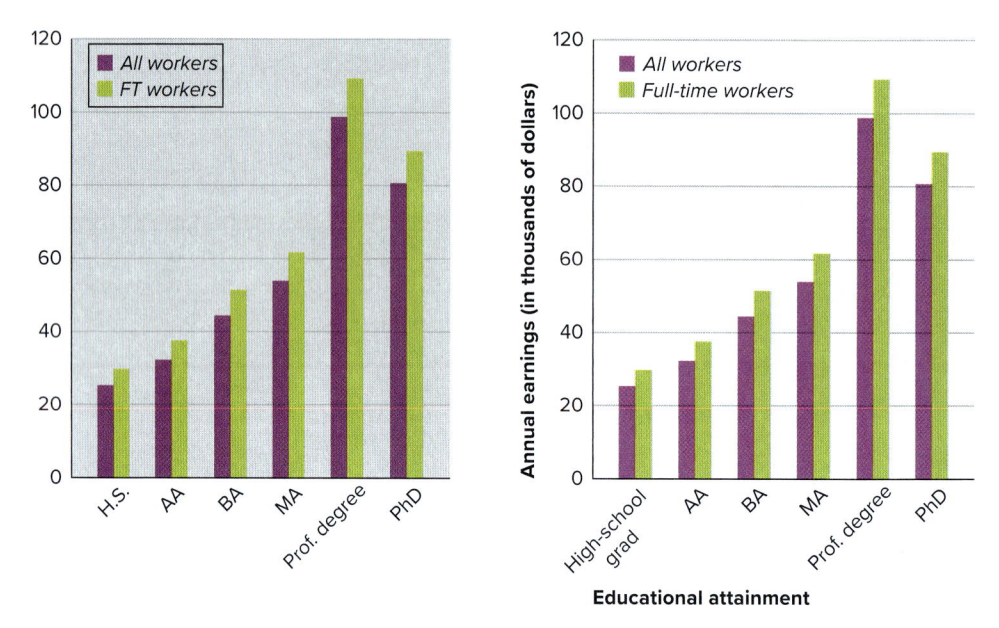

FIGURE 5.5 Clarity and precision The bar graph at left will be more difficult for readers to interpret than the graph at right: "Full-time" is abbreviated to FT and "high-school" to H.S., which could be confusing; no indication is given that the dollar amounts are in thousands; and the shading and the box around the legend make the figure unnecessarily busy.

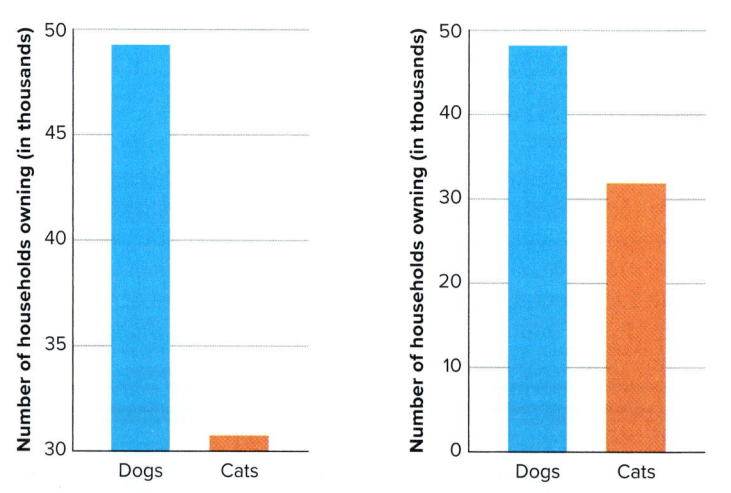

FIGURE 5.6 Distortion in scale By starting the vertical scale at 30,000, the graph at left distorts the difference in the number of households. The graph at right more accurately depicts the differences.

Writing Matters • Revising Visuals **5d** 85

FIGURE 5.7 Manipulative images in advertising
Published in magazines in 1950s, this deodorant ad not only preys on women and projects insecurity, it also undermines women in the workplace.

Quick Reference: Matching Visual Evidence to Claims

- **Tables** display large amounts of information, data that include decimals, or information on multiple variables that are difficult to convey in a graph.
- **Pie charts** convey significant divisions in a single entity that add up to 100 percent.
- **Bar graphs** compare two or more variables.
- **Line graphs** show changes among variables over time.
- **Diagrams** model processes or locations.
- **Maps** represent geographic locations; may also include data.
- **Photographs** provide readers with a reference point or an example, or depict a process (two or more photographs needed).
- **Movie stills** provide a reference point, offer an example, or show a process (two or more stills needed).
- **Advertisements** provide a reference point or an example, present a claim and related image(s), and use rhetorical appeals to persuade or even manipulate readers; may include data (which must be tested).
- **Screenshots** provide a reference point or an example from an electronic resource, such as a website.

6 Revising, Editing, Proofreading, and Formatting

IN THIS CHAPTER

REVISING GLOBALLY

a. Gaining perspective, 86

b. Revising your draft, 87

c. Reconsidering your title, 90

REVISING LOCALLY

d. Choosing words carefully, 91

e. Editing sentences, 91

REVISING WITH OTHERS

f. Peer revising, 93

g. Revising with a tutor or instructor, 95

PROOFREADING AND FORMATTING

h. Proofreading, 96

i. Formatting, 98

j. Creating and submitting a portfolio, 106

Student Models
Final Draft of a Researched Essay (MLA style, annotated)
Michael Wedd, "Rethinking Alternative Energy," 99–105;
Personal Statement,
Rachana Ky, 108–10

Krista Kennedy

Before electronic navigational systems became commonplace, lighthouses were an essential part of navigational safety for sailors. Located on coastlines, they shone a clear, bright beam out to sea, alerting sailors to nearby land. After you have drafted a first version of your writing project, begin the process of revising, editing, and proofreading so your readers can see clear signals of coherence and meaning throughout your text.

REVISING GLOBALLY: ANALYZING YOUR OWN WORK

Revising globally means learning to re-see—looking at the big picture to address elements like thesis, evidence, audience, context, genre, and ethical responsibilities. The first step toward assessing these aspects of your writing is to take a break so you can see your work with fresh eyes. Then you can be more objective as you adjust focus and organization, make changes to address your audience more effectively, and develop your ideas more fully.

6a Gaining Perspective

Writers generally feel a sense of "ownership" toward the texts they compose. This helps them produce an authentic voice and a commitment to the ideas they express. Yet that sense of ownership can hold a writer back from making needed changes. To gain objectivity, writers can draw on a wide range of techniques, such as those described in the Quick Reference box on the next page.

> **Quick Reference — Seven Ways to Gain Objectivity about Your Draft**
>
> 1. **Allow time between drafts.** A few days or even a few hours between drafts can provide the needed distance from your draft.
> 2. **Clear your mind.** Do something to get your mind off your project, such as going for a run or playing a quick game of Fortnite.
> 3. **Learn from other readers.** Having others read and respond to your draft will give you a sense of what your text is (and is not) communicating.
> 4. **Analyze the work of a fellow writer.** Most tutors and teachers will tell you that they learn as much from the coaching experience as do the people whom they coach.
> 5. **Listen to your draft being read aloud.** Every time your reader stumbles, pauses, or has to reread a passage, mark the spot. Then figure out what caused the hesitation, and revise accordingly.
> 6. **Outline your draft.** Once your outline is complete, read it through carefully. If any sections seem unconnected to the thesis or to the sections before or after, reorganize.
> 7. **Compare your text to others in a similar context and genre.** When writing in an unfamiliar context or genre, reading professional texts may help you see what does and does not work in your own writing.

> *More about*
> Peer revising, 93–95

6b Revising Your Draft

Begin revising by rereading the text. Read your project through to the end before making any changes. Then reread and take notes. As you work through each paragraph, focus on the global issues of thesis, evidence, organization, and development. Most writers revise for just one issue at a time, rereading for each issue. At this stage you should skip over local issues such as spelling and punctuation; do not let them distract you.

1. Thesis and introduction

Because writers often discover and develop their ideas as they compose, the first draft of the thesis may not capture the evolving project's main idea. (Often, the true thesis appears in the conclusion of the first draft.) This might mean you should adjust your evidence to your thesis. More frequently it means you should revise your thesis to match the evidence offered in your draft. Check too, to be sure that the introduction indicates your purpose—your reasons for writing—and your attitude toward your material. Are you skeptical? Enthusiastic? Hesitant? Confident? Still figuring it out?

> *More about*
> Drafting a thesis, 35–36
> Revising a thesis, 37–38
> Drafting an introduction, 68–70

In addition to revising your thesis, consider your introduction. Is the length proportionate to the whole project? A three-paragraph introduction is fine for a seven-page paper, but if the whole project is only a few paragraphs long, the introduction should be very short. Does the introduction provide necessary background, a relevant anecdote, or compelling statistics that will give the audience a context for your thesis?

2. Evidence and counterevidence

> **More about**
> Organizing arguments, 174–76

Rereading your draft, you may have had concerns about the evidence for your thesis. Perhaps the draft is unconvincing or overly general, or the evidence came from only one perspective. Perhaps you did not have enough evidence. If you need more or better evidence, go back to the idea-generating stage, do additional research, or search for diverse viewpoints on your topic. Perhaps your draft talked only about the evidence for your thesis but ignored counterevidence. An effective argument shows both evidence and counterevidence, and it explains why the writer believes the evidence is more credible than the counterevidence.

3. Audience

> **More about**
> Audience, 18–21
> Introduction, 68–70
> Development, 45–47, 64–68
> Connotation, 20–21, 606
> Level of formality, 20–21, 599
> Conclusions, 70–72

After rereading your text, consider how your readers will react. Will you win them over? Look at your introduction. Will it make your audience want to keep reading? Next, consider the evidence and counterevidence in your body paragraphs. Will it inform or persuade the people who will be reading your project? Now consider your word choice. Is the language appropriate to those people? An academic or business audience will expect a more formal tone but will not need you to define specialized terms; a general audience may be more engaged by an informal tone and may need specialized terms clearly defined. Is the language free of bias? Finally, review your conclusion. Will it provide readers with a feeling of closure? Tailor the conclusion to the needs of your readers. For a long or complex text, readers may need a summary; for a persuasive one, readers may want to take action, so offer any suggestions you might have.

4. Organization

> **More about**
> Unity, 53–57
> Coherence, 58–62
> Transitions, 59–60, 807

Rereading your draft may have alerted you to problems with organization. When revising, make sure that your project is both unified and coherent. In a unified text, all the paragraphs support the thesis, and all the details in each paragraph support the paragraph's main idea.

Writing Responsibly: The Big Picture

A useful way to think about revising is to focus on your responsibilities to your diverse audience, your topic, other writers, and yourself:

- Have you provided your audience with a worthwhile reading experience?
- Have you covered your topic fully and creatively?
- Have you represented borrowed ideas accurately and acknowledged all your sources, whether you have quoted, summarized, or paraphrased?
- Have you developed a stance that readers will find credible, represented your ideas clearly and powerfully, and written in a voice that is a reflection of your best self?

to SELF

Self Assessment

As you revise, check your draft for the following elements. If the answer to any question is no, make the revisions necessary.

Introduction
- ☐ **Thesis** Does my thesis state my main claim? Does my thesis match the evidence in my draft? Does the introduction indicate my purpose and attitude toward my topic?
- ☐ **Evidence and counterevidence** Does my introduction indicate the complexity of my topic and how I will support my thesis?
- ☐ **Audience** Does my introduction provide needed background information? Will the introduction be engaging or compelling for the people reading my project?
- ☐ **Organization** Does my introduction give readers a sense of how the body of my project will develop my ideas?

Body Paragraphs
- ☐ **Thesis** Does my whole draft explain why I believe the thesis? Is each body paragraph relevant to my thesis? Is the evidence in each paragraph relevant to the paragraph's topic?
- ☐ **Evidence and counterevidence** Is the evidence I supply relevant? Do I supply enough evidence? Is the evidence compelling? Do I show counterevidence to my thesis? Do I cite my sources?
- ☐ **Audience** Will my readers need more (or less) information? Are my tone and word choices appropriate for this audience?
- ☐ **Organization** Does my organizational pattern suit my evidence? Does each paragraph lead logically to the next?

Conclusion
- ☐ **Thesis** Is my conclusion focused on a relevant issue that shows the importance of my topic? Does it reinforce my purpose?
- ☐ **Evidence and counterevidence** Does my conclusion avoid introducing new supporting evidence?
- ☐ **Audience** Does my conclusion provide an action plan, a reflection, or a necessary summary?
- ☐ **Organization** Does my conclusion follow logically from the body paragraphs?

Writing Matters • Revising, Editing, Proofreading, and Formatting

> **More about**
> Relevance, 53, 263–64
> Generating ideas, 25–31
> Developing paragraphs, 64–68
> Finding information (ch. 13), 237–62

When revising, be prepared to delete ideas, facts, and even whole paragraphs—no matter how much you like them—if they do not support your thesis.

In a coherent text, the relationship among the paragraphs is clear and logical. Sometimes a text lacks coherence because the writer has not included transitional words and phrases that signal the relationships among ideas. Sometimes it lacks coherence because a step in the argument has been omitted or the ideas are not fully supported. It may lack coherence because the relationships among the paragraphs are unclear.

6c Reconsidering Your Title

Once you have revised your draft globally, revisit the title. It should prepare your audience for what they will read in your text. For most college projects, your title should accurately reflect not only the topic but also your approach to it:

Note how these writers use a descriptive phrase to make their titles more specific.

- Fast Fashion: An Unethical Industry that Harms Workers and the Environment
- Inmate Access to Technology: Safer Prisons and More Successful Reentries to Society

Note how these writers indicate their approach in their titles.

- A Critical Analysis of on Rene Brooks's "Time Blindness"
- Rhetorical Analysis of Konstantin Ivanov's "The Way Is Open for Humans" (poster)

Make It Your Own

Review a writing project you have gotten back from an instructor, and write a paragraph explaining how you fulfilled your responsibilities as a writer. (See "The Big Picture," p. 89.) Are there any global issues you would revise now if you had the opportunity? Explain.

REVISING LOCALLY: EDITING WORDS AND SENTENCES

persona The apparent personality of the writer as conveyed through tone and style

Your writing is a reflection of you—your ideas and your attitude toward your topic and audience. Revise locally to make your words and sentences reflect your meaning and create a *persona* that is open-minded, free of bias, and appropriate for your purpose, audience, context, and genre.

6d Choosing Your Words with Care

When revising, reconsider your word choices. Each word should reflect your intended meaning; it should have accurate **denotation.** Choose a word that expresses your exact meaning: If readers have to guess your intent, they may not guess correctly, and they may be annoyed by having to figure it out.

In addition to denotations, words have **connotations**—emotional associations that affect readers' interpretations. Compare *freedom fighter* with *terrorist*. Both words have the same denotation; both refer to people who use violence to achieve political ends. The connotative difference, however, is enormous, showing the writer's attitude toward the fighter.

Next, consider the level of formality that is appropriate to your audience, context, and genre: A text message to a friend may be filled with slang and acronyms, but this informality is rarely appropriate in academic or professional writing. Trying too hard to sound formal can also go wrong: Writers who intend to sound sophisticated by trotting out a word like *progenitor* to mean *parent* may instead make themselves sound pompous.

All writing benefits from avoiding biased language—language that unfairly or offensively characterizes groups or individuals.

Finally, consider whether you have combined general, abstract language with specific, concrete words; explaining broad issues requires abstract language, but specific words will make your writing more compelling.

> **More about**
> Denotation, 20–21, 605, 608–9
> Connotation, 20–21, 606, 608–9
> Levels of formality, 20–21, 599
> Biased language, 600–3
> General and specific language, 606–8

6e Editing Your Sentences

When revising, reconsider the structure of your sentences:

1. Are they grammatically correct?
2. Are they varied, and do they emphasize the most important information?
3. Are they as concise as they can be without losing meaning or affecting style?

In most contexts (academic and business, in particular), readers expect sentences to be formed according to the conventions of English grammar. Nongrammatical sentences may confuse, distract, or even annoy readers. Edit your prose to conform to standard written English.

Once you are sure your sentences are clear and correct, shape them to reflect your emphases. A good way to begin editing for style is to read your draft out loud—or better still, get a friend to read it to you. Listen to the rhythm of your sentences. Do they all sound alike? If so, your sentences probably use the same sentence structure, or they all begin the same way.

> **More about**
> Common sentence problems (Grammar Matters tutorial preceding ch. 33), 628–33
> Sentence types, 657–58
> Sentence variety, 587
> Writing concisely (ch. 26), 557–64
> Style, 557–626 (part 7)
> Grammar, 627–756 (part 8)
> Punctuation and mechanics, 801–82 (part 10)

> **More about**
> Writing concisely (ch. 26), 558–64
> Coordination and subordination (ch. 27), 565–77
> Parallelism (ch. 28), 578–85
> Variety and emphasis (ch. 29), 586–95

To improve the situation, consider the information in your sentences. Combine related information in a single sentence by putting the most important information in the independent (main) clause, with additional information in the subordinate (dependent) clause. If the information is of equal weight, use compound sentences and parallel structures to emphasize this balance. Where appropriate, use questions, commands, and exclamations for variety or emphasis.

In addition to writing varied sentences, hone them to eliminate clutter, and polish them to highlight your ideas. Try these strategies to revise for wordiness:

- Eliminate empty expressions, intensifiers, roundabout expressions, and redundancies.
- Eliminate ineffective repetition.
- Favor the active voice.

Writing Responsibly: Making Your Text Long Enough without Wordiness

When your text is too short, you may be tempted to pad it with wordy sentences, but that might make it hard (and boring) to read. Instead, try these tips:

- Revisit your thesis: Is it too narrow? If so, explore strategies for broadening it.
- Check your evidence: Have you offered facts, statistics, expert testimony, and examples to support your thesis? If not, return to the library or its website to search for more information. Have you explained your evidence so that your audience will understand it? Have you specified exactly how your evidence supports your thesis?
- Analyze your counterevidence: Are you showing your audience the whole range of perspectives or only the data that support your thesis? Most audiences will appreciate knowing not just why you believe your thesis but also why you believe it even though there are other reasonable interpretations of the issue.

to TOPIC

> **More about**
> Empty phrases, 559
> Roundabout and redundant expressions, 560–61
> Ineffective repetition, 561
> Using the active voice, 562, 593–94

Writing concisely for the web is particularly important, as most users prefer pages that are easy to scan.

Because not every writer makes the same kinds of errors, individualized checklists are useful. To create your own, try the following:

1. Review the last five texts that you have produced, looking for the kinds of common sentence errors noted in the Grammar Matters tutorial preceding chapter 33 (part 8).
2. List the issues that you, your peers, your tutor, or your instructor find.
3. Reorganize the list so that the types of errors you make most frequently are at the top.

Each time you write, use the top five items on your editing checklist to guide your local revisions. Over time, you are likely to make fewer of these errors.

NOTE Instructors often use symbols to indicate the most common mistakes. Learn these symbols so that you can correct errors your instructor identifies and improve your draft.

> **More about**
> List of editing symbols,

REVISING WITH OTHERS

As writers, we can be touchy. We pour ourselves into our texts and feel hurt that others might not understand or appreciate what we have written. Little wonder, then, that we often feel defensive when others read our work before it is finished. Yet paradoxically, getting feedback from a real, live audience is one of the best ways to make sure readers—who do not have you standing by to explain—will understand your writing, will be convinced by your evidence, will be persuaded by your conclusion, and will form a high opinion of you as a responsible, authoritative writer.

6f Revising with Peers

One way to get feedback from readers is to solicit comments from your peers. In business, this might mean sharing your text with coworkers online or via email. In school, this usually means sharing your draft with your classmates face to face or through a class blog or wiki. Whether in a business or academic context, the role of writer and peer editor carries its own responsibilities.

1. The writer's role

When readers respond to your text, adopt a stance that is both engaged and receptive:

- **Talk.** Before readers begin to comment, explain what you are trying to accomplish and what you would like help with.
- **Listen.** As others respond to your draft, listen instead of arguing or defending. If readers seem uninformed or inattentive, figure out how you can revise the text so that even an uninformed or inattentive reader can understand what you are trying to say.

Peer Review with Multilingual Students Students are sometimes uneasy about working in peer groups. Yet participating in these groups can reduce everyone's concerns, as they realize everyone makes mistakes, and everyone benefits from feedback from a diverse group of readers. Group work helps non-native speakers of English become more familiar with the rules and idiosyncrasies of English—resolving difficult issues of idiom and word choice, for example—and more trustful of native speakers' natural abilities with their language.

Native English-speaking students may also be hesitant to work in groups with peers from different language backgrounds. However, workplaces, like college, are increasingly globalized. Native speakers of English benefit from hearing the perspectives of multilingual peers whose diverse experiences with language and culture may provide insightful perspectives on topic, interpretation, organization, word choice, grammar, and style.

- **Question.** If your readers are not addressing your concerns or are speaking in generalities, ask them to point to specific passages. Ask yourself what underlying issue they are trying to get at. Do not settle for a disappointing response.
- **Write.** Take notes as your readers talk. What they say may be vivid at the time, but you will be surprised by how quickly you might forget the details.
- **Evaluate.** You are the person who must make the final decision. Be open to advice, but also evaluate the advice you receive. Is it sound advice? How much will it help your project? How well will it work for you as a writer?

2. The peer reviewer's role

As a reader of a classmate's draft, keep the following guidelines in mind:

- **Stay positive.** Tell the writer what is working well, along with what could be improved (Figure 6.1).
- **Talk to the writer.** Listen and respond to the writer's concerns, whether conducting the session face to face or asynchronously.
- **Look at the big picture, but be specific.** Focus on what the writer is trying to achieve, but back up general comments by pointing to specific passages in the text and explaining as best you can how they might work better for you as a reader.
- **Be a reader and a fellow writer—not a teacher, editor, or critic.** Your job is not to judge the text or to rewrite it, but to participate in its composition by helping the writer recognize and resolve issues.

Writing Matters • Revising with a Tutor or an Instructor 6g 95

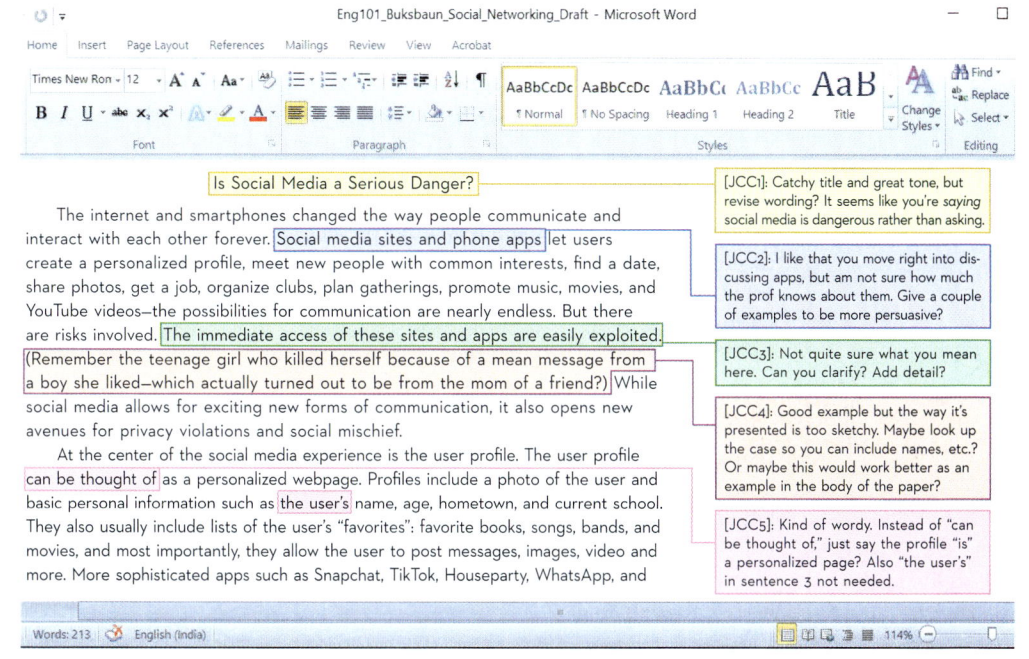

Is Social Media a Serious Danger?

The internet and smartphones changed the way people communicate and interact with each other forever. Social media sites and phone apps let users create a personalized profile, meet new people with common interests, find a date, share photos, get a job, organize clubs, plan gatherings, promote music, movies, and YouTube videos—the possibilities for communication are nearly endless. But there are risks involved. The immediate access of these sites and apps are easily exploited. (Remember the teenage girl who killed herself because of a mean message from a boy she liked—which actually turned out to be from the mom of a friend?) While social media allows for exciting new forms of communication, it also opens new avenues for privacy violations and social mischief.

At the center of the social media experience is the user profile. The user profile can be thought of as a personalized webpage. Profiles include a photo of the user and basic personal information such as the user's name, age, hometown, and current school. They also usually include lists of the user's "favorites": favorite books, songs, bands, and movies, and most importantly, they allow for the user to post messages, images, video and more. More sophisticated apps such as Snapchat, TikTok, Houseparty, WhatsApp, and

Comments:
- [JCC1]: Catchy title and great tone, but revise wording? It seems like you're *saying* social media is dangerous rather than asking.
- [JCC2]: I like that you move right into discussing apps, but am not sure how much the prof knows about them. Give a couple of examples to be more persuasive?
- [JCC3]: Not quite sure what you mean here. Can you clarify? Add detail?
- [JCC4]: Good example but the way it's presented is too sketchy. Maybe look up the case so you can include names, etc.? Or maybe this would work better as an example in the body of the paper?
- [JCC5]: Kind of wordy. Instead of "can be thought of," just say the profile "is" a personalized page? Also "the user's" in sentence 3 not needed.

FIGURE 6.1 Electronic peer review If conducting peer review electronically, remember that there is a person on the receiving end of your comments. Stay positive, helpful, and friendly, and link each comment to something specific in the text.

6g Revising with a Tutor or an Instructor

Many colleges sponsor a writing center that offers free tutoring or online services such as NetTutor. Many instructors also allow students to submit a rough draft of their projects for comment. Take full advantage of these opportunities, and when you do, follow these guidelines:

> **More about**
> Time management, 24, 223–24

- **Be prepared.** Bring a copy of your assignment, your textbook or handbook, any sources you are using, and whatever writing you might have already done on the assignment, even if that writing is very informal or a work in progress.

- **Be open to advice.** Bring your own list of issues or concerns about the text or project, but also be receptive to broader issues or suggestions. Your tutor or instructor may have concerns that go beyond your list and that require you to reconsider your assumptions, revise your thesis, or conduct additional research.

- **Be an active participant.** If the tutor or instructor makes a suggestion you do not understand, ask for an explanation (and take notes). If you disagree with a suggestion, figure out the underlying issue and an alternative resolution. Then revise.

> ### Work Together
>
> Exchange with a classmate a writing project you are working on or recently completed. Explain what you are trying to accomplish, and listen to your classmate's comments, asking for clarification and taking notes. Now respond to your classmate's draft. Remember to point to specific words, sentences, and paragraphs.
>
> ### Make It Your Own
>
> Using comments you received from your classmate, revise your draft. After completing the process, write a paragraph discussing which of your peer's suggestions made the biggest difference in your revision, and why. If you did not find the process helpful, discuss what you and your classmate might have done to make it more productive.

PROOFREADING AND FORMATTING

> **More about**
> Using a dictionary, 615–17
> Usage glossary, G15–G20
> Homonyms and near homonyms, 618–19

6h Proofreading

When revising, your focus is on your ideas and how you express them; when proofreading, you focus on correcting errors.

To proofread effectively, divorce yourself from the draft you know so well, so that you can see the text as it actually appears on the page. An effective way to achieve this distance is to print out your draft and read the hard copy line by line from the bottom up. Mark each correction on the printout as you read; enter them one by one, and then double-check that you did not introduce additional errors while making corrections. Another option for proofreading is to work in teams: One person reads the text (including punctuation marks) out loud, while the other person marks errors on the printout.

Writing Responsibly: Beware the Spelling Checker!

While spelling checkers and autocorrect can be very helpful in catching typos, they cannot always distinguish between homonyms (such as *they're, their*) or other frequently confused words (such as *lay, lie; affect, effect*). They may even lead you astray, suggesting words that are close to the word you mistyped (such as *defiant* for the misspelled *definate*) but worlds away from the word you intended (*definite*). Writers have a responsibility to use words that communicate what they want to say and to not leave the reader guessing. Do not rely completely on automated spelling correction; also use a dictionary to double-check the program's suggestions, check usage in the usage glossary, and proofread your text carefully yourself. Only you can know what you *meant* to say!

to SELF

Self Assessment: A Checklist for Proofreading

Before you submit your text to your instructor, check the following elements. If you answer no to any of the questions, make the necessary revisions.

Spelling

- ☐ Did you spell-check your project?
- ☐ Did you read through the text carefully, looking for misused words?
- ☐ Did you check specifically for words you frequently confuse or misspell?

Punctuation

- ☐ Did you check sentence punctuation, especially use of the comma and the apostrophe?
- ☐ Did you make sure that all quotations have quotation marks or block indentation, that you provided end punctuation for all your sentences, and that end punctuation and in-text citations are correctly placed?
- ☐ Did you check specifically for errors you regularly make such as comma splices or fused sentences?

Other Errors

- ☐ Did you make sure that remnants of previous corrections—an extra word, letter, or punctuation mark—do not remain?
- ☐ Did you check that you have included all in-text citations where needed (for summaries, paraphrases, quotations, or ideas you have borrowed for a research project)?
- ☐ Did you check that all in-text citations are included in the reference list or list of works cited, and make sure that all formats are correct and consistent?

Proofreading When English Is Not Your First Language If you have difficulty proofreading a project, try reading it aloud; this may help you recognize errors. Also, ask your instructor if you can have a friend, classmate, or tutor help you proofread. A visit to the writing center may result in some helpful tips or practice, as well.

Make It Your Own

Customize the proofreading checklist in the Self-Assessment on the preceding page to reflect your own needs by adding the errors you have made on your last two or three writing projects.

Work Together

Working in pairs, trade printed copies of a writing project. Ask your classmate to read the text aloud while you mark corrections. When the process is complete for one text, trade roles with your partner and repeat the process.

> **More about**
> Visual design (ch. 9), 184–98
> MLA format, 379–82
> APA format, 426–30

6i Formatting an Academic Text

The Quick Reference box on this page provides guidelines for formatting an academic text. More coverage of formatting and incorporating visuals appears elsewhere in this book.

> **More about**
> Prewriting and earlier drafts of "Rethinking Alternative Energy":
> Freewriting, 27
> Brainstorming, 27–28, 32
> Cluster diagramming, 28–29
> Journalists' questions, 29–30
> Thesis, 35–38
> Tree diagram, 39–40
> Outline, 41–43
> First draft, 47–50

Quick Reference — Formatting Academic Texts

- Leave 1- to 1.5-inch margins.
- Indent the first line of each paragraph by half an inch.
- Use a standard font, such as 11-point Calibri or 12-point Times New Roman.
- Use headings, headers, page numbers, and paragraph indents to help readers navigate the text easily.
- Format headings of the same level the same way throughout the project.
- Use figure and table numbers to help readers navigate back and forth from text to visual.
- Use a style guide that is appropriate to your discipline.
- Keep your design simple; focus on content.

Student Model Final Draft of a Researched Essay

You have seen the essay by Michael Wedd (Columbia College) as it developed, from freewriting and brainstorming, to drafting a thesis statement, outlining, and first draft. Now consider his final draft. If you compare this to his earlier draft, you will see how he has revised globally and locally to tighten his thesis, develop his evidence, and make his introduction and conclusion more compelling.

Wedd 1

Michael Wedd

Professor Dunn

English 102

5 Oct. 2021

Rethinking Alternative Energy

    The rise of alternative energy industries has been challenging, controversial, and turbulent. With the availability of many alternative energy systems globally, it is worth pausing for a minute to ask some questions. Conversations are taking place at many levels of government and society about the costs and the benefits of alternative energy. The problematic relationships between alternative energy industries and the environment they claim to protect are a focus of these debates.

    Environmentalists are conflicted when it comes to alternative energy. Most agree that fossil-fuel-based power plants damage the climate and make life harder for many of the world's species. However, which types of alternative energies are best remains a difficult question. A major benefit of sources such as wind, sun, and water is that they are in practically limitless supply and produce harvestable energy every day. Despite the clear benefits of these sources, some environmental activists, government regulators, and members of the public are concerned about the associated risks. The structures needed to produce these energies can have grave effects on their surrounding environments, ecosystems, wildlife, and in the case of nuclear power plants, on human beings, too (Cherry; Deverakonda; "Former Japanese PM"; McCurry). Despite how pressing the issue of climate change is, we must consider not only the benefits but also the costs of producing the alternative energies we deploy. If alternative energy ends up putting the environment—and in some cases humanity directly—in jeopardy, then we need to rethink the ways in which we use it.

Wind energy seems to be a harmless, passive, and effective way of producing energy, but upon closer inspection it has its drawbacks. [Topic sentence] Wind turbines kill birds, bats, and other airborne creatures at an alarming rate. The American Bird Conservancy (ABC), a group whose mission is to protect bird species and their habitats throughout the Americas, targets wind turbines as a growing threat to birds. An ABC report states that "[t]he United States now has 48,000 wind turbines installed from coast to coast, with many more planned. Those turbines killed nearly 600,000 birds in 2012, from Golden Eagles to migratory songbirds" ("Bird Strikes"). Wind turbines, which are being built increasingly larger to increase their productivity, reach hundreds of feet into the air and threaten birds, some of which are endangered. The group predicts that by 2030, "a ten-fold increase in turbines is expected to boost annual bird mortality to 1.4 to 2 million." Wind turbines put bats at great risk, too. Steven Cherry, a reporter with The Iowa Center for Public Affairs Journalism—a state-wide political watchdog group—highlighted some of these risks. He explains, "Wind turbine blades catch the [bats] in a vortex wake that ruptures their lungs, causing them to drown in their blood, experts have found." He lists the Northern long-eared bat, an endangered species, as a common casualty. Audubon, a science, conservation, and bird protection organization that supports wind turbines, wants more to be done to reduce the industry's negative impact on birds and bats. They argue that wind power facilities need to "consult with wildlife experts . . . to help inform study and siting decisions" and to seek technological solutions to protect animals. Further, Audubon stresses that the government must apply "strong enforcement of existing laws that protect wildlife, including the Endangered Species Act, the Bald and Golden Eagle Protection Act, and the Migratory Bird Treaty Act." If these measures are not taken, "314 species stand to lose more than 50 percent of their current ranges by 2080 ("Audubon's Position"). Until there are more protections in place, wind turbines should not be marketed as a safe, "clean" form of alternative energy while their blades are bloodied by hundreds of thousands of airborne creatures annually in the United States alone.

Solar energy is another alternative that at first seems benign but is actually putting airborne wildlife in grave danger. At the $2.2 billion Ivanpah solar facility in the California desert, which is part of the largest solar energy complex in the world, birds are being scorched mid-flight and plummeting to earth like meteorites. A report by the *Pulitzer Center* states that "[u]nsuspecting birds fly through Ivanpah's airspace, where the superheated air between the heliostats [mirrors] and the [boiling] towers can reach temperatures as high as 900 degrees Fahrenheit. Flesh catches fire as the birds are ignited in midair" (Deverakonda). Researchers with the US Fish & Wildlife Service, who visited Ivanpah in 2012, were quoted as referring to the complex as a "mega-trap" for a number of wildlife species (Deverakonda). Solar energy is one of the most abundant and seemingly limitless sources of harvestable energy in our solar system, but the ways in which we are capturing it are producing high risks for a number of animal species.

The most controversial of these alternative energy sources is the atom. According to the U.S. Department of Energy, nuclear energy is more reliable than wind, solar, and other energy sources, and provides more than half of the country's clean energy (2). Nuclear energy also accounts for significant portions of the world's alternative energy portfolio, but recent events cast a dark shadow on the industry. Japan's 2011 Fukushima nuclear meltdown is still in recent memory. Its physical effects are predicted to reach decades into the future, and its psycho-social effects could last much longer. Japan's powerful nuclear lobby is attempting to rekindle their reactors, though, despite the long shadow cast by Fukushima's triple-meltdown. *The Guardian* reports, "Japan's revamped Nuclear Regulation Authority (NRA) said the new safety checks meant there would be no repeat of the Fukushima catastrophe" (McCurry). Naoto Kan, former prime minister of Japan, believes that the Japanese government is not taking the dangers of nuclear power seriously enough, though. He was quoted in *Deutche Welle*, a German broadcasting service, saying, "[u]nfortunately, I have the impression that neither the Japanese public nor the experts have learned the right lessons from the disaster. If the accident had been a bit more severe, we would have had to evacuate ... [an area of] 250 kilometers for a long period of time" ("Former Japanese PM"). But many years after Fukushima, the consequences of the accident continue to impact Japan and the world. For example, devising a plan for what to do with the contaminated, radioactive water that leaked from the damaged reactors continues to be a problem. One controversial option is to release it into the Pacific Ocean (Yamaguchi). Nuclear energy holds potential as an alternative source, but with the aftershocks of both the Chernobyl crisis of the 1970s and 1980s and the more recent Fukushima disaster still affecting people and whole ecosystems today, we must carefully consider the dangers of nuclear power before embracing it as the clean energy of the future. Clearly, environmentally conscious citizens acknowledge how important it is to check global warming and diversify our energy portfolio, but it is crucial that we also protect the flora and fauna with which we share this planet. It is not enough to be environmentally conscious about the sources from which we draw our energy; we must also consider the ways in which we harvest from those sources, and the tangible effects that alternative energy infrastructure can have on its surroundings. Instead of merely replacing fossil-fuel sources with renewable ones, it is also important that we ask whether it is possible to scale back energy consumption as well. It will be a long time before alternative energy production can meet the accelerating global demand. The solution to this problem will have to include ways of not only increasing renewable energy production safely but also reducing global consumption substantially.

Works Cited

> List of works cited follows MLA style.

"Audubon's Position on Wind Power." *Audubon*, 2019, audubon.org/conservation/audubons-position-wind-power.

"Bird Strikes." *American Bird Conservancy*, 2016, abcbirds.org.

Cherry, Steven. "Wind Energy Industry Spun into Bat Preservation Effort." *The Iowa Center for Public Affairs Journalism*, 30 June 2015, iowawatch.org/2015/06/30/wind-energy-industry-spun-into-in-bat-preservation-effort.

Deverakonda, Akshay. "The Fall of Icarus: Ivanpah's Solar Controversy." *Pulitzer Center on Crisis Reporting*, 5 Mar. 2015, pulitzercenter.org/stories/fall-icarus-ivanpahs-solar-controversy.

"Former Japanese PM Naoto Kan: 'Fukushima Radically Changed My Perspective.'" *Deutsche Welle*, 25 Feb. 2015, p.dw.com/p/1EgOv.

McCurry, Justin. "Japan Restarts First Nuclear Reactor since Fukushima Disaster." *The Guardian*, 11 Aug. 2015, theguardian.com/environment/2015/aug/11/japan-restarts-first-nuclear-reactor-fukushima-disaster.

U.S. Department of Energy. *The Ultimate Fast Facts Guide to Nuclear Energy*. Jan. 2019, energy.gov/sites/prod/files/2019/01/f58/Ultimate%20Fast%20Facts%20Guide-PRINT.pdf.

Yamaguchi, Mari. "Fukushima Nuclear Plant Out of Space for Radioactive Water." *AP News*, 9 Aug. 2019, apnews.com/c0f1423e672b4887a9820e2d56224059.

> **EXERCISE 6.1 Assessing a revision**
>
> Compare the final version of Michael Wedd's essay (above) with the earlier version (pp. 47–50). Which changes are global and which are local? Is there anything more that you would suggest he do with this essay before submitting it? Explain.

6j Creating and Submitting a Portfolio

Some instructors (and prospective employers) may ask you to submit a writing portfolio. A portfolio may contain any of the following:

- A collection of texts that show your best work
- A collection of texts (such as a proposal, a formal report, a set of instructions, a website) that demonstrate the range of work you have produced
- A collection of texts from a single project (such as journal entries, reflections, freewriting and brainstorming, outline, first draft, revised draft) that show your writing process

What you include depends on the portfolio's purpose, audience, and context: You may create a portfolio of your best work to demonstrate your writing skills for admission to a course (a creative writing course, for example). When applying for a job, you may create a portfolio showing the range of writing you have done. Or you may create a portfolio to demonstrate the process you followed for a composition class.

As you select the contents, consider your audience:

- What kinds of writing projects will interest your audience?
- How many examples will your audience expect you to include? Will they want to see multiple examples of the same type of work, or is one example sufficient? Will they be interested in work you have created in electronic media, or will they focus exclusively on your writing?
- How will they want you to submit the portfolio—electronically or in print?

In addition, most portfolios contain some version of the following:

Title page or home page For a printed portfolio, include a title page with the following information:

- Title (for example, "One Writer's Journey through Sophomore Composition" or "Portfolio for Application to Stockbridge Writers' Group")

- Identifying information (name, course, contact information)
- Date of submission

For an electronic portfolio, include this information in a separate document or on the home page.

Table of contents or menu with hyperlinks For a printed portfolio, include a table of contents listing the items in the order in which they are arranged, number the pages sequentially, and provide page references in your table of contents. An electronic portfolio should include a menu with hyperlinks to the contents.

Personal statement Whether submitted electronically or in print, a portfolio usually includes a personal statement that describes the contents of the portfolio and explains your choice and arrangement of selections and what the selections demonstrate about you as a writer. For portfolios submitted electronically, consider embedding links to your writing selections from your personal statement as well as from the menu. Much of the arrangement will depend on the purpose of the portfolio. If you want to show your development as a writer, consider arranging the contents chronologically. If you want to display a range of your writing, consider Nestorian order, with your second-best examples at the beginning; the least impressive material in the middle; and your very best at the end, where it will leave a lasting impression. If you are concerned about a possibly inattentive audience who won't read the whole portfolio, journalists' order might be effective, with your portfolio contents moving from your most to your least impressive material.

Make It **Your Own**

Review three recent writing projects and consider what they reveal about you as a writer. Think about the process you used to write them, the choices you made as you worked on them, and your level of satisfaction with the finished pieces. Then write a two-page reflective essay that could be used as the basis for a personal statement to introduce them in a portfolio. Use specific examples from these texts to support your claims.

Submission Submitting a printed portfolio is straightforward: You assemble the contents, make sure each page is clearly labeled with your name and a brief title, place the contents in a folder or three-ring binder with your identifying information on the front, double-check the contents against the table of contents, and hand it in.

Submitting an electronic portfolio offers more options: You might create an electronic folder that contains your documents and attach the folder—zipped, if necessary—to an email. Alternatively, you might create a website, post the contents to a server, and send the URL to recipients. Consult your recipient in advance to determine what will be the most welcome method of electronic submission.

> More about
> Creating a website, 203–10

Student Model Personal Statement

Consider the following personal statement. Notice how Syracuse University student Rachana Ky lists the items he included in his writing portfolio, briefly describes his reasons for selecting them, and points out what he believes are the strengths of each.

Dear Professor Howard:

    Here is my writing portfolio, the culmination of the semester's work. The selections I have included are the literacy development essay and ethnography from Writing 205 (Sophomore Composition) and a paper on the Parthenon from Architecture 133 (History of Architecture). The purpose of including these papers is to show how I write on a range of assignments, from the personal to the purely academic. The literacy development essay was based on my own life experience. The ethnography describes my observations in the weight room but is more objective than the literacy development essay. The Parthenon essay is the most objective of the three, focusing on a topic about which I have no personal knowledge.

    Each of these three pieces of work reflects different qualities or characteristics that reveal me as a writer. The literacy development essay describes my intellectual growth. This piece was written for a broad audience. To show my own growth, I used simple, direct language in the early parts of the essay and more sophisticated language later. My development is best reflected through the verb choices: From simple forms of "to be" and "learned," I moved on to "flogged," "balked," and "superseded."

    My ethnography strives to capture the mood of the weight room, and I used descriptive language to convey the smell of body odor, the feel of extreme exertion, and the look of the sweaty, muscular bodies. I also tried to capture the different mind-sets of those using the weight room, from steroidal bodybuilders to svelte women striving for better abs.

    The paper on the Parthenon shows my writing when it is limited to the language of architecture. It describes the Parthenon, what it meant to the people who built it, and the history of the building (what remains and how pieces of it were dispersed across the Western world). I notice that in this essay, my word choices were fairly simple, but I was still able to get my point across without using all the fancy words used by architecture critics.

I believe the introduction to each paper is strong. In general, when I cannot come up with a good start to a paper, I notice that I have problems developing the rest of the essay, so I work hard to develop an introduction that creates a sense of what my paper will discuss and how. The first two samples in particular, where I was not limited to following a certain style, have particularly engaging introductions that, I hope, have captured the reader's imagination.

I look forward to hearing your thoughts about the enclosed.

Rachana

Rachana Ky

Text Credits

Pg 100–105: Courtesy of Michael Wedd; Pg 109–110: Courtesy of Rachana Ky

Part Two

Reasoning
Matters
Reading, Thinking, and Arguing

7 Thinking and Reading Critically 112
8 Applying Analysis and Crafting Arguments 143

7 Thinking and Reading Critically

IN THIS CHAPTER

a. Comprehending, 112

b. Reflecting, 119

c. Preparing to write, 127

Student Models

For **Joe Fernandez paper, Summary of an Article,** 115; **Double-Entry Reading Journal,** 125; **Claims and Evidence Analysis, Joe Fernandez** on René Brooks's "Time Blindness," 129; **Critical Analysis Essay, Joe Fernandez,** "A Critical Analysis of René Brooks's 'Time Blindness,'" 135; **Annotations to an Image,** 126; **Aidan Kelley,** "A Rhetorical Analysis of Konstantin Ivanov's 'The Road Is Open to Humans' (poster)," 130

Professional Models

Essay, Bahar Gholipour, "How Accurate Is the Myers-Briggs Personality Test?," 116; **Article, René Brooks,** "Time Blindness: Timely Advice for Dealing with It" (annotated by Joe Fernandez), 121

When you read critically, you peel back a text to uncover its meaning. You begin with comprehension, just getting the gist of the text. Next comes reflection, when you annotate and analyze the text. As you prepare to write, you explore not only what is written but also what is left unstated, and you draw on your own experience and other texts to hone your evaluation. The process of peeling a text, as you would the layers of an onion, is what drives and deepens the intellectual process.

7a Comprehending

In our day-to-day lives, we read constantly, and the texts range from brief tweets to thousand-page books. Some texts, like street signs (Figure 7.1), are simple messages of just a few words or images; they are designed to communicate information quickly, simply, and clearly.

Most of the readings assigned in college were written to inform or educate readers about an issue or topic. They may also

Writing Responsibly | Engaging with What You Read

When conducting research, you have a responsibility to engage with the texts you read. If you are struggling, begin by determining what barrier is keeping you from making a connection with the text: Is the language too challenging? Is the topic unfamiliar or too familiar? Is your concentration poor because you did not eat lunch? Then try to overcome the barrier: Use a dictionary to learn the unfamiliar vocabulary; consider the material as a recapitulation of an important topic; eat a sandwich.

to TOPIC

have a secondary purpose: to persuade readers to accept a position on that issue or topic. Because most college-level reading assignments attempt to engage you in the complexities of an issue, you should read the text systematically. You will get the most out of complex texts if you preview the text, read through it quickly to get the gist, write a brief summary, and, most importantly, enjoy what you read!

Reading for Comprehension Many people think the key to better reading is to read slower. Native and non-native English speakers may slow their *speech* to help their listeners comprehend, but the same idea may not work for *reading*. In fact, research shows that reading faster can help increase your comprehension, because you associate ideas more readily.

1. Preview the text.

The more you know about a text before you begin reading, the more efficiently you will be able to read. Unless you are reading a work of literature—a novel, a poem, or a play—you should resist the urge to dive in and read the text from beginning to end. Instead, start by *previewing:*

- **Note the title and subtitle.** The title sets the stage for the work and may reveal its topic, its approach, and even its tone.

- **Read the abstract, introduction, conclusion, and sidebars**. Many scholarly journals place an ***abstract***, or summary, at the beginning of each article; abstracts also appear in article database entries. Other texts may offer overviews of main ideas and important questions in introductions, prologues, conclusions, boxes, or sidebars. Textbook chapters often conclude with study questions that provide a framework for thinking about key topics.

- **Read first sentences and paragraphs.** In short texts, read the first sentence of each paragraph; in longer texts, read the first paragraph of each section. From this you will gain a preliminary sense of the topic and argument of the text.

- **Read the headings and subheadings.** If the text is organized into sections with headings, skim them for an outline.

- **Scan figures and illustrations.** Figures may signal important ideas. Visuals convey complex processes quickly and are often accompanied by a succinct explanation (Figure 7.2).

FIGURE 7.1 Everyday texts Street signs convey information through words, shapes, and images. They are simple, so we can act on them immediately, almost without thinking.

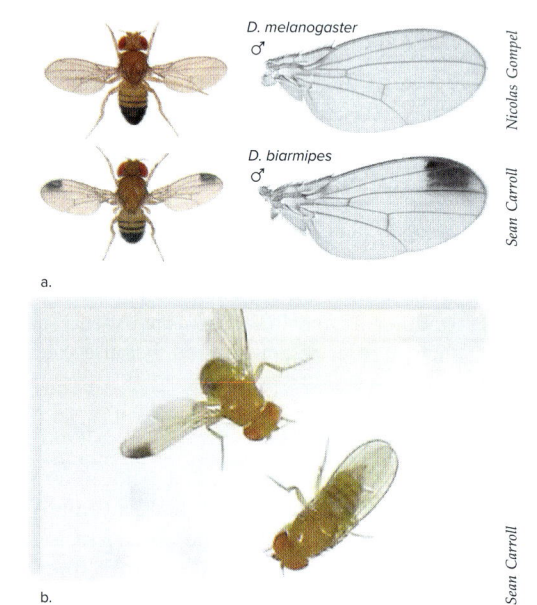

114 **7a** Reasoning Matters • Thinking and Reading Critically

FIGURE 7.2 **Preview figures and illustrations** Previewing figures, illustrations, and captions in the source you are considering can provide insight. This illustrated figure and caption, by Sean Carroll and Nicolas Gompel, describes a distinguishing characteristic of an insect, pointing to an emphasis on evolution.

Wing spot in *Drosophila biarmipes* **a.** Male *D. biarmipes* have a spot on the leading edge of their wings that is not present in their close relative, *D. melanogaster*. **b.** *D. biarmipes* males flash the spot on their wings to attract the attention of females during a courtship dance.

2. Get the gist.

> *More about*
> Paraphrasing and patchwriting, 285, 292–94

patchwriting Using the language or sentence structure of the source; not putting the content into fresh words

After previewing the text, read the whole thing from beginning to end to get the *gist,* or basic idea. If the text you are reading is persuasive or argumentative, the gist may be expressed in a *thesis statement*. Often this will be signaled in the introduction and then developed and expanded throughout the text. As you read, circle words or phrases you have questions about, but press on without looking them up—yet. When you have finished, close the book and write down what you remember. Try to *paraphrase*, to state the ideas in your own words, rather than quoting from the text. If you can accurately paraphrase the text's major points without quoting or *patchwriting,* you have grasped its literal meaning. If you cannot, read the text again, close the book, and try again to paraphrase.

3. Summarize the text.

When you feel you have a good (though not necessarily perfect) grasp of the text, *summarize* it. A paraphrase may be as long as (or longer than)

the passage it restates, but a summary shortens it by restating only the main idea (the *thesis*) and major supporting points (the *evidence*). Your summary should be at least 50 percent shorter than the text it restates; many summaries are only 10 percent (or less) as long as the original. The summary below captures the main idea and major supporting points of the René Brooks article that Joe Fernandez writes about later in this chapter. The original editorial, which starts on page 121, is about 1,830 words; this summary is about 170 words, a bit less than one-tenth of the original.

Student Model
Joe Fernandez, "A Critical Analysis of René Brooks's 'Time Blindness,'" 135–39

Student Model Summary of an Article

Student Joe Fernandez summarizes René Brooks's article "Time Blindness" (pp. 121–125).

> In an article published on her blog, *Black Girl, Lost Keys: Educating and Motivating Women with ADHD*, René Brooks argues that time blindness, a symptom of ADHD, is something that should be recognized by society, better understood by neurodiverse and neurotypical people, and managed through the use of specific strategies. She defines time blindness as "the inability to gauge the passage of time" and identifies lateness as a major side effect of time blindness, one that can jeopardize personal and professional relationships. Brooks points out the difficulties that neurotypicals have in "seeing" or acknowledging time blindness and discusses how that feels to those who are time blind. Time blindness, she says, is best approached with empathy and humor. While time blindness can affect people's lives negatively, there is a benefit (the ability to hyperfocus on something you love to do) and plenty of concrete ways to manage it. In her final paragraphs, Brooks gives specific advice for coping with time blindness and offers readers plenty of positive encouragement.

For any complex reading assignment, writing a summary will help you to remember the main points of the text, and the summary you create can also provide a useful reference when you write about the text. As you compose your summary, avoid patchwriting: The more you can write about a topic in your own words, the better you will understand it.

> **More about**
> Synthesis, 133

4. Enjoy the text.

You are most likely to comprehend a text when you enjoy it, and you are far more likely to enjoy it if you *think about* the text as you read. Engage with it as you would with a message from a friend or with the trailer for a new movie. The pleasure of reading often comes from noticing the details: a nice turn of phrase, a subtle joke, or a clever comparison. Enjoyment does not require total agreement with—or even a complete understanding of—every word on the page. It does require active engagement and an open mind. Allowing yourself to take pleasure in reading can also improve your academic performance and your ability to connect (or *synthesize*) what you read with material from other classes and your own life.

EXERCISE 7.1 Comprehending and engaging with the text

Look at the title of the article below, and then write a sentence indicating what you think the essay will be about, based on the title alone. Next, read the essay and summarize the text. Identify the author's point of view on the topic and give an example to support your claim. Finally, write one or two sentences explaining what you found surprising, interesting, or challenging about this essay, and why.

Professional Model Essay

How Accurate Is the Myers-Briggs Personality Test?
By Bahar Gholipour

There are two types of people in the world: those who believe in the Myers-Briggs personality test and those who don't.

Except that's not true. Grouping people into 2, 3, or 16 categories, which is the aim of a lot of personality tests, has never quite worked. And even in the case of the Myers-Briggs Type Indicator (MBTI), which is simultaneously the most popular personality test in the world and the most frequently debunked, nonexperts and psychologists alike take varying positions about the value of the tool.

About 1.5 million people take the test online each year, and more than 88% of Fortune 500 companies, as well as hundreds of universities, use it in hiring and training, according to The Myers-Briggs Company, a California-based firm that administers the MBTI. Even fictional characters, from Disney princesses, to Harry Potter, and Darth Vader have been assigned an MBTI type.

Despite the popularity of the test, many psychologists criticize it—hardly a few months go by without a harsh take-down of the MBTI in the media, where a psychologist will say that the Myers-Brigg is unscientific, meaningless, or bogus. But there are others who take a milder view of the test.

"Many personality psychologists consider the MBTI to be a somewhat valid measure of some important personality characteristics but one that has some important limitations," said Michael Ashton, professor of psychology at Brock University in Ontario.

What is the MBTI?
The MBTI was invented in 1942 by Katharine Cook Briggs and her daughter, Isabel Briggs Myers. Cook, always a keen observer of people and their differences, was inspired by the work of psychologist Carl Jung and his theories; for example, the concepts of introversion and extroversion. The mother and daughter devoted their lives to developing the type indicator, hoping to help people understand their tendencies and choose appropriate jobs. The test uses 93 questions to assess the following traits:

- Introvert (I) versus Extrovert (E)
- Intuitive (N) versus Sensory (S)
- Thinking (T) versus Feeling (F)
- Judging (J) versus Perceiving (P)

Based on the combination of traits people fall into, the test ultimately assigns them one of the 16 labels, such as INTJ, ENFP, and so on.

Why do psychologists doubt it?
Psychologists' main problem with the MBTI is the science behind it, or lack thereof. In 1991, a National Academy of Sciences committee reviewed data from MBTI research and noted "the troublesome discrepancy between research results (a lack of proven worth) and popularity."

The MBTI was born of ideas proposed before psychology was an empirical science; those ideas were not tested before the tool became a commercial product. But modern psychologists demand that a personality test pass certain criteria to be trusted. "In social science, we use four standards: Are the categories reliable, valid, independent and comprehensive?" Adam Grant, University of Pennsylvania professor of psychology, wrote on LinkedIn. "For the MBTI, the evidence says not very, no, no, and not really."

Some research suggests the MBTI is unreliable because the same person can get different results when retaking the test. Other studies have questioned the validity of the MBTI, which is the ability of the test to accurately link the "types" to outcomes in the real world—for example, how well people classified as a certain type will perform in a given job.

The Myers-Briggs Company says the studies discrediting the MBTI are old, but their results are still being perpetuated in the media. Since those early criticisms, the company says it has done its own research to refine the test and assess its validity. "When you look at validity of the instrument [the MTBI], it is just as valid as any other personality assessment," Suresh Balasubramanian, the company's general manager, told *USA Today*.

Some of the test's limitations, however, are inherent in its conceptual design. One limitation is the MBTI's black-and-white categories: You are either an extrovert or introvert, a judger or a feeler. "This is a shortcoming, because people don't fall neatly into two categories on any personality dimension; instead, people have many different degrees of the dimension," Ashton told Live Science. And, in fact, most people are close to the average, and relatively few people are at either extreme. By placing people into tidy boxes, we are separating people who are in reality more similar to each other than they are different.

The MBTI may be missing even more nuances by assessing only four aspects of personality differences. "Several decades ago, personality researchers had determined that there were at least five major personality dimensions, and more recent evidence has shown that there are six," Ashton said. "One of those dimensions involves how honest and humble versus deceitful and conceited someone is, and the other dimension involves how patient and agreeable versus quick-tempered and argumentative someone is."

Not entirely useless
Some of the shortcomings of the MBTI stem from the complex, messy nature of human personality. Neat categories of MBTI make personality look clearer and more stable than it really is, according to David Pincus, a professor of psychology at Chapman University in California. Psychologists prefer other tools, namely the Big Five, which assesses personality based on where an individual lies on the spectrums of five traits: agreeableness; conscientiousness; extraversion; openness to experience; and neuroticism. The Big Five model has a better record of scientific validation than the MBTI, experts say.

Still, the MBTI is not entirely useless.

People are drawn to tests like MBTI out of a desire to understand themselves and others. "The four dimensions from which the MBTI types are derived are all useful ones for describing people's personalities," Ashton said.

And even when the MBTI's results don't quite match your intuition about yourself or are just wrong, they can still provide insight. Many people who've taken the MBTI have noticed this effect. As a former employee at Bridgewater Associates (a hedge fund almost as famous for having employees take personality tests as it is for its $120 billion in assets) wrote in *Quartz*, the MBTI labels never seemed to fully describe a person. Instead, the real value of the test seemed to be in the push "to reconcile the gaps between what the test results tell us, and what we know to be true about ourselves."

In this sense, the MBTI can serve as a starting point for self-exploration by giving people a tool and a language to reflect on themselves and others.

The test is "a portal to an elaborate practice of talking and thinking about who you are," Merve Emre, an associate professor of English at Oxford University in the United Kingdom, wrote in "The Personality Brokers," a review of the MBTI's history.

Ultimately, it's not the MBTI label, but the power of introspection that drives the insights and sometimes fuels the motivation to take steps to change one's condition.

Live Science, 19 May 2019.

Make It Your Own

Find a photograph in a printed or online newspaper (or use one from this book), and write a one- or two-paragraph description of it. Be sure to indicate your first impression and what the photo depicts. Then insert a copy of the image after your description so that readers will see the description *before* they see the image.

Work Together

Trade descriptions with a classmate. Without looking at the photograph, try to form a mental picture of the image. Now look at the photograph. Discuss how well the description captured the image and what you would change. Did the description change what you noticed or how you responded to the image?

7b Reflecting

Once you have the gist of a text, let *reflection* help lead you to full comprehension. Annotating the text is a good starting place for reflection; writing about the text in your reading journal may spur reflection, too.

1. Annotate the text.

A useful first step in reflecting upon a text is to reread it with a pencil or pen in hand (or a computer at the ready). Careful annotations will also be useful later, when you are studying for an exam or composing a project that discusses the text. As you annotate, focus on some or all of the following:

- **Definitions.** Look up and write down definitions of unfamiliar words.
- **Concepts.** Underline the most important, interesting, or difficult concepts.

> **Tech** **Annotating Online Texts**
>
> When you read from a screen instead of a page, consider saving the text to your hard drive, flash drive, or cloud server so you can annotate it in your word processor or PDF reader.

> **More about**
> Tone, 20–21, 159, 599, 604–6, 607
> Bias, 600–3
> Avoiding logical fallacies, 176–79
> Note taking, 286–87
> Working bibliography, 230–36

- **Tone.** Note the writer's tone—sarcastic, sincere, witty, self-confident.
- **Biases.** Look for the writer's biases and unstated assumptions (and your own). Does the text ignore or misrepresent important counterevidence? Does it contain loaded or hurtful language?
- **Fallacies.** Is the text illogical or misleading?
- **Responses.** Jot down your own reactions and insights, as well as any questions you have about the text.
- **Connections.** Make connections with other texts you have read or with your own experiences.

Read footnotes and any text in parentheses: They seldom contain the main claims or supporting evidence, but they can provide key background information, references to additional scholarship on a topic, and juicy tidbits the writer felt moved to share.

Self Assessment

When annotating an image, analyze the following elements. Be sure to answer each of these questions and take the suggested steps to offer a thorough critique.

- ☐ **Tone.** Does it strike you as warm, amused, angry, dispassionate? Point to specific parts of the image that convey the tone.
- ☐ **Responses.** What responses does the image elicit from you, and why? Again, tie your responses directly to elements of the image.
- ☐ **Biases.** Do you detect any assumptions or biases? If so, explain what they are and how the visual indicates them.
- ☐ **Connections.** Does this image remind you of another visual or printed text? If so, in what ways? (Be specific.) Identify any connections between the visual and your own experience.

Professional Model Article (annotated by a student)

The following article by René Brooks was originally published on her blog, *Black Girl Lost Keys: Educating and Motivating Women with ADHD* (blackgirllostkeys.com).* Student writer Joe Fernandez analyzes and annotates the article with his questions and comments in preparation for writing about it (see pp. 136–140).

Time Blindness: Timely Advice for Dealing with It

By RENÉ BROOKS

[*What is it? What kind of pain does it cause?*]

Time blindness is a pain where a pill won't reach.

Seriously.
There are many complexities in life, but few are as frustrating to the person with ADHD as their relationship with time. I'm no different. Time rules our lives. Yet our neurodiverse brains slip in and out of time, treating it like the concept it is.

[*Attention Deficit and Hyperactivity Disorder.*]

[*Neurodiverse? ADHD brains are somehow different from other brains?*]

Unfortunately, like most social concepts, time is here and it isn't going anywhere. That means many people with ADHD have to survive in a world that isn't best suited to the time blind.

[*So some people are unable to "see" time?*]

[*Lateness is a problem, one that others resent. The writer establishes that her lateness is not about dominance.*]

Why are people with time blindness always late?
People get super touchy about time. An article I recently read said that people show up late to establish dominance. Okay, maybe in the neurotypical world that's a thing, but if I show up late it is likely because I was walking the dogs or got sucked into some other task and didn't take note of the time. My behavior isn't part of a nefarious plot, just a daily function of my ADHD. Time blindness can be frustrating, but you can improve your relationship with time.

["*Neurotypical*" *is the opposite of "Neurodiverse"?*]

["*Nefarious plot*" *offers imagery and humor. The writer is frustrated with time blindness, but she approaches it in an inviting and positive way for her readers.*]

[*Here she makes clear that people with ADHD who may suffer from time blindness are her primary audience.*]

What is time blindness?
Time blindness refers to the inability to gauge the passage of time. Have you ever planned to spend five minutes on a task only to realize a whole hour has passed? Ever delayed replying to an email, not realizing it's been two weeks since you received the original message? Or gone out for just a few minutes only to return home hours later? These are common occurrences for someone who is time blind.

[*I can relate in a way. As a student I sometimes have trouble managing time. But time blindness seems to be a problem of a different level.*]

---

*Please note that the version of Brooks's article that appears here has been edited and shortened. For the full version of her article, see blackgirllostkeys.com/adhd/time-blindness-timely-advice/.

122 7b Reasoning Matters • Thinking and Reading Critically

Left margin notes	Main text	Right margin notes
The writer is making a case that time blindness is a serious problem, one that can be difficult for others to understand.	**Neurotypicals struggle to understand time blindness** Though the diagnosis and symptoms indicate how serious time blindness is, it is a difficult concept to convey to someone who is neurotypical. Gauging time seems effortless to them, almost like breathing. The idea that a person with time blindness may not know their dinner is about to burn, something that cannot be fixed by being "more careful," is foreign to them. If you've ever tried to explain time blindness to someone who doesn't have it, you know how skeptical people can be. They listen and eye you suspiciously as they try to decide if you are serious or drawing a long bow at their expense. Ironically, after a period of time observing an ADHD person and seeing the consequences of time blindness, they usually believe there is a problem.	*Yikes, time blindness is potentially dangerous. Putting dinner in the oven and losing track of time could cause a fire and injuries.*
Part of being time blind is not being believed by others. The words "skeptical" and "suspicious" indicate that the responses of others can be alienating.		*"Drawing a long bow" means exaggerating or telling a tall tale.*
	What are some of the negative consequences of time blindness? Time blindness can cause big trouble in our lives. Being late for meetings, not showing up for school on time, and keeping friends waiting are things that can happen when you live with time blindness. As a result, people are often too annoyed with us to understand our predicament. They can become so frustrated by our lateness that they no longer see it as a symptom we are forced to deal with, but as a problem that personally offends them. When people begin to take your ADHD personally it can cause serious damage to your relationships. Employers especially can be unforgiving, as time blindness to the untrained eye can look like a willful disregard for the time of others. Without a proper understanding of how they can support the person with ADHD with their time blindness, people begin to exclude that person from activities. People may make rude comments about the tardiness of a person who is time blind. Or insult them by saying things like "I don't trust you to be on time" or "we already KNOW you're going to be late" and other insensitive remarks that don't take into account that the most frustrated person isn't them, but the person with ADHD. Hearing people make such remarks when I've already explained to them how ADHD works lets me know that I can't trust them. In order to be my friend, coworker, or associate, I need you to have a sense of humor. I need a level of empathy that doesn't involve trying to "improve" me by scolding me for not being on time. I have a mother already, and she raised me well. I'm not taking any new applications.	*It's ironic that it takes time to see how time blindness works.*
By referring to time blindness as a "predicament" and something that "we are forced to deal with," the writer reveals the emotional strain caused by of this symptom of ADHD.		*When others are "personally" offended, or take ADHD and time blindness "personally," it harms relationships.*
Not only can time blindness hurt personal relationships, it can jeopardize workplace / professional ones, too. At work, some are "unforgiving," lack "proper understanding," and maybe most painfully, become exclusionary.		*The writer's wordplay ("time blindness to the untrained eye") helps maintain a lightness in tone, even when "willful disregard" is part of the same sentence.*
		One of the solutions the writer offers is for others to approach her with humor and empathy. *She uses humor (as she uses wordplay) to get her point across.*
	The word "disability" does not appear in this article, but aren't ADHD and the related symptom of time blindness considered to be disabilities? I wonder why the writer chooses not to frame things that way. *It's clearly frustrating that others may not "see" or understand her symptoms.*	

Reasoning Matters • Reflecting   **7b**   123

The writer provides a link to a presentation by Russell Barkley. Who is he? Is he an authority on time blindness?

Here the incredible Russell Barkley gives a great overview of what time blindness is and what it means for those of us with ADHD.

Are there any benefits to being time blind?

As much havoc as time blindness has brought into my life, there have been some benefits. For example, I feel sorry for people who cannot lose themselves in something. To be able to sink into a good book and forget the world, or to be swept away by a project you feel passion for, are among the good things in life. In fact, I feel the most alive when I operate outside of the constraints of minutes, hours, and seconds.

This is the writer's first mention of "focus" except for references to "ADHD."
Of course the ability or inability to focus is an important issue. I just hadn't been thinking about that until now.

Hyperfocus is one of those time blindness–related things that makes me feel glad, despite its drawbacks. For people with ADHD, being able to focus on something when we want to isn't always possible. That's why in those moments when I am able to, I can't help but ride the hyperfocus wave and enjoy it. Hyperfocus isn't something you want to rely on routinely to get tasks done because it is so fickle. However, when you ARE able to get hyperfocus to align with your best interests, it can be magical.

The writer's consistent voice, tone, and style help readers absorb her thoughts on a serious topic.

How time blindness turns your life into extremes

There are two times in the time blind world: *now* and *not now*. That means the doctor's appointment you have next week, your cousin's wedding that is in a month, and that project that is due three months from now are not on your radar. Those are *not now*.

This paragraph provides a transition to the final section of the article, where the writer offers solutions and strategies for managing time blindness.

People with ADHD can find their lives in a wreck because of the fallout from tasks that require preparation and focus. Since we are always cleaning up the mess from the last disaster, we fall behind for future tasks. We become hamsters on a wheel, running at top speed, but never seeming to progress. Everybody wants to feel that their efforts are paying off, but despite working really hard to succeed in life skills, we often feel like we are failing.

Certain aspects of life require that we're able to work a plan. Our time blindness, once it is managed, can become much less of a factor in trying to live well. While it doesn't go away, we can learn skills to control it.

Externalize: to take something outside of its usual boundaries.

What are some strategies for dealing with time blindness?

The name of the game when you are ready to begin managing time blindness is to externalize. When your brain can't estimate the passage of time, it is totally okay to find some device, tool, or technology to give you a hand. These tools are there to supplement what your brain can't do: mark the passage of time.

The specific strategies in this bulleted section give readers concrete ways to cope with ADHD and time blindness.

- **Use an analog watch.** We're in the digital age, but sometimes it is good to be old-fashioned. For people with ADHD, it can be

---

I wasn't thinking there were benefits to time blindness, but I'm glad there are.

Being "swept away," feeling "passion," and feeling "alive" sounds amazing.

Hyperfocus comes at a cost, but in the best circumstances, it is also "magical."

The writer introduces another symptom of time blindness: Problems with planning that lead to feelings of failure.

The phrase "hamsters on a wheel" reflects the feeling of being overwhelmed as a result of time blindness and problems with making plans.

Readers with time blindness are reminded that their challenges are caused by their brains and are not the result of a personal shortcoming.

difficult to visualize time, but analog watches can help make it possible.
- While digital clocks only show you what the present time is, analog clocks allow you to physically see how much time has elapsed in an hour and how much time is left in an hour.
- Being able to "see" the time can help you to track it outside of the present moment.
■ **When trying to stay on task, use a nudge alarm.** When we are working on a project or even just goofing off, it can be difficult to keep track of time. An alarm or a chime will help.
- I often have a timer set that will go off in 15-minute intervals to help me not lose track of the time that is slipping by.
■ **Stop hyperfocus before it starts.** So there I was, getting ready to start my day when I sat down to watch just ONE episode of a TV show. A TV show I really, REALLY like. You know what happened next. Several hours later, there I was still watching the show and being very annoyed with myself for not getting my work done.
- Hyperfocus happens to us so naturally that we can't help ourselves. Once we get into a task we love, it is not shocking to find we can't tear ourselves away. Do your best to stay away from these kinds of tasks before you have to do something important.

In closing, the writer again draws on her own experience to encourage her audience.

It has taken me a few years of tweaking my relationship with time, but these days I'm so often on time that it throws off the people in my life. Recently my best friend, who I've known long before my diagnosis, shared with me that she has stopped adding a time buffer to our plans because now I show up on time and she's not ready!

Her friendly and optimistic tone, evident throughout the article, is especially uplifting in the final paragraphs.

Who would have ever thought I'd be able to show up on time? If *I* can overcome time blindness, I feel like there's big-time hope for you.

Until next time,

René

EXERCISE 7.2 Annotating a text

Using the annotations to the René Brooks's article above as a model, annotate the essay by Bahar Gholipour (pp. 116–119).

2. Keep a reading journal.

Articulating your responses in a *reading journal* is a good way to build a deeper understanding and a sense of taking part in—not just taking in—what you read. A journal entry can do any of the following:

- Freewrite your reactions to what you are reading. Analyze the writer's purpose: Is it to entertain, inform, persuade?
- Reflect on passages that seem important to you.

- Talk back to or argue with what you are reading.
- Synthesize ideas from the text with ideas of your own or ideas from other sources.

> **More about**
> Purpose, 15–17
> Generating ideas, 25–31
> Outlining, 41–44
> Synthesizing, 133

A double-entry reading journal can provide a column for quotations, summaries, or paraphrases and a column for your responses. This technique can help you keep your own ideas separate from the ideas you have found in the text.

The entries from the reading journal below reflect one student's thoughts about the Bahar Gholipour essay that appears in Exercise 7.1.

Student Model Double-Entry Reading Journal

Below, a student reads and responds to passages from the article by Bahar Gholipour (pp. 116–119) in preparation for writing about it.

Reading Journal Entries for Bahar Gholipour's "How Accurate Is the Myers-Briggs Personality Test?"

Quotation	Response to Quotation
"About 1.5 million people take the test online each year…Even fictional characters, from Disney Princesses, to Harry Potter and Darth Vader have been assigned an MBTI type." (par 3)	*The line about Disney Princesses, Harry, and Darth made me laugh. It's a great way to establish how popular the MBTI (Myers-Briggs Type Indicator) is, regardless of its critics. The author uses humor to make her point and sets the tone for the essay.*
Summary	Response to Summary
The mother-daughter team who created the MBTI back in the early 1940s wanted to help people know themselves better and figure out their best career match. (par 5)	*The origin of the personality test is interesting. I may do a little background research on the women who created it and the time period in which they did so.*
Paraphrase	Response to Paraphrase
A critique of the MBTI (by David Pincus) is that it doesn't take into account the "messy nature of human personality," and instead makes it seem "clearer and more stable than it really is." (para 13)	*I like the idea of our personalities being "messy" and complex. Is part of what makes us so obsessed with the MBTI that we want to simplify things or feel more in control of ourselves somehow? I wonder if there are studies on what motivates us to take personality tests.*

EXERCISE 7.3 Writing a journal entry

Using the journal entry on this page as a model, write a journal entry on either the Gholipour article (pp. 116–119) or the Brooks article (pp. 121–124). If you quote any material, note where it comes from, in case you need to cite it later.

EXERCISE 7.4 Writing about an image

Find a striking photograph online or in a magazine, newspaper, or textbook. Using the sample below as a model, write a journal entry about the image, relating your thoughts, feelings, and reactions to the photograph as a whole or to specific parts of it.

Student Model Annotations to an Image

Below, a student analyzes a photograph and annotates it with questions and observations.

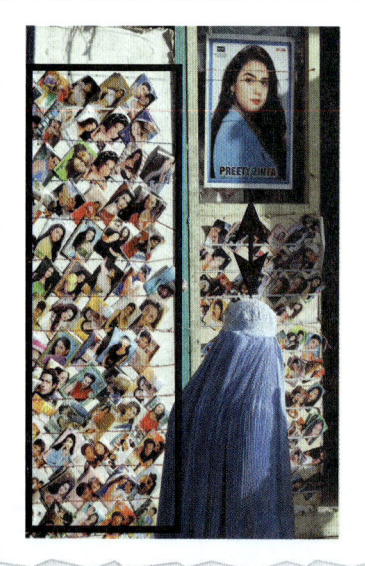

The colors are vibrant and the robe concealing the woman in the foreground is almost the same shade of blue as the blouse that Preety Zinta wears in her portrait.

Is the subject the covered woman in the foreground, the portrait of Zinta, or the glamour shots in the background? Zinta almost looks like the covered woman's reflection and her set expression reveals very little.

What is the woman in the foreground is thinking? Does she want to uncover her head (like Zinta) or is she shocked by Zinta's flowing hair and red lipstick? The contrast makes a point about the way women are perceived and treated in various cultures.

> **Quick Reference** — **Steps in Developing Critical Understanding**
> - **Analyze.** Divide a text into its component parts to understand *how* it reaches its audience.
> - **Interpret.** Dig below the surface to draw conclusions based on the author's assumptions, motives, and omissions, as well as the circumstances in which the text was written.
> - **Synthesize.** Connect ideas in a text to relevant ideas in other texts or experiences; analyze the relationships among ideas or draw comparisons and contrasts.
> - **Critique.** Evaluate based on evidence gathered through careful reading, analysis, interpretation, and synthesis.

7c Preparing to Write

Reading critically prepares you for the next step: writing. Having something interesting to say about a reading selection will come from *analyzing* the text carefully; *interpreting* the text to find or create a new, deeper meaning; *synthesizing* what you have learned from the text with what you have learned elsewhere; and *critiquing,* or evaluating, the text.

> **More about**
> Analysis, 64–65, 67
> Evaluating claims, 146–49
> Evidence, 45–47
> Analyzing works of literature (ch. 22), 486–509

1. Analyze.

To comprehend a text fully, **analyze** it: Take it apart, consider its components, figure out how the parts fit together, and assess how the text as a whole persuades its audience. When you are reading a nonfiction text such as a report, an essay, an editorial, or an article, a systematic look at how the text works will significantly increase your understanding of the text.

An essential component of any analysis is the ***rhetorical superstructure*** of the text—its claims and evidence. This sort of analysis also provides a sound basis for any further analysis you might want to do. Consider the following:

- The major claims the text makes. Do you agree with the claims? Why or why not?
- The evidence (such as examples, facts, statistics, or expert testimony) offered for the claims. How accurate and sufficient is this evidence?
- The presence or absence of counterevidence. Does the text inform its audience of weaknesses in its claims or evidence, or does it explain alternative perspectives or interpretations? How is the counterevidence treated? Is it ignored—no counterevidence at all? Is it acknowledged, but declared less persuasive or important than the evidence? Is it acknowledged and rejected out of hand? Is it acknowledged and then argued with, to discredit or refute it? How ethical do you deem the source's treatment of counterevidence?

> **More about**
> Purpose, 15–17
> Audience, 18–21
> Organization: classical, Rogerian, Toulmin, 174–76
> Rhetorical appeals (logos, ethos, pathos), 150–55
> Tone, 20–21, 159, 599, 604–6, 607
> Style, 557–626 (part 7, Style Matters)
> Reliability, 265–69, 270–71
> Summary writing, 295–97
> Citation indexes, 269

In addition to identifying and analyzing claims and evidence, you will gain an increasingly deep understanding of a text by conducting rhetorical analysis and intertextual analysis. **Rhetorical analysis** helps you focus on the manner in which the text presents its material, as well as the persuasive moves it makes. The following basic issues in rhetorical analysis may reveal the purpose of the text and the author's relationship to the audience:

- The logical pattern used in the text, which provides information about the author's purpose. Exploratory arguments are likely to use *inductive logic*, citing particular examples and then drawing a general conclusion. Persuasive arguments are likely to use *deductive logic*, offering generally accepted truths from which conclusions can be drawn about specific instances. Taking into account the audience, context, and purpose of this text, how appropriate is the logical pattern?

- The presentation of the argument. Does it draw on classical, Rogerian, or Toulmin structure? What does its structure suggest about the author's purpose?

- The presence or absence of logical fallacies. Logical fallacies are sometimes an indication of an author who is inexpert on the topic, an author who assumes the audience already agrees with the claims of the text, or an author who is trying to confuse the issue and manipulate the audience.

- The rhetorical appeals used in the text. Where can you see appeals to the audience's appreciation for *logos* (rational, logical claims or evidence), *ethos* (showing the expertise or credibility of author of the text), or *pathos* (drawing on the audience's emotions or sympathy)? When you consider the audience, context, and purpose of this text, how appropriate do these rhetorical appeals seem?

- The tone and style of the text. Answering a few basic questions can give you insight into the author's attitude toward the topic or audience: How formal or informal is the style? Do the word choices indicate that the audience is expected to have advanced knowledge of the topic, or is the text written to be accessible to a non specialist audience?

Intertextual analysis will help you understand the author's trustworthiness and relationship to the audience. Conduct intertextual analysis by looking at issues such as these:

- The sources the author draws on (if any). How reliable are they, and what is the author's attitude toward them?
- Other sources that draw on this one. From a *citation index* such as that provided by *Google Scholar* and many library databases, you can find out whether your source is being cited by others.
- The author's expertise on this topic. This question is especially important if the author is not naming or citing their sources.

Student Model Claims and Evidence Analysis

In the following analysis of the Brooks article (p. 121) student Joe Fernandez identifies the main claims of the text and the evidence provided in support of those claims:

Claims

1. Time blindness, a symptom of Attention Deficit and Hyperactivity Disorder (ADHD) is a major problem for those who have it (the neurodiverse) and one that many people (neurotypicals) do not acknowledge.
2. Time blindness can be understood by all and managed through the use of specific strategies.

Evidence

- The time blind are often late, something that hurts personal and professional relationships.
- Some neurotypical people take personally the lateness of a person who is time blind and in response may exclude that person from activities.
- Empathy and humor go a long way in understanding and supporting those who are time blind.
- While some who have time blindness have difficulties planning, something that can cause feelings of failure, they can learn skills to manage and cope.
- Using an analog watch, setting alarms, and estimating the time to complete a task (imagining it as a "worst-case scenario") helps people with time blindness cope and succeed.
- The writer notes that she has succeeded in overcoming lateness and time blindness by following the guidelines she provides in the article.

Student Model Rhetorical Analysis of an Image

In this rhetorical analysis of a 1960 poster celebrating the Soviet Union's successful launch of satellites into space, Syracuse University student Aidan Kelley explores what the poster persuades viewers of, and how it does that work.

Aidan Kelley

Professor Howard

Writing 205

3 Feb. 2021

A Rhetorical Analysis of Konstantin Ivanov's

"The Road Is Open to Humans" (poster)

Created by graphic artist Konstantin Ivanov (1921-2003), the poster titled "The Road Is Open to Humans," was released in 1960 following the successful launches of *Sputnik I* and *II*, the first satellites launched into space by any country. While the poster precedes actual human spaceflight, artist Ivanov works to convince his audience that based on the progress of its people, the Soviet Union will surely lead mankind into a new era of space exploration.

Ethos

Ivanov's poster reflects the sentiment among Cold War nations at the time that the "space age" would be the inevitable future for civilization. First and foremost, the artist uses visuals to present the Soviet Union as the sole force driving this progress. Most obviously, the rocket ship displayed is marked with the Communist symbol of a sickle and hammer, as well as the red star, which came to be associated with the Communist Party of the Soviet Union. The rocket itself is cradled by a large, fit, unidentified man. Though he is not a famous figure, this individual appears to be of Slavic descent and is wearing work clothes. Given this portrayal, he represents the strength of the workers of the Soviet Union, and is meant to persuade the public that they are part of what makes Soviet space progress possible.

Kelley 2

> In addition to the visual analysis of the poster that he provides in the main text, Kelley also annotates the image itself.

Ivanov's use of simple, bold lines and colors grab viewers' attention and convey action.

The rocket cradled by the figure, which furthers the image's **ethos**, is illustrated with the red star and hammer and sickle that signify the Soviet Communist Party. The spiraling trail of the rocket shows that it has already completed two successful missions around the Earth **(logos).**

The figure's determined expression and upward tilt of chin and body point to the future, establishing part of the **ethos** of the image. His body and clothing are meant to reflect the Soviet worker, or "everyman." He appeals to the **pathos** of viewers, evoking a sense of pride in his/their accomplishments and a sense that the space program is, quite literally, in good hands.

Inside the rocket are two dogs that the Soviet program had successfully sent into space, persuading viewers that the "road" forward has been established, an appeal to **logos**. The sweet-looking pups also appeal to viewers' emotions (**pathos**), and urge viewers to associate warmth and safety with the space program.

> Kelley provides source information in the caption of Fig. 1, so no works cited page is needed.

Fig. 1. "The Road Is Open to Humans!" by Konstantin Ivanov. Source: Konstantin Ivanov. "The Road is Open to Humans!" *Memorial Museum of Cosmonautics*, 1960, https://kosmo-museum.ru.

Pathos

Ivanov uses key visual elements to connect with viewers through emotion. The dogs in the image were well-known to the 1960 Soviet audience; they portray Belka and Strelka, the world's first successful space pups. In the poster, they look friendly and unintimidating, inviting viewers to associate feelings of fondness and sympathy with the Soviet space program. However, much of the emotion of the poster is conveyed and evoked by the man holding the rocket. Though he has a strong build and a stern expression, the figure holds the rocket (and the dogs within it) gently in his hands. This gesture suggests that the Soviets are being careful about taking dogs, and soon humans, into space, and that they're doing so responsibly. The figure's confidence, body language, and steady gaze into space, into a perhaps glorious future, invites viewers to feel hopeful, proud, and confident about the Space Age and the opportunities it offers.

131

Kelley 3

Logos

Ivanov does not only invoke sentiment, he refers directly to past space flight achievements of the Soviet Union to persuade audiences. The dogs in the image serve not only to stir emotion in viewers, but to remind them of recent successes. Because of the widespread fame of the USSR's space program, the public would recognize Belka and Strelka, two dogs who were sent into space together aboard *Korabl-Sputnik II*, and the first animals to return from space alive. Though multiple dogs had died in previous rocket tests, including the famous case of Laika aboard *Sputnik II*, this poster plays off of a definitive success to logically persuade its audience that more successful missions will be conducted in the near future. Another aspect of the poster that appeals to logos and conveys success are the white streaks or paths that encircle the Earth, indicating that the rocket has completed two journeys.

2. Interpret.

> **More about**
> Identifying
>   assumptions,
>   158–59
> Identifying
>   stakeholders,
>   265–66
> Interpreting,
>   308–11

After analyzing the text to determine how it works, consider the significance or meaning of the elements you have identified, and draw inferences about what may be below the surface of the text. Use the following questions to help guide your *interpretation* of a text:

- What assumptions does the writer make about the subject or audience? Why are such assumptions significant?
- What does the text omit (evidence, opposing views), and what might these omissions indicate?
- What conclusions can you draw about the author's attitude from the tone? What motives can you infer from the author's background or previous publications?
- Who published this text or sponsored the research, and what influence might these sponsors have on the way the information, arguments, or evidence is presented?
- In what context was the text written—place, time, cultural environment—and how might this context have influenced the writer?

3. Synthesize.

College assignments often ask you to **synthesize**—to connect what you have read to ideas in other texts or to the world around you. You may begin to synthesize early on, as you read and annotate the text. You will probably develop these connections in your reading journal and as you draft and revise your project.

To synthesize, ask yourself the following questions:

- What else have you read or experienced that this text may explain, illustrate, clarify, complicate, or contradict?
- How do the author's other writings amplify, clarify, complicate, or contradict the selection you are writing about?
- What outside forces (historical events, socioeconomic forces, cultural shifts) might influence or underlie the text?
- What claims or points in each text do you find especially compelling? How do compelling points in one text connect to ideas in the other(s)?
- What claims could these texts, taken together, provide evidence for?
- How is your understanding of a topic enhanced or your thinking changed by putting these texts together? What might others gain by seeing these texts together?

> **More about**
> Synthesizing, 308–11
> Comparing and contrasting, 65–66

Writing Responsibly — Drawing Inferences

An inference is only as good as what it is based on. Inferences based on facts are fair; those based on personal values and beliefs or on a faulty understanding of the text are apt to be one-sided and unfair. Aim for the former and avoid the latter.

to TOPIC

Writing Responsibly — Understanding Criticism

In everyday speech, *criticism* is often used simply to mean "finding fault." But in academic disciplines, *criticizing* means "evaluating a work's merits based on a careful and fair analysis." Approach the task of critique skeptically yet with an open mind, and provide evidence for the judgments you make. If you are used to thinking about published texts as absolutely authoritative sources of information, it is important for you to realize that *all* texts present only partial views that can always be challenged.

to OTHER WRITERS

4. Critique.

A *critique* is a well-informed evaluation. It may be positive, negative, or a bit of both. A movie review, for example, is a critique; it provides readers with an evaluation to help them decide whether to see the film. A reviewer's opinion alone is usually not enough to sway a would-be audience member. The reviewer must also provide evidence for the judgment by describing the performances, the screenplay, or the director's vision. Similarly, critiques written for college courses offer judgments based on careful analysis of the text's component parts. They may also be informed by other texts, your own knowledge and experience, or both.

Self Assessment: Preparing to Write about a Visual

When exploring a visual, especially if writing about it, ask yourself the following questions. Does evidence support your answers?

Analysis

- **Parts and patterns.** What are the relationships among the parts? Does the image include or imply a comparison or contrast, a cause or effect?
- **Purpose.** Is the visual's purpose to inform, persuade, entertain, or express emotion? If the visual is persuasive, what does it claim and how does it support this claim?
- **Attitude.** What is the artist's attitude toward the subject or audience? On what basis can you make this inference?
- **Context.** Where is the image set? When was it created? Who produced or sponsored it, and why? How do accompanying words inform your reading?

Interpretation

- **Assumptions.** What values does the image assume or promote? How do those values match, contrast with, or challenge those of its audience?
- **Omissions.** Is something missing? Has the visual been cropped to eliminate background? If so, how does this affect your understanding?
- **Audience.** Who is the intended audience? Where was the visual originally published, or where did you find it? How was the image received by its original audience?

Synthesis

- **Other sources.** How is this image similar to or different from others that you know? Have you read or studied anything that could help you understand this visual?
- **Background.** What knowledge or personal experiences do you have that might deepen your understanding?

Critique

- **Aims.** Based on your analysis, what were the artist's aims, and were they achieved?
- **Claims.** What claims is the artist making, and are you persuaded?
- **Authority.** What expertise or experience does the artist bring?

Professional Model
Review, 508–9

As you prepare to write a critique, consider the following issues:

- **The writer's aims.** What are the author's goals? Are they achieved? Are they worth achieving?

- **The writer's claims.** What are the writer's claims? How much are you persuaded by them? Why?

- **The writer's evidence.** How credible is the evidence? How reliable and relevant is the evidence? How sound is the reasoning?

- **The writer's authority.** What expertise or life experience does the writer bring to the topic, and is it relevant?

Also consider your own goals and position:

- **Your aims, claims, and evidence.** Why are you writing the critique? What claims are you making? What evidence will you use to support those claims?
- **Your authority.** What authority do you have, and why might readers value your judgment and evaluation? You may not be an expert, but your opinion can be interesting and persuasive if it is based on thoughtful analysis.
- **Your audience.** What are your readers' interests and knowledge about the subject? What background information will you need to provide? Will they be sympathetic to your claims, or will you have to work hard to persuade them?

> **More about**
> Claims, 146–49
> Evidence, 45–47
> Authority, 153, 265–69
> Relevance, 263–64
> Reliability, 265–69
> Audience, 18–21

EXERCISE 7.5 Analyzing a speech

Analyze the speech by John F. Kennedy on pages 74–76. In two or three paragraphs, describe the speaker's assumptions and attitude. Also consider how circumstances (the "son of Boston" leaving his home state of Massachusetts for Washington, DC; the recent presidential election) might have affected its reception.

Work Together

In groups of three or more, compare your syntheses. How effectively do your classmates' syntheses draw connections between the two texts? In what ways are they similar to and different from your own? Discuss the strategies you used to complete this synthesis and any revisions that could make them more effective. Make a note of strategies you might use in the future.

Student Model Critical Analysis Essay

In the essay that follows, Joe Fernandez (Syracuse University) analyzes René Brooks's article "Time Blindness" and draws on his classroom experiences to create this critical response.

Fernandez 1

Joe Fernandez

Professor Howard

Writing 205

16 Mar. 2021

A Critical Analysis of René Brooks's Article "Time Blindness:
Timely Advice for Dealing with It"

> **Introduction: Brief summary of article to which the student is responding**

Modern life tends to involve a full calendar. Whether it's work, school, or life events, we all have a lot of places to be and things we need to do by a certain time. There are deadlines to meet and reservations to attend. I thought about this as I read the article about adults with ADHD who suffer from time blindness. The author, René Brooks, defines time blindness as "the inability to gauge the passage of time" and explains how it affects a person's ability to estimate the time required to complete a task, meet a deadline, or arrive somewhere on time. The author also makes the point that the time blind are often misunderstood and frustrated. Central to this is that "neurotypical" people may find it difficult to understand and accept time blindness; for example, a person with time blindness who often runs late to work, class, or meetups with friends is not doing so intentionally and is in fact very frustrated by her own lateness. Finally, the author outlines strategies that have helped her deal with and overcome time blindness.

> **Thesis: Acknowledges strengths of the article but also notes a problem**

Brooks does a great job describing major aspects of time blindness, from what it is and how it feels to ways to manage it. She successfully details her points in a way that is persuasive and informative. My main critique, however, is that the article would be more effective with the addition of a scientific source or two.

Brooks's discussion of the negative consequences experienced by time blind people is effective, especially because she refers to struggles that she's had such as being late for meetings and feeling singled out and vulnerable in the workplace, and because she brings in the perspective of a neuropsychologist. She makes a solid case that there are social and professional costs to time blindness. A particularly detrimental consequence of time blindness and frequent tardiness is that neurotypical people "begin to exclude the ADHD person from activities" and say hurtful things that reveal their lack of trust and confidence. The author offers further proof that time blindness is a real problem by linking to a video featuring Russell Barkley, who gives an overview of ADHD, time blindness, and an ADHD person's relationship with time. Overall, Brooks has helped me understand the challenges that people with time blindness face and clued me in to what neurotypical people like me can do to better support them.

Topic sentence: Analyzes author's approach to explaining time blindness and its impact

Evidence supports topic sentence

However, there is one area in which the article falls a bit short for me and likely for other science-minded readers who don't know much about ADHD; it does not include the data or brain imagery that would help me visualize the causes and effects of ADHD and time blindness from a neuroscience point of view. Including information from a peer-reviewed journal article, for example, could have helped me really "get" what ADHD and time blindness are. Further, while the Russell Barkley video is a major piece of evidence that expands on the article's description of time blindness, Brooks does not quote from it or work it into her discussion, and does not explain who he is beyond being "incredible." Some quick research reveals he holds a PhD in Clinical Psychology, is a Clinical Professor of Psychiatry at the Virginia Commonwealth University Medical Center, and has published widely on ADHD ("About Russell A. Barkley").

Topic sentence: Challenges author's choices about sources

Providing a little context for Barkley would make clear he is a trustworthy source, and bringing in another source or two could help anchor the article in neuroscience. However, this may be beyond the scope of the piece, and distract too much from the author's purpose.

[Topic sentence: Analyzes another strength of the article] Brooks is at her most informative and persuasive when she talks about ways to cope with and manage time blindness. Even though I don't have time blindness, I can relate to some of the issues she raises. This is especially true right now as I am writing this paper during a pandemic; my schedule has changed dramatically and more of my time is being allocated for multiple tasks. I have gone from a nine-to-five schedule with on call duties requiring me to work the occasional night or weekend, to working 100% at home while taking care of my children. Given that my wife is an ICU nurse and that we no longer have childcare help, I have become the primary stay-at-home parent. This means I must juggle my work schedule while taking care of my two- and four-year-olds. It is a blessing to spend time with them, but it does make my life and work balance more difficult. Brooks lays out five tools in her article, and I now use three of them daily.

[Topic sentence: Analyzes another strength of the article] One of Brooks's tools that has helped me the most is to do the same thing at the same time each day. She writes that this is valuable "because doing the same task at the same time day after day ingrains it in my mind and produces a rhythm for my day." I couldn't agree more with this statement. The second most valuable tool for me is using a nudge alarm or timer to help stay on task. This is especially helpful when doing activities with my kids. It helps separate the day into different tasks and keeps the house rolling. Another of her tools is one that I find helpful for myself; that is to stop hyperfocus before it starts. I can very easily become immersed in my favorite tasks and lose track of time. Brooks says it is helpful to save such tasks until after the important ones are completed, which is a great piece of advice. She also says if you can't resist a given task, "go in there with an alarm and an UNSHAKEABLE commitment to doing the task at hand once the time has elapsed." I think these tools can help everyone whether we have time blindness or not. In addition, Brooks recommends using an analog watch because it helps you visualize the passage of time while digital watches or cell phones do not. Lastly, I also value thinking of the worst-case scenario when estimating how long something will take. As Brooks notes, we should not just budget for how long a drive may take, but also add in time to stop for gas or a cup of coffee.

Overall, with or without the addition of sources that I've recommended, "Time Blindness" is a very-well written article that presents valuable details, scenarios, and advice that can help many people. Specifically, it can help people without time blindness to understand it, and help people who suffer from time blindness to manage it. Brooks does a wonderful job explaining time blindness, drawing on her personal experience, expertise, and the expertise of others; inviting empathy and humor; offering encouragement; and making a solid case for learning more about ADHD and time blindness.

> Conclusion: Acknowledges the overall success of the article

Works Cited

Brooks, René. "Time Blindness: Timely Advice for Dealing with It." *Black Girl Lost Keys*, 2 Mar. 2020, blackgirllostkeys.com/adhd/time-blindness-timely-advice.

"About Russell A. Barkley, Ph.D." *Russell A. Barkley, PhD.: Dedicated to Education and Research on ADHD*, www.russellbarkley.org/about.html.

EXERCISE 7.6 Writing a critique

Find an editorial in a printed or an online newspaper. First, read the editorial using the techniques discussed in this chapter and write a summary noting the editorial's main idea and major supporting points. Then write a paragraph-long critical response to it using analysis, interpretation, synthesis, and critique.

EXERCISE 7.7 Interpreting a graphic

Bar graphs like the one here regularly appear in newspapers and magazines with no accompanying story. Based on the graphic alone, write a one- to two-paragraph story to accompany it.

What is the main claim of the graphic? What evidence does it use to support its main claim?

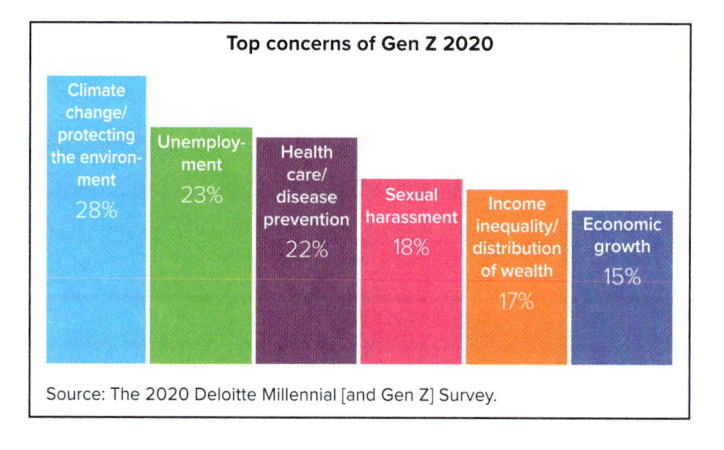

Top concerns of Gen Z 2020

- Climate change/protecting the environment: 28%
- Unemployment: 23%
- Health care/disease prevention: 22%
- Sexual harassment: 18%
- Income inequality/distribution of wealth: 17%
- Economic growth: 15%

Source: The 2020 Deloitte Millennial [and Gen Z] Survey.

Text Credits

Pg 116: Gholipour, Bahar, How Accurate Is the Myers-Briggs Personality Test? *Live Science*, May 19, 2019, https://www.livescience.com/65513-does-myers-briggs-personality-test-work.html; **Pg 121:** Brooks, René, "Time Blindness: Timely Advice For Dealing With It." *Black Girl Lost Keys*, March 2, 2020, blackgirllostkeys.com/adhd/time-blindness-timely-advice/; **Pg 131:** Source: A Rhetorical Analysis of Konstantin Ivanov's, "The Road Is Open to Humans" (poster) By Aiden Kelley; **Pg 137:** Source: Fernandez 1, A Critical Analysis of René Brooks' Article, "Time Blindness".

Reasoning Matters • Preparing to Write   **7c**   141

Writing Responsibly

Understanding and Representing the Entire Source

> **Make It Your Own!** For a research project to be worthwhile, it should represent the overall arguments of its sources—more than just a few sentences—so that readers can understand what the sources were saying and how they fit together.

Each time you write from sources, push yourself to work with them in more substantial ways. Take the time to read each source—the entire source—carefully. Next, **summarize** it, as a way of processing the information: Restate, concisely and in fresh language, the main claims (and the most important supporting evidence) of an entire source. Then when you draft your research project, blend in summaries of your important sources, so that your readers understand how they, too, contribute to your discussion.

You can also draw from sources by quoting or paraphrasing brief passages. But if you simply paste a quotation into your draft, how much do you or your audience actually understand the source or even the passage you are quoting? **Paraphrasing** is a better alternative, because it pushes you to think about the passage: to know the material well enough to restate it in your own words. Changing just a few words in the passage, however, is not paraphrasing; it is **patchwriting**: a mixture of your words and the source's. This is an error interpreted by many readers as plagiarism.

Because quoting and patchwriting do not require much comprehension and are easy to do, inexperienced college writers may rely on them too heavily. Frequently, too, the quotations come from the first few pages of the source—which some students feel is all they have to read. Researchers with the Citation Project found that the majority of college writers' citations came from the first two pages of the source (see chart) and felt the quality of these projects suffered. That is because, in most sources, the first few pages discuss only general findings, while the insightful, detailed examples and evidence that are important to a good analysis or argument are deeper in the text.

When a writer provides only isolated quotations from sources ("dropped quotations"), the result may be uninformative, like this passage from a project about social media and individual identity:

Page Cited
DATA FROM **The Citation Project**

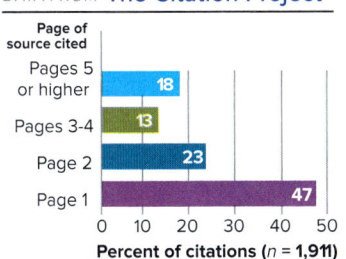

Page of source cited	Percent of citations
Pages 5 or higher	18
Pages 3-4	13
Page 2	23
Page 1	47

Percent of citations (*n* = 1,911)

Researchers found that although most college writers quote from the first pages of a source, the best research projects drew from the entire source.

First draft

> [Student's voice] People value their personal lives and try to separate their private and public selves. Many are aware of being different people in the workplace, in school, on a date. All this may be changing, though. [Quotation] "The fact that the Internet never seems to forget is threatening, at an almost existential level, our ability to control our identities; to preserve the option of reinventing ourselves and starting anew; to overcome our checkered pasts" (Rosen). [Parenthetical citation]

142 7c Reasoning Matters • Thinking and Reading Critically

Notice how, in this draft, readers are given no information about the source; they are presented only with one sentence from it. This causes the reader to wonder: Does the writer understand the source, or has she simply found a "killer quote" that supports her argument? Because the writer provides only the isolated quotation, it is not even clear what her purpose is in including it.

Now consider how this passage is transformed by adding a summary and contextualized quotations:

Revised draft

[Summary of the parts of the source relevant to the student's argument — Student's voice]
People value their personal lives, and many deliberately work to keep their private and public selves separate. Many of us are aware, too, of being different people in the workplace, in school, on the athletic field, on a date. Some value these differences, happy to switch from dedicated intellectual in the classroom to enthusiastic player on the soccer field.

[Summary of the remainder of the source]
All this may be changing, though. [Signal phrase providing information about the author] Writing in *The New York Times*, journalist Jeffrey Rosen points out that we may no longer be in control of the multiple identities that were previously taken for granted. In our online lives, what we post on Facebook and Twitter can easily merge with what we post on a school blog, in our comments on a news story, or in our pictures on *Flickr*. Rosen explains that even in untagged pictures, our faces can be identified through facial-recognition technology. He also describes the privacy-protecting laws that are in development and the companies that offer services to clean up our online reputations.

[Student's voice] Most central to my research, though, is his explanation for this claim: [Quotation (no page reference because source is unpaginated)] "The fact that the Internet never seems to forget is threatening, at an almost existential level, our ability to control our identities; to preserve the option of reinventing ourselves and starting anew; to overcome our checkered pasts."

Source: Rosen, Jeffrey. "The Web Means the End of Forgetting." *The New York Times,* 21 July 2010, www.nytimes.com/2010/07/25/magazine/25privacy-t2.html.

The writer has shown responsibility to her source, her topic, and her audience. Because she has taken the time to read and understand the source, she is able to summarize it to show what its main claims are. Her audience now knows how the quotation was used in the source and how it supports her argument. With this brief summary, the writer has also explained her ideas clearly and established a "conversation" between herself, her source, and her audience—that is, rather than just "using" sources, she is thinking about them, interacting with them, and giving her audience enough information that they can do the same.

Self Assessment

Review and revise your work with each source. Have you done the following?

- ☐ Read, understand, and accurately represent the whole source. Did you look for the details deeper in the source?
- ☐ Summarize the main ideas of the source. Did you put the source's ideas in your own words, fairly and accurately? ▶ *Paraphrasing, 292–94*
- ☐ Incorporate your summary into your source analysis. Did you use the best examples and evidence?
- ☐ Locate the most relevant passages. Did you cite from *throughout* the source?
  ▶ *Critical reading, 112–40*

8 Applying Analysis and Crafting Arguments

IN THIS CHAPTER

a. Persuading, exploring, and affirming, 143

b. Making claims, 146

c. Choosing evidence rhetorically, 150

d. Considering alternative viewpoints, 156

e. Discovering assumptions and common ground, 158

f. Organizing arguments: Classical, Rogerian, Toulmin, 174

g. Avoiding logical fallacies, 176

h. Using tone and style effectively and ethically, 181

Student Model
Exploratory Argument,
Brianna Davids, "Inmate Access to Technology: Safer Prisons and More Successful Reentries to Society," 159

> **More about**
> Crafting a thesis, 35–38, 147, 303–4
> Claims of judgment, 148–49
> Tone, 20–21, 159, 599, 604–6, 607
> Diction, 18–19, 604–6

Our culture often confuses *arguing* with *fighting*. While arguments can indeed lead to fights, they usually do not. We are also accustomed to hearing about "both sides" of an argument, which is a misleading concept: arguments are discussions that usually have *many* sides, many points of view, many pros and cons that cannot easily be weighed against each other, and that may not produce a "winner" and a "loser." This chapter introduces several different forms of argument, ranging from exploration to persuasion, that are appropriate in academic and professional settings, and it explains how you can enter into argument as a critical thinker, not just a fighter.

8a Persuading, Exploring, and Affirming

In general conversation, an argument is a form of verbal fighting: there are winners and losers. Someone is proven right; someone else is proven wrong. In a gentler version of this image, someone is "persuaded" by someone else. In reality, arguments can take several forms: arguments that result in winners and losers; arguments aiming to persuade an audience; arguments that aim for greater understanding of complex issues; and arguments intended to establish who are and are not members of a group.

1. Arguing to win

We are all familiar with arguing to win. This is what happens in formal debates, where one arguer is declared the winner and

FIGURE 8.1 Arguing to persuade This advertisement argues that taking your lunch to work saves money over time; it first asserts this claim, then backs it up with evidence.

the opposition's claims are refuted, proven wrong or insufficient. Pay attention to the news stories following a political debate: predictably they will themselves debate who won the debate! College assignments that ask you to "take a stand" on an issue and "refute the opposition" are inviting this sort of argument from you.

2. Arguing to persuade

Arguing to persuade can be seen as a more tempered version of arguing to win. In this sort of argument, one "wins" by persuading the audience to agree, even though the audience may at first oppose the arguer's point of view. This sort of argument is familiar in political campaigns, too, as candidates work to persuade potential voters that they have the best solution to such compelling issues as health care, good roads, social inequalities, and international relations. It is also familiar in advertising, such as in the "takeout" ad in Figure 8.1. College assignments that ask you to take up an issue and find the best solution to it are inviting this sort of argument from you.

Notice the tone of certainty in the following conclusion from an argument meant to persuade:

> The modern-day educational system, which is more practical and structured [than it is] centered on personal understanding, is a product of the needs of a mass-educated society. Rising tuition costs and higher expectations . . . contribute to the feeling that deeper understanding is secondary to the grades received. Students rush through their college years without taking the time to explore avenues of thought that could broaden their perspectives. . . . To educate people on a large scale, the education community sacrifices some of what made education so powerful, by shifting the focus from true understanding to academic achievement.
>
> –Dung Nguyen, from "The True Purpose of College and Higher Education," *Delta Winds: A Magazine of Student Essays,* A Publication of San Joaquin Delta College.

3. Arguing to learn

Although it is at the heart of academic work, arguing to learn receives less attention than do the oppositional models of arguing to win or arguing to persuade. Arguing to learn is exploratory, not oppositional; it seeks to understand complex issues. In this sort of argument, one takes for granted that no single perfect solution exists. Instead, the arguer and the audience need to come to a shared understanding of the complexity and difficulty of an issue or problem. In writing this sort of argument, your purpose is to discover the available possible solutions, to weigh their pros and cons, and perhaps to recommend one as especially promising, and explain both the reasons for your choice (your evidence) as well as doubts you have about your choice (your counterevidence).

Notice the investigative quality of this paragraph drawn from an exploratory argument (see full paper on pages 159–174).

> When addressing the public's and prison administrator's resistance to ICT (information and communications technology), it is important to discuss prisoner access to technology in terms of the benefits it offers to guards, inmates, and society at large. While prisons in the US, including those run by the Federal Bureau of Prisons, do not currently have incentives and earned privileges (IEP) programs, European prisons are structured around an IEP with five aims: (1) to provide privileges that are earned through good behavior but that are revoked in cases of ill behavior; (2) to encourage responsible behavior; (3) to encourage hard work and constructive activities; (4) to encourage progress throughout sentencing; and (5) to create a controlled, disciplined, and safe environment for prisoners and staff (Liebling 1). These privileges are not handed out loosely: Prisoners must continually prove themselves to prison staff in order to be rewarded. Such rewards include higher pay, longer or more frequent visitation, additional temporary releases, and access to living in the "better parts" of the prison (Liebling 1). The use of incentives and earned privileges could go a long way in terms of answering the questions and doubts that the general public may have, especially if prison public relations and the media were able to explain the program and its benefits to the public.
>
> –Brianna Davids, Syracuse University, from "Inmate Access to Technology: Safer Prisons and More Successful Reentries to Society," used with permission.

4. Arguing to affirm group beliefs

Arguments on social media are often not for the purpose of winning, persuading, or exploring. Instead, they are for the purpose of announcing one's own point of view to others who share it. Such arguments affirm the already-solidified beliefs of a group. They characteristically make no attempt to examine all the evidence and all the possible interpretations of it; if counterevidence is included in arguments to affirm group beliefs, it is thoroughly discredited, sometimes savagely. *Ad hominem* attacks on those who do not share one's point of view frequently appear in arguments to affirm group beliefs. Such attacks are intended to demonstrate not only what one believes but why those who disagree should not be trusted. Such arguments appeal to a sense of group rightness and virtue while demonizing those outside the group. In the United States, calling members of the Republican party "deplorables" or the Democrats "elitists" or "snowflakes" is a biased argument that affirms group beliefs and demonizes opponents. Because they close down critical thinking, arguing simply to affirm group beliefs is inappropriate in academic writing.

8b Making Claims

> **More about**
> Prejudice, 148–49

Just about every text—speeches, advertisements, websites, journal or magazine articles—has a main point or thesis that makes a claim (Figure 8.2). When faced with any kind of text, begin your critical evaluation by determining whether the thesis makes a claim of *fact, opinion,* or *belief,* or whether it simply expresses a *superstition, stereotype,* or *prejudice.*

1. Making claims of fact

A text whose main claim is a statement of fact is *informative* (or *expository*):

> **More about**
> Informative purpose, 16, 37–38

Susan B. Anthony and Martha Carey Thomas worked for women's voting rights in the United States.

Denmark became a constitutional monarchy in 1849.

The square root of 4 is 2.

FIGURE 8.2 Sugar Shock Claims can be advanced visually as well as in writing. This visual makes a claim about the relationship between sugary sodas and health. Bring the same critical acumen to assessing the claims made through visuals that you bring to assessing print texts.

> **Quick Reference** — **Devising an Arguable Thesis**
>
> In an argument, the thesis makes a claim of judgment or value:
>
> **Claim of Judgment (Opinion)**
> The use of email in the workplace reduces personal interactions among colleagues.
>
> **Claim of Value (Personal Belief)**
> Electronic communications ruin interpersonal relationships.
>
> **Claim of Fact**
> Email has surpassed the telephone as the most popular way to communicate in the workplace.
>
> Also, consider qualifying your position with words like *often*, *sometimes*, *some*, and *most* to avoid committing yourself to a stronger position than you can effectively defend. Do not, however, use these qualifiers as a way of making claims that cannot be supported.

A *claim of fact* is not debatable and cannot be the central claim in an argument. For this reason, claims of fact are sometimes called *weak claims*.

Superstitions are claims with no basis in fact:

> A wish made on a falling star will come true.
>
> If she wears her lucky hat, she'll pitch a perfect game.
>
> If you don't forward this email to five friends, you'll suffer 10 years of bad luck.

2. Making claims of value

Values are fundamental principles that an individual or a group holds to be inarguably true; they are based on a moral or religious belief system:

> Humans should not eat animals.
>
> All people should be treated fairly under the law.
>
> Stealing is unjustifiable.

People tend to defend their beliefs with great passion, and *claims of value*, like the three statements above, are frequently at the heart of persuasive texts. As you craft your own argument or read the arguments of others, carefully assess the relationship between a claim of value and the assumptions (or warrants) underlying it.

> More about
> Warrants, 176

3. Making claims of judgment

The holder of an opinion regards it as the most plausible answer *for now,* based on an evaluation of the available information:

> Graduates with engineering degrees are likely to find high-paying jobs.
>
> The healthiest diet is low in carbohydrates.
>
> The Adam Ezra Group is destined to have a number-one hit song.

Supplied with identical facts, not everyone will hold the same opinion. For this reason, the main claim of an argumentative text is often based on an opinion, or ***claim of judgment.*** Sometimes it makes a ***claim of policy*** (a claim about what we should do or how we should solve a problem). Sometimes it makes a ***claim of causation*** (a claim about the causes or effects of a problem).

When opinions are not provisional or temporary, they become ***prejudices,*** usually expressed in stereotypes:

> Athletes are poor students.
>
> Women are too emotional to be president.
>
> Blondes are dumb.

> **More about**
> Counterevidence, 151–52
> Sweeping generalizations, 177

Prejudice is by its very nature unfair because it ascribes qualities to an individual based on generalities about a group, generalities that are themselves often inaccurate. Whenever you suspect that a prejudice is operating as a claim, examine the evidence—and more importantly, the counterevidence—for

---

Writing Responsibly — **Choosing an Engaging Topic**

In addition to making sure your topic is arguable, you should ask yourself the following questions:

1. Is my topic fresh?
2. Do I have something to add?
3. Is it worth reading (and writing) about?

Thinking critically about saturated topics (such as abortion and gun control) is difficult. Instead of articulating your own argument, you can easily wind up offering a rehash of other people's.

The topics about which you can write most interestingly are those on which you have a distinctive perspective. Almost any eighteen-year-old can write passionately about the legal drinking age, for example, but to justify resuscitating tired topics, you must have something original to add. Whatever topic you choose, you will have your best shot at engaging your readers and doing justice to your topic when you write about something you and your readers find compelling.

to TOPIC

the claim. Often a prejudice is based on overgeneralization with counter-evidence ignored or suppressed. A claim based on prejudice never makes an ethical thesis in an argument.

When writing an argument, ask yourself whether your thesis is one with which reasonable people might disagree. A claim of fact (or a widely held opinion) is not debatable; reasonable people would not disagree about the number of Electoral College votes needed to win a US presidential election (270) or about the temperature at which water boils at sea level (212 degrees Fahrenheit).

Because claims of value (personal conviction or belief) depend on shared assumptions, they are often difficult to support with persuasive evidence. Writers typically find it difficult, if not impossible, to conduct an open-minded exploration of such issues. Writing about claims of value is an important way of exploring and sharing your beliefs, but if your assignment is to craft a persuasive argument, focusing on a claim of value can make your task extremely difficult.

EXERCISE 8.1 Assessing claims

Determine whether each of the following topics makes a claim of judgment, a claim of fact, or a claim of value. Explain each of your answers in a sentence or two.

> **EXAMPLE**
>
> It is illegal in this town for grocery stores to use plastic bags.
>
> *This is a claim of fact because it can be verified.*

1. Grocery stores should charge customers for plastic bags to encourage people to recycle their old bags or to use canvas sacks instead.
2. Expecting customers to provide their own bags is ridiculous.
3. In some areas of the country, subsidizing solar energy is a waste of government money.
4. Solar panels have become much less expensive over the last 10 years.
5. It is too difficult to be a vegetarian.

EXERCISE 8.2 Assessing thesis statements

Determine whether the following thesis statements are arguable or not, and explain why.

> **EXAMPLE**
>
> Theodore Roosevelt's sickly and weak physical condition as a child had a critical influence on many of his later personal and political decisions.

> *This is arguable because we have extensive factual information about Roosevelt's childhood physical condition as well as his later personal and political decisions, and a writer can form a knowledgeable and defensible opinion about the importance of the connection between them.*

1. Using animals for drug experimentation is barbaric, cruel, and immoral.
2. Exposure to secondhand smoke significantly increases the risk of lung cancer and heart disease in nonsmokers, as well as several respiratory illnesses in young children.
3. Bilingual education is not effective in areas with large non-English-speaking populations of the United States.
4. Advertisements cause significant harm to people and our society as a whole.
5. Many invasive plants now threatening native species in the United States were deliberately planted by home gardeners.

Make It **Your Own**

Draft an arguable thesis for one of the topics in Exercise 3.1 (p. 36) or 3.2 (p. 39). If you prefer, select a different topic.

8c Choosing Evidence Rhetorically

An argument will be only as persuasive as the explanations and evidence, or *grounds*, that support the claim. Support can appeal to your readers' intellect, it can draw on the authority of a figure they respect, or it can appeal to their emotions. Each of these is a *rhetorical appeal.* The ancient Greeks called these appeals logos, ethos, and pathos. Each has a place in responsible writing. As you develop your evidence, you have a responsibility, to your audience and to yourself, to make rhetorical appeals that your audience will find appropriate and persuasive.

1. Logos: appealing to your readers' intellect

Logos refers to evidence that is rational and consistent; it appeals to readers by engaging their logical powers. Academic writing, such as the excerpt from Rachel Bateman's essay below, relies heavily on reasoned support and concrete evidence:

> Research suggests that violence in the media adversely affects a particularly vulnerable subset of children (usually males): those with Attention Deficit Disorder or information-processing disorders. These children

have a hard time understanding the moral context of violence when it is used as entertainment; they may not differentiate enough between an action sequence in a movie and a face-to-face interaction in their daily lives (Gerteis, 1993). Television viewing of children with these disorders should be carefully monitored, and role-models—parents, doctors, and teachers—should work with these kids to help them better understand the meaning and consequences of real-life violence.

—Rachel Bateman, University of Kansas,
"A Closer Look at the Causes of Violence"

A logical appeal can effectively reach a wide range of readers—from sympathetic to hostile—by reinforcing or challenging opinions with reasoned support.

Visuals that provide strong, quantifiable evidence—facts, data, statistics—appeal to the reader's intellect. This evidence may be displayed in a graph, chart, or map or in a before-after photo pair (Figure 8.3). They are effective for convincing a skeptical audience and are appropriate in all types of texts, especially academic texts, where logical reasoning is highly valued.

Two methods of reasoning, deductive and inductive, can help you structure a logos-based argument.

Exploratory arguments are likely to use ***inductive logic:*** They cite particular examples or specific instances and then draw a conclusion or claim. For instance, imagine that, over a period of months or years, you take exams, sometimes after a good night's sleep and sometimes after staying up late cramming. Reflecting back on your experience, you draw the conclusion that you get better grades on tests after getting a good night's sleep before an exam. This is inductive reasoning. ***Counterevidence***, material that contradicts or offers alternatives to your claim, plays an essential role in

FIGURE 8.3 Melting Glacier at Glacier National Park, Montana These photos of Boulder Glacier, taken in 1913 (left) and in 2012 (right), make a logical appeal. They provide factual (verifiable) evidence for climate change.

exploratory argument. An argument that assesses a complex situation but includes only the evidence that supports its thesis is not exploratory; rather, it attempts to hide the messiness of the situation. Only by dealing with the whole range of evidence can an exploratory argument arrive at a plausible recommendation.

To incorporate both evidence and counterevidence into your argument, explain each item thoroughly, and explain why you find the evidence more persuasive than the counterevidence. As you are drafting your argument, keep your mind open: if, as you are brainstorming and drafting your project, you realize that the counterevidence actually is more persuasive than the evidence, you can change your thesis.

Persuasive arguments are likely to use ***deductive logic***. They start from a general premise to draw conclusions about specific instances. Continuing with the example from the section above, consider this general premise: "Test-takers do their best work after a good night's sleep." From this premise, you might draw the conclusion that, before your next psychology exam, you should get a good night's sleep. If the general premise is true, then the conclusion is inescapable, but is the general premise true?

Imagine that you have not read the assigned chapters and that you have put off studying for the exam. In that case, all the sleep in the world is unlikely to improve your performance, and studying for the exam late into the night might be your best option. When writing or assessing arguments based on deductive logic, be sure to consider alternative explanations for the conclusion and to examine carefully the assumptions underlying the premises.

In this excerpt from his journal, student William Archer (Colgate University) explores two possible ways to understand the Vietnam War in the context of a class discussion of tragedy. He begins with a question, considers the evidence, and weighs his findings to arrive at a tentative position:

> Should the Vietnam War be viewed more as a Greek or Christian tragedy? Viewing the war as a Christian tragedy would suggest that if certain things had been done differently, a more positive outcome might have resulted; officials made mistakes (moral and strategic) that led to their downfall (and the deaths of soldiers), and those mistakes could have been avoided. Viewing the war as a Greek tragedy would imply that nothing those involved did could have made any difference; officials had character flaws and destinies that ultimately led to their downfall.
>
> There is valid evidence to support either claim. Someone could take the Christian tragedy outlook and argue that had the United States chosen to maintain democratic principles instead of overthrowing President Diem, then we might have avoided the war altogether. Others could take the

Greek tragedy outlook and claim that under our government's built-in fear of the spread of communism, war in Southeast Asia was inevitable.

For now, I view the war more as a Greek tragedy; given the historical context following World War II, a proxy war between key powers was bound to happen somewhere in the region. I wonder what would have happened if the United States had chosen a different Southeast Asian nation to "draw the line" with?

—William Archer, Colgate University

Academic writing like Archer's is frequently exploratory in its early stages and becomes persuasive as the argument develops. Working this way often yields a more thoughtful, considered position than does beginning from a predetermined thesis.

Exploratory versus Persuasive Approaches to Argument For personal or cultural reasons, you may be more comfortable seeking consensus than stating an opinion. Seek help in formulating a Rogerian or Toulmin argument, or if you want to write an exploratory argument, check with your instructor to be sure this approach is acceptable.

Logos and Ethos in the United States In academic and business writing in the United States, argument relies primarily on rational appeals. Mentioning highly revered traditional authorities or sources (such as important political figures or religious works) is useful only if your audience consists entirely of fellow believers. For a broader audience, evaluate the arguments and supporting evidence of these authorities, and include their work as support only if it directly contributes to your argument.

2. Ethos: Appealing to your own credibility and that of your sources

Establishing a credible *ethos*—good character, sound knowledge, or good reputation—encourages readers to have confidence in what you say. Kate Laffan, for example, establishes her credentials in the very first paragraph of her article:

According to *The New Republic* magazine in June this year, "You will have to make sacrifices to save the planet," while the US newspaper *Metro* asks, "What would you give up to end climate change?" These headlines, read from my desk in London where I carry out research in environmental psychology, present us with stark choices: between self and society, well-being and morality.

—Kate Laffan, "Going Green Is All About What You Gain, Not What You Give Up," *Aeon*

> **Writing Responsibly**
>
> **Establishing Yourself as a Responsible Writer**
>
> As a writer, you can establish your ethos not only by offering your credentials, but also by providing readers with sound and sufficient evidence drawn from recognized authorities on the topic. By adopting a reasonable tone and treating alternative views fairly, you demonstrate that you are a sensible person. By editing your prose carefully, you establish your respect for your readers.
>
> to SELF

> *More about*
> Making a presentation (ch. 11), 212–20
> Tone, 20–21, 159, 599, 604–6, 607

Ethical appeals (ethos) can be very effective with wavering readers. When people are undecided about an issue, they often want to learn more about it from an expert or a person of good character who has considered all possibilities and provides sound judgments.

3. Pathos: Appealing to your readers' emotions

Using *pathos* to support a claim means stirring the audience's emotions in an effort to elicit sympathy and, thus, agreement. Pathos often relies on examples, stories, or anecdotes to persuade readers. It also uses a tone that stimulates readers' feelings. Visuals that appeal to the readers' emotions or beliefs (Figures 8.4 and 8.5) make an emotional (or *pathetic*) appeal. Use pathos cautiously: Arguments that appeal solely to readers' emotions can be manipulative, sometimes even unethical, unless they are accompanied by appeals to logos. In addition, many academic disciplines respect only logos and ethos as rhetorical appeals.

Emotional appeals sometimes use visuals, especially photographs, because of the immediate impact they can have on the hearts of audience members. Photographs that tug on the readers' emotions are common in advertising but rare in academic or business writing, where judgments are more likely to be made on the basis of logos and ethos.

FIGURE 8.4 Loss of sea ice poses a threat to the polar bear This photograph makes a strong emotional appeal—we fear for the safety and well-being of the polar bear—but it would be out of place in an academic text without statistics that show a clear relationship between diminishing polar bear populations and reduced ice coverage caused by climate change.

Reasoning Matters • Choosing Evidence Rhetorically **8c** **155**

FIGURE 8.5 Visual pathos Organizations with a mission to promote health and well-being often use pathos to persuade viewers. This advertisement by a US government agency features an image of a happy, connected family, an image that supports the claim that parents can keep their children from drinking or using drugs.

Substance Abuse and Mental Health Services Administration (SAMHSA)

→ **EXERCISE 8.3 Assessing logos, ethos, and pathos**

Examine the evidence René Brooks offers in her article (pp. 121). Identify whether the rhetorical appeals are to logos, ethos, or pathos. Then examine the evidence in Joe Fernandez's critique of the Brooks article (pp. 136) in the same way. Finally, write a paragraph explaining which of these two texts you find more persuasive and why.

Writing Responsibly: Preparing Oral Arguments

Appeals to logos and ethos are usually appropriate when you are writing formal arguments for college courses. When you are delivering a speech, presentation or other form of oral argument, your audience is likely to notice and remember vivid appeals to pathos.

Support these emotional appeals with appeals to logos and ethos. After telling a moving story about an individual, use statistics or an expert's opinion to show how the issue affects others. Without appeals to logos and ethos, an appeal to pathos can be merely manipulative.

to AUDIENCE

Student Models
Illustrated projects: 131, 161, 170, 385, 387, 388, 438, 463

EXERCISE 8.4 Assessing visual appeals

Write a paragraph in which you argue that illustrations in one of the student projects in this book make rhetorical appeals to logos, ethos, or pathos.

8d Considering Alternative Viewpoints

To address an issue in all its complexity, you must consider alternative viewpoints. When reading or writing an argument, consider *counterevidence:* the doubts you or other reasonable people might have or the objections that opponents might raise. When writing an argument, ask tutors, friends, or colleagues to help you brainstorm alternative positions or search for alternative voices in print and online sources. One-sided arguments are characteristic of advertising and propaganda, but they have no place in your academic writing, where knowledge-building and critical thinking are valued.

Responses to alternative viewpoints can take several approaches:

- You can provide counterevidence that refutes the opposition. Consider a supporting paragraph from Brianna Davids's argument about inmates and technology:

> While some information and communication technologies (ICTs) such as secured tablets and video kiosks have been introduced to America's prisoners very slowly over the past few years, **[Refutation]** there is an ongoing debate here and elsewhere on whether prisoners should have access to these technologies at all (Kerr and Willis 12-13). The main issues surrounding the debate are public perception of what prison is "for," and objections regarding prison safety and security. **[Counterevidence]** However, research suggests that there are many benefits to giving prisoners access to technology. For example, studies have found that technology not only reduces violence in prison, it prepares inmates for the digitally advanced world outside of prison, and lowers their rate of reoffending once they are released (McDougall et al. 457).

–Brianna Davids, Syracuse University, from "Inmate Access to Technology: Safer Prisons and More Successful Reentries to Society"

Student Model
Exploratory Argument: 159–74

- You can acknowledge alternative views and explain why your position is still the most reasonable *despite* this counterevidence. In the introduction to her essay, Shona Sequiera creates an appealing tension by indicating what both her counterevidence and her evidence will be:

  > Although *Their Eyes Were Watching God* has been widely criticized for painting too romantic a picture of African American life, Hurston's heroine Janie is ultimately able to transcend oppressive stereotypes and successfully come into her own. Her journey towards self-identity and self-knowledge harbors the celebratory ethnic notion that black is not just a color but a culture as well.

  [Concession: "Although *Their Eyes Were Watching God* has been widely criticized for painting too romantic a picture of African American life,"]
  [Explanation of why opposing position is less important than the writer's]

  —Shona Sequiera, Connecticut College, "Transcending Stereotypes in Hurston's *Their Eyes Were Watching God*"

- You can revise your thesis to include concessions, exceptions, or qualifiers such as *some* or *usually*:

  > While the media may have an effect on some young adults, bursts of violence, like those at Columbine High School, Virginia Tech, and Northern Illinois University, are far more complex and have many more underlying causes than anti–media violence activists usually acknowledge: Mental illness, alienation, availability of weapons, and defects in school security are also components of the motivation to become violent.

  [Concession: "While the media may have an effect on some young adults,"]
  [Qualifier: "usually"]

  —Rachel Bateman, University of Kansas, "A Closer Look at the Causes of Violence"

> **EXERCISE 8.5 Assessing the strength of a conclusion**
>
> Reread the student essay by Joe Fernandez that appears at the end of Chapter 7 (pp. 135–139). Does the writer include enough evidence to persuade you of his claim? Does he consider evidence that undermines his claim? How reasonable is his tone? Write a paragraph discussing these issues. Draw specific evidence from the essay to support your claims.

1. Evaluating alternative viewpoints

When reading an argument, consider whether the author has taken alternative viewpoints into consideration, how well the author incorporates counterevidence, and how reasonably and respectfully the author treats that counterevidence. If the source does not mention alternative viewpoints or dismisses them as invalid, be especially careful in your evaluation. *Confirmation bias* is a constant danger when you are reading arguments: it is easy to accept an argument as true and valid because you already agree with its claims. Similarly, when an argument goes against your prior beliefs, it is easy to dismiss it as wrong. Approach arguments as a critical thinker. Evaluate them carefully, opening your mind to the possibility of learning something new or adjusting your prior beliefs.

2. Dealing with hate speech, misinformation, disinformation, and trolls

Looking for diverse points of view in the sources you are reading and choosing is important for good critical thinking and decision-making. However, this work requires a cautious approach whenever you are reading and researching contemporary issues, where you may encounter hate speech, misinformation, and disinformation.

> **More about**
> Identifying misinformation, disinformation, and fake news, 270–71
> Evaluating for relevance and reliability, 263–69
> Evaluating online texts, 271–74
> Evaluating visual sources, 274–76

You will find a bright line between "diverse points of view" and hate speech, which characterizes the work of online trolls, many of which are actually bots. Hate speech may employ ad hominem attacks and verbal cruelty, but it goes beyond these tactics to generalize about entire demographics based on factors like gender, race, nationality, political affiliation, and religion. Hate speech makes these generalizations and then relegates the identified group to second-class citizenship or even non-human status. It is intended to elicit hatred toward its target, often to harass or intimidate the identified group. Nothing about critical thinking and decision-making requires you to consider hate speech in the category of "alternative viewpoints."

Less obvious are sources that circulate misinformation and disinformation, but it is equally important that you eliminate them from the alternative viewpoints you are exploring in your reading and research. (See also Chapter 14: Evaluating Information.)

8e Discovering Assumptions and Common Ground

In order to persuade an audience of the truth of a claim, the writer must move it to accept certain common assumptions. For Brianna Davids to convince us that inmates and society would benefit from the integration of information and communication technologies (ICTs) in US prisons, we must first assume that there are problems in prison and also in communities when inmates are released without necessary life and work skills, problems that include a high risk of reoffending, all of which is bad. If you do not share these basic assumptions, then you will not be convinced that rethinking prison life in America is worth the time and trouble. When W.E.B. DuBois said in 1903, "The problem of the twentieth century is the problem of the color-line—the relation of the darker to the lighter races of men in Asia and Africa, in America and the islands of the sea," he may have assumed that his statement would lead to social change. That would depend, however, on whether his audience *wanted* equality between the races. DuBois knew that some of the audience did not agree with that principle, so his book, *The Souls of Black Folk*, offers evidence in support of the need for change.

As you read and write arguments, consider carefully the assumptions, or *warrants,* that underlie the claims being made: On what common ground must both reader and writer stand before they can discuss a topic productively? What must both writer and audience agree is true without argument or evidence? What information should you share that might help move your audience to endorse your principles?

Writing Responsibly: The Well-Tempered Tone

In public discourse, the "zinger," or clever put-down, is often used to silence an opponent. Sarcasm also thrives: Some take a sarcastic tone toward whatever they oppose. But if you want your argument (and yourself) to be taken seriously, especially in academic and business circles, and if you want to persuade people who do not already agree with you, establishing a fair, even-tempered tone and avoiding sarcasm are crucial. Use sound evidence, not snide comments, to make your point.

to SELF

EXERCISE 8.6 Identifying main claim and evidence

Read (or reread) the essay "How Accurate Is the Myers-Briggs Personality Test?" (Bahar Gholipour, pp. 116–119), identify the main claim, and assess the evidence provided in support of this claim.

Student Models
Persuasive arguments, 136, 383, 497, 517

Student Model Exploratory Argument

In the following exploratory argument, Brianna Davids, a student at Syracuse University, first looks at the issue of the lack of technologies in US prisons, specifically, the lack of information and communications technologies (ICTs) and then uses her analysis as the basis of a claim that ICTs are beneficial to inmates and society.

Davids 1

Brianna Davids

Professor Howard

Writing 205

18 November 2021

Inmate Access to Technology:

Safer Prisons and More Successful Reentries to Society

> Introduction: Explains why topic matters

In the US, the country with the most prisoners in the world (see fig. 1), inmates do not have the level of access to technology that one might expect. While some information and communication technologies (ICTs) such as secured tablets and video kiosks have been introduced to America's prisoners very slowly over the past few years, there is an ongoing debate here and elsewhere on whether prisoners should have access to these technologies at all (Kerr and Willis 12-13). The main issues surrounding

> Background: Describes debate and research around purpose of prison, role of technology

the debate are public perception of what prison is "for" and objections regarding prison safety and security. However, research suggests that there are many benefits to giving prisoners access to technology. For example, studies have found that technology not only reduces violence in prison, it prepares inmates for the digitally advanced world outside of prison, and lowers their rate of reoffending once they are released (McDougall et al. 457). In this paper, I will examine the question of whether the benefits

> Counterevidence: Describes alternative perspective

to prisoners outweigh public attitudes and prison safety concerns, ultimately making a case for doing more to introduce technology to prisons to better the lives of prison guards, inmates, released prisoners, and the public.

> Evidence: Describes research, expert opinions, examples

Prisons may be presented as "luxurious" by the media, but in reality the conditions and practices within prisons make them criminogenic. That is, prisons themselves are

Rates of Incarceration per 100,000

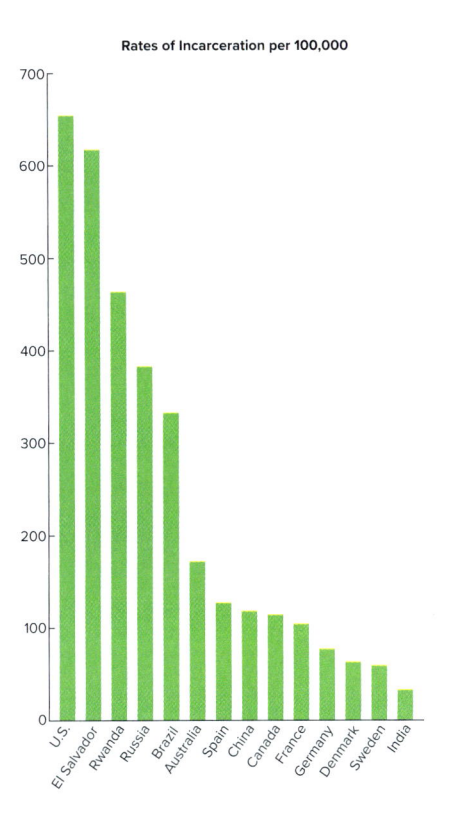

[Bar chart showing incarceration rates by country: U.S. ~650, El Salvador ~620, Rwanda ~460, Russia ~380, Brazil ~330, Australia ~170, Spain ~130, China ~120, Canada ~115, France ~105, Germany ~78, Denmark ~63, Sweden ~58, India ~33]

Fig. 1. The US incarcerates more people than any other country. According to the Sentencing Project: "There are 2.2 million people in the nation's prisons and jails—a 500% increase over the last 40 years. Changes in law and policy, not changes in crime rates, explain most of this increase. The results are overcrowding in prisons and fiscal burdens on states, despite increasing evidence that large-scale incarceration is not an effective means of achieving public safety." From "Criminal Justice Facts."

Source: "Criminal Justice Facts," by Sentencing Project, https://www.sentencingproject.org/criminal-justice-facts/

> Evidence: Shows U.S. leads the world in he number of people it imprisons

places that produce crime, something that is counter to what they are meant to do, which is decrease the likelihood that inmates will reoffend (McDougall et al. 457). Cynthia McDougall and colleagues also found that crime in prison stems from the lack of control incarcerated individuals experience, which leads to distress and an increased likelihood of criminal behavior including violence, abuse, and retribution. Giving prisoners more control over managing basic tasks, they discovered, lessens feelings of unfairness and isolation and can offset aspects of the toxic culture so prevalent in prisons. For example, some prisons in the UK allow inmates to manage basic tasks such as managing finances, ordering from the commissary, and visiting with loved ones by video. Prisoners in the UK are also given opportunities for learning how to use digital technology, something that benefits them educationally and in terms of their futures (McDougall et al. 458). The use of these technologies is not taken lightly, and there has been a long, ongoing debate on prisoner access that began with an early technology.

According to Yvonne Jewkes, who has written about the impact of prison on identity and wellbeing, in-cell television was one of the first technologies to spark a lively debate about whether prisoners should have access to technology. The introduction of in-cell television changed the nature of imprisonment, and was

> Evidence: Describes early debate around technology in prisons

implemented in the UK in 1991, and as early as 1985 in other European countries. Prior to this, shared prison televisions were set to a type of community-access channel. However, at prisons that provided access to multiple televisions and channels, there were fewer arguments over the channel being watched (Jewkes 1). Although the debate about in-cell television has died down, the questions it raised are relevant to today's debates about the use of digital technologies.

Davids 4

    Information and communications technologies are being provided and used very differently in prisons throughout the world. While other countries have central government bodies that oversee their prisons, the US does not. While a Federal Bureau of Prisons, under the Department of Justice (DOJ) does exist, it oversees a fraction of prisoners, holding only 165,575 of the total 2.2 million imprisoned inmates in America (Federal Bureau, "Population Statistics"; "Criminal Justice Facts"). Because there is no single government entity that oversees America's correctional institutions, be they local sheriff-run jails or state- or privately run penitentiaries, there are no established guidelines for inmate access to technology or to specific ICTs. However, in Australia, inmates use technology for a variety of purposes. They are allowed to email up to five approved contacts; videoconference for legal proceedings, family visitations, and consultations with medical and mental health professionals; pursue educational services such as online college; access employment programs for finding a job outside of prison; participate in rehabilitation programs; and use kiosks to schedule appointments, find employment, transfer earnings, receive messages, and more (Kerr and Willis 4–11). As Aysha Kerr and Matthew Willis found, having control over these tasks helps to reduce inmate stress and create a more positive prison atmosphere for the inmates, something that also makes the lives of prison guards safer and easier.

    The sentencing phase of their criminal case is extremely stressful for inmates. In this context, feelings of anger and powerlessness can be exacerbated by their lack of access to information and the social aspects of the digital world. Other stressors, such as the distance between a prison and a prisoner's family, and the relocation from one prison to another, can make it very difficult for an inmate's loved ones

> Evidence: Provides context for how US prisons function

> Evidence: Describes inmate access to technology elsewhere in the world

> Evidence: Explains inmates' experience

to come for visitation days. As a substitute method of staying in touch, ICT could bring these families together via video chat or email. According to Eva Marie Toreld and colleagues, "the digital society has made digital communication a vital part of everyday life," and giving prisoners access to that communication reduces frustration and improves their success in reintegrating into society (337).

> *Writer's claim backed by quote from expert / authority*

Further, giving inmates access to ICT for keeping in touch with family is a great motivator for good behavior. McDougall and colleagues found that when the uses of digital technology are geared toward inmate interests, such as talking to family, inmates become more motivated to use digital technology for other purposes, including those that will benefit them educationally (460). The use of ICT improves prisoner behavior and boosts their feelings of worth and personal control, while at the same time it also benefits staff, freeing them from some administrative tasks, and allowing them to focus on other important aspects of their work, such as rehabilitation (McDougall et al. 459). McDougall and colleagues also found that prisoners like tablets, preferring to use them for taking psychological evaluations, rather than using pen and paper. The use of tablets (which offer restricted use of the internet and select materials) fosters in inmates a more constructive attitude toward prison (McDougall et al. 460). With a more positive attitude, prisoners are able to better focus on improving and educating themselves throughout their sentence so that they can be prepared for life outside of prison.

> *Evidence: Presents benefits of inmate use of technology*

If the overall goal of prisons is to be effective in reducing crime, then that goal requires staff to prepare inmates for successful lives outside of prison. To function in today's society, inmates need to understand and use technology in many areas of day-to-day life, including work, school, and home, and in relation to health, well-being,

> *Writer's claims about role of prison and inmate technology supported with evidence from research*

and social connections. Not allowing prisoners to access such technologies isolates and excludes them from crucial services and connection. It hinders their education, rehabilitation, and preparation for reentry into society (Bagaric and Hunter). In Spain, for example, prisoners are not allowed to access the internet or any other digital technology, including educational and vocational material. Most of the prisoners are illiterate and have poor social skills, and without exposure to technology throughout imprisonment, they face obstacles in finding employment and securing a stable income upon release (Barreiro-Gena and Novo-Corti 1173). In Norway, on the other hand, the expectation is that prisoners have the same basic rights that the general population has, according to Toreld and colleagues, and that life inside the cell should be as normalized as possible in relation to "life outside." But, as is the case in Spain, prisons in Norway ban internet use and restrict telephone use as well. Toreld and colleagues argue that such restrictions generate a prison population that is less educated and functional than the population outside prison walls. To be "digitally active," that is, to be an active citizen in a digital society, one must possess technological knowledge and skills while learning to adapt to constant change in the process. Without access to technology, inmates are unable to fully function in society (Toreld et al. 336–37). Further, without access to normalizing activities, prisoners may easily fall into old habits upon release and reoffend.

Among the objections to allowing prisoners access to ICTs is the assumption that prisoner access to digital technology is dangerous and leads to more criminal behavior in and outside of prison. However, McDougall and colleagues found that such access reduces the chances that an individual will reoffend. Their quantitative study in the UK looked at thirteen prisons where staff had introduced prisoners to digital technology and increased that access over a period of seven years.

> Writer addresses alternative perspective

They discovered that inmates' use of digital technology—especially through their sentencing when access to legal materials is crucial—reduced the rate of reoffending, specifically within the first year of release.

> Supports claim with quotation from authority

Quantitative results were supported by a prisoner survey and usage data. Prison disciplinary offenses were significantly reduced over a two-year period, and reoffending in the first year after release was reduced by 5.36% compared to a 0.78% reduction in comparison prisons. The prisoner survey and usage data suggested that prisoners felt much more in control of their lives in prison and much more confident in coping with technology in the outside world. The changes created by the introduction of digital technology offer the opportunity to make prisons more efficient for staff, and places of improved learning and rehabilitation for prisoners, contributing to a safer society (McDougall et al. 1).

As McDougall and colleagues note, by reducing criminal behavior and creating a safer environment through technology access, prison staff can better focus on the goals of educating and rehabilitating individual inmates so that they can leave prison as contributing members of society. However, it will take work to persuade the public and prison administrators and staff of these proven benefits.

> Acknowledges legitimacy of counterevidence

Admittedly, the objections of prison officials have merit: granting prisoners access to digital technologies and "the outside world" can increase the risk that they will plan and engage in criminal behavior or obtain prohibited materials. For example, in Australia, prisoners have "misuse[d] computers to make improvised weapons, conceal physical and digital contraband, engage in clandestine communication, and compromise systems" (Kerr and Willis 12). While criminal activities do occur, research shows that only "a minority [of inmates] will use their new skills for 'anti-social purposes'" (Toreld et al. 337). Further, prison staff have easily managed security issues by isolating local servers, allowing access to "offline versions" of educational sites, providing access to approved content, and restricting connectivity (Martinez). And for prison staff, the use of digital technologies, including RFIDs, camera systems, GPS, and internet restriction apps to monitor behaviors has been effective and serves to remind inmates that they are being surveilled (Reisdorf and Jewkes 778). In the US, a stated goal for high-security prisons is the "close control of inmate movement," something that technology certainly makes easier (Federal Bureau, "About Our Facilities").

> Evidence: Describes benefits of inmate technology use

Public objections to introducing ICT to prisoners are based largely on the assumption that prisons should do more to punish and less to rehabilitate. According to Yvonne Jukes, even when prisons successfully launched in-cell television in Europe, there was significant backlash from the public based on a "get tough" attitude. Opponents maintained that inmates did not deserve television and should instead be punished for their crimes through deprivation, so much so that one Nordic governor responded by requiring the removal of all in-cell televisions in 1995. However, in 1997, leadership changed and in-cell television was implemented once again. Jewkes also describes the debate around prison TV as one sparked by the media itself. Much of the reporting, she says, inaccurately portrayed prison life and mischaracterized the way incentives and earned privileges work in European prison. The media instilled in viewers a mistaken belief in the "luxurious" aspects of prison life that criminals did not deserve (Jewkes 2). However, if members of the public were to learn exactly how incentives and earned privileges can work there could be a sea change in how they view prison life.

> Acknowledges legitimacy of counterevidence

> Describes backlash against inmate technology use

When addressing the public's and prison administrators' resistance to ICT, it is important to discuss prisoner access to technology in terms of the benefits it offers to guards, inmates, and society at large. While prisons in the US, including those run by the Federal Bureau of Prisons, do not currently have incentives and earned privileges (IEP) programs, European prisons are structured around an IEP with five aims: (1) to provide privileges that are earned through good behavior but that are revoked in cases of ill behavior; (2) to encourage responsible behavior; (3) to encourage hard work and constructive activities; (4) to encourage progress throughout sentencing; and (5) to create a controlled, disciplined, and safe environment for prisoners and staff (Liebling 1). These privileges are not handed out loosely: Prisoners must continually prove themselves to prison staff in order to be rewarded. Such rewards include higher pay, longer or more frequent visitation, additional temporary releases, and access to living in the "better parts" of the prison (Liebling 1). The use of incentives and earned privileges could go a long way in terms of answering the questions and doubts that the general public may have, especially if prison public relations and the media were able to explain the program and its benefits to the public.

For one thing, even though the Federal Bureau of Prisons (BOP) in the US does not currently offer inmates access to technology—except for approved online sources and library materials for understanding the law and preparing legal documents—the BOP notes the benefits of prisoner access to communications technology. Its web page on prisoner communications states, "Studies show that when inmates maintain relationships with friends and family, it greatly reduces the risk they will recidivate" (Federal Bureau, "Stay in Touch"). However, with some exceptions, such as the states of New York and California,

US prisons have been extremely slow to "update" their systems or move forward with tools for inmates such as access to online education and health care professionals, as well as videoconferencing that would allow them to connect with family.

One of the reasons that US prisons are slow to adopt technology is that some of the earliest providers (such as GTL) were exploitative of inmates, requiring them to pay exorbitant prices for access (Martinez). According to the CEO of a newer company that supplies tablets to inmates, another reason is that few prison administrators in the US understand technology and its benefits, especially in regard to inmate enrichment, preferring to rely on dated tools. "They're a lot more comfortable buying pepper spray than they are in investing in technology," Grewe says (qtd. in Martinez).

> Restates problem regarding adoption of inmate technology

Despite the apparent reticence of the US prisons to adopt technology, there are companies such as Edovo (see fig. 2) and APDS developing digital tools to improve prisoners' reentry success and decrease the rate of recidivism. With the world's highest incarceration numbers, the US has not done well in terms of preventing former inmates from reoffending. According to the PEW Center, forty percent of those released from prison will reoffend within three years of their release (Martinez). The Bureau of Justice Statistics reports that eighty-three percent of state prisoners are re-arrested at least once after release, with an average of five re-arrests.

> Evidence: Describes digital tools available to prisons

Among the causes of recidivism is that, upon release, most of the formerly incarcerated return to the environments and cycles of poverty and violence that fostered their original criminal activity (Armstrong). Mia Armstrong writes, "Reducing recidivism requires constructing an alternate reality—and technology can help," including training and controlled access to social media, which promotes "positive social behavior." Further,

> Evidence: Indicates that technology can reduce recidivism

Davids 11

Edovo's stated purpose is to improve lives by providing digital tools to prisons. Its main audience is likely prison administrators and staff, but the needs of others (inmates and their families), of "everyone," are also indicated.

Edovo counters the problems it has identified with solutions that include safe and free access to communication and to educational content, helpful service and custom options, and the resulting benefits of safer prisons and better rehabilitation. The solutions, broken out into three categories, promise advantages to prison administrators, staff, and inmates.

The organization identifies the lack of real inmate rehabilitation as a problem, presumably one Edovo can solve.

This problem is broken out into three issues that center on communication—limited access to it, high fees and poor service, and the impact of both on recidivism.

These features reflect and are meant to address the worries that administrators and staff (and even members of the public) have regarding the integration of information and communication technologies (ICTs) into prisons.

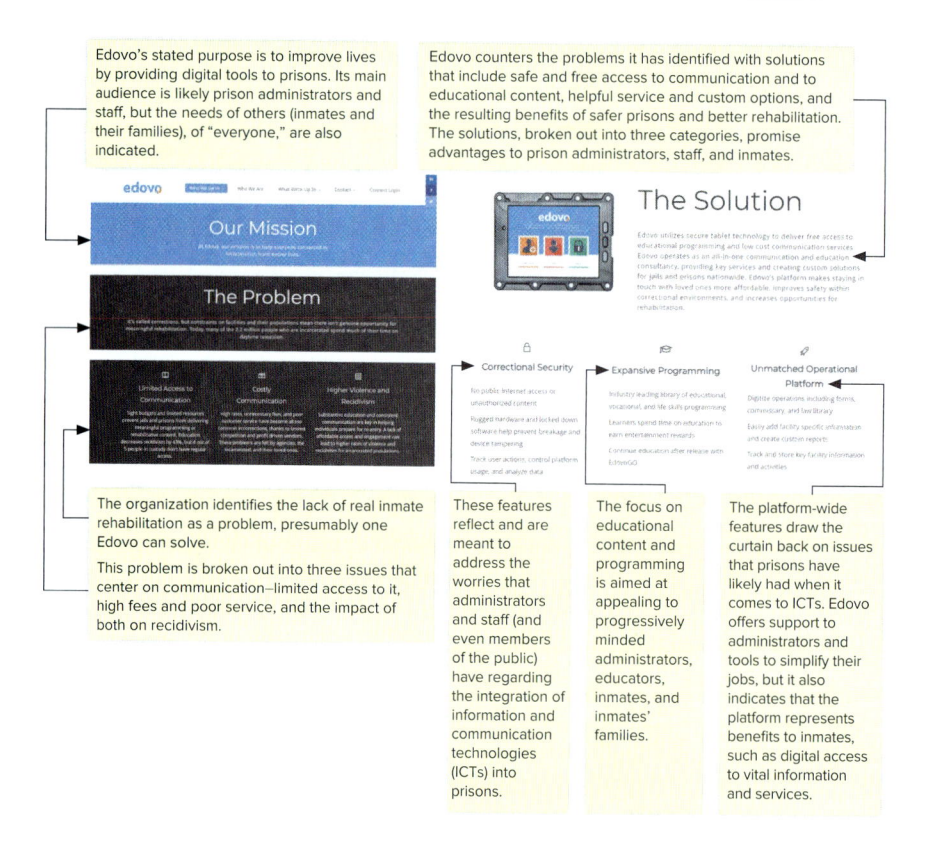

The focus on educational content and programming is aimed at appealing to progressively minded administrators, educators, inmates, and inmates' families.

The platform-wide features draw the curtain back on issues that prisons have likely had when it comes to ICTs. Edovo offers support to administrators and tools to simplify their jobs, but it also indicates that the platform represents benefits to inmates, such as digital access to vital information and services.

Fig. 2. The tablet maker Edovo lays out the problems that inmates and prison staff face and offers its products as a solution for improving prison safety and providing opportunities for rehabilitation ("Our Mission"). Founded in 2014, Edovo states its goal as "building technology solutions to support positive outcomes for incarcerated individuals and their families, correctional facilities, and affected communities," with a "firm belief in a smarter, safer justice system for all" ("Who We Are").

digital literacy is key for inmates because it gives them the opportunity to reimagine their lives, to find employment beyond unskilled work, and to gain new confidence and independence, according to a 2015 study done at Portland State University (Armstrong). Clearly such benefits to prisoners are worth the time and money required to integrate aspects of today's technologies into prison life. Imagine a country in which prisoners are truly rehabilitated and become productive members of society upon release. Among many other benefits, this could do much to right the wrongs of the US criminal justice system and reward those who want to live better lives.

> Evidence: Supports claim that technology and reduced recidivism provide benefits

To move forward on this issue in the US, we need to overcome the objections of prison administrators, perhaps by suggesting that they consider the model IEP aims and successes of UK and other European prisons. Even better would be the creation of a government institution or non-governmental organization that oversees all detention facilities, one that can institute a system that benefits prison staff and inmates. We also need to overcome the objections of members of the public who may be skeptical about integrating technology into US prisons. This goal could be achieved by pointing to successes in other countries; sharing information; carefully planning, monitoring, and evaluating the introduction of digital tools in prisons in an ongoing way; and educating and persuading people, through the media, about the benefits of these tools to prisons, inmates, and society as a whole.

> Conclusion: Shows complexity of the issue
>
> Argues for technology solutions in prison
>
> Returns to thesis

While introducing informational and communications technologies (ICTs) poses a slight security risk, as noted, and the public may push back on the idea that inmates "deserve" tools for rehabilitating themselves, it is still crucial that we recognize the benefits of treating individuals in prison humanely. Through technology, we can help

> Acknowledges risk (counterevidence) while restating thesis and supporting it with evidence

reduce their frustration, improve their physical and mental health, provide education and tools for success, prepare them for the digitally advanced world outside of prison, and reduce their risk of going back to prison. All of these factors can help change prisons from violent criminogenic institutions into places that provide inmates with the chance to better themselves and become citizens who benefit their communities. ICTs should be implemented in more prisons, perhaps starting in a limited way and based on data from existing successful programs, such as those in Europe. They should also be constantly evaluated and studied, and they should be implemented based on the incentives and earned privileges (IEPs) model of the European programs. Further, prison administrators and staff should get the education and ongoing training they will need to institute ICTs at their facilities, with careful attention paid to how inmates are rewarded, so that they, too, are set up for success.

Works Cited

Sources: Authoritative, reflect a diversity of perspectives and publications

Armstrong, Mia. "How Prisons Can Use Tech to Slow Their Ever-Revolving Doors." *Slate*, 26 June 2018, slate.com/technology/2018/06/how-prisons-can-use-tech-to-help-reduce-recidivism.html.

Bagaric, Mirko, and Dan Hunter. "Give Prisoners Internet Access for a Safer and More Humane Community." *The Conversation*, 15 Nov. 2016, theconversation.com/give-prisoners-internet-access-for-a-safer-and-more-humane-community-68543.

Barreiro-Gena, Maria, and Isabel M. Novo-Corti. "Collaborative Learning in Environments with Restricted Access to the Internet: Policies to Bridge the Digital Divide and Exclusion in Prisons through the Development of Skills of Inmates." *Computers in Human Behavior*, vol. 51, 27 Feb. 2015, https://doi.org/10.1016/j.chb.2015.01.076.

"Criminal Justice Facts." The Sentencing Project, 2020, www.sentencingproject.org/criminal-justice-facts.

Edovo. "Our Mission." 2020, www.edovo.com.

---. "Who We Are." 2020, www.edovo.com/who-we-are.

Federal Bureau of Prisons. "About Our Facilities." 2020, www.bop.gov/about/facilities/federal_prisons.jsp.

---. "Population Statistics." 2020, www.bop.gov/about/statistics/.population_statistics.jsp. Accessed 11 Nov. 2021.

---. "Stay in Touch." 2020, www.bop.gov/inmates/communications.jsp.

Jewkes, Yvonne. "The Use of Media in Constructing Identities in the Masculine Environment of Men's Prisons." *European Journal of Communication*, vol. 17, no. 2, 1 June 2002, pp. 205–25. *SAGE Journals*, https:// doi.org/10.1177/0267323102017002693.

Kerr, Aysha, and Matthew Willis. "Prisoner Use of Information and Communications Technology." *Trends and Issues in Crime and Criminal Justice*, no. 560, 2 Oct. 2018, pp. 4–13. *Australian Institute of Criminology*, aic.gov.au/publications/tandi/tandi560.

Liebling, Alison. "Prison Officers, Policing, and the Use of Discretion." *Theoretical Criminology*, vol. 4, no. 3, 1 Aug. 2000, pp. 333–57. *SAGE Journals*, https://doi.org/10.1177/1362480600004003005.

Davids 16

Martinez, Juan. "Jail Tech: Phones, Tablets, and Software behind Bars." *PC Magazine*, 7 Nov. 2016, www.pcmag.com/news/jail-tech-phones-tablets-and-software-behind-bars.

McDougall, Cynthia, et al. "The Effect of Digital Technology on Prisoner Behavior and Reoffending: A Natural Stepped-Wedge Design." *Journal of Experimental Criminology*, vol. 13, 12 Oct. 2017, pp. 445-82. *SpringerLink*, https://doi.org/10.1007/s11292-017-9303-5.

Reisdorf, Bianca C., and Yvonne Jewkes. "(B)Locked Sites: Cases of Internet Use in Three British Prisons." *Information, Communication, and Society*, vol. 19, no. 6, 2 Mar. 2016, pp. 771-86. *Taylor and Francis Online*, https://doi.org/10.1080/1369118X.2016.1153124.

Toreld, Eva Marie, et al. "Maintaining Normality When Serving a Prison Sentence in the Digital Society." *Croatian Medical Journal*, vol. 59, no. 6, pp. 335-39. *NCBI*, https://doi.org/10.3325/cmj.2018.59.335.

8f Organizing Arguments: Classical, Rogerian, and Toulmin Models

> **More about**
> Organizing, 39–44
> Explaining and supporting your ideas, 45–47
> Purpose, 15–17
> Audience, 18–20

As with any writing, an argument is most effective when it is carefully organized. The following are three widely used models for organizing arguments. Each one serves certain purposes of argument.

Before choosing a structure, study the following models; one may work well for your project. If you combine elements from more than one, do it for rhetorical reasons rather than convenience; organize your argument with your purpose and audience foremost in your mind.

1. The classical model

The *classical model* of argumentation derives from the work of ancient Greek and Roman orators. It is well suited to persuasive arguments and is composed of five parts, usually presented in this order:

1. **Introduction.** Acquaint readers with your topic, give them a sense of why it is important and why you are qualified to address it, suggest the purpose of your argument, and state your main claim (or *thesis*) in one or two sentences.

2. **Background.** Provide whatever basic information your audience will need to understand and appreciate your position. You might include a brief review of major sources on the subject or offer a chronology of relevant events.

3. **Evidence.** This is the heart of your argument, and it should be the longest section in your project—at least 50 percent of the whole. In it, explain to readers why you believe what you do, and offer well-chosen evidence to support your claims. Depending on your rhetorical situation, you might appeal to your readers through their logic (*logos*), through their respect for you and your sources (*ethos*), or through their emotions (*pathos*). Support your argument with *logos*, *ethos*, or *pathos* depending on rhetorical considerations such as your purpose, your audience, and the genre in which you are writing. If your project is multimedia, you might want to include information graphics to support logical appeals. A well-chosen and accurately formatted list of works cited will help your appeals to *ethos*, especially if, in your text, you point to the strong credentials of your sources. Images and videos can effectively move an audiences's emotions, as they identify with (or reject) what they see.

4. **Counterevidence.** Describe and explain alternative viewpoints, treating opponents fairly.

5. **Conclusion.** Leave readers with a strong sense of why they should agree with you: suggest solutions, call for action, or reemphasize the value of your position. If your argument is complex, it may also be helpful to summarize it briefly here.

> **More about**
> Deduction,
> 152–53

2. The Rogerian model

The purpose of *Rogerian* argument is to build common ground on complex issues, not to "win" an argument. It was developed by Carl Rogers, a twentieth-century psychologist who hoped this method would make discussion more productive. The Rogerian model is composed of the same five parts as the classical model, but in a different order:

1. **Introduction**
2. **Background**

3. **Counterevidence**
4. **Explanations and evidence**
5. **Conclusion**

In a Rogerian argument, the counterevidence appears before the evidence because the presentation of counterevidence helps establish the complexity of the issue. Instead of refuting the counterevidence, the writer explores its legitimacy first and then explains why he or she nevertheless believes the thesis.

3. The Toulmin model

The model for arguments developed by philosopher Stephen *Toulmin* includes five parts, but the parts are somewhat different from those of classical and Rogerian argument:

1. **Claim:** your thesis, the central argument
2. **Grounds:** the reasons you believe the claim and evidence supporting your claim
3. **Warrants:** any assumptions that explain how the grounds support the claim
4. **Backing:** supporting evidence for the warrants; they require their own supporting evidence because they are themselves claims
5. **Rebuttal:** counterevidence and your response to it

> **More about**
> Revising, 86–96
> Claims of value, judgment, 147–49
> Explanations and evidence, 45–47
> Appeals, 150–55
> Counterevidence, 151–52, 156–58
> Persuading, exploring, and affirming, 143–46

Like classical argument, the Toulmin model is persuasive. Like classical argument, Toulmin presents the main claim and evidence before counterevidence. One distinctive feature of Toulmin argument is that it places counterevidence last, and it also refutes the counterevidence, leaving less doubt that the main claim is the best perspective. It also recognizes that assumptions underlie all claims and brings those assumptions to the surface, making the search for common ground easier (or at least clarifying the terms of the discussion).

8g Avoiding Logical Fallacies

When assessing an argument that seems persuasive, keep an eye out for logical *fallacies*. Familiarizing yourself with logical fallacies will help you avoid them as you write your own argument, and it will help you evaluate the trustworthiness of sources you are consulting. Because inductive arguments depend on examples and the conclusions you draw from them, fallacies like the following can creep in:

- **Hasty generalization (jumping to conclusions).** *Look at her, running that stop sign! She's a terrible driver!*

    A hasty generalization occurs when a general conclusion is based on insufficient evidence: Since even the best drivers occasionally make mistakes, this one piece of evidence is not enough to incriminate this driver.

- **Sweeping generalization.** *Women are terrible drivers! My girlfriend ran a stop sign the other day and almost got us both killed!*

    Sweeping generalizations apply a claim to *all* cases when it actually applies to only a few or maybe to none. Stereotypes are often based on a sweeping generalization. (Whenever words like *all*, *every*, and *none* are used in an argument, take a closer look; these often signal that a sweeping generalization is coming.)

- **False analogy.** *Our candidate's victories over his enemies during the war will ensure his victory over his political opponents in the election.*

    A false analogy draws a connection between two items or events that have few or no relevant common characteristics. This false analogy does not explain how the two things resemble each other: Why would a military victory guarantee a political victory? Is the political process really like a military campaign? Are opposition candidates really like enemy soldiers?

Writing Responsibly: Visual Claims and Visual Fallacies

In academic writing, you might use a visual to *support* a claim, but you should be cautious about using a visual to *make* a claim. Visual claims are effective sales tools (they are common in advertisements), but they are likely to commit a visual fallacy, such as *overgeneralization*—drawing a conclusion based on too little evidence. (Is it reasonable to assume that *all* women using a certain brand of soap will look like a movie star simply because one celebrity claims to use the product?) This ad may also commit the fallacy of false authority. (Is the actress an authority on whose expertise we can rely when buying soap?) As this vintage ad indicates, such consumer-manipulating arguments are not new.

to TOPIC

- **Stacking the deck (special pleading).** *Got dandruff? Our shampoo contains MarvEll, guaranteed to end your dandruff problems!*

  An argument that stacks the deck focuses only on supporting evidence and ignores counterevidence that casts reasonable doubt on it. In this case, the dandruff-killing properties of the shampoo may also make your hair brittle, but the ad would not mention that fact.

- **False authority.** *My mother says that ice cream is more nourishing than a bowl of oatmeal.*

  Unless your mother is a nutritionist, her word alone is insufficient. An argument that appeals to a false authority draws evidence from someone who is *not* an expert on the topic.

- **Bandwagon appeal.** *Mom and Dad, you* have *to buy me an SUV; all my friends have one!*

  The bandwagon appeal implies that the majority opinion is the right opinion and invites you to climb aboard. Some bandwagon appeals may be based on poll results, lending them the impression of reliability. But poll results merely report what the majority of respondents *believe* to be true. Many European Americans in 1860 believed that holding other people in slavery was acceptable, which goes to show that the majority can be wrong.

The power of deductive arguments depends on the validity of the conclusion or the appeal of the premises, so watch out for arguments based on dubious logic or hidden or missing premises:

- **Begging the question (circular reasoning).** *You must believe me because I never lie.*

  An argument that begs the question uses the conclusion (in a disguised form) as one of the premises in the argument. In this example, the second half of the sentence repeats the conclusion rather than offering a premise from which it can be derived.

- **Non sequitur (irrelevant argument).** *You can solve a lot of problems with money, so the rich must be much happier than we are.*

  A non sequitur (which means "it does not follow" in Latin) draws a conclusion from a premise that does not follow logically. The conclusion in the statement above equates money with happiness, but research shows that the two do not go hand in hand.

- ***Post hoc, ergo propter hoc* (false cause)**. *This ring must be lucky: I wore it for the first time today, and I pitched a perfect game.*

  Post hoc, ergo propter hoc means "after this, therefore, because of this" in Latin. In a *post hoc* fallacy, the speaker wrongly assumes that the first event caused the second: Just because the player wore a ring while pitching a perfect game does not mean that the ring is "lucky"; maybe she was just having a good day or the other team's hitters were weak.

- **Either-or fallacy (false dilemma)**. *You're either for us or against us!*

  The either-or fallacy allows, misleadingly, for only two choices or sides in an argument, never allowing for other options, never acknowledging compromise or complexity. (A visual false dilemma occurs in the image shown in Figure 8.6.)

FIGURE 8.6 **Either-or fallacy on a website** This image from an anti–gun-control website suggests that there are only two ways to protect yourself. A third option might be to call the police. (Source: http://bbvm.wordpress.com/2009/03/12/two-ways-to-shield-yourself-from-a-violent-attack-see-women-of-caliber/)

Self Assessment

As you revise your argument, consider the following features. If your answer to any of these questions is no, make the necessary revisions.

- ☐ **Claim.** Do you take an arguable position based on an opinion or belief on which reasonable people could disagree? Have you modified it to avoid making a stronger claim than you can effectively support? Does your introduction show why your topic is important?

- ☐ **Evidence.** Do you supply evidence in support of your claim? Do you use rational, ethical, or emotional appeals that are appropriate to your topic, purpose, and audience? Do you use visuals, where appropriate, to make or support claims?

- ☐ **Counterevidence.** Have you acknowledged alternative interpretations of your evidence, as well as evidence that undermines your claims? Have you explained why your position is the most reasonable, despite these objections?

- ☐ **Organization.** Have you followed an appropriate model of argument, such as a classical, Rogerian, or Toulmin model? Is the organizational structure appropriate to your overall aim—persuasion or exploration?

- **Red herring.** *Reporter: "Mayor, what do you have to say about the dangerous decay of the city's flood walls?" Mayor: "I'm proud of the accomplishments in my administration: We have a much larger, better equipped police force than when I took office."*

  According to the *Oxford English Dictionary*, a red herring is a smoked fish with a distinctive odor used to train dogs to follow a scent. As early as 1884, it was used to mean an irrelevance used to distract attention from the real issue. In the example above, the mayor is trying to dodge a difficult question by changing the subject.

- **Ad hominem (personal attack).** *His views on how to resolve the parking problem on campus are ridiculous! What would you expect from a member of a frat that has its own parking lot?*

  An ad hominem (personal) attack attempts to undermine an opposing viewpoint by criticizing the motives or character of the individual offering the alternative view. When writers use ad hominem attacks, they focus their critiques on aspects of a person's character without connecting character flaws to the issues in question.

- **Guilt by association.** *Tiffany is the most treacherous person I ever met. If Makoto is Tiffany's friend, he can't be trusted.*

  Guilt by association dismisses or condemns people because of the relationships they have. Even if Tiffany is indeed untrustworthy, that does not mean everyone who befriends her is also untrustworthy.

- **Projection (cunning projection).** *I'm rubber, you're glue, whatever you say bounces off me and sticks to you.*

  The children's taunt is a form of projection, a logical fallacy also known as *cunning projection*. The speaker attributes their own failings to an opponent, which diverts the audience's attention from the speaker to the opponent. Especially if the speaker is charismatic, the audience can actually be led to attribute the flaw to the opponent of the person whose flaw it actually is.

- **Subtweeting**. *A person whom I won't name but who was at last night's gathering. . . .*

  Twitter is an invention of the twenty-first century, and so are tweets. Hence, "subtweeting" is not a classic fallacy, yet its tactics have long been part of discourse. In a subtweet (regardless of whether it happens on *Twitter* or elsewhere), the speaker complains about or criticizes another person without naming them but does so in a way that enables the audience to identify the target. Subtweeting, because it does not name its target, also denies that target the opportunity to defend themselves. If the target is not named, defending themselves makes them look even guiltier.

- **Gaslighting**. *You must be crazy; that never happened.*

    Gaslighting is a form of manipulation; when it takes place between two people who are in a relationship, gaslighting is a form of emotional abuse. The speaker persuades the target that their observation, experience, or memory is wrong. Gaslighting can occur not only in personal relationships but in discourse addressed to large groups. In this case, the speaker "reinvents history," telling the audience a nonfactual version of events that benefits the speaker and that the audience is expected to accept.

- **Slippery slope.** *If we exempt one person from the physical education requirement, everybody will want an exemption.*

    The slippery slope fallacy implies that one event will initiate an unstoppable sequence of events. But as any skier can tell you, a slippery slope does not always mean that you will slide uncontrollably to the bottom of the hill. It is not impossible to exempt some students (those with a good excuse) while requiring the rest to take gym.

> **EXERCISE 8.7 Locating logical fallacies in political websites**
> Locate three logical fallacies in the websites of political figures—the president, your city's mayor, a senator from your home state, a candidate running for an upcoming election. (Go beyond the home page, deeper into the site, at least twice.) In a paragraph, name the fallacy and explain how the text (or visual) commits it.

8h Using Tone and Style Effectively and Ethically

Disagreement is an integral part of contemporary culture; we encounter it daily in school, at work, online, and amongst our friends. We might call these disagreements "arguments," but often they are simply quarrels based almost exclusively on appeals to *ethos* and *pathos*. The comments that are posted in response to virtually any article online illustrate this sort of discourse. On the ESPN sports website, for example, readers will see *logos* as commenters cite the statistics of a player, team, or match, but they will also see a great many ad hominem and red herring logical fallacies when commenters attack the character or lifestyle of the person with whom they disagree.

Show respect for the people, situations, and cultures you are writing about, even if you disagree with or disapprove of them. Check yourself for any of these stylistic indications that you are not exercising reasoned judgment:

- Adopting a tone of superiority
- Using profane language
- Adopting a sarcastic tone
- Using demeaning put-downs
- Using derisive name-calling

When you are writing about something or someone you disagree with, state your opinions plainly and explain the reasons for your disapproval.

Work Together

Exchange your revised project with a fellow student. Read each other's work carefully. Does it commit any of the fallacies listed on pages 176–181? If so, mark them and explain what makes them fallacies. If the project is fallacy-free, explain why its claims are logical.

Make It Your Own

Write a paragraph reflecting on the material in this chapter and your responses. What did you learn about effective argumentation and logic by reading and evaluating other people's writing? What surprised you? Have you noticed the use of ethos, logos, or pathos in your daily life, or caught any logical fallacies? If so, what effect did these things have on the argument being made? Has your opinion of argument changed as a result of your increased understanding of it? End with a checklist of five specific issues to check as you revise future projects.

Text Credits

Pg 144: Dung Nguyen, from "The True Purpose of College and Higher Education," *Delta Winds: A Magazine of Student Essays*, A Publication of San Joaquin Delta College; Pg 145, 156, 160: Brianna Davids. Inmate Access to Technology: Safer Prisons and More Successful Reentries to Society.

Part Three

Media Matters

Designing, Writing, and Presenting

9 Designing Accessible Print and Digital Documents 184
10 Writing for Multiple Media 199
11 Presenting with Multiple Media 212

9 Designing Accessible Print and Digital Documents

by Rebecca Moore Howard and Krista Kennedy

IN THIS CHAPTER

a. Understanding the four principles of design (CRAP), 184

b. Understanding universal, empathy-driven design, 186

c. Understanding the principles of accessible design (POUR), 187

d. Planning your design project, 188

e. Applying traditional, universal, and accessible design principles, 190

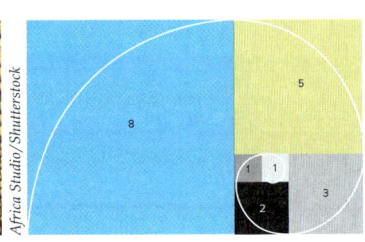

Africa Studio/Shutterstock

The seed patterns of the sunflower are an example of the golden spiral, a mathematical sequence found in nature, in our bodies, and in much of what we create. The spiral is part of the golden ratio, an approach that humans have long applied to creating art and architecture (since the times of ancient Egypt and Greece) because it ensures compositional balance.

Design is everywhere. Once you begin to notice its patterns and variations, you'll see evidence of it in your everyday life. As you engage with print, digital, or any other kind of content, pay attention to how it is presented. How well does it reflect the design principles outlined in this chapter? How might you improve the designs of others? These questions will get you thinking like a designer. Just as you write with your readers in mind, design your work so that it can be easily accessed and understood by all members of your audience.

9a Understanding the Four Principles of Design (CRAP)

The well-known author of *A Non-Designer's Design Book,* Robin Williams, explains how the four principles of design (memorably known as the CRAP design principles) work:

1. **Contrast** among design elements calls attention through difference.

2. **Repetition** of a design element lends unity (oneness).

3. **Alignment,** arrangement in a straight line (vertical, horizontal, or diagonal), creates connections among parts and ideas.

4. **Proximity** (or nearness) suggests that content is related.

Media Matters • Understanding the Four Principles of Design (CRAP) **9a** 185

The use a few bold colors (black, yellow, blue), the use of white space, and the contrast between the style of the portrait and logo images draws attention through difference.

The presentation of information in a vertical/horizontal grid helps readers see the relationships among parts and ideas.

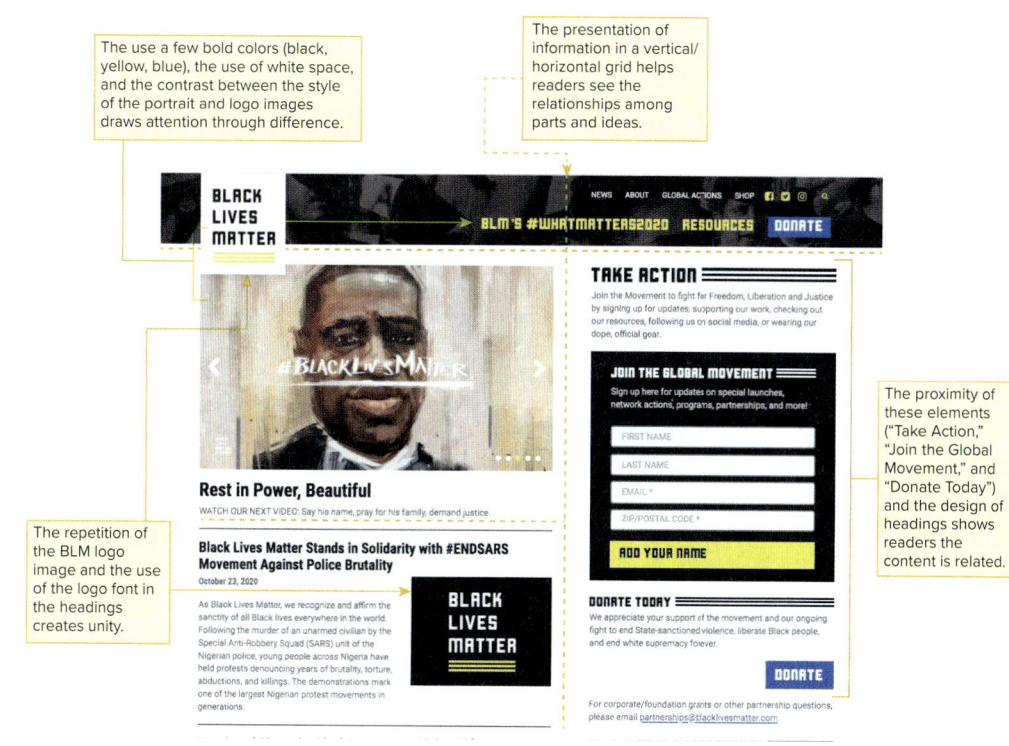

The proximity of these elements ("Take Action," "Join the Global Movement," and "Donate Today") and the design of headings shows readers the content is related.

The repetition of the BLM logo image and the use of the logo font in the headings creates unity.

FIGURE 9.1 Analysis of the effectiveness of webpage design: *Black Lives Matter*
The creators of the *Black Lives Matter* website use font size, color, alignment, and white space to highlight information and make the page attractive. The home page for an active organization is by necessity crowded with information, so they provide clear headers, boxes, and forms to make the page easier to navigate. Placing navigation links in proximity and using clear terms helps users understand which links will take them to specific information types.
Source: https://blacklivesmatter.com

In effective designs, such as those evident in Figures 9.1 and 9.2, these four principles work together to direct readers to the most important information and to highlight relationships among the elements on the page or screen.

EXERCISE 9.1 Analyzing a design

Find a web page, a brochure, or an advertisement (in print or online) that you think makes good use of words and graphics, and in two or three paragraphs explain how it uses the four principles of design: contrast, repetition, alignment, and proximity (CRAP).

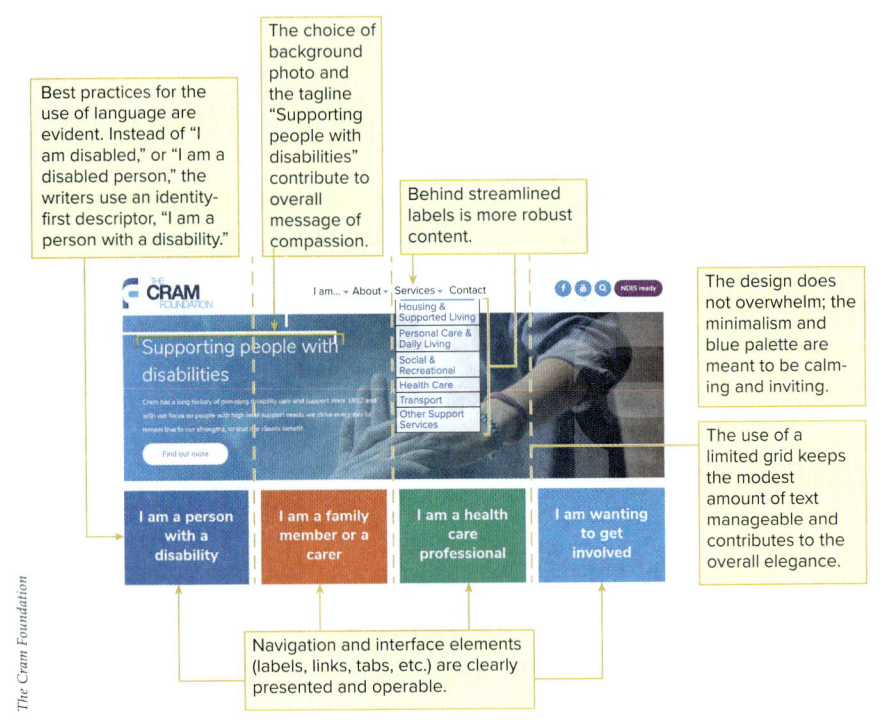

FIGURE 9.2 Analysis of the accessibility of a website design: *The CRAM Foundation*. The creators of the CRAM Foundation's website use contrast, proximity, and alignment to provide an interface that is understandable, perceivable, and operable. Clearly labeled link descriptions on contrasting backgrounds make it easier for persons who are blind or neurodivergent to locate and understand links, whether or not they are using screen readers. The color scheme also ensures that persons who are color blind can perceive the information and operate the links. Clear alignment makes the site more usable for all persons, especially those who view the world with a neurodiverse perspective.
Source: https://www.cramfoundation.com.au.

9b Understanding Universal, Empathy-Driven Design

Good designers practice what Adithya Kumar calls "empathy-driven design," design that works to comprehend the situations of your readers.[1] An empathy-driven approach to your writing and the design of your projects means creating documents that meet the needs of all of your readers, including those with limited vision or who are blind, with limited hearing or are deaf, who are neurodivergent, and those with other disabilities.

---

[1] https://uxdesign.cc/design-philosophy-ee40bbcecc67#.b3moo3mku

Universal design principles are the best way to create designs that are accessible to as many members of your audience as possible. It is not a special requirement for a minority audience, but a fundamental requirement for designs that will be usable and even pleasurable for all of your readers. For example, providing well-edited closed captions with your video will enable persons who are deaf to enjoy your project as well as reach the estimated 92% of viewers who watch video without sound on their mobile devices.[2] Including accessible image captions (known as "alt text") for the images in your project not only makes it accessible to persons who are blind who use screen readers but also adds more keywords that improve the search engine optimization (SEO) of your document, making it easier for search engines to find.

> **Tech** Using Alt Text
>
> You can tell if a digital image includes alt text descriptions by hovering over it with your mouse. For information on creating alt text see: https://webaim.org/techniques/alttext/

A note on language. The person, not the disability, should always come first. Use language that emphasizes abilities and conveys a positive message rather than language that focuses on a person's disabilities or limitations. For example, use:

- "person with [who has] a disability" instead of "disabled person;"
- "child with a congenital disability" or "child with a birth impairment" instead of "impaired child;" and
- "person with mental illness" instead of "mentally ill person."

9c Understanding the Principles of Accessible Design (POUR)

The World Wide Web Consortium, or W3C, recommends the following central principles of accessible design.[3] Together, these core principles form the acronym POUR. Accessible content should be:

1. **Perceivable:** All users must be able to perceive the information that is being presented. This means that information must be perceivable via multiple senses.
2. **Operable:** Navigation elements and interface components such as links and tabs must be operable.

---

[2] https://www.nexttv.com/news/mobile-videos-often-watched-without-audio-study-finds#:~:text=A%20survey%20of%20U.S.%20consumers,and%20ad%20buyer%20Publicis%20Media%20.

[3] https://www.w3.org/TR/UNDERSTANDING-WCAG20/intro.html

Media Matters • Designing Accessible Print and Digital Documents

3. **Understandable:** Elements of the interface and ways of operating them must be understandable.
4. **Robust:** Content must be sufficiently robust that it can be reliably interpreted by a range of users and their assistive technologies.

Designing for the POUR principles means providing multiple ways for readers to access your texts. For instance, you will likely provide captions for all of your images, tables, or charts. As you think in terms of universal design, you will ensure that these captions include rich descriptions. In order to make the images themselves truly accessible in a digital document, you'll use your content management system's alt-text function in order to provide a description that will be embedded along with the image itself so that when a screen reader encounters it or a user hovers over the image, that alt text will be made available to the user. In some cases you may choose to write your own alt text to provide deeper context (as the student writers on page 190 do).

> **EXERCISE 9.2** Analyzing accessibility
>
> Find a web page, a brochure, or an advertisement (in print or online) and in two or three paragraphs explain how it does or does not demonstrate the use of the POUR principles.

9d Planning Your Design Project

To figure out how best to apply the four principles of design to your project, begin with a careful consideration of your rhetorical situation:

> *More about*
> Purpose, 15–17
> Audience, 18–20
> Context and genre, 22

- **Topic.** What is your topic, and how can you reflect that topic through your design?
- **Audience.** Who will your audience be, what kind of expectations do they bring with them, and what kind of relationship do you have (or want to have) with them?

> **Quick Reference** Learning How Persons with Disabilities Use the Web
>
> Use these resources from the Center for Persons with Disabilities to learn more about the ways that specific types of disabilities shape the way readers use the web.
> 1. **Visual** Disabilities and web use: https://webaim.org/articles/visual/
> 2. **Auditory** Disabilities and web use: https://webaim.org/articles/auditory/auditorydisabilities
> 3. **Cognitive** Disabilities and web use: https://webaim.org/articles/cognitive/
> 4. **Motor** Disabilities and web use: https://webaim.org/articles/motor/

- **Purpose.** Is your purpose to inform, to persuade, to express yourself, or to entertain, and how should this be reflected in your design?
- **Context.** In what context (academic, business, public) or setting (over the internet, in person) will your project be received, and how might this affect its design?
- **Genre.** What type of project (résumé, business letter, essay, lab report) will best fulfill your purpose, and what design conventions are associated with this genre?
- **Circulation**. Will this document be distributed in print or digitally? If digitally, in what sort of media? Should it operate on a variety of electronic devices? Consider audience and context as you make these decisions.
- **Accessibility.** What elements need to be included in order to make your project accessible to all potential readers? How will including these elements shape your workflow and time management?

Next determine how the pieces of information you want to convey relate to one another:

> **More about**
> Organizing, 39–44

- What information is most and least important?
- Does some of the information support a broader claim or provide evidence for this claim?
- How might you convey or reinforce your ideas visually?

EXERCISE 9.3 Analyzing a document

Return to the web page, brochure, or advertisement that you used in Exercise 9.1. Analyze its purpose, audience, context, and genre. What (if any) principles of design can you identify at work in the document? What design principles would you recommend be applied in a revision of the document? Do you think a person who has vision loss or hearing loss could effectively use this text?

Make It Your Own

For an organization you are involved with or endorse, plan a promotional web page, brochure, or advertisement to solicit members or advertise an event. How will the purpose of your document affect its design? What audience will you appeal to? What information will they need, or what information will persuade them to join or attend an event?

Media Matters • Designing Accessible Print and Digital Documents

> **More about**
> Colors, 195–96
> Fonts, 192–94
> Visuals, 77–85, 196–98
> White space, 194

9e Applying Traditional, Universal, and Accessible Design Principles

Once you have organized your project, you are ready to begin designing it.

Student Model: A Well-Designed Document

This student report, created for online spaces, is designed to be accessible for all audience members, including persons who are neurodivergent or have loss of vision. It adheres to the principles of CRAP and POUR design, with contextual alt-text descriptions of visuals and a palette that makes the content perceivable for those with color blindness. Note that the report has been annotated by the coauthors of this chapter.

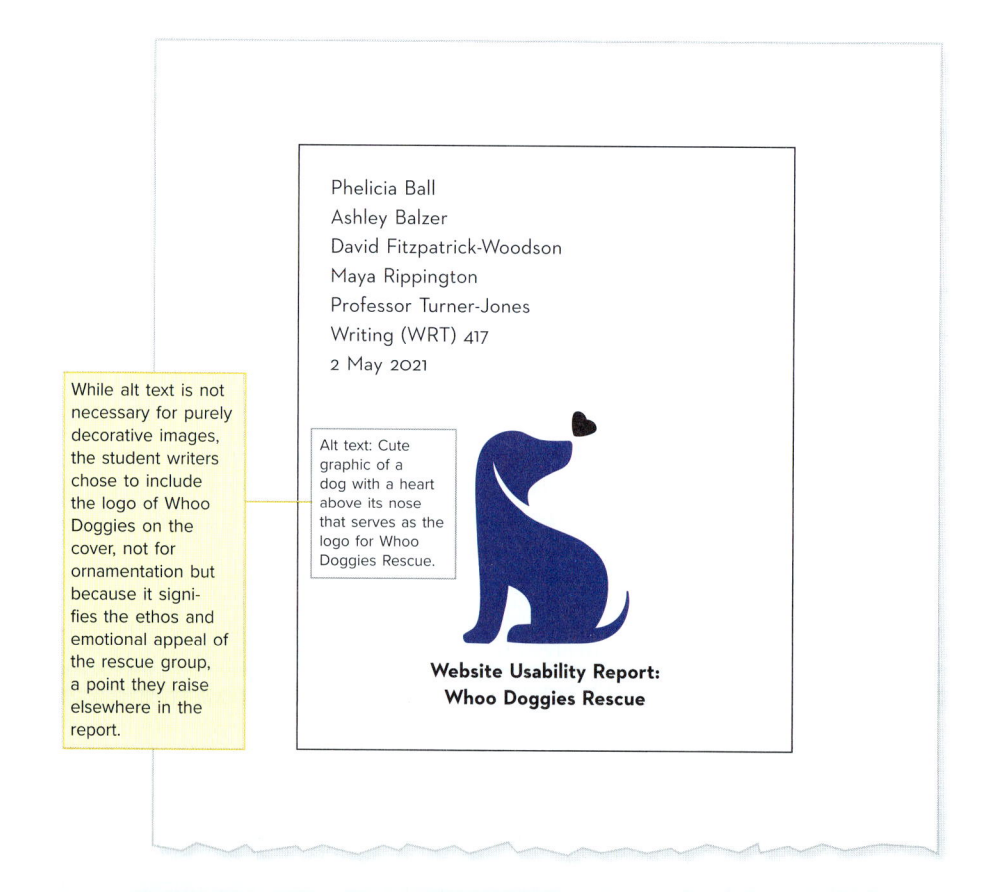

Phelicia Ball
Ashley Balzer
David Fitzpatrick-Woodson
Maya Rippington
Professor Turner-Jones
Writing (WRT) 417
2 May 2021

> While alt text is not necessary for purely decorative images, the student writers chose to include the logo of Whoo Doggies on the cover, not for ornamentation but because it signifies the ethos and emotional appeal of the rescue group, a point they raise elsewhere in the report.

> Alt text: Cute graphic of a dog with a heart above its nose that serves as the logo for Whoo Doggies Rescue.

**Website Usability Report:
Whoo Doggies Rescue**

> Clear headings in three levels and the use of white space between them, as well as the use of contrast and color, help make the report accessible.

> The students' use of the page grid makes the content manageable and understandable for varied audiences.

Ball, Balzer, Fitzpatrick-Woodson, Rippington 1

Results

Based on our three main research questions regarding the Whoo Doggies' website, as well as our findings from in-person interviews and the Qualtrics survey, we concluded the following.

1. How successful were users in completing forms?

> Consistent use of styles make this document accessible for those using screen readers.

Adoptees: More than the volunteers, the adoptee users had difficulty navigating the site, reporting a lack of alignment of text on the application form and the faulty search option for identifying and learning about the dogs. Therefore, they were not as likely to want to go further with the application. That said, there was a 100% success rate in locating the adoption forms on the site.

Adoptee Qualtrics quotes: "Some parts of the application are awkwardly worded."

"The lack of alignment between the text and type fields makes this form very challenging."

"It's simple and easy to navigate. A+"

Adoptee in-person quotes: "The adoption form is too long. I don't have the time or patience to fill it out."

"I have 20:20 vision and can barely read the form. Won't this be a problem for others?"

Volunteers: Overall, these users had a better experience than the adoptees. However, more than one third reported difficulty in finding and completing the volunteer form.

> Alt text: Pie graph showing whether respondents would volunteer for Whoo Doggies based on their reviews of the group's website.
>
> 45% "Already volunteer."
> 18% "Might not."
> 16% "Definitely yes."
> 12% "Probably not."
> 6% "Probably yes."
> 3% "Definitely not."

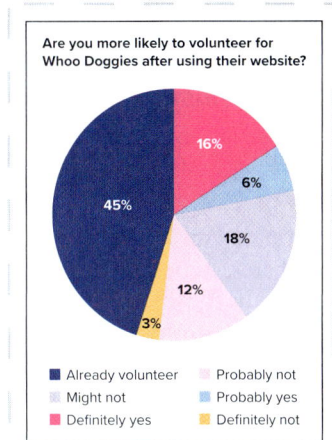

Fig. 1. is based on the results of a question asked in our Volunteer Qualtrics Survey. (See Methods, Qualtrics Testing: Volunteer Survey for more.)

> The alt text for Figure 1 provides the pie graph's data concisely. While graphs are less accessible to persons with disabilities than charts, offering concrete alt text helps make them understandable.

Student model courtesy of Phelicia Ball, Ashley Balzer, David Fitzpatrick-Woodson, and Maya Rippington.

1. Create an overall impression.

Start by considering the overall impression you want to give the reader: Should the design be conservative or trendy, serious or playful? Let your decision about the style of your project guide you in your choice of colors, fonts, and visuals.

2. Plan the layout.

Next consider the overall *layout,* the visual arrangement of text and images. An effective layout should use proximity, alignment, repetition, and contrast to make the relationships among the elements clear. Keep your layout simple, and use it to direct the reader's eye to the most important pieces of information. Creating a clear layout ensures that your project is accessible to readers who use screen magnification as well as readers who are viewing your page on the smaller screens of mobile devices. Neurodiverse readers who need visual consistency to enhance their comprehension will appreciate your attention to this aspect, as well as almost anyone else who needs to efficiently access the information you provide.

3. Format the document.

Once you have sketched your layout, you are ready to create a cohesive and attractive design by using the following elements:

Fonts Word processors give writers a wide range of fonts (or typefaces) to choose from. Serif fonts (fonts with a little tail on the ends of letters, like Cambria and Times New Roman) are easier to read when printed on paper, while sans serif fonts (such as Arial and Calibri) are easier to read on screen and are preferred for web publishing.

> *More about*
> Using italics and underlining, 865–68

In addition to selecting the font family, you can set your font in a variety of styles, including **boldface,** *italics,* or underlining. Since *italics* and underlining often have a specific meaning, avoid using them except when necessary. Apply the core design principles of repetition and contrast to your font choices: repeat the same font for consistency and use a different font to produce contrast. Consistently using a limited set of fonts will improve accessibility for all of your readers. Be aware that many of the screen readers used by readers with vision loss often ignore styles as well as specialty fonts.

Writing **Responsibly** / Selecting Fonts with Readers in Mind

Not all readers have perfect vision. If your audience might include members over 40 (or under 12), use a font size of at least 12 points to make the reading experience easier and more pleasant. If your audience might include low-vision or Blind readers, increase your font size even more.

to AUDIENCE

Use color or boldface for emphasis and contrast, but do so consistently and sparingly: The more they are used, the less attention they will call to themselves. Color will also pose difficulties for persons who have loss of vision, or low vision, a variant of color blindness. The American Foundation for the Blind estimates that around 10% of all adults experience some form of visual disability.[4] Careful use of color will also make your project more accessible to neurodivergent readers who may easily experience migraines or other issues triggered by visual elements.

As you plan your use of color, consider the following best practices:

- Avoid light shades of color.
- Provide solid color backgrounds.
- Create high contrast.
- Do not overlay text on images without providing accessible captions or alt text.

Writing Responsibly: Establishing a Consistent Font

When you copy material from a source, you have the responsibility of citing the source, indicating that it is a direct quotation, and providing full information about the source in a bibliography. When you cut and paste your direct copy from an electronic source, you also have the responsibility of converting its font to the one you are using for your main text. Otherwise, when the font suddenly shifts from black to blue, or from Times to Arial, the audience may be distracted from your message.

to OTHER WRITERS

> **More about**
> Using information responsibly
> (ch. 15), 279–301

When choosing a font size, make sure it will be easy to read (especially if you are using it for the body of your project). Generally, 12-point type for your body text will be legible to most readers, but print out a page of text to check the font size: 12-point type in one font may look larger than 12-point in another.

The font you choose can also add contrast, or it can group items through repetition: If most of your text is in a serif font, a sans serif font (or the same font in bold or a different color) can call attention to a heading. Use the same style, size, color, and type of font for all the headings at the same level and for all text of the same type. Ensure consistency by using the Styles option on your word processing program. Using Styles will also ensure that screen readers used by persons with loss of vision are able to differentiate between titles and body text.

> **More about**
> Page layout:
> MLA style
> (ch. 18), 379–82
> APA style (ch. 19), 426–30
> *Chicago* style
> (ch. 20), 458–59
> CSE style (ch. 21), 482–83

---

4 https://www.afb.org/research-and-initiatives/statistics

Keep in mind, too, that the fonts you use (especially in headings) can reinforce the overall impression you are trying to create. A typeface such as 𝔒𝔩𝔡 𝔈𝔫𝔤𝔩𝔦𝔰𝔥, for example, might be appropriate in a poster announcing the first meeting of the Shakespeare Society. Be careful: for a text-heavy document, legibility is more important than drama. More than a few words in an ornate font like *Edwardian Script* or **Haettenschweiler** will be hard to read. Setting lengthy passages on a website in a serif font may also make the text difficult to read on screen, though such fonts can be used effectively for headings online. With digital documents, you will also need to establish legible contrast between background and text.

NOTE For college writing, check the style guide for your discipline to make sure these design decisions will be acceptable.

FIGURE 9.3 Using white space to group elements To group information into a unit for readers, add white space above a heading or around a figure and its caption.

White space The portion of a page or screen with no text or images, the *white space,* does not literally have to be white (Figure 9.3). The margins at top, bottom, left, and right of a page provide white space, as does the extra space before a paragraph or around a heading. Extra white space above or around text or a graphic organizes elements into a section. Using the same amount of white space around headings at the same level or visuals of the same type lends consistency to your layout. Adding extra white space lends emphasis and ensures that areas or sections of the page are easy to identify and locate. It makes it easier for all readers (especially those who are neurodiverse) to locate and focus on information.

> **More about**
> Parallelism
> (ch. 28), 580–87

Headings Writers often use headings and subheadings to group text and guide readers. They can help readers comprehend a text's structure at a glance. This is particularly true for readers with vision loss, who may use their screen reader to jump from header to header in order to obtain an overview of your project's structure. By creating effective headers, you will help all readers get a sense of your main ideas, and they can then return to the ones they find most interesting or useful. The principles of repetition and contrast are crucial with headings:

- Set all headings of the same level in the same font, style, and color, and align them in the same way on the page or screen:

    First-level heading (title)

    Second-level heading (major section)

    Third-level heading (subsection)

- Use the same grammatical structure for all headings of the same level. For example, use all *-ing* phrases (*Containing the Economic Downturn, Bailing Out Wall Street*) or all *noun* phrases (*Economic Downturn Ahead, Wall Street Bailout*).
- Distinguish among heading levels by setting all headings of the same level in a specific font, style, or color or by placing them differently on the page (flush left, centered).

Lists Another strategy for grouping related items (and for adding white space) is to use lists. Keep lists succinct to allow readers to skim them for information. They can be particularly effective in web pages to summarize and break up blocks of text on the screen. When creating lists, regardless of your medium, remember to do the following:

- Keep list items parallel (use all phrases or all sentences, for example).
- Keep the number of items in a list small (four to six).
- Begin list items with a bullet, not a hyphen or other symbol, and align all items at left.
- Use numbered lists to indicate steps in a process and bulleted lists to group related information.

While lists are common in professional writing (as in résumés and *PowerPoint* presentations), they are used sparingly in most academic writing.

Color Color, through contrast, calls the reader's attention to what is important in the text: Headings; bullets or numbers in lists; boxes, charts, and graphs; or illustrations often appear in color so that readers will notice them. Use color judiciously:

- Use a limited color palette. Too many colors in close proximity will create a hodgepodge effect.
- Use a pleasing color palette. Analogous colors, those adjacent to each other on a color wheel (Figure 9.4), create a softer, more harmonious look. Complementary colors, those opposite each other on the color wheel, contrast with each other, each making the other color look brighter.
- Use readable color combinations. Make sure elements in color contrast enough with their background that they are legible.

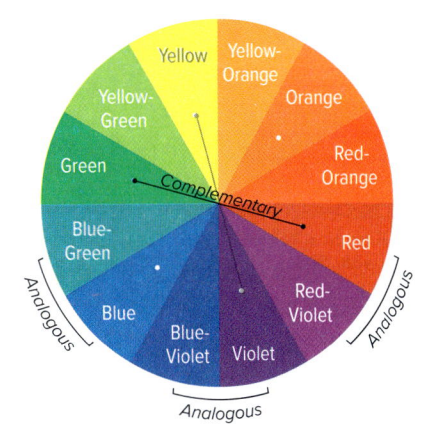

FIGURE 9.4 The color wheel Colors opposite each other on the color wheel are complementary; colors adjacent to each other are analogous.

- Use appropriate colors. Consider the associations colors and combinations of colors carry: pastels for new babies, bright yellow and black for warnings, green for nature. Consider your audience carefully as you choose colors; their associations vary from one culture to another. White, for example, is the color for weddings in the United States; in China, it is red.

- Use colors consistently. The repetition of colors will group items of the same type.

- **Important:** Do not use color alone to convey information. Most people with a color-vision disability are unable to distinguish between red and green because both colors appear as gray to them. A smaller number are unable to distinguish between blue and yellow. To be sure that readers who are color blind can obtain important information, avoid the red/green or blue/yellow color combination, or use labels or underlining in addition to color.

> *More about*
> Visual arguments (ch. 8), 143–82
> Visuals in college writing assignments, 77–78

4. Add visuals.

Visuals are the first thing readers notice when they look at a text. For this reason, they are integral to documents geared toward the general public and must thus catch the eye of potential readers. Visuals are appropriate in some academic genres—in economics, for example, graphs are used frequently—but they are not customary in all academic disciplines. Ideally, any visuals you include in a document should be visually compelling. This does not mean that you should choose images just because they will capture the reader's attention. To be effective, images must be compelling *and* must expand your readers' understanding of your text. They must also be appropriate to your writing situation.

> *More about*
> Incorporating visuals, 350, 381–82 (MLA), 428–29 (APA)
> Choosing the right type of visual, 77–81
> Revising visuals, 82–85
> Academic writing, 488–538
> Professional writing, 539–58

Place visuals on a page as soon as possible after the text discussion that refers to them. In academic and professional writing, include a reference to the figure or table in your text, numbered in order of appearance (such as figure 1 or table 2). The overall effect is usually best if images are placed at the top or bottom of the page and are either centered or placed flush with the left or right margin.

Each of your images should have a caption that includes the figure or table number and is both informative and accessible. It should not merely function as a title of sorts for the image, but instead provide a description of the content or argument in the image. Including descriptions ensures that your information will be useful for all of your readers, from those who are better at processing information textually rather than visually to those with visual loss who rely entirely on your description to understand the image's meaning. If you are creating a web page, you will need to include an alt-text image description (Figure 9.5) along with your accessible caption. Your Content Management System (CMS) such as *Wix, SquareSpace,* or *WordPress* provides information on how to include this element in their Help files. Image descriptions should start with the words "Image Description" to let readers know what it is, particularly those who are using screen readers. The text that follows should provide an efficient description of the content and the function of the image.

If you include video content in your web page, make sure that it has quality closed captions that are free of typos and algorithmically generated errors. While auto-captioning provided by services such as *YouTube* has improved in recent years, it still introduces a number of nonsensical errors, especially for accented voices, that at best are distracting and at worst completely obscure meaning. There are many options for incorporating high-quality captions that range from uploading a transcript that *YouTube* will auto-sync to using a free captioning platform like *Amara* to hiring a professional captioner.

FIGURE 9.5 **Alt Text: Harriet Tubman standing, hands folded at waist, looking at camera.**

National Portrait Gallery, Smithsonian Institution

Quick Reference: Creating Accessible Print and Web Documents

Use these resources to learn more about creating accessible print and web documents.

1. **Principles of Universal Design:** www.udll.com/media-room/articles/the-seven-principles-of-universal-design/
2. **Creating Accessible Documents:** www.washington.edu/accessibility/documents/
3. **Introduction to Web Accessibility:** www.w3.org/WAI/fundamentals/accessibility-intro/
4. **Creating Accessible Images:** webaim.org/techniques/images/
5. **Creating Accessible PDFs:** helpx.adobe.com/acrobat/using/creating-accessible-pdfs.html
6. **10 Free Tools to Make Your Video Captioning Process Easier:** blog.amara.org/2018/05/02/10-free-tools-to-make-your-captioning-process-easier-in-2018/

Quick Reference: Including Images and Graphics

	Images	**Graphics**
Type	Photographs, drawings and sketches, screenshots, film stills.	Tables, flowcharts, pie charts, line and bar graphs, diagrams, timelines, maps.
Purpose	Depict or explain an event, object, or process, or illustrate a concept.	Convey complex information in an easily readable form.
Audience	Use images to draw readers in.	Use graphics to help readers understand complex data, trends, processes.
Context and Genre	In academic and professional contexts and genres, use images to provide evidence, to help readers grasp a point, or to provide an example. In personal and public writing, use images for these purposes, as well as to capture interest, make an argument, or reinforce a point.	In every context and genre, use graphics to help readers understand complex data quickly.

EXERCISE 9.4 Analyzing layout

Return once again to the design you analyzed in Exercises 9.1, 9.2, and 9.3. In one or two paragraphs, analyze its layout. Consider its overall impression (trendy or conservative, playful or serious); its use of white space, lists, color, and headings to create proximity, alignment, repetition, and contrast; its use of fonts and visuals, and how the visuals function (do they reinforce product identity, provide an example, offer additional information, further the argument, demonstrate a process?). Has your assessment of the document's purpose, audience, context, and genre changed as you studied it more closely?

Make It Your Own

Using the plan you developed for the Make It Your Own exercise on page 189, sketch the web page, brochure, or advertisement you planned. Consider the overall impression that would be most appropriate given your writing situation.

Work Together

In groups of three or four, critique the documents you produced in the Make It Your Own exercise above. How well has each designer used proximity, alignment, repetition, and contrast? How well does each design express the purpose of the group or event? How well does it appeal to the target audience?

10 Writing for Multiple Media

IN THIS CHAPTER

a. Writing and answering email, 199

b. Creating websites and web pages, 203

c. Writing in social media, 210

Like contemporary artists, writers today have an array of media to choose from: pen and paper, email, text message, website, blog, tweet, *Snapchat, Instagram*. From these many choices, they must select the medium that will be most appropriate to their message, their purpose, and their audience. They must also choose a medium that will help them meet their responsibilities as writers. This chapter offers guidelines for matching medium to message, for deciding on the most appropriate style and tone, and for fulfilling your responsibilities to yourself and your readers.

10a Writing and Answering Email

Writers today have a wide range of choices for informal messaging on applications such as *Snapchat* and *Twitter*, in addition to the texting enabled by cell phone apps. If your boss or instructor initiates a conversation on one of these informal platforms, you should of course feel free to reply in that medium. Unless your boss or instructor indicates otherwise, though, choose email as your most appropriate means of professional communication. Email offers a convenient and speedy way to communicate in writing, but its very speed creates the need for special care. Before you press the Send button, consider whether you have selected and arranged your words to create an appropriate ***tone.*** If you have doubts, revise your message or consider making a phone call or paying a visit in person instead.

> **More about**
> Tone, 20–21, 159, 599, 604–6, 607
> Business emails, memos, 542–43
> Acronyms, 598–99, 873

1. Write email.

To deal efficiently with the volume of email most of us get, even personal email should take on the characteristics of the traditional business memo: limiting the number of recipients, providing an appropriate subject line, getting right to the point, and sticking to a single topic.

Recipients Include in the To line only those recipients who need to take action on the message; include in the cc line anyone who must be kept informed but from whom you do not need a reply.

Subject line Provide a short, descriptive title in the subject line of your email: "A question about tomorrow's assignment." The subject line should reflect the content of the message; alter it, in a reply or when forwarding a message, only when doing so is necessary or useful.

Salutation Many professional communities use formal salutations ("Dear Dr. Mansfield") in their emails; others do not. Pay attention to emails you have previously received from the people to whom you are writing, and follow their lead. When in doubt, include the formal salutation.

Task-Oriented Emails Get Right to the Point The tone of an email should be appropriate to the task. An email to a professor or business associate should not be as informal as a note to a friend. Indeed, in formal settings in the United States, emails that are task oriented frequently dispense with formalities and personal touches and get right to the point following the greeting. In some cultures, such messages would be considered rude. Members of some professional communities in the US view them as efficient and timesaving.

Quick Reference: Consider Your Writing Situation When Composing Email

Purpose and Focus

The primary purpose of most email messages is to inform, so focus on a single issue, state it briefly in the subject line, repeat it in the first paragraph, and keep the email brief.

Audience and Context

While email is generally somewhat informal, adjust your tone and level of formality to the context in which you are writing and in which your words will be read. Unless you are writing to a close friend, avoid emojis, emoticons, gifs, stickers, and conversational acronyms—IMO for "in my opinion" or FWIW for "for what it's worth"—and nonstandard capitalization, grammar, punctuation, and spelling. If you are replying to an earlier message, select "reply" rather than starting a new email, to avoid creating filing problems for your audience.

Writing Responsibly: Maintaining Confidentiality in Email

You may have noticed the bcc ("blind carbon copy") option in the header of your email messages. Any recipient you list in this line will receive a copy of your message but will not be identified to other recipients. Sending blind copies can be ethical or unethical: Use the Bcc option to keep the email addresses of recipients private, as when sending a message to a group of people who do not know one another. Do not blind-copy a recipient to deceive your correspondent into believing a message is confidential. So your readers will not mistakenly believe they are the only recipient of a message, mention in the body of the message that it is being shared with others. If you wish to forward another's email, first obtain permission.

to OTHER WRITERS

Organization and length State your purpose in the first paragraph, and keep the paragraphs short. If an email must be long, use numbered lists, headings, and transitions to make the organization clear and to help the recipient quickly grasp the content.

Style To avoid embarrassing mistakes, treat the writing context as being slightly more formal than you think it is.

Design Some email programs allow for text styling such as boldface and italics; others allow only plain text. When you are not sure whether your recipient will see formatting, use the following conventions:

1. For book titles and other text you would normally italicize, place an underline before and after the title: _Lone Survivor_ by Marcus Luttrell.
2. For emphasis, place an asterisk before and after the word to be highlighted: *Recommendations*.
3. Place URLs on a separate line to make it easy for your readers to copy and paste them into the address bar of their web browser.
4. Avoid special characters, like dashes, that may disappear or become garbled in transmission.

> **More about**
> URLs, 271–73
> Block style letters, 538–39
> Font types and styles, 192–94
> Discussion groups, 245

Some discussion groups require that messages be sent in plain text. In general, format paragraphs in block style, with no indention of the first line, and separate paragraphs with a blank space. Choose a standard sans serif font such as Arial or Verdana in a 12-point font size. Keep the font black. Some organizations have house style requirements for fonts. If your organization has a style guide, check it for guidelines concerning email font and design.

Closing If your email begins with a formal salutation, provide a pleasant or complimentary closing ("Yours truly," "Best wishes," "Sincerely"), as well.

Contact information After your name, list contact information such as your mailing address, phone number, Twitter name, or website address.

> **More about**
> Spelling (ch. 32), 618–26
> Punctuation (chs. 47–53), 793–857
> Capitalization (ch. 54), 858–64

Revision Edit for grammatical and typographical errors and be sure you included your attachments. If your emotions are involved, delay sending for an hour or even a day, until you are calm and reasonable. Hostile email can establish you as an unreasonable person; it may also circulate beyond your intended recipients, doing even more harm.

Archiving Consider whether sent messages need to be preserved. You may find it helpful to "tag" emails—establish topical archive folders for your correspondence (Figure 10.1). Merely saving email messages in your inbox will make them difficult to find later and may use up limited storage space.

2. Answer email.

Answering email messages involves not only the issues related to writing email but also the following:

Timing Read and reply to your email regularly—every day, if possible. If replying to a particular email will take more time than you have, send an immediate reply so that the sender knows you received the message, and indicate when you will respond. If you are going to be away from email for a day or more, add an auto-reply message to alert correspondents.

Context Before answering, read all the messages that have been sent to you on that topic. If your email program allows, sort your messages by subject to be

---

Writing Responsibly — Making Considerate Attachments

When your recipients receive your email with attachments, they may download it to their computers. Before you attach your file, give it a name that will make sense when it appears on the recipients' hard drive. Often this will mean including your name in the file name, along with a label identifying the text, such as "Rivera Graphs.doc." In the body of your email, name and describe your attachments; otherwise your recipients may be hesitant to open them for fear of phishing and viruses. While you may be able to email large files as attachments, your recipients' servers may not accommodate them. Consider zipping (compressing) big files or sending them through a free third-party program such as *Dropbox*, *Google Drive*, *Windows OneDrive*, or *Hightail*.

to OTHER WRITERS

Writing Responsibly: Understanding Email and Privacy

Email is never private. A confidential message to a close friend may get forwarded to others, intentionally or accidentally; messages sent from a company computer may be read by your boss or your company's compliance team; and even deleted messages can be accessed by hackers or the government. For your own peace of mind, do not write messages that might harm your reputation or those of others.

to SELF

sure that you have read everything in the thread you are responding to. So that your recipient has a context for what you are saying, quote pertinent passages from the email to which you are responding, or refer your reader to an earlier message in the thread.

Recipients Most people get more email than they can handle, so always consider carefully before selecting "reply all." Does everybody on the list really need to be included?

> **EXERCISE 10.1 Analyzing an email message**
>
> Analyze an email message you wrote to a boss, an instructor, or an older family member (parent or grandparent): Is it focused on a single topic? Does it include an appropriate subject line? Is the message logically organized? Is it of an appropriate length? Is the tone appropriate given the recipient of the message? Does the message avoid errors of grammar, spelling, punctuation, and mechanics? In one or two paragraphs, explain how you might revise the message. Next, rewrite the email for a different audience and, asking the same questions, describe the differences.

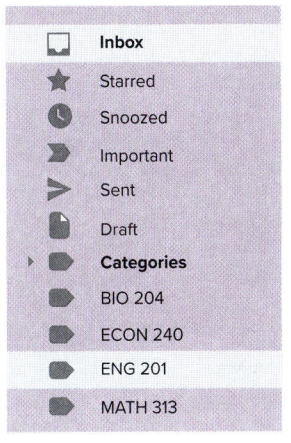

- Inbox
- Starred
- Snoozed
- Important
- Sent
- Draft
- **Categories**
  - BIO 204
  - ECON 240
  - ENG 201
  - MATH 313

FIGURE 10.1 Folders for archived email

10b Creating Websites and Web Pages

"Writing for the web" can involve a wide range of social media work, such as maintaining a Twitter feed, writing content for a blog, or creating new Snapchat content. Or it can mean creating a *website*, a collection of files located at a single address, or URL, on the World Wide Web.

1. Plan your site.

Every website begins with a *home page*, the page designed to introduce visitors to the site. Many writers turn to a blogging platform such as

WordPress to host not only a traditional blog but also websites. However you create your website, the home page should include the website's title, the date the site was created or last updated, contact information, a copyright or Creative Commons notice, and clear navigation to site content, either through navigation bars or a site map.

Unlike print documents in which reading traditionally proceeds *linearly* (the document is arranged so that all readers begin at page 1 and read through to the end), most websites are *networked* (users may enter the site at any page and follow their own path through the site). Just how easy it is for users to find their way around your site depends on its structure and on the navigation tools you provide.

Site structure When creating a website, consider how the various pages will relate to one another and how users will move among them. A site that includes a home page and a handful of *web pages*—documents that, like the home page itself, may include text, audio and still images, and database files—with loosely related content may work best with a hub-and-spoke structure (Figure 10.2). If your website will offer a series of pages with related content, a hierarchical arrangement, with links from home page to lower-level pages and from page to page, may be more useful (Figure 10.3).

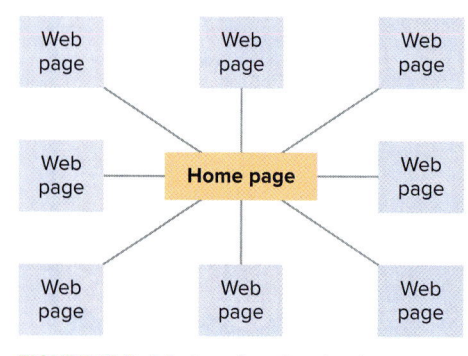

FIGURE 10.2 A hub-and-spoke structure

> ### Quick Reference — Creating a Website? Consider Your Rhetorical Situation
>
> **Purpose and Focus**
>
> Readers scan websites quickly, so keep your sentences brief and clear and your focus tight. Images, sound files, and design should reflect your purpose and capture readers' attention.
>
> **Context and Audience**
>
> Consider any restrictions of your host (site sponsor) as you plan your site. Consider, too, the needs and expectations of a culturally diverse global audience, including readers whom you did not anticipate. Avoid language or content that you or others might find embarrassing or offensive.
>
> **Genre**
>
> If you will be providing information that will remain current for a long time, create a website that you update once or twice a year; if your site requires daily or weekly updates, create a blog; if you want readers to contribute to the site's content, create a wiki.

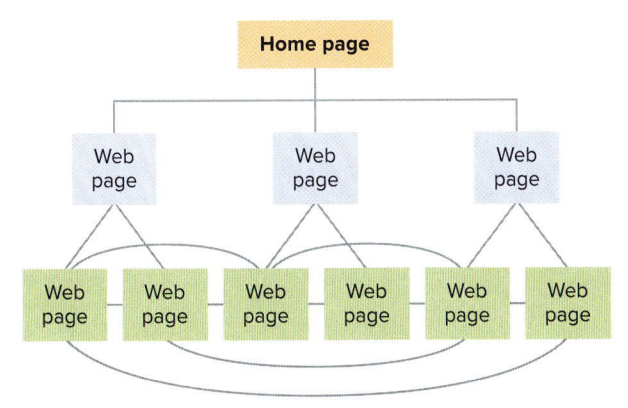

FIGURE 10.3 A hierarchical, treelike structure, with additional links

Navigation tools Navigation tools include the following:

- **Menus.** Placed at the top, bottom, left, or right side of the web page, menus list main sections of your website and are consistent from page to page.
- **Breadcrumb trails.** Used to show the path you took to the page you are on, breadcrumb (or "click") trails offer users an easy way to jump back to higher-level pages.
- **Links.** Used to jump from place to place on a web page or from web page to web page, links appear as highlighted words or images on a web page.

The website shown in Figure 10.4 offers these navigation tools.

Home page While the contents of your home page will depend on the purpose, audience, context, and genre of your site, users will benefit from the following:

- **Title.** The home page (and each additional web page) should include a title that clearly and succinctly indicates the type of information your site will include.
- **Date created, last updated.** Providing a copyright date or indicating when you last updated the site lets readers know how current your site is and enables users to create a complete bibliographic citation. This will not be necessary on blogs because the reverse chronological structure places the most recent update at the top.

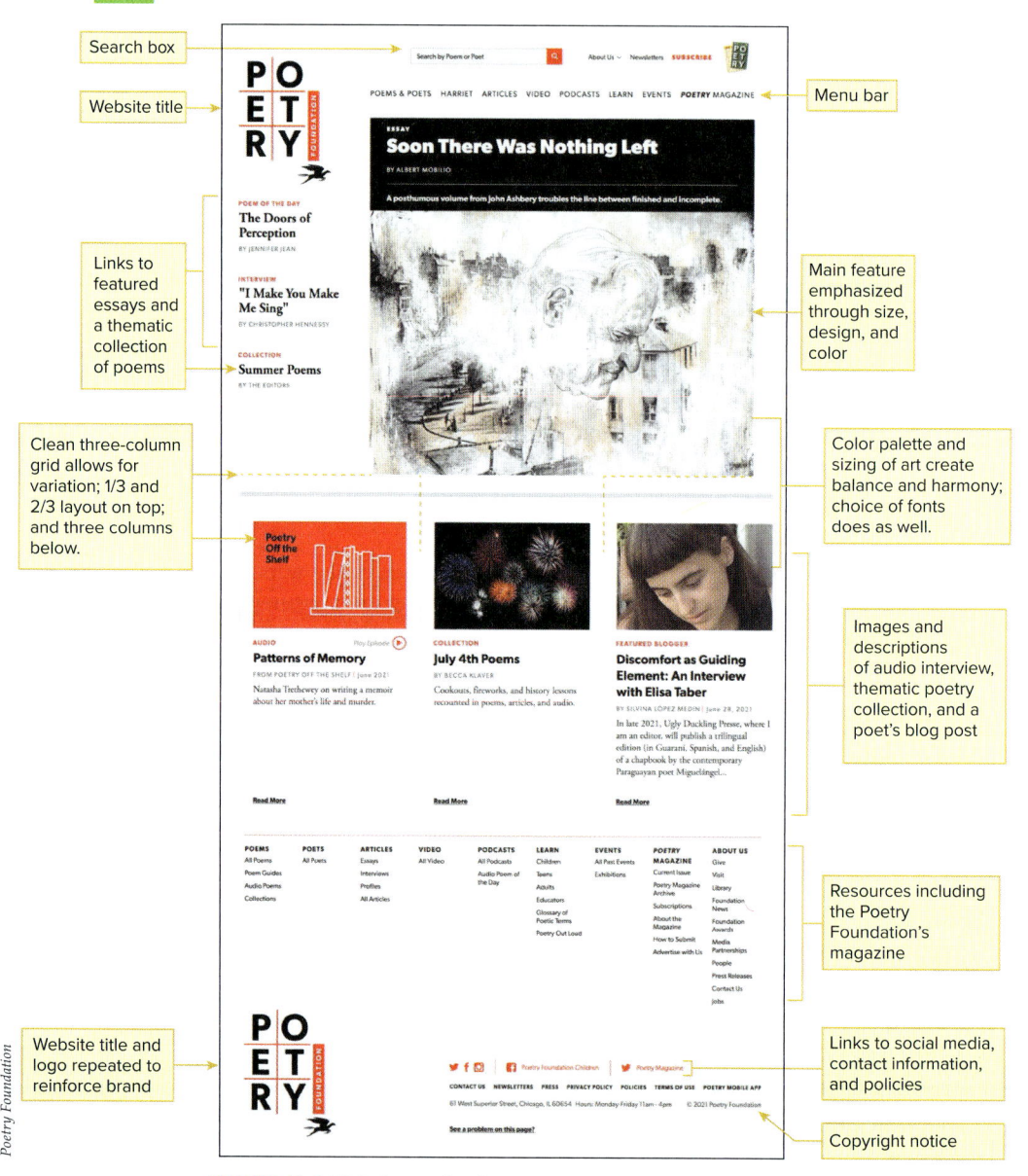

FIGURE 10.4 Website navigation tools, helpful features The *Poetry Foundation* website, a winner of a Webby award ("Honoring the Best of the Internet," webbyawards.com), provides simple navigation, a clear design, and an elegant structure that organizes content by poet, poem, theme, media type, and other categories.

FIGURE 10.4 Continued

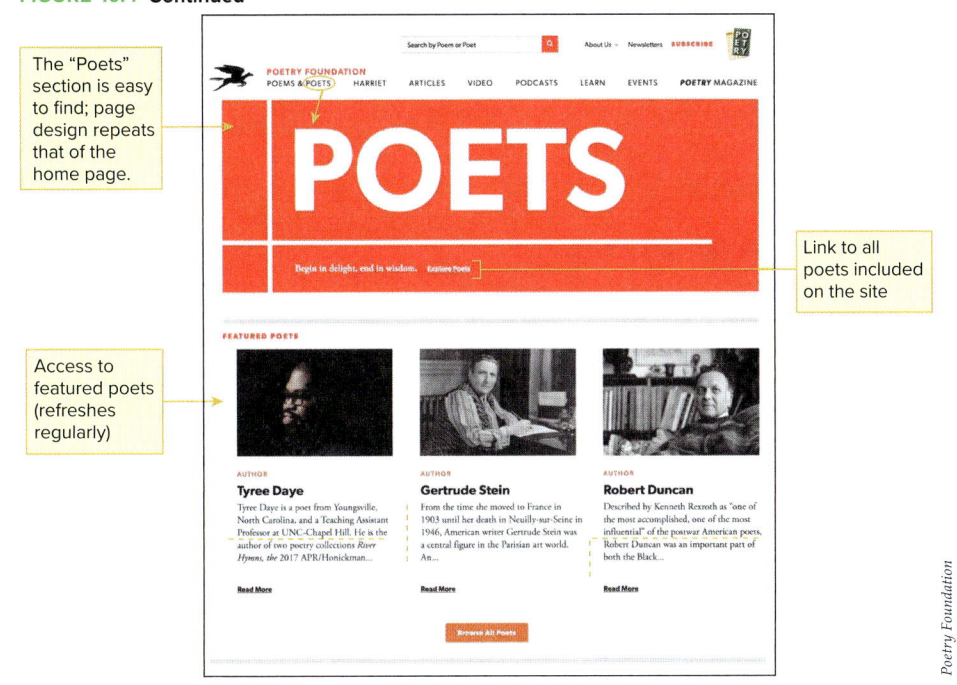

The "Poets" section is easy to find; page design repeats that of the home page.

Link to all poets included on the site

Access to featured poets (refreshes regularly)

Poetry Foundation

- **Link to a site map**. A site map is a table of contents for the site; it helps users find the information they are looking for quickly and easily.
- **Search function.** A natural-language search box that provides an alternative to the site map or navigation bar.
- **Link to contact information.** Provide a link to your basic contact information, including an email address, your name, and your role. To avoid possible cyberstalking, reveal only as much information as you are willing for the entire world to know, and establish a separate email address exclusively for correspondence from your website.
- **Copyright or Creative Commons notice.** All material published on the web is automatically protected by copyright. Remind readers of this fact by including a copyright notice: "Copyright © 2022 Paul Jefferson." For the copyright date, use the year in which you created or last updated the page. An increasingly popular alternative notice is a Creative Commons License. Browse the *Creative Commons* website (http://creativecommons.org/) to learn more about this project.

> **EXERCISE 10.2 Examining the navigation tools and home page of a website**
>
> Analyze your school's website or another website you visit regularly. In a paragraph or two, discuss the strengths and weaknesses of the site's structure and navigation tools. What tools do you use regularly, and why? Now study the website's home page. Which elements discussed in this chapter are included? Which would you like to see added, and why?

2. Design your site.

> *More about*
> Four principles of design, 184–85

> **PDF** Portable Document Format; created by Adobe, PDF format allows a document to be opened in different systems without losing its formatting

Communicating on the web is inescapably visual, and the design of your website will influence both how clear and accessible your site is and how receptive users are to your message. To make your site visually effective, plan it carefully and apply the principles of design (proximity, alignment, repetition, and contrast). When choosing a template, evaluate the available options carefully and select one that follows the four principles of design.

Incorporating image, sound, and video files Web pages more easily attract an audience when they include multimedia files—images, graphics, sound, or video. Images and graphics should do more than ornament the page, however; they should also provide useful information, set an appropriate tone, or suggest useful perspectives on the content of the page. They should also reflect a culturally diverse population. When adding images and graphics to your site, consider how much is enough. A visually bland web page can fail to stir readers' interest; a visually cluttered page can distract them.

Since not every site visitor will actually play the files (and some may not be able to see or hear the files), provide a written description of any that are crucial to your point. A description may also pique visitors' curiosity enough for them to click the link or file you provide. Most video files can and should be hosted elsewhere (*YouTube* and *Vimeo* are two possibilities) and embedded on your site to push content across multiple platforms.

Choosing dynamic templates Keep in mind that your audience may be accessing your site from a variety of devices. Choose a dynamic template that will automatically scale for users who are accessing your site via phone or tablet.

Ensuring accessibility Design your site so that it is accessible to all users. For audience members who are blind and using screen readers, provide text descriptions of images that the reader screen can pick up. For audience members who are deaf, caption your videos. The free captioning tool Amara is one option, and the basic captioning function offered by *YouTube* will let you upload a transcript and sync the text to the dialogue. If you are attaching PDFs to your site, keep in mind that they are inaccessible to users who are blind: they are an image of text rather than text itself, so screen readers cannot read them. *WebAIM.org* offers helpful details on designing for PDF accessibility. You can also optimize your PDFs so a screen reader can access them.

> **Tech** — **Use a Lower Resolution to Avoid Memory-Hogging Image Files**
>
> Including high-resolution image files or a large quantity of lower-resolution image files can make loading a web page so time-consuming that visitors become exasperated and give up. Avoid this problem by reducing the size of your images. Most image files will look fine online at 72 dots per inch, and .jpg and .gif are generally acceptable image file types.

3. Revise and edit your website.

A website full of errors will undermine your credibility with readers long before they ever assess the content on your site, so check your website carefully before bringing it "live":

- Since most readers scan websites for information, make sure your prose is clear and concise.
- Check that visual, audio, and multimedia files add value and meaning and are not merely ornamental, intended just to catch the eye.
- Check that your design is attractive and consistent.
- Check that image, audio, and other media files load properly.
- Check all links to make sure they work.
- Ask friends to read pages: Users with different platforms, browsers, and devices may run into different problems.
- Test the usability with specific strategies for catching issues. Give several friends specific tasks to perform on your website to see whether they can find and access the information you want your site to convey.
- Edit and proofread your site carefully for errors in spelling, grammar, punctuation, and mechanics. Whether consciously or unconsciously, readers' opinions of writers' credibility can be affected by the quality (or lack) of editing and proofreading.

> *More about*
> Writing concisely (ch. 26), 558–64
> Deciding to illustrate, 77–78
> Designing printed and electronic documents (ch. 9), 184–98
> Evaluating websites, 271–74
> Editing and proofreading, 90–93, 96–98

> **Writing Responsibly** — **Checking Accessibility**
>
> As you work online, avoid *ableism*. Always design your project so that its text, image, audio, and video components are accessible to all users. It may be helpful to run your material through an accessibility checker. The Assistive Technology Resource Center (atrc.colostate.edu) provides a list of programs, some of which are free.
>
> to AUDIENCE

4. Maintain your website.

Once your website is up and running, check it every month or so:

- Make sure the site continues to run on different browsers.
- Delete, replace, or repair broken links at least once a month.
- Make sure image files appear; if a small icon appears instead, check that the image file is in your server folder and that its URL is typed correctly (including the file extension, such as .jpg or .gif).

10c Writing in Social Media

Online communication is woven deeply into the fabric of contemporary life: email, texting, wikis, blogs, and an array of social apps, from *Twitter* to *TikTok* to *Snapchat,* are in classrooms, professional settings, and homes. The very familiarity of these media can lull writers into making errors that they later regret. Writers must always adapt their style and tone to their *rhetorical situation*; now the medium and the app are part of a writer's rhetorical situation, too. In fact, given the networked nature of social media today, you may find it useful to think beyond rhetorical situations to **rhetorical ecologies** that account for the circulation and migration of information. As writers move from *Instragram* to their mail apps, the style and tone of what they write must also make the instantaneous change. Moreover, members of your audience may repost your message to an entirely different app, contextualizing it differently. The nature of the conversations taking place within an app can vary dramatically, as well; compare a *Twitter* thread about a celebrity's love life with a *Twitter* conversation about copyright law to see the differences.

> **More about**
> Rhetorical situation, 8

> **More about**
> Ad hominem and other logical fallacies, 176–81

Writing Responsibly — Flaming

The quick interactivity and the anonymity of online media present a special challenge: keeping your temper. **Flaming**—writing a scathing response to someone with whom you disagree—is a great temptation, but it shuts down reasoned discourse, instead encouraging ad hominem attack. Flaming may convey a sense of power for your having found a biting way to put down an opponent, but it also minimizes the likelihood of anyone's listening to or being influenced by you.

to OTHER WRITERS

Many of the principles described in *sections 10a* and *10b* for email and website writing also apply to these other forms of online writing. Think about your purpose, and tailor your writing style and tone to your intended audience. Before sending or posting your message, consider how your audiences might interpret it, and make any necessary adjustments.

The goal of online discussions, as with live discussions, is to learn collaboratively through give and take; however, because participants are not physically present, the temptation to go off on a tangent may be great. To avoid this, focus on responding directly to the comments of other participants and summarizing the discussion before moving on. Your online voice can be casual, but strive to keep your comments clear and to maintain a voice that is friendly and polite, even when you disagree.

When participating in a discussion in *asynchronous media* (media that do not require participants to sign on at a specific date and time), take advantage of the opportunity to reflect on and proofread your comments before posting them. Asynchronous discussions usually require participants to make a commitment to sign on regularly and to make comments at least once a week.

In *synchronous media* such as text messaging and chat, where communication occurs in real time, participants must make a commitment to sign on at a specific time and to focus attention on the discussion while it is occurring. Reflection and careful proofreading are not possible, but synchronous discussions are useful for brainstorming and for developing a sense of community.

> *More about*
> Discussion lists, 245
> Blogs, 245
> Documenting posts to discussion lists, 367 (MLA), 421 (APA), 455 (*Chicago*), 481 (CSE)
> Citing blogs and blog posts, 367–69 (MLA), 421–22 (APA), 455 (*Chicago*), 481 (CSE)

> *More about*
> Collaborative writing projects, 32–34, 51

11 Presenting with Multiple Media

IN THIS CHAPTER

a. Identifying purpose, audience, context, genre, 213

b. Devising a topic and thesis, 214

c. Organizing the presentation, 214

d. Preparing and rehearsing the presentation, 215

e. Delivering the presentation, 219

f. Speaking responsibly, 219

In this TED talk, Stella Young challenges common misperceptions about disability and those with disabilities. As the editor of *Ramp Up*, an Australian publication about disability, and as a performer who addressed that topic through comedy, Young educated diverse audiences on disability perceptions and rights. In this comic performance, she makes a serious point: too often, disabled people are regarded as useful only for the purpose of inspiring abled people, often through images in advertising and social media. She calls these images *inspiration porn*. "And I use the term *porn* deliberately," Young says, "because [these images] objectify one group of people for the benefit of another group of people." Millions have watched this TED talk online and been instructed (as well as entertained) by it. Very few of us ever have an opportunity to reach out to such a large audience on such an important topic. Still, we are often called on to present our ideas at school, at work, and in our communities. If we can present them clearly and compellingly, using multiple media when they will help us reach listeners, we, too, can effect change.

11a Identifying Your Purpose, Audience, Context, and Genre

As with any writing project, begin planning your presentation by considering the possibilities for your *purpose, audience, context,* and *genre*. In an academic or business context, your primary *purpose* is likely to be the same as for a written text: to present information or to persuade others to accept your position or to take action. Even more so than a written text, an oral presentation is likely also to have a secondary purpose: to engage the imagination or emotions of the audience so that members can more readily identify with and remember the key points.

When addressing classmates or colleagues, you will probably have a sense of the needs and expectations of your *audience*. When addressing an unfamiliar group, ask yourself why the group has assembled and what they hope to get out of your presentation. It may be useful to ask the event organizers what kind of audience to expect.

An integral part of crafting your presentation with your audience in mind is to anticipate what that audience's physical needs might be. Because audience members' disabilities may not always be visible to you, prepare all your presentations inclusively:

- Ask yourself how legible your presentation will be to someone whose vision is impaired.
- If you are showing slides, describe what is on each one, for the benefit of audience members who are blind.
- Caption your videos for the benefit of audience members who are deaf.
- Provide lyric sheets for songs.

In addition, search online for the latest advice about accessible presentations, such as that offered by the Web Accessibility Initiative.

The *context,* or setting, in which you deliver your presentation will affect the kinds of equipment you will need, the types of multimedia aids you create, and the relationship you can establish with your audience. When addressing a small group in a college classroom, for example, you will probably not need any special equipment, whereas in larger settings you may need a projector, a sound system, and special lighting.

Finally, consider the *genre* of your presentation. As a college student, you may be asked to contribute to or lead a class discussion, or to give a presentation online or in person to a class, student group, or social service organization. In business, you may be asked to train colleagues or make a sales pitch to potential customers in person or online.

> **More about**
> Purpose, 15–17
> Audience, 18–20
> Context and genre, 22

Contributing to Class Discussion In US schools, active participation in class is an important part of the learning experience, and it may even play a role in instructors' grades. If you are uncomfortable with the idea of speaking in class, let your instructor know. If students in your class seem uncomfortable when they speak, remember that you are responsible for being an effective listener as well as a speaker. That means listening patiently and respectfully at all times.

11b Devising a Topic and Thesis

> *More about*
> Devising a topic, 25
> Narrowing, expanding a topic, 31–32
> Devising a thesis, 35–38

A presentation, like a written text, begins with an appropriate topic and a well-focused thesis. Your topic and approach should engage you and your audience and offer special insight. Craft a thesis that conveys your purpose and that will engage and guide your audience.

11c Organizing the Presentation

It is more difficult for people to understand and remember ideas they have heard than those they have read. Organize your talk to help your audience hold your main points in memory while the presentation unfolds.

1. Introduction

> *More about*
> Introductions, 68–70

Use your introduction (10–15 percent of your presentation) to develop a rapport with your audience and to establish the key points of your presentation. Your introduction should accomplish the following:

- Specify your topic and approach, and convey why it should matter to your audience.
- Engage your audience: A compelling anecdote, startling statistics, or an apt quotation are all good opening gambits.
- Establish your credentials: Knowledge, experience, or the research you have conducted all give you special expertise.
- Provide a brief overview of your main points so that the audience will know in advance what they should be listening for.

2. Body

The body (75–85 percent of your presentation) should explain the points that you previewed in your introduction. It should be clearly and logically organized, so listeners know where you are going and where you have been. Use transitions such as "first," "second," and "third" to guide your audience, and provide a brief summary of the main points you made earlier ("As I explained a few minutes ago ...") and a preview of the points you are about to discuss ("Next I will show how ...").

For each claim you make, supply appropriate, relevant evidence, such as specific examples drawn from your reading or your experience. Facts and statistics can be very effective as long as you do not burden your audience with more numbers than it can process. (Presenting statistics in information graphics can help.) Engaging anecdotes or stories that use concrete, descriptive language, on the other hand, are more easily remembered.

> **More about**
> Organizing, 39–44, 53–57, 304–7
> Transitions, 59–60
> Explaining and supporting ideas, 45–47, 64–68, 308–11
> Using visuals as evidence, 78–81
> Finding information (ch. 13), 237–62

3. Conclusion

Keep your conclusion brief (5–10 percent of your presentation). Use it to reinforce the main point of the presentation: Repeat the main idea and key points, end with a brief but powerful statement, or return to the opening anecdote, example, or statistic.

> **More about**
> Conclusions, 70–72

11d Preparing and Rehearsing the Presentation

For an oral presentation, the following methods of delivery are common, and many presenters combine them when appropriate:

- **Speaking off the cuff.** If you are an expert on a topic about which your audience knows little, you may be able to speak engagingly and informatively with little special preparation.
- **Reading a written presentation aloud.** If your material is highly technical or if you are anxious about speaking, reading your presentation may work. Since you will lose eye contact with the audience and risk losing their attention, build in opportunities to speak without a script to engage your listeners.
- **Speaking from your notes.** Speaking from notes will keep you organized and prevent you from forgetting important points while allowing you to make eye contact with the audience.

1. Prepare a speaking outline.

When speaking from notes, create a speaking outline by jotting notes on a topic outline about where to pause, when to increase the urgency in your voice, and when to advance to the next slide or visual aid. Add content notes, too, but keep them brief, including only as much information as you need to remind yourself of the point you want to make.

2. Use language effectively.

Well-chosen language can help listeners understand and remember your main points. As you draft and rehearse your presentation, do the following:

> **More about**
> Abstract versus concrete language, 606–8
> Eliminating wordiness, 559–61
> Figures of speech, 608–10
> Parallelism (ch. 28), 578–85
> Repetition (intentional), 592–93

- Use clear, familiar language.
- Choose concrete words. When abstract words are needed, support them with concrete examples.
- Eliminate wordiness.
- Keep sentences concise.
- Include vivid figures of speech, such as metaphors and similes, that link an unfamiliar notion to a familiar or striking one.
- Use parallelism and repetition to emphasize your main points.

3. Create visual, audio, and multimedia aids.

> **More about**
> Using visuals as support, 78–81
> Designing for accessibility (ch. 9), 183–98

Visual, audio, and multimedia aids can enhance your presentation by clarifying or providing additional information, by showing what you are describing, and by countering stage fright (directing attention away from you). When using visual or multimedia aids during a presentation, make sure the aids are relevant, that you explain them clearly and succinctly, that you do not provide so many that the audience pays attention to them rather than to you, and that you speak to your audience, not to your visual aids.

Presentation software such as *Microsoft PowerPoint, Google Slides,* or *Apple Keynote* usefully projects visual, audio, and multimedia aids. However, overuse of presentation software or poor preparation of slides can overwhelm or distract the audience. (For advice on the effective use of presentation software, see the Self Assessment box on the next page.)

4. Rehearse your presentation.

Practice your presentation out loud in front of a mirror, a group of friends or family, or a video camera. Reading the slides word for word can bore your audience, so learn your material well. Use at least two or three practice sessions to make sure of the following:

- You are comfortable with the content of your presentation.
- Your presentation is the right length (long enough but not too long).
- Your delivery is polished: You are familiar with the pronunciation of all words and names, you know when to pause or gesture, and you are comfortable making eye contact with the audience (or with yourself in the mirror).
- You deploy and discuss visual aids with grace.
- You have good posture and avoid nervous fidgeting and irritating mannerisms (such as the repetition of "um" or "like").

If possible, rehearse in the space where you will be making your presentation to determine how loudly you will have to speak, to test placement of visual aids or screens, and to check your equipment.

> **More about**
> Visual design (ch. 9), 183–98
> Matching visual to information, 78–81

Adjusting Your Gestures to Appeal to a Multicultural Audience Gestures vary from culture to culture. As you prepare to give formal presentations, pay attention to the gestures commonly made by classmates or other peers who represent your prospective audience. How do they differ from gestures you are accustomed to? Are you aware of any gestures you should not use while speaking to a multicultural audience?

Quick Reference — Overcoming Presentation Anxiety

The following tips may help you get through your presentation with a minimum of nerves.

- Envision your success: Picture yourself calm and relaxed at the podium or screen; imagine yourself giving a successful presentation.
- Take several slow, deep breaths, or tighten and relax your muscles just before you take the podium.
- Ignore your racing heart or clammy hands. Instead, use the adrenaline surge to add energy to your presentation.
- Focus on your message: Get excited about what you have to say, and you will bring the audience with you.
- Accept the fact that you may stumble, and be prepared to go on.

Self Assessment: Ten Steps to Using Presentation Software Effectively

When preparing a presentation, reflect on your work. Ask yourself the following questions, revising and practicing as necessary.

- ☐ **Did you review your outline to determine where slides would enhance your presentation?** Do not overwhelm your presentation by creating a slide for every moment.
- ☐ **Did you begin with a title slide?** This slide should include the title of your presentation, your name, and any other useful identifying information, such as your college or business affiliation and your *Twitter* handle.

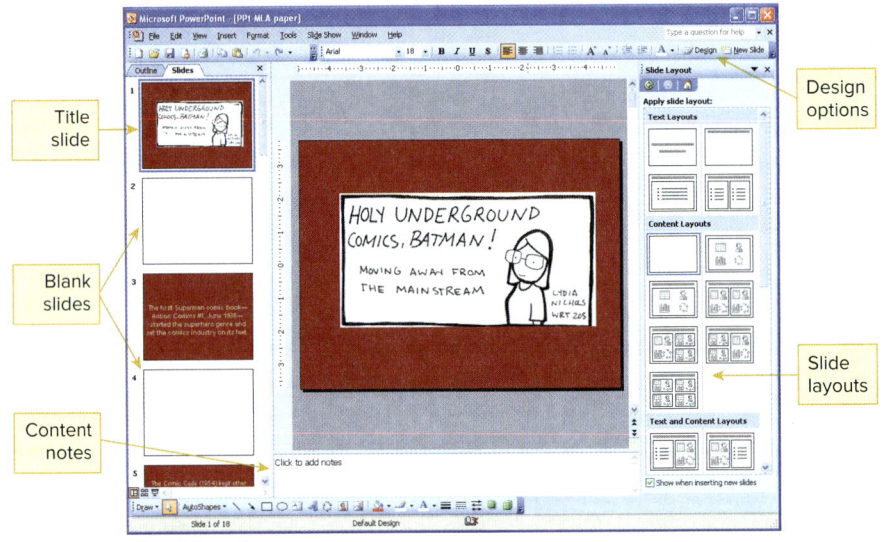

Microsoft Corporation

- ☐ **Did you keep text brief, design uniform, and content varied?** The audience should be listening to you, not reading your slides. To make slides easy to absorb, maintain a consistent design. To enhance interest, vary the other components (images, information graphics, video clips).
- ☐ **Did you add blank slides?** Go to a blank slide when no illustration is relevant.
- ☐ **Did you check that slides are visually pleasing?** Keep slides uncluttered and balanced; limit your use of animations (the way text or images enter a slide).
- ☐ **Did you proofread your slides?** Make sure all text is clear, and correct all misspellings and all mistakes of grammar, punctuation, and mechanics.
- ☐ **Did you learn your software's commands?** Keystroke commands allow you to advance or return to slides, use the animation effects, and end the slide show.
- ☐ **Did you practice your presentation with your slides in advance?** Use animations to bring information forward, and do not leave slides up after you have moved on to the next topic.
- ☐ **Did you check your equipment in advance?** Make sure that cords are long enough, that you can lower the lights and cover windows, and so forth.
- ☐ **Did you practice giving your presentation without your slides?** Murphy's Law—whenever something *can* go wrong, it *will* go wrong—applies to presentation software. If the power fails or your computer dies, you should still be able to go on with the show.

11e Delivering the Presentation

When the time comes to make your presentation, approach the podium, wait for your audience to settle down, and then begin:

> **More about**
> Designing for accessibility (ch. 9), 183–98

- **Connect with the audience.** Introduce yourself, thank the audience for attending, and smile.
- **Maintain eye contact with the audience.** As you speak, look out at the audience, turning to the left, the right, and center, so all members of the audience feel included.
- **Control your pacing, volume, and tempo.** Speak slowly and clearly. Pause between sections of your presentation. Vary the tone of your voice. If you sense that you are losing your audience, slow your pace, increase your volume, or step closer to the audience.
- **Avoid ableism.** Assume that some members of your audience have loss of vision or hearing. Speak loudly and clearly. Make your graphics large enough to be easily read, and don't choose a background design that interferes with readability.

Writing Responsibly — Listening Actively

When attending a presentation, be fair to the speaker by listening actively:

- Give the speaker your undivided attention.
- Make an effort to understand the speaker's point of view.
- Set aside prejudices based on the speaker's appearance, accent, rate of speech, or apparent level of comfort.
- Listen for the speaker's main points.
- Identify and assess the evidence presented.

to OTHER WRITERS

11f Speaking Responsibly

As you prepare your presentation, keep your responsibilities as a speaker in mind:

- **Know your material and your purpose.** For an informative speech, be sure your information is current and your examples pertinent. For a persuasive speech, adopt a position that you believe in, one for which you can offer compelling, concrete evidence.

> *More about*
> Biased language, 600–3
> Logical fallacies, 176–81
> Patchwriting, 285, 292–94
> Signal phrases, 314, 315, 335–36 (MLA), 399–400 (APA)
> Revising visuals, 82–85
> Contextualizing sources, 314–16

- **Acknowledge counterevidence and alternative interpretations.** Do not alter quotations unfairly or misuse statistics. Avoid words and images that manipulate your audience or that rely on logical fallacies.

- **Use signal phrases.** Since your audience will not have access to your written text, acknowledge sources with signal phrases such as "In a 2020 research study titled 'Beyond Telephone Polling,' Alison Ling shows. . ." and be prepared to provide a list of works cited if requested.

- **Practice before presenting.** Respect the time and attention of your audience by practicing your presentation until you can deliver it with confidence and grace.

Work Together

With two to four classmates, listen to a complete speech posted on *YouTube* or a website such as *American Rhetoric* (http://americanrhetoric.com/). As you listen, take notes on the main point of the speech, the organization of the speech, the transitions or other signposts the speaker uses, and the speaker's language and delivery. Compare your notes. What did you notice that other group members did not (and vice versa)?

Part Four

Research Matters

Finding, Evaluating, and Citing Sources

- **12** Planning a Research Project 222
- **13** Finding Information 237
- **14** Evaluating Information 263
- **15** Overcoming Fear of Plagiarizing 279
- **16** Writing the Research Project 302
- **17** Citing Rhetorically 312

Writing Responsibly: Citation Tutorials
Choosing and Unpacking Complex Sources 256–57
Blending Voices in Your Text 290–291
Acknowledging Indirect Sources 300–301
Explaining Your Choice of Sources 326–27

12 Planning a Research Project

IN THIS CHAPTER

a. Analyzing purpose, audience, and method of development, 222

b. Setting a schedule, 223

c. Choosing and narrowing a research topic, 224

d. Drafting research questions and hypotheses, 225

e. Choosing sources strategically, 227

f. Establishing a research log, 228

g. Building and annotating a working bibliography, 230

> **More about**
> Purpose, 15–17
> Audience, 18–20

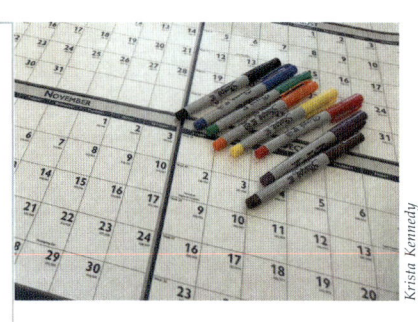

One of the most destructive myths about writing is the "single-draft masterpiece." Most writers, even the most celebrated and successful, go through multiple drafts of what eventually may become a masterpiece. Writers who work on deadlines know there are preliminary steps to take before the actual drafting can get underway. They work with calendars, planners, and to-do lists to produce a project as complex as a researched paper.

12a Analyzing the Assignment's Purpose, Audience, and Method of Development

Most research projects will have one of these purposes:

- **To inform.** Explain an issue, compare proposed solutions, or review the research on a specific topic.
- **To persuade.** Argue for a claim.
- **To inquire.** Explore a complex topic, searching for the best possible solution.

Study your assignment carefully and talk with your instructor to figure out which purpose your project is intended to serve. If your purpose is *to discover and describe the features of your topic* (the merits and risks of nuclear power generation, for example), you should not be making an argument on the topic. If you are asked *to explore a topic, take a position, and defend it* (researching nuclear power generation, say, and deciding whether it is necessary), you will need to include description but focus on making an argument. If you are asked *to explore a situation and make a recommendation* (such as on a state initiative to build a nuclear power plant), your research will be inquiry-based. Again, you will need to describe the situation, but your focus will be on weighing the pros and cons and then recommending a *provisional* course of action, one based on the best information available but subject to revision as new information comes to light.

Sometimes, college research assignments specify the method of development to use, such as comparison-contrast or cause-effect. One of the most frequently used methods of development is *analysis*—the writer divides the issue, proposal, or event into its component parts; explains how the parts work together; and discusses the implications.

As a writer, you have a responsibility to shape your project with the needs and expectations of your audience in mind, so consider who that audience will be. For most college assignments, your audience will include your instructor and perhaps your fellow students. Your instructor will want to see not only that you understand the material covered in class but also that you can interpret it, analyze it, and think creatively and critically about it. Fellow students may need you to define terms or provide background.

> **More about**
> Arguing for a claim, 146–49
> Methods of development, 64–68
> Interpretation, analysis, synthesis, and critique, 66–67, 127–35, 307–11
> Generating ideas, 25–31

Quick Reference — Factors in Planning a Research Project

- When is the project due?
- How long is the project to be?
- What type of research is required?
- What types of sources are more useful: scholarly books and articles only, or a mix of scholarly and popular sources?
- How many sources will you need to answer your research questions fully and accurately?
- On what criteria will the project be evaluated?
- What other work and activities will compete for your time and attention?

12b Setting a Schedule

Set a schedule for your research project that allows time for each of the following steps:

> **More about**
> Setting a realistic schedule, 24

- Analyzing the assignment, taking its scope and purpose into consideration
- Analyzing your audience to determine what your audience will expect from you
- Choosing a topic that is appropriate to your assignment and your audience
- Narrowing your topic to one that can be fully explored within the time you have available to devote to it
- Framing research questions and developing a hypothesis that will structure and focus your research project
- Deciding whether to use a citation management system such as *Zotero* or *EasyBib*, and experimenting with the system to familiarize yourself with it and to check its accuracy

- Familiarizing yourself with the library databases available for your research
- Developing a preliminary list of keywords for your source searching
- Setting up a working bibliography in which you will keep track of the information you will need for documenting your sources later
- Conducting database searches for sources that might help you answer your research questions
- Annotating your working bibliography so that you can remember what these sources cover and how you expect to use them

Following these steps will allow you to approach your research project with clarity and confidence.

> **Tech** **Using an Assignment Calculator**
>
> To set a realistic schedule, try using an online assignment calculator like the one offered by the University of Minnesota Libraries (www.lib.umn.edu/apps/ac). Such tools divide the writing process into steps and suggest a date by which each step should be completed. Check your own library's website to see whether a time management calculator is provided, or search for one by typing "assignment calculator" into the search box of a search engine such as Bing or Google.

> **Make It Your Own**
>
> For a research project you have been assigned, answer the questions in the Quick Reference box on the previous page, and then set up a schedule for each stage of your research project. Be sure to leave time for other assignments and for unexpected delays.

12c Choosing and Narrowing a Research Topic

> **More about**
> Generating ideas, 25–31
> Narrowing a topic, 31–32

When the choice is up to you, select a topic that will interest your readers and you, ideally one about which you already have some knowledge and insight. Idea-generating techniques such as freewriting and brainstorming can help you devise a topic that will be of interest to your readers, and they can help you narrow your topic so that you can write about it specifically and insightfully. For college research projects, conducting preliminary research or reviewing assigned reading or class notes may be the most helpful in choosing and narrowing your topic. You might put your general topic into the search box of a library catalog or database to see what topics arise in the results. A search in the database *PsycARTICLES* on "peer influence," for example, generated topics from smoking and group initiation to copycat crime among juvenile offenders.

If you are choosing a topic that you want to learn more about, consider whether the purpose of your assignment is to write an informative, a persuasive, or an exploratory research project. If your topic is one you do not know much about, your research will include familiarizing yourself with the basic data and issues surrounding that topic. That will work well if your purpose is to inform your audience of what you have learned. If, however, your purpose is to persuade an audience of one position on your topic or to explore the complexities of the topic and make recommendations, you will need to conduct additional research. Unless you have been given an information-based assignment or have a lot of free time to devote to this project, you may want to choose a topic you are already familiar with.

Make It **Your Own**

Use two or more of the idea-generating techniques in chapter 2, *section 2c,* to devise and narrow a research topic for this or another class.

12d Drafting Research Questions and Hypotheses

Inexperienced researchers too often think of research as gathering and compiling information on a topic. While such tasks are assigned in college and the workplace, most of your college research assignments are likely to ask you to explore a complex topic and come to your own conclusions or recommendations about it. Key to success in this sort of exploratory research is drafting good research questions and hypotheses, and using those questions and hypotheses to guide your entire research process.

Student Models
Research projects:
Brianna Davids, "Inmate Access to Technology" (ch. 8), 159–74
Isabel Beck, "Fast Fashion" (ch. 18), 383–96
Robyn Worthington, "Nature versus Nurture" (ch. 19), 430–38

1. Draft possible research questions.

After you have tentatively chosen a topic and as you begin finding, previewing, and reading sources, your most urgent task is to develop a list of questions about your topic that these sources raise or might help you answer. These are your possible *research questions*. As you draft possible questions, keep these criteria in mind:

- Ask questions of quantity and degree, not binary yes/no questions:

    DRAFT   Does digital technology make its users more intelligent?

    REVISION   What effects does digital technology have on its users' intelligence?

- Limit the scope of your question as much as possible:

    DRAFT What effects does digital technology have on its users' intelligence?

    REVISION What effects does the use of digital technology have on college students' intelligence?

- Reframe your question when you find your sources are trending toward specific inquiries:

    DRAFT What effects does the use of digital technology have on college students' intelligence?

    REVISION What effects does the use of laptops in class have on college students' learning?

- Let your question suggest the importance of your inquiry:

    DRAFT What effects does the use of laptops in class have on college students' learning?

    REVISION Do the benefits of using laptops in class outweigh the negative effects on college students' learning?

2. Draft your hypotheses.

As you generate questions, also record what you think your answer might be. These anticipated answers are the *hypotheses* that your research will test. For most of your college research assignments, your task is not to find the "right" answer to a research question, but to develop your own answer to a complex issue or problem.

These examples show research questions and hypotheses for Isabel Beck's project on the ethics of fast fashion and for Robyn Worthington's project on the impact of birth order on our personalities.

See **Isabel Beck**, "Fast Fashion" (ch. 18)

Research question: What is the impact of fast fashion on garment workers and the environment?

Hypothesis: When we purchase fast fashion we contribute to the exploitation and harming of garment workers and the destruction of the environment.

Research question: What is the relationship between birth order and personality formation?

Hypothesis: The differences in personalities among siblings may be caused by a combination of nature (birth order) and nurture (environmental factors).

See **Robyn Worthington,** "Nature versus Nurture" (ch. 19)

Make It *Your Own*

Create three to five questions that could guide your research on the topic you devised and narrowed in the Make It Your Own activity on page 225. Remember that your questions must be answerable through research. If they are too broad, revise them to be more specific. Then turn one of your questions into a hypothesis.

Writing *Responsibly* — Using Printed Sources

With so much information available online, you might think that you no longer need to consult printed materials. However, many classic and scholarly books are not yet available digitally, and your library may not subscribe to the electronic versions of important newspapers, magazines, and scholarly journals. Dedicate yourself to finding the best information available, whether you access it through a search engine, through an online database like *Academic Search Premier* or *Web of Science*, or through trips to your library's stacks. Most libraries display the latest issues of journals and magazines together in a section of the library called "current periodicals." Ask a librarian to point you to them. Additionally, most libraries are able to get access to materials they don't own from other libraries via Interlibrary Loan.

to TOPIC

12e Choosing Research Sources Strategically

Your research project must reflect real research, instead of just creating the appearance of it. The sources you choose are key to fulfilling your responsibilities to your audience, your topic, and yourself. When choosing sources, ask yourself these questions:

- Have you visited your library and its subscription databases (not just *Google*) to see what kinds of resources are available?
- Have you consulted, for background, general reference sources that provide basic facts about your topic?

Research Matters • Planning a Research Project

> **More about**
> Reliability, 265–69
> Scholarly versus popular sources, 266–67
> Counterevidence, 156–58
> Finding online sources, 242–44, 245
> Finding articles in journals, magazines, and newspapers, 246–51
> Finding books, 251–54
> Finding government documents, 254–55
> Finding multimedia sources, 255, 258
> Field research: interviews, observational studies, surveys, 259–62

- Have you consulted, for an authoritative overview, specialized reference sources that discuss the debates and issues about your topic?
- Have you found in-depth analyses and arguments written by experts on your topic, and have other experts on the topic peer reviewed the source before publication?
- Have you located—after finding a journalist, blogger, or website discussing research results—the original research report or article itself, instead of settling for secondhand information?
- Are your sources either up to date or classics that established the principles for studying the topic you are researching?
- Have you consulted enough sources to develop a broad understanding of your topic?
- Have you consulted sources that offer a variety of perspectives on your topic, rather than just searching for sources that agree with your hypothesis?
- Have you consulted the best sources, even if they are not available online?
- Have you conducted experiments, observations, surveys, or interviews, when relevant, to develop information of your own?

You may need help to determine whether a source is up to date or reliable or to locate sources online or in your library's print collection. When you do, consult a research expert: a reference librarian.

Make It Your Own

For the research hypothesis you devised in the Make It Your Own activity on page 227, make a list of sources that would allow you to uncover useful information. Write a paragraph about these sources, answering the questions following the bullets in *section 12e*.

12f Establishing a Research Log

A *research log* is a journal in which you record research questions and hypotheses; your working thesis; your search terms; information from sources; your interpretation, analysis, synthesis, and critique of sources; and your ideas for where to go next.

1. Set up the research log.

A research log can be compiled in any of the following media: index cards, a notebook, or a file in a computer, tablet, or phone.

Before you set up your research log, consider the advantages and disadvantages of each medium: Although some may think index cards are old-fashioned in the digital age, they are easy to arrange in outline order or to "storyboard" when it comes time to write. Notebooks are easy to carry around and more difficult to lose than note cards. Keeping notes on index cards or in a notebook forces you to interact with your sources, rather than just cutting and pasting information into a word processing file. Keeping a research log on a computer (especially a laptop or tablet) or phone makes it possible to search your notes electronically, to rearrange them into outline order, and to copy material from your notes directly into your project. A phone is likely to be with you at all times, and you can sync note-taking apps such as *OneNote* and *Evernote* with your computer.

> **More about**
> Keeping an idea journal or commonplace book, 26
> Keeping a reading journal, 124–25
> Annotating, 119–24
> Making notes, 286–87
> Avoiding patchwriting, 285, 292–94
> Research questions and hypotheses, 225–27
> Search terms (keywords), 242
> Interpretation, analysis, synthesis, and critique, 66–67, 127–35, 307–11

> **Tech** Back Up Your Electronic Research Log
>
> Do not be a victim of a computer crash: If you keep your research log in electronic form, be sure to back up your files after every session, and store the backup files in a separate place—on a cloud server, for example. If you cannot save your files to a second device, email the files to yourself or print out the new material after each session.

2. Define the components of a research log.

Divide your research log into sections for different categories of notes:

- The research assignment
- Purpose statement and audience profile
- Your research schedule
- A list of possible research questions
- Your working hypothesis
- Notes taken while reading sources
- Your own ideas
- Your working bibliography

> **Make It Your Own**
>
> Using the information you have generated in the other Make It Your Own activities in this chapter (pp. 225, 227, 228), establish a research log.

> **More about**
> Taking notes to avoid plagiarism, 286–87
> Patchwriting, 292–94

Writing Responsibly: Avoiding Accidental Plagiarism

The wonderful ease of cutting and pasting from digital sources is matched by the terrible ease of falling into unintentional plagiarism. If you are maintaining an electronic research log, it is especially important to mark clearly what you have copied directly from a source and what you have paraphrased, summarized, or commented on. Consider supplementing your electronic research log with a folder for printouts and photocopies, and check your text against it.

to SELF

12g Building and Annotating a Working Bibliography

Start your research by gathering potential sources and reviewing them to discover whether they are relevant and reliable. Then set up a *working bibliography* to record those that might be useful. Annotate each entry so that you can remember why you thought the source was worth examining.

1. Identify the components of a working bibliography.

> **DOI (digital object identifier)** A permanent tag that does not change over time or from database to database

> **permalink** A stable URL that is not subject to change

A working bibliography should include the information you will need for locating and documenting your sources. You will want to note the following: names (author, editor, publisher), titles (book, article, journal, website), sources (DOI, permalink, URL), version (issue, volume), and dates (publication, access). See the Quick Reference box on the next page for additional guidance.

As you construct the entries in your working bibliography, follow the documentation style that you will use in your project. Scholars in literature typically use MLA style (ch. 18), scholars in psychology and other social sciences typically use APA style (ch. 19), scholars in the humanities (except for literature) typically use *Chicago* style (ch. 20), and scholars in the sciences typically use CSE style (ch. 21). (If you are not sure which documentation style to use, consult your instructor.) Using the appropriate style in the planning stage will save you time later, when you are formatting your finished project.

> **More about**
> Publication information, 330–33 (Documentation Matters tutorial preceding ch. 18)
> Digital object identifiers (DOI), 231, 366, 409, 410, 420

Saving a copy of an efile or photocopying a printed document is prudent in case the source becomes unavailable later. Some instructors may also require you to submit copies of your sources with your final project. A PDF generally captures an article as it looked (or would have looked) in print, while an HTML copy provides the text, often without the formatting, page numbers, or illustrations. If both a PDF and an HTML file are available, select the PDF, which will enable you to cite the page numbers of the article and see any illustrations. The PDF will also be downloadable and can be saved, printed, or sent via email, but the HTML version will often not be formatted for printing or saving.

Quick Reference — Components of a Working Bibliography

To locate and document...	include in the working bibliography...
a printed book or an article or chapter in a printed book	the call number, the name of the author or editor, the title of the book, the title of the article or chapter (if relevant), the publisher, the place of publication, and the date of publication.
an ebook or an article or chapter in an ebook	all of the above minus the call number, plus the DOI or URL.
a printed article	the name of the author, the title of the article, the title of the journal, the volume and issue number of the journal, the year of publication, and the page numbers of the article.
an article accessed through a database	all of the above, plus the name of the database, the DOI or, if there is no DOI, the URL (preferably a permalink if available) for the journal's home page, and the date you last accessed the file. If no page numbers are provided, include paragraph numbers or section name.
an article in an online journal	all of the above.
a web page, wiki entry, or entry in a blog or discussion list	the name of the author, the title of the web page or entry title, the title of the website or blog, the sponsor, and the publication date or the date you last accessed the file.

2. Recognize the title of the source and name of the publisher.

For many projects, you will be using sources found through library databases or on the web. As you construct your working bibliography, you may be challenged to figure out the title of your source or the name of the publication. Often it is difficult to identify which is the name of the publication and which is the sponsor of the publication. This is even more confusing when the sponsor is identified as "Publisher" (as in Figure 12.3, p. 234). Another problem arises when the name of a subsection of the publication looks like the name of the publication or the title of the source.

Tech — Citation Management Software

Citation management software—such as the proprietary *Mendeley* and *RefWorks* and the open source *Zotero*—can format the entries in your bibliography no matter what documentation style you choose. *Zotero* and *Mendeley* also allow users to discover and share citations with one another via bibliographies and groups. Your library may make such software available to you for free. Use the documentation chapters in this handbook to test your program for accuracy; not every program performs to perfection, and you are the writer and the person responsible for providing your audience with error-free documentation that does not cause confusion.

The following strategies should be helpful in your search for accurate information to include in your working bibliography:

- **Explore links.** Links labeled "about" or "contact us" often contain key information. You can also try clicking on the website logo.
- **Look for a bibliographic entry.** Many library databases not only provide you with the source itself but also with a bibliographic entry in your choice of citation style—APA or MLA, for example—for use in your bibliography. Figure 12.1 shows a search result from a library database. It seems clear that the source title is "Disinformation by Design: The Use of Evidence Collages and Platform Filtering in a Media Manipulation Campaign."

ProQuest

Basic Search   Advanced Search   Publications   Browse   Databases (67)

‹ Back to results   ‹ 3 of 5,445 ›

Disinformation by Design: The Use of Evidence Collages and Platform Filtering in a Media Manipulation Campaign

Krafft, P M; Donovan, Joan.
Political Communication; Washington Vol. 37, Iss. 2, (Mar 2020): 194-214.
DOI:10.1080/10584609.2019.1686094

Bibliographic information, including the name of the publication (the journal Political Communication) in which the article appears

Volume number

Issue number

Abstract/Details

Abstract

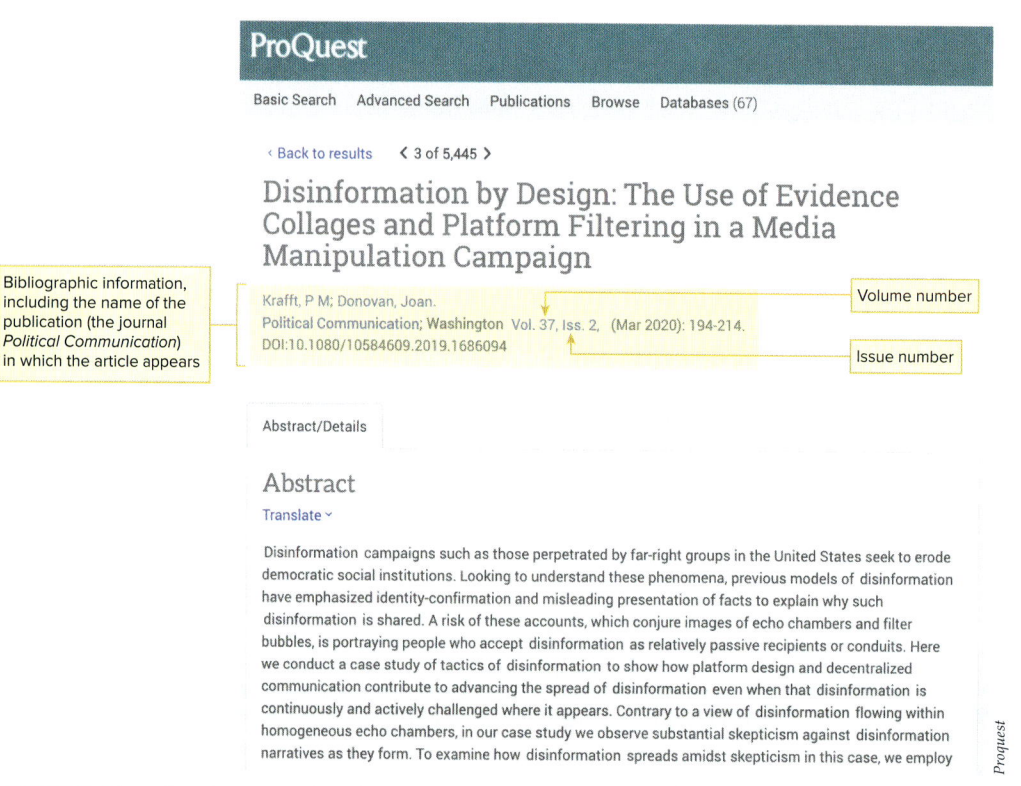

Translate ˅

Disinformation campaigns such as those perpetrated by far-right groups in the United States seek to erode democratic social institutions. Looking to understand these phenomena, previous models of disinformation have emphasized identity-confirmation and misleading presentation of facts to explain why such disinformation is shared. A risk of these accounts, which conjure images of echo chambers and filter bubbles, is portraying people who accept disinformation as relatively passive recipients or conduits. Here we conduct a case study of tactics of disinformation to show how platform design and decentralized communication contribute to advancing the spread of disinformation even when that disinformation is continuously and actively challenged where it appears. Contrary to a view of disinformation flowing within homogeneous echo chambers, in our case study we observe substantial skepticism against disinformation narratives as they form. To examine how disinformation spreads amidst skepticism in this case, we employ

Proquest

FIGURE 12.1 Locating the name of the publication in the bibliographic information In this journal article retrieved from a database, it is only in the bibliographic information that the name of the publication, *Political Communication*, appears.

The name of the publication, however, is not as clear. Is it *ProQuest*? Fortunately, a bibliographic citation immediately follows the title, and that identifies the publication as the journal *Political Communication*.

- **Look for a click path**. Many online publications have a small bar that shows where the current page appears in the site's organization. The current page usually will be on the right-hand side of the click path, with increasingly larger categories to the left (Figure 12.2).

- **Look for a volume and issue number.** The name of the publication usually accompanies this information (Figures 12.3 and 12.4).

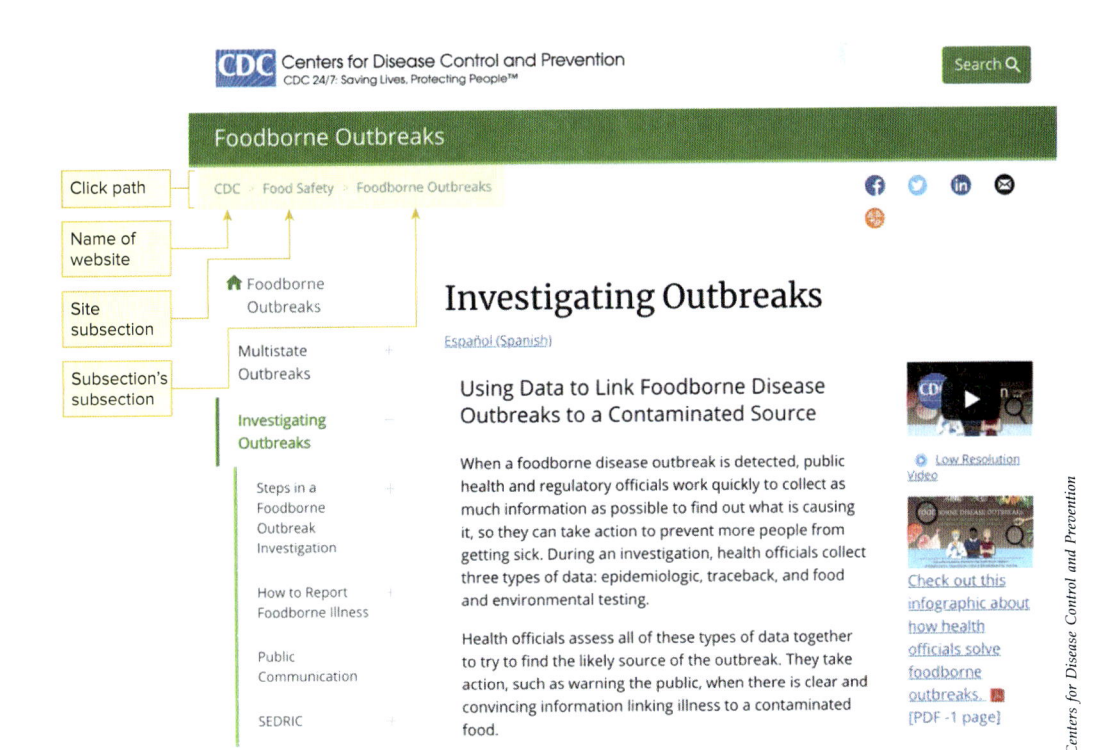

FIGURE 12.2 Locating the publisher by following the click path The name of the website *Centers for Disease Control and Prevention* (abbreviated to *CDC*) is the first item on the left of the click path, followed by the name of the site subsection, "Food Safety," and that subsection's subsection, "Foodborne Outbreaks." The title of this source, "Investigating Outbreaks," appears below the click path.

Research Matters • Planning a Research Project

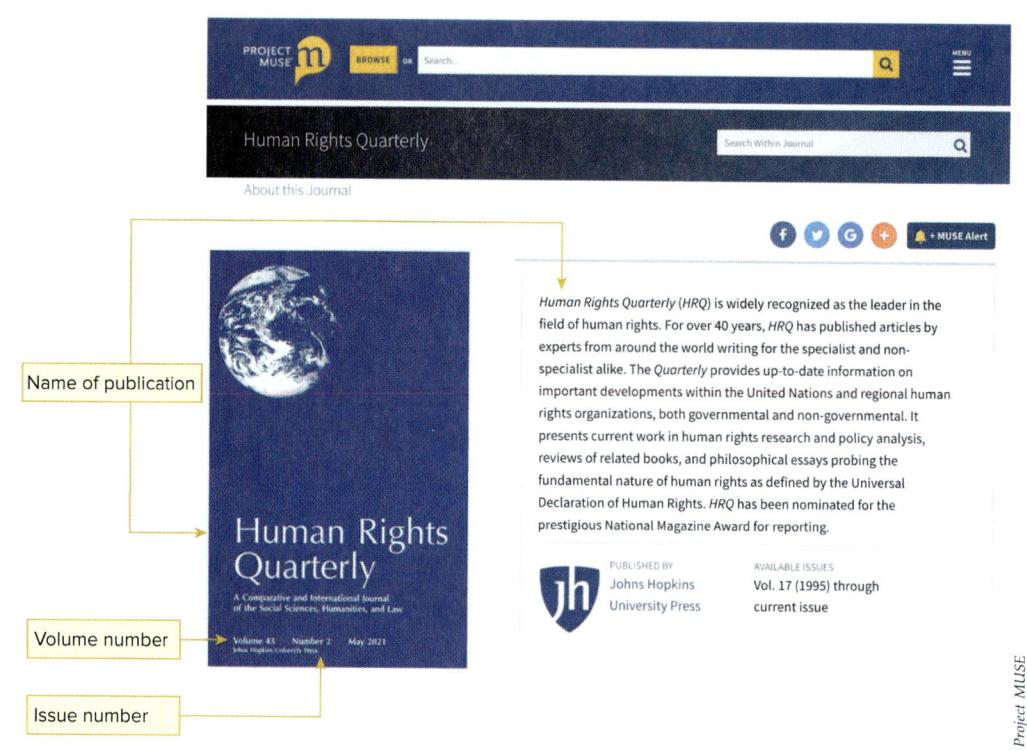

FIGURE 12.3 Locating the name of the publication in database results When you are citing a scholarly article, the "publisher" in the entry of your bibliography is the name of the journal, not the press that publishes the journal. Interpreting database results requires your being alert to the difference. As is the case with many database results, this one shows an image of the publication cover. On it is the name of the scholarly journal *Human Rights Quarterly*. If you are citing an article from *Human Rights Quarterly*, this title is the information you need. Below it is the notation "Published by: The Johns Hopkins University Press." Don't let that name confuse you. (Click on that link, and you will find a list of all the scholarly journals published by that press.)

- **Look for the name of an organization or a college.** An organization or a university is usually the sponsor of the publication, rather than the name of the publication itself. Once you have eliminated the sponsor, keep looking around the page for the name of the publication. Figure 12.3 shows the process.

Research Matters • Building and Annotating a Working Bibliography 12g 235

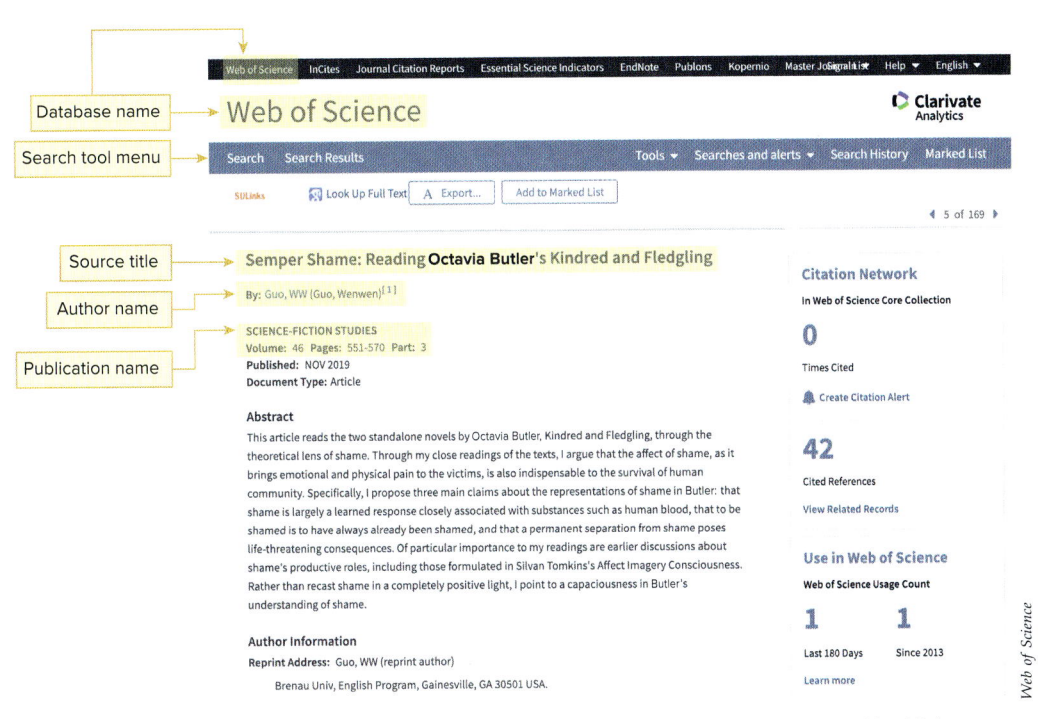

FIGURE 12.4 **Locating the title of a source** At the top of the screen is the database name, *Web of Science*. Below that are site menus. Under them is the title of the source, "Semper Shame: Reading Octavia Butler's Kindred and Fledgling," followed by the author's name; the publication name, *Science-Fiction Studies*, follows, along with additional publication information.

- **Look at the top of the page.** Websites often place the sponsor's or database's name at the top, followed by the name of the publication, and then by the title and author of the source (Figure 12.4).

3. Annotate the working bibliography.

An annotated entry in a working bibliography includes not only the information you will need to document and locate the source, but also a brief note that summarizes the source and indicates how you might use it in your project. Annotating sources now will save you time later when you begin synthesizing and reporting your research.

Research Matters • Planning a Research Project

Student Model
Research project:
Isabel Beck, "Fast Fashion" (ch. 18)

Below is a sample entry from a working bibliography for Isabel Beck's research project:

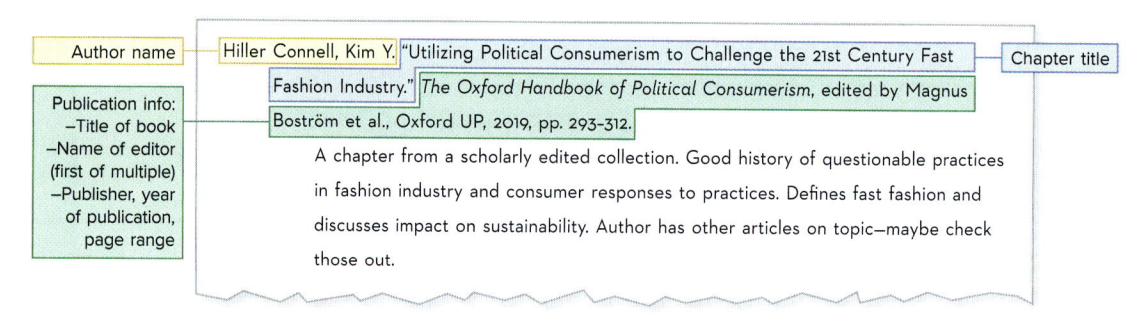

> [Author name] Hiller Connell, Kim Y. [Chapter title] "Utilizing Political Consumerism to Challenge the 21st Century Fast Fashion Industry." [Publication info: Title of book] *The Oxford Handbook of Political Consumerism*, [Name of editor (first of multiple)] edited by Magnus Boström et al., [Publisher, year of publication, page range] Oxford UP, 2019, pp. 293-312.
>
> A chapter from a scholarly edited collection. Good history of questionable practices in fashion industry and consumer responses to practices. Defines fast fashion and discusses impact on sustainability. Author has other articles on topic—maybe check those out.

> **More about**
> Finding information (ch. 13), 237–62
> Scholarly versus popular sources, 266–67

Make It **Your Own**

For the research project that you have been working on through the Make It Your Own assignments in this chapter, create a working bibliography of at least 10 sources. Choose a mix of source types, including at least three books, three scholarly articles, and one or more newspaper or magazine articles, reference works, websites, pamphlets, government documents, or visual, multimedia, or audio sources. Then locate and annotate the five most promising sources, recording complete publication information and taking preliminary notes on what the source covers and how it might be useful to your research project.

13 Finding Information

IN THIS CHAPTER

a. Searching rhetorically, 237

b. Finding reference works, 238

c. Finding information on the web, 242

d. Finding reliable interactive media, 245

e. Finding articles using databases and indexes, 246

f. Finding books, 251

g. Finding government information, 254

h. Finding multimedia sources, 255

i. Conducting field research, 259

> **More about**
> Reliability, 265–69
> Scholarly versus popular sources, 266–67

Your research may usefully begin with a simple web search that offers brief, easy-to-read sources that give you basic facts about your topic. Relying solely on these can unfortunately lead to a shallow project whose pieces do not fit together. Push further: search for more detailed sources that help you answer your research question. Look for a balance of general sources which provide background, specialized sources which provide disciplinary context, and sources offering popular opinion and expert insights.

13a Searching Rhetorically

As you conduct your search for information, keep these principles in mind:

- **Be observant.** Explore the menu in whatever database you are using.
- **Be curious.** Make use of the Help menu when you have questions.
- **Be patient.** Never settle for the first results you see.
- **Learn the basics of your topic.** Search for sources that provide basic background information on your topic.
- **Learn the complexities of your topic.** Search for sources that explain the complexities and controversies about your topic; it's hard to write exclusively from simplistic information.
- **Embrace controversy.** Search for sources that provide multiple viewpoints on your topic, rather than ones that just agree with your research hypothesis.

- **Pursue your own answers.** Search for sources that will help you come up with your own answer to your research question, rather than sources that answer it for you.

- **Broaden your understanding.** Deliberately search for sources whose authors speak from a wide spectrum of positions, perspectives, and places, and are varied in terms of gender, nationality, and race.

- **Slow down.** Look for the good stuff, not the quick stuff.

13b Finding Reference Works

Unless you are already an expert on your research topic, your search for sources should include both general and specialized reference works such as dictionaries, encyclopedias, biographical sources, bibliographies, almanacs, yearbooks, and atlases. General reference sources, written for newcomers to the topic, can do the following:

- Introduce you to your topic and help you determine whether it will sustain your interest.
- Provide an overview and basic facts.

Your search should also include specialized, subject-specific reference works written for researchers wanting in-depth understanding of the topic. These can

- introduce you to the issues and debates on your topic
- help you get a sense of subtopics you might want to explore
- highlight scholars, thinkers, or other figures important to your topic
- provide lists of reliable sources on the topic
- introduce and define special terminology, which will help you develop a list of keywords that you can use in further searching for sources

> *More about*
> Searching a library catalog, 251–54

You will find reference works listed in your library's catalog. You may also be able to link to electronic reference sources through your library's home page or databases. As you search reference works, you may have to generate keywords for increasingly general search terms: If you cannot find good overview sources on "bats AND wind turbines," for example, you may have to search separately for "dangers of alternative energy sources" or "wildlife AND alternative energy." If you cannot find good overview sources on "ghostwriting," you might try the larger category of "plagiarism" or the even larger category of "ethics." Reference sources on related issues that include your topic may help you understand and explain the context for your research or its importance.

1. Use dictionaries and encyclopedias.

In addition to whatever online tools they may use, most writers keep a collegiate dictionary at hand to verify spellings, look up definitions, and gather additional brief information about words. An *unabridged* dictionary provides more: more words, more examples of usage, more complete descriptions of the word's roots in other languages. The most extensive unabridged dictionary is the *Oxford English Dictionary* (or *OED*), a multivolume work providing the entire history of English words and showing the ways in which their meanings have changed over time. Unabridged dictionaries, including the *OED*, may be available in print or online.

Specialized dictionaries are written for students and scholars in specific academic fields. In addition to defining terms, subject-specific dictionaries may also provide a comprehensive introduction to the topic, as well as a list of further resources. If, for example, you want a deeper understanding of what *absolutism* means to a political scientist, you can turn to a source like the *Blackwell Dictionary of Political Science*, which offers a long paragraph explaining the term, followed by three recommended sources on the topic.

Encyclopedias such as the *Concise Columbia Electronic Encyclopedia* and *Wikipedia* are available for free online. Others, such as *The New Encyclopedia Britannica*, are available in print but may be free of charge through your library's website.

General encyclopedias provide a useful introduction to your topic, and some may offer a list of further resources. Specialized encyclopedias, on the other hand, provide not only an introduction to the topic but also a sense of

> **More about**
> Selecting a dictionary, 613–15
> Using a dictionary, 615–17

> **More about**
> Reliability, 265–69

Writing Responsibly: Using *Wikipedia* Responsibly

Wikipedia is an online encyclopedia created and revised by users. Its ongoing updates make its entries more up to date than those in most other encyclopedias. Most *Wikipedia* updates, however, are done by a relatively small number of people whose average age is 32, which means most entries are not validated by experts—unlike a source such as the *Encyclopedia Britannica*. Further, the source is not balanced in terms of sex and gender representation; according to a 2018 study, 90 percent of contributors identify as male, 8.8 percent as female, and 1 percent as nonbinary (see *Wikipedia*, "Gender Bias on *Wikipedia*"). As for dependability and accuracy, *Wikipedia* admits it "is not considered to be a reliable source, as not everything in *Wikipedia* is accurate, comprehensive, or unbiased" (see *Wikipedia*, "Researching with *Wikipedia*"). Approach *Wikipedia* with care, and verify the information you find there. Although *Wikipedia* is not an authoritative source for most college-level research projects, the "References" and "Sources" lists following each entry may provide authoritative sources and jumping off points for further research. For example, the references for the entry "Gender Bias on *Wikipedia*" link to articles from scholarly and professional journals, including *Information, Communication, & Society*, *Women's Studies Journal*, and *MIT Technology Review*.

to TOPIC

how scholars in the field approach the topic. They are also likely to provide a brief list of authoritative sources. If your library makes *Reference Universe* or *Credo Reference* available, you can search across many of the library's reference works online and the contents of much of its print reference holdings.

Quick Reference: Dictionaries and Encyclopedias

Specialized Dictionaries
- *The Bedford Glossary of Critical and Literary Terms*
- *Dictionary of 20th-Century World Politics*
- *Dictionary of American History*
- *Dictionary of American Literary Characters*
- *Grove Dictionary of Art*
- *Public Policy Dictionary*

Specialized Encyclopedias
- *The Advertising Age Encyclopedia of Advertising*
- *Cambridge Encyclopedia of the English Language*
- *Encyclopedia of African-American Culture and History*
- *Encyclopedia of American Cultural and Intellectual History*
- *Encyclopedia of Bioethics*
- *Encyclopedia of Government and Politics*
- *Encyclopedia of Latin American History and Culture*
- *Encyclopedia of Religion*
- *Garland Encyclopedia of World Music*
- *McGraw-Hill Encyclopedia of Engineering*
- *McGraw-Hill Encyclopedia of Science and Technology*
- *Routledge Encyclopedia of Philosophy*
- *Women's Studies Encyclopedia*

2. Refer to almanacs and yearbooks.

Almanacs and yearbooks are annual publications offering facts and statistics, such as when each phase of the moon will occur and annual per capita income of nations. The best-known general-purpose almanac is the *World Almanac and Book of Facts,* which has been published annually since 1923. Subject-specific almanacs and yearbooks, such as the *Almanac of American Politics* and the *Yearbook of Immigration Statistics,* provide a wide body of statistical and tabular data on specific topics. Today, much of the information once most readily found in an almanac or yearbook is now available online at sites such as the *CIA World Factbook* and the Research Tools page at the *Economist* magazine's website. Your library may also subscribe to statistical databases such as *ProQuest Statistical Insight, Data-Planet Statistical Datasets,* or *Historical Statistics of the United States.*

Quick Reference

Almanacs and Yearbooks
- *Almanac of American Politics*
- *Americana Annual*
- *Britannica Book of the Year*
- *Congressional Quarterly Almanac Plus*
- *Facts on File Yearbook*
- *Information Please Almanac*
- *Statistical Abstract of the United States*
- *UNESCO Statistical Yearbook*

3. Check out biographical reference works.

Biographical reference sources can provide you with the facts and events of people's lives (both the famous and the fairly obscure), such as their education, their accomplishments, and their current position. They can also help you understand the historical context in which people lived or in which their works were produced. Numerous biographical resources are available to researchers; two of the most commonly consulted are the *American National Biography* and the *Oxford Dictionary of National Biography* (British).

> **Quick Reference**
>
> **Biographical Reference Sources**
> *Baker's Biographical Dictionary of Musicians*
> *Biographical Dictionary of American Indian History to 1900*
> *Cambridge Biographical Encyclopedia*
> *Cambridge Dictionary of American Biography*
> *Fifty Major Thinkers on Education*
> *McGraw-Hill Encyclopedia of World Biography*
> *Mexican American Biographies: A Historical Dictionary, 1836–1987*
> *Notable American Women: A Biographical Dictionary*
> *Notable Black American Women*
> *Webster's New Biographical Dictionary*
>
> **Bibliographical Resources**
> *Bibliographic Guide to Education*
> *Bibliographic Guide to Psychology*
> *Bibliographic Guide to the History of Computing, Computers, and the Information Processing Industry*
> *Film Research: A Critical Bibliography*
> *Information Sources in the Life Sciences*
> *Information Sources of Political Science*
> *International Bibliography of the Social Sciences*
> *MLA International Bibliography of Books and Articles on the Modern Languages and Literatures*
> *Sociology: A Guide to Reference and Information Sources*

Writing Responsibly Going beyond Reference Sources

Because both general and specialized reference works provide background information to orient you to your topic, they are an essential starting point in your research. For a college-level research project, however, reference works are only the beginning; to fulfill your responsibilities to your topic and audience, you must go beyond these sources to find books, articles, and websites that treat your topic in depth.

to TOPIC

4. Use bibliographies.

Bibliographies list sources on a particular topic, providing the information needed to locate the source. They often provide an abstract or brief summary of each source, so you can tell whether it is likely to be relevant to your research.

13c Finding Information on the Web

Engines like *Google* and *Bing* search billions of web pages for whatever words the user enters and then return links in order of relevance, as determined by the search engine's criteria. (*Google,* for example, ranks its results based on a frequently changing, proprietary algorithm that considers factors such as the number of other pages that link to a site, its purpose, as well as advertising.) The results retrieved can differ based on the criteria the search engine uses to rank relevance, as well as on the web pages it indexes. For that reason, running a search on multiple engines is a good idea. A list of alternative search engines appears in the Quick Reference box on page 243.

Before using a search engine for the first time, read about how it works. Look for links (often at the bottom of the page) called "About" or "Help" to find answers to frequently asked questions (FAQs) or for advice about how best to conduct a search on that site. Look, too, for advanced search options; these will help you focus your search.

1. Use keywords.

The most common way to begin a web search is with a simple keyword search. A search on *Google* using the term "fast fashion" (the topic of Isabel Beck's project at the end of chapter 18) yielded more than 2.5 billion hits (Figure 13.1).

> **More about**
> Relevance,
> 263–64

This kind of searching is very easy, and it yields plenty of results—too many. No one could look at all 2.5 billion results, and most are not even relevant. To narrow the results to a more manageable number, and to focus more closely on sites that will be relevant to your research, you can group terms using quotation marks or use a combination of terms. A search on "fast fashion" and "history," for example, reduced the number of hits from 2.5 billion to 1.9 million—still too many but a definite improvement.

2. Use advanced search options.

You can narrow search results further with advanced search options (Figure 13.2), which can limit results by language, file type (*Word,* rich text, PDF, *PowerPoint,* or *Excel*), website or top-level domain (cnn.com or harvard.edu; org, .gov, .edu, or .com), and other options. Limiting the search on "'underground comics' history" to sites with the domain .edu, for example, reduced the number of hits to 1,420.

3. Use metasearch engines.

Because search engines index different web pages and use different methods to rank sites, using more than one engine increases your odds of finding

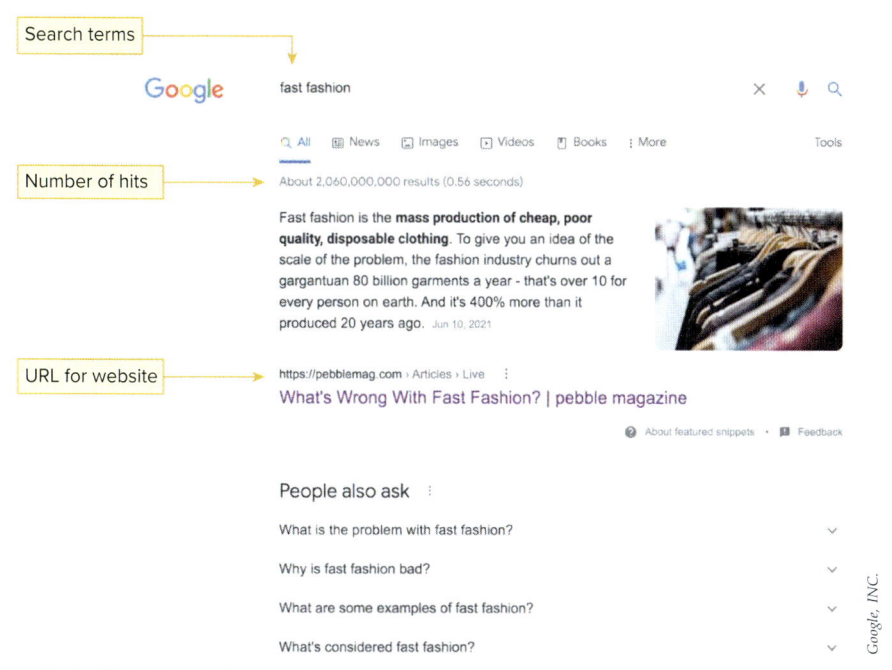

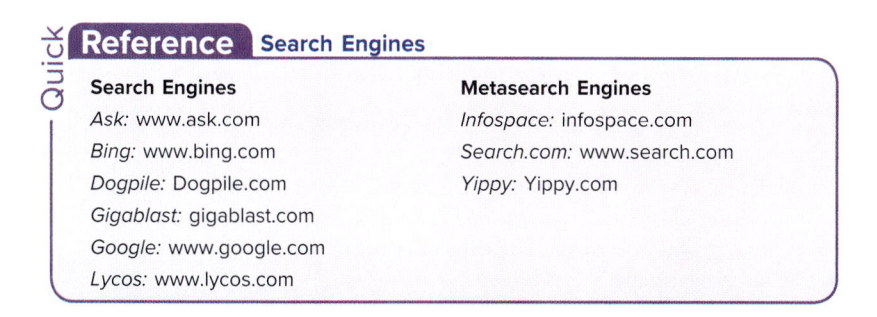

FIGURE 13.1 A simple keyword search on Google

Callouts: Search terms; Number of hits; URL for website

useful resources. To search multiple sites simultaneously, use ***metasearch engines,*** which return the top search results from several search engines at once, with duplicate entries deleted. (A list of metasearch engines appears in the Quick Reference below.) A search using the terms "fast fashion" and "history" on *InfoSpace,* for example, produced a few hundred hits (not 2.5 billion).

> **More about**
> Devising a topic, 25, 224–25
> Narrowing or broadening a topic, 31–32

Quick Reference Search Engines

Search Engines
Ask: www.ask.com
Bing: www.bing.com
Dogpile: Dogpile.com
Gigablast: gigablast.com
Google: www.google.com
Lycos: www.lycos.com

Metasearch Engines
Infospace: infospace.com
Search.com: www.search.com
Yippy: Yippy.com

Research Matters • Finding Information

To conduct an advanced search, go to https://www.google.com/advanced_search.

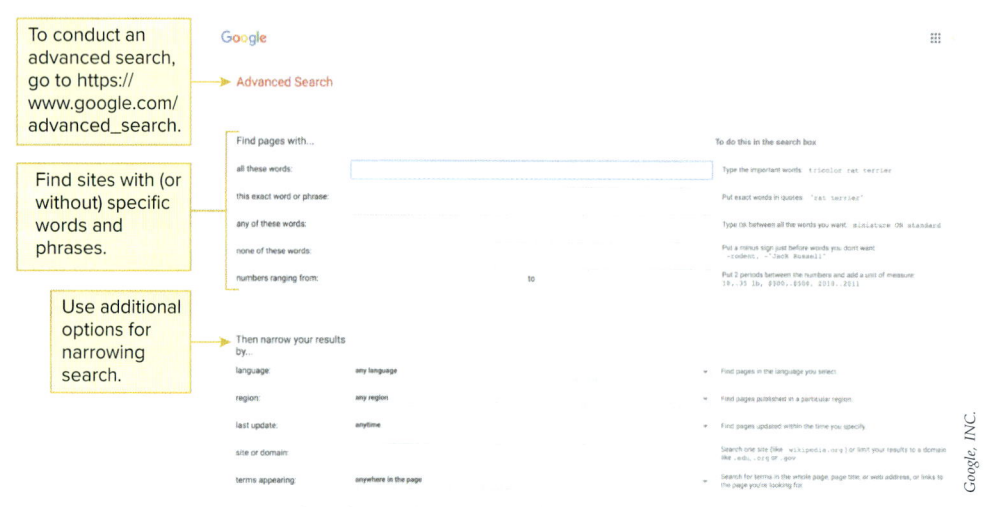

Find sites with (or without) specific words and phrases.

Use additional options for narrowing search.

FIGURE 13.2 **An advanced search on Google**

> **EXERCISE 13.1 Conducting a simple keyword search**
>
> Using the topic you selected for the Make It Your Own activity on p. 225, generate three or more keywords and use them to conduct keyword searches on two of the search engines listed in the Quick Reference box on the previous page. Write a paragraph comparing your results: Did each search engine generate the same number of results? How do the top 10 results differ? What about the next 10?

> **EXERCISE 13.2 Conducting an advanced keyword search**
>
> Return to the same search engines you used in Exercise 13.1 and use the same keywords, but this time select the advanced search feature to narrow your search to sites within the domains .edu, .gov, and .org. Write a paragraph comparing the results from the advanced search with those from the simple search you conducted in Exercise 13.1.

Make It **Your Own**

Review the sources generated in Exercises 13.1 and 13.2 and create a working list of sources you might use for a project on the topic. Write a paragraph explaining why this combination of sources seems appropriate.

Make It **Your Own**

For a research project you are developing, create a list of keywords. Use the advanced search option of one of the search engines listed in the Quick Reference box on page 243 to help you find .edu, .gov, or .org sources for these keywords. Bookmark any sources that seem as if they will be useful, and make a note of the search term and the title in your research notebook. Write one sentence about why that source might be useful for your project.

13d Finding Reliable Interactive Media

In addition to conventional websites, a variety of other digital sources—including blogs, discussion lists, and groups on social networking sites like *Facebook,* *Reddit,* and *Twitter*—can offer insight into your topic when experts contribute content.

Of course, not all blogs, discussion lists, and groups are equally authoritative, and some spread misinformation, disinformation, and extremist content. Evaluate the reliability of such sites by finding out the qualifications of the writers, and verify the information you glean from such sources by consulting additional sources.

To find a blog or discussion list on your topic, use a specialized search engine (such as *Blogarama* and *Google Groups*). You can also enter your keyword with "blog," "listserv," "newsgroup," or "chat room" in a search engine.

News alerts and RSS feeds collect news stories on topics you specify. Registering for alerts at sites such as *Google* (www.google.com/alerts) will bring daily updates on your chosen topics to your email box. To read RSS feeds, use a website like *Feedly* or *Inoreader* to subscribe to site feeds.

Sites for sharing information, whether in print or other media, are born or expire (or at least fade in popularity) almost every day; as this book goes to press, *YouTube, Pocket, Pinterest,* and *Instagram* are widely used for sharing information and media files on topics of common interest, but new possibilities constantly arise.

> **More about**
> Evaluating information (ch. 14), 263–78
> Misinformation, disinformation, and fake news, 270–71

> **More about**
> Documenting a blog, 367–69 (MLA), 421–22 (APA), 455 (*Chicago*), 481 (CSE)
> Documenting a discussion list, 367 (MLA), 421 (APA), 455 (*Chicago*), 481 (CSE)
> Reliability, 265–69
> Netiquette, 544

EXERCISE 13.3 Researching electronic sources

Find a blog or discussion group on the topic you explored in Exercises 13.1 and 13.2. Who are the contributors to this site? Conduct a web search to learn about the site's contributors.

13e Finding Articles in Journals and Other Periodicals Using Databases and Indexes

Periodical is the umbrella term for magazines, newspapers, and scholarly journals that are issued at regular intervals—daily, weekly, monthly, quarterly. A search engine such as *Google* or *Ask* can point you to articles published online in magazines, newspapers, and some journals, but many articles in academic journals are not available for free on the web, and many magazines and newspapers require subscriptions before you can access their content. For a comprehensive listing of articles published in periodicals, turn to the databases available through your college library's website. (You may be prompted to sign in.)

Library databases are organized so that you can search for articles by author, title, subject, date, and other fields. Some databases provide only an *abstract*, or summary, but many provide the complete text, either in a *PDF* (sometimes called "full text PDF") file, which shows the article more or less as it would have appeared in print, or in an *HTML* (sometimes called "full text") file, which provides the text but may not include the formatting or illustrations that would have appeared in the printed text.

1. Choose an appropriate database.

Most college libraries provide a wide variety of databases. Most will offer an all-purpose database like *ProQuest Central*, *Academic Search Premier*, or *Academic OneFile* that indexes both popular magazines and scholarly journals, as well as discipline-specific databases, such as *Education Source*, *PsycARTICLES*, and *Science Direct*. They may also offer *Nexus Uni*, formerly known as *LexisNexis Academic*, which indexes news reports from around the world. A reference librarian can help you learn which databases available at your library will best suit your research needs.

> **More about**
> Writing situation, 14–22

Writing Responsibly | Really Reading Real Sources

As you choose your sources, it may seem efficient to select only those that are short and easy to read. Resist this temptation; fulfill your responsibility to your topic by pushing beyond easy, basic information. If you controlled for page length in your source selection, you would be writing your research project from uninsightful sources that would produce shallow, uninteresting claims. Instead, when your source selection is finished, include substantial sources that treat complex questions in complex ways. Reading these sources will be a greater challenge, but you will be able to produce richer, more successful writing from them.

to TOPIC

Tech Using *Google Scholar*

Google Scholar (scholar.google.com) allows users to search the web for scholarly materials—articles in academic journals, theses, books, and abstracts.

Pros

- *Google Scholar* can help you locate material that you would otherwise need both your library's catalog and subscription databases to find.
- It may even link to your own library's digital holdings (see the preferences settings in *Google Scholar*).
- It links to many citation management software types.
- It identifies other books, websites, documents, and publications that have cited the source and provides links to them.
- It can help you find missing information about your source. If you have the author and title, *Google Scholar* can often provide the journal name, volume number, page number, and URL.

Cons

- *Google* has its own definition of *scholarly*, so some hits may be to works your instructor may not consider authoritative.
- *Google Scholar* does not allow you to filter your results by subject or discipline, so you may find many irrelevant results.
- You may be shifted to sites where you will be asked to pay for full-text versions of the source. (Always check your library's holdings or try *interlibrary loan*—a system for borrowing from another library—before paying for access.)
- Because of *Google's* search and ranking methods, the most recent sources may not be included, or they may appear at the end of the list. (You can include a date range in Advanced Scholar Search.)

> **More about**
> Evaluating sources (ch. 14), 263–78

When searching for articles, be sure to consider the types of sources that are most appropriate to your topic and writing situation. In particular, consider whether you should use popular sources, scholarly sources, or a combination of the two.

For Robyn Worthington, writing for her psychology class, *PsycARTICLES* (a database that indexes articles from psychology journals) was a good starting place for her periodicals search. For Isabel Beck, researching the ethics of fast fashion, a general database (such as *ProQuest Central* or *Academic Search Premier*), which indexes both popular and scholarly sources, was a good place to start.

2. Search the database.

Searching a database is much like using a search engine such as *Google* or *Bing*. You type in a search term and hit Enter (or Return) to generate a list of articles that include your keywords. Unlike a search engine, however, the database

> **Student Model**
> Research projects:
> "Inmate Access to Technology," Brianna Davids (ch. 8), 159–74
> "Fast Fashion," Isabel Beck (ch. 18), 383–96
> "Nature versus Nurture," Robyn Worthington (ch. 19), 430–38

limits its search to selected publications, and because you are provided with full information about these sources, it is easier to assess their reliability.

To make sure the results of a database search are relevant, narrow your search by combining search terms and using the advanced search options the database makes available. Typing "fast fashion" in the search box of a database like *Academic Search Premier* generates a list of over 25,000 items—fewer than with a *Google* search but still far too many to be helpful. As with a web search engine, combining terms ("fast fashion" AND "history") narrows the search. The search could be narrowed further by using the database's advanced search or filtering options. The menu bars on the left and right in Figure 13.3 show some of the options for narrowing a search.

NOTE Databases differ from vendor to vendor and are updated frequently, so check your library's Help screens or ask a librarian for advice.

If narrowing your search by combining terms and using the database's narrowing options is not getting you the results you need, try the following:

- Conduct your search again with alternative or refined search terms. Check your database's subject or topics list (sometimes called Thesaurus) for the terms with which your topic was indexed and use those terms in your search.

- Narrow (or expand) your search using Boolean logic. (See the Quick Reference box on the next page.)

- Return to the library's database menu to run your search on other databases.

> **More about**
> Creating a working bibliography, 230–36

As you find promising sources, create entries for them in your working bibliography, or follow directions on the database for emailing entries to yourself.

Just as metasearch engines allow you to send your keyword search out to several search engines simultaneously, some database vendors allow you to search simultaneously through all their databases. Increasingly, libraries are also offering *federated searching*, also known as *discovery services*, allowing

> **More about**
> Relevance, 263–64
> Citation management programs, 231

Tech Hidden Benefits of Library Databases

In addition to their superiority in finding sources, a library database may be linked to citation management software such as *Mendeley* or *Zotero*. When you choose a source in the database, the software makes a bibliographic entry in whatever style—MLA, APA, and so forth—you select.

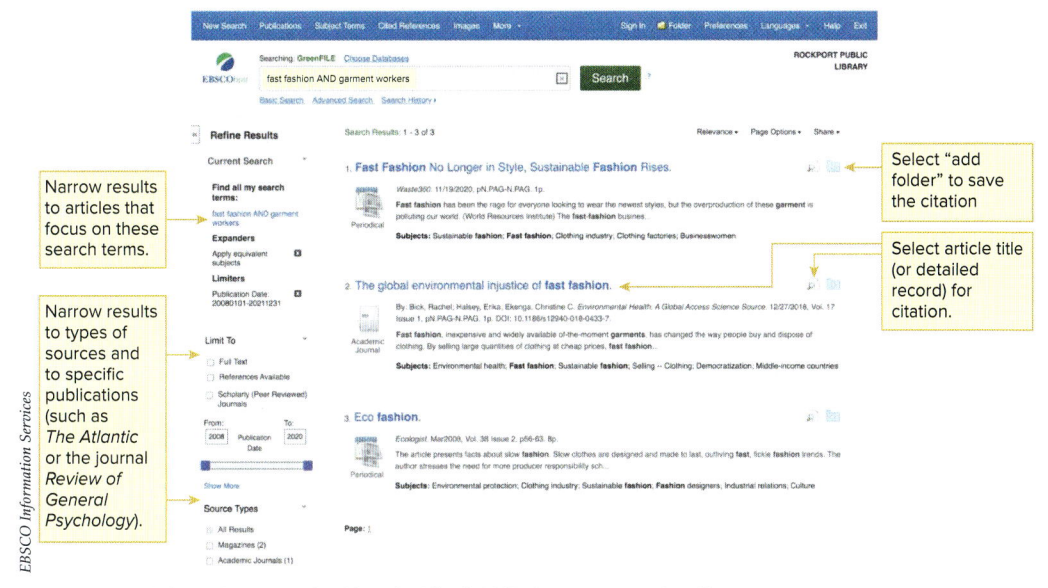

Research Matters • Finding Articles in Journals and Other Periodicals Using Databases and Indexes   13e   249

FIGURE 13.3 Search results for "fast fashion" AND "garment workers"

you to search across many databases simultaneously. Check your library's website to see what multiple-database searching options are available to you.

3. Find copies of articles.

After generating a list of promising-looking articles from your database search, you are ready to retrieve copies of the articles. Some articles you can access directly from the database search page (look for links saying something like "Find It in Full Text") and you can then print them, download them to your hard drive, or email them to yourself. The first article from the search screen in Figure 13.3, for example, is available online.

Tech | HTML versus PDF

Articles accessed through a database are often available in both HTML and PDF versions. The HTML (often called *full text*) version will download much more quickly, but the PDF (often called *full text PDF*) version may be a duplicate of the article as it appears in the publication, including illustrations and page numbers, which you can then include in your reference list or list of works cited.

Quick Reference: Conducting a Boolean Search

Most databases (and search engines like *Google* and *Bing*) narrow a search with Boolean logic, which relies on the words *and, not,* and *or* to expand or narrow a search and parentheses or quotation marks to group words. Most databases also use wildcard characters (* or ?) to stand in place of letters, allowing you to search for different forms of a word at the same time. Check Help screens or consult a reference librarian to learn how to use Boolean logic in searching your library's databases.

AND — Fast Fashion AND Ethics — Narrows a search by retrieving items that include *both* terms.

OR — Fast Fashion OR Ethics — Expands a search by retrieving items that include *either* term.

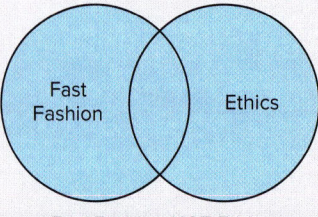

NOT — Fast Fashion NOT Ethics — Narrows a search by retrieving items that include one term but not the other.

" " — "ethical consumption" — Quotation marks group terms to retrieve pages with these words in this order.

( ) — (clothes OR clothing) AND (factories) — Parentheses group terms so complex alternatives can be retrieved.

* / ? — work* (or work?) to search for work, worker, and working simultaneously — Wildcard characters allow you to search for more than one version of a word at the same time by replacing the letters that are different in each word with an asterisk (*) or a question mark (?).

For some articles, however, only an abstract will be available through the database; in a few cases, only a bibliographic citation may be available. While it may be tempting to skip articles that you cannot have delivered instantly to your desktop, you may miss out on important sources of information. To find articles you cannot link to from the database, consult your library's website (or a librarian) for a list of journals available through your library or through interlibrary loan. The interlibrary loan system allows you to borrow materials from other libraries by making a request through your home library.

EXERCISE 13.4 Conducting a database search

Using one or more keywords that you generated in Exercise 13.1, conduct a search using a general database such as *ProQuest Central* or *Academic Search Premier*. Now conduct the same search using an appropriate subject-specific database. (Ask your instructor or a librarian for help in determining which databases might be appropriate.) Compare the results: How many articles were returned on each search? How many of the same articles were listed on the first two pages of results?

EXERCISE 13.5 Locating an article

For one of the searches you performed in Exercise 13.4, find an article that is not available as a link from the database results page. Then write a paragraph describing the steps you took to find it.

13f Finding Books Using Library Catalogs

While reference works can give you an overview or direct you to other sources, it is in books that you are most likely to find extensive, in-depth treatments of your topic—especially in the humanities and some social sciences. One or two well-chosen books, supplemented by a selection of journal articles and other sources, can round out your research and deepen your understanding of your topic.

1. Search the catalog.

Libraries index all their holdings in catalogs, which in most cases you can access through your library's website. Most library catalogs allow users to search for resources by author, title, and subject heading. Some include additional search options such as call number or keyword (Figure 13.4). Because catalogs differ from library to library, check the Help or Search

Research Matters • Finding Information

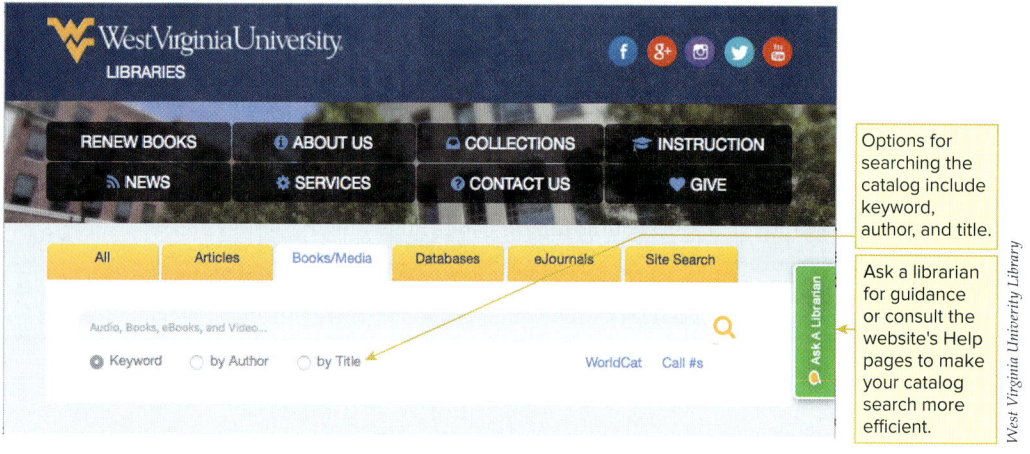

FIGURE 13.4 A library website Students at West Virginia University and other colleges and universities around the country can search for print and digital sources from their library's catalog.

Options for searching the catalog include keyword, author, and title.

Ask a librarian for guidance or consult the website's Help pages to make your catalog search more efficient.

West Virginia University Library

Tips screen before beginning a search. You may find it useful to conduct a "keyword anywhere" search, using your search terms. Most library catalogs include tables of contents for anthologies and edited books, so a keyword search may yield useful results, even when the term does not appear in the item's title or author fields.

NOTE Some catalogs may require you to specify the category (such as author or title) in which you wish to search. If you do not, the program may default to a category you are not expecting. For example, if you are looking for books *about* Herman Melville and do not specify that you are searching by subject, your library's program may default to searching for books *by* Melville and provide you with a list of books by him as well as about him.

> **More about**
> Keyword searching, 242

Search a library's catalog much as you do a search engine or a periodical database: Type a keyword or a combination of words in the search box and hit Enter. Whereas *Google* and other web search engines allow you to use any keyword related to your topic, library catalogs use a preset list of subject headings to index library books. When searching a library's catalog by subject, use these preset headings. To find the subject headings the library has used, go to a catalog entry for a book on your topic that you have already identified as relevant. The book's record will list the subject headings used (Figure 13.5).

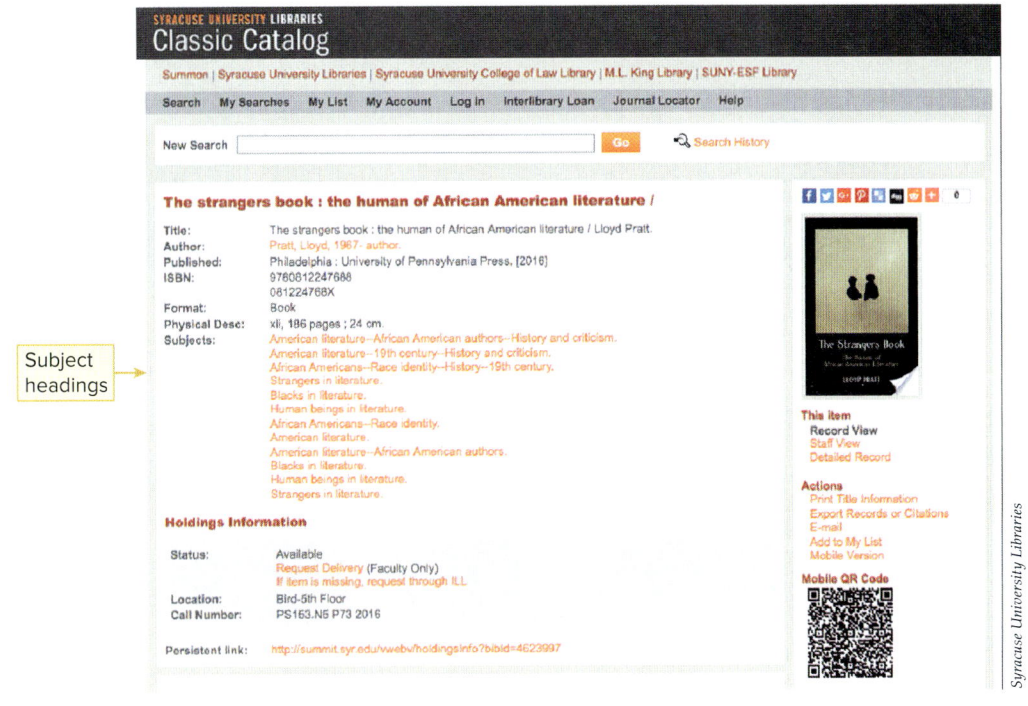

FIGURE 13.5 Finding subject headings in a library record

Clicking on them will bring you to a list of related subject headings and to other books cataloged using the same terms. Repeat the process with other useful books to add subject terms.

2. Browse the stacks or the catalog.

Many researchers enjoy browsing library stacks to find books on their topic: Since books on a topic all share the first part of a call number, they are shelved close together. If you are free to wander in your library's stacks, check for other books on your topic shelved close to those you have identified as relevant. If your library catalog allows it, search for other books on your subject by inserting the first part of a relevant book's call number in the catalog's search box. (The screenshot in Figure 13.6 shows a search for items whose call number begins with PN 6725.) Or the results page in an online catalog search on your library's website might show you sources on related topics.

13g Research Matters • Finding Information

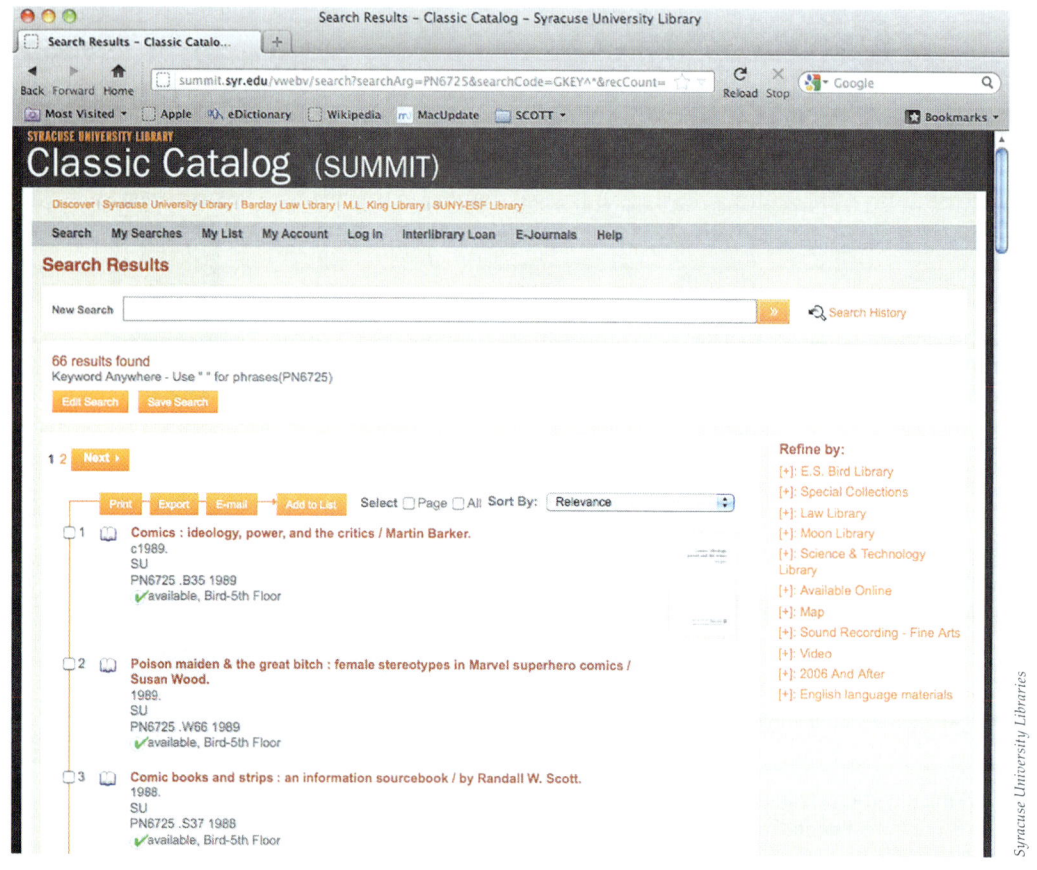

FIGURE 13.6 Browsing by call number

EXERCISE 13.6 Using the library catalog

Using the keywords you generated in Exercise 13.1, find a book using your library's catalog. Then refine your search using the subject headings and call number. Write a paragraph describing the process and analyzing your results.

13g Finding Government Information

Although you will usually rely on books and articles in your college research, government publications can provide you with rich resources, including congressional records, government reports, and legal documents.

> **Quick Reference** — **Accessing Government Information Online**
>
> The websites for the following all provide access to government documents and datasets online:
>
> European Union
> USA.gov
> FedWorld Information Network
> Library of Congress
> National Institutes of Health
> Organization for Economic Cooperation and Development
> State and Local Government on the Net
> United Nations
> US Bureau of Labor Statistics
> US Census Bureau
> US Government Printing Office

The federal government makes more than 300,000 documents available online, free of charge, from all three branches of the government—executive, legislative, and judicial. Most state and local governments also post their documents on the web, as do many governments around the world. If you are researching a social, legal, or political issue or if you need up-to-date statistics about almost any group, you may find valuable information in government publications. To locate government documents, conduct an advanced web search limited to the domain .gov or search databases such as *ProQuest Congressional* and *LexisNexis Congressional*.

13h Finding Multimedia Sources

Photographs, graphs, charts, and drawings have long been a staple of research in disciplines such as art history, film studies, history, geography, geology, political science, sociology, and psychology. With research in all disciplines now being shared through multimedia presentations and websites, the use of multimedia resources has also expanded. To find culturally diverse multimedia resources, start with your library's catalog. Besides the video clips you can find on *YouTube* and *Hulu,* you may also find appropriate multimedia resources online at the sites hosted by the organizations listed in the Quick Reference box on this page. Increasingly, academic libraries are offering access to streaming media subscription services like *Academic Video Online, Kanopy, American History in Video,* and *Naxos Music Library.* Check your library's website to see what options are available.

NOTE Because you need to cite your media sources, remember to add them to your working bibliography.

> *More about*
> Working bibliography, 230–36

Writing Responsibly
Choosing and Unpacking Complex Sources

Make It Your Own! Research projects that rely heavily on short, simple sources tend to be simplistic and awkward. If you find, read, and write about lengthy, complex sources, you will produce superior scholarship.

Everyone wants to be efficient, yet college writers trying to save time may inadvertently do themselves and their audience a disservice when they write. While incorporating research into their projects, too many writers choose only short, simple sources that can be read quickly (see chart), and the quality of their writing suffers.

Researchers with the Citation Project were struck by the extent to which the quality of students' research projects was reduced by the shallowness of their sources. More than half of the projects' citations were to a source no longer than five pages, resulting in projects that were simplistic and unimpressive. They lacked the complex information and in-depth opinions that are essential to good research and interesting writing.

Length of Source Cited
DATA FROM **The Citation Project**

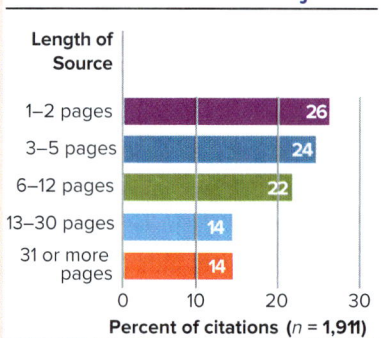

Length of Source	Percent of citations
1–2 pages	26
3–5 pages	24
6–12 pages	22
13–30 pages	14
31 or more pages	14

Percent of citations (n = **1,911**)

Researchers found that while most college research writers choose short, simple sources, the best writers work from lengthy, complex sources that bring details and insight—and not just basic facts—to the topic.

Writers relying on short sources work with too small a toolbox. Their projects will have very little to say if there is very little to draw on. Sources that are more extensive, in contrast, explore the interesting complexities and important debates about their topic. Such sources give writers—and the writers' audience—things to think about and talk about. They provide essential research material that leads to rich analysis and well-grounded argument.

Simply choosing lengthy sources is not enough, however. You should also "unpack" your sources—share with your audience the complexities and insights of your sources. Note how, in the following example, from an article on unnecessary medical procedures, complexity is lacking when the writer simply drops a quotation into his text and lets it speak for him:

First draft

[Student's voice] Whenever people go to the doctor, they should be aware of the risks of unnecessary medical testing. [Signal phrase] A doctor from San Francisco says, [Quotation] "[M]ost experts agree that overuse needs to be curbed. If it isn't, we could face a future public health problem of rising cancer rates, thanks to our medical overzealousness" [Parenthetical citation] (Parikh).

Research Matters • Finding Multimedia Sources 13h

The writer offers a quotation that supports his argument, and he has cited the quotation correctly. He has also provided some information about the writer of the source. However, because this quotation stands alone, readers of this student's project may think that the source made this statement as a simple directive: *Overuse of medical tests should stop.* In fact, the source offered a detailed review of the reasons for the overuse of CT scans, as well as a thoughtful set of recommendations.

Such information deserves to be represented. It is part of your responsibility to your audience and topic to show the whole picture that the source offers. Consider how much more interesting, informative, and persuasive the passage becomes when it provides more information and context:

Revised draft

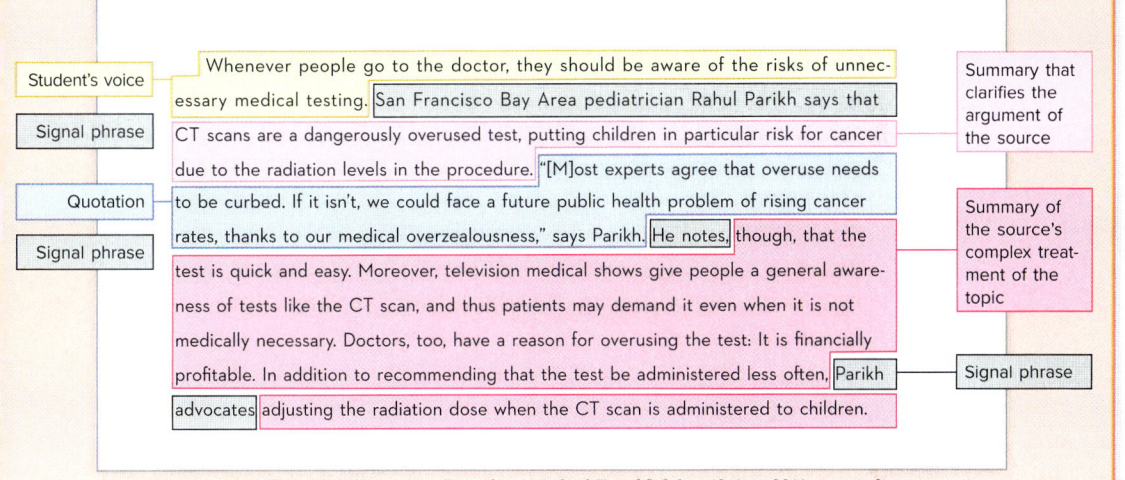

> Whenever people go to the doctor, they should be aware of the risks of unnecessary medical testing. San Francisco Bay Area pediatrician Rahul Parikh says that CT scans are a dangerously overused test, putting children in particular risk for cancer due to the radiation levels in the procedure. "[M]ost experts agree that overuse needs to be curbed. If it isn't, we could face a future public health problem of rising cancer rates, thanks to our medical overzealousness," says Parikh. He notes, though, that the test is quick and easy. Moreover, television medical shows give people a general awareness of tests like the CT scan, and thus patients may demand it even when it is not medically necessary. Doctors, too, have a reason for overusing the test: It is financially profitable. In addition to recommending that the test be administered less often, Parikh advocates adjusting the radiation dose when the CT scan is administered to children.

- Student's voice
- Signal phrase
- Quotation
- Signal phrase
- Summary that clarifies the argument of the source
- Summary of the source's complex treatment of the topic
- Signal phrase

Source: Parikh, Rahul. "How TV Illustrates a Disturbing Medical Trend." *Salon,* 18 Apr. 2011, www.salon.com/2011/04/18/poprx_unncessary_tests.

Notice that in the first draft, it sounds as if the doctor quoted is talking about all medical testing; the second draft shows that in fact Parikh was talking about a specific test, the CT scan. Choosing extensive sources, paying attention to the complexity of the material, and incorporating that complexity into your project not only increases the sophistication of your own writing; it can also save you from misrepresenting the source.

Self Assessment

Review your work with each source, revising as necessary, to be sure you:

- ☐ Choose lengthy, detailed sources. Did you find material that provides insights and debates on the topic? ▶ *Finding information, 237–62*
- ☐ Discuss the complexities of your sources' treatment of their topic. Did you go beyond simple, basic facts? ▶ *Analyzing, interpreting, synthesizing, and critiquing, 127–35*
- ☐ Explain any material you quote. Did you give background on every source?
  ▶ *Relevance and reliability, 263–69*

Research Matters • Finding Information

Quick Reference: Multimedia Resources

Academy of American Poets (poets.org)
American Rhetoric: The Power of Oratory in the United States (americanrhetoric.com)
Internet Archive (archive.org)
Library of Congress (loc.gov)
MIT OpenCourseWare (ocw.mit.edu)
National Aeronautics and Space Administration (NASA) (nasa.gov)
National Park Service (nps.gov)
New York Public Library (nypl.org)
Perry Castañeda Library Map Collection, University of Texas (legacy.lib.utexas.edu)
Smithsonian (si.edu)

Make It Your Own

For a research assignment for this or another class, create a working bibliography of at least 10 items. Include at least one of each of the following:

- Website
- Article in a scholarly journal
- Article in a newspaper
- Article in a magazine
- Subject-specific reference book
- Book
- Government publication
- Media resource

Which are available online? Which can you locate in your library?

Work Together

In small groups or as a class, take a tour of the library. (You will need to arrange this in advance.) Come prepared with a topic, and ask a librarian for advice on how best to conduct a database search or find resources on your topic in the library's catalog. Explore the library's multimedia offerings, and check out at least one book on your topic. Finally, prepare a brief report listing at least three things you learned about the library that you did not know before your visit.

13i Conducting and Reporting Field Research

Field research is often part of a research project in which the writer begins by reviewing information from secondary sources (reports of others' research) and then adds to the body of information by conducting a fresh inquiry. The most common types of field research are interviews, observational studies, and surveys.

1. Interviews

Expertise and the knowledge that comes with experience can often be gained only through an interview. Media such as email, text messaging, video chat, and even the telephone extend your range of possible interviewees, but face-to-face interviews give you an opportunity to read the other person's body language (facial expressions and bodily gestures), which can provide insight and direction for follow-up questions.

Instructors with special expertise in your subject make good subjects for an interview; government agencies, businesses, and public service organizations can also connect you with experts. When researching cultural or historical events, consider interviewing participants such as attorneys in a legal case, your soldier-cousin for her experience in Iraq, organizers of a demonstration for immigrants' rights.

These tips can help you make the best use of your time:

Before the Interview

- Consider your purpose, and shape your questions accordingly.
- Select your interviewee with care, and contact that person for an appointment.

Writing Responsibly / Conducting Interviews Fairly

- To project professionalism, show up for the interview on time and prepared.
- Ask only for information that your expert alone could provide, not information you could easily gather on your own.
- Tell the interviewee up front how you will use the information you gather, and get their written consent.
- Ask for permission to record the interview, and confirm any quotations you may want to use.
- Offer the interviewee an opportunity to review your notes or your draft document. (You need not change your notes or document in response, but you should acknowledge any difference of opinion.)

to SELF

- Conduct background research on the topic and on the person whom you are interviewing, and develop 10–15 open-ended questions. (Ask, "How would you rate the job the president of the Student Senate is doing, and why?" *not*, "Is the president of the Student Senate doing a good job?") Avoid questions that prompt an interviewee to provide a particular answer. (Ask, "How do you think the stock market will react in the coming year, and why?" *not*, "How far will the stock market fall in the coming year?")

During the Interview

- Set your interviewee at ease, but remain politely neutral.
- Use your prepared questions and listen carefully to the answers; also listen for surprises and ask follow-up questions.
- Take extensive notes or, if permitted, record the interview.
- Avoid interrupting the interviewee or talking about yourself.

After the Interview

- Reflect on your notes while the interview is still fresh, recording your thoughts and any additional questions you would like to ask; then phone or email the interviewee once for follow-up. (Multiple follow-up messages are likely to annoy.)
- Make a transcript of the interview, and send a copy to your interviewee for comment or confirmation.
- Send a thank-you note within 24 hours of your interview, and then send the interviewee a copy of your finished project with a note of appreciation.

Writing Responsibly — Avoiding Manipulation and Bias in Observations

- Ask permission to observe organized groups. Let the group's leader decide whether all should be informed, but reveal your purpose if asked.
- Resist manipulating the site or the community to get the results you want.
- Move around the scene to change your perspective.
- Provide groups the opportunity to read and respond to your study before you submit it. (You need not change your report, but you should acknowledge differences of opinion.)
- Alert your readers to the limitations of your study or to ways your own experiences and perspectives may have influenced your observations.

to TOPIC

2. Observational studies

Observational studies are common in the social sciences, particularly in psychology, sociology, and anthropology. Consider the following before beginning an observational study:

- **Your hypothesis.** What do you expect to learn? You can refine your hypothesis as your observations continue, but starting out with a hypothesis will help guide your observations and note taking.

> **More about**
> Devising a hypothesis, 226–27

- **Your role.** Will you participate in the group or observe the group from outside? The role you play will influence your perspective and affect your observations. Consider the steps you can take to minimize bias.

- **Your methods.** Establish categories for the observations you expect, and adjust them in response to your observations. Make notes immediately after a research session rather than during it, so your presence will be less obtrusive.

3. Surveys

Surveys are used frequently in politics and marketing but are useful in many types of research to assess beliefs, opinions, and behavior. When developing a survey, consider these issues:

- **Your hypothesis.** What do you expect to learn from your survey?
- **Your target population.** What group will you reach, and how will you contact them? Strive to include a broad and representative range of respondents.
- **Your survey.** What type of questions will you ask, how many questions will you include, and how will you administer the survey?

Tech Online Surveys

Web-based survey tools allow you to conduct surveys online. The following are among the most popular:

- Google Docs
- SurveyMonkey
- SurveyGizmo
- Zoomerang

Each allows users to create and send out a basic survey to a limited number of respondents for free.

You might also consider conducting your survey with the help of social media such as *Facebook* or *Twitter*.

Most surveys offer true-false, yes-no, and multiple-choice questions because these are easier to tabulate. Still, a few open-ended questions may deepen your sense of the respondents' feelings, and quotations can be used in your project. Whatever type of questions you ask, be sure your answer options are fair and that they offer an adequate range of choices. Because respondents are not likely to spend more than a few minutes answering questions, surveys should be brief: one to two pages is a reasonable limit.

> ### Writing Responsibly
> **Reporting Results Fairly**
>
> As you integrate the results of your field research into your larger project, explain how you chose your research participants, how many you invited, and how many agreed to participate. Do not, however, name or indirectly identify your participants unless they have agreed to their identity being made public.
>
> When you quote from an interview or survey, indicate how typical the quotation is. Did you choose it just because it supports your thesis, or is it typical of the majority of responses?
>
> *to AUDIENCE*

14 Evaluating Information

IN THIS CHAPTER

a. Evaluating for relevance, reliability, and diversity, 263

b. Misinformation, disinformation, and fake news, 270

c. Evaluating digital texts: websites, blogs, wikis, discussion forums, and social media, 271

d. Evaluating visual sources, 274

This young bald eagle had a successful hunt for its dinner and now holds the fish firmly as it flies to its dining room. Yet the eagle is inspecting the fish as it flies: measuring it? Making sure it has a good grip on the fish? Deciding whether the fish is one meal or two? Whatever its purpose, the eagle demonstrates that finding materials (think of your research sources as your fish!) isn't enough; one must evaluate them carefully, too.

Brian E. Kushner/Shutterstock

14a Evaluating for Relevance, Reliability, and Diversity

Evaluating sources means assessing how *relevant*, or useful, a source is to your research and determining the source's *reliability*—how much you can believe it.

1. Relevance

The first step in source evaluation is to determine its relevance—its usefulness to your research. This step does not require you to read the entire source; a good preview should be enough:

- **Check the publication date.** Recently published works are most likely to be of the greatest relevance, as they will probably provide the most up-to-date information. Be alert, though, to classics; they contain information or ideas on

abstract A summary of the text's main claims and most important supporting evidence

> **More about**
> Previewing a text, 113–14
> Finding the copyright date, 330–33 (Documentation Matters tutorial preceding ch. 18)
> Primary versus secondary sources, 489–91

which researchers still rely. Classics will be cited frequently by other reliable sources; your instructor can also help you identify them.

- **Read the abstract, foreword, introduction, or lead** (first paragraph in a newspaper article). These usually provide a summary, overview, or key facts discussed in detail in the source.

- **Read the headings and subheadings.** These will provide an outline of the source. If the source is a book, its table of contents may provide an outline of the book.

- **Scan figures and illustrations.** These may signal important ideas and explain complex processes.

- **Read the conclusion.** The conclusion (the last few paragraphs in a periodical article or final chapter of a book) often reiterates the central idea and argument, important questions, and major findings.

- **Consult the index.** Check it for key terms in your research.

When you have finished your preview, put the current version of your research question in front of you and ask these questions:

- Does the source provide background information that will help you understand the issues involved in your research?

- Does the source provide evidence for the hypothesis in your current version of your research question?

- Does the source complicate or contradict your hypothesis? If so, don't rule it out; it can help you explain the whole scene of your research, and it may help you reconsider or revise your hypothesis.

- Does the source offer a detailed exploration of the debates about your issue, or does it offer just basic facts or a condensed overview? You may need some brief overviews to gain a preliminary understanding of the issues, but you cannot write an insightful argument based only on simplified sources.

- Is the source a report of others' research? The summaries of scientific research that are published in magazines and newspapers are written for a general audience and written by journalists who are usually themselves not experts on the topic. You will benefit from reading such introductions, but your project and your audience will benefit from your tracking down the research report that the journalist is working from. Make that research report, not the journalist's account of it, the focus of your attention.

2. Reliability

How reliable is your source; how much can you and your audience trust it? Before you can make this judgment, you need to read the source carefully. If you have done the previewing described in the advice above for determining relevance, you are likely to find this whole-text reading much quicker, with much greater comprehension, than if you just started reading the source "cold," with no prior understanding of its claims and materials. After you have read the whole text, go through the following steps to determine its reliability. Keep in mind that no source will pass all these tests. Judging reliability is instead a matter of weighing the answers to your reliability tests, figuring out *how much*, not "whether," you can trust the source:

- **How did you find the source?** Sources located through your college library are more likely to be reliable than are sources located through a *Google* search because library sources are selected in consultation with subject-matter experts, in response to reviews, or after considering where the source was published. A source published solely on the web (unless in a scholarly journal published online) is not likely to have been subjected to the same level of scrutiny. *Google* searches will return such sites, but library databases will not. Finding a source on a library database is not a guarantee of reliability, but it is one indicator. In contrast, a clickbait source—an ad masquerading as a news story about how to lose

---

Quick Reference | Judging Reliability

Your path to the source. Did you locate the source on an open *Google* search, through a library database, or by some other means?

Scholarly work. Was the source published in a scholarly journal or book, or in a popular magazine, newspaper, or book?

Peer review. Was the source vetted by an editorial board or peer reviewers?

Citations. Does the text cite sources, so that you can locate them yourself?

Presentation. Is the text clearly written, well organized, and carefully edited and proofread?

Expertise. Is the author an authority on the subject?

Purpose. Is the purpose of the source to inform its audience, or is it to persuade them to buy a product? Will the author or publisher have a vested interest in the topic?

Objectivity. Do tone, logic, quality of the evidence, and coverage of the opposition suggest that the source is unbiased?

Evidence. Does the source offer sound evidence for its claims?

Counterevidence. Does the source consider other points of view and discuss them fairly?

Scholarly reception. How many others are using the source, and how do they respond to it?

15 pounds in 1 day or about 10 reasons Nick Jonas should be secretary of state—is unlikely to pass any reliability tests.

- **Is it a scholarly source?** The intended audience of a source significantly affects the reliability of the source. A *scholarly source* is intended for an audience of experts on the topic. Although it may be challenging for you to read, it will contain the most detailed, insightful information that is well worth your effort. Scholarly sources include articles published in academic journals and books published by scholarly presses. They usually include citations to other sources and full bibliographic information, either in notes or in a bibliography. Scholarly sources include *College English, The Journal of American History, The Lancet, Nature,* and *Transgender Studies Quarterly*.

    In contrast, articles in magazines and books published by the *popular press* are selected for a general audience and are intended to raise enough interest to inspire a large number of people to read the publication. Often these articles include advertisements that sometimes accompany an "objective" story. Popular sources may be fact-checked, but they are seldom reviewed by experts. Popular sources include *Essence, The New York Times, Newsweek, People,* and *Vanity Fair*.

    Between scholarly and popular sources are intellectual periodicals such as the *Chronicle of Higher Education, The New Yorker,* and *Scientific American*. They have most of the characteristics of the popular press but are aimed specifically at educated audiences who wish to stay well informed. Articles in such periodicals are typically much longer and more detailed than those in the general popular press. Although they are not peer reviewed and usually do not include citations or a bibliography, articles in such periodicals are usually carefully prepared and fact-checked and are generally more reliable than those in the popular press.

- **Is the source peer reviewed?** The most reliable indicator of source reliability is *peer review*. Before they are published, scholarly sources are sent for review to one or more experts in the field who check the accuracy and importance of the source and make recommendations about its publication. These expert reviewers ensure that the source meets the ethical standards of the discipline, that its methods are sound, and that it contributes to the scholarly conversation in the field. On the home page of a peer-reviewed periodical, you will find the words *peer review* or *editorial board*. If the source is published by a university press, it will be peer reviewed, but not all peer-reviewed sources are published by university presses.

> **More about**
> Biographical reference works, 241

Quick Reference: Typical Characteristics of Scholarly and Popular Sources

Scholarly

- Articles are written by scholars, specialists, researchers
- Use technical terminology
- Tend to be long—typically, ten pages or more
- Include citations in the text and a list of references
- Are reviewed by other scholars before publication
- Acknowledge any conflicts of interest (such as research support from a pharmaceutical company)
- Generally look serious; unlikely to include color photographs, but may include charts, graphs, and tables
- Published by professional organizations

Popular

- Articles are written by journalists or professional writers
- Avoid technical terminology
- Tend to be brief—as little as one or two pages
- Seldom include citations or a list of references
- Generally fact-checked but not reviewed by panel of experts
- Less likely to acknowledge potential conflicts of interest
- Often published on glossy paper with eye-catching color images
- Published by commercial companies

Writing Responsibly: Keeping an Open, Inquiring Mind

Read sources with an open mind, use reliable sources, avoid exaggerated claims and logical fallacies, and criticize unreasonable or poorly supported conclusions but not the people who hold them. As a researcher, you have a responsibility to avoid bias. Consider all sides of an argument, especially those that challenge the positions you hold. Use difficult sources, too: Do not reject a source because it is written for a more expert audience than you. Find the time to study it carefully and gain at least a provisional understanding of it.

to TOPIC

Peer review is an excellent indicator, but not a foolproof test of reliability. Unfortunately, research has revealed that some unscrupulous "scholarly" journals have faked peer review, instead rushing submissions to publication with no peer review whatsoever. Moreover, some journals send submissions for peer review to scholars with no particular expertise in the topic or methods of the submitted article. Such problems are in the minority, but the fact that they exist means researchers cannot use peer review as an absolute guarantee of source reliability.

- **Does the text cite its sources?** Most scholarly articles and books and some popular books will include a bibliography, and some journal databases will list the article's sources in the citation.

> **More about**
> Tone, 20–21, 159, 599, 604–6, 607
> Opinion versus belief, 146–47
> Types of evidence, 45–47
> Bias, 600–3

> **More about**
> Exploratory arguments, 144–45
> Reasoning logically, 146–49
> Using evidence as support, 45–47, 64–68
> Citing sources, 334–96 (MLA style, ch. 18), 397–438 (APA style, ch. 19), 439–69 (*Chicago* style, ch. 20), 470–84 (CSE style, ch. 21)
> Choosing a citation style, 491, 511–12

Reputable newspapers and magazines will check a writer's sources, even though they often go unnamed, identified only as a "White House source" or a "source close to the investigation."

- **What sources does the text cite?** In US academic writing, sources written by US white men are cited disproportionately to those written by women, international writers, and writers of color. This trend creates an echo chamber that excludes diverse points of view. Deep evaluation of a source should include attention to how broad is the range of voices that contributes to knowledge-building in the source.

- **Is the source well written and edited?** Has the writer approached the task with a sense of responsibility—by writing, organizing, editing, and proofreading the material carefully? Is the page design easy to follow? Are the visuals appropriate to the audience and purpose and free from manipulation or distortion?

- **Is the author an expert on the topic?** Does the author have advanced training in the subject? You can determine this by reading about the author in a biographical reference work, by finding other works the author has published, by considering the author's academic background, by searching the author's name online, or by determining whether the author has been cited in the footnotes or bibliographies of other reliable sources.

- **Does the author or publisher have a vested interest?** How does the author stand to benefit from the work? Most authors will benefit in some way: through sales of the book or through the prestige of publishing. But consider whether the author or publisher will benefit in some other way: Is the source promoting a product or process from which its author will benefit financially? Will the author or publisher gain adherents to a political position? Check the author's or publisher's website for advertisements and to see whether a mission statement reveals an agenda. The author's or publisher's social media feeds may also offer clues. If you discover the author holds very different political, religious, or cultural views than your own, don't immediately reject the source. Read it carefully, critically, and fairly.

- **Does the tone seem objective?** Does the source have an objective tone, make reasonable claims supported by logical evidence, include counterevidence, and treat it with respect? Authors may care deeply and write passionately about their subject, but if they characterize groups unfairly or offensively or treat the individuals in a group as if they are all the same, then you should suspect bias.

Writing Responsibly — Online Plagiarism

The ease with which users can cut and paste information from one site into another means you must be wary of online sites, especially if they are self-sponsored. Unreliable sites frequently copy directly from other, more reliable sites. If you suspect plagiarism, copy a passage and paste it into a search engine's search box. Do any of your hits use the same (or very similar) language? The best way to avoid using material plagiarized from another site is to evaluate sites carefully for reliability.

to SELF

- **How do other scholars respond to the source?** Using a *citation index* can reveal how others have responded to the source. You can turn to *Google Scholar* or to library databases such as *Web of Science, Proquest,* and *Scopus* for good citation indexes, and their "help" menus will show you how to navigate them (see Figure 14.1). Citation indexes can help you answer questions such as these: Are other scholars using your source as evidence for their own claims? Are they arguing with it? Citation indexes can also reveal how many scholars have cited the source, which can give you an idea of its influence. However, very recent sources, from the previous three years, may not yet have many citations. The same is true of very narrowly focused topics: an article on pandemics is likely to have a much wider audience than will one about cultivating hostas in New England backyards.

3. Diversity

In addition to the necessity of evaluating sources for relevance and reliability, researchers today are often encouraged and even expected to evaluate their sources for diversity. Diversity evaluation requires expansive, creative thinking from researchers as they decide what "diversity" means for their project.

As you find and evaluate your sources, pay attention to who is writing and who is publishing them. Do a little research on the authors and publishers themselves. Your objective should be to gather a real range of ideas, standpoints, and perspectives to help you answer your research question.

Diversity evaluation involves not just single sources but also the interaction among them: when you look at your growing list of sources, are they all being written from similar perspectives or by similar people? Sometimes diversity evaluation intersects with issues of counterevidence and confirmation bias: have you perhaps unconsciously chosen nondiverse sources because they all agree with what you already believe?

Learn a little about the authors of your sources, paying attention to categories such as gender, race, nationality, disability, and politics. As you gather

> **More about**
> Confirmation and confirmation bias, 157–58, 274
> Counterevidence, 156–58

author information, think critically about how hard it is to "know" what another person's gender, race, nationality, disability, religion might be. But if you do a bit of quick research on your authors, you should be able to get a general sense of who they are and how similar to or different from each other they are. If you find that all your sources tick the same box, consider researching more deeply, searching for a wider range of positions or perspectives on your topic.

For your particular research project, think about other possible forms of diversity. If you are working on a politically oriented topic, for example, what range of perspectives is represented in your sources? If your research is about a particular group of people, whose voices are represented in your sources? Are they all from outside the group, or are some of these sources written by members of the group you are studying? Ask yourself these questions:

- **What kinds of evidence does the source offer for its claims?** Are the rhetorical appeals appropriate for the audience and purpose? Is the author depending too much on their own authority? Is the author making generalized claims based only on emotional or anecdotal evidence? Is the author offering enough factual evidence for generalized claims?

- **Does the source consider other points of view?** Does the source ignore or dismiss counterevidence? Or does the source consider multiple points of view on a complex issue and then explain why the author believes or advocates one of those points of view?

14b Misinformation, Disinformation, and Fake News

Researchers working online today must be alert to the possibility of fake news, which are stories containing inaccuracies or lies. Researchers Whitney Phillips and Ryan Milner suggest we think of "polluted information" instead of "fake news."* *Polluted information* may take the form of *misinformation*—inaccuracies posted by well-meaning people who mistakenly believe they are correct. Or it may take the form of *disinformation*—deliberate lies or distortions of the facts. Simply choosing well-respected sources such as *The Los Angeles Times* or *Harper's* magazine is not enough because misinformation may be disguised to look as if it comes from a reputable publisher. If a source fails any of the following tests, you should reject it:

- If the source comes to you through social media, open it up on the web. Explore the website: Is it a full news source, with tabs leading you to a variety of topics, or does it have just a few sensational stories?

---
* Phillips, Whitney, and Ryan M. Milner. *You Are Here: A Field Guide for Navigating Polluted Information.* MIT Press, 2021.

- If the source appears to be published by a respected source like *Time* magazine or *The Washington Post*, open a new tab on your browser, search for that publication, and open its website. Now compare the website URL with the URL of the article you have found. If they are altogether different, the source is fake. If extra characters precede the URL of the source, it is fake. If you can't find your source on the publisher's website, it is fake.

- Evaluate whether the information in the source actually provides evidence for the claim in the headline. If it doesn't, the source is **clickbait**, designed to accumulate "hits" rather than to inform readers.

- Conduct a fact check. Do other reputable sources offer the same information? Sometimes one publisher has a "scoop" before any of the others, but its advantage won't last for long: News circulates quickly online.

Don't rely on a source just because it has been posted by someone you respect. Smart people can be deceived by polluted information, so you must always verify sources for yourself. Don't accept a source just because it says something you want to hear, something you want to be true. Confirm that all your sources are real. Websites such as *FactCheck.org, Politifact.com, OpenSecrets.org, Snopes.com, TruthOrFiction.com,* and *HoaxSlayer.com* are your best friends in this task.

14c Evaluating Digital Texts: Websites, Blogs, Wikis, Discussion Forums, and Social Media

Anyone can create a website, post a blog, or contribute to an open wiki or discussion forum. This freedom makes the web exciting, but it also means researchers should evaluate online sources with special care. In addition to the general criteria listed above, consider these factors when evaluating websites:

> *More about*
> Websites, 203–10, 245
> Interactive media, 210–11, 245

URL A site's **URL** (short for *universal resource locator,* its web address) appears at the top of the browser window (Figure 14.1). Every item on the web has a URL, and all URLs end with an extension, or *domain,* that indicates the type of site it is. The most common domains are these:

- **.com** (commercial): sites hosted by businesses
- **.edu** (educational): sites sponsored by colleges and universities
- **.gov** (governmental): sites sponsored by some branch of federal, state, or local government

Research Matters • Evaluating Information

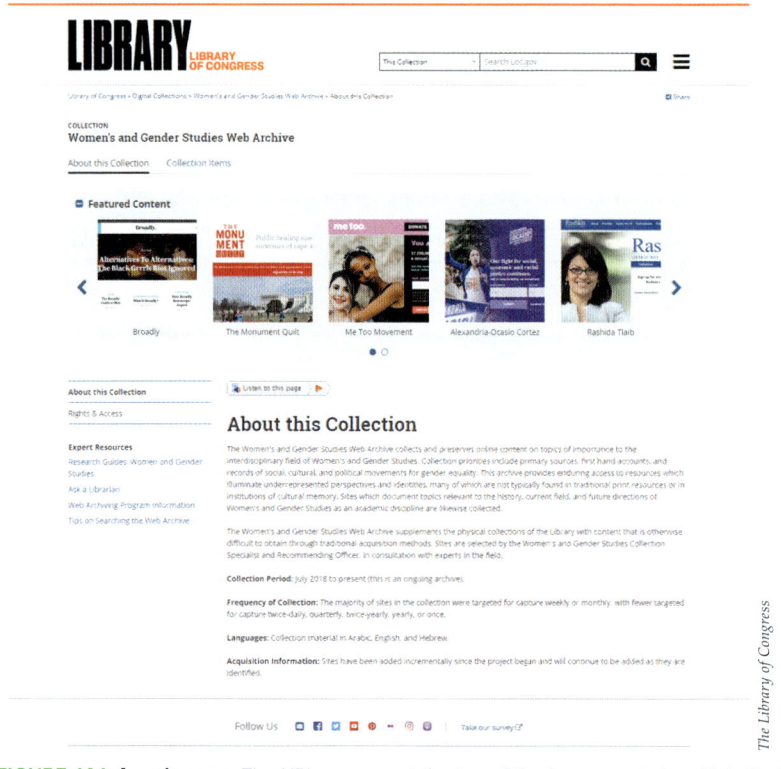

FIGURE 14.1 **A web page** The URL appears at the top of the browser window. Note that the Library of Congress's website indicates the sponsoring organization prominently and provides links to pages providing information about the organization and site.

The Library of Congress

- **.net** (network): typically, sites sponsored by businesses selling internet infrastructure services (such as internet providers) but also sometimes chosen by businesses that want to appear technologically sophisticated or organizations that want to indicate that they are part of a network

- **.org** (organization): usually sites sponsored by nonprofit groups (though sometimes the nonprofit status of these groups may be questionable)

Sites featuring .org, .gov, and .edu domains indicate some connection to an educational, governmental, or nonprofit organization, but your evaluation of a

> **Tech — Identifying Personal Websites**
>
> A URL that includes a personal name (jsmith) plus a tilde (~) or percent sign (%) or words like "users" or "members" is likely to be personal (not sponsored by a larger organization). Before using information from a personal site, investigate the author's credentials carefully.

website should never end with its URL. Businesses usually offer information intended to sell products or services, yet commercial sites can nevertheless be highly informative. A site ending in .edu may just as easily have been constructed and posted by a student as by an expert, and much of the information posted on university websites is designed to entice new students and is thus a type of advertising. Nonprofit organizations are not trying to sell a product, but they are usually seeking support. Government sites, too, while predictably a source of highly reliable information, are unlikely to publish information that will undermine the administration's agenda. The reliability of information from all sites (indeed, all texts, whether in print or online) must be evaluated with care.

Sponsor As with any publication, the credentials of a website's creator are an important factor in assessing reliability, but websites frequently lack an identified author. Instead, they have *sponsors*—corporations, agencies, and organizations that are responsible for creating content and making it available. To determine who sponsors a site, jump to the home page, link to pages called "About" or "Contact us," or click on the website's logo (see Figure 14.1). Often, deleting the portion of the URL following the domain (.com, .edu, .org) will take you to the home page. If the website yields little information, try conducting a web search on the site's name; you might even try including the word "scam" or "fraud" in that search. You can also go to the *WhoIs* site (whois.net) to search for registration and history information about your website.

Open or moderated? The reliability of online discussion forums depends in large part on their contributors. Sources to which anyone can contribute should be screened carefully; nonexpert enthusiasts can inadvertently post inaccurate misinformation, and people can deliberately post distorted disinformation. For example, *Wikipedia* once had to block certain web addresses on Capitol Hill to prevent congressional staffers from altering—and falsifying—the biographies of their bosses or their bosses' political opponents.

Wikis and web forums in which prospective contributors are screened by the site's owner, or *moderator,* are more likely to be reliable. The wiki *Encyclopedia of Life,* for example, promises to provide reliable information because it will be created and moderated by a consortium of highly regarded scientific institutions. Some scholars are even writing wiki textbooks to which they invite other experts to contribute.

Social media Evaluating information derived from social media requires special care. As an information source, social media have several benefits, among them speed: news travels fastest on social media. For that reason, most mainstream news outlets maintain social media feeds to extend the circulation of their message. Speed comes at a cost, though: in their haste to "break" the latest news, even the most reliable news outlets can occasionally print inaccuracies or even misinformation. Especially when your information comes from social media, verify it. Check to see if others have picked up and verified the story. When one source posts breaking news, the others will quickly pick it up and make sure it's accurate. When in doubt, always go to a news validator like *Snopes.com* or *FactChecker.com*.

If your social media source is not a reputable organization or individual, be especially wary. What evidence is being offered for the claim? Especially if the social media post is saying something that affirms what you already believe, you must take great care. The danger here is called *confirmation bias*: We are all susceptible to information that affirms our beliefs, so it is especially important to be skeptical of such information and to conduct all the reliability tests that you would for other online information.

14d Evaluating Visual Sources

> *More about*
> Visual arguments,
> 144, 146, 151,
> 177, 179, 196–98

Visual texts such as information graphics (tables, graphs, flowcharts) and photographs convey their messages powerfully yet sometimes so subtly that uncritical viewers may accept their claims without even realizing that a claim is being made. As with printed texts, researchers need to evaluate visual texts carefully to determine whether the source is both relevant and reliable. To determine relevance and reliability, consider the following:

- What are the credentials of the visual's creator?
- How authoritative is the source in which the visual appeared?
- On what date was the image created or the photograph taken?
- What purpose(s) does the visual serve? Is it to entertain, to inform, or to persuade?
- Who is its intended audience?
- How accurate are the title, headings, labels, and any other text that appears with the visual? How does the text influence how you "read" the visual? How relevant is the visual to the accompanying text?

> *More about*
> Purpose, 15–17
> Avoiding
>   distortion,
>   manipulation,
>   83, 154–55

- What is in the foreground and background, and what is your eye drawn to?
- To what social, ethnic, political, or national groups do the creator of the visual and the subjects depicted in the visual belong, and is this relevant?
- What emotions does the visual depict? What emotions does it elicit from you or other viewers?
- Has the visual been manipulated or cropped to omit or distort information? (See Figure 14.3.)

1. Information graphics

In addition to the questions above, which apply to all visuals, information graphics such as charts, graphs, and tables require additional considerations:

- What do the data represent?
- What relationships does the graphic show?
- How up-to-date is the information in the graphic?
- Are the data complete? Are there any gaps in years covered or groups represented?
- Are the data presented fairly?
- Is the relation of the pie slices in a pie chart, lines in a line graph, or bars in a bar chart to the data they represent clear and consistent?
- Is the source of the data unbiased?

2. Memes

A meme is a thematic cultural artifact that is widely shared online, usually through social media; a meme can be a phrase or a captioned image or video that is modified creatively, often for comic or satirical effect (see Figure 14.2), though sometimes as a way to spread negative and even hateful messages. Memes are valuable for demonstrating what sorts of ideas and social commentary exist in contemporary life. They reveal (for better or worse) the attitudes and beliefs of creators who are seldom identified, including those who imitate, revise, and amplify a meme because they find it amusing or instructive.

While memes may reflect the thinking, humor, and anxieties of the day, perhaps even entertaining, informing, and persuading viewers, memes are not themselves reliable sources about their topic. Instead, they are interesting sources about people's attitudes, not about the topic itself.

Should you refer to a meme as a reliable source in your paper? No. However, you may want to present a meme as an item for analysis. For example, if you were writing a paper about social responses to the COVID-19 pandemic, you might include a meme on the topic and then annotate and apply rhetorical analysis to it.

> **More about**
> Memes. Memes can be cruel in their treatment of their topic, committing a range of logical fallacies described in chapter 8.

FIGURE 14.2 The "Grumpy Cat" meme surfaced circa 2012 Various iterations of "Grumpy Cat" portrayed a frowning cat's supposed disapproval and dissatisfaction with various life situations.

FIGURE 14.3 The power of an image Although many Americans knew that President Roosevelt had been partially paralyzed by polio, only two photographs were taken of the President in a wheelchair. Were photographers protecting FDR's privacy, or suppressing important information?

EXERCISE 14.1 Evaluating reliability

Using the criteria discussed in *section a* in this chapter, write a paragraph in which you rate the reliability of the article excerpted below. Explain why you rated the article as you did.

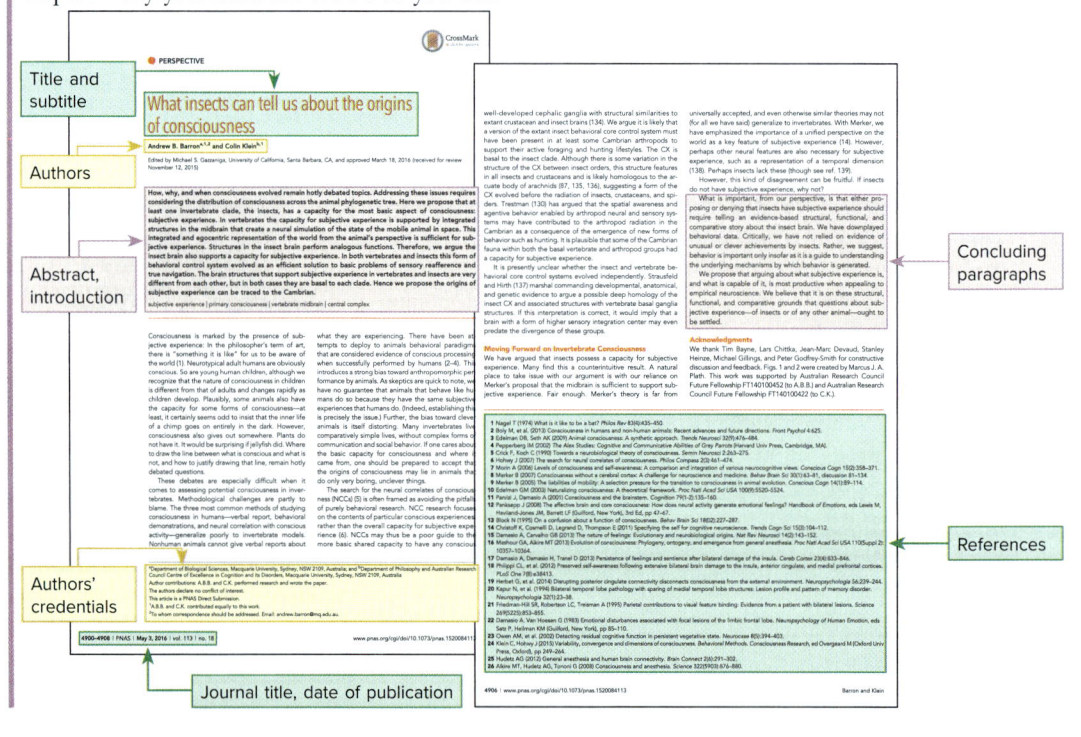

Research Matters • Evaluating Visual Sources

→ EXERCISE 14.2 Evaluating web pages

Using the criteria discussed in *sections 14a* and *14b,* evaluate the two web pages shown on this page. Which would you consider the more reliable source on plagiarism, and why?

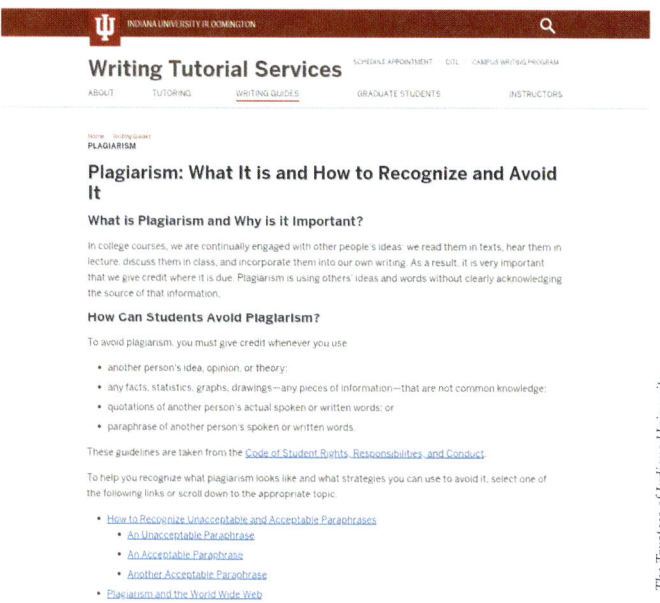

INDIANA UNIVERSITY BLOOMINGTON

Writing Tutorial Services

ABOUT | TUTORING | WRITING GUIDES | GRADUATE STUDENTS | INSTRUCTORS

SCHEDULE APPOINTMENT | CITL | CAMPUS WRITING PROGRAM

Home › Writing Guides
PLAGIARISM

Plagiarism: What It is and How to Recognize and Avoid It

What is Plagiarism and Why is it Important?

In college courses, we are continually engaged with other people's ideas: we read them in texts, hear them in lecture, discuss them in class, and incorporate them into our own writing. As a result, it is very important that we give credit where it is due. Plagiarism is using others' ideas and words without clearly acknowledging the source of that information.

How Can Students Avoid Plagiarism?

To avoid plagiarism, you must give credit whenever you use

- another person's idea, opinion, or theory;
- any facts, statistics, graphs, drawings—any pieces of information—that are not common knowledge;
- quotations of another person's actual spoken or written words; or
- paraphrase of another person's spoken or written words.

These guidelines are taken from the Code of Student Rights, Responsibilities, and Conduct.

To help you recognize what plagiarism looks like and what strategies you can use to avoid it, select one of the following links or scroll down to the appropriate topic:

- How to Recognize Unacceptable and Acceptable Paraphrases
  - An Unacceptable Paraphrase
  - An Acceptable Paraphrase
  - Another Acceptable Paraphrase
- Plagiarism and the World Wide Web
- Strategies for Avoiding Plagiarism
- Terms You Need to Know (or What is Common K

How to Recognize Unacceptable and

Here's the ORIGINAL text, from page 1 of *Lizzie Bord*
Joyce Williams et al.:

The rise of industry, the growth of cities, and the expa
developments of late nineteenth century American hi
a feature of the American landscape in the East, they
provided jobs for a rising tide of immigrants. With ind
Fall River, Massachusetts, where the Bordens lived) w
commerce and trade.

Here's an UNACCEPTABLE paraphrase that is **plagia**

The increase of industry, the growth of cities, and the
nineteenth century America. As steam-driven companies b
they changed farm hands into factory workers and provid
feed the growth of large cities like Fall River where t
and trade as well as production.

The Trustees of Indiana University

---

p.org

Understanding Plagiarism
Preventing Plagiarism
Teaching about Plagiarism
Plagiarism Checking
Plagiarism Research
Plagiarism Policy

Article

What is Plagiarism?

Published May 18, 2017

Many people think of plagiarism as copying another's work or borrowing someone else's original ideas. But terms like "copying" and "borrowing" can disguise the seriousness of the offense:

According to the Merriam-Webster online dictionary, to "plagiarize" means:

- to steal and pass off (the ideas or words of another) as one's own
- to use (another's production) without crediting the source
- to commit literary theft
- to present as new and original an idea or product derived from an existing source

In other words, plagiarism is an act of fraud. It involves both stealing someone else's work and lying about it afterward.

But can words and ideas really be stolen?

According to U.S. law, the answer is yes. The expression of original ideas is considered intellectual property and is protected by copyright laws, just like original inventions. Almost all forms of expression fall under copyright protection as long as they are recorded in some way (such as a book or a computer file).

All of the following are considered plagiarism:

- turning in someone else's work as your own
- copying words or ideas from someone else without giving credit
- failing to put a quotation in quotation marks

Plagiarism.org

→ EXERCISE 14.3 Evaluating a graph

Using the criteria discussed in *section 14c*, write a paragraph evaluating the graph below. Be sure to support your assessment with specific evidence.

PINCHED FOR TIME: MORE WOMEN THAN MEN
Percentage of Americans Who Always Feel Rushed

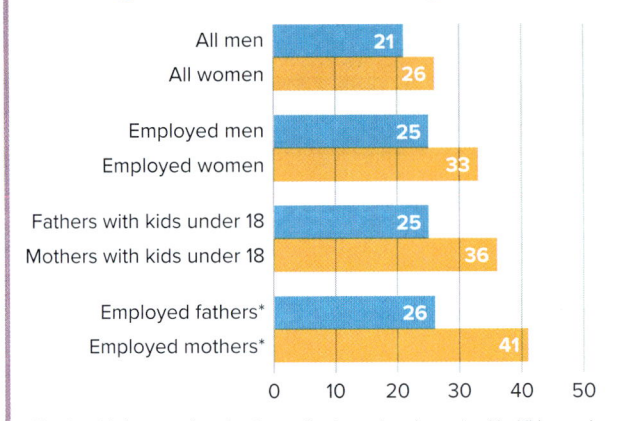

All men	21
All women	26
Employed men	25
Employed women	33
Fathers with kids under 18	25
Mothers with kids under 18	36
Employed fathers*	26
Employed mothers*	41

*Employed fathers, employed mothers refers to employed parents with children under age 18. Employed does not include people who identify as retired but also work for pay.
Source: Pew Research Center

Make It Your Own

Using the criteria in this chapter, write a paragraph evaluating three sources in the working bibliography that you began in the Make It Your Own exercise in chapter 12, page 236, or that you found for a research project in this or another class.

Work Together

In small groups, discuss your evaluations from Exercises 14.1, 14.2, and 14.3. Where do you agree or disagree in your evaluations, and why?

Text Credit

Pg. 276: Barron, Andrew B. and Klein, Colin, "What Insects Can Tell Us About the Origin as of Consciousness," *Proceedings of the National Academy of Sciences,* May 3, 2016, Vol 113, No. 18. Copyright © 2016 National Academy of Sciences. Used with permission.

15 Overcoming Fear of Plagiarizing: Paraphrase, Summary, and Rhetorical Note-Taking

IN THIS CHAPTER

a. Researching rhetorically, 280

b. Understanding plagiarism, 280

c. Taking notes rhetorically, 286

d. Citing accurately, 287; Writing Responsibly Blending voices in your text, 290

e. Paraphrasing elegantly, 292

f. Summarizing eloquently, 295

g. Quoting strategically, 297; Writing Responsibly Acknowledging indirect sources, 300

Student Models
Summary of a Source, 296; Reading Note: Integrating Borrowed Ideas and Words, 299

> **citation** The acknowledgment of sources in the body of a research project

Krista Kennedy

At one time it was commonplace for people to grow their own food and "can" it in glass jars. The practice is still widespread, though not at the scale of 100 years ago. In this contemporary photo of home-canned food, each jar has a white label on the lid. These labels tell the user what is in the jar and when it was canned. Growing one's own tomatoes, cooking homemade tomato sauce, and canning it is a memorable experience. Yet memory fails. When was that sauce canned, and what ingredients are in there? Thus, the labels are essential.

Imagine conducting your research using similar labels. With each source you encounter, you put it on a list—a "shelf"—and on the individual "jar," you put a label that tells you what the source is, where you found it, and what use you think you might make of it. As a result, your research process will be much less chaotic. You will have good records to help you remember what you have and why. And when you compose your research project, you will be able to use the information on your "labels" to show your audience what that process was. And you will have protected yourself from inadvertent plagiarism.

Plagiarism. The word strikes fear in the hearts of students, instructors, and writers throughout the world. Everyone fears they might plagiarize accidentally and then be judged and punished in life-altering ways. Many writers report that fear of plagiarism makes them unwilling to paraphrase material from their sources. Some students put a *citation* at the end of every sentence that contains ideas from a source in an attempt to protect themselves from charges of plagiarism. With all those citations cluttering up

> **documentation** Information in a reference list (APA), list of works cited (MLA), footnote, or bibliography (*Chicago* style), that allows readers to locate the sources cited in the text.

the paragraphs, the result can be nearly unreadable. (Note that each citation should correspond with *documentation* at the end of the paper. These entries appear in a works cited or reference list.) Meanwhile, instructors fear that their students might be cheating, that they might be deceptively claiming to have written something that actually came from a concealed source.

Plagiarism is a problem when it happens, but it is also a problem when the fear of it prevents writers from enjoying the challenges, discoveries, and excitement of researching and writing from sources. This chapter is intended to help you understand what plagiarism is. It is also intended to help you avoid it. Most of all, it is intended to help you feel confident when you write from sources, so that you can derive actual pleasure from the experience.

15a Researching Rhetorically

Ideally, you write from sources so that avoiding plagiarism isn't even an issue. Writing from sources can be a way of expanding your brain, expanding your world. Writing from sources is a conversation in which you are in charge but in which you are also in dialogue with what you are reading in those sources. Writing from sources is a deeply social act, one that can put you in a real conversation not only with your sources but with your audience as well.

Your sources are more than jars on a shelf. They are ideas and arguments written by humans. Approach your writing as a collaboration, a conversation, with those humans. In this chapter and throughout this book you will find advice on how to make that collaborative conversation visible to your audience and how to make your audience part of the conversation, as well. Instead of looking for "killer quotes" in your sources, look for the voices in them, and invite those voices into your writing.

15b Understanding Plagiarism

Are you a burglar stealing those jars of canned goods, trying to sneak away undetected? Or are you a cook drawing from various jars to create new dishes? Problems of plagiarism occur when writing from sources is less a creative exploration than a desperate raid.

The term *plagiarism* refers to a variety of missteps and transgressions. The first of these involves intentional misdeeds by the writer, but the other four can happen accidentally. Nevertheless, many college policies state that the writer's intentions are not part of adjudicating cases of plagiarism.

If portions of work you submit to a college class are classified as plagiarism, it may not matter whether you did it intentionally. For this reason, you need to take responsibility for knowing what counts as plagiarism.

1. Ghostwriting and contract cheating

In many situations, submitting work under one's own name that someone else composed is considered ethical. Many politicians, corporate executives, and public figures are called upon to deliver written texts and speeches that they do not have time to write themselves. For them, hiring a *ghostwriter* (often called a speechwriter) is an acceptable practice. The person for whom the text was written gets the credit as "author," while the ghostwriter is paid for the actual writing. In the best-case scenario, the credited author provides the ghostwriter with ideas and material for the text. Once the text is drafted, the credited author revises it to be sure it matches their intentions.

Regardless of how the process is conducted, it is never acceptable for students to submit work that has been written by someone else—neither one's mother, one's roommate, someone hired for the task, nor a writer hired by a website selling "plagiarism-free" term papers. ***Contract cheating,*** in which a student hires another person to take an entire course in the student's name, can be seen as an extended form of illicit ghostwriting. In a college setting, ghostwriting is an extreme form of plagiarism because college assignments are intended to give students experience in writing and are usually counted as part of the final grade in a course. The purpose of the assignment is not for students to produce a text by any means possible; it is for the students to *learn* through the experience of producing the text themselves. Having someone else do the writing prevents that learning.

Three motivations explain most incidents of college ghostwriting and contract cheating: The credited author is desperately behind schedule and cannot handle all of their responsibilities. Or the credited author lacks confidence in their expertise and ability to do the assigned work. Or the credited author only wants the credential of having taken the course and has no interest in learning anything from it.

The first of these scenarios explains why this book, along with so many college instructors, emphasizes the need for learning time management skills and techniques. If you nevertheless find yourself unable to complete an assignment on time, talk to the instructor about an extension. Don't hand in a project under your name that someone else wrote, in part or in its entirety.

The second of these scenarios explains why writing centers and learning centers are offered at so many colleges. It also explains why instructors hold office hours. If you lack confidence in your expertise and ability to do assigned work, seek out the support that the course and your college offer to you. Asking for help does not identify you as a weak writer, but rather as a writer who has things to learn. College is the place to do that.

The third of these scenarios is a tragedy. College can at times seem unnecessarily annoying or difficult, and some of the classes you are required to take may seem irrelevant to your plans for the future. Yet you can take charge of your learning. Trust your college to have a reason (beyond sadism) to require you to take courses you might otherwise not choose. Find aspects of each course that *are* useful for you. Find things in the course that you might benefit from knowing. Take responsibility for yourself and your learning, and give your classes a chance.

2. Self-plagiarism

Many college students are surprised, and sometimes outraged, to learn that submitting one's own work to multiple sites (such as multiple publishers or multiple college classes) without informing those sites and gaining their permission is widely considered a form of plagiarism. In your college classes and in any writing you may do for publication, talk with the instructors or publishers beforehand so you know what their policies are and whether you can make multiple submissions of the same work. This advice holds true for entire writing projects, and it is also true for extensive duplication within texts. If you are copying several sentences or paragraphs from a project written for one class, pause before you paste that material into a project for another class. If it is a very short passage, quote yourself using language such as this: "In a blog post for my psychology class last year, I noted that—" and also include your psychology piece in your list of works cited, with your name as author, along with the title of your blog post (and your blog), the class it was submitted to, and the date of submission. If the duplication is substantial, ask your instructor for permission to reuse it. Most instructors are open to the idea that a student might extend work from one class into another, broadening and deepening an inquiry begun elsewhere.

3. Lack of citation

Knowing what and how to cite enables you to communicate to your audience the conversation you are having with your sources. In a sense, citation is a way of showing off how much you have worked and how much you know. In contrast, not knowing what and how to cite puts you at risk of plagiarism; missing or faulty citation accounts for a substantial number of college plagiarism cases. Citation is needed whenever you quote, paraphrase, or summarize a source.

a. What you do have to cite. You must document quotations, paraphrases, summaries, and information that is unlikely to be known by nonexperts:

- **Quotations.** Enclose short quotations in quotation marks, and indent long quotations as a block. Name the author either in a signal phrase ("Professor Jones argues") or in a parenthetical citation, and include the page number. (In some styles, you may include this information in a footnote or an endnote.) Then document the source in your bibliography, references list, or list of works cited.

- **Paraphrases and summaries.** Provide a citation each time you use a source, even when you are not quoting. As with quotations, cite the author and page number in the text, and include full source information in your bibliography, references list, or list of works cited.

- **Ideas and information.** Acknowledge the source of any information or ideas that are *not* common knowledge (see *section 3b below*). As with quotations, paraphrases, and summaries, cite the author and page number in your text and provide full source information in your bibliography, references list, or list of works cited. Information from the internet needs to be cited just as much as information gleaned from a journal article or book.

> **More about**
> Using quotation marks (ch. 51), 834–42
> Using block indention for long quotations, 339, 380–81 (MLA), 426 (APA)
> Citing sources, 334–52 (MLA), 397–407 (APA), 439–57 (*Chicago*), 470–82 (CSE)
> Documenting sources, 352–77 (MLA), 408–25 (APA), 439–57 (*Chicago*), 470–82 (CSE)

b. What you do not have to cite. You do *not* have to cite ***common knowledge*** (unless it is included in a quotation)—even if you learned the information from a source. Common knowledge is general information that is available in a number of different sources and that is considered factual and incontestable. Here are some examples:

Facts

- On average, the Earth is about 93 million miles from the sun.
- Labor organizer "Mother" Jones worked on behalf of the United Mine Workers of America.

Dates

- The spring equinox occurred on March 20 in 2021.
- US women won the right to vote on August 26, 1920, when the Nineteenth Amendment was passed.

> **More about**
> Citing media illustrations, 350, 374–76 (MLA), 422–24 (APA), 456–57 (*Chicago*)

Writing Responsibly — Using Illustrations and Avoiding Plagiarism

The web contains a variety of images, videos, and sound files that you can download to your word processor: A click of the mouse, and they are yours. Or are they? Keep full records of who created them, where you found them, and on what date you downloaded them so that you can cite them fully.

to OTHER WRITERS

Events

- James Earl Ray was convicted of the assassination of civil rights leader Martin Luther King Jr.
- Francis Crick, James Watson, and Maurice Wilkins are credited with discovering the structure of DNA.

Cultural Knowledge

- The composer Wolfgang Amadeus Mozart was a child prodigy.
- Elvis Presley made the song "Hound Dog" a smash hit, although he did not write it.

Everything outside of these categories should be cited in the text of your project and documented in a footnote or in your bibliography, references list, or list of works cited.

4. Lack of quotation marks

Whenever you are using ideas or language from a source, you must cite the source. Whenever you are copying word for word, you *also* need to quote it. Failure to both cite and quote direct copying can raise questions about plagiarism in your writing. A ***quotation*** is someone else's words transcribed exactly, using quotation marks or block indentation to signal that the language is from a source. Quotation marks and block indentation tell your audience when you are switching from your own voice to someone else's.

> The writer frames the quotation with quotation marks to make clear which words are hers and which are from her source.

> She names the source authors and gives a page number in parentheses.

BRIEF QUOTATION (MLA STYLE)

According to researchers, "the digital society has made digital communication a vital part of everyday life," and giving prisoners access to that communication reduces frustration and improves their success in reintegrating into society (Toreld et al. 337).

BLOCK QUOTATION (MLA STYLE)

The researchers discovered that inmates' use of digital technology, especially through their sentencing when access to legal materials is crucial, reduced the rate of reoffending.

> Quantitative results were supported by a prisoner survey and usage data. Prison disciplinary offenses were significantly reduced over a two-year period, and reoffending in the first year after release was reduced by 5.36% compared to a 0.78% reduction in comparison prisons. The prisoner survey and usage data suggested that prisoners felt much more in control of their lives in prison and much more confident in coping with technology in the outside world. (McDougall et al. 1)

Because the quotation is longer than 4 lines (per MLA), the writer presents it as a block, without quotation marks.

She names the source authors and gives a page number in parentheses. Note that in a block quote, the period comes before the source.

When taking notes, copy quotations word for word. Then when you transfer the quotation to the text of your writing project, you may want to revise it a little to make it flow more smoothly into the place where you are inserting it. If you delete any portion of a sentence copied from a source, use ellipses to indicate where the deleted words were. Put brackets around any words that you insert into the copied sentence.

5. Patchwriting

A *paraphrase* restates someone else's ideas in fresh words and sentences. *Patchwriting* occurs when a writer attempts to paraphrase but sticks too closely to the language or sentence structures in the source. Writers who are inexperienced with paraphrasing often patchwrite by replacing some terms with synonyms, deleting a few words, or altering the grammar slightly, but they do not put the passage fully into fresh words and sentences. Patchwriting commonly occurs as writers work with sources on complex, unfamiliar topics.

At one time, patchwriting was widely regarded as an ethical transgression and thus was treated as plagiarism. Increasingly, scholars are recognizing patchwriting as a reading and writing issue, not an ethical one. You need to know, though, that there is still disagreement on this matter, and some readers still regard patchwriting as plagiarism.

No matter how your readers categorize it, no one thinks of patchwriting as good writing. Experienced writers rewrite their patchwriting, turning it into an effective paraphrase; in the process, they push themselves toward a better understanding of the source.

15c Taking Notes Rhetorically

> **More about**
> Establishing a research log, 228–30

> **More about**
> Annotating, 119–24
> Summarizing, 114–15, 295–97
> Quoting, 297–99, 311
> Analyzing, 127–32, 308–11
> Interpreting, 132, 308–11
> Synthesizing, 133, 308–11
> Critiquing, 133–35

Of course you want to avoid plagiarizing. Yet trying to avoid plagiarism is a negative approach to writing. It focuses your attention on avoiding error rather than producing a worthwhile text that you benefit from writing and that your audience benefits from reading. Keeping the rules of plagiarism in mind and observing them in your work is an essential thing to do. A positive, rhetorical approach to your writing will help you tamp down the plagiarism worries and avoid plagiarism at the same time.

Taking a rhetorical approach to your writing involves taking charge of your sources, interacting with them, and inviting your audience into the conversation you are having with them. To interact with your sources, search for ideas and information rather than "killer quotes." As you search for sources and read them, work rhetorically by taking notes in your research log. In each note, record the source and page number so you can easily cite it when you draft your project. To take rhetorical notes, consider making some of the following moves:

- *Summarize.* What claims does your source seem to be making? Write a few sentences summarizing the source's claims. You will be able to use this material when you draft your project, to help your audience understand the nature of your sources.

- *Analyze.* What sorts of evidence does this source offer for its claims?

- *Evaluate.* For you as a reader, how appropriate and convincing is this evidence?

> **More about**
> Evaluating sources for reliability, 265–69

- *Respond.* What connections do you see between this source and your own experiences?

- *Synthesize.* What connections do you notice between this source and others you have read?

- *Paraphrase.* When you encounter important passages, resist the urge just to cut and paste them into your notes. Instead, paraphrase them in your own words. This will help you understand the material better, and when you incorporate your paraphrases into your project, it will make your writing much more readable.

- *Quote.* When you encounter an important passage that is written in an especially compelling way, copy it down exactly, and when possible, note the page it came from. Using some quotations in your writing is fine, but you should avoid weighing your project down with them and drowning out your own voice.

Writing Responsibly: Highlighting versus Making Notes

While highlighting is a useful way to signal important information in a source, it is not a substitute for writing your own notes about a text. Highlighting can help you mark what is important, but annotating will push you to engage with the text and save you from leafing through page after highlighted page, looking for a passage that you faintly recall having read. So even though it may seem more time-consuming than highlighting, making notes will actually serve you better in the long run.

to SELF

15d Citing Accurately

A *citation* names the author of source material. When you are working with a paginated source, the citation also includes the number of the page from which you derived the source material. Insert a citation at the end of every passage (but not every sentence) of source material in your project.

- **If you are writing in MLA style,** your parenthetical citation should include the source author's last name. When the source is paginated, end your citation with the number of the page on which the quotation appeared in the source. Place your citation in parentheses at the end of each passage of source material.

   IN-TEXT PARENTHETICAL CITATION (MLA STYLE, FOR PARAPHRASE)

   Research shows that when consumers learn about how their clothes are made, and the impact of that production on people and the environment, they are more willing to purchase slow fashion or sustainable clothing items (Hiller-Connell 303).

   *Student Model from **Isabel Beck,** "Fast Fashion" (ch. 18), 383–96*

- **If you are writing in APA style,** your parenthetical citation should include the source author's last name, followed by the year the source was published. When you are quoting from a paginated source, end your citation with the number of the page on which the quotation appeared in the source. (In APA style, citations to paraphrases and summaries do not require a page reference.) Place your citation in parentheses at the end of each passage of source material.

   IN-TEXT PARENTHETICAL CITATION (APA STYLE, FOR PARAPHRASE)

   Darwin's theory of evolution, specifically his principle of divergence, has been used as a possible explanation for the differences in sibling personality (Sulloway, 1996).

   *Student Model from **Robyn Worthington,** "Nature versus Nurture" (ch. 19), 430–38*

Research Matters • Overcoming Fear of Plagiarizing: Paraphrase, Summary, Note-Taking

IN-TEXT PARENTHETICAL CITATION (APA STYLE, FOR QUOTING A SOURCE)

Darwin theorized that "given enough time, species tend to evolve multiple forms that diverge in character, a process called adaptive radiation" (Sulloway, 1996, p. 85).

- **If you are working in *Chicago* author-notes style,** your in-text citation will be a superscript number corresponding to a footnote or an endnote. Chapter 20 provides examples and details.

- **If you are writing in CSE citation-sequence or CSE citation-name style,** your in-text citation will be a superscript number corresponding to an entry in a list of references. Chapter 21 provides examples and details.

The purpose of citation is to include your audience in the conversation you are having with your sources. Ideally, your project will include not just quotations from your sources but also paraphrases and summaries of those sources. You need to cite all three of these—quotations, paraphrases, and summaries. You also need to cite sources of information that are not *common knowledge.* Each citation needs to be *framed* so your audience knows where your use of source material begins and ends.

1. Citing quotations

A *quotation* is someone else's words transcribed exactly, with quotation marks or block indentation to signal that it is from a source. Enclose short quotations in quotation marks, and indent long quotations as a block. Place a citation at the end of the quotation. Quotation marks make clear where the source material begins, but a *signal phrase* at the beginning of the quotation will help your audience understand why you are including this quotation and what significance they might draw from it.

IN-TEXT QUOTATION (APA STYLE)

The stereotype effect, as defined by researcher Monica Biernat (2003), is "a finding that individual members, comparable in all ways except their category membership, are judged in a direction consistent with group-level expectations or stereotypes" (p. 1019).

The writer frames the quotation with quotation marks to make clear which words are hers and which are from her source.

The writer gives the author's name in a signal phrase and the publication year (2003) and page number (p. 1019) as parenthetical citations. APA requires a page number (or numbers) when quoting from a source, if they are available.

Student Model from **Robyn Worthington,** "Nature versus Nurture" (ch. 19), 430–38

BLOCK QUOTATION (APA STYLE)

Rohrer et al. (2015) reported the following:

> All in all, we did not find any effect of birth order on extraversion, emotional stability, agreeableness, conscientiousness, or imagination, a subdimension of openness. There was a small, but significant, decline in self-reported intellect, a second subdimension of openness. The effect on intellect persisted after controlling for IQ scores, indicating that there is a genuine birth-order effect on intellect that goes beyond objectively measured intelligence and can be observed in adults. (p. 14227)

Additional testing, then, may help determine the usefulness of the theory of birth order and personality.

The writer names the author in a signal phrase followed by the publication year in parentheses and the page number in a parenthetical citation following the end punctuation of the quote.

Because the quotation is longer than 40 words (per APA), the writer presents it as an indented block with no quotation marks.

2. Citing paraphrases and summaries

Cite all paraphrases and summaries of sources. The citation goes at the end of the paraphrase or summary. However, your audience also needs to know where the paraphrase or summary begins. Introducing the passage with a signal phrase answers that need, and it also helps your audience understand why you are including this paraphrase or summary and what significance they might draw from it.

The writer introduces her paraphrase with a signal phrase naming the author.

If source had page numbers (or numbered paragraphs), the writer would have placed one in parentheses before the period, per MLA style.

Student Model from **Isabel Beck,** "Fast Fashion" (ch. 18) 383–96

PARAPHRASE (MLA STYLE)

According to Conca, we wear fast fashion items fewer than five times and keep them for just 35 days.

SUMMARY (MLA STYLE)

The researchers found that when shown a desirable object for sale, the nucleus accumbens, or pleasure sensors, in the test subjects' brains lit up; the more the person wanted the item, the more activity the brain scanner picked up (Knutson et al. 148).

The writer summarizes the result of a study and gives the author name and corresponding page number, per MLA style.

Research Matters • Overcoming Fear of Plagiarizing: Paraphrase, Summary, Note-Taking

Writing Responsibly

Blending Voices in Your Text

> **Make It Your Own!** Good researched writing is more than collecting the ideas of others; it is instead an exploration of how the sources have helped researchers develop their own ideas. You will produce better work if, as you draft your project, you let your audience see *your* thinking.

Whenever you write from sources, you are blending the voices of your sources with one another and with your own. Although *voice* sometimes refers to the difference between passive and active voice, it also refers to who is talking in the text—the writer or the source.

Your audience wants to know whose voice it is "hearing." When you quote, it knows you are importing the voice of the source. When you **paraphrase** (rewrite the information in fresh language), your audience hears you talking. But when you **patchwrite** (copy from sources and make minor changes to its language, but not actually paraphrase), you lead your audience to the mistaken belief that it is hearing you when in fact it is neither your voice nor the source's, but rather an inappropriate mixture of the two. To blend voices successfully, you need to avoid patchwriting and show the beginning and end of your use of sources.

Some readers consider it plagiarism when a writer patchwrites. Regardless of whether readers classify it as plagiarism, they do not consider patchwriting good writing. The following passage from a source discussing the history of child psychology, followed by a student's first-draft writing from that source, illustrates the issue:

Passage from source

> In the 1910s and later, as child psychology became an academic discipline, teachers increasingly looked to educational researchers rather than librarians as the central experts in children's reading.

Patchwriting

> From the 1910s on, child psychology became a discipline, and teachers more and more thought that educational researchers rather than librarians were the main experts in children's reading (248).

The patchwriting follows the original sentence, deleting a few words and substituting some others, but is still dependent on the language and arrangement of the source sentence. Not knowing that this is a blend of two voices—the writer's and the source's—the reader is misled to think this is the student's voice.

Paraphrase

> Child psychology emerged as an academic discipline in the early twentieth century, prompting teachers to look to researchers for expertise about children's reading. Librarians were no longer the primary authority on the topic (248).

The paraphrase appropriately uses keywords from the original, such as *discipline* and *child psychology,* but it otherwise uses fresh language and fresh sentence arrangement to restate the source.

Ground your own writing in paraphrase and summary, include some quotation, and avoid patchwriting altogether. This will allow your voice, rather than those of your sources, to dominate your text. This strategy requires your conscious effort and practice. Writing true paraphrase is an advanced skill that many college writers do not practice (see chart), but those who master this skill write the most successful research projects.

To let your audience know when you are paraphrasing or summarizing, use a signal phrase at the beginning of the source use and a parenthetical citation at the end. If your use of sources is lengthy, you can also occasionally mention the source or the author as you write, just to remind your audience that they are reading your summary or paraphrase of a source:

Students' Use of Sources
DATA FROM **The Citation Project**

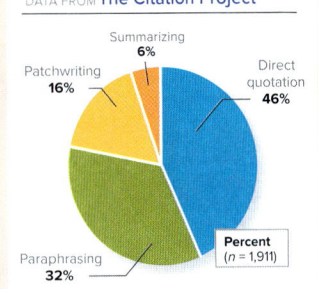

- Summarizing 6%
- Patchwriting 16%
- Direct quotation 46%
- Paraphrasing 32%

Percent (*n* = 1,911)

Researchers found that while most college research writers use quoting and patchwriting, the best projects were by those who use summary and paraphrase.

Marking where the source use begins and ends

Signal phrase at beginning of source use: Kathleen McDowell explains that **[Paraphrase of a sentence from the source:]** the academic discipline of child psychology, which emerged in the early twentieth century, looked to researchers for expertise about children's reading. Librarians were no longer the leading authorities on the topic. **[Summary of two pages in the source:]** Both librarians and child psychologists were interested in children's reading patterns, but for different reasons. The librarians, **[Signal phrase within the source use:]** McDowell says, wanted to understand what sorts of texts would interest children so they could get them into the library. Child psychologists, in contrast, wanted to understand the children themselves. Both groups collected information about children's reading, but they did it in different ways. The librarians observed children's reading and reported on their observations, while the child psychologists conducted scientific research **[Parenthetical citation at end of source use:]** (248–49).

Source: McDowell, Kathleen. "Toward a History of Children as Readers, 1890–1930." *Book History,* edited by Ezra Greenspan and Jonathan Rose, vol. 12, Penn State UP, 2009, pp. 240–65.

Self Assessment

Review your work with each source, revising as necessary, to be sure you:

- ☐ Use paraphrase and summary. Did you avoid overreliance on quotations? ▶ *Summarizing, 295–97; paraphrasing, 292–94; patchwriting, 285, 292–94*
- ☐ Paraphrase while avoiding patchwriting. Did you restate source material in fresh language and fresh sentences? ▶ *Taking notes and avoiding plagiarism, 286*
- ☐ Use signal phrases and parenthetical citations. Did you let your audience know where your paraphrase and summary begins and ends? ▶ *Voice, 316–18*

15e Paraphrasing Elegantly

Each time you read a source and encounter an important passage, paraphrase it in your research log. You will find this difficult at first, but the more you do it, the easier it will be and the more you will understand your sources. When you include some of these paraphrases in your written project, your audience will find them much easier to read than quotations, because you will not be switching back and forth between your voice and that of the source.

As you paraphrase a passage, *close the source.* If you are looking at the source and asking yourself, "How else can I say this?" you are just playing with words, not restating an idea. Looking at the source while trying to paraphrase it also increases your chances of patchwriting instead of paraphrasing by working too closely with the language and structure of the source. To write an effective, even eloquent paraphrase, follow these steps:

1. **Read the source until you feel you understand it.** Think about the overall meaning of the passage you are borrowing. Figure out whether there are any key terms that must be retained in your paraphrase.
2. **Close the text and walk away.** Do something else for a few minutes or a few hours.
3. **Come back to your desk and write what you remember.** If you cannot remember anything, repeat steps 1 and 2.
4. **Check your paraphrase against the source** to make sure you have correctly represented what it said. If you have closely followed any of the source language (other than key terms), either copy exactly and supply quotation marks or revise your note.

Self Assessment

When you paraphrase, check for these elements. Have you done *all* of the following?

- ☐ Used synonyms rather than the words of the source where possible; use key terms and technical language from the source when no synonym is reasonable.
- ☐ Quoted specialized terms the first time used but not thereafter.
- ☐ Used different sentence structures from those in the original passage. If you find yourself borrowing the sentence structures of your source, try dividing or combining sentences or varying their length and structure to alter their rhythm and blend them into your own text.
- ☐ Started the paraphrase with a signal phrase and ended it with a citation.
- ☐ Documented the source in your bibliography, reference list, or list of works cited.

> **More about**
> Varying sentence length and structure, 587

If you are not sure whether you are paraphrasing successfully or patchwriting, compare your work with the following examples, and if necessary, revise:

Passage from Source

With these caveats, we argue more limitedly that digital technology offers new avenues of aesthetic experimentation for comic artists and that the internet has given some comic artists a modest prosperity that they would not have without the internet as a means of distribution. (Sean Fenty et al. "Webcomics: The Influence and Continuation of the Comix Revolution." *ImageTexT*, vol. 1, no. 2, 2004, par. 2, www.english.ufl.edu/imagetext/archives/v1_2/group/.)

Note with Patchwriting

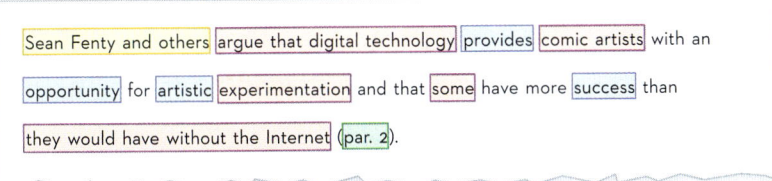

Sean Fenty and others argue that digital technology provides comic artists with an opportunity for artistic experimentation and that some have more success than they would have without the Internet (par. 2).

| First author + and others |
| Picks up language from source |
| Uses synonym or word in another form |
| Paragraph reference (use only when source numbers its paragraphs) |

Note without Patchwriting

According to Sean Fenty and others, comic artists use the computer to experiment and the internet to publish their works, allowing them more creative options and earning them more money than they made in the pre-Internet era (par. 2).

Notice that the patchwritten note relies heavily not only on the language but also on the sentence structure of the source. The note without patchwriting captures the main ideas of the passage without borrowing sentence structures or more than a few keywords from the original.

Here is another example:

Passage from Source

Until recently, the Church was one of the least studied aspects of the Cuban revolution, almost as if it were a voiceless part of Cuban society, an institution and faith that had little impact on the course of events. (Super, John C. "Interpretations of Church and State in Cuba, 1959-1961." *The Catholic Historical Review*, vol. 89, no. 3, 2003, pp. 511-29.)

Note with Patchwriting

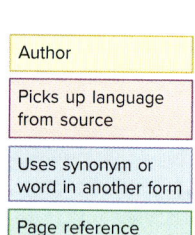

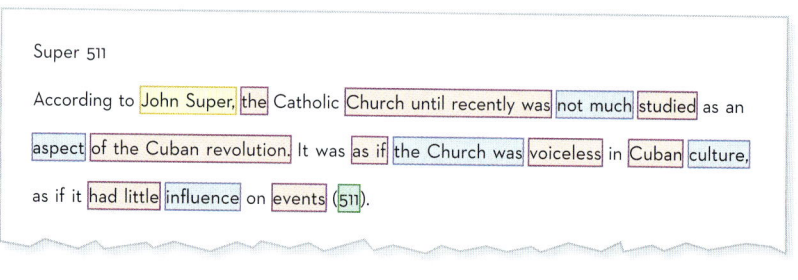

Super 511

According to John Super, the Catholic Church until recently was not much studied as an aspect of the Cuban revolution. It was as if the Church was voiceless in Cuban culture, as if it had little influence on events (511).

- Author [John Super]
- Picks up language from source [the, Church, Cuban, events]
- Uses synonym or word in another form [aspect, as if, voiceless, had little influence]
- Page reference [511]

Note without Patchwriting

John Super argues that scholarship on the Cuban revolution is only beginning to recognize the influential role of the Church (511).

The revised note still retains key terms from the source: "Cuban revolution" and "Church" appear in both the original passage and the revised note because there can be no synonyms for proper nouns (names). But the passage no longer draws heavily on the source's sentence structure, organization, or word choices.

Taking notes in English If you are a non-native writer of English, your English language skills will benefit from your making the effort to paraphrase and summarize. In the interests of time, you may have to quote more frequently than you paraphrase or summarize. When that is the case, choose your quotations strategically: quote the most complex source material, and paraphrase or summarize the more accessible material.

Make It Your Own

From a source for a research project (or from another college-level text), choose three sentences you consider important. Then paraphrase them following the guidelines in *section 15e*. Attach a copy of the source to your paraphrase.

> **Work Together**
>
> In groups of two or three, compare the original source with the paraphrases that each group member wrote for the Make It Your Own exercise above. Did group members paraphrase accurately? Did they avoid patchwriting? Discuss any sentences that may lean too heavily on the language or sentence structure of the original source. What might the writer do to avoid patchwriting? If the paraphrase avoids patchwriting, identify the paraphrasing strategies each writer used.

15f Summarizing Eloquently

Like a paraphrase, a summary should be in your words, not those of the source. A summary is different from a paraphrase in that it compresses the material from the source, stating the source ideas much more succinctly. Summaries can be written in a variety of ways for a variety of purposes, but all your summaries should restate and compress the main claims of the source. In addition, it is often useful to summarize the major evidence the source provides for its claims. In most cases the summary should not include your own ideas or commentary; your own views should appear separately in your project. If you need to mix source summary with commentary, insert signal phrases and citations strategically so your audience knows who is speaking at all times—you, or the source.

In general, a summary should be at least 50 percent shorter than the material you are summarizing, but most summaries go far beyond that: A single paragraph, for example, might summarize a 25-page essay. Your summary should be only as long as needed to capture the main claim and major supporting evidence accurately. To summarize a source eloquently, follow these steps:

1. **Read the source,** and identify key and unknown words. Look up words that you do not know. For short sources, one or two careful readings may be enough; for longer or more complex sources, you may need to reread the source several times.
2. **Annotate the source.** Underline or highlight the thesis or main ideas. For a longer source, creating an outline may be helpful.
3. **Write down the main claims** (without looking at the source). For each group of supporting paragraphs, write a one- or two-sentence summary in your own words.
4. **Combine your sentences into a paragraph,** editing to omit repetition and using transitions to make logical connections between sentences clear.

> **More about**
> Transitions, 59–60
> Placing signal phrases and page references, 314, 335–36, 399–400

5. **Check your summary against the source.** Have you used fresh words and sentence structures? If not, this may be a sign that you do not yet understand the source. Go back and read the material again, and revise any patchwriting out of your draft.

Student Model Summary of a Source

Below is an example of an effective summary of an original source:

Passage from Source

Before exploring these connections, however, webcomics must be more clearly defined. Many people are only familar with webcomics through Scott McCloud's explanation of them in *Reinventing Comics,* where he took on the role of a spokesperson for webcomics. While McCloud offered an initial study on webcomics, this paper does not operate within a McCloudian definition of comics, where he expounds upon their potential to revolutionize all comics production. In this paper, the term *webcomics* must be distinguished from hyperbolic proclamations about the internet as an inevitable site of radical aesthetic evolution and economic revolution for comics. The problems with McCloud's claims about the liberatory and radical properties of the internet have been addressed by others, like Gary Groth in his article for *The Comics Journal,* "McCloud Cuckoo Land." Our argument does not claim that the internet is a superior comic medium, free of those "tiny boxes" and "finite canvases" that seem to trouble McCloud (online). Further, we recognize that the internet has not offered a level playing field, free of corporate domination, "a world," to quote McCloud's *Reinventing Comics,* "in which the path from selling ten comics to selling ten thousand comics to selling ten million comics is as smooth as ice" (188, Panel 1). With these caveats, we argue more limitedly that digital technology offers new avenues of aesthetic experimentation for comic artists and that the Internet has given some comic artists a modest prosperity that they would not have without the internet as a means of distribution. (Sean Fenty et al. "Webcomics: The Influence and Continuation of the Comix Revolution." *ImageTexT,* vol. 1, no. 2, 2004, par. 2, www.english.ufl.edu/imagetext/archives/v1_2/group/.)

Summary

Scott McCloud claims that the Internet will free underground comic artists from the restrictions of print distribution and make it possible for underground comic artists to reach huge audiences. Sean Fenty, Trena Houp, and Laurie Taylor, on the other hand, focus on the possibilities for experimentation on the web and argue that the web provides better opportunities to make money publishing underground comics than does print. (par. 2)

Notice that the writer of the summary captures the main idea of the source in her own words and sentence structures. Her summary is about one quarter the length of the original material.

Self Assessment

When you summarize, check for these elements. Have you done *all* of the following?

- ☐ Made clear that you are writing a summary of a source, not your own ideas.
- ☐ Cited the source you are summarizing.
- ☐ Rearranged the ideas of the source so that they make sense in your own text. For example, if the source presents a cause and its effects, you can present the effects first and the causes second, if that will work better in your project.
- ☐ Provided transitions to clarify relationships among ideas.
- ☐ Kept your own ideas, examples, and interpretations out (unless you were asked to analyze, respond, or interpret in addition to summarizing).
- ☐ Included page citations wherever you are summarizing an identifiable part of the source.
- ☐ Maintained the balance of the ideas in the source, without emphasizing one more than it was emphasized in the source.
- ☐ Made sure that your omissions and deletions do not alter or distort the meaning of the source.
- ☐ Documented the source in your bibliography, reference list, or list of works cited.

15g Quoting Strategically

Quotations allow the voices of your sources to emerge within your writing. When you are working with primary sources such as interviews and surveys that you have conducted or works of creative literature you are studying, you may have reason to quote frequently or extensively, to attune your audience to the voice of the source. Otherwise, quote sparingly, choosing to paraphrase much more often than quoting.

Quote from a source under the following circumstances:

- When your source uses particularly vivid or engaging language
- When you want to reproduce a subtle idea that might be difficult to paraphrase or summarize without distortion
- When your source conveys technical information that is difficult to paraphrase
- When you want to convey ideas in an expert's own words
- When you want to analyze or highlight the specific language used in your source (as when studying a work of literature or a historical document)
- When you want to emphasize an important point

When taking notes, copy quotations word for word, and double-check them against the source. Whether you transcribe a quotation or cut and

> **More about**
> Using quotation marks (ch. 51), 834–42
> Indention for longer quotations, 339, 380–81 (MLA), 426 (APA)
> Deciding when to create or borrow visuals, 82
> Obtaining permission, 10–11, 259
> Ellipses in quotations, 840, 854–55
> Brackets in quotations, 840, 851
> Interviews, 259–60
> Surveys, 261–62
> Writing about literature (ch. 22), 486–509

paste it into your notes, put quotation marks around it to avoid any confusion later. In your writing project, adjust quotations to integrate them into your own sentences, using ellipses to signal cuts and brackets to indicate any words you have added or changed. In your notes, the quotation should appear exactly as it did in the source.

If you find that you are copying a lot of quotations but are paraphrasing little and summarizing even less, you may not be fully comprehending what you are reading. In these situations, try the following:

> **More about**
> Evaluating sources (ch. 14), 263–78

- Read the source again.
- Look up words you do not understand.
- Consult reference sources that can provide background knowledge.
- Discuss the source with your instructor, classmates, or friends.

Work to understand the whole source rather than just quoting from the sections that you believe you understand or that you think sound authoritative. Understanding the difficult parts is important, for they may well change the meaning of what you thought at first you understood.

Writing Responsibly · Using Quotations Fairly

We have all seen ellipsis-laden quotations praising a new movie, and we have all wondered whether a crucial word or words might have been omitted: "This is the . . . movie of the year!" could well have been "This is the *worst* movie of the year!" in the original review. That is one reason to be skeptical when reading such advertisements. (Another is the advertiser's desire for the movie to succeed at the box office.)

In academic writing, you can adjust a quotation to bring the punctuation or grammar into line with your own text, or to remove extraneous information, as long as your changes are indicated with ellipses or brackets and you do not distort the author's point. Protect your credibility and be fair to your source by altering quotations accurately.

to OTHER WRITERS

Student Model Reading Note: Integrating Borrowed Ideas and Words

The following reading note correctly uses quotation marks to signal material taken word for word from the source, yet it indicates that the writer does not fully understand what she is writing about.

Draft Note

> Milne 140
>
> The "free-black community . . . of Five Points" is not reflected in "the areas of Block 160 that were excavated." "All that survived . . . were the remains of their ancestors interred in the mostly forgotten burying ground, a few intriguing and unusual items discarded in the defunct privies and cisterns, and a handful of church addresses." But "it is probable that many members of this community remained in the neighborhood, living 'off-the-grid.' . . . "

This note is merely a string of quotations, sewn together with a few of the note-taker's own words. It is difficult to read and lacks the researcher's insight and critical judgment. Rereading the source in order to gain a better understanding of it enabled the writer to summarize with much less quotation. The following revision is much easier to read, as well:

Revised Note

> Milne 140
>
> Very few items belonging to members of the African American population in Five Points have been excavated, most likely because members of this community were not part of mainstream society—they were "living 'off the grid'" (140)—not because they had all moved away.

> **More about**
> Integrating borrowed ideas and words, 311, 313–16

Writing Responsibly

Acknowledging Indirect Sources

Make It Your Own! Confusing direct and indirect sources is a common problem. Fortunately, the procedures for correctly representing indirect sources in your research projects are not hard to learn, and following them will subtly enhance your writing.

When you cite sources, you do not just inform your audience about where you obtained your information; you let your audience know who is speaking in the source. If your source quotes or uses ideas from another writer, that other writer is for you an indirect source[1]: You are not reading that other writer yourself but are reading what he or she said. If you want to use that material from the indirect source, you should acknowledge the indirect source as well as the source that was talking about it. This is a sophisticated technique that takes practice to master; researchers with the Citation Project discovered that citing indirect sources accurately was a challenge for first-year college writers, separating them from experienced writers.

The following example, from a project exploring the Graduate Equivalency Diploma (GED) alternative to traditional high schools, shows how the problem occurs:

Student's first draft

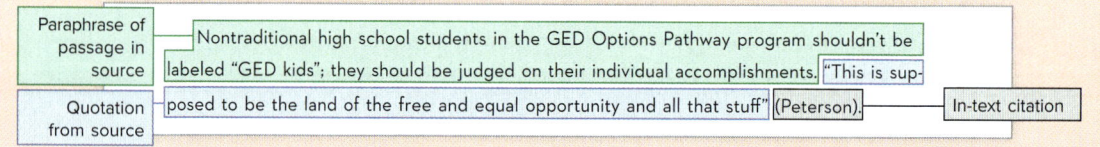

> [Paraphrase of passage in source] Nontraditional high school students in the GED Options Pathway program shouldn't be labeled "GED kids"; they should be judged on their individual accomplishments. [Quotation from source] "This is supposed to be the land of the free and equal opportunity and all that stuff" (Peterson). [In-text citation]

Peterson, who is cited in the sample above, is the writer of the newspaper story in which the quotation appears. However, Peterson does not speak the sentence in quotation marks. That sentence is being spoken by another source, whom Peterson is quoting in the following passage:

Passage from source

> The program does use the Graduate Equivalency Degree, or GED, as a tool. The students all have to pass the test's five sections, but when they complete the program they earn a regular high school diploma. This is an important point for Robbins, and she stresses that her students will get to graduate with their classes.
>
> "In fact, I'm trying to get everybody to quit calling them those GED kids," she said. "Number one, they've labeled them. That irritates me. [Quoted passage] This is supposed to be the land of the free and equal opportunity and all that stuff. Don't label my kids. Let them prove what they can do. Let the test scores speak."

When you are drawing on material from a source that is quoting, paraphrasing, or summarizing another, your citations should accurately indicate who is speaking and should also indicate where

---

[1] The terms *indirect source* and *indirect quotation* are often used interchangeably.

Research Matters • Quoting Strategically 15g 301

you found the material. This can be accomplished in a parenthetical citation, a signal phrase, or a combination of the two:

Parenthetical citation: Name the speaker, write "qtd. in" (quoted in), then name the source's author

| Paraphrase of passage in source | Students in the GED Options Pathway program should not be labeled "GED kids"; they should be judged on their individual accomplishments. | Parenthetical citation identifies speaker and source |
| Quotation from source | "This is supposed to be the land of the free and equal opportunity and all that stuff" (Robbins, qtd. in Peterson). | |

Signal phrase: Name both the speaker and the source in your text

| Signal phrase identifies source and speaker | Journalist Erica Peterson reports teacher Anastasia Robbins's beliefs: Students in the GED Options Pathway program should not be labeled "GED kids"; they should be judged on their individual accomplishments. | Paraphrase of passage in source |
| | "This is supposed to be the land of the free and equal opportunity and all that stuff," says Robbins. | Quotation |

Combination of signal phrase and parenthetical citation:

| Signal phrase identifies the speaker | Teacher Anastasia Robbins believes that students in the GED Options Pathway program should not be labeled "GED kids"; they should be judged on their individual accomplishments. | Paraphrase of passage in source |
| Quotation | "This is supposed to be the land of the free and equal opportunity and all that stuff" (qtd. in Peterson). | Parenthetical citation identifies speaker and source |

Source: Peterson, Erica. "W.Va. Program Gives High-Risk Students an Option." *West Virginia Gazette,* 24 Apr. 2011, www.wvgazettemail.com/News/201104240499.

Providing the name of the person being quoted (regardless of whether it is a person who was interviewed or another author) is all you need for acknowledging your indirect source; that name should not be in the list of works cited at the end of your project, since you did not read the original article or interview that person. The source you were reading, though, should be both cited in your project and included in your list of works cited.

Self Assessment

Review your work to be sure that whenever you worked from an indirect source, you:

- ☐ Cited the direct source. Did you name the source in which you found the material and include only the direct source in your list of works cited? ▶ *Direct versus indirect sources, 347–48 (MLA)*
- ☐ Used parenthetical citation, signal phrases, or a combination of both to acknowledge the name of the speaker in the indirect source and the author of the source in which you found the material. Did you make clear who is speaking? ▶ *Signal phrases, 314–15*

Text Credits

Pg. 290, 293, 296: From The UF Visual Rhetoric Research Group: Sean Fenty, Trena Houp and Laurie Taylor, "Webcomics: The Influence and Continuation of the Comix Revolution" *ImageTexT,* Vol. 1 No. 2 Winter 2005. Copyright © 2004 Sean Fenty, Trena Houp and Laurie Taylor. Used with permission.

16 Writing the Research Project

IN THIS CHAPTER

a. Drafting a thesis statement, 303

b. Organizing your ideas, 304

c. Drafting your research project, 307

d. Revising, proofreading, formatting, and publishing your project, 311

Student Models
From **Isabel Beck,** "Fast Fashion":
 Thesis Statement, 304;
 Outline, 306; **Supporting Claims,** 309

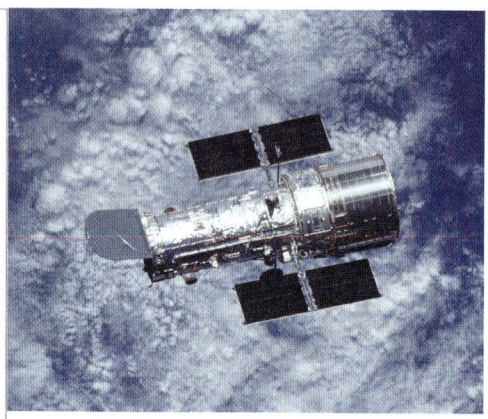

The Hubble Space Telescope, taking pictures of the cosmos since 1990, has provided enough data to keep scientists busy for years, long after the telescope stops functioning. So far, scientists have published over 17,000 articles based on what they have learned from Hubble (nasa.gov/hubble). These articles have given us a clearer idea of the age of our universe, a better understanding of how galaxies evolve, and information about what happens when stars collapse. Until these articles were published, the Hubble merely provided pretty pictures to the rest of us.

Like the scientific articles published from the Hubble data, your college research projects are an opportunity to share what you have read and studied; they are an opportunity to provide your audience with a synthesis of the information you have gleaned from a variety of sources and to present what you have learned, filtered through the lens of your understanding. They are the culmination of your research and an expression of yourself.

> **Reference** **Drafting the Research Project**
>
> - **Thesis.** Draft a one- or two-sentence thesis statement that grows out of your research question and hypothesis. Revise your thesis as you draft your project.
> - **Organization.** List and explain the reasons you believe your thesis statement or why you think it is the most reasonable way to address a difficult issue. Sort research notes into separate piles for each of your reasons. Draft an outline that organizes your material so that your audience can follow your logic and maintain interest to the end.
> - **Analysis, interpretation, synthesis, critique.** Divide ideas into their component parts and think about what they mean. Then combine ideas from sources with your own ideas to come up with something fresh. Decide how well sources have achieved their authors' goals and whether those goals were worthwhile.
> - **Evidence and counterevidence.** Incorporate evidence, making sure it is relevant. Use summaries, paraphrases, and a few quotations as support. Acknowledge contradictory evidence and explain why your position is still reasonable despite this. (If your position does *not* seem reasonable in light of the counterevidence, revise your thesis!) Make sure you provide enough evidence—and the appropriate types of evidence—to persuade your audience.
> - **Citation and documentation.** Cite your sources in the body of your text. Use quotation marks for all direct copying. Replace any patchwriting with paraphrase. Document sources in a list of works cited.

> **More about**
> Assessing the writing situation, 14–22, 222–23
> Devising a thesis, 35–38, 225–27
> Choosing a topic, 25, 224–25
> Using evidence, 45–47
> Finding information (ch. 13), 237–62
> Acknowledging alternative views, 156–58
> Organizing, 39–44, 53–57, 174–76, 304–7
> Drafting, 45–47, 307–11
> Summary, paraphrase, and quotation, 292–99, 311
> Avoiding patchwriting, 285, 292–94

16a Drafting a Thesis Statement

As you began your research, you chose and defined a *topic* that would be appropriate to your purpose and of interest to your audience. You then framed *research questions* and turned them into a *hypothesis* that you tried to test and confirm through your research. Now, with research data in hand, you are ready to draft a *thesis statement* that will serve as the focus of your project. You may find that the final version of your research hypothesis makes a good thesis statement.

This thesis should be a one- or two-sentence statement that grows out of your research hypothesis (or hypotheses), revised in light of what you learned through your research process. It should be a statement that you are prepared to explain, using the information you gleaned from sources and your own ideas, and it should convey your *purpose,* your reasons for conducting this research.

Student Model Thesis Statement for "Fast Fashion" by Isabel Beck

Read the research question, hypothesis, and thesis statement for the student research essay by Isabel Beck:

> **Research question:** What is fast fashion, and what impact does it have on people and the environment?
>
> **Hypothesis:** The production of fast fashion, which is the creation of cheap, trendy clothing made at high speed to mimic high-end fashion, ❶ drives consumers to purchase low-quality, disposable clothing; endangers ❷ workers with low pay and poor factory conditions; and hurts the environment ❸ with pollution and the overuse of natural resources.
>
> **Thesis statement:** By choosing to purchase smaller quantities of durable, responsibly made clothing, consumers can decrease the negative impact of fast fashion on garment workers and the environment while also saving money.

Hypothesis defines terminology and answers research question by listing three distinguishing traits.

Thesis statement makes purpose clear: positions consumers as potential solvers of problems created by fast fashion. It argues that consumers have the power to improve the world when they make better choices.

> Student Model
> Research project, Isabel Beck, "Fast Fashion" (ch. 18), 383–96

As you draft your research project, you may discover that the counterevidence is overwhelming or that the body of your draft offers a different answer to your research question than the one in your thesis. (Frequently, the true thesis will come to you as you draft the conclusion to your first draft.) So be prepared to revisit your thesis as you draft, revising or even replacing it as necessary.

Make It Your Own

For a research project that you are working on, draft (or revise) a thesis statement. Does the thesis statement concisely assert your main claim? Will it appeal to your audience? Does it convey your purpose?

> More about
> Research log, 228–29
> Annotating, 119–24
> Generating ideas, 25–31
> Making notes, 124–27, 286, 297–99

16b Organizing Your Ideas

The process of organizing your ideas begins with assembling the materials you will need. These include the following:

- Your research log and any other notes you have taken
- Any photocopies or printouts of sources

Research Matters • Organizing Your Ideas

- A copy of your thesis statement
- Any supplies you may need (flash drives, pens, pencils, highlighters, stick-on notes, index cards, a notebook)

1. Organize your ideas and notes.

With your preliminary thesis statement drafted and supplies at hand, you are ready to begin organizing your ideas and notes.

1. Start by listing the reasons you believe your thesis is true. While these reasons may be derived from your research sources, they should be *your* reasons, stated in your own words. (The strategies for generating ideas can help.)
2. Review the notes you took while reading sources: Do they provide evidence that supports your reasons for believing your thesis? Organize your notes according to which of your reasons they support: Separate index cards into piles, or cut and paste notes into separate computer files for each supporting point.
3. Review your notes again, looking for counterevidence that undermines your thesis or that points to alternative interpretations. Organize this material and consider how it might change your own point of view. If (as is usually the case) your understanding of your topic has changed during the course of your research, revise your preliminary thesis to reflect your current beliefs.
4. Assess your evidence: The size of a computer file or stack of index cards will indicate how much information you have collected in support of each of your reasons for believing the thesis. If a set of notes looks skimpy, find more supporting evidence, revise your thesis, or delve deeper into your reasons for believing your thesis.

2. Outline your project.

After you have organized your ideas and notes, outline your project to determine the most effective order for presenting your ideas. Some writers prefer

> **More about**
> Scratch outlines, 41–42
> Sentence outlines, 42–44
> Topic outlines, 42–44

Writing Responsibly — **Acknowledging Counterevidence**

While sorting your notes, be sure to retain *counterevidence*—evidence that *undermines* your claims. If some of your research contradicts or complicates your thesis or supporting reasons, do not suppress it. Instead, revise your thesis or supporting reasons on the basis of this counterevidence, or acknowledge the counterevidence and explain why the reasons for believing your thesis are more convincing than those that challenge it. Your audience will appreciate your presentation of multiple perspectives.

to AUDIENCE

a sentence outline because it aids drafting. (Each sentence in the outline becomes the topic sentence of a paragraph.) Others, eager to start writing, prefer a scratch (informal) outline that simply lists their reasons and the major supporting points in order of presentation. Still others prefer a topic outline: It is quicker to write than a sentence outline, but its formal structure of roman numerals and letters makes the structure of the draft clearer.

Student Model Research project, Isabel Beck, "Fast Fashion" (ch. 18), 383–96

Student Model Outline for "Fast Fashion" by Isabel Beck

The outline below shows the structure of the first part of Isabel Beck's research project. Note that the roman numeral sections list Beck's reasons; the capital letter and arabic numeral sections list the evidence in support of her reasons.

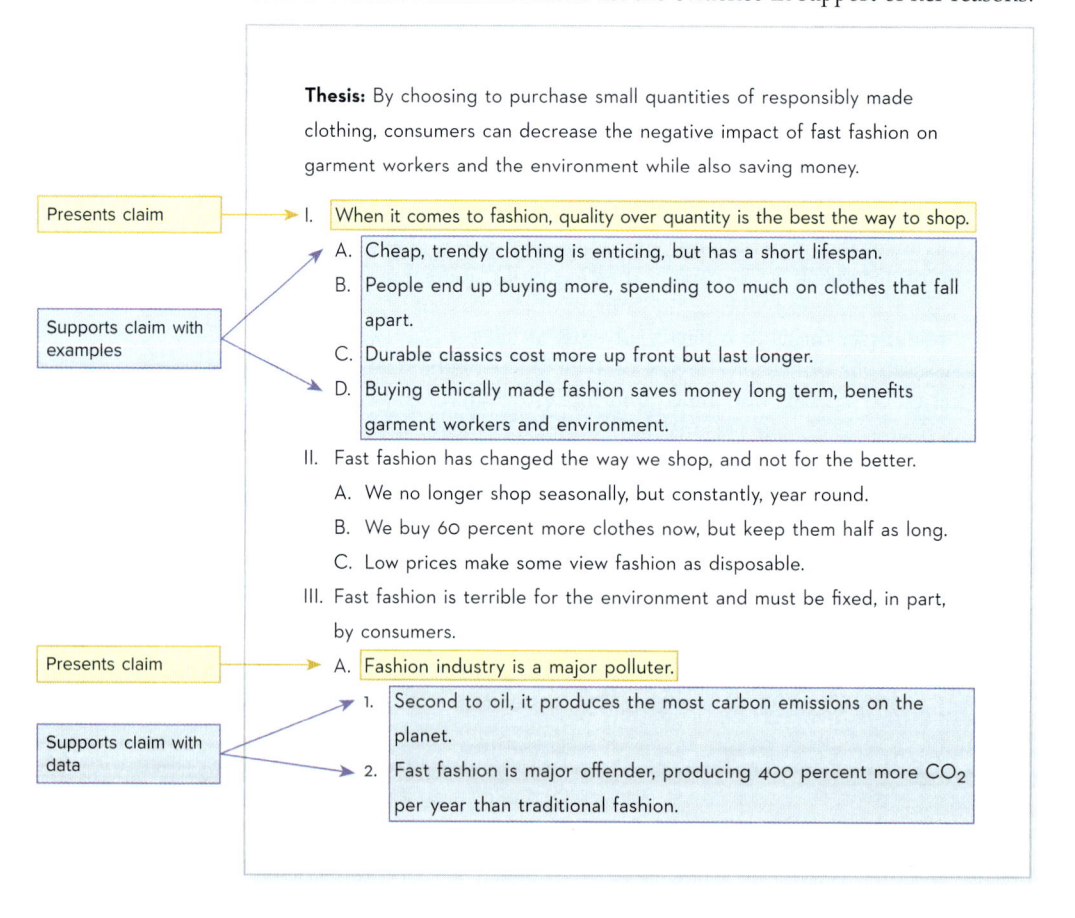

Thesis: By choosing to purchase small quantities of responsibly made clothing, consumers can decrease the negative impact of fast fashion on garment workers and the environment while also saving money.

I. When it comes to fashion, quality over quantity is the best way to shop. *[Presents claim]*
   A. Cheap, trendy clothing is enticing, but has a short lifespan.
   B. People end up buying more, spending too much on clothes that fall apart.
   C. Durable classics cost more up front but last longer.
   D. Buying ethically made fashion saves money long term, benefits garment workers and environment.
   [Supports claim with examples]

II. Fast fashion has changed the way we shop, and not for the better.
   A. We no longer shop seasonally, but constantly, year round.
   B. We buy 60 percent more clothes now, but keep them half as long.
   C. Low prices make some view fashion as disposable.

III. Fast fashion is terrible for the environment and must be fixed, in part, by consumers.
   A. Fashion industry is a major polluter. *[Presents claim]*
      1. Second to oil, it produces the most carbon emissions on the planet.
      2. Fast fashion is major offender, producing 400 percent more CO_2 per year than traditional fashion.
      [Supports claim with data]

>
> B. The fashion industry needs to slow down.
>   1. We have changed how we buy food, slowing down to consider sustainability, carbon footprint, animal welfare, etc. when making choices; similar changes can be applied to fashion, too.
>   2. Slow fashion is an ethically focused, eco-friendly movement but is a hard sell for those shopping on the cheap at Forever21, H&M.
> IV. Fast fashion violates basic human rights and needs significant overhaul.
>   A. The humanitarian consequences of fast fashion are serious.
>   1. Human rights violations include human trafficking, underage labor, slavery.
>   2. Major global brands turn a blind eye to rampant labor abuses.
>   B. The collapse of an eight-story garment factory at Rana Plaza in Bangladesh was a preventable disaster.
>   1. In 2013, 1,134 died; 2,500 were injured.
>   2. Global brands (Zara, Walmart, Benetton, Mango) produced clothing in Rana Plaza factories despite obvious safety issues.
>   3. Disaster brought some change, forced brands toward more ethical supply chains.
> V. Fast fashion breeds gender-based violence that we must address.
>   A. (and so on)

Make It **Your Own**

For a research project that you are working on, do the following:

- List the evidence (including visual evidence, if any) that makes you believe your thesis.
- Decide on the best order in which to present your material, and make an outline (sentence, scratch, or topic) from which to work.

16c Drafting Your Research Project

When drafting your research project, your goal is to draw on information in sources to support your own ideas, weaving that information into your sentences and paragraphs so that it supports your ideas without overwhelming them. Draw on your analysis of sources, your own interpretations of what you have read, and your synthesis of ideas from sources. To support your claims, incorporate summaries, paraphrases, and quotations from your notes, using signal phrases to identify the sources of borrowed ideas and to provide context for your sources.

> ### Make It **Your Own**
>
> For a research project that you are working on, compose a first draft. As you write, reread the tips in the Quick Reference box below as necessary. You will revise this draft later, so you should not worry about errors and gaps in the draft.

1. Use analysis, interpretation, and synthesis to evaluate and support your claims.

When you read sources and took notes, you analyzed your material to divide it into its component parts, and you interpreted what you read to determine its meaning. You also synthesized sources: You may have identified ideas in one source that were supported by information in others, described areas

> **Quick Reference** Writing the First Draft
>
> *More about*
> Drafting, 44–47
>
> As you begin writing, keep in mind that you are composing a draft—what you write will be revised—so do not worry about whether you are saying it "right." A few writers' tricks will help you produce that first draft:
> - Keep your thesis statement in front of you to help you stay focused as you write.
> - Start with the sections that are easiest to write, and then organize and fill in the gaps later.
> - Begin writing without looking at your sources or notes. Then consult sources and notes for evidence to support what you have drafted.
> - When incorporating quotations, paraphrases, or summaries, identify which source the material comes from (including the page number) to avoid having to track down this information later and, perhaps, plagiarizing inadvertently.
> - Draft with a notepad next to you or another file open on your computer so you can jot down ideas that come to you while drafting.
> - Include visuals that support your points and that help your audience understand what you are writing about.

of agreement (or disagreement) among sources, or explained which sources were most persuasive and why. The work you have already done to analyze, interpret, and synthesize sources is what you will draw on as you draft your research project. Use it to show readers how your sources support, complicate, or destabilize your thesis; do not expect your audience to figure this out without your help.

Student Model
Research project: Isabel Beck, "Fast Fashion" (ch. 18), 383–96

Student Model Supporting Claims from "Fast Fashion" by Isabel Beck

Examine the paragraph below from Isabel Beck's essay on the ethics of fast fashion to see how she uses analysis, interpretation, and synthesis to support her own claims.

Beck 5

The humanitarian consequences of fast fashion are also an important issue arising from this practice. What many people may not know about the fast-fashion industry is that it is a breeding ground for human rights violations, human trafficking, underage labor, and even slavery. A 2018 World Report from the Human Rights Watch describes rampant labor rights abuses and asserts that global brands that order products made in factories are obligated to make sure workers in those factories are safe and protected from abuse (Stauffer). A quick Google search for *human rights violations fast fashion* produces a shocking 128,000,000 results, many with grim headlines about the "life or death" epidemic. In 2013, an eight-story garment factory collapsed in Bangladesh; 1,134 people died and approximately 2,500 were injured (see fig. 3). The Rana Plaza accident is considered the deadliest structural failure in modern history. It also created controversy within the fashion industry; a number of Western companies, including Zara, Walmart, Benetton, and Mango all produced apparel in Rana Plaza factories. The incident brought to light

Sentence 1: Beck's claim (topic sentence) offers her interpretation

Sentences 2, 3, and 4 synthesize information from sources to support her claim.

Sentence 1 continues her synthesis of information supporting the claim made in sentence 1 of the previous paragraph.

Beck 6

> A visual of the factory tragedy underscores the seriousness of the accident and supports Beck's earlier claim about the negative impact of fast fashion on people. Beck's caption offers an interpretation of what the reader is seeing.

Fig. 3. Rana Factory Collapse. The Rana Plaza tragedy was a turning point that drew international attention to the plight of garment workers who produce fast fashion.

Source: Sk Hasan Ali. "Dhaka, Bangladesh, April 24, 2013." *Shutterstock,* 24 April 2013, www.shutterstock.com/image-photo/dhaka-bangladesh-april-24-2013-top-797806180.

the unethical and unsafe working conditions of factory workers and prompted major fashion retailers to take action and overhaul their supply chains in favor of more ethical practices (Stauffer).

Instead of merely stringing together material from sources, Beck integrates her own ideas with information from sources to craft paragraphs that readers will find persuasive. She analyzes her sources (a report by a nonprofit; information on a humanitarian disaster that sparked change), interprets which support her claim, and synthesizes evidence to make her case.

2. Use summary, paraphrase, and some quotations to support your claims.

Use quotations sparingly, so that your research project will not seem like a series of quotations strung together with a few words of your own. Put borrowed ideas into your own words by either paraphrasing or summarizing. Use quotations only when the language is particularly vivid or technical, when you want to demonstrate the ethos (credibility) of the speaker, or when you are analyzing the language of the source. In the sample paragraph on the previous page, Isabel Beck uses a combination of quotation and summary to support her claims.

NOTE When summarizing or paraphrasing, work to avoid patchwriting, and when quoting, use quotation marks or indent longer quoted passages as a block.

> **More about**
> Quoting, paraphrasing, or summarizing, 292–99
> Signal phrases, 314, 335, 399
> Avoiding patchwriting, 285, 292–94
> Quotation marks (ch. 51), 834–42

3. Acknowledge your sources.

Even while working on your first draft, you should acknowledge information you have gathered from sources—quotations, paraphrases, summaries, illustrations, data, or other information—by citing them in the text and providing full documentation in a list of works cited, a reference list, or a bibliography. Both citation and documentation are necessary to avoid plagiarism and demonstrate your ethos as a writer. No matter which citation and documentation style you use, your entries should be complete and consistent so that readers can locate your sources and enter into the conversation you have contributed to in your research project.

> **More about**
> Citing sources, 334–52 (MLA), 397–407 (APA), 439–57 (Chicago), 470–82 (CSE)
> Documenting sources, 352–77 (MLA), 408–25 (APA), 439–57 (Chicago), 470–82 (CSE)

16d Revising, Proofreading, Formatting, and Publishing Your Project

Once you have composed a first draft, however rough it may be, you can begin the process of shaping and polishing it—the process of *revision*. First, attend to big-picture (global) issues, such as clarifying your purpose, making sure your project is cohesive and unified, and making sure your ideas are fully developed. Next, attend to local issues, such as making sure your word choices reflect your meaning and are at the appropriate level, that you have varied your sentences, and that your prose is concise.

Once revision is complete, edit your text to correct errors of grammar, punctuation, and mechanics. Then proofread carefully—remember that spell-check software can help, but it cannot replace a careful human proofreader. Finally, format your project following the requirements of your discipline.

> **More about**
> Global revision, 86–90
> Local revision (editing), 90–93
> Peer review, 90–95
> Proofreading, 96–98
> Formatting, 379–82 (MLA), 426–30 (APA), 458–59 (Chicago), 482–83 (CSE)

17 Citing Rhetorically

IN THIS CHAPTER

a. Integrating source material responsibly, 313

b. Showing source boundaries, 314

c. Emphasizing your voice, 316

d. Providing context, 318

e. Integrating altered quotations, 322

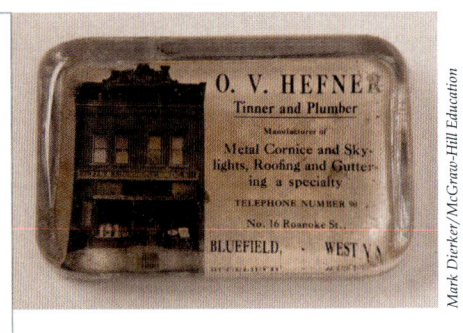

When you research a topic, you explore sources that express a variety of perspectives; you choose those that enhance your understanding of the topic; and then you describe those sources' ideas in ways that will allow your audience to understand what the sources have contributed to your point of view.

Source citations are necessary in a researched project; inadequate citation can open your work to charges of plagiarism. Chapter 15 explains how to avoid such disasters.

Because of writers' worries about plagiarism, it is easy to become so focused on avoiding charges of plagiarism that you lose sight of the other purposes of citation. The *rhetorical* use of citation establishes meaning and connection between the writer, the audience, the project, and its sources. If you want your writing from sources to have a smooth flow that is easily read, understood, and appreciated, think of citations not just as plagiarism insurance but as a key part of your conversation with your sources and your audience.

For your audience, the clarity of your project comes when you go beyond just identifying the source. When you cite rhetorically, you use informative signal phrases, show source boundaries, emphasize your own voice, provide context for the source, and integrate altered quotations smoothly. Rhetorical citation makes your conversation with sources, like the image or message in a glass paperweight, "transparent": Others can see how your ideas developed and how you are relating to your sources and the information in them.

17a Integrating Source Material Responsibly

When writing from sources, your most basic responsibility is to let your audience know whenever your text is drawing on a source. This protects you from charges of plagiarism. It also fulfills a responsibility to your audience, by letting readers know who is speaking in your text. It fulfills a responsibility to yourself, as well: Careful citation increases your writerly ethos; it makes you a more credible, respected writer. In MLA style, *in-text citation*—whether through parenthetical references, signal phrases, or a combination of the two—accomplishes all of this.

> **More about**
> Using information responsibly (ch. 15), 279–301
> In-text citation, 335–52 (MLA style, ch. 18)
> Ethos, 153–54

Having a Conversation with Sources You may consider published sources to be authorities, but an important aspect of academic writing is learning how to be critical even of authoritative material. You are free to agree or disagree with any source, but it is important that you use sources to support your claims, rather than simply repeating a source's language and ideas.

1. Parenthetical citations

You can cite your sources by using the author's last name and relevant page number(s) in a *parenthetical citation*.[1] Place that citation at the end of the material from your source:

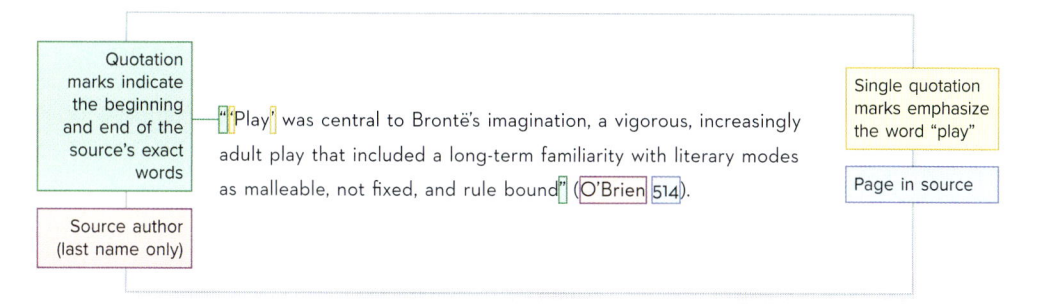

"'Play' was central to Brontë's imagination, a vigorous, increasingly adult play that included a long-term familiarity with literary modes as malleable, not fixed, and rule bound" (O'Brien 514).

- Quotation marks indicate the beginning and end of the source's exact words
- Source author (last name only)
- Single quotation marks emphasize the word "play"
- Page in source

When you are paraphrasing or summarizing material, you should also use parenthetical citation to acknowledge that your material comes from a source:

---
[1] The terms *parenthetical citation, parenthetical note,* and *parenthetical reference* are often interchangeable.

> She might not have composed a lot of poems, but what Brontë has left us is intriguing. Her poetry features tensions between the ordinary and the grand. In her poems, what might at first seem simple proves to be complicated (O'Brien 511).

[Source author (last name only): O'Brien]
[Page in source: 511]

2. Signal phrases

To incorporate borrowed material smoothly into your prose, introduce it with a *signal phrase.* One part of the signal phrase is an identification (usually the name) of the writer from whom you are borrowing. The other part is a verb; choose one that conveys your sense of the writer's intention.

> **More about**
> Verb tense, 702–7

In choosing your signal verb, consider the attitude or position of the writer you are quoting. Is the writer making a claim? Is the writer agreeing or disagreeing or even conceding a point? Or is the writer's position neutral? It is easy to choose a neutral verb, such as *writes, says,* or *comments.* Whenever possible, though, go beyond these neutral verbs to indicate the writer's attitude:

> Oscar Wilde quipped, "A poet can survive everything but a misprint."

For the quotation above, *quipped* (which means "uttered a witty remark") is clearly appropriate, given the cleverness of the sentence quoted. *Snarled,* on the other hand, would not be appropriate: Although Wilde's quip may have an edge to it, few would agree that the comment conveys the anger or viciousness associated with the verb *snarl.*

To maintain your audience's interest, vary the signal words you use, while avoiding verbs that might misrepresent the writer's intentions. (A list of signal verbs appears in the Quick Reference box on p. 315.) You can also vary your placement of the signal phrase:

> E. M. Forster asked, "How do I know what I think until I see what I say?"
>
> "How do I know what I think," E. M. Forster asked, "until I see what I say?"
>
> "How do I know what I think until I see what I say?" E. M. Forster asked.

> **More about**
> Paraphrasing, 292–94
> Summarizing, 295–97
> Using quotation marks, 297–99, 834–42

17b Showing Source Boundaries

When the material from your source is a quotation, it is easy for the audience to see the source boundaries: The quotation marks indicate where your use of source material begins and ends. When you are paraphrasing or

Quick Reference: Signal Verbs

Neutral Signal Verbs

analyzes	introduces
comments	notes
compares	observes
concludes	records
contrasts	remarks
describes	reports
discusses	says
explains	shows
focuses on	states
illustrates	thinks
indicates	writes

Writers in literature and the other humanities typically use present tense verbs in signal phrases; writers in the sciences use the present or past tense, depending on the context.

Signal Verbs That Indicate:

Claim/Argument

argues	finds
asserts	holds
believes	maintains
charges	points out
claims	proposes
confirms	recommends
contends	suggests
demonstrates	

Disagreement

complains	questions
contradicts	refutes
criticizes	rejects
denies	warns
disagrees	

Concession

- acknowledges
- admits
- concedes
- grants

Agreement

- agrees
- concurs
- confirms
- supports

---

summarizing the source, the place where you begin to use source material may not be clear. Signal phrases help solve the problem; you can place a signal phrase at the beginning of the source material and a parenthetical reference at the end.

Consider this example:

> She may not have composed a lot of poems, but what Brontë has left us is intriguing. Lee O'Brien's article argues that Brontë's poetry features tensions between the ordinary and the grand. In her poems, what may at first seem simple proves to be complicated (511).

Signal phrase includes source author (full name on first reference) — "Lee O'Brien's article argues"

Page in source — (511)

In the example above, it is clear that the first sentence is the writer's statement of their own ideas and the second and third sentences are a paraphrase from the O'Brien source. Notice that when the author's name is included in the signal phrase, it does not need to be included in the parenthetical reference.

1. Unpaginated source material

Many sources are accessed electronically and have no page numbers. For an unpaginated source, include only the author's last name in the parenthetical reference:

> "In her poetry, Emily Brontë achieves a remarkable effect by the energy and sincerity, and often by the music, with which she portrays her stoicism, independence, and compassion in stanzas which in many instances are the commonplace vehicles used by mere rimers" (Allingham).

[Source author (last name only): Allingham]

When you are quoting from the source, the quotation marks show where the copying begins and ends.

When you are paraphrasing or summarizing from an electronic source with no page numbers, however, you must work subtly with the material to show your audience where the source use begins and ends. Usually you can do this by using the author's name in the parenthetical reference, and describing the author in a signal phrase:

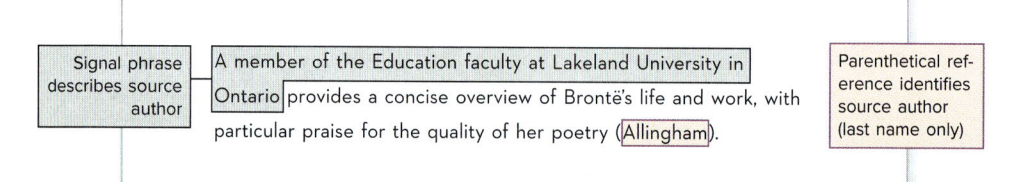

> A member of the Education faculty at Lakeland University in Ontario provides a concise overview of Brontë's life and work, with particular praise for the quality of her poetry (Allingham).

[Signal phrase describes source author: "A member of the Education faculty at Lakeland University in Ontario"]
[Parenthetical reference identifies source author (last name only): Allingham]

17c Emphasizing Your Voice

Just as important as signaling source boundaries is the need to signal your own voice. Your audience wants to know clearly when it is *you* talking.

In the following example it is not clear where the student writer stops drawing from the O'Brien source and begins to state her own ideas:

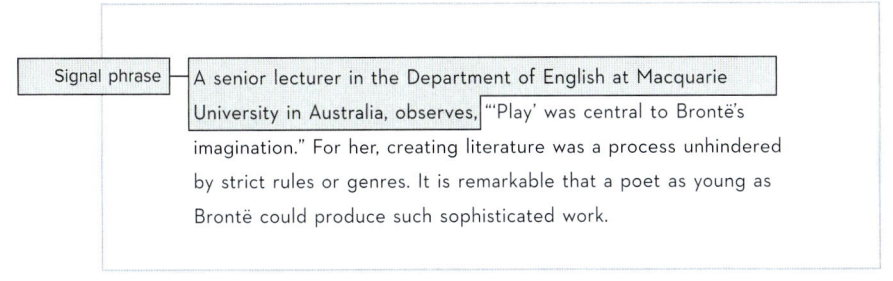

> [Signal phrase] A senior lecturer in the Department of English at Macquarie University in Australia, observes, "'Play' was central to Brontë's imagination." For her, creating literature was a process unhindered by strict rules or genres. It is remarkable that a poet as young as Brontë could produce such sophisticated work.

The use of a signal phrase with a parenthetical reference clarifies the beginning and end of the information from O'Brien; what follows the parentheses is the student writer's own observation:

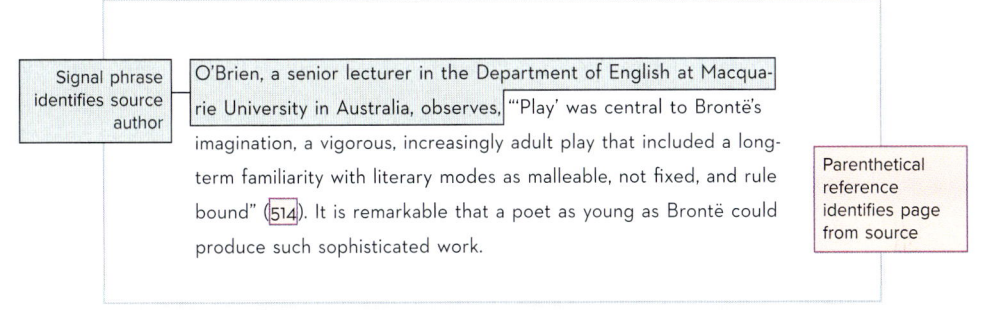

> [Signal phrase identifies source author] O'Brien, a senior lecturer in the Department of English at Macquarie University in Australia, observes, "'Play' was central to Brontë's imagination, a vigorous, increasingly adult play that included a long-term familiarity with literary modes as malleable, not fixed, and rule bound" (514). [Parenthetical reference identifies page from source] It is remarkable that a poet as young as Brontë could produce such sophisticated work.

An alternative way to mark the beginning and end of information from a source is to describe the author in the signal phrase and then name the author and provide a page reference in the concluding parentheses:

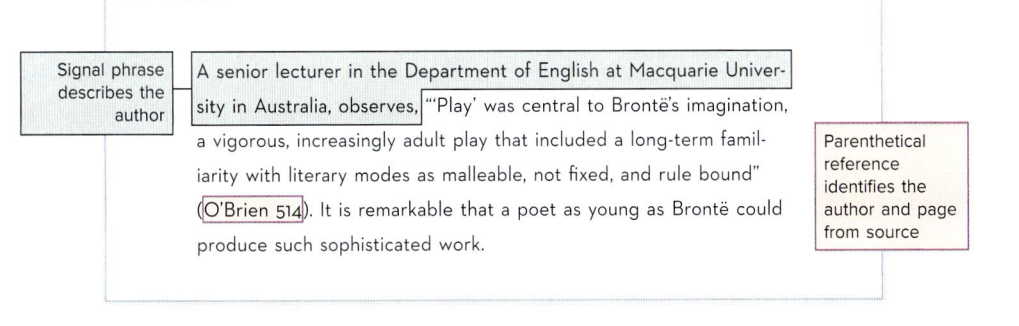

> [Signal phrase describes the author] A senior lecturer in the Department of English at Macquarie University in Australia, observes, "'Play' was central to Brontë's imagination, a vigorous, increasingly adult play that included a long-term familiarity with literary modes as malleable, not fixed, and rule bound" (O'Brien 514). [Parenthetical reference identifies the author and page from source] It is remarkable that a poet as young as Brontë could produce such sophisticated work.

> **More about**
> First-person pronouns, 492–93, 735–36

The final sentence in this passage is an interesting one, and the student writer wants to emphasize that it is their own insight. That could be done with first-person singular phrases such as "I believe" or "in my opinion." In some genres and writing situations (including many college assignments), however, first-person singular is inappropriate. Fortunately, there are more sophisticated ways to handle the task. One option is to speak in the first-person plural, subtly drawing the audience into the conversation:

> O'Brien, a senior lecturer in the Department of English at Macquarie University in Australia, observes, "'Play' was central to Brontë's imagination, a vigorous, increasingly adult play that included a long-term familiarity with literary modes as malleable, not fixed, and rule bound" (514). We cannot ignore how remarkable it is that a poet as young as Brontë produced such sophisticated work.

Parenthetical reference shows end of source material

First-person plural suggests shift to student writer's voice

It is even more effective to comment upon the source or its information:

> O'Brien, a senior lecturer in the Department of English at Macquarie University in Australia, observes, "'Play' was central to Brontë's imagination, a vigorous, increasingly adult play that included a long-term familiarity with literary modes as malleable, not fixed, and rule bound" (514). Her assessment of Brontë highlights the value of youthful creativity. We cannot ignore how remarkable it is that a poet as young as Brontë produced such sophisticated work.

Parenthetical reference shows end of source material

Transition to student writer's interpretation of source material

In this version, the writer's voice is implicitly clear. The phrase *Her assessment of Brontë* points to the previous material, and then the writer provides an interpretation. Demonstrative pronouns (*this, that, these, those*) can also be used as a transition to the student writer's discussion of source material.

17d Providing Context

Readers appreciate knowing not only when you are speaking and when your sources are, but also *who* your sources are and why you chose them.

Rhetorical citations provide this information smoothly: Your citations can explain why you chose the source, what kind of source it is, when the source was published, and what its argument is.

1. Explain your choice of sources.

Unless your readers are familiar with your sources, they may have no reason to respect them and thus no reason to believe your claims. You can avoid this problem with rhetorical citations that not only name your source but also indicate why you respect the source, as this student writer does:

> **More about**
> Evaluating sources (ch. 14), 263–78

[Signal phrase includes student writer's opinion of the source] → Gretchen Frazee offers a helpful description of the Greenwood section of Tulsa, Oklahoma, in 1921: "Leading up to the attacks, Tulsa's black residents were prosperous, in part because of an oil boom that boosted the city and state's economies."

In the example above, the writer establishes that the source can be respected for its thorough treatment of the topic.

NOTE Because her source is digital and unpaginated, the student provides no page number in the signal phrase or in a parenthetical citation.

The selection below acknowledges the shortcomings of the source while also asserting its usefulness:

[Signal phrase becomes extended explanation of student writer's opinion of the source] → Although she is not a historian, Gretchen Frazee has college training in journalism and workplace experience as a news producer. She offers a carefully researched description of the scene of the worst known incident of racial violence in the history of the United States, in the Greenwood section of Tulsa, Oklahoma, in 1921: "Leading up to the attacks, Tulsa's black residents were prosperous, in part because of an oil boom that boosted the city and state's economies."

2. Identify the type of source.

Is your source a newspaper column? A blog? A scholarly article? The differences among types of sources are important. If you want up-to-the-minute information, a newspaper or blog is likely to have it. If you want carefully researched, accurate information, a scholarly journal article is a good choice. Your audience wants to know that you have made appropriate source choices, and you can provide such information in rhetorical citations:

> [Signal phrase describes and identifies source author and her credentials] Gretchen Frazee, deputy digital editor of *PBS NewsHour*, offers a carefully researched description of the scene of the worst known incident of racial violence in the history of the United States, in the Greenwood section of Tulsa, Oklahoma, in 1921: "Leading up to the attacks, Tulsa's black residents were prosperous, in part because of an oil boom that boosted the city and state's economies."

3. Identify the date of publication.

For many issues, the date of publication is important. For example, readers need to know whether the description of an historical event was written at the time of that event or significantly later:

> [Signal phrase includes publication date of time-sensitive information] Writing in 2020, ninety-nine years after the event, Gretchen Frazee describes the scene of the worst-known incident of racial violence in the history of the United States, in the Greenwood section of Tulsa, Oklahoma, in 1921: "Leading up to the attacks, Tulsa's black residents were prosperous, in part because of an oil boom that boosted the city and state's economies."

When your source is a research report, mentioning the year of publication also helps your readers decide whether the data and findings are current or dated.

4. Identify the larger discussion in the source.

For the most successful, persuasive writing from sources, you need to *read* the sources, rather than just pulling sentences from them. That allows you not only to position the quotation, paraphrase, or summary in your text, but also to indicate how it contributed to the source text's discussion. Build a brief source summary into rhetorical citation:

> **More about**
> Critical reading (ch. 7), 111–42
> Avoiding plagiarism (ch. 15), 279–301

> [Extended signal phrase includes summary of the source] Gretchen Frazee's account of the 1921 Tulsa Race Massacre emphasizes the peace and prosperity of "Black Wall Street," the Greenwood section of Tulsa, Oklahoma, before the attacks that left more than three hundred African Americans dead: "Leading up to the attacks, Tulsa's black residents were prosperous, in part because of an oil boom that boosted the city and state's economies."

The phrase "emphasizes the peace and prosperity of 'Black Wall Street,' the Greenwood section of Tulsa, Oklahoma, before the attacks that left more than three hundred African Americans dead" summarizes the source.

Citation is not only ethical but rhetorical; in addition to protecting you against charges of plagiarism, it also creates a sophisticated, readable document that audiences are likely to trust.

EXERCISE 17.1 Integrating and identifying source material

Read Isabel Beck's essay "Fast Fashion: An Unethical Industry that Harms Garment Workers and the Environment" (pp. 383–96) and note how she integrates her source material. Use one of four different-colored highlighting markers to identify each of the different rhetorical moves she uses:

- Parenthetical references that are the only acknowledgment of the source in the sentence (that is, any sentences that have no signal phrases or other cues; just the parenthetical reference)
- Signal phrases
- Phrases that clearly signal her own voice speaking
- References to context: explaining her choice of source, the type of source, or the date of publication

Research Matters • Citing Rhetorically

> When you have finished highlighting, use what you have learned in this chapter to evaluate how Beck integrates her sources. What changes would you recommend if she were to revise this essay? Include the page reference in this book where she can read an explanation of each change you suggest.
>
> ### Make It Your Own
>
> Choose a source-based project you have already written or a draft in progress, and working on a printout of your project, use one of four different-colored highlighting markers to identify each of the four different rhetorical moves described in Exercise 17.1.
>
> ### Work Together
>
> When you have completed the highlighting, exchange your work with another student and use that paper's highlighting and what you have learned so far in this chapter to evaluate the ways the student has integrated sources. For any revisions you recommend, be sure to include the page reference in this book where an explanation can be found.
>
> Now review your own work and the comments and suggestions made by your audience and look for patterns. Which types of signals do you use most? Which do you use least? Make a checklist of issues and use it to help you revise in the future.
>
> If this is a project you are currently drafting, revise to include some of these rhetorical cues in the sections where you seem to have the least transparency regarding sources. Before you look at your project again, write a brief reflection on this process. What did you learn about how sources can be used effectively by reading and evaluating someone else's work? Did your fellow student use any strategies that you think you might try? Did they use sources in a way that you would prefer to avoid?

17e Integrating Altered Quotations

Sometimes you may need to alter a quotation so that it fits into your sentence. For example, you might delete words from one source's quotation because those words do not help you make your point. As long as the

Research Matters • Integrating Altered Quotations

meaning is not significantly changed, you may do any of the following to fit quoted material more smoothly into your own sentences:

- Quote short phrases rather than full sentences.
- Add or change words for clarity.
- Change capitalization.
- Change grammar.

All added or changed words should be placed in square brackets; deleted words should be replaced with ellipses. The example below shows a responsible alteration of a quotation:

> **More about**
> Using ellipses in quotations, 840, 854–55
> Using square brackets in quotations, 840, 851

> **More about**
> Acknowledging indirect sources, (ch. 15) 300–1

Quotation Integrated into Student Text

Certain portions of the Comic Book Code were incredibly specific and controlling, such as the rule that forbade "[t]he letters of the word 'crime' on a comics magazine . . . [to] be appreciably greater in dimension than the other words contained in the title" (qtd. in "Good Shall Triumph over Evil").

Original Quotation

The letters of the word "crime" on a comics magazine shall never be appreciably greater in dimension than the other words contained in the title.

> "qtd. in" indicates that the quotation was found in the source "Good Shall Triumph over Evil," but that source was quoting another source.

A capital letter was changed to a lowercase letter, double quotation marks were changed to single, one word was added and a couple of others were omitted, but the overall meaning of the passage remains the same.

Imagine, however, that the writer had made these changes instead:

Quotation Unfairly Altered

Certain portions of the code allowed some flexibility. Consider, for example, the rule that allowed "[t]he letters of the word 'crime' on a comics magazine . . . [to] be appreciably greater in dimension than the other words contained in the title" (qtd. in "Good Shall Triumph over Evil").

Original Quotation

The letters of the word "crime" on a comics magazine shall never be appreciably greater in dimension than the other words contained in the title.

Clearly this alteration of the quotation is not acceptable, as it changes the meaning of the passage completely.

EXERCISE 17.2 Integrating quotations

Read the passage below. Then, in the following quotations, circle the numbers for those that alter the quotation fairly, and cross through the numbers of those that change the meaning of the quotation.

> The meeting of Normans and Anglo-Saxons at Hastings was the most decisive battle of the Middle Ages and one of the determining days in the making of the West. Hastings changed Britain, which had been dominated since the end of Roman rule by invading tribes from the Continent and the North—Angles, Saxons, and Vikings. This day more than any other turned Britain away from its Scandinavian past and toward Europe. Hastings inaugurated the era of the knight, the social dominance of those who fought with lance on horseback.
> —Howard R. Bloch, *A Needle in the Right Hand of God.*
> Random House, 2006, p. 7.

1. Bloch maintains that the Battle of Hastings "turned Britain away from its Scandinavian past" and from Europe as well (7).
2. The Battle of Hastings, notes Bloch, gave the "invading tribes from the Continent and the North" new power over Britain (7).
3. "[T]hose who fought with lance on horseback" became dominant after the Battle of Hastings, observes Bloch (7).
4. Bloch concludes that the fight between the Romans and the invading tribes from the Continent and the North was "the most decisive battle of the Middle Ages" (7).

Self Assessment

As you revise projects that use sources, review your draft, revising as necessary, to be sure you:

- ☐ Cite your sources. Have you named any from which you are paraphrasing, summarizing, or quoting?
- ☐ Use signal verbs. Have you conveyed the attitude of your source?
- ☐ Use signal phrases and parenthetical references. Have you shown where each source use begins and ends, even when it is unpaginated?
- ☐ Emphasize your own insights. Have you commented on or analyzed the source, rather than just repeating it?
- ☐ Provide relevant contextual information. Have you identified the type of source, its date of publication, and its publisher?
- ☐ Reveal your reasoning. Have you explained why you chose and trusted your sources?

Make It Your Own

Choose a source-based project you have already written or a draft in progress, and use the material in this chapter and the tips in the Self-Assessment box above to help you review the ways you use and incorporate source material. Make a note of changes that would strengthen your use of source material, and add any new items you identify to the checklist in the Self-Assessment.

Writing Responsibly

Explaining Your Choice of Sources

Make It Your Own! When college writers share their opinion of their sources, their text is more interesting and convincing. Rather than just quoting from your sources, tell *why* you are quoting them, and your writing will be more persuasive.

In much of your college writing, you select and work with sources: You decide how to use sources to help convey your thesis. Your basic responsibility is to acknowledge those sources, cite them correctly, and provide full publication information about them at the end of your project. When you talk *about* your sources—tell what you think of your source and its information—you invite your audience into your thinking processes and portray yourself as an experienced academic writer.

When college writing instructors involved in the Citation Project studied research projects from US colleges, they noticed how few students talked about their sources. Most of the projects just pulled out information—usually a brief quotation—from sources, as if all the sources were alike. The nature of the sources and the student's thoughts about them remained invisible to the audience. The following example, from a project on sexism and sexual violence, shows the drab result:

First draft

> [Student's voice] Hostility toward women can be seen even in the ancient West. [Tom Stevenson observes,] [Quotation] "Livy's underlying message, it would seem, is that Roman men have to regulate public contributions by prominent women, and not accept female advice too easily, without prolonged consideration" [Citation] (189).

The material from the Stevenson source is accurately quoted and cited, and the sentences flow. But the passage provokes questions rather than insights. Who are Stevenson and Livy? Where did this source come from? Why did the writer choose it? Why should the writer's audience respect Stevenson's opinions? What else did the source say? What was the context in which the quotation appeared? These are the kinds of questions readers ask, and answering them will bring your text to life:

Revised draft

> [Student's voice] Hostility toward women can be seen even in the ancient West. [Tom Stevenson,] [Citation] a classics scholar at the University of Queensland, writes in the scholarly journal *Classical World* that [Credentials of author and publisher] the Roman historian Livy described women who supported their menfolks' success, which might seem to be a compliment to the women. But notice that the women aren't having their own successes. Furthermore, all of Livy's women are either described too briefly, or they are flawed. [Summary of the remainder of the source] Even as Stevenson provides this analysis, he also cautions against being too simplistic [Counter-evidence]

Research Matters • Integrating Altered Quotations   17e   327

Revised draft continued

> about Livy's portrayal of women; some of their faults were because their men were flawed. Still, Stevenson concludes, "Livy's underlying message, it would seem, is that Roman men have to regulate public contributions by prominent women, and not accept female advice too easily, without prolonged consideration" (189).

— Citation / Quotation

Source: Stevenson, Tom. "Women of Early Rome as *Exempla* in Livy, *AB Urbe Condita*, Book1." *Classical World*, vol. 104, no. 2, winter 2011, pp. 175–89.

Now, not only is the material from the source accurately quoted and cited, but Livy has been identified, and Stevenson's credentials and the authority of the publication have been established, along with a description of his argument.

Sometimes you choose to use a source because you like its argument or presentation of information, even if it may not be particularly scholarly. In these cases, too, you should let your audience know why you have chosen the source:

> [Information about why the writer chose this source] One good way to understand the treatment of women in contemporary society is to consult news media. They are not reports of research written by experts, but rather are sources that reflect and shape popular opinion. *Time* magazine publishes an article on date rape because it believes this is an issue that readers will or should care about. It also reports on current events. [Summary of some information in the source] So it is *Time* that reports on a congressional bill intended to reduce sexual violence in colleges. [Student's voice] Why is the bill needed? The answer is in the shocking numbers the magazine cites: "One in five college women will be the victim of a sexual assault (and 6% of men)" (Webley). — Quotation / Citation

Source: Webley, Kayla. "It's Not Just Yale: Are Colleges Doing Enough to Combat Sexual Violence?" *Time*, 18 Apr. 2011, time.com/time/nation/article/0,8599,2065849,00.html.

Self Assessment

Review your work with each source. Have you done the following?

- ☐ Identify the source's author and their credentials. Did you show what makes you trust them? ▶ *Applying analysis and crafting arguments, 143–82*
- ☐ Identify the publisher of the source and its credentials. Did you show what makes you trust this organization? ▶ *Finding information, 237–62*
- ☐ Consider the date of publication. Did you provide and comment on the publication date, if it affects your trust in the source?
- ☐ Summarize the source. Did you indicate how the selection you have drawn from contributed to the argument the source was making? ▶ *Evaluating information, 263–78*
- ☐ Provide additional discussion. Did you help your audience understand the reasons you chose this source and your selections from it?

Text Credits

Pg. 314: Forster, E. M., *Aspects of the Novel* (Edward Arnold, 1927). **Pg. 324: 17.2** Bloch, R. Howard, *A Needle in the Right Hand of God: The Norman Conquest of 1066 and the Making and Meaning of the Bayeux Tapestry* Random House, 2006, p. 7.

Part Five

Documentation Matters

- **18** Documenting Sources: MLA Style 334
- **19** Documenting Sources: APA Style 397
- **20** Documenting Sources: *Chicago* Style 439
- **21** Documenting Sources: CSE Style 470

Documentation Matters | Documenting a Source: MLA Style and APA Style

Book (Printed)

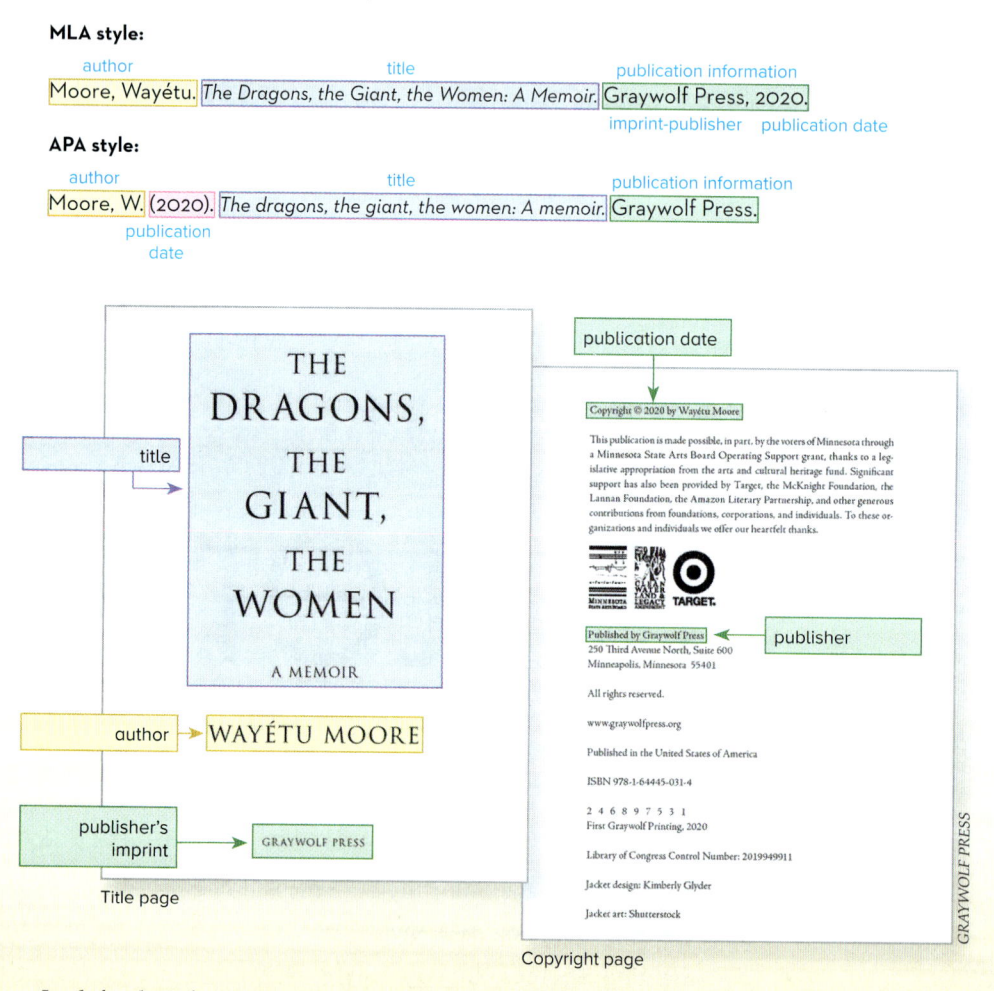

MLA style:

<u>author</u>   <u>title</u>   <u>publication information</u>
Moore, Wayétu. *The Dragons, the Giant, the Women: A Memoir.* Graywolf Press, 2020.
                                                         imprint-publisher   publication date

APA style:

<u>author</u>   <u>title</u>   <u>publication information</u>
Moore, W. (2020). *The dragons, the giant, the women: A memoir.* Graywolf Press.
         publication
         date

Title page

- title: THE DRAGONS, THE GIANT, THE WOMEN — A MEMOIR
- author: WAYÉTU MOORE
- publisher's imprint: GRAYWOLF PRESS

Copyright page

- publication date: Copyright © 2020 by Wayétu Moore

This publication is made possible, in part, by the voters of Minnesota through a Minnesota State Arts Board Operating Support grant, thanks to a legislative appropriation from the arts and cultural heritage fund. Significant support has also been provided by Target, the McKnight Foundation, the Lannan Foundation, the Amazon Literary Partnership, and other generous contributions from foundations, corporations, and individuals. To these organizations and individuals we offer our heartfelt thanks.

- publisher: Published by Graywolf Press
  250 Third Avenue North, Suite 600
  Minneapolis, Minnesota 55401

All rights reserved.

www.graywolfpress.org

Published in the United States of America

ISBN 978-1-64445-031-4

2 4 6 8 9 7 5 3 1
First Graywolf Printing, 2020

Library of Congress Control Number: 2019949911

Jacket design: Kimberly Glyder

Jacket art: Shutterstock

GRAYWOLF PRESS

Look for the information you need to document a printed book on the book's title page and copyright page. (For more about documenting a book, see pp. 352–61 for MLA style, pp. 408–15 for APA style.)

MLA and APA

Journal Article (Printed)

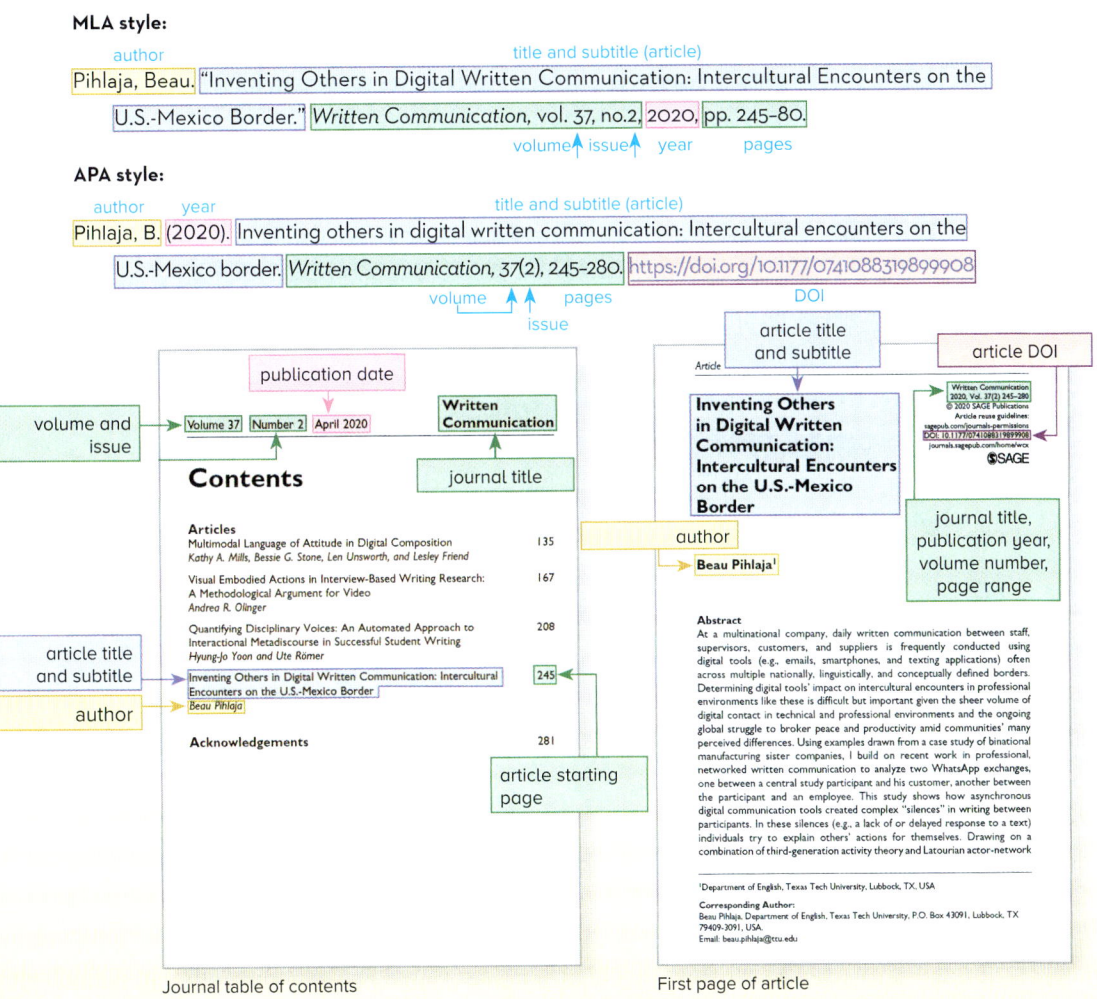

MLA style:

[author] Pihlaja, Beau. [title and subtitle (article)] "Inventing Others in Digital Written Communication: Intercultural Encounters on the U.S.-Mexico Border." *Written Communication*, vol. 37, no. 2, 2020, pp. 245-80.
[volume] [issue] [year] [pages]

APA style:

[author] Pihlaja, B. [year] (2020). [title and subtitle (article)] Inventing others in digital written communication: Intercultural encounters on the U.S.-Mexico border. *Written Communication, 37*(2), 245-280. [DOI] https://doi.org/10.1177/0741088319899908
[volume] [issue] [pages]

Journal table of contents

- volume and issue: Volume 37, Number 2, April 2020
- publication date: April 2020
- journal title: Written Communication

Contents

Articles

Multimodal Language of Attitude in Digital Composition — 135
Kathy A. Mills, Bessie G. Stone, Len Unsworth, and Lesley Friend

Visual Embodied Actions in Interview-Based Writing Research: A Methodological Argument for Video — 167
Andrea R. Olinger

Quantifying Disciplinary Voices: An Automated Approach to Interactional Metadiscourse in Successful Student Writing — 208
Hyung-Jo Yoon and Ute Römer

[article title and subtitle] Inventing Others in Digital Written Communication: Intercultural Encounters on the U.S.-Mexico Border — 245 [article starting page]
[author] Beau Pihlaja

Acknowledgements — 281

First page of article

Article

[article title and subtitle] **Inventing Others in Digital Written Communication: Intercultural Encounters on the U.S.-Mexico Border**

[journal title, publication year, volume number, page range] Written Communication 2020, Vol. 37(2) 245–280
© 2020 SAGE Publications
Article reuse guidelines:
sagepub.com/journals-permissions
[article DOI] DOI: 10.1177/0741088319899908
journals.sagepub.com/home/wcx
SAGE

[author] Beau Pihlaja[1]

Abstract

At a multinational company, daily written communication between staff, supervisors, customers, and suppliers is frequently conducted using digital tools (e.g., emails, smartphones, and texting applications) often across multiple nationally, linguistically, and conceptually defined borders. Determining digital tools' impact on intercultural encounters in professional environments like these is difficult but important given the sheer volume of digital contact in technical and professional environments and the ongoing global struggle to broker peace and productivity amid communities' many perceived differences. Using examples drawn from a case study of binational manufacturing sister companies, I build on recent work in professional, networked written communication to analyze two WhatsApp exchanges, one between a central study participant and his customer, another between the participant and an employee. This study shows how asynchronous digital communication tools created complex "silences" in writing between participants. In these silences (e.g., a lack of or delayed response to a text) individuals try to explain others' actions for themselves. Drawing on a combination of third-generation activity theory and Latourian actor-network

[1]Department of English, Texas Tech University, Lubbock, TX, USA

Corresponding Author:
Beau Pihlaja, Department of English, Texas Tech University, P.O. Box 43091, Lubbock, TX 79409-3091, USA.
Email: beau.pihlaja@ttu.edu

Find what you need to document a journal article on the cover or table of contents of the journal and on the first and last pages of the article. (For more, see pp. 361–65 for MLA style, pp. 415–19 for APA style.)

331

MLA and APA

Journal Article from an Online Database

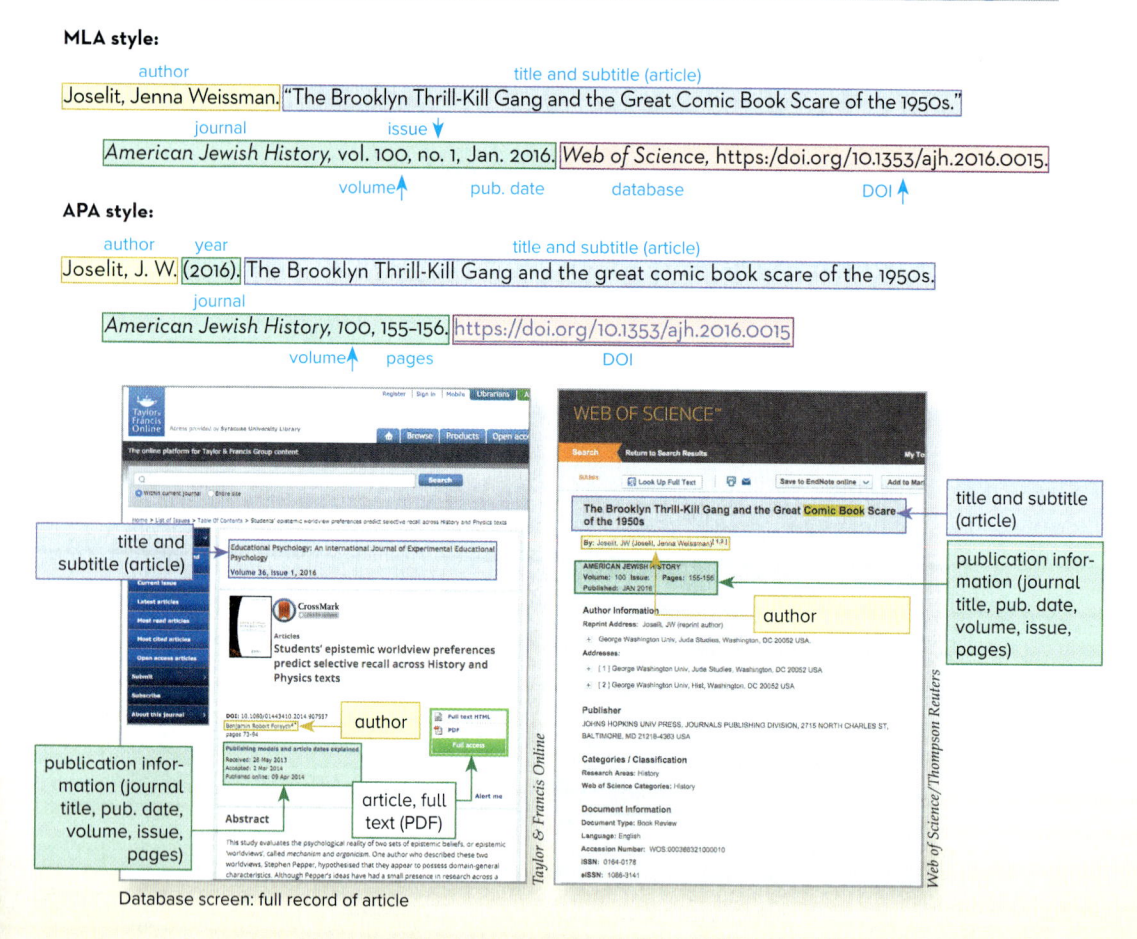

MLA style:

Joselit, Jenna Weissman. "The Brooklyn Thrill-Kill Gang and the Great Comic Book Scare of the 1950s." *American Jewish History*, vol. 100, no. 1, Jan. 2016. Web of Science, https://doi.org/10.1353/ajh.2016.0015.

APA style:

Joselit, J. W. (2016). The Brooklyn Thrill-Kill Gang and the great comic book scare of the 1950s. *American Jewish History, 100*, 155–156. https://doi.org/10.1353/ajh.2016.0015

Database screen: full record of article

Find what you need to document an article from a database on the search results screen, the full record of the article, or the first and last pages of the article itself. (For more, see pp. 362–64 for MLA style, pp. 416–18 for APA style.)

332

MLA and APA

Short Work on a Website

MLA style:

author — Clifton, Lucille. | title of short work (poem) — "Bouquet." | title of website (journal) — *The Paris Review*, | pub. date — Summer, 2000,
URL for short work (poem) — https://www.theparisreview.org/poetry/7548/bouquet-lucille-clifton.

While access dates are optional, it is helpful to include them in an MLA-style citation if the work has no pub. date.

APA style:

author — Clifton, L. | pub. date — (Summer, 2000). | title of short work (poem) — Bouquet. | URL for short work (poem) — https://www.theparisreview.org/poetry/7548/bouquet-lucille-clifton

---

the **PARIS REVIEW** ← title of website (journal)

bouquet ← title of short work (poem)

author → Lucille Clifton

ISSUE 233, SUMMER 2020 ← publication information

text of poem → i have gathered...

The Paris Review

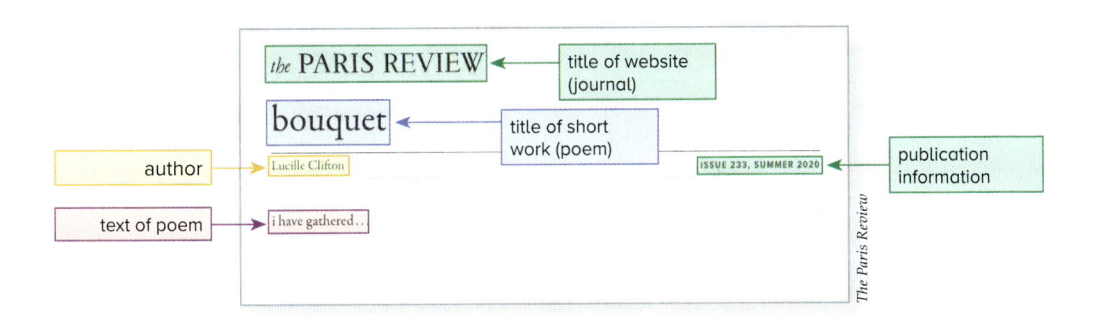

Frequently, the information you need to create a complete entry in the list of works cited is missing or difficult to find on web pages. Look at the top or bottom of the web page or home page or for a link to an "About" or "Contact Us" page. (For more, see pp. 366–70 for MLA style, pp. 419–22 for APA style.)

333

18 Documenting Sources: MLA Style

IN THIS CHAPTER

a. In-text citations, 335

b. Works-cited list, 352

c. Informational notes, 378

d. Formatting, 379

**Student Model
Research Project:
MLA Style, Isabel Beck,
"Fast Fashion," 383**

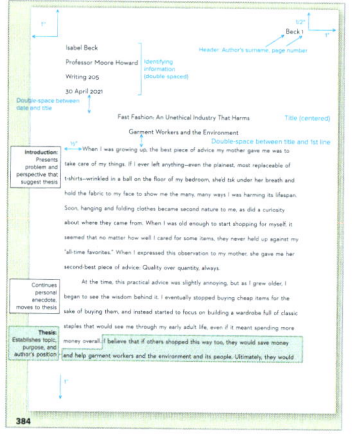

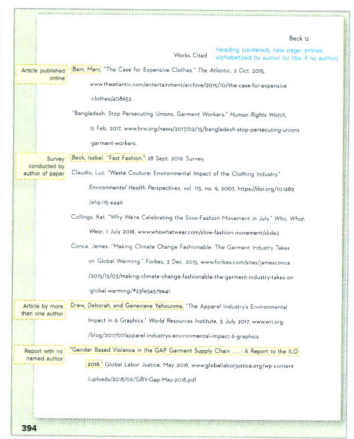

Developed by the Modern Language Association (MLA), MLA style guidelines are used by many researchers in the humanities—especially in languages and literature—to cite and document sources and to format researched projects in a uniform way. These guidelines are revised every few years to accommodate changes in research, writing, and publishing technologies. The *MLA Handbook* (9th ed.) requires that writers acknowledge sources in two ways:

- **Citation:** In the body of your project, provide an in-text citation for each source used.
- **Documentation:** At the project's end, provide a list of all the works you cited in the project.

In-text citations appear in the body of your project. They mark each use you make of a source, regardless of whether you are quoting, paraphrasing, summarizing, or drawing ideas from it. They also alert readers to a shift between *your* ideas and those you have borrowed.

18a Creating MLA-Style In-Text Citations

You can cite a source in your text by using a signal phrase and page reference (in parentheses) or a parenthetical citation:

- *Signal phrase.* Include the author's name and an appropriate verb in your sentence before the borrowed material, and put the page number(s) in parentheses after the borrowed material. Provide the author's full name the first time you mention a source; for subsequent citations you can use just the author's surname. You should never use the author's first name alone.

> While encouraging writers to use figurative language, **journalist Constance Hale cautions** [signal phrase] that "a metaphor has the shelf life of a fresh vegetable" (**224**) [page no.], illustrating the warning with her own lively metaphor.

[Qualifications of source author]

Using a signal phrase allows you to integrate the borrowed material into your sentence, to put the source in context by adding your own interpretation, and to describe the qualifications of the source author. For these reasons, most summaries, paraphrases, and quotations should be introduced by a signal phrase.

> **More about**
> Documenting a Source: MLA Style and APA Style, 330–33 (*Documentation Matters* tutorial preceding this chapter)
> Popular academic styles per discipline, 491, 511–12
> APA style (ch. 19), 397–438
> *Chicago* style (ch. 20), 439–69
> CSE style (ch. 21), 470–84

> **More about**
> Signal verbs (ch. 17), 312–28

Writing Responsibly — Citing and Documenting Sources

When you cite and document sources, you demonstrate how thoroughly you have researched your topic and how carefully you have thought about your sources, which encourages your audience to believe you are a credible researcher. In your citations and documentation you acknowledge any material that you have borrowed from a source and you join the conversation on your topic by adding your own interpretation. Accurate entries in the body of your project and list of works cited allow your audience to find and read your sources so that they can evaluate your interpretation and learn more about the subject themselves. Accurate entries also demonstrate the care with which you have written your research project, which further reinforces your credibility, or ethos.

to AUDIENCE

- ***Parenthetical citation.*** Include in parentheses the author's surname plus the page number(s) from which the borrowed material comes:

> While figurative language can make a passage come alive, be aware that metaphors have "the shelf life of a fresh vegetable" (Hale 224).
>
> *parenthetical note*

Parenthetical citations are useful when you are citing more than one source, when you are establishing facts, or when the author's identity is not relevant to the point you are making.

> *More about*
> Creating works-cited entries, 352–77

NOTE The works-cited entry is the same whether you use a signal phrase or a parenthetical citation:

> *author* — Hale, Constance. *title* — *Sin and Syntax.* *publication info* — Broadway, 2001.

1. Include enough information to lead readers to the source in your list of works cited.

Whether you are using a signal phrase or a parenthetical citation, in-text citations should provide enough information for readers to locate the source in the ***list of works cited.*** In most cases, providing the author's full name or surname and a page reference is enough. Occasionally, however, you may need to provide more information:

> Example 6, 343

- If you cite more than one source by the same author, mention the title of the work in the text or include a shortened form of the title in the in-text citation. (You may also want to mention the title of the work, if it is relevant to the point you are making.)

> Example 7, 343

- If you refer to sources by two different authors who have the same surname, be sure to include the authors' first initials in any parenthetical in-text citation.

> Example 8, 343
> Example 16a, 349

Occasionally, you may need to include less information. For example, you would omit a page number when you are summarizing an entire source, when your source is just one page long, or when your source, such as a web page, is not paginated.

Quick Reference: General Principles of In-Text Citation

- Cite not only direct quotations but also paraphrases, summaries, and information gathered from a source, whether printed or online.
- In most cases, include the author's full name and a page reference. Use only the author's surname for additional in-text references or in parenthetical references. For one-page and unpaginated sources (such as websites), provide only the author's name.
- Place the name(s) either in a signal phrase or in a parenthetical citation. A signal phrase makes it easier to integrate borrowed information or the author's credentials into your own prose. Use a parenthetical citation when establishing facts or citing more than one source at a time.
- For two or more sources by the same author, include the title—either a complete title in the text or an abbreviated title in the parenthetical citation.
- Whenever you add a title or an abbreviated title, insert a comma between the surname and the title, but not between the title and the page number. In parenthetical citations, do not insert punctuation between the author's surname and the page number.

> **More about**
> What you do and do not need to cite, 283–84
> Signal phrases, 312–28
> Signal verbs (list), 315
> Integrating borrowed material into your text, 313–16

2. Place in-text citations to avoid distracting readers and show them where borrowed material starts and stops.

When you incorporate a quotation, paraphrase, summary, or idea from a source into your own text, carefully consider the placement of the in-text citation, keeping the following goals in mind:

- To make clear exactly which material is drawn from the source
- To avoid distracting your reader

Tech: Page References and Web Pages

Despite the term *web page*, most websites do not have page numbers in the sense that printed books do. Your browser may number the pages when you print a web page from a website, but this numbering appears only on your printed copy. Different computers and printers break pages differently, so your printed page 5 might be someone else's page 4 or 6. For this reason, in-text citations of most web pages include only the author's name. If a website numbers its paragraphs, provide that information in place of a page reference.

Signal phrase When using a signal phrase, bookend the borrowed information: Insert the author's name before, and the page number after, the cited material. For a source with more than two authors, a phrase such as *and others* or *and colleagues* is included.

> [signal phrase] Brian Knutson and colleagues found that when shown a desirable object for sale, the nucleus accumbens, or pleasure sensors, in the test subjects' brains lit up ([page number] 148).

> **More about**
> Phrases, 651–54
> Clauses, 654–56
> Sentences, 657–58

Parenthetical citation When using a parenthetical citation, place the note at a natural pause—at the end of a phrase, clause, or sentence—right after the borrowed material and before any punctuation.

Following a sentence

> Research shows that when consumers learn about how their clothes are made, and the impact of that production on people and the environment, they are willing to purchase slow fashion or sustainable clothing items (Hiller-Connell 303).

Following a clause (unpaginated source)

> The Rana Plaza factory disaster, the deadliest structural failure in modern history, created controversy within the fashion industry (Stauffer), especially when word got out that Western companies produced apparel there.

Following a phrase (unpaginated source)

> The Rana Plaza factory disaster, the deadliest structural failure in modern history and one that shook the fashion industry (Stauffer), revealed the complicity of Western companies.

Block quotations When the text you are quoting takes up more than four lines of your project, indent the borrowed material as a block by one-half inch from the left margin, and place the parenthetical citation one space after the closing punctuation mark. No quotation marks should be used when indenting quoted material as a block.

> **More about**
> Block quotations, 346, 380–81

Example

> signal phrase
> Howard and Kennedy assert that parents and school officials tend to ignore hazing until an incident becomes public knowledge. They describe a concrete incident that demonstrates their claims:
>
> > 1/2" In general, the Bredvik school community (parents, teachers, coaches, and students) condoned or ignored behaviors that could be called "hazing" or "sexual harassment." However, when the incident was formally brought to the attention of the larger, public audience, a conflict erupted in the community over how to frame, understand, and react to the event. (347-48)

3. Adjust in-text citations to match your source.

The exact form of an in-text citation depends on the source. Does it have one author, several authors, or no authors? Is the source paginated? Is the source a novel, a story in an anthology, or a *PowerPoint* presentation? The examples below cover the most common source types. (A list of in-text citation examples in MLA style appears on page 341.) For more unusual sources, study the general principles as outlined here and in the *MLA Handbook,* 9th ed. (available in any library), and adapt them to your special circumstances.

> **More about**
> Integrating supporting material, 313–14
> When to use signal phrases, 314, 315

Writing Responsibly: Using Signal Phrases to Demonstrate Your Relationship with Sources

As you consider using a source, think about *why* you want to use it. Does it provide a supporting reason or illustration? Does it provide an authoritative voice? Does it make a point that contrasts with your own? Then include a signal phrase that reflects your answer to that question.

> Tom Bergin, who covers the oil and gas industry for *Reuters,* provides one example of the consequences of offshore drilling.
>
> Neurobiologist Catherine Levine agrees with this point of view.
>
> The views of meteorologist John Coleman contrast dramatically with those of the majority of climate scientists.

to TOPIC

MLA In-Text Citations Index

1. One author
2. Two authors
3. Three or more authors
4. Group, government, or corporate author

1. One author

a. Signal phrase

[Thomas Cahill cautions] responsible historians against disparaging the Middle Ages. Medieval Europe's reputation as a time of darkness, ignorance, and blind faith is "largely (if not wholly) undeserved" ([310]).
page no.

b. Parenthetical citation

The Middle Ages are often unjustly characterized as a time of darkness, ignorance, and blind faith ([Cahill] [310]).

2. Two authors Include the full names (at first mention) or surnames of the two authors in your signal phrase; include only the surnames in the parenthetical citation. Use *and,* not an ampersand (&), in the parenthetical citation.

To write successfully about their families, authors must have motives beyond merely exposing secret histories ([Miller and Paola] [72]).

Quick Reference: Examples of MLA-Style In-Text Citations

1. One author 340
   a. Signal phrase 340
   b. Parenthetical note 340
2. Two authors 340
3. Three or more authors 341
4. Group, government, or corporate author 342
5. Unnamed author 342
6. Two or more sources by the same author 343
7. Two or more authors with the same surname 343
8. Entire source (including a one-page source) 343
9. Selection from an anthology 344
10. Multivolume source 344
11. Literary source 344
    a. Novel 345
    b. Poem 345
    c. Play 346
12. Sacred text 346
13. Motion picture, television or radio broadcast, podcast 347
14. Indirect source 347
15. Dictionary or encyclopedia entry 348
16. Website or other online source 349
    a. Without page, paragraph, screen, or slide numbers 349
    b. With paragraph, screen, or slide numbers 349
    c. In a PDF file 349
17. Personal communication (email, letter, interview) 350
18. Table, chart, or figure 350
19. Government document 351
20. Legal source 351
21. Multiple sources in one sentence 351
22. Multiple sources in one citation 351
23. Audio or video source 352

MLA In-Text Citations Index

1. One author
2. Two authors
3. **Three or more authors**
4. Group, government, or corporate author
5. Unnamed author

3. Three or more authors For sources with three or more authors, add *and others* or *and colleagues* after the first author's full name (at first mention) or surname in your signal phrase. Insert the Latin phrase **et al.** following the first author's surname in the parenthetical citation.

et al. Abbreviation of the Latin phrase *et alii*, "and others"

> 1st author's surname + *and others* in signal phrase
> Visonà and others stress that symbols used in African art are not intended to be iconic but instead to suggest a wide variety of meanings. The authors liken this complexity to "a telephone line that carries multiple messages simultaneously" (19).

NOTE *Al.* is an abbreviation, so it requires a period; *et* is a complete word, so it does not. Do not italicize this Latin phrase in your citation.

> Symbols used in African art are not intended to be iconic but rather to suggest a complex range of meanings (Visonà et al. 19).
>
> [1st author + et al.]

> Example 3, 353

Do the same in your list of works cited.

MLA In-Text Citations Index

2. Two authors
3. Three or more authors
4. **Group, government, or corporate author**
5. **Unnamed author**
6. Two or more sources by the same author
7. Two or more authors with the same surname

4. Group, government, or corporate author When a government agency, corporation, or other organization is listed as the author, use that organization's full name in the signal phrase in your in-text citation.

> [government agency as author]
> The Federal Emergency Management Agency indicates that Kansas City is located in a region of frequent and intense tornado activity (4).

Include the complete name in a parenthetical citation if it consists of a short noun phrase; otherwise, shorten the name to the briefest phrase possible. For example, the *National Association of Social Workers* would be *National Association* in a parenthetical reference.

5. Unnamed author If the author is unnamed and the work is alphabetized by title in the list of works cited, use the title in your in-text citation. Abbreviate long titles in parenthetical citations.

> One nineteenth-century children's book vows that "when examined by the microscope, the flea is a pleasant object," and the author's vivid description of this sight—a body "curiously adorned with a suit of polished armor, neatly jointed, and beset with a great number of sharp pins almost like the quills of a porcupine"—may win readers' curiosity, if not their sympathy (*Insects* 8).
>
> [title]

> Example 4, 354

If you do abbreviate the title, start your abbreviation with the word by which the title will be alphabetized in your list of works cited. Also, only if the author is listed specifically as "Anonymous" should you use that designation.

Documentation Matters • Creating MLA-Style In-Text Citations

6. Two or more sources by the same author When you draw on two or more sources by the same author, differentiate between those sources by including titles.

> In her book *Nickel and Dimed*, [book title] social critic Barbara Ehrenreich demonstrates that people cannot live on the then-current minimum wage (60). Perhaps, as she notes in her blog entry "'Values' Voters Raise Minimum Wages," [blog entry title] they will be a little better able to hold their own in the six states (Arizona, Colorado, Montana, Missouri, Nevada, Ohio) that have recently raised their minimum wage.

A lengthy title should be abbreviated in the parenthetical citation. For example, the title of Ehrenreich's blog entry would be shortened to "'Values' Voters."

7. Two or more authors with the same surname When you cite sources by two different authors with the same surname, differentiate them by including their first names each time you mention them in a signal phrase, or by including their first initials in a parenthetical citation.

> Including citations is important not only because they give credit but also because they "organize a field of inquiry, create order, and allow for accountability" (S. Rose 243). This concern for acknowledging original sources dates back to the early eighteenth century: Joseph Addison was one of the first to argue for "the superiority of original to imitative composition" (M. Rose 114).

8. Entire source (including a one-page source) Mention an entire source—whether it is a film or a website, a book or an article, a painting or a cartoon—using the information that begins the entry in your list of works cited.

> The film *The Lady Eve* asks whether love is possible without trust.

> Example 41b, 372

MLA In-Text Citations Index

4. Group, government, or corporate author
5. Unnamed author
6. **Two or more sources by the same author**
7. **Two or more authors with the same surname**
8. **Entire source**
9. Selection from an anthology
10. Multivolume source

> Example 10, 357

MLA In-Text Citations Index

8. Entire source
9. Selection from an anthology
10. Multivolume source
11. Literary source
12. Sacred text

9. Selection from an anthology If your source is a selection from an anthology, reader, or other collection, your citation should name the author of the selection—not the editor of the anthology. In the example below, William Faulkner is the author of the selection "A Rose for Emily," a story that appears in a literature anthology edited by Robert DiYanni.

> Southern fiction often explores the marked curiosity that women of stature and mystery inspire in their communities. [author of selection] William Faulkner's "A Rose for Emily," for example, describes the title character as "a tradition, a duty, and a care; a sort of hereditary obligation upon the town . . ." (79).

> Example 15b, 359

10. Multivolume source If you use information from more than one volume of a multivolume work, your in-text citation must indicate both the volume and the page from which you are borrowing. (This information can be omitted if you use only one volume of the work, since your works-cited entry will indicate which volume you used.)

> Esteemed journalist [author] Ida Tarbell writes that in 1847 Abraham Lincoln was a popular man of "simple, sincere friendliness" who was an enthusiastic—though awkward—bowler ([vol. no.] 1: [pg. no.] 210).

11. Literary source Because many classics of literature—novels, poems, plays—are published in a number of editions (printed and digital) with pagination that varies widely, your citation should provide your readers with the information they will need to find the passage, regardless of which edition they are reading.

a. Novel Include the chapter number (with the abbreviation *ch.*) after the page number from your edition. Include only the chapter number for a digital book that has no stable page numbers.

> Joyce shows his protagonist's dissatisfaction with family, faith, and country through the adolescent Stephen Daedalus's first dinner at the adult table, an evening filled with political and religious discord (274; ch. 1).
>
> _{pg. no. ch. no.}

Use arabic (2, 9, 103), not roman (ii, ix, ciii), numerals, regardless of what your source uses.

If the novel has chapters grouped into parts or books, include both the part or book number and the chapter number, using the appropriate abbreviation (*pt.* for *part* or *bk.* for *book*).

> Even though New York society declares the Countess Olenska beyond her prime, Newland Archer sees in her the "mysterious authority of beauty" (Wharton 58; bk. 1, ch. 8).

MLA In-Text Citations Index

9. Selection from an anthology
10. Multivolume source
11. **Literary source**
12. Sacred text
13. Motion picture, television or radio broadcast, podcast

b. Poem For poetry, use line numbers, rather than page or location numbers. With the first reference to line numbers, use the word *line* or *lines*; omit it thereafter.

> Shakespeare ends Sonnet 55 with a gesture to his lover (lines 13–14), but it seems an afterthought to a sonnet that meditates on death: "Like as the waves make towards the pebbled shore, / So do our minutes hasten to their end" (1–2).
>
> _{1st ref ... later ref}

For long poems that are divided into sections (books, parts, numbered stanzas), provide section information as well, omitting the section type (such as *book* or *part*) and separating the section number from the line number(s) with a period. If you provide more than four lines of the poem, treat the material as you would a block quotation.

MLA In-Text Citations Index

10. Multivolume source
11. Literary source
12. **Sacred text**
13. Motion picture, television or radio broadcast, podcast
14. Indirect source

Use arabic (*1, 5*), not roman (*i, viii*), numerals, and omit spaces.

> More about block quotations, 380–81

Use arabic (*1, 5, 91*), not roman (*i, v, xci*), numerals for act, scene, and line numbers, and omit spaces after periods between numbers.

No space

Lord Byron's *Don Juan* (1818–1824) begins with a cheeky criticism of heroism, indicating the poem's irreverent outlook on life that is to come.

> I want a hero: an uncommon want,
>
> When every year and month sends forth a new one,
>
> Till, after cloying the gazettes with cant,
>
> The age discovers he is not the true one;
>
> Of such as these I should not care to vaunt, . . . (1.1–5)
>
> ↑ lines

c. Play When citing plays, use act, scene, and line numbers (in that order), not page numbers or location numbers (used in digital editions). Do not label the parts. Instead, separate them with periods.

> When the ghost of Hamlet's father cries, "Adieu, adieu, adieu! remember me," Hamlet wonders if he must "remember" his father through vengeance (1.5.91).

12. Sacred text Cite sacred texts (such as the Bhagavad-Gita, the Talmud, the Qur'an, and the Bible) not by page number but by book title (abbreviated in parenthetical citations), chapter number, and verse number(s), and separate each section with a period. Do not italicize titles of sacred books or put them in quotation marks, and do not italicize the name of the sacred text, unless you are referring to a specific edition.

> *sacred text*
> In the Bible's timeless love poetry, the female speaker concludes her description of her lover with this proclamation: "This is my beloved and this is my friend, / O daughters of Jerusalem" (Song of Sol. 5.16).
>   *book   ch. verse*

>   *specific edition*
> *The New Oxford Annotated Bible* offers a moving translation of the love poetry in the
>   *book*
> *Song of Solomon.* The speaker ends her description of her lover with this proclamation:
>   *ch. verse*
> "This is my beloved and this is my friend, / O daughters of Jerusalem" (5.16).

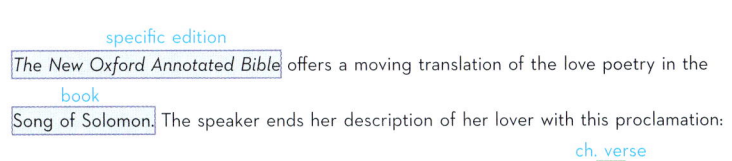

13. Motion picture, television or radio broadcast, podcast The information you include in an in-text citation for a motion picture, a television or radio broadcast, or podcast depends on what you are emphasizing in your project. When you are emphasizing the work itself, use the title; when you are emphasizing the director's work, use the director's name; when you are emphasizing an actor's work, use the actor's name. Start your works-cited entry with whatever you have used in your in-text citation.

>   *title*
> While *The Lady Eve* is full of slapstick humor, it is mainly remembered for its snappy
> dialogue, at once witty and suggestive.

>   *actor's name*
> Barbara Stanwyck's portrayal of Jean Harrington is at once sexy and wholesome.

14. Indirect source When you can, avoid quoting from a secondhand source. When you cannot use the original source, mention the name of the person you are quoting in your sentence. In your parenthetical citation, include *qtd. in* (for *quoted in*) plus the name of the author of the source in which you found the quotation.

> Handel's stock among opera-goers rose over the course of the twentieth century. In 1912,
>   *author quoted*
> an English music critic, H. C. Colles, maintained that "it would be difficult, if not impossible,
>   *source of quotation*
> to make any one of Handel's operas tolerable to a modern audience" (qtd. in Orrey 62).
> Today, however, Handel's operas are performed around the world.

MLA In-Text Citations Index

11. Literary source
12. Sacred text
13. **Motion picture, television or radio broadcast, podcast**
14. **Indirect source**
15. Dictionary or encyclopedia entry
16. Website or other online source

❯ Example 41b, 372

MLA In-Text Citations Index

13. Motion picture, television or radio broadcast, podcast
14. Indirect source
15. **Dictionary or encyclopedia entry**
16. Website or other online source
17. Personal communication

> **More about**
> Parts of a dictionary entry, 615–17

In your list of works cited, include the *indirect* source (*Orrey*), not the source being quoted (*H. C. Colles*).

15. Dictionary or encyclopedia entry In the citation of a dictionary or encyclopedia entry, omit the page number on which you found the item. For a dictionary entry, place the defined word in quotation marks, followed by the abbreviation *def.* Follow this with the letter or number of the definition you wish to reference.

> Another definition of *honest* is "respectable" ("Honest," def. 6), but what, if anything, does truth have to do with respectability?

In the parenthetical citation for an encyclopedia entry, include the entry's full title in quotation marks.

> The study of ethics is not limited to philosophers, as its "all-embracing practical nature" makes it an applicable or even necessary course of study in a wide variety of disciplines, from biology to business ("Ethics").

If you are citing two entries with the same title from different reference sources, add an abbreviated form of the reference work's title to each entry.

> While the word *ethics* is commonly understood to mean "moral principles" ("Ethics," def. 4, *Random House Webster's*), to philosophers it is "the evaluation of human conduct" ("Ethics," *Philosophical Dict.*).

16. Website or other online source Cite electronic sources such as websites, online articles, ebooks, and emails as you would print sources, even though many of these sources do not use page numbers.

a. Without page, paragraph, screen, or slide numbers Unless there is another stable numbering system at work (such as numbered paragraphs, screens, or slides), cite the author without a page reference.

> When first published in 1986, Alan Moore's *Watchmen* revolutionized the comic book. Today, even its harshest critics acknowledge the book's landmark status (Shone). *[author only]*

You may credit your source more elegantly by mentioning the author in a signal phrase and omitting the parenthetical citation altogether.

> Reading Alan Moore's *Watchmen* in 2005, critic Tom Shone found it "underwhelming," *[signal phrase]* but he admitted that in 1986 the comic book was "unquestionably a landmark work."

b. With paragraph, screen, or slide numbers If an electronic source numbers its paragraphs, screens, or slides, and the numbers do not change, you can reference these numbers as you would pages (with an appropriate identifying abbreviation or word—*par.* or *pars.*, *screen* or *screens*). Place a comma after the author's name if it also appears in the parenthetical citation.

> The internet became an outlet for direct distribution through artist websites, making independent titles not only more accessible to consumers but also more affordable for individual artists to produce and market (Fenty et al., par. 1).

c. In a PDF file Online documents offered as a PDF (portable document format) file include all the elements of the printed document, including the page number. Since pages are fixed, you can and should cite page numbers.

MLA In-Text Citations Index

14. Indirect source
15. Dictionary or encyclopedia entry
16. **Website or other online source**
17. Personal communication
18. Table, chart, or figure

> *More about*
> PDF files, 208–9, 230, 246, 249

MLA In-Text Citations Index

15. Dictionary or encyclopedia entry
16. Website or other online source
17. Personal communication
18. Table, chart, or figure
19. Government document
20. Legal source

> Examples 46–50, 374–76

17. Personal communication (email, letter, interview) As with other unpaginated sources, when citing information from a letter, an email message, an interview, or other personal communication, you should include the author's name in a signal phrase or parenthetical citation. Also indicate the type of source you are citing.

> Many people have asked why teachers cannot do more to prevent school shootings; in an [email] *[source type]* to this author, one instructor responds: "As creative writing teachers untrained in psychology, can we really determine from a student's poetry whether they are emotionally disturbed—even a threat to others?" ([Fox]). *[author of email]*

18. Table, chart, or figure If a copy of the visual you are discussing is *not* included in your project, include relevant information in the text (artist's name or table title, for example), and include an entry in your list of works cited.

> There is no experience quite like standing in front of a full-size painting by [Jackson Pollock]. His paintings have an irresistible sense of movement to them, the particular quality of which is unique to his work. This is especially evident in [One (Number 31, 1950)], which once hung on the fourth floor of [New York's Museum of Modern Art].

Table 1
The Demise of the Three-Decker Novel

Year	No. of 3-deckers published
1894	184
1895	52
1896	—
1897	4
1898	0

Source: Information from [John Feather], [*A History of British Publishing*]. [Crown Helm, 1988, p. 125.]

FIGURE 18.1 Table in MLA style

If a copy of the visual *is* included in your project, reference it in your text. Include the source information in a table's source note (Figure 18.1). Use the abbreviation *Fig.* (or the label *Figure* if preferred) and a number for other types of visuals and place the caption below the figure. Include full source information in the caption if you do not cite the source in the text, set up like a works-cited entry but with the author's given name first (see the figure caption on p. 388).

19. Government document Provide enough information in the signal phrase or parenthetical citation for readers to locate the government source in the list of works cited.

> Just as the nation was entering World War II, the United States War Department published a book about reading aerial photographs.

> Example 51, 376

20. Legal source Laws, acts, and legal cases are typically referred to by name either in your sentence or in a parenthetical citation. Laws and acts are neither italicized nor enclosed in quotation marks.

> Example 52, 376

> In 2008 the U.S. Congress passed the Combat Bonus Act.

Legal cases are italicized in your text as well as in the parenthetical citation.

> In 1963 the Supreme Court ruled that poor defendants should receive legal representation, even if they could not pay for it themselves (*Gideon v. Wainright*).

21. Multiple sources in one sentence When you use different information from multiple sources within a single sentence, give separate citations in the appropriate places.

> Other common themes of underground comics include sex and sexual identity, politics, and social issues (Daniels 165), as shown in Crumb's work, which is well known for its satirical approach to countercultural topics (Heller 101-02).

MLA In-Text Citations Index

17. Personal communication
18. Table, chart, or figure
19. Government document
20. Legal source
21. Multiple sources in one sentence
22. Multiple sources in one citation
23. Audio or visual source

22. Multiple sources in one citation When you draw information from more than one source, follow the borrowed material with a list of all relevant sources, separated by semicolons.

Documentation Matters • Documenting Sources: MLA Style

> Entire source—no page reference

Jamestown was once described as a failed colony populated by failed colonists, but new findings suggest that the colonists were resourceful survivors (Howard; Lepore 43).

MLA In-Text Citations Index

20. Legal source
21. Multiple sources in one sentence
22. Multiple sources in one citation
23. **Audio or visual source**

> Example 40d, 372

23. Audio or video source For a source displayed in an audio or a video player, provide the time in the page number position. Hiddleston's name appears in the author position in the corresponding works-cited entry.

> Tom Hiddleston's interpretation of Hamlet's famous soliloquy has a resigned, world-weary tone, especially as he evokes the idea of death as "the undiscovered country" (01:59–02:03).

MLA Works-Cited Entries

1. **One author**
2. Two authors
3. Three or more authors

> Annotated visual of where to find author, title, and publication information, in tutorial preceding this chapter, 330–33

18b Preparing an MLA-Style List of Works Cited

The list of works cited, which comes at the end of your research project, includes information about the sources you have cited in your text. (A bibliography that includes sources you read but did not cite in your research project is called a *list of works consulted.*) Your list of works cited provides readers with the information they need to locate the material you used in your project. (See the Quick Reference box on pp. 354–55 for a list of MLA-style examples included in this chapter.)

Books—Printed and Electronic

In a printed book, most or all of the information you need to create an entry in the list of works cited appears on the title and copyright pages, which are located at the beginning of the book. In an online or e-book, print and electronic publication information often appears at the top or bottom of the first page or screen or is available through a link.

1. One author

a. Printed The basic entry for a printed book looks like this:

> Author's surname, First name. *Title: Subtitle.* Publisher, date of publication.

Here is an example of an entry in a list of works cited:

<u>author</u>   <u>title</u>   <u>publication information</u>
Morrison, Toni. *Home*. Alfred A. Knopf, 2012.
                              <u>pub.</u> <u>date</u>

Many Chinese, Japanese, and Korean names begin with the surname and do not need to be reversed or separated by a comma.

b. Database When you are documenting a book you accessed through a database or an archive, add the name of the database and include the DOI (digital object identifier) or a permalink, if available. Otherwise, provide the complete URL for that book within the database.

> Farmer, Philip José. *The Green Odyssey*. Ballentine, 1957.
> <u>database</u>
> *Project Gutenberg*, https://www.guteneberg.org/ebooks/50571.
>   <u>URL</u>

c. Ebook The citation for an electronic version of a book is the same as for a printed book except for the inclusion of *E-book ed.*

> Morrison, Toni. *Home*. E-book ed., Alfred A. Knopf, 2012.

2. Two authors List authors in the order in which they appear on the title page. Only the first author should be listed with surname first.

> <u>author 1</u>   <u>author 2</u>
> Valle, Jan W., and David J. Connor. *Rethinking Disability: A Disability Studies Approach to Inclusive Practices*. Routledge, 2019.
>
> <u>author 1</u>   <u>author 2</u>
> Anderson, Poul, and Karen Anderson. *Innocent at Large*. Project Gutenberg, 3 Apr. 2016, www.gutenberg.org/files/51650/51650-h/51650-h.htm.

3. Three or more authors List the first author and add *et al.*

> Akmajian, Adrian, et al. *Linguistics: An Introduction to Language and Communication*. MIT, 2017.
>
> Collinson, Diané, et al. *Fifty Eastern Thinkers*. Routledge, 2000, https://doi.org/10.4324/9780203005408.

MLA Works-Cited Entries

1. One author
2. **Two authors**
3. **Three or more authors**
4. Unnamed (anonymous) author
5. Author using a pen name

> **More about**
> *et al.*, 341

> Example 3, 341–42

Reference: Examples of MLA-Style Works-Cited Entries

Books—Printed and Electronic

1. One author 352
   a. Printed 352
   b. Database 353
   c. Ebook 353
2. Two authors 353
3. Three or more authors 353
4. Unnamed (anonymous) author 354
5. Author using a pen name (pseudonym) 356
6. Two or more works by the same author 356
7. Group or corporate author 356
8. Edited book or anthology (printed or online) 356
9. Author and editor or translator 357
10. One or more selections from an edited book or anthology 357
11. Edition other than the first 358
12. Imprint (division) of a larger publishing company 358
13. Introduction, preface, foreword, or afterword 358
14. Entry in a reference work 358
    a. Printed 359
    b. Online 359
    c. CD or DVD 359
15. Multivolume work 359
    a. Multiple volumes 359
    b. One volume 359
16. Book in a series 359
17. Republished book 360
18. Title within a title 360
19. Sacred text 360
20. Missing publication information 360
21. Pamphlet, brochure, or press release 361
22. Conference proceedings 361
23. Dissertation 361

Periodicals—Printed and Electronic

24. Article in a scholarly journal 362
    a. Printed 362
    b. Accessed through a database 362
    c. Online 363
25. Article in a magazine (weekly, monthly) 363
    a. Printed 363
    b. Accessed through a database 363
    c. Online 363
26. Article in a newspaper 364
    a. Printed 364
    b. Accessed through a database 364
    c. Online 365
27. Article on microform 365
28. Review (printed or online) 365
29. Editorial (printed or online) 365
30. Letter to the editor (printed or online) 365

Other Electronic Sources

31. Website 366
32. Web page or short work on a website 366
33. Home page (academic) 367
    a. Course 367
    b. Department 367
34. Discussion list posting 367
35. Article on a wiki 367

MLA Works-Cited Entries

4. Unnamed (anonymous) author

4. Unnamed (anonymous) author Start the entry with the title.

Terrorist Hunter: The Extraordinary Story of a Woman Who Went Undercover to Infiltrate the Radical Islamic Groups Operating in America. HarperCollins, 2003.

36. Social media post (on a blog, *Facebook, Instagram, Reddit, TikTok, Twitter*) 367
    a. Elements of social media entries 367
    b. Author names 368
    c. Post as title 368
    d. Description as title: image 368
    e. Description as title: meme 368
    f. Comment on a post 369
    g. Publisher's name 369
    h. Date of post 369
    i. URL 369
37. Consumer network post and review (on *Yelp, TripAdvisor, Etsy, eBay*) 370
    a. Consumer review networks 370
    b. Shopping networks 370
38. App (for an e-device) 370
39. Video game (for devices such as *Xbox, Wii*) 370

Audio and Visual Sources

40. Motion picture 371
    a. Film 371
    b. Video or DVD 371
    c. Internet download 371
    d. Online video clip 372
41. Television or radio broadcast, podcast 372
    a. Series 372
    b. Episode 372
    c. Single program 372
    d. Podcast 373
42. Musical or other audio recording 373
    a. CD, LP, audiobook 373
    b. Song or selection from a CD or an LP or a chapter from an audiobook 373
    c. Compressed music file (MP3, MP4) 373
    d. Online sound file or clip 373
43. Live performance 374
    a. Ensemble 374
    b. Individual 374
44. Musical composition 374
45. Lecture, speech, or debate 374
46. Table 374
47. Work of art 374
    a. Original work 375
    b. Reproduction of a work of art 375
48. Comic or cartoon 375
    a. Cartoon or comic strip 375
    b. Comic book or graphic novel 375
49. Map or chart 375
50. Advertisement 376

Miscellaneous Sources—Printed and Electronic

51. Government document 376
    a. Printed 376
    b. Online 376
52. Legal source 376
53. Letter (published) 376
    a. Single letter 376
    b. Collection of letters 377
54. Interview 377
55. Personal correspondence 377
    a. Letter 377
    b. Email 377
    c. Memorandum 377
    d. Text message 377
56. Diary or journal 377
    a. Single entry, published 377
    b. Single entry, unpublished 377
    c. Diary or journal, published 377

Alphabetize the entry in your list of works cited using the first significant word of the title (not an article like *a, an,* or *the*). Only if the author is listed specifically as "Anonymous" should you use that designation in the works-cited entry (and in your text).

MLA Works-Cited Entries

4. Unnamed (anonymous) author

Anonymous. *Go Ask Alice.* Prentice Hall, 1971.

MLA Works-Cited Entries

3. Three or more authors
4. Unnamed (anonymous) author
5. **Author using a pen name**
6. **Two or more works by the same author**
7. Group or corporate author
8. **Edited book or anthology**
9. Author and editor or translator
10. One or more selections from an edited book or anthology

5. Author using a pen name (pseudonym) If the author is using a pen name (or *pseudonym*), document the source using the author's pen name and insert the author's actual name in parentheses following the pseudonym.

Keene, Carolyn (Edward Stratemeyer). *The Secret of the Old Clock*. Grosset & Dunlap, 1930.

6. Two or more works by the same author Alphabetize the entries by the first important word in each title. Supply the author's name only with the first entry. For subsequent works, replace the author's name with three hyphens.

Ritter, Kelly. *Before Shaughnessy: Basic Writing at Yale and Harvard, 1920–1960.*

Southern Illinois UP, 2009.

---. *Reframing the Subject: Instructional Film and Class-Conscious Literacies.* U of

Pittsburgh P, 2015.

7. Group or corporate author Treat the sponsoring organization as the author.

corporate author
Blackfoot Gallery Committee. *The Story of the Blackfoot People: Nitsitapiisinni.* Firefly

Books, 2002.

8. Edited book or anthology When citing the book as a whole, treat the editor as the author and insert the word *editor* (or *editors* if there is more than one editor) after the name. For more than two editors, use the first editor's name (surname first), followed by a comma and the words *et al., editors.*

Hazen, Kirk, editor. *Appalachian Englishes in the Twenty-First Century.* West Virginia U, 2020.

Pedersen, Isabel, and Andrew Iliadis, editors. *Embodied Computing: Wearables,*

Implantables, Embeddables, Indigestibles. MIT, 2020.

Sarto, Guida, et al., editors. *The Cambridge Companion to Boccaccio.* Cambridge UP,

2015. *University Publishing Online*, https://dx.doi.org/10.1017/CCO9781139013987.

9. Author and editor or translator List the author first. After the title, include the words *Edited by* or *Translated by* (as appropriate) before the editor's or translator's name. If the book was accessed online, add the information shown in item 1b–c.

> Larsson, Asa. *Sun Storm.* Translated by Marlaine Delargy. Delacorte Press, 2006.

10. One or more selections from an edited book or anthology If your source is a selection (such as a chapter, a story, a poem, or an image) in an edited book or anthology, think of that book or anthology as a *container,* and provide full information about both your source and its container. Start your entry with the selection's author and title.

> [author] [title (selection)]
> Faulkner, William. "A Rose for Emily." *Literature: Reading Fiction, Poetry, and Drama,*
> [pages (selection)]
> edited by Robert DiYanni, 6th ed., McGraw-Hill, 2007, pp. 79-84.

When documenting a longer work, such as a novel or a play, that is included in the anthology or collection, italicize the work's title.

> [title (selection)]
> Ives, David. *Sure Thing. Literature: Reading Fiction, Poetry, and Drama.* . . .

If you are citing more than one selection in the anthology or collection, include an entry for the collection as a whole.

> DiYanni, Robert D., editor. *Literature: Reading Fiction, Poetry, and Drama,* 6th ed., McGraw-Hill, 2009.

Then, for each selection you use, include only the author and title, the surname of the anthology's editor, and the page numbers of the selection.

> Faulkner, William. "A Rose for Emily." DiYanni, pp. 79-84.

For a scholarly article included in an edited book, provide the article's original publication information as the first part, or *container,* of the entry, and then the publication information for the edited book as the second container.

> [original publication info]
> Stock, A. G. "Yeats and Achebe." *The Journal of Commonwealth Literature,* vol. 5, no. 3,
> [reprint publication info]
> 1970, pp. 105-11. *Things Fall Apart,* by Chinua Achebe, edited by Francis Abiola Irele,
> Norton Critical Edition, W. W. Norton, 2008, pp. 271-77.

If the book was accessed online, add the information shown in item 1b–c.

MLA Works-Cited Entries

7. Group or corporate author
8. Edited book or anthology
9. **Author and editor or translator**
10. **One or more selections from an edited book or anthology**
11. Edition other than the first
12. Imprint (division) of a larger publishing company

▸ Example 8, 356

▸ Example 24 a–c, 362–63

MLA Works-Cited Entries

9. Author and editor or translator
10. One or more selections from an edited book or anthology
11. **Edition other than the first**
12. **Imprint (division) of a larger publishing company**
13. **Introduction, preface, foreword, or afterword**
14. **Entry in a reference work**
15. Multivolume work
16. Book in a series

11. Edition other than the first Insert the edition number (*2nd ed.*, *3rd ed.*) or edition name (*Rev. ed.* for "revised edition") before the publication information. The edition number or name should appear on the title page.

> Feather, John. *The Information Society: A Study of Continuity and Change.* 6th ed.,
> Facet Publishing, 2013.

12. Imprint (division) of a larger publishing company Name only the main publisher.

> Betcherman, Lita-Rose. *Court Lady and Country Wife: Two Noble Sisters in*
> *publisher*
> *Seventeenth-Century England.* HarperCollins Publishers, 2005.

13. Introduction, preface, foreword, or afterword Begin with the name of the person who wrote this section of the text. Then provide a descriptive label (such as *Introduction* or *Preface*), the title of the book, and the name of the book's author. (If the author of the section and the book are the same, use only the author's surname after the title.) Include the page numbers for the section.

> Howard, Rebecca Moore. Foreword. *Authorship Contested: Cultural Challenges to the*
> *Authentic, Autonomous Author,* edited by Amy E. Robillard and Ron Fortune,
> Routledge, 2016, pp. xii–xiii.

If this section has a title, include it after the author's name; the descriptive label is optional but generally omitted.

> *afterword's title*
> Burton, Larry W. "Countering the Naysayers: Independent Writing Programs as
> Successful Experiments in American Education." *A Field of Dreams: Independent*
> *Writing Programs and the Future of Composition Studies,* edited by Peggy O'Neill,
> et al., Utah State UP, 2002, pp. 295–300.

14. Entry in a reference work Format an entry in a dictionary or an encyclopedia as you would a selection from an edited book or anthology. For signed articles, include the author's name. (Articles in reference works often carry the author's initials only, so you may need to cross-reference the initials with a list of contributors in the front or back of the book.) If an article is unsigned, begin with its title.

a. Printed For a standard dictionary definition, include an abbreviation for the part of speech in italics (*N.* or *Adj.*, for example) and the number of the definition if there is more than one.

> "Culture, N. (2)." *The American Heritage Dictionary of the English Language*, 4th ed.,
>
> Houghton Mifflin, 2000, p. 442.
>
> Green, Michael. "Cultural Studies." *A Dictionary of Cultural and Critical Theory*,
>
> Blackwell Publishers, 1996.

b. Online For online reference works, include the full URL of the site you referenced.

> "Culture, *N* (5)." *Merriam-Webster Online Dictionary*, 2016, www.merriam-webster.com
>
> /dictionary/culture.

c. CD or DVD Although CDs have largely been replaced by the Internet, you may still need to use them. If the CD or DVD is published in versions rather than editions, include the version number before the publication information. Including the medium (CD, DVD) is not necessary, but if your source contains multiple discs, include the disc number you used (such as *disc 1*) after the publication date.

> Cooley, Marianne. "Alphabet." *World Book Multimedia Encyclopedia*,
>
> *version*
> version 6.0.2, World Book, 2002.

15. Multivolume work

a. Multiple volumes Indicate the span of years in which the volumes were published, as well as the total number of volumes, followed by the abbreviation *vols.* Specify the volume from which you borrowed a particular passage or idea in your in-text citation.

> *pub. dates*
> Tarbell, Ida M. *The Life of Abraham Lincoln*. Lincoln Memorial Association, 1895–1900.
> *no. of vols.*
> 2 vols.

b. One volume If you used only one volume, include the number of the volume you used before the publication information, and give only the publication date of that volume.

> *vol. used*   *pub. date*
> Tarbell, Ida M. *The Life of Abraham Lincoln*. Vol. 1, Lincoln Memorial Association, 1895.

16. Book in a series
If the book you are citing is part of a series, the series title will usually be noted on the book's title page or on the page before the

---

MLA Works-Cited Entries

13. Introduction, preface, foreword, or afterword
14. Entry in a reference work
15. **Multivolume work**
16. Book in a series
17. Republished book
18. Title within a title

> Example 10, 344

MLA Works-Cited Entries

14. Entry in a reference work
15. Multivolume work
16. Book in a series
17. Republished book
18. Title within a title
19. Sacred text
20. Missing publication information
21. Pamphlet, brochure, or press release
22. Conference proceedings

title page. Insert the series title (with no quotation marks or italics) after the publication date. If books in the series are numbered, include the number following the series title.

> Todorov, Tzvetan. *Mikhail Bakhtin: The Dialogical Principle*. Translated by Wlad Godzich, U of Minnesota P, 1995. *[series title]* Theory and History of Literature *[no.]* 13.

17. Republished book If a book has been republished, its original date of publication will appear on the book's copyright page. If the original publication date may be of interest to your readers, include it before publication information for the version you consulted. If the book was edited or an introduction was added, include that information before the republication information.

> Burroughs, William S. *Naked Lunch*. *[orig. pub. date]* 1959. *[editors]* Edited by James Grauerholz and Barry Miles, *[repub. info.]* Grove Press, 2001.

18. Title within a title Omit italics from any title that would normally be italicized when it falls within the main title of a book.

> Birmingham, Kevin. *[book title]* The Most Dangerous Book: The Battle for *[title within title]* Ulysses. Penguin Books, 2014.

If the title within the title would normally appear in quotation marks, retain the quotation marks and italicize both titles.

19. Sacred text Italicize the title of the edition you are using. Editors' and translators' names follow the title.

> *The New Oxford Annotated Bible*. New Revised Standard Version, edited by Michael D. Coogan et al., 3rd ed., Oxford UP, 2010.

> *The Holy Qur'an*. Edited and translated by Abdullah Yusuf Ali, 10th ed., Amana Publications, 1997.

20. Missing publication information Provide as much information about your source as you are able to locate. The following source does not include printed page numbers, named authors, or a publication date. Therefore, these items are not included in the citation.

> "Healing in Action: A Toolkit for Black Lives Matter Healing Justice and Direct Action." Black Lives Matter. https://blacklivesmatter.com/wp-content/uploads/2018/01/BLM_HealingAction_r1.pdf.

21. Pamphlet, brochure, or press release Follow the format for print or online book entries. For a press release, include day, month, and year of publication, if available. Include the type of publication at the end of the entry.

"Statement: Beverly Cleary." *New York Public Library*, 26 Mar. 2021, www.nypl.org/press

/press-release/march-26-2021/statement-beverly-cleary. Press release.

22. Conference proceedings Include the title of the conference, the sponsoring organization (if its name is not cited in the conference title), and the date and location of the conference, if that information is not already included in the publication's title.

Bizzell, Patricia, editor. *Proceedings of the* Rhetoric Society of America:
Rhetorical Agendas: Political, Ethical, Spiritual. 28–31 May 2004,
U of Texas–Austin. Erlbaum, 2005.

For a paper delivered at a conference, provide the name of the speaker, the title of the talk, and the date as well as the location, if applicable.

Lindquist, Julie. "Writing and Teaching in a Time of COVID: Uncommon Reflections on

Learning and Loss." CCCC Virtual Annual Convention, 9 Apr. 2021.

23. Dissertation Italicize the title. Include the year of submission and the school to which the dissertation was submitted (abbreviate *University* to *U*). Place *PhD Dissertation* at the end of the entry, followed by online publication information, if available.

Brackins, Genevieve. *Mothering Amidst and Beyond Hegemony in Margaret Atwood's*

The Handmaid's Tale and Toni Morrison's Beloved. 2014. Florida State U,

PhD Dissertation. *ProQuest*, fsu.digital.flvc.org/islandora/object/fsu%3A253602.

Periodicals—Printed and Electronic

Newspapers, magazines, and scholarly journals are types of *periodicals* that publish collections of texts such as stories, articles, poems, and images at regular intervals—daily, monthly, or at set intervals during the year. Most researchers

---

MLA Works-Cited Entries

19. Sacred text
20. Missing publication information
21. Pamphlet, brochure, or press release
22. Conference proceedings
23. Dissertation
24. Article in a scholarly journal
25. Article in a magazine

MLA Works-Cited Entries

22. Conference proceedings
23. Dissertation
24. **Article in a scholarly journal**
25. Article in a magazine
26. Article in a newspaper

> Annotated visual of where to find author, title, publication, and other information, tutorial on pages preceding this chapter, 330–33

today find articles in periodicals by searching their library's *databases*—online indexes that provide citation information as well as an abstract (or summary) and sometimes an electronic copy of the article itself—in either PDF or HTML format. (A PDF file shows the article more or less as it would have appeared in print; an HTML file includes the text of the article but not the illustrations or formatting of the print version.) As you construct your works-cited entry for a selection in a periodical, think of that periodical as the selection's *container*, and provide full information about both the selection and the container. Include not only the title of the article (in quotation marks) but also the title of the periodical (in italics). The other publication information you include depends on the type of periodical you are documenting.

24. Article in a scholarly journal The information you need to create an entry for a printed journal article is on the cover or in the table of contents of the journal and on the first and last page of the article. For articles downloaded from a database, the information you need appears on the screen listing the articles that fit your search terms, on the first and last page of the file you download, or in the full record for the article you select. For articles that appear in journals published solely online, you may find the information you need on the website's home page, in the journal's table of contents, or on the first screen of the article.

a. Printed The basic entry for an article in a printed journal looks like this:

Surname, First name. "Article Title." *Journal Title*, vol. #, (issue) no. #, year, pp.

Here is a sample entry:

Weaver, Karen. "Trophies, Treasure, and Turmoil: College Athletics at a Tipping Point." *Change*, vol. 47, no. 1, 2015, pp. 36–45.

b. Accessed through a database When you document an article from a scholarly journal that you accessed through an online database, add the name of the database (in italics), and add the DOI for the article, preceded by *https://doi.org/*. If a DOI is not available, provide a permalink for the article, if possible, or the URL, copied and pasted from the browser window.

Weaver, Karen. "Trophies, Treasure, and Turmoil: College Athletics at a Tipping Point." *Change*, vol. 47, no. 1, 2015, pp. 36–45. *Taylor & Francis Current Content Access*, https://doi.org/10.1080/00091383.2015.996090.

c. Online To document an online journal article, follow the model for a printed journal article. After the publication information, add a comma and provide a complete DOI for the article preceded by *https://doi.org/*, or a permalink or URL if a DOI is not available. (The parts that are different from a printed journal article are highlighted.)

> Rousseau, Stéphanie, and Eduardo Dargent. "The Construction of Indigenous Language Rights in Peru: A Language Regime Approach." *Journal of Politics in Latin America*, vol. 11, no. 2, 2019, pp. 161-80. https://journals.sagepub.com/doi/full/10.1177/1866802X19866527.

25. Article in a magazine (weekly, monthly)

a. Printed Provide the issue's publication date (month and year or day, month, and year) and the page range for the article. Include the magazine's volume or issue number if they are available.

> Fuller, Alexandra. "Her Heart Inform Her Tongue: Language Lost and Found." *Harper's Magazine*, *pub. date* Jan. 2012, *pgs.* pp. 60-64.

> Gladwell, Malcolm. "Thresholds of Violence." *The New Yorker*, 19 Oct. 2015, pp. 30-37.

If the article appears on nonconsecutive pages (the first part appears on p. 2 but the rest of the article is continued on p. 10), include a plus sign after the first page number (2+).

b. Accessed through a database

> Fuller, Alexandra. "Her Heart Inform Her Tongue: Language Lost and Found." *Harper's Magazine*, Jan. 2012, pp. 60-64. *database* EBSCOhost, www.ebsco.com/ezproxy/fuller_01/12.

c. Online

> Carr, Nicholas. "Is Google Making Us Stupid?" *website* *The Atlantic*, July-Aug. 2008, www.theatlantic.com/magazine/archive/2008/07/is-google-making-us-stupid/306868/.

> Thomas, June. "Is Social Acceptance Killing Queer Cinema?" *website* *Slate*, 27 Nov. 2015, slate.com/human-interest/2015/11/gay-movies-two-hollywood-reporter-critics-think-2015s-queer-films-are-terrible.html.

MLA Works-Cited Entries

23. Dissertation
24. Article in a scholarly journal
25. Article in a magazine
26. Article in a newspaper
27. Article on microform

> Annotated visual of where to find author, title, publication, and other information, tutorial on pages preceding this chapter, 330–33

> More about
> Title capitalization, 861–62

MLA Works-Cited Entries

24. Article in a scholarly journal
25. Article in a magazine
26. **Article in a newspaper**
27. Article on microform
28. Review (printed or online)

26. Article in a newspaper The information you need to create an entry for a printed newspaper article is on the masthead of the newspaper (at the top of the first page) and on the first and last page of the article. For newspaper articles downloaded from a database, the information you need appears on the screen listing the articles that fit your search terms or on the first and last page of the article itself. Articles that appear in online versions of the newspaper usually contain all the information you need at the top of the first screen. Use conventional capitalization of titles even when your original source does not.

a. Printed For an article in a daily newspaper, include the date (day, month, year). If the paper paginates sections separately, include the section number, letter, or name immediately before the page number.

Richtel, Matt, and Julie Bosman. "To Serve the Young, eBook Fans Prefer Print." *The New York Times*, 21 Nov. 2011, p. B1.
  _{date   section & pg.}

If the work appears in a named or numbered section of the newspaper, add the section name before or the number after the abbreviation *sec.* If no author is listed, begin the entry with the title of the article. If the article continues on a nonconsecutive page, add a plus sign after the first page number (*A20+*). If the newspaper's masthead specifies an edition (such as late edition or national edition), include that information after the title.

Keller, Julia. "Viral Villainy." *Chicago Tribune*, final ed., 22 Mar. 2009, sec. 6, pp. 1+.
  _{edition   section, nonconsecutive. pg.}

If the name of the city in which the newspaper is published does not appear in the newspaper's title, include it in brackets after the title.

Speciale, Samuel. "Majority of Students Apply to Only One College, Federal Study Says." *Gazette-Mail* [Charleston], 26 Nov. 2015, p. B1.

For well-known national newspapers (such as *The Christian Science Monitor*, *USA Today*, and *The Wall Street Journal*), no city or state is needed. If you are unsure whether the newspaper is well known, consult your instructor or a reference librarian.

b. Accessed through a database For a newspaper article accessed through a database, add the database name and include the full DOI or URL for the article.

Maiman, Bruce. "In Praise of Common Courtesy." *The Sacramento Bee*, 15 Apr. 2014, p. 11A. Access World News, sacbee.com/opinion/op-ed/bruce-maiman.
  _{database}

c. Online For an online newspaper article, include the full DOI or URL.

Marris, Emma. "The Case against Zoos." *The New York Times,* [website] 11 June 2021,

www.nytimes.com/2021/06/11/opinion/zoos-animal-cruelty.html.

> IMPORTANT: Do not italicize a website name unless it is also the name of a periodical.

27. Article on microform Many libraries still store old issues of periodicals on microform, a photograph of a periodical viewed through a microform reader. An entry for an article on microform is the same as for a printed article.

If your source is preserved on microform in a reference source such as *News-Bank,* add the title of the reference source, italicized, and any access numbers (such as fiche and grid numbers) following the publication information.

> Example 24a, 362
> Example 25a, 363
> Example 26a, 364

28. Review (printed or online) Begin with the reviewer's name (if provided), followed by the title of the review. If the title of the work being reviewed is not indicated by the title of the review or the review itself is not titled, include the label *Review of* followed by the title and author of the work being reviewed. Finally, include the title of the periodical and its publication information. If the review was accessed online, add information as shown in item 24b–c, 25b–c, or 26b–c.

[reviewer] Grover, Jan. [title (review)] "Unreliable Narrator." Review of [title (book)] *Love Works Like This: Opening One's Life to a Child,* by [author] Lauren Slater. *Women's Review of Books*, vol. 19, nos. 10-11, 2002, p. 40.

MLA Works-Cited Entries

24. Article in a scholarly journal
25. Article in a magazine
26. Article in a newspaper
27. **Article on microform**
28. **Review**
29. **Editorial**
30. **Letter to the editor**
31. Website
32. Web page or short work on a website

29. Editorial (printed or online) Often editorials are unsigned. When that is the case, begin the entry with *Editorial Board,* followed by the title of the editorial and the periodical's publication information. For a signed editorial, style as shown in 24a, 25a, or 26a. Add *Op-ed* at the end of the entry for a signed newspaper editorial.

Editorial Board. "Making Tax Season Worse." *Columbus Dispatch,* 28 Feb. 2015, p. 11A.

If the editorial was accessed online, add information as shown in item 24b–c, 25b–c, or 26b–c.

30. Letter to the editor (printed or online) Begin with the author's name, followed by the label *Letter to the editor* and the publication information.

[letter author] Park, John. [label] Letter to the editor. *Time,* 5 Dec. 2011, p. 9.

> Example 24a–c, 362–63
> Example 25a–c, 363
> Example 26a–c, 364–65

If the letter to the editor has a title, add it (in quotation marks) after the author's name. If the letter to the editor was accessed online, add information as shown in item 24b–c, 25b–c, or 26b–c.

> Annotated visual of where to find author, title, and publication information, tutorial on pages preceding this chapter, 330–33

MLA Works-Cited Entries

29. Editorial
30. Letter to the editor
31. **Website**
32. **Web page or short work on a website**
33. Home page (academic)
34. Discussion list posting

Other Electronic Sources

While it is usually easy to find the information you need to create a complete entry for a book or an article in a periodical, websites can be a bit trickier. Most of the information you need will appear on the site's home page, usually at the bottom or top of the page, or on the web page you are documenting. Sometimes you may need to look further: Click on links such as "About us" or "More information." Frequently, websites do not provide complete information, so include as much as you can. Provide the most stable means of accessing the source that is available. A DOI (digital object identifier) is the most stable and should be preceded by *https://doi.org,* which you can add to any DOI that consists only of a number. If the source indicates a permalink instead, use that URL in your entry. If neither a DOI nor a permalink is available, provide the regular URL.

31. Website The basic entry for a website looks like this:

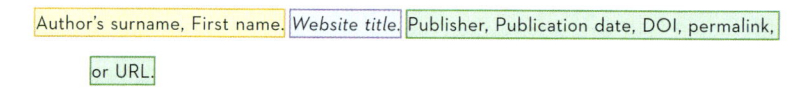

Author's surname, First name. *Website title.* Publisher, Publication date, DOI, permalink, or URL.

Here is a sample entry:

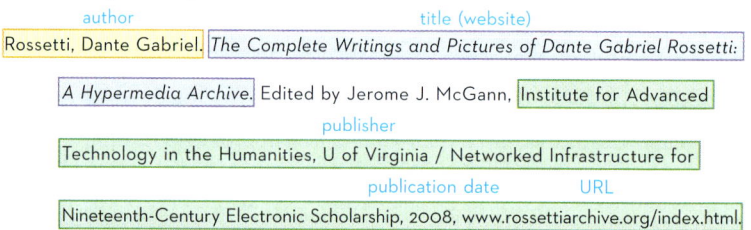

Rossetti, Dante Gabriel. [author] *The Complete Writings and Pictures of Dante Gabriel Rossetti:* [title (website)] *A Hypermedia Archive.* Edited by Jerome J. McGann, Institute for Advanced Technology in the Humanities, U of Virginia / Networked Infrastructure for [publisher] Nineteenth-Century Electronic Scholarship, 2008, www.rossettiarchive.org/index.html. [publication date] [URL]

If no author or editor is listed, begin with the website's title.

32. Web page or short work on a website If your source is part of a larger website, think of the larger site as a *container*, and provide full information about both your source and its container.

Callaghan, Jennefer. "Adorno, Theodor." [page title] *Postcolonial Studies @ Emory.* Dept. of English, Emory U, Oct. 2017, scholarblogs.emory.edu/postcolonialstudies/2014/06/01/65.

33. Home page (academic)
a. Course

"Philosophy of the Program: The Basics Underscoring the Approach to Composition Classes at Labette Community College." *Department of English*, Labette Community College, 2014, www.labette.edu/english/philosophy.html.

b. Department

English Dept. U of California–Santa Barbara, 2013, www.English.ucsb.edu/.

34. Discussion list posting
Treat the subject line (*thread*) as the title, and include the name of the list and the date of the posting.

Hubenschmidt, Holly. Comment on "Suggestions for Credit Bearing Information Literacy Course" thread. *Infolit*, 1 Oct. 2020, lists.ala.org/sympa/arc/infolit/2020-10/msg00002.html.

35. Article on a wiki
Usually wikis are written and edited collaboratively, so there is no author to cite. Instead, begin the entry with the article title. When a wiki article is signed, begin the entry with the author's name.

"History of Sweatshop Protests at SU, 2000–2001." *SyrGuide*. 11 June 2014, syrguide.com/guide/2014/06/11/history-of-sweatshop-protests-at-su-2000-2001.

36. Social media post (on a blog, *Facebook*, *Instagram*, *Reddit*, *TikTok*, *Twitter*)

a. Elements of social media entries Construct bibliographic entries for social media using these elements, in this order: author, title, publisher (platform name or blog title), date, URL.

Hughes, Akilah [@AkilahObviously]. "I made a bunch of cookies today," *Twitter*, 25 Dec. 2020, twitter.com/AkilahObviously/status/1342350307443949568.

MLA Works-Cited Entries

31. Website
32. Web page or short work on a website
33. **Home page (academic)**
34. **Discussion list posting**
35. **Article on a wiki**
36. **Social media post (on a blog, Facebook, Instagram, Reddit, TikTok, Twitter)**
37. Consumer network post and review (on Yelp, TripAdvisor, Etsy, eBay)
38. App (for an e-device)

MLA Works-Cited Entries

34. Discussion list posting
35. Article on a wiki
36. **Social media post (on a blog, Facebook, Instagram, Reddit, TikTok, Twitter)**
37. Consumer network post and review (on Yelp, TripAdvisor, Etsy, eBay)
38. App (for an e-device)

b. Author names

For posts on platforms such as *Twitter* and *Instagram*, provide the author's account name followed by the author's online handle in square brackets. If the name and handle are almost the same, you can omit the handle as long as you provide the URL. (A lengthy post can be shortened with ellipses—see also 36c.)

<u>author account name</u>
<u>Dr. Gen</u> [<u>@drchingona</u>]. "Most people know Bless Me Ultima. . . ." *Instagram*, 30 June 2020,
          <u>online handle</u>
    www.instagram.com/p/CBdvqemJNmW/.

c. Post as title

With the exception of blog posts, most social media entries, on platforms such as *Facebook*, *Instagram*, and *Twitter*, do not have a title. If the post is 140 characters or less (which is the case for many tweets), use the entire post as the title in your works cited entry. If it is longer than 140 characters, you can use ellipses to shorten it (see 36b).

                                        <u>title (entire post)</u>
Seys, Madeleine. <u>"I choose to use Dr because it is an ungendered title that is not connected to my age or relationship status. And because I worked hard to earn it."</u> *Twitter*, 8 Jul. 2020, twitter.com/MadeleineSeys/status/1281030397342564352.

d. Description of post as title: image

If the post is a meme or other image with no title or accompanying text, provide a description of the image; do not put quotation marks around your description:

                <u>title (description of image)</u>
Alvarez, Steven. <u>Shoes on a wire.</u> *Instagram*, 12 Jul. 2020. www.instagram.com/p/CCn8IVXBKht/?utm_source=ig_web_button_share_sheet.

e. Description of post as title: meme

If the post is a captioned meme, use the caption as the title of the source:

                                <u>title (description of image)</u>
Patterson, David. <u>"Vermeer's Lugubrious, *The Swoon* (Hoerst Is Gone and the Wifi Password Is Lost)."</u> *Facebook*, 5 May 2020, www.facebook.com/david.patterson.3114.

f. Comment on a post

For a comment on a social media post, begin the title with the words *Comment on* followed by the title of the post being commented on:

                                              title (of post being commented on)

Wise, Alicia. [Comment on] ["The Problem Solvers You Don't Know about Yet: Valuing

    Disability in the Publishing Industry."] *The Scholarly Kitchen*, 29 July 2019,

    scholarlykitchen.sspnet.org/2019/07/29/guest-post-the-problem-solvers-you

    -dont-know-about-yet-valuing-disability-in-the-publishing-industry.

g. Publisher's name

Use the italicized name of the social media platform (such as *TikTok* or *Twitter*) or the blog as the publisher.

                                        publisher (name of social media platform)

Love baking_Dave [@lovebaking778]. "Creative Cake." [*TikTok*,] 27 Dec. 2020,

    https://www.tiktok.com/@lovebaking778.

h. Date of post

Use the actual date of the post. If you are citing a thread, provide the date range, the first and last dates in the thread.

    u/Youknowwhatmaybe. "Elephant finds plastic ribbon and has the best day ever."

           date

    Reddit, [12 Dec. 2020], https://www.reddit.com/r/aww/comments/kl5rg8/elephant

    _finds_plastic_ ribbon_and_has_best_day.

i. URL

Conclude your entry with the URL of the post, followed by a period. When the platform (such as *Facebook*) doesn't provide a URL for individual posts, use the URL for the author's page.

    Weinstein, Liz. "First batch of bacon jam scones = completed. Need to make some

        adjustments, but think I have a winner on my hands here." *Facebook*, 18 June

                  URL

    2020, [https://www.facebook.com/liz.weinstein].

MLA Works-Cited Entries

34. Discussion list posting
35. Article on a wiki
36. **Social media post (on a blog, Facebook, Instagram, Reddit, TikTok, Twitter)**
37. Consumer network post and review (on Yelp, TripAdvisor, Etsy, eBay)
38. App (for an e-device)

MLA Works-Cited Entries

35. Article on a wiki
36. Social media post (on a blog, Facebook, Instagram, Reddit, TikTok, Twitter)
37. Consumer network post and review (on Yelp, TripAdvisor, Etsy, eBay)
38. App (for an e-device)
39. Video game
40. Motion picture
41. Television or radio broadcast, podcast

37. Consumer network posts and reviews (on *Yelp, TripAdvisor, Etsy, eBay*)

a. Consumer review networks Networks such as *Yelp, TripAdvisor,* and *Zomato* allow users to critique venues, products, and services. To cite such a source, follow the guidelines for social media (item 36). Below is a consumer's *Yelp* review of a restaurant.

author — Amy S.
title — Review of Dancing Yak,
publisher — *Yelp,*
date — 21 Dec. 2020,
URL — www.yelp.com/biz/dancing-yak-san-francisco-10?hrid=RDV6lwlmPy6tT9 kjTZqSw&utm_campaign=www_review_share.

b. Shopping networks Shopping networks such as *Etsy* and *eBay* allow users to buy and review products of independent sellers. To cite a shopping network post or review, follow the instructions for a social media post. Below is a seller's post for a product.

author — FreeYoMindCollective.
title (description of image) — Feminist button, destroy the patriarchy, not the planet,
publisher — *Etsy,*
date — 1 Dec. 2020,
URL — www.etsy.com/listing/859711200/feminist-button-destroy-the-patriarchy?.

38. App (for an e-device)

Minecraft Version 1.16.1, Mojang AB.

39. Video game (for devices such as *Xbox* or *Wii*)

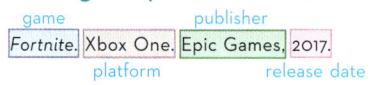

game — *Fortnite.*
platform — Xbox One.
publisher — Epic Games,
release date — 2017.

Audio and Visual Sources

The information you need to create an entry for most audio and visual sources will appear on the cover, label, or program of the work or in the credits at the end of a film. The person you list in the "author" position—the director, performer, artist, or composer—will vary depending on what you have emphasized in your research project. If you are writing about a director's body of work, put the director's name first; if you are writing about a performance, put the performer's name first. If it is the work itself that you are writing about, put the title of the work first. (This decision should be mirrored in your in-text citation.) However you choose to organize the entry, indicate the role of those whom you list, using phrases such as *performance by, directed by,* and *conducted by.*

As with any other entry, italicize the titles of complete or longer works (such as albums, films, operas, and original works of art) and place quotation marks around the titles of shorter works or works published as part of a larger whole (such as songs on a CD or a single episode of a television show). Publication information includes the name of the distributor, production company, or network, as well as the date on which the audio or visual was created, recorded, or broadcast. If you found the audio or visual source online and there is no date of publication, also include the date on which you accessed it.

MLA Works-Cited Entries

38. App (for an e-device)
39. Video game
40. **Motion picture**
41. Television or radio broadcast, podcast
42. Musical or other audio recording

40. Motion picture
a. Film

       title   director   distributor, release date
Da 5 Bloods. Directed by Spike Lee, Netflix, 2020.

If other artists besides the director are relevant to your project, list them between the director and the distributor.

                                             performers
Da 5 Bloods. Directed by Spike Lee, performances by Delroy Lindo and Chadwick Boseman,
        composer
    musical score by Terence Blanchard, Netflix, 2020.

If your project stresses the director, performer, or other contributor, place that information at the beginning of the citation.

   contributor   [contribution]
Blanchard, Terence, musical score. *Da 5 Bloods.* Directed by Spike Lee, performances by

    Delroy Lindo and Chadwick Boseman, Netflix, 2020.

b. Video or DVD
Include the original release date, when relevant, after the title.

             orig. release
The Lady Eve. 1941. Directed by Preston Sturges, performances by Barbara Stanwyck and
                        distributor
    Henry Fonda, Universal Home Entertainment, 2006.

c. Internet download (from *Netflix, Amazon Prime,* or other movie source)
Include the source you used to download the video, as well as the film's URL.

A Fall from Grace. Directed by Tyler Perry, performances by Crystal Fox, Phylicia Rashad,
                    source   URL
    Cicily Tyson, 2020. *Netflix,* www.netflix.com.

MLA Works-Cited Entries

38. App (for an e-device)
39. Video game
40. Motion picture
41. **Television or radio broadcast, podcast**
42. Musical or other audio recording
43. Live performance

d. Online video clip (from YouTube or other video source) Cite a video clip on *YouTube* or a similar site as you would a web page. If the name of the uploader appears, include it after the website (*uploaded by*). Since these types of videos are not always stable, you may want to include the date you accessed the material.

performer — Hiddleston, Tom. *video clip title* — "Tom Hiddleston Reads Hamlet's Soliloquy (Act 3, Scene 1)." *website* — *YouTube*, uploaded by Zsuzsanna Uhlik, *date posted* — 31 May 2019, *URL* — www.youtube.com/watch?v=FRtG0h7gxsI. *date accessed* — Accessed 7 May 2021.

41. Television or radio broadcast, podcast If your source is an episode in a series, think of that series as a *container*, and provide full information about both your source and its container. Start your entry with the title of the series or episode. Follow that with a list of the relevant contributors and include the network on which the series or episode aired. Because the director may change from episode to episode, other contributors, such as the creator or producer, may be more relevant. Include the date of the program. If your project emphasizes an individual, begin with that person's name.

a. Series

series title — *Will & Grace*. Created by David Kohan and Max Mutchnick, directed by James Burrows, performances by Erik McCormack and Debra Messing, *network* — NBC, *broadcast dates* — 21 Sept. 1998-23 Apr. 2020.

b. Episode

episode title — "October Surprise." *series title* — *The Politician*, performance by Theo Germaine, season 1, episode 3, Netflix, 2019. *Netflix*, www.netflix.com.

c. Single program

Persuasion. By Jane Austen. Adapted by Simon Burke, performances by Julia Davis and Rupert Penry-Jones, PBS, 13 Jan. 2008.

d. Podcast For a podcast, add the full URL for the file.

> Crespi, Sarah, and Lizzie Wade. "How Past Pandemics Reinforced Inequality, and
>
> Millions of Mysterious Quakes beneath a Volcano." *Science*, 14 May 2020,
>
> www.sciencemag.org/podcast/how-past-pandemics-reinforced-inequality-and
>
> -millions-mysterious-quakes-beneath-volcano.

[URL annotation points to the URL]

MLA Works-Cited Entries

39. Video game
40. Motion picture
41. Television or radio broadcast, podcast
42. **Musical or other audio recording**
43. Live performance
44. Musical composition

42. Musical or other audio recording Begin with whichever part of the entry is more relevant to your project—the name of the composer or performer, or the title of the CD or song. Place the title of shorter works, such as a song, in quotation marks. Italicize the titles of longer works, such as the title of an opera, but not the titles of symphonies identified only by form, number, and key, such as Brahms's Symphony no. 1 unless it is the title of an album, as in the second example below.

a. CD, LP, audiobook

> Adamo, Mark. *Little Women*. Performances by Stephanie Novacek et al., conducted
>
> by Patrick Summers, Ondine, 2001.

[prod. co. & release date annotation points to "Ondine, 2001."]

> Brahms, Johannes. *Symphony no. 1*. Performance by Chicago Symphony Orchestra,
>
> conducted by Georg Solti, Decca, 1992.

b. Song or selection from a CD or an LP or a chapter from an audiobook

> Eilish, Billie. "You Should See Me in a Crown." *When We Fall Asleep, Where Do We Go?*,
>
> Darkroom Interscope, 2019.

c. Compressed music file (MP3, MP4)

> The Head and the Heart. "Honeybee." *Living Mirage*, Reprise, 2019, www.pandora.com
>
> /station/play/3951239479175828731.

> Example 32, 366

d. Online sound file or clip For a sound recording accessed online, combine the format for a web page with the format for a sound recording.

> "The General Prologue, The Knight's Portrait, II, 43–78." *The Riverside Chaucer,* 3rd ed.,
>
> Houghton Mifflin, 2000. *Baragona's Literary Resources,* alanbaragona.wordpress.com
>
> /the-criyng-and-the-soun/the-general-prologue-the-knights-portrait-ii-43-78-baragona/.

MLA Works-Cited Entries

41. Television or radio broadcast, podcast
42. Musical or other audio recording
43. Live performance
44. Musical composition
45. Lecture, speech, or debate
46. Table
47. Work of art
48. Comic or cartoon
49. Map or chart

43. Live performance The entry for a performance is similar to that for a film. Include the venue and city of the performance and the date of the performance you attended. Include the names of important contributors after the title. If the performance is untitled, include a descriptive label.

a. Ensemble

Hamill, Kate. *Pride and Prejudice*. Directed by Jason O'Connell, performances by Jeff Gonzalez et al., [group] Syracuse Stage, [perf. date] 20 Mar. 2019.

b. Individual

[performer] Benet, Eric. "Eric after Dark." 1 July 2020, ericafterdark.com.

44. Musical composition To document a musical composition itself rather than a specific performance, recording, or published version of it, include only the composer and the title of the work (in italics unless the composition is identified only by form, number, and key).

[composer] Schumann, Robert. [untitled symphony] Symphony no. 1 in B-flat major, op. 38, 1841.

45. Lecture, speech, or debate Treat the speaker as the author; place the title in quotation marks (if there is one); and indicate the occasion and sponsoring organization (if relevant), location, date, and mode of delivery (such as *Lecture* or *Address*). If the lecture, speech, or debate is untitled, replace the title with a brief descriptive label.

[speaker] Barnhart, Edwin. [title] "Exploring the Mayan World." [sponsor/lecture series] The Great Courses, [date] 17 Jul. 2020, [URL] www.thegreatcoursesplus.com/exploring-the-mayan-world. [label] Lecture.

> Example 18, 350

46. Table For a table included in your project, place source information in a note below the table. For a table that you are discussing but that does not appear in your project, include an entry in your list of works cited following the model below. Include an access date if the table is likely to be updated.

[title] "Senate Salaries since 1789." [website] United States Senate, www.senate.gov/artandhistory/history/common/briefing/senate_salaries.htm. [label] Table. Accessed 13 Apr. 2020.

> Example 18, 350

47. Work of art For a work of art included in your project, place source information in the figure caption. For a work that you discuss but that does not appear in your project, include an entry in your list of works cited following the models below.

a. Original work

artist · title · date of production · location

Pollock, Jackson. *One (Number 31)*. 1950, Museum of Modern Art, New York City.

b. Reproduction of a work of art

Basquiat, Jean-Michel. *Hollywood Africans*. 1983, Museum of Fine Arts, Boston.

Writing the Future: Basquiat and the Hip-Hop Generation Exhibition Catalogue, by J. Faith Almiron et al., edited by Liz Munsell and Greg Tate, MFA Publications, 2020.

48. Comic or cartoon For a cartoon reproduced in your project, provide source information in the caption. For cartoons that you discuss without providing a copy of the image in your project, include an entry in your list of works cited following these models:

a. Cartoon or comic strip

artist · title · publication information

Spiegelman, Art. *Maus*. Pantheon Books, 1991.

b. Comic book or graphic novel
When a graphic novel is collaboratively written and the contributors have distinctly different roles, begin your bibliographic entry with the name and role of the contributor whom your project emphasizes:

author · title · illustrator

Sasturain, Juan, writer. *Perramus*. Illustrated by Alberto Breccia,

pub. info.

Fantagraphics, 2020.

If your project does not emphasize just one collaborator, begin the bibliographic entry with the title of the graphic novel, followed by the major contributors and their roles:

Perramus. Written by Juan Sasturain, illustrated by Alberto Breccia, Fantagraphics, 2020.

49. Map or chart For a map or chart reproduced in your project, provide source information in the caption. For a map or chart discussed but not included in your project, include an entry in your list of works cited following the model below.

"The Invasion of Sicily: Allied Advance to Messina (23 July–17 August 1943)." *The West Point Atlas of American War,* edited by Vincent J. Esposito, vol. 2, Frederick A Praeger, 1959, p. 247.

MLA Works-Cited Entries

45. Lecture, speech, or debate
46. Table
47. Work of art
48. Comic or cartoon
49. Map or chart
50. Advertisement
51. Government document

> Example 18, 350

MLA Works-Cited Entries

48. Comic or cartoon
49. Map or chart
50. Advertisement
51. Government document
52. Legal source
53. Letter (published)
54. Interview
55. Personal correspondence

> Example 7, 356
> Example 19, 351

50. Advertisement For an advertisement reproduced in your project, provide source information in the caption. For an advertisement discussed but not included in your project, include an entry in your list of works cited following the models below.

> Advertisement for Earthlink Cable Internet. *Metro*, 17 Apr. 2007, p. 11.
>
> *date accessed*
> Advertisement for Infiniti. *Yahoo.com*. Accessed 20 Apr. 2016.
>
> Advertisement for Tide detergent. *YouTube*, https://www.youtube.com/watch?v=YvjuL6Bci6M.

Miscellaneous Sources—Printed and Electronic

51. Government document If no author is listed, use the name of the governing nation and the government department and agency (if any) that produced the document, as you would for a work with a corporate author.

> *nation* *department*
> United States, War Department. *Advanced Map and Aerial Photograph Reading*.
>
> Government Publishing Office, 1941.

For congressional documents, you can include the number and session of Congress and the number and type of document as supplemental information at the end of the entry.

a. Printed

> United States, Congress, House. Combat Bonus Act. Government Publishing Office, 2008.
>
> 110th Congress, 2nd session, House Report 6760.

b. Online

> United States, Congress, House. Combat Bonus Act. Library of Congress, 31 July 2008,
>
> www.congress.gov/bill/110th-congress/house-bill/6760.

52. Legal source

> United States, Supreme Court. *Gideon vs. Wainwright*. 18 Mar. 1963. *FindLaw*,
>
> caselaw.findlaw.com/us-supreme-court/372/335.html.

53. Letter (published)

> Example 10, 357

a. Single letter Cite a single letter as you would a selection from an edited book or anthology but add the recipient's name, the date the letter was written, and the letter number (if there is one).

Brooks, Phillips. "To Agnes." 24 Sept. 1882. *Children's Letters: A Collection of Letters Written to Children by Famous Men and Women*, edited by Elizabeth Colson and Anna Gansevoort Chittenden, Hinds, 1905, pp. 3-4.

[author: Brooks, Phillips.] [recipient: "To Agnes."] [date written: 24 Sept. 1882.]

b. Collection of letters Cite as you would an edited book or anthology.

> Example 8, 356

54. Interview Treat a published interview as you would an article in a periodical. Treat an interview broadcast on radio or television or podcasted as you would a broadcast. For an unpublished interview you conducted, include the name of the person interviewed, a label such as *Personal interview with the author* or *Telephone interview with the author,* and the date on which the interview took place.

> Examples 24–25, 362–63
> Example 41, 372–73

Wentworth, Alicia. Personal interview with the author. 11 Feb. 2020.

[person interviewed: Wentworth, Alicia.] [label: Personal interview with the author.] [date: 11 Feb. 2020.]

55. Personal correspondence To document personal correspondence, such as a letter, include a descriptive label such as *Letter to the author.* Include the format of the letter, such as *Manuscript* or *Typescript,* at the end of the entry if that information is pertinent.

a. Letter

Green, D'Nice. Letter to the author. 13 Nov. 2019.

[letter writer: Green, D'Nice.] [label: Letter to the author.] [date written: 13 Nov. 2019.]

b. Email

Gomez, Cecilia. E-mail to Rebecca Howard. 12 Apr. 2021.

[email author: Gomez, Cecilia.] [E-mail to Rebecca Howard.] [date sent: 12 Apr. 2021.]

c. Memorandum Very few institutions send out printed memos anymore, but if you need to document one, treat it as you would an email message.

d. Text message

Grimm, Laura. Text message to the author. 14 June 2020.

56. Diary or journal

a. Single entry, published Treat an entry in a published diary or journal like an article in an edited book or anthology, but include a descriptive label (*Diary entry*) and the date of composition after the entry title. If the entry has no title, use the descriptive label and date as the title.

b. Single entry, unpublished

Zook, Aaron. "Sketches for *Aesop's Foibles* (new musical)." Journal entry. 1 May 2016.

[author: Zook, Aaron.] [title: "Sketches for *Aesop's Foibles* (new musical)."] [label: Journal entry.] [entry date: 1 May 2016.]

> Example 10, 357

c. Diary or journal, published Treat a complete diary or journal as you would an edited book or anthology.

> Example 8, 356

MLA Works-Cited Entries

51. Government document
52. Legal source
53. Letter (published)
54. Interview
55. Personal correspondence
56. Diary or journal

18c Using MLA Style for Informational Notes

In addition to in-text citations, MLA style allows researchers to include informational notes to provide relevant, but potentially distracting, content or to provide bibliographic information about one or more sources. MLA style recommends using a list of endnotes at the end of the project. Word-processing programs generally style numbers that identify informational notes in the text as well as the corresponding numbers in the list of endnotes as superscript (above-the-line) arabic numbers. Include an entry for each source mentioned in the notes in your list of works cited.

Use *content notes* to provide information that clarifies or justifies a point in your text, but avoid notes that include interesting digressions that could distract your readers. Isabel Beck's essay at the end of this chapter includes a content note. You can also use content notes to acknowledge the contributions of others (tutors, classmates, and so on) to the preparation of your project.

Bibliographic notes can add information about a source or point readers to other sources on the topic. If several sources provide the same information, cite the most valuable source in your text, and list the others in a bibliographic note. Then include the full citation of all these sources in your list of works cited.

A 2018 World Report from the Human Rights Watch describes rampant labor rights abuses and asserts that global brands that order products made in factories are obligated to make sure workers in those factories are safe and protected from abuse (Stauffer).[1] . . . In his 2019 statement to members of the U.S. Congress, Roeun reported that poverty wages have forced Cambodian garment workers to eat less (to the point of malnutrition) and work more (6 days a week, for 60 hours per week). When you combine that with the stifling heat of the un-airconditioned factories, the results, Rouen says, are "regular incidences of mass fainting."[2]

Notes   Heading (centered), new page

^{½"} [1] In his 2018 report, Stauffer also notes that in the $2.4 trillion apparel industry that employs millions of workers, factory owners punish those who affiliate with a union; force overtime; fire pregnant women; and ignore the sexual harassment of women in the workplace. The worst abuses take place in unauthorized subcontracted factories that are not monitored in any way.

[2] Roeun goes on to say that during failed negotiations for an increased minimum wage for workers, the Garment Manufacturers Association in Cambodia (GMAC), a collection of factory owners, insisted that the figure remain unchanged. Further, any boosts to wages have been accompanied by cutting employees and raising production targets. For example, in factories that supply products to H&M, Gap, and Levi-Strauss, in 2012, 105 workers made 1,500 pairs of pants per day; however in 2018, 55 workers were expected to make 2,300 pairs of pants per day.

18d Formatting a Paper in MLA Style

The care with which you cite and document your sources reflects the care you have taken in writing your research project. Continue that care by formatting your project in the way your readers expect. For most writing projects in literature and composition, follow the MLA's formatting guidelines.

1. Margins and spacing

Set one-inch margins at the top, bottom, and sides of your paper. Double-space the entire paper, including long quotations, the list of works cited, and any endnotes. Indent the first line of each paragraph by half an inch, and do not add an extra space between paragraphs. Use a hanging indent for each entry in the list of works cited: The first line should be flush with the left margin with subsequent lines indented half an inch. (For more on creating a hanging indent in a word processing program, see the Tech box on page 381.)

Student Model
Research project, MLA style, 383–96

> **Tech** **Creating a Header**
>
> Most word processing software allows you to insert a header. In Microsoft Word, select "Header" from the Insert tab. Any information you type into the header space will then appear at the top of every page of your manuscript. You can also choose to insert page numbers to paginate your project automatically.

> *More about*
> Choosing a typeface and type size, 192–94

2. Typeface

Choose a standard typeface, such as Times New Roman or Arial, in an easily readable size (usually 12 points).

3. Header

MLA style requires that each page of your project include a header, consisting of your surname and the page number. Place the header in the upper right-hand corner, a half inch from the upper edge and one inch from the right edge of the page.

4. Identifying information

No title page is required for individual projects in MLA style. Instead, include the following identifying information in the upper left-hand corner of the first page of your research project, one inch from the top and left edges of the paper:

- Your name
- Your instructor's name
- The number of the course in which you are submitting the paper
- The date

If your instructor requires a title page, ask for formatting instructions or follow the model on page 431. If your project was a collaborative effort, provide a separate title page that lists all the authors as well as the rest of the identifying information in the upper left-hand corner, and then center the title in the middle of the page.

> *More about*
> Crafting a title, 90

5. Title

Center the title of your project and insert it two lines below the date. Do not put quotation marks around your title or italicize it. Double-space again before beginning to type the first paragraph of your research project.

> *More about*
> Block quotations, 339, 346, 836
> Sample block quotations, 339 (prose), 346 (poetry)

6. Long quotations

Set quotations of prose longer than four lines of your text as a block: Omit the quotation marks, and indent the entire quotation one-half inch from the

Tech: Indentation

The major style guides (MLA, APA, *Chicago*, CSE) were initially written before the widespread use of personal computers, when most writers still worked on typewriters. To create a paragraph or hanging indent on a typewriter, the typist would hit the space bar five times or set a tab. Now, just about everyone creates writing projects on a computer, where paragraphs and hanging indents are created using the Ruler or Paragraph Dialog box.

Ruler

Move the top triangle to the right to create a paragraph indent

Move the bottom triangle to the right to create a hanging indent

Paragraph Dialog Box

Microsoft Corporation

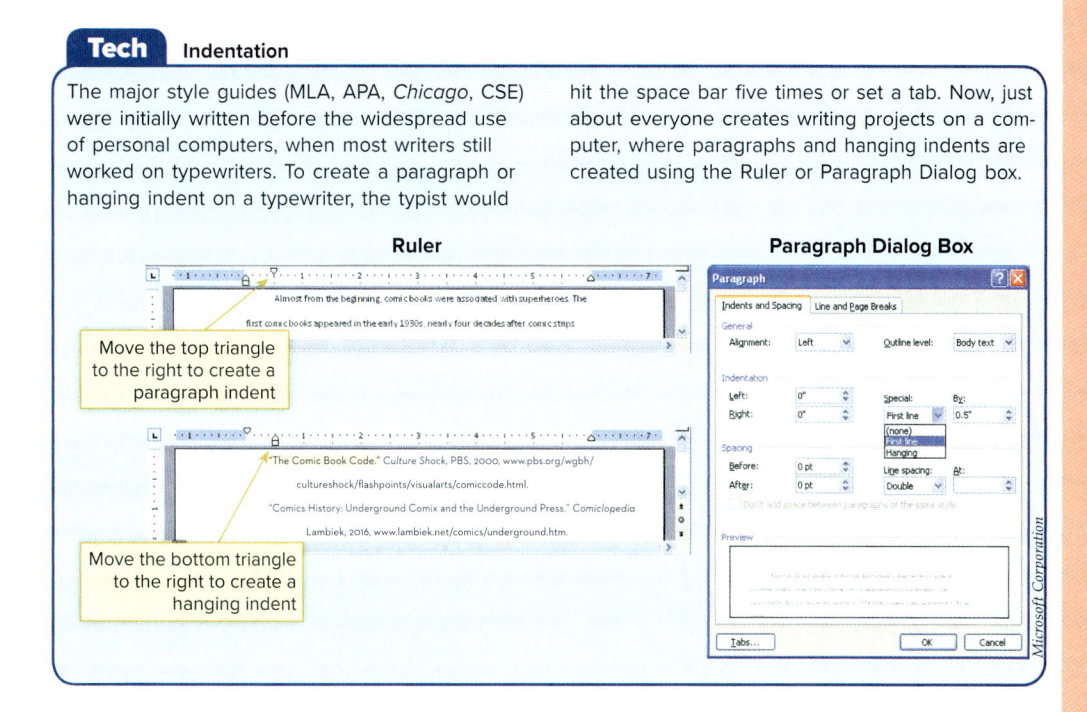

left margin of your text. When quoting four or more lines of poetry, indent all the lines one-half inch from the left margin; keep the same indentation and line breaks that were in the original poem, and include the line numbers of the passage quoted. If a line of the poem is too long to fit on a single line of your page, indent the continuation by an extra quarter of an inch.

7. Tables and figures

Tables and figures (photographs, cartoons, graphs, and charts) are most effective when they appear as close as possible after the text in which they are first discussed. (If placing figures and tables appropriately is awkward, consider including them in an appendix at the end of your project.) Labeling your tables and figures, both in the text and in your caption, will help readers connect your discussion with the illustration:

> Sample tables and figures, 77–85, 385, 387, 388

- Refer to the visual in your text using the word *table* or the abbreviation *fig.*, and number tables and figures in a separate sequence using arabic numerals (table 1, table 2; fig. 1, fig. 2). MLA style uses lowercase for in-text references to tables and figures unless they begin a sentence: "Table 1 presents 2010 data, and table 2 presents 2012 data."

> **Writing Responsibly** **Of Deadlines and Paperclips**
>
> Instructors expect students to turn in thoughtful, carefully proofread, and neatly formatted papers on time—usually in class on the due date. Another expectation is that the writer will clip or staple the pages of the paper *before* it is submitted. Do justice to yourself by being fully prepared.
>
> to SELF

- Accompany each illustration with the word *Table* or the abbreviation *Fig.*, the appropriate number, and a brief, explanatory title. Customarily, table numbers and titles appear above the table, and figure numbers and titles appear below the figure. Generally, they use the same margins as the rest of the paper and are double-spaced.

- If additional information is needed, provide an explanatory caption after the number and title. (Remember that your text should explain what the figure or table demonstrates. That information should not be repeated in the caption.)

- If you borrow the illustration or borrow information needed to create the illustration, cite your source. Any photographs or drawings you create yourself should identify the subject but do not need a citation. Citations usually appear below the table in a source note or in the figure caption. If you document the illustration in a figure caption or source note, you do not need to include an entry in your list of works cited.

8. Printing and binding

If you are submitting a hard copy of your project, print it using a high-quality printer (make sure it has plenty of ink), on opaque 8½ × 11–inch white paper. Most instructors do not want you to enclose your project in a binder. Unless your instructor tells you otherwise, staple or paperclip the pages together in the upper left-hand corner.

9. Portfolios

Many instructors ask students to submit the final draft of the research project in a portfolio, which may include an outline, preliminary notes and drafts, a working or annotated bibliography, and a personal statement describing their writing process and what they have learned from the experience.

> **More about**
> Outlining, 41–44, 305–7
> Note taking, 119–24, 286–87, 297–99
> Writing a first draft, 45–47
> Working or annotated bibliography, 230–36

Student Model Research Project: MLA Style: "Fast Fashion," by Isabel Beck

In the student model research project that follows, Isabel Beck fulfills her responsibilities to her topic and audience. She uses critical analysis to support her claim that fast fashion is dangerous and unethical, and she provides definitions, statistics, and evidence to fill in the background her readers might lack. Her research draws on a variety of print and online sources, personal experience, and field research (an original survey), and she uses visuals to support some of her points.

Following is the assignment prompt to which Isabel Beck responded:

Due May 2

Length: 3000-5000 words

In this essay, you'll pull together all the work you've done this semester on your project, as well as sources on research methods and background issues that we've shared as a class.

Genre: The genre of this entry is your choice: you can write it in a reflective tone; as a humanities-style research paper; as a qualitative research report; or something else you discuss with me.

Argument: Whether you decide to work in the mode of a Toulmin, Classical, or Rogerian argument, you need to clearly be making an argument.

What to include: The following list is not an outline for your essay, but rather a list of elements that you'll need to incorporate:

1. The current version of your research question
2. An explanation of what prompted you to pose and pursue your research question
3. A thesis statement that provides your current answer to your research question
4. Evidence that leads you to believe your thesis
5. Counterevidence: sources and perspectives that pull against your thesis; doubts you have about your thesis
6. Explanation of and reflection on the methods you used to explore your research question. How well did these work? What would you do differently if you were to start this research over?

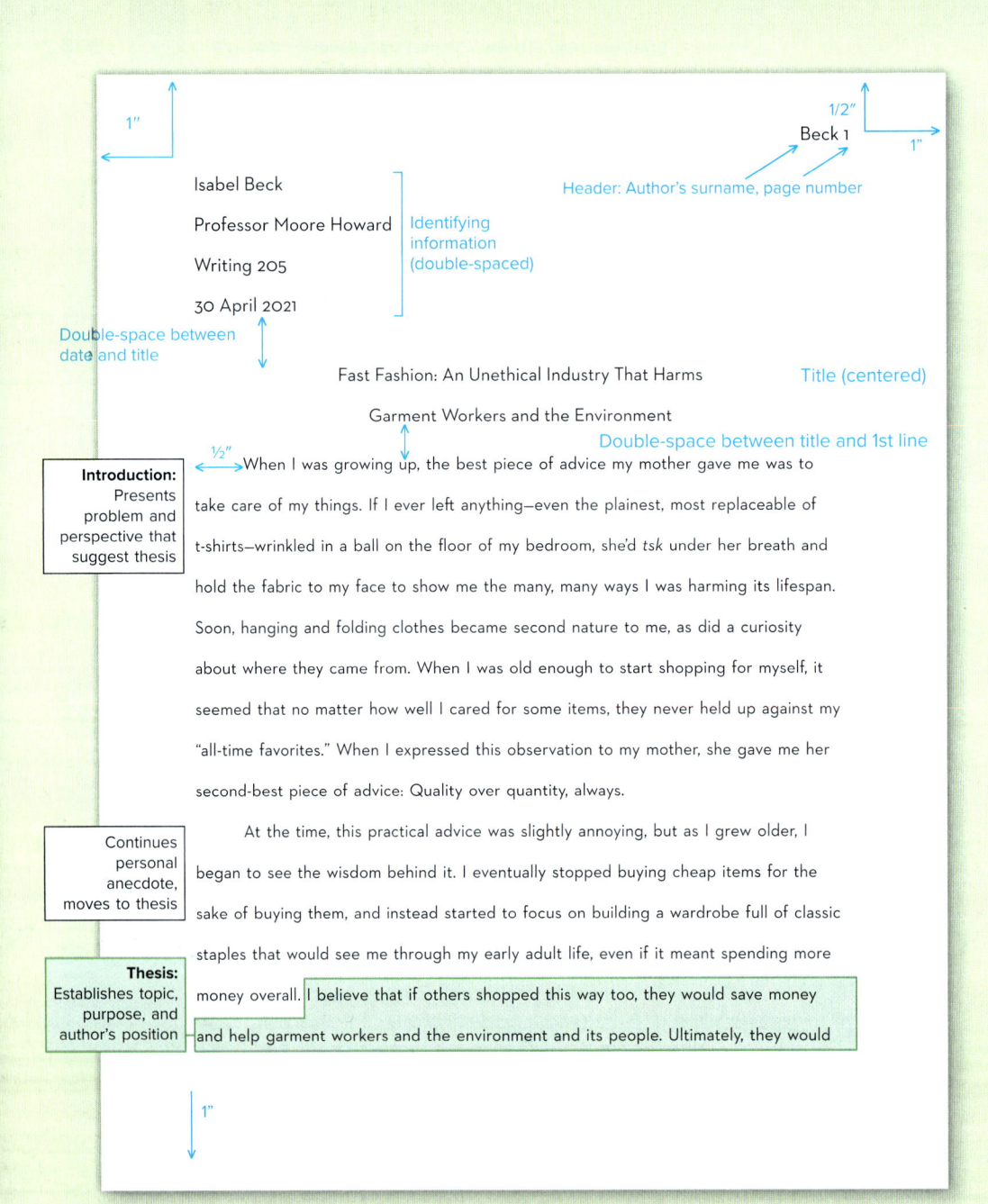

Isabel Beck

Professor Moore Howard

Writing 205

30 April 2021

Fast Fashion: An Unethical Industry That Harms Garment Workers and the Environment

When I was growing up, the best piece of advice my mother gave me was to take care of my things. If I ever left anything—even the plainest, most replaceable of t-shirts—wrinkled in a ball on the floor of my bedroom, she'd *tsk* under her breath and hold the fabric to my face to show me the many, many ways I was harming its lifespan. Soon, hanging and folding clothes became second nature to me, as did a curiosity about where they came from. When I was old enough to start shopping for myself, it seemed that no matter how well I cared for some items, they never held up against my "all-time favorites." When I expressed this observation to my mother, she gave me her second-best piece of advice: Quality over quantity, always.

At the time, this practical advice was slightly annoying, but as I grew older, I began to see the wisdom behind it. I eventually stopped buying cheap items for the sake of buying them, and instead started to focus on building a wardrobe full of classic staples that would see me through my early adult life, even if it meant spending more money overall. I believe that if others shopped this way too, they would save money and help garment workers and the environment and its people. Ultimately, they would see a better return on their investment. In order for better shopping habits to become widespread, however, as consumers, we need to understand the consequences of supporting the fast-fashion industry.

Fast fashion is the opposite of durable and classic. *Good on You*, an app that allows users to search for a fast-fashion retailer and rate it based on how socially responsible it is, defines fast fashion as "cheap, trendy clothing that samples ideas from the catwalk or celebrity culture and turns them into garments in big stores at breakneck speed." Indeed, clothes shopping used to be a relatively biannual affair: something that happened with the changing of the seasons, or out of wardrobe necessity. The existence of fast fashion, however, has turned shopping into something more akin to entertainment than anything else.

Topic sentence: Prepares reader for contextual information

Signal phrase identifies source and establishes credibility

As fig. 1 indicates, fast fashion increases the number of fashion seasons from two (spring/summer and fall/winter) to fifty. We're buying sixty percent more clothing

Topic sentence: Introduces visual; Paragraph gives evidence

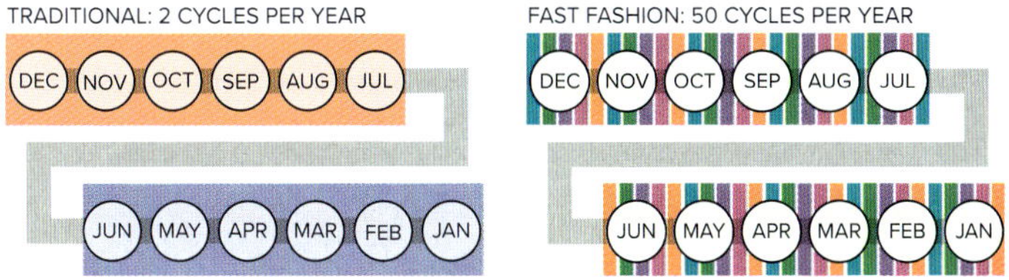
TRADITIONAL: 2 CYCLES PER YEAR
DEC NOV OCT SEP AUG JUL
JUN MAY APR MAR FEB JAN
FAST FASHION: 50 CYCLES PER YEAR
DEC NOV OCT SEP AUG JUL
JUN MAY APR MAR FEB JAN

Fig. 1. Traditional vs. "Fast" Fashion. This graph shows at a glance the differences between the standard two-cycle fashion year and the fast-fashion cycle that breaks down to approximately one cycle per week in a given year. This is not sustainable (Drew and Yehounme).

Caption identifies figure, explains visual, connects with author's claim / argument, and cites source.

Sources: True Cost, World Resources Institute

than we used to. And because fast fashion is cheap and flimsy, we keep such garments for half as long as we would keep better-made clothes (Drew and Yahounme).

The negative effects of the fast fashion industry are far-reaching. First and foremost, it is terrible for the environment. An article from the *Environmental Health Perspectives* journal titled "Waste Couture: [The] Environmental Impact of the Clothing Industry," asserts that "globalization has made it possible to produce clothing at increasingly lower prices, prices so low that many consumers consider this clothing to be disposable . . . some call it 'fast fashion'" (Claudio). But there are consequences; according to Forbes, the fashion industry is responsible for "10% of global carbon emissions and remains the second largest industrial polluter, second only to oil." Making things worse for the industry and environment are fast fashion garments. On average, we wear fast fashion items fewer than five times and keep them for just thirty-five days; these same items produce over four hundred percent more carbon emissions per item per year than do higher-quality garments that are worn fifty times and kept for a full year (Conca).

In recent years, Americans have begun to place due emphasis on the origins and healthfulness of our food, asking questions about sustainability, environmental footprint, and animal welfare. What if we navigated clothes shopping with the same level of care and concern? Would it have any effect on the status of what *Newsweek* has named an "environmental crisis"? (Wicker). Maybe. Much like the "slow food" movement that has been a response, of sorts, to fast food, "slow fashion" is on the rise. Slow fashion is about "consuming and creating fashion consciously and with integrity . . . it connects social and environmental awareness with the pleasure of wearing beautiful, well-made, and lasting clothing (as compared to the immediate gratification of fast fashion)," according to *Who, What, Wear* (Collings).

Fig. 2. Kat Collings writes that slow fashion is "the intersection of ethical, eco, and lasting fashion." Slow fashion, she says, "is about consuming and creating fashion consciously and with integrity."

A major component of slow fashion is that it is ecologically minded and manufactured using techniques that are eco-friendly; if everyone on the planet were to become more conscious consumers and support a movement such as slow fashion, a change would surely be seen in the amount of waste and energy generated by fast fashion production (see fig. 2). The problem is that it is hard to get consumers to make a change because doing so requires more effort and a higher up-front cost than does shopping at a big-name discount store such as Forever 21 or H&M (Collings).

> Paragraph explains the benefits of the writer's proposal and concludes with counterevidence

The humanitarian consequences of fast fashion are also an important issue arising from this practice. What many people may not know about the fast-fashion industry is that it is a breeding ground for human rights violations, human trafficking, underage labor, and even slavery. A 2018 World Report from the Human Rights Watch describes rampant labor rights abuses and asserts that global brands that order products made in factories are obligated to make sure workers in those factories are safe and protected from abuse (Stauffer). A quick *Google* search for *human rights violations fast fashion* produces a shocking 128,000,000 results, many with grim headlines about the "life or death" epidemic.

> Sentence 1: Beck's claim (topic sentence) offers her interpretation

> Sentences 2, 3, and 4 synthesize information from sources to support her claim.

> A visual of the factory tragedy underscores the seriousness of the accident and supports Beck's earlier claim about the negative impact of fast fashion on people. Beck's caption offers an interpretation of what the reader is seeing.

Fig. 3. Rana Factory Collapse. The Rana Plaza tragedy was a turning point that drew international attention to the plight of garment workers who produce fast fashion.

Source: Sk Hasan Ali. "Dhaka, Bangladesh, April 24, 2013." *Shutterstock*, 24 April 2013, www.shutterstock.com/image-photo/dhaka-bangladesh-april-24-2013-top-797806180.

> Sentence 1 continues her synthesis of information supporting the claim made in sentence 1 of the previous paragraph.

In 2013, an eight-story garment factory collapsed in Bangladesh, 1,134 people died and approximately 2,500 were injured (see fig. 3). The Rana Plaza accident is considered the deadliest structural failure in modern history. It also created controversy within the fashion industry; a number of Western companies, including Zara, Walmart, Benetton, and Mango all produced apparel in Rana Plaza factories. The incident brought to light the unethical and unsafe working conditions of factory workers and prompted major fashion retailers to take action and overhaul their supply chains in favor of more ethical practices (Stauffer).

Even so, abuse is still the norm, especially for female workers, as is documented in two reports from Global Labor Justice that focus on gender-based violence in garment supply chains for GAP and H&M ("Gender Based Violence in the GAP Garment Supply Chain"; "Gender Based Violence in the H&M Garment Supply Chain"). According to the reports, more than 540 workers at factories that supply the two retailers have described instances of threats and abuse that were recorded between January and May of 2018 in Bangladesh, Cambodia, India, Indonesia, and Sri Lanka. These claims are just one set of allegations pertaining to what Tola Moeun, director of a Cambodian human and labor rights organization, calls a daily reality. In his 2019 statement to members of the U.S. Congress, Moen reported that poverty wages have forced Cambodian garment workers to eat less (to the point of malnutrition) and work more (six days a week, for sixty hours per week). When you combine hunger and overwork with the stifling heat of the unairconditioned factories, the results, Moeun says, are "regular incidences of mass fainting."[2]

Outside of the major tragedies that have occurred in the industry, many factories still cut corners on a regular basis to reduce production costs. Not only is the minimum wage for most workers approximately sixty-seven dollars a month in countries including Bangladesh, but the workers are exposed to materials containing pesticides, toxic chemicals, ammonia, and formaldehyde, all of which have been linked to brain damage, fetal damage, and sterility in humans ("Bangladesh"; Plell). In short, the safety and comfort of garment workers hasn't historically been the biggest concern of fast-fashion corporations, but events such as the 2013 Rana Plaza incident have highlighted some of the gross human rights violations of many factory owners, causing the media to take notice and raise public awareness of these issues.

> Transition connects with previous claims, introduces a new one, and forecasts the conclusion of the essay

The third and final argument against fast fashion has to do with the financial implications of shopping for these products. Fast fashion is known to be notoriously cheap, and certain items are even viewed as disposable. Fast fashion garments certainly are cheap *in the moment*. At some large chain retailers, basic clothing items such as tank tops are sold for as little as one dollar. When prices are that low, it's easy to view the purchase as meaningless, because it's so affordable it doesn't even matter if the item falls apart or looks bad. And while very cheap clothing may seem like a dream come true at first, the old saying that "You get what you pay for" is truly relevant here; the low cost of these items is made possible only by their extremely low quality. So, while it may be no big deal to spend fifteen dollars on a blouse one time, what happens when that blouse falls apart and you're forced to buy another? How many times is it "no big deal" to spend fifteen dollars on a blouse before the repeated cost becomes a significant financial loss? The better choice, of course, is to spend a bit more for an item that's made to last, preferably one that's made in a socially responsible manner.

> Identifies the authoritative source of new information

An article in *The Atlantic*, "The Case for Expensive Clothes," actually encourages readers to splurge on every item of clothing they purchase: "The goal is to spend above $150 on each item of clothing" (Bain). But why? "It's enough that it [$150] causes me to seriously hesitate . . . it forces me to think about just how much I want that item of clothing, how much I'll wear it, and whether I think the value it offers is worth a significant cost . . . it's an investment, rather than the cheap buzz of getting something new." The writer makes a good point about getting a "cheap buzz": the reason fast fashion is so

> Offers a quotation and then comments on its significance

addictive is neurological. In 2007, a team of researchers from Stanford, MIT, and Carnegie Mellon looked at the brains of test subjects as they made decisions while out shopping for clothes. The researchers found that when shown a desirable object for sale, the nucleus accumbens, or pleasure sensors, in the test subjects' brains lit up. The more the person wanted the item, the more activity the brain scanner picked up (Knutson et al. 148).

In addition to the research on traditional vs. fast fashion that I conducted in my university's library and on the internet, I also conducted field research in the form of a survey. I hypothesized that others would have had similar experiences to my own when it comes to fast fashion—that they would (1) be aware of its horrible environmental and humanitarian impact, and (2) be familiar with the never-ending cycle of spending money on clothing with little return on the investment because of the garments' poor quality. In order to develop my survey, I turned to Heidi Julien's "Survey Research" to help me understand how to get the best results from this method of research (303).

> Explains her research methods

I distributed my survey, which consisted of ten questions, via multiple platforms and means, with *SurveyMonkey* hosting the survey. First, I used social media to distribute the survey to other college students (many of whom attend Syracuse University) as well as family and friends. I not only posted a link to the survey on my personal *Facebook* page where my 2,624 friends could see it, but I also published the link in various groups that I belong to, including the "Syracuse University Class of 2020" page, which has 1,111 members, and my sorority's *Facebook* group, which has 189 members. Thirteen students in my Research & Writing course also responded to my survey.

The results of my survey indicated that "fast fashion" is not a widely used term, and therefore is not necessarily familiar to the average person. It needs to be

> Reflects on the value of her research methods

carefully and accurately defined, as I have done at the beginning of this paper. The results of my survey also serve as counterevidence to my thesis; I expected that most respondents would be well-informed about the negative environmental and humanitarian costs of fast fashion and that they'd report experiencing major issues with the quality of their clothing. This was not the case: approximately seventy-four percent of respondents have experienced poor quality with fast-fashion garments only one to three times; fifty-seven percent were not aware of fast fashion's damaging impact on the environment; and thirty-seven percent did not know about fast fashion's connection to human rights violations in recent years (Beck). These responses were not what I was expecting, and they shook up the preconceived notions I had going into my field research. The results also made me more aware of my own biases about this issue as I navigated through the remainder of my research (Heshmat). I drew from Raymond Nickerson's "Confirmation Bias: A Ubiquitous Phenomenon in Many Guises" to understand and account for these biases once I realized that they had been present in my initial research (178).

> Explains how her research has changed her beliefs

Though the apparel industry will likely continue to be a source of environmental pollution, efforts including the slow-fashion movement can help reduce the effects of our carbon footprint and secure safe factories for garment workers. Research shows that when consumers learn about how their clothes are made, and the impact of that production on people and the environment, they are more willing to purchase slow-fashion or sustainable clothing items (Hiller Connell 303). The average person can avoid contributing to the harsh fast-fashion industry through self-education and by using applications like *Good on You* to see which retailers are practicing socially responsible brand ownership and which ones are not. When consumers purchase clothing from independent and/or sustainable clothing brands, they deny financial support to larger corporations whose money could be better spent ensuring that their practices don't ruin the environment and people's lives.

Notes

[1] In his 2018 report, Stauffer also notes that in the $2.4 trillion apparel industry that employs millions of workers, factory owners punish those who affiliate with a union; force overtime; fire pregnant women; and ignore the sexual harassment of women in the workplace. The worst abuses take place in unauthorized subcontracted factories that are not monitored in any way.

[2] Roeun goes on to say that during failed negotiations for an increased minimum wage for workers, the Garment Manufacturers Association in Cambodia (GMAC), a collection of factory owners, insisted that the figure remain unchanged. Further, any boosts to wages have been accompanied by cutting employees and raising production targets. For example, in factories that supply products to H&M, Gap, and Levi-Strauss, in 2012, 105 workers made 1,500 pairs of pants per day; however in 2018, 55 workers were expected to make 2,300 pairs of pants per day.

Beck 12

Works Cited

Bain, Marc. "The Case for Expensive Clothes." *The Atlantic,* 2 Oct. 2015, www.theatlantic.com/entertainment/archive/2015/10/the-case-for-expensive-clothes/408652.

"Bangladesh: Stop Persecuting Unions, Garment Workers." *Human Rights Watch,* 15 Feb. 2017, www.hrw.org/news/2017/02/15/bangladesh-stop-persecuting-unions-garment-workers.

Beck, Isabel. "Fast Fashion." 28 Sept. 2019. Survey.

Claudio, Luz. "Waste Couture: Environmental Impact of the Clothing Industry." *Environmental Health Perspectives,* vol. 115, no. 9, 2007, https://doi.org/10.1289/ehp.115-a449.

Collings, Kat. "Why We're Celebrating the Slow-Fashion Movement in July." *Who, What, Wear,* 1 July 2018, www.whowhatwear.com/slow-fashion-movement/slide2.

Conca, James. "Making Climate Change Fashionable: The Garment Industry Takes on Global Warming." *Forbes,* 3 Dec. 2015, www.forbes.com/sites/jamesconca/2015/12/03/making-climate-change-fashionable-the-garment-industry-takes-on-global-warming/#23fe5a579e41.

Drew, Deborah, and Genevieve Yehounme. "The Apparel Industry's Environmental Impact in 6 Graphics." *World Resources Institute,* 5 July 2017, www.wri.org/blog/2017/07/apparel-industrys-environmental-impact-6-graphics.

"Gender Based Violence in the GAP Garment Supply Chain . . . : A Report to the ILO 2018." *Global Labor Justice,* May 2018, www.globallaborjustice.org/wp-content/uploads/2018/06/GBV-Gap-May-2018.pdf.

Beck 13

"Gender Based Violence in the H&M Garment Supply Chain . . . : A Report to the ILO 2018." *Global Labor Justice*, May 2018, www.globallaborjustice.org/wp-content /uploads/2018/05/GBV-HM-May-2018.pdf.

Good on You: Ethical Fashion. Good on You, Ltd., 2019. App. — App for e-device

Heshmat, Shahram. "What Is Confirmation Bias?" *Psychology Today*, 23 Apr. 2015, www.psychologytoday.com/us/blog/science-choice/201504/what-is-confirmation -bias.

Hiller Connell, Kim Y. "Utilizing Political Consumerism to Challenge the 21st Century Fast Fashion Industry." *The Oxford Handbook of Political Consumerism*, edited by Magnus Boström, et al., Oxford UP, 2019, pp. 293-312. — Chapter from an edited collection (print book)

Julien, Heidi. "Survey Research." *The SAGE Encyclopedia of Qualitative Research Methods*, edited by Lisa M. Given, SAGE, 2008, pp. 846-48. — Entry from a specialized encyclopedia (print book)

Knutson, Brian, et al. "Neural Predictors of Purchases." *Neuron*, vol. 53, no. 1, 2007, pp. 147-56. — Article from an academic / scientific journal (print)

Moeun, Tola. "Labor and Human Rights in Cambodia." Center for Alliance of Labor and Human Rights (CENTRAL), 9 Sept. 2019, https://www.central-cambodia .org/archives/3125. Statement. — Statement by a named author

Nickerson, Raymond S. "Confirmation Bias: A Ubiquitous Phenomenon in Many Guises." *Review of General Psychology*, vol. 2, no. 2, 1998, pp. 175-220.

Plell, Andrea. "There Are Hidden Chemicals in Our Clothing." *Remake*, 5 Jan. 2018, www.remake.world/stories/news/there-are-hidden-chemicals-in-our-clothing/.

Beck 14

[Report by a named author] Stauffer, Brian. "World Report 2018: Soon There Won't Be Much to Hide: Transparency in the Apparel Industry." *Human Rights Watch*, 6 Apr. 2018, www.hrw.org/world-report/2018/essay/transparency-in-apparel-industry.

Wicker, Alden. "Fast Fashion Is Creating an Environmental Crisis." *Newsweek*, 1 Sept. 2016, www.newsweek.com/2016/09/09/old-clothes-fashion-waste-crisis-494824.html.

Text Credit

Pg. 347: The Comprehensive Bible: Containing the Old and New Testaments [...], Song of Sol. 5.16". **Pg. 384:** Courtesy of Isabel Beck.

19 Documenting Sources: APA Style

IN THIS CHAPTER

a. In-text citations, 397

b. Reference list, 408

c. Informational notes, 425

d. Formatting, 426

Student Model
Research Project: APA Style, Robyn Worthington, "Nature versus Nurture" 430

> *More about*
> Documenting a Source: APA Style (Documentation Matters tutorial preceding ch. 18), 330–33
> MLA style (ch. 18), 334–96
> *Chicago* style (ch. 20), 439–69
> CSE style (ch. 21), 470–84

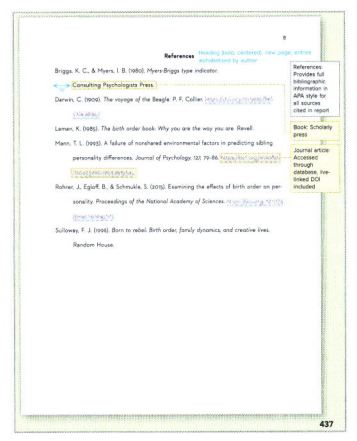

Developed by the American Psychological Association, APA style is used by researchers in psychology and many other social science disciplines, such as education, social work, and sociology. The *Publication Manual of the American Psychological Association* (7th ed., © 2020) requires that sources be cited in two ways:

- **In-text citations:** In the body of your project, provide an in-text citation for each source used.
- **Reference list:** At the project's end, document each source in a reference list.

19a Creating APA-Style In-Text Citations

In-text citations appear in the body of your project. They mark each use you make of a source, regardless of whether you are quoting, paraphrasing, or drawing on an idea. In-text citations

397

should include just enough information for readers to locate the source in your reference list, which appears at the end of the project. They should also alert readers to shifts between *your* ideas and those you have borrowed from a source.

Writing Responsibly: Citing and Documenting Sources

When you cite and document sources, you demonstrate how thoroughly you have researched your topic and how carefully you have thought about your sources, which encourages your audience to believe you are a credible researcher. In your citations and documentation, you acknowledge any material that you have borrowed from a source, and you join the conversation on your topic by adding your own interpretation. Accurate entries in the body of your project and list of references allow your audience to find and read your sources so that they can evaluate your interpretation and learn more about the subject themselves. Accurate entries also demonstrate the care with which you have written your research project, which further reinforces your credibility, or ethos.

to AUDIENCE

Quick Reference: General Principles of In-Text Citation

- Cite not only direct quotations but also paraphrases, summaries, and information gathered from a source, whether printed or online.
- Include the author's surname and the year of publication. You may place the name(s) in a signal phrase or in a parenthetical citation.
- Place parenthetical citations after the borrowed material; if the author is named in a signal phrase, insert the year of publication, in parentheses, immediately following the author's name and the page reference at the end of the borrowed passage.
- For works with no author, use the first few words of the title in the author position.
- For works with two authors, use the word *and* before the second author in a signal phrase; replace the word *and* with an ampersand (&) in a parenthetical citation. For works with three or more authors, include only the name of the first author listed in the source, followed by "et al.," which means "and others."
- Include a page or paragraph number when borrowing specific information but not when summarizing an entire source.

1. Place in-text citations so that readers know where borrowed material starts and stops.

When you incorporate a quotation, a paraphrase, a summary, or an idea from a source into your own prose, carefully consider the placement of the in-text citation, keeping the following goals in mind:

- To make clear exactly which material is drawn from the source
- To avoid distracting your reader

You can cite a source in your text in two ways:

a. *Signal phrase*. Include the author's name (often just the surname) and an appropriate verb in your sentence, and place the date of publication, in parentheses, immediately following the author's name.

> Psychologist G. H. Edwards (1992) found that subtypes or subcategories of beliefs emerge from within gender categories.

> **More about**
> What you do and do not need to cite, 283–84
> Signal phrases (ch. 17), 312–28
> Integrating borrowed material into your text, 313–16

A signal phrase often makes it easier for readers to determine where your ideas end and borrowed material begins. It also allows you to integrate the borrowed material into your sentence and to put the source in context by adding your own interpretation and the qualifications of the source author. For these reasons, most of your summaries, paraphrases, and quotations should be introduced by a signal phrase.

b. *Parenthetical citation*. In parentheses, provide the author's surname, followed by a comma and the year in which the source was published. Place the note immediately after the borrowed material.

> Subtypes or subcategories of beliefs emerge from within gender categories (Edwards, 1992).

Parenthetical citations are most appropriate when citing more than one source or establishing facts.

NOTE The reference list entry is the same, regardless of whether you use a signal phrase or a parenthetical citation:

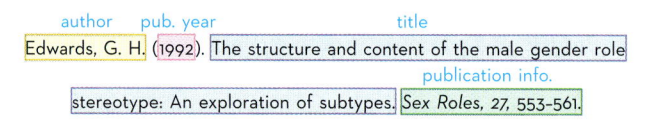

> author   pub. year   title
> Edwards, G. H. (1992). The structure and content of the male gender role
>   publication info.
> stereotype: An exploration of subtypes. *Sex Roles, 27,* 553-561.

> **More about**
> Creating reference list entries, 408-25

Provide enough information in your in-text citation for readers to locate the source in the reference list. In most cases, the author's surname and the date of publication are sufficient. Occasionally, you may need to provide more information. When citing works by authors with the same surname, also include the authors' initials. (See Examples 1–2 and 11, 401–402 and 405; see Example 7, 404.)

> While subtypes or subcategories of beliefs may emerge from within gender categories (Edwards, G. H., 1992), broader categories of beliefs emerge from within cultural groups (Edwards, C. P., 1988).

Quick Reference: Examples of APA-Style In-Text Citations

1. One author, paraphrase or summary 401
   a. Signal phrase 401
   b. Parenthetical citation 401
2. One author, quotation 401
   a. Signal phrase 402
   b. Parenthetical citation 402
3. Two authors 402
4. Three or more authors 403
5. Group or corporate author 403
6. Unnamed (anonymous) author 404
7. Two or more sources in one citation 404
8. Two or more sources by the same author in one citation 404
9. Two or more sources by the same author in the same year 405
10. Two or more authors with the same surname 405
11. Reprinted or republished work 405
12. Sacred or classical source 406
13. Indirect source 406
14. Website or other online source 406
15. Personal communication (email, letter, interview) 407

When quoting from a source, include page numbers. (See Example 2, 401–2.)

> The stereotype effect occurs when "individual members . . . are judged in a direction consistent with group-level expectations . . ." (Biernat, 2003, p. 1019).

2. Adjust in-text citations to match your source.

The exact form of an in-text citation depends on the type of source you are citing. The examples that follow cover the most common types. For more unusual sources, study the general principles outlined here and adapt them to your special circumstances or consult the *Publication Manual of the American Psychological Association,* 7th ed. (available in any library).

1. One author, paraphrase or summary The APA does not require that writers include a page reference for summaries and paraphrases, but your instructor may. If your instructor does want you to include a page reference, follow the model for a quotation on the next page.

a. Signal phrase

> From her interviews with vegans, Cherry (2015) found that the majority had adopted that lifestyle before the age of 18.

signal phrase

b. Parenthetical citation

> The majority of vegans participating in a sociological study reported having adopted that lifestyle before the age of 18 (Cherry, 2015).

APA In-Text Citations

1. One author, paraphrase or summary
2. One author, quotation
3. Two authors
4. Three or more authors

2. One author, quotation If you are borrowing specific language from your source, include the author's name, the year of publication, and a page reference.

NOTE The APA suggests, but does not require, that writers include a page reference for summaries and paraphrases when readers may need help finding the cited passage. Your instructor may require that you always include one, so be sure to ask. If your instructor *does* want you to include a page reference, follow examples 2a–b.

a. Signal phrase In a signal phrase, insert the year of publication immediately after the author's name and a page reference at the end of the cited passage. This not only provides source information but also makes clear what part of your text comes from the source.

> As Roach (2013) explains, "Humans are better equipped for sight than for smell. We process visual input ten times faster than olfactory" (p. 26).

b. Parenthetical citation In a parenthetical citation, include all three pieces of information at the end of the passage cited.

> "Humans are better equipped for sight than for smell. We process visual input ten times faster than olfactory" (Roach, 2013, p. 26).

APA In-Text Citations

1. One author, paraphrase or summary
2. One author, quotation
3. **Two authors**
4. Three or more authors
5. Group or corporate author

3. Two authors List two authors by surnames in the order listed by the source; be sure to use this same order in your reference list entry. In a signal phrase, spell out the word *and* between the two surnames; in a parenthetical citation, replace the word *and* with an ampersand (&).

> signal phrase (*and* spelled out)
> Wood and Bourke (2020) describe recent research that "has focused on biological explanations for gender variations in pain response" (p. 9).

> Recent research, the authors explain, "has focused on biological explanations
> parenthetical citation (ampersand)
> for gender variations in pain response" (Wood & Bourke, 2020, p. 9).

4. Three or more authors When a source has three or more authors, provide the last name of the first author listed in the source and include "et al." (meaning "and others") following that author's name in your in-text citation.

> Research studies conducted by Reichenberger et al. (2020) used the Salzburg Stress
>
> Eating Scale to correlate stress and food intake.

NOTE *al.* is an abbreviation, so it requires a period; *et* is a complete word, so it does not. There should be no punctuation between the author's name and *et al.*

---

5. Group or corporate author Provide the full name of the group in your signal phrase or parenthetical citation. If you are going to cite this source again in your project, use the group's name in a signal phrase and insert an abbreviation of the name in parentheses. In subsequent in-text references, use only the abbreviation.

> full name   acronym
> In 2003 the National Commission on Writing in America's Schools and Colleges (NCWASC)
>
> demanded that "the nation's leaders . . . place writing squarely in the center of the
>
> school agenda, and [that] policymakers at the state and local levels . . . provide the
>
> resources required to improve writing" (p. 3). The NCWASC also noted that . . .

Alternatively, include the full name in a parenthetical citation, and insert the abbreviation in square brackets afterward.

APA In-Text Citations

2. One author, quotation
3. Two authors
4. **Three or more authors**
5. **Group or corporate author**
6. Unnamed (anonymous) author
7. Two or more sources in one citation

> If writing is to improve, our society "must place writing squarely in the center of the school agenda, and policymakers at the state and local levels must provide the resources required to improve writing" (National Commission on
>   full name   abbreviation
> Writing in America's Schools and Colleges [NCWASC], 2003, p. 3).

6. Unnamed (anonymous) author When no author is listed for a source, use the first few words of the reference list entry (usually the title) instead.

> On average, smokers shave about 12 minutes off their life for every
>   title
> cigarette smoked ("A Fistful of Risks," 1996, pp. 82–83).

Set titles of articles or parts of books in quotation marks and titles of books and other longer works in italics.

7. Two or more sources in one citation When the information you are drawing on comes from more than one source, follow the borrowed material with a list of all relevant sources, separated by semicolons. List the sources in alphabetical order, the same order in which they appear in the reference list.

> Introducing domestic animals into the prison environment has beneficial effects on female inmates (Cooke & Farrington, 2015; Jasperson, 2010).

8. Two or more sources by the same author in one citation When citing two or more sources by the same author in a single citation, name the author once but include all publication years, separating them with commas.

> Weber-Wulff's work explored the reliability of plagiarism detection software (2016, 2019).
>
> *pub. year 1 — pub. year 2*

> Plagiarism-detecting software does not detect all text matches (Weber-Wulff, 2016, 2019).
>
> *pub. year 1 — pub. year 2*

9. Two or more sources by the same author in the same year When your reference list includes two or more publications by the same author in the same year, add a letter following the year (*2006a, 2006b*). Use these year-and-letter designations in your in-text citations and in your reference list. (See Example 6, 411.)

> For history students whose first language is not English, a writing-to-learn pedagogy has a positive effect on the acquisition of historical reasoning (Smirnova, 2015b).
>
> *letter assigned*

10. Two or more authors with the same surname If your reference list includes works by different authors with the same surname, include the authors' initials to differentiate them.

> Rehabilitation is a viable option for many juvenile offenders, whose immaturities and disabilities can, with institutional support and guidance, be overcome as the child matures (M. Beyer, 2006).
>
> *first initial + surname*

If a source has more than one author, include initials for the first author only.

11. Reprinted or republished work Include both dates in your in-text citation, with the original date of publication first.

APA In-Text Citations

7. Two or more sources in one citation
8. Two or more sources by the same author in one citation
9. **Two or more sources by the same author in the same year**
10. **Two or more authors with the same surname**
11. Reprinted or republished work
12. Sacred or classical source
13. Indirect source

> Danon-Boileau (2005/2006) took a cross-disciplinary approach to the study of language disorders in children.

(orig. year: 2005/2006; reprint year: 2006)

12. Sacred or classical source Cite sacred texts, such as the Bible, the Talmud, or the Qur'an, in the body of your research project using standard book titles, chapter numbers, and verse numbers, and indicate the version you used.

> In the Song of Solomon, the female speaker concluded her description of her lover with this proclamation: "His mouth is most sweet: yea, he is altogether lovely / This is my beloved, and this is my friend, O daughters of Jerusalem" (5:16, Revised Standard Version).

(5:16 = ch.:verse; Revised Standard Version = version)

For classical works, cite the year of the translation or version you used: (Plato, trans. 1968).

13. Indirect source When you can, avoid quoting from a secondhand source (source material you have learned about through its mention in another source). When you cannot locate or translate the original source, mention the original author's name in a signal phrase. In your parenthetical citation, include *as cited in* followed by the name of the author of the source in which you found the information, and conclude with the year of that source's publication.

> Bonilla-Silva (as cited in Utheim, 2014) located the origin of US "colorblind racism" in the 1960s.

In the reference list, provide only the source you used: For the example above, include a reference list entry for Utheim, not Bonilla-Silva.

14. Website or other online source Frequently, the information you need to create a complete in-text citation is missing. Electronic sources may lack fixed page numbers: Page 5 in one browser may be page 4 or 6 in another.

Use page numbers only when they are fixed, as in a PDF file. When paragraph numbers are provided, include those (with the abbreviation *para.*) instead of a page number.

> **More about**
> PDF files, 208–9, 230, 246, 249

> The Internet has also become an outlet for direct distribution of underground comics through artist websites, making independent titles more affordable to market (Fenty, Houp, & Taylor, 2004, para. 1).

When the source includes neither fixed page numbers nor paragraph numbers, cite the source by author name and publication date only. If the author is unnamed, use the first few words of the title. (See Examples 27–28, 420–21.)

> Cell-phone use while driving can impair performance as badly as drinking alcohol does ("Driven to Distraction," 2006, para. 1).

If no date is provided, use *n.d.* for *no date.*

> Barrett (n.d.) unwittingly revealed the sexism prevalent on college campuses in the early 1960s through his account of a football game.

15. Personal communication (email, letter, interview) For sources such as personal email messages, interviews, and phone calls that your readers cannot retrieve and read, mention the communication in your text or provide a parenthetical citation, but do not include an entry in the reference list (unless your instructor requires you to).

> The author herself was much more modest about the award (S. Alexievich, personal communication, April 13, 2016).

> **APA** In-Text Citations
>
> 13. Indirect source
> 14. Website or other online source
> **15. Personal communication (email, letter, interview)**

19b Preparing an APA-Style Reference List

The reference list, which comes after the body of your research project, lists the sources you have cited in your text. The format of each entry in the list depends in part on the type of source you are citing, such as a printed book, an article in an electronic journal or accessed through a database, or an audio recording. (See the Quick Reference box on pp. 408–409 for a list of APA-style reference list examples.)

Books—Printed and Electronic

> See the annotated visual showing where to find author, title, publication, and other information in the tutorial preceding ch. 18, 330–33.

In a printed book, the information you need to create a reference list entry appears on the title and copyright pages at the beginning of the book. In an online book or ebook, print and electronic publication information appears at the top or bottom of the first page or is available through a link.

NOTE APA no longer includes the physical location (city and state) of a publisher.

Quick Reference: Examples of APA-Style Reference List Entries

Books—Printed and Electronic
1. One author 409
   a. Printed 409
   b. Ebook and book with a DOI 409
2. Two authors 410
3. Three to twenty authors 410
4. Twenty-one or more authors 411
5. Unnamed (anonymous) author 411
6. Two or more books by the same author 411
7. Two or more authors with the same surname and first initial 412
8. Group or corporate author 412
9. Author and editor or translator 412
10. Edited book or anthology 413
11. Selection from an edited book or anthology 413
12. Edition other than the first 413
13. Introduction, preface, foreword, or afterword 413
14. Entry in an encyclopedia or other reference work 413
    a. Printed 414
    b. Online 414
15. Multivolume work 414
16. Republished book 414
17. Sacred or classical source 414
18. Dissertation or thesis 414
    a. Published (from a database, with no DOI) 415
    b. Published (not from a database, with a DOI) 415
    c. Unpublished 415
    d. Abstracted in DAI 415

Periodicals—Printed and Electronic
19. Article in a scholarly journal 416
    a. Printed 416
    b. Online or accessed through a database 416
20. Special issue of a journal 417
21. Article in a magazine 417
    a. Printed 417
    b. Online or accessed through a database 417
22. Article in a newspaper 417
    a. Printed 418
    b. Online or accessed through a database 418
23. Review (printed or online) 418

1. One author

a. Printed The basic entry for a printed book (with no DOI) looks like this:

Author's surname, Initial(s). (Year of publication). *Title: Subtitle.* Publisher.

Here is a sample citation for a book (with no DOI):

Pollock, J. (2012). *Crime and justice in America: An introduction to criminal justice.* Anderson Publishing.

b. Ebook and book with a DOI Works published electronically or made accessible online are often tagged with a digital object identifier (DOI). Unlike a URL that may change or stop working, a DOI is a permanent identifier that will not change over time or from database to database. If the ebook you are documenting is tagged with a DOI, use that identifier instead of publication information or URL, and add a description of the source type in brackets after the title. If no DOI has been assigned, replace publication information with the URL from which the electronic file can be obtained.

> **APA** Reference List Entries
>
> **1.** One author
> **2.** Two authors
> **3.** Three to twenty authors
>
> For books, only first word of title and subtitle (plus names) are capitalized.
>
> **More about**
> Digital object identifiers, 231, 409, 410, 420
> URLs, 271–73

---

24. Letter to the editor (printed or online) 419
25. Abstract (printed or online) 419

Other Electronic Sources
26. Website 420
27. Short work from a website 420
28. Discussion list posting 421
29. Article on a wiki 421
30. Blog or other social media post 421
    a. Blog post 421
    b. Comment on a blog post 422
    c. Social media post 422
31. Computer software 422
32. Presentation slides 422

Audio and Visual Sources
33. Motion picture 422
34. Online video or video blog (vlog) 423
35. Television or radio broadcast 423
    a. Series 423
    b. Episode 423
    c. Podcast 423
36. Musical or other audio recording 423
    a. Album or audiobook 423
    b. Selection or song 423
37. Lecture, speech, conference presentation, or poster session 423
38. Map 424

Miscellaneous Sources—Printed and Electronic
39. Government publication 424
    a. Printed 424
    b. Online 424
40. Report (nongovernmental) 424
41. Data set 424
42. Fact sheet, brochure, pamphlet 424
43. Conference proceedings 425
44. Legal source (printed or online) 425
45. Interview (published or broadcast) 425
46. Personal communication (email, letter, interview) 425

If you accessed the source on a device such as a Kindle or Nook, no URL should be included.

To find out whether your source has a DOI, go to https://www.crossref.org/ and use the "Search Metadata" option.

NOTE According to the seventh edition of the APA manual, all DOIs and URLs should be live-linked and include the prefixes "http://," "https://," and/or "www.," if available. No punctuation follows URLs and DOIs.

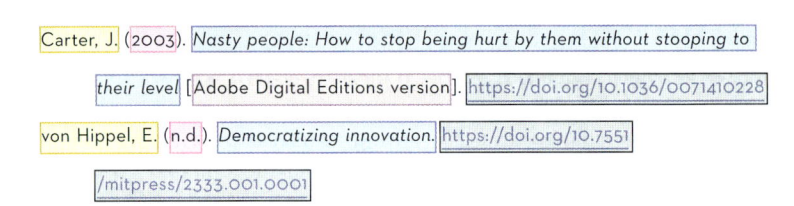

Carter, J. (2003). *Nasty people: How to stop being hurt by them without stooping to their level* [Adobe Digital Editions version]. https://doi.org/10.1036/0071410228

von Hippel, E. (n.d.). *Democratizing innovation.* https://doi.org/10.7551/mitpress/2333.001.0001

If no publication date available, use n.d.

2. Two authors When there are two authors, list them in the order in which they appear on the title page.

Propen, A., & Schuster, M. (2017). *Rhetoric and communication perspectives on domestic violence and sexual assault.* Routledge. https://doi.org/10.4324/9781315229164

Use an ampersand (&) between names.

3. Three to twenty authors When the book has three to twenty authors, list all their names.

James, J., Burks, W., & Eigenmann, P. (2011). *Food allergy.* Saunders. https://doi.org/10.1016/C2009-0-42473-5

Use an ampersand (&) between the last two names.

APA Reference List Entries

1. One author
2. **Two authors**
3. **Three to twenty authors**
4. Twenty-one or more authors
5. Unnamed (anonymous) author

Tech Citing Sources: Digital Object Identifiers (DOIs) and URLs

Because URLs change and links break, many sources (including print) now include a digital object identifier (DOI), a permanent code that makes URLs unnecessary. Whenever a source has a DOI, include it at the end of your citation; use the URL only when no DOI is given. Include any prefixes such as "https://," "http://," and/or "www.," and, for the ease of your readers, live-link DOIs and URLs. Note that APA no longer requires the phrase "Retrieved from."

When your citation ends with a DOI or URL, do not add a period after it. Allow your word-processing program to automatically break DOIs and URLs across lines; do *not* add hyphens or spaces. To check for a source's DOI, go to https://www.crossref.org/ and select "Search Metadata."

4. Twenty-one or more authors When the book has twenty-one or more authors, list the first nineteen authors followed by three ellipsis points and the last author's name.

5. Unnamed (anonymous) author Start the entry with the title followed by the publication date. Alphabetize the entry in the reference list using the first significant word in the title (not an article such as *a, an,* or *the*).

> *O: A Presidential Novel.* (2011). Simon & Schuster.

6. Two or more books by the same author For multiple books by the same author (or authors), arrange the entries in order of publication (from least to most recent).

> Hawhee, D. (2005). *Bodily arts: Rhetoric and athletics in ancient Greece.* University of Texas Press. https://doi.org/10.7560/705845

> Hawhee, D. (2017). *Rhetoric in tooth and claw: Animals, language, sensation.* University of Chicago Press. https://doi.org/10.7208/chicago/9780226398204.001.0001

When books were written by the same author(s) in the same year, alphabetize the entries by title and add the letter *a* following the publication date of the first entry, *b* following the publication date of the second entry, and so on. (See Example 9, 405.)

> Dobrin, S. I. (2011a). *Ecology, writing theory, and new media: Writing ecology.* Routledge. https://doi.org/10.4324/9780203134696

> Dobrin, S. I. (2011b). *Postcomposition.* Southern Illinois University Press.

Works written by a single author should be listed *before* sources written by that same author plus a coauthor, regardless of publication dates.

> Kress, G. (2009). *Multimodality: A social semiotic approach to contemporary communication.* Routledge. https://doi.org/10.4324/9780203970034

APA Reference List Entries

3. Three to twenty authors
4. **Twenty-one or more authors**
5. **Unnamed (anonymous) author**
6. **Two or more books by the same author**
7. Two or more authors with the same surname and first initial
8. Group or corporate author

APA Reference List Entries

5. Unnamed (anonymous) author
6. Two or more books by the same author
7. **Two or more authors with the same surname and first initial**
8. **Group or corporate author**
9. **Author and editor or translator**
10. Edited book or anthology
11. Selection from an edited book or anthology

Kress, G., Jewett, C., Ogborn, J., & Tsatsarelis, C. (2015). *Multimodal teaching and*

learning: The rhetorics of the science classroom. Bloomsbury. https://doi.org

/10.5040/9781472593764

When citing multiple sources by an author and various coauthors, alphabetize entries by the surname of the second author.

Sternberg, R., Grigorenko, E., & Jarvin, L. (2009). *Teaching for wisdom, intelligence,*

creativity, and success. Skyhorse Publishing. https://doi.org/10.4135/9781483350608

Sternberg, R., & Sternberg, K. (2016). *Cognitive psychology* (7th ed). Wadsworth.

7. Two or more authors with the same surname and first initial When your reference list includes sources by two different authors with the same surname and first initial, differentiate them by including their first names in brackets.

Cohen, A. [Andrew]. (1994). *Assessing language ability in the classroom*. Heinle.

Cohen, A. [Anne]. (1973). *Poor Pearl, poor girl! The murdered girl stereotype in*

ballad and newspaper. University of Texas Press.

8. Group or corporate author List the sponsoring organization as the author. Use the full name, and alphabetize it in the reference list according to the name's first significant word (ignoring articles such as *a, an,* or *the*). If the same group or corporation is also listed as the publisher, replace the name of the publisher with the word *Author.*

RAND Corporation. (2018). *Spotlight: 2018-2019* Author. https://doi.org/10.7249/CP531-2018

9. Author and editor or translator If the source originally appeared earlier than the edited or translated version, add the date of original publication at the end of the entry. If the work has an editor, use the abbreviation *Ed.* For a translator, use the abbreviation *Trans.*

Alvtegen, K. (2010). *Shame* (S. Murray, Trans.). Felony and Mayhem.

(Original work published 2006)

10. **Edited book or anthology** Put the editor's name in the author position.

> Brownell, K., & Gold, M. (Eds.). (2012). *Food and addiction: A comprehensive handbook.* Oxford University Press. https://www.doi.org/10.1093/med:psych/9780199738168.001.0001

For a book with a single editor, change the abbreviation to *Ed.*

11. **Selection from an edited book or anthology** Begin with the selection's author, followed by the publication date of the book and the selection's title (with no quotation marks or other formatting). Then insert the word *In,* the editors' names, and the title of the book or anthology (italicized). Next include page numbers for the entire selection (even if you used only part of it). Conclude the entry with the publication information for the book in which the selection appeared.

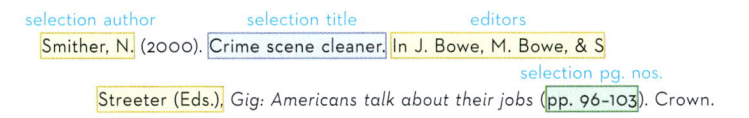

> *selection author*   *selection title*   *editors*
> Smither, N. (2000). Crime scene cleaner. In J. Bowe, M. Bowe, & S.
>   *selection pg. nos.*
> Streeter (Eds.), *Gig: Americans talk about their jobs* (pp. 96–103). Crown.

12. **Edition other than the first** Insert the edition number (*2nd ed., 3rd ed.*) or edition name (*Rev. ed.* for "revised edition") after the book's title. (The edition number or name usually appears on the title page.)

> Finsterbusch, K. (2018). *Taking sides: Clashing views on social issues* (12th ed.). McGraw-Hill.

13. **Introduction, preface, foreword, or afterword** The seventh edition of the *Publication Manual of the APA* does not provide an example of an entry for an introduction, preface, foreword, or afterword, but based on other examples, such an entry might look like the one below:

> *foreword's author*   *label*   *book's author*   *book's title*
> Andretti, M. (2008). Foreword. In D. Daly, *Race to win: How to become a*
>   *pg. nos. (foreword)*
> *complete champion* (pp. 2–3). Quayside-Motorbooks.

14. **Entry in an encyclopedia or other reference work** Format an entry in a reference work as you would a selection from an edited book. For signed articles, include the author's name. (Articles in reference works often carry

---

APA Reference List Entries

9. Author and editor or translator
10. Edited book or anthology
11. Selection from an edited book or anthology
12. Edition other than the first
13. Introduction, preface, foreword, or afterword
14. Entry in an encyclopedia or other reference work
15. Multivolume work
16. Republished book

the author's initials only, so you may need to cross-reference the initials with a list of contributors in the front or back of the book.) If an article is unsigned, begin with its title. (See Example 11, 413.)

a. Printed

entry author   *entry title*
Bretag, T. (2016). Educational integrity in Australia. In T. Bretag (Ed.), *Handbook of academic*
                   entry page nos.
integrity (pp. 23-38). Springer. https://doi.org/10.1007/978-981-287-098-8

b. Online

Kontos, A. (2014). Assimilation. In Eklund, R., & Tenenbaum, G. (Eds.), *Encyclopedia of*
                                                 URL
sport and exercise psychology. https://us.sagepub.com/en-us/nam
/encyclopedia-of-sport-and-exercise-psychology/book237359

APA Reference List Entries

13. Introduction, preface, foreword, or afterword
14. Entry in an encyclopedia or other reference work
15. **Multivolume work**
16. **Republished book**
17. **Sacred or classical source**
18. **Dissertation or thesis**
19. Article in a scholarly journal
20. Special issue of a journal

15. Multivolume work
For a multivolume work with multiple DOIs, break out each volume in your reference list.

Van den Buick, J. (Ed.). (2021). *The International encyclopedia of media psychology.* (Vol. 1). Wiley-Blackwell. https://doi.org/10.1002/9781119011071

Van den Buick, J. (Ed.). (2021). *The international encyclopedia of media psychology.* (Vol. 2). Wiley-Blackwell. https://doi.org/10.1002/9781119011071

16. Republished book

Huxley, E. (2006). *Red strangers.* Penguin Group. (Original work published 1939)

17. Sacred or classical source
Sacred texts, such as the Bible, the Talmud, or the Qur'an, ancient sources, such as Plato's *Republic,* or classical literature, such as Shakespeare's *King Lear,* are all cited as books. (See Example 12, 406.)

Plato. (1871). *The Republic* (B. Jowett, Trans.). The Internet Classics Archive. https://classics.mit.edu/Plato/republic.html (Original work published ca. 360 B.C.E)

18. Dissertation or thesis
Indicate in brackets whether the work is a doctoral dissertation or a master's thesis. If the dissertation or thesis was accessed

through a database service, include the name of the database from which it was obtained and provide any identifying number and the DOI, if available, live-linked. For a work from a database, and with no DOI, include the URL *only* if the database is open to all readers, as is the case for item a. If the work was obtained from a university or personal website, include the URL.

a. Published (from a database, with no DOI)

> Weill, J. M. (2016). *Incarceration and social networks: Understanding the relationships that support reentry* (Publication no. 95F6457A85534232) [Doctoral dissertation, University of California]. EbscoHOST: Open Dissertations. https://www.escholarship.org/uc/item/6z15h0jj

b. Published (not from a database, with a DOI)

> Grzanka, P. R., Santos, C. E., & Moradi, B. (2017). Intersectionality research in counseling psychology. [Doctoral dissertation]. *Journal of Counseling Psychology, 64*(5), 453-457. http://dx.doi.org/10.1037/cou0000237

c. Unpublished

> Luster, L. (1992). *Schooling, survival and struggle: Black women and the GED* [Unpublished dissertation]. Stanford University.

d. Abstracted in DAI
If you used the abstract in the *Dissertation Abstracts International* database, include that information in the entry. Remember, though, that reading the abstract is no substitute for reading the actual source.

> Kelley, E. (2008). Parental depression and negative attribution bias in parent reports of child symptoms. *Dissertation Abstracts International: Section B. Sciences and Engineering, 69*(7), 4427.

Periodicals—Printed and Electronic

A periodical is a publication issued at regular intervals—newspapers are generally published every day, magazines every week or month, and scholarly journals four times a year. For periodicals, include not only the title of the

---

APA Reference List Entries

17. Sacred or classical source
18. **Dissertation or thesis**
19. Article in a scholarly journal
20. Special issue of a journal

> See the annotated visual showing where to find author, title, publication, and other information in the tutorial preceding ch. 18, 330–33.

> More about
> Formatting author information: Examples 1–11, 401–5

article (with no quotation marks or italics) but also the title of the periodical (in italics, all important words capitalized). Other publication information you include depends on the type of periodical you are citing.

19. Article in a scholarly journal The information needed to create a reference list entry for a printed journal article appears on the cover or in the table of contents of the journal and on the first and last page of the article. For articles downloaded from a database, the information appears on the search results screen, in the full record of the article, or on the first and last page of the downloaded file. For articles that appear in journals that are published solely online, the needed information may be on the website's home page, in the journal's table of contents, or on the first page of the article.

a. Printed The basic citation for an article in a printed journal looks like this:

Author's surname, Initial(s). (Year of publication). Article title. Journal Title, vol no., pages. DOI, if available, live-linked, no punctuation follows

Here is an example of an actual citation of a printed journal article with a DOI:

Wright, S. (2011). Invasive species and the loss of beta diversity. Ethics and the Environment, 16, 79-98. https://doi.org/10.2979/ethicsenviro.16.1.75

> More about
> Digital object identifiers (DOIs), 409, 410, 420
> PDFs, 208–9, 230, 246, 249

If the article is published in a journal that starts each issue with page 1, provide the issue number after the volume number (not italicized, in parentheses).

Sui, C. (2007). Giving indigenous people a voice. *Taiwan Review, 57*(8), 40.

b. Online or accessed through a database Whenever a DOI is provided, whether for a source accessed online or in print, include it at the end of your reference list entry.

APA Reference List Entries

18. Dissertation or thesis
19. Article in a scholarly journal
20. Special issue of a journal
21. Article in a magazine

Luo, Y. (2011). Do 10-month-old infants understand others' false beliefs? *Cognition, 121,* 289-298. DOI https://doi.10.1016/j.cognition.2011.07.011

For an article in an online journal that does *not* provide a DOI, include its URL.

Janyam, K. (2011). The influence of job satisfaction on mental health of factory workers. *The Internet Journal of Mental Health, 7*(1). http://www.ispub.com/journal/the_internet_journal_of_mental_health/

20. Special issue of a journal

Lowe, B., Souze-Monteiro, D., & Fraser, I. (Eds.) (2015). Changing food consumption behaviors [Special issue]. *Psychology & Marketing*, 32(5), https://doi.org/10.1002/mar.20793

21. Article in a magazine

a. Printed Provide the full publication date of the issue (year, month, and day or year and month). If the volume and issue number of the magazine are available, include that information as you would for a journal article. (See Example 20, above.) If the article has a DOI, include it, live-linked. Note that the following two examples do not have DOIs.

Greene, K. (2011, December). Our data, ourselves. *Discover*, 42–47.

Donadio, R. (2020, October). Mob justice. *The Atlantic*, 326(3), 22–25.

b. Online or accessed through a database Include the article's DOI. If there is no DOI, include the URL only if it gives access to all readers.

Washington, H. (2015, November). Catching madness. *Psychology Today*. https://www.psychologytoday.com/magazine/archive

If the magazine is available in a printed edition but the article is only available online, include the phrase *Supplemental material* in brackets after the article's title.

Daniller, A. (2007, December). Psychology research done right [Supplemental material]. *GradPSYCH*. http://gradpsych.apags.org

22. Article in a newspaper

The information you need to create a reference list entry for a printed newspaper article is on the masthead of the newspaper (at the top of the first page) and on the first and last page of the article. For newspaper articles downloaded from a database, the information you need appears on the search results screen, the full record of the article, or the article itself. For articles that appear online, the information you need is usually at the top of the first page of the article. Include "*The*" if it is part of the newspaper's name.

APA Reference List Entries

19. Article in a scholarly journal
20. Special issue of a journal
21. Article in a magazine
22. Article in a newspaper
23. Review (printed or online)
24. Letter to the editor (printed or online)

APA Reference List Entries

21. Article in a magazine
22. Article in a newspaper
23. **Review (printed or online)**
24. Letter to the editor (printed or online)
25. Abstract (printed or online)

a. Printed

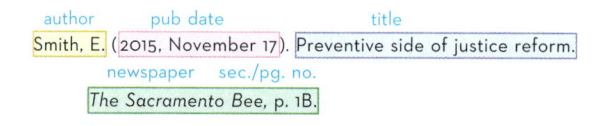

> author — pub date — title
> Smith, E. (2015, November 17). Preventive side of justice reform.
> newspaper — sec./pg. no.
> *The Sacramento Bee,* p. 1B.

If the pages of the article are not continuous, provide all page numbers.

> Apuzzo, M., & Lipton, E. (2015, November 25). Rare alliance on sentencing begins to fray. *The New York Times,* pp. A1, A17.

To cite a newspaper article downloaded from a database, follow the model for a printed newspaper article, but omit the page numbers, and change the comma after the newspaper's title to a period.

b. Online or accessed through a database
Follow the format for a printed newspaper article, but omit the page reference and include the article's URL if it can be accessed by all readers.

> Cutter, L., & McLachlan, B. (2021, January 29). In this age of disinformation, media literacy is a necessary skill for Colorado students. *The Denver Post.* https://www.denverpost.com/2021/01/29/disinformation-social-media-media-literacy-for-colorado-students/

23. Review (printed or online) Follow the model for the type of periodical in which the review appeared. In the author position, insert the name of the author of the review; if the review is titled, insert that title in the title position (no italics or quotation marks); and add in brackets the label *Review of the book* (or *Review of the film,* and so forth) followed by the title and author of the reviewed work. End with publication information for the periodical in which the review appeared. (See Examples 20–23, 417–18.)

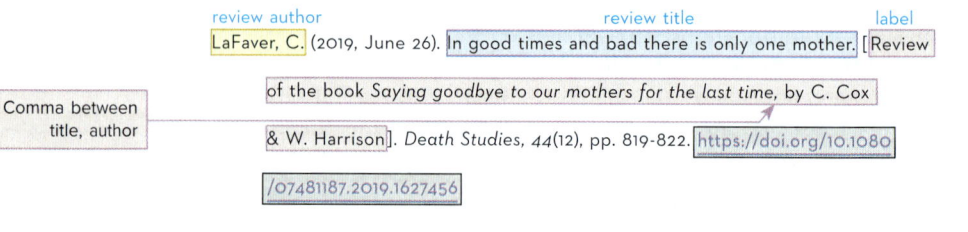

> review author — review title — label
> LaFaver, C. (2019, June 26). In good times and bad there is only one mother. [Review of the book *Saying goodbye to our mothers for the last time,* by C. Cox & W. Harrison]. *Death Studies, 44*(12), pp. 819-822. https://doi.org/10.1080/07481187.2019.1627456

Comma between title, author

If the review is untitled, substitute the label *Review of the book,* the book's title, and the book's author in brackets.

> Hurdley, R. (2011, September). [Review of the book *Gripes: The little quarrels of couples,* by J. Kaufmann]. *Cultural Sociology, 5,* pp. 452–453. https://doi.org/10.1177/17499 755110050030704

Comma between title, author

24. Letter to the editor (printed or online) Follow the model for the type of periodical in which the letter appeared, and insert the label *Letter to the editor* in brackets following the letter's title. (See Examples 20–23, 417–18.)

letter author | *label*

> Probollus, K. (2019, January 31). A woman's plea: Let's raise our voices [Letter to the editor]. *The New York Times.* https://www.nytimes.com/2019/01/31/opinion /letters/letters-to-editor-new-york-times-women.html

If the letter is titled, put that information (no italics or quotation marks) right before the *Letter to the editor* label.

25. Abstract (printed or online) It is always better to read and cite the article itself. However, if you relied only on the abstract, or summary, cite only the abstract to avoid misrepresenting your source and your research.

> Ghazi, A., Pakfetrat, A., Hashemy, S., Boroomand, F., & Javan-Rashid, A. (2020). Evaluation of antioxidant capacity and cotinine levels of saliva in male smokers and non-smokers [Abstract]. *Addiction and Health, 12*(4), p. 244.

> Tebeaux, E. (2011, January). Technical writing and the development of the English paragraph 1473–1700 [Abstract]. *Journal of Technical Writing and Communication, 41,* 219–253. http://doi.org/10.2190/TW.41.3.b

Other Electronic Sources

While it is usually easy to find the information you need to create a complete citation for a book or an article in a periodical, websites can be a bit trickier. Most of the information you need will appear on the site's home page, usually at the bottom or top of that page, or on the web page you

APA Reference List Entries

22. Article in a newspaper
23. Review (printed or online)
24. **Letter to the editor (printed or online)**
25. **Abstract (printed or online)**
26. Website
27. Short work from a website

> See the annotated visual showing where to find author, title, publication, and other information in the tutorial preceding ch. 18, 330–33.

APA Reference List Entries

24. Letter to the editor (printed or online)
25. Abstract (printed or online)
26. **Website**
27. **Short work from a website**
28. Discussion list posting
29. Article on a wiki

are citing. Sometimes, however, you may need to look further. Click on links with titles such as "About us" or "More information." Frequently, websites do not provide complete information, in which case include as much information in your entry as you can.

26. Website In general, when mentioning an entire website in a research project, you do not have to include an entry in your reference list. However, if you quote or paraphrase content from the site or interact with it in a substantial way, include it, following this model:

Author's surname, Initial(s). (Copyright date or date last updated). Website title.

DOI, live-linked; if no DOI, give URL, live-linked

Here is an example of an actual citation:

Kynard, C. (2021). Education, liberation, & Black radical traditions for the 21st century.

http://carmenkynard.org/

(See Example 15, 407.)

If no author is cited, move the title to the author position. If the web page is untitled, add a description in brackets. If no date is provided, insert *(n.d.)* following the author's name. (See Example 14, 407.)

27. Short work from a website Provide the title of the article or other short work (with no formatting) and the URL for the specific page you are citing.

National Eating Disorders Association. (2018). Binge eating disorder. *(article title)*

URL
https://www.nationaleatingdisorders.org/learn/by-eating-disorder/bed

---

Tech — Checking URLs and DOIs in Your Reference List

DOIs. If your entry includes a DOI, check its accuracy before submitting your project by visiting https://www.crossref.org/ or https://www.doi.org and inserting the DOI into the search box.

URLs. Before submitting your project, test all URLs. If a URL no longer works, search for the work online by title or keyword; you may find it "cached" on the web even though the owner of the original site has taken the work down. Then use the URL for the cached version in your bibliographic entry.

Note: APA now requires DOIs and URLs to be live-linked.

Documentation Matters • Preparing an APA-Style Reference List   **19b**   **421**

Wulf, K. (2016, January 27). The importance of academic (history) writing. *The Scholarly Kitchen.* https://scholarlykitchen.sspnet.org/2016/01/27/the-importance-of-academic-history-writing/

28. Discussion list posting Treat the subject line (or *thread*) as the title, and include the label *Discussion list post* (in brackets).

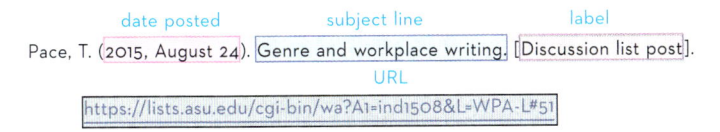

Pace, T. (2015, August 24). Genre and workplace writing. [Discussion list post]. https://lists.asu.edu/cgi-bin/wa?A1=ind1508&L=WPA-L#51

29. Article on a wiki Cite a wiki article as you would an article from a website, but be sure to give its archived version. For example, for an article from *Wikipedia,* select "View history," then the time and date of the version you've sourced. If there is no link to an archived version, give the URL and retrieval date. Because wikis are written and edited collaboratively, there is no author to cite; begin with the article's title. If the date of the most recent update is not noted, include the abbreviation *n.d.* (*no date*) in its place. Always include the wiki's title preceded by "In."

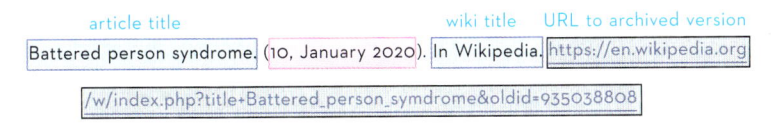

Battered person syndrome. (10, January 2020). In Wikipedia. https://en.wikipedia.org/w/index.php?title+Battered_person_symdrome&oldid=935038808

30. Blog or social media post Include a screen name if the author's name is not provided.

a. Blog post

Brooks, R. (2021, January 11). 5 truths about growing up a fat girl [Blog post]. Black girl lost keys. https://blackgirllostkeys.com/trauma/5-truths-about-growing-up-a-fat-girl/

APA Reference List Entries

26. Website
27. Short work from a website
28. Discussion list posting
29. Article on a wiki
30. Blog or social media post
31. Computer software
32. Presentation slides

b. Comment on a blog post

comment author [avatar]   date posted   subject line (thread title)
Medicinehorse179. (2015, November 17). Re: No more type I/II error confusion
    label   URL
[Blog comment]. http://mindhacks.com/

c. Social media post

Lippman, L. (2018, June 10). That's sunburn [Facebook post]. https://www.facebook.com/lauralippman

31. Computer software Provide an entry for computer software only if it is unfamiliar to your readers and it is necessary to a computation you have made.

title   label
Power Researcher [Computer software]. Uniting Networks.

If the software you are citing is available in more than one version, add a version number in parentheses between the title of the software and the identifying label.

32. Presentation slides

label
Ball, C. E. (2016). *The big tent of multimodal composition* [PowerPoint]. SlideShare. https://www.slideshare.net/s2ceball/the-big-tent-of-multimodal-composition

Audio and Visual Sources

The information you need to create an entry for most audio and visual sources appears on the cover, label, or program of the work or in the credits at the end of a film or television show. As with other citations, italicize the titles of longer works, such as albums and films, and do not format or add quotation marks to the titles of shorter works, such as single songs or single episodes of television programs.

33. Motion picture

release   title
Grazer, B. (Producer), & Howard, R. (Director). (2001). *A beautiful mind*
distributor
[Motion picture]. Warner Bros.

> **More about**
> Reliability, 265–69

APA Reference List Entries

29. Article on a wiki
30. Blog or social media post
31. Computer software
32. **Presentation slides**
33. **Motion picture**
34. Online video or video blog (vlog)
35. Television or radio broadcast

34. Online video or video blog (vlog)

if no author identified, begin entry with source title

25 things psychology tells you about yourself. (2014, December 8). [Video].

https://www.youtube.com/watch?v=ic9fnTpoYdk

35. Television or radio broadcast
a. Series (accessed through online stream)

Rae, I. (Executive producer). (2016-present). *Insecure* [Television series]. HBO.

https://www.hbo.com/insecure

b. Episode (accessed on television)

Benioff, D., and Weiss, D. B. (Writers and Directors). (2019). The iron throne.

[Television series episode]. In D. Benioff and D. B. Weiss (Producer),

Game of Thrones. HBO.

c. Podcast

Vedantam, S. The science of compassion [Audio podcast]. *The Hidden Brain*.

http://www.npr.org/series/423302056/hidden-brain

36. Musical or other audio recording
a. Album or audiobook

Rockefeller, J. (2014, November 11). *The introvert personality: The advantage of*

introverts in an extrovert world [Audio book]. http://www.audible.com/pd

/The-Introvert-Personality-Audiobook/B00PG3RN3G

b. Selection or song

     writers   © date   performers

Dilly, D., & Wilkin, M. (1959). The long black veil [Album recorded by H. Dickens

& A. Gerrard]. *On Pioneering women of bluegrass*. Smithsonian/Folkways Records.

37. Lecture, speech, conference presentation, or poster session

Guilko, T. (2015, October 4). *From baby boomers to Generation Y: Motivation across*

the ages [Paper presentation]. The British Psychological Society's Division on

Occupational Therapy Conference, Oxford, UK.

APA Reference List Entries

33. Motion picture
34. Online video or video blog (vlog)
35. Television or radio broadcast
36. Musical or other audio recording
37. Lecture, speech, conference presentation, or poster session
38. Map
39. Government publication

38. Map

U.S. Census Bureau, Geography Division (Cartographer). (2001). Mean center of

population for the United States: 1790 to 2000 [Demographic map].

http://www.census.gov/geo/www/cenpop/meanctr.pdf

Miscellaneous Sources—Printed and Electronic

39. Government publication
a. Printed

Child Welfare Information Gateway. (2015). *Adoption options: Where do I start?*

U.S. Department of Health and Human Services, Children's Bureau.

If the source includes a publication number, add that information in parentheses after the title.

b. Online

U.S. General Accounting Office. (1993, September 21). *North American Free Trade Agreement:*

A focus on the substantive issues (Publication No. GAO/T-GGD-93-44). http://www

.gpoaccess.gov/gaoreports/search.html

(See Example 8, 412)

40. Report (nongovernmental)

Head, A. (2014, July 29). *Trends from the lifelong learning interviews with recent graduates.*

Project Information Literacy Progress Report. http://www.projectinfolit.org/publications

41. Data set

U.S. Department of Justice, Federal Bureau of Investigation. (2007, September). *2006*

Crime in the United States [Data set]. http://www.data.gov/raw/310

42. Fact sheet, brochure, pamphlet

Information Services Department, Hong Kong Special Administrative Region Government.

(2015, February). *Agriculture and fisheries* [Fact sheet]. http://www.gov.hk/en

/about/abouthk/factsheets/

If no author is listed, move the title to the author position. If no publication date is available, insert *n.d.* (for *no date*) in its place.

43. Conference proceedings Cite conference proceedings either as an edited book or as the special issue of a journal, depending on how they were published. (See Examples 10 and 20 on 413 and 417.)

44. Legal source (printed or online)

    case title   *U.S. Reports* decision
    (abbreviated)   vol.   no.   date   URL

Lynn v. Alabama, 493 U.S. 945 (1989). *Open Jurist.* http://openjurist.org/493/us/945/lynn-v-alabama

45. Interview (published or broadcast)

  interview subject   broadcast date

Hoffman, B. (2015, November 28). What information do intelligence agencies need to keep US safe? Interview by S. Simon. http://www.npr.org/sections/interviews/

46. Personal communication (email, letter, interview) Cite personal communications that are not available to the public in the body of the research project, but do not include an entry in the reference list (unless required by your instructor).

19c Using APA Style for Informational Notes

In addition to in-text citations, APA style allows researchers to include informational notes. These notes may provide supplementary information, acknowledge any help the writer received, or call attention to possible conflicts of interest.

To add supplementary information, include a superscript (above-the-line) arabic number in the text and at the beginning of the note (either at the bottom of the page for a footnote or in a list of notes at the end of the project).

The participants in each condition were told at the beginning of the experiment that they were participating in a memory-recall task. They were to identify what they could remember from a clip from the movie *Pretty Woman* (Milchan et al., 1990),[1] a stereotypical "chick-flick."

APA Reference List Entries

41. Data set
42. Fact sheet, brochure, pamphlet
43. Conference proceedings
44. Legal source (printed or online)
45. Interview (published or broadcast)
46. Personal communication (email, letter, interview)

> **Notes**
>
> ←½"→ ¹This romantic comedy starring Julia Roberts and Richard Gere (dir. Garry Marshall) was extremely popular, grossing nearly $464 million worldwide, according to the site Box Office Mojo (http://www.boxofficemojo.com /movies/?id=prettywoman.htm). Nevertheless, participants had not seen the film before participating in the experiment.

> **Sample title page, 431**

Add notes to acknowledge help or possible conflicts of interest to the title page, four lines below the date.

19d Formatting a Paper in APA Style

> **Student Model**
> Research project, APA style: "Nature versus Nurture: Does Birth Order Shape Personality?" by Robyn Worthington 430–38

The care with which you cite and document your sources reflects the care you have taken in writing your research project. Continue that care by formatting your project in the way your readers expect. For most writing projects in the social sciences, follow the APA's formatting guidelines. The *Publication Manual of the APA* offers guidance for student projects as well as for writers submitting projects for publication in scholarly journals.

1. Margins and spacing

- Set margins of at least one inch at the top, bottom, and left- and right-hand sides of your paper.
- Indent the first line of each paragraph half an inch.

> **More about**
> Block quotations, 836

- Indent quotations of forty or more words as a block, half an inch from the left margin.
- Double-space the entire paper, including the abstract, title page, block quotations, footnotes, figure numbers and titles, and the reference list. Set the text so that the right margin is uneven (ragged), and do not hyphenate words at the ends of lines.

> **Sample reference list, 437**

- Use a hanging indent for each reference list entry: The first line should be flush with the left margin with subsequent lines indented half an inch.

> **More about**
> Choosing a typeface and type size, 192–94

2. Typeface and page number

Use a standard typeface such as Times New Roman or Arial in a readable size (usually 12 points). Include the page number half an inch from the top and one inch from the right edge of the page. Use your word processor's (such as Microsoft Word's) header feature to number the pages automatically.

3. Title page

- Insert the title, typed in upper- and lowercase letters, centered on the top half of the page. The title should be in bold type.
- Insert a blank line and then type your name.
- Papers for submission to a scholarly journal include the author's university or college affiliation; student writers usually include the course number, the name of the instructor to whom the project will be submitted, and the date of submission, each centered on separate lines.
- If you need to acknowledge help you received—for example, in conducting your research or interpreting your results—include a note on the title page, four lines below the identifying information.

> **More about**
> Crafting a title, 90
> Notes acknowledging help or conflicts, 425–26

> Sample title page, APA style, 431

4. Abstract

The abstract generally includes a one-sentence summary of the most important points in each section of the project:

> Sample abstract, APA style, 431

- Introduction—problem you are investigating
- Methods—number and characteristics of the participants and your research methods

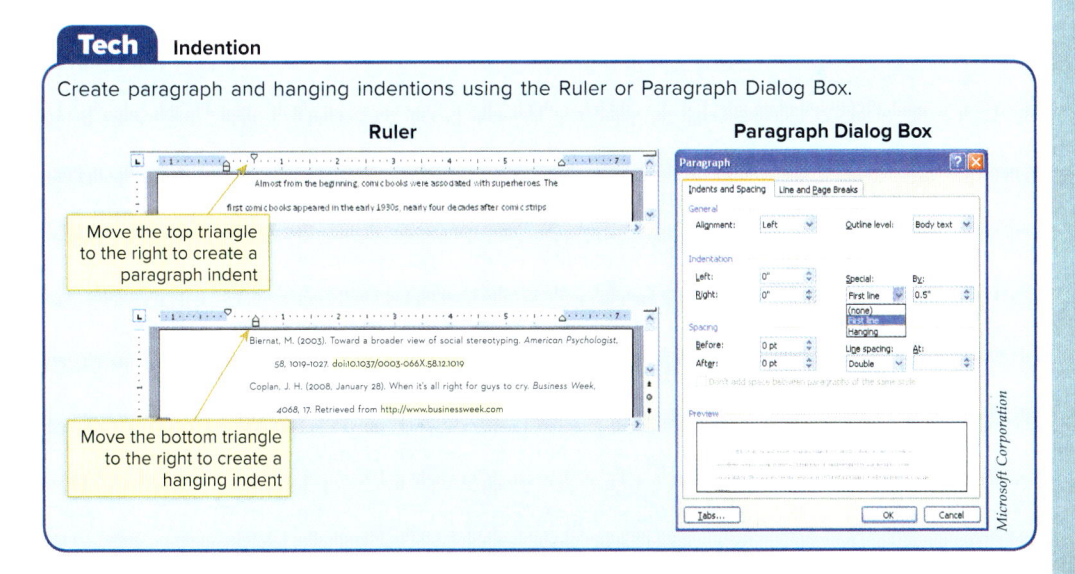

Tech | Indention

Create paragraph and hanging indentions using the Ruler or Paragraph Dialog Box.

Ruler

Move the top triangle to the right to create a paragraph indent

Move the bottom triangle to the right to create a hanging indent

Paragraph Dialog Box

Microsoft Corporation

> **Tech** Creating a Header
>
> Word processing programs allow you to insert a header automatically. In Microsoft Word, select "Header and Footer" under the View menu. If you have any questions about creating a header, consult your program's Help directory.

- Results—your outcomes
- Discussion—implications of your results. This section concludes your text.

The abstract follows the title page and appears on its own page, headed with the word *Abstract* centered at the top of the page and in bold type. The abstract should be no more than 150–250 words.

5. Tables and figures

- Refer to tables and figures in the text, using the word *Table* or *Figure* followed by the number of the table or figure in sequence. (The first figure is Figure 1; the first table is Table 1.) Discuss the significance of tables and figures in the text, but do not repeat the information that appears in the table or figure itself.

> Sample figure captions, APA style, 438

- Each figure should include a figure number and title. The word *Figure* and the number assigned in the text (both in bold type) should appear above the figure. The title (in italics) should appear on a line below the figure number. It should identify the figure briefly. If you borrowed the figure or the data to create the figure, include the source information below the figure, preceded by the word *Note* (in italics, followed by a period).

- Include the word *Table* and the table number (no italics) on one line and, on the next line, the table title (in italics). The table itself should appear below the table number and title. If you borrowed the table or the data to create the table, include source information below the table, preceded by the word *Note* (in italics, followed by a period).

> Sample figure, APA style, 438

- In research projects submitted for publication, tables should appear, each on a new page, after the reference list or endnotes (if any). Figures (graphs, charts, photographs, maps, and so on) should appear, each on a new page, following the tables. In college research projects, however, your instructor may prefer to see tables and figures in the body of your research project, as close as possible following their first mention in the text. Check with your instructor before formatting your project.

TABLE 19.1

Occupations Projected to Have the Most Openings Each Year, on Average, 2019–29

Occupation	Occupational openings, projected 2019–29 annual average	Median annual wage, 2019
General and operations managers	204,400	$100,780
Registered nurses	175,900	73,300
Software developers; software quality assurance analysts and testers	131,400	107,510
Project management specialists; business operations specialists; all other	128,000	73,570
Accountants; auditors	125,700	71,550
Elementary school teachers	103,200	59,670
Management analysts	87,100	85,260
Market research analysts; marketing specialists	84,200	63,790
Personal service managers; entertainment and recreation managers; all other	74,500	110,630
Secondary school teachers	71,100	61,660

Note. Bachelor's degrees are required for all of the above jobs. Adapted from *Bachelor's Degree to Enter Occupations Projected to Have the Most Openings Each Year, on Average, 2019-29,* by U.S. Bureau of Labor Statistics and Office of Occupational Statistics and Employment Projections, 2019 (https://stats.bls.gov/careeroutlook/2020/article/education-level-and-openings.htm#s 4). In the public domain.

> When you use or adapt a table that is in the public domain, for example, a table like this one (published by the US government), you need to credit your source but do not need to request permission.

> For works that are held by copyright holders (that is, not in the public domain or created by the government), you do not need to request permission unless you are publishing your work in a commercial context. As a college writer, it is enough to credit the copyright holder as is done here.

> This table was adapted from a table created by two governmental agencies.

6. Reference list

- Center the heading "References" at the top of the page.
- Use a hanging indent for each reference list entry: The first line should be flush with the left margin, with subsequent lines indented half an inch.
- Alphabetize the entries in the reference list by the surname of the author or, if no author is listed, by the first important word in the title (ignoring *A, An,* or *The*).
- Italicize all titles of books and websites, but do not enclose titles of articles or book chapters in quotation marks.

> **More about**
> Italics with titles, 865–66

Writing Responsibly — Of Deadlines and Paperclips

Instructors expect students to turn in thoughtful, carefully proofread, and neatly formatted papers on time—usually in class on the due date. Another expectation is that the writer will clip or staple the pages of the paper *before* the paper is submitted. Do justice to yourself by being fully prepared.

to SELF

> **More about**
> Capitalization, 861–62
> Proper nouns, 860–61

- Capitalize the first word, the first word following a colon or a dash, and proper nouns in titles of books, articles in periodicals, websites and web pages, films, and so on. Capitalize all major words in journal titles: *Psychology, Public Policy, and Law; Monitor on Psychology.*

7. Printing, paper, and binding

Print your project using a high-quality printer (make sure it has plenty of ink), on opaque, 8½ × 11–inch white paper. Most instructors do not want you to enclose your paper in a binder, but if you are in doubt, ask. If it is not submitted in a binder, paperclip or staple the pages together.

Student Model Research Project: APA Style

> **More about**
> Writing in the sciences and social sciences (ch. 23), 510–29
> Appendixes, 515

In the sample student research project that follows, Robyn Worthington examines the relationship between birth order and personality. She fulfills her responsibilities to topic and audience by drawing on a variety of relevant and reliable sources to provide the background that her readers will need, by including visuals that help her readers understand her project, and by following the format for an APA-style research project, the format her readers expect.* By acknowledging her sources, she fulfills her responsibility to the other writers from whom she has borrowed information. By conducting her primary research with care, by acknowledging the limitations of her project, and by revising, editing, and proofreading her project carefully, she demonstrates her own credibility as a researcher and writer.

---

*The following paper reflects the guidelines of the *Publication Manual for the American Psychological Association*, 7th edition (2020).

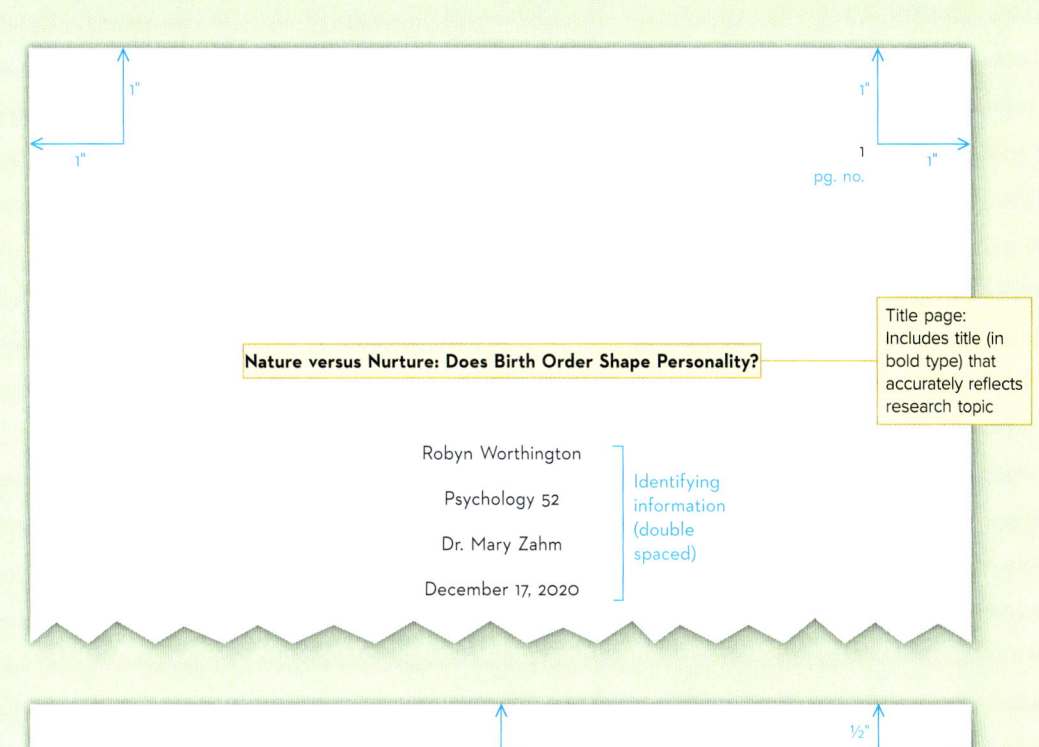

Nature versus Nurture: Does Birth Order Shape Personality?

Robyn Worthington

Psychology 52

Dr. Mary Zahm

December 17, 2020

Abstract

Psychological researchers agree that the personalities of siblings differ, but there is much disagreement about the reasons for the differences. Many variables have been studied, including age range, birth order, gender, and nonshared environmental factors. This study examines the extent to which birth order affects personality and attempts to show a correlation. A revised sample of 51 participants completed a Myers-Briggs Type Indicator Test. Results show a significant relationship between birth order and introversion/extraversion, but they do not support the hypothesis fully.

3

Introduction

As the mother of three boys, I have been stunned by the differences in their personalities. Despite having the same parents and the same home environment, their personality differences are great. Researchers in psychology agree that siblings differ, but there is much disagreement about the reasons for the differences. Variables such as age range, birth order, gender, and nonshared environmental factors have been studied as possible causes. This study investigates a possible correlation between birth order and personality.

Darwin's theory of evolution, specifically his principle of divergence, has been used as a possible explanation for the differences in sibling personality (Sulloway, 1996, p. 85). Darwin theorized that "given enough time, species tend to evolve multiple forms that diverge in character, a process called adaptive radiation" (Sulloway, 1996, p. 85). In the nineteenth century, naturalist Charles Darwin (1909) observed that a species of finches living in isolation and competing for resources developed biological variations that made them successful competitors. "One might really fancy," he said in *The Voyage of the Beagle* "that, from an original paucity of birds in this archipelago, one species had been taken and modified for different ends" (p. 399). One factor in adaptive radiation is development in different environmental niches. According to Sulloway (1996), the family environment is not a single environment but a collection of microenvironments. The oldest child comes into an (intact) family of two; the family environment the next child experiences includes two parents and a sibling with whom the second child must compete; the third child finds a family with two parents and two siblings with each of whom the third child must compete, and so on. In short, as each child is born, the family environment changes, including the way that the parents interact with each child and the way the children interact with each other, and this difference in family environment can affect personality (Leman, 1985). By developing diverging personalities, younger siblings avoid competing with older, bigger, more experienced siblings on the same grounds (Sulloway, 1996).

Certain characteristics of personality have been associated with birth order. Oldest, or first borns, have been characterized as ambitious high achievers who are usually confident, organized, and conservative (Leman, 1985; Sulloway, 1996). Both Leman and Sulloway suggest that children born second tend to diverge as much as possible from the first born, taking on a totally different set of characteristics. They are noted as being more sociable, more cooperative, and more open to experience than their conservative older siblings, who have a tendency to relate strongly with their parents. Youngest children tend to be charming, affectionate, outgoing, and used to being the center of attention; they may also be spoiled and impatient (Leman, 1985).

Gender, age range, and nonshared environment are also thought to be factors in personality differences in siblings. In a study of university psychology students, Tammy Mann (1993) predicted that nonshared environmental factors would account for personality differences more than other factors. However, the results showed that the family constellation variables of age, birth order, and gender may be more firmly associated with personality differences in siblings than the nonshared environment. In fact, 27% of the correlations between constellation variables and sibling personality differences were statistically significant (Mann, 1993).

Not all empirical studies have successfully demonstrated the theory of birth order and personality that Sulloway draws from Darwin; some have produced negative findings (Roher et al., 2015). Additional testing, then, may help determine the usefulness of the theory.

Methods

This study used Darwin's theory of evolution as well as the theory proposed by Frank Sulloway concerning birth order and personality as models. The hypothesis to be tested is that birth order would account for the differences in personality among siblings. Birth order was defined as either oldest, middle, youngest, or only child. Personality was assessed by the Myers-Briggs Type Indicator (Briggs & Myers, 1980), in the categories of extraversion/introversion, sensing/intuition, thinking/feeling, and judging/perceiving.

The initial sample consisted of 70 randomly selected adolescents and adults from whom 55 surveys were returned. For statistical calculations, only-children were eliminated from the sample, as their number was too few. The revised sample consisted of 51 people ranging in age from 14 to 90 years of age. All were European American and considered themselves as having middle-class backgrounds. Of the 51 subjects, 16 reported being an oldest sibling, 17 reported being a middle sibling, and 18 reported being a youngest sibling.

The Myers-Briggs Type Indicator Test was distributed to the participants along with a background questionnaire (Appendix) on which subjects supplied personal data, including birth order. The surveys were collected, scored, and labeled with four letters that corresponded to the participants' personality type:

E (extraversion) or I (introversion)

N (intuitive) or S (sensing)

F (feeling) or T (thinking)

J (judging) or P (perceiving)

The information collected was statistically evaluated by establishing a null and an alternate hypothesis for each personality trait. The scores were placed in a contingency table, and the calculations were performed and evaluated using the chi-square test for goodness of fit.

Results

A statistically significant relationship between birth order and personality traits was found in one of the four areas. Calculations revealed a significant relationship between extraversion/introversion at the .005 (0.5%) level of significance. Of the 16 oldest children, 14 preferred introversion, 10 out of 17 middle siblings showed a preference for extraversion, and 12 out of 18 youngest siblings showed a preference for extraversion. (See Figure 1.) In all other areas, the calculations fell short of a reliable level of significance. In the traits of sensing/intuition, thinking/feeling, and judging/perceiving, the test values were below 1, too low for even a .005 (0.5%) level of significance.

> Results: Explains outcomes (with visual representation of results) and discloses shortcomings

Discussion

While this study demonstrated a significant relationship between birth order and the traits of extraversion/introversion, the data collected do not support the hypothesis that birth order accounts for differences in other aspects of personality in siblings. The variables involved may be too difficult to assess using the statistical methods of this study. Other characteristics, such as gender and number or spacing of children, all influence the way that parents relate to their children and the way that siblings relate to each other, so these factors, too, are likely to affect personality. Other factors include genetics and nonshared environmental experiences such as playgroups and nursery school/day care, friends, teachers, and so forth—all of which may have an impact on personality.

> Discussion: Interprets results

With so many variables, assessing the causes of personality differences in siblings is extremely difficult. Based on the results of this study, I have concluded that personality development is not likely the result of any one factor but, instead, a combination of many. Further, since this study included only middle-class European Americans, it cannot be assumed to be representative of the population as a whole. Future research might include a cross-sectional study of various ethnic and socioeconomic groups as a better representation of the population. An interesting result of the study was that, when the personality traits were divided by gender, 24 out of 31 females demonstrated a preference for the trait of feeling to that of thinking. Future research might include a study of the effect of gender on personality differences or personality differences among siblings based on gender.

> Conclusion: Summarizes findings, acknowledges shortcomings, suggests new avenues for research

References

Briggs, K. C., & Myers, I. B. (1980). *Myers-Briggs type indicator.* Consulting Psychologists Press.

Darwin, C. (1909). *The voyage of the Beagle.* P. F. Collier. https://doi.org/10.5962/bhl.title.98662

Leman, K. (1985). *The birth order book: Why you are the way you are.* Revell.

Mann, T. L. (1993). A failure of nonshared environmental factors in predicting sibling personality differences. *Journal of Psychology, 127,* 79–86. https://doi.org/10.1080/00223980.1993.9915545

Rohrer, J., Egloff, B., & Schmukle, S. (2015). Examining the effects of birth order on personality. *Proceedings of the National Academy of Sciences.* https://doi.org/10.1073/pnas.1506451112

Sulloway, F. J. (1996). *Born to rebel: Birth order, family dynamics, and creative lives.* Random House.

9

Figure 1
Preference for Extraversion/Introversion among Siblings

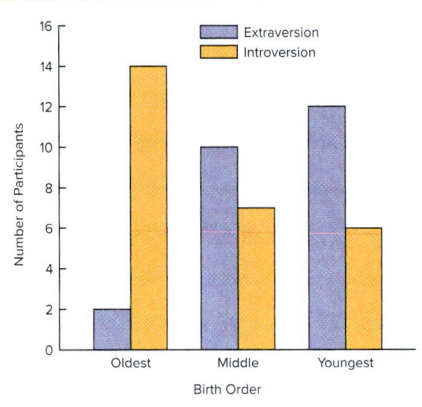

> Figure number in bold type; figure title below it in italics

> Figure follows reference list

[Bar chart showing Number of Participants by Birth Order (Oldest, Middle, Youngest) for Extraversion and Introversion:
- Oldest: Extraversion 2, Introversion 14
- Middle: Extraversion 10, Introversion 7
- Youngest: Extraversion 12, Introversion 6]

10

Appendix
Background Questions

Date of birth: _____

Sex: M _____ F _____

How many siblings do you have? _____ (Brothers _____ Sisters _____)

What is your birth order? Oldest _____ Middle _____ Youngest _____ Only child _____

How many years separate you from the siblings who were born just before and/or just after you?   A brother _____ years older   A sister _____ years older

A brother _____ years younger   A sister _____ years younger

As a young child, did you attend day care or nursery school? Yes _____ No _____

If yes, how old were you when you first attended? _____

How many years did you attend? _____

Text Credits

Pg. 397, 431: Worthington, Robyn, Bristol Community College, "Nature versus Nurture: Does Birth Order Shape Personality?"

20 Documenting Sources: *Chicago* Style

IN THIS CHAPTER

a. Notes and bibliography entries, 440

b. Tables and figures, 458

c. Formatting, 458

Student Model
Research Project: *Chicago* **Style,** Sara Sweetwood, "The Rise and Fall of Bound Feet in China" 459

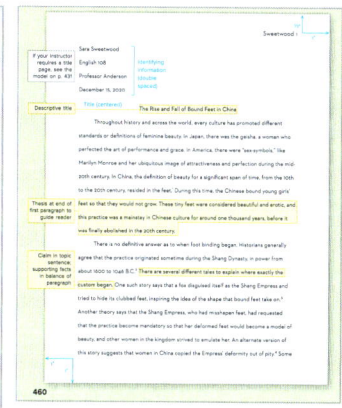

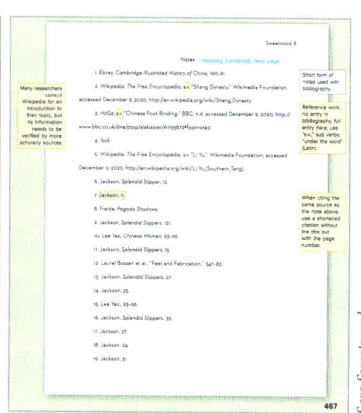

Written by editors at the University of Chicago Press, the *Chicago Manual of Style* (17th ed., 2017) provides advice to help writers and editors produce clear and consistent copy for their readers. Many writers in the humanities and social sciences (in history, economics, and philosophy, for example) follow the guidelines provided by the *Chicago Manual* for citing and documenting sources.

Editors at the University of Chicago Press recognize that readers from different disciplines may have different expectations about how in-text citations and bibliography entries should look, so the *Chicago Manual* provides an author-date system similar to that of the American Psychological Association (APA) and the Council of Science Editors (CSE) for writers in the sciences. It also provides a note and bibliography system for writers in the humanities and social sciences. If your readers (including your instructor) expect you to use the author-date system, consult the *Chicago Manual* itself or follow the style detailed in the APA chapter in this book.

This chapter includes examples of the most common types of *Chicago*-style notes and bibliography entries. For more information or for examples of less common types of sources, consult the *Chicago Manual* itself. You can also subscribe to the *Chicago Manual* online.

> **More about**
> MLA style (ch. 18), 334–96
> APA style (ch. 19), 397–438
> CSE style (ch. 21), 470–84

439

Reference: Examples of *Chicago*-Style Note and Bibliography Entries

Books—Printed and Electronic
1. One author 442
   a. Printed 442
   b. Database 442
   c. Ebook 443
2. Two or three authors 443
3. Four through ten authors 444
4. Unnamed (anonymous) author 444
5. Two or more works by the same author 444
6. Group or corporate author 445
7. Editor (no author) 445
8. Author and editor or translator 445
9. Selection from an edited book or anthology 446
10. Edition other than the first 446
11. Introduction, preface, foreword, or afterword by a different writer 447
12. Entry in an encyclopedia or dictionary 447
    a. Printed (note) 447
    b. Online (note) 447
13. Multivolume work 448
14. Book in a series 448
15. Sacred text (notes) 448
16. Dissertation or thesis 449

Periodicals—Printed and Electronic
17. Article in a scholarly journal 449
    a. Printed 449
    b. Accessed through a database 450
    c. Online 451
18. Article in a magazine 451
    a. Printed (note) 451
    b. Accessed through a database 451
    c. Online 451
19. Article in a newspaper (signed) 452
    a. Printed 452
    b. Accessed through a database 452
    c. Online 453
20. Article or editorial in a newspaper (unsigned) 453
21. Review 453
22. Letter to the editor 453

Other Electronic Sources
23. Website (entire) 454
24. Web page, short work from a website, or wiki article 454
25. Discussion list or blog posting 455
26. CD-ROM 455

Audio and Visual Sources
27. Motion picture (film, video, DVD) 455
28. Music or other audio recording 456
29. Podcast 456
30. Performance 456
31. Work of art (note) 456

Miscellaneous Sources—Printed and Electronic
32. Government publication 457
33. Interview (published or broadcast) 457
    a. Printed or broadcast 457
    b. Online 457
34. Personal communication 457
    a. Letter (note) 457
    b. Email (note) 457
35. Indirect source 457

---

footnote Note that appears at the bottom of the page

endnote Note that appears in a list of notes at the end of the project

20a Creating *Chicago*-Style Notes and Bibliography Entries

The note system offered by the *Chicago Manual* allows you to include full bibliographic information in a footnote or an endnote or to use an abbreviated footnote or endnote with a bibliography. The University of Chicago Press recommends using abbreviated notes with a bibliography.

Writing Responsibly: Citing and Documenting Sources

When you cite and document sources, you demonstrate how thoroughly you have researched your topic and how carefully you have thought about your sources, which encourages your audience to believe you are a credible researcher. In your citations and documentation you acknowledge any material from which you have quoted, paraphrased, summarized, or drawn information, and you join the conversation on your topic by adding your own interpretation. Accurate entries in the body of your project and bibliography allow your audience to find and read your sources so that they can evaluate your interpretation and learn more about the subject themselves. Accurate entries also demonstrate the care with which you have written your research project, which further reinforces your credibility, or ethos.

to AUDIENCE

Examples of the *complete* form of notes and bibliography entries for different types of sources appear in the next section. An *abbreviated* note typically includes enough information for readers to recognize the work and find it in the bibliography. It usually includes the author's surname, a shortened version of the title that includes the title's keywords in the same order as they appear on the title page, and the page number you are citing. Here is an example of an abbreviated note and a bibliography entry for the same book:

NOTE (ABBREVIATED)   1. Vancouver, *Voyage of Discovery,* 283.

BIBLIOGRAPHY   Vancouver, George. *A Voyage of Discovery to the North Pacific Ocean and Round the World, 1791–1795.* Edited by W. Kaye Lamb. London: Hakluyt Society, 1984.

A complete bibliographic note or bibliography entry includes three parts: the author's name, the title of the work, and the publication information (print, electronic, or both). The information you include in each of these parts will differ depending on the type of source you are citing. There are many models, but every variation cannot be covered, so be prepared to adapt a model to your special circumstances.

> Annotated visual of where to find author and publication information (Documentation Matters tutorial preceding ch. 18), 330–33

> *More about*
> Formatting notes (*Chicago* style), 458
> Formatting bibliographies (*Chicago* style), 459

Tech: Creating Footnotes and Endnotes

Most word processing programs, including Microsoft Word and Google Docs, allow you to insert footnotes and endnotes easily. This automated system for inserting footnotes will automatically renumber all the notes in your project if you add or delete one. However, the software for managing notes may not provide many formatting options, so check with your instructor in advance to make sure the software's default format is acceptable.

Chicago Note & Bibliography Entries

1. One author
2. Two or three authors
3. Four through ten authors

Books—Printed and Electronic

In a printed book, the information you need to create a note and bibliography entry (with the exception of the page numbers) is on the title and copyright pages, at the beginning of the book. In an online or ebook, print and electronic publication information usually appears on the first few screens.

1. One author

a. Printed The basic note for a printed book looks like this:

> Ref. No. Author's first name Surname, Title: Subtitle (Place of Publication: Publisher, date of publication), page(s).

Here is a sample note:

> 1. Michael W. Twitty, *The Cooking Gene: A Journey Through African American Culinary History in the Old South* (New York: Amistad, 2017), 96-98.

The basic bibliography entry for a printed book looks like this:

> Author's surname, First Name. Title: Subtitle. Place of publication: Publisher, date of publication.

Here is a sample of a bibliography entry:

> Twitty, Michael W. *The Cooking Gene: A Journey Through African American Culinary History in the Old South.* New York: Amistad, 2017.

The *Chicago Manual* allows for either full publishers' names (the name minus words like *Incorporated* or *Publishers*) or abbreviated versions (*Wiley* instead of *John Wiley & Sons,* for example). Be consistent within your research project. This chapter uses full names.

If the book is self-published or published online, sometimes there is no place of publication. *Chicago* style permits the place to be left out.

b. Database

Here is a sample note for a book accessed from a database with no place of publication provided:

> 2. W. E. B. Du Bois, *The Souls of Black Folk* (1903; Project Gutenberg, 2019), chap. 1, https://www.gutenberg.org/files/408/408-h/408-h.htm.

Here is the corresponding bibliography entry:

Du Bois, W. E. B. *The Souls of Black Folk*. Reprint of the 1903 edition, Project Gutenberg, 2019. https://www.gutenberg.org/files/408/408-h/408-h.htm.

If the online book is *not* available in print or is not yet in final form and might change by the time your readers seek it out, provide your access date immediately before the DOI or URL. Separate the access date from the surrounding citation by commas in a note and by periods in a bibliography entry.

> **Tech — Guidelines for Formatting URLs**
>
> In *Chicago* style, if a URL will not fit on a single line, break it after a colon (:) or a double slash (//), before or after an ampersand (&) or equals sign (=), and before a dot or other punctuation mark.

c. Ebook

Sample note:

3. Charles C. Mann, *1491: New Revelations of the Americas before Columbus* (New York: Alfred A. Knopf, 2005), Adobe Reader Digital Edition, chap. 3.

Sample bibliography entry:

Mann, Charles C. *1491: New Revelations of the Americas before Columbus*. New York: Alfred A. Knopf, 2005. Adobe Reader Digital Edition.

2. Two or three authors

Sample notes:

4. David Gold and Catherine Hobbs, *Educating the New Southern Woman: Speech, Writing, and Race at the Public Women's Colleges, 1884–1945* (Carbondale: Southern Illinois University Press, 2013).

5. Laura Brubeck, Jacob Smith, and Neil Verma, *Indian Sound Cultures, Indian Sound Citizenship* (Ann Arbor: University of Michigan Press, 2020), 119.

Sample bibliography entries:

Gold, David, and Catherine Hobbs. *Educating the New Southern Woman: Speech, Writing, and Race at the Public Women's Colleges, 1884–1945*. Carbondale: Southern Illinois University Press, 2013.

Chicago Note & Bibliography Entries

1. One author
2. **Two or three authors**
3. Four through ten authors
4. Unnamed (anonymous) author

> **Chicago** Note & Bibliography Entries
>
> 1. One author
> 2. Two or three authors
> 3. **Four through ten authors**
> 4. **Unnamed (anonymous) author**
> 5. **Two or more works by the same author**
> 6. Group or corporate author
> 7. Editor (no author)
>
> Examples 1–3, 442–44

The first author is the only author listed surname first.

Brueck, Laura, Jacob Smith, and Neil Verma. *Indian Sound Cultures, Indian Sound Citizenship.* Ann Arbor: University of Michigan Press, 2020.

3. Four through ten authors

Sample note:

1st author plus et al. ("and others" in Latin) in note

6. Lawrence Niles et al., *Life Along the Delaware Bay: Cape May Gateway to a Million Shorebirds* (Piscataway, NJ: Rutgers University Press, 2012), 87.

Sample bibliography entry:

4–10 authors in bibliography entry

Niles, Lawrence, Joanna Burger, Amanda Dey, and Jan Van der Kam. *Life Along the Delaware Bay: Cape May Gateway to a Million Shorebirds.* Piscataway, NJ: Rutgers University Press, 2012.

For sources with more than ten authors, include only the first seven in the bibliography, followed by *et al.*

4. Unnamed (anonymous) author

If no author is listed, begin with the title.

Sample note:

7. *Terrorist Hunter: The Extraordinary Story of a Woman Who Went Undercover to Infiltrate the Radical Islamic Groups Operating in America* (New York: Ecco, 2003), 82.

Sample bibliography entry:

Terrorist Hunter: The Extraordinary Story of a Woman Who Went Undercover to Infiltrate the Radical Islamic Groups Operating in America. New York: Ecco, 2003.

5. Two or more works by the same author

Your note will be the same as for any book by one or more authors. In your bibliography, alphabetize the entries by the first important word in the title, and replace the author's name with three dashes in entries after the first.

Sample bibliography entries:

Inoue, Asao. *Antiracist Writing Assessment Ecologies: Teaching and Assessing Writing for a Socially Just Future.* Anderson, SC: Parlor Press, 2015.

———. *Labor-Based Grading Contracts: Building Equity and Inclusion in the Compassionate Writing Classroom*. Fort Collins: Colorado State University Open Press, 2019.

6. Group or corporate author
Sample note:

    group as author
    8. Blackfoot Gallery Committee, *The Story of the Blackfoot People: Nitsitapiisinni* (Richmond Hill, ON: Firefly Books, 2002), 15.

Sample bibliography entry:

    group as author
Blackfoot Gallery Committee. *The Story of the Blackfoot People: Nitsitapiisinni.* Richmond Hill, ON: Firefly Books, 2002.

7. Editor (no author)
Sample note:

    9. R. K. Ashdowne, ed., *Dictionary of Medieval Latin from British Sources, fascicule XVII, Syr-Z* (New York: Oxford University Press, 2013), 22.

Sample bibliography entry:

Ashdowne, R. K., ed. *Dictionary of Medieval Latin from British Sources, fascicule XVII, Syr-Z.* New York: Oxford University Press, 2013.

NOTE When the abbreviation *ed.* appears after a name, it means *editor*, so for more than one editor, change the abbreviation from *ed.* to *eds.*

8. Author and editor or translator
Sample notes:

    10. John Locke, *The Second Treatise of Government*, ed. Thomas P. Peardon (Indianapolis: Oxford University Press, 1990), 124.

    11. Adania Shibli, *We Are All Equally Far from Love*, trans. Paul Starkey (Northhampton, MA: Interlink Books, 2012), 71.

Chicago Note & Bibliography Entries

4. Unnamed (anonymous) author
5. Two or more works by the same author
6. Group or corporate author
7. Editor (no author)
8. Author and editor or translator
9. Selection from an edited book or anthology
10. Edition other than the first

Sample bibliography entries:

Edited by, Translated by, in bibliography

Locke, John. *The Second Treatise of Government*. Edited by Thomas P. Peardon.

Indianapolis: Oxford University Press, 1990.

Shibli, Adania. *We Are All Equally Far from Love*. Translated by Paul Starkey.

Northhampton, MA: Interlink Books, 2012.

NOTE When the abbreviation *ed.* appears before a name, it means *edited by*, so do not add an *-s* when there is more than one editor.

9. Selection from an edited book or anthology
Sample note:

12. Elizabeth Kleinfeld, "Just Read the Assignment: Using Course Documents to Analyze Research Pedagogy," in *Points of Departure: Rethinking Student Source Use and Writing Studies Research Methods,* ed. Tricia Serviss and Sandra Jamieson (Fort Collins, CO: Utah State University Press, 2017), 230.

Sample bibliography entry:

Kleinfeld, Elizabeth. "Just Read the Assignment: Using Course Documents to Analyze Research Pedagogy." In *Points of Departure: Rethinking Student Source Use and Writing Studies Research Methods,* edited by Tricia Serviss and Sandra Jamieson, 227–244. Fort Collins, CO: Utah State University Press, 2017.

Include a page range in a bibliography entry only for a work contained within a longer work, such as a chapter in a collection.

10. Edition other than the first
Sample note:

13. Patricia S. Daniels, Stephen G. Hyslop, and Douglas Brinkley, eds., *National Geographic Almanac of World History*, 3rd ed. (National Geographic, 2014), 72.

Sample bibliography entry:

> Daniels, Patricia S., Stephen G. Hyslop, and Douglas Brinkley, eds. *National Geographic Almanac of World History*. 3rd ed. Washington, DC: National Geographic, 2014.

11. Introduction, preface, foreword, or afterword by a different writer

Sample note:

> 14. Sister Helen Prejean, introduction to *Lead Me On, Let Me Stand: A Clergyman's Story in White and Black*, by William H. Barnwell (Columbia: University of South Carolina Press, 2015), 7.

Sample bibliography entry:

> Prejean, Sister Helen. Introduction to *Lead Me On, Let Me Stand: A Clergyman's Story in White and Black*, by William H. Barnwell, 3–12. Columbia: University of South Carolina Press, 2015.

introduction pgs.

Include a page range in a bibliography entry only for a work contained within a longer work, such as an introduction to a book.

12. Entry in an encyclopedia or dictionary

For a well-known reference work such as the *American Heritage Dictionary* or the *Encyclopedia Britannica*, a bibliography entry is not necessary.

a. Printed (note)

> 15. *The American Heritage Dictionary of the English Language*, fifth ed., s.v. "plagiarism."

s.v. Abbreviation of the Latin phrase *sub verbo*, "under the word"

b. Online (note)
Unless a "last updated" date appears on the site, include an access date before the URL.

> 16. *The American Heritage Dictionary of the English Language*, s.v. "plagiarism," accessed July 23, 2020, https://ahdictionary.com/word/search.html?q=plagiarism.

URL

Chicago Note & Bibliography Entries

9. Selection from an edited book or anthology
10. Edition other than the first
11. **Introduction, preface, foreword, or afterword by a different writer**
12. **Entry in an encyclopedia or dictionary**
13. Multivolume work
14. Book in a series

13. Multivolume work

Sample notes:

17. Robert Caro, *The Years of Lyndon Johnson*, vol. 3, *Master of the Senate* (New York: Alfred A. Knopf, 2002), 4.

18. George Brown Tindall and David E. Shi, *America: A Narrative History*, 8th ed. (New York: W. W. Norton, 2003), 2:123.

Sample bibliography entries:

Caro, Robert. *The Years of Lyndon Johnson*. Vol. 3, *The Master of the Senate*. New York: Alfred A. Knopf, 2002.

Tindall, George Brown, and David E. Shi. *America: A Narrative History*. 8th ed. 2 vols. New York: W. W. Norton, 2003.

14. Book in a series

Sample note:

19. Cedric Burrows, *Rhetorical Crossover: The Black Presence in White Culture*, Pittsburgh Series in Composition, Literacy, and Culture (PA: University of Pittsburgh Press, 2020), 132.

Sample bibliography entry:

Burrows, Cedric. *Rhetorical Crossover: The Black Presence in White Culture*. Pittsburgh Series in Composition, Literacy, and Culture. PA: University of Pittsburgh Press, 2020.

15. Sacred text (notes)

20. 1 Kings 3:23–26 (King James Version).

21. Qur'an 17:1–2.

Sacred texts are not usually included in the bibliography.

16. Dissertation or thesis For an unpublished dissertation or thesis, place the title in quotation marks; titles of published dissertations or theses are italicized. Include the type of document (*PhD diss., MA thesis*), the university where it was submitted, and the date of submission.

Sample note for an unpublished dissertation:

> 22. Jessica Davis Powers, "Patrons, Houses and Viewers in Pompeii: Reconsidering the House of the Gilded Cupids" (PhD diss., University of Michigan, 2006), 43–57, ProQuest (AAI 3208535).

Sample bibliography entry for an unpublished dissertation:

> Powers, Jessica Davis. "Patrons, Houses and Viewers in Pompeii: Reconsidering the House of the Gilded Cupids." PhD diss., University of Michigan, 2006. ProQuest (AAI 3208535).

Periodicals—Printed and Electronic

A periodical is a publication issued at regular intervals—newspapers are generally published every day, magazines every week or month, and scholarly journals four times a year. For periodicals, include not only the title of the article (in quotation marks) but also the title of the periodical (in italics). The type of publication information you include depends on the type of periodical you are citing.

17. Article in a scholarly journal The information you need to create a note and bibliography entry for a printed journal article appears on the cover or title page of the journal and on the first and last page of the article. For articles downloaded from a database, the information appears on the screen listing the articles that fit your search terms, on the full record of the article, or on the first and last page of the file you download. For articles that appear in journals published solely online, you will find the publication information on the website's home page, in the journal's table of contents, or on the first page of the article.

a. Printed The basic note for an article in a printed journal looks like this:

> Ref. No. Author's first name and Surname, "Title of Article," *Title of Journal* Vol. no., issue no. (Year of publication): Pages.

Chicago Note & Bibliography Entries

15. Sacred text (notes)
16. Dissertation or thesis
17. Article in a scholarly journal
18. Article in a magazine
19. Article in a newspaper (signed)

▸ Annotated visual of where to find author, title, and publication information (Documentation Matters tutorial preceding ch. 18), 330–33

▸ *More about*
Formatting author information: Examples 1–6, 442–45

Months (May) or seasons (Winter) may be included before the year of publication, but they are not required. If a journal is paginated by volume—for example, if issue 1 ends on page 175 and issue 2 begins on page 176—the issue number may be omitted.

Here is a sample note for a printed journal article with an issue number:

> 23. Bishupal Limbu, "Democracy, Perhaps: Collectivity, Kinship, and the Politics of Friendship," *Comparative Literature* 63, no. 1 (2011): 92.
> vol. no. issue no.

Here is a sample bibliography entry:

> Limbu, Bishupal. "Democracy, Perhaps: Collectivity, Kinship, and the Politics of Friendship." *Comparative Literature* 63, no. 1 (2011): 92–6.

b. Accessed through a database Most researchers locate journal articles through subscription databases available through their college library. Frequently, articles indexed in such databases are also available in HTML or PDF format through the database. If the article you are citing is available in PDF format, include the page numbers you are citing in your note and the page range in your bibliography entry. If the article is available only in HTML format, add a subhead or paragraph number to your note if this will help readers locate the passage you are citing. To cite an article accessed through a subscription database, add the name of the database and reference number (if any) at the end of your entry, or include the URL if stable. More and more academic journals are also adding digital object identifiers (DOIs); if the article you are citing includes a DOI, add it in place of the database information.

Sample note:

> 24. Amal Alhadabi and Aryn C. Karpinski, "Grit, Self-Efficacy, Achievement Orientation Goals, and Academic Performance in University Students," *International Journal of Adolescence and Youth* 25, no. 1 (2020): 525, doi: 10.1080/02673843.2019.1679202.
> DOI

Sample bibliography entry:

> Alhadabi, Amal, and Aryn C. Karpinski. "Grit, Self-Efficacy, Achievement Orientation Goals, and Academic Performance in University Students." *International Journal of Adolescence and Youth* 25, no. 1 (2020): 519–535. doi: 10.1080/02673843.2019.1679202.

Chicago Note & Bibliography Entries

16. Dissertation or thesis
17. **Article in a scholarly journal**
18. Article in a magazine
19. Article in a newspaper (signed)

HTML Hypertext markup language, the coding system used to create websites and web pages

PDF Portable document format, a method for sharing documents without losing formatting

DOI Digital object identifier, a permanent identifier given to electronic sources

c. Online Online journals may not provide page numbers. Provide a sub-heading or paragraph number (if the article provides them), and include the DOI (if there is one) or the URL for the article (if there is not).

Sample note:

> 25. Pamela Saunders, "Cripping Kairos: The Risky Rhetorical Performance of Autism Disclosure for the College Student," *Disability Studies Quarterly* 40, no. 2 (2020), [URL] https://dsq-sds.org/article/view/7072/5569.

Sample bibliography entry:

> Saunders, Pamela. "Cripping Kairos: The Risky Rhetorical Performance of Autism Disclosure for the College Student." *Disability Studies Quarterly* 40, no. 2 (2020). [URL] https://dsq-sds.org/article/view/7072/5569.

18. Article in a magazine Omit volume and issue numbers, and replace the parentheses around the publication date (month and year or month, day, and year) with commas. Page numbers may be omitted.

a. Printed (note)

> 26. Marian Smith Holmes, "The Freedom Riders," *Smithsonian*, February 2009, 72.

> Holmes, Marian Smith. "The Freedom Riders." *Smithsonian*, February 2009, 70–75.

b. Accessed through a database

Sample note:

> 27. Victor Davis Hanson, "Today's Revolutionaries Aren't Like Their 60s Predecessors," *National Review*, July 23, 2020, Access World News.

Sample bibliography entry:

> Hanson, Victor Davis. "Today's Revolutionaries Aren't Like Their 60s Predecessors." *National Review*, July 23, 2020. Access World News.

c. Online

Sample note:

> 28. Peter Dreier, "Feminist Activist Bella Abzug Paved the Way for Women Politicians," *Teen Vogue*, July 24, 2020, [article URL] https://www.teenvogue.com/story/who-was-bella-abzug-womens-rights-activist.

Sample bibliography entry:

> Dreier, Peter. "Feminist Activist Bella Abzug Paved the Way for Women Politicians." *Teen Vogue*, July 24, 2020. https://www.teenvogue.com/story/who-was-bella-abzug-womens-rights-activist.

19. Article in a newspaper (signed) Because page numbers may differ from edition to edition, use the edition name and section letter or number (if available) instead. A bibliography entry may be omitted.

a. Printed

If the city in which the newspaper is published is not identified on the newspaper's masthead, add it in parentheses; if it might be unfamiliar to readers, add the state, also.

Sample note:

> 29. Jim Kenneally, "When Brockton Was Home to a Marathon," *Enterprise* (Brockton, MA), April 20, 2006, sec. 1.

Sample bibliography entry:

> Kenneally, Jim. "When Brockton Was Home to a Marathon." *Enterprise* (Brockton, MA), April 20, 2006, sec. 1.

For well-known national newspapers (such as the *Christian Science Monitor, USA Today,* and the *Wall Street Journal*), no city or state is needed. If you are unsure whether the newspaper is well known, consult your instructor or a reference librarian.

b. Accessed through a database

Sample note:

> 30. Stanley Coren, "Dogs, An Archaeologist's Best Friend," *Dallas Morning News*, June 4, 2020, PressReader.

Sample bibliography entry:

> Coren, Stanley. "Dogs, An Archaeologist's Best Friend." *Dallas Morning News*, June 4, 2020. PressReader.

c. Online

Sample note:

> 31. Chris Talbott, "Everett Illustrator Matthew Southworth and Seattle Author Garth Stein Sync Up for Debut Graphic Novel *The Cloven*," *Seattle Times*, 24 July 2020, https://www.seattletimes.com/entertainment/books/everett-illustrator-matthew-southworth-and-seattle-author-garth-stein-sync-up-for-debut-graphic-novel-the-cloven/.

[article URL]

Sample bibliography entry:

> Talbott, Chris. "Everett Illustrator Matthew Southworth and Seattle Author Garth Stein Sync Up for Debut Graphic Novel *The Cloven*." *Seattle Times*, 24 July 2020. https://www.seattletimes.com/entertainment/books/everett-illustrator-matthew-southworth-and-seattle-author-garth-stein-sync-up-for-debut-graphic-novel-the-cloven/.

20. Article or editorial in a newspaper (unsigned) When no author is named, place the newspaper's title in the author position in your bibliography entry. (*Chicago* style does not require a bibliography entry for unsigned newspaper articles or editorials, but your instructor might.)

21. Review

Sample note:

> 32. Anthony Tommasini, review of *Siegfried*, by Richard Wagner, conducted by Fabio Luisi, Metropolitan Opera, New York, *New York Times*, October 29, 2011, sec. C.

Sample bibliography entry:

> Tommasini, Anthony. Review of *Siegfried*, by Richard Wagner, conducted by Fabio Luisi, Metropolitan Opera, New York. *New York Times*, October 29, 2011, sec. C.

22. Letter to the editor Omit the letter's title, page numbers, and the edition name or number.

Sample note:

> 33. John A. Beck, letter to the editor, *Los Angeles Times*, March 16, 2010.

Sample bibliography entry:

> Beck, John A. Letter to the editor. *Los Angeles Times*, March 16, 2010.

Chicago Note & Bibliography Entries

18. Article in a magazine
19. Article in a newspaper (signed)
20. Article or editorial in a newspaper (unsigned)
21. Review
22. Letter to the editor
23. Website (entire)
24. Web page, short work from a website, or wiki article

Other Electronic Sources

> Annotated visual of where to find publication information (Documentation Matters tutorial preceding ch. 18), 330–33

Although it is usually easy to find citation information for books and articles in periodicals, websites can be a bit trickier. Most of the information you need will appear at the bottom or top of the web page or on the site's home page. Sometimes, however, you may need to look further. Click on links such as "About us" or "More information." Frequently, websites do not provide complete information, so provide as much information as you can. If no author is listed, place the site's sponsor in the "author" position. If key information is missing, include a phrase describing the site, in case the URL changes.

23. Website (entire) Typically, writers draw on specific articles, short works, or pages from a website (see example 24). However, there may be instances in which you will cite an entire website. The basic note for a website looks like this:

> Ref. No. Website Title, Author (if provided), Sponsoring Organization, last update or access date if last update not provided, URL.

Here is a sample note for a website:

> *Sponsor in position of author*
> 34. Literary Hub, Grove Atlantic and Electric Literature, accessed January 1, 2021, https://lithub.com/.

The bibliography entry for the note above looks like this:

> *Sponsor in position of author*
> Grove Atlantic and Electric Literature. Literary Hub. Accessed January 1, 2021. https://lithub.com/.

Chicago Note & Bibliography Entries

22. Letter to the editor
23. Website (entire)
24. Web page, short work from a website, or wiki article
25. Discussion list or blog posting
26. CD-ROM

Include an access date only when the publication date or last update is not indicated. *Chicago* style does not require an entry in the bibliography for web content, but if your instructor does, follow the example above.

24. Web page, short work from a website, or wiki article When referring to a specific page or article on a website or wiki, place that page's title in quotation marks. For a wiki article, begin with the article's title.

Sample note:

> 35. "The Restoration and 18th Century," British Literature Wiki, University of Delaware, accessed May 26, 2020, https://sites.udel.edu/britlitwiki/the-restoration-and-the-18th-century/.

Sample bibliography entry:

British Literature Wiki, University of Delaware, "The Restoration and 18th Century." Accessed May 26, 2020. https://sites.udel.edu/britlitwiki/the-restoration-and-the-18th-century/.

25. Discussion list or blog posting Discussion list entries, blog posts, and social media entries need not be included in the bibliography.

26. CD-ROM If there is more than one version or edition of the CD-ROM, add that information after the title.

Sample note:

36. *History through Art: The 20th Century* (San Jose, CA: Fogware Publishing, 2000), CD-ROM, chap. 1.

Sample bibliography entry:

History through Art: The 20th Century. San Jose, CA: Fogware Publishing, 2000. CD-ROM.

Audio and Visual Sources

The information you need to create notes and bibliography entries for most audio and visual sources appears on the cover, label, or program or in the credits at the end of a film or a television show. Begin with the author, director, conductor, or performer, or begin your citation with the name of the work, depending on what your project emphasizes. The *Chicago Manual* provides few models of audiovisual sources. Those below are based on the principles explained in *Chicago*.

27. Motion picture (film, video, DVD)
Sample note:

37. *Honeyland*, directed by Tamara Kotevska and Ljubomir Stefanov (2019; North Macedonia: Trice Films), film.

Sample bibliography entry:

Honeyland. Directed by Tamara Kotevska and Ljubomir Stefanov. 2019. North Macedonia: Trice Films. Film.

Chicago Note & Bibliography Entries

23. Website (entire)
24. Web page, short work from a website, or wiki article
25. Discussion list or blog posting
26. CD-ROM
27. Motion picture (film, video, DVD)
28. Music or other audio recording
29. Podcast

28. Music or other audio recording

Sample note:

> 38. Johannes Brahms, *Piano Concerto no. 1 in D minor, op. 15,* Berliner Philharmoniker, conducted by Claudio Abbado, Philips Classics Productions BMG D153907, 1986, compact disc.

Sample bibliography entry:

> Brahms, Johannes. *Piano Concerto no. 1 in D minor, op. 15.* Berliner Philharmoniker. Claudio Abbado (conductor). Philips Classics Productions BMG D153907, 1986, compact disc.

29. Podcast

Sample note:

> 39. Melvyn Bragg, host, "The Indian Mutiny," *In Our Time,* BBC Radio 4, podcast audio, February 18, 2010, www.bbc.co.uk/programmes/b00qprnj.

Sample bibliography entry:

> Bragg, Melvyn, host. "The Indian Mutiny." *In Our Time,* BBC Radio 4, February 18, 2010. Podcast audio. www.bbc.co.uk/programmes/b00qprnj.

30. Performance

Sample note:

> 40. Jay O. Sanders, *Titus Andronicus,* dir. Michael Sexton, Anspacher Theater, New York, November 29, 2011.

Sample bibliography entry:

> Sanders, Jay O. *Titus Andronicus.* Directed by Michael Sexton. Anspacher Theater, New York, November 29, 2011.

31. Work of art (note) If a reproduction of the work appears in your project, identify the work in a figure caption. If you discuss the work but do not show it, cite it in your notes but do not provide an entry in your bibliography. If the reproduction is taken from a book, follow the model for a selection from an edited book or anthology.

> 41. Alexander Calder, *Two Acrobats*, 1929, wire sculpture, Menil Collection, Houston.

Miscellaneous Sources—Printed and Electronic

32. Government publication For documents published by the Government Printing Office (or GPO), including the publisher is optional. If you omit the publisher, change the colon after the location to a period.

33. Interview (published or broadcast)
a. Printed or broadcast
Sample note:

> 42. Barack Obama, interview by Maria Bartiromo, *Closing Bell*, CNBC, March 27, 2008.

Sample bibliography entry:

> Obama, Barack. Interview by Maria Bartiromo. *Closing Bell*, CNBC, March 27, 2008.

b. Online
Sample note:

> 43. Barack Obama, interview by Maria Bartiromo, *Closing Bell*, CNBC, March 27, 2008, www.cnbc.com/id/23832520.

Sample bibliography entry:

> Obama, Barack. Interview by Maria Bartiromo. *Closing Bell*. CNBC, March 27, 2008.
>
> www.cnbc.com/id/23832520.

34. Personal communication Unless your instructor requires it, no bibliography entry is needed for a personal communication.
a. Letter (note)

> 44. Roberto James, letter to the author, August 13, 2019.

b. Email (note)

> 45. Donita Williams, email message to the author, January 13, 2021.

35. Indirect source If you do not have access to the original source, your note and bibliography entry should name both the original source and the source from which you borrowed the material.

Chicago Note & Bibliography Entries

30. Performance
31. Work of art (note)
32. Government publication
33. Interview (published or broadcast)
34. Personal communication
35. Indirect source

20b Using *Chicago* Style for Tables and Figures

The *Chicago Manual* recommends that you number tables and figures in a separate sequence (*Table 1, Table 2, Figure 1, Figure 2*) both in the text and in the table title or figure caption. Tables and figures should be placed as close as possible after the text reference. For tables, provide a brief identifying title and place it above the table. For figures, provide a caption that includes any information about the figure that readers will need to identify it, such as the title of a work of art, the artist's name, the work's location, and a brief description. If the figure or table, or information used to create the figure or table, comes from another source, provide a source note. Source notes for tables generally appear below the table, while source information for figures appears at the end of the figure caption.

20c Formatting a *Chicago*-Style Research Project

> **More about**
> MLA-style formatting, 379–82
> Formatting college projects, 98

The *Chicago Manual* provides detailed instructions about manuscript preparation for authors submitting their work for publication, but it does not offer formatting instructions for college projects. Follow the formatting instructions provided in Chapter 9 or Chapter 18, or consult your instructor.

1. Format notes.

> While acknowledging that not all scholars agree, Mann observes, "If Monte Verde is correct, as most believe, people were thriving from Alaska to Chile while much of northern Europe was still empty of mankind and its works."[8]

The *Chicago Manual* recommends numbering bibliographic notes consecutively throughout the project, using superscript (above-the-line) numbers. Type the heading "Notes" at the top of a new page following the end of the text, and type the notes below the heading. (You may need to insert a page break if your word processor has automatically created endnotes on the last page of your paper.)

2. Format the bibliography.

To begin your list of works cited, type the heading "Bibliography," "References," or "Works Cited" at the top of a new page. (Ask your instructor which heading is preferred.) Entries should be formatted with a hanging indent: Position the first line of each entry flush with the left margin, and indent subsequent lines by half an inch. Entries should be alphabetized by the author's surname.

> **More about**
> Hanging indent,
> 379, 381, 426

Writing Responsibly: Of Deadlines and Paperclips

Instructors expect students to turn in thoughtful, carefully proofread, and neatly formatted papers on time—usually in class on the due date. They also expect writers to clip or staple the pages of the paper *before* submitting. Do justice to yourself by being fully prepared.

to SELF

Student Model Research Project: *Chicago* Style

The research project that follows was written by Sara Sweetwood for a history course at Pace University. Sweetwood fulfills her responsibilities to topic and audience by drawing on a variety of relevant and reliable sources to make her case. She fulfills her responsibility to the writers from whom she borrows information and ideas by citing them in abbreviated notes in the text and by providing a complete entry for each work in the list of works cited at the end of the project. She demonstrates her credibility as a researcher and a writer by providing evidence to support her claims and by revising, editing, and proofreading her project carefully.

Sweetwood 1

Sara Sweetwood

English 108

Professor Anderson

December 15, 2020

The Rise and Fall of Bound Feet in China

    Throughout history and across the world, every culture has promoted different standards or definitions of feminine beauty. In Japan, there was the geisha, a woman who perfected the art of performance and grace. In America, there were "sex-symbols," like Marilyn Monroe and her ubiquitous image of attractiveness and perfection during the mid-20th century. In China, the definition of beauty for a significant span of time, from the 10th to the 20th century, resided in the feet.[1] During this time, the Chinese bound young girls' feet so that they would not grow. These tiny feet were considered beautiful and erotic, and this practice was a mainstay in Chinese culture for around one thousand years, before it was finally abolished in the 20th century.

    There is no definitive answer as to when foot binding began. Historians generally agree that the practice originated sometime during the Shang Dynasty, in power from about 1600 to 1046 B.C.[2] There are several different tales to explain where exactly the custom began. One such story says that a fox disguised itself as the Shang Empress and tried to hide its clubbed feet, inspiring the idea of the shape that bound feet take on.[3] Another theory says that the Shang Empress, who had misshapen feet, had requested that the practice become mandatory so that her deformed feet would become a model of beauty, and other women in the kingdom strived to emulate her. An alternate version of this story suggests that women in China copied the Empress' deformity out of pity.[4] Some attribute the practice to Emperor Li Yu, who ruled from 961 to 976 C.E.[5] Li Yu, supposedly attracted to small feet, asked one of his concubines, named Yao Niang, to wrap her feet in bindings and perform a dance on the tips of her toes. She was a talented dancer and other members of the nobility began to wrap their feet as well in the hope that Li Yu would give them attention as he did to her.[6]

The practice stayed within rich women and the nobility until the early 17th century, when it eventually worked its way down the social ladder and soon "millions of Chinese women of all socioeconomic backgrounds" were binding their feet. (See Figure 1.) Because the process was lengthy and expensive, a typical lower class family would only bind the feet of their eldest daughter, while the younger ones would work on farms as laborers.[7] As Adele Fielde, a Baptist missionary who lived in China in the 1800s, said, "near the coast, even in the farmsteads and among the most indigent, everyone has bound feet. It is not [. . .] a sign of wealth, for [. . .] the poorest follow [the custom]. [. . .] Taking all of China together, probably nine-tenths of the women have bound feet."[8]

The practice probably became so widespread for a variety of reasons. First, the painful process forced the women to walk in a delicate manner, called the "lotus gait," that men found erotic and ladylike.[9] It also essentially handicapped the women, forcing them to rely on a maid's help to perform basic tasks and thus prevented infidelity and promoted reliance on the husband.[10] "A woman who was kept physically restricted was, presumably, less likely to be mentally independent. Her very helplessness conveyed an elevated status to her husband and his family. Anyone who could afford a 'helpless' wife must be a successful man, regardless of his actual social or economic reality."[11] It is hypothesized that having bound feet became a status symbol because it proved that a family was not in need of a woman's labor, and could instead afford the lengthy process.[12]

Foot binding often began as early as the age of four and as late as age twelve, though the average age to start the process was six. The practice was started so early in a girl's life because younger feet were softer, made up of pre-bone cartilage, and therefore were more easily breakable. Normally, the process commenced in the frigid wintertime temperatures when the feet were numb and less susceptible to pain, because the first few months were said to be the most excruciating.[13] The toes, save for the biggest, would be broken and then pressed to the bottom of the foot. The feet were then bound tightly with cotton wrappings in this position.[14] Both the feet and the bandages were routinely soaked in an herb and animal blood mixture that was believed to soften the feet. The girls were kept in these wrappings for varying, gradually increasing lengths of time. Young girls could be punished if they attempted to remove these bandages.[15] Gradually, the feet were forced into smaller and smaller pairs of shoes until the desired size was reached, which normally occurred after two years of binding.[16] One very important aspect of foot binding was the idyllic standard known as the "golden lotus," referring to a perfectly bound foot that measured three inches or less in length. Women strived to attain this measurement. A perfectly bound foot would "be shaped like the bud of a lotus flower—full and round at the heel and coming to a thin point at the front."[17] Women who fulfilled the required dimensions to earn the title of having perfect feet were more desired by men.[18]

The process of binding feet was also riddled with superstitions. There were several dates commonly chosen for their relation to deities. Before beginning the process of foot binding, it was customary for mothers to consult a diviner or astrologer to determine

Figure 1. For a thousand years in China, until the mid-20th century, many women of all classes had bound feet, conforming to an idealized standard of beauty.

the luckiest day to begin.[19] One was the twenty-fourth day of the eighth lunar month, the birthday of a goddess called the Little-footed Miss. Another date chosen was the nineteenth day of the second lunar month, the birthday of Kuan Yin, goddess of mercy. Another popular date in some areas of China was in the seventh lunar month, during the corn and hemp festival. It is hypothesized that people believed that beginning foot binding on this date was lucky because the foot would resemble the slender shape that the stalks of corn and hemp have.[20] Before binding the feet, the mother would place the tiny shoes meant for bound feet at the altar of these goddesses. She would light incense and candles, and offer fruits and dumplings, which the daughter would subsequently eat. It was believed that eating these dumplings would help her feet resemble the supple and small qualities of the food.[21]

This practice was not without health consequences for those subjected to it. Because the tight bindings and curled toes prevented proper blood flow, it was common for the toes to become necrotic. This could result in the loss of appendages, or in severe circumstances, gangrene, potentially leading to death. Toenails that were not trimmed could cut into the skin and cause infection, as bacteria was easily formed underneath the tight bandaging.[22] The process caused young girls excruciating pain, as it required repeatedly breaking and tightly binding the toes. It crippled young girls, and left them partially disabled for the remainder of their lives:

> The [process] permanently changed the feet so that later unbinding could not restore their natural form. Foot binding greatly inhibited the mobility of Chinese girls and women for the rest of their lives. It permanently stopped their running, slowed their walking, and reduced their balance. As they aged, many women could only walk with canes.[23]

Sister Ann Colette Wolf worked in China from 1946 to 1967 in a school established by missionaries called the Sisters of Providence. On encountering employees with bound feet, she wrote, "It was pitiful to see them walk. [. . .] Usually a person had to employ two women to do the work which one woman could have done if she had not been so crippled."[24]

A study conducted by historians examined the effects bound feet had on older women later in life.[25] The historians surveyed about 200 women aged seventy years and older living in and around Beijing. The study found that women with bound feet were more likely to have fallen during the past year. They also had greater history of fractures, and were more likely to be unable to squat or stand from a chair unassisted. In the end, the historians concluded that, "over the centuries, foot binding produced severe lifelong disability for many millions of women. The deformities of foot binding linger on as a common cause of disability in elderly Chinese women."

After being a prominent part of Chinese culture for one thousand years, the abolition of foot binding was a lengthy process. It began in the 18th century with some influential Chinese writers and scholars, like Kung Tzu-chen and Li Ruzhen, calling for an end to the practice. Li Ruzhen said, "I thought that all women must have been unfilial, and their mothers bound their feet to protect them from the death penalty. I had no idea they were bound for beauty. If we cut off someone's nose to make it smaller, wouldn't that person be considered deformed?" [26] An increase in contact with foreigners brought with it an influx in the exchange of ideas. Westerners traveling to China protested against the practice. In the late 1890s, Chinese scholar Kang Yu Wei led the No Bind Feet Society, imploring fathers to prevent their sons from marrying bound footed women. Kang Yu Wei wrote a letter to the Empress Dowager in which he talked about how the foreigners photographed women with bound feet and dispersed it among themselves, condemning the practice as barbaric.[27]

Another step forward towards ending foot binding came in 1905, when the Empress Dowager Ci-xi put in place several reforms, including advocating that the practice be brought to an end, as it was cruel and damaging to the health of girls.[28] In 1912, the Qing Dynasty fell and a new Nationalist government formed. The leader Sun Yat-sen amplified the pressure to end bound feet. Although some relented in the cities, the practice carried on in more rural areas. In 1928, the anti-foot binding agenda was enhanced by several new edicts that were put in place by the Nationalist government. The first called for all school textbooks to contain a chapter on the ban on the practice. Girls under the age of fifteen were ordered to cease binding their feet. Another incentive to end foot binding was the offering of monetary rewards for removed bindings, while families with bound footed girls were fined.[29] Although these reforms decreased the number of foot bindings, it was not until 1949 when the Chinese Communists came into power that foot binding was formally abolished. The practice, they said, resulted in the loss of otherwise healthy workers.[30] A huge challenge the new government faced was incorporating those with bound feet into the workforce. It remedied this by splitting up the type of work assigned. Those who were able bodied were assigned tasks like planting and harvesting in the fields, while those who were not as healthy were assigned less physical jobs like weeding plants and clearing out waste.[31]

> Conclusion: Provides brief summary and reiterates significance of cultural practice

With the government ban on foot binding still in effect today, the practice has come to a stop, and there is no reason to think it will ever return. Despite its prominence in China for a thousand years, foot binding eventually came to be viewed as cruel and unhealthy. Thus, a practice that once defined womanly beauty and dictated marriages and courtships is today just another footnote in Chinese history.

Notes

1. Ebrey, *Cambridge Illustrated History of China*, 160-61.

2. *Wikipedia: The Free Encyclopedia,* s.v. "Shang Dynasty," Wikimedia Foundation, accessed December 9, 2020, http://en.wikipedia.org/wiki/Shang_Dynasty.

3. *H2G2,* s.v. "Chinese Foot Binding," BBC, n.d. accessed December 9, 2020, http://www.bbc.co.uk/dna/ptop/alabaster/A1155872#footnote2.

4. Ibid.

5. *Wikipedia: The Free Encyclopedia,* s.v. "Li Yu," Wikimedia Foundation, accessed December 9, 2020, http://en.wikipedia.org/wiki/Li_Yu_(Southern_Tang).

6. Jackson, *Splendid Slipper*, 12.

7. Jackson, 11.

8. Fielde, *Pagoda Shadows*.

9. Jackson, *Splendid Slippers*, 121.

10. Lee Yao, *Chinese Women*, 93-96.

11. Jackson, *Splendid Slippers*, 15.

12. Laurel Bossen et al., "Feet and Fabrication," 347-83.

13. Jackson, *Splendid Slippers*, 27.

14. Jackson, 35.

15. Lee Yao., 93-96.

16. Jackson, *Splendid Slippers*, 35.

17. Jackson, 27.

18. Jackson, 24.

19. Jackson, 31.

20. Jackson, 28.

21. Jackson, 31.

22. *H2G2*, "Chinese Foot Binding."

23. Bossen et al., "Feet and Fabrication," 348.

24. Wolf, *Sisters of Providence*.

25. Cummings, et. al., "Consequences of Foot Binding among Older Women in Beijing, China," 1677-79.

26. Jackson, *Splendid Slippers*, 140-43.

27. Jackson, 144-45.

28. Jackson, 152.

29. Jackson, 154.

30. Jackson, 157.

31. Snow, *Red Star over China*.

Sweetwood 10

Works Cited

Bossen, Laurel, et al. "Feet and Fabrication: Footbinding and Early Twentieth-Century Rural Women's Labor in Shaanxi." *Modern China* 37, no. 4 (2011): 347-83. Academic Search Premier.

"Chinese Foot Binding." *H2G2*. BBC, n.d. Accessed Dec. 9, 2016. http://www.bbc.co.uk/dna/ptop/alabaster/A1155872#footnote2.

Cummings, Steven R., Xu Ling, and Katie Stone. "Consequences of Foot Binding among Older Women in Beijing, China." *American Journal of Public Health* 87, no. 10 (1997): 1677-79. Academic Search Premier. Accessed Nov. 18, 2016.

Ebrey, Patricia Buckley. *Cambridge Illustrated History of China*, 2nd ed. New York: Cambridge University Press, 2010.

Fielde, Adele M. *Pagoda Shadows: Studies from Life in China*, 6th ed. Boston: W. G. Corthell, 1890.

Jackson, Beverley. *Splendid Slippers: A Thousand Years of an Erotic Tradition*. Berkeley: Ten Speed, 1997.

Lee Yao, Esther S. *Chinese Women: Past and Present*. Mesquite, TX: Ide House, 1983.

"Li Yu." *Wikipedia: The Free Encyclopedia*. Wikimedia Foundation. Accessed Dec. 9, 2016. http://en.wikipedia.org/wiki/Li_Yu_(Southern_Tang).

"Shang Dynasty." *Wikipedia: The Free Encyclopedia*. Wikimedia Foundation. Accessed Dec. 9, 2016. http://en.wikipedia.org/wiki/Shang_Dynasty.

Snow, Edgar. *Red Star over China*. New York: Bantam, 1968.

Wolf, Sister Ann Colette. *Against All Odds: Sisters of Providence, Mission to the Chinese*. St.-Mary-of-the-Woods, Indiana: St. Mary's, 1990.

Entires arranged alphabetically

Online article: Stable URL provided

Journal article: Accessed through a database

Book (printed): Scholarly press

Book (printed): Popular press

Text Credits

Pg. 439, 460: Courtesy of Sara Sweetwood. Pg. 458: Mann, Charles C., 1491: New Revelations of the Americas Before Columbus (New York: Alfred A. Knopf, 2005) p. 173

21 Documenting Sources: CSE Style

IN THIS CHAPTER

a. In-text citations, 470

b. Reference list, 472

c. Formatting, 482

Student Model
Research Project: CSE-Style Reference List, 483

> **More about**
> MLA style
>   (ch. 18), 334–96
> APA style
>   (ch. 19), 397–438
> *Chicago* style
>   (ch. 20), 439–69

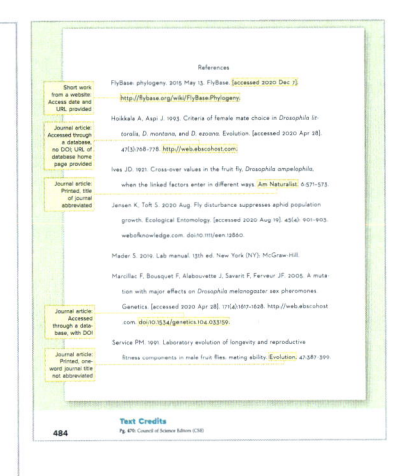

Writers in the sciences customarily use formatting and documentation guidelines from *Scientific Style and Format: The CSE Manual for Authors, Editors, and Publishers* (8th ed., 2014) published by the Council of Science Editors (CSE). CSE style requires that sources be cited briefly in the text and documented in a reference list at the end of the project. The goal of providing in-text citations and a list of references is to allow readers to locate and read the sources for themselves and to distinguish the writer's ideas from those borrowed from sources.

21a Creating CSE-Style In-Text Citations

In-text citations, which appear in the body of your project, identify any material borrowed from a source, whether it is a quotation,

---

Writing Responsibly — Citing and Documenting Sources

When you cite and document sources, you acknowledge any material from which you have quoted, paraphrased, summarized, or drawn information, and you join the conversation on your topic by adding your own interpretation, data, methods, and results. Simultaneously, you give interested readers (including your instructor) a way to join the conversation. Accurate entries allow your audience to find and read your sources so that they can evaluate your research and learn more about the subject themselves. Accurate entries also demonstrate the care with which you have written your project, which reinforces your credibility, or ethos.

to AUDIENCE

a paraphrase, a summary, or an idea. The CSE offers three formats for citing sources in the body of the project:

- Name-year
- Citation-sequence
- Citation-name

The *name-year system* requires you to include the last name of the author and the year of publication in parentheses whenever the source is cited:

Ethylene is the result of a chemical reaction created in an electrolyzer (Cossier 2020).
[author] [date]

If you use the author's name in your sentence, include just the year of publication in parentheses:

Christoffel (2007) argues that public health officers adopted the strategies
[author] [date]
they did because they were facing a crisis.

The name-year system tells readers immediately who wrote the source and how current it is, which is particularly crucial in the sciences. This system involves many rules for creating in-text citations (for example, how to create in-text citations for several authors, with organizations as authors, and so on), which can make it difficult to apply the rules consistently.

The *citation-sequence* and *citation-name systems* use a superscript number (the same number for a source each time it is cited) to refer the reader to a list of references at the end of the project.

Some testing of the River Invertebrate Prediction and Classification System (RIVPACS) had already been conducted[1]. Biologists in Great Britain then used environmental data to establish community type[2], and two studies developed predictive models for testing the effects of habitat-specific sampling[3,4]. These did not, however, account for the earlier RIVPACS research[1].

> Place reference numbers before punctuation marks. When drawing information from multiple sources, include multiple citations, separated by commas (no space between commas and reference numbers).

Tech — Creating Superscript Numbers

The footnoting function in your word processing program will not work for inserting reference numbers for the citation-sequence or citation-name systems because it will only insert the reference marks in sequence (1, 2, 3, . . .), whereas the CSE system requires that you use the same superscript number for a source each time you cite it. Instead, insert superscript numbers manually, without using your word processing program's footnote function, and type your list of references separately. (Use the Help function of your word processor to learn about inserting superscript numbers.)

When using the citation-sequence system, arrange the sources in your reference list in order of first mention in your research report and then number them. (The first work cited is number 1, the second work cited is number 2, and so on.) When using the citation-name system, alphabetize sources and then number them. (The first work alphabetically is number 1, the second work alphabetically is number 2, and so on.)

The citation-sequence and citation-name systems need no rules about how to form in-text citations, but they do require readers to turn to the reference list to see the name of the author and the source's date of publication. Since the word processor's footnoting system cannot be used, numbering (and renumbering) of notes must be done by hand. To avoid the confusion that can arise during revision and editing, consider using a simplified author-date system while drafting the research project and inserting the numbers for the citation-sequence or citation-name system in the final draft.

Check with your instructor about which system to use, and use it consistently. If your instructor does not have a preference, consider the advantages and drawbacks of each system before making your choice.

21b Preparing a CSE-Style Reference List

A research report or project in CSE style ends with a list of cited references. How you format those references depends on the type of source and the system you use.

Reference — Examples of CSE-Style Reference List Entries

Books—Printed and Electronic
1. One author 473
    a. Printed 473
    b. Online 473
2. Two or more authors 474
3. Group or corporate author 474
4. Edited book 475
5. Selection from an edited book or conference proceedings 475
    a. Selection from an edited book 475
    b. Conference paper (published) 475
    c. Conference paper (unpublished) 476
6. Dissertation 476

Periodicals—Printed and Electronic
7. Article in a scholarly journal 477
    a. Printed 477
    b. Accessed through a database 477
    c. Online 478

8. Article in a magazine 478
    a. Printed 478
    b. Accessed through a database 478
    c. Online 479
9. Article in a newspaper 479
    a. Printed 479
    b. Accessed through a database 479
    c. Online 480

Miscellaneous Sources—Printed and Electronic
10. Website (entire) 480
11. Short work from a website 481
12. Discussion list, blog, or other social media posting 481
13. Email message 481
14. Technical report or government document 482

Books—Printed and Electronic

In a printed book, you can find most or all of the information you need to create a reference list entry on the copyright and title pages at the beginning of the book. In an online or ebook, print and electronic publication information often appears at the top or bottom of the first page or is available through a link.

> Annotated visual of where to find author and publication information (Documentation Matters tutorial preceding ch. 18), 330–33

1. One author

a. Printed The basic format for a printed book looks like this:

Name-year system

Author's surname First and Middle Initials. Date of publication. Title: subtitle. Edition. Place of publication: Publisher.

> No punctuation between surname and initials and no period or space between initials

Citation-sequence and citation-name systems

Ref. No. Author's surname First and Middle Initials. Title: subtitle. Edition. Place of publication: Publisher; date of publication.

NOTE Book titles are neither italicized nor underlined in CSE style.

Here are samples of reference list entries:

Name-year system

Shaw S. 2020. The next great migration: the beauty and terror of life on the move. New York (NY): Bloomsbury.

Citation-sequence and citation-name systems

1. Shaw S. The next great migration: the beauty and terror of life on the move. New York (NY): Bloomsbury; 2020.

b. Online

If an online source has been updated, include "updated (year month day);" preceding the date of access, all in one set of brackets.

Name-year system

Stroup A. 1990. A company of scientists: botany, patronage, and community at the seventeenth-century Parisian Royal Academy of Sciences.

CSE Reference List Entries

1. **One author**
2. Two or more authors
3. Group or corporate author

CSE Reference List Entries

1. One author
2. **Two or more authors**
3. Group or corporate author
4. Edited book
5. Selection from an edited book or conference proceedings

Berkeley (CA): University of California Press; [accessed 2020 Mar 2].
http://ark.cdlib.org/ark:/13030/ft587006gh/.

Citation-sequence and citation-name systems

2. Stroup A. A company of scientists: botany, patronage, and community at the seventeenth-century Parisian Royal Academy of Sciences. Berkeley (CA): University of California Press; 1990; [accessed 2020 Mar 2]. http://ark.cdlib.org/ark:/13030/ft587006gh/.

2. Two or more authors

Name-year system

Gabr H, El-Kheir W. 2021. Stem cell therapy: practical considerations. London (GB): Academic Press.

Follow the order of authors on the title page. No *and* before last author.

Citation-sequence and citation-name systems

3. Gabr H, El-Kheir W. Stem cell therapy: practical considerations. London (GB): Academic Press; 2021.

If the source has more than ten authors, list the first ten; after the tenth author, insert the words *et al.*

3. Group or corporate author

Name-year system

Institute of Medicine Committee on the Use of Complementary and Alternative Medicine by the American Public. 2005. Complementary and alternative medicine in the United States. Washington (DC): National Academies Press.

Citation-sequence and citation-name systems

4. Institute of Medicine Committee on the Use of Complementary and Alternative Medicine by the American Public. Complementary and alternative medicine in the United States. Washington (DC): National Academies Press; 2005.

4. Edited book

Name-year system

> Vogt T, Dhamen W, Binev P, editors. 2012. Modeling nanoscale imaging in electron microscopy. New York (NY): Springer.

Citation-sequence and citation-name systems

> 5. Vogt T, Dhamen W, Binev P, editors. Modeling nanoscale imaging in electron microscopy. New York (NY): Springer; 2012.

5. Selection from an edited book or conference proceedings
a. Selection from an edited book

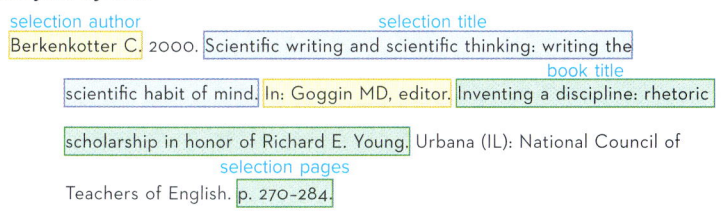

Name-year system

> Berkenkotter C. 2000. Scientific writing and scientific thinking: writing the scientific habit of mind. In: Goggin MD, editor. Inventing a discipline: rhetoric scholarship in honor of Richard E. Young. Urbana (IL): National Council of Teachers of English. p. 270–284.

Citation-sequence and citation-name systems

> 6. Berkenkotter C. Scientific writing and scientific thinking: writing the scientific habit of mind. In: Goggin MD, editor. Inventing a discipline: rhetoric scholarship in honor of Richard E. Young. Urbana (IL): National Council of Teachers of English; 2000. p. 270–284.

b. Conference paper (published)

To cite a paper published in the proceedings of a conference, add the number and name of the conference, the date of the conference, and the location of the conference (separated by semicolons and ending with a period) after the title of the book and before the publication information.

Name-year system

> Arduser L. 2019. Death care and technical communication: what mortuary science can offer. In: Carnegie T, editor. CPTSC 2019. Proceedings of the 2019 CPTSC Annual

---

CSE Reference List Entries

2. Two or more authors
3. Group or corporate author
4. **Edited book**
5. **Selection from an edited book or conference proceedings**
6. Dissertation
7. Article in a scholarly journal

Conference; West Chester (PA): Council for Programs in Technical and Scientific Communication. p. 29-30.

Citation-sequence and citation-name systems

7. Arduser L. Death care and technical communication: what mortuary science can offer. In: Carnegie T, editor. CPTSC 2019. Proceedings of the 2019 CPTSC Annual Conference; West Chester (PA): Council for Programs in Technical and Scientific Communication; 2019. p. 29-30.

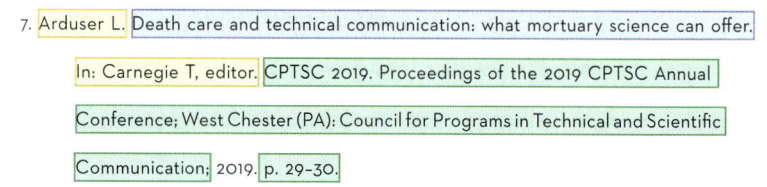

c. Conference paper (unpublished)

To cite a paper delivered at a conference, but not published in the conference proceedings, follow this model:

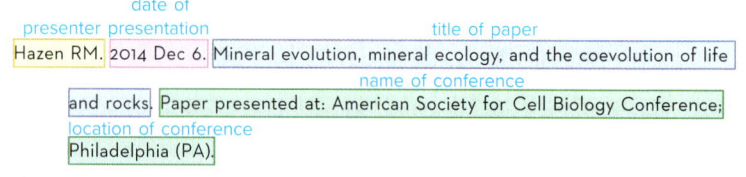

Name-year system

presenter — Hazen RM.
date of presentation — 2014 Dec 6.
title of paper — Mineral evolution, mineral ecology, and the coevolution of life and rocks.
name of conference — Paper presented at: American Society for Cell Biology Conference;
location of conference — Philadelphia (PA).

Citation-sequence and citation-name systems

8. Hazen RM. Mineral evolution, mineral ecology, and the coevolution of life and rocks. Paper presented at American Society for Cell Biology Conference; 2014 Dec 6. Philadelphia (PA).

6. Dissertation
For dissertations published by University Microfilms International (UMI), include the access number.

Name-year system

Song LZ. 2003. Relations between optimism, stress and health in Chinese and American students [*content designator* — dissertation]. [*location* — Tucson (AZ)]: University of Arizona. *access information* — Available from: UMI, Ann Arbor, MI; *access no.* — AAI3107041.

Citation-sequence and citation-name systems

9. Song LZ. Relations between optimism, stress and health in Chinese and American students [dissertation]. [Tucson (AZ)]: University of Arizona; 2003. Available from: UMI, Ann Arbor, MI; AAI3107041.

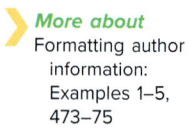

Periodicals—Printed and Electronic

The information needed to document a printed journal article is on the cover or table of contents of the journal and the first and last pages of the article. For articles downloaded from a database, the information you need appears on the screen listing the articles that fit your search terms, on the full record of the article, or on the first (and last) page of the file you download. For journal articles published online, the information you need appears on the website's home page, on that issue's web page, or on the first screen of the article.

7. Article in a scholarly journal
a. Printed

The basic citation for an article in a scholarly journal looks like this:

Name-year system

> Author's surname First and Middle Initials. Year of publication. Article Title: subtitle.
>
> Journal Title abbreviated. Vol. number(Issue number):page numbers.

Citation-sequence and citation-name systems

> Ref. No. Author's surname First and Middle Initials. Article Title: subtitle.
>
> Journal Title abbreviated. Year of publication;Vol. number(Issue number):
>
> page numbers.

Here is a sample citation of each type:

Name-year system

> Cox L. 2007. The community health center perspective. Behav Healthc. 27(3):20-21.

Citation-sequence and citation-name systems

> 10. Cox L. The community health center perspective. Behav Healthc. 2007; 27(3):20-21.

b. Accessed through a database Most researchers locate journal articles through subscription databases available through their college library. Frequently, articles indexed in such databases are available in HTML or PDF format through a link from the database. As yet, the CSE does not provide a model for an article accessed through an online database, but since most library databases are by subscription, readers will probably find the URL of the database's home page more useful than a direct link to the article itself. If a DOI is available, include it.

> Annotated visual of where to find author and publication information (Documentation Matters tutorial preceding ch. 18), 330–33

CSE Reference List Entries

5. Selection from an edited book or conference proceedings
6. Dissertation
7. **Article in a scholarly journal**
8. Article in a magazine
9. Article in a newspaper

Journal titles: Omit punctuation, articles (*an, the*), and prepositions (*of, on, in*), and abbreviate most words longer than 5 letters (except 1-word titles like *Science* and *Nature*).

DOI Digital object identifier, a permanent identifier assigned to electronic articles

CSE Reference List Entries

6. Dissertation
7. Article in a scholarly journal
8. **Article in a magazine**
9. Article in a newspaper
10. Website (entire)

Name-year system

Bullock, J. 2020. Suicide: rewriting my story. N Engl J Med. [accessed 2020 May 17]; 382(13):1196-1197. https://www.proquest.com/. doi:10.1056/NEJMp1917203.

access date — *URL (database home page)* — *DOI*

Citation-sequence and citation-name systems

11. Bullock, J. Suicide: rewriting my story. N Engl J Med. 2020 [accessed 2020 May 17]; 382(13):1196-1197. https://www.proquest.com. doi:10.1056/NEJMp1917203.

c. Online When a subscription is not required to access the article, provide a direct URL to the article; otherwise, provide the URL to the journal's home page. If a DOI is provided, include it.

Name-year system

Patten SB, Williams HVA, Lavorato DH, Eliasziw M. 2009. Allergies and major depression: a longitudinal community study. Biopsychosoc Med. [accessed 2020 Feb 5];3(3). www.bpsmedicine.com/content/3/1/3. doi:10.1186/1751-0759-3-3.

URL — *DOI*

Citation-sequence and citation-name systems

12. Patten SB, Williams HVA, Lavorato DH, Eliasziw M. Allergies and major depression: a longitudinal community study. Biopsychosoc Med. 2009 [accessed 2020 Feb 5];3(3). www.bpsmedicine.com/content/3/1/3. doi:10.1186/1751-0759-3-3.

8. Article in a magazine
a. Printed

Name-year system

Schulz K. 2015 Oct 19. Pond scum. New Yorker. p. 40-45.

Citation-sequence and citation-name systems

13. Schulz K. Pond scum. New Yorker. 2015 Oct 19; p. 40-45.

b. Accessed through a database

Name-year system

Schulz K. 2015 Oct 19. Pond scum. New Yorker. [accessed 2020 Apr 23]; p. 138-149. www.newsbank.com.

CSE Reference List Entries

7. Article in a scholarly journal
8. Article in a magazine
9. **Article in a newspaper**
10. Website (entire)
11. Short work from a website

Citation-sequence and citation-name systems

14. Schulz K. Pond scum. New Yorker. 2015 Oct 19 [accessed 2020 Apr 23]; p. 138–149. www.newsbank.com.

c. Online
Name-year system

Le Page M. 2020 Jul 27. Birdwatching AI can recognise individual birds from behind. NewScientist. [accessed 2020 Jul 28]. https://www.newscientist.com /article/2249879-birdwatching-ai-can-recognise-individual-birds-from-behind/.

Citation-sequence and citation-name systems

15. Le Page M. Birdwatching AI can recognise individual birds from behind. NewScientist. 2020 Jul 27 [accessed 2020 Jul 28]. https://www.newscientist.com /article/2249879-birdwatching-ai-can-recognise-individual-birds-from-behind/.

9. Article in a newspaper
a. Printed
Name-year system

Stern J. 2015 Dec 5. How terror hardens us. New York Times (Late Ed.). Sect. Sun. Rev.:1.

Citation-sequence and citation-name systems

16. Stern J. How terror hardens us. New York Times (Late Ed.). 2015 Dec 5; Sect. Sun. Rev.:1.

b. Accessed through a database
Name-year system

Stern J. 2015 Dec 5. How terror hardens us. New York Times. [accessed 2020 Feb 7]. Sun. Rev.:1. www.lexisnexis.com.

Citation-sequence and citation-name systems

17. Stern J. How terror hardens us. New York Times. 2015 Dec 5 [accessed 2020 Feb 7]; Sun. Rev.:1. www.lexisnexis.com.

c. Online
Name-year system

LaFee S. 2006 May 17. Light can hold fatal attraction for many nocturnal animals. San Diego Union-Tribune. [accessed 2020 May 20]. [about 11 paragraphs]. www.signonsandiego.com/news/science/.

Providing the length of a source is optional

Citation-sequence and citation-name systems

18. LaFee S. Light can hold fatal attraction for many nocturnal animals. San Diego Union-Tribune. 2006 May 17 [accessed 2020 May 20]. [about 11 paragraphs]. www.signonsandiego.com/news/science/.

Include URL of article if available; if not, use URL of home page.

Miscellaneous Sources—Printed and Electronic

The information needed to document a website or web page usually appears at the top or bottom of the home page or web page. You may also need to look for a link to a page labeled "About us" or "Contact us." Frequently, information needed for a complete reference list entry is missing, in which case provide as much information as you can.

Annotated visual of where to find author, title, and publication information (Documentation Matters tutorial preceding ch. 18), 330–33

10. Website (entire)
Name-year system

In the name-year system, include as much as possible of the following information:

Author. Title of website. Publication date. Edition. Place of publication: Publisher; [Date updated; Date accessed]. URL.

In the following example, the site has no author, so the reference list entry begins with the name of the site's sponsor.

MIT news. 2020 Apr 17. [Accessed 2020 May 19]. https://news.mit.edu/.

Citation-sequence and citation-name systems

When referencing an entire website, the only difference between the name-year system and the citation-sequence and citation-name systems is that the citation-sequence and citation-name entries add a reference number at the beginning of the entry.

19. MIT News. 2020 Apr 17 [accessed 2020 May 19]. https://news.mit.edu/.

CSE Reference List Entries

8. Article in a magazine
9. Article in a newspaper
10. **Website (entire)**
11. Short work from a website
12. Discussion list, blog, or other social media posting

11. Short work from a website
When documenting a short work, or specific document or page from a website, use the following models:

Name-year system

article author — Trafton A. 2020 Jul 22. *article title* — Chemists make tough plastics recyclable. *website* — MIT News. [accessed 2020 Jul 25]. *URL* — http://news.mit.edu/2020/tough-thermoset-plastics-recyclable-0722.

Citation-sequence and citation-name systems

20. Trafton A. Chemists make tough plastics recyclable. MIT News. 2020 Jul 22 [accessed 2020 Jul 25]. http://news.mit.edu/2020/tough-thermoset-plastics-recyclable-0722.

12. Discussion list, blog, or other social media posting

Name-year system

Bolden C. *date/time posted* — 2015 Jul 17, 10:47 am [accessed 2019 Aug 27]. Request for observations of parasites in fisheries. *medium* — [discussion list]. *disc. list* — FISH-SCI. http://segate.sunet.se/cgi-bin/wa?A0=FISH-SCI.

Citation-sequence and citation-name systems

21. Bolden C. Request for observations of parasites in fisheries. [discussion list]. FISH-SCI. 2015 Jul 17, 10:47 am [accessed 2019 Aug 27]. http://segate.sunet.se/cgi-bin/wa?A0=FISH-SCI.

13. Email message

Name-year system

email author — Martin SP. *date/time sent* — 2012 Nov 18, 3:31 pm. *date accessed* — [accessed 2020 Nov 20]. *subject line* — Revised results [email]. *email recipient* — Message to: Lydia Jimenez.

Citation-sequence and citation-name systems

22. Martin SP. Revised results [email]. Message to: Lydia Jimenez. 2012 Nov 18, 3:31 pm [accessed 2020 Nov 20].

CSE Reference List Entries

9. Article in a newspaper
10. Website (entire)
11. **Short work from a website**
12. Discussion list, blog, or other social media posting
13. Email message
14. Technical report or government document

CSE Reference List Entries

11. Short work from a website
12. Discussion list, blog, or other social media posting
13. Email message
14. **Technical report or government document**

14. Technical report or government document If no author is listed, use the name of the governing nation and the government agency that produced the document, and include any identifying number.

Name-year system

Department of Health and Human Services (US). 1985 May. Women's health: report of the Public Health Service Task Force on Women's Health Issues. [publisher unknown]. PHS:85-50206.

Citation-sequence and citation-name systems

23. Department of Health and Human Services (US). Women's health: report of the Public Health Service Task Force on Women's Health Issues. [publisher unknown]; 1985 May. PHS:85-50206.

> **More about**
> Writing an abstract, 427–28
> Formatting college papers, 98
> Formatting in APA style, 426–30

21c Formatting a CSE-Style Research Project

The CSE does not specify a format for the body of a college research report, but most scientific reports include the following sections:

- Abstract
- Introduction
- Methods
- Results
- Discussion
- References

Ask your instructor for formatting guidelines, refer to the general formatting guidelines provided in chapter 9, or follow the formatting guidelines for APA style in chapter 19.

Start a new page for your reference list, and title it "References."

Name-year system List entries in alphabetical order by author's surname. If no author is listed, alphabetize by the first main word of the title (omitting articles such as *the*, *a*, and *an*). Do not number the entries.

Citation-sequence system Number your entries in order of their appearance in your project. Each work should appear in your reference list only once, even if it is cited more than once in your project. Double-check to make sure that the numbers in your reference list match the numbers in your text.

Citation-name system Alphabetize the entries in your reference list first (by the author's surname or the first main word of the title if no author is listed). Then number them. Each work should appear in your reference list only once, even if it is cited more than once in your project. Double-check to make sure that the numbers in your reference list match the numbers in your text.

Student Model Research Project: CSE-Style Reference List

The sample reference list on page 484 is taken from a laboratory report by Alicia Keefe, University of Maryland. Keefe fulfilled her responsibility to the writers from whom she borrowed information and ideas by supplying a complete citation for each source. She fulfilled her responsibility to her reader by formatting the entries using the name-year system in CSE style, in keeping with her reader's expectations.

Writing Responsibly Of Deadlines and Paperclips

Instructors expect students to turn in thoughtful, carefully proofread, and neatly formatted projects on time—usually in class on the due date. They also expect writers to clip or staple the pages of the paper *before* the project is submitted. Do justice to yourself by being fully prepared.

to SELF

References

FlyBase: phylogeny. 2015 May 13. FlyBase. [accessed 2020 Dec 7]. http://flybase.org/wiki/FlyBase:Phylogeny.

Hoikkala A, Aspi J. 1993. Criteria of female mate choice in *Drosophila littoralis, D. montana,* and *D. ezoana.* Evolution. [accessed 2020 Apr 28]. 47(3):768-778. http://web.ebscohost.com.

Ives JD. 1921. Cross-over values in the fruit fly, *Drosophila ampelophila,* when the linked factors enter in different ways. Am Naturalist. 6:571-573.

Jensen K, Toft S. 2020 Aug. Fly disturbance suppresses aphid population growth. Ecological Entomology. [accessed 2020 Aug 19]. 45(4): 901-903. webofknowledge.com. doi:10.1111/een.12860.

Mader S. 2019. Lab manual. 13th ed. New York (NY): McGraw-Hill.

Marcillac F, Bousquet F, Alabouvette J, Savarit F, Ferveur JF. 2005. A mutation with major effects on *Drosophila melanogaster* sex pheromones. Genetics. [accessed 2020 Apr 28]. 171(4):1617-1628. http://web.ebscohost.com. doi:10.1534/genetics.104.033159.

Service PM. 1991. Laboratory evolution of longevity and reproductive fitness components in male fruit flies: mating ability. Evolution. 47:387-399.

Text Credits

Pg. 470: Council of Science Editors (CSE)

Part Six

Genre Matters

Writing in and beyond College

- **22** Writing in Literature and the Other Humanities 486
- **23** Writing in the Sciences and Social Sciences 510
- **24** Preparing for and Taking an Essay Exam 530
- **25** Professional and Civic Writing 537

22 Writing in Literature and the Other Humanities

IN THIS CHAPTER

a. Approach, 486

b. Resources, 489

c. Citing and documenting sources—MLA and *Chicago* style, 491

d. Language, 491

e. Writing about fiction, 494

f. Writing about poetry, 501

g. Writing about drama, 507

Student Models
Textual Analysis, Jewel Andrews, "A Close Reading of Shelley's 'Poetical Essay on the Existing State of Things,'" 488; **Writing about Fiction: Interpretive Analysis,** Jordan Williams, "A Close Reading of Mohsin Hamid's *The Reluctant Fundamentalist*," 496; **Writing about Poetry: Explication, Jewel Andrews,** "My View on a Long-Lost but Timeless Poem: Shelley's 'Poetical Essay on the Existing State of Things,'" 501

Professional Model
Writing about Drama: Review of a Play, Jenny Lower, "This 116-Year-Old Russian Play Pulses with 21st-Century Urgency," 507

There is rarely one right way to interpret or appreciate literature, art, music, or events in history. Instead, the texts studied in these humanities disciplines offer readers multiple rewarding opportunities to explore the many ways of being human.

22a Adopting the Approach of Literature and the Other Humanities

Whether focused solely on the text and the reader's experience of it or on its social, historical, or cultural contexts, writing in the humanities is an act of interpretation. Yet while those who study the humanities produce multiple meanings, each interpretation must be based on evidence from or about the text.

1. Read actively and reflectively.

Understanding works of literature and other texts in the humanities is not merely a matter of extracting information, but it does begin with reading to gain a basic understanding of the text. Begin by summarizing: What is the main point of the work? In literature, this is the *theme*. A summary will help you get to the heart of the matter, but keep in mind that literary analysis must do more than summarize what the text says.

Next, annotate or make notes about the work. Some of your notes may provide perspectives on the work that you can use later when writing. The notes in Figure 22.1 (p. 488), for example, show the beginnings of themes that Jewel Andrews explores in her analysis of Percy Bysshe Shelley's "Poetical Essay on the Existing State of Things."

Finally, allow yourself to enjoy what you are reading. If you make an effort to appreciate the language, note insights, or make connections to something in your own experience, you will get more out of your reading.

2. Analyze the text.

Understanding a historical event or work of literature, philosophy, or art involves analysis, dividing the work or event into its component parts to see how they work together.

Usually you will need to study the text again (and again) to identify the elements from which it is constructed and to determine how these parts work together. The Quick Reference box on page 489 lists some of the elements that a literary analysis should take into consideration.

3. Adopt a critical framework.

Coming to terms with a text requires more than comprehension and analysis. It also requires *interpretation* (determining what the elements *mean*), *synthesis* (connecting the text to what you already know and to other works you have read), and sometimes *critique* (evaluating the methods and effects of a work). You may compare two or more texts as an aid to understanding, or you may adopt a critical, theoretical approach to the work.

In introductory classes in literature and the other humanities, students are often expected to take a ***formalist approach***, looking closely at the work itself (the primary source) to understand how it functions. Examples of other popular approaches are outlined in the Quick Reference box on page 490.

> **Student Model**
> Explication: "My View on a Long-Lost but Timeless Poem: Shelley's 'Poetical Essay on the Existing State of Things,'" Jewel Andrews, 501, 503–5

> **More about**
> Summarizing, 114–15, 295–97
> Annotating, 119–24
> Reading journal, 124–25
> Enjoying what you read, 116

> **More about**
> Analysis, 127–29, 308–9

> **More about**
> Interpretation, 132, 308–9
> Synthesis, 133, 308–9
> Critique, 133–35

Writing Responsibly / Reading with Study Guides

SparkNotes and similar study guides, long a staple of college bookstores and now available online, may tempt struggling students to substitute the guide for the text itself. Do not succumb! You not only deprive yourself of a learning experience, but you may also find that the study guide leaves you unprepared for the sophisticated level of understanding your instructor expects. If you are having difficulty making sense of a text, discuss the work with classmates, read essays about or reviews of the work at your college library, watch a reading or a performance of the work, or seek advice from your instructor.

to SELF

Student Model Textual Analysis

In the following close reading, student Jewel Andrews analyzes the text of the poem "Poetical Essay on the Existing State of Things," by Percy Bysshe Shelley, laying the groundwork for her paper on pages 503–506.

**A Close Reading of Shelley's
"Poetical Essay on the Existing State of Things"**

Why "essay" and not "poem"?

DESTRUCTION marks thee! o'er the blood-stain'd heath

Is faintly borne the stifled wail of death;

Millions to fight compell'd, to fight or die

Thought-provoking: "the sternly wise, the mildly good"

In mangled heaps on War's red altar lie.

Lots of use of the word "red" (= blood)

The sternly wise, the mildly good, have sped

To the unfruitful mansions of the dead.

Dramatic phrase! "Unfruitful mansions of the dead"

Whilst fell Ambition o'er the wasted plain

Triumphant guides his car—the ensanguin'd rein

"car" probably means "chariot"?

Glory directs; fierce brooding o'er the scene,

Did regular people really talk like this in Shelley's time, or is he playing with words for rhythm and rhyme?

With hatred glance, with dire unbending mien,

Fell Despotism sits by the red glare

Of Discord's torch, kindling the flames of war.

For thee then does the Muse her sweetest lay

Pour 'mid the shrieks of war, 'mid dire dismay;

For thee does Fame's obstrep'rous clarion rise,

Abbreviates words, often by removing syllables. To keep a tight rhythm?

Does Praise's voice raise meanness to the skies.

Are we then sunk so deep in darkest gloom,

That selfish pride can virtue's garb assume?

Does real greatness in false splendour live?

Lots of unnatural-sounding word order to make it rhyme.

When narrow views the futile mind deceive,

When thirst of wealth, or frantic rage for fame,

"legal murders" and "titled idiot"— great phrasing!

When legal murders swell the lists of pride;

When glory's views the titled idiot guide,

Then will oppression's iron influence show

The great man's comfort as the poor man's woe.

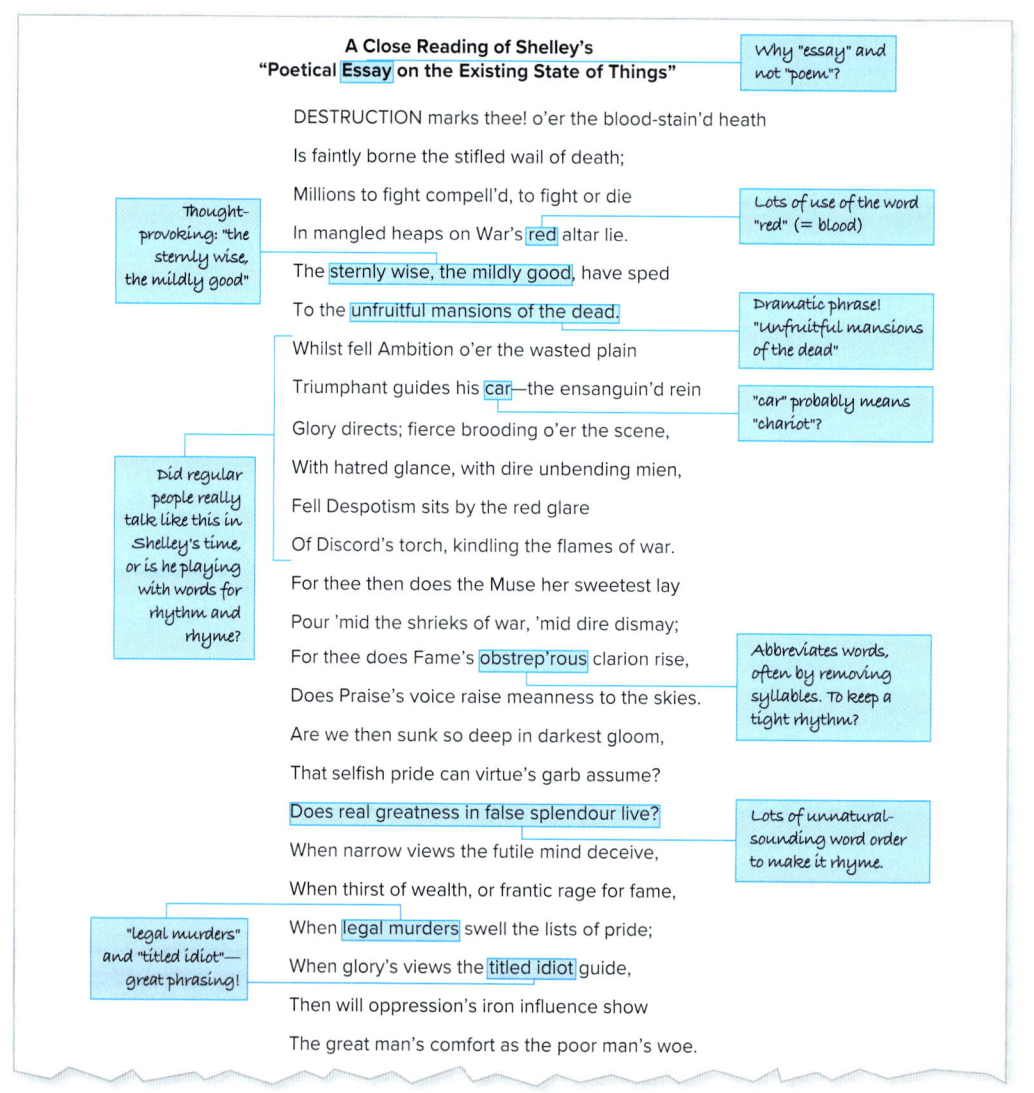

FIGURE 22.1 Notes from a close reading of a poem

Quick Reference: Elements of Literature

When writing about a work of literature, consider the following elements and ask yourself these questions:

Genre. Into what broad category, or *genre* (fiction, poetry, drama), does the work fit? Into what narrower category (mystery, sci-fi; sonnet, ode; comedy, tragedy) does the work belong? What expectations are set up by the genre, and how does the work adhere to or violate these expectations?

Plot. What happens? Does the plot unfold chronologically (from start to finish), or does the text use flashbacks or flash-forwards? Does the plot proceed as expected, or is there a surprise?

Setting. Where and when does the action occur? Is the setting identifiable? If not, what hints does the text give about the where and when? Are time and place consistent, or do elements from other times or places intrude?

Character. Who is the *protagonist,* or main character? Who are the supporting characters? How believable are the characters? Do they represent types or individuals?

Point of view. Who is telling the story—one of the characters or a separate narrator? What point of view does the narrator take—the first-person (*I*) or third-person (*she, he, it*)? Does the narrator have special insight into the characters or recount events as an outsider?

Language/style. What level of diction (formal, informal, colloquial, dialect) does the text use, and why? How are words put together? Does the text contain long, complex sentences or short, direct ones? Does the text contain figurative language (such as metaphor and simile), or is the writing more literal?

Theme. What is the main point of the story? If you were to tell the story as a fable, what would its moral be?

Symbol. Do any of the characters, events, or objects represent something more than their literal meaning?

Irony. Is there a contrast between what is said and what is meant, between what the characters know and what the reader knows?

Allusion. Does the work contain references to literary and cultural classics or sacred texts?

Before adopting a critical approach, consider the issues you have discussed in class or in other classes you are taking. A psychology class, for example, may provide a theory that will help you explain the behavior of a character; an economics class may help you understand the market forces affecting the plot; a women's studies class may provide methods of interpretation that will give you new perspectives on historical events.

22b Using the Resources of Literature and the Other Humanities

As you prepare to write about a text, ask your instructor whether you should consult outside sources. *Primary sources* for studying a literary work include the work itself; they may include the author's letters or email messages, diaries, interviews, annotated manuscripts, or performances (live

Quick Reference: Critical Approaches to Literature

Biographical approach. Focus on the author's life to understand the work. Does the work reflect the trajectory of the author's own life or perhaps depict a working out in literature of something the author was unable to work out in reality?

Deconstructionist approach. Focus on gaps, discontinuities, or inconsistencies in the text that reveal or challenge the assumptions of the dominant culture. What do these inconsistencies communicate that the author may not have intended?

Feminist approach. Focus on the power relations between women and men (or elements in the work that take on gender traits). Does the work reinforce traditional power relations or challenge them?

Marxist approach. Focus on the power relations among social classes (or among elements that take on class characteristics). Does the work reinforce the status quo or challenge it?

New historicist approach. Focus on the social-historical moment in which the work was created. How does the work reflect that historical moment?

Postcolonial approach. Focus on the power relations between colonizing and colonized peoples (or on elements in the work that reflect traditional power dynamics). Does the work reinforce or challenge those power relations?

Queer approach. Focus on the power relations between "normal" and "deviant." How differently can a text be read when the reader rejects this dichotomy?

Reader response approach. Focus not on the author's intentions or the text's meaning but on the experience of the individual reader. How does the individual reader construct meaning in the act of reading?

---

or recorded). To write about Percy Bysshe Shelley's poem "Poetical Essay on the Existing State of Things," Jewel Andrews not only analyzed the poem but also explored the online exhibit "Shelley's Ghost: Reshaping the Image of a Literary Family," which has videos, podcasts, interactive media, and artifacts such as digital scans of historical documents and Shelley's original notebooks and manuscripts. Writers, academics, and civic leaders often visit college campuses; sitting in on a talk or even interviewing such people is an opportunity to include a primary source that will inform your research on a topic. Primary sources in the other humanities might include any of the following:

- In film studies, a classic film like *Citizen Kane* (1941) or a popular movie like *Spotlight* (2015); a director's annotated script; or a series of storyboards, comic-strip-like sketches showing the main characters, action, and shot sequences in a film

- In classics, a lyric poem by the ancient Greek poet Sappho, a history of ancient Rome by Livy (59 BCE–17 CE), or a vase depicting an important event in classical history

- In art history, a painting, sculpture, or other artistic production or a video of an artist at work

Genre Matters • Using the Language of Literature and the Other Humanities **22d** **491**

- In philosophy, a text like Plato's *Meno* or a lecture by a philosopher like Peter Singer
- In history, a historical document, such as the Mayflower Compact (1620), or court records detailing an event like the My Lai massacre during the Vietnam War

Secondary sources are works about the author, period, text, or critical framework you are using. They provide information about the primary source you are studying. Use secondary sources to develop and support, not to substitute for, your own interpretation. For example, if you were writing about Zora Neale Hurston's *Their Eyes Were Watching God* (1937), you might use the framework provided by the documentary *Ethnic Notions,* a secondary source, to assess the main character in the novel, your primary source. You can find secondary sources by searching your library's catalog, specialized databases (such as the *MLA International Bibliography, Historical Abstracts,* the *Arts and Humanities Citation Index,* or the *Philosopher's Index*), the *Book Review Digest,* and the *Literary Criticism Index.*

> **Student Model**
> Interpretative analysis: "A Close Reading of Mohsin Hamid's *The Reluctant Fundamentalist,*" Jordan Williams, 497–501

> **More about**
> Finding information, (ch. 13) 237–62

22c Citing and Documenting Sources— MLA and *Chicago* Style

Whenever you borrow ideas or information or quote from a work, you must cite the source in the text and document it in a bibliography or list of works cited. While there are other style guides, most writers in literature and the other humanities use either the style detailed in the *MLA Handbook,* 9th edition, or in the *Chicago Manual of Style,* 17th edition. Ask your instructor which you should use.

> **More about**
> In-text citation (MLA), 335–52
> Works-cited list (MLA), 352–77
> Notes and bibliography (*Chicago*), 440–57

22d Using the Language of Literature and the Other Humanities

Each discipline uses language distinctively, and your writing will be most effective when it follows conventions that are accepted in the discipline in which you are writing.

1. Use the specialized vocabulary of the discipline correctly.

Most academic disciplines in the humanities use specialized vocabulary. Learning that vocabulary will help you understand sources and communicate effectively with your audience. To master this new language, consult discipline-specific dictionaries and encyclopedias, such as *The Penguin*

> **More about**
> Finding subject-specific reference works, 240

Dictionary of Literary Terms and Literary Theory, The Columbia Dictionary of Modern Literary and Cultural Criticism, or *The Oxford Encyclopedia of British Literature.* Consider the terms in context, and ask your instructor for help.

2. Use past and present tense correctly.

> **More about**
> Tense, 702–7

Writers in the humanities, including literary studies, usually choose the present tense when writing about the work being studied (the events, characters, and setting) or the ideas of other scholars, and they use the present or past tense (as appropriate) when discussing actual events, such as the author's death or a historical or cultural event from the time that the work was published.

Present Tense

> Uses present tense to discuss the work studied

These witches and ghosts are real, and often present, for Haun's characters, and "witch doctors" have busy practices fending them off. Dreams and visions are carefully noted and heeded, and the natural world is festooned with warning signs.

—Lisa Alther, "The Shadow Side of Appalachia: Mildred Haun's Haunting Fiction"

Past Tense

> Uses past tense to discuss past events

Margaret Lindsey, defamed as a sorceress (incantatrix) by three men in 1435, successfully purged herself with the help of five women; her accusers were warned against making further slanders under pain of excommunication.

—Kathleen Kamerick, "Shaping Superstition in Late Medieval England"

3. Use first and third person correctly.

> **More about**
> Person, 680–81

The use of the first person (*I, we*) or third person (*he, she, it, they, Elena, the conflict*) pronoun varies from one humanities discipline to another. In part, this reflects a difference in emphasis: Are writers emphasizing their arguments or the evidence on which they are based? In philosophy, the goal is often to advance one's own perspective:

> First person (*I*)

I begin, in Section 1, by clarifying the kind of groups and the type of collective rights that I shall be concerned with.

—Steven Wall, "Collective Rights and Individual Autonomy"

In literary studies, the emphasis is on the work of literature, so writers use the third person whenever reasonable. Compare these two versions of a sentence from Jewel Andrews's essay on Shelley's poem "Poetical Essay on the Existing State of Things":

FIRST PERSON	THIRD PERSON
When I first read the poem, I thought Shelley was writing about the brutality and tragedy of war in general, but a closer look made it clear to me he's taking aim at Britain's involvement in the Napoleonic Wars against the French.	A first reading of the poem suggests that he is writing about the brutality and tragedy of war in general, but a closer read . . . makes it clear he's taking aim at Britain's involvement in the Napoleonic Wars against the French.

The version in the third person shifts the emphasis from the writer to the poem and is thus less personal and more persuasive. (Notice also that it shifts to the present tense.)

4. Use the active voice.

In the humanities, writers typically use the active voice:

ACTIVE Janie's relationship with her third husband, Tea Cake, plays a key role in transforming her concept of racial identity.

PASSIVE A key role in transforming her concept of racial identity was played by Janie's relationship with her third husband, Tea Cake.

Use of the active voice promotes a clear, concise style and specifies who did what to whom. Of course, some circumstances may require the passive voice, as when the "who" is unknown or when you want to emphasize the action rather than the actor.

> *More about*
> Active versus passive voice, 562, 593–94

5. Use the author's full name at first mention and surname only thereafter.

In writing about the works of others, provide the author's complete name ("Mohsin Hamid") the first time it is mentioned; subsequently, use the author's surname ("Hamid") only, unless this will cause confusion. (When writing about the Brontë sisters, for example, you may need to specify whether you are discussing Charlotte or Emily Brontë.) You may use the first name when writing about a fictional character, but it is not customary to refer to an author by first name.

> *More about*
> Capitalizing titles, 861–62
> Quotation marks versus italics for titles, 837, 865–66

6. Include the work's title in your title.

When writing about a work of literature or another text (a painting or film, for example), provide the title of the work in the title or subtitle of your

> **More about**
> Capitalizing titles, 861–62

project and again in the first paragraph of your text. Capitalize the title correctly and use italics or quotation marks as needed.

22e Writing about Fiction

> **More about**
> Analyzing assignments, 23–24, 222–23, 533

A common assignment in the humanities is the *interpretive analysis,* which calls on the writer to study one or more elements of a text; in literature, a writer might study a character or the setting; in philosophy, a writer might study the use of a particular word or concept (*freedom, free will*); in history, a writer might study the repercussions of a historical event. In some disciplines (such as literature, philosophy, or film), a writer might analyze a single primary source or compare one or more primary sources. Often (particularly in history and art history), students will be asked to draw on secondary as well as primary resources in addition to providing their own analysis.

> **Student Models**
> Interpretive analysis: "A Close Reading of Mohsin Hamid's *The Reluctant Fundamentalist,*" Jordan Williams, 497–501
> Explication: "My View on a Long-Lost but Timeless Poem: Shelley's 'Poetical Essay on the Existing State of Things,'" Jewel Andrews, 488, 503–506

Another writing assignment that is common in literature and the performing arts is the *critique* or review: an assessment of a work of literature or art or of a performance (a play, concert, or film). Some disciplines, such as literature or philosophy, may call on students to *explicate* a text, or provide a close reading (line by line or even word by word). Often, a close reading will focus on one or more of the elements of literature. (See the Quick Reference box on p. 489.)

> **Professional Model**
> Review: "This 116-Year-Old Russian Play Pulses with 21st-Century Urgency," Jenny Lower, 508–9

Of course, many writing assignments in college will combine assignment types: To write an academic essay about a work of literature, follow the steps in the writing process discussed in part 1 (pp. 7–110) and the specific recommendations in the sections below.

1. Devise a literary thesis.

Narrow your focus to an idea you can develop fully in the assigned length. To devise a topic in literature, ask yourself questions about the elements of the work:

- What are the central conflicts among or within characters?
- What aspects of the plot puzzled or surprised you, and why?
- How might the setting (time and place) have influenced the behavior of the characters?
- Did the writer use language in a distinctive (or difficult or obscure) way, and why?
- What worlds, peoples, or cultures are evoked in this work, and what attitudes toward them are expressed or implied?

- What images recurred or were especially powerful, and why?
- What other works did you think about as you were reading this one, and why?

Then answer one of your questions. Your answer can be your **working thesis**.

As you draft your paper, you should analyze or interpret (not merely summarize) the text, as these contrasting examples demonstrate:

SUMMARY THESIS	In this poem, Shelley evokes the suffering and tragedy of war.
INTERPRETIVE/ ANALYTICAL THESIS	In this poem, Shelley uses symbolism and rhythm to denounce the actions of his government and evoke the devastating toll of war.

To support the first thesis, the writer could merely report the poem's main point. To support the second thesis, however, the writer must analyze the poem's symbolism and rhythm and then use that analysis to explain her interpretation of the poem's central conflict.

2. Support your claims with evidence from the text.

As with any writing project, you can use idea-generating techniques like brainstorming, freewriting, and clustering to figure out what your thesis is and why you believe it. Then turn back to the text: What details from the work illustrate or support your reasons? These are the *evidence* your readers will need. Consider this passage from Jewel Andrews's essay:

> The 172-line "Poetical Essay" is full of the poet's outrage at the state of the world. A first reading of the poem suggests that he is writing about the brutality and tragedy of war in general, but a closer read plus research on Shelley and his writing makes it clear he's taking aim at Britain's involvement in the Napoleonic Wars against the French, and at the imprisonment of an Irish journalist critical of British military operations. Shelley sets the tone right away: "Millions to fight compell'd, to fight or die / In mangled heaps on War's red altar lie" (lines 3–4) and, in a takedown of the privileged ruling class into which he was born, he taunts: "When glory's views the titled idiot guide" (24). The lines "Ye cold advisers of yet colder kings, / To whose fell breast no passion virtue brings" (37–38) make it clear whose side he is on.

[Topic sentence: States claim]

[Evidence: Uses quotations and summary from the poem and explains their relevance]

Andrews argues that Shelley uses powerful symbolism to depict the barbarity of war and the cold arrogance of the aristocracy, and she offers concrete evidence from the text—some quoted, some summarized—to support her claim. Note that Andrews does not merely drop the evidence from the poem into her essay but instead explains its relevance.

> **More about**
> Writing ethically (ch. 1), 7–13,
> Writing Responsibly boxes (listed on the last pages facing inside back cover)
> Planning (ch. 2), 14–34
> Organizing and drafting (ch. 3), 35–51
> Crafting and connecting paragraphs (ch. 4), 52–76
> Drafting and revising visuals (ch. 5), 77–85
> Revising, editing, proofreading, and formatting (ch. 6), 86–110

> **More about**
> Devising a thesis, 35–38

> **More about**
> Idea-generating techniques, 25–31

> **More about**
> Incorporating evidence, 45–47, 307–11

3. Support your claims with evidence from outside the text.

Depending on your approach, you may also draw on evidence from outside the text. For example, if you were writing a paper about *Their Eyes Were Watching God* (Zora Neale Hurston), you could draw your critical framework from a documentary film. You could also draw counterevidence from a secondary source, an essay in a scholarly collection.

Student Model Writing about Fiction: Interpretive Analysis

The essay that follows by Jordan Williams, a student at Syracuse University when she wrote the paper, offers an interpretation of the main character in Mohsin Hamid's novel *The Reluctant Fundamentalist*.

Williams 1

Jordan Williams

Professor Lester

English 207

1 May 2020

A Close Reading of Mohsin Hamid's *The Reluctant Fundamentalist*

In *The Reluctant Fundamentalist*, author Mohsin Hamid provides an alternative view of America through the eyes of his protagonist, a Pakistani man named Changez. Changez's unique immigrant experience in the U.S. centers not on places, events, or customs, but on his relationship with a woman who is, to him, a physical representation of America. Far from being an American dream tale, Changez's story lacks the optimism and sense of opportunity that are perpetuated in myths about American life. Instead, when he returns to Lahore he shares what he experienced without joy, and in a somber tone.

    Being an immigrant and moving to a country with different cultural norms can disrupt our sense of who we are. This theme is very important in the novel as both Changez and Erica struggle to maintain their identities while relying on someone else to keep them whole. Erica's attachment to the deceased Chris increasingly takes over her life, and as time goes on, she idolizes him and fantasizes about the time they had together. The degree of her infatuation is evident when in Greece as she tells Changez, "I kind of miss home, too. Except my home was a guy with long, skinny fingers" (28). Similarly, Changez lacks a real sense of home in America, except for what he experiences with Erica. As she fades away from reality and eventually disappears altogether, he loses his tenuous connection to and foundation in America. Even when he returns home to Lahore, Changez feels disconnected and confused about his identity,

Williams 2

telling a stranger that he "brought something of [Erica] to Lahore—or perhaps it would be more accurate to say that [he] lost something of [himself] to her that [he] was unable to relocate in the city of [his] birth" (172). In a parallel to Erica's idealization of Chris, Changez speaks very solemnly about Erica, a person who once brought him such great joy as their lives intertwined and she became a part of him and his experience. Nostalgia and loss are other encompassing themes of the novel; they drive major events and divert the focus away from the love story that Hamid teasingly vows to tell. At its essence, the novel is Changez's nostalgia-filled conversation with a stranger, one in which he recalls his feelings and frustrations toward Erica who insists on obsessing over a dead man and fails to move forward with her life. For Changez, Erica's nostalgia for Chris is infuriating and gets in the way of his desires: "[B]ut he is *dead*, I wanted to shout! It was all I could do not to kiss her then; perhaps I should have" (136). Despite his critique of her behavior, Changez sees similarities in his own as he tells the stranger, "I had been telling you earlier, sir, of how I left America. The truth of my experience complicates that seemingly simple assertion; I had returned to Pakistan, but my inhibition of your country had not entirely ceased" (172). As Erica obsesses over Chris, Changez obsesses over Erica, and his realization of her death comes on gradually; little by little he sees she is less and less like the person he had known before the attack on New York City on September 11, 2001. His loss of Erica is profound, and he can only speak of it with a complete stranger. Destructive nostalgia, the painful longing for those who are lost, is the basis for the ultimate downfall of both Erica and Changez.

Another aspect of the novel is Hamid's use of language and imagery. As Changez discusses his losses with the stranger, he uses words that relate to water, an entity that may signify transformation, movement, or lack of control. Changez says: "[T]he effect of this [the loss of Erica] was to pull and tug my moods; waves of mourning washed over me, sadness and regret prompted at times by an external stimulus, and at other times by an internal cycle that was almost *tidal*, for want of a better word" (172). Changez's water-centric description of his emotions relates to the ocean and its advancing and receding waves, suggesting Erica's back-and-forth feelings for him. Interestingly, their relationship began at the beach, and as the tide rolled in and out along the shores of Greece, so did their connection.

At the beginning of their friendship, Erica invites Changez to fancy parties and pulls him in with her kindness and charm, so much so that during his time in Manila they remained in communication on a weekly basis. Changez becomes infatuated, partly because of his own inexperience. His upbringing in Lahore led him to think of Erica as something of a girlfriend. After all, in his childhood, "relationships were often conducted over fleeting phone calls, messages through friends, and promises of encounters that never happened" (69). As he becomes more attached to Erica, things escalate to a more intimate relationship. However, the intimacy only goes so far and is not satisfying. Changez describes Erica as distant, saying that she is "struggling against the current that pulled her within herself, and her smile contained the fear that she might slip into her own depths, where she would be trapped, unable to breathe" (86). While she is accepting of him, she cannot be fully invested in him.

The unpredictable ebb and flow of their relationship reaches a crisis; Erica backs away from Changez but he keeps trying to contact her. He copes with moods and her everchanging acceptance and rejection of him until she ultimately releases him, saying, "I could see I was pulling you in, and I didn't want you to get hurt" (134). From Changez's point of view, Erica, unable to break free from her losses, is swept away by waves of sadness and grief.

If Erica represents America in the novel, then her emotions and treatment of Changez have a heavy impact on his American experience and sense of self. When Changez recounts his story, he does so with a tone that shifts between fond remembrance, adoration, anguish, and betrayal. He faces all of these emotions as he "responded to the gravity of an invisible moon at [his] core, and [he] undertook journeys [he] had not expected to take" (172). For example, when Changez accompanies Erica to New York City's high class parties, he feels a sense of belonging that had been foreign to him. "I felt at home[...]," he says. "Whatever the reason, it made me smile, and Erica, seeing me smile, smiled back" (51).

However, Changez's sense of home is in jeopardy. When the city crumbles with the September 11th attacks, so does Erica. While signs reading "We are America," indicate unity and solidarity in the face of fear and tragedy, Erica struggles to cope (79). By not fleeing to the Hamptons, Erica attempts to stand in allegiance with her city, but both she and her city are shaken, and feeling overwhelmed she backs away from her friendship with Changez. Upset by Erica's abandonment, Changez is unable to complete his job for Underwood Samson; when he returns for Erica he finds she has vanished. It's the ultimate rejection. Both the loss of his job and abandonment by Erica are too great for Changez; he recounts that during his last few days in New York he "was an incoherent and emotional madman, flying off into depression" (167). Changez is left bewildered and emotionally scarred.

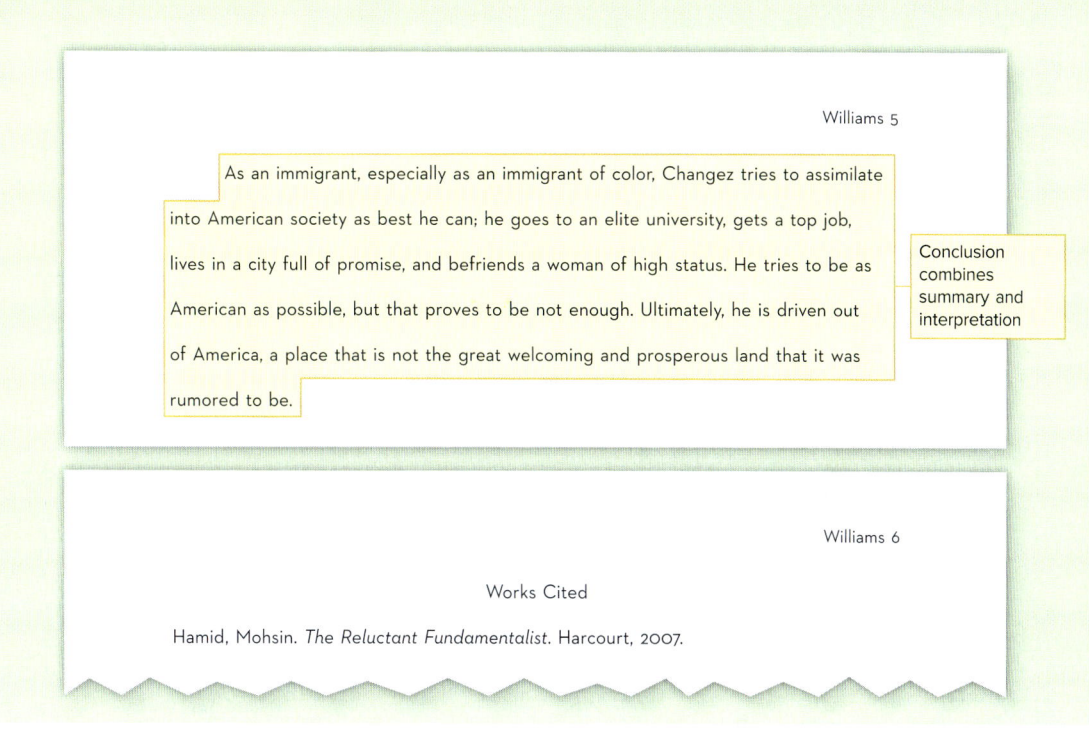

> As an immigrant, especially as an immigrant of color, Changez tries to assimilate into American society as best he can; he goes to an elite university, gets a top job, lives in a city full of promise, and befriends a woman of high status. He tries to be as American as possible, but that proves to be not enough. Ultimately, he is driven out of America, a place that is not the great welcoming and prosperous land that it was rumored to be.

Conclusion combines summary and interpretation

Works Cited

Hamid, Mohsin. *The Reluctant Fundamentalist*. Harcourt, 2007.

22f Writing about Poetry

While the shape of the poem on the page can be important, poetry is traditionally a spoken art form. When writing about poetry, start by reading the poem aloud or listening to the poet read the work. In addition to the issues that apply to writing about literature generally, pay special attention to the sound, structure, and language of the work. (For more information on writing about poetry, see the Quick Reference box on the next page.)

Student Model Writing about Poetry: Explication

The essay that begins on page 503 was written by Jewel Andrews. Andrews draws evidence from a close reading of the poem "Poetical Essay on the Existing State of Things" (see Figure 22.1) to support her claim that poet Percy Bysshe Shelley uses symbolism and rhythm to persuade readers to accept his view of war. To build her case, Andrews also draws on other primary sources, including videos, podcasts, and interactive media relating to the poet and artifacts and historical documents that belonged to Shelley.

Quick Reference — Writing about Poetry

When writing about a poem, consider the following elements and ask yourself these questions:

Sound

Rhythm. Is the rhythm part of the traditional form of the poem? If not, which words are stressed, and how is this relevant to the poem's meaning?

Rhyme. Is the rhyme scheme part of the traditional form of the poem? If not, what is the purpose of the rhyme scheme? If the poem does not rhyme, are there any other sounds linking words or lines in the poem?

Alliteration/Assonance/Consonance. Does the poem use alliteration (the repetition of a consonant sound at the beginning of a stressed syllable) to link lines or words within a line? Does the poem use assonance or consonance, the repetition of a vowel or consonant sound, to link lines or words in a line? What effects do these choices have on the reader or listener?

Structure

Verse form. Is the poem written in a traditional verse form (such as the sonnet or the limerick), or is the form open, or free? Does the verse form relate to the meaning of the poem?

Line length. Are the poem's lines of regular length, or do lengths vary from line to line or from stanza to stanza? Do sentences carry over from line to line, or does each line express a complete thought? If line lengths are irregular, does length emphasize or deemphasize a thought?

Stanzas. Are lines grouped into regular (or irregular) stanzas? If so, does the stanza convey a single unit of thought, or does an idea or sentence continue across stanzas?

Language

Imagery. What sensory "pictures" does the poem call to mind—the stifling warmth of a July day in the Deep South? The luxuriant springtime riot of mountaintop flowers? What is the relationship between the images the poem calls forth and the ideas it conveys?

Figurative language. Simile (a comparison using *like* or *as*—"My love is like an ice pick"), metaphor (a comparison that does not use *like* or *as*—"My love is an ice pick"), and a host of other figures of speech create images in the reader's mind. Can you identify any figures of speech in the poem and, if so, how do they affect meaning?

Connotation. Poets choose words for their connotative (implicit) as well as for their denotative (literal) meanings. Consider the emotional difference between the verbs *gripe* and *lament*. Both mean "to complain," but, oh, the difference between the two. Note the connotations of the words in the poem you are studying and how they help create the overall effect of the poem.

Repetition. Poets may choose to repeat an important word or phrase. If a word or phrase is repeated (as is the word *and* in "The Raven"), consider its significance. How does this repetition affect your understanding and experience of the poem?

The last stanza from Edgar Allan Poe's "The Raven" (lines 103–8) demonstrates the issues of sound, structure, and language:

> And the ráven, never flítting, still is sítting,
>   still is sítting
> On the pállid bust of Pállas just above my
>   chamber door;
> And his eyes´ have all the see´ming of a
>   démon's that is drea´ming,
> And the lámp-light o'er him strea´ming
>   throws his shádow on the floor;
> And my soul´ from out that shádow that
>   lies floa´ting on the floor
>   Shall be lífted—nevermore´!

Andrews 1

Jewel Andrews

Professor Sewell

English 110

5 May 2021

My View on a Long-Lost but Timeless Poem:

Shelley's "Poetical Essay on the Existing State of Things"

Ask someone today to describe the work of nineteenth-century English poet Percy Bysshe Shelley and you might hear "sentimental" or, worse, "corny." To our twenty-first-century ears, his elaborate verse can sound overripe. But Shelley (1792–1822), one of the greatest Romantic poets of his or any era, was far from mushy: born a wealthy aristocrat, his radical political and social views made him an outcast in his own country, and he fled to Italy with his wife, Mary Shelley (who later wrote *Frankenstein*). Shelley's political poetry expressed his passionate views on war, poverty, imperialism, and the failure of governments. In his "lost" poem "Poetical Essay on the Existing State of Things"—rediscovered in 2006 and made available to the public in 2015, roughly 200 years after he wrote it at age 18[1]—Shelley uses symbolism and rhythm to denounce the actions of his government, ridicule those in power, and evoke the devastating toll of war.

The 172-line "Poetical Essay" is full of the poet's outrage at the state of the world. A first reading of the poem suggests that he is writing about the brutality and tragedy of war in general, but a closer read plus research on Shelley and his writing makes it clear he's taking aim at Britain's involvement in the Napoleonic Wars against the French, and at its imprisonment of an Irish journalist critical of British military operations ("Out of the Attic"). Shelley sets the tone right away: "Millions to fight compell'd, to fight or

Andrews 2

die / In mangled heaps on War's red altar lie" (lines 3-4) and, in a takedown of the privileged ruling class into which he was born, he taunts: "When glory's views the titled idiot guide" (24). The lines "Ye cold advisers of yet colder kings, / To whose fell breast no passion virtue brings" (37-38) make it clear whose side he is on.

[Uses quotation and summary as evidence, and explains relevance]

Shelley employs the color red throughout to symbolize blood and death: "War's red altar lie" (4), "Fell Despotism sits by the red glare" (11), and "To snatch at fame, to reap red murder's spoil" (43). Similarly, he uses words and phrases like "shrieks of war," "legal murders," and "tenfold grief" to bring to life fearful images of suffering and misery.

[Topic sentence]

As well as the blood and death symbolism, Shelley conjures up vivid pictures of social tyranny: "Then will oppression's iron influence show / The great man's comfort as the poor man's woe" (25-26) and "Must starving wretches torment, misery bear?" (48). The potent phrase "Oppression's iron influence" is paired with "great man's comfort" to depict the power and privilege of the ruling classes, while the "starving wretches" who must "bear" their "torment" and "misery" summon up the powerlessness of the poor and downtrodden.

[Topic sentence] [Explains significance of symbol]

In addition to symbolism, Shelley employs rhythm and rhyme to convey a sense of anger and urgency. When read aloud, the tight rhythmic pattern of the couplets is obvious. For example, lines 51-52 ("Yet shall the vices of the great pass on, / Vices as glaring as the noon-day sun") and 103-104 ("Though hot with gore from India's wasted plains, / Some Chief, in triumph, guides the tightened reins") have an almost chanting, marching cadence, a beat that reinforces the theme of the battlefield. The poet's reference to India indicates his strong anti-colonial feelings at a time when the British Empire's global reach was enormous. According to British poet Michael Rosen in an interview in *The Guardian*, Shelley "spends a good few lines on pointing out the oppression

[Topic sentence (begins second half of essay)]

of British imperialism in India" (qtd. in Flood). This can be seen in lines like "The fainting Indian, on his native plains / Writhes to superior power's unnumbered pains" (145-146).

    Throughout the poem, Shelley uses powerful symbolism and rhythm to articulate his staunch political positions and disgust at the status quo. His words and phrasing are not always easy to understand—after all, he was writing two hundred years ago, when the use of inverted sentences (in which the verb comes before the subject) and archaic words like "meed" (which means "a deserved share or reward") was common. But reading and analyzing the poetry of Percy Bysshe Shelley is well worth the effort; beyond his eloquent phrasing and sharp use of symbolism and meter, this poem, and his other political poems such as "The Masque of Anarchy" and "Men of England," are as relevant today as they were when they were written.[2] Let Shelley—who famously said in an essay called "A Defence of Poetry" that "poets are the unacknowledged legislators of the world"—have the last word: "Poetry is a sword of lightning, ever unsheathed, which consumes the scabbard that would contain it."

> Conclusion: Thesis restated, importance of poem's theme reiterated

> Provides closure by circling back to poet

Notes

[1] "Poetical Essay" was purchased by the University of Oxford's Bodleian Libraries, which has uploaded a digital copy that can be accessed through its website.

[2] The online exhibition "Shelley's Ghost: Reshaping the Image of a Literary Family" is a partnership of the Bodleian Libraries and the New York Public Library.

Works Cited

Flood, Alison. "Lost Shelley Poem Execrating 'Rank Corruption' of Ruling Class Made Public." *The Guardian*, 10 Nov. 2015, www.theguardian.com/books/2015/nov/10/lost-shelley-poem-execrating-rruling-class-public-poetical-essay-on-the-existing-state-of-things.

"Out of the Attic: Fresh Light on the Young Revolutionary." *The Economist*, 14 Nov. 2015, p. 54.

Shelley, Percy Bysshe. "A Defence of Poetry." 1821. *Poetry Foundation*, 13 Oct. 2009, www.poetryfoundation.org/learning/essay/237844.

Shelley, Percy Bysshe. "Poetical Essay on the Existing State of Things." 1811. *Shelley's Poetical Essay*, Bodleian Libraries, 2015, https://poeticalessay.bodleian.ox.ac.uk.

Works Consulted

> Typically not required, but if your instructor wishes to see works you consulted other than those cited in your project, follow this format.

Clark, Nick. "Percy Bysshe Shelley Lost Poem to Go Public at University of Oxford." *The Independent*, 10 Nov. 2015, www.independent.co.uk/arts-entertainment/art/news/poetical-essay-on-the-existing-state-of-things-lost-poem-by-percy-bysshe-shelley-to-go-on-display-a6729206.html.

Martyris, Nina. "How Percy Shelley Stirred His Politics into His Teacup." *NPR*, 4 Aug 2015, www.npr.org/sections/thesalt/2015/08/04/429363868/how-percy-shelley-stirred-his-politics-into-his-tea-cup.

Rich, Adrienne. "Legislators of the World." *The Guardian*, 18 Nov. 2006, www.theguardian.com/books/2006/nov/18/featuresreviews.guardianreview15.

22g Writing about Drama

Like students of fiction, students of drama focus on character, plot, language, symbols, and the theme (or main point) of the work. Unlike fiction, plays are written to be acted. When writing about drama, you may be asked to go beyond the words on the page, to watch a performance of a play and to critique it in a review. When writing about a performance, offer an assessment not only of the actors' performances and the director's staging, but also of the set, costumes, props, lighting, and sound design, analyzing whether they helped to create a distinctive overall effect. Some issues to consider when critiquing a play are listed in the Quick Reference box below.

> **More about**
> Elements of literature, 489

Professional Model Writing about Drama: Review of a Play

In the review that follows, Jenny Lower of the *LA Weekly* offers a supportive review of the play *Uncle Vanya*, focusing her attention on the ways in which the cast, director, costumes, props, and even the translation contribute to its success. She attends to the needs of her entire audience: For those new to the famous play, the title and introduction of Lower's review offer background information, and the body of her review provides plot summary. For Lower's more experienced theatergoing audience, she offers comparisons with other productions of the play. The model features the added interest of showing how summary can be woven into a review, rather than presented as a single block of information.

Quick Reference | Writing about Drama

When writing about drama, consider the following elements and ask yourself these questions:

Actors' performances. How well did the actors depict the characters? Did they bring something more to the character than you had recognized on the printed page? Did they build on an unspoken motive, a lie, or an omission from the dialogue?

Direction. How effective was the director in shaping the overall production? Were the design elements consistent with the script and performances? Were the pacing and mood of the performance appropriate?

Stage set. Were the stage sets realistic or abstract? Did they reinforce the setting (the place and time) of the play, or were they in contrast to the conventional setting? How effective were the stage sets in reinforcing the themes of the play?

Costumes. Were the costumes appropriate to the characters? Were they appropriate to the period in which the play was set, or were they in contrast to that period? How effective were the costumes in advancing the themes?

Props. What stage properties (props) were used, and what symbolic value might they have?

Lighting and sound design. How effective was the lighting in contributing to the mood of the play? Did music underscore scene changes or contribute to the mood? Was sound used to create appropriate atmospheric effects? How effective were lighting and sound design in reinforcing the themes of the play?

This 116–Year–Old Russian Play Pulses with 21st–Century Urgency

By Jenny Lower

Linda Park is engrossing as the beautiful Yelena, who starts trouble in *Uncle Vanya* at Antaeus Theatre Company.

Boredom is contagious in Anton Chekhov's *Uncle Vanya*, now receiving an energetic revival at the Antaeus Company. The locus of the ennui is Yelena (Linda Park), the gorgeous, restless young wife of Serebryakov (Lawrence Pressman), an elderly professor who has retired to his family's provincial estate.

"You infected us all with your uselessness," complains Astrov (Jeffrey Nordling), a rugged country doctor who all but abandons his patients to bask in Yelena's beauty. He's a proto-environmentalist and a vegetarian, and one of two men infatuated with her.

In the hands of a less able cast and director, all this lethargy and squandered potential could have led to a production that engulfs the audience in torpor as well, as plenty of dismal Chekhovian stagings prove. But Robin Larsen's lively staging reveals the humor and urgency of this 116-year-old play. She is aided by playwright Annie Baker's contemporary translation, crafted from a literal Russian translation, which lends warmth and relevance to the language.

This Vanya resonates, in part thanks to Baker's work, with jarringly modern concerns.

Vanya (Don R. McManus) is the erstwhile brother-in-law of Yelena's husband, and the play's most pathetic figure. Unlike Astrov, Vanya causes no stirrings in Yelena's heart. After 25 years of working the estate like a peasant to finance the professor's life in the city, his proletariat admiration for the family scholar has hardened to contempt.

He has no wife, no children, and no intellectual legacy, despite mental power he claims could have allowed him to become "a Schopenhauer or a Dostoevsky." Then there's Vanya's niece and Serebryakov's daughter from his first marriage, Sonya (Rebekah Tripp), self-sufficient and practical, in love these six years with Astrov, who barely notices her.

Apart from Astrov's rants about the degradation of the Russian forests, we hear class turmoil in Vanya's disgust that Serebryakov has never raised his salary, and in his fury when the professor reveals his plan to sell the estate out from under Vanya and Sonya in order to purchase a vacation home in Finland. Where will they live?

Yet many of the play's key moments, serious though they are, tremble on the brink of hilarity.

When McManus (sharing the role with Arye Gross; all parts are partner–cast) finally locates the

Genre Matters • Writing about Drama   **22g**   509

Critique: A moment when the production almost spins out of control	passion that has escaped Vanya for so long, he erupts in an enraged gesture so grandiose in its futility that the scene slips briefly into farce.	McManus and Tripp are especially powerful in the climactic encounter, reeling from their separate heartaches, as Serebryakov's plan to dismantle their life's work slowly worms into their consciousness.	Critique: Praise for the director's control and actors' performances
Critique: Praise for the performance of one actor	Park's Yelena exhibits operatic indifference, her self-absorption never more comically absolute than when Sonya suggests ways she might occupy herself. And poor Sonya's trust in her step-mother is so misplaced, it's difficult not to muster a pitying laugh when Yelena's offer to appraise the doctor's feelings for her step-daughter leads, as it must, to a declaration of love for herself.	There is heartbreak in the way Nordling's eyes follow Park in the final scene as she shrouds her hair with a scarf. Lynn Milgrim as the indulgent nurse Marina and Morlan Higgins, returning to the stage after a three-year absence as the pockmarked neighbor Waffles, lend a steadying presence. Higgins helps ease the transitions with wistful musical interludes strummed on his mandolin.	Support: The effects of costuming
Support: Partial plot summary			Background information about one of the actors
	But Larsen never allows these scenes to lose their poignancy.		Support: The effects of a prop

Work Together

In groups of three or four, discuss the differences between the review above (pp. 508–9) and one of the student papers in this chapter (pp. 497–501, 503–5). How does the difference in purpose, audience, context, and genre affect the tone, the type of evidence provided, and the focus of the writing project?

Text Credits

Pg. 495: Source: Jordan Williams; **Pg. 501**: Courtesy of Laura Sewell; **Pg. 506**: Lower, Jenny, "This 116-Tear Old Russian Play Pulses with 21st-Century Urgency" LA Weekly, October 21, 2015. Copyright ©2015 by Jennifer Lower. Used with permission.

23 Writing in the Sciences and Social Sciences

IN THIS CHAPTER

a. Approach, 510

b. Research methods, 511

c. Citing and documenting sources—APA and CSE style, 511

d. Language, 512

e. Common writing assignments, 513

Student Model
Research Report, Emily Durand, "A Field Research Report on the Mental Health of College Students: What Support Should Institutions Provide?," 516

Serhii Bobyk/Alamy Stock Photo

Federico Caputo/Alamy Stock Photo

A scientist—a biologist, nurse, or physicist, for example—focuses on the characteristics, systems, and processes of the natural world, whether of people, plants, or planets. A social scientist—an anthropologist, economist, or sociologist, for example—focuses on people, on who they are and how they work together, as individuals and in groups. What unites the sciences with the social sciences is a reliance on *empirical* (experimental, observational) research.

23a Adopting the Approach of the Sciences and Social Sciences

The search for verifiable data anchors the writing produced by both scientists and social scientists. Writing is integral to the work of these disciplines because it is the basic tool for keeping records and sharing results. Researchers make their notebooks and reports useful to other researchers by doing the following:

- Explaining their methods clearly and carefully so that others can repeat the experiment
- Describing data accurately and thoroughly (including the data that disprove or undermine the hypothesis)
- Placing their findings in the context of research conducted by others
- Offering reasonable conclusions based on those data

23b Using the Research Methods of the Sciences and Social Sciences

The research on which scientists base their claims is *primary:* They collect data by conducting tests—experiments, observational studies, and surveys, questionnaires, and interviews—to challenge their hypotheses. Scientists usually collect *quantitative* (numerical) data, while social scientists may collect quantitative or *qualitative* (descriptive) data.

Quantitative data, which might include the temperature at which a liquid vaporizes or the number of subjects who answer a question in the same way, can be gathered through experiments, surveys, questionnaires, and interviews. For quantitative data to be meaningful, it must be based on careful measurements and observations, and it must be gathered from a sample that is both representative of the group and large enough that unusual responses will not skew the results. Any scientist who conducts the same experiment should achieve the same results.

Qualitative (nonnumerical) data provide information about the experiences of individuals. This information may be drawn from interviews, observation, or both, and it often takes the form of a case study or ethnography. Qualitative data might include reports on the feeling a medication induces or descriptions of a subject's behavior. For qualitative research to be useful, the data must be based on a rich understanding of the phenomenon or issues being studied and must provide great detail. Qualitative data must be organized carefully for the researcher to make sense of the information.

> **More about**
> Observational studies, 261
> Surveys, 261–62
> Interviews, 259–60

23c Citing and Documenting Sources—APA and CSE Style

Whenever you borrow ideas or information or quote from a work, you must cite the source. While there are a variety of style guides, many scientists use the style developed by the Council of Science Editors to document their sources,

> **More about**
> APA style (ch. 19), 397–438
> CSE style (ch. 21), 470–84

Writing Responsibly — Presenting Data Accurately

Writing in the *Quarterly Journal of Medicine,* editor and neurologist Christopher Martyn explains the importance of accurately representing research:

> Time, energy and public money are wasted when researchers follow false leads . . . [E]very time a case of fraud hits the headlines, the reputation of scientists and scientific research takes a knock. In biomedical research, patients may even be harmed, if conclusions are drawn from fraudulent clinical studies (244).

When conducting an experiment, be especially careful to record data accurately. You are far more likely to receive a bad grade for falsifying data than for acknowledging that your experiment did not achieve the desired result.

to TOPIC

while social scientists often use the style devised by the American Psychological Association. Ask your instructor which you should use. All academic documentation styles require you both to cite sources in your text and to provide full bibliographic information in a reference list at the end of your project.

23d Using the Language of the Sciences and Social Sciences

> **More about**
> Figures of speech, 608–10
> Writing concisely (ch. 26), 557–64

Since the goal of scientists and social scientists is to convey information, writers in these disciplines concentrate on making their language as clear and precise as possible. Your writing will be most effective when it follows conventions for writing that are accepted in the discipline in which you are writing.

1. Learn the discipline's vocabulary.

Even at the introductory level, most writing in the sciences and social sciences requires that you learn some specialized terminology and use it with precision. You can learn vocabulary from the context or from the word parts (prefixes, roots, and suffixes) that form the term. The following resources can provide comprehensive explanations:

> **More about**
> Searching an online library catalog, 251–54

- Discipline-specific dictionaries and encyclopedias: Since each discipline will have its own terminology, search your library's catalog for appropriate reference sources using the words *dictionary* or *encyclopedia* and the name of the discipline (such as *sociology* or *biology*). Some discipline-specific reference works may be available via your library's website.

- Textbooks: Most textbooks in the sciences and social sciences set key terms in boldfaced or italic type and define them at first use. Check for an index or glossary at the back of the book or for a list of key terms in the margins or at the end of each chapter.

- Your instructors: Pay attention in lectures not just to what your instructors *say* but also to how they *use* words. Instructors may also define key terms or list them on slides, handouts, or the board.

The following excerpt from a student's report demonstrates both an understanding of and comfort with the specialized vocabulary of her discipline:

[Specialized words] The Mars Global Surveyor (MGS) [magnetometer] experiment was most useful due to its examination of [magnetic properties] present in Mars's crust. The most constructive portion was gained when the spacecraft altitude was below 200 km to as low as 101 km during the first 10 minutes of [periapsis] (the period during which MGS was closest to the planet's surface).

—Molly Patterson, Colgate University, Untitled report for Geology 105

2. Use the third person and passive voice to describe how research was conducted.

> More about
> Person, 680–81
> Active versus passive voice, 562, 593–94

Scientists and social scientists write research reports so that other researchers can follow their procedures and produce an identical result. Since (in principle) the individual conducting the research is unimportant, researchers in the sciences typically use the third person and passive voice to describe how research was conducted:

> The materials consisted of two PsyScope computer programs run on Macintosh computers and a paper and pencil questionnaire. The participant was first assigned a room for experiment one (conditioning manipulation). The participant was then given the informed consent form, which was signed prior to the start of the experiment. The lights were turned off and the participant read the instruction. The experimenter asked if there were any questions.
>
> —Amy M. Ehret, Illinois State University, "Effects of Stigma on Approach and Avoidance Behaviors in Social Situations"

[Third person] [Passive voice]

Some social scientists use the first person (*I, we*) when discussing observations they made as a participant or the conclusions they drew from their research. Social scientists typically avoid the passive voice when describing the actions of participants.

3. Use the past tense to discuss methods and present tense to discuss implications.

> More about
> Tense, 702–7

Scientists and social scientists use the past tense to discuss methods of data collection or the behavior of research participants, and they use the present tense to discuss the implications of their research. This is neatly demonstrated in the sentence below:

> Since this study included only middle-class Caucasians, it is not representative of the population as a whole.
>
> —Robyn Worthington, Bristol Community College, "Nature versus Nurture: Does Birth Order Shape Personality?"

[Past tense] [Present tense]

23e Writing Assignments in the Sciences and Social Sciences

> Student Model
> Research report "Nature versus Nurture," Robyn Worthington (ch. 19), 430–38

Common types of writing projects in the sciences and social sciences include the following:

- Literature review: In a literature review, writers summarize research on a specific topic, analyze and evaluate the sources and

More about
Summarizing,
114–15, 295–97
Analyzing,
127–29, 308–9
Evaluating
sources
(ch. 14), 263–78
Synthesizing,
133, 308–9

the research on which these studies were based, and synthesize sources to develop a thorough understanding of the topic.

- Research or laboratory notebook: In a research or laboratory notebook, writers record in precise detail (1) the materials (including sketches of setups if complex) in the order used; (2) a chronological list of the procedures followed; and (3) the results (raw data, clearly labeled and logically organized), including any graphs or calculations.
- Research or laboratory report: In a research or laboratory report, writers provide a detailed description of research, including methods, results, and discussion.

Unlike a humanities research project, a research or laboratory report in the sciences and social sciences usually follows a standard format:

Title page Titles should succinctly and accurately describe the project. The title should avoid playfulness or puns and should convey as briefly as possible the most important aspects of the report. The title page should include the following information:

- Title
- Subtitle (if any)
- Author's name (the *byline*)
- Instructor's name and course number
- Date of submission
- Author notes

More about
Author notes,
425–26

Abstract A brief summary of the report, the *abstract* usually includes a one-sentence summary of the most important points in each section of the report. Abstracts are typically 150–250 words long.

Introduction The introduction provides necessary background, such as a brief review of other, closely related studies, indicates the purpose of conducting the research, and states the limits of what the research is intended to show.

Methods The methods section provides the following:

- Information about participants or subjects, including the number of participants and any relevant demographic information about them
- A description of the methods used to collect information (for example, face-to-face interview, online questionnaire, or telephone survey) or to conduct the experiment

- The equipment used (if any)
- The methods of recording data

The methods section must provide enough detail that others could repeat the study or experiment and achieve the same results.

Results The results section provides details of your outcomes. Information graphics are used to convey results succinctly.

Discussion The discussion section of the report offers readers an interpretation of the results, showing how the data collected support (or fail to support) the hypothesis. The discussion indicates the limitations of the data (what they do not indicate), and it relates the results to those of earlier researchers. (Do the data confirm, undermine, or extend earlier research?) The discussion concludes with an analysis of the implications of the research.

References The reference list includes secondary sources and begins on a new page, with the heading (the word *References*) centered at the top of the page.

Tables and figures Tables follow the reference list; figures follow tables. Each table or figure appears on a separate page.

Appendixes Appendixes include any figures, tables, photographs, or other materials that amplify but are not central to the discussion. Appendixes should be mentioned in the main body of the text so that readers know to consult them. Each appendix should include only one figure, set of data, and so on, but a report can include several appendixes. If more than one appendix is included, each should be assigned a letter (Appendix A, Appendix B, and so on). Arrange the appendixes in the order in which they are mentioned in the text, and give each appendix a succinct, descriptive title, such as "Appendix A: Background Questions."

> **More about**
> Matching graphic to information, 78–80
> Numbering figures and tables, 428–29 (APA)

> **More about**
> Creating an APA-style reference list, 408–25
> Creating a CSE-style reference list, 472–82

Work Together

Read the research report on pages 516–29. Then in groups of three or four, discuss the differences between the research report and one of the student projects in the previous chapter (pp. 497–501, 503–5). How do the approach, language, and structure of the two writing projects differ?

Student Model Research Report

The research report that follows describes a study on the mental health of college students and the role of college administrators and faculty conducted by Emily Durand, a student at Syracuse University. Durand's study follows APA style.

Following is the assignment prompt to which Emily responded.

Assignment: Final Research Report

Due January 20, 2021
Length: 3000-5000 words

Your final research report needs to have the following components. Please note that this list is not an outline for your entry, but rather a list of elements that you'll need to incorporate:

1. The current version of your research question
2. An account of how your research question has/has not changed as you've worked on this project
3. An explanation of what prompted you to pose and pursue your research question
4. A thesis statement that provides your current answer to your research question
5. Evidence that leads you to believe your thesis
6. Counterevidence: sources and perspectives that pull against your thesis; doubts you have about your thesis
7. Explanation of and reflection on the methods you used to explore your research question. How well did these work? What would you do differently if you were to start this research over?
8. Bread-crumb trail: Don't rely on your audience's attention. As we read what you've written, we need to be reminded occasionally of what your overall argument is. Your transitions, then, need to hinge each sentence together and each paragraph together; and you need to show explicitly how what you're writing at any given point relates to your argument.
9. Citations to sources you're using in the body of your entry
10. A list of works cited (or, if you're using APA style, a References list), presented in the citation system you've chosen—MLA or APA

A Field Research Report on the Mental Health of College Students:

What Support Should Institutions Provide?

Emily Durand

Writing 303

Professor Rebecca Moore Howard

January 19, 2021

Abstract

The way colleges treat students with mental health disabilities is problematic. I've explored this issue by reviewing relevant research and administering my own student survey. My literature review indicated that colleges tend not to hold faculty and staff accountable for students' well-being; with some not even recognizing the need for mental health counseling. My survey of 56 respondents ranging in age from 18 to 28, with half reporting a mental health disability or concern, indicated that students struggle to cope with personal and academic stressors that may exacerbate their illnesses. Academic advisors tend to be more effective than professors in helping students cope with stress. Further research into the use of specific teaching strategies and universal design is warranted.

Introduction: A Statement of the Problem

[Uses first person to emphasize personal experience] Throughout the semester I have researched what college institutions can do to be more inclusive of those with mental health concerns and disabilities. As a student with several mental health disabilities, I have encountered a variety of discriminatory acts throughout my time in college. [Introduction: explains issues under consideration, indicates importance of the research] My own circumstances prompted me to investigate what other students have experienced and how administrators, faculty, and staff, including at other institutions, handle the mental health concerns of their students. I felt it was important to identify not only the negative experiences others were having but the positive ones, too, so that institutions might be more inclined to learn from and use them as models for their own practices. [Shifts to third person] This type of research has the potential to inform college administrators and advocates who are working on policy changes within their own institutions. Further, this research may also benefit students with mental health concerns, and perhaps serve as a point of reference for the wider disability advocate community.

Literature Review

[Topic sentence] Much of the research on the mental health of college students showed that the onus is on students themselves to recognize their problems and seek counseling. [Literature review: describes previously published research] Institutions and their employees tend not to hold themselves as accountable as one might expect. One source, Eisenburg and Chung (2012), looked at how colleges can improve the efficacy of their counseling services; however, some institutions questioned whether they should be responsible for providing such support to students. As a result, much of the following literature review consists of a synthesis of resources, scholarly and nonscholarly; the sources are generally informative on the issue but not specific to the question of institutional responsibility. There is little doubt from Robotham and Claire's (2006) research, however, that academic expectations are stressful for students and negatively impact their mental health, whether for a specific period of time, or in an ongoing, constant way. In addition, students' various intersecting identities can impact the degree to which their mental health symptoms manifest, as Bostwick and their colleagues (2014) showed.

In addition to experiencing stressors such as moving away from home, forming new relationships, and adjusting to new responsibilities, college students must also cope with major academic stressors. [Topic sentence] Not only are they learning to navigate syllabi and course requirements, perhaps under the looming threat of losing financial aid, but college students are also figuring out how to plan for deadlines, improve their time management skills, and learn the art of communicating with faculty and staff. In this context, some enter college with existing mental health disabilities that may become exacerbated, while others develop new mental health problems and struggle to proceed with their studies.

It is important to note that students are protected, as the Understood Team (2018) explained, under a variety of laws designed to prevent discrimination against those with disabilities, including mental health disabilities. However, Baker (2014) showed that colleges have been known to take discriminatory action against students with mental health disabilities, in some cases effectively ending their educations. When students were asked in a survey conducted by the National Alliance on Mental Illness (2012), 64% said they were no longer enrolled in college because of a mental health issue. This evidence showed that there are real consequences for students [Topic sentence]

[Counterevidence: the project includes and discusses research that does not support the writer's thesis]

5

[Topic sentence] and colleges, and that funding initiatives to support students' mental health is both necessary and worthwhile.

[Counterevidence: arguments against the writer's recommended solution] That said, many colleges have problems supporting or even addressing their students' mental health. As Baker (2014) explained in her article, some administrators say they should not be expected to provide a multitude of counseling services to students. Doing so is unrealistic, they argue. How can they possibly attend to the needs of every student with a mental health problem? Some say that students with mental health problems may present too much of a danger to themselves or others, and are a liability to the institution. As a result, many colleges respond by forcing students to leave campus if they exhibit self-harming behaviors or suicidal ideation. Yes, the logistics of funding, providing counseling, and training faculty and staff are difficult, but not making these a priority is, by default, discriminatory.

[Topic sentence] A major problem with research on the mental health of college students is that sources generally do not discuss factors such as race, class, and gender discrimination. **[Explains shortcomings of previously published research]** Something that Williams' and Mohammed's literature review (2008) confirmed is that discrimination negatively impacts a person's stress levels. Therefore, it is reasonable to hypothesize that students who experience discrimination suffer more stress in college than those who do not. In response, it is crucial that institutions find ways to confront discrimination and provide real support for the mental health of their students so that they can be well and on track to learn and succeed.

[Offers solution for problem] The survey conducted by the National Alliance on Mental Illness (2012) showed that students feel unsupported by their institutions because faculty and staff lack the training to talk about mental health. Colleges can address this problem by providing employees with trauma and mental health training that can benefit students in distress. When institutions are proactive (rather than reactive) in regard to mental health, faculty and staff can focus on the job of preparing students for the next step in their journeys.

Methodology

My original field plan was to perform observational research on what other colleges are doing to help students with mental health concerns. However, I decided that it would be more powerful to conduct my own survey. For one thing, logistically speaking, survey research is cost-effective and time-efficient, and because I conducted the survey online, it was easy to distribute it widely. I shared it across social media platforms where others reshared it; I also shared it with members of my writing class.

As I designed my survey, it was important to me that participants had as much control as possible over their responses; therefore, I did my best to create a trauma-informed, inclusive survey. I allowed fill-in responses for age and gender and provided "Prefer not to answer" options wherever possible. I provided a combination of quantitative and qualitative questions, and an open-ended question where participants could add anything else that they felt was relevant to share. I did attempt to make the language accessible, as I was relying on the reading and digital literacy of participants for the success of the survey. However, some of the questions, I have realized, could have been better worded, especially for those who may not know what "counts" as disability. Many, for example, do not even realize mental illness may qualify as a disability.

> Methodology: Explains how the research was conducted

> Describes but does not acknowledge sampling limitations; these methods do not yield a sample that represents a larger demographic group

> Offers details on how she conducted her research

> Discusses shortcomings of the writer's field research

Another issue with my survey is that I did not make clear whether I was asking about mental health and/or other kinds of disabilities. The *SAGE Encyclopedia of Qualitative Research Methods* (Julien, 2008) stressed the importance of removing jargon from survey questions, so in future surveys I will be sure to use different, more accessible language, perhaps asking an accessibility and usability expert (or experts) to review my questions before I launch the survey. Although one of the goals of my survey for this project was to investigate how students with diagnosed and undiagnosed mental illnesses responded, in future surveys I may place more emphasis on the symptoms that people experience and be more clear about what constitutes stress.

Also, as suggested by Julien (2008), I opened with more quantitative questions to develop trust among participants so that they would feel more inclined to respond to the open-ended questions near the end. However, there may have been a lower response rate to the open-ended question, not only because they required more time to respond to but also because they were at the end.

Survey Questions

> Includes details about the research

The questions were as follows:

1. What is your gender?
2. What is your age?
3. Do you have one or more mental health concerns or disabilities?
4. If applicable, is your mental health concern/disability diagnosed or undiagnosed?

5. In the past two weeks, how often were you stressed as a result of professors' academic expectations (assignments, deadlines, etc.)?

6. In the past two weeks, how often were you stressed as a result of advisors' academic expectations (such as suggestions on courses or other tasks)?

7. Based on your college experience(s), how would you rate the way your professor(s) handled your mental health concern(s)?

8. Based on your college experience(s), how would you rate the way your advisor(s) handled your mental health concern(s)?

9. What experiences, if any, would you like to share regarding how faculty and staff have been helpful regarding your mental health concern(s)?

10. What experiences, if any, would you like to share regarding how faculty and staff have been unhelpful regarding your mental health concern(s)?

11. Do you feel that faculty or staff in colleges could be doing something different to better help students with mental health concerns and disabilities? If yes, please share any suggestions you have.

12. Is there anything else you would like to add?

For questions five and six, I felt it was important to include numerical options given that qualifiers such as "sometimes," or "always," are highly subjective. I did also include, however, more subjective response options for questions seven and eight as a scale from "Poorly" to "Very Well." In general, I felt that a combination of a variety of questions and responses was important, given the complex nature of the subject of mental health.

> Explains how research decisions were made

Findings

Fifty-six people participated in the survey. Of these, 80.4% of respondents identified as female, 17.9% as male, 5.4% as nonbinary, 3.6% as gender nonconforming, and 1.8% as transgender. Participants' ages broke down as follows: 41.1% of participants were 21 years old, 23.2% were 22, 21.4% were 20, and the rest ranged from 18 to 28. Approximately half (29) responded that they had a mental health concern or disability, while 28% responded that they did not; 10.7% said they may have a mental health concern or disability, and 12.5% said they were not sure. Out of these 29 participants, 21 reported that their mental health concern was diagnosed and 6 reported that their concern had not been professionally evaluated. Others who were unsure of their mental health disability mostly reported that their concern was undiagnosed.

In response to the question, "In the past two weeks, how often were you stressed as a result of professors' academic expectations (assignments, deadlines, etc.)?" no participants chose the "Never" response. Results were mostly evenly distributed across all other response options (1-2 times, 2-3 times, 3-4 times, 4-5 times, Over 5 times), with the mode (23.2%) choosing the "Over 5 times" response. Approximately one-third of respondents chose "Never" in response to the question, "In the past two weeks, how often were you stressed as a result of advisors' academic expectations (such as suggestions on courses or other tasks)?" Approximately another third chose "1-2 times," while the remaining participants were mostly evenly distributed among the other response options (2-3 times, 3-4 times, 4-5 times, Over 5 times).

Survey responses to the question, "Based on your college experience(s), how would you rate the way your professor(s) handled your mental health concern(s)?" resulted in a solid bell curve between "Poorly" and "Very Well," with a "1" response corresponding to the most poor and a "5" response corresponding to the best responses.

Survey responses to the question, "Based on your college experience(s), how would you rate the way your advisor(s) handled your mental health concern(s)?" also resulted in a bell curve shape, with more participants leaning toward "Very Well" rather than "Poorly" compared to how professors handled their mental health concerns.

The response rate to the open-ended questions dropped by approximately half. Some recognizable themes did appear, however, among participants. One of the most common was that professors did not make any effort to learn about students' lives and, as a result, many students' concerns went unaddressed unless they disclosed their mental health problem. Participants made statements such as, "Professor didn't know until I talked," "They never ask," and, "I feel like they are unaware of how overwhelmed I feel sometimes." Also as a result, many participants responded that they would appreciate more one-on-one communication as a potential solution. Another major theme was that, according to student respondents, professors tended not to accommodate students' disabilities, even if they were legally required to do so. In instances where professors were legally required to accommodate student disabilities, they tended not to see mental health as being as significant as physical health, and universal design accommodations were rarely implemented. The other primary theme that students noted as an issue was a lack of investment into counseling resources or that counseling resources were unhelpful even when present.

There were numerous responses to the question of how helpful faculty and staff had been to students. Responses seemed dependent on the individual faculty or staff member; although some responded qualitatively that professors were more helpful, quantitatively there were more participants who said advisors handled mental health concerns best. Some of the most common responses were regarding professors who made the effort to check in with students individually, and those who, when alerted to students' mental health concerns, allowed extensions and absences.

A few respondents said that their professors should not bear the primary responsibility for students with mental health disabilities, while others, including some who identified as having mental health concerns, said professors should not provide "special" exceptions to students.

Discussion

> Discussion: Reflects on the value of the research findings

My survey helped answer my questions in a number of ways. First, the fact that participants on average said that professors and faculty handled their students' mental health concerns in, at best, a mediocre way, is significant. The responses showed that, while there are some exceptional individuals on the faculty and staff who work very well with students, all would benefit from a more systematic and trained response to students in mental health crises. The indication was that required trainings could be highly beneficial for faculty and staff because it would make them better equipped to handle students' mental health concerns. It is also significant that participants said they were never *not* stressed in the previous two weeks due to professors' expectations; this finding warrants further investigation into universal design and how it can favorably impact students' stress levels. Because stress coincides with higher levels of cortisol, and cortisol causes higher rates of health problems, the chronic stress associated with college is not something to be taken lightly.

The themes noted in the findings section of this paper are helpful to me as a basis for my recommendations regarding universal design. That said, my field research results warrant further analysis, especially regarding the correlation between students' diagnosed mental illnesses and the quality of response from faculty and staff. My research has also raised more questions to pursue. For instance, what would motivate faculty and staff to participate in trainings to be more informed about and inclusive of students with mental health concerns?

> Suggests followup research that would be useful

My research indicates the need for colleges to incorporate more universal design as a way to counter students' chronic stress and integrate more responsive measures when it comes to the mental health of their students. My hope is that others may further the inquiries I've made, perhaps putting together for faculty and staff some background information and teaching strategies for addressing and even preventing student mental health problems. The goal is for colleges to provide a safer, higher-quality learning experience overall.

> Conclusion: offers conclusions to be drawn from the research

References

Baker, K. M. J. (2014, February 11). How colleges flunk mental health. *Newsweek*, https://www.newsweek.com/2014/02/14/how-colleges-flunk-mental-health-245492.html

Bostwick, W. B., Meyer, I., Aranda, F., Russell, S., Hughes, T., Birkett, M., & Mustanski, B. (2014). Mental health and suicidality among racially/ethnically diverse sexual minority youths. *American Journal of Public Health*, *104*(6), 1129-1136. https://doi.org/10.2105/ AJPH.2013.301749

Eisenberg, D., & Chung, H. (2012). Adequacy of depression treatment among college students in the United States. *General Hospital Psychiatry*, *34*(3), 213-220. https://doi.org/10.1016/j.genhosppsych.2012.01.002

Gruttadaro D, & Crudo, D. National Alliance on Mental Illness. (2012). College students speak: A survey report on mental health. Johns Hopkins University, https://www.sprc.org/resources-programs/college-students-speak-survey-report-mental-health; https://diversity.jhu.edu/diversity-leadership-council/

Julien, H. (2008). Survey research. In L. M. Given (Ed.), *The SAGE encyclopedia of qualitative research methods: Vol. 2* (pp. 846-848). SAGE Publications, https://us.sagepub.com/en-us/nam/the-sage-encyclopedia-of-qualitative-research-methods/book229805

Lee, A. (2021). IDEA, Section 504, and the ADA: Which laws do what, https://www.understood.org/en/school-learning/your-childs-rights/basics-about-childs-rights/at-a-glance-which-laws-do-what

Robotham, D., & Julian, C. (2006). Stress and the higher education student: A critical review of the literature. *Journal of Further and Higher Education, 30*(2), 107–117. https://doi.org/10.1080/03098770600617513

Williams, D. R., & Mohammed, S. A. (2009). Discrimination and racial disparities in health: Evidence and needed research. *Journal of Behavioral Medicine, 32*(1), 20–47. https://doi.org/10.1007/s10865-008-9185-0

Text Credits

Pg. 511: Source: Amy M. Ehret, Illinois State University, "Effects of Stigma on Approach and Avoidance Behaviors in Social Situations"; **Pg. 515:** Courtesy of Emily Durand.

24 Preparing for and Taking an Essay Exam

IN THIS CHAPTER

a. Preparing, 530

b. Previewing, 532

c. Writing an effective answer, 533

Student Model
Effective Essay Exam Response, Taiji Okada, "*Big Lewbowski:* A Variation on Film Noir with a Different Kind of Hero," 535

Long before marathon runners cross the finish line, they get ready for the 26.2-mile race. They practice regularly, eat well, and learn the terrain ahead of time. They also use strategy, knowing how to pace themselves and when to turn up the heat. And they do not panic if someone else dashes ahead. Runners know that being prepared is crucial to running a good race.

Students who succeed on essay exams have many of these attributes. They prepare by reviewing their notes and answering practice questions, and they have a test-taking strategy that allows them to get to the finish line. All of this preparation—not cramming the night before—is what leads to a good grade.

24a Preparing for an Essay Exam

You begin to prepare for any college test by reading, taking notes, listening, and working on your assignments. An essay exam, however, requires some special preparation.

1. Take good notes and review them often.

Stay up to date on your reading assignments, and take good notes:

- Highlight and underline important terms and concepts, but do not overdo it—highlighting everything means you must reread everything.

- Write down your thoughts and questions, and connect what you are reading to other ideas or situations.

- Note any statements in the text that seem especially important or interesting—or that might show up on an essay exam.

> *More about*
> Annotating, 119–24
> Taking notes, 286–87
> Keeping a reading journal, 124–25
> Summarizing, 114–15, 295–97
> Outlining, 41–44, 305–7

> **Tech** Note-Taking Technologies
>
> Experiment with a variety of note-taking technologies: index cards that can later be sorted, arranged, and labeled; a big notebook that's hard to lose; a smaller, more portable sketch pad or bullet journal; cloud tools like *Google Docs;* an app such as *Evernote* or *OneNote* for a hand-held device; or a laptop on which you can type quickly. As you experiment, pay attention to the pros and cons of your note-taking technology. Recent research suggests you will comprehend and remember the most if you take notes by hand. Other research suggests that using a laptop or hand-held device in class can open you up to distractions such as *Snapchat* and *Instagram*. There is no such thing as multitasking; it's just switching quickly from one task to another, without your full attention being on any of them. If the laptop or device is within view of your classmates, you may be distracting them from class, too.

- For complicated texts, write outlines or summaries that will help you figure out what is going on, keep track of the development of ideas, and recall the material later on.
- When taking notes in class, focus on the major points your instructor is making—do not try to write down every detail.

Keep all your notes in a reading journal. As you review them, focus on the most important ideas and information. Using a highlighter or a pen in a new color, take notes *on* your notes, marking the big topics or drawing connections among major ideas. Reviewing your notes regularly (not just the day before an exam) will help you absorb and retain important concepts and identify material you are likely to be asked about.

Study Groups An alternative to coming up with questions on your own is to work in small study groups. Each member could devise a question or an outline for the rest of the group, or members might work together to come up with questions and answers. Study groups work well when members share their ideas and learn from one another; they fail when some members rely too heavily on others to do their thinking for them. Group work can be a challenge when members do not share the same goals, experiences, or cultural or linguistic backgrounds. Before any project starts, be sure to discuss members' expectations.

2. Devise and answer practice questions.

After reviewing your notes, consider the terms and concepts that seem essential, and identify issues or patterns that have arisen repeatedly in readings and lectures. Then brainstorm questions based on these terms, concepts, issues, and patterns. As you brainstorm, be sure to include questions that you fear will be asked, as well as ones you hope will be on the exam. For each of the questions you develop, devise a brief outline and draft a practice answer.

3. Understand the rules for the exam.

Regardless of how you study, you also need to know what will be required and what will be allowed. Consult the course syllabus as well as any preparatory materials the instructor has provided. If these don't answer the following questions, ask your instructor:

- Is use of a dictionary, thesaurus, or writer's handbook permitted during the exam? What about phones, tablets, or laptops?
- How many questions will there be? Will different questions be worth different numbers of points, or will all questions be equally weighted?
- Is partial credit available for partial answers or for an outline of an answer?
- Are sample questions and answers available?

24b Previewing the Exam

When you sit down to take an essay exam—or any test, for that matter—you may have the impulse to start writing immediately. It is a good idea, though, to take a few minutes to look over the exam, decide on a strategy, and make sure you understand the questions.

1. Read the exam, and develop a test-taking strategy.

The first step in writing a successful exam is to read the entire exam before writing anything. As you read, develop a strategy for taking the test:

- Determine how many points are assigned to each question, and set a time limit for answering each part. Give yourself more time for the questions that are worth more points: Finishing a 50-point question is more important than finishing a 10-pointer.
- Check off the questions that you find easy and can complete quickly. Starting with some of those may give you momentum.
- Leave yourself a little time to read through your answers to add or clarify information; to correct errors of spelling, usage, and grammar; and to rewrite illegible words.

Quick Reference: Common Verbs on Essay Exams

What Is the Question?

1. **Analyze** the architectural style of Frank Lloyd Wright.
2. **Compare and contrast** the major economic problems of the North and South during the Civil War.
3. **Define** the terms *denotation* and *connotation*, and discuss these terms in regard to the word *mother*.
4. **Describe** how bees build a hive.
5. **Evaluate** the playing style of tennis champion Serena Williams.
6. **Illustrate** the effects of climate change on mammals of the Arctic, including the walrus and the polar bear.
7. **List** and **explain** the four main causes of financial inequality.
8. **Summarize** Carl Rogers's humanist approach to psychology.

What Am I Supposed to Do?

1. **Name** the elements of his style, and then **critically examine** those elements and the style as a whole.
2. Name the economic problems, and explain how they were **similar and different** in the North and South.
3. Give the **main characteristics** of the terms. **Show that you understand** the definitions by applying them to *mother*.
4. Create, in words, a **step-by-step** picture of what bees do.
5. State what you think of Williams's tennis style, and give specific and concrete **evidence** for your opinion(s).
6. Give specific **examples** of the effects on the animals named and at least one additional animal.
7. **Jot down** the causes and **tell clearly** how each results in financial inequality.
8. Give the **main points** of his approach, and keep your answer **concise.**

2. Analyze the questions: What do they ask you to do?

When you read an exam question, it may be easier to identify the topic than to know what you are supposed to *do* with it. *Compare* is quite different from *define* or *summarize,* so pay close attention to the verbs and do what they tell you. (See the Quick Reference box above for sample question analyses.)

Be alert for two-part questions; make sure you answer both parts. Ask your instructor to clarify any question that is vague or confusing.

Asking for the answer (or even a hint) is inappropriate (and probably unsuccessful), but asking your instructor to define an unfamiliar word (as long as it is not a key term) is perfectly reasonable.

More about
Analyzing the assignment, 23–24, 222–23
Writing about literature (ch. 22), 486–509
Writing in the sciences and social sciences (ch. 23), 510–29
Comparison-contrast, 65–66
Definition, 67–68
Summarizing, 114–15, 295–97

24c Writing an Effective Answer

To structure an essay exam answer, follow the same rules that guide you when you write any other essay.

1. Respond to the question, provide support, organize logically, and review your work.

Writing an effective answer means answering the question you are asked, providing sufficient supporting evidence, and organizing your response clearly and logically, then reviewing your work. Use these tips for showing off what you have learned.

> *More about*
> Informal (scratch) outlines, 41–42
> Thesis statements, 36–38
> Transitions, 59–60
> Supporting your ideas, 45–47

- Write a thesis statement, one or two sentences that express your main point and that respond directly to the question.
- Outline the points you want to make. Jot down the evidence you will use.
- Draft your answer. Start with your thesis and use your outline to fill in your explanation of the thesis.
- Leave ample margins on each side of the page and several blank lines below each answer, in case you decide to add information later on.
- When you have finished your draft, reread it, correcting any problems with coherence, correctness, and legibility.

Quick Reference — What an Effective Answer Does—and Does Not Do

An effective answer . . .	An effective answer does not . . .
- has a clear thesis that answers the question that was asked	- answer the question you hoped would be asked
- provides ample and accurate supporting evidence	- stick in information on the topic that is unrelated to the question
- answers the question parts in the order they were asked	- pad the answer by repeating what you have already said
- uses the method of development suggested by the question (such as analysis, comparison-contrast, definition)	- make personal judgments that the question does not ask for

---

Writing Responsibly — Using Your Computer during an Essay Exam

Check with your instructor in advance of an essay exam to see whether you can write your exam on a laptop. The computer will allow you to present a readable copy: You can use cut-and-paste to revise and reorganize your answer and run a spell-check program to catch and correct the most obvious typos. It would be inappropriate—and unfair to your classmates—to do anything other than write, so avoid the temptation to consult online sources; open only your word processing program and leave your browser closed.

to OTHER WRITERS

Student Model Effective Essay Exam Response

The sample answer on page 536 responds directly to the exam question by comparing The *Big Lebowski* and *The Big Sleep* and by including the core concept "film noir" in the answer. Notice that this writer fulfills his responsibility to his reader (and to himself) by demonstrating that he understands the issues discussed in class and can synthesize information from films he has seen to support his claims.

Essay Exam Question

Identify and compare/contrast the films from which the stills below are taken. Be sure to include in your discussion at least one of the core concepts we have discussed in class, such as genre, dialogue, film noir, and so on. (30 points)

Okada 1

Taiji Okada

Professor Ingrid Reyes

English 202

May 14, 2021

Big Lewbowski: A Variation on Film Noir with a Different Kind of Hero

Though *The Big Lebowski* is generally considered a parody of film noir detective stories such as *The Big Sleep*, this 1998 cult classic might also be categorized as a contemporary variation on the style. As the still photos show, the differences are obvious: gonzo comedy aside, *Lebowski* chiefly differs in the nature and quality of its hero. Instead of the occasionally superhuman wit and capability of Philip Marlowe, we have The Dude, called by the film's narrator "one of the laziest people on the planet Earth." However, though The Dude's ineptitude is largely played for laughs, much of the humor derives from discomfort and even dread; his insufficiency as a hero only heightens the sense of alienation.

At the beginning of *The Big Sleep*, Marlowe is made to sit in an orchid hothouse, where he proceeds to grow more physically uncomfortable with every passing moment, but he is able to speak his client's language, anticipate his interests and needs, and ultimately earn the general's quiet admiration. The Dude, in contrast, is so out of his depth that he seems incapable of scoring a single point against anyone he meets. When The Dude finds himself in a shadow-drenched room, the viewer may not feel an immediate sense of dread, but it does seem clear that the protagonist has little hope of prevailing. In a particularly revealing scene, The Dude's "client" taunts him with the failure of his generation's ideals, and our hero has no real answer.

These two scenes reveal the core of the typical noir hero: the individual who loses, over and over again, and who is compelled to absorb these defeats and continue on, often with a diminished sense of self. The hero responds by creating a persona to act as surrogate for this loss—one as the hard-boiled detective (Marlowe) and the other as the hyper-passive Dude.

25 Professional and Civic Writing

IN THIS CHAPTER

a. Business letter formats, 537

b. Business letters, 540

c. Business memos, 542

d. Job application letters, 543

e. Résumés, 547

f. Reports and proposals, 552

g. Press releases, 554

Student Models
Job Application, 546;
Traditional Résumé, 548;
Scannable, Optimized Résumé, 550

Professional Models
Business Letter: Apology, 541;
Business Memo, 543; Report, 553; Press Release, 554

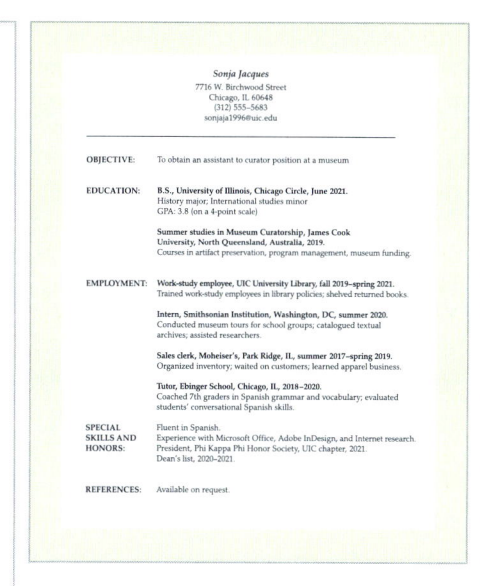

If you bought a bag of apples at the grocery store on Wednesday and discovered on Thursday that most of them were rotten, you would probably complain to the produce manager and ask for a refund. If this kind of thing happened often, you might write a letter to the store's owner. If you found something rotten in a government agency or corporation, you might write a letter to the editor of your city's newspaper to bring the problem to the attention of your community. If you found an issue that you could help resolve, you might offer a proposal for solving the problem and promote your program with a press release. Business writing, then, is more than memos or résumés and cover letters. It is something we all do, whether as employees or as citizens.

25a Using Business Letter Formats

Regardless of what you do after college, you will need to know how to write a good business letter. In company settings, you might need to communicate with suppliers, customers, or members of another department, for example. In your personal life, you may need to write a business letter to request information, thank someone, or comment on a product or service.

The formality of the context can serve as a guide in determining which format to use when communicating—whether through email, an email attachment, or a printed letter. Sending printed, mailed letters used to be the most common way to communicate about business issues—and for most of US history, it was the only way. Today, however, it is common for professional communications to be sent by email.

A short message such as a letter to the editor or clarification with a business or customer over an easily repaired problem might be conveyed in the body of an email. If the issue requires follow-up action or is likely to be circulated among a group, it is better to send a letter as an attachment that can be downloaded. More formal communications, or communications that should remain private (such as salary or legal issues) are best relayed in printed form, distributed through the US Postal Service or a private shipping company such as UPS or FedEx.

Whether sending letters by conventional mail or email, be considerate of your reader's time and present information courteously and concisely. These guidelines can help you write an effective business letter:

- **State your purpose in the first paragraph**. Readers in the workplace want to see at a glance what the letter is about.
- **Be clear and specific throughout the letter**. A vague, muddled, or repetitious letter may be ignored.
- **Keep your paragraphs short**. This will help your reader grasp your major points quickly.
- **Adopt a positive yet somewhat formal tone**. Make sure the tone fits the audience and purpose.
- **Reread and edit your letter**. Clarify your points, reduce wordiness, and correct all errors. Grammatical and typographical errors may severely diminish your credibility with your reader.

1. Use a standard letter format.

Whatever the purpose of your business letter, follow one of two standard formats:

Professional Models
Business Letters: Full block style, 541
Modified block style, 546

1. **Full block style**. Align all text with the left-hand margin. This is the best choice when you are writing a letter on letterhead stationery.

2. **Modified block style**. Align the following elements just to the right of the center of the page: return address, date, closing, and signature. Align everything else with the left-hand margin.

In addition to using an appropriate letter style, follow these design guidelines:

- Use 8½ × 11–inch white or off-white paper. You may also use letterhead stationery, especially if you are communicating as a representative of a company or an organization.
- Single-space your paragraphs and insert an extra line of space between them; do not indent paragraphs.
- Use a standard size (number 10) envelope, and fold the letter horizontally in thirds. Don't forget to attach a stamp!
- Follow standard practice for addressing the envelope: addressee's full name, title, and address (with zip code) in the middle of the envelope; and your name and address in the upper left-hand corner. Use your computer's software to generate a neatly typed envelope or address label.

2. Include standard elements.

As you type your letter, incorporate the typical elements of a business letter:

Return address and date If you are using letterhead stationery with a pre-printed address, add just the date. Otherwise, include your full address. Spell out the names of months.

Inside address Give the name, title (if appropriate), and full address of the person to whom you are writing. Spell out words like *Street* or *Road,* but use the two-letter postal abbreviations for states.

Salutation In some instances, you may address a letter to a company or organization (*Dear Habitat for Humanity*) or to a job title (*Dear Shipping Department Manager*), but it is preferable to address your letter to an actual person, even if you have to contact the company to determine who that person is. Also, use appropriate titles (abbreviated before the name), such as *Mr., Ms., Dr., Gen., Prof.,* or *Rev.* Professional titles supersede gender-specific titles. For example, if you were writing to a female minister, you would address the letter to *Rev. Aldrich,* not *Ms. Aldrich.* If you have the person's name but do not know the gender, use the whole name: *Dear Pat Gonzalez.*

> **More about**
> Titles before and after names, 871
> Abbreviating titles, 871

Body Type each paragraph flush with the left margin and put a line of space between paragraphs. Do not use paragraph indention.

Closing and signature Using the formality of the letter as a guide, choose an appropriate closing phrase, such as *Sincerely, Yours truly,* or *Best regards.* Four lines (two double spaces) below the closing, type your full name, and sign in the space above.

Additional information Below your name, include other kinds of information, such as *Cc.* if you are sending a copy to someone in addition to the addressee or *Enc.* if you are enclosing items with the letter.

Sample business letter, block style The letter in full-block style on page 541 (Figure 25.1) is on letterhead stationery that includes the company's address and other contact information. If this letter had been written on plain paper, a return address would be needed directly above the date. Most items and all paragraphs are separated by two lines (one double space), but below the date and below the closing, four lines of space are required.

25b Writing Business Letters

The letters you write as an employee or in your personal life will have a variety of purposes. On Monday you may be a businessperson writing a letter of apology to a customer, and on Tuesday you might be a private citizen writing a letter of complaint. It is helpful, then, to look at some guidelines for writing different kinds of business letters.

1. Letters of complaint

When writing a letter of complaint, your challenge is to exercise restraint. Be reasonable and informed, and get to the point. Effective complaint letters do not cast the recipient of the letter in a negative light. When writing a letter of complaint, follow these four steps:

1. Describe the problem at the outset, and include details.
2. Explain the importance of the problem and why the recipient should be involved in the solution.
3. State your hopes for the solution to the problem.
4. If you have had positive experiences with the person or organization in the past, mention that; it will help your cause.

2. Letters of apology

In the workplace, you may receive letters from customers who are complaining about the service you offer or the product you provide. In a letter of apology (Figure 25.1), your goal is to fix or make up for the problem,

Professional Model Business Letter: Apology

REBECCA'S RESTAURANT
550 N. Wabash, Chicago, IL 60611   312-268-8539   www.rebeccasrest.com

October 10, 2021

(4 line spaces)

Ms. Lauren Grayson
6243 North Sheridan Road   *Inside address*
Chicago, IL 60610

Dear Ms. Grayson: *Salutation*

Gives reason for letter and offers apology
I am responding to your letter of September 28 about the difficulties you had in trying to purchase a gift certificate for your friends, the Websters. First let me say that I apologize and can assure you that the employee you spoke to on the phone apologizes as well.

Explains company policy
We do offer our guests the option of purchasing gift certificates via fax. The only things we require are faxed copies of identification and a credit card, and a filled-out gift certificate form—all of which you supplied. It is also our policy to keep guest information confidential at all times. In this instance, however, it is clear that we failed to execute our procedures.

Explains action taken and repeats apology
I have spoken to the employee involved and explained the importance of our system and guest satisfaction. I am enclosing a $75 gift certificate as a token of my apology.

Furthermore, I have sent a $75 gift certificate to the Websters, in the hope that they also accept our apologies and understand how important our guests are to us here at Rebecca's.

Closes cordially
Please feel free to contact me personally if you ever need anything in the future. I will do my best to help you in any way I can.

Sincerely,   *Closing*

(4 line spaces)

Christopher Juarez   — *Signature*

Christopher Juarez
General Manager

Enc.   *Enclosure indicated*

— Body

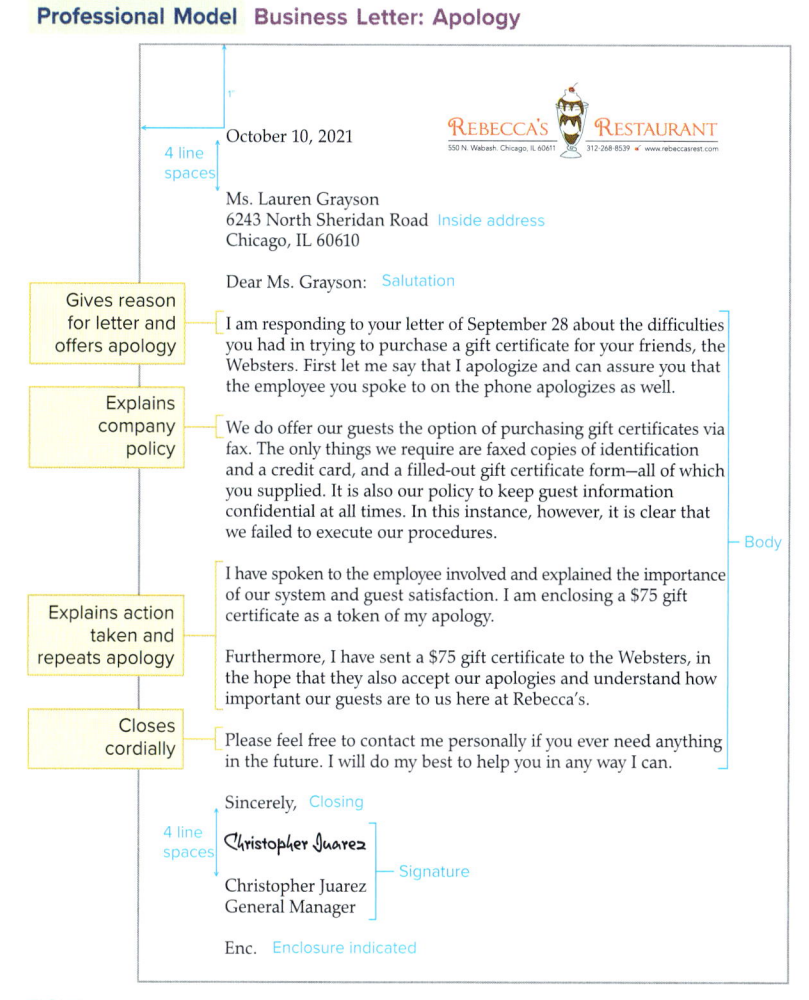

FIGURE 25.1 Sample letter of apology (full block style)

reassure your customers that they are important, and restore the reputation of your company or organization.

Follow these steps in writing a letter of apology:

1. State the problem in the first paragraph, and apologize for it.
2. Explain your company's policy (if appropriate), and admit that correct procedures were not followed.

> **Writing Responsibly** — **Letters to the Editor**
>
> When private citizens write a letter to the editor of a newspaper or magazine, they often feel strongly about something—a previous article in the publication, a political candidate, or a local problem. If you write such a letter, keep your emotions in check. Make your point, get your facts straight, assume a courteous tone, and avoid personal attacks against the publication or writer. Most publications now accept such letters via email; read your submission over carefully and adjust the tone before hitting send.
>
> to AUDIENCE

3. Tell the customer what you have done to correct the problem within your company, and what you are doing to make things right with the customer.
4. Repeat your apology, and offer further assistance if needed.

3. Letters of rejection

When you must turn down a request, a bid on a project, or a job application, your task is not only to communicate the bad news but also to maintain goodwill with the person to whom you are writing. An effective letter of rejection will do the following:

1. Begin with a positive statement, thanking the recipient for taking the time to apply for the job, submit the proposal, or do whatever the person has done.
2. Give the reason(s) for the rejection in a clear yet kind way.
3. Conclude the letter with an expression of goodwill that is particular to the recipient.

Professional Model
Business memo (email), 543

25c Writing Business Memos

On any given workday, you may write a memo to convey information to the advertising department, to raise a question with your supervisor, or to explain a new procedure to coworkers. You may write thousands of memos during your lifetime; they are the typical communication tool people use within a company or organization. Printed memos may be distributed, but they are now most frequently sent via email (Figure 25.2). A few tips to help you write an effective memo follow.

> **More about**
> Writing and answering email, 199–203, 544

1. Use a standard memo format.

Insert the information in the sections of your email's header *To, From, Date,* and *Subject*. (If you are sending a printed memo, type these headings at the top of the page or use the memo template that comes with your word

Professional Model Business Memo

Awards for Resident Advisors

To: Santos Maria
Cc: Carter Jane
Bcc:

- **Recipients**
- **Specific subject line** — Awards for Resident Advisers
- **Main point stated in 1st paragraph** — Our resident advisers are on the front line of student affairs, dealing day to day with conflicts among students, difficulties new students face in adjusting to college life, and the enforcement of college policies. So this year, in conjunction with the Student Housing Office, we are recognizing the contribution resident advisers make by conferring a Resident Adviser of the Year award.

Candidates should demonstrate the following qualities:

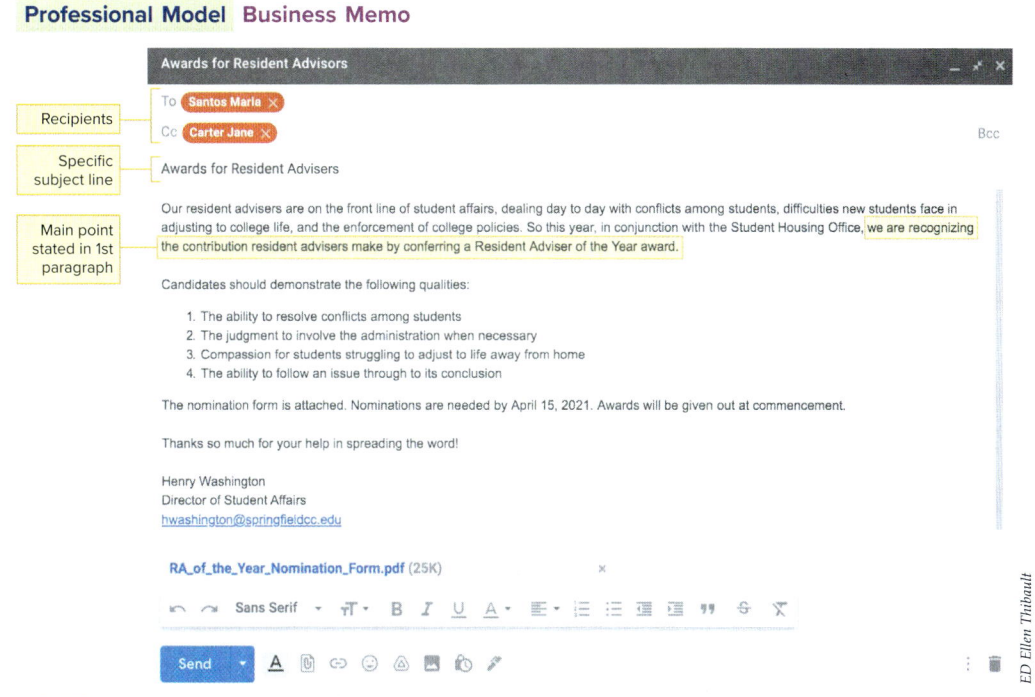

1. The ability to resolve conflicts among students
2. The judgment to involve the administration when necessary
3. Compassion for students struggling to adjust to life away from home
4. The ability to follow an issue through to its conclusion

The nomination form is attached. Nominations are needed by April 15, 2021. Awards will be given out at commencement.

Thanks so much for your help in spreading the word!

Henry Washington
Director of Student Affairs
hwashington@springfieldcc.edu

RA_of_the_Year_Nomination_Form.pdf (25K)

FIGURE 25.2 Sample memo (emailed)

processing program.) All memos should include a subject line that accurately summarizes the content of the message. If recipients are being copied, list them in the *Cc* line. Attachments to emailed memos usually appear in the header; for printed memos with attachments, add *Enc.* at the end of the message.

2. Get right to the point.

Use a tone appropriate for your reader, but be clear, specific, and concise. In your first paragraph, name the issue the memo is addressing and explain briefly why you are writing. In subsequent paragraphs or in a list, add any necessary details. A numbered or bulleted list is particularly effective in memos because it helps readers "see" your points or questions clearly. Conclude on a positive note, and thank the recipient if appropriate.

25d Writing Job Application Letters

A letter of application (Figure 25.3) is essentially a sales letter: Your goal is to sell yourself to a prospective employer and to get an interview. To do

Quick Reference: Email Etiquette

Following email etiquette (or *netiquette*) can make you more effective in social as well as professional settings. Here are fifteen tips for writing effective email:

1. **Use accurate subject lines, and focus on a single topic.** Doing so will help your recipients manage their email, and it will help you find your message later.
2. **Get right to the point, and keep messages brief.** Consideration for your reader's time is key.
3. **Maintain an appropriate tone.** Remain cordial and avoid *flaming* (or launching a personal attack).
4. **Include salutations (or greetings) and complimentary closings only in the most formal contexts.** Most email messages do not require a formal salutation or closing.
5. **Follow the rules of capitalization.** Avoid writing all but the most informal messages in all lowercase (or all capital) letters. (Words in all capital letters are the equivalent of shouting.)
6. **Ask permission before sharing an email message with someone to whom it was not addressed.** Sending along a message without asking permission may be unfair to the original sender.
7. **Reply promptly when your action is needed.** You may not always be able to answer swiftly, but do acknowledge receipt of the message, and let the sender know when to expect a full reply.
8. **Avoid hitting "reply all" unless every recipient will be interested in the reply.** With the quantity of email circulating today, most recipients will appreciate *not* being included if the message is not directed toward them.
9. **Avoid "spamming" friends and colleagues.** Messages promising bad luck if you do not send the message on to five (or more) friends are commonplace on the internet, but you can choose *not* to comply. Also refrain from forwarding memes and political stories; these are better suited to social media rather than cluttering people's inboxes.
10. **Copy portions of previous messages, or reference the email string for clarity.** If readers will need information from an earlier message, either copy and paste a portion of the message or refer the reader to a specific message.
11. **Never represent someone else's words as your own.** Acknowledge your use of any words or ideas you have borrowed from others. Usually, you need not provide a formal citation, but you should include the writer's name and any information needed to locate the source.
12. **Include your contact information with every message.** Make sure recipients know how to contact you in ways besides email: Provide a telephone number and mailing address with each message.
13. **Edit your messages**. Email should not be confused with text messaging; it is much more formal and should be clear and correct.
14. **Pause before sending!** While the temptation to shoot off an angry message is sometimes great, avoid it. Treat the email recipient with courtesy, even when you are annoyed.
15. **Archive your messages.** If you are likely to need to refer to a message you have sent or received, archive it in an appropriate folder or in the cloud.

so, your letter should be enthusiastic yet formal. Before you begin to write, learn something about the company or organization. You can then reveal a bit of your knowledge in your letter, which will show the recipient that you are serious about the job. Like other types of professional correspondence,

Writing Responsibly: Personal Emails and Text Messages at Work

When you send email on computers that are the property of a business or organization, the correspondence is considered the property of the organization and is subject to search should there be a suspicion of abuse. In addition, government workers' written communications may be made public through the Freedom of Information Act. Write responsibly at work, and assume that your email (or text messages) may be viewed by others.

to SELF

letters of application should follow some common guidelines concerning format and content:

- Use one of the two standard letter formats: block format (Figure 25.1) or modified block format (Figure 25.3), and limit the letter's length to a single page.
- Address the letter to a specific person, even if you have to phone the company to determine who that is.
- Start by mentioning the specific job you are applying for and how you learned about it.
- In the next paragraph or two, explain why you are applying for this job, and list your specific qualifications.
- Point out the items in your résumé that are a good "fit" for this job, but do not just repeat the résumé.

> **More about**
> Conciseness (ch. 26), 558–64
> Flaming, 210
> Tone, 20–21, 159, 599, 604–6, 607
> Capitalization (ch. 54), 858–64

Conducting Global Business in the United States Here are a few tips that may help you get a job and be successful at it:

- *Take advantage of your language skills.* Because many corporations operate globally and have clients from diverse backgrounds, be sure to mention—on your résumé and in a job interview—any languages besides English in which you are fluent.
- *Do not include personal information (such as age, religion, marital status) or a photograph on your résumé.* It is not the custom in the United States to include personal information or a photograph with a job application, and US employers are legally barred from assessing job qualifications on the basis of these factors.
- *Be direct and concise in your business writing.* Although your culture of origin or your other writing experiences may suggest a more indirect approach, follow the advice in this chapter if you are writing to a US organization.

Student Model: Job Application

Modified block style: Return address and date align right of center

7716 W. Birchwood Street
Chicago, IL 60648

July 1, 2021

Mr. Aaron Gieseke
Recruitment, Human Resources
Museum of Science and Industry
57th Street and Lake Shore Drive
Chicago, IL 60637

Addresses specific person formally

Dear Mr. Gieseke:

Mentions specific job and shows familiarity with museum

I am applying for the entry-level position of assistant to the curator, which you posted on CareerBuilder.com. Since childhood, I have been delighted by the museum's extraordinary exhibits, from Colleen Moore's Fairy Castle to the walk-through heart and chick hatchery. I would welcome the opportunity to put my skills and knowledge to work at your renowned institution.

Highlights educational ties to job

Two years ago, I was fortunate to take several in-depth courses in museum curatorship at James Cook University. With European curators as teachers, I came to understand the many facets of running a museum, including preserving artifacts and tapping sources of funding. I also learned about the myriad jobs that go on behind the scenes and decided that museum life was where I wanted to be in my professional life.

Links work experience to job and shows knowledge of museum

This decision was reinforced many times over while I was an intern at the Smithsonian last summer. I especially enjoyed working with researchers on new interactive exhibits and using my Spanish language skills with international visitors. Inasmuch as the Museum of Science and Industry was the first to initiate interactive exhibits and welcomes thousands of overseas travelers each year, I believe my qualifications are ideal for the job.

Asks for interview and gives contact information

My résumé is enclosed. I would be delighted to meet with you for an interview at any time. You may phone me at (312) 555–5683 or email me at sonjaja1996@uic.edu. I look forward to hearing from you.

Modified block style: Closing and signature align with return address

Sincerely,

Sonja Jacques

Sonja Jacques

Enc.

FIGURE 25.3 Sample job application letter (modified block style)

- Conclude by asking for an interview and providing information about how you may be reached.
- Edit and proofread your letter carefully: A job application letter must be well written and contain no errors.

Throughout the letter, you need to walk a fine line: Do not be too modest about your accomplishments, but do not exaggerate your qualifications, either.

25e Writing Résumés

A *résumé* is a brief document that summarizes your work and educational experience for a prospective employer. Like a job application letter, it is a tool for selling yourself and obtaining an interview. Thus, in drafting a résumé, keep your audience and purpose in mind: Who will read this résumé? What will they want to know? Especially for those new to the workforce, focus on the skills you have acquired from your work experience. For example, you might explain that you "maintained good customer relations" and "presented a positive corporate image" in your job at a fast-food restaurant. If you are changing careers—from computer programming to advertising, for example—revise your résumé accordingly.

> Sample résumés:
> Traditional, 548
> Scannable, 550

Tell the truth on your résumé, but cast the information in a positive light. Also think about what you have done that is appropriate for this particular job. You may have nearly forgotten the tutoring you did at your campus literacy center when you were a first-year student, but that experience is relevant if you are applying for a teaching position.

Quick Reference: Designing a Print Résumé

- Leave plenty of white space; avoid a crowded look to make your résumé more readable.
- Use a slightly different design for your name and contact information to make your résumé more attractive and attention getting (Figure 25.4).
- Use a table format for other sections, aligning items on the left and setting off headings in boldface or capitals. You may want to use the résumé template that comes with your word processing software or add other design elements. However, be careful not to overdesign the document—keep it simple and easy to read.
- Single-space all sections, and put an extra line of space between them.
- Proofread your résumé until you are sure the document has no grammatical or typographical errors.
- Use a standard font, such as Times New Roman, and print your résumé on 8½ × 11-inch white or off-white paper. Use black ink only.

Student Model Traditional Résumé

Name and contact information set off from rest of résumé

Sonja Jacques
7716 W. Birchwood Street
Chicago, IL 60648
(312) 555-5683
sonjaja1996@uic.edu

OBJECTIVE: To obtain an assistant to curator position at a museum

Education first, as typical for recent graduate

EDUCATION: **B.S., University of Illinois, Chicago Circle, June 2021.**
History major; International studies minor
GPA: 3.8 (on a 4-point scale)

Summer studies in Museum Curatorship, James Cook University, North Queensland, Australia, 2019.
Courses in artifact preservation, program management, museum funding.

EMPLOYMENT: **Work-study employee, UIC University Library, fall 2019–spring 2021.**
Trained work-study employees in library policies; shelved returned books.

Intern, Smithsonian Institution, Washington, DC, summer 2020.
Conducted museum tours for school groups; catalogued textual archives; assisted researchers.

Sales clerk, Moheiser's, Park Ridge, IL, summer 2017–spring 2019.
Organized inventory; waited on customers; learned apparel business.

Tutor, Ebinger School, Chicago, IL, 2018–2020.
Coached 7th graders in Spanish grammar and vocabulary; evaluated students' conversational Spanish skills.

SPECIAL SKILLS AND HONORS:
Fluent in Spanish.
Experience with *Microsoft Office, Adobe InDesign,* and internet research.
President, Phi Kappa Phi Honor Society, UIC chapter, 2021.
Dean's list, 2020–2021.

REFERENCES: Available on request.

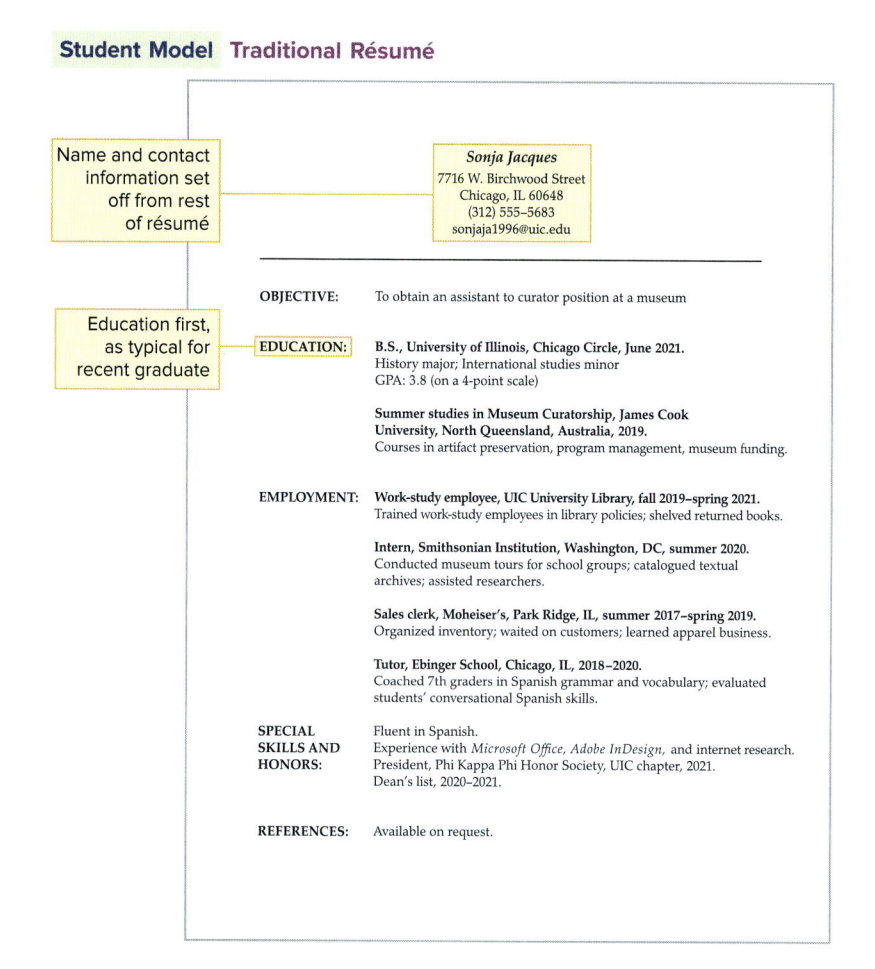

FIGURE 25.4
Sample printed résumé

> **More about**
> Document design (ch. 9), 184–98

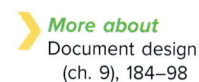

1. Traditional print résumés

A résumé (Figure 25.4) arranges information in standard categories and a familiar sequence to make it easy for prospective employers to glean your qualifications quickly. This is not the place to demonstrate your flair for creative writing or flamboyant design. (The Quick Reference box on page 547 includes some basic guidelines for designing and formatting a print résumé.) Here are some tips to help you keep the content of your résumé on track:

- Arrange each section in reverse chronological order, with most recent job or degree first. If there are major gaps in your work history, or if you have changed careers, you may want to organize your résumé according to the skills that are particularly relevant to the job you are applying for. Keep in mind, however, that most employers prefer to read résumés in reverse chronological order.

- Use active verbs and parallel construction throughout. For example, if you use *managed* for the first verb, you might use *organized* and *researched* thereafter.

- Limit your résumé to one page unless your work experience is extensive. Most recent college graduates should write a one-page résumé.

> **More about**
> Active versus passive voice, 562, 593–94
> Parallelism (ch. 28), 578–85

Most résumés include the following sections:

Contact information List your full name, mailing address, phone number, and email address at the top of the résumé. If you have separate home and school addresses, give them both, but make it clear to the recipient (perhaps in your cover letter) how and when you can be contacted at each location.

Career objective Indicate the specific position you are applying for or your career objective. Instead of *position in publishing,* say *entry-level editorial position in children's publishing.*

> **More about**
> Portfolios, 106–7

Education List the degrees you hold (college and above), the institutions that granted them, the date you received them (or anticipate receiving them), and your major and minor. Mention any honors such as being on the dean's list, and include your grade-point average if it is high (say, 3.5 or above on a 4-point scale). Include certificates, such as teaching certification.

Employment history Give the names and addresses of employers, titles of jobs, primary duties, and dates of employment.

Skills, awards, or memberships List computer skills (such as proficiency in *InDesign, Excel,* or *Photoshop*) and other skills that are relevant to the job, such as fluency in a foreign language. Include awards and memberships that are pertinent. For example, if you were applying for a job at a community organization, you would want to state that you served as a volunteer and on the board of directors of Big Brothers Big Sisters.

References Provide names, mailing addresses, phone numbers, and email addresses of three to six people who have agreed to serve as your references, or at the bottom of your résumé add *References available on request.* In either case, be sure to obtain permission to list someone as a reference in advance.

Student Model Scannable, Optimized Résumé

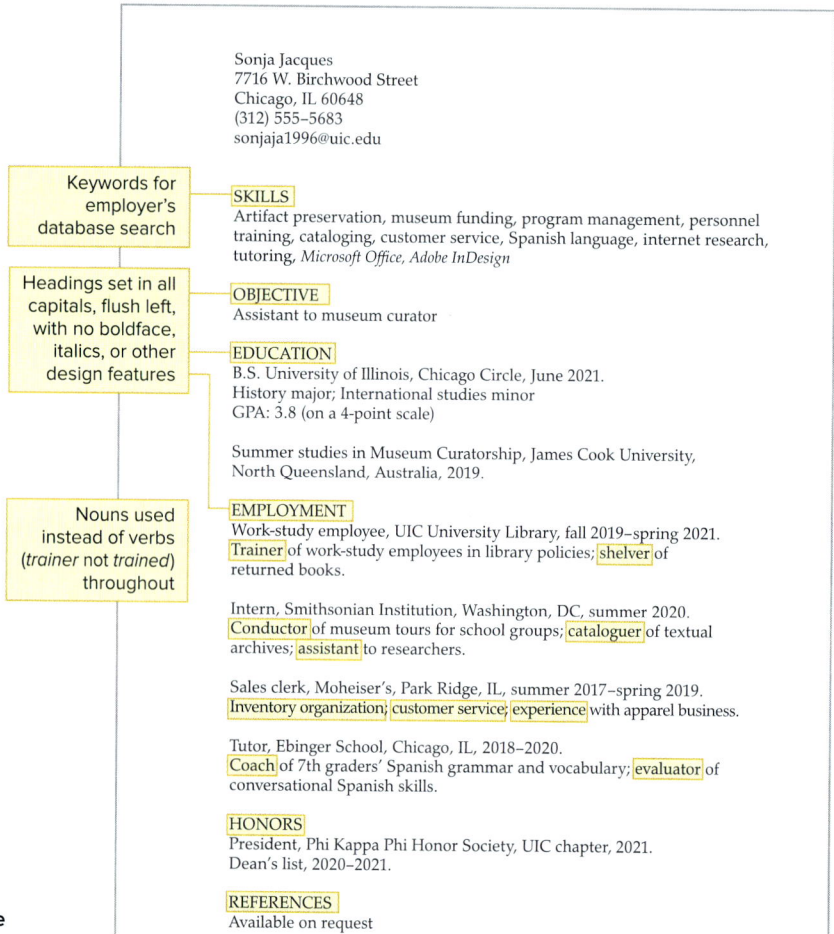

Sonja Jacques
7716 W. Birchwood Street
Chicago, IL 60648
(312) 555-5683
sonjaja1996@uic.edu

SKILLS — *Keywords for employer's database search*
Artifact preservation, museum funding, program management, personnel training, cataloging, customer service, Spanish language, internet research, tutoring, *Microsoft Office, Adobe InDesign*

OBJECTIVE — *Headings set in all capitals, flush left, with no boldface, italics, or other design features*
Assistant to museum curator

EDUCATION
B.S. University of Illinois, Chicago Circle, June 2021.
History major; International studies minor
GPA: 3.8 (on a 4-point scale)

Summer studies in Museum Curatorship, James Cook University, North Queensland, Australia, 2019.

EMPLOYMENT
Work-study employee, UIC University Library, fall 2019–spring 2021. **Trainer** of work-study employees in library policies; **shelver** of returned books.

*Nouns used instead of verbs (*trainer* not *trained*) throughout*

Intern, Smithsonian Institution, Washington, DC, summer 2020. **Conductor** of museum tours for school groups; **cataloguer** of textual archives; **assistant** to researchers.

Sales clerk, Moheiser's, Park Ridge, IL, summer 2017–spring 2019. **Inventory organization; customer service; experience** with apparel business.

Tutor, Ebinger School, Chicago, IL, 2018–2020.
Coach of 7th graders' Spanish grammar and vocabulary; **evaluator** of conversational Spanish skills.

HONORS
President, Phi Kappa Phi Honor Society, UIC chapter, 2021.
Dean's list, 2020–2021.

REFERENCES
Available on request

FIGURE 25.5
Sample scannable résumé

Writing Responsibly — Representing Yourself

When the job ad calls for a "claims adjuster" and you've done that work but with the title "claims specialist," feel free to list "claims adjuster" under your Skills section. But if you've just been an intern who's done errands for claims adjusters, don't list "claims adjuster" as a skill. A résumé that represents you falsely might get you a job—for a short while—and a reputation in the industry that you wouldn't want to live with.

2. Scannable, optimized electronic résumés

If you are going in person to apply for a job, you may want to take a traditional print résumé with you. Otherwise, you are far more likely to be transmitting your résumé electronically, within the text of an email message, as an email attachment, or on your website. Your prospective employer may want to scan your résumé into a database of applicants. To meet this requirement, a traditional print résumé needs to be revised and redesigned so that it is easily scannable (see Figure 25.5):

- Make your electronic résumé machine readable, in case your prospective employer uses an applicant tracking system (ATS). Adecco, a website for employers and job seekers, offers useful tips for machine-readable résumés.

- Position all copy flush with the left margin. Use only capitals to set off headings. Eliminate italics, boldface, and all other design or format features.

- Wherever possible, change your skills from verbs (*supervised*) to concise nouns (*supervisor of*). If you have the job description, try to use the keywords it mentions. (Employers frequently use keywords to screen out inappropriate applications.)

- Especially when they receive numerous applications, employers may use a pattern-recognition software that scans résumés to see who has the basic qualifications named in the job ad. It is advisable to modify your résumé for each job, "optimizing" it with a section located near the top of the résumé titled "Skills" that includes keywords matched to the job ad.

- Below your contact information, list keywords from your résumé, such as titles of positions you have held (*assistant manager*) or skills you possess (*Spanish*).

- When your résumé is complete, email it to yourself first, to make sure it is error-free and the layout is readable.

NOTE Conventions for electronic or scannable résumés change over time and may vary from company to company. Check with your prospective employer to make sure your résumé fits the company's requirements.

Make It Your Own

Find an appealing job ad in a local newspaper or website, or find a posting in your school's job center. Then draft a résumé for the position following the recommendations in the section above.

Work Together

In groups of three or four, review each other's résumés. How could you rephrase the career objectives to tailor them more specifically to the job description? How might you revise the résumé to make it more appealing to the target audience?

> **Student Models**
> Research projects:
> "Fast Fashion," Isabel Beck, 383–96
> "Inmate Access to Technology," Brianna Davids, 159–74
> "A Field Research Report on the Mental Health of College Students," Emily Durand, 516–28
> "Nature Versus Nurture," Robyn Worthington, 430–38

25f Writing Reports and Proposals

As a student, you may have written reports about research you have conducted. You may have written proposals as well, perhaps suggesting to your college administration that campus parking be expanded. In this case, you would have done some research on parking problems to back up your suggestions. When you write as an employee or as a volunteer, reports and proposals have these same attributes: They provide information for a specific purpose, they usually involve research and analysis, and they may suggest some kind of change. Proposals, in particular, offer solutions for problems and seek funding for the project.

Reports and proposals may vary greatly in length, from a single page to more than a hundred pages. Long reports and proposals usually follow specific formats (which are dictated by the organization you are writing for), they include a table of contents, and they are divided into sections (with subheadings) such as the following:

- **Abstract, executive summary, or overview.** A one-paragraph summary of the entire report or proposal. It highlights the purpose, major findings, and conclusions or recommended actions.

- **Introduction or statement of the problem.** A discussion of the topic or problem that explains succinctly what is at issue and why it is important.

- **Research methods and results.** A clear description of how you gathered information and what you discovered from your research. If appropriate, use graphs or tables to bolster your written explanation.

- **Conclusion or proposed solution.** A discussion of the relevance of your report or of the specific solution you are proposing.

> **More about**
> Choosing the appropriate information graphic, 78–80
> Revising information graphics, 82–85
> Persuasive arguments, 144, 150–53
> Tone, 20–21, 159, 599, 604–6, 607

Professional Model Report

NATIONAL STRATEGY FOR THE COVID-19 RESPONSE AND PANDEMIC PREPAREDNESS

JANUARY 2021

Executive Summary

✶ ✶ ✶ ✶ ✶

We can and will beat COVID-19. America deserves a response to the COVID-19 pandemic that is driven by science, data, and public health — not politics. Through the release of the National Strategy for the COVID-19 Response and Pandemic Preparedness, the United States is initiating a coordinated pandemic response that not only improves the effectiveness of our fight against COVID-19, but also helps restore trust, accountability and a sense of common purpose in our response to the pandemic.

On January 9, 2020, the World Health Organization announced that there were 59 cases of coronavirus-related pneumonia. Just one year later, the United States has experienced over 24 million confirmed COVID-19 cases and over 400,000 COVID-19 deaths. America has just 4% of the world's population, but 25% of the world's COVID-19 cases and 20% of all COVID-19 deaths. And our nation continues to experience the darkest days of the pandemic, with record numbers of cases, hospitalizations and deaths. Over 77,000 Americans lost their lives to COVID-19 in December, and across our nation businesses are closing, hospitals are full, and families are saying goodbye to their loved ones remotely.

The National Strategy provides a roadmap to guide America out of the worst public health crisis in a century. It outlines an actionable plan across the federal government to address the COVID-19 pandemic, including twelve initial executive actions issued by President Biden on his first two days in office:

The National Strategy is organized around seven goals:

1. Restore trust with the American people.
2. Mount a safe, effective, and comprehensive vaccination campaign.
3. Mitigate spread through expanding masking, testing, data, treatments, health care workforce, and clear public health standards.
4. Immediately expand emergency relief and exercise the Defense Production Act.
5. Safely reopen schools, businesses, and travel while protecting workers.

FIGURE 25.6 Sample report
Source: https://www.whitehouse.gov/wp-content/uploads/2021/01/National-Strategy-for-the-COVID-19-Response-and-Pandemic-Preparedness.pdf

For a proposal, be sure to help readers see that your solution is preferable to other possible solutions and that it is feasible in terms of financing, staffing, or other potential roadblocks.

(The cover and first page of the executive summary of a report on the response to the COVID-19 pandemic appear in Figure 25.6.)

As you draft a report or proposal, maintain an objective tone, and include only relevant and reliable information. Keep your purpose and audience in mind. It is not unusual for reports and proposals to be read by many different people (such as managers, sales representatives, and accountants). When this is the case, think about their various concerns and questions. For example, if you are proposing that the sales staff have larger, more expensive cars, how will you justify the extra cost to the financial experts?

25g Writing Press Releases

Press, or *media, releases,* like the one shown in Figure 25.7, are brief articles that announce events to newspapers, magazines, and online media outlets. If you work in the advertising or marketing department of an organization, part of your job might be writing press releases. Similarly, you could write them as a volunteer for a local charity or sporting club. Regardless of the organization they are written for, press releases follow a standard format because reporters and editors need to read them quickly and decide whether to use the information they contain. Here are some guidelines to follow when drafting a press release:

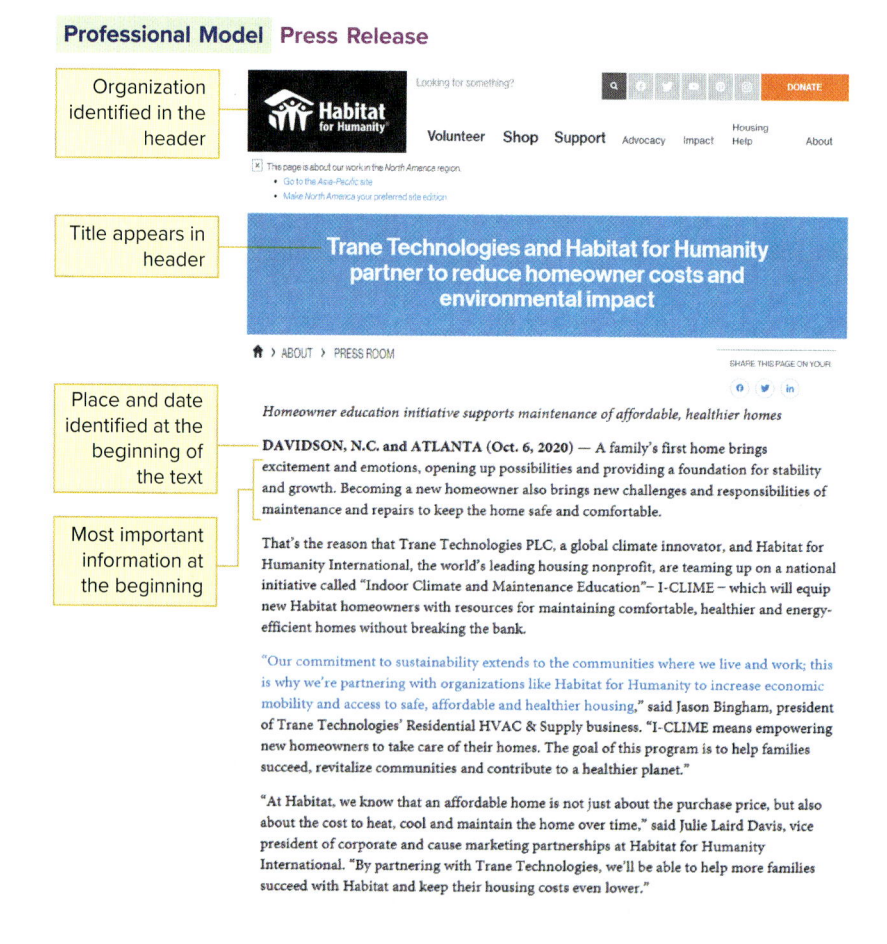

Professional Model Press Release

Organization identified in the header

Habitat for Humanity

Looking for something?   DONATE
Volunteer Shop Support Advocacy Impact Housing Help About

This page is about our work in the North America region.
- Go to the Asia-Pacific site
- Make North America your preferred site edition

Title appears in header

Trane Technologies and Habitat for Humanity partner to reduce homeowner costs and environmental impact

> ABOUT > PRESS ROOM   SHARE THIS PAGE ON YOUR

Homeowner education initiative supports maintenance of affordable, healthier homes

Place and date identified at the beginning of the text

DAVIDSON, N.C. and ATLANTA (Oct. 6, 2020) — A family's first home brings excitement and emotions, opening up possibilities and providing a foundation for stability and growth. Becoming a new homeowner also brings new challenges and responsibilities of maintenance and repairs to keep the home safe and comfortable.

Most important information at the beginning

That's the reason that Trane Technologies PLC, a global climate innovator, and Habitat for Humanity International, the world's leading housing nonprofit, are teaming up on a national initiative called "Indoor Climate and Maintenance Education"– I-CLIME – which will equip new Habitat homeowners with resources for maintaining comfortable, healthier and energy-efficient homes without breaking the bank.

"Our commitment to sustainability extends to the communities where we live and work; this is why we're partnering with organizations like Habitat for Humanity to increase economic mobility and access to safe, affordable and healthier housing," said Jason Bingham, president of Trane Technologies' Residential HVAC & Supply business. "I-CLIME means empowering new homeowners to take care of their homes. The goal of this program is to help families succeed, revitalize communities and contribute to a healthier planet."

"At Habitat, we know that an affordable home is not just about the purchase price, but also about the cost to heat, cool and maintain the home over time," said Julie Laird Davis, vice president of corporate and cause marketing partnerships at Habitat for Humanity International. "By partnering with Trane Technologies, we'll be able to help more families succeed with Habitat and keep their housing costs even lower."

I-CLIME will launch in Charlotte, N.C., with a series of educational resources for Habitat homebuyers focused on topics including preventative maintenance, appliance care and warranties, as well as strategies for energy efficiency and indoor air quality. Habitat for Humanity and Trane Technologies expect the partnership to expand to additional markets in 2021 to benefit hundreds of families, helping to reduce the energy intensity and greenhouse gas emissions for those households served.

Trane Technologies employees will also volunteer with Habitat for Humanity on local home builds, as well as support fundraising and in-kind giving. These efforts are part of the company's 2030 Sustainability Commitments that include a pledge to reduce its customers' carbon emissions by 1 gigaton — 2% of the world's annual emissions, bring its own operations to carbon neutral, and create community opportunities through investments in education and workforce development, housing and comfort, and food and wellness.

About Habitat for Humanity

Driven by the vision that everyone needs a decent place to live, Habitat for Humanity began in 1976 as a grassroots effort on a community farm in southern Georgia. The Christian housing organization has since grown to become a leading global nonprofit working in local communities across all 50 states in the U.S. and in more than 70 countries. Families and individuals in need of a hand up partner with Habitat for Humanity to build or improve a place they can call home. Habitat homeowners help build their own homes alongside volunteers and pay an affordable mortgage. Through financial support, volunteering or adding a voice to support affordable housing, everyone can help families achieve the strength, stability and self-reliance they need to build better lives for themselves. Through shelter, we empower. To learn more, visit habitat.org.

About Trane Technologies

Trane Technologies is a global climate innovator. Through our strategic brands Trane and Thermo King, and our environmentally responsible portfolio of products and services, we bring efficient and sustainable climate solutions to buildings, homes and transportation. www.tranetechnologies.com.

FIGURE 25.7 Sample press release
Source: www.habitat.org/newsroom/2020/trane-technologies-and-habitat-humanity-partner-reduce-homeowner-costs-and

- Use your organization's letterhead, if possible, and include all pertinent contact information (address, phone number, email address, website URL, and so on).
- At the top of the first page, type *For Immediate Release* and the date.
- Include an article title in bold or capital letters.
- To enable editors to cut your release for length easily, put the most important information up front and less important details toward the end.
- Use an objective tone, and make sure the content is factual and newsworthy.

Make It Your Own

Draft a press release announcing a student activity on campus (real or imagined). Make sure to include the most important information in the first paragraph and to provide information that is newsworthy.

Work Together

Exchange press releases with a classmate, and take turns role-playing the position of editor of a local newspaper. Would you publish your partner's press release? Why or why not?

Part Seven

Style Matters
Writing Engagingly

- **26** Writing Concisely 558
- **27** Using Coordination and Subordination 565
- **28** Using Parallelism 578
- **29** Engaging Readers with Variety and Emphasis 586
- **30** Choosing Appropriate Language 596
- **31** Choosing Effective Words 604
- **32** Using the Dictionary and Spelling Correctly 613

26 Writing Concisely

IN THIS CHAPTER

a. Eliminating wordiness, 559

b. Eliminating repetition, 561

c. Avoiding indirect constructions, 562

d. Consolidating, 563

> **More about**
> Sentence length and variety, 587

Young children just learning to play soccer tend to swarm around the ball, each one duplicating the effort of the others, so that they move the ball toward the goal uncertainly. With practice and time, however, players learn to work together efficiently to control the ball. Every player counts; none wastefully duplicates the work of another.

Wordy writing is like young children's soccer: The point gets made haltingly if at all. Sentences crowded with unnecessary words compel readers to separate what matters from what does not. *Concise* writing, in contrast, is like the play of a practiced team: Each point is made forcefully and without duplication of effort.

Every word counts. Consider this example:

WORDY The fact is that there is only one thing that should make us experience the emotion of fear and that is to all intents and purposes the emotion of fear itself.

CONCISE The only thing we have to fear is fear itself.

—Franklin Delano Roosevelt, first inaugural address

Writing Responsibly: Conciseness versus the Too-Short Paper

Effective writing should be concise but not necessarily brief. Concise writing provides readers with all the information they need without distractions, but it does not skimp on essential detail. It may take a long sentence to express a complex thought. Do not shortchange your readers—or your ideas—by omitting necessary detail.

to AUDIENCE

Style Matters • Eliminating Wordy Expressions w **26a** 559

The first sentence is crowded with wordy expressions (*the fact is*), redundancies (*the emotion of fear*), and roundabout constructions (*there is only one thing*). The second, concise and direct, helped rally Americans to confront the Great Depression.

> **Quick Reference** Strategies for Writing Concisely
> - Cut wordy expressions. (559)
> - Cut ineffective or unnecessary repetition. (561)
> - Revise roundabout constructions. (562)
> - Consolidate phrases, clauses, and sentences. (563)

Most of us write inadvertently wordy first drafts. As you revise, look for opportunities to tighten your prose. The Quick Reference box above offers some strategies.

26a Eliminating Wordy Expressions

First-draft writing sometimes contains common but wordy expressions that pad and clutter sentences. As you revise, prune these away.

Conciseness What one culture considers wordy, another may consider elegant. Not only culture but also context affects what readers expect: In literary contexts and even in some personal writing, US readers sometimes appreciate rich, expansive sentences. In academic contexts, however, US readers usually prefer writing that is concise and to the point.

1. Empty phrases

Some wordy expressions, like *to all intents and purposes, in fact, the fact is,* and *in the process of,* carry no information, and you can delete them.

▸ My roommate was ~~in the process of~~ applying for the job, but ~~in fact~~ it had already been filled.

Similarly, intensifiers—modifiers like *absolutely, actually, definitely, really,* and *totally*—may add little meaning to the words they modify.

▸ The tourists were ~~absolutely~~ thrilled. None of them had ~~actually~~ seen a polar bear before.

Phrases built around words like *aspect, character, kind, manner,* and *type* are also often mere filler.

▸ They ~~are the kind of people who~~ have always ~~behaved in a generous manner.~~ *been generous.*

2. Roundabout expressions

Some wordy expressions say in many words what is better said with one.

Wordy Expression	Concise Alternative
at the present time	now (or delete entirely)
at that point in time	then (or delete entirely)
until such time as	until
at all times	always
at no time	never
most of the time	usually
in this day and age	today
due to the fact that	because
in spite of the fact that	although, even though
has the ability to	can
in the event that	if
in the neighborhood of	around

▶ ~~Due to the fact that~~ *Because* the housing market is ~~weak at this point in time,~~ *weak,* many homeowners are waiting to sell until ~~such time as~~ conditions improve.

3. Redundant expressions

Some wordy expressions are ***redundant,*** stringing together two or more words that say the same thing.

Wordy Expression	Concise Alternative
blue in color	blue
in close proximity	close
each and every	each (or every)
end result	result
few/many in number	few/many
final outcome	outcome
past history	history
plans for the future/ future plans	plans
repeat again	repeat
round in shape	round
sum total	total

> **Tech** **Style Checkers and Wordiness**
>
> Although they might occasionally flag an inappropriate roundabout construction, computer style checkers are generally unreliable judges of wordiness. Rely on readers—yourself, your instructor, writing center tutors, your friends—to help you determine what is and is not acceptable.

▸ The presenter's mistakes were ~~few in number,~~ *few,* but they cost her the *company* contract, and she plans ~~for the future~~ never to repeat them ~~again~~.

26b Eliminating Ineffective or Unnecessary Repetition

Ineffective or unnecessary repetition can dull your prose and tire your readers.

1. Repetition and redundancy

As you revise your writing, look for words repeated unnecessarily, whether exactly or in varied form.

DRAFT   Biographer Robert Caro's [informative] overview provides particularly revealing [information] about the Johnson administration.

REVISION   Biographer Robert Caro's informative overview is particularly revealing about the Johnson administration.

Redundancy, another form of unnecessary repetition, is not restricted to the kind of stock phrases listed in the previous section; it happens whenever one expression duplicates the meaning of another.

▸ The portrait is ~~a likeness~~ of Frida Kahlo.

A portrait *is* a likeness of a particular person.

2. Elliptical constructions

Sometimes grammatically necessary words can be omitted from a sentence when the context makes their meaning and function clear, and you can take advantage of such *elliptical constructions* to tighten your prose.

▸ On Friday mornings Ghazala does assigned readings, and on Friday ~~afternoons she does~~ *afternoons,* research.

26c Avoiding Indirect Constructions

Certain sentence patterns tend toward wordiness and indirection. These include *expletive constructions,* sentences in the *passive voice,* and sentences built around weak verbs.

> **More about**
> Expletive constructions, 759–60

1. Sentences that begin with *There are..., It is...*

Expletive constructions are sentences that begin with expressions like *there are, there is,* or *it is.* (Do not confuse *expletive* in this sense with its other sense of *swear word* or *curse.*) Revising to eliminate expletives will often make a sentence more direct and concise.

DRAFT There are several measures that institutions can take to support students.

REVISION Institutions can take several measures to support students.

2. Passive voice

> **More about**
> Passive versus active voice, 593–94, 709–11

In an active-voice sentence, the subject performs the action of the verb. In a passive-voice sentence, the subject receives the action.

ACTIVE <u>Jared</u> (subj.) <u>photographed</u> (verb) the bear.

PASSIVE <u>The bear</u> (subj.) <u>was photographed</u> (verb) by Jared.

Rewriting to use the active voice usually makes sentences more concise and direct.

DRAFT A motion was proposed by the committee chair that the vote be delayed until the cost of the program could be accurately determined by the finance subcommittee.

REVISION The committee chair proposed to delay the vote until the finance subcommittee could accurately determine the program's cost.

3. Sentences built around nouns derived from verbs

If the sentence is built around a weak verb such as *is, are, were,* or *was* (all forms of the verb *to be*), sometimes replacing the verb can produce a more concise and vivid result.

DRAFT The <u>destruction</u> (noun) of the town by the tornado <u>was</u> (verb) complete.

REVISION The tornado <u>destroyed</u> (verb) the town.

26d Consolidating Phrases, Clauses, and Sentences

You can often make your writing more concise by reducing *clauses* to *phrases* and clauses or phrases to single words.

> **clause** A word group with a subject and a predicate
> **phrase** A group of related words that lacks a subject, predicate, or both

DRAFT   Scientists cite glaciers, which have been retreating, and the polar ice caps, which have been shrinking, as evidence of global climate change.

REVISION   Scientists cite retreating glaciers and shrinking polar ice caps as evidence of global climate change.

Sometimes you can also combine two or more sentences into one more concise, effective sentence.

DRAFT   Scientists note that glaciers have been retreating and the polar ice caps have been shrinking. Most of them now agree that these phenomena are evidence of global climate change.

REVISION   Most scientists now agree that retreating glaciers and the shrinking polar ice caps are evidence of global climate change.

➔ EXERCISE 26.1 Editing for conciseness

Use the strategies described in this chapter to make the following passage concise and direct.

> It is a fact that citizen, or amateur, scientists have the ability to contribute to the work of professional scientists. They can be of use in many different scientific fields of endeavor. For example, in the area of biology, citizen scientists can report the observations that they make. They have the ability to report observations about bird migration, seasonal change, and other factors that they can view in the vicinity of their own backyards. The widespread, detailed data provided by amateurs can help scientists bring their studies to completion.
>   In the area of astronomy, discoveries that are very significant have been made by amateurs. These include the very first sightings of many comets. They also include important observations of variable stars. Variable stars are stars that change in brightness over time. There are organizations and even awards for amateur astronomers. This shows how important their work is.

Make It Your Own

Reread a piece of your writing, ideally a recent or current project, and look for sentences that could be made more concise. If you find any, make a note of the problem and how you could fix it, then add this to your list of areas to consider as you revise your prose.

Work Together

Working with two or three classmates, read a piece of each other's writing and identify where and how your classmates' sentences could be made more concise. Compare your results with those of the others in the group. What did each of you see that others did not? Write a few sentences reflecting on how this collaborative activity might help you revise your own work in the future.

Text Credit

Pg. 558: Franklin Delano Roosevelt, First Inaugural Address, March 4, 1933.

27 Using Coordination and Subordination

IN THIS CHAPTER

a. Coordinating terms, phrases, and clauses, 566

b. Coordinating effectively, 567

c. Subordinating information, 570

d. Combining coordination and subordination, 575

This photo, taken in the atrium of the National Gallery of Art in Washington, DC, shows a giant sculpture by Alexander Calder—a 920-pound, 76-foot-long mobile made of multicolored metal rods and plates. Despite its size and weight, the sculpture sweeps gracefully overhead. Calder achieved this elegant effect by carefully coordinating elements of equal weight and balancing heavy elements with a series of lighter subordinate elements that descend in a branching cascade from the cable that secures the mobile to the ceiling. The subordinated and coordinated elements combine to convey Calder's visual message.

Writers can similarly use coordination and subordination to craft sentences that best convey their intended meaning. *Coordination* establishes the equal weight or importance of two or more sentence elements.

equal weight
▶ We entered the museum, and a dramatic sight confronted us.

equal weight
▶ The mobile is made of rods and plates.

Tech **Style Checkers and Coordination and Subordination**

Using coordination and subordination requires you to figure out the logical relationships among the ideas you want to express and to decide on their relative importance, so that you can make these relationships clear to your audience. A computer style checker cannot do that for you.

565

Subordination establishes the supporting or modifying role of one or more sentence elements.

▶ Heavy elements balance lighter elements that descend in a branching cascade from the cable that secures the mobile to the ceiling.

(main idea — modifying subordinate idea — modifying subordinate idea)

27a Coordinating Terms, Phrases, and Clauses

Coordination can link or contrast two or more equally important words, *phrases,* or *clauses*.

> **phrase** A group of related words that lacks a subject, a predicate, or both
> **clause** A word group with a subject and predicate. An ***independent clause*** can stand alone as a sentence; a ***subordinate clause*** cannot.

1. Terms and phrases

To coordinate terms and phrases requires either a coordinating conjunction (such as *and, but, for, nor, or, so,* or *yet*) or a correlative conjunction (such as *both…and, either…or,* or *neither…nor*). Usually no punctuation separates two coordinated words or phrases.

> **More about**
> Coordinating and correlative conjunctions, 643

▶ Both Steven Spielberg and George Romero attended the New York Film Academy.

▶ London's Theatre Royal in Drury Lane has staged performances by the Shakespearean actor Edmund Kean and by the Monty Python comedy troupe.

Commas usually separate more than two terms or phrases in a coordinated series.

▶ From John Webster's point of view in 1612, the greatest playwright might have been George Chapman, William Shakespeare, or Ben Jonson.

2. Independent clauses

> **More about**
> Punctuating coordinated independent clauses, 671–79

To coordinate two independent clauses, use a comma and a coordinating conjunction, a semicolon, or a semicolon and a conjunctive adverb such as *for example, however, in addition,* or *therefore*.

- Today we consider Shakespeare to be the greatest English playwright, but his contemporaries regarded him as just one among many.

- Outkast's album *Speakerboxx/The Love Below* was a huge success; it remains the best-selling hip-hop album of all time.

- The play received glowing reviews and won a Tony award; however, it closed after only a short run.

27b Coordinating Effectively

Coordinating elements in a sentence gives them equal importance or weight. How you coordinate those elements shows your readers the relationship among them.

1. Using conjunctions to coordinate

Conjunctions differ in meaning, and some can have more than one meaning, depending on context (see the Quick Reference box on the next page).

A conjunction whose meaning does not match the relationship between coordinated elements might confuse readers and obscure the writer's point. In the following sentence, for example, changing *and* to *but* reveals what the writer intended to emphasize: the contrast between Einstein's youth and his accomplishments.

- Einstein was still young, ~~and~~ *but* he had revolutionized physics.

2. Using a semicolon to coordinate independent clauses

Use a semicolon to join two independent clauses that have a logical connection to each other. The second clause can contrast with the first, provide an example of it, or give a reason for it.

> More about
> Semicolons,
> 820–26

CONTRAST	During the polar winter, the sun never rises; during the polar summer, it never sets.
EXAMPLE	The movie was a financial success; it set a record for opening-day box office receipts.
EXPLANATION	She wanted to be sure to have the assignment done for tomorrow; Spanish is her favorite class.

Quick Reference: Conjunctions and Their Meaning

Meaning	Conjunctions	Examples
addition	and, both...and	**Both** advances in ship design **and** the introduction of the magnetic compass helped make possible the European voyages of discovery.
sequence	and	The lawyer turned **and** faced the jury.
cause and effect	so, for, (sometimes) and	The housing market has softened, **so** sellers have had to lower their prices.
choice	or, whether...or, either...or, nor, neither...nor	Tournament games can be played on neutral courts **or** home courts. **Neither** ESPN **nor** any other network wants to show empty arenas.
contrast	but, yet	The police raided the house, **but** the suspect had fled. The poll indicates support for the law **yet** doubt about its chance for passage.
	not just...but, not only...but also	**Not just** the NCAA **but** the teams and fans should have a voice in the decision. [In addition to contrasting the coordinated elements, these conjunctions emphasize one over the other, suggesting that the first is commonplace and expected, the second new and noteworthy.]

When you join clauses with a semicolon and a conjunctive adverb, the conjunctive adverb specifies the relationship.

▸ During the polar winter, the sun never rises**; in contrast,** during the polar summer, it never sets.

3. Avoiding inappropriate coordination

Coordination is inappropriate when it combines elements that are not of equivalent importance or weight. The coordinating conjunction in the following sentence, for example, puts an incidental fact—Einstein's year of birth—on an equal footing with a statement about his early accomplishments. The revision subordinates the minor information in a modifying phrase.

	coordinating conjunction
INAPPROPRIATE COORDINATION	Albert Einstein was born in 1879, and by 1905 he had published four important scientific papers.
	modifying phrase
REVISED	Albert Einstein, born in 1879, had published four important scientific papers by 1905.

4. Excessive coordination

In everyday speech, people often coordinate long strings of sentences with *and* and other conjunctions. What is acceptable in speech, however, quickly becomes tedious, even confusing, in writing. As you edit, look for such ***excessive coordination.***

EXCESSIVE COORDINATION	Steven Spielberg graduated from Saratoga High School, in Saratoga, California, in 1965, and he applied to the University of Southern California's film school three times, but he was rejected each time, so he finally decided to attend California State University at Long Beach, and while he was at Cal State he started an unpaid internship at Universal Studios, and an executive was impressed by his talent, so in 1969 he was allowed to direct a television episode there, and by 1975 he was directing films like *Jaws*, and that was his first big hit as a movie director, so perhaps in the end he was lucky to have been rejected by USC.
REVISED	Steven Spielberg, who graduated in 1965 from Saratoga High School in Saratoga, California, applied to the University of Southern California's film school three times and was rejected each time. Finally, he decided to attend California State University at Long Beach. While he was at Cal State, he started an unpaid internship at Universal Studios. An executive there was impressed by his talent, so in 1969 he was allowed to direct a television episode there. By 1975, he was directing films like *Jaws*, his first big hit as a movie director. Perhaps, in the end, he was lucky to have been rejected by USC.

EXERCISE 27.1 Eliminating inappropriate and excessive coordination

Edit the following sentences to eliminate excessive or inappropriate coordination.

EXAMPLE

Your parents probably encouraged you to start the day with a good ~~breakfast, so~~ *breakfast, and* now a five-year study suggests they were ~~right, but the~~ *right. The* study found that the more likely adolescents are to eat breakfast, the less likely they are to be overweight.

1. The study was conducted in the public schools of the Minneapolis–St. Paul area, and researchers found that there was a direct relationship between eating breakfast and body mass index (BMI), yet the more often an adolescent had breakfast, the lower was his or her BMI.

2. The adolescents studied were an average of 15 years old at the start of the study, and those who ate breakfast consumed more carbohydrates and fiber, received fewer calories from fat, so got more exercise.

3. The relationship between breakfast eating and BMI was consistent throughout the study's entire five years, but the researchers controlled for age, sex, race, socioeconomic status, smoking, and concerns about diet and weight.

4. The study only observed an association between breakfast-eating habits and body mass, yet it did not prove a causal relationship, and nevertheless, one of the authors said that the research provided some useful guidance for healthy eating.

5. He noted that eating a healthy breakfast would encourage healthy eating for the rest of the day, yet it might help to lessen the urge for fast food or vending-machine food, and parents could also contribute, he added, by setting a good example and having a good breakfast themselves.

27c Identifying Important Ideas and Supporting Information with Subordination

Unlike coordination, which links equal ideas, subordination indicates which part of the sentence contains your important ideas, and which parts contain supporting examples, explanations, and details. Putting information in a subordinate structure de-emphasizes it, showing that it is supporting material rather than a major idea.

> |———— main idea ————||———— main idea ————|
> ▸ The evidence is conclusive; my client is innocent.
>
> Coordination gives each idea equal weight.
>
> |———— subordinated idea ————||——— main idea ———|
> ▸ As the evidence proves conclusively, my client is innocent.
>
> The emphasis is on the client.
>
> |———— main idea ————||———— subordinated idea ———|
> ▸ The evidence proves conclusively that my client is innocent.
>
> The emphasis is on the evidence.

Subordination can also clarify the logical relationship among a series of ideas. The revised version of the following passage clarifies the chronological relationship among the facts listed in the draft, and it emphasizes the most significant fact—that comic books did not become widely popular until 1938.

DRAFT The first comic books appeared in the early 1920s. Nearly four decades earlier, comic strips had begun appearing in the major newspapers. Comic books did not gain widespread popularity until June 1938. Writer Jerry Siegel and artist Joe Shuster debuted their character Superman in June 1938.

REVISED Although comic books first appeared in the 1920s, which was nearly four decades after comic strips had begun to appear in the major newspapers, they did not gain widespread popularity until June 1938, when writer Jerry Siegel and artist Joe Shuster debuted their character Superman.

1. Subordinating techniques

To subordinate information within a sentence, put it in a subordinate clause, reduce it to a modifying phrase or word, or include it in an appositive.

- **Subordinate clause.** Subordinate clauses begin with a *subordinating* word, usually either a subordinating conjunction (such as *after, although, because, before, that,* or *when*) or a relative pronoun (such as *that, what, which, who,* or *whose*).

  > , whose reign was from 1473 to 1458 BCE,
  > ▸ Hatshepsut was one of only a few women to rule ancient Egypt.
  >   ∧
  > ~~Her reign was from 1473 to 1458 BCE.~~

> **More about**
> Subordinating conjunctions and relative pronouns, 654–56, 662–63

> **Quick Reference** — **Subordination and Punctuation**
>
> In most cases, a comma follows a subordinate structure that begins an independent clause.
>
> > After the 1965 Newport festival, fans complained about Dylan's switch from acoustic to electric guitar.
>
> A subordinate structure that interrupts or ends an independent clause may or may not be set off with punctuation, depending on whether the information in it is **essential** (restrictive) or **nonessential** (nonrestrictive). A structure is essential if it specifically identifies the word or words it modifies. No punctuation sets off interrupting or concluding restrictive structures.
>
> > Athletes who win Olympic gold medals often earn money by endorsing products.
>
> A structure is nonessential if the meaning or identity of the word or words it modifies is clear without it. A comma or other punctuation usually sets off interrupting or concluding nonessential structures. (See pp. 811–13.)
>
> > Michael Phelps, the most decorated Olympian of all time, is a published author.

- **Modifying phrase or word.**

    > ▶ <u>Enticed by months of clever advance marketing,</u> millions
    > ^
    > M̶i̶l̶l̶i̶o̶n̶s̶ of people bought the new multimedia smartphone within days of its release. T̶h̶e̶y̶ ̶h̶a̶d̶ ̶b̶e̶e̶n̶ ̶e̶n̶t̶i̶c̶e̶d̶ ̶b̶y̶ ̶m̶o̶n̶t̶h̶s̶ ̶o̶f̶ ̶c̶l̶e̶v̶e̶r̶ ̶a̶d̶v̶a̶n̶c̶e̶ ̶m̶a̶r̶k̶e̶t̶i̶n̶g̶.̶

- **Appositive.**

    > ▶ The sculpture sweeps <u>, a giant mobile made of multicolored metal rods and plates,</u> gracefully overhead. I̶t̶ ̶i̶s̶ ̶a̶ ̶g̶i̶a̶n̶t̶ ̶m̶o̶b̶i̶l̶e̶ ̶m̶a̶d̶e̶ ̶o̶f̶ ̶m̶u̶l̶t̶i̶c̶o̶l̶o̶r̶e̶d̶ ̶m̶e̶t̶a̶l̶ ̶r̶o̶d̶s̶ ̶a̶n̶d̶ ̶p̶l̶a̶t̶e̶s̶.̶

> **appositive** A noun or noun phrase that renames a preceding noun or noun phrase

2. Choosing a subordinating term

Understanding the meaning of subordinating terms is essential to using subordination effectively (see the Quick Reference box on the next page).

Use a subordinating term whose meaning matches the relationship you intend to convey between a subordinate element and the element it modifies. The following sentence uses a term referring to cause in a context that calls for a term referring to purpose. Revising requires either changing the term or rewording the clause.

> **DRAFT** He ran for mayor because he could bring the town's budget under control.

REVISED He ran for mayor so that he could bring the town's budget under control.

or

He ran for mayor because he wanted to bring the town's budget under control.

Be particularly careful with the subordinating conjunctions *as* and *since*, which can refer ambiguously to both cause and time.

DRAFT As she was applying the last coat of varnish, Leena declared the restoration complete.

REVISED While she was applying the last coat of varnish, Leena declared the restoration complete.

or

Because she was applying the last coat of varnish, Leena declared the restoration complete.

Quick Reference: Subordinating Terms and Their Meaning

Meaning	Conjunctions	Examples
time	after, as, before, since, until, when, whenever, while	Comics grew in popularity after Superman appeared in 1938.
place	where, wherever	Home is where the heart is.
cause or effect	as, because, since, so that	Because of the water main break, traffic came to a standstill.
condition	even if, if, provided that, since, unless	If you finish the job today, you can take a vacation day tomorrow.
purpose	in order that, so that, that	She finished the job quickly so that she could have a day off.
identification	that, when, where, which, who	Svetlana Alexievich is the author who won the Nobel Prize for literature in 2015.
contrast or comparison	as, although, as if, even though, though, whereas	Although Einstein was still a young man, he had revolutionized physics.

3. Avoiding illogical subordination

State key ideas in an independent clause, and put illustrations, examples, explanations, and details in subordinate structures. Illogically subordinating a main idea to a supporting idea can confuse readers. The following sentence subordinates the idea of Einstein's accomplishments to the idea of his youth, illogically implying that he was young in spite of his accomplishments rather than accomplished in spite of his youth.

ILLOGICAL SUBORDINATION	Einstein was still young, although he had revolutionized physics.
REVISED	Although he was still young, Einstein had revolutionized physics.

4. Avoiding excessive subordination

Excessive subordination—stringing together too many subordinate structures—can make a sentence hard to read. The string of subordinate structures in the following sentence leaves readers unsure by the end where they began. The revision into two sentences clarifies the information the writer wants to convey.

EXCESSIVE SUBORDINATION	San Francisco, although generally an ideal habitat for peregrine falcons, is not entirely so, as became clear when rescuers had to remove falcon eggs from a nest on the Bay Bridge, despite the parents' protests, because once hatched, the fledglings would probably have drowned while learning to fly.
REVISED	San Francisco, although generally an ideal habitat for peregrine falcons, is not entirely so. Rescuers had to remove falcon eggs from a nest on the Bay Bridge, despite the parents' protests, because once hatched, the fledglings would probably have drowned while learning to fly.

EXERCISE 27.2 Eliminating excessive or illogical subordination

Edit the following passage to eliminate excessive or illogical subordination.

> An increasing number of high school seniors, although possessing excellent grades and good prospects for gaining admittance into the colleges of their choice, are opting for another alternative called a "gap year," which involves spending the year after graduating from high school doing something other than going to college. One recent graduate said she worked so hard in high school that she felt as if she had been continually running a marathon, without enough time for her three college-level physics courses, her clarinet practice, her band competitions, and her volunteer work, all of which often left her exhausted at the end of the day. She was accepted at several colleges, although she spent her gap year teaching English in Japan. This woman, who felt so pressured by her high school schedule that she chose to postpone college, has plenty of company, which includes a young man working on a farm in Costa Rica, a man who cares for injured sled dogs in Canada, a woman who builds guitars in England, and a woman who studies ballet in New York City, all activities that, according to the man in Costa Rica, "give you a break from being a student so you can reclaim the person inside." Even if many young people feel that their gap year gives them a refreshing, stimulating, and maturing change, they are delaying their start at college.

27d Using Coordination and Subordination Together

Used together, coordination and subordination can add grace and variety to your writing and help readers identify the points you want to emphasize. In this passage from a paper on Shakespeare's views on war in his play *Henry V*, student Jonathan Adler holds readers' interest and guides them to his concluding point by using both coordination and subordination in sentences of varied length.

> *More about*
> Variety and emphasis, 586–95

> Instead of glorifying war, Shakespeare shows us in *Henry V* that war is costly and that it has consequences. For his own security, however, Shakespeare had to disguise these views about war; speaking out against the government during his time was a risky thing to do. This need for disguise is where his dark comedy or satire comes in. In comedy and satire he can hide his anti-war sentiments while at the same time expressing them and mocking the entire process of going to war.
>
> —Jonathan Adler, Syracuse University

coord Style Matters • Using Coordination and Subordination

Coordination and Subordination Mastery of subordination is considered a sign of sophistication in American academic writing, but this is not true of all languages or cultures. If academic style in your native language or your style in other contexts favors coordination over subordination, you may need to make a conscious effort to use more subordinated structures in your writing. If your style favors subordination over coordination, you may have a tendency to oversubordinate your sentences in academic English. Your goal should be to strike a balance between both coordination and subordination.

EXERCISE 27.3 Combining sentences with coordination and subordination

Use coordination and subordination to combine sentences in the following passages in the way that seems most effective to you. Try to vary the coordination and subordination techniques you use.

1. Every holiday season, some people complain about the need to exchange gifts. Many are annoyed by the crowds, the expense, the materialism, and the overall stress of finding and buying suitable presents.

2. There are people who even refuse to take part in gift giving during the holidays. Some psychologists say that these people may be passing up an important opportunity to bond with their family and friends.

3. People's gift lists indicate who is important and unimportant in their lives, researchers note. A partner can use gift giving to show interest, strengthen a relationship, or even signal that the connection should end.

4. A recent study examined gift giving by pet owners. Researchers heard from owners why they gave their pets gifts. Owners said they wanted to make the pets happy. They also wanted to improve their pets' care and make them feel more comfortable.

5. Especially noteworthy is that the pets cannot return the gifts they receive. The act of giving itself makes the pet owners feel good. Simply knowing they are taking care of their pets gives them pleasure.

Make It **Your Own**

Reread a piece of your writing, ideally a recent or current project, and identify coordinate and subordinate structures. Look for any that need to be revised. If you find any, make a note in the margins of the paper identifying which section of this chapter explains the appropriate revision and add this to your list of areas to consider as you revise your prose.

Text Credit

Pg. 575: Jonathan Adler, Syracuse University.

28 Using Parallelism

IN THIS CHAPTER

a. Using paired and series items, 579

b. Maintaining parallelism in comparisons, 581

c. Including function words, 581

d. Maintaining parallelism in lists and outlines, 582

e. Using parallelism for emphasis, 584

Piero di Cosimo (Florentine, 1462–1521), Portraits of Giuliano and Francesco Giamberti da Sangallo, 1482–1485

These fifteenth-century portraits by Piero di Cosimo have two nearly matching, or parallel, parts. Each half of the diptych consists of similar—but not identical—features: paintings of two men, dark Florentine costumes, and idealized Italian landscapes in the background. The portraits are the same size, identically framed. Within this structure, however, the images differ: the faces, hair, clothing, caps, and background are all unique, and the men look at each other rather than in the same direction. Still, there are enough parallels in the composition that the portraits of the father-and-son architects Giuliano and Francesco Giamberti da Sangallo work as a pair, together suggesting the stature and humanity of the two subjects.

The artist uses visual parallelism to convey his subjects' connectedness despite their individuality. Similarly, writers use grammatical *parallelism*—the expression of equally important ideas in similar grammatical form—to increase the clarity of their writing and to emphasize important points. Abraham Lincoln, for example, deployed parallelism to powerful effect as he urged his fellow citizens to persevere in the Civil War in this closing passage from the Gettysburg Address:

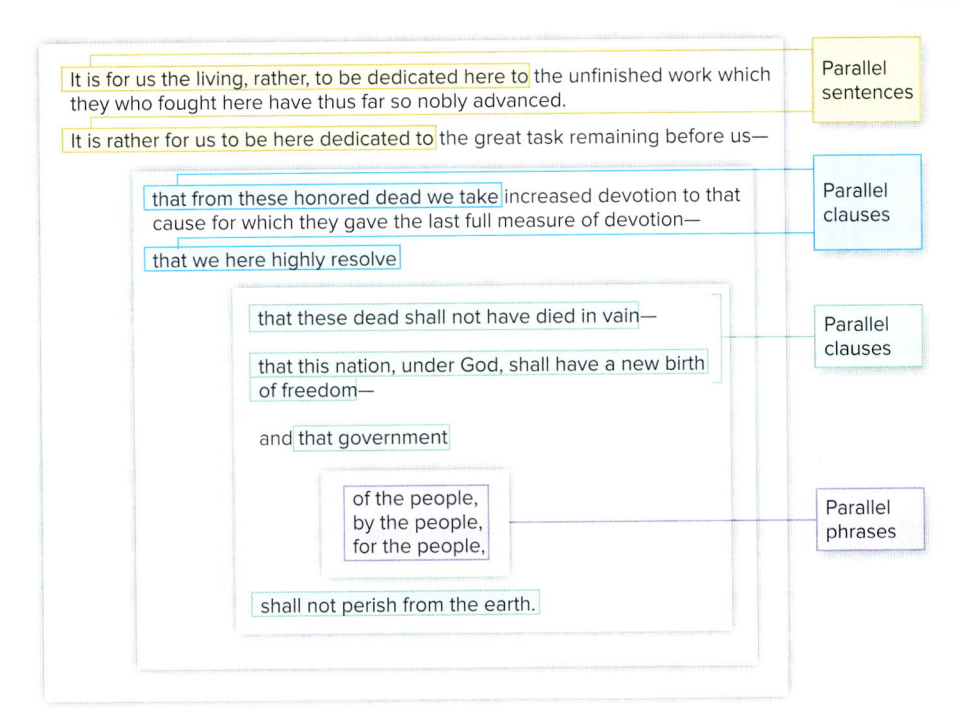

Style Matters • Using Parallelism for Paired Items and Items in a Series

```
It is for us the living, rather, to be dedicated here to the unfinished work which    ─ Parallel sentences
they who fought here have thus far so nobly advanced.
It is rather for us to be here dedicated to the great task remaining before us—
    that from these honored dead we take increased devotion to that    ─ Parallel clauses
    cause for which they gave the last full measure of devotion—
    that we here highly resolve
        that these dead shall not have died in vain—                    ─ Parallel clauses
        that this nation, under God, shall have a new birth
        of freedom—
        and that government
            of the people,                                              ─ Parallel phrases
            by the people,
            for the people,
        shall not perish from the earth.
```

28a Using Parallelism for Paired Items and Items in a Series

For clarity and to avoid awkwardness, use parallel form to express paired ideas and items in a series. Join subordinate clauses with similarly structured clauses, join phrases with similarly structured phrases, and join individual terms with other terms of the same form.

1. Items paired with a conjunction such as *and* or *but*

The English language has seven coordinating conjunctions: *and, but, for, nor, or, so,* and *yet*.

> More about
> Coordinating conjunctions, 643

▶ Too many girls learn at a young age to be passive and ~~that they should be~~ deferential.

The original uses *and* to pair an infinitive phrase (*to be passive*) with a subordinate clause (*that they should be deferential*); the revision uses *and* to join a pair of adjectives (*passive* and *deferential*).

▸ The course always covers the twentieth century through World War II but sometimes ~~touching~~ ^*also touches*^ on the beginning of the Cold War ~~is possible also~~.

In the revision, the verbs *covers* and *touches on* are in parallel form.

Deceptive Parallelism Parallel structure is found in most languages, so the concept will probably not be unfamiliar to you. Use caution, however, to ensure that items that seem parallel are all grammatically equivalent. For example, in "He spoke only positively and friendly about his previous professor," *positively* and *friendly* appear parallel, but *positively* is an adverb whereas *friendly* is an adjective. To be parallel, the sentence requires restating along these lines: "He had only positive and friendly things to say about his previous professor."

2. Items paired with correlative conjunctions

> **More about**
> Correlative conjunctions, 643

Conjunctions such as *both . . . and, either . . . or, neither . . . nor,* and *not only . . . but also* are **correlative conjunctions.** They come in pairs, and they link ideas of equal importance. Readers expect items linked by a correlative conjunction to be parallel. To be parallel, however, the items linked by the correlative conjunctions must have the same grammatical form.

FAULTY PARALLELISM   The defense attorney not only convinced the jury that her client had no motive for committing the crime, but also was nowhere near the scene of the crime when it occurred.

This suggests that the defense attorney, not her client, was nowhere near the crime scene.

STILL FAULTY   The defense attorney convinced the jury not only that her client had no motive for committing the crime, but also was nowhere near the scene of the crime when it occurred.

A clause beginning with *that* follows *not only,* so a clause beginning with *that* should follow *but also.*

REVISED   The defense attorney convinced the jury not only that her client had no motive for committing the crime, but also that he was nowhere near the scene of the crime when it occurred.

3. Items in a series

Like paired items, three or more equivalent items in a series should be in parallel form.

FAULTY PARALLELISM   The detectives secured the crime scene, examined it for clues, and the witnesses were then called in for questioning.

REVISED The detectives |secured| the crime scene, |examined| it for clues, and then |called in| the witnesses for questioning.

> **Tech** **Parallelism and Computer Style Checkers**
>
> A computer's style checker cannot identify ideas that merit parallel treatment in an otherwise grammatical sentence.

28b Maintaining Parallelism in Comparisons

When you compare two items with *than* or *as,* the items should be in the same grammatical form.

> **More about**
> Clear comparisons, 729–31
> Including function words, 753–54

▶ Getting into debt is unfortunately much easier than ~~to get~~ *getting* out of it.

28c Including Function Words to Maintain Parallelism

Words such as articles (*a, an, the*), conjunctions, and prepositions indicate the relationships among other words in a sentence. They should be included or repeated as needed in linked items for clarity and grammar as well as for parallelism.

▶ The trail leads over high mountain passes and *through* dense forests.

Trails lead *over* passes but *through* forests.

➔ EXERCISE 28.1 Correcting parallelism errors

Correct any errors in parallelism in the following sentences.

EXAMPLE

This spot offers a good view not only of herons but ~~you can~~ also *of* see egrets.

1. Many types of wading birds, some rare, are attracted to this island to rest during migration, to feed, and they nest here as well.
2. Perhaps surprisingly, this habitat is located not in a national park or wildlife refuge but it is found in the middle of New York harbor.
3. However, until 10 or 15 years ago, the area was inhospitable to wildlife because it was missing one crucial factor: not food or shelter but the presence of clean water.

4. Starting with the Clean Water Act of 1972 and accelerating within the last fifteen years with state legislation, regional planning, and as more federal funds were appropriated, the water in the harbor has become hospitable to wildlife.

5. Today, more than 2,000 pairs of shorebirds, including not only several species of herons, snowy egrets, but also great egrets, and glossy ibis nest on the different islands.

Writing Responsibly: Using Parallelism to Clarify Relationships among Ideas

An important component of the writing process is figuring out the *relationships* among your ideas and making those relationships clear to your readers. As you revise, ask yourself questions like these: What is the cause and what is the effect? What items are truly a part of the group and what items are not? Which ideas are important and which ideas provide supporting information?

Using parallelism can help you emphasize for your reader that certain ideas are of equal importance. (Coordination and subordination, discussed in the previous chapter, can also help you emphasize that ideas or information are of equal or unequal importance.)

Experimenting with some of the techniques you are learning in this chapter, and in other chapters in this part, can lead to new insights about your topic.

to AUDIENCE

28d Maintaining Parallelism for Items in Lists and Outlines

Each item in a list or an outline should be in the same grammatical form as the others.

1. Items in a list

Whenever you have a list of three or more items, those items should be in the same grammatical form. The following list is difficult to read in its draft form because the first and third items begin with independent clauses, whereas the other three begin with a noun followed by a bit of commentary. The revision puts them all in the noun followed by commentary form.

DRAFT LIST	REVISED
Among the top 10 most healthful foods, these are my favorites:	Among the top 10 most healthful foods, these are my favorites:
1. <u>Avocados are delicious unadorned.</u> I also enjoy them sliced in half with the hole filled with a mixture of olive oil and lime juice.	1. <u>Avocados.</u> They are delicious unadorned. I also enjoy them sliced in half with the hole filled with a mixture of olive oil and lime juice.

Style Matters • Maintaining Parallelism for Items in Lists and Outlines // **28d** **583**

2. <u>I like nuts because they are so portable.</u>

3. <u>Berries.</u> All of them are delicious, except blackberries.

4. <u>Yogurt.</u> I avoid the kind with fruit on the bottom.

5. <u>Garlic.</u> I like it, but it doesn't like me.

2. <u>Nuts.</u> I like them because they are so portable.

3. <u>Berries.</u> All of them are delicious, except blackberries.

4. <u>Yogurt.</u> I avoid the kind with fruit on the bottom.

5. <u>Garlic.</u> I like it, but it doesn't like me.

2. Items in outlines

Maintain parallelism in outlines and headings by keeping all items at the same level in the same form. In the original version of the following outline, three of the top-level headings—I, II, and IV—are noun phrases whereas III is a question. Likewise, under heading I, the first subheading begins with a noun whereas the second and third are **gerund** phrases, and under heading IV, the last item is an independent clause. Revising the outline so that the headings are parallel makes it easier to understand.

> **gerund** The *-ing* form of a verb used as a noun

DRAFT OUTLINE

I. Types of literary fraud
    A. Plagiarism
    B. Forging documents
    C. Misrepresenting the facts
II. Examples of literary fraud
    A. Kaavya Viswanathan
    B. Clifford Irving
    C. James Frey
III. Why do people commit literary fraud?
    A. Financial gain
    B. Personal glory
    C. Insecure
    D. Weak writing skills
    E. Busy schedule

REVISED OUTLINE

I. Types of literary fraud
    A. Plagiarism
    B. Forgery
    C. Misrepresentation
II. Examples of literary fraud
    A. Kaavya Viswanathan
    B. Clifford Irving
    C. James Frey
III. Motives for literary fraud
    A. Financial gain
    B. Personal glory
    C. Insecurity
    D. Weak writing skills
    E. Busy schedule

IV. Problems with literary fraud	IV. Problems with literary fraud
A. Copyright infringement	A. Copyright infringement
B. Breach of faith	B. Breach of faith
C. Readers take actions based on erroneous assumptions	C. Reader actions based on erroneous assumptions

> **More about**
> Parallelism and emphasis, 592–93

28e Using Parallelism to Create Emphasis

Placing ideas in parallel form highlights their differences and similarities.

▸ All the images are copies of the same original, the same size, and ~~they have equal space between them~~ *all are equally spaced* within a grid of rows and columns.

As the passage from Lincoln's Gettysburg address at the beginning of this chapter illustrates, parallelism can be a forceful tool for emphasizing important ideas. John F. Kennedy provides another example in his famous Inaugural Address. Notice how the President's parallelisms generate an almost musical cadence that drives us toward his concluding point.

> Let every nation know, whether it wishes us well or ill, that we shall pay any price, bear any burden, meet any hardship, support any friend, oppose any foe to assure the survival and the success of liberty.
>
> —John F. Kennedy

EXERCISE 28.2 Parallelism and emphasis

Use parallelism to combine and emphasize the ideas in the following groups of sentences.

EXAMPLE

The ancestor of the modern horse was a species that evolved in North America about 4 million years ~~ago. It~~ *ago,* spread to Eurasia over the Bering land ~~bridge. Horses~~ *bridge, and then* became extinct in North America at the end of the last Ice Age about 12,000 years ago.

Style Matters • Using Parallelism to Create Emphasis // **28e**

1. Scientists have long debated where and when the horse was domesticated. They have also debated where and when dogs and the pig were domesticated. The time and place of the domestication of other animals, such as cattle, sheep, and goats, is much clearer.

2. Dogs were domesticated before horses. Cattle were domesticated before horses. Goats were domesticated before horses. Pigs were domesticated before horses. Sheep were domesticated before horses.

3. Scientists now believe that horses were domesticated about 6,000 years ago in Central Asia. This conclusion is based on DNA evidence. It is also based on evidence obtained from archaeological remains. It is also based on studies of contemporary nomadic peoples whose lifestyles may resemble those of the people who first domesticated the horse.

4. All the evidence about horse domestication points to a complicated process. This process went on over a long time. This process occurred at many different places. This process was further complicated by climate changes during the last Ice Age, which altered the wild horses' habitat and forced them to migrate north.

Make It **Your Own**

Reread three pieces of your recent writing and identify examples of parallelism. Look for faulty parallelism, and if you find any, make a note in the margins of the paper identifying which section of this chapter explains the appropriate revision. Add this to your list of areas to consider as you revise your prose.

Text Credits

Pg. 579: Abraham Lincoln, The Gettysburg Address, November 19, 1863. **Pg. 584:** John F. Kennedy, Inaugural Address, January 20, 1961.

29 Engaging Readers with Variety and Emphasis

IN THIS CHAPTER

a. Varying sentence length, structure, 587

b. Varying sentence openings, 587

c. Creating emphasis with rhythm, 590

d. Creating emphasis with punctuation, 591

e. Using questions, commands, exclamations, 592

f. Using strategic repetition, 592

g. Choosing emphatic verbs, 593

h. Choosing active or passive voice, 593

In this painting, *At the Opera*, artist Mary Cassatt captures our interest with a variety of visual elements, among them the large figure of the woman in the foreground; the more sketchily rendered figures in the background; the curving form of the balconies; the bright points of red and white; and the contrasting large, dark areas. Cassatt also structures the painting to emphasize certain elements over others and to direct our attention to a story unfolding within the scene. Our eyes go first to the woman in the foreground; then we follow her gaze through her opera glasses and let the curve of the balcony railing draw our attention to the upper left, where a male figure also is looking through opera glasses—not toward the stage, however, but at the woman in the foreground.

Writers also use variety and emphasis to capture and hold their readers' attention and to direct those readers to the subtleties of the story being told. Speakers use intonation, tone of voice, and timing to avoid monotony and emphasize or de-emphasize particular words or phrases. Writers use variety and emphasis to help readers "hear" the words of the text in their mind's ear.

Quick Reference Achieving Variety and Emphasis

- Vary sentence length and structure. (587)
- Vary sentence openings. (587)
- Use rhythm strategically. (590)
- Choose appropriate punctuation. (591)
- Introduce questions, commands, and exclamations when appropriate. (592)
- Use strategic repetition. (592)
- Choose emphatic verbs and favor the active voice. (593)

29a Varying Sentence Length and Structure

Ask yourself whether your sentences are all the same length and type, or whether they vary. Confronting readers with page after page of sentences of the same or similar length—long, short, or in between—can tire them and make it hard for them to recognize important details. To hold readers' attention and direct it to the points you want to emphasize, vary the length of your sentences and include a mix of sentence structures: *simple, compound, complex,* and *compound-complex.*

Short sentences deliver information concisely and dramatically. They are most emphatic, however, when they are mixed with longer sentences. In the following passage, too many short sentences in a row create a choppy effect, leaving the reader with the impression that each point is equally important. The revision combines most of the short sentences into longer sentences that clarify the relationship among the ideas the writer wants to convey. The writer's main point is now dramatically isolated in the one short sentence that remains.

> **simple sentence** One independent clause and no subordinate clauses
> **compound sentence** Two or more independent clauses and no subordinate clauses
> **complex sentence** One independent clause with at least one subordinate clause
> **compound-complex sentence** Two or more independent clauses with one or more subordinate clauses

DRAFT   The whole planet is at risk. We need to put a stop to the wild spread of this disease. The key is education. First, we should educate those living with the virus. Then we should let them educate the world. They can help us win this war against HIV. They can help other people understand that everyone is vulnerable.

REVISION   With the whole planet at risk, we need to put a stop to the wild spread of this disease. The key is education. First, we should educate those living with the virus; then we should let them educate the world. They can help us win this war against HIV by helping other people understand that everyone is vulnerable.

29b Varying Sentence Openings

Ask yourself whether the subjects and verbs usually come at the beginning of your sentences. In the default structure of an English sentence, the subject comes first, then the verb, and then the direct object, if there is one. Reflecting this structure, most sentences start with the subject. However, a long string of subject-first sentences can make your text monotonous. Use modifying clauses and phrases to vary your sentence openings and to emphasize important information.

> **adverb** A word that modifies a verb, an adjective, another adverb, or an entire phrase or clause and that specifies how, where, when, and to what extent or degree

Adverbs and adverbial phrases and clauses   Where you place an ***adverb***, and the phrases and clauses that function as adverbs, affects the rhythm of a sentence and the information it emphasizes.

ADVERBIAL SUBORDINATE CLAUSE

- Stocks can be a risky investment because they can lose value.
- Because they can lose value, stocks can be a risky investment.
- Stocks, because they can lose value, can be a risky investment.

> **More about**
> Sentence structure, 645–59

ADVERBIAL PREPOSITIONAL PHRASES

- We were in the same lab for physics class last semester.
- Last semester, we were in the same lab for physics class.
- For physics class, we were in the same lab last semester.

NOTE Moving an adverb can sometimes alter the meaning of a sentence. Consider these two examples:

- The test was surprisingly hard.
- Surprisingly, the test was hard.

In the first, *surprisingly* modifies *hard,* suggesting that the writer found the test harder than expected; in the second, *surprisingly* modifies the whole clause that follows it, suggesting that the writer expected the test to be easy.

---

adjective A word that modifies a noun or pronoun with descriptive or limiting information

participial phrase A phrase in which the present or past participle acts as an adjective

Adjectival phrases The placement of *adjectives* and most adjectival phrases and clauses is less flexible than the placement of adverbs. However, participles and *participial phrases,* which act as adjectives, can often come at the beginning of a sentence as well as after the terms they modify.

- New York City's subway system, flooded by torrential rains, shut down at the height of the morning rush hour.
- Flooded by torrential rains, New York City's subway system shut down at the height of the morning rush hour.

subject complement An adjective, pronoun, or noun phrase that follows a linking verb and describes or refers to the subject of the sentence

An adjective phrase that functions as a *subject complement* can also sometimes be repositioned at the beginning of a sentence.

- The Mariana Trench is almost seven miles deep, making it the lowest place on the surface of the earth.
- Almost seven miles deep, the Mariana Trench is the lowest place on the surface of the earth.

> **More about**
> Placement of adjectives, 724–31

Appositives and absolute phrases An *appositive* is a noun or noun phrase that renames another noun or noun phrase. Because they designate the same thing, the appositive and the original term can switch positions.

> - The governor, **New York's highest official,** ordered an investigation into the subway system's failure.
> - **New York's highest official,** the governor, ordered an investigation into the subway system's failure.

An *absolute phrase,* consisting of a noun or pronoun with a participle, modifies an entire independent clause. It can often fall either before or after the clause it modifies.

> - **The task finally completed,** the workers headed for the parking lot.
> - The workers headed for the parking lot, **the task finally completed.**

Transitional expressions A *transitional expression* relates the information in one sentence to material that precedes or follows. Its placement affects the emphasis that falls on other parts of the sentence. The second passage below, for example, calls more attention to Superman's distinctiveness than the first does.

> More about Transitional expressions, 59–60

> - Most comic book characters from the 1930s quickly fell into obscurity. **However,** Superman was not one of them.
> - Most comic book characters from the 1930s quickly fell into obscurity. Superman, **however,** was not one of them.

EXERCISE 29.1 Varying sentence openings

Revise the following sentences to begin with something other than the subject.

EXAMPLE

Soaring in search of food, ravens
~~Ravens~~ patrol the misty blue sky high above the valley, ~~soaring in search of food.~~

1. The Canaan Valley, one of the highest valleys east of the Mississippi, was designated a National Natural Landmark in 1974.
2. This ecosystem, with its many species of plants and animals, is an example of northern forest.
3. It seems out of place, located here in West Virginia, a Mid-Atlantic state.
4. The valley is more than 3,000 feet deep and enjoys cool summers and snowy winters.
5. The valley is likely to remain wild and natural for many years to come because it is protected by federal and state governments.

29c Creating Emphasis with Rhythm

Sentences, like music, have rhythm, and within that rhythm, some beats get more stress than others. Readers readily notice the beginning of a sentence, where they usually find the subject, and they notice the end, where everything wraps up. Take advantage of readers' habits by slotting important or striking information into those positions. In the following example, the writer changed the subject of the sentence from *ready availability* to the more significant *free news* and moved *financial ruin* to the end, dramatically underscoring the seriousness of the challenge newspapers face.

DRAFT   The ready availability of free news on the internet threatens financial ruin for traditional newspapers.

REVISED Free news, readily available on the internet, threatens traditional newspapers with financial ruin.

A common way to organize information in longer sentences is with a cumulative or loose structure. A *cumulative sentence* begins with the subject and verb of an independent clause and accumulates additional information in subsequent modifying phrases and clauses.

▸ That's the news from Lake Wobegon, where all the women are strong, all the men are good-looking, and all the children are above average.

—Garrison Keillor, tag line from the radio show *A Prairie Home Companion*

A *periodic sentence,* in contrast, reserves the independent clause for the end, preceded by modifying details. The effect is to build suspense that highlights key information when it finally arrives.

▸ Through the center of town, up the strip, past the housing developments and shopping malls, street lights giving way to the thin streaming illumination of the headlights, trees crowding the asphalt in a black unbroken wall: that was the way to Greasy Lake.

—T. Coraghessan Boyle, "Greasy Lake"

An *interrupted periodic sentence* begins with the subject of the independent clause but leaves the conclusion of the clause to the end, separating the two parts with modifying details. In the following example, the subject of the sentence is highlighted in yellow, and the predicate is highlighted in blue.

▸ The archaeologist Howard Carter, peering through the small opening to the main chamber of Tutankhamen's tomb at treasures hidden from view for more than three millennia, when asked what he saw, replied "wonderful things."

An *inversion* is a sentence in which, contrary to normal English word order, the verb precedes the subject. Inverted sentences call attention to themselves. Used sparingly, they can help you emphasize a point or create a sense of dramatic tension.

▸ Into the middle of town [rode] [the stranger].
                               verb   subj.

Developing an Ear for Sentence Variety Many of the sentence structures that add variety to written English are uncommon in conversation and as a result may not come naturally to you even if you are fluent in conversational English. To develop an ear for sentence variety in your academic writing, try going through this chapter and imitating some of the structures it describes with examples of your own. Ask an instructor or another skilled writer of English to check your work to see if you have produced effective sentences.

29d Creating Emphasis with Punctuation

One way to draw your readers' attention to significant material is to place it at the end of a sentence after a colon or dash.

> **More about**
> Colons, 852–54
> Dashes, 847–49

▸ According to photographer William Klein, the advertising campaign for fashion designer John Galliano wasn't just influenced by Klein's visual techniques[—]it stole them.

▸ The judge had two words for Galliano's use of Klein's signature visual style[:] copyright infringement.

You can also draw attention to nonessential phrases or clauses within an independent clause when you set them off with dashes instead of commas.

> **More about**
> Essential and nonessential modifiers, 811–13

▸ The judge had two words[—]copyright infringement[—]for Galliano's use of Klein's signature visual style.

The punctuation between two independent clauses can affect the way readers perceive the relationship between them. A dash (as we have just seen) or a period creates a more emphatic separation than a semicolon or a comma and coordinating conjunction.

> **More about**
> Periods, 843–44
> Semicolons, 820–26
> Commas, 802–19

▸ The jury convicted the defendants[.] The judge sentenced them to life.

▸ The jury convicted the defendants[;] the judge sentenced them to life.

▸ The jury convicted the defendants[, and] the judge sentenced them to life.

29e Using Questions, Commands, and Exclamations

> **More about**
> Sentence categories, 657–58

Most sentences are *declarative*: They make a statement—declare something—about their subjects. Other types of sentences include questions, commands, and exclamations. When used sparingly, these can add variety to prose and draw attention to important ideas. Overused, they sound gimmicky or childish.

Questions in academic writing tend to be **rhetorical**; they are meant to call attention to an issue, not to elicit an answer.

> ▸ [F]or all our focus on happiness it is by no means clear that we are happier as a result. Might we not even say that our contemporary concern is something of an inauspicious sign, belying a deep anxiety and doubt about the object of our pursuit? Does the fact that we worry so much about being happy suggest that we are not?
>
> —Darrin M. McMahon, "The Pursuit of Happiness in Perspective"

> **More about**
> Person, 492–93

Commands are a type of second-person sentence: The subject of a command, even when unstated, is always *you*. The second person is best reserved for addressing the reader directly, and commands, in particular, are useful for describing a process or conveying advice.

> ▸ Your feminist premise should be: I matter. I matter equally.
>
> —Chimamanda Ngozi Adichie, *Dear Ijeawele, or a Feminist Manifesto in Fifteen Suggestions*

Exclamations are emphatic statements or expressions of strong emotion. Interjections are exclamatory words that stand alone within a sentence. Both are usually punctuated with exclamation marks, and both are rare in academic writing.

> ▸ "I wish I knew all about her!" said Dorothea. "I wonder how she bore the change from wealth to poverty. I wonder whether she was happy with her husband!"
>
> —Mary Ann Evans [George Eliot], *Middlemarch: A Study of Provincial Life*

29f Using Strategic Repetition

Redundancy and other forms of unnecessary repetition can add clutter and bore readers. Repetition is sometimes necessary, however, for clarity and to maintain parallelism.

Writers can also use repetition strategically for emphasis, calling attention to important ideas. Repetition for emphasis works especially well within parallel structures, as in this sentence from a student project.

▸ Some children are never told that they are adopted, never given the opportunity to search for their biological parents.

—Jessica Toro, Syracuse University

> **More about**
> Parallelism, 578–85

Toro could have used *or* instead of the second *never,* but the repetition dramatically underscores her concern about the consequences of a particular policy toward adopted children.

29g Creating Emphasis with Emphatic Verbs

Verbs that describe an action directly are often more emphatic than verbs like *be, have,* or *cause* that combine with nouns or adjectives to describe an action indirectly.

▸ Many economists ~~have a belief~~ *believe* that higher gasoline taxes would ~~be beneficial to~~ *benefit* the economy in the long run. The increased costs would ~~have a stimulating effect on~~ *stimulate* research into alternative energy sources and eventually ~~cause a reduction in~~ *reduce* both carbon emissions and our dependence on oil.

29h Choosing the Active or Passive Voice

> **More about**
> Voice in verbs, 695, 709–11
> Passive voice and wordiness, 562

In an active-voice sentence, the subject performs the action of the verb; in a passive-voice sentence, the subject receives the action of the verb. Active-voice sentences are usually more emphatic, direct, and concise than their passive-voice counterparts.

ACTIVE VOICE: EMPHATIC

▸ Rising oil prices stimulate research into alternate energy sources.

PASSIVE VOICE: UNEMPHATIC

▸ Research into alternative energy sources is stimulated by rising oil prices.

However, if you want to emphasize the recipient of an action over the performer, or agent, of the action, the passive voice can be an appropriate choice.

In this famous sentence from his address to the nation on December 8, 1941, for example, President Franklin Delano Roosevelt used the passive voice to focus on the United States as the victim of the attack on Pearl Harbor.

> Yesterday, December 7th, 1941—a date which will live in infamy—the United States of America was suddenly and deliberately attacked by naval and air forces of the Empire of Japan.

Because it can allow the agent to remain unidentified, the passive voice can also be an appropriate choice when the identity of the agent is unknown or unimportant.

> According to the coroner, the victim had been murdered between 3 and 4 in the morning.

The identity of the murderer is unknown.

> *The Second Sex*, a major work in feminist philosophy, was first published back in 1949.

The focus is on the date of publication, not the specific identity of the author.

Similarly, in science writing, the passive voice allows the description of procedures without constant reference to the individuals who carried them out.

> The effects of human activities on seagrasses were studied at Sandy Neck and Centerville beaches from 31 March 2016 to 30 March 2019.

Writing Responsibly: Voice and Responsibility

Because the passive voice allows the agent of an action to remain unnamed, it lends itself to misuse by people avoiding responsibility for their own or others' mistakes and misdeeds. Consider, for example, the classic dodge of the cornered politician or bureaucrat: "Mistakes were made."

Be on the lookout for this evasive use of the passive voice in your own writing and the writing of others. It is a usage that comes all too readily to hand when we need to convey unflattering or damaging information about ourselves or those we represent.

to TOPIC

EXERCISE 29.2 Emphatic verbs, active verbs

Revise each of the following sentences, replacing indirect expressions with emphatic verbs and, when appropriate, changing verbs from passive to active voice.

EXAMPLE

Many people ~~have a lack of awareness about~~ *are not aware of* how paperback books ~~gained in popularity~~ *became popular* in the United States.

1. Decades before the internet and digital communications, soldiers in World War II lacked small, portable sources of entertainment during their down time.
2. In the late 1930s, just before the US joined the Allied forces, paperback books began to be available on the US market.
3. Armed Services Editions (ASEs) were distributed to the soldiers during the war.
4. These popular paperbacks came home with the soldiers returning from war and became known to the general population.
5. By 1949, sales of paperback books were greater than sales of hardcopies in the US.

Make It **Your Own**

Reread three pieces of your recent writing and edit them for variety and emphasis using the strategies covered in this chapter. If you find many sentences needing revision, add variety and emphasis to your list of areas to consider as you revise your prose.

Work **Together**

Working in a small group, review three examples of different types of writing—such as an advertisement, an informational text, and a short story—and analyze the authors' use of the strategies covered in this chapter. What did each of you see that others did not? Write a few sentences reflecting on how this collaborative activity might help you revise your own work in the future.

Text Credits

Pg. 592: Source: Evans, and Mary Ann. 1873. Middlemarch: A Study of Provincial Life by George Eliot.

30 Choosing Appropriate Language

IN THIS CHAPTER

a. Using language in context, 596

b. Avoiding biased, hurtful language, 600

A murmuration is an amazing sight. Although these starlings are flying in what looks like a big, messy-looking bunch, somehow they swoop and turn together, with none of them wandering off, none of them bumping into each other. Researchers have concluded that these birds navigate by "playing telephone" with the seven nearest birds. The communication is always accurate, never inappropriate. They use appropriate language to navigate swiftly away from predators such as nearby falcons. As you write, think of yourself as a starling, sending messages in appropriate language to your immediate readers and thus, possibly, to a large group.

30a Using Language in Context

We all adjust our language to suit our audience and purpose. No form of the language is intrinsically better or more correct than another, but certain forms have become standard for addressing a broad audience in an academic setting or in the workplace. In this context, using appropriate language usually means the following:

- Avoiding nonstandard dialects
- Avoiding regionalisms, colloquialisms, and slang
- Avoiding overly technical terminology (jargon and neologisms)
- Adopting a straightforward tone, one that is neither overly informal nor pompously inflated

1. Nonstandard dialects

A *dialect* is a variant of a language with its own distinctive pronunciation, vocabulary, and grammar. A linguist once quipped that the only difference between the standard form of a language and its other dialects is that the standard form has an army and a navy. The standard form, in other words, became standard because it is the dialect of the elite and powerful.

> **More about**
> The grammar of Standard American English (ch. 33), 634–59

Nonstandard dialects of English are not "bad" English, as a few people still erroneously believe. If you speak a dialect like Appalachian English or African American English and you are addressing an audience of peers from your community, then your home dialect *is* appropriate. If you are addressing a broader audience or writing in an academic or workplace context, however, the written dialect known as Standard American English, or Edited English, is usually the preferred choice.

2. Regionalisms, colloquialisms, and slang

Regionalisms are expressions that are characteristic of particular areas. Saying the car "needs washed" is acceptable in Pittsburgh but not in Boston. The expression "I might could do it" might be acceptable in Pikeville, Kentucky, but not in Des Moines, Iowa. Regionalisms can be appropriate in conversation or informal writing but are usually out of place in formal academic writing.

▸ Many scientists believe that we might ~~could~~ *be able to* slow global warming if we can reduce carbon emissions.

Colloquialisms are informal expressions common in speech but usually out of place in formal writing.

▸ An R rating designates a movie that is not appropriate for ~~kids~~ *children* under 17 who are not accompanied by ~~a grown-up~~ *an adult*.

Used judiciously, however, the occasional colloquialism can add verve to your writing.

> The musicians were only kids, none of them more than 10 years old, but they played like seasoned professionals.

Writing Responsibly: Avoiding Online Shortcuts

In text messages and social media, writers have developed a host of acronyms and abbreviations—like *BTW* for "by the way" and *IMO* for "in my opinion"—that save time and space on the tiny screens of mobile phones. With the possible exception of the most informal emails, these expressions are almost never appropriate in other contexts, particularly not in academic or business writing. The same applies to emoticons and emojis like :-) and 👍, as well as other shortcuts such as writing entirely in lower case without punctuation, as in *i saw her this am.*

to SELF

Slang is the extremely informal, inventive, often colorful (and sometimes off-color) vocabulary of a particular group. In general, slang is inappropriate in formal writing, but as with colloquial language, when used sparingly and judiciously, it can enliven a sentence and help emphasize an important point.

3. Neologisms and jargon

The world changes. Technology advances, new cultural trends emerge, and new research alters our understanding of ourselves and gives rise to new fields of study. As these changes occur, people necessarily invent new words and expressions—*neologisms.* Some neologisms gain wide use and establish themselves as acceptable vocabulary for formal writing. Other neologisms, however, soon disappear or never advance from informal to formal usage. When you consider using a neologism, ask yourself whether a more familiar synonym might do the job. If the neologism is necessary but you are not sure your audience will be familiar with it, define it.

> Some instructors use wikis*, websites that allow a group of users to create and edit content collectively,* as tools for teaching collaborative writing.

The term *jargon* refers to the specialized vocabulary of a particular profession or discipline. Doctors speak of *adenomas* and *electroencephalograms.* Automobile mechanics speak of *camber angles* and *ring-and-pinion gears.* Lawyers speak of *effluxions of time* and *words of procreation.* English professors speak of *discursive historicity* and *terministic screens.* For an audience of specialists, this kind of insider vocabulary can efficiently communicate concepts that might otherwise take several sentences, even paragraphs, to explain. If you are addressing other specialists, jargon may be appropriate. If you are addressing a general audience, however, it is usually inappropriate and should generally be avoided. When a specialized term is needed, define it.

▶ The tenants lost the apartment ~~due to the effluxion of time on their lease.~~ *when their lease expired.*

4. Appropriate formality

When you speak or write to close friends and intimates from your own age group, your language will probably—and appropriately—be relaxed and informal, sprinkled with dialect, slang, and colloquial expressions. Writing for most college courses or in the workplace, however, requires a formal tone and clear, straightforward language free of slang and colloquialisms. Clear and straightforward, however, should not mean simpleminded or condescending. Use challenging vocabulary if it aptly expresses your meaning, but do not try to impress your readers by inflating your writing with fancy words mined from a thesaurus.

> **More about**
> Using a thesaurus, 614–15

INAPPROPRIATELY INFORMAL	Tarantino is always ripping scenes from earlier flicks to use in his own.
POMPOUS	It is a characteristic stylistic mannerism of the auteur Quentin Tarantino to allusively amalgamate scenic quotations from the repertory of his cinematic forebears in his own oeuvre.
APPROPRIATE	In his movies, the director Quentin Tarantino routinely alludes to scenes from earlier movies.

EXERCISE 30.1 Editing for language in context

Edit the following passage to establish appropriate formality for a college paper and to eliminate inappropriate regionalisms, colloquialisms, slang, and jargon.

> There are many reasons why folks are now trying essentially to effect a truncation of their consumption of meat. Some believe that having less meat will make them healthier. Some are desirous of losing weight by cutting their intake of fat. Some are doing it merely to be copycats. Regardless of the motivation, nutrition experts say that reducing meat consumption is not rocket science and can be effectuated by following some simple steps.

To begin with, chill out about getting enough protein. Plants supply protein too, and some, such as spinach and lentils, proffer greater quantities of protein per calorie than a cheeseburger does. Per capita, Americans currently scarf up about a half pound of meat per day. The biggest bump in the road can be cooking more meat than you need, so start buying less meat than you usually do. When you have less meat on hand, you'll eat less of it. Have a go at planning meals with meat on the side of the plate instead of smack dab in the middle. Ramp up the amount of vegetables you buy, and dig up recipes for yummy vegetable dishes. Promulgate some rules for yourself; for example, you may want to have meatless breakfasts and lunches, and then eat whatever you like for dinners. Buckle down on this, and you'll soon find that meat plays a smaller role in your meals.

Writing Responsibly: Euphemisms and Doublespeak

We use **euphemisms** in place of words that might be offensive or emotionally painful. We speak to mourners about a relative who has *passed away*, and we excuse ourselves saying we have to go *to the bathroom* without referring to specific bodily functions.

The polite or respectful use of euphemisms, however, can easily shade into a more evasive reluctance to address harsh realities. Why use *correctional institution*, for example, when what you mean is *prison* or *jail*? Why use *inaccuracies* when what you mean is *lies*?

Euphemisms that are deliberately deceptive, used to obscure bad news or sanitize an ugly truth, are called **doublespeak**. A company that announces that it is *downsizing*, not that it is about to lay off half of its workforce, is using doublespeak. *Terrorists* who call themselves *freedom fighters* are using doublespeak.

When reading, ask yourself: Does this word obscure or downplay the truth? When writing, think carefully about your motives: Are you using a euphemism (or doublespeak) to avoid hurting someone's feelings, or to evade responsibility for an uncomfortable truth?

to AUDIENCE

30b Avoiding Biased or Hurtful Language

> More about
> Stereotyping,
> 148–49, 176–77

Biased language unfairly or offensively characterizes a particular group and, by extension, its individual members. It can be as blatant as a hatefully uttered racial, ethnic, or gendered slur, but it can also be subtle and unintentional, as in thoughtless stereotyping or an inappropriately applied label.

A **stereotype** is a simplified, uncritical, and often negative generalization about an entire group of people: *Blondes are ditzy; athletes are weak students; lawyers are unscrupulous; politicians are dishonest.* Even when they seem positive, stereotypes lump people together in ways that offensively ignore their individuality. In an article in the *New York Times,* for example, Chinese American writer Vivian S. Toy remembers among her "painful experiences of being different" that a college adviser once recommended that she switch her major to biology "since Chinese are better suited for the sciences."

We label people whenever we call attention to a particular characteristic about them. **Labeling** is appropriate when it is relevant.

▶ Laura Grimm was the first female athletic director in the Western Pennsylvania Interscholastic Athletic League.

Labeling is inappropriate, and usually offensive, when it is irrelevant.

▶ Muhammad Ali, an African American, was a famous boxer.

To appreciate how irrelevant the label "African American" is in that last sentence, consider the following:

▶ Babe Ruth, a man, was a famous baseball player.

1. Gender bias

English has no pronouns that designate an individual person without also designating that person's gender (*she, he, her, him, hers, his, herself, himself*). This lack creates problems when a writer uses the singular to refer generically to a whole class of people or to people in general.

▶ The sensible student is careful what [*he? she?*] posts about [*himself? herself?*] on social networking sites such as *Instagram* or *Twitter.*

Until about the 1970s, the conventional solution to this problem was to use the masculine pronoun as the generic pronoun. In other words, depending on context, *he* referred either to a particular male human or to "he or she," a generic human of either gender. On the other hand, *she* always meant "female," never "she or he." Similarly, the terms *man* and *mankind* could refer generically to humanity as a whole, but *woman* and *womankind* only to women. For several decades, such gendered usages have been in revision. Since the 1970s, writers have been searching for and trying out various gender-neutral alternatives to the generic masculine singular pronoun.

***Avoid generic* he**   One way to avoid the generic *he*—and often the most graceful way—is to change the number of the noun from singular to plural; then a plural pronoun works smoothly.

▶ ~~The sensible student is~~ *Sensible students are* careful what ~~he posts~~ *they post* about ~~himself~~ *themselves* on social networking sites such as *Instagram* or *Twitter.*

> **More about**
> Pronoun-antecedent agreement, 689–93

As a second option, writers and major publishers such as the *Washington Post* have begun to use *they, them,* and *their* to refer to singular nouns. For years this usage was considered an agreement error. Now, in an era that recognizes male, female, nonbinary, and transgender identities, the plural pronoun agrees not only with singular nouns but also with contemporary social values. Moreover, in our globalized social interactions, writers cannot necessarily know from hearing a person's name whether that is a male- or female-identifying name. Much less can they know the gender identity of a source's author. *They, them,* and *their* solve the problem and are now not only accepted but recommended as a generic singular pronoun:

- The sensible student is careful what they post about themselves on social networking sites such as *Instagram* or *Twitter*.

A third, more traditional alternative is to use *he or she* (or *she or he*).

- The sensible student is careful what he or she posts on social networking sites.

Be sparing with this option, however; used many times in quick succession, it becomes awkward. You can usually avoid *he* or *she* by revising.

AWKWARD	The sensible student is careful what <u>he or she</u> posts about <u>himself or herself</u> on the social networking sites <u>he or she</u> frequents.
IMPROVED	The sensible student is careful about posting personal information on social networking sites.

Avoid generic man Replace terms like *man, men,* and *mankind* used to represent all human beings with gender-neutral equivalents such as *humanity, humankind,* or *humans*.

- <s>Man is the only animal</s> to have ventured into space.
  Humans are the only animals

Replace occupational names that have the term *man* in them with gender-neutral alternatives.

- <s>Congressmen</s> have excellent health insurance.
  Members of Congress

Avoid gender stereotypes and inappropriate gender labeling Some occupations with gender-neutral names are stereotypically associated with either men or women. Avoid perpetuating those stereotypes with inappropriate gender labeling.

▶ Nursing is an ancient, honorable profession. ~~Women~~ *People* who choose it can expect a rewarding career.

▶ ~~Women~~ *Job seekers* with children may want to apply to companies that offer flexible hours to working ~~mothers~~ *parents*.

▶ ~~Ladies~~ *Women* and men will be evaluated according to the same criteria.

2. Cultural labels

Use cultural labels with care. Racial and ethnic labels are appropriate only when race or ethnicity is relevant to the topic under discussion. The same is true for references to disabilities, sexual orientation, or other personal characteristics. When you do use labels, avoid terms that may give offense; instead, call people what they want to be called. When referring to a transgender person, use whichever pronoun that person prefers. And be aware that acceptable labels can become outdated and offensive. A label that used to be acceptable may take on negative connotations over time. People from Asia are *Asians,* not *Orientals* (a term many find disparaging). *Native American* and *American Indian* (or just *Indian*), on the other hand, are generally acceptable to the people they designate. The term *African American* is now widely accepted as a designation for Americans of African descent. Ongoing debate surrounds the use of the terms *Hispanic* and *Latino* to describe those descended from Spanish-speaking peoples of the Western Hemisphere. The term *Latinx* has entered the debate as a gender-neutral option. The words *gay* and *lesbian* are preferable to *homosexual.* The best choice in all cases is to be as specific as context permits. If what you mean is *Vietnamese,* or *Japanese,* or *Inuit,* or *Lakota,* or *Mexican American,* or *Dominican American,* or *Catalan,* or *Sicilian,* then use those terms, not the more general *Asian,* or *Native American, or Hispanic,* or *European.* Pay attention, too, to changing conventions of capitalization: *Black* (not *black*) is now in wide use, as is *Deaf.* Increasingly, publishers are capitalizing *White,* as well.

31 Choosing Effective Words

IN THIS CHAPTER

a. Finding the right word, 604

b. Choosing compelling words and figures, 606

c. Mastering idioms, 610

d. Avoiding clichés, 610

Darren McCollester/Getty Images

In the late 1960s, antiwar demonstrations were in the news regularly, accompanied by images of young protestors. Their arguments in their speeches were complex, variously based in ethics, humanitarianism, politics, and self-preservation. Their chants and protest signs, however, were simple: "End the war." In addition to the literal meaning of that sentence, it carried emotional associations, as well; "end the war" also means "stop the killing." Today's protests for Black Lives Matter and the reform of racist institutions, for civil rights for LGBTQ individuals, for women's reproductive rights, and for voter rights, to name a few issues, are just as political and emotional as those of the past. Protests continue to demonstrate that, whether in the streets or on the page, language matters.

31a Diction: Finding the Right Word

Diction, or the choice of words to best convey an idea, requires attention to both literal meaning and emotional associations. The literal meaning of a word, its dictionary definition, is its ***denotation***.

> **More about**
> Commonly confused words, 619, G15–G20

Style Matters • Diction: Finding the Right Word

> **Tech** Word Choice and Grammar and Style Checkers
>
> The grammar and style checkers in most word processing programs offer only marginal help with effective word choice. They often cannot distinguish an incorrectly used word from a correctly used one—*affect* from *effect*, for example—nor can they differentiate the emotional associations of words whose literal meaning is similar.

When you use a word, be sure its denotation matches your intended meaning. Be particularly careful, for example, not to misuse words that are similar in pronunciation or spelling.

▶ Calling someone a Scrooge ~~eludes~~ *alludes* to a Charles Dickens story about a selfish man.

To *elude* is to evade or escape; to *allude* is to make an indirect reference.

▶ The psychology of perception includes the study of optical ~~allusions~~ *illusions*.

An *allusion* is an indirect reference; an *illusion* is a mistaken perception.

Be careful, too, with words that differ in meaning even though they are otherwise closely related.

▶ Many people owe their lives to the ~~heroics~~ *heroism* of volunteer firefighters.

Heroics are melodramatic, excessive acts; *heroism* is courageous, potentially self-sacrificing behavior.

➡ EXERCISE 31.1 Denotation

Consult a dictionary, style guide, the Quick Reference box on p. 609, or the Glossary of Usage at the end of this book as needed to find and correct any misused words in the following sentences.

EXAMPLE

The reporter tried but failed to ~~illicit~~ *elicit* a comment about climate change from the candidate.

1. Most scientists now except human activity as a cause of global warming.
2. Melting glaciers and rising sea levels are often sited as affects of global warming.

3. People in coastal areas may have trouble adopting to rising sea levels.
4. Another eminent result of global warming may be the breakup of ice shelves in Antarctica.
5. The strength of any one hurricane, however, cannot feasibly be attributed to global warming.

The secondary meanings of a word—the psychological or emotional associations it evokes—are its **connotations.** The word *walk,* for example, has many synonyms, including *amble, saunter, stride,* and *march.* Each of these, however, has distinctive connotations, as their effect in the following sentence suggests:

The candidate {ambled / sauntered / walked / strode / marched} to the podium to address her supporters.

The verb *walk* in this context is emotionally neutral, but the others all have connotations that suggest something about the candidate's state of mind. *Amble* suggests a relaxed aimlessness, whereas *saunter* suggests a jaunty self-confidence. *Stride* and *march* both suggest purposefulness, but *march,* with its military associations, also carries a hint of aggressiveness.

A word's connotations can also vary from reader to reader. To some people, for example, the word *wilderness* evokes a place of great danger; to others, a place of excitement; and to still others, a treasure to be preserved.

31b Choosing Compelling Words and Figures

Some words are general, some specific, and others fall between:

← more general		more specific →
consume	eat	devour
fruit	apple	Granny Smith
mountain	California peak	Mt. Whitney

In addition, some words are concrete, designating things or qualities that can be seen, heard, felt, smelled, or touched; and others are abstract, designating concepts like *justice, capitalism,* or *democracy.*

Writing Responsibly — Word Choice and Credibility

The denotation and connotation of the words you choose can powerfully influence the tone of your writing, the effect you have on your readers, and what your readers conclude about you. Highly charged vocabulary, as in the following examples, might lead readers to question the writer's reliability:

- Hippie tree huggers are threatening the jobs of thousands of hardworking loggers.
- Conscientious activists are trying to protect endangered forests from rapacious, tree-murdering logging companies.

In academic writing, you will enhance your credibility if you describe conflicting positions in even-toned language:

- Environmentalists discuss their conflict with the logging industry in terms of the threat industry practices pose to a critical resource; the logging companies, contending that they are responsible forest stewards, describe the conflict in terms of their contribution to local economies.

Once you have looked at the issue fairly, nothing prevents you from then supporting one of these positions and challenging the other.

to AUDIENCE

1. Compelling words

Bring your writing to life by combining general and abstract language with the specific and concrete. Use general and abstract language to frame broad issues, and specific, concrete language to capture readers' attention and help them see things through your eyes. Using general language without specifics leaves readers to fill in the blanks on their own, and using specific language without the general and abstract leaves readers wondering what the point is.

The first of the two following descriptions of the Badwater ultramarathon lacks specific language that can tell us how long the race is, why it is challenging, or exactly where it takes place. The second fills in those details with concrete words—like "hottest spot in America," "stinking water hole," "135 miles," "Death Valley," "piney oasis," "8,300 feet up the side of Mt. Whitney," and "asphalt and road gravel." With these specifics, the writer David Ferrell evokes the challenges of the race without recourse to the abstract word *challenging*.

GENERAL AND ABSTRACT	Badwater is a long, physically challenging race over a partially paved course that begins in a geological depression and ends partway up a mountain.
CONCRETE AND SPECIFIC	Badwater is a madman's march, a footrace through the summer heat of the hottest spot in America. It extends 135 miles from a stinking water hole on the floor of Death Valley to a piney oasis 8,300 feet

up the side of Mt. Whitney. The course is nothing but asphalt and road gravel. Feet and knees and shins ache like they are being whacked with tire irons. Faces turn into shrink-wrap.

—David Ferrell, "Far Beyond a Mere Marathon"

2. Figures of speech

In the example above, notice how Ferrell, in addition to providing concrete specifics, also uses striking comparisons and juxtapositions to paint a vivid picture of the rigors of the race and to suggest the mind-set required to compete in it. He calls the race "a madman's march," for example, and conjures up a beating with a tire iron and an image of a shrink-wrapped face to convey the physical punishment contestants endure. These are examples of *figurative language,* or *figures of speech,* the imaginative use of language to convey meaning in ways that reach beyond the literal meaning of the words involved.

Among the most common figures of speech are similes and metaphors. A *simile* is an explicit comparison between two unlike things, usually expressed with *like* or *as*: "Feet and knees and shins ache like they are being whacked with tire irons." A *metaphor* is an implied comparison between two unlike things stated without *like, as,* or other comparative expressions: "Faces turn into shrink-wrap." (A list of common figures of speech appears in the Quick Reference box on p. 609.)

3. Inappropriate figures of speech and mixed metaphors

Used judiciously, figures of speech can spice up your writing. Used in the wrong context or piled inconsistently one on the other in *mixed metaphors,* they can be jarring, even silly. The original simile in the following example incongruously invokes the image of a pole vaulter, an athlete who goes mostly up and down, to describe a speeding train, which travels mostly horizontally. The revision, comparing the train to a race horse, is more apt.

▶ The new high-speed train, like a champion ~~pole vaulter,~~ *thoroughbred,* made it from Boston to Washington in record time.

Mixed metaphors—which combine multiple, conflicting images for the same concept—confuse readers.

MIXED METAPHOR   Confronted with the tsunami of data available on the Internet, researchers, like travelers caught in a blinding desert sandstorm, may have trouble finding the nuggets of valuable information buried in a mountain of otherwise worthless ore.

Quick Reference: Figures of Speech

Figure and Definition	Examples
simile: An explicit comparison between two unlike things, usually expressed with *like* or *as*	▸ Feet and knees and shins ache like they are being whacked with tire irons. —David Ferrell ▸ Only final exams, like the last lap of a long race, lay between the members of the senior class and their diplomas.
metaphor: An implied comparison between unlike things stated without *like, as,* or other comparative expressions	▸ Faces turn into shrink-wrap. —David Ferrell ▸ After crossing the finish line of their last exams, seniors looked forward to that moment on the victory stand when the president of the college would bestow a diploma on them.
analogy: An extended simile or metaphor, often comparing something familiar to something unfamiliar. Well-constructed analogies can be particularly effective for explaining difficult concepts.	▸ What that means [that the universe is expanding] is that we're not at the center of the universe, after all; instead, we're like a single raisin in a vast lump of dough that is rising in an oven where all the other raisins are moving away from each other, faster and faster as the oven gets hotter and hotter. —David Perlman, "At 12 Billion Years Old, Universe Still Growing Fast"
personification: The attribution of human qualities to nonhuman creatures, objects, ideas, or phenomena	▸ The plague that rampaged through Europe in the fourteenth century selected its victims indiscriminately, murdering rich and poor in equal proportion.
hyperbole: Deliberate exaggeration for emphasis	▸ That little restaurant on Main Street makes the best pizza on the planet.
understatement: The deliberate use of less forceful language than a subject warrants	▸ The report of my death was an exaggeration. —Mark Twain, clearly alive and well, responding to an obituary about him in a London paper
irony: The use of language to suggest the opposite of its literal meaning or to express an incongruity between what is expected and what occurs	▸ I come to bury Caesar, not to praise him. —Mark Antony, in Shakespeare's play *Julius Caesar,* in a speech that praises the murdered leader effusively

The preceding sentence, seeking to emphasize the challenges of online research, invokes tsunamis, sandstorms, mountains, and mining.

REVISED   As they mine the mountain of data available on the Internet, researchers may have trouble identifying the nuggets of valuable information buried with the otherwise worthless ore they dig up.

The revision elaborates a single metaphor that compares finding useful information online to mining for precious minerals.

31c Mastering Idioms

Idioms are expressions whose meaning does not depend on the meanings of the words that compose them. Each idiom is a unified package of meaning with its own denotations and connotations. The following sentence, for example, would make no sense if you tried to interpret it based on the literal meaning of the words *call, on,* and *carpet:*

> ▸ The directors called the CEO on the carpet for the company's poor sales in 2020.

Of course, the expression *call on the carpet* has nothing to do with calls or carpets. It is an idiom that, understood as a whole, means *to reprimand* or *scold.*

> **More about**
> Specialized dictionaries, 614–15

Most dictionaries list idiomatic uses of particular words. The entry for the word *call* in the *Merriam-Webster Online Dictionary,* for example, provides definitions for the idioms *call for, call forth, call into question, call it a day,* and *call it quits,* among others. For more detailed information on the history and meaning of particular idioms, consult a specialized dictionary such as the *American Heritage Dictionary of Idioms.*

Idioms, Prepositions, and Phrasal Verbs Because idioms can be understood only as a whole, you have to learn them as a whole, just as you would any unfamiliar word. Pay particular attention to the way prepositions combine with other words in idiomatic ways. A ***phrasal verb***, for example, is a combination of a verb with one or more prepositions that has a different meaning than the verb alone.

> **More about**
> Prepositions, 793–800
> Phrasal verbs, 776–78

> Raisa *saw* the flat tire on her car. [She looked at it.]
>
> Raisa *saw to* the flat tire on her car. [She had it repaired.]

31d Avoiding Clichés

A ***cliché*** is a figure of speech, idiom, or other expression that has grown stale from overuse (see the Quick Reference box on the next page for some examples). Clichés come quickly to mind because they express common wit and wisdom in widely recognized phrases. For the same reason, they provide an easy substitute for fresh thought and expression. They may help you frame a subject in the early drafts of a paper, but they can also make your writing sound trite and unimaginative. You should edit them out as you revise your work. As the following example indicates, writing that is loaded with clichés is often also loaded with mixed metaphors.

CLICHÉ-LADEN As the campaign pulled into the home stretch and the cold hard fact of the increasingly nip-and-tuck polls sank in, the candidates threw their promises to stay on their best behavior to the wind and wallowed in the mire of down-and-dirty attack ads.

REVISED As Election Day neared and the polls showed the race tightening, the candidates abandoned their promises of civility and released a barrage of unscrupulous attack ads.

Quick Reference Dodging Deadly Clichés

When you encounter clichés like these in your writing, delete them or replace them with fresher images of your own.

best thing since sliced bread	hit the nail on the head	smart as a whip
beyond a shadow of a doubt	a hundred and one percent	straight and narrow
cold, hard fact	in the prime of life	think outside the box
cool as a cucumber	just desserts	throw [something] to the wind
down and dirty	nip and tuck	tried and true
down the home stretch	no way, shape, or form	wallow in the mire
easier said than done	on their best behavior	without a moment's hesitation
face the music	one foot out the door	zero tolerance
faster than greased lightning	plain as the nose on your face	
green with envy	slow as molasses	

What Is the Difference between an Idiom and a Cliché? The only thing that separates an idiom from a cliché is the frequency with which it is used. If you are a native English speaker, be alert to idioms that appear often in popular sources and in conversation, and try to avoid those in academic and professional writing. If you are not a native English speaker, you may not recognize an idiom as a cliché if you have not encountered it often in your reading. If you have questions about clichés and idioms, ask your instructor or consult a dictionary of idioms, such as *McGraw-Hill's Dictionary of American Idioms and Phrasal Verbs* or the *Longman American Idioms Dictionary*.

EXERCISE 31.2 Avoiding clichés and mixed metaphors

Edit the following sentences to eliminate clichés and mixed metaphors.

EXAMPLE

Mayor Wyndham has been reelected regularly because people feel that she is ~~tried and true~~ reliable and does not do anything unexpected.

1. Her new proposal hit the town council like a ton of bricks.
2. She wanted to have the county reroute the main road to the capital smack dab through town, forcing traffic to run a gauntlet through our commercial center.
3. Store owners, who have recently seen their sales sink like a stone, thought the plan hit the nail on the head and were happy as clams.
4. However, most townspeople flooded the mayor's office with an avalanche of angry calls and emails opposing the proposal.
5. Opponents insisted that in no way, shape, or form would they take to a proposal that threatened the peace and quiet that had attracted them to the town in the first place.

Make It Your Own

Review one of your recent writing projects and identify any passages that include misused words, words with an inappropriate connotation, words that are overly general or abstract mixed metaphors, or clichés. If you find many areas needing revision, add them to your list of areas to consider as you revise your prose.

Text Credits

Pg. 608: Ferrell, David, "Far Beyond a Mere Marathon," *Los Angeles Times*, August 23, 1997. **Pg. 608:** Perlman, David, "At 12 Billion Years Old, Universe Still Growing Fast" *SFGate* May 26, 1999. **Pg. 608:** Mark Twain, in a letter to Frank E. Bliss, November 4, 1897. **Pg. 608:** William Shakespeare, *Julius Caesar* (1599).

32 Using the Dictionary and Spelling Correctly

IN THIS CHAPTER

a. Choosing a dictionary, 613
b. Using a dictionary, 615
c. Avoiding common spelling problems, 618
d. Remembering spelling rules, 620
e. Forming plurals, 623
f. Improving your day-to-day spelling, 625

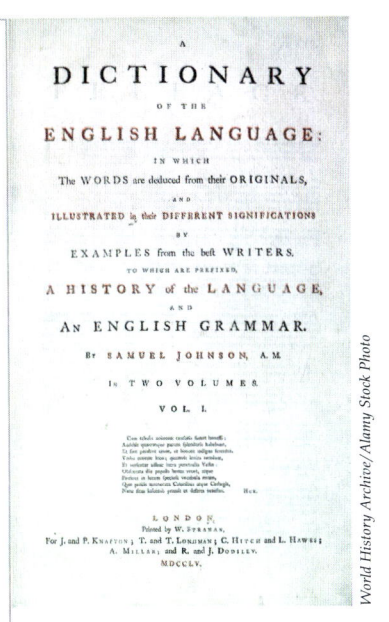

Samuel Johnson's *Dictionary of the English Language* (1755), although not the first ever published, established many of the conventions still found in dictionaries today, nearly four centuries later. Johnson identified a core vocabulary of some 43,500 words; labeled each word's part of speech; briefly traced its origins; provided a concise, elegant (and sometimes humorous) definition of the word in all its senses; and accompanied each definition with an illustrative quotation. Johnson hoped to define and fix a standard of proper spelling and usage, but his dictionary, like those that have followed it, also reflects the state of the language in the time and place in which it was created.

32a Choosing a Dictionary

Dictionaries today come in a variety of forms, both printed and electronic, large and small, general purpose and specialized.

1. Abridged dictionaries

Sometimes referred to as "desk dictionaries," these handy volumes contain information on approximately 200,000 words. Examples include *The American Heritage College Dictionary, Merriam-Webster's Collegiate Dictionary,* the *Random House Webster's College Dictionary,* and *Webster's New World College Dictionary. The American Heritage College Dictionary* is available online at *Yahoo! Education.*

Merriam-Webster's Collegiate Dictionary is available online as the *Merriam-Webster Online Dictionary*. Most word processing programs also include a built-in dictionary with many features of an abridged dictionary.

2. Unabridged dictionaries

Unabridged dictionaries provide detailed information for half a million words in the English language. The most comprehensive unabridged dictionary is the 20-volume *Oxford English Dictionary* (known as the *OED*). Others include *Random House Webster's Unabridged Dictionary* and *Webster's Third New International Dictionary, Unabridged.*

Both the *OED* and *Webster's Third New International* are available online for a fee. You should be able to find an unabridged dictionary in the reference section of any library, however, and many libraries provide access to online versions.

Dictionaries for Second-Language Learners In addition to translation dictionaries and standard abridged and unabridged dictionaries, you may also want to consult an all-English dictionary tailored for the second-language learner, such as *Heinle's Newbury House Dictionary of American English,* the *Longman Dictionary of American English,* or the *Oxford Dictionary of American English.* To understand American slang and idioms, consult a dictionary such as *McGraw-Hill's Dictionary of American Slang and Colloquial Expressions.* Since slang and idioms change rapidly, you should also consult native English-speaking peers.

3. Specialized dictionaries

Specialized dictionaries focus on a particular aspect of English vocabulary.

- Dictionaries of usage provide guidance about the use of particular words or phrases. Examples include *The American Heritage Book of English Usage* (available online at Bartleby.com) and *Right, Wrong, and Risky: A Dictionary of Today's American English Usage.* *The New Fowler's Modern English Usage* provides guidance on British as well as American usage.

- Subject-specific dictionaries explain the specialized terminology of particular fields and professions. Examples include *The Dictionary of Anthropology, Black's Law Dictionary,* and *A Dictionary of Business and Management.*

- Thesauruses and synonym dictionaries provide lists of words that are equivalent to or that overlap in meaning with one another (*synonyms*), as well as words that have contrasting meanings (*antonyms*).

>More about
Subject-specific dictionaries, 239–41

>More about
Denotation and connotation, 20–21, 604–6

Writing Responsibly: Choose Accurate Synonyms

When you consult a thesaurus, check both the meanings (*denotations*) and the associations (*connotations*) of the words you find there. A carelessly chosen synonym can distort the information you intend to convey. Suppose, for example, that you wanted to replace *intimidate* in the sentence "The professor's brilliance intimidated her students."

Looking in a thesaurus, you might find both *overawe* and *bludgeon* listed as synonyms. *Overawe* is an appropriate substitute, probably more precisely reflecting the effect of the professor on her students than *intimidate*. *Bludgeon*, in contrast, inaccurately conjures visions of a bloody crime scene.

to TOPIC

They can help you find just the right word for a particular context or an alternative to a word you have been overusing. Examples include *Merriam-Webster's Dictionary of Synonyms* and *The New American Roget's College Thesaurus*. Note also that most word processing programs have a built-in thesaurus.

32b Using a Dictionary

Figure 32.1 shows the entry for the word *respect* in the *Merriam-Webster Online Dictionary*, the online counterpart to the eleventh edition of *Merriam-Webster's Collegiate Dictionary*. Although most online and printed abridged dictionaries present the same kinds of information, each has its own format and system of abbreviations.

1. Spelling, word division, and pronunciation

Entries begin with the word correctly spelled followed by acceptable variant spellings, if any. Dots show the division of the word into syllables, indicating where to put a hyphen if you must break the word between lines of text. Next, the pronunciation of the word is given. The print version has a key to pronunciation symbols; the online version has a link to this key, but it also gives the pronunciation in an audio link.

> More about
> Hyphenation,
> 877–82

> More about
> Regular and
> irregular verbs,
> 696–97
> Regular and
> irregular plurals,
> 623–25

2. Grammatical functions and forms

Labels indicate the part of speech and other grammatical aspects of a word. Most dictionaries specify the forms of irregular verbs (*draw, drew, drawn*) but not of regular verbs like *respect,* and they provide irregular plurals (*woman, women*) but not regular plurals (*dogs*). The entry shown in Figure 32.1 includes a definition of the plural form *respects* because it has a usage that does not apply to the singular form.

616 | **32b** | sp | Style Matters • Using the Dictionary and Spelling Correctly

First entry (as noun) → **respect** noun
- Save Word
- re·spect | \ ri-ˈspekt \ ← **Pronunciation with audio link**

Definition of *respect* (Entry 1 of 2)

1 : a relation or reference to a particular thing or situation
  // remarks having *respect* to an earlier plan
2 : an act of giving particular attention : CONSIDERATION
3 a : high or special regard : ESTEEM
  b : the quality or state of being esteemed
  c : **respects** *plural* : expressions of high or special regard or deference
     // paid our *respects*
4 : PARTICULAR, DETAIL
  // a good plan in some *respects*

→ **Definitions and links to related online entries**

in respect of
chiefly British : with respect to : CONCERNING

in respect to
: with respect to : CONCERNING

with respect to
: with reference to : in relation to

Idioms with links to related online entries ↑

Second entry (as verb) → **respect** verb
re·spect | \ ri-ˈspekt \
respected; respecting; respects

Definition of *respect* (Entry 2 of 2)

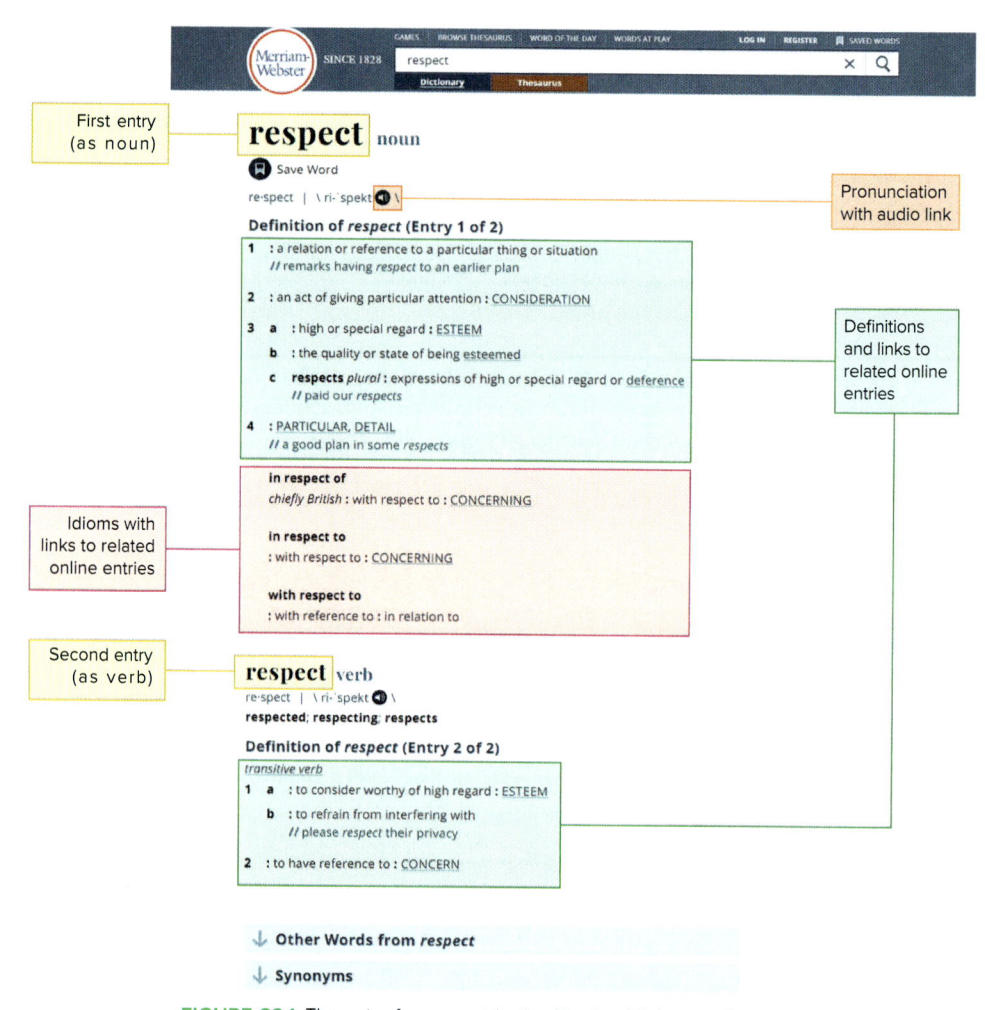

transitive verb
1 a : to consider worthy of high regard : ESTEEM
  b : to refrain from interfering with
     // please *respect* their privacy
2 : to have reference to : CONCERN

↓ Other Words from *respect*

↓ Synonyms

FIGURE 32.1 The entry for *respect* in the *Merriam-Webster* online dictionary at https://www.merriam-webster.com/.

3. Definitions and examples

> **More about**
> Idiomatic expressions, 610

If a word has more than one definition, each is numbered, and any additional distinctions within a definition are labeled with a letter. Several definitions in the entry for *respect* as a noun include examples of the word used

↓ **Choose the Right Synonym**

↓ **More Example Sentences**

↓ **Learn More about** *respect*

Other Words from *respect*
Verb
respecter *noun*

Synonyms for *respect*

Synonyms: Noun
reference, regard

Synonyms: Verb
admire, appreciate, consider, esteem, regard

⟶ Synonyms for *respect* (noun and verb)

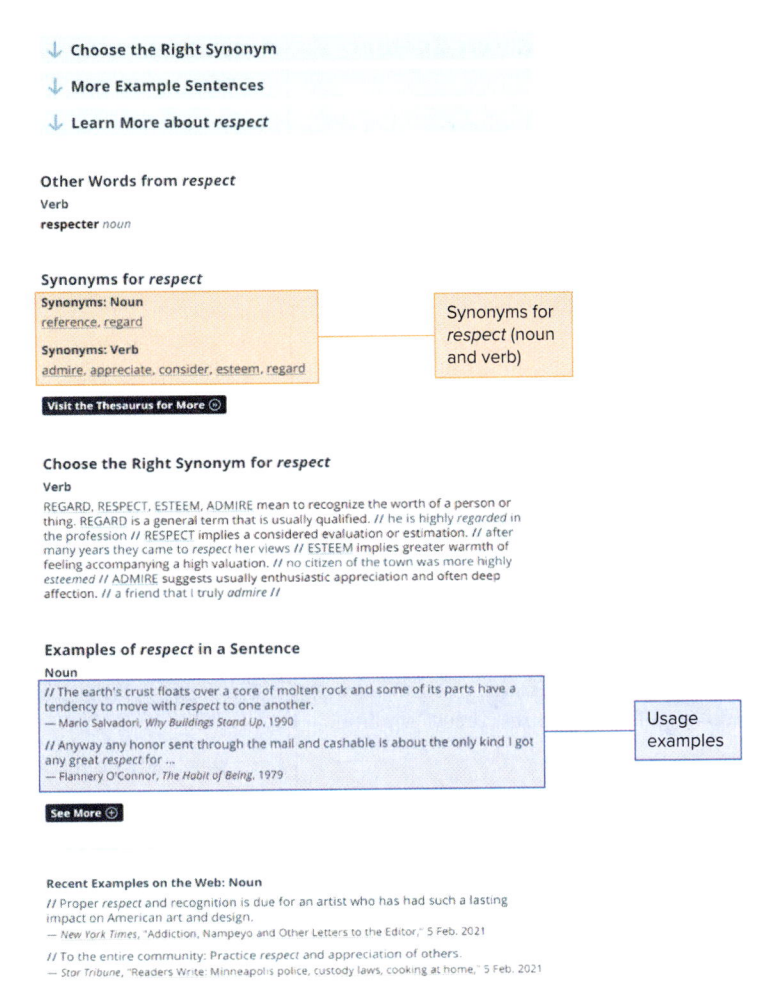

Visit the Thesaurus for More ⊕

Choose the Right Synonym for *respect*
Verb
REGARD, RESPECT, ESTEEM, ADMIRE mean to recognize the worth of a person or thing. REGARD is a general term that is usually qualified. // he is highly *regarded* in the profession // RESPECT implies a considered evaluation or estimation. // after many years they came to *respect* her views // ESTEEM implies greater warmth of feeling accompanying a high valuation. // no citizen of the town was more highly *esteemed* // ADMIRE suggests usually enthusiastic appreciation and often deep affection. // a friend that I truly *admire* //

Examples of *respect* **in a Sentence**
Noun
// The earth's crust floats over a core of molten rock and some of its parts have a tendency to move with *respect* to one another.
— Mario Salvadori, *Why Buildings Stand Up*, 1990

// Anyway any honor sent through the mail and cashable is about the only kind I got any great *respect* for ...
— Flannery O'Connor, *The Habit of Being*, 1979

⟶ Usage examples

See More ⊕

Recent Examples on the Web: Noun
// Proper *respect* and recognition is due for an artist who has had such a lasting impact on American art and design.
— *New York Times*, "Addiction, Nampeyo and Other Letters to the Editor," 5 Feb. 2021

// To the entire community: Practice *respect* and appreciation of others.
— *Star Tribune*, "Readers Write: Minneapolis police, custody laws, cooking at home," 5 Feb. 2021

FIGURE 32.1 (*Continued*)

in context. At the end of the entry are the definitions of several idiomatic expressions that include *respect*.

4. Synonyms and usage

Most dictionaries list synonyms for the entry word; in online dictionaries, clicking on a synonym will take you to the full entry for that word. Usage labels offer guidance on how to use a word appropriately.

> **More about**
> Usage in "A Glossary of Usage,"
> G15–G20

32c Avoiding Common Spelling Problems

For most people, spelling does not come easily. Even voracious readers and expert writers need to review common spelling problems, such as spelling from pronunciation, confusing homonyms, and confusing different forms of the same word.

Using a Bilingual Dictionary as an Aid to English Spelling If your first language has, like Spanish, a more phonetic spelling system than English has, a bilingual or translation dictionary can help you find the spelling of English words. For example, if you think *physician* begins with the letter *f*, you will have a hard time finding the correct spelling in an English dictionary, but if you look up *médico* in a Spanish-English dictionary, you will immediately find the proper spelling.

1. The unreliability of pronunciation

The word *Wednesday* is pronounced without the first *d* and the second *e* ("Wensday"). The letters *ow* in *sow* are pronounced as in *cow* when *sow* is used as a noun meaning "female pig." When *sow* is used as a verb meaning "to plant seeds," however, the letters *ow* are pronounced like the *ew* in *sew*. As these examples indicate, you cannot rely on the way an English word sounds to guide you to its correct spelling.

2. Homonyms and other problematic words

Many spelling errors result from confusion over homonyms and near-homonyms like those in the Quick Reference box on page 619.

- *Homonyms* are groups of words that sound exactly alike but have different spellings and meanings, such as *to/too/two* and *cite/sight/site*.

- *Near-homonyms* are groups of words such as *personal/personnel* and *conscience/conscious* that are close but not the same in pronunciation. Near-homonyms also include groups such as *breath/breathe* and *advice/advise* that are different forms of the same word.

> **More about**
> Confusing words and phrases in "A Glossary of Usage," G15–G20

There is no easy formula for mastering these words. If any of them give you trouble, try to memorize their spellings and meanings, and always check for them as you proofread your writing.

Quick Reference: Some Homonyms and Near-Homonyms

accept (to take willingly)
except (to exclude)

advice (counsel)
advise (to offer counsel)

affect (to influence; feeling)
effect (to cause; a result)

all ready (fully prepared)
already (by this time)

allude (to mention indirectly)
elude (to avoid)

allusion (an indirect reference)
illusion (a deceptive or false perception)

altar (a raised structure for religious ritual)
alter (to change)

are (form of *be*)
our (relating to us)

ascent (upward advance)
assent (to concur)

bare (unclothed; to make known)
bear (an animal; to support)

board (a piece of wood; to get on a vehicle)
bored (uninterested)

brake (stopping mechanism)
break (to wreck; a pause)

capital (seat of government)
capitol (building for the legislature)

cite (to acknowledge a source)
sight (something to see)
site (a place)

complement (to complete)
compliment (an admiring remark)

conscience (moral awareness)
conscious (awake, mindful)

council (a governing or advisory group)
counsel (advice; to advise)

descent (downward movement)
dissent (disagreement)

desert (desolate area; to abandon)
dessert (a meal's last course)

device (a contrivance)
devise (to contrive)

discreet (prudent, unpretentious)
discrete (distinct)

elicit (to bring out)
illicit (illegal)

eminent (highly regarded)
imminent (about to happen)
immanent (inherent)

fair (attractive; impartial)
fare (a price for transportation)

forth (forward)
fourth (following *third*)

gorilla (a great ape)
guerrilla (a fighter in unconventional warfare)

grate (to grind or irritate)
great (large or superior)

hear (to perceive sound)
here (at this place)

hole (an opening)
whole (complete)

incidence (rate of occurrence)
incidents (occurrences)

its (possessive of *it*)
it's (*it is* or *it has*)

lead (a metal; to go ahead of)
led (past tense of *lead*)

meat (edible animal flesh)
meet (to encounter)

passed (past tense of *pass*)
past (before the present)

patience (calm persistence)
patients (people under medical care)

peace (tranquility)
piece (a part)

personal (private; individual)
personnel (employees)

plain (not complicated)
plane (aircraft; carpenter's tool)

presence (being in attendance)
presents (gifts)

principal (most significant; chief)
principle (rule or tenet)

rain (precipitation)
reign (monarch's period of rule)
rein (strap used to control an animal; to restrain)

raise (to lift)
raze (to demolish)

respectfully (with respect)
respectively (in the order given)

right (correct; opposite of *left*)
rite (ceremony or ritual)
wright (one who fashions a thing)
write (to form words on a surface)

road (street)
rode (past tense of *ride*)

stationary (immobile)
stationery (writing paper)

than (compared to)
then (at that time; therefore)

their (possessive of *they*)
there (in that place)
they're (*they are*)

to (toward)
too (also)
two (number after *one*)

waist (midriff; narrow part)
waste (garbage; to squander)

weak (not strong)
week (seven days)

wear (to have on)
where (in what direction or place)
were (past tense of *be*)

weather (condition of the atmosphere)
whether (word that introduces choices or alternatives)

which (what one)
witch (sorcerer)

who's (*who is* or *who has*)
whose (possessive of *who*)

your (possessive of *you*)
you're (*you are*)

Use American Rather Than British Spelling Multilingual writers who began their study of English outside the United States may be accustomed to British spelling. Some writers also believe that British spellings (for example, *-our*, as in *colour; -ise*, as in *realise;* and *-lled*, as in *dialled*) are more formal. If you are writing for a US audience, however, use American style. The following list shows examples of the differences, but if you are unsure about a word, consult an American dictionary.

AMERICAN	BRITISH
airplane	aeroplane
labor/mold	labour/mould
theater/center	theatre/centre
labeled/modeled	labelled/modelled
defense	defence
plagiarize/analyze	plagiarise/analyse
program	programme
toward	towards

32d Remembering Spelling Rules

Mastering a few key rules—and noting their exceptions—can improve the accuracy of your spelling.

Writing Responsibly — Spelling Errors

A misspelled word is not an important issue when you are texting friends, but in other situations it may signal that you are careless about details. If you misspell *accountant* in a job-application letter to a financial firm, for example, the recipient may wonder how accurate you are about numbers. If you misspell a name, people may interpret it as a sign of indifference or disrespect.

to SELF

1. The *ie/ei* rule

The traditional rule—"*i* before *e* except after *c* or when sounded like *ay* as in *neighbor* and *weigh*"—will help you spell words like *believe, receive,* and *sleigh* correctly.

I BEFORE *E*	diesel, piece, pier, retrieve, shield, siege
E BEFORE *I* AFTER *C*	ceiling, conceit, conceive, deceit, perceive, receipt
EI SOUNDS LIKE *AY*	beige, deign, eighteen, reindeer, sleigh, veil

Exceptions: *feisty, forfeit, heifer, height, heir, neither, protein, sovereign, seize, their, weird*

> **EXERCISE 32.1 Spelling *ie* and *ei* words**
>
> Correct any misspellings in the following sentences.
>
> **EXAMPLE**
>
> When Angie ~~recieved~~ the ~~reciept~~ for her rental deposit, she knew she had reached a milestone in her life.
> (received) (receipt)
>
> 1. It was her first apartment, and the cielings were 18 feet high!
> 2. With that hieght, she could retreive her tall sculpture from her parents' backyard and install it in her apartment.
> 3. Of course, creating such an oversized sculpture had been a conciet, but she had always beleived that art should have no boundaries.
> 4. Now that fiesty conviction in the form of a huge peice of biege metal would take palpable shape in the very first home of her own.

2. Prefixes

Prefixes attach to the beginning of a root word to modify its meaning. Prefixes have no effect on the spelling of the rest of the word, even if the last letter of the prefix and the first letter of the root word are the same. For example, *re-* combines with *wind* to form *rewind*, *dis-* combines with *inherit* to form *disinherit*, and *mis-* combines with *statement* to form *misstatement*. In some cases, however, a hyphen separates a prefix from the rest of the word, as in *anti-inflammatory*.

> **More about**
> Prefixes and hyphenation, 878–79

3. Suffixes

Suffixes attach to the end of a root word to change its meaning and grammatical form. The suffix *-ly*, for example, changes the adjective *sweet* to the adverb *sweetly*. Unlike prefixes, suffixes often affect the spelling of the preceding root.

> **More about**
> Suffixes and hyphenation, 878–79

Words that end with a silent *e* In most instances, drop the silent *e* if the suffix starts with a vowel:

observe → observant   response → responsible   revoke → revoked

Retain the silent *e* if the suffix starts with a consonant:

hope → hopeful   love → lovely   polite → politeness

Exceptions: *advantageous, argument, duly, enforceable, judgment, serviceable*

Words that end with y For most words that end with a consonant and *y*, change the *y* to an *i* when you add a suffix:

| apology → apolog<u>ize</u> | deny → den<u>ies</u> |
| heavy → heav<u>ier</u> | merry → merr<u>iment</u> |

Retain the *y* if the suffix is *-ing*, if a vowel precedes the *y*, or if the word ending in *y* is a proper name:

| spy → spy<u>ing</u> | play → play<u>ful</u> | McCoy → McCoy<u>s</u> |

Suffixes *-cede, -ceed,* ***and*** *-sede* To avoid confusing these three suffixes, remember these facts:

1. *Supersede* is the only English word that ends in *-sede*.
2. *Exceed, proceed,* and *succeed* are the only words that end in *-ceed*.
3. All other similar words use the suffix *-cede: accede, concede, precede, secede*.

Suffixes *-ally* ***versus*** *-ly* ***and*** *-efy* ***versus*** *-ify* When a word ends in *ic*, use the suffix *-ally*. In all other instances, use *-ly*:

| bas<u>ic</u> → basic<u>ally</u> | mag<u>ic</u> → magic<u>ally</u> |
| brisk → brisk<u>ly</u> | confident → confident<u>ly</u> |

Only four words use the suffix *-efy: liquefy, putrefy, rarefy, stupefy*. All other such words use the suffix *-ify: beautify, certify, justify, purify*.

Words that end with a consonant Do not double a final consonant if the suffix begins with a consonant (*commitment, fearless, kinship, poorly*). For suffixes that begin with a vowel, follow these guidelines:

- **One-syllable root words.** Double the final consonant if only one vowel precedes it:

  | bit → bit<u>ten</u> | chat → chat<u>ty</u> | skip → skip<u>ping</u> |

  For other one-syllable words, do not double the consonant:

  | chart → chart<u>ed</u> | droop → droop<u>ing</u> | speak → speak<u>er</u> |

- **Multisyllable words.** Double the final consonant if only one vowel precedes the final consonant and if the final syllable of the root is accented in the new word containing the suffix:

  | ad**mit** → ad**mit**<u>tance</u> | con**cur** → con**cur**<u>rent</u> |
  | con**trol** → con**trol**<u>led</u> |

For multisyllable words that do not meet these criteria, do not double the final consonant:

devil → devilish	parallel → parallelism
erupt → erupted	proclaim → proclaiming

In *devilish* and *parallelism,* the accent is on the first syllable of the root word; the final *t* in *erupt* is preceded by a consonant; and the final *m* in *proclaim* is preceded by two vowels.

EXERCISE 32.2 Adding suffixes

Correct any misspelled words in the following list, and circle those that are spelled correctly.

changeable	truly	beginning	tragicly
deploing	argueable	replys	running
supercede	regreted	optimally	angrily
principally	soly	sponsored	

32e Forming Plurals

Most English nouns form the plural by adding the suffix *-s* or *-es*. Some nouns, however, like *child* (plural *children*) and *man* (plural *men*), have irregular forms, and some compound nouns form the plural on a word that is not the last one in the compound.

Tech — Use Spelling Checkers Cautiously

Although the features of a spell checker are helpful, you cannot depend on them alone to guarantee error-free spelling.

- Spelling checkers do not differentiate homonyms and commonly confused words, such as *descent, dissent* or *too, two*. If you type a correctly spelled word that happens not to be correct for the context, a spelling checker will not mark it wrong.
- If you misspell a word, a spelling checker may suggest replacing it with the wrong word. For example, if you type *retify* for *rectify,* the checker's first recommendation might be *ratify,* which is clearly the wrong word.
- A spelling checker will alert you to many situations in which you need to capitalize, but it will not alert you to the unnecessary use of capitals, as in *Shakespeare is an Important British writer.*

Spelling checkers, then, are a useful tool but not a replacement for a dictionary and careful proofreading.

> **More about**
> Capitalization, 858–64

1. Regular plurals

- To form the plural of most English nouns, add an -s.

  letter → letters   shoe → shoes   Erickson → the Ericksons

- To form the plural of nouns that end with s, sh, ch, x, or z, add -es.

  miss → misses   dish → dishes   latch → latches

  box → boxes   fez → fezzes   Davis → the Davises

- To form the plural of some nouns that end with f or fe, change the f to a v and add -s or -es.

  loaf → loaves   scarf → scarves   thief → thieves

  knife → knives   wife → wives

- However, words that end in ff or ffe and some words that end in f or fe form the plural just with the addition of an -s.

  bluff → bluffs   giraffe → giraffes

  chief → chiefs   safe → safes

- To form the plural of nouns that end with o, add -s if the o is preceded by a vowel or if the word is a proper noun.

  duo → duos   ratio → ratios   video → videos

  Add -es if the o is preceded by a consonant.

  echo → echoes   potato → potatoes   veto → vetoes

  Some exceptions: *autos, ponchos, sopranos, tacos*

- To form the plural of words that end with y, add -s if the y is preceded by a vowel or if the word is a proper noun.

  decoy → decoys   essay → essays   Hagarty → the Hagartys

  Change the y to i and add -es if the y is preceded by a consonant.

  berry → berries   enemy → enemies   family → families

2. Irregular plurals

The only way to learn irregular plurals is to memorize them. Many nouns have irregular plurals that have survived from earlier forms of English.

woman → women   child → children   deer → deer

foot → feet   ox → oxen   sheep → sheep

mouse → mice

Other English nouns with irregular plurals were borrowed from languages such as Greek, Latin, and French and retain the plural form of the original language.

analysis → analyses	criterion → criteria	phenomenon → phenomena
alumna → alumnae	medium → media	tableau → tableaux
alumnus → alumni	nucleus → nuclei	

For many such words, a regularized plural form is acceptable as an alternative to the irregular form: *index, indices/indexes; fungus, fungi/funguses*

3. Plurals of compound nouns

To form the plural of compound nouns composed of separate or hyphenated words, add *-s* or *-es* to the main noun in the compound.

| brigadier generals | chiefs of staff | runners-up |

If there is no main noun, add *-s* or *-es* at the end: *singer-songwriter*s.
For compounds that are spelled as one word, add *-s* or *-es* at the end.

| keyboards | spaceships | touchdowns |

An exception: *passersby*

EXERCISE 32.3 Forming plurals

Write the plural form of each of the following singular nouns.

buzz	rally	half	ploy
mother-in-law	domino	study	tooth
handcuff	moose	studio	goose
spoof	person	tomato	

32f Improving Your Day-to-Day Spelling

Writers who have mastered all the rules in this chapter may still occasionally misspell some words. Here are a few tips for further reducing misspellings in your work:

- If you tend to misspell the same word or types of words repeatedly, keep track of them in a vocabulary log and check for them specifically when you proofread.
- Use a dictionary often, and keep one handy next to your computer.

- Remember that pronunciation may lead you astray in your spelling. Although you may say "goverment," do not forget that *govern* is the root word, so the word is spelled *government,* with an *n*.
- Use a spelling checker with caution (see the Tech box on p. 623), and proofread carefully.

Make It **Your Own**

With the spelling checker on, type this sentence into a blank word processing document:

> Fore score and seven yours ago, are fathers brought fourth on this continence anew nation, conceived in liberty and dedicated to the preposition that awl men our created equal.

Now compare the sentence to the first sentence of Abraham Lincoln's Gettysburg Address:

> Four score and seven years ago, our fathers brought forth on this continent a new nation, conceived in liberty and dedicated to the proposition that all men are created equal.

How many errors did your spelling checker catch? Introduce two or more similar errors into other famous passages (or into passages from a textbook or a newspaper or magazine article), and see how dependably the spelling checker catches them. For famous quotations, consult *Bartlett's Familiar Quotations,* available in print and also as an app at www.bartlettsquotes.com, *The Yale Book of Quotations,* or *The Oxford Dictionary of Quotations,* available in print and also online by subscription at www.oxfordreference.com.

Work **Together**

With a classmate, exchange printouts (double-spaced) of the sentences with the errors you introduced in the Make It Your Own exercise above. Correct the sentences by hand; then check your work against the original sources.

Text Credits

Pg. 626: The Gettysburg Address, Abraham Lincoln November 19, 1863.

Part Eight

Grammar Matters
Writing with Clarity

33 Understanding Grammar   634
   Grammar Tutorial: Identifying Common Sentence Errors   628
34 Avoiding Sentence Fragments   660
35 Avoiding Comma Splices and Fused Sentences   671
36 Maintaining Agreement   680
37 Using Verbs   694
38 Understanding Pronoun Case and Reference   712
39 Using Adjectives and Adverbs   724
40 Avoiding Confusing Shifts   732
41 Avoiding Misplaced and Dangling Modifiers   740
42 Avoiding Mixed and Incomplete Constructions   749

Grammar Matters | Identifying Common Sentence Problems

Recognizing and Correcting Fragments (660–70)

A fragment is an incomplete sentence punctuated as if it were complete.

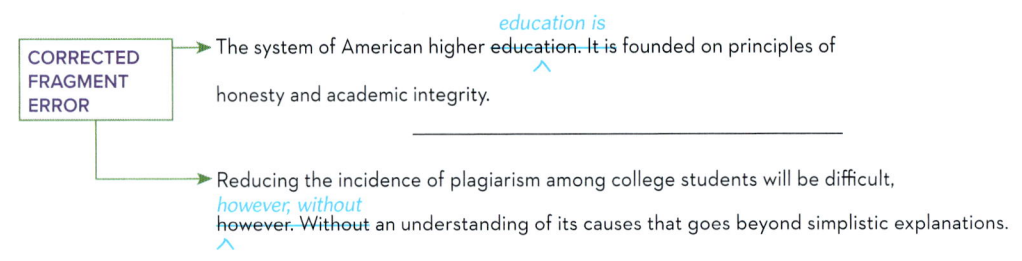

CORRECTED FRAGMENT ERROR

→ The system of American higher ~~education. It is~~ *education is* founded on principles of honesty and academic integrity.

→ Reducing the incidence of plagiarism among college students will be difficult, ~~however. Without~~ *however, without* an understanding of its causes that goes beyond simplistic explanations.

Maintaining Subject-Verb Agreement (680–89)

A verb and its subject agree when they match each other in person (first, second, or third) and number (singular or plural).

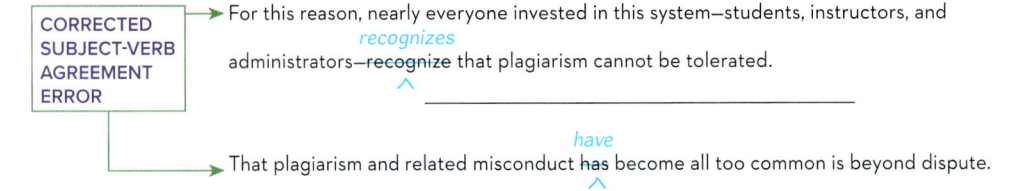

CORRECTED SUBJECT-VERB AGREEMENT ERROR

→ For this reason, nearly everyone invested in this system—students, instructors, and administrators—~~recognize~~ *recognizes* that plagiarism cannot be tolerated.

→ That plagiarism and related misconduct ~~has~~ *have* become all too common is beyond dispute.

Maintaining Pronoun-Antecedent Agreement (689–93)

A pronoun agrees with its antecedent (the word the pronoun replaces) when they match each other in person (first, second, or third), number (singular or plural), and gender (masculine, feminine, or neuter) while avoiding gender bias.

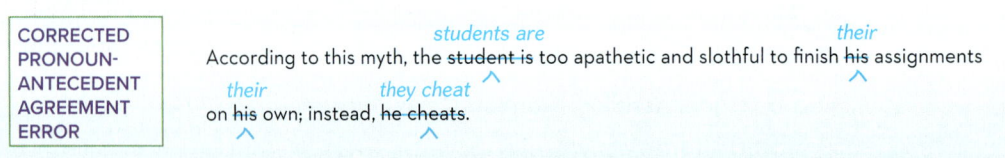

CORRECTED PRONOUN-ANTECEDENT AGREEMENT ERROR

According to this myth, the ~~student is~~ *students are* too apathetic and slothful to finish ~~his~~ *their* assignments on ~~his~~ *their* own; instead, ~~he cheats~~ *they cheat*.

628

Recognizing and Correcting Fused (Run-On) Sentences (671–79)

In a fused (or run-on) sentence, one independent clause incorrectly follows another with no punctuation or joining words between them.

CORRECTED FUSED SENTENCE ERROR

Practices among higher education students are not much ~~better according to~~ *better. According to* research by Donald L. McCabe, a professor at Rutgers University who has done extensive work on cheating, 38% of college students admitted to committing forms of plagiarism in the previous year (Rimer 7).

Recognizing and Correcting Comma Splices (671–79)

In a comma splice, two independent clauses are incorrectly joined by a comma alone, without a coordinating conjunction such as *and* or *but*.

CORRECTED COMMA SPLICE ERROR

It is late at night, *and* a student sits staring at a computer.

Using Irregular Verb Forms Correctly (694–702)

Regular verbs form the past tense and past participle by adding -*ed* to the base form; irregular verbs do not.

CORRECTED VERB FORM ERROR

A paper is due the following morning, and research needs to be done, notes need to be ~~took~~ *taken*, and, in the end, an essay needs to be ~~wrote~~ *written* and edited.

Avoiding Unclear Pronoun Reference (719–22)

Pronoun reference is clear when readers can effortlessly identify a pronoun's antecedent (the word the pronoun replaces).

CORRECTED PRONOUN REFERENCE ERROR

→ Undeniably, some ~~of it~~ *plagiarism* occurs because students find *it* ~~plagiarizing~~ easier than simply doing the work required.

→ The argument that laziness is ~~its main cause, however, is~~ *the main cause of plagiarism, however, is* at best incomplete and seems, moreover, to be fed by unfair stereotypes of ~~them~~ *students* as bored by academic rigor and more interested in video games or social media than in the hard work of learning.

629

Grammar Matters | Identifying Common Sentence Problems (continued)

Student Model **First Draft with Sentence Problems**

Why Some Students Cheat:
The Complexities and Oversimplifications of Plagiarism (Draft 1)

Sentence fragment — The system of American higher education. It is founded on principles of honesty and academic integrity. For this reason, nearly *everyone* invested in this *— Lack of subject-verb agreement* — system—students, instructors, and administrators—*recognize* that plagiarism cannot be tolerated. People also agree that a lot of plagiarism is occurring. Reducing the incidence of plagiarism among college students will be difficult, however. *Without an* *— Sentence fragment* — *understanding of its causes that goes beyond simplistic explanations.*

That *plagiarism and related misconduct has become* all too common is *— Lack of subject-verb agreement* — beyond dispute. A survey published in *Who's Who among American High School Students* (reported by Newberger) indicated that 15 percent of top-ranked high schoolers plagiarize. Practices among higher education students are not much *— Fused sentence* — better according to research by Donald L. McCabe, a professor at Rutgers University who has done extensive work on cheating, 70% of college students "copied almost word for word from a source and submitted as their own work" (41). A study by Stephen Hard and colleagues showed that plagiarism was common among the 411 students who participated in their research.

There is a commonly held myth about how most plagiarism occurs. It is late at *— Comma splice* — night, a student sits staring at a computer. A paper is due the following morning, and research needs to be done, *notes need to be took, and, in the end, an essay needs* *— Incorrect verb forms* — *to be wrote and edited.* The student, overwhelmed, succumbs to the temptations of plagiarism—"cutting and pasting" from sources, downloading an essay from the internet, *— Pronoun-antecedent agreement error: gender bias* — or simply buying a paper from another student. *According to this myth, the student is* *too apathetic and slothful to finish his assignment on his own; instead, he cheats.*

Undeniably, some of *it* occurs because students find *it* easier than simply doing the *— Incorrect pronoun references* — work required. The argument that laziness is *its* main cause, however, is at best incomplete and seems, moreover, to be fed by unfair stereotypes of *them* as bored by academic rigor, more interested in video games or social media than the hard work of learning.

In fact, some plagiarism grows from the opposite of these characteristics. High-achieving students, for example, fear what a bad grade will do to their

630

Student Model First Draft with Sentence Problems

otherwise stellar GPAs. Such students may treat the attainment of impressive marks as a necessity and will betray the very academic system they revere in order to sustain their average.

Other students plagiarize more from lack of interest in a particular course than general idleness. Students who view writing papers as hoops they must jump through to graduate, for instance, were more likely to have downloaded a paper from an online "paper mill" than to write one themselves. For them, a college writing class is something to be endured rather than an opportunity for learning. — *Shift in tense*

Students draw a distinction between their interests and their academic assignments, and plagiarism is rationalized by them as a way to escape an "unfair" academic obligation. Websites such as *EduBirdie*, which will write a paper to order, cater students like these, who consider at least some aspects of academia essentially useless. — *Shift in voice* / *Incomplete construction*

Many other instances of plagiarism are committed by students whom it turns out have honest intentions but are ignorant of citation methods. Michael Gunn, a British student, copied quotations from Internet sources in numerous papers over several years and was shocked to learn that this qualified as plagiarism (Baty). Even recognizing the importance of citation may not know how to cite their sources correctly. A student who omits the source of a paraphrase in a paper would probably be surprised to learn that him, her, or they is often considered as guilty of plagiarism as the student who downloads an essay. — *Pronoun case error* / *Mixed construction error* / *Pronoun case error*

The internet has compounded confusion with regard to citation. The internet is a place of free exchange and information movement rapidly from computer to computer. In this environment, ownership and citation become hazy. As John Leland, a reporter for *The New York Times*, writes, "Culture's heat now lies with the ability to cut, paste, clip, sample, quote, recycle, customize, and re-circulate." Many students—for example by highlighting it, copying it, and pasting it into a word processing document—find it easy and "natural" to take text from an online source. Having trouble keeping track of everything they have read, however, the chances increase of students accidentally plagiarizing by forgetting to cite a copied text. So, too, does the likelihood of "patchwriting," the substitution of synonyms or the shuffling of sentences in a borrowed text without putting the information fully into the writer's own words (Howard 233). Finally, some students will also be tempted to commit intentional plagiarism, choosing to leave a block of copied text uncited. — *Adverb problem* / *Misplaced modifier error* / *Dangling modifier error*

631

Grammar Matters | Identifying Common Sentence Problems (continued)

Avoiding Confusing Shifts in Tense and Voice (732–34)

Shifts from one tense to another or from the active to the passive voice are confusing when they occur for no clear reason.

CORRECTED SHIFT IN TENSE ERROR

Students who view writing papers as hoops they must jump through to graduate, for instance, ~~were~~ *are* more likely to ~~have downloaded~~ *download* a paper from an online "paper mill" than to write one themselves.

CORRECTED SHIFT IN VOICE ERROR

Students draw a distinction between their interests and their academic assignments, and ~~plagiarism is rationalized by them~~ *they rationalize plagiarism* as a way to escape an "unfair" academic obligation.

Avoiding Incomplete Constructions (753–55)

A phrase or clause is incomplete if it is missing any words required for idiomatic and grammatical clarity.

CORRECTED INCOMPLETE CONSTRUCTION ERROR

Websites such as *EduBirdie*, which will write a paper to order, cater *to* students like these, who consider at least some aspects of academia essentially useless.

Avoiding Mixed Constructions (749–53)

A mixed construction is a sentence with parts that do not fit together grammatically or logically.

CORRECTED MIXED CONSTRUCTION ERROR

Even ~~recognizing~~ *students who recognize* the importance of citation may not know how to cite their sources correctly.

Distinguishing Adjectives and Adverbs (724–31)

Adjectives modify nouns or pronouns; adverbs modify verbs, adjectives, other adverbs, and entire phrases and clauses.

CORRECTED ADVERB ERROR

The internet is a place of free exchange and information ~~movement rapidly~~ *the rapid movement of* from computer to computer.

He, She, They, Who or *Him, Her, Their, Whom*? Matching Pronoun Case to Function (712–19)

A case problem occurs when the form of a pronoun—subjective, objective, or possessive—does not correspond to its grammatical role in a sentence.

CORRECTED PRONOUN CASE ERROR

Many other instances of plagiarism are committed by students ~~whom it turns out~~ *who, it turns out,* have honest intentions but are ignorant of citation methods.

A student who omits the source of a paraphrase in a paper would probably be surprised to learn that ~~him, her, or they is~~ *they are* often considered as guilty of plagiarism as the student who downloads an essay.

Avoiding Misplaced Modifiers (740–44)

A misplaced modifier is an ambiguously, confusingly, or disruptively placed modifying word, phrase, or clause.

CORRECTED MISPLACED MODIFIER ERROR

Many students—~~for~~ *find it easy and "natural" to take text from an online source—for* example by highlighting it, copying it, and pasting it into a word processing document—~~find it easy and "natural" to take text from an online source~~.

Avoiding Dangling Modifiers (745–47)

A dangling modifier does not clearly modify the subject or any other part of a sentence, leaving it to the reader to infer the intended meaning.

CORRECTED DANGLING MODIFIER ERROR

~~Having~~ *Because students can have* trouble keeping track of everything they have read, however, the chances increase ~~of students' accidentally plagiarizing~~ *that they will plagiarize accidentally* by forgetting to cite a copied text.

633

33 Understanding Grammar

IN THIS CHAPTER

PARTS OF SPEECH

a. Nouns, 635
b. Pronouns, 637
c. Verbs, 639
d. Adjectives, 640
e. Adverbs, 641
f. Prepositions, 642
g. Conjunctions, 643
h. Interjections, 644

SENTENCE STRUCTURE

i. Subjects, 645
j. Predicates, 647
k. Sentence patterns, 648
l. Phrases, 651
m. Clauses, 654
n. Sentence types, 657

The rules of baseball, which give the game meaning and structure, have become second nature to proficient players. Most of these rules are inflexible: A player who ran around the bases carrying the ball would not be playing baseball. Some rules vary, however: Until the Covid-19 pandemic, in the American League but not in the National League, teams could designate another player to bat instead of the pitcher.

Languages, too, have rules—*grammars*—that structure words so they can convey meaning. Just as baseball players have internalized the rules of the game, so have we all internalized the grammar of our native language. Most rules of grammar are inflexible. Any English speaker, for example, would recognize a statement like *throw Maria ball the base first to* as ungrammatical. Some aspects of grammar, however, can vary over time, from region to region, and from group to group.

The form of English that is preferred today in academic settings and in the workplace in the United States is known as **Standard American English.** Although it is not better or more correct than other varieties, Standard American English is what readers expect to encounter in academic and business writing in the United States. This chapter reviews the rules of Standard American English grammar, and the chapters that follow it in part 8 focus on particular aspects of grammar and usage that many writers find troublesome.

> **More about**
> Common sentence problems, 628–33 (*Grammar Matters* tutorial preceding this chapter)

Writing Responsibly: Why Grammar Matters

Sometimes a writer uses nonstandard grammar as a way of drawing attention to issues of culture and power, or as a way of asserting the legitimacy of nonstandard dialects. In academic settings, though, writers have a responsibility to use language their readers regard as grammatically correct. A shared standard of grammar eases communication and demonstrates your respect for your readers.

to AUDIENCE

PARTS OF SPEECH

The term *parts of speech* refers to the functions words play in a sentence. English has eight parts of speech:

- nouns
- pronouns
- verbs
- adjectives
- adverbs
- prepositions
- conjunctions
- interjections

The same word can have more than one function, depending on the context in which it appears.

▶ Many students work to help pay for college. [*Work* is a verb.]
▶ Mastering calculus requires hard work. [*Work* is a noun.]

33a Nouns

Nouns name ideas (*justice*), things (*chair*), qualities (*neatness*), actions (*judgment*), people (*Albert Einstein*), and places (*Tokyo*). They fall into a variety of overlapping categories:

- ***Proper nouns*** name specific places, people, or things and are usually capitalized: *Nairobi, Hudson Bay, Greta Thunberg,* the *Taj Mahal.* All other nouns are ***common nouns,*** which name members of a class or group: *turtle, sophomore, skyscraper.*

- ***Collective nouns*** name a collection that can function as a single unit: *committee, administration, family.*

- ***Concrete nouns*** name things that can be seen, touched, heard, smelled, or tasted: *planet, liquid, symphony, skunk, pepper.*

Quick Reference: The Parts of Speech

Parts of Speech	Functions	Examples
Nouns	name ideas, things, qualities, actions, people, and places	**Sarah** usually drives her blue **car** to **work**, but, alas, it needs expensive **repairs**.
Pronouns	rename or take the place of nouns or noun phrases	Sarah usually drives **her** blue car to work, but, alas, **it** needs expensive repairs.
Verbs	express action, occurrence, or state of being	Sarah usually **drives** her blue car to work, but, alas, it **needs** expensive repairs.
Adjectives	modify nouns or pronouns with descriptive or limiting information, answering questions such as *What kind? Which one?* or *How many?*	Sarah usually drives her **blue** car to work, but, alas, it needs **expensive** repairs.
Adverbs	modify verbs, adjectives, and other adverbs as well as entire phrases and clauses, answering such questions as *How? Where? When?* and *To what extent or degree?*	Sarah **usually** drives her blue car to work, but, alas, it needs expensive repairs.
Prepositions	relate nouns or pronouns to other words in a sentence in terms of time, space, cause, and other attributes	Sarah usually drives her blue car **to** work, but, alas, it needs expensive repairs.
Conjunctions	join words, phrases, and clauses to other words, phrases, or clauses and specify the way the joined elements relate to each other	Sarah usually drives her blue car to work, **but**, alas, it needs expensive repairs.
Interjections	express strong feeling but otherwise serve no grammatical function	Sarah usually drives her blue car to work, but, **alas**, it needs expensive repairs.

- *Abstract nouns* name qualities or ideas that cannot be perceived by the senses: *mercy, fear.*
- *Countable* (or *count*) *nouns* name things or ideas that can be counted. They can be either **singular** or **plural**: *cat/cats, assignment/assignments, idea/ideas.*
- *Uncountable* (or *noncount*) *nouns* name ideas or things that cannot be counted and do not have a plural form: *homework, knowledge, pollution.*

> **More about**
> Count and noncount nouns,
> 767–69, 771–74

Countable and Noncountable Nouns In many languages the classification of nouns as count or noncount affects the way they combine with articles (*a, an, the*) and other determiners (*my, your, some, many, this, these*). Awareness of the effect of this aspect of nouns on sentence grammar will help you avoid errors.

Most nouns form the plural with the addition of a final *-s* or *-es*: *book/books, beach/beaches, country/countries*. A few have irregular plurals: *woman/women, life/lives, mouse/mice*. For some nouns, the singular and the plural forms are the same: *deer/deer, fish/fish*.

Nouns indicate possession with a final *s* sound, marked in writing with an apostrophe: *Rosa's idea, the students' plan*.

> **More about**
> Noun plurals, 623–25

> **More about**
> Apostrophes and possession, 827–31

33b Pronouns

Pronouns rename or take the place of nouns or **noun phrases**. The noun that a pronoun replaces is called its **antecedent**. The Quick Reference box on page 638 summarizes the types of pronouns and their functions.

> **noun phrase** A noun and its modifiers

> **More about**
> Pronouns, 689–93, 712–23
> Singular *they* and *their*, 602

EXERCISE 33.1 Identifying nouns and pronouns

Circle the nouns and underline the pronouns in the following sentences.

EXAMPLE

On his way to pick up his aunt at the airport, Bradley found himself stuck in traffic.

1. Making the situation even worse, the driver behind him kept honking their horn.

2. Bradley felt his car shake a bit and realized that the driver behind him had bumped his rear fender slightly while pulling out to change lanes.

3. The other driver was out of sight by the time Bradley reminded himself to get the car's license number.

4. He arrived at the airport a few minutes late, saw that his car's fender was unharmed, scanned the monitor for information about incoming flights, and learned that many, including his aunt's, were an hour behind schedule.

Quick Reference: Pronouns and Their Functions

Type and Function	Forms	Examples
Personal pronouns take the place of specific nouns or noun phrases.	Singular: *I, me, you, he, him, she, her, it, they, them* Plural: *we, us, you, they, them*	Yue bought the tickets for Adam, and she gave them to him before the concert.
Possessive pronouns are personal pronouns that indicate possession.	Singular: *my, mine, your, yours, his, her, hers, its, their, theirs* Plural: *our, ours, your, yours, their, theirs*	Adam gave one of the tickets to his roommate.
Reflexive pronouns refer back to the subject of a sentence.	Singular: *myself, yourself, himself, herself, itself, oneself* Plural: *ourselves, yourselves, themselves*	Laetitia reminded herself to return the books to the library.
Intensive pronouns rename and emphasize their antecedents.	Same as reflexive pronouns	Dr. Collins herself performed the operation.
Demonstrative pronouns rename and point to nouns or noun phrases. They can function as adjectives as well as nouns.	Singular: *this, that* Plural: *these, those*	Yameng visited the Forbidden City. That was his favorite place in China. That place was his favorite.
Relative pronouns introduce subordinate clauses that describe the pronoun's antecedent.	*who, whom, whoever, whomever, what, whose, whatever, whichever, that, which*	I. M. Pei is the architect who designed the East Wing of the National Gallery.
Interrogative pronouns introduce questions.	*who, whoever, whom, whomever, what, whatever, which, whichever, whose*	Who designed the East Wing of the National Gallery?
Indefinite pronouns do not refer to specific people or things.	Singular: *anybody, anyone, anything, each, either, everybody, everyone, everything, much, neither, nobody, no one, nothing, one, somebody, someone, something* Singular or plural: *all, any, more, most, some* Plural: *both, few, many, several*	Everybody talks about the weather, but nobody does anything about it. —Attributed to Mark Twain
Reciprocal pronouns refer to the individual parts of a plural antecedent.	*each other, one another*	The candidates debated one another many times before the primary.

33c Verbs

Verbs express action (*The quarterback throws a pass*), occurrence (*The play happened in the second half*), or state of being (*The fans are happy*). Verbs also carry information about time (tense), as well as person, number, voice, and mood.

> **More about**
> Verb forms,
> 694–700

Two kinds of verbs combine to make up a *verb phrase: main verbs* and **helping** (or **auxiliary**) **verbs.** Main verbs carry the principal meaning of a verb phrase. Almost all verb constructions other than the present and past tense, however, require a combination of one or more helping verbs with a form of the main verb. Some helping verbs (forms of *be, have,* and *do*) also function as main verbs. Others, called **modal verbs** (*can, could, may, might, must, shall, should, will, would,* and *ought to*), function only as helping verbs.

Modal Auxiliaries Modal auxiliaries can pose special problems for multilingual students because other languages use very different grammatical strategies to express intention, possibility, or expectation. For more on their meaning and use, see pages 782–84.

Helping verbs always precede the main verb in a verb phrase.

		verb phrase		
	The player	hit	a long home run.	main verb
helping verbs	The home run	may have broken	a distance record.	main verb
helping verbs	The children	have been playing	for two hours.	main verb

NOTE Do not confuse *verbals* with complete verbs. Verbals are verb forms functioning as nouns, adjectives, or adverbs, not as verbs.

> **More about**
> Verbals, 652–53, 661

- The potters *fired* the vessels in their kiln. [*Fired* is a verb.]
- The *fired* clay is rock hard. [*Fired* is a verbal, in this case an adjective modifying *clay.*]

EXERCISE 33.2 Identifying verb phrases

Underline the verb phrases in the following sentences, and circle the main verb in each. Note that some sentences may have more than one verb phrase.

1. Rennie has been to the zoo more often this year than ever before.
2. Her twin nieces began walking recently, and since then their favorite activity has been going to the zoo with Aunt Rennie.

3. This spring the twins were excited about the newly arrived pandas.
4. By the time Rennie and the twins finally got to the zoo, the pandas had become accustomed to visitors and were chewing calmly on some bamboo.

33d Adjectives

> **More about**
> Adjectives,
> 725–31

Adjectives modify nouns or pronouns with descriptive or limiting information. They answer questions such as *What kind? Which one?* or *How many?*

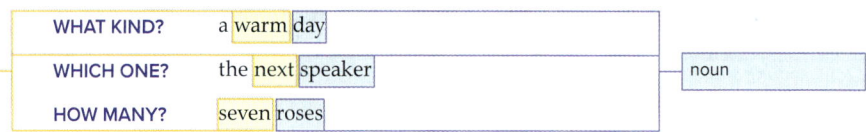

WHAT KIND?	a *warm* day
WHICH ONE?	the *next* speaker
HOW MANY?	*seven* roses

Adjectives most commonly fall before nouns in a noun phrase and after *linking verbs* as *subject complements*.

▸ The *young* musicians played a *rousing* concert.

▸ They were *enthusiastic*.
 pro- link. adj.
 noun verb

> **linking verb** A verb that conveys a state of being linking a subject to its complement
> **subject complement** An adjective, pronoun, or noun phrase that follows a linking verb and describes or refers to the sentence subject

Many adjectives change form to express comparison: *young, younger, youngest; enthusiastic, more/less enthusiastic, most/least enthusiastic.*

Possessive, demonstrative, and indefinite pronouns that function as adjectives—as well as the articles *a, an,* and *the*—are known as **determiners** because they specify or quantify the nouns they modify. Determiners always precede other adjectives in a noun phrase. Some, like *all* and *both,* also precede any other determiners.

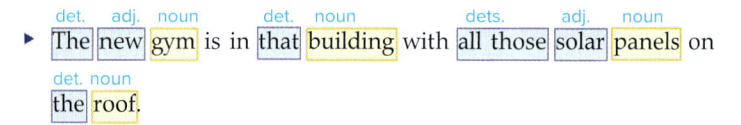

▸ *The new* gym is in *that* building with *all those solar* panels on *the* roof.
  det. adj. noun   det. noun   dets. adj. noun
  det. noun

> **More about**
> Comparative adjectives,
> 729–31

The Ordering of Adjectives The ordering of adjectives in noun phrases and the use of articles and other determiners in English can be challenging for multilingual writers. English sentences tend to place adjectives before nouns, while adjective placement in other languages varies, and some languages do not use articles at all. For more on these topics, see pages 786 and 768–74.

33e Adverbs

Adverbs modify verbs, adjectives, and other adverbs, as well as entire phrases and clauses. They answer such questions as *How? Where? When?* and *To what extent or degree?*

> **More about**
> Adverbs, 724–31

HOW? ⟨adverb⟩ Embarrassingly, my cell phone ⟨verb⟩ rang ⟨adv.⟩ loudly.

The adverb *loudly* modifies the verb *rang*. The adverb *embarrassingly* modifies the whole sentence.

WHEN? Dinner is ⟨adv.⟩ finally ⟨adj.⟩ ready.

The adverb *finally* modifies the adjective *ready*.

WHERE?
EXTENT? ⟨verb⟩ Stop ⟨adv.⟩ right ⟨adv.⟩ there!

The adverb *right* modifies the adverb *there,* which modifies the verb *stop*.

Like adjectives, many adverbs change form to express comparison: *far, farther, farthest; frequently, more/less frequently, most/least frequently.*

> **More about**
> Comparative adverbs, 729–31

A ***conjunctive adverb*** is a transitional expression that can link one independent clause to another. The conjunctive adverb modifies the second clause and specifies its relationship to the first. A period or semicolon, not a comma, should separate independent clauses linked with a conjunctive adverb.

▸ Writers have several options for joining independent clauses; a comma alone, however, is not one of them.

Quick Reference Common Conjunctive Adverbs

accordingly	however	otherwise
also	indeed	similarly
anyway	instead	specifically
as a result	likewise	still
besides	meanwhile	subsequently
certainly	moreover	suddenly
finally	nevertheless	then
for example	next	therefore
furthermore	nonetheless	thus
hence	now	

gram • Grammar Matters • Understanding Grammar

> **More about**
> Adjective and adverb phrases, 652–53, 743–44
> Adjective and adverb clauses, 655–56

NOTE In addition to individual words, whole phrases and clauses can function as adjectives and adverbs within sentences.

EXERCISE 33.3 Identifying adjectives and adverbs

Underline the adjectives and circle the adverbs in the following sentences.

1. Grace Rosario had always liked to have a tidy bedroom.
2. She decided to ask Maritza gently if they could have a little chat about neatness.
3. The two were good friends as well as roommates, so they agreeably worked out a compromise.
4. They split their small room into equal halves, and each cleaned her half as thoroughly as she wished.

33f Prepositions

Prepositions relate nouns or pronouns to other words in a sentence in terms of time, space, cause, and other attributes.

- The lecture begins [at] noon [in] the auditorium.

As the Quick Reference box on the next page indicates, prepositions can consist of more than one word.

EXERCISE 33.4 Identifying prepositions

Underline the prepositions in each of the following sentences.

1. Many people drink coffee despite worrying about the health risks.
2. Over the last twenty years, research has shown that coffee is safe in moderation, and it may even offer some health benefits.
3. According to some studies, regular coffee drinkers have a lower incidence of type 2 diabetes than people who do not drink coffee.
4. However, because the main ingredient in coffee is caffeine, a mildly addictive stimulant, excessive use is not recommended.

> **Quick Reference** — **Common One-Word and Multiword Prepositions**

about	at	far from	near	past
above	because of	for	near to	since
according to	before	from	next to	through
across	behind	in	of	to
after	below	in addition to	off	toward
against	beneath	in case of	on	under
ahead of	beside	in front of	on account of	underneath
along	between	in place of	on behalf of	until
among	by	in spite of	on top of	up
around	by means of	inside	onto	upon
as far as	close to	inside of	out of	with
as to	down	instead of	outside	within
as well as	during	into	outside of	without
aside from	except	like	over	

33g Conjunctions

Conjunctions join words, phrases, and clauses to other words, phrases, or clauses and specify the way the joined elements relate to each other.

- *Coordinating conjunctions* (*and, but, or, for, nor, yet,* and *so*) join grammatically equivalent elements, giving them each equal significance.

  ▸ Ingenious and energetic entrepreneurs can generate effective but inexpensive publicity. [The conjunction *and* pairs two adjectives; the conjunction *but* contrasts two adjectives.]

- *Correlative conjunctions* are pairs of terms that, like coordinating conjunctions, join grammatically equivalent elements. Common correlative conjunctions include *either . . . or, neither . . . nor, both . . . and, not only . . . but also,* and *whether . . . or.*

  ▸ Rami Malek has won both an Academy Award and a Golden Globe.

- *Subordinating conjunctions* link subordinate clauses to the independent clauses they modify.

  ▸ The party could not begin until the guest of honor had arrived.

> **More about**
> Independent and subordinate clauses, 654–56

> **Quick Reference** — **Common Subordinating Conjunctions**
>
> | | | | |
> |---|---|---|---|
> | after | before | since | when |
> | although | even if | so that | where |
> | as | even though | though | while |
> | as if | if | unless | |
> | because | once | until | |

➤ EXERCISE 33.5 Identifying conjunctions

Underline the conjunctions in the following sentences, and label the type of conjunction (coordinating, correlative, or subordinating) each is.

1. Photography was Randall's hobby, so he volunteered to take photos at the community service club's fundraising car wash.

2. He said he would send the story and photos not only to the local newspaper but also to the school's TV station.

3. After the car wash, Randall had to decide whether to download the photos to his computer or ask to use his friend Amita's computer, which was faster and had more memory than his.

4. Although he decided to ask Amita, he ended up using his own computer anyway because hers needed repairs.

5. In the end, once he had followed up his photo story submission with phone calls, both the newspaper and TV station decided to run the story.

33h Interjections

Interjections are words like *alas, bah, oh, ouch,* and *ugh* that express strong feeling—of regret, contempt, surprise, pain, or disgust, for example—but otherwise serve no grammatical function.

- ▸ Ugh! That's the worst coffee I ever tasted.
- ▸ "Bah," said Scrooge.

SENTENCE STRUCTURE

All English sentences have two basic parts: a subject and a predicate. The *subject* is the thing the sentence is about. The *predicate* states something about the subject.

> |—— subject ——| |———— predicate ————|
> ▸ Digital technology transformed the music industry.

English sentences fall into one of four functional categories:

- *Declarative sentences* (the most common type) make a statement.
  - ▸ Digital technology transformed the music industry.
- *Imperative sentences* give a command.
  - ▸ Hire a social media manager if you want to market your product successfully.
- *Interrogative sentences* ask a question.
  - ▸ Has digital technology made print books obsolete?
- *Exclamatory sentences* express strong or sudden emotion.
  - ▸ How I hate updating my apps manually!

33i Subjects

The *simple subject* of a sentence is a noun or pronoun. The *complete subject* consists of the simple subject plus any modifying words or phrases.

> |— complete subject —|
>   simple
>   subject
> ▸ *Two robotic vehicles* began exploring Mars in January 2004.

A *compound subject* contains two or more simple subjects joined by a conjunction.

> |———————— compound subject ————————|
>   ss   conj   ss
> ▸ *The six-wheeled, solar-powered Spirit and the identical Opportunity* landed within three weeks of each other.

In imperative sentences (commands), the subject, *you,* is unstated.

▸ [*You*] Learn about space exploration at www.nasa.gov.

> ### Quick Reference — Finding the Subject
>
> The complete subject of a sentence is the answer to the question "Who or what did the action or was in the state defined by the verb?"
>
> |— complete subject —| verb
> - Two robotic vehicles landed safely on Mars in January 2004.
>
> What landed on Mars in January 2004? Two robotic vehicles did. The subject is *two robotic vehicles*.
>
> |————— complete subject —————| verb
> - The scientists and engineers who designed the rovers cheered.
>
> Who cheered? The scientists and engineers who designed the rovers did. The subject is *the scientists and engineers who designed the rovers*.
>
> The subject usually precedes the verb, but it is not always the first element in a sentence. In the following sentence, for example, the phrase *in July 2007* modifies the rest of the sentence but is not part of the subject.
>
> |— subject —| verb
> - In July 2007, Martian dust storms restricted the activity of the rovers.

In interrogative sentences (questions), the subject falls between a helping verb and the main verb or, if the main verb is a form of *be,* after the verb.

helping verb | |—subject—| | main verb
- Did | the rovers | find evidence of water on Mars?

verb | |——— subject ———|
- Were *Spirit* and *Opportunity* more durable than expected?

> **More about**
> Word order and emphasis,
> 590–91

Writers occasionally invert normal word order and place the subject after the verb for emphasis.

verb | |——— subject ———|
- Out of the swirling dust emerged the hardy Mars rover.

The subject also follows the verb in sentences that begin with *there* followed by a form of *be.* In these **expletive constructions,** the word *there* functions as a placeholder for the delayed subject.

v | |— subject —|
- There are two vehicles roaming the surface of Mars.

English Word Order In English, word order is less flexible than in many other languages, and the position of a word often affects its grammatical function and meaning. English sentences tend to place subjects before verbs and verbs before their objects. English readers expect this order, so using other word orders can cause confusion.

More about
English word order, 757–66

33j Predicates

The *simple predicate* of a sentence is the main verb and any helping verbs. The *complete predicate* is the simple predicate together with any objects, complements, and modifiers.

▸ Polynesian mariners <u>settled</u> the Hawaiian Islands.
   [simple pred. | complete predicate]

▸ The first settlers <u>may have arrived</u> as early as the fourth century CE.
   [simple pred. | complete predicate]

A *compound predicate* is a complete predicate with two or more simple predicates joined by a conjunction.

▸ Polynesian mariners <u>navigated</u> thousands of miles of open ocean and <u>settled</u> the islands of the South Pacific.
   [simple pred. ... complete predicate ... sp]

➔ EXERCISE 33.6 Identifying subjects and predicates

For each of the following sentences, underline and label the simple subject and simple predicate; then circle and label the complete subject and complete predicate.

1. Carlynn had never gone on a camping trip before.
2. Everyone else was diligently working to set up the campsite.
3. Carlynn's cousin Marilupe handed Carlynn a hatchet and told her to find some dead wood for the campfire.
4. Later, an exhausted Carlynn and a still energetic Sara stacked the wood and assembled some large rocks in a circle.

5. Then Marilupe amazed Carlynn as well as everyone else by demonstrating how to start a fire without matches.

33k Verb Types and Sentence Patterns

There are three kinds of verb, *intransitive, linking,* and *transitive,* and they combine with other elements in the predicate in five basic sentence patterns.

1. Subject → intransitive verb

Intransitive verbs require no object and can stand alone as the only element in a predicate. They are often modified, however, by adverbs and adverbial phrases and clauses.

▶ The volcano *erupted*.
  (subj. — verb [intrans.])

▶ The volcano *erupted* suddenly in a powerful blast of ash and steam.
  (subj. — verb [intrans.] — adverbial modifiers)

Quick Reference — Five Sentence Patterns

1. subject → intransitive verb

   ▶ The lights dimmed.
     (s — iv)

2. subject → linking verb → subject complement

   ▶ The audience fell silent.
     (s — lv — sc)

3. subject → transitive verb → direct object

   ▶ The orchestra played the overture.
     (s — tv — do)

4. subject → transitive verb → indirect object → direct object

   ▶ The show gave the audience a thrill.
     (s — tv — io — do)

5. subject → transitive verb → direct object → object complement

   ▶ The applause made the actors happy.
     (s — tv — do — oc)

2. Subject → linking verb → subject complement

A *subject complement* is an adjective, pronoun, or noun phrase that describes or refers to the subject of a sentence. A *linking verb* connects the subject to its complement. Linking verbs express states of being rather than actions. The verb *be,* when used as a main verb, is always a linking verb. Other verbs that can function as linking verbs include *appear, become, fall, feel, grow, look, make, prove, remain, seem, smell, sound,* and *taste.*

▸ The Oscar is a coveted award.
    |— subj. —| vb. |— subj. comp. —|
               link.

▸ The patient felt better.

3. Subject → transitive verb → direct object

Transitive verbs have two *voices:* active and passive. *Transitive verbs* in the *active voice* require a *direct object*—a pronoun or noun phrase that receives the action of the verb.

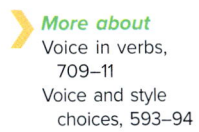

▸ The undersea volcano created a new island.
   |——— subject ———| trans. vb. |— do —|
                         active

> **More about**
> Voice in verbs, 709–11
> Voice and style choices, 593–94

The *passive voice* reverses the role of the subject, making it the recipient of the action of the verb. An active-voice sentence can usually be transformed into a passive-voice sentence of the same meaning. The subject of the passive-voice version is the direct object of the active-voice version.

▸ A new island <u>was created</u> by the undersea volcano.
   |— subject —| trans. verb
               passive

In the passive voice, the agent of the action can be left unstated.

▸ A new island <u>was created</u>.

NOTE Many verbs can be either transitive or intransitive.

TRANSITIVE My sister *won* the Scrabble game.
                          |——— do ———|

INTRANSITIVE My sister always *wins.*

When in doubt about the usage of a verb, check a dictionary.

4. Subject → transitive verb → indirect object → direct object

Some transitive verbs can take an *indirect object* as well as a direct object. The indirect object, which precedes the direct object, identifies the beneficiary of the action of the verb.

s	tv	io	do
▸ Juan	lent	Ileana	his notes.
▸ The donor	bought	the library	a new computer center.

Often, the indirect object can also be stated as a prepositional phrase that begins with *to* or *for* and follows the direct object.

▸ Juan lent his notes *to Ileana.*

▸ The donor bought a new computer center *for the library.*

Verbs that can take an indirect object include *ask, bring, buy, call, find, get, give, hand, leave, lend, offer, pass, pay, promise, read, send, show, teach, tell, throw,* and *write.*

> *More about*
> Indirect objects,
> 761–63

Indirect Objects The use of indirect objects is highly idiomatic in English. The verbs that take them are similar to others that do not. Likewise, in some situations an indirect object before the direct object is interchangeable with a prepositional phrase after it, but in others only one or the other is acceptable. Learning how to use indirect objects effectively, then, requires exposure to a broad variety of English-language situations and texts.

---

5. Subject → transitive verb → direct object → object complement

An *object complement* is an adjective or noun phrase that follows the direct object and describes the condition of the object or a change that the subject has caused it to undergo.

s	tv	do	oc
▸ The fans	considered	the umpire's call	mistaken.
▸ *Time* magazine	named	Greta Thunberg	2019 Person of the Year.

EXERCISE 33.7 Identifying objects and complements

In the following sentences, underline the objects and complements. Then write DO above each direct object, IO above each indirect object, SC above each subject complement, and OC above each object complement.

1. Before he died, my grandfather wrote my mother a long letter.
2. It is actually a family history in letter form.
3. In it, my grandfather describes his own parents' arduous journey from their homeland to their new home in America.
4. The story makes me grateful for their courage.

33l Phrases

A *phrase* is a group of related words that lacks a subject, a predicate, or both. Phrases function in various ways within sentences, but cannot function as sentences by themselves. A phrase by itself is a *fragment*, not a sentence.

fragment An incomplete sentence punctuated as if it were complete

1. Noun phrases

A *noun phrase* consists of a noun together with any modifiers. Noun phrases function as subjects, objects, and complements within sentences.

▸ *Sam's mouth-watering apple pie* emerged piping hot from the oven. [noun phrase/subject]

▸ The guests devoured *Sam's mouth-watering apple pie*. [noun phrase/direct object]

▸ The high point of the meal was *Sam's mouth-watering apple pie*. [noun phrase/subj. comp.]

An *appositive phrase* is a noun or noun phrase that renames a noun or noun phrase and is grammatically equivalent to it.

▸ The high point of the meal, *Sam's mouth-watering apple pie*, emerged piping hot from the oven. [appositive]

2. Verb phrases

A *verb phrase* consists of a main verb and all its helping verbs. Verb phrases function as the simple predicates of sentences and clauses.

▸ By Election Day, the candidates *will have been campaigning* for almost two years. [verb phrase: *will have been campaigning*]

3. Prepositional phrases

A *prepositional phrase* is a preposition followed by the *object of the preposition:* a pronoun or noun and its modifiers. Prepositional phrases function as adjectives and adverbs.

▸ The train arrives in an hour. [The prepositional phrase *in an hour* functions as an adverb modifying the verb *arrives*.]

▸ She recommended the book about Einstein. [The prepositional phrase *about Einstein* functions as an adjective modifying the noun *book*.]

EXERCISE 33.8 Identifying prepositional phrases

In the following sentences, underline each prepositional phrase, write above it the type (adjective or adverb), and circle the words it modifies.

1. Roger said he was a little nervous before he stepped into the canoe.
2. Miguel told Roger to sit in the front of the canoe.
3. Miguel, who had been on many canoe trips before, expertly steered from the canoe's back seat.
4. The trip down the river was safe and exciting for both Roger and Miguel.

4. Verbal phrases

Verbals are verb forms that function as nouns, adjectives, or adverbs. Although they may have objects and complements, verbals lack the information about tense, person, and number required of a complete verb.

A *verbal phrase* consists of a verbal and any modifiers, objects, or complements. There are three kinds of verbal phrases: gerund phrases, infinitive phrases, and participial phrases.

Gerunds A *gerund* is the present participle (or *-ing* form) of a verb used as a noun; and like nouns, gerunds and gerund phrases can function as subjects, objects, and complements.

▸ *Increasing automobile fuel efficiency* will reduce carbon emissions. [gerund phrase/subject]

▸ The mayor recommends *improving the city's mass transit system.* [gerund phrase/dir. obj.]

Infinitives An *infinitive* is the *to* form of the verb (*to decide, to eat, to study*). Infinitives and infinitive phrases can function as adjectives and adverbs as well as nouns.

▸ The goal of the law is *to increase fuel efficiency.* [noun phrase/subj. comp.]

▸ Congress passed a law *to increase* fuel efficiency. [adjective phrase]

▸ *To reduce traffic congestion,* the city improved its mass transit system. [adverb phrase]

Infinitive versus Gerund after the Verb Some verbs can be followed by a gerund but not an infinitive, others by an infinitive but not a gerund, and still others by either a gerund or an infinitive. Lists of verbs and what can follow them do exist, but learning specific examples is a matter of experience with a broad variety of English-language situations and texts.

> **More about**
> Infinitive versus gerund after verbs, 779–81

Participial phrases In a *participial phrase* the present participle or past participle of a verb acts as an adjective. The present participle ends in *-ing.* The past participle of regular verbs ends in *-ed,* but some verbs have irregular past participles.

> **More about**
> Irregular past participles, 697–99

- *Surveying the disheveled apartment,* Grace Rosario wondered whether it would be possible to room with Maritza.

- *Deeply concerned,* she asked, "How long have you lived alone?"

EXERCISE 33.9 Identifying verbal phrases

In the following sentences, underline each verbal phrase. Then write above it the type (gerund, infinitive, or participial).

1. Seeking economic opportunity or freedom from political or religious repression, millions of immigrants came to the United States between the end of the Civil War and the early 1920s.
2. Many of the newcomers intended to return to their homelands.
3. Most immigrants during this period came from southern and eastern Europe, replacing the Irish and German immigrants who had predominated before the Civil War.
4. Leaving home and settling in a new environment must have been difficult.
5. Not always welcomed in their new communities, immigrants often settled together in ethnic enclaves.

5. Absolute phrases

Absolute phrases modify entire sentences rather than particular words within sentences. They usually consist of a pronoun or noun phrase followed by a participle. Set off by commas, they can often fall flexibly before, after, or within the rest of the sentence.

▶ *All our quarrels forgotten,* we sat before the fire and talked quietly.

When the participle in an absolute phrase is a form of *be,* it is often omitted as understood.

▶ *Her interview [having been] successful,* she was offered the job on the spot.

33m Independent and Subordinate Clauses

A *clause* is a word group with a subject and a predicate. An *independent* (or *main*) *clause* can stand alone as a sentence.

|—— independent clause ——|
▶ Sam's pie won first prize.

A *subordinate* (or *dependent*) clause is a clause within a clause.

> ▸ Sam baked the pie that won first prize.
> [independent clause: entire sentence; sub. clause: that won first prize]

That is, a subordinate clause functions inside an independent clause (or another subordinate clause) as a noun, adjective, or adverb but cannot stand alone as a sentence. A subordinate clause by itself is a *fragment*. A subordinating word—either a *subordinating conjunction* (see the Quick Reference box on p. 644) or a *relative pronoun* (see the Quick Reference box on p. 638)—usually signals the beginning of a subordinate clause.

> **More about**
> Subordinate clause fragments, 667–68
> Punctuating subordinate clauses, 805–6, 812–13

1. Adjective clauses

Like adjectives, **adjective clauses** (also called *relative clauses*) modify nouns or pronouns. They usually begin with a relative pronoun that immediately follows the word the clause modifies and refers back to it.

> ▸ Sam baked the pie *that* won first prize.
> [s v do]

> ▸ The donor *who* paid for the library's new computer center is a recent graduate.
> [s v do]

In both of these examples, the relative pronoun is the subject of the subordinate clause, and the clause follows normal word order, with the subject before the verb. When the relative pronoun is the direct object, however, it still comes at the beginning of the clause, reversing normal word order.

> ▸ The candidate *whom* we supported lost the election.
> [do s v]

> **More about**
> *Who* versus *whom*, 717–19

Adjective clauses can also begin with the subordinating conjunctions *when* and *where*.

> ▸ Redditch, Worcestershire, is the town *where Harry Styles was born.*

It is sometimes acceptable to omit the relative pronoun that introduces an adjective clause when the meaning of the clause is clear without it.

> ▸ The candidate [*whom*] *we supported* lost the election.

> **More about**
> The meaning of subordinating conjunctions, 573

2. Adverb clauses

Adverb clauses usually begin with a subordinating conjunction, which specifies the relation of the clause to the term it modifies. Like adverbs, adverb clauses can modify verbs, adjectives, and adverbs as well as whole phrases and clauses.

▸ The baby boom began *as World War II ended.*

  The adverb clause modifies the verb *began.*

▸ The economy grew faster *than many Americans thought it would.*

  The adverb clause modifies the adverb *faster.*

▸ The 1950s were an affluent decade, *although the general prosperity did not extend to all.*

  The adverb clause modifies the preceding independent clause.

3. Noun clauses

Noun clauses do not modify other parts of a sentence but instead replace noun phrases as subjects, objects, or complements within an independent clause. Noun clauses can begin with a relative pronoun as well as with certain subordinating conjunctions, including *how, if, when, whenever, where, wherever, whether,* and *why.*

▸ *Whoever crosses the finish line first* wins the race. [subject]

▸ Home is *where the heart is.* [subject comp.]

▸ The evidence proves *that the defendant is not guilty.* [direct object]

33n Sentence Types

Sentences fall into four types depending on the combination of independent and subordinate clauses they contain. Including a mix of types and choosing the appropriate type for the information you intend to convey can help you hold your readers' attention and emphasize important points.

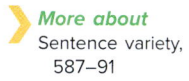

> **More about**
> Sentence variety, 587–91

1. Simple sentences

A *simple sentence* has only one independent clause and no subordinate clauses.

▸ |———————— independent clause ————————|
Serena Williams has won twenty-three Grand Slam singles titles.

A simple sentence need not be short or even uncomplicated. A sentence with a compound subject, a compound predicate, or both is still a simple sentence as long as it has a single complete subject, a single complete predicate, and no subordinate clauses.

▸ |———————————————————————— independent
Sisters Serena Williams and Venus Williams each won Grand Slam
clause ————————————————|
singles titles and dominated women's professional tennis.

2. Compound sentences

A *compound sentence* has two or more independent clauses but no subordinate clauses. A comma and a coordinating conjunction, a semicolon, or a semicolon and a conjunctive adverb usually join the clauses.

> **More about**
> Avoiding comma splices and fused sentences (ch. 35), 671–79

▸ |———————— independent clause ————————|
Serena Williams won twenty-three Grand Slam singles titles, and
|———————— independent clause ————————
in 2017, *Forbes Magazine* included her among the one hundred
— independent clause —|
highest paid athletes.

▸ |———————— independent clause ————————|
Williams was the subject of the documentary *Being Serena*;
|———————— independent clause ————————|
she also made a cameo appearance in the 2018 film *Ocean's 8*.

3. Complex sentences

A *complex sentence* consists of a single independent clause with at least one subordinate clause.

▶ |———————— subordinate clause ————————|
After she defeated the sixth seed in the 1998 Australian Open, Serena
|———————— independent clause ————————|
Williams lost to her sister Venus Williams in the second round.

▶ |———————————————————————————— independent
          |— subordinate clause —|
Venus and Serena Williams, who are sisters, have played against
clause ————————————————————————|
each other in fifteen Grand Slam singles matches.

4. Compound-complex sentences

A *compound-complex sentence* has two or more independent clauses with one or more subordinate clauses.

▶ |———————— independent clause ————————|
Professional tennis has long been a white dominated sport, and
|———————————————————————————— independent
          |—— subordinate clause ——|
Venus and Serena Williams, who are African American, have
clause ————————————————————|
experienced a number of racist criticisms.

> ### ➔ EXERCISE 33.10 Identifying sentence types
>
> Next to each of the following sentences, write the type of sentence it is: simple, compound, complex, or compound-complex.
>
> 1. Lindsay practices her breathing exercises every day with her husband, Larry, who coaches her enthusiastically.
>
> 2. Lindsay and Larry attend weekly childbirth classes, meet other expectant parents, learn about the stages of labor, and practice massage and relaxation techniques.
>
> 3. One couple, although friendly to Lindsay and Larry, often interrupt the instructor, so Larry is sometimes annoyed by them.

4. Lindsay and Larry will be first-time parents, but they are learning important information by attending the classes.

5. As they learn more, Lindsay and Larry gain confidence as prospective parents; however, the childbirth video made them nervous at first.

Make It **Your Own**

Write down five sentences from a reading assignment or from a newspaper article. Identify the independent and dependent clauses in each sentence, and label each sentence as simple, compound, complex, or compound-complex.

Work **Together**

Exchange your sentences and your analysis of them with those of another student, and check each other's work. Consult your professor if you disagree about any sentences.

Text Credits

Pg. 630, 632: Courtesy of Tom Hackman.

34 Avoiding Sentence Fragments

IN THIS CHAPTER

a. Recognizing fragments, 660

b. Correcting fragments, 664

c. Using intentional fragments, 669

An open drawbridge is not a complete bridge; it is two bridge fragments, neither of which, by itself, will get travelers all the way across the river. Similarly, a sentence *fragment* is not a complete sentence. It may begin with a capital letter and end with a period (or a question mark or an exclamation point), but it is missing one or more essential elements of a complete sentence. It takes readers only partway through the writer's thought, leaving them searching for the missing pieces. Although writers may use them intentionally in certain contexts, fragments are almost always out of place in academic and business writing.

> **subject** A noun or pronoun that names the topic of a sentence
> **complete verb** A main verb together with any helping verbs needed to indicate tense, voice, and mood

34a Recognizing Fragments

A sentence must have at least one ***independent clause,*** which is a group of related words that has a ***complete verb*** and a ***subject*** but does not start with a subordinating term such as *although, because, who,* or *that.* A word group punctuated like a sentence that does not satisfy these conditions is a fragment, not a sentence.

> **Quick Reference** — **Identifying Fragments**
>
> To determine whether a word group is a fragment or a sentence, ask yourself these questions:
>
> 1. **Does it have a complete verb?** — If the answer is no, it is a fragment.
> 2. **Does it have a subject?** — If the answer is no, it is a fragment.
> 3. **Does it begin with a subordinating word (such as *when*) and express an incomplete thought?** — If the answer is yes, it is a fragment.

1. No verb

A *complete verb* consists of a main verb together with any helping verbs needed to express tense, mood, and voice. If a word group lacks a complete verb, it is a *phrase*, and if that phrase is punctuated as a sentence, it is a phrase fragment.

> **More about**
> Verbs (ch. 37), 694–711

FRAGMENT (NO VERB)	Her beautiful new sports car.
SENTENCE	Her beautiful new sports [subj. *car*] [complete verb *was smashed*] beyond repair.

Verbals are words that look like verbs—they are derived from verbs—but they lack the information about tense that is required of a complete verb. Instead, they function as nouns, adjectives, or adverbs. Verbals can include past participles (the *-ed* form in most verbs), present participles (the *-ing* form), and infinitives (the *to* form). By themselves, verbal phrases are fragments, not sentences.

> **More about**
> Verbals, 652–53, 661

FRAGMENT	An [verbal *inspired*] teacher [verbal *making*] a difference in her students' lives.
SENTENCE	An [verbal *inspired*] teacher, [subj. *she*] [verb *is making*] a difference in her students' lives.

2. No subject

The subject of a sentence is the answer to the question "Who or what did the action defined by the verb?" If a word group lacks a subject, it is a phrase. If the phrase is punctuated like a sentence, it is a phrase fragment.

	verb
FRAGMENT	Serves no purpose.
	subject verb
SENTENCE	The bread machine in my kitchen serves no purpose.

> **More about**
> Imperatives, 707

Imperatives (*commands*) look like they do not have a subject. Actually their unstated subject is understood to be *you,* and they are sentences, *not* fragments.

	verb
IMPERATIVE SENTENCE	Come here right now!

Including a Stated Subject Unlike in most other languages, all sentences in formal English except commands always require an explicitly stated subject. See chapter 43, "Understanding English Word Order and Sentence Structure."

> **More about**
> Subordinate clauses, 654–56

3. Begins with a subordinating term

A subordinate clause and an independent clause both have a subject and verb, but a subordinate clause begins with a subordinating term, either a subordinating conjunction or a relative pronoun (see the Quick Reference box on the next page). The subordinating term links the subordinate clause to another clause, where it functions as a noun, adjective, or adverb. A subordinate clause cannot stand alone as a sentence, and if it is punctuated like one, it is a subordinate clause fragment.

	subordinator
FRAGMENT	When the drawbridge closes.
	subordinator
SENTENCE	We will cross the river when the drawbridge closes.
	subordinator
FRAGMENT	Which made driving hazardous.
	subordinator
SENTENCE	The storm left a foot of snow, which made driving hazardous.

Be careful to distinguish between relative pronouns used to introduce a subordinate clause and the same words used as interrogative pronouns to introduce questions. Questions beginning this way are complete sentences.

Grammar Matters • Recognizing Fragments   frag   **34a**   **663**

FRAGMENT	*relative pronoun* **Who** will be attending.
SENTENCE	*interrogative pronoun* **Who** will be attending?

Quick Reference: Subordinating Terms

Subordinating Conjunctions

after	before	since	unless	whereas
although	even if	so that	until	while
as	even though	than	when	why
as if	if	that	whenever	
because	once	though	where	

Relative Pronouns

| that | who | whom | whose | which |
| what | whoever | whomever | whatever | whichever |

➔ EXERCISE 34.1 Identifying fragments

Identify each of the following word groups as a sentence or a fragment; then further label each fragment as a phrase fragment or a subordinate clause fragment.

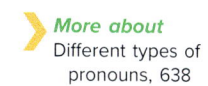

EXAMPLE

Which have women heads of state. *[fragment, subordinate clause]*

1. In 2006, Michelle Bachelet became the first female president of Chile.
2. Who would have predicted such a turn of events just a few years earlier?
3. Not many observers at the time.
4. Because Chile was for many years a bastion of gender conservatism.
5. Electing Bachelet changed all that.
6. The voters went to the polls.
7. With an open mind.
8. The people of Chile were excited.

> **More about**
> Different types of pronouns, 638

9. Waving flags and banners, honking horns, blowing whistles, and chanting slogans.
10. Which is a promising sign for the future.

34b Correcting Fragments

Once you have identified a fragment, you have two options for correcting it:

1. Connect the fragment to a related independent clause.

  ▶ The first mission to Pluto was launched in 2006. Arrived in 2015. → *and arrived*

  ▶ Archaeologists sift through the dust slowly. Looking for personal belongings buried with the deceased. → *, looking*

2. Convert the fragment into an independent clause.

  ▶ The first mission to Pluto was launched in 2006. Arrived in 2015. → *It arrived*

  ▶ Archaeologists sift through the dust slowly. Looking for personal belongings buried with the deceased. → *; they are looking*

These options apply to both phrase fragments and subordinate clause fragments. Either option can fix a fragment; deciding on the best one is a stylistic choice that depends on the context in which the fragment occurs.

Writing Responsibly — Sentence Fragments and Context

Although writers sometimes use them deliberately in certain contexts (see 34c), for a variety of reasons you should avoid sentence fragments in your academic or business writing. One is that fragments can create ambiguities, as in the following example:

▶ Our small town has seen many changes. Some long-time stores went out of business. Because the new mall opened. There are now more options for family entertainment.

Did the new mall put stores out of business, provide new entertainment options, or both? To clarify this ambiguity, the writer would need to attach the fragment to the preceding sentence or the following sentence, or rewrite these sentences in some other way.

Another reason to avoid fragments is that readers may interpret them as the result of carelessness or a lack of competence, which would undermine your efforts to present yourself authoritatively.

to TOPIC

> **Tech** **Grammar Checkers and Sentence Fragments**
>
> The grammar checkers in word processing programs may miss some fragments and, in some cases, may incorrectly flag imperatives as fragments. Although your grammar checker can help you, you will still need to edit your prose carefully for fragments.

1. Phrase fragments

Phrase fragments lack a subject, a complete verb, or both. As you edit your writing, watch for fragments based on certain kinds of phrases in particular. These include prepositional phrases, verbal phrases, appositive phrases, the separate parts of compound predicates, and items in lists and examples.

Prepositional phrases A *prepositional phrase* consists of a preposition (such as *as, at, for, from, in addition to, to,* or *until*) followed by a pronoun or noun and its modifiers. You can usually correct a prepositional phrase fragment by attaching it to an adjacent sentence.

> ▶ The Kenyon College women won the NCAA Division III swimming championship ~~again that year. For~~ **for** the seventeenth consecutive year.

> **More about**
> Prepositions and prepositional phrases, 642–43, 652, 793–800

Verbal phrases Although verbals are derived from verbs, **verbal phrases** can function as adjectives, adverbs, or nouns within a sentence but not as sentences on their own. In the following example, *stranding* is a verbal.

> ▶ The car had run out of ~~gas. Stranding~~ **gas, stranding** us in the middle of nowhere.

Appositive phrases An *appositive phrase* is a noun or *noun phrase* that renames a preceding noun or noun phrase and is grammatically equivalent to it. Appositives become fragments when they are separated by a period from the phrases they rename.

> **More about**
> Appositives, 651

> **noun phrase** A noun together with any modifiers

> ▶ The family eagerly awaited the highlight of the ~~meal. Beatriz's~~ **meal, Beatriz's** perfect molé verde.

Compound predicates A *compound predicate* consists of two or more complete verbs, together with their objects and modifiers, that are joined by a

> **More about**
> Compound predicates, 647

coordinating conjunction (such as *or, and,* or *but*) and that share the same subject. A fragment results when the last part of a compound predicate is punctuated as a separate sentence.

▶ By the end of May, the band members hated each other. ~~But~~ still *but* had six weeks left to tour.

> **More about**
> Punctuation for lists, 848, 852

Lists and examples Lists become fragments when they are separated from the sentence to which they belong. To correct list fragments, link them to the sentence by rephrasing the passage or replacing the period with a colon or a dash.

FRAGMENT	Three authors are most commonly associated with the Beat movement. Allen Ginsberg, Jack Kerouac, and William Burroughs.
REVISED	Three authors are most commonly associated with the Beat movement: Allen Ginsberg, Jack Kerouac, and William Burroughs.

or

The three authors most commonly associated with the Beat movement are Allen Ginsberg, Jack Kerouac, and William Burroughs.

Examples or explanations that begin with transitional words such as *for example, in contrast,* and *in addition* can be sentences; they are fragments, however, if they are punctuated like a sentence but lack a subject or a complete verb, or otherwise consist of only a subordinate clause. In the following example, the writer corrected a phrase fragment by rephrasing and attaching it to the preceding sentence.

▶ People today have access to many sources of news and ~~opinion. For~~ *opinion, including, for* example, the Internet and cable television as well as broadcast television and print newspapers and magazines.

The writer of the next example corrected a subordinate clause fragment by deleting the subordinating word *that,* which turns the fragment into a sentence.

▶ Certain facts underscore the rapid growth of the Internet. For ~~example that~~ web browsers did not become widely available until *example,* the mid-1990s.

EXERCISE 34.2 Correcting sentence fragments

Correct each sentence fragment below and write at the end what kind of fragment it is (prepositional phrase, verbal phrase, appositive phrase, compound predicate, list or example).

EXAMPLE

The most unforgettable character I know is my ~~grandfather. Jacob~~ *grandfather, Jacob* Black. *[appositive phrase]*

1. Even though he was only five feet four inches tall, he was a championship boxer. During high school.
2. Boxing was what many young men pursued. Back in the 1940s.
3. Later, he joined the army. Becoming a first sergeant in the quartermaster corps.
4. He was responsible for setting up army camps in Korea. Also for supervising supplies, cooking, and recreation.
5. He must have been a pretty tough guy in those days. Not the warm and loving grandpa I knew later on.

2. Subordinate clause fragments

A subordinate clause has a subject and a verb but begins with a subordinating word or phrase—a subordinating conjunction or a relative pronoun—and cannot stand alone as a sentence. When you correct a subordinate clause fragment, be sure to consider the relationships among the ideas you are expressing before deciding whether to transform the subordinate clause into an independent clause or to connect it to a related independent clause. Subordinating conjunctions, for example, specify the relationship between the information in a subordinate clause and the clause it modifies. If that relationship is important, you will probably want to correct the fragment by connecting it to the independent clause to which it relates.

> *More about*
> Subordination and subordinating conjunctions, 570–76

▶ *Twitter* continues to gain popularity as a source of information~~. Because~~ *because* it can publish late-breaking news as soon as it occurs.

The correction retains the subordinating conjunction *because* and with it important information about the cause-and-effect relationship between the two parts of the sentence. That information would have been obscured if the writer had simply deleted the subordinating conjunction to change the fragment into a separate sentence: *It can publish late-breaking news as soon as it occurs.*

In other cases, revising a subordinate clause fragment into a separate sentence by deleting the subordinating word can produce a clearer, less awkward result than would attaching it to another sentence.

▸ Horses and camels have something in common. ~~That the~~ **The** ancestors of both originated in the western hemisphere and migrated to the eastern hemisphere.

> **More about**
> Punctuating subordinate clauses and other subordinate structures, 811–13

A subordinate clause that begins with a subordinating conjunction is usually set off by a comma if it comes at the beginning of a sentence but not if it comes at the end. The punctuation of a subordinate clause that begins with a relative pronoun depends on whether the clause is ***essential*** (it specifically identifies the word or words it modifies) or ***nonessential*** (the identity of the word or words it modifies is clear without it).

→ EXERCISE 34.3 Correcting subordinate clause fragments

Correct each fragment below and write at the end whether the fragment begins with a subordinating conjunction or a relative pronoun.

EXAMPLE

Northern Florida is dotted with natural ~~springs. That~~ **springs that** are direct outlets of a huge aquifer, or groundwater source. *[relative pronoun]*

1. The springs discharge millions of gallons of cool, clean, fresh water each day. Because the aquifer is very close to the surface.

2. The area contains many rivers, lakes, and ponds. That are fed from the springs.

3. Although the area still seems rural and remote. The water attracts many vacationers.

4. For many years people came to visit area tourist attractions. That included "mermaid" shows and glass-bottom boat rides.

5. Today, however, the region has gained a reputation for ecotourism. Because it abounds with state parks, water trails, and campgrounds.

34c Using Intentional Fragments Effectively and Judiciously

Writers sometimes use fragments not in error but intentionally for emphasis or to reflect how people actually speak. Exclamations and the answers to questions often fall into this category.

▸ Another loss! Ouch!

▸ What caused this disaster? The collapse of our running game.

Intentional fragments are also common in advertising copy, and many writers use them for effect when the context makes their full meaning clear.

▸ All science. No fiction.

—Toyota advertisement

▸ Man is the only animal that blushes. Or needs to.

—Mark Twain, *Following the Equator*

Consider your writing situation, your context and genre, and especially your audience before deciding to use a sentence fragment deliberately. If your purpose is careful reporting or analysis, you should probably avoid the intentional sentence fragment because it can create ambiguity (see the Writing Responsibly box on p. 664). In academic or business writing, where clarity of expression is highly prized, fragments are frowned upon and can undermine your authority. On the other hand, if your purpose is expressive or you are writing in an informal context or genre (for example, in a blog or for a fanzine), the occasional intentional fragment can be highly effective.

EXERCISE 34.4 Correcting sentence fragments

Identify and correct any sentence fragments in the following paragraph.

On January 2, miners of the morning shift reported for work. As usual beginning the descent to the coal seam deep underground. Not all had descended into the mine when the explosion happened. There were two crews. One still aboveground. The explosion occurred at 6:31 a.m. Causing a power outage throughout the mine. Which filled with smoke. And deadly carbon monoxide. A mine rescue team was called. But not until 8:04 a.m. Because it took the mine supervisors that long to ascertain what had happened. Meanwhile, the trapped miners had only a limited supply of oxygen. Distraught families gathered aboveground waiting for news. At last a shout rang out. "Alive!" A collective sigh of relief and thanksgiving was audible. As family members waited to see their loved ones once again.

Make It Your Own

Reread three texts you have written recently or a draft you are working on and look for sentence fragments. If you find any, make a note of what kind they are and correct them; then add this error to your list of areas to consider as you revise your prose.

Work Together

Exchange texts and analyze your classmate's writing for sentence fragments. Underline any you find and make a note of what kind they are. Compare your results with those of the others in the group. What did each of you see that others did not? Were some types of fragments easier to find than others? If so, make a note of any you had difficulty finding and add them to your revision checklist.

35 Avoiding Comma Splices and Fused Sentences

IN THIS CHAPTER

a. Correctly joining independent clauses, 671

b. Identifying comma splices and fused sentences, 672

c. Recognizing when comma splices and fused sentences occur, 673

d. Correcting comma splices and fused sentences, 675

> *More about*
> Clauses, 654–56

> *More about*
> Coordination, 565–77

How things are joined together is important, whether those "things" are pipes or sentences. If they are not correctly connected, they work poorly or not at all. A blowtorch is a good tool for reconnecting leaky pipes; correct punctuation is a good tool for repairing the comma splices and run-ons in "leaky" sentences. If clauses are incorrectly joined with a comma alone (a ***comma splice***), the comma is too weak to show the connection between the two thoughts. If the clauses crash into one another with no separating punctuation (a *fused*, or *run-on, sentence*), readers will not know where one thought ends and the other begins.

©Krista Kennedy

35a Correctly Joining Independent Clauses

An *independent clause* can stand on its own as a sentence. Related independent clauses can follow one another as separate sentences, each ending in a period.

▶ The blues singer Alberta Hunter retired in the 1950s. She made a successful comeback in the 1970s.

Alternatively, you can join (or *coordinate*) independent clauses in a compound sentence with a variety of coupling mechanisms that let readers know one clause is ending and another beginning. Of these, two are the most common:

- A comma and a coordinating conjunction (*and, but, or, nor, for, so, yet*)

671

- The blues singer Alberta Hunter retired in the 1950s, **but** she made a successful comeback in the 1970s.

- A semicolon
  - The blues singer Alberta Hunter retired in the 1950s; she made a successful comeback in the 1970s.

You can also use a colon or a dash between independent clauses when the first clause introduces the second or the second elaborates on the first. (The colon is usually more appropriate in formal writing.)

- The blues singer Alberta Hunter retired in the 1950s: she made a successful comeback in the 1970s.

35b Identifying Incorrectly Joined Independent Clauses: Comma Splices and Fused Sentences

When a writer improperly joins two independent clauses with a comma alone, the result is a *comma splice*.

COMMA SPLICE
|———————— independent clause ————————|
The *House of Mirth* was Edith Wharton's second novel,
|———————— independent clause ————————|
it reflects and criticizes class privilege in 1905.

When a writer runs two independent clauses together with no punctuation between them, the result is a *fused sentence* (also called a *run-on sentence*).

FUSED SENTENCE
|———————— independent clause ————————|
The *House of Mirth* was Edith Wharton's second novel
|———————— independent clause ————————|
it reflects and criticizes class privilege in 1905.

Writing Responsibly — Clarifying Boundaries

Comma splices and fused sentences obscure the boundaries between linked ideas. If you leave them uncorrected in your writing, you burden readers with a task that should be yours: to identify where one idea ends and another begins and to specify how those ideas relate to each other.

to AUDIENCE

Quick Reference: Identifying Comma Splices and Fused Sentences

When two independent clauses are joined by	The result is
A comma and coordinating conjunction	**Not** a comma splice or fused sentence
A semicolon	**Not** a comma splice or fused sentence
A colon or dash	**Not** a comma splice or fused sentence
A comma alone	A **comma splice**—revise
No punctuation at all	A **fused sentence**—revise

35c Recognizing When Comma Splices and Fused Sentences Tend to Occur

To avoid comma splices and fused sentences in your own work, pay attention to situations in which they are particularly likely to occur:

1. When the second clause begins with a conjunctive adverb (such as *for example, however,* or *therefore*) or other transitional expression

   COMMA SPLICE The blues singer Alberta Hunter retired in the 1950s, however, she made a successful comeback in the 1970s.

   REVISED The blues singer Alberta Hunter retired in the 1950s; however, she made a successful comeback in the 1970s.

2. When the grammatical subject of the second clause is a pronoun whose antecedent is the subject of the first clause

   COMMA SPLICE The *House of Mirth* was Edith Wharton's second novel, it reflects and criticizes class privilege in 1905.

   REVISED The *House of Mirth* was Edith Wharton's second novel, and it reflects and criticizes class privilege in 1905.

Tech: Comma Splices, Fused Sentences, and Grammar Checkers

Grammar checkers in word processing programs do not reliably identify comma splices or fused sentences. They catch some, but they miss many more.

3. When the first clause introduces the second or the second explains or elaborates on the first

FUSED SENTENCE	Alberta Hunter began her career at the bottom singing in bordellos, she worked her way up to the top clubs in Chicago.
REVISED	Alberta Hunter began her career at the bottom: singing in bordellos, she worked her way up to the top clubs in Chicago.

4. When one clause is positive and the other negative

COMMA SPLICE	Wharton's novel doesn't just depict class privilege, it also reflects an ambiguous antisemitism.
REVISED	Wharton's novel doesn't just depict class privilege; it also reflects an ambiguous antisemitism.

→ EXERCISE 35.1 Identifying comma splices and fused sentences

In each of the following sentences, underline the independent clauses. Then write CS after each comma splice, write FS after each fused sentence, and circle the numbers of sentences that are correct as is.

EXAMPLE

This is our dog her name is Dusty. *[FS]*

1. Dusty is a mutt, she is not a purebred dog.
2. Some people think she is a German shepherd others just ask what kind of dog she is.
3. I always say she is just a dog.

Writing Responsibly: Is a Comma Splice Ever Acceptable?

Comma splices often show up in compound sentences composed of two short, snappy independent clauses in parallel form, particularly when one is advertising:

   Buy one, get one free.

It can appear, too, in the work of experienced writers, who may use it deliberately because they feel a period, semicolon, or comma and coordinating conjunction would be too disruptive a separation in sentences like these:

You're not a man, you're a machine.

—George Bernard Shaw, *Arms and the Man*

Go ahead, make my day.

—Joseph C. Stinson, screenplay to *Sudden Impact*

However, this usage looks like an error and will confuse readers, and thus it is best avoided in academic writing.

to AUDIENCE

4. Dogs like Dusty are called a variety of names, mongrel is probably the most common.
5. Mutt and mixed-breed are other common names that are used for these dogs.
6. Mixed-breed dogs have fewer genetic disorders than do purebred dogs the inbreeding of purebreds has created genetic problems.
7. For example, German shepherds often have hip problems, collies often have eye diseases.
8. One type of mixed-breed is the crossbreed, a deliberate cross between two purebred strains.
9. As for Dusty, she certainly looks like a German shepherd she also looks like a Norwegian elkhound.
10. To me, she is the world's greatest dog, I love her very much.

35d Correcting Comma Splices and Fused Sentences

The Quick Reference box on this page lists five strategies for correcting comma splices and fused sentences. The strategy you choose should depend on the logical relationship between the clauses and the meaning you intend to convey.

1. Separate sentences

Correcting a comma splice or fused sentence by dividing the independent clauses into separate sentences makes sense when one or both of the clauses are long or when the two clauses do not have a close logical relationship.

▶ My friends and I began our long-anticipated trip to Peru in early July ~~we~~ *. We* arrived in Lima on Saturday morning and flew to Cuzco that same day.

Quick Reference — Ways to Correct Comma Splices and Fused Sentences

1. Use a period to divide the clauses into separate sentences. (675)
2. Join the clauses correctly with a comma and coordinating conjunction. (676)
3. Join the clauses correctly with a semicolon. (676)
4. Join the clauses, if appropriate, with a colon or dash. (676)
5. Change one independent clause into a subordinate clause or modifying phrase. (677)

Use a period also when the second clause is a new sentence that continues a quotation that begins in the first clause.

▶ "We must not be enemies," Abraham Lincoln implored the South in his first inaugural address, "Though passion may have strained, it must not break our bonds of affection."

2. Coordinating conjunction

> **More about**
> The meaning of coordinating conjunctions, 567–68

When you join independent clauses with a comma and a coordinating conjunction (*and, but, or, nor, for, so,* or *yet*), choose the conjunction that best fits the logical relationship between the clauses.

▶ We needed to adjust to the altitude before we began hiking in the Andes we spent three days sightseeing in Cuzco.
, so

3. Semicolon

> **More about**
> Coordinating with a semicolon, 567–68, 820–22

Join two independent clauses with a semicolon when they have a clear logical relationship, either of contrast, example, or explanation.

▶ Most languages spoken in Europe belong to the Indo-European language family, a few, such as Basque, Finnish, and Hungarian, do not.
;

Using a semicolon in combination with a conjunctive adverb or other transitional expression can clarify the relationship between the clauses.

▶ Most languages spoken in Europe belong to the Indo-European language family, Basque, Finnish, and Hungarian are exceptions.
; however,

4. Colon or dash

> **More about**
> Punctuating for emphasis, 591
> Colons, 852–54
> Dashes, 847–49

You can use a colon or, less commonly, a dash to join independent clauses when the first clause introduces the second or the second explains or elaborates on the first. This usage can create a more emphatic separation between the clauses than would a semicolon.

- The message is clear**;** smoking kills.

- Don't get kicked out of school**—** learn to study effectively.

5. Subordinate clause or modifying phrase

You can correct a comma splice or fused sentence by turning one of the independent clauses into a subordinate clause or by reducing the information in it to a modifying phrase. Note, however, that putting information in subordinate clauses and phrases usually de-emphasizes it in relation to the information in the independent clause it modifies.

> **More about**
> Subordination and emphasis, 570–76

COMMA SPLICE	Spanish, like French and Italian, is a Romance language**,** it derives from Latin, the language of the Romans.
REVISED: SUBORDINATE CLAUSE	Spanish, like French and Italian, is a Romance language |———— subordinate clause ————| because it derives from Latin, the language of the Romans.
REVISED: MODIFYING PHRASE	|———— modifying phrase ————| Spanish, a Romance language like French and Italian, derives from Latin, the language of the Romans.

EXERCISE 35.2 Correcting comma splices and fused sentences

Choose one of the methods described above to correct each comma splice or fused sentence. Circle the numbers of any sentences that are correct as is.

EXAMPLE;

Disaster films are almost as old as film itself**;** the first was made in 1901.

1. Obviously, disasters are natural subjects for films they are dramatic and visually interesting.
2. Early disaster movies focused on natural events such as fires, floods, and earthquakes, later ones showed human-made tragedies.
3. The first modern disaster movies were made in the 1950s, they focused on airplane crashes.
4. The golden age of disaster movies was probably the 1970s, the most popular of all was *Airport*, released in 1970.

5. It was followed by numerous sequels as well as by other hugely successful examples of the genre, such as *The Towering Inferno*.

6. Since that time, the summer blockbuster has remained everyone's idea of a good time it usually includes enough romance and drama, as well as special effects, to please everyone.

7. The genre even spawned its own subgenre, the disaster spoof, represented by the hits *Airplane* and *Airplane II*.

8. With the increasing sophistication of computerized special effects in the 1990s disaster films enjoyed a huge revival they had flagged in popularity in the 1980s.

9. However, real disasters like the attack on the World Trade Center may have changed all that how much fun is it to see a film like *Snowpiercer*?

10. Other disaster films that refer to real events, such as *Deepwater Horizon,* which focused on the explosion of an oil rig off the coast of Louisiana, have been successful only time will tell whether the genre will survive.

EXERCISE 35.3 Correcting comma splices and fused sentences

Revise the following passage to correct any comma splices or fused sentences.

Opera is an art form that combines music, lyrics, and dialog, so is musical comedy, however. Then what is the difference between them? Perhaps it is their origins opera arose in the seventeenth century primarily in Italy as an attempt to revive classical Greek drama. Musical comedy arose in the United States in the twentieth century out of vaudeville and other plotless musical shows such as burlesque and reviews. Regardless, there is a great deal of overlap between the two forms today although the famous composer and lyricist Stephen Sondheim says that if something is performed in an opera house, it is an opera, but if it is performed in a theater, it is a musical comedy, today many works are performed in both places.

Make It **Your Own**

Choose a text you have recently written or are writing. On one page of that text, underline each independent clause and check each sentence to be sure it is not a fused sentence or a comma splice; if it is, revise the sentence accordingly and add this error to your revision checklist.

Work **Together**

Exchange your revised pages with a classmate and double-check each other's work. Where do you have differences of opinion? Review this chapter to resolve any differences.

Text Credits

Pg. 674: Shaw, George Bernard, *Arms and the Man* (1894). **Pg. 674:** Stinson, Joseph C. (screenplay), *Sudden Impact* (Warner Bros. 1983).

36 Maintaining Agreement

IN THIS CHAPTER

SUBJECT-VERB AGREEMENT

a. How subjects and verbs agree, 680
b. Intervening words, 682
c. Compounds, 683
d. Indefinite pronouns, 685
e. Collective nouns, 685
f. Numbers, 686
g. Singular nouns that end in -s, 687
h. Titles, words as words, and gerund phrases, 687
i. *Who, which,* or *that,* 688
j. Subject after verb, 688
k. Linking verbs, 689

PRONOUN-ANTECEDENT AGREEMENT

l. Indefinite words, 690
m. Collective nouns, 692
n. Compounds, 692

In many languages, the grammatical form of some words in a sentence must match the form of other words. When the forms match, the reader can easily understand the sentence; when they do not, the effect can be like trying to force a square peg into a round hole, leaving the reader distracted or confused. In English, subjects and verbs require this kind of matchup, or ***agreement,*** as do pronouns and the words to which they refer.

SUBJECT-VERB AGREEMENT

A verb and its subject have to agree, or match each other, in person and number. ***Person*** refers to the form of a word that indicates whether it corresponds to the speaker or writer (*I, we*), the person addressed (*you*), or the people or things spoken or written about (*he, she, it, they, Alice, milkshakes*). ***Number*** refers to the form of a word that indicates whether it is singular, referring to one thing (*a student*), or plural, referring to more than one (*two students*).

36a Understanding How Subjects and Verbs Agree

With just a few exceptions, it is only in the present tense that verbs change form to indicate person and number. Even in the

Tech Grammar Checkers and Subject-Verb Agreement

Grammar checkers in word processing programs can alert you to many subject-verb agreement problems, but they can also miss errors and can flag some constructions as errors that are not. Make your own informed judgment about any changes the computer might recommend.

present tense, they have only two forms. One form, which ends in -s, is for third-person singular subjects; the other is for all other subjects.

	Singular		Plural	
	subject	verb	subject	verb
First Person	I	vote	we	vote
Second Person	you	vote	you	vote
Third Person	he, she, it, the student	vote*s*	they, the students	vote
	they	vote		

> **More about**
> The forms of regular and irregular verbs, 694–700

Most nouns form the plural with the addition of an *-s* (*dog, dogs*) or *-es* (*coach, coaches*).

In other words, an *-s* on a noun makes the noun plural; an *-s* on a present-tense verb makes the verb singular.

	Noun	Verb
Singular	The dog	bark*s*
Plural	The dog*s*	bark

> **More about**
> Regular and irregular plural nouns, 623–25

NOTE Nouns with irregular plurals include *woman* (plural *women*), *foot* (plural *feet*), *child* (plural *children*), and *phenomenon* (plural *phenomena*).

---

1. Agreement with *be* and with helping verbs

Unlike any other English verb, *be* has three present-tense forms (*am, are, is*) and two past-tense forms (*was, were*). In **verb phrases** that begin with a form of *be, have,* or *do* as a helping verb, the subject agrees with the helping verb.

	⊢——— subject ———⊣	⊢—— verb phrase ——⊣
SINGULAR	The *price* of oil	*has* been fluctuating.
PLURAL	Commodity *prices*	*have* been fluctuating.
SINGULAR	The *price*	*was* fluctuating.
PLURAL	*Prices*	*were fluctuating.*

> **verb phrase** A *main verb* together with any *auxiliary,* or *helping, verbs.* The main verb carries the principal meaning of the phrase; the auxiliaries provide information about tense, voice, and mood.

> **More about**
> Forms of *be, have,* and *do,* 697, 699

The modal auxiliaries—*can, could, may, might, must, shall, should, will, would,* and *ought to*—have only a single form; they do not take an *-s* ending for third-person singular subjects.

	⊢ subject ⊣	⊢ verb phrase ⊣
SINGULAR	The *price*	*can* change.
PLURAL	*Prices*	*can* change.

> **More about**
> Modal auxiliaries, 782–84

Writing Responsibly — Dialect Variation in Subject-Verb Agreement

The rules of subject-verb agreement are not the same in all dialects of English. In various communities in the English-speaking world, you might hear people say things like *"The cats is hungry," "We was at the store," "That coat needs washed,"* or *"She be walking to school."* In the contexts in which they occur, these variations are not mistakes; they reflect rules that are different from those of Standard American English. Still, the subject-verb agreement rules of Standard American English are what most readers in the United States expect to encounter.

to AUDIENCE

2. Subject-verb agreement pitfalls

> *More about*
> Identifying sentence subjects,
> 645–47

The basic rules of subject-verb agreement may be clear, but writers (and speakers) nonetheless often trip over them. As the Quick Reference box on the next page indicates, these errors usually involve problems identifying the subject of a sentence and determining whether it is singular or plural.

36b Ignoring Words That Intervene between the Subject and the Verb

In English, the subject of a sentence is usually near the verb. As a result, writers sometimes mistakenly treat words that fall between the subject and the verb as if they were the subject. The writer of the following sentence mistook the singular noun phrase *Order of the Phoenix* for the true subject, the plural noun *members*. The revision corrects the agreement error.

FAULTY   The **members** of the **Order** of the Phoenix **is** dedicated to thwarting Voldemort.

REVISED   The **members** of the **Order** of the Phoenix **are** dedicated to thwarting Voldemort.

NOTE When a singular subject is followed by a phrase that begins with *as well as, in addition to, together with,* or some similar expression, the verb is singular, not plural.

> Harry Potter, together with the other members of the Order of the
> Phoenix, ~~are~~ *is* determined to thwart Voldemort.

Grammar Matters • Distinguishing Plural from Singular Compound Subjects   agr   **36c**   **683**

Quick Reference: Avoiding Subject-Verb Agreement Pitfalls

1. Ignore words that intervene between the subject and the verb. (682)
2. Distinguish plural from singular compound subjects. (683)
3. Distinguish singular from plural indefinite pronouns. (685)
4. Understand collective noun subjects. (685)
5. Find agreement when the subject is a measurement, a number, or the word *number*. (686)
6. Recognize that some nouns that end in *-s* are singular. (687)
7. Treat titles, words as words, and gerund phrases as singular. (687)
8. Match the number of a relative pronoun subject (*who, which, that*) to its antecedent. (688)
9. Match the verb to the subject when the subject follows the verb. (688)
10. Match a linking verb with its subject, not its subject complement. (689)

36c Distinguishing Plural from Singular Compound Subjects

A *compound subject* consists of two or more subjects joined by a *conjunction* (*Jack and Jill, one or another*).

> **conjunction** Part of speech that joins words, phrases, or clauses to other words, phrases, or clauses and specifies the way the joined elements relate to each other

1. Compounds joined by *and* or *both . . . and*

Most compound subjects joined by *and* or *both . . . and* are plural.

▸ *Twitter and Instagram are* two popular social networking websites.

▸ *Both Twitter and Instagram allow* users to post links to photos and videos.

A compound subject joined by *and* is singular, however, if the items in the compound refer to the same person or thing.

▸ The winner *and* next president *is* the candidate with the most electoral votes.

A compound subject joined by *and* is also singular if it begins with *each* or *every*.

▸ *Each* paper *and* exam *contributes* to your final grade.

However, if it is followed by *each,* a compound joined by *and* is plural.

▸ The research paper *and* the final exam *each contribute* 25 percent toward your final grade.

2. Compounds joined by *or, nor, either . . . or, neither . . . nor*

When a compound subject is joined by *or, nor, either . . . or,* or *neither . . . nor,* the verb agrees with the part of the compound that is closest to the verb.

▸ *Neither* the coach *nor* the players <u>were</u> worried by the other team's early lead.

> The second part of the compound is plural, so the verb is plural.

Applying this rule can produce an awkward result when the first item in a compound is plural and the second is singular. Reversing the order often resolves the problem.

AWKWARD	*Neither* the players *nor* the coach <u>is</u> happy about last night's loss.
REVISED	*Neither* the coach *nor* the players <u>are</u> happy about last night's loss.

Sometimes the result is so awkward that the only solution is to reword the sentence. This happens particularly when the subject includes the pronouns *I, we,* or *you* and the verb is a form of *be.*

AWKWARD	*Neither* Carla *nor* I <u>am leaving</u> until the job is finished.
REVISED	Carla *and* I <u>are not leaving</u> until the job is finished.
	or
	Neither Carla *nor* I <u>will leave</u> until the job is finished.

▸ EXERCISE 36.1 Making subjects and verbs agree

Underline the subject in each of the following sentences, and then circle the verb that agrees with it.

EXAMPLE

Mr. Jefferson's <u>computer</u>, as well as its programs, ((is)/ are) out of date.

1. The members of the panel (agrees/agree) that he needs a new computer.
2. Many students today (has/have) their own very fast computers.
3. Both Ms. Lopez and Mr. Handler (is/are) installing new software on their computers.
4. Mr. Jefferson's old computer (prevents/prevent) him from using that software.
5. His new computer and software (is/are) scheduled to arrive next week.

Quick Reference — **Common Indefinite Pronouns**

Always singular: *another, anybody, anyone, anything, each, either, everybody, everyone, everything, much, neither, nobody, no one, nothing, one, somebody, someone, something*

Always plural: *both, few, many, others, several*

Variable: *all, any, more, most, some*

36d Distinguishing Singular and Plural Indefinite Pronouns

Indefinite pronouns (see the Quick Reference box below) refer to unknown or unspecified people, quantities, or things. Most indefinite pronouns always take a singular verb.

▸ *Everybody talks* about the weather, but *nobody does* anything about it.

—Attributed to Mark Twain

Some indefinite pronouns (*both, few, many, others, several*) always take a plural verb.

▸ *Many* of us *make* New Year's resolutions, but *few* of us *keep* them.

Some indefinite pronouns (*all, any, more, most, some*) are either singular or plural, depending on context.

▸ *Some* of these questions *are* hard.

▸ *Some* of this test *is* hard.

In the first sentence, *some* takes a plural verb because it refers to the plural noun *questions;* in the second sentence, *some* takes a singular verb because it refers to the singular noun *test.*

36e Understanding Collective Noun Subjects

A ***collective noun*** designates a collection, or group, of individuals: *audience, chorus, committee, faculty, family, government.* In US English, a collective noun is singular when it refers to the group acting as a whole.

▸ The *faculty is* revising the general education requirements.

The group acts as a whole.

A collective noun is plural when it refers to the members of the group acting individually.

▶ The *faculty are* unable to agree on the new requirements.
   The individual members of the group disagree among themselves.

If this usage sounds odd to you, however, you can reword the sentence with a clearly plural subject.

▶ The *members* of the faculty *are* unable to agree on the new requirements.

36f Finding Agreement When the Subject Is a Measurement, a Number, or the Word *Number*

Numbers, fractions, and units of measure take a singular verb when they refer to an undifferentiated mass or quantity.

▶ Over *140 billion barrels* of gasoline *was* consumed in the United States in 2019.

▶ *One-third* of the applicant pool *is* fully qualified for the job.

▶ *Seven thousand dollars is* too high a price for that car.

Numbers, fractions, and units of measure take a plural verb when they refer to a collection of individual people or things.

▶ The year 2019 saw *more than 600,000 immigrants become* naturalized citizens of the United States.

▶ *About a third* of the applicants with a college education *are* fully qualified for the job.

▶ *More than 300 applications* for the job *were* filed with the employment service.

The word *number* is plural when it appears with *a* but singular when it appears with *the*.

▶ *A number* of voters *are* in favor of the transportation bond.

▶ *The number* of voters in favor of the transportation bond *is* low.

36g Recognizing Nouns That Are Singular Even Though They End in -s

Some nouns that end in -s are singular. Examples include diseases like *diabetes* and *measles*.

▸ *Measles is* a contagious disease.

Words like *economics, mathematics,* and *physics* are singular when they refer to an entire field of study or body of knowledge.

▸ *Economics is* a popular major at many schools.

They are plural, however, when they refer to a set of individual traits related to the field of study.

▸ *The economics* of the music industry *are* changing rapidly.

36h Treating Titles, Words as Words, and Gerund Phrases as Singular

The titles of books, articles, movies, and other works; the names of companies and institutions; the names of countries; and words treated as words are all singular even if they are plural in form.

▸ *Harry Potter and the Order of the Phoenix was* the fifth book in J. K. Rowling's popular series.

▸ *The Centers for Disease Control and Prevention helps* protect the nation's health.

▸ *The United States is* one of the world's largest food exporters.

▸ *Fungi is* one of two acceptable plural forms of the word *fungus; funguses is* the other.

Gerunds and gerund phrases are also always singular.

▸ *Conducting excavations is* just one part of an archaeologist's job.

> **gerund** The present participle (*-ing* form) of a verb used as a noun

36i Matching a Relative Pronoun (*Who, Which,* or *That*) to Its Antecedent When the Pronoun Is the Subject of a Subordinate Clause

> **More about**
> Pronouns and their antecedents, 689–93, 719–22

A relative pronoun (*who, which,* or *that*) that functions as the subject of a subordinate clause is singular if its **antecedent** (the word it refers to) is singular, but it is plural if its antecedent is plural.

▶ People *who live* in glass houses should not throw stones.

▶ The cactus is a plant *that thrives* in a hot, dry environment.

Be careful with antecedent phrases that include the expressions *one of* or *only one of. One of* usually signals a plural antecedent; *only one of* signals a singular antecedent.

▶ Barack Obama is *one of several presidents* of the United States *who were elected* to two terms.

Several presidents were elected to two terms, and one of them was Obama. The pronoun *who* refers to the plural noun *presidents.*

▶ Franklin D. Roosevelt is *the only one* of those presidents *who was elected* to more than two terms.

Only one president, Roosevelt, was elected to more than two terms. The pronoun *who* refers to that particular one and is singular.

36j Finding Agreement When the Subject Follows the Verb

> **More about**
> Inverted word order, 591

If you reverse normal order and put the subject after the verb for emphasis or dramatic effect, be sure the verb agrees with the actual subject, not a different word that precedes the verb.

▶ Onto the tennis court *stride the defending champion and her challenger.*

The subject is the plural compound *the defending champion and her challenger,* not the singular term *tennis court.*

The subject also follows the verb in sentences that begin with *there* followed by a form of *be* (*there is, there are, there was, there were*).

There are
▶ ~~There's~~ more people registered to vote than actually vote on Election Day.

The subject, *people,* is plural, so the verb should be plural.

36k Matching a Linking Verb with Its Subject, Not Its Subject Complement

A *linking verb* (such as *was* or *were*) connects the subject of a sentence to a *subject complement*, which describes or refers to the subject. When either the subject or the subject complement is singular but the other is plural, make sure the verb agrees with the subject.

> **More about**
> Linking verbs and subject complements, 649

▶ One influential voting bloc in the election ~~were~~ *was* young voters.

The subject is the singular noun *bloc*, not the plural noun *voters*.

EXERCISE 36.2 Making subjects and verbs agree

Underline the subject in each of the following sentences and circle the verb. If the verb agrees with the subject, do nothing else. If the subject and verb do not agree, write the correct form of the verb above the error.

EXAMPLE

The traffic (sound) very loud. *sounds*

1. The number of vehicles using Reynolds Road have nearly doubled in a year.
2. Mr. Ojiba is the only one of the Town Council members who agrees with the proposal to install traffic-slowing speed bumps in the road.
3. A significant number of residents is opposed to installing traffic lights.
4. There was no other solution proposed to the Council.
5. The road provides a much more direct route into the city.
6. Everyone want there to be a solution to this problem.

PRONOUN-ANTECEDENT AGREEMENT

Pronouns rename or take the place of nouns, noun phrases, or other pronouns. The word or phrase that a pronoun replaces is its *antecedent.* Pronouns and their antecedents must agree in person (first, second, or third), number (singular or plural), and gender (neuter, feminine, or masculine). The antecedent usually appears before the pronoun but sometimes follows it. The two pronouns in the following example have the same antecedent—*Emma*—which follows the first pronoun and precedes the second.

▶ In *her* haste, *Emma* shut down the computer without saving *her* work.

NOTE If a subject prefers a gender-neutral pronoun such as *they* or *her*, you should respect that preference: *Emma shut down the computer without saving their work.*

A Possessive Pronoun Agrees with Its Antecedent, Not the Word It Modifies
In English, a possessive pronoun (such as *his, hers,* or *its*) agrees with its antecedent, not the word it modifies. In the following example, *father* is the antecedent, so the pronoun should be masculine.

▸ The father beamed joyfully at ~~her~~ *his* newborn daughter.

As with subject-verb agreement, the basic rule of pronoun-antecedent agreement—match the pronoun to its antecedent in person, number, and gender—is uncomplicated. However, writers are often uncertain how to apply the rule, as the Quick Reference box on the next page summarizes.

> **Tech** Grammar Checkers and Pronoun-Antecedent Agreement
>
> Grammar checkers in word processing programs cannot identify pronoun-antecedent agreement errors.

36l Matching Pronouns with Indefinite Pronoun and Generic Noun Antecedents

> *More about*
> Singular and plural indefinite pronouns, 685

Antecedents that are singular but have a plural sense are among the most common sources of pronoun-antecedent confusion. These include the following:

▸ *Indefinite pronouns* such as *each, everybody,* and *everyone* that are singular even though they refer to groups.

▸ *Generic nouns*—that is, singular nouns used to designate a whole class of people or things rather than a specific individual. In this sentence, for example—*The aspiring doctor faces years of rigorous training*—the expression *aspiring doctor* generically designates all would-be doctors.

1. Singular indefinite pronoun or generic noun antecedents

A pronoun with a singular indefinite pronoun or generic noun antecedent should usually be singular. Do not let the plural sense of the antecedent distract you.

▸ The dog is a domesticated animal, unlike ~~their~~ *its* cousin the wolf.

The antecedent is the singular generic noun *dog,* so the pronoun should be singular too.

> **Reference** Avoiding Pronoun-Antecedent Agreement Pitfalls
>
> 1. Match pronouns with indefinite pronoun and generic noun antecedents. (690)
> 2. Match pronouns with collective noun antecedents. (692)
> 3. Match pronouns with compound antecedents. (692)

This rule creates a problem, however, when the indefinite antecedent refers to both women and men. Correct agreement requires a singular pronoun, but using *he* as a substitute for either *man* or *woman* results in gender bias.

> **More about**
> Avoiding gender bias, 601–3

GRAMMATICALLY CORRECT BUT GENDER-BIASED AGREEMENT

In past downturns *the affluent consumer* continued to spend, but now even *he* is cutting back.

Writers often try to avoid this conflict with a gender-neutral plural pronoun such as *they*. This usage has long been common in everyday speech, and now it is considered appropriate for formal writing, as well.

UNBIASED AND GRAMMATICALLY CORRECT AGREEMENT

In past downturns, *the affluent consumer* continued to spend, but now even *they* are cutting back.

Because *they* is newly accepted as a generic singular pronoun, some readers are still surprised when they see it. You can also avoid both gender bias and faulty agreement by rephrasing according to one of these strategies:

1. Make both the antecedent and the pronoun plural.

   ▶ In past downturns, ~~the affluent consumer~~ *affluent consumers* continued to spend, but now even ~~he is~~ *they are* cutting back.

2. Rephrase the sentence without the pronoun.

   ▶ ~~In past downturns, the~~ *Even the* affluent consumer *, who* continued to spend ~~but now even he~~ is cutting back. *in past downturns,* *now*

2. Plural or variable indefinite pronoun antecedents

Although most indefinite pronouns are singular, some (*both, few, many, others, several*) are always plural.

▶ *Both* of the candidates released *their* income tax returns.

Others (*all, any, more, most, some*) are singular or plural, depending on the context.

▶ When the teacher surprised the *students* with a pop quiz, she discovered that *most* had not been doing *their* homework.

▶ Although some of the river's *water* is diverted for irrigation, *most* still makes *its* way to the sea.

36m Matching Pronouns with Collective Noun Antecedents

Collective nouns (for example, *audience, chorus, committee, faculty, family, government*) are singular when they refer to a group acting as a whole.

▶ *My family* traces *its* roots to West Africa.

Collective nouns are plural when they refer to the members of a group acting individually.

▶ *The billionaire's family* fought over *their* inheritance.

36n Matching Pronouns with Compound Antecedents

Compound antecedents joined by *and* are usually plural and take a plural pronoun.

▶ Back in 2012, *Clinton and Obama* were the leading candidates for *their* party's nomination.

Pronouns with compound antecedents joined by *or, nor, either . . . or,* or *neither . . . nor* agree with the nearest antecedent. To avoid awkwardness when one of the antecedents is plural and the other singular, put the plural antecedent second.

▶ *Neither the coach nor the players* worried that *their* team might lose.

Grammar Matters • Matching Pronouns with Compound Antecedents

When the antecedents differ in gender or person, however, the results of the "nearest antecedent" rule can be so awkward that the only solution is to reword the sentence:

AWKWARD   It was clear after the New Hampshire primary that either Barack Obama or Hillary Clinton would find herself the Democratic Party's nominee for president.

REVISED   It was clear after the New Hampshire primary that either Barack Obama or Hillary Clinton would be the Democratic Party's nominee for president.

EXERCISE 36.3 Editing for pronoun-antecedent agreement

Edit the following sentences to correct errors in pronoun-antecedent agreement and avoid gender bias.

EXAMPLE

Zoe and her parents felt as though something was missing from ~~her~~ *their* family.

1. Nearly every home in their neighborhood had their own dog, cat, or other type of pet.
2. That is why the Conyer family was slowly walking through the animal shelter, looking over every animal as Zoe, Robert, and their parents passed his cage.
3. Some of the dogs they passed barked frantically, but others just lay idly in his or her cages.
4. Then Robert pointed to a puppy enthusiastically pawing at their cage and whining to attract the family's attention.
5. That's when they found Molly, a cheerful, agreeable, and gentle dog who immediately immersed itself in the life of the Conyer family.

Make It **Your Own**

Reread several papers that you have recently written and note where you handled agreement issues well. If you see areas in need of revision, edit them and add this issue to your revision checklist.

37 Using Verbs

IN THIS CHAPTER

VERB FORMS

a. Basic verb forms, 694

b. Regular and irregular verbs, 696

c. Complete verbs, 697

d. *-s* or *-es*, *-d* or *-ed* endings, 700

e. *rise/raise, sit/set, lie/lay*, 701

TENSE

f. Verb tenses, 702

g. Uses of the present tense, 705

h. Tense sequence, 706

MOOD

i. Verb moods, 707

j. The subjunctive, 708

VOICE

k. Verb voice, 709

l. Active versus passive, 710

Just as an engine is the driving force of a train, a verb is the driving force of a sentence. Verbs specify the action (*Sylvia won the race*), occurrence (*She became a runner in high school*), or state of being (*She was tired after the track meet*) that affects the subject. Verbs also provide information about time (***tense***), the identity of the subject (***person*** and ***number***), whether the subject is acting or being acted on (***voice***), and the attitude or manner of the writer or speaker (***mood***) (see the Quick Reference box on the next page).

VERB FORMS

37a Understanding the Basic Forms of Verbs

With the exception of the verb *be*, all verbs have five forms: base, *-s* form, past tense, past participle, and present participle.

	Base Form	-s Form	Past Tense	Past Participle	Present Participle
Regular Verb	campaign	campaigns	campaigned	campaigned	campaigning
Irregular Verb	choose	chooses	chose	chosen	choosing

Quick Reference: What Information Do Verbs Reveal?

Verbs provide information about tense, person and number, voice, and mood.

- **Tense.** When does the action occur? In the **present** (*laugh/laughs*), **past** (*laughed*), or **future** (*will laugh*)?
- **Person.** Does the verb form tell you that the subject is speaking (*I laugh*), spoken to (*You should laugh*), or spoken about (*He laughs*)?
- **Number.** Are the subject and its accompanying verb **singular** (*He laughs*) or **plural** (*They laugh*)?
- **Mood.** Is the verb *indicative,* stating or questioning something about the subject (*He laughs*)? Is it *imperative,* giving a command (*Douse the coach!*)? Is it *subjunctive,* expressing a possibility (*If the coach were doused again, she might lose patience with her players*)?
- **Voice.** Is the verb *active,* with the subject performing the action (*He laughs*), or *passive,* with the subject being acted upon (*The coach is doused with water by her players*)?

- The *base form* is what you find when you look up a verb in the dictionary. Use it with a plural noun or the pronouns *I, we, you,* or *they* to express a present or habitual action, occurrence, or state of being.
    - ▶ Presidential candidates *campaign* every four years.
    - ▶ I usually *choose* candidates based on their policies.

- The *-s form* is the base form plus *-s* or *-es*. Use it with a singular noun or a singular pronoun (*he, she, it*) to express present or habitual action, occurrence, or state of being.
    - ▶ My favorite senator always *campaigns* in our town.
    - ▶ She *chooses* positive messages instead of negative ones.

> **More about**
> Verb tenses, 702–7
> Voice, 709–11

- The past-tense form of regular verbs such as *campaign* is the base form plus *-d* or *-ed*; the past-tense forms of irregular verbs such as *choose* vary. Use the past tense with singular or plural subjects to express past action, occurrence, or state of being.
    - ▶ The mayor *campaigned* downtown yesterday.
    - ▶ Some people *chose* to protest his appearance.

- The past participle is the same as the past tense in most verbs but varies in some irregular verbs. Use the past participle in combination with forms of *have* to form the perfect tenses and with forms of *be* to form the passive voice.
    - ▶ The candidate *has campaigned* nonstop.
    - ▶ Our town *was chosen* by the candidate for his last campaign stop.

- The present participle of all verbs, regular and irregular, is formed by adding -*ing* to the base form. Use the present participle with forms of *be* to form the progressive tenses.

▶ Senator Chung *is campaigning* here today.

▶ They *have been choosing* new furniture.

NOTE Past and present participles sometimes function as ***verbals***, not verbs. Past participles, for example, can sometimes be modifiers (*an educated public*), and present participles can be modifiers (*her opening statement*) or nouns (*campaigning is exhausting*).

> **More about**
> Verb forms as modifiers, 652–53

> **verbal** A verb form that functions as a noun, adjective, or adverb

37b Using Regular and Irregular Verb Forms Correctly

The vast majority of English verbs are ***regular***, meaning that their past-tense and past-participle forms end in -*d* or -*ed*:

Base	Past Tense	Past Participle
climb	climb**ed**	climb**ed**
analyze	analyz**ed**	analyz**ed**
copy	copi**ed**	copi**ed**

However, about two hundred English verbs are ***irregular***, with past-tense and past-participle forms that do not follow one set pattern:

Base	Past Tense	Past Participle
build	built	built
eat	ate	eaten
see	saw	seen

The forms of irregular verbs can easily be confused.

▶ My wool shirt ~~shrunk~~ *shrank* when I washed it in hot water.

Tech **Grammar Checkers and Verb Problems**

Grammar checkers in word processing programs will spot some errors that involve irregular or missing verbs, verb endings, and the subjunctive mood, but they will miss other errors and may suggest incorrect solutions. You must look for verb errors yourself and carefully evaluate any suggestions from a grammar checker.

Grammar Matters • Combining Main Verbs with Helping Verbs to Form Complete Verbs

If you are unsure whether a verb is regular or irregular or what form you should use in a particular situation, consult a dictionary or the Quick Reference box on page 698. In the dictionary, you will find any irregular forms listed in the entry for the base form of a verb.

EXERCISE 37.1 Choosing the correct irregular verb

In the following sentences, fill in the blank with the correct form of the word in parentheses.

EXAMPLE

The *Titanic* __sank__ (sink) after it __struck__ (strike) an iceberg.

1. Today, ships with special hulls _____ (cut) through new ice to _____ (take) tourists to _____ (see) Antarctica.
2. One photographer on an arctic cruise _____ (say) she _____ (take) a photograph of Gentoo penguins that _____ (have) bright orange beaks.
3. She _____ (write) in her journal that she _____ (see) their big tails _____ (swing) from side to side as they walked.
4. When a naturalist _____ (tell) them these birds may _____ (become) extinct because the temperature has _____ (rise), reducing the _____ (freeze) area where they live, she _____ (feel) very sad.

37c Combining Main Verbs with Helping Verbs to Form Complete Verbs

Almost all verb constructions other than the present and past tenses require the combination of a ***main verb*** with one or more ***helping verbs*** (or ***auxiliary verbs***) in a ***verb phrase.*** The most common helping verbs are *be, have,* and *do,* all three of which can also function as main verbs (they <u>are</u> hungry; she <u>had</u> lunch; they <u>did</u> the dishes). *Be,* unlike any other English verb, has eight forms.

FORMS OF *BE*

Base		*be*
Present Tense	I	*am*
	we, you, they	*are*
	he, she, it	*is*
Past Tense	I, he, she, it	*was*
	we, you, they	*were*
Past Participle		*been*
Present Participle		*being*

Quick Reference: Common Irregular Verbs

Base Form	Past Tense	Past Participle	Base Form	Past Tense	Past Participle
arise	arose	arisen	leave	left	left
be	was/were	been	lend	lent	lent
bear	bore	borne, born	let	let	let
beat	beat	beaten	lie (recline)†	lay	lain
become	became	become	lose	lost	lost
begin	began	begun	make	made	made
bid	bid	bid	mean	meant	meant
bite	bit	bitten, bit	pay	paid	paid
blow	blew	blown	prove	proved	proved, proven
break	broke	broken	quit	quit	quit
bring	brought	brought	read	read	read
build	built	built	ride	rode	ridden
burst	burst	burst	ring	rang	rung
buy	bought	bought	rise	rose	risen
catch	caught	caught	run	ran	run
choose	chose	chosen	say	said	said
come	came	come	see	saw	seen
cost	cost	cost	send	sent	sent
cut	cut	cut	set	set	set
dig	dug	dug	shake	shook	shaken
dive	dived, dove	dived	shoot	shot	shot
do	did	done	shrink	shrank	shrunk
draw	drew	drawn	sing	sang	sung
drink	drank	drunk	sink	sank	sunk
drive	drove	driven	sit	sat	sat
eat	ate	eaten	sleep	slept	slept
fall	fell	fallen	slid	slid	slid
feel	felt	felt	speak	spoke	spoken
fight	fought	fought	spend	spent	spent
find	found	found	spread	spread	spread
flee	fled	fled	spring	sprang, sprung	sprung
fly	flew	flown	stand	stood	stood
forget	forgot	forgotten, forgot	steal	stole	stolen
freeze	froze	frozen	strike	struck	struck, stricken
get	got	gotten, got	swim	swam	swum
give	gave	given	swing	swung	swung
go	went	gone	take	took	taken
grow	grew	grown	teach	taught	taught
hang (suspend)*	hung	hung	tear	tore	torn
have	had	had	tell	told	told
hear	heard	heard	think	thought	thought
hide	hid	hidden	throw	threw	thrown
hit	hit	hit	wake	woke, waked	waked, woken
hold	held	held	wear	wore	worn
keep	kept	kept	win	won	won
know	knew	known	wind	wound	wound
lay	laid	laid	write	wrote	written
lead	led	led			

*Hang is regular—hang, hanged, hanged—when used to mean "kill by hanging."
†Lie is regular—lie, lied, lied—when used to mean "to be untruthful."

Grammar Matters • Combining Main Verbs with Helping Verbs to Form Complete Verbs

FORMS OF *HAVE* AND *DO*

Present Tense (Base and -s Form)	I, you, we, they he, she, it	*have* *has*	*do* *does*
Past Tense		*had*	*did*
Past Participle		*had*	*done*
Present Participle		*having*	*doing*

The *modal verbs*—*can, could, may, might, must, shall, should, will, would,* and *ought to*—function only as helping verbs. Modals indicate ability, intention, permission, possibility, desire, and suggestion. They do not change form to indicate number or tense.

Modal Verbs English modal verbs have a range of meanings and unusual grammatical characteristics that you may find challenging. For example, they do not change form to indicate number or tense:

> More about Modals, 782–84

▸ In a close election, one or two votes ~~cans~~ *can* make a difference.

The main verb carries the principal meaning of the verb phrase; the helping verbs, if any, carry information about tense and voice. A ***complete verb*** is a verb phrase with all the elements needed to determine tense, voice, and mood. Main verbs can stand alone as complete verbs only in their present-tense and past-tense forms.

▸ The candidates [complete verb / main verb] campaigned until Election Day.

Main verbs in other forms (past or present participles) require helping verbs.

▸ The candidates [complete verb: helping verbs *have been* / main verb *campaigning*] for almost two years.

Sometimes in informal speech you can drop needed helping verbs, and some dialects allow certain constructions as complete verbs that Standard English does not allow. Helping verbs can sometimes be contracted (*they've voted already, we'll register tomorrow*) but in formal writing should never be omitted entirely.

▸ The candidates *have* been campaigning for almost two years.

CAUTION Do not use *of* for *have* in a verb phrase with a modal. When you use informal contractions like *could've* or *might've* in speech, remember that they mean *could have* and *might have*.

37d Including *-s* or *-es*, *-d* or *-ed* Endings When Required

> **More about**
> Subject-verb agreement, 680–89

Sometimes when speaking informally, you can omit the verb endings *-s, -es, -d,* or *-ed* or blend the sound of an ending inaudibly with the initial sound of the following word. Some dialects do not always require these endings. In formal writing, include them, or not, as standard usage requires.

> ▸ My dad ~~say~~ *says* I am ~~suppose~~ *supposed* to mow the lawn. I also ~~needs~~ *need* to trim the hedges. Before he ~~move~~ *moved* to Phoenix, my brother ~~use~~ *used* to do the mowing.

> **More about**
> Phrasal verbs, 776–78

Phrasal Verbs Phrasal verbs, such as *ask out* and *give in,* combine a verb with one or more prepositions or adverbs known as particles. The verb and particle combination of a phrasal verb has a distinct meaning, one that is different from the stand-alone words that form it. Because phrasal verbs are idiomatic, native English speakers are usually comfortable using them spontaneously. But that does not mean they can explain why one "gets on" a plane but "gets in" a rowboat.

EXERCISE 37.2 Correcting verb endings

In the following sentences, correct any verbs that have the wrong or missing verb endings *-s, -es, -d,* or *-ed*.

EXAMPLE
In our first year of college, many of us ~~mix~~ *mixed* studying with partying, but not one of us ~~do~~ *does* that now.

1. Tonight, Eyal and Aaron wants to see the movie, but Franco and I are determine to get our papers finish before we goes out.
2. I use to do my work at the last minute, so I never revise my papers.
3. Last semester I declare my major, so now I am concern about my grades.

4. My roommate say she go to the Writing Center, and they have always helps her.

5. I schedule an appointment for next week, before we go to the party.

37e Distinguishing *Rise* from *Raise*, *Sit* from *Set*, *Lie* from *Lay*

The forms of *rise* and *raise*, *sit* and *set,* and *lie* and *lay* are easily confused. One verb in each pair (*rise, sit,* and *lie*) is **intransitive,** meaning that it does not take a direct object. The other verb in each pair (*raise, set,* and *lay*) is **transitive,** meaning that it does take a direct object (underlined in the following examples).

> More about
> Transitive and intransitive verbs, 648–50

- *Rise* means "to move or stand up." *Raise* means "to cause something (the direct object) to rise."
    - ▶ The plane *rises* into the air. The pilot *raises* the landing gear.
- *Sit* means "to be seated." *Set* means "to place or put something (the direct object) on a surface."
    - ▶ The passengers in coach *sit* in cramped seats. The attendants *set* drinks on their trays.
- *Lie* means "to recline." *Lay* means "to place or put something (the direct object) on a surface."
    - ▶ The passengers in first class *lie* in fully reclining seats. During the landing, the pilot *lays* the plane gently on the runway.

Quick Reference Distinguishing *Rise* from *Raise*, *Sit* from *Set*, and *Lie* from *Lay*

Base Form	-s Form	Past Tense	Past Participle	Present Participle
rise (to get up)	rises	rose	risen	rising
raise (to lift)	raises	raised	raised	raising
sit (to be seated)	sits	sat	sat	sitting
set (to place)	sets	set	set	setting
lie (to recline)	lies	lay	lain	lying
lay (to place)	lays	laid	laid	laying

A further difficulty with *lie* and *lay* is their confusing overlap of forms: The past tense of *lie* is *lay*, whereas the past tense of *lay* is *laid*. Changing the previous example to the past tense illustrates the issue.

▶ The passengers in first class ~~laid~~ *lay* in fully reclining seats. During the landing, the pilot ~~lay~~ *laid* the plane gently on the runway.

→ EXERCISE 37.3 Using *rise/raise*, *sit/set*, and *lie/lay* correctly

In the following paragraph, correct any errors involving *rise/raise*, *sit/set*, and *lie/lay*.

> Senna began her daily exercise routine as soon as she raised from bed. She seldom laid in bed long after her alarm went off. She usually set the alarm to go off at 4:30 a.m. Most of her neighbors were still laying in their beds when she was rising barbells over her head. Each time she rose a weight, she held it up for several seconds, then gently sat it down. She would also set on the floor and later lay down flat for some stretching exercises. After these warm-ups, Senna went out for a run and watched the sun raise over the lake. As she ran, she tried not to rise her knees too high, and she never let her arms lay idly at her side. Home again from her run, she would sometimes lay down again for a few minutes before beginning her workday.

TENSE

37f Understanding Which Verb Tense to Use

Verb *tenses* provide information about the time in which an action or event occurs—past, present, or future—about whether or not the action is ongoing or completed, and about the time of one action relative to another.

1. Simple tenses

Use the ***simple present tense*** for current or habitual actions or events and to state general truths. Accompanied by a reference to a future event, the simple present can also indicate a future occurrence (also see *section 37h*).

CURRENT ACTION	Hernando *opens* the door to his classroom.
HABITUAL ACTION	He *enjoys* teaching second-graders.
GENERAL TRUTH	Earth *is* the third planet from the sun.
FUTURE OCCURRENCE	Winter *ends* in two weeks.

Use the *simple past tense* for completed actions or occurrences.

- The bell *rang*. Hernando *asked* his students to be quiet.

Use the *simple future tense* for actions that have not yet occurred.

- He *will give* them a spelling test this afternoon.

2. Perfect tenses

The perfect tenses generally indicate the completion of an action before a particular time. Use the *present perfect tense* for an action that started in the past but is now completed or for an action that started in the past but is ongoing.

COMPLETED ACTION   I *have read* all the Harry Potter books.

ONGOING ACTION   I *have read* books all my life.

Use the *past perfect tense* for actions completed by a specific time in the past or before another past action.

- Because the students *had studied* hard for their test, they knew most of the spelling words.

    The studying—*had studied* (past perfect)—came before the knowing—*knew* (simple past).

Use the *future perfect tense* for an action that will be completed by a definite time in the future.

- By the time the semester ends, Hernando's students *will have improved* their spelling grades.

3. Progressive tenses

The progressive tenses indicate ongoing action. Use the *present progressive tense* for an action that is ongoing in the present.

- Matilda *is learning* Spanish.

Use the *past progressive tense* for an action that was ongoing in the past.

- Last night, Yue *was practicing* for her recital.

Quick Reference: An Overview of Verb Tenses and Their Forms

Simple Tenses

Tense	Form	Example
Simple present	base or -s form	I *learn* something new every day.
Simple past	past tense form	I *learned* Spanish many years ago.
Simple future	*will* + base form	I *will learn* to ski next winter.

Perfect Tenses

Tense	Form	Example
Present perfect	*has/have* + past participle	I *have learned* to water ski already.
Past perfect	*had* + past participle	I *had learned* to water ski by the time I was nine.
Future perfect	*will have* + past participle	I *will have learned* how to skydive by September.

Progressive Tenses

Tense	Form	Example
Present progressive	*am/is/are* + present participle	I *am learning* about Japanese food.
Past progressive	*was/were* + present participle	I *was learning* to make sushi yesterday.
Future progressive	*will be* + present participle	I *will be learning* new skills next week.
Present perfect progressive	*have/has been* + present participle	I *have been cooking* seriously since I was a teenager.
Past perfect progressive	*had been* + present participle	I *had been preparing* simple dishes even before then.
Future perfect progressive	*will have been* + present participle	I *will have been enjoying* this hobby for two decades by the end of the year.

Use the ***future progressive tense*** for an ongoing action that will occur in the future.

▸ Elena *will be working* as a publishing company intern next summer.

Use the ***present perfect progressive tense*** for an ongoing action that began in the past.

▸ Hernando *has been working* on his master's degree in education since 2019.

Use the *past perfect progressive tense* for an ongoing past action that is now completed.

▸ Until this semester, he *had been taking* education courses at night.

Use the *future perfect progressive tense* for an ongoing action that will be finished at a definite time in the future.

▸ By the end of August, Hernando *will have been studying* education for more than six years.

Do Not Use the Progressive Tenses with All Verbs Certain verbs, typically those that convey a mental process or a state of being, are not used in the progressive tenses. Examples include *appreciate, belong, contain, envy, fear, know, like, need, owe, own, remember, resemble, seem,* and *want.*

▸ She ~~is seeming~~ *seems* angry with her boyfriend. He ~~was owing~~ *owed* her an apology.

37g Following Conventions for the Use of the Present Tense

The present tense is conventionally used for describing works of art, for describing events in literary works, and for stating scientific facts.

▸ In the series *Sylvia Plath: Girl Detective*, producers Mike Simses and Kate Simses ~~brought~~ *bring* us a cheerful character who ~~was~~ *is* not at all depressed.

▸ Watson and Crick discovered that DNA ~~had~~ *has* a double helix structure.

   Although the discovery was in the past, it remains true.

In general, use the present tense to introduce a quotation, paraphrase, or summary.

▸ As Harriet Lerner ~~noted,~~ *notes,* "Anger is neither legitimate nor illegitimate, meaningful nor pointless. Anger simply is."

> **More about**
> APA documentation style, 397–438

EXCEPTION The APA documentation style calls for the use of the past tense or the past perfect tense for reporting findings or introducing cited material.

> ▸ Chodoff (2002) ~~claims~~ *claimed* that in their efforts to put a diagnostic label on "all varieties and vagaries of human feelings," psychiatrists ~~risk~~ *risked* medicalizing "the human condition itself."

37h Using Tense Sequence to Clarify Time Relationships

> **More about**
> Inappropriate shifts in tense, 732–33

When a sentence contains two separate actions, readers need a clear idea of the time relationship between them. Writers communicate this information through their choice of tenses, or *sequence of tenses.* Change verb tenses when there is reason to do so, but do not shift tenses unnecessarily.

In a sentence with two past actions, for example, use the simple past tense for both verbs if the actions occurred simultaneously.

> ▸ When he *arrived* at the station, the train *departed.*
>
> He arrived and the train departed at the same time.

If the actions happened at different times, use the past perfect tense for the action that occurred first.

> ▸ By the time he *arrived* at the station, the train *had departed.*
>
> The train departed before he arrived.

1. Infinitives and tense sequence

An *infinitive* consists of *to* followed by the base form of the verb (*to listen, to go*). Use this form, the *present infinitive,* for an action that occurs after or simultaneously with the action of the main verb.

> ▸ Ivan is known to be a good student.
>
> The knowing and the being happen together.
>
> ▸ Everyone expects Ivan to ace the exam.
>
> The expectation is about Ivan's future performance on the exam.

Use the *perfect infinitive—to have* and the past participle (*to have listened, to have gone*)—for an action that happened before the action of the main verb.

▶ Ivan is said *to have studied* all weekend.

    The studying took place before the talk about it.

2. Participles and tense sequence

Use the present participle (*listening, going*) to express action that happens simultaneously with the action of the main verb, regardless of the tense of the main verb.

▶ *Handing* her son Robbie a cup of coffee, Mona offered him some brownies.

Use the past participle (*listened, gone*) or the present perfect participle (*having listened, having gone*) to express action that happens before the action of the main verb.

▶ *Discouraged* by her daughter's aloofness, Mona asked her son to help.

    Mona was discouraged before she asked.

▶ *Having mediated* their disagreements for years, Robbie refused to intervene.

    Robbie mediated before he refused.

MOOD

37i Understanding Verb Mood

The *mood* of a verb indicates whether a speaker or writer views what is said as a fact, a command, or a possibility. Most English sentences are in the *indicative mood,* which states facts or opinions and asks questions.

▶ Our research papers *are* due tomorrow morning.

▶ *Did* you *say* the deadline had changed?

The *imperative mood* issues commands, gives instructions, or makes requests. The subject of an imperative sentence (*you*) is usually left unstated.

▶ *Hand in* your papers by Friday afternoon.

▶ *Turn* left at the third stoplight.

▶ Please *pass* the salt.

The *subjunctive mood* expresses possibility (or impossibility), as in hypothetical situations, conditions known to be untrue, wishes, suggestions, and requirements.

- If I *were* finished, I could go to bed.
- The doctor suggests that he *get* more exercise.

37j Using the Subjunctive Mood Correctly

The subjunctive has three tenses: present, past, and past perfect. The present subjunctive is always the base form of the verb, regardless of the person or number of the subject: *Ramon asks that his teacher give* (not *gives*) *him an extension*. The past subjunctive of *be* is *were*: *I wish I were* (not *was*) *finished*. For all other verbs, the past subjunctive is identical to the past tense. Similarly, the past perfect subjunctive is identical to the past perfect indicative.

> **Writing Responsibly** — Using the Subjunctive in Formal Writing
>
> Because the subjunctive has been fading from everyday usage, the indicative may seem more acceptable to you. Most readers, however, still expect to find the subjunctive used in formal writing.
>
> - I wish that I ~~was~~ *were* finished.
>
> to AUDIENCE

The subjunctive has been fading from everyday usage, and as a result, the indicative (*I wish I was finished*) may seem an acceptable alternative to you. Most readers, however, expect to find the subjunctive used appropriately (*I wish I were finished*) in formal writing.

Clauses with verbs in the subjunctive are always subordinate clauses. They include *conditional clauses* that begin with *if, as if,* or *as though* and describe a condition known to be untrue. Conditional clauses put forward a set of circumstances and modify a main clause that states what follows from those circumstances.

- If I *were* taller, I would try out for basketball.
- The candidate acts as though he *were* already the winner.

If the main clause includes a modal auxiliary such as *would, could,* or *should,* do not use a similar construction in the *if* clause.

- If I ~~would have been~~ *were* an aspiring actor, I would audition for that part.

Verbs in the main clause that express a wish, request, recommendation, or demand also trigger the subjunctive in the subordinate clause.

- The hikers wished their campground ~~was~~ *were* not so far away.

- Citizens are demanding that the government ~~fixes~~ *fix* the economy.

- Senators have requested that the president ~~is~~ *be* more responsive to the middle class.

- Alicia's adviser recommended that she ~~takes~~ *take* calculus.

EXERCISE 37.4 Using the subjunctive mood correctly

In each of the following sentences, circle the correct verb form.

EXAMPLE

If Cally (was /(were)) a morning person, she would be more alert for her 8:00 a.m. classes.

1. The professor requests that students (be/are) in their chairs at the beginning of class.
2. He reacts to tardiness as if it (was/were) a personal insult.
3. One student's adviser recommended that she (get/gets) more sleep and breakfast.
4. If this class (were/was) part of her major, she would be more inclined to do so.
5. She just wishes the semester (were/was) over.

VOICE

37k Understanding Voice

The term *voice* refers to the role of the subject in a sentence. Only transitive verbs—verbs that take a direct object—can be in the passive voice. In the *active voice,* the subject is the actor and the direct object is acted on.

ACTIVE VOICE   Omar hit the ball out of the park.

Omar is the subject, and *the ball* is the direct object.

In the ***passive voice***, the subject is acted on. To change an active-voice sentence into the passive voice, make the direct object the subject, combine the appropriate form of *be* with the past participle of the main verb, and identify the actor in a phrase beginning with *by*.

> **PASSIVE VOICE**   The ball was hit out of the park by Omar.

The passive voice also permits you to leave the actor unidentified.

> **PASSIVE VOICE**   The ball was hit out of the park.
> **(AGENT UNIDENTIFIED)**

To change the passive voice to active, make the subject into the direct object and the actor into the subject, and change the verb from the passive form to its active form.

▸ Omar's ~~baseball career was enhanced by his~~ generosity off
  enhanced his baseball career.
  the field.*/*

If the passive-voice sentence leaves the actor unidentified, you will need to supply one.

Americans elected the
▸ ~~The~~ country's first African American president ~~was elected~~ in 2008.

37l Choosing between the Active and Passive Voice

> **More about**
> Style and voice,
> 593–94

The active voice is usually preferable to the passive voice because it is the livelier and more direct of the two. The passive voice, in contrast, can deaden prose and obscure a writer's point.

In certain situations, however, the passive voice can be the appropriate choice:

- When the recipient of an action is more important than the actor or the identity of the actor is unimportant

    ▸ The song "Glory" was given the award for Best Original Song by the Academy of Motion Pictures Arts and Sciences.

    The writer wants to focus on the song, not on who gave the award.

- In reports of scientific procedures

    ▸ Five hundred patients *were treated* with Cytoxan over a six-month period.

    The purpose of a scientific report is to describe what happened, not to focus on the scientists who conducted the research.

- When the actor is unknown or cannot be identified
  ▶ Our home *was burglarized* while we were on vacation.

EXERCISE 37.5 Changing passive voice to active

Revise each of the following sentences, changing the passive voice to the active voice.

EXAMPLE

Passive: The stage directions for the play were adapted by the director.

Active: *The director adapted the stage directions for the play.*

1. The costumes and props had been designed in order to increase the play's grandeur.
2. Taylor's performance was made more compelling than it otherwise would have been by the brilliant staging of the scene.
3. Because the play's scenes were rehearsed by the actors every day, excitement about the play spread across the campus.
4. Folding chairs were brought by the maintenance crew so the unexpected attendees on opening night could sit.

Make It Your Own

Write a paragraph about a true or fictional event that did not go according to plan. Write what you or the protagonist expected to happen, why things went wrong, how it turned out, and, finally, what might have been done differently.

Work Together

Exchange your paragraph with a classmate and circle each other's verbs. If you see any that need to be revised, underline them and in the margin write the pages in this chapter that discuss the issue. When you have both finished, review the recommended revisions and write a brief reflection about how they might make your paragraph easier to understand. If you found this activity difficult, add verbs to your revision checklist.

38 Understanding Pronoun Case and Reference

IN THIS CHAPTER

PRONOUN CASE

a. In subject complements, 714

b. In compounds, 714

c. In appositives, 716

d. For *we* and *us* before nouns, 716

e. With infinitives, 716

f. With *-ing* words, 717

g. In comparisons, 717

h. *Who* and *whom*, 717

CLEAR PRONOUN REFERENCE

i. Ambiguous reference, 720

j. Broad reference, 720

k. Implied reference, 721

l. *You*, 721

m. Indefinite *they* and *it*, 721

n. Reference to people with *who* and *whom*, 722

> *More about*
> Subjects and objects, 645–51

When you play an online multiplayer game like *Fortnite,* you may be interacting with dozens of other players who could be located almost anywhere in the world. Neither you nor they are physically present in the game. Instead, you all have virtual stand-ins—avatars—to represent you.

Like avatars, pronouns are stand-ins. They represent other words—their ***antecedents***—in speech or writing. Also like avatars, they sometimes change form, depending on the role you want them to play within a sentence.

PRONOUN CASE

Nouns, and the pronouns that represent them, can play various roles within a sentence. They can be subjects:

	subject	
NOUN	The Steelers	lost.
PRONOUN	They	lost.

712

They can be objects (including direct objects, indirect objects, and objects of prepositions):

	subject		direct object
NOUN	The Bears	beat	**the Steelers.**
PRONOUN	We	beat	**them.**

They can indicate possession:

	possessive			possessive	
NOUN	**Chicago's**	team	beat	**Pittsburgh's**	team.
PRONOUN	**Our**	team	beat	**their**	team.

> **More about**
> Indicating possession with apostrophes, 827–31

The term *case* refers to the different forms a noun or pronoun takes—*subjective, objective,* or *possessive*—depending on which of these roles it serves. Nouns do not change much—they have the same form as subjects that they do as objects, and they indicate possession with an *s* sound that is marked in writing with an apostrophe (*Chicago's team*). In contrast, most *personal pronouns* and some *relative* and *interrogative pronouns* are shape shifters—they have distinct forms for many of their roles:

> **personal pronouns** Pronouns that take the place of nouns or noun phrases
> **relative pronouns** Pronouns that introduce subordinate clauses that describe the pronoun's antecedent
> **interrogative pronouns** Pronouns that introduce questions

		Subjective Case	Objective Case	Possessive Case
Personal Pronouns				
	1st person	*I*	*me*	*my, mine*
Singular	2nd person	*you*	*you*	*your, yours*
	3rd person	*he*	*him*	*his*
		she	*her*	*her, hers*
		it	*it*	*its*
	1st person	*we*	*us*	*our, ours*
Plural	2nd person	*you*	*you*	*your, yours*
	3rd person	*they*	*them*	*their, theirs*
Case-Variant Relative and		*who*	*whom*	*whose*
Interrogative Pronouns		*whoever*	*whomever*	

Some case errors are easy for native speakers of English to detect because they sound wrong.

▸ Hermione is one of Harry's best friends, and ~~her~~ *she* often gives ~~he~~ *him* sound advice.

In many situations, however, the ear is an unreliable guide to proper case usage.

case Grammar Matters • Understanding Pronoun Case and Reference

38a Using the Subjective Case for Subject Complements

A pronoun that functions as a *subject complement* following a form of *be* used as a main verb should be in the subjective case, not the objective case.

> **subject complement**
> An adjective, pronoun, or noun phrase that follows a linking verb and describes or refers to the sentence subject

▸ Asked who spilled the milk, my sister confessed that the guilty one was ~~her~~. *she.*

If this usage sounds overly formal, try reversing the subject and subject complement.

▸ Asked who spilled the milk, my sister confessed that the guilty *she was* ~~one was her~~. *one.*

38b *She and I* or *Her and Me*? Keeping Track of Case in Compounds

Pronouns that are part of compound subjects or subject complements should be in the subjective case.

▸ My friends and ~~me~~ *I* [compound subject] chat online while we play video games.

Pronouns that are part of compound objects should be in the objective case.

▸ My parents call my brothers and ~~I~~ *me* [compound dir. obj.] every weekend.

Pronouns that are part of compound possessives should be in the possessive case.

▸ My father often gets ~~me~~ *my* [compound possessive] and my brother's names confused.

Grammar Matters • *She and I* or *Her and Me*? Keeping Track of Case in Compounds   case   **38b**   715

> **Quick Reference**   **Editing for Case in Compounds**
>
> To determine the correct case of a pronoun in a compound, isolate the pronoun from the rest of the compound; then read the result aloud to yourself. If the pronoun sounds wrong, replace it with the one that sounds right.
>
> Faulty   [My friends and] me chat online while we play video games.
> Revised   My friends and I chat online while we play video games.
>
> *Me chat online* is clearly wrong. Replacing the objective pronoun *me* with the subjective pronoun *I* corrects the problem.
>
> Faulty   My parents call [my siblings and] I every weekend.
> Revised   My parents call my siblings and me every weekend.
>
> *My parents call I* is clearly wrong. Replacing the subjective pronoun *I* with the objective pronoun *me* corrects the problem.
>
> Faulty   My father often gets me [and my brother's] names confused.
> Revised   My father often gets my and my brother's names confused.
>
> *My father gets me names confused* is clearly wrong. Replacing the objective pronoun *me* with the possessive pronoun *my* corrects the problem.

➔ EXERCISE 38.1 Pronoun case in subject complements and compounds

Circle the correct pronoun from each pair in parentheses.

EXAMPLE

When we were about 12, Sofia and (**I** / me) were intensely interested in rocketry.

1. Actually it was (she/her) who first joined the rocketry club, and then she got me involved.

2. We got so good at building and launching model rockets that other kids would call (she or I/her or me) whenever they had problems.

3. As we got older and our interests changed, (she and I/her and me) gradually lost our fascination with rocketry.

4. Now that I'm in college, one of (me/my) and my roommate's favorite pastimes has become rocketry.

38c Keeping Track of Pronoun Case in Appositives

appositive phrase A noun or noun phrase that renames a preceding noun or noun phrase and is grammatically equivalent to it

The case of a pronoun in an *appositive phrase* should reflect the function of the phrase the appositive renames.

▶ The two most talented actors in our school, Valentino and ~~her~~ *she*, always get the best roles in school productions.

> The phrase *The two most talented actors in our school* is the subject of the sentence, so the pronoun in the appositive phrase should be in the subjective case (*she*).

▶ The director always wants the best artists, ~~she~~ *her* and ~~I~~ *me*, to work on the scenery.

> The appositive phrase is renaming the object *the best artists,* so the pronouns in the phrase should be in the objective case (*her* and *me*).

38d Deciding between *We* and *Us* before Nouns

In expressions that combine *we* or *us* with a noun, use *we* with nouns that function as subjects or subject complements and *us* with nouns that function as objects. To decide which is which, say the sentence to yourself with the pronoun alone.

▶ ~~Us~~ *We* gamers live vicariously in the game world through our avatars.

> *Us live vicariously* is clearly wrong. The subjective pronoun *we* should replace the objective pronoun *us*.

▶ Our avatars act vicariously in the game world on behalf of ~~we~~ *us* gamers.

> *Avatars act on behalf of we* is clearly wrong. The objective pronoun *us* should replace the subjective pronoun *we*.

38e Using the Objective Case Both before and after an Infinitive

infinitive The *to* form of a verb (*to decide, to eat, to study*)

Both the subject and object of an *infinitive* should be in the objective case.

▶ I asked *her* to recommend *me* for the job.

> Both *her,* the subject of the infinitive *to recommend,* and *me,* its direct object, are in the objective case.

38f Deciding on Pronoun Case with the *–ing* Form of a Verb

In most cases, use the possessive form of a noun or pronoun with a ***gerund*** (the present participle, or *-ing* form of a verb used as a noun).

> **More about**
> Gerunds, 653

▶ Professor Kimani, I appreciate ~~you~~ *your* taking time to advise me on my résumé.

Use the objective form of a noun or pronoun, however, when the *-ing* word functions as a modifier rather than a noun.

PRONOUN IS THE MODIFIER   Margo is an Albert Pujols fan. She admires *his* playing.

PRONOUN IS MODIFIED   Margo saw *him* playing in the World Series.

38g Clarifying Pronoun Case in Comparisons with *Than* or *As*

In comparisons with *than* or *as,* the choice of pronoun case can sometimes result in two otherwise identical sentences with significantly different meanings.

▶ Hassina likes her new car more than I.
▶ Hassina likes her new car more than me.

In the first sentence, the subjective case (*I*) signals a comparison between Hassina's and the writer's fondness for Hassina's car (she thinks better of it than the writer does). In the second sentence, the objective case (*me*) signals a comparison between Hassina's fondness for her car and her fondness for the writer (she thinks better of her car than of the writer). To avoid confusing readers in situations like this, identify which pronoun your meaning requires by supplying any words needed to make the comparisons explicit.

▶ Hassina likes her new car more than I *do.*
▶ Hassina likes her new car more than *she likes* me.

38h Using *Who, Whom, Whoever,* and *Whomever*

The pronouns *who, whom, whoever,* and *whomever* have two jobs. As ***relative pronouns*** they introduce **subordinate clauses.** As ***interrogative pronouns*** they introduce questions.

> **subordinate clause**
> A word group with a subject and predicate that cannot stand alone as a sentence but instead functions within a sentence as a noun, adjective, or adverb

- Use *who* or *whoever* for the subject of a subordinate clause or question.

  ▸ Tiger Woods, *who* began playing as a toddler, dominated golf in his early adulthood. [subordinate clause; subj.]

  ▸ *Who* began playing golf as a toddler? [question; subj.]

- Use *whom* or *whomever* for the object of a subordinate clause or question. Notice, however, that contrary to normal word order, in which direct objects follow verbs, *whom* and *whomever* usually come at the beginning of a clause or question.

  ▸ Woods, *whom* many golf fans still admired, fell out of the list of top golfers after his back surgery. [subordinate clause; dir. obj.]

  ▸ *Whom* do many golf fans admire? [question; dir. obj.]

- The case of a relative pronoun is determined by its role in a clause, not the role of the clause in the sentence. The relative pronoun in the following example is the subject of its clause and so should be in the subjective case—*whoever*—even though the clause as a whole is the object of the preposition *to*.

  ▸ In professional golf, the winner's prize goes to ~~whomever~~ *whoever* completes the course in the fewest strokes.

Writing Responsibly — Case and Tone

Many people now ignore the distinction between *who* and *whom*, using only *who*. In academic and business writing, however, many readers will assume that you do not understand correct usage if you use *who* when *whom* is called for. Even if *whom* and *whomever* sound inappropriately formal, even old-fashioned, to your ear, consider what your reader's expectations are and adjust your usage accordingly.

to AUDIENCE

- Match the pronoun to its verb, not to the verb of an intervening clause. In the following example, the pronoun should be the subjective case *who* because it is the subject of *was,* not the object of *know.*

  > *who*
  > Thomas Edison, ~~whom~~ many people know was the inventor of the lightbulb, was also the inventor of the phonograph.

EXERCISE 38.2 Distinguishing *who, whom, whoever, whomever*

Circle the correct pronoun from each pair in parentheses.

EXAMPLE

Ayrton, (who / whom) grew up in southern California, was visiting New York City for the first time.

1. It was the middle of winter, and taxis seemed to stop for (whoever/whomever) stood furthest into the street, but not for him.
2. (Whoever/Whomever) would have guessed that when Ayrton slipped on some ice and fell on his back, everybody on the street would surround him and reach down to help him up?
3. These were not the uncaring people (who/whom) he had assumed New Yorkers were.
4. He was soon back on his feet thanks to a tough-looking older man (who/whom) Ayrton invited to join him for a coffee.

CLEAR PRONOUN REFERENCE

Pronoun reference involves the clarity of the relationship between a pronoun and its antecedent. With clear pronoun reference, readers can easily identify the antecedent of a pronoun.

> Mario talked to his sister Roberta about her career plans.
>
> The pronoun *his* clearly refers to Mario; the pronoun *her* clearly refers to Mario's sister.

Pronoun reference is unclear when readers cannot be certain what a pronoun's antecedent is.

▸ Mario talked to Paul about his career plans.

> Did Mario and Paul talk about Mario's career plans or Paul's? Without more information, readers will be uncertain.

38i Avoiding Ambiguous Reference

The reference of a pronoun is ambiguous when it has two or more equally plausible antecedents.

▸ Mario talked to Paul about his career plans.

One way to resolve ambiguous reference is to replace the pronoun with the appropriate noun.

▸ Mario talked to Paul about Paul's career plans.

To avoid repeating the noun, rephrase the sentence in a way that eliminates the ambiguity.

▸ Paul talked about his career plans with Mario.

> The position of the pronoun *his* associates the plans clearly and unambiguously with Paul, not Mario.

38j Avoiding Confusingly Broad Reference with *It, This, That,* and *Which*

When pronouns such as *it, this, that,* and *which* refer broadly to an entire clause, sentence, or series of sentences, readers may be uncertain about what specific information the pronouns cover.

■ Who owns Antarctica? Several countries—including Argentina, Australia, Chile, France, New Zealand, Norway, the United Kingdom, and the United States—all claim or reserve the right to claim all or part of the continent. ~~This makes it~~ *These competing claims make the question of ownership* difficult to answer.

> The revision specifies what information the writer meant by *this* and *it*.

38k Avoiding Implied Reference

A pronoun should have a clearly identifiable antecedent, not an unstated, or implied, antecedent. In the following example, the only word that could serve grammatically as the antecedent to *they* is *stories,* but stories are not places. The writer's intended antecedent is implied in the adjective *small-town,* as the revision makes clear.

DRAFT From her stories of her small-town childhood, they seem like great places to grow up.

REVISED Her stories of her childhood make small towns seem like great places to grow up.

Similarly, in the next example, the antecedent to *he—Einstein—*is implied, confusingly, in the possessive form *Einstein's.*

▸ According to Einstein's theory of relativity, ~~he showed that~~ mass and energy are interchangeable.

38l Reserving *You* for Directly Addressing the Reader

In formal writing, reserve the pronoun *you* (and the implied *you* of commands) to address the reader directly, as in "you, the reader." Do not use *you* as a substitute for indefinite words such as *anybody, everybody,* or *people.*

▸ Before computers and the Internet, ~~you~~ *people* got ~~your~~ *their* news mostly from print newspapers, radio, and television.

38m Avoiding the Indefinite Use of *They* and *It*

In formal writing, the pronouns *they* and *it* need specific antecedents. Avoid using these pronouns to refer to unspecified people or things.

▸ At Hogwarts School of Witchcraft and Wizardry, ~~they~~ *students* use owls, not email, for sending messages.

▸ ~~In the~~ *The* beginning of the chapter~~, it~~ compares pronouns to computer-game avatars.

38n Designating People with *Who*, *Whom*, and *Whose*, Not *That* and *Which*

When you are speaking, you are as likely to use *that* as you are to use *who* or *whom* to refer to people. In formal writing, however, you should usually use only *who* and *whom* to refer to people.

▶ According to his website, people ~~that~~ *who* have special needs will be served by the Jordan Spieth Family Foundation.

Use *that* and *which* for animals and things.

▶ The stray cats ~~who~~ *that* live in the alley sometimes howl at night.

For pets and other named animals, however, *who* or *whom* is often more appropriate than *that* or *which*.

▶ Our cat Juniper, ~~which~~ *who* is now twelve years old, is still healthy and spry.

The possessive pronoun *whose* is also best reserved for people but can apply to animals and things when avoiding it requires the awkward use of the phrase *of which*.

▶ The polar bear is an animal ~~the~~ *whose* habitat ~~of which~~ is threatened by global warming.

EXERCISE 38.3 Editing for pronoun reference

Edit the following passage to eliminate problems with pronoun reference.

> Everyone who knew Colin identified him as someone that loved music. When you wanted to know about a band's background, you would ask Colin, who had made a life's work of studying the histories of musicians and composers. When Sydnee Sandford, a popular host on his college's radio station, interviewed Colin about the 1960s rock musicians that she was featuring on her show, he became instantly famous on campus. That is what started it. A week later, the radio station manager told Colin that they would like to know if he wanted his own radio program. It appealed to him, but he also understood that he was a person that was quite shy and uncomfortable with public speaking. Based on his past experiences at speaking before audiences, they caused him to avoid giving her an answer. Sensing his obvious discomfort,

she pointed out that she herself was also shy and had long been terrified of public speaking. She said that her answer was that you would discuss on your show and interview others about what interested you the most. Colin remembered how easy it was to talk on her show because he enjoyed the topic.

Colin's show aired at 3 to 4 a.m., and the only person the taste of which in music he used as a guide was himself. Soon he attracted a huge listenership on campus.

Make It **Your Own**

Write a true or fictional paragraph about giving someone a birthday present. Consider writing about deciding what to give, how you found the present, and how the recipient reacted. Use at least six different pronouns, with at least one from each of the three pronoun cases: subjective, objective, and possessive.

Work **Together**

Exchange your paragraph with a classmate and circle each other's pronouns. If you see any that need to be revised, underline them, and in the margin write the pages in this chapter that discuss the issue. When you have both finished, review the recommended revisions and write a brief reflection about how they might make your paragraph easier to understand. If you found this activity difficult, add pronouns to your revision checklist.

39 Using Adjectives and Adverbs

IN THIS CHAPTER

a. Differentiating adjectives and adverbs, 724

b. Using adjectives as subject complements, 725

c. Choosing *bad* or *badly*, *good* or *well*, 726

d. Using negatives correctly, 728

e. Avoiding nouns as adjectives, 728

f. Using comparative forms, 729

The clothing, jewelry, and hairstyles we choose—our modifiers—send a message to others about how we want them to perceive us. A flamboyant dress, a tattoo, eye-catching jewelry, and flowing hair send one impression; a tailored business suit sends another. Similarly, we send readers a message about how we want our words to be understood by our choice of adjectives and adverbs to modify them.

39a Differentiating Adjectives and Adverbs

Adjectives modify (or describe) nouns and pronouns, answering questions such as *What kind? Which one?* or *How many? Adverbs* modify verbs, adjectives, other adverbs, and entire phrases, clauses, and sentences; they answer questions such as *How? Where?* or *When?*

Although many adverbs end in the suffix *-ly*, many do not (*later, often, quite, seldom*), and dozens of adjectives do (*elderly, lowly, scholarly*). The only reliable way to distinguish an adjective from an adverb is not from its form but from its function (see the Quick Reference box on p. 725).

> **More about**
> The characteristics of English adjectives, 786–87

English Adjectives Do Not Have Plural Forms In English, adjectives do not change form to agree with the words they modify.

Traditions can provide ~~goods~~ *good* foundations for innovation.

724

> **Quick Reference** — **The Functions of Adjectives and Adverbs**
>
> **Adjectives modify:**
>
> | | |
> |---|---|
> | Nouns | *sunny* day |
> | Pronouns | someone *responsible* |
>
> **Adverbs modify:**
>
> | | |
> |---|---|
> | Verbs | spoke *forcefully* |
> | Adjectives | *painfully* loud |
> | Adverbs | *very* cautiously |
> | Phrases | *finally* over the finish line |
> | Clauses and sentences | *Eventually,* the story ended. |

39b Using Adjectives, Not Adverbs, as Subject Complements after Linking Verbs

Linking verbs express a state of being rather than an action or occurrence. They link the subject to a *subject complement,* which describes or refers to the subject. In other words, the subject complement modifies the subject, not the verb; it can be an adjective or a noun, but not an adverb.

The verb *be,* when used as a main verb, is always a linking verb.

▸ The *solution* is <u>simple</u>.

> The adjective *simple* modifies the subject, *solution*.

Other verbs, such as *appear, become, feel, look, prove, sound,* and *taste,* may function as linking verbs in one context and action verbs in another. A word following one of these verbs should be an adjective if it modifies the subject and an adverb if it modifies the verb.

> **More about**
> Linking verbs and subject complements, 649

▸ *Maria* looked <u>anxious</u> to the dentist.

> *Looked* is a linking verb and the adjective *anxious* is a subject complement that describes Maria's state of mind as the dentist perceived it.

▸ Maria *looked* <u>anxiously</u> at the dentist.

> *Looked* is an action verb modified by the adverb *anxiously,* which describes the manner in which Maria performed the action of looking.

39c Choosing *Bad* or *Badly*, *Good* or *Well*

> **Tech**
>
> **Grammar Checkers and Adjective-Adverb Problems**
>
> Grammar checkers in word processing programs catch some adjective and adverb errors but miss many others. A grammar checker, for example, missed errors such as *The Patriots played bad, the boat rocked gentle*, and *Tomás looked well in his tuxedo*.

In casual speech, we commonly mingle adjectives and adverbs. In writing, however, adjectives are used to modify nouns and pronouns, and adverbs are used to modify verbs, adjectives, or other adverbs. Do not confuse *bad* with *badly*, *good* with *well*, or *real* with *really*. Use the adjective form of these pairs for subject complements. Include *-ly* endings when needed, and use an adjective, not an adverb, to modify a direct object.

- *Bad* is an adjective; *badly* is an adverb.
  - ▶ The Patriots played ~~bad~~ *badly* in the fourth quarter.

    Badly modifies the action verb *played*.

  - ▶ The quarterback feels ~~badly~~ *bad* about the loss.

    Feels is a linking verb; *bad* modifies *quarterback*.

- The word *good* is an adjective, and *well* is its adverb counterpart. *Well* is an adjective, however, when it is used to mean "healthy."
  - ▶ Leah did ~~good~~ *well* on her final exams.

    The adverb *well* modifies the verb *did*.

  - ▶ Tomás looks ~~well~~ *good* in his tuxedo.

    Looks is a linking verb; the adjective *good* modifies *Tomás*.

  - ▶ After a late-night graduation party, Leah is not feeling ~~good~~ *well*.

    Well is used as an adjective because it refers to health.

- Do not confuse the adjective *real* with the adverb *really*.
  - ▶ The actors are ~~real~~ *really* enthusiastic about tonight's performance.

> **More about**
> Conciseness
> (ch. 26), 558–64

NOTE Intensifiers like *really* often add little or no meaning to a sentence and can usually be dropped in the interest of conciseness.

Grammar Matters • Choosing *Bad* or *Badly*, *Good* or *Well*

- Do not confuse adverbs that end in *-ly* with their adjective counterparts that do not.

  ▸ You should play ~~gentle~~ *gently* with small children.

  The adverb *gently* modifies the verb *play*.

- Never use an adverb to modify a direct object. When a modifier follows a direct object, ask yourself, "What word is being modified?" If the answer is "the verb," then the modifier should be an adverb, but if the answer is "the direct object," then the modifier is an ***object complement*** and should be an adjective or noun.

  > **More about**
  > Direct objects and object modifiers, 648–50, 761–63

  ▸ The divorce left *Kayla cautious* about future relationships.

  The adjective *cautious* modifies the direct object *Kayla*.

  > **object complement**
  > An adjective or noun phrase that follows the direct object and describes the condition of the object or a change the subject has caused it to undergo

  ▸ She *conducted* herself *cautiously* with potential new friends.

  The adverb *cautiously* modifies the verb *conducted*, not the direct object *herself*.

▸ EXERCISE 39.1 Correcting common adjective-adverb problems

Revise the following sentences to correct any adjective or adverb errors.

EXAMPLE

Most people are ~~real~~ *really* surprised to learn that Bennett and Raul are roommates and even ~~well~~ *good* friends.

1. Raul takes unusual good care of his clothes and dresses fashionable.
2. Bennett feels indifferently about clothes and dresses real sloppy.
3. Of course, Raul always keeps his side of their room awful messily.
4. Bennett, on the other hand, puts absolute everything careful in its proper place.
5. Despite these stark differences, the two of them get along real good.

39d Using Negatives Correctly

In a sentence with a *double negative,* two negative modifiers describe the same word. Because one negative cancels the other, the message becomes positive. In Standard American English, double negatives can be acceptable, but only to emphasize a positive meaning. The sentence *It is not unlikely that the attorney will be disbarred,* for example, means that the attorney's disbarment is likely. Although some dialects allow the use of double (and more) negatives to emphasize a negative meaning, and many people use them that way in casual speech, you should avoid them in formal writing. Remember that the negative word *not* is part of contractions such as *couldn't* and *shouldn't* and that words like *barely, hardly*, and *scarcely* have a negative meaning.

▶ Students ~~shouldn't~~ *should* never park in a faculty-only lot.

▶ I ~~can't~~ *can* hardly argue with facts like those.

39e Avoiding Long Strings of Nouns Used as Adjectives

One noun can often function as an adjective to modify another: *government worker, traffic violation, college course.* Multiple nouns strung together this way, however, can be cumbersome and confusing.

CONFUSING   The *teacher education policy report* will be available tomorrow.

REVISED   The *policy report on teacher education* will be available tomorrow.

Order of Adjectives in a Series When more than one adjective modifies a noun, the adjectives usually need to follow a specific order:

▶ a ~~European~~ *European* stunning racehorse

Charts like the one on page 787 may help you learn what that order is, but to follow that order reliably, you will need consistent exposure to a broad range of English-language situations and texts. For guidance on ordering multiple adjectives, see page 787.

39f Using Comparative and Superlative Adjectives and Adverbs

Most adjectives and adverbs have three forms for indicating the relative degree of the quality or manner they specify: positive, comparative, and superlative. The *positive form* is the base form—the form you find when you look the word up in the dictionary.

POSITIVE   Eyal is *tall*.

The *comparative form* indicates a relatively greater or lesser degree of a quality.

COMPARATIVE   Eyal is *taller* than Martin.

The *superlative form* indicates the greatest or least degree of a quality.

SUPERLATIVE   Eyal is the *tallest* player on the team.

Regular adjectives and adverbs form the comparative and superlative with either the suffixes *-er* and *-est* or the addition of the words *more* and *most* or *less* and *least*. A few adjectives and adverbs have irregular comparative and superlative forms (see the Quick Reference box on the next page). If you are not sure whether to use *-er/-est* or *more/most* for a particular adjective or adverb, look it up in a dictionary. If the entry shows *-er* and *-est* forms, use them. If no such forms are listed, use *more* or *most*.

1. Comparative or superlative

Use the comparative form to compare two things, the superlative to compare three or more.

▸ Between John Oliver and Margaret Cho, I think Cho is the ~~funniest.~~ *funnier.*

▸ Of all comedians ever, I think Wanda Sykes is the ~~funnier.~~ *funniest.*

2. Redundant comparisons

Do not combine the comparative words *more/most* with adjectives or adverbs that are already in comparative form with an *-er* or *-est* ending.

▸ Trains in Europe and Japan are ~~more~~ faster than trains in the United States.

> **Quick Reference** — Forming Comparatives and Superlatives

Regular Forms

	Positive	Comparative	Superlative
Adjectives	bold	bolder/less bold	boldest/least bold
	helpful	more/less helpful	most/least helpful
Adverbs	far	farther	farthest
	realistically	more/less realistically	most/least realistically

Irregular Forms

	Positive	Comparative	Superlative
Adjectives	bad	worse	worst
	good	better	best
	little	less (quantity)/littler (size)	least (quantity)/littlest (size)
	many	more	most
	much	more	most
	some	more	most
Adverbs	badly	worse	worst
	well	better	best

3. Complete comparisons

> More about
> Complete comparisons, 754–55

Make sure your comparisons are logical and that readers have all the information they need to understand what is being compared to what.

▶ The nurses' test scores were higher. *than those of the pre-med students.*

The original makes us ask, "Higher than what?" The addition clarifies the comparison.

4. Absolute terms

Expressions like *more unique* or *most perfect* are common in everyday speech, but if you think about them, they make no sense. *Unique, perfect,* and other words such as *equal, essential, final, full, impossible, infinite,* and *unanimous* are absolutes, and absolutes are beyond compare. If something is unique, it is by definition one of a kind. If something is perfect, it cannot be improved upon. In formal writing, then, avoid using absolute terms comparatively.

▶ Last night's performance of the play was the ~~most perfect~~ *best* yet.

EXERCISE 39.2 Revising for problems with adjectives and adverbs

In the following paragraphs, correct any errors in adjective or adverb usage.

It was her last year of college, and Aaqilah was finding life to be extreme exhilarating and real overwhelming at the same time. She had worked hardest in the previously three years to complete her required courses so that this year she could be more selective about the courses she took. That is why, although she was a chemistry major, she was taking several courses that scarcely had nothing to do with chemistry. She was furthering her study of Russian and was doing a lot of translating between Russian and English, which was terrible stressful at times. Her opera course was a purely delight, and she also loved studying European history from 1500 to 1789, although that required an immense amount of reading.

She was also enjoying her extracurricular activities, but she couldn't barely fit them all into her demanding schedule. Playing flute in the wind ensemble was fun, especially since she was the more accomplished musician in the group. However, playing in the band for the musical was bad taxing because the score was highly intricate.

Make It **Your Own**

Write a paragraph describing what you would have in your dream house if you were fabulously rich. Use at least six adjectives and six adverbs in your descriptions of your house's features, making at least two of the adjectives or adverbs comparative or superlative.

Work **Together**

Exchange your paragraph with a classmate and circle each other's adjectives and adverbs. If you see any that need to be revised, underline them and in the margin write the pages in this chapter that discuss the issue. When you have both finished, review the recommended revisions and write a brief reflection about what effect they would have on your paragraph. If you found this activity difficult, add adjectives and adverbs to your revision checklist.

40 Avoiding Confusing Shifts

IN THIS CHAPTER

a. Avoiding shifts in tense, 732

b. Avoiding shifts in mood and voice, 733

c. Avoiding shifts in person and number, 735

d. Avoiding shifts in direct and indirect discourse, 737

When NASCAR drivers round the curves or head into the straightaway, they need to shift gears, but an expert driver shifts only when doing so will provide a clear advantage. Similarly, good writers try not to jar their readers with unnecessary shifts in style or grammar.

40a Avoiding Awkward Shifts in Tense

> More about
> Verb tenses, 702–7

Verb tenses place events in a sentence in time. Sentences with more than one verb may require a shift in tense from one to another if the verbs refer to events that occur at different times.

▸ Yesterday *was* snowy, and today *is* cloudy and cold, but according to the weather report, the weekend *will be* warm and sunny.

The sentence contrasts past, present, and future weather conditions.

Readers can be confused, however, by shifts in tense that do not correspond to shifts in time. Avoid such inappropriate shifts, especially when you are telling a story or describing a sequence of events.

▸ The guide waited until we had all reached the top of the pass; then she ~~leads~~ *led* the way down to the river and ~~makes~~ *made* sure everybody ~~is~~ *was* safe in camp.

Convention dictates the use of the present tense for writing about literary events and characters as well as about films, plays, and other similar works.

> In Madame Defarge, the principal villain of *A Tale of Two Cities*, Charles Dickens ~~depicted~~ *depicts* the cruel ironies of the French Revolution.

40b Avoiding Awkward Shifts in Mood and Voice

Two other characteristics of verbs are mood and voice; as with tense, shifts in mood and voice should help make clear what the writer intends to convey.

> **Tech** Catching Confusing Shifts
>
> The grammar and style checkers in word processing programs are unreliable for differentiating appropriate and confusing shifts. One style checker, for example, had no objection to this absurd statement: "Yesterday it will rain; tomorrow it snowed two feet." On the other hand, the same style checker flags every occurrence of the passive voice, regardless of whether it is appropriate to the passage in which it appears.

1. Shifts in mood

English verbs have three moods: indicative, imperative, and subjunctive. Most sentences are consistently in the indicative mood, which is used to state or question facts and beliefs. You may, however, inadvertently shift inappropriately between the imperative mood—used for commands, directions, and entreaties—and the indicative mood when explaining a process or giving directions.

> Dig a narrow hole about six inches deep, place the tulip bulb firmly at the bottom of the hole, and then ~~you can~~ fill the hole with dirt.

The subjunctive mood is used in certain situations to express a wish or demand or to make a statement contrary to fact. Although many of us often replace it with the indicative in everyday speech, readers expect to encounter it in formal writing.

> *More about*
> Mood, 707–9

> If the presidential primary ~~was~~ *were* held earlier in the year, our state's voters would have a greater voice in the outcome of the race.

2. Shifts in voice

Avoid shifting needlessly between the active voice, in which the subject performs the action of the verb (*I wrote the paper*) and the passive voice, in which the subject receives the action (*The paper was written by me*).

More about
Voice, 593–94, 709–11

shift Grammar Matters • Avoiding Confusing Shifts

As originally written, the following passage started out in the active voice (*British consumed, Italians favored*) but then shifted to the passive voice for no reason:

▶ During the eighteenth century, the British consumed most of their carbohydrates in the form of processed sugar. The Italians favored pasta, whereas sourdough bread ~~was preferred by the French.~~ *the French preferred*

EXERCISE 40.1 Correcting verb shifts in tense, mood, and voice

Correct the following sentences to make the verbs consistent in tense, mood, and voice. Check for shifts both within and between sentences. If a sentence needs no revision, circle its number.

EXAMPLE

After she mowed the lawn and pulled some weeds, Kris ~~relaxes~~ *relaxed* on the porch watching the hummingbirds until supper ~~is~~ *was* ready.

1. As most birdwatchers know, hummingbirds can do many things that other birds could not do.

2. With their wings being beaten an astonishing 50 times a second or more, hummingbirds sometimes fly as fast as 60 miles per hour.

3. Because hummingbirds expend so much energy, they needed to eat often, usually every 20 minutes.

4. With the highest metabolic rate of any animal, they burn energy faster than tigers, elephants, and all other birds.

5. Hummingbirds' most amazing feature, though, is their ability to fly in any direction—including upside down—something no other bird was capable of doing.

6. When birdwatchers study hummingbirds up close, the uniqueness of the species can be fully appreciated.

7. In addition, get a good view of the birds' long bills and stunning iridescent feathers.

8. Given hummingbirds' constant need for food, which they obtain from nectar and flowers, one would expect to have found them only in warm climates.

9. However, if birdwatchers are able to travel around the country, they would discover some species in chilly locales, such as the Rocky Mountains and Alaska.

10. Many hummingbirds migrate to warmer areas during winter months, but they returned to cooler areas in the spring and summer.

40c Avoiding Awkward Shifts in Person and Number

Person refers to the identity of the subject of a sentence and the point of view of the writer. In the first person (*I, we*), the writer and subject are the same. In the second person (*you*), the reader and subject are the same. In the third person (*he, she, it, they, Marie Curie, electrons*), the subject is the writer's topic of discussion, what the writer is informing the reader about. *Number* refers to the quantity (singular or plural) of a noun or pronoun.

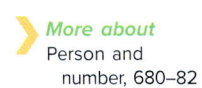

> **More about**
> Person and number, 680–82

1. Shifts in person

Many situations require a shift in person. You might be telling a story in the first person, for example, but you will almost certainly have to relate some parts of it in the third person.

▸ We approached the spooky old house with trepidation. The front door creaked open. We stepped inside.

Arbitrary shifts in person, in contrast, are distracting to readers. The writer of the following passage, for example, began in the first person but shifted jarringly to the second person. The revision establishes a consistent first-person point of view.

▸ When I get together with my friends in the tech club, we usually discuss the latest apps. ~~You~~ *We* tend to forget, though, that a garden spade and a ballpoint pen are also technological tools and that thousands of nonelectronic items become part of ~~your~~ *our* technological world every year.

Most academic writing is in the third person. The second person, including commands, is best reserved for addressing readers directly, telling them how to do something or giving them advice. (You have probably noticed that this handbook often addresses you, the reader, in just this way.) Be consistent, however, and avoid shifting arbitrarily between second and third person.

▶ To train your dog properly, ~~people~~ *you* need plenty of time, patience, and dog biscuits. You should start with simple commands like "sit" and "stay."

2. Shifts in number

> **More about**
> Avoiding gender bias, 601–3, 690–91

When the antecedent is a singular generic noun (*person, doctor*) or indefinite pronoun (*anyone, everyone*) writers can choose between several options: the generic plural *they,* a change in the number of the noun, or the singular *he* or *she*.

GENERIC PLURAL	When a person witnesses a crime, they should report it to the police.
	In traditional usage, pairing the plural pronoun *they* with a singular antecedent (*person*) was considered an error. In contemporary usage it is usually accepted.
PLURAL THROUGHOUT	When people witness a crime, they should report it to the police.
HE OR SHE	When a person witnesses a crime, he or she should report it to the police.
	This option can become tiresome if overused.

As you proofread your work, look for illogical shifts in number between two related nouns. As originally written, for example, the following sentence suggests that the passengers shared a single computer.

▶ All passengers had to open their ~~computer~~ *computers* for a security inspection.

EXERCISE 40.2 Correcting shifts in person and number

Correct the following sentences so that they are consistent in person and number.

EXAMPLE

historians
Although a~~ historian~~ may understand past migrations, they do not have all

the answers to current urban expansions.

1. During the nineteenth century, miners, merchants, and entrepreneurs flocked to the thriving river town of Galena, Illinois, to seek your fortune.
2. Galena was indeed "the west" in those days because you could not yet find any major cities west of the Mississippi River.
3. A Galenian can boast that their city, once the lead-mining capital of the world, was also home to Ulysses S. Grant and nine Civil War generals.
4. A Galenian is also likely to be proud of their town's renowned collection of original nineteenth-century architecture.
5. The mines are long closed, and the river resembles a meandering stream, but Galena remains a historic treasure where a visitor can step into yesterday, escape their busy life, and you can relax.

40d Avoiding Awkward Shifts in Direct and Indirect Quotations and Questions

Direct quotations reproduce someone's exact words and must always be enclosed in quotation marks: *My roommate announced, "The party will start at 8 p.m."* **Indirect quotations** report what someone has said but not in that person's exact words: *My roommate announced that the party would start at 8 p.m.*

Abrupt shifts between direct and indirect quotations, like the one in the following example, are awkward and confusing. Both of the revised versions are clearer and easier to follow than the original. In this instance, however, direct quotation is the best choice because Berra's own words express his humor most effectively.

> **More about**
> Punctuating direct and indirect quotations, 834–37, 839–41
> Quoting sources, 297–99, 335–40
> Direct and indirect sources, 300–1

shift Grammar Matters • Avoiding Confusing Shifts

AWKWARD SHIFT	Yogi Berra said that you should go to other people's funerals or "otherwise, they won't come to yours."
REVISED: DIRECT QUOTATION	As Yogi Berra said, "You should always go to other people's funerals. Otherwise, they won't come to yours."
REVISED: INDIRECT QUOTATION	Yogi Berra said that you should go to other people's funerals because, otherwise, they won't come to yours.

> **More about**
> Punctuating direct and indirect questions, 843–44

Abrupt shifts between direct and indirect questions are confusing. A ***direct question*** is stated in question (interrogative) form and ends with a question mark: *When does the library open?* An ***indirect question*** reports a question in declarative form and ends with a period: *I wonder when the library opens.*

AWKWARD SHIFT	The author asks how much longer can the world depend on fossil fuels and whether alternative sources of energy will be ready in time.
REVISED: DIRECT QUESTION	The author asks two questions: How much longer can the world depend on fossil fuels, and will alternative sources of energy be ready in time?
REVISED: INDIRECT QUESTION	The author asks how much longer the world can depend on fossil fuels and whether alternative sources of energy will be ready in time.

> ### EXERCISE 40.3 Revising confusing shifts

Revise the following passage to eliminate confusing shifts.

> In a taste test described in *The New York Times,* a cross section of the country's population sampled thousands of products in several locations, and store brands were given high marks by the testers. When the testers tried both national and store brands for such products as cereal, cream, pizza, and chicken nuggets, the researchers determine that the store brands were preferred over national brands by testers. While the testers did favor some national-brand products, such as chicken nuggets, cheese pizza, chocolate ice cream, and potatoes au gratin, the testers overwhelmingly prefer store-brand raisin bran. Store-brand frozen broccoli and chocolate chip cookies were also winners.

Grammar Matters • Avoiding Awkward Shifts in Direct and Indirect Quotations and Questions

> Although store brands have achieved a near equality with national brands in the minds of many consumers, shoppers are still careful in their choices. A shopper might ask, why shouldn't I buy a store brand if it tastes as good as a name brand? But if you find the store brand isn't good enough, you wouldn't buy it even if it was a lot cheaper.

Make It **Your Own**

Write a five- or six-sentence paragraph describing your favorite vacation, real or imaginary. Include in your paragraph as many types of awkward shifts in tense, mood, voice, person, and number as you can. You may include shifts both within and between sentences. Label this paragraph "Version A." Then rewrite your paragraph, eliminating the awkward shifts. Label this "Version B."

Work **Together**

Exchange Version A with a classmate and edit each other's paragraph to eliminate the unnecessary shifts. Compare your corrections with your classmate's Version B. Discuss and resolve any differences. If you found this activity difficult, add it to your revision checklist.

Text Credits

Pg. 738: Berra, Yogi, *When You Come to a Fork in the Road, Take It*. Hyperion, 2002, p. 163.

41 Avoiding Misplaced and Dangling Modifiers

IN THIS CHAPTER

MISPLACED MODIFIERS

a. Avoiding confusing or ambiguous placement, 741

b. Avoiding disruptive placement, 743

DANGLING MODIFIERS

c. Identifying dangling modifiers, 746

d. Correcting dangling modifiers, 747

Since 1886, the Statue of Liberty has dominated New York harbor, holding aloft a torch in the hand of her outstretched right arm. In 1876, however, while work on the rest of the statue continued in France, the arm and torch stood incongruously at the Philadelphia Centennial Exhibition, displayed there, and later in New York's Madison Square Park, to help raise funds for the construction of the statue's pedestal. This photograph of the display may strike you as strange because this huge piece of sculpture does not belong in a park; it is supposed to be attached appropriately to the rest of the statue. Similarly, when you misplace modifiers in your sentences, you may inadvertently confuse or surprise your readers.

MISPLACED MODIFIERS

A modifying word, phrase, or clause is misplaced if readers have to figure out what it modifies or if they stumble over it while trying to comprehend the sentence. Look for such *misplaced modifiers* as you revise your drafts.

> **Tech** Misplaced Modifiers and Grammar and Style Checkers
>
> The grammar and style checkers in word processing programs usually cannot tell what a modifier is supposed to modify, so they rarely flag those that are at a confusing distance from their intended targets or that seem ambiguously to modify more than one term. They do flag most split infinitives and some other disruptive modifiers.

41a Avoiding Confusing or Ambiguous Placement

Place modifiers so that they clearly refer to the words you intend them to modify and only those words.

1. Modifiers confusingly separated from the words they modify

We tend to associate modifiers with the words closest to them. A modifier positioned far from its intended target might appear to modify some other part of the sentence instead—and might confuse or amuse your readers.

▸ The couple moved to a bigger apartment *because they needed more space* after their first child was born ~~because they needed more space~~.

The couple's need for space did not cause the birth of their child.

▸ For more than four years, the two rovers *that landed in January 2004* had been exploring the surface of Mars ~~that landed in January 2004~~.

The rovers landed, not the surface of Mars.

➔ EXERCISE 41.1 Correcting confusingly placed modifiers

Revise the following sentences so that all modifiers are clearly and logically positioned.

EXAMPLE
Mr. Doyle walked down Main Street to Town Hall, the building that housed all the town's administrative offices, with determination.

Mr. Doyle walked with determination down Main Street to Town Hall, the building that housed all the town's administrative offices.

1. Because it was a quiet, peaceful, and relaxing town, he knew that a lot of people had chosen to move there, and he knew that like him they didn't like the changes.

2. He had decided to go to Town Hall and formally protest the installation of a traffic light on Reynolds Road in the main intersection of town, dressed in his finest suit.

3. He went straight to the main desk, walking through the large, ornate doors of the building.

4. He was there to protest the proposed traffic light, he told the receptionist, which was a direct threat to the town's long-standing harmony and tranquility.

5. The receptionist said that after holding several public meetings on the issue, he was very sorry but the Town Council had already voted for the traffic light.

2. Squinting modifiers

A *squinting modifier* confuses readers by appearing to modify both what precedes it and what follows it.

DRAFT   People who study hard <u>usually</u> will get the best grades.

The sentence is ambiguous: Do people who make a practice of studying hard get the best grades, or do the best grades usually (but not always) go to people who study hard? The following revisions show that the sentence can be clarified in two different ways:

REVISION   People who <u>usually</u> study hard will get the best grades.

REVISION   People who study hard will <u>usually</u> get the best grades.

3. Ambiguous limiting modifiers

Limiting modifiers include qualifying words such as *almost, even, exactly, hardly, just, merely, only, scarcely,* and *simply*. Always place these words in front of the words you intend to modify. Do not place them in front of a verb unless they modify the verb. Otherwise, you risk ambiguity.

In the following example, the ambiguous placement of the limiter *just* leaves the reader with a variety of possible interpretations. If *just* is understood to modify *offers,* the sentence makes the unlikely suggestion that the only class the math department offers is Calculus III at night on Thursdays. The revisions provide three equally likely alternative readings.

AMBIGUOUS   The math department just offers Calculus III at night on Thursdays.

REVISED   At night on Thursdays, the math department offers just Calculus III. [That is the only math course you can take on Thursday nights.]

REVISED   On Thursdays, the math department offers Calculus III just at night. [That is the only time you can take the class on Thursdays.]

REVISED   The math department offers Calculus III at night just on Thursdays. [That is the only day you can take the class at night.]

41b Avoiding Disruptive Placement

A modifier is disruptive when it awkwardly breaks the flow among grammatically connected parts of a sentence.

1. Separation of subject from verb or verb from object

Long adverbial phrases and clauses tend to be disruptive when they fall between subjects and verbs (as in the first example below), within verb phrases (as in the second example), or between verbs and their objects (as in the third example).

▸ *Game of Thrones*, ~~well after its last episode aired in May 2019,~~ continued to elicit admiring commentary and analysis ⟨*well after its last episode aired in May 2019.*⟩

▸ ~~The~~ show might ~~, if it maintains a large following,~~ dominate ⟨*If it maintains a large following, the*⟩ streaming video for years to come.

▸ The show has won ~~, despite its frequent use of nudity and violence,~~ a variety of awards and acclaim ⟨*, despite its frequent use of nudity and violence.*⟩

An adjective phrase or clause that modifies the subject of a sentence is not usually disruptive when it falls between subject and verb. On the contrary, it would likely be misplaced in any other location.

▸ The two Mars rovers, *which both landed in January 2004,* were designed to last only 90 days.

2. Split infinitives

An infinitive consists of *to* and the base form of a verb (*to share, to jump, to remember*). An infinitive splits when a modifier is inserted between the *to* and the verb. Grammarians have traditionally considered infinitives to be indivisible units and split infinitives to be improper. Although many authorities now consider them acceptable, split infinitives can be awkward and often should be revised, particularly in formal writing.

▸ Grant's strategy was to ~~relentlessly~~ attack *relentlessly* Lee's army despite the heavy losses the Union army suffered as a result.

Sometimes, however, a modifier is less awkward when splitting an infinitive than in any other spot in a sentence. If the adverb *relentlessly* were placed anywhere else in the following sentence, for example, it would not clearly and unambiguously modify only the word *attack*. Placed before the infinitive or at the end of the sentence, it could be understood to modify *urged;* placed after the infinitive, it could be understood to modify *retreating*.

▸ Lincoln urged his generals to *relentlessly* attack retreating enemy forces.

Writing Responsibly: Misplaced Modifiers in the Real World

Misplaced modifiers can sometimes cause real distress. A confusing instruction like the one below from the website of the Federal Emergency Management Agency (FEMA) might bewilder a homeowner struggling to recover from a natural disaster.

> You will need your social security number, current and pre-disaster address, phone numbers, type of insurance coverage, total household annual income, and a routing and account number from your bank *if you want to have disaster assistance funds transferred directly into your bank account*. [Emphasis added.]

As written, this suggests that an applicant for relief needs all of the listed items in order to have disaster assistance deposited directly into a bank account. Here is what the writer probably meant to say:

> You will need your social security number, current and pre-disaster address, phone numbers, type of insurance coverage, total household annual income, and, *if you want to have disaster assistance funds transferred directly into your bank account*, a routing and account number from your bank.

to TOPIC

EXERCISE 41.2 Correcting disruptive modifiers

In the following sentences, move any disruptive modifiers, and revise any awkward split infinitives.

EXAMPLE

Amber's laptop, ~~ever since she'd bought it,~~ had worked flawlessly ^ *ever since she'd bought it.*

1. Over the last week, however, she had been, mainly with the keyboard, having problems with it.
2. Often, when she hit the *r* key, she would see an *x* on her screen, and hitting, even when tapping gently and carefully, the *o* key gave her a *b* on the screen.
3. The technical support specialist with whom she spoke finally, after talking Amber through several troubleshooting routines, instructed her to mail the computer to a repair facility.
4. She worried that the repair process, leaving her to indefinitely rely on her library's computers, would take a long time.
5. When the repaired computer, two weeks later, arrived in the mail, Amber discovered that the repair staff had considerately replaced not only the laptop's keyboard, but its motherboard as well, and the computer worked better than ever.

DANGLING MODIFIERS

Consider the following sentence:

▶ While paddling the canoe toward shore, our poodle swam alongside.

Who or what is paddling the canoe? Surely not the poodle, yet that is what the sentence seems, absurdly, to suggest. The problem here is that the phrase *while paddling the canoe toward shore* does not actually modify the subject, *poodle,* or anything else in the sentence. It dangles, unattached, leaving it to the reader to infer the existence of some unnamed human paddler. Correcting this ***dangling modifier*** requires either making the paddler the subject of the sentence (as in the first revision that follows) or identifying the paddler in the modifier (as in the second revision).

> ▸ While paddling the canoe toward shore, our poodle ~~swam~~ alongside.
>   *I saw* *swimming*

> ▸ While ~~paddling~~ the canoe toward shore, our poodle swam alongside.
>   *I paddled*

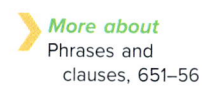

41c Identifying Dangling Modifiers

Dangling modifiers have the following characteristics:

> **verbal** Verb form that functions as a noun, adjective, or adverb

- They are most often phrases that include a *verbal* (a gerund, an infinitive, or a participle) that has an implied but unstated actor.
- They occur most often at the beginnings of sentences.

> **More about**
> Phrases and clauses, 651–56

- They appear to modify the subject of the sentence, so readers expect the implied actor and the subject to be the same.
- They dangle because the implied actor and the actual subject of the sentence are different.

DANGLING INFINITIVE PHRASE

To learn about new products, the company's sales meeting occurs annually in August. [Meetings do not learn.]

DANGLING PARTICIPIAL PHRASE

Hoping to boost morale, an attractive resort hotel is usually selected for the meeting. [Resorts cannot hope.]

DANGLING PREPOSITIONAL PHRASE WITH GERUND OBJECT

After traveling all day, the hotel's hot tub looked inviting to the arriving sales reps. [The sales reps traveled, not the hot tub.]

41d Correcting Dangling Modifiers

Simply moving a dangling modifier will not correct it.

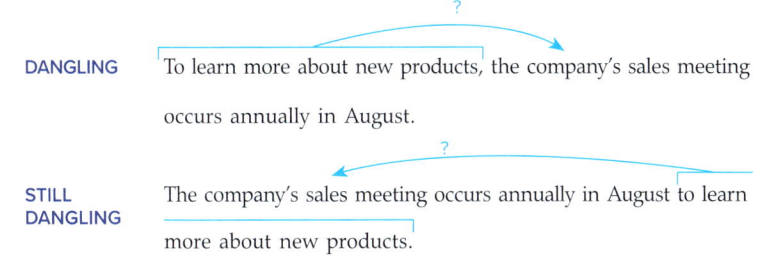

DANGLING To learn more about new products, the company's sales meeting occurs annually in August.

STILL DANGLING The company's sales meeting occurs annually in August to learn more about new products.

To correct a dangling modifier, first determine the identity of the modifier's unstated actor. You then have two options:

1. Rephrase to make the implied actor the subject of the sentence.
2. Rephrase to include the implied actor in the modifier.

Use the approach that works best given the purpose of the sentence in your draft.

MAKING THE IMPLIED ACTOR THE SUBJECT

To learn about new products, the company's sales meeting ~~occurs~~ *sales reps attend* *annual* ~~annually~~ in August.

Hoping to boost morale, an attractive resort hotel ~~is usually selected~~ *management usually selects* for the meeting.

In both these cases, the implied actor—*sales reps* in the first, *management* in the second—was missing entirely from the original sentence.

INCLUDING THE IMPLIED ACTOR IN THE MODIFIER

As the sales reps arrived after ~~After~~ traveling all day, the hotel's hot tub looked inviting to *them.* ~~the arriving sales reps.~~

In this case, the implied actor, *sales reps,* appeared in the original sentence but needed to be repositioned.

EXERCISE 41.3 Correcting dangling modifiers

Revise the following sentences to eliminate dangling modifiers.

EXAMPLE

As soon as Derek stepped aboard,
~~On stepping aboard,~~ the boat began to roll back and forth.

1. To avoid seasickness in the bobbing boat, focusing on the distant shoreline was a great help.

2. Having little hope of actually catching anything, expectations for success were low.

3. Having dropped his line into the water, a tug indicated that he had a bite.

4. Reeling in the fish, everyone cheered because the first-timer had made the first catch.

5. Catching a few more fish and not getting seasick, the trip was clearly a success.

Make It Your Own

Reread several papers that you have recently written and note where you handled modifiers well. Circle any confusingly placed, ambiguous, disruptive, or dangling modifiers and edit them using the information in this chapter. If you found several, add this issue to your revision checklist.

42 Avoiding Mixed and Incomplete Constructions

IN THIS CHAPTER

MIXED CONSTRUCTIONS

a. Correcting mixed constructions, 749

b. Correcting mismatched subjects, predicates, 751

INCOMPLETE CONSTRUCTIONS

c. Adding essential words, 753

d. Avoiding incomplete comparisons, 754

This Queen Anne mansion (built in 1885) is an example of a whimsical style of Victorian architecture characterized by ornate and oddly placed windows, turrets, and chimneys; multiple winding stairs that lead to unexpected balconies or doors; and intricate carvings and colorful decorations designed to make the house resemble a large, off-kilter wedding cake. While there are elements of balance, the style purposely rebels against symmetry, making it somewhat dizzying to behold. As you edit your writing, look for sentences that similarly start in one direction but turn disorientingly in another, leaving readers unsure where you have taken them. Look, too, for sentences that omit words readers need to grasp fully your intended meaning.

MIXED CONSTRUCTIONS

When a sentence begins one way and then takes an unexpected turn—in grammar or logic—the result is a *mixed construction.* To find and correct mixed constructions in your drafts, keep your eye on the way your sentences begin, and make sure every predicate has a grammatically and logically appropriate subject.

42a Recognizing and Correcting Grammatically Mixed Constructions

Grammatically mixed constructions can occur when a writer treats an introductory phrase or clause that cannot function as the subject of a sentence as if it were the subject. The following example starts with a long prepositional phrase (underlined) that the writer mistakenly uses as the subject of the sentence. A prepositional phrase,

mix Grammar Matters • Avoiding Mixed and Incomplete Constructions

although it can modify the subject or other parts of a sentence, cannot be the subject. The result is a *sentence fragment,* not a sentence.

> **sentence fragment** An incomplete sentence punctuated as if it were complete

MIXED As a response by pandemic-weary Americans to the disruption of their social lives added family members, new pets, to their homes in 2020.

Fixing a sentence like this requires identifying a grammatical subject and isolating it from the introductory phrase. Here is one possible revision (with the subject underlined):

REVISED As a response to the disruption of their social lives, <u>pandemic-weary Americans</u> added family members, new pets, to their homes in 2020.

Here is a more concise alternative that eliminates the introductory phrase altogether:

REVISED <u>Pandemic-weary Americans</u> added family members, new pets, to their homes in 2020.

> **More about**
> Clauses, 654–56
> Relating ideas with subordination, 570–76

In the next example, the writer follows a subordinate clause (*Because they were staying home more*) with the verb *provoked,* which has no subject. The editing changes the first part of the sentence into a noun phrase subject for *sparked.*

▸ ~~Because they were staying home more~~ ^The increased time at home^ sparked renewed interest in the care and training of a pet.

Mixed constructions also occur when a writer treats a modifying phrase or clause as if it were the predicate of a sentence. Look for this kind of mixed construction, especially in sentences that begin with the phrase *the fact that.* The following example begins with a subject, *the fact,* followed by a long adjective *that* clause that modifies the subject but cannot at the same time be the predicate of the sentence.

> **subject complement** An adjective, pronoun, noun, or noun phrase that follows a linking verb and refers to the subject of the sentence

MIXED The fact that furry friends can bring joy and comfort even in tumultuous times.

One way to revise this sentence is to add the verb *is,* making the *that* clause into a **subject complement.**

REVISED The fact is that furry friends can bring joy and comfort even in tumultuous times.

> **More about**
> Eliminating wordy expressions, 559–61

Better yet is simply to eliminate the phrase *the fact that,* a wordy expression that adds no information to the sentence.

Grammar Matters • Recognizing and Correcting Mismatched Subjects and Predicates

REVISED   Furry friends can bring joy and comfort even in tumultuous times.

When drafting a project, you may find yourself not only mixing constructions but also confusingly mixing up several ideas in the effort to get your thoughts down. Clarifying snarls like these may require you to pull the ideas apart and sort them into separate sentences.

MIXED   While these new family members have grown up expecting a lot of attention to provide years of companionship, then with love and patience adapt to the change in routine that would affect animals to make them anxious and clingy.

REVISED   These new family members have grown up expecting a lot of attention. Veterinarians warn that sudden changes to routine affect pets, and animals could become anxious and clingy. But with love and patience, they can adapt to the changes and provide years of companionship.

42b Recognizing and Correcting Mismatched Subjects and Predicates

The error of *faulty predication* occurs when a subject and predicate are mismatched—when they do not fit together logically. For example, the original subject of the following sentence, *recommendation,* does not work with the verb *insisted*. Recommendations cannot insist; doctors can.

▸ The ~~doctor's recommendation~~ *doctor* insisted that Wei visit a chiropractor immediately.

Many instances of faulty predication involve a mismatch between the subject and subject complement in sentences in which the verb is a form of *be* or other **linking verb**.

MISMATCHED   Only <u>students</u> who are absent because of illness or a family emergency will be <u>grounds</u> for a makeup exam.

REVISED   Only students who are absent because of illness or a family emergency will be permitted to take a makeup exam.

linking verb A verb that connects a subject to a subject complement

Two forms of expression involving the verb *be* that have become commonplace in everyday speech are examples of faulty predication and should be avoided in formal writing. These are the use of *is where* or *is when* in definitions and the use of *the reason is . . . because* in explanations.

1. Is where, is when

Using the expressions *is when* and *is where* creates illogical definitions if the terms defined do not involve a place (*where*) or a time (*when*).

▶ A tornado is ~~where~~ *a violent storm in which* high winds swirl around in a funnel-shaped cloud.

  A tornado is a storm, not a place.

▶ A friend is ~~when~~ someone *who* cares about you and has fun with you.

  A friend is a person, not a time.

The expressions result in grammatical mismatches, too, because *where* and *when* introduce adverb clauses, which cannot function as subject complements.

2. The reason . . . is because

Explanations using the expression *the reason . . . is because* are similarly mismatched both logically (*the reason* and *because* are redundant) and grammatically (*because* introduces an adverb clause, which cannot function as a subject complement). The following example shows two simple ways to fix this kind of faulty predication—by changing the subject of the sentence or by substituting *that* for *because*.

▶ ~~The reason~~ I wrote this paper ~~is~~ because my instructor required it.

▶ The reason I wrote this paper is ~~because~~ *that* my instructor required it.

> **More about**
> Including a stated subject and eliminating redundant subject and object pronouns, 758–59, 760

Obligatory Words and Unacceptable Repetitions in English Unlike some languages, formal written English requires a stated subject in all sentences except commands.

▶ ~~Rained~~ *It rained* all day yesterday.

On the other hand, formal written English does not permit the use of a pronoun to emphasize an already stated subject or direct object.

▶ Maria, ~~she~~ forgot to take her umbrella.

INCOMPLETE CONSTRUCTIONS

As you draft sentences, you may unintentionally leave out grammatically or logically essential words. Sometimes these omissions result in sentence fragments. Often, however, they create seemingly minor but nonetheless distracting grammatical or idiomatic bumps. As you proofread and edit your drafts, be especially alert for such missing words in compound and other constructions and in comparisons.

42c Adding Essential Words to Compound and Other Constructions

In compound constructions, the omission of *nonessential* repetitions can often help tighten prose.

> **More about**
> Writing concisely
> (ch. 26), 558–64

▶ Investigators wondered about the causes of the fire and [about] who might have been involved. They questioned six officials and then [they] arrested two.

Such *elliptical constructions* work, however, only when the stated words in one part of a compound match the omitted words in other parts. When grammar or idiom requires different words—different verb forms, different prepositions, or different articles, for example—those words should be included.

> **elliptical construction** A construction in which otherwise grammatically necessary words can be omitted because their meaning is understood from the surrounding context

▶ The candidate claimed that she always had *supported* and always would support universal health care coverage.

The word *supported* is needed because *had support* would be ungrammatical.

▶ On the campaign trail and *in* debates, her opponent for the nomination insisted that his plan was better than hers.

In this situation, the word *debates* requires the preposition *in*, not *on*.

► A yearning for change, ^an unsettled economy, and ^the character of the candidates themselves combined to sustain high voter turnout during the primary season.

> The word *unsettled* requires a different form of the indefinite article (*a, an*) than *yearning,* and in this situation the word *character* requires the definite article (*the*) rather than the indefinite article.

Occasionally, you may need to repeat a modifier for clarity.

► The candidates asked their loyal backers and ^their opponents to support the winner, whoever that might be.

> The repeated *their* makes clear that the adjective *loyal* applies only to *backers* and not to *opponents.*

Although you can often omit the word *that* without obscuring the meaning of a subordinate clause, sometimes you need to include it to avoid confusion.

■ I know ^that Sharita, who is a sympathetic person, will not be terribly upset about the stains on the silk shirt ~~that~~ I borrowed from her.

> In the original, without the first *that, Sharita* could be understood as the object of *know* rather than the subject of the long subordinate clause that follows. On the other hand, the *that* at the end of the sentence can be eliminated because no such ambiguity affects the subject (*I*) of the clause it introduces.

42d Avoiding Incomplete or Ambiguous Comparisons

> **More about**
> Comparisons, 729

Comparisons show how two items are alike or different. For comparisons to be clear, the items they juxtapose must be logically equivalent. The original version of the following sentence confusingly compares a group of people, children, to a process, growing up. The editing makes the two sides of the comparison equivalent.

► Children who grow up on farms are more active than ~~growing up in~~ ^those who grow up in big cities.

To be complete, comparisons must fully specify what is being compared to what.

► Lemon eucalyptus is better at deterring ticks. ^than tea tree oil

Grammar Matters • Avoiding Incomplete or Ambiguous Comparisons

Be careful how you use the terms *any* and *any other* when you compare one item to others that belong to the same category.

▶ Mount Everest is higher than any ^*other*^ mountain in the world.

Mount Everest is a mountain in the world, so without the modifier *other,* the sentence suggests that Mount Everest is higher than itself.

▶ Aconcagua, the highest mountain in South America, is higher than any ~~other~~ mountain in North America.

The sentence compares a mountain in South America to mountains in North America, not to other mountains in South America.

Be sure, also, to include any information you need to avoid ambiguity in your comparisons. In its draft form, the following comparison has two possible interpretations, as the revisions make clear.

DRAFT	Scientists are better informed about the face of Mars than the lower mantle of Earth's layers.
REVISED	Scientists are better informed about the face of Mars than <u>they are about</u> the lower mantle of Earth's layers.
REVISED	Scientists are better informed about the face of Mars than <u>about</u> the lower mantle of Earth's layers.

When you use the word *as* in a comparison, be sure to use it twice.

▶ Stephen King's horror stories are ^*as*^ scary as Edgar Allan Poe's.

➔ EXERCISE 42.1 Correcting incomplete constructions

Revise the following sentences to eliminate incomplete constructions. Some sentences may be revised in more than one way.

EXAMPLE
Traveling by airplane was once more convenient than ^*traveling by*^ train.

1. Yuko understood, from what she heard on the news, air travel had become more difficult in recent years.

2. The airline Yuko chose for her trip to Los Angeles had a more reliable on-time record than any air carrier.

3. She thought she had been careful about her flight planning as she possibly could have been.

4. Unfortunately, she could not have planned for a sudden severe storm during her flight, resulting disruptions in the country's air travel system, and unexpected landing of her flight at Albuquerque, New Mexico, at midnight.

5. She learned that the plane would need repairs and the airline unable to continue the flight to Los Angeles for days.

6. Yuko knew Helen, who sat next to her on the plane, was willing to rent a car and drive the rest of the way to Los Angeles.

7. After an all-night drive, an exhausted Yuko concluded that, whenever available, train travel would be better.

Make It **Your Own**

Reread several papers that you have recently written and note where you handled sentence constructions well. If you see examples of mixed or incomplete constructions, or ambiguous comparisons, edit them and add this issue to your revision checklist.

Part Nine

Language Matters

Guidance for Multilingual Writers

43 Understanding English Word Order and Sentence Structure 758

44 Using Nouns and Noun Determiners 767

45 Managing English Verbs 776

46 Managing Adjectives and Adverbs 786

47 Using Prepositions 793

43 Understanding English Word Order and Sentence Structure
by Ted E. Johnston and M. E. Sokolik

IN THIS CHAPTER

a. Observing standard word order, 758

b. Including a stated subject, 758

c. Managing *there* and *it* constructions, 759

d. Eliminating redundant pronouns, 760

e. Direct objects, indirect objects, and object complements, 761

f. Observing word-order patterns in questions, 763

g. Observing inverted word order, 764

> *More about*
> Sentence types, 645
> Word order in questions, 763–64

clause A word group with a subject and a predicate. An *independent clause* can stand alone as a sentence; a *subordinate clause* cannot.

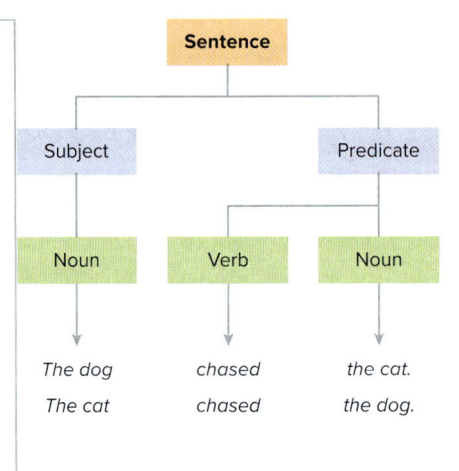

```
                    Sentence
                   /        \
              Subject      Predicate
                |          /       \
              Noun       Verb      Noun
                ↓          ↓         ↓
             The dog    chased    the cat.
             The cat    chased    the dog.
```

English is a word-order language, which means that the position of a word in a sentence often determines its grammatical function. As a result, *The dog chased the cat* means something different from *The cat chased the dog.* This chapter describes and explains word order and related aspects of English sentence structure.

43a Observing Standard Word Order

In declarative sentences (as opposed to questions or commands), standard word order is subject-verb-object (or S-V-O). That is, the subject comes first, then the verb, and then the direct object, if there is one, or any other words that make up the predicate.

FAULTY WORD ORDER   *verb* ? ?   Chased the cat the dog.

STANDARD WORD ORDER   *subject verb object*   The dog chased the cat.

43b Including a Stated Subject

Except for commands, English sentences and *clauses* require a subject to be stated, even if the identity of the subject is clear from a previous sentence or clause. In the following example, the

758

pronoun *he,* referring to the subject of the first sentence, can serve as the subject of both clauses of the second sentence.

▶ Nico has a hard life for a ten-year-old. ^(He is)Is just a boy, but ^(he)is expected to work like a man.

Similarly, a subordinate clause requires a stated subject even if its subject is a pronoun or another noun phrase that obviously refers to the same entity as the subject of the clause that precedes it.

▶ Lucy asked for directions because ^(she)was lost.

In commands, the subject is unstated but is understood to be "you."

▶ [you] Leave now!

43c Managing *There* and *It* Constructions

Expletives are words that are empty of content; that is, they do not refer to anything. In English, the words *there* and *it* are often used as expletives.

In *there* constructions, *there* precedes a form of *to be. There,* however, is not the subject. The subject follows the verb, and the verb is either singular or plural, depending on the subject. The expletive *it,* on the other hand, is always the singular subject of its clause. *It* constructions are often used to indicate an environmental condition or some aspect of time. The verb in expletive *it* constructions is often a form of *be,* but other verbs can be used, especially those related to process (for example, *start, continue, end*). The expletives *there* and *it* cannot be omitted from such clauses, even though they do not refer to anything.

▶ ^(There are)Are not enough reasons to support your argument.

▶ I am not pleased that ^(there)is a fly in my soup.

▶ When ^(it)was almost 3:00 p.m., ^(it)started hailing really hard.

In a similar construction, the pronoun *it* is not empty, but refers to content that follows the verb. In the following sentence, for example, *it* refers to *to drive during a snowstorm*. In either case, empty or meaningful, *it* is the subject and cannot be omitted.

▶ ~~Is~~ *It is* dangerous to drive during a snowstorm.

43d Eliminating Redundant Subject and Object Pronouns

Although English requires a stated subject in all clauses except commands, the use of a pronoun to reemphasize an already stated subject is not acceptable in writing, even though such constructions often occur in informal speech.

▶ Rosalinda, ~~she~~ left early for the airport. [subject / redundant subject]

Similarly, when *which* or *that* begins a clause and serves as the clause's subject or direct object, do not also add *it* to serve as the subject or direct object. In the following sentences, for example, both *which* and *it* refer redundantly to the movie *Minari;* to correct the sentences requires eliminating one or the other pronoun.

▶ Last night I saw *Minari*, which ~~it~~ impressed me very much. [subject / redundant subject]

or

▶ Last night I saw *Minari*; ~~which~~ it impressed me very much.

▶ I liked *Minari*, which many of my friends liked ~~it~~ too. [direct object / redundant object]

or

▶ I liked *Minari*; ~~which~~ many of my friends liked it too.

Language Matters • Direct Objects, Indirect Objects, and Object Complements

EXERCISE 43.1 Using standard word order and including a subject

In the following sentences, correct word-order errors involving subjects or omissions of *it* or *there*.

EXAMPLE

It was
~~Was~~ obvious the students hadn't studied for the test.

1. Without a doubt, is nothing more breathtaking than seeing a double rainbow after a storm.
2. I am excited by this letter, which I received it late yesterday.
3. Was still too early to plant the tomatoes, so died all of them.
4. We read that are several new dance clubs opening this weekend.
5. We left the office because was after five o'clock.
6. Don't you think is a little silly to argue about who is the better cook?
7. My aunt and uncle, they are both working in California as computer programmers.
8. Is completely impossible to dislike that professor!
9. This is an uplifting story because has such an optimistic ending.
10. I read a controversial article that it claims North and South America were settled much earlier than previously thought.

43e Structuring Sentences with Direct Objects, Indirect Objects, and Object Complements

Direct objects, indirect objects, and object complements can follow a transitive verb.

1. Direct and indirect objects

A ***direct object*** receives or carries the action of a transitive verb. Certain transitive verbs—such as *ask, find, give, order, send, show, teach, tell,* and *write*—can also take an ***indirect object,*** which names the recipient of the direct object. The indirect object goes after the verb and before the direct object.

> More about
> Direct and indirect objects,
> 648–50

          subject verb indirect   direct
                          object   object
▸ She sent Michiko a book on Scandinavian cuisine.

Alternatively, the recipient of the direct object can be identified in a phrase beginning with a preposition, usually *to,* that follows the direct object.

> subject verb   direct   preposition indirect
>   object   object
> ▸ She sent a book on Scandinavian cuisine to Michiko.

When the direct object is a personal pronoun, the verb must be followed by a prepositional phrase, not an indirect object.

> ▸ She sent ~~Michiko~~ it. → *to Michiko.*

Several common verbs do not take indirect objects even though the actions they refer to are similar to those of verbs that do. These verbs include *answer, carry, change, close, complete, deliver, describe, explain, keep, mention, open, propose, put, recommend, repair* (or *fix* when it means *repair*), and *say*. With these verbs, the function of the indirect object can be performed only by a prepositional phrase beginning with *to* (or sometimes *for*) that follows the direct object.

> ▸ The doctor explained ~~my father~~ the dangers of secondhand smoke. → *to my father.*

> ▸ The professor opened ~~us~~ the door to understanding. → *for us.*

2. Object complements

An *object complement* follows a direct object and describes a condition of the object or a change in the object that the subject has caused the object to undergo.

>   direct object
>   object complement
> ▸ Some workers here make my job impossible.

Placing an object complement before the direct object will either make a sentence ungrammatical or change its meaning. The following sentence, as originally written, was ungrammatical.

> ▸ The players have just elected ~~their team captain~~ Paul. → *their team captain.*

The following sentences, in contrast, are both grammatical but have different meanings.

> We need to keep all the ~~happy~~ workers.
>   *adjective*

> We need to keep all the workers ~~happy~~.
>   *object complement*

The first sentence, with the adjective *happy* before the direct object, recommends retaining the workers who are already happy, but not necessarily those who are not. The second, with *happy* in the object complement position after the direct object, recommends taking action to make sure that not one of the workers feels unhappy.

EXERCISE 43.2 Using objects and object complements

Correct any errors related to indirect objects or object complements in the following sentences. Next to sentences with an error, write IO if the problem is related to indirect objects and OC if it is related to object complements. Mark any correct sentences OK.

EXAMPLE

We want the ~~closed~~ door, *closed,* please.   OC

1. We painted the yellow walls because yellow is a cheerful color.
2. She sent me a very informative email.
3. I consider his inappropriate remarks and refuse to respond to them.
4. The owner described me the house in great detail.
5. The president appointed me his new assistant.
6. Frank has a build very muscular.
7. I had an extra blanket, so I gave a homeless man it.
8. We ordered the carpet baby blue, not the beige one.
9. The last treatment did to the patient more harm than good.
10. The teacher explained the students the assignment one more time.

43f Observing Word-Order Patterns in Questions

In questions, unlike declarative statements, a verb nearly always precedes the subject.

To form a question with one-word forms of the verb *be,* simply invert subject and verb.

    subject verb   verb subject

▸ The grapes are ripe.   Are the grapes ripe?

In all other cases, a question requires a helping verb as well as a main verb. The subject goes after the first helping verb in a verb phrase and before the rest of the verb phrase.

   subject helping main   helping subject main
              verb   verb   verb   verb

▸ They have left for New York.   Have they left for New York?

   subject helping main   helping   subject main
              verb   verb   verb   verb

▸ The children can go with us.   Can the children go with us?

   subject   helping helping main   helping   subject   helping main
               verb   verb   verb   verb   verb   verb

▸ The painters should have finished. Should the painters have finished?

To form a question with one-word verbs other than forms of *be,* use the appropriate form of *do* as the helper.

    subject   verb   helping verb subject   main verb

▸ The prisoner escaped.   Did the prisoner escape?

Questions that begin with question words like *what, who,* and *why* normally follow the same word order as other questions.

   helping verb subject   main verb

▸ What is the engineer saying about the project?

If the question word is the subject, however, the question follows subject-before-verb word order.

   subject   verb   direct object

▸ Who is saying these things about the project?

43g Observing Inverted Word Order When Certain Conjunctions or Adverbs Begin a Clause

When they appear at the beginning of a sentence or clause, certain adverbs, adverb phrases, correlative conjunctions (such as *neither . . . nor* and *not only . . . but also*), and the conjunction *nor* by itself require inverted word order similar to that used in questions.

- Neither ~~the parents~~ *the parents* have called the principal, nor ~~they~~ *they* have informed the school board.

- The twins don't bowl, nor *do* they play tennis.

Negating or limiting adverbs such as *rarely, seldom, no sooner,* and *no longer* also require inverted word order when they start a sentence or clause. Such sentences have a formal tone.

- Seldom ~~the dancers~~ *the dancers* have had the opportunity to perform in public.

Moving the adverb to the interior of the sentence cancels the inversion.

> **More about**
> Adverbs, 724–31, 788–89

- The dancers have *seldom* had the opportunity to perform in public.

Usually, this less formal, noninverted version of such sentences is preferable to the inverted version.

EXERCISE 43.3 Working with word-order inversions

In the following sentences, correct any word-order errors related to inversions. Mark any correct sentences OK.

EXAMPLE

Neither we *do* want to go to the party, nor we *do* want to help pay for it.

1. Neither he takes classes at the university, nor he works.
2. Jossette has been working on her research project?
3. When Chen bought his new computer?
4. We rarely went to dinner with friends.
5. Rarely it rains in the desert.
6. Goes she often to parties?
7. Couldn't Fatima have done something sooner about the error?
8. Why smoking should be banned in bars?
9. Not only she works hard, but she also studies hard.
10. Mark neither reads French nor speaks it.

Make It Your Own

In an issue of a newsmagazine such as *Time,* the *Economist, U.S. News and World Report,* or the *Week,* find two examples each of sentences with indirect objects, object complements, and inversions involving *not only, neither/nor,* or some other initial adverb or adverbial phrase. Copy the sentences and underline the components in each sentence, identifying the feature. Write two examples of your own for each type of sentence patterned on the examples you found.

Work Together

In small groups, check the examples group members wrote in the Make It Your Own activity above. Does everyone agree with the results? Why or why not? Ask your instructor if you are uncertain about any of the examples.

44 Using Nouns and Noun Determiners
by Ted E. Johnston and M. E. Sokolik

IN THIS CHAPTER

a. Understanding different types of nouns, 767

b. Using nouns with articles and other determiners, 768

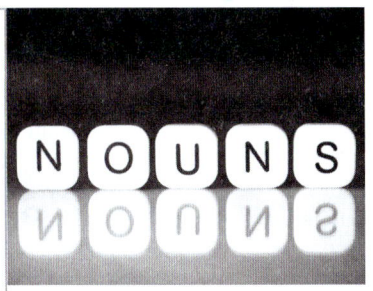

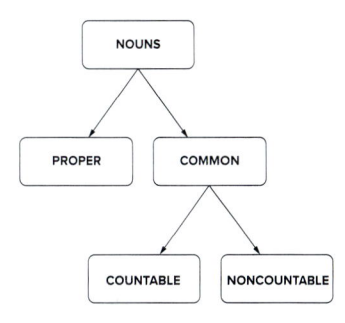

B Calkins/Shutterstock

Using English nouns correctly and effectively requires that you recognize the types of nouns and the determiners that accompany them.

44a Understanding Different Types of Nouns

> *More about*
> Types of nouns, 635–37

To use a noun correctly, you need to know whether it is a *proper noun* or a *common noun*, and, if it is a common noun, whether it is *count* or *noncount*. A **common noun** identifies a general category and is usually not capitalized: *woman, era, bridge, corporation, mountain, war*. A **proper noun** identifies someone or something specific and is usually capitalized: *Audre Lorde, Middle Ages, Golden Gate Bridge, Burger King, Himalayas, World War II*.

> *More about*
> Forming noun plurals, 623–25

Count nouns name discrete, countable things. **Noncount nouns** (also called **noncountable nouns** or **mass nouns**) usually name entities made of a continuous substance or of small, indistinguishable particles, or they refer to a general quality. A *drop*, a *grain*, and a *suggestion*, for example, are count nouns, but *water, sand,* and *advice* are noncount nouns.

- Count nouns can be singular (*drop*) or plural (*drops*). Most noncount nouns are singular, even those that end in -s, and thus should be matched with singular verbs. Noncount nouns cannot be preceded by a number or any other term that would imply countability (such as *a, an, several, another,* or *many*), nor can they be made plural if they are singular.

▸ Aerobics ~~help~~ *helps* me to relax.

Here are some examples of contrasting count and noncount nouns:

Count	Noncount
car/cars	traffic
dollar/dollars	money
noodle/noodles	spaghetti
pebble/pebbles	gravel
spoon/spoons	silverware

- Many nouns can be noncount in one context and count in another.
  ▸ While speaking of *love* [noncount], my grandmother recalled the three *loves* [count] of her life.

  In the opening phrase, *love* is an abstraction. In the main clause, *loves* refers to the people the grandmother has loved.

- All languages have count and noncount nouns, but a noun that is count in one language may be noncount in another.

44b Using Nouns with Articles (*a, an, the*) and Other Determiners

The *articles* *a, an,* and *the* are the most common determiners. Other determiners include possessives (*my, your, Ivan's*), numbers (*one, five, a hundred*), and other words that quantify (*some, many, a few*) or specify (*this, those*).

1. Articles with common nouns

The main function of the *indefinite articles,* *a* and *an,* is to introduce nouns that are new to the reader. The *definite article,* *the,* usually precedes nouns that have already been introduced or whose identity is known or clear from the context. Noncount nouns and plural count nouns also sometimes appear with no article (or the *zero article*).

Language Matters • Using Nouns with Articles (*a, an, the*) and Other Determiners

Quick Reference: Some Common Noncount Nouns

Although there is no hard-and-fast way to distinguish noncount from count nouns, most noncount nouns do fall into a few general categories.

Abstractions and Emotions	advice, courage, happiness, hate, jealousy, information, knowledge, love, luck, maturity, patriotism, warmth
Mass Substances	air, blood, dirt, gasoline, glue, sand, shampoo, water
Food Items	beef, bread, corn, flour, gravy, pork, rice, salt, sugar
Collections of Related Items	cash, clothing, equipment, furniture, graffiti, information, jewelry, luggage, mail, traffic
Games and Other Activities	aerobics, baseball, checkers, homework, news, Pilates, poker, pool, soccer, tennis, volleyball
Weather-Related Phenomena	cold, drizzle, frost, hail, heat, humidity, lightning, rain, sleet, snow, sunshine, thunder
Diseases	arthritis, chicken pox, diabetes, influenza, measles
Fields of Study	botany, chemistry, mathematics, physics, sociology

- Use *a* before a consonant sound (*a cat*) and *an* before a vowel sound (*an elephant*). Do not be misled by written vowels that are pronounced as consonants (*a European tour*) or written consonants that are pronounced as vowels (*an hour early*). Be especially careful with words that begin with *h* (*a hot stove, an honorary degree*) and *u* (*a uniform, an upheaval*).

- Use *a* or *an* only with singular count nouns. A singular count noun *must* be preceded by an article or some other determiner even if other modifiers come between the determiner and the noun.

  ▶ A friend of mine bought an antique car on *eBay*.

- Never use *a* or *an* with a noncount noun.

  ▶ A~~good~~ advice is hard to find.
      Good

- Use *a* or *an* when you first introduce a singular count noun if the specific identity of the noun is not yet known to the reader or is not otherwise clear from the context. Use *the* for subsequent references to the same noun.

- ▸ A friend of mine bought [an] antique [car] on *eBay*. She restored [the] [car] and sold it for [a] tidy [profit]. [The] [profit] came in handy when she took [a] [vacation].

  The is appropriate for *car* in the second sentence because it refers to the same car introduced in the first sentence. The word *profit* in the second sentence takes *a* because it is making its first appearance there. The third sentence continues the process.

- Use *the* with both count and noncount nouns whose specific identity has been previously established or is clear from the context.
  - ▸ We admired [the] antique [car] that my friend bought on *eBay*.

    The modifying clause *that my friend bought on eBay* identifies a specific car.

  - ▸ She sold it for [a] tidy [profit] and used [the] [money] for [a] [vacation].

    The context clearly identifies the money with the profit.

  - ▸ My friend is traveling around [the] [world] for three months.

    The noun *world* logically refers to the planet we live on—not, say, Mars or Venus.

  - ▸ Vicky is [the] [fastest] [runner] on her team.

    The superlative *fastest* refers specifically to one person.

- No article is used to introduce noncount nouns or plural count nouns used generically—that is, to make generalizations.
  - ▸ Good [advice] is hard to find.
  - ▸ Good [teachers] can change lives.

- Both the definite and indefinite articles can introduce singular nouns used generically. Sometimes either is appropriate:
  - ▸ [The] good [teacher] can change lives.
  - ▸ [A] good [teacher] can change lives.

  Sometimes the generic meaning is clear with only one or the other:

  - ▸ Thomas Alva Edison invented *the* ~~a~~ lightbulb.

> **More about**
> Superlatives,
> 729–30

2. Articles with proper nouns

Proper nouns in English almost never occur with the indefinite article (*a*, *an*), and most occur with no article:

▸ Ruby grew up in Lima, Peru, but now lives in Wichita, Kansas.

There are many exceptions, however:

- Certain place names always occur with *the*: *the* Bronx, *the* Philippines, *the* Northeast, *the* Pacific Ocean.
- The names of ships (including airships) conventionally occur with *the*: *the* Queen Mary, *the* Challenger.
- Many product names can be used with *a* or *the* or sometimes both: *the* Cheerios, *an/the* iPhone, *a/the* Toyota.
- Many multiword proper nouns occur with *the*: *the* United States, *the* Brooklyn Bridge, *the* Department of State, *the* Civil Rights Act. Others do not, however. The city of Chicago, for example, is home to both *the* Wrigley Building (with article) and *Wrigley Field* (no article).
- Most plural proper nouns occur with *the*: *the* United Nations, *the* Chicago Cubs.

EXERCISE 44.1 Using articles correctly

Insert *a*, *an*, *the*, or no article as appropriate in the blanks in the following paragraph.

I'd only been there ___ hour or so, but I needed ___ little break from ___ crowd. I slipped away from ___ heat of ___ party and ___ crush of bodies on ___ dance floor, escaping to ___ cool spot in ___ garden. Under ___ ancient willow tree, I lay in ___ cool grass, slipped off my satin slippers, and stared up at ___ silvery moon.

3. Nouns and other determiners

As with articles, the use of other determiners with nouns depends on the kind of noun in question, particularly whether it is singular or plural, count or noncount. In all cases, determiners precede any other adjectives that modify a noun.

> **More about**
> Order of adjectives, 786–87

Possessive nouns or pronouns Use possessive nouns (*Julio's*) and possessive pronouns (*my, our, your, his, her, their, its, whose*) with any count or noncount noun.

singular count	plural count	noncount
Ann's book	*Ann's* books	*Ann's* information
her book	*her* books	*her* information

This, that, these, those The demonstrative pronouns *this, that, these,* and *those* specify, or single out, particular instances of a noun. Use *this* and *that* only with noncount nouns and singular count nouns. Use *these* and *those* only with plural count nouns.

singular count	plural count	noncount
this book	—	*this* information
that book	—	*that* information
—	*these* books	—
—	*those* books	—

Quantifying words or phrases Use numbers only with count nouns: *one shirt, two shirts.* See the Quick Reference box on the next page for a list of other quantifying words and how they work with different kinds of nouns in most contexts.

***Few versus* a few *and* little versus* a little** The determiners *few* and *a few* (for count nouns) and *little* and *a little* (for noncount nouns) all indicate a small quantity, but they have significant differences in meaning. *Few* means a negligible amount, whereas *a few* means a small but significant number. Likewise, *little* means *almost none,* whereas *a little* means *some.*

- Kiara has few good friends.
  She is almost friendless.
- Kiara has a few good friends.
  She has significant companionship.
- Luis provided little help before the party.
  He didn't do his share.
- Luis gave me a little help after everyone left.
  He made himself useful.

Language Matters • Using Nouns with Articles (*a, an, the*) and Other Determiners

Quick Reference: Matching Nouns with Quantifying Words and Phrases

Quantifying Word or Phrase	Singular Count Nouns	Plural Count Nouns	Noncount Nouns	Examples
any, no	✓	✓	✓	You can read any book on the list. Have you read any books this summer? Do you have any information about the reading list?
another, each, every, either, neither	✓	no	no	I read another book last week.
the other	✓	✓	✓	The other book is a murder mystery. I haven't finished the other books on the reading list. The other information is the most reliable.
a couple of, a number of, both, few, a few, fewer, fewest, many, several	no	✓	no	The professor assigned fewer books last term.
a lot of, lots of, all, enough, more, most, other, some	no	✓	✓	Some books are inspiring. Some information is unreliable.
little, a little, much, a great deal of, less, least	no	no	✓	I need a little information about the course requirements.

Indicating extent or amount with noncount nouns Because a noncount noun is always singular, do not make it plural or add a determiner that implies a plural form. For example, do not use a determiner such as *a large number of, many,* or *several* immediately before a noncount noun. Instead, use a determiner such as *a great deal of, less, little, much,* or *some*—or revise the sentence another way.

44b art Language Matters • Using Nouns and Noun Determiners

► The city is doing ~~researches~~ *some* on the proposal.

The modifier *some* is appropriate for the noncount noun *research* because it does not imply plurality.

► Gina bought two ~~breads~~ *loaves of* at the store.

In the edited version, *two* modifies the count noun *loaves*.

► We do not have many ~~violences~~ *incidents of violence* in our neighborhood.

► A ~~large number~~ *great deal* of information is available on your topic.

A large number of, which suggests plurality, cannot be used with *information,* a noncount noun.

EXERCISE 44.2 Editing for noun and determiner usage

Correct any errors resulting from the improper use of nouns and determiners in the following passage.

A great deal of students showed up at the class party this past weekend. Everyone seemed to have fairly good time despite few major problems that I am now being blamed for. However, whenever we plan this kinds of events in future, we need much more people to help. So little people actually helped that I essentially had to do all work on my own. Therefore, I refuse to take a blame for all things that went wrong. Everyone should be aware that other person (who will remain nameless) who had agreed to help me organize event didn't do his share of job. Not surprisingly, biggest problem we had was that there were not enough supplies. For example, we had less sodas than we needed, so some guests had to drink lot of water because it was so hot that evening. Another examples was that we didn't have as many ice as we needed, and there weren't enough plastic glasses or napkins. I had to send someone out to buy much of this items using my own moneys.

Language Matters • Using Nouns with Articles (*a*, *an*, *the*) and Other Determiners — art 44b

Make It Your Own

Write five sentences with plural references using noncount nouns from five of the categories in the Quick Reference box on page 769. For example, you might write, "The recipe calls for *five cups of flour*." Next, referring to the Quick Reference box on page 773, write three sentences with count nouns and three with noncount nouns using different quantifiers. For example, you might write, "I read *a couple of* science fiction *novels* over spring break."

Work Together

In small groups, exchange your work on the exercise above. Discuss your differences, and consult your instructor if you need help arriving at a consensus.

45 Managing English Verbs
by Ted E. Johnston and M. E. Sokolik

IN THIS CHAPTER

a. Using phrasal verbs, 776

b. Using gerunds and infinitives, 779

c. Using participles as adjectives, 781

d. Using helping verbs, 782

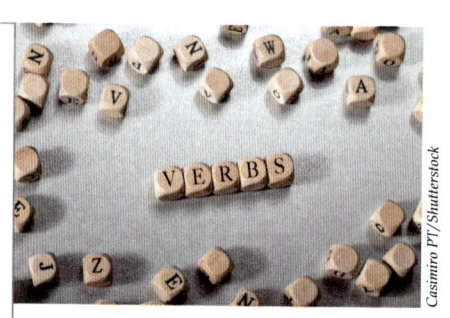

Verbs can express an action or occurrence (*The dog jumps for the Frisbee*) or indicate a state of being (*The dog is frisky*). In many languages, verbs can have several forms. For example, they may change to indicate the identity of a subject or an object or the time frame in which an event happens. English verbs, in contrast, have only a few forms, but these combine with other words to accomplish the same functions.

45a Using Phrasal Verbs

Phrasal verbs—sometimes called *multiword verbs*—consist of a verb and one or two **particles.** The particle takes the form of a preposition or an adverb, and it combines with the verb to create a new verb with a new meaning. For example, the verb *throw* means to project something through the air. The phrasal verb *throw out* consists of the verb *throw* and the particle *out*; it means to dispose of something.

> **More about**
> Verbs and verb phrases, 652, 680–81, 694–700

▸ Segundo [threw] his old notebook on his bed.
       verb

▸ Segundo [threw] [out] his old notebook.
     phrasal verb particle

The meaning of a verb-and-particle combination differs from the meaning of the same words in a verb-and-preposition combination. The phrasal verb *look up*, for example, means to consult or find something in a reference work, which is different from the meaning of *look* followed by a phrase that happens to begin with the preposition *up*.

	phrasal verb particle
PHRASAL VERB	Svetlana looked up the word in the dictionary.
	verb preposition
VERB WITH PREPOSITIONS	Svetlana looked up the steep trail and began to hike.

A transitive phrasal verb is *separable* if its direct object can fall either between the verb and the particle (separating them) or after the particle.

phrasal verb
particle direct object
▸ She looked up the address online.

direct object particle
▸ She looked the address up online.
↑—phrasal verb—↑

Quick Reference — Some Common Phrasal Verbs and Their Meanings

SEPARABLE		INSEPARABLE	
ask out	invite for a date	add up to	total
calm down	make calm, become calm	barge in on	interrupt unannounced
give up	surrender	call on	visit, or ask for a response directly
hand in	submit		
hand out	distribute	come across	find accidentally
look up	find something in a reference work	drop in	visit unannounced
		get out of	evade an obligation, exit
put back	return to original position	give in	surrender
put down	criticize meanly; suppress	grow up	mature
		hint at	suggest
take back	return; retract	look down on	disdain
take off	remove	look up to	admire
take on	assume responsibility for	put up with	tolerate
		run into	encounter; collide
take up	begin a hobby or activity	stand in for	substitute for
		turn up	show up, arrive
throw out	dispose of		

Language Matters • Managing English Verbs

If the direct object of a separable phrasal verb is a pronoun, it must come between the verb and the particle.

I decided to hand ~~in it~~. *it in.*

A phrasal verb is *inseparable* if no words can fall between the verb and the particle.

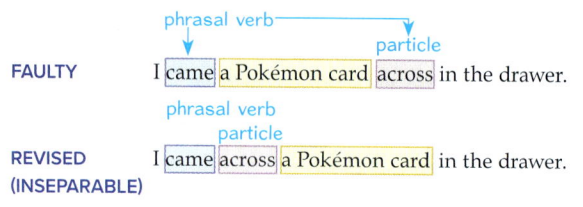

FAULTY   I |came| a Pokémon card |across| in the drawer.

REVISED (INSEPARABLE)   I |came|across| a Pokémon card in the drawer.

The meaning of a phrasal verb changes when the particle changes (see the Quick Reference box on page 777). The phrasal verb *take on*, for example, means "to assume responsibility for."

▶ She |took| |on| the editing of the podcast.

The phrasal verb *take back*, in contrast, means "to return" or "to retract."

▶ She |took| all her toys |back| to the playroom.

EXERCISE 45.1 Using phrasal verbs correctly

Put a check by the sentences that use verbs and phrasal verbs incorrectly, and then revise those sentences so they are correct.

EXAMPLE

After the accident, the EMT calmed down ~~him~~. *him* ✓

1. I hear that Olivia is sick. Who is going to stand in for her?
2. I cannot find my phone. Have you come it across?
3. The director handed the script out yesterday.
4. Is there any way for us to get this mess out of?
5. If you do not understand a word, look up it.
6. That snowsuit looks too warm. Why don't you take off it?

7. Will you take these back to the store?
8. I ran an old friend into at the movie theater.

45b Using Gerunds and Infinitives after Verbs and Prepositions

A *gerund* is the *-ing* form of a verb used as a noun (*listening, eating*). An *infinitive* is the base form of a verb preceded by *to* (*to listen, to eat*).

1. Gerunds and infinitives after verbs

- Only gerunds can follow some verbs, and only infinitives can follow others.

    ▸ The congresswoman recommended ~~to submit~~ *submitting* the proposal for a vote.

    ▸ Rosa Parks refused ~~sitting~~ *to sit* in the back of the bus.

- Some verbs can be followed by either gerunds or infinitives. For some of these verbs, the choice of gerund or infinitive has little effect on meaning, but for a few the difference is significant.

    SAME MEANING
    The sunflower [continued]*(verb)* to grow *(infinitive)*.
    The sunflower [continued]*(verb)* growing *(gerund)*.

    DIFFERENT MEANINGS
    Juan [remembered]*(verb)* to email *(infinitive)* his paper to his professor.
    [He didn't forget to do it.]

    Juan [remembered]*(verb)* emailing *(gerund)* his paper to his professor.
    [He recalled having done it already.]

- Some verbs that can be followed by an infinitive can also be followed by an infinitive after an intervening noun or pronoun.

    ▸ Yue [wanted]*(verb)* to study *(infinitive)* the violin.

    ▸ Yue's partner [wanted]*(verb)* [her]*(pronoun)* to study *(infinitive)* the violin.

- Certain verbs, however, take an infinitive only after an object noun or pronoun.

  ▸ The bandleader [*verb:* urged] the wedding guests to join the conga line. [*infinitive*]

A few verbs (for example, *feel, have, hear, let, look at,* and *see*) require an **unmarked infinitive**—the base verb alone, without *to*—after an intervening noun or pronoun.

  ▸ Paolo let his children ~~to go~~ go to the carnival.

  ▸ Mia heard a monkey ~~to howl~~ howl late at night.

Quick Reference: Gerund or Infinitive after Selected Verbs

Some verbs that can be directly followed by a gerund but not an infinitive

admit	discuss	imagine	practice	risk
avoid	enjoy	mind	quit	suggest
consider	escape	miss	recall	tolerate
deny	finish	postpone	resist	understand

Some verbs that can be directly followed by an infinitive but not a gerund

agree	claim	hope	offer	refuse
appear	decide	manage	plan	wait
ask	expect	mean	pretend	want
beg	have	need	promise	wish

Some verbs that can be directly followed by a gerund or an infinitive with little effect on meaning

begin	hate	love	start
continue	like	prefer	

Some verbs for which choice of gerund or infinitive affects meaning

forget	remember	stop	try

Some verbs that take an infinitive only after an intervening noun or pronoun

advise	command	force	persuade	tell
allow	convince	instruct	remind	urge
cause	encourage	order	require	warn

2. Gerunds after prepositions

Only a gerund, not an infinitive, can be the object of a preposition.

▸ The article is about ~~to travel~~ *traveling* to outer space.

45c Using Participles as Adjectives

Both the present participle and the past participle of a verb can function as adjectives, but they convey different meanings, especially if the base verb refers to an emotion or state of mind such as anger or boredom. The ***present participle*** (or *-ing* form) usually describes the cause or agent of a state of affairs. The ***past participle*** (the *-ed* form in regular verbs) usually describes the result of the state of affairs.

> **More about**
> Regular and irregular verb forms, 694–700, 698

State of Affairs	Cause	Result
Physics class *bored* me today. *verb*	The class was *boring*. *adj.*	I was *bored*. *adj.*
Dr. Sung's lecture *interested* me. *verb*	The lecture was *interesting*. *adj.*	I was *interested*. *adj.*

→ EXERCISE 45.2 Using gerunds, infinitives, and participial adjectives

Use the verbs in parentheses to correctly complete each sentence. The first one is done as an example. Some may have more than one correct solution.

1. That movie was really *boring* (bore). I fell asleep after 20 minutes.
2. Andy was _____ (astonish) to see a rare bird in his backyard.
3. Martine advised Hugo _____ (see) the museum exhibit. Our friends begged us not _____ (drive) there in the icy weather.
4. We had to postpone _____ (give) our parents an anniversary party because my mother had to work Saturday.
5. We enjoy _____ (cook) for our friends.
6. The customer inquired about _____ (purchase) a new air fryer.
7. Nik admitted _____ (borrow) his roommate's new guitar without _____ (ask).
8. Sophia continued _____ (watch) TV during dinner.
9. The sergeant commanded the troops _____ (march) up the hill.

More about
Verb forms,
694–700
Subject-verb
agreement,
680–89

45d Using Helping Verbs for Verb Formation

Most English verb constructions, other than the present and past tenses, consist of a main verb with one or more helping (auxiliary) verbs. The main verb carries the principal meaning, and the helping verbs carry information about time, mood, and voice. There are two kinds of helping verbs: *simple* and *modal*.

- The simple helping verbs—*have, do,* and *be*— can also function as main verbs, and like other main verbs, they can change form to indicate person and tense.

- The modal helping verbs—including *can, could, may, might, must, ought to, shall, should, will,* and *would*—carry information about attributes of the main verb such as ability, intention, permission, possibility, desire, and suggestion (see the Quick Reference box on the next page). Unlike simple helping verbs, modal helping verbs do not change form to indicate number or tense.

  ▶ All the athletes at the Olympics can swim fast, but Michael
     can
     Phelps ~~cans~~ swim faster than any of the others.

  ▶ Simone Biles should practice for half a day today, and she
     should have practiced
     ~~shoulded practice~~ for half a day yesterday, too.

NOTE When you hear such contractions as *should've* or *could've* in speech (or similar contractions with other modals), remember that the contracted word is *have* (*should have, could have*), not *of*.

- In a verb phrase, helping verbs almost always precede the main verb, and modals precede any other helping verbs.

              modal simple
            helping helping   main
             verb   verb   verb

  ▶ In June, Chen [will] [have been] [living] in Seattle for 10 years.

- When forming verbs, include needed auxiliaries.

  is
  ▶ Demetrio taking six courses this semester.

  have
  ▶ My dogs been seeing the new veterinarian for months.

Language Matters • Using Helping Verbs for Verb Formation

Quick Reference: Modals and Meaning

Modals	Meaning	Examples
can, could	Used to indicate ability, possibility, and willingness and to request or grant permission	DeRay <u>can</u> paint wonderful watercolors. [ability] You <u>can</u> leave rehearsal early today. [grant permission] <u>Could</u> we meet at the festival? [request permission] I'm so hungry I <u>could</u> eat a horse. [possibility] I <u>could</u> work your shift if you need me to. [willingness]
may, might	Used to request and grant permission and to offer suggestions. For requests, *might* has a more hesitant and polite connotation than *may,* but they are otherwise usually interchangeable.	<u>May</u> I have your keys, please? [request permission] <u>Might</u> I borrow your Ferrari this weekend? [more polite request for permission] It <u>may/might</u> rain this afternoon. [possibility] You <u>may/might</u> want to bring a swimsuit. [suggestion]
must	Expresses necessity, prohibition (in the negative), and logical probability	Concert goers <u>must</u> pass through security before entering the stadium. [necessity] Passengers <u>must not</u> leave their seats while the seatbelt sign is illuminated. [prohibition] We <u>must</u> be on our final approach. [logical probability]
shall, should, ought to	*Should* and *ought to* express advisability and expectation, usually interchangeably. *Shall* expresses intention as well as advisability, but in American English it usually appears only in questions.	<u>Shall/Should</u> we eat in or go out for dinner tonight? [advisability] We <u>should/ought to</u> eat out less to save money. [advisability] The *pad thai* <u>should/ought to</u> arrive in twenty minutes or so. [expectation]
will, would	*Will* expresses intention, willingness, and expectation. *Would* expresses intention, willingness, typical or repeated action, and logical assumption, and it is also used for polite requests.	I <u>will</u> finish the gift wrapping if you want. [willingness] I <u>will</u> apply to graduate school next year. [intention] The vaccine <u>will</u> arrive soon. [expectation] <u>Would</u> you mind opening the window? [request] Amalia decided she <u>would</u> audition for the musical. [intention] When preparing dinner, he <u>would</u> always sing along to his favorite tunes. [repeated action] That alarm you're hearing <u>would</u> be the monthly test of the emergency system. [logical probability]

- In general, never follow a modal with another modal, and always follow a modal with the base form of a simple helping verb or main verb.

  > Tomás should ~~can~~ *be able to* finish his calculus homework before the movie starts.

  > Yuki must ~~to~~ take three more courses to graduate.

EXERCISE 45.3 Using modal helping verbs

The following email message has six errors in the use of modals and helping verbs. Edit the message to correct these errors. The first error has been found for you.

Hi, Max,

I hope everything is going well. I *am* ~~writing~~ to ask you a favor. We want to organize an auction for the baseball team. If you might could contribute a little time, that would to be great! We need someone who cans contact potential donors, assign starting bids for items, and mail out publicity. We think we might raise as much as $10,000 for team uniforms if we can get enough volunteers. I really hope you will to help us out. Do you think you come on Saturday for a short meeting?

Thanks in advance!

Alex

Make It **Your Own**

Review a recent piece of writing you completed for one of your classes. Print a new copy and circle all the verbs, gerunds, infinitives, and participial adjectives. Note any that you find confusing or that were marked by your instructor as incorrectly used. Make notes about their correct use by consulting this book, your instructor, or your college writing center.

Work Together

The use of modals affects how polite (or impolite) a piece of writing is considered to be. Working with a partner, consider the following pairs of sentences. Decide which in each pair is more polite, and discuss why. Does it depend on your audience? Be prepared to discuss your conclusions with your class.

1. a. Can you open the window?
   b. Would you mind opening the window?
2. a. Might I have a bite of your cake? It looks delicious.
   b. Could I have a bite of your cake?
3. a. Can I get a letter of recommendation from you?
   b. May I ask you to write me a letter of recommendation?

46 Managing Adjectives and Adverbs
by Ted E. Johnston and M. E. Sokolik

IN THIS CHAPTER

a. Placing adjectives in the proper order, 786
b. Choosing the correct prepositions, 787
c. Placing adverbs correctly, 788
d. Dealing with confusing adverbs, 790

adjectives & adverbs

Adjectives modify nouns and pronouns. *Adverbs* modify verbs, adjectives, other adverbs, and entire phrases, clauses, and sentences. This chapter will help you use adjectives and adverbs correctly and place them appropriately in your sentences.

> **More about**
> Articles and other determiners, 768–74
> Cumulative versus coordinate adjectives, 809–10

46a Placing Adjectives in the Proper Order

- Most adjectives have only one form, regardless of whether the noun they modify is singular or plural.

  ▸ Serena wants a *white* *dress*, but these *white* *dresses* are not to her liking.
  (adjective + singular noun; adjective + plural noun)

- Adjectives usually come before a noun (*Serena has a white dress*) or after a **linking verb** (*Serena's dress is white*).

- When multiple adjectives cumulatively modify the same noun, the kind of information they convey determines their proper order (see the Quick Reference box on the next page).

linking verbs *Be* and other verbs that express a state of being rather than an action and connect a subject to its subject complement

NOTE More than three adjectives in a sequence can be awkward. Instead, vary your sentences to distribute the adjectives without confusing your readers.

Quick Reference: Putting Cumulative Adjectives in Standard Order

Article or Other Determiner	Overall Evaluation or Opinion	Size	Shape or Other Intrinsic Aspect	Age	Color	Essence: Nationality, Material, or Purpose	Noun
two		big			red	rubber	balls
an	exciting			new		mystery	novel
my		tiny	helpless	newborn			kitten
those	funny			old	black-and-white		sitcoms
the	delicious		round			French	pastry

46b Choosing the Correct Prepositions with Adjectives

On a particular day, you might be excited *by* a new song, mad *at* a friend, or happy *about* the weather. As these phrases reveal, you need to be careful when combining adjectives and prepositions. When in doubt, consult a dictionary to make sure you are using the proper *idiom.* The editing in the following paragraph gives additional examples of correct idiomatic usage:

> More about
> Idioms, 610
> Prepositions, 793–800

Ally is delighted [adjective] ~~in~~ *with* [preposition] her midterm grades. She had been nervous [adjective] ~~of~~ *about* [preposition] her performance in biochemistry. Ally is grateful [adjective] ~~at~~ *to* [preposition] her instructors. When she struggled, they were not disappointed [adjective] ~~at~~ *in* [preposition] her, and they were proud [adjective] ~~about~~ *of* [preposition] her when she succeeded. She is dedicated [adjective] ~~with~~ *to* [preposition] completing her nursing degree.

EXERCISE 46.1 Using adjectives correctly

Correct problems with adjective order or prepositions used after adjectives in the following sentences. (The Quick Reference box above will help you with some of these.) If a sentence has no problems, circle its number.

EXAMPLE

The ~~new~~ ridiculous *new* parking regulations are hurting students financially.

1. In our new cozy kitchen, we have a blue round table from Ikea.
2. The artist gave a historical lengthy overview of Abstract Expressionism.
3. The mayor is devoted for eliminating racist violence in our city.
4. There used to be a red big leather sofa in the lobby.
5. The lawyer's final masterful defense of her client was thought-provoking.
6. Everyone should be alarmed with attacks on democracy.
7. My economical new hybrid car helps me cope with the price of gas.
8. The witness said he saw a green old van leave the scene of the crime.
9. That gray-haired wise doctor still maintains a practice private.
10. The residents are worried from the possibility of another hurricane.

46c Placing Adverbs Correctly

- An adverb cannot be located between a verb and its object.

    ▶ Susan [plays] [beautifully] the [piano], *beautifully*.
          verb   adverb   object

    In this sentence, *beautifully* fits correctly only at the end, after *piano*, the direct object.

- Many adverbs, primarily those related to time (such as *often* and *frequently*), may be placed either before the subject or verb or after the direct object.

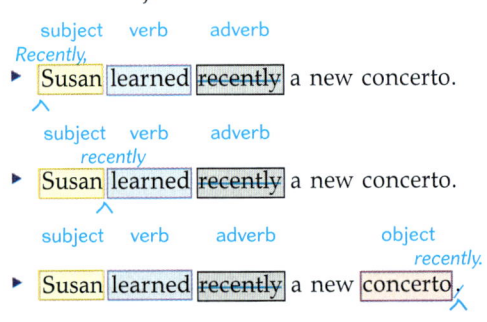

    Recently,
    ▶ [Susan] [learned] [recently] a new concerto.
       subject verb   adverb

    recently
    ▶ [Susan] [learned] [recently] a new concerto.
       subject verb   adverb

    recently.
    ▶ [Susan] [learned] [recently] a new [concerto],
       subject verb   adverb   object

- When a main verb has no helping verbs, the adverb should precede it. When the main verb has helping verbs, the adverb should usually be placed between the first helper and the main verb.

    ▶ Taiji [effortlessly] [finished] the races by remaining positive and focused.
           adverb   verb

Language Matters • Placing Adverbs Correctly

```
           adverb      first      second     main
                       helping    helping    verb
                       verb       verb
                       effortlessly
```
▶ Taiji [effortlessly] has [been] [winning] races by remaining positive and focused.

Some adverbs (but not all) can be placed between the second helper and the main verb.

```
           adverb      first      second     main
                       helping    helping    verb
                       verb       verb
                                  effortlessly
```
▶ Taiji [effortlessly] has [been] [winning] races by remaining positive and focused.

- In most instances, place an adverb first if it modifies the entire sentence.

  adverb
  ▶ [Surprisingly], he has decided to change his major to psychology.

- When certain negative adverbs or adverb phrases begin a sentence, they require a change in the standard subject-verb order. Included in this group are *not only, at no time, never, rarely,* and *seldom*.

  > **More about**
  > Inverted word order when certain negative adverbs start a sentence, 764–65

  have
  ▶ Seldom I ~~have~~ been so proud of my brother.

EXERCISE 46.2 Putting adverbs in the right place

Correct any adverb placement problems in the following sentences. Circle the number of any sentences that are already correct.

EXAMPLE
       unintentionally
The doctor gave me ~~unintentionally~~ the wrong information.

1. The children played fast and furiously the game and then fell instantly asleep.
2. Walid is doing well in math now that he is doing diligently the homework.
3. Rarely does the manager promote new employees so quickly.
4. We should consider always the suggestions of our employees rather than implementing suddenly changes.
5. Not only Tamika works on Saturday, but also on Sunday.

6. Young Ralph has sadly never learned to read.
7. The judge soon should make her decision.
8. Do you really think that Ivan treats Marissa unfairly?

46d Dealing with Confusing Adverbs

Certain English adverbs seem similar but actually have significantly different connotations and functions. Often-confused words include *too* with *so*, *too* with *either*, *not* with *no*, *hard* with *hardly*, and *such* with *so*.

1. Too and so

To give an adjective a negative or more negative meaning, use *too* in most instances. To intensify any adjective, use *so* or *very* or a similar adverb.

▶ The professor realized her first test had been so [*too*] difficult
                                        adverb adjective

and was surprised to find us still too [*so*] excited about the class.

2. Too and *either*

When following up a statement about one subject's action with a statement about another subject's doing likewise, use *either* after a verb that is grammatically negative (as with *won't* or *hasn't*), and use *too* after a verb that is grammatically positive. Remember that unless verbs such as *avoided* or *refused* are used with a negative adverb (such as *not*), they are grammatically positive, even though by themselves they have negative meanings.

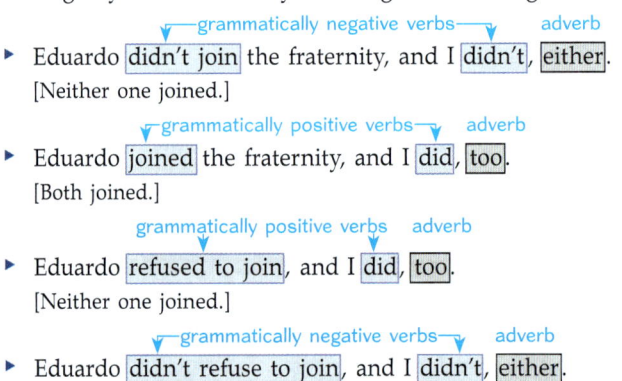

▶ Eduardo didn't join the fraternity, and I didn't, either.
   [Neither one joined.]

▶ Eduardo joined the fraternity, and I did, too.
   [Both joined.]

▶ Eduardo refused to join, and I did, too.
   [Neither one joined.]

▶ Eduardo didn't refuse to join, and I didn't, either.
   [Both were willing to join.]

3. *Not* and *no*

Because *no* is an adjective, it can only modify a noun. The adverb *not*, however, can modify an adjective, a verb, or another adverb. The expression *not a (an)* can replace the adjective *no* in front of a noun.

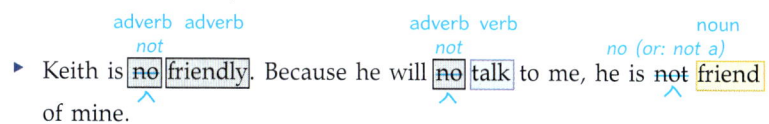

▶ Keith is ~~no~~ friendly [adverb: *not*]. Because he will ~~no~~ talk [adverb: *not*] to me, he is ~~not~~ friend [noun: *no (or: not a)*] of mine.

4. *Hard* and *hardly*

The word *hard* can be either an adjective or an adverb. As an adverb, it means *intensely* or *with great effort*. The adverb *hardly* means *just a little* or *almost not at all*.

▶ Juan got an *A* after he studied hard [adverb] for the exam. Laura got a *D* because she hardly [adverb] looked at her notes.

5. *Such* and *so*

Such a (an), *such*, or *so* can emphasize a type or a quality. Use *such a (an)* before an adjective that precedes a concrete noun: *She is such a wise person.* Use *such* by itself directly in front of an abstract noun: *Such wisdom is rare.* To intensify any freestanding adjective, as in the case of a subject complement, use *so*: *She is so wise.*

➔ EXERCISE 46.3 Correcting easily confused adverbs

Correct any adverb errors in the following sentences, and circle the number of those sentences that have no errors.

EXAMPLE

Jack didn't go to the party, and I didn't, ~~too~~. [*either*]

1. We worked hardly on this project, and all we got was a *C*.
2. We don't feel guilty about this decision, and you shouldn't, too.
3. The waiters here are so slow; we may never get our food.
4. April is not millionaire, but she is so generous person.
5. I really admire that he helps his elderly parents too much.
6. We have come so far to give up now.

Make It **Your Own**

Review a text that you were assigned to read in one of your classes, and find examples of cumulative adjectives used before a noun. Look for strings of two, three, or more adjectives not separated from one another by commas, being sure to include any noun determiners. Use the Quick Reference box on page 787 to account for the order in which the adjectives appear. Do any examples violate the usual order?

Work **Together**

Join with several other students and compare the examples of cumulative adjectives you analyzed in the exercise above. Consult your instructor if your group disagrees about the analysis of any of the examples.

47 Using Prepositions
by Ted E. Johnston and M. E. Sokolik

IN THIS CHAPTER

a. Recognizing prepositions, 793
b. The functions of prepositions, 794
c. Using prepositions correctly, 798
d. Necessary and unnecessary prepositions, 799

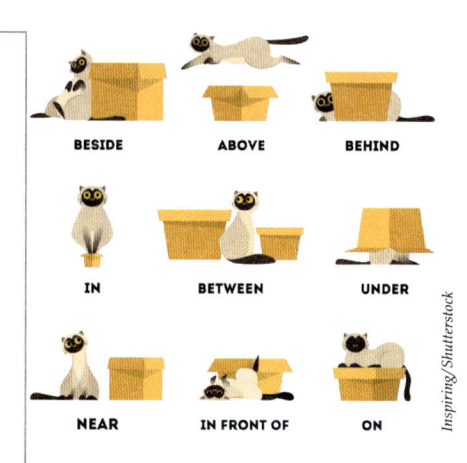

Prepositions specify a relationship between other words or phrases. They are seemingly insignificant words (*for, at, with, under, over*), yet they serve important functions. They provide important information about relationships between other words and phrases: "The mayor worked *against* the proposal"; "the laptop is *inside* my backpack."

To help you learn correct preposition use in English, this chapter explains how to identify prepositions (*section 47a*), how to determine the function they serve (*47b*), and how to use them idiomatically (*47c* and *d*).

47a Recognizing Prepositions

Although there are fewer than one hundred single-word prepositions in use in English, many additional multiword prepositions function in similar ways. The Quick Reference box on the next page lists some of the most common of both.

→ EXERCISE 47.1 Recognizing prepositions

Identify the prepositional phrases in the following sentences. Underline the prepositional phrase, and circle each preposition.

EXAMPLE

A small air carrier might assume responsibility (for) the freight (from) the customer.

1. The Dehkhoda Institute, which is devoted to the teaching of Farsi, was founded in 1945.

793

> **Quick Reference** — Common Single-Word and Multiword Prepositions
>
> **Single-Word Prepositions**
>
> | | | | |
> |---|---|---|---|
> | about | beneath | like | to |
> | above | beside | near | toward |
> | across | between | of | under |
> | after | by | off | underneath |
> | against | down | on | until |
> | along | during | onto | up |
> | among | except | out | upon |
> | around | for | outside | with |
> | at | from | over | within |
> | before | in | past | without |
> | behind | inside | since | |
> | below | into | through | |
>
> **Multiword Prepositions**
>
> | | | | |
> |---|---|---|---|
> | according to | by means of | in front of | on account of |
> | ahead of | close to | in place of | on behalf of |
> | as far as | due to | in spite of | on top of |
> | as to | far from | inside of | out of |
> | as well as | in accordance with | instead of | outside of |
> | aside from | in addition to | near to | |
> | because of | in case of | next to | |

2. The black-backed jackal is an African canine with a foxlike appearance.
3. The first cricket test match was played in 1877 between Australia and England.
4. In November, snow fell on the coast, which is rare so early in the season.
5. The citywide depression lasted for two centuries, through famine and war, until the 1990s.

47b The Functions of Prepositions

Every preposition has multiple possible functions depending on the context in which it occurs. As a result, it is often easier to understand prepositions in terms of their function than to try to memorize what each one means.

Language Matters • The Functions of Prepositions **prep 47b** 795

The most basic use for a preposition is to indicate *location*. Other important functions are to indicate *time*, to indicate *condition* or *degree*, to specify *cause* or *reason*, and to designate *possession*, *attribute*, or *origin*.

> **Quick Reference — Identifying Functions of Prepositions**
>
> Common functions of prepositions include the following:
>
> 1. To indicate *location* (795)
> 2. To indicate *time* (795)
> 3. To indicate *condition* or *degree* (796)
> 4. To specify *cause* or *reason* (796)
> 5. To designate *possession*, *attribute*, or *origin* (797)

1. Location

The most basic prepositions for indicating location are *at, on,* and *in.*

- *At* specifies a general point of orientation.
    - ▶ Meet me at the station.

- *On* specifies contact between two things.
    - ▶ The book is on the table.
    - ▶ The clipboard hangs on the wall.

- *In* specifies that one thing is contained within another.
    - ▶ The solution is in the beaker.
    - ▶ Liz is in San Francisco.

NOTE Many locations operate like *surfaces* or *containers*. Generally, use *in* for locations that seem like containers and *on* for locations that seem like surfaces.

CONTAINER	He sat in his car. [**Not:** *He sat on his car,* which would mean he was on top of it.]
SURFACE	He sat on the bus. [Buses, trains, and airplanes are usually considered surfaces because people can walk around on them.]
CONTAINER	We walked in the hallway.
SURFACE	We walked on the sidewalk.

2. Time

The most common prepositions for relating things to a moment or a period of time are *at, in, on,* and *by.*

- *At* designates a particular point in time.
    - ▶ Let's meet at 4:00 p.m.
    - ▶ The party ended at midnight.

- *In* can designate either a future time or a particular period.
    - ▶ I'll leave in 10 minutes.
    - ▶ We'll finish the job in April.

- *On* designates a particular day or date.
- *By* indicates *no later than*.

▸ His birthday is on Friday.
▸ Her birthday is on the twelfth.
▸ Turn in your essay by 3:00 p.m.
▸ They decided to leave by 5:00 a.m. to avoid rush hour.

3. Condition/Degree

Prepositions of condition or degree indicate the state of the object. Some common prepositions in this category are *of, on, in, about,* and *around.*

- *In* or *on* can specify a condition. These uses are often idiomatic.

▸ The house is on fire.
▸ She is on vacation.
▸ Charlie is not in trouble.
▸ Darlene left her desk in perfect order.

- *Of* is used in phrases indicating fractions or portions.

▸ Three of the books are required for the course.
▸ One of those coats is mine.

- *Around* or *about* can indicate approximation.

▸ That medication costs around twenty dollars.
▸ I walked about ten miles.

4. Cause/Reason

Prepositions showing cause include *from, of, for,* and *because of.*

- *From* indicates cause or explains a condition.

▸ We were wet from the rain.
▸ We were tired from walking all day.

- *For* often indicates a cause and answers the question *Why?*

▸ Oregon is famous for its forests.
▸ He got an award for selling more cars than anyone else.

- *Of* and *because of* both show a reason.

▸ The patient died of pneumonia.
▸ I sneezed because of my cold.

5. Possession/Attribute/Origin

The most common prepositions showing possession, attribute, or origin are *of, from,* and *with.*

- Possession is typically shown with *of.*
  - ▸ That song is one [of] Lizzo's.
  - ▸ The director [of] the movie is Bong Joon-ho.

- An attribute can be indicated by *with.*
  - ▸ He is a director [with] real talent.
  - ▸ He is the one [with] the Palme d'Or award.

- *From* can show origin.
  - ▸ Bong is [from] Daegu, South Korea.
  - ▸ The award came [from] the Cannes Film Festival.

NOTE Indicating possession with *of* instead of *'s* or *s'* is often awkward.

AWKWARD	the bike of Bob
PREFERRED	Bob's bike

EXERCISE 47.2 Determining the function of a preposition

Write the function of the underlined preposition in the space to the right of each sentence. Choose from *Location, Time, Condition/Degree, Cause/Reason,* or *Possession/Attribute/Origin.*

EXAMPLE

She bought the car with greater fuel efficiency. attribute

1. The construction was completed in 2012. _____
2. In 1946, Margolin moved to Lebanon. _____
3. Bellatrix is described as a tall woman with pale skin. _____
4. Let's meet at the library to study tonight. _____
5. We were dying of thirst. _____
6. He's having a birthday party in July. _____
7. Hearing loss is estimated to begin at age thirty. _____
8. There are no students from Texas here. _____

47c Using Prepositions Correctly

Certain verbs or nouns will suggest the use of particular prepositions. It may help to memorize these phrases:

- *give* something *to* someone
- *take* something *from* someone
- *sell* something *to* someone
- *buy* something *from* someone
- *lend* something *to* someone
- *borrow* something *from* someone
- get *married* or *engaged to* someone
- *fill* something *with* something
- *shout to* someone (in greeting)
- *shout at* someone (in anger)

> **More about**
> Passive voice, 562, 593–94
> Direct and indirect objects, 649–50, 761–62

In addition, some prepositions serve a particular grammatical function. For example, in passive constructions, the preposition *by* identifies who or what did something.

- The car was repaired by Hassina.

Similarly, indirect objects, when placed after rather than before a direct object, are usually preceded by *to:*

- Luis gave the present to his father.

EXERCISE 47.3 Using prepositions correctly

Insert the correct preposition into the blanks below. In some cases, more than one preposition may be acceptable.

EXAMPLE

He came from a small village in the middle of the country.

1. Our sense ___ identity—___ who we are and what we have done—is tied ___ our memories.
2. *The Big Knife* is a 1955 film directed and produced ___ Robert Aldrich and based ___ the play ___ Clifford Odets.

3. Ronald and Reginald Kray were identical twin brothers and the foremost organized crime leaders ___ London ___ the 1950s and 1960s.

4. The original manuscripts ___ Oscar Wilde today are found ___ many collections, but ___ far the largest collection is found ___ the William Andrews Clark Memorial Library ___ UCLA.

5. Tortell is a Catalan pastry stuffed ___ marzipan, which ___ some special occasions is topped ___ glazed fruit. It is traditionally eaten ___ January 6.

47d Necessary and Unnecessary Prepositions

Unfortunately, there is no rule of grammar to tell when a preposition is needed. Consider these examples:

- I like to listen *to* Afrobeat music.
- She was looking *at* the waterfall.

Similarly, there is no rule for determining when one is not needed:

- ~~In~~ *One* block from the school, there is a coffee shop.
- We were discussing ~~about~~ climate change in class.

To make things more complicated, sometimes a phrase is acceptable with or without a preposition.

- I've lived here for six years.
- I've lived here six years.

One strategy for mastering these usages, some of them idiomatic, is to notice in your reading when you encounter unfamiliar constructions involving prepositions. Some students keep a grammar log or other notebook to help them remember these constructions.

EXERCISE 47.4 Distinguishing between necessary and unnecessary prepositions

Correct the following passage for preposition usage. Cross out any prepositions that are not needed, insert any that are missing, and leave unchanged any that are correctly used. There are 13 preposition errors in the passage, not including the one in the example.

EXAMPLE

Flip the Frog is an animated cartoon character created ^by an American cartoonist, Ub Iwerks, who also helped ~~with~~ to create another famous character—Mickey Mouse.

Flip starred a series cartoons distributed by MGM from 1930 to 1933. Apart Flip, the series had many other characters, including Flip's dog and a mule named of Orace.

Flip's first appearance was in a cartoon called by *Night*. Iwerks animated this short feature while working his friend Walt Disney in 1930. After a number disagreements between them, Iwerks left Disney and went on to accept an offer to open a cartoon studio his own a salary of $300 a week. Disney at the time couldn't match with this offer. The first cartoon series Iwerks was expected to create featured on a character called Tony the Frog, but Iwerks didn't like the name and had it changed Flip.

Make It Your Own

In a paper you have recently written or are now writing, look for preposition errors. How many do you find? What functions of these prepositions do you recognize (location, time, etc.)? How would you fix the errors?

Work Together

For a paper you have recently written or are now writing, exchange texts with a classmate and analyze your classmate's writing for prepositional errors. How many do you find? How would you correct them? (If your partner is a native speaker of English, you may find very few errors. If this is the case, note any preposition usages that are unfamiliar to you and discuss their meaning with your partner.) Be prepared to discuss what you gained from this exercise.

Part Ten

Detail
Matters
Punctuation and Mechanics

- **48** Using Commas 802
- **49** Using Semicolons 820
- **50** Using Apostrophes 827
- **51** Using Quotation Marks 834
- **52** Using End Punctuation 843
- **53** Using Other Punctuation 847
- **54** Capitalizing 858
- **55** Italics and Underlining 865
- **56** Using Abbreviations 869
- **57** Using Numbers 874
- **58** Using Hyphens 877

48 Using Commas

IN THIS CHAPTER

a. In compound sentences, 802

b. After introductory elements, 805

c. With conjunctive adverbs and transitional phrases, 807

d. With interjections and similar elements, 807

e. To separate items in a series, 808

f. To separate coordinate adjectives, 809

g. To set off nonessential elements, 811

h. With quotations, 813

i. With numbers, names and titles, place names and addresses, and dates, 814

j. To avoid ambiguity, 817

k. Not between subjects and verbs, verbs and objects, 817

compound sentence Two or more independent clauses linked by a comma and a coordinating conjunction or a semicolon

independent clause A word group that includes a subject and a predicate that can stand alone as a sentence

Artfury/Shutterstock

Commas function as dividers within—but not between—sentences. The rules for comma placement are fairly straightforward. A list of the rules writers use most often appears in the Quick Reference box on the next page.

Writing Responsibly — Commas and Clarity

Incorrect use of commas can have us saying something we do *not* mean and thus confusing our readers. Consider this example, with and without commas:

This sentence . . .	*means . . .*
Writing to my mother is a terrible chore.	I find writing to my mother a real pain!
Writing, to my mother, is a terrible chore.	My mother finds writing a real pain!

to AUDIENCE

48a Using Commas in Compound Sentences

In a *compound sentence* a comma and *coordinating conjunction* work together: The comma marks the break between the two *independent clauses,* and the coordinating conjunction joins them into a single sentence. When a coordinating conjunction combines two independent clauses, place a comma *before* it (not *after* it):

▶ *independent clause* | *independent clause*
My heart is in San Francisco**,** but my body is in New York.
coordinating conjunction

Detail Matters • Using Commas in Compound Sentences 48a 803

Quick Reference: Common Comma Do's and Don'ts

***Do* use a comma . . .**

. . . to separate independent clauses joined by a coordinating conjunction. (802)

                                      coordinating
           independent clause   conjunction independent clause

▶ Hip-hop music was born in the 1970s, but it continues to flourish.

. . . to set off introductory elements from an independent clause. (805)

          subordinate clause   independent clause

▶ Although it was born in New York City, rap has become popular around the world.

. . . to separate three or more items in a series. (808)

                                         ①   ②   ③

▶ Some early hip-hop artists include Grandmaster Flash, Run DMC, and LL Cool J.

. . . to separate coordinate (but not cumulative) adjectives. (809)

                            coordinate adjectives

▶ Hip-hop soon grew to have a huge, enthusiastic audience outside the New York club scene.

. . . to set off nonessential elements. (811)

                            nonessential clause

▶ The Zulu Nation, now known as the Universal Zulu Nation, was formed in in the 1970s to attract kids toward hip-hop and away from gangs.

***Do not* use a comma . . .**

. . . following a coordinating or subordinating conjunction. (802, 803)

▶ Run DMC was popular enough to be featured on the game Guitar Hero,
   subordinating conjunction
   although, one of the two songs the group played are by the band Aerosmith.

. . . to separate paired elements. (804)

▶ Scholars have long been writing about hip-hop music, and culture.

. . . to separate independent clauses not joined by a coordinating conjunction. (804)

▶ LL Cool J's *Radio* was perhaps the first mainstream rap hit, it went platinum within five months.

. . . preceding the first item or following the last item in a series. (803)

                                                    ①   ②   ③

▶ Hip-hop has also merged with musical styles such as, hip house, nu soul, reggaetón,
         ④
   and merenrap, to create exciting sounds.

. . . between a subject and its verb or a verb and its object or complement. (817)

   subject verb   direct object
▶ LL Cool J, had, eight platinum records in a row.

Detail Matters • Using Commas

> **Quick Reference** — The Seven Coordinating Conjunctions
>
> and   but   or   nor
> for   so   yet

NOTE Unless readers will be confused, the comma can be omitted when the two independent clauses are very short:

▸ *no comma:* I sing in Italian but I speak only English.

Do not use a comma before the conjunction if both parts cannot stand on their own as sentences:

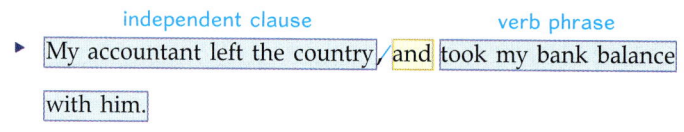

▸ [*independent clause*] My accountant left the country, and [*verb phrase*] took my bank balance with him.

> **More about**
> Comma splices (ch. 35), 671–79
> Semicolons (ch. 49), 820–26

Paired items should not be separated by a comma:

▸ Both [*pair:* my purse, and my bank account] are empty.

When the clauses are long and already punctuated with commas, readers might find the sentence clearer if you replace the comma before the coordinating conjunction with a semicolon:

▸ Comic books are gradually becoming more respectable as works of serious fiction, with graphic novels such as *Maus* and *Watchmen* earning tremendous critical acclaim; yet some people still refuse to take them seriously.

NOTE Without a coordinating conjunction, a comma between two independent clauses creates a ***comma splice.***

➔ EXERCISE 48.1 Correcting commas in compound sentences

Correct the sentences below by adding or deleting commas. (Some may already be correct.)

EXAMPLE

The dollar has dropped against the euro͵so tourists have flocked to the United States to shop.

1. The US dollar continues to be weak against both the euro, and the pound.
2. The yen remains strong against the US dollar but it fell against the Australian dollar as markets opened this morning.
3. The yen, and the yuan are strengthening.
4. The currencies of Latin America continue to be weak relative to the euro, but they are holding their own against the US dollar.
5. Japanese, and American travelers who visit Europe this summer will feel the pinch, but Australian, and Chinese visitors should find Europe a bargain.

48b Using a Comma after Introductory Elements

A word, phrase, or subordinate clause introducing an independent clause is usually followed by a comma. There are two exceptions:

- Exception 1: Do not insert a comma after the introductory element in an inverted sentence, where an introductory word group immediately precedes the verb.

    introductory word group   verb
    ▸ Into the deep, dark ocean dove Dr. Kathy Sullivan.

- Exception 2: Do not insert a comma after an introductory word group that acts as the subject of the sentence.

    subject   verb
    ▸ Exploring deep, dark oceans is what she does.

When the introductory element is very brief, some writers omit the comma. If readers might be confused, even for a moment, include it:

- Before eating, the missionaries said grace.

1. Insert a comma after introductory clauses.

When a *subordinate,* or dependent, clause introduces an independent clause, place a comma between the two.

    subordinate clause
▸ Although Banksy remained an elusive figure, his popularity continued to grow.

> **subordinate clause**
> A word group that lacks a subject or predicate or that begins with a subordinating word or phrase; a word group that cannot stand alone as a sentence

> *subordinate clause*
> ▸ [Because she was the first African American woman to earn a PhD in economics and a lawyer who worked for racial and economic justice], Sadie Tanner Mossell Alexander (1898–1989) should be remembered and celebrated.

2. Insert a comma after introductory phrases.

Insert a comma following an introductory *phrase* to signal the start of the main clause:

participial phrase
▸ [Lacking Mozart's natural abilities], Salieri formed an obsessive hatred for his rival.

prepositional phrase
▸ [In an unguarded moment], the politician muttered an unprintable phrase into the live microphone.

absolute phrase
▸ [A vegetarian for many years], he suddenly craved bacon.

> **phrase** A group of related words that lacks a subject, predicate, or both; it cannot stand alone as a sentence, but it can function *in* a sentence as a noun, a verb, or a modifier

> **More about**
> Participial phrases, 653
> Prepositional phrases, 652
> Absolute phrases, 654

EXERCISE 48.2 Inserting commas after introductory elements

Supply a comma as needed after introductory elements in the sentences below. (You will not need to add a comma in every sentence.)

EXAMPLE

With the largest scholarly and research collection in the world, the Library of Congress gives us access to an ever-growing body of knowledge on every subject imaginable.

1. After the founding of Congress in 1789 President John Adams approved a $5,000 budget for the Library of Congress.
2. According to the library's website founding members of Congress valued rigorous classical education and saw it as foundational to democracy.
3. In fact the members of Congress already had access to the New York Society Library and Free Library of Philadelphia.
4. In 1812 Thomas Jefferson sold his personal library to Congress.
5. During the Progressive Era the Librarian of Congress happily hired more staff, planned more events, and added to the library's multimedia collections.

48c Using Commas to Set Off Conjunctive Adverbs and Most Transitional Phrases

Transitional expressions and *conjunctive adverbs* are usually set off by commas.

> ▶ The basking shark, *in fact*, consumes only zooplankton and small fish. [transition]

> ▶ It may end up as dinner for an orca or a tiger shark, *however*. [conjunctive adverb]

When the transitional expression or conjunctive adverb is used to link independent clauses, place a semicolon before it.

> ▶ The whale shark is the largest fish in today's oceans; *nevertheless*, it presents no threat to humans. [conjunctive adverb]

transitional expressions Words and phrases that show the relationship between sentences

conjunctive adverb A transitional expression that can link one independent clause to another; it modifies the second clause and specifies its relationship to the first

48d Inserting Commas to Set Off Interjections, Contrasting Information, Expressions of Direct Address, Parenthetical and Conversational Expressions, and Tag Questions

> ▶ *Wow*, that wind farm is gorgeous! [interjection]

> ▶ Some people, *sadly*, think the industrial look of a wind farm is ugly. [interjection]

> ▶ The current energy situation requires us to revise, *not cling to*, traditional notions of beauty. [contrasting information]

> ▶ *Professor Kinney*, how much do you know about offshore wind farming? [direct address]

> ▶ The first US offshore wind farm, *it turns out*, was on Nantucket Sound. [parenthetical expression]

> - **No,** it isn't a single-handed solution to our energy problems.
>
>   *[conversational expression]*
>
> - Wind farms will nevertheless make a big contribution, **won't they**?
>
>   *[tag question]*

48e Using Commas to Separate Items in a Series

Place a comma between each item in a series of three or more.

> - Our new house will feature **solar panels**, **a hilltop windmill**, and **rainwater conversion**.

Some writers omit the comma before the coordinating conjunction (*and* in this example) in a series, but readers may find the final comma (known as the *Oxford comma*) helpful in distinguishing paired and unpaired elements. The managing editor of the *Chicago Manual of Style* likes to quote this hypothetical dedication, which highlights the potential problems that can be caused by omitting the serial comma:

> - I dedicate this book to my parents, Mother Teresa and the Pope.

To Use or Not to Use the Serial, or Oxford, Comma English-speaking nations may share a common language, but their rules for using it sometimes differ. British writers have more or less dispensed with the serial comma (except to avoid confusion), while Americans (except for journalists) continue to use it. When writing for a US audience, use the serial comma.

> *More about*
> Using semicolons in a series, 823

When the items in the series are long or contain internal commas, substituting semicolons for commas can make the sentence easier to read:

> - Phillis Wheatley was born in Senegal in 1753; was sold into slavery to a Boston, Massachusetts, family; studied Greek, Latin, and English; and became the first published African American writer.

Detail Matters • Using Commas to Separate Coordinate, Not Cumulative, Adjectives

EXERCISE 48.3 Using commas with conjunctive adverbs, transitional phrases, interrupting words and phrases, and items in a series

Supply commas as needed in the sentences below. (You will not need to add a comma in every sentence.)

EXAMPLE

My goodness‸did I have a horrible cold last week!

1. I originally thought my sneezing was due to an allergy; however my doctor pointed out the difference between the symptoms of an allergy and a cold.
2. A telltale sign for example is how quickly the symptoms develop.
3. Allergy symptoms start immediately, but cold symptoms, on the other hand, take a day or longer to develop and gradually worsen.
4. Allergies nearly always cause itchiness in the eyes nose and throat, while a cold usually does not.
5. My obvious cold symptoms according to my doctor were fever aches and chest congestion.

48f Using Commas to Separate Coordinate, Not Cumulative, Adjectives

Coordinate adjectives each modify the noun or pronoun they precede and are of equal weight; ***cumulative adjectives***, by contrast, modify not only the noun or pronoun they precede but also the next adjective in the series. Hence, the order of coordinate adjectives does not matter, but the order of cumulative adjectives does.

Consider the example below:

▶ The girl struggled to hide her brooding⸲ moody nature from the [coordinate adjectives] sympathetic⸲ insightful child psychologist she visited weekly. [cumulative adjectives]

> **More about**
> Adjective order,
> 786–87

While you could reverse *brooding* and *moody* or *insightful* and *sympathetic,* you could not reverse *insightful* and *child*: A *child insightful psychologist* does not make sense.

Detail Matters • Using Commas

> **Quick Reference** — **Testing for Coordinate and Cumulative Adjectives**
>
> To determine whether two or more adjectives should be separated by a comma, try these two tests:
>
> 1. **Place the word *and* between the two adjectives.** If the phrase still makes sense, then the adjectives are coordinate, and you should put a comma between them:
>
>   Yes: sexy and exciting boyfriend
>   No: enormous and shoulder bag
>
> 2. **Reverse the order.** If the meaning remains the same no matter what order they appear in, then the adjectives are coordinate, and you should insert a comma between them:
>
>   Yes: sexy, exciting boyfriend = exciting, sexy boyfriend
>   No: enormous shoulder bag ≠ shoulder enormous bag

EXERCISE 48.4 Using commas with coordinate and cumulative adjectives

Add commas as needed in the sentences below.

EXAMPLE

How likely is it that a curious, adventurous sixth grader will take up smoking?

1. As part of a revealing study, researchers interviewed 1,195 sixth graders and then spoke to them several times over the next four years.
2. The study suggested that two characteristics indicate a heightened identifiable risk level for becoming a smoker.
3. The clearest key indication for future smoking is that it is easy to get cigarettes.
4. The other demonstrated major characteristic is that young people tend to become smokers if they have friends who smoke.
5. Furthermore, combining these two characteristics is a strong indicative risk factor.

Detail Matters • Using Commas to Set Off Nonessential Appositives, Phrases, and Clauses **48g**

48g Using Commas to Set Off Nonessential Appositives, Phrases, and Clauses

Words, phrases, or clauses that add information to a sentence but do not identify the person, place, or thing being described are **nonessential** (or *nonrestrictive*) **elements** and are set off by commas from the rest of the sentence. Elements that identify the person, place, or thing being described are **essential** (or *restrictive*) and are *not* set off by commas. Consider the following sentence:

> My coworker [essential element: Philip], [nonessential element: whom I had never seen without a tie], arrived at the office this morning wearing a toga.

Philip picks out one coworker from among the rest, so that element is essential. The nonessential clause—*whom I had never seen without a tie*—provides important information about Philip, but it does not identify him from among the writer's colleagues, so it is nonessential.

Compare the sentence above to this sentence:

> My coworker, [nonessential element: Philip], showed up at work this morning wearing yoga pants.

In this sentence, *Philip* is set off by commas, suggesting that the writer has only one colleague, so identifying him by name is not essential.

> **More about**
> Essential and nonessential elements, 668

1. Use commas with nonessential appositives.

An *appositive* renames a preceding noun phrase. When it identifies, or specifies, the noun phrase, it is essential and is not set off by commas:

> The Roman emperor [noun phrase] Claudius [essential appositive noun] suffered from an ailment that caused him to limp and to stammer uncontrollably.

In this case, *Claudius* distinguishes this Roman emperor from all the other Roman emperors, so it is essential and should not be set off by commas.

When the appositive adds information but does not identify, it is nonessential and is set off by commas.

> The fourth Roman Emperor [noun phrase], Claudius [nonessential appositive noun], suffered from an ailment that caused him to limp and to stammer uncontrollably.

> **appositive** A noun or noun phrase that renames the noun, pronoun, or noun phrase that precedes it

Because there was only one *fourth Roman emperor,* the name *Claudius* is nonessential.

2. Use commas with nonessential phrases.

A phrase that acts as an adjective, modifying a noun, pronoun, or noun phrase, can also be essential or nonessential: If it identifies what it is describing, then it is essential and should *not* be set off by commas; if it does not identify, then it is nonessential and *should* be set off by commas.

▶ The girl, asked by her father to behave, said, "I am being haive."
   (noun) (nonessential phrase)

▶ The girl asked by her father to behave is my niece.
   (noun) (essential phrase)

3. Use commas with nonessential clauses.

A subordinate (or dependent) clause can also act as an adjective, modifying a noun, pronoun, or noun phrase. When it identifies the noun, pronoun, or noun phrase, it is essential and is *not* set off by commas; when it does not, it is nonessential and *is* set off by commas.

Adverb clauses The placement of an adverb clause indicates whether it is essential or nonessential: If it appears at the beginning of the sentence, it is generally nonessential and set off by a comma; if it appears in the middle of the sentence, it is generally essential and is not set off by commas:

▶ Because he found the politics required to win an Academy Award demeaning, George C. Scott refused to accept an Oscar for his performance in the movie *Patton.*
   (nonessential adverb clause) (noun)

▶ George C. Scott refused to accept an Academy Award for his performance in the movie *Patton* because he found the politics required to win an Oscar demeaning.
   (noun) (essential adverb clause)

That clauses versus which clauses Subordinate clauses beginning with the word *that* are always essential and thus never set off by commas.

▶ Produce that has been genetically modified differs from its non–GM counterpart by a human-made alteration to its DNA.
   (essential clause)

The word *which* is primarily used to introduce nonessential clauses, although using it with essential clauses is increasingly accepted.

▸ Genetically modified produce, [which is sold in grocery stores throughout the United States], is still looked on with suspicion by many consumers.

(nonessential clause)

NOTE Outside of the United States, some writers do not see a need to make a distinction between *which* and *that*.

EXERCISE 48.5 Using commas with appositives, phrases, and clauses

Correct the errors in the following sentences by inserting or deleting commas as necessary.

EXAMPLE

Lyme disease‸a bacterial infection‸was named for the town in Connecticut where it was first identified.

1. The malady, Lyme disease, is transmitted by deer ticks.
2. A person can become infected by deer ticks, that wait in tall grass for someone or something to latch onto.
3. When someone gets Lyme disease he or she will sometimes develop a reddish rash that looks like a spreading bull's-eye.
4. Lyme disease is difficult to diagnose because many people, who have it, do not remember getting bitten by a tick.
5. There is a good protective measure completely covering the arms and legs whenever walking in tall grass that can help a person avoid deer ticks and the Lyme disease that they carry.

48h Using Commas with Quotations

In most cases, separate a *direct quotation* from a *signal phrase* with a comma:

▸ After learning that he had been appointed poet laureate, [Charles Simic exclaimed], "I'm almost frightened to get out of bed—too much good luck in one week."

(signal phrase)

---

direct quotation The exact words someone has used; direct quotations must be placed in quotation marks to avoid plagiarism

signal phrase A noun or pronoun plus an appropriate verb identifying the writer from whom you are borrowing words or ideas

Exceptions

- When the quotation begins the sentence and ends with a question mark or an exclamation point, no comma should be added.
  - "When shall we three meet again, in thunder, lightning, or in rain?"[no comma] asks the first witch in Shakespeare's *Macbeth*.

- When the quotation is integrated into your own sentence, omit the comma:
  - Friar Lawrence warns Romeo that [no comma] "these violent delights have violent ends."

- When the signal phrase is incorporated into a complete sentence that makes sense without the quotation, use a colon before the quotation:
  - Hamlet exits the graveyard scene with a veiled threat: "The cat will mew, and dog will have his day."

Indirect quotations should not be set off by commas.

- New poet laureate Charles Simic confessed that having so much good luck worried him.

> **indirect quotation**
> A quotation that has been paraphrased (put into the writer's own words), instead of taken word-for-word from the source

48i Using Commas with Numbers, Names and Titles, Place Names and Addresses, and Dates

Numbers, names and titles, place names and addresses, and dates are each punctuated according to specialized conventions, some of which vary from one community or discipline to another.

> *More about*
> Numbers (ch. 57), 874–76

1. In numbers

The following conventions are standard in most American English usage:

- In four-digit numbers, using a comma to mark divisions of hundreds is optional, except with years, when no comma should be included:
  - The company paid $9347 [no comma] for those supplies in 2020.
  - The company paid $9,347 for those supplies in 2020.

- In five-digit numbers, a comma is used to mark divisions of hundreds.
  - Workers have filed 93,471 unemployment claims since January.

2. Between personal names and titles

Use a comma to separate a personal name from a title that follows it:

- Send the request to Janet Wanjigi, director of the Center for Drug Evaluation and Research.

Use no comma when a title precedes the name or when the "title" consists of roman numerals:

▶ Send the request to **Doctor** Janet Wanjigi.

▶ My son will be named Albert Farnsworth **IV**.

The titles Jr. and Sr. may appear with or without commas. Note that the Modern Language Association (MLA) requires commas in this situation.

▶ Robert Downey, Jr., played Iron Man in the *Avengers* from 2008 to 2019.

                no commas
▶ Robert Downey Jr. played Iron Man in the *Avengers* from 2008 to 2019.

3. In place names and addresses

Use a comma to separate names of cities from states, provinces, regions, or countries:

▶ Boston, Massachusetts, was the birthplace of Benjamin Franklin. Famous as an American patriot, Franklin also lived for several years in London, England, and Paris, France. He died at age 84 in Philadelphia, Pennsylvania.

Do *not* place a comma between the name of a state and the zip code:

▶ The Franklin Institute, founded to honor Benjamin Franklin, is
                                                     no comma
located at 222 North 20th Street, Philadelphia, Pennsylvania 19103.

4. In dates

Use commas to set off dates in which the day follows the month and when dates include the time of day or the day of the week:

▶ I will never forget that my son was born at 5:17 a.m., Tuesday, March 17, 2019.

No comma is needed in dates when only the month and year are used or when the day *precedes* the month:

- My niece was born in February 2015. [no comma]
- Her exact birth date is 13 February 2015. [no comma]

EXERCISE 48.6 Using commas with numbers, names, places, and dates

In the following sentences, add commas as necessary to mark numbers, names and titles, place names and addresses, and dates. (Not all sentences will need correction.)

EXAMPLE

The board of directors met on Tuesday, June 5, 2016, at 3:00 p.m., in the institute's new offices in Swansea, Massachusetts.

1. Yvonne Gesinghaus, MD, disagrees with the board's decision.
2. According to Dr. Gesinghaus "We should spend the $10500 on research, not on a party in San Antonio Texas."
3. Nevertheless, she requests that we send an invitation to William Green Sr. 217 Adamson Parkway Seattle WA 90107.
4. His invitation must go out by 7 October 2021.
5. The next meeting of the board of directors has been rescheduled to Monday January 10 2022.
6. The finance officer told Dr. Gesinghaus that the meeting on Monday will start promptly at 5 p.m.
7. Also, please change your records to reflect her new job title: Yvonne Gesinghaus Director of Research and Development.
8. The foundation she now works for is located in a suburb of Fall River Massachusetts.
9. The new director's annual salary will be $165000.
10. The increase will take effect in January 2022.

48j Using Commas to Avoid Ambiguity

A comma can separate ideas that might otherwise be misinterpreted, and it can mark places where words have been deleted.

1. To separate ideas

When two ideas could be misread as a single unit, add a comma to separate the two:

▶ My friends who can afford to,take taxis frequently.

2. To replace omitted words and avoid repetition

Replace a repeated word with a comma after its first use:

▶ I vacationed in the Adirondacks, my brother, ~~vacationed~~ in British Columbia.

48k Avoiding Commas between Subjects and Verbs, Verbs and Objects, and Prepositions and Objects

A single comma should not separate a subject from its verb, a verb from its object or a preposition from its object unless another rule calls for it:

▶ The Senate finance committee/ is the focus of much attention. *(subject / verb)*

▶ The committee must explain/ its decision to a nervous public. *(verb / object)*

▶ Three interns drafted the proposal for/ significant carbon reduction. *(preposition / object)*

➔ EXERCISE 48.7 Using commas to resolve ambiguity

Correct the following sentences by inserting or deleting commas as necessary. (Not all sentences will need correction.)

EXAMPLE

The members who want to,contribute their time to painting the club's meeting hall.

1. Fiona is painting a wall, and Helena the baseboards.
2. Those who can stay and keep painting through the second shift.

3. Although most members never help, those who do devote a great deal of their spare time to it.
4. The members who do enjoy a sense of satisfaction that they have made a difference.
5. Jason worked ten hours this week, Alika eight, and Jesse fifteen.

EXERCISE 48.8 Avoiding unnecessary commas

Delete any unnecessary commas from the following sentences.

EXAMPLE

Current treatments for multiple myeloma include/ chemotherapy, radiation, and stem-cell transplantation, but/ other treatments are under development.

1. In April 2007, researchers at the Mayo Clinic, discovered that a byproduct of wood mold, chaetocin, kills multiple, myeloma, cells more effectively than current treatments, such as thalidomide, or stem-cell transplantation.
2. The doctor, who led the study told reporters, that the team had found chaetocin to cause myeloma cell, death in mice and, that it had also provided new avenues for research.
3. This cancer of the bone marrow cells, is currently incurable, but this new research on chaetocin holds, promise for a cure.
4. Chaetocin kills myeloma cells in mice by, accumulating in the cancer cells, slowing the growth of myeloma cells, and causing biological changes in cancer cells that led to, their death.
5. Dr. Bible, who led the team of researchers, noted that treatments were still several years off, but expected that his team's discovery would help patients in the future.

EXERCISE 48.9 Using commas correctly

Add or delete commas as needed in the paragraph below.

EXAMPLE

Americans,instead of losing their spirit of creativity,seem to be getting more inventive/ than ever.

The United States Patent Office, was so overwhelmed that it had a backlog of 700000 applications and its average review time was thirty-one months. In an attempt to deal with the flood of applications the office proposed new rules. The new rules made inventors provide more information; in addition the agency would also allow expanded public review of applications. What's more and this may be of greater concern to inventors the office began approving a smaller percentage of applications. In 2007 it approved approximately fifty percent of applications which was down from seventy-two percent in 2000. To improve the chances of approval inventors, need to be sure that their inventions are both new, and useful. The description of an invention whether it is simple, or highly complex should also be understandable, and written clearly. At the turn of the twenty-first century American inventiveness was not only thriving but it was also more competitive than ever before.

Make It **Your Own**

Review your use of commas in a recent writing project of two or more pages. Add commas where needed and cross through unnecessary ones. Then analyze the impact these changes would have on your reader. (Refer to the sections in this chapter as needed.)

Work **Together**

Exchange your work on Exercise 48.9 with a partner. Check your classmate's use of commas. Do you see any errors? If so, refer to sections in this chapter to help you explain the effect these errors had on you as a reader. (Be specific.)

Text Credits

Pg. 813: Simic, Charles, quoted in "Simic Reflects on Poet Laureate Honor" NPR Weekend Edition Sunday, August 5, 2007. **Pg. 814:** Shakespeare, William, *Macbeth* (1605). **Pg. 814:** Shakespeare, William, *Romeo and Juliet* (1594). **Pg. 814:** Shakespeare, William, *Hamlet* (1600).

49 Using Semicolons

IN THIS CHAPTER

a. Linking independent clauses, 820

b. Using before a conjunctive adverb or transitional phrase, 822

c. Marking a series with internal commas, 823

d. Repairing a comma splice, 823

e. Avoiding overuse, 824

Although there are other uses of the semicolon, its main function is to link two independent clauses into a single sentence. The comma and a coordinating conjunction also play this role, so what makes the semicolon useful? It is the signal the semicolon sends to the reader; it tells the reader that the clause that follows will specify consequences, restate meaning, or introduce a contrast.

A list of the most important rules for using semicolons appears in the Quick Reference box on the next page.

Writing Responsibly — Sending a Signal with Semicolons

Writers who do not understand the role of the semicolon may use it to connect independent clauses randomly, and this can lead readers to see a connection between ideas that the writer did not intend or cannot explain. Consider this sentence: *Angelina is working in New York; Jamal has a headache.* The semicolon here suggests that there is a logical relationship between the two clauses, that one is the cause or effect of the other, when in fact the two may reflect mere coincidence. Avoid conveying more than you meant; use the semicolon with care.

to TOPIC

49a Using a Semicolon to Link Independent Clauses

When two ***independent clauses*** are closely related and parallel, a semicolon emphasizes their relationship.

> independent clause 1
> Adjusting to life in a new country does not come easily;
> independent clause 2
> I learned that firsthand.

independent (or main) clause
A word group that contains a subject and a main verb and that does not begin with a subordinating conjunction, relative pronoun, or relative adverb

820

Detail Matters • Using a Semicolon to Link Independent Clauses **; 49a** **821**

> **Reference** Common Semicolon Do's and Don'ts
>
> ***Do* use a semicolon . . .**
>
> **. . . to link two closely related independent clauses when the second clause specifies the consequence of the first, restates its meaning, or introduces a contrast. (820)**
>
> ▶ In 1911, Italian nationalist Vincenzo Peruggia stole the *Mona Lisa* from the Louvre in France; he believed fervently that da Vinci's painting should be displayed in Italy.
>
> **. . . when a conjunctive adverb or transitional phrase links them. (822)**
>
> ▶ Peruggia was arrested while trying to sell the painting to a Florence art gallery; however, his mission was not entirely in vain.
>
> **. . . to distinguish items in a series with internal commas. (823)**
>
> ▶ Before arresting Peruggia, authorities questioned Guillaume Apollinaire, a French poet; Pablo Picasso, a Spanish painter and founder of cubism; and various Louvre employees.
>
> **. . . to repair a comma splice. (823)**
>
> ▶ Before the *Mona Lisa* was restored to Paris, it was exhibited in museums across Italy; as a result, Peruggia was hailed as a national hero and served only a brief prison term.
>
> ***Do not* use a semicolon . . .**
>
> **. . . to link an independent clause to anything except another, related independent clause. (822)**
>
> ▶ During his trial, [independent clause] Peruggia leapt to his feet; [phrase] raging at the prosecutor, the judge, and even his own lawyer.
>
> ▶ [independent clause] Peruggia claimed he was motivated only by patriotism; [subordinate clause] even though he had demanded a "reward" of half a million lire.
>
> **. . . to introduce a list. (823)**
>
> ▶ Despite an outcry, the *Mona Lisa* was returned to France after visiting the following Italian cities; [list] Naples, Rome, Florence, Venice, and Milan.

A semicolon replaces a comma and coordinating conjunction:

▶ Summer traffic to Jones Beach can be slow, [coordinating conjunction] so you might want to take the train instead.

▶ Summer traffic to Jones Beach can be slow; [no coordinating conjunction] you might want to take the train instead.

> **More about**
> Parallelism (ch. 28), 578–85
> Commas (ch. 48), 802–19
> End punctuation (ch. 52), 843–46
> Dashes, 847–49
> Colons, 852–54
> Coordinating conjunctions (list), 804

A semicolon is often used when the second clause emphasizes the consequences of the first, restates the first, or offers a contrast with the first:

▶ [clause 1: My mother's taste is always changing]**;** [clause 2: emphasizes consequences: just when I think I know what she likes, she proves me wrong.]

▶ [clause 1: When the French arrived, this area was very different from what it has become]**;** [clause 2: restates clause 1: Detroit was once a deep forest.]

▶ [clause 1: People think of Franklin Delano Roosevelt as the architect of the New Deal]**;** [clause 2: contrasts clause 1: he actually designed buildings, too.]

Do not use a semicolon to link a phrase or a subordinate clause to an independent clause; instead, use a comma.

▶ [clause: That Marvel film proved successful]~~;~~**,** [phrase: grossing $22 million in the first night].

49b Using a Semicolon before a Conjunctive Adverb or Transitional Phrase Linking Two Independent Clauses

> **More about**
> Conjunctive adverbs (list), 641
> Transitional words and phrases (list), 61

When a conjunctive adverb (such as *therefore, however,* and *furthermore*) or a transitional phrase such as *on the other hand* or *for example* comes between two independent clauses, precede it with a semicolon (and follow it with a comma).

▶ *Get Out* and *Us* introduced the world to the genius of Jordan Peele**;** [conjunctive adverb: moreover]**,** they were entertaining films.

When the conjunctive adverb or transitional phrase is placed within one of the independent clauses rather than between them, retain the semicolon between the clauses and insert a comma before and after the conjunctive adverb or transitional phrase:

▶ Film is a popular form of entertainment**;** it can be**,** [transitional phrase: in addition]**,** a means of exploring literature's classic themes in contemporary contexts.

49c Using a Semicolon to Mark a Series with Internal Commas

Ordinarily, commas are used to mark items in a series:

▶ You can create an off-grid home by [building with straw bales]{item 1}, [using solar power]{item 2}, and [generating additional energy with windmills on the property]{item 3}.

However, when the items are especially long or complex or when an item in the series has internal punctuation, use semicolons.

▶ The architectural firm of Hanover, Harvey, and Witkins recommends creating an off-grid home by [building with straw bales]{item 1}; [packing them tightly, which makes them flame-resistant]{item 2}; [utilizing solar power]{item 3}; and [generating additional energy through windmills on the property]{item 4}.

Do not use a semicolon to introduce a list; instead, use a colon.

▶ I used the following in my "green" home~~;~~: straw bales, solar panels, and water-conserving fixtures.

49d Repairing a Comma Splice

One way to repair a *comma splice* is to replace the comma between the two independent clauses with a semicolon.

> **comma splice** Two independent clauses joined by a comma alone

▶ Reporters Without Borders fights restrictions placed on journalists~~,~~; the group also raises awareness about this increasingly important issue.

Sometimes a comma splice occurs because a comma is placed before a conjunctive adverb or transitional phrase that links two independent clauses. To correct it, replace the comma with a semicolon:

▶ Most people don't think of babies as prospective employees~~,~~; however, in Hollywood infants can become working actors at fifteen days old.

49e Avoiding Overuse

> **More about**
> Sentence variety, 586–91

complex sentence
One or more subordinate clauses linked to an independent clause

Use semicolons sparingly to avoid suggesting that everything in the passage is of equal importance. Overusing semicolons can also be a sign that you need to vary your sentence structures. You can turn some independent clauses into phrases or create *complex sentences* by turning some of your independent clauses into subordinate clauses.

DRAFT

According to *The Los Angeles Times*, [independent clause 1: the earliest known gunshot victim in the Americas died in 1536]; [independent clause 2: archaeological exploration in Peru has uncovered a pierced skull.] [independent clause 3: The Inca warrior was shot by Spanish conquistadors.] [independent clause 4: Historical records verify that a battle took place at the location in which the skull was found]; [independent clause 5: the battle is now known as the "siege of Lima."] [independent clause 6: As many as seventy-two victims' remains have been found]; [independent clause 7: most were not shot]; [independent clause 8: most were bludgeoned to death.]

REVISION

According to *The Los Angeles Times*, the earliest known gunshot victim in the Americas died in 1536. Archaeological exploration in Peru has uncovered the pierced skull of an Inca warrior [subordinate clause: who was shot by Spanish conquistadors]. Historical records verify that the skull was found at the site [phrase: of a battle now known as the "siege of Lima."] As many as seventy-two victims' remains have been found. Most were not shot but were instead bludgeoned [phrase: to death].

- Combines independent clauses 2 and 3; clause 3 becomes a subordinate clause introduced by the relative pronoun *who*.
- Combines independent clauses 4 and 5; clause 5 becomes a phrase.
- Combines independent clauses 7 and 8; clause 8 becomes a phrase.

EXERCISE 49.1 Correcting the use of semicolons

Add or delete semicolons or replace them with a different punctuation mark to correct or improve the sentences below. (Some sentences may be correct.)

EXAMPLE

About sixty-five percent of Americans say the government is not doing enough to deal with climate change*;* an even greater percentage say we should be funding and creating more alternative energy sources.

1. Wide-scale tree planting is one way to absorb carbon emissions; and this solution is favorable to ninety percent of Americans calling for the planting of one trillion trees.
2. Most Americans want tougher restrictions on power plant emissions, moreover, according to a recent survey, they want higher taxes placed on corporations and greater fuel efficiency for vehicles.
3. About sixty-three percent of Americans surveyed identified climate change as having a great impact on their communities apparently, Midwesterners reported this effect at a lower rate than did people in the Northeast, South, and West.
4. The study shows that in regard to alternative energies, Americans want to see more solar panel farms and more wind turbine farms such as those in their communities however they do not approve of expanding nuclear power, fracking, and offshore drilling.
5. Researchers noted that conservative Republicans' drive to expand offshore drilling, fracking, and coal mining gives them a specific disadvantage when it comes to millennial and Gen Z voters; something that will likely affect the future of the party.

EXERCISE 49.2 Using semicolons correctly

Add or delete semicolons or replace them with a different punctuation mark to correct or improve the paragraph below.

EXAMPLE

Many elderly people worry that they may lose certain mental abilities, such as memory*;* recently, researchers have uncovered some potentially useful methods of maintaining mental sharpness.

In general, the idea is for the aging to get plenty of mental and physical stimulation just as physical exercise strengthens muscles, mental exercise strengthens the brain. The brain needs novelty; new challenges; and continued stresses to maintain or increase its strength, this type of stimulation creates new nerve cells and connections between them. It is common for some cells of an elderly person's brain to deteriorate, however; the newly developed brain tissue may compensate for the lost brain cells. So those who knit should try ever more complicated patterns, those who like listening to opera should try to learn the libretto, and those who like crossword puzzles should try new kinds of puzzles; such as Sudoku and double crostics. Also important for keeping mentally sharp is to pursue stimulating activities with other people, these can include taking classes; playing bridge; or participating in a reading group.

Make It **Your Own**

Review your use of semicolons in a recent writing project of two or more pages. Add semicolons where needed and cross through unnecessary ones. Then analyze the impact these changes would have on your reader. (Refer to the sections in this chapter as needed.)

Work **Together**

Exchange Exercise 49.2 with a partner. Check your classmate's use of semicolons. Do you see any errors? If so, refer to sections in this chapter to help you explain the effect these errors had on you as a reader. (Be specific.)

50 Using Apostrophes

IN THIS CHAPTER

a. Using apostrophes to indicate possession, 827

b. Using apostrophes in contractions, abbreviated years, 831

c. Moving away from using apostrophes with plurals of abbreviations, dates, numbers, and words or letters as words, 831

Apostrophes replace missing letters in contractions (*can't, ma'am*). Apostrophes also make nouns and indefinite pronouns possessive (*Edward's* or *somebody's horse*). Centuries ago, English speakers indicated possession with a pronoun (*Edward his horse*), so, in fact, today's possessive form (*Edward's horse*) is also an age-old contraction. A list of the most important rules for using apostrophes appears in the Quick Reference box on the next page.

50a Using Apostrophes to Indicate Possession

In English, you can indicate possession (ownership) in nouns and indefinite pronouns by using the preposition *of*:

▶ Many admired the commitment of the volunteers. But the involvement of everybody is needed to make real progress.

Writing Responsibly — Contractions in Formal Writing

Contractions and other abbreviations provide useful shortcuts in speech and informal writing, and they are finding their way into more formal academic and business writing. They are still not fully accepted, however. To determine whether contractions will be acceptable to your readers or will undermine your authoritative tone, check with your instructor, look for contractions in academic journals in your field, or consult reports or business letters written by other company employees. If you are in any doubt, spell out the words.

to SELF

827

Detail Matters • Using Apostrophes

> **Quick Reference** — **Common Apostrophe Do's and Don'ts**
>
> ***Do* use an apostrophe . . .**
>
> **. . . to indicate possession** (with singular and plural nouns and indefinite pronouns). **(827)**
>
> ▶ The book's cover promised "a thrilling read," but we were skeptical.
> ▶ Everyone's taste is different.
> ▶ Most of their houses' exteriors are beautifully designed.
> ▶ She borrowed Socrates' book, not Jess's.
>
> **. . . to form a contraction or abbreviate a year. (831)**
>
> ▶ Didn't you forget your anniversary last year?
> ▶ They graduated back in '09.
>
> ***Do not* use an apostrophe . . .**
>
> **. . . with possessive pronouns, especially *its*. (829)**
>
> ▶ Now that they've shared their playlist, I want to share our~~'~~s.
> ▶ Sadly, it~~'~~s sales are lagging.
>
> **. . . with plurals. (830)**
>
> ▶ I've got load~~'~~s of song~~'~~s in my brain just itching to get out.
>
> **. . . with dates, letters, and numbers. (831)**
>
> ▶ The members of her club were born in the 1990~~'~~s.
>
> **. . . with verbs ending in -s. (830)**
>
> ▶ My mom still hope~~'~~s to sell downloads to members of her book club.

You can also do so by adding an apostrophe, with or without an *-s*:

▶ Many admired the [students]' commitment. But [everybody]'s involvement is needed to make real progress.
  (noun) *(indefinite pronoun)*

1. With singular nouns and indefinite pronouns (but not personal pronouns)

Singular *nouns* and *indefinite pronouns* add an apostrophe and an *-s* to indicate possession. Singular nouns ending in *-s* require only an apostrophe.

▶ The factory's smokestacks belched black smoke, irritating everyone's lungs.
▶ The thesis' introduction was far too long.

---

noun A word that names ideas, things, qualities, actions, people, and places

indefinite pronouns Pronouns that do not refer to specific people or things, such as *all, anybody, either, everybody, few, many, either, no one, someone*

Detail Matters • Using Apostrophes to Indicate Possession

> **Tech** **Apostrophes and Spelling or Grammar Checkers**
>
> Be wary of apostrophe-related "errors" identified by your device's spelling or grammar checker. These programs usually do a good job of automatically inserting apostrophes in contractions such as *don't*, but too often they erroneously change *its* to *it's*, and they do not automatically insert apostrophes for possessive proper nouns such as *Matthew's*. Pay attention to the program's suggestions, but always double-check them for accuracy.

For most singular proper nouns that already end in -s, add an -'s:

▸ Dolores(s) asthma was particularly aggravated.

Add an apostrophe alone to a singular proper noun only when adding an -'s would make the word difficult to pronounce:

▸ Socrates(') pneumonia became so serious he had to be hospitalized.

Personal pronouns are *never* made possessive by adding an apostrophe. Be sure to use the possessive form, *not* a contraction.

▸ We regret that ~~you're~~ (your) new power plant will have to close, but ~~they're~~ (their) health is more important.

> **personal pronouns**
> Pronouns that replace specific nouns or noun phrases, such as *I, me, he, him, she, her, it, we, us, you, they, them*

Be especially careful with *its*:

- *It's* (*it is*) is a contraction like *don't* (*do not*) and *can't* (*cannot*).
- *Its* is a **possessive pronoun** like *his* and *hers*.

If you tend to confuse *it's* and *its,* remember that the contraction *always* takes an apostrophe, but the personal pronoun *never* does:

▸ Buca di Beppo is celebrated for [its] (possessive pronoun) lasagna, so [it's] (contraction) a good idea to call ahead for reservations.

> **possessive pronouns**
> Pronouns that indicate ownership, such as *my, his, yours, mine,* and *theirs*

2. With plural nouns

To make plural nouns possessive, first form the plural and then the possessive. When the plural form ends in -s, just add an apostrophe; when it does not end in -s, add an apostrophe and -s.

Singular	Plural	Possessive
lady	ladies	ladies'
person	people	people's

- By midnight, the ladies' maids were exhausted.
- I'm often amazed by people's consideration for the well-being of others.

This rule applies to family names that end in *-s,* too: Make the name plural and then possessive.

- The ~~William's~~ *Williamses'* parties always ended at dawn.

NOTE Just because a word ends with an *-s* does not mean that it needs an apostrophe. Delete apostrophes from plural nouns and singular verbs:

- Your dog*'*s bark wildly, but my cat remain*'*s placid.
  [noun (plural)] [verb (singular)]

3. To indicate joint or individual ownership or possession

First, decide whether the apostrophe indicates *joint* or *individual ownership.* When the nouns share possession, make only the last noun possessive:

- Giorgione and Titian's painting *Portrait of a Venetian Gentleman* (c. 1510) is on view at the National Gallery of Art in Washington, DC.

  Giorgione and Titian painted the portrait collaboratively.

When the nouns each possess the same object, quality, or event, make each noun possessive:

- Giorgione's and Titian's paintings of Venus are important milestones in the art of the High Renaissance.

  Each produced paintings of Venus that are important milestones.

4. With compound nouns

While number (singular or plural) is usually attached to the core noun in a compound noun, the possessive is attached to the last noun:

- Jeremiah is driving his sisters-in-law crazy.
  [core noun (plural)]

  Jeremiah has more than one sister-in-law, and he is driving them all crazy. Attach number to the core noun, *sister.*

Detail Matters • Not to Form Plurals of Abbreviations, Letters, and More

▶ Jeremiah is driving his [sister-in-law]'s car.
   core noun (singular) — sister-in-law; *last noun* — law

   Jeremiah is using the car belonging to his sister-in-law; attach possession to the last noun, *law*.

▶ Jeremiah has his [sisters-in-law]'s unwavering support.
   core noun (plural) — sisters; *last noun* — law

   Jeremiah has more than one sister-in-law, and he has their unwavering support; attach the plural to the core noun (*sisters*) and possession to the last noun (*law's*).

50b Using Apostrophes in Contractions and Abbreviated Years

An apostrophe can stand in place of missing letters or numbers in a contraction or in an abbreviated year.

- I am — I'm
- He is, she is — He's, she's
- It is/has — It's
- They are — They're
- You are — You're
- Cannot — Can't
- Could not — Couldn't
- Would not — Wouldn't
- Let us — Let's
- Who is — Who's
- 2020 — '20

50c Moving Away from Using Apostrophes to Form Plurals of Abbreviations, Dates, Numbers, and Words or Letters Used as Words

Only a few years ago, -'s was a common way of creating the plural for abbreviations, dates, and words or characters used as words. These practices are now in flux, but using apostrophes for this purpose has generally fallen out of favor. Unless the style guide you use instructs otherwise, do not use apostrophes to form these plurals.

▶ My brother has stayed in more YMCA's than anyone else I know.

▶ Van Gogh's paintings were first exhibited in the late 1880's.

▶ Now he minds the *p*'s and *q*'s of students in composition classes.

▶ His students give him 5's on his evaluations.

50c Detail Matters • Using Apostrophes

NOTE The Modern Language Association (MLA) still recommends the use of an apostrophe with the plurals of letters and letter grades:

> Now he minds the *p*'s and *q*'s of students in composition classes.
> He got two B's and three C's.

Use an apostrophe to form a plural letter if its absence might cause confusion.

CONFUSING	You've dotted your *t*s and crossed your is.	*may be misread as* is
CLEAR	You've dotted your *t*'s and crossed your *i*'s.	

➔ EXERCISE 50.1 Correcting apostrophes

Supply or delete apostrophes as appropriate. You might have to add or delete letters to spell the word correctly. (Some sentences may be correct.)

EXAMPLE

The tenors' voice crack's whenever he thinks about PhD's in musicology assessing his performance.

1. It was one of his biggest crowd's since his heyday in the early 2000's.
2. Many of the audience member's were fans who gave the performance 10's.
3. The auditorium resounded with they're *bravo*'s and *more*'s.
4. Personally, I think singer's who can't hit the high notes should issue IOU's with each performance.
5. This singer's high C's are always flat, and he deserve's boos for how he manage's the tempo of his concerts.
6. My two sisters and brothers-in-laws applause was among the most enthusiastic of the entire audience.
7. At our' dinner after the concert, my sister's were in agreement over their appreciation of the tenor, and Suzie's and Amber's praise for the tenor was fervent and wholehearted.
8. I didn't want to hurt Suzies and Ambers feelings, so I kept my criticisms about the tenor to myself ' during dinner.

9. On the way to our's car I tugged my husband Yusefs arm and I told him how shocked I was at my sisters's not noticing the tenor's lack of professionalism.
10. Yusef smiled and said, "Your wise to let you're sisters' savor the performance, but I think you should be honest but tactful at next weeks concert when we sit in the Jones' special box at the opera house."

EXERCISE 50.2 Using apostrophes correctly

In the following paragraph, add or delete apostrophes as necessary. You might have to add or delete letters to spell the word correctly.

One of Adam Smiths contributions to modern economic's is the distinction between use value and exchange value. Writing in the 1700's, Smith defined *use value* as the ability to satisfy peoples wants. In Smiths analysis, *exchange value* is the amount of good's or service's that people are willing to pay for something. His economics can help us understand our's. Smiths pointing out the difference between use value and exchange value can help contemporary economist's understand that value doesnt just derive from price. Jeremy Reiss essay clearly reflects this understanding.

Make It Your Own

Review your use of apostrophes in a recent writing project of two or more pages. Add apostrophes where needed and cross through unnecessary ones. Then analyze the impact these changes would have on your reader. (Refer to the sections in this chapter as needed.)

Work Together

Exchange Exercise 50.2 with a partner. Check your classmate's use of apostrophes. Do you see any errors? If so, refer to sections in this chapter to help you explain the effect these errors had on you as a reader. (Be specific.)

51 Using Quotation Marks

IN THIS CHAPTER

a. Setting off direct quotations, 834
b. Indicating titles of short works, 837
c. Indicating words used in a special sense, 837
d. Misusing quotation marks, 838
e. Punctuating quotations, 839
f. Altering quotations: ellipses and brackets, 840
g. Introducing and identifying quotations, 840

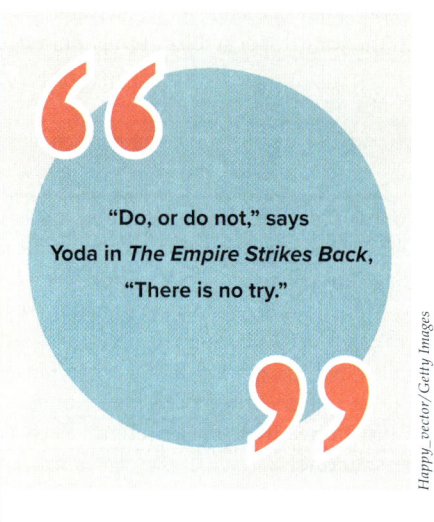

> "Do, or do not," says Yoda in *The Empire Strikes Back*, "There is no try."

Indicating who said what is an important use of quotation marks. When we fail to indicate that words were spoken or written by others—whether accidentally or on purpose—we open ourselves up to charges of plagiarism. Misusing quotation marks can also confuse or annoy your readers. Learning when to use—and when *not* to use—quotation marks is an important part of a writer's responsibilities. A list of the most important rules for using quotation marks appears in the Quick Reference box on the next page.

51a Setting Off Direct Quotations

Double quotation marks (" ") indicate the beginning and end of direct quotations (someone's exact words, whether written or spoken):

> ▸ Of grappling with the unknown, Albert Einstein wrote this: "The most beautiful thing we can experience is the mysterious. It is the source of all true art and all science."

Single quotation marks (' ') indicate quotations within quotations:

> ▸ Barbara Jordan, the first Black woman to represent a Southern state in Congress, felt that when the Constitution was written she "was not included in that 'We, the people.'"

Quick Reference: Common Quotation Mark Do's and Don'ts

Do use quotation marks . . .

. . . to set off direct quotations. 834

▶ Eisenhower once said that any person "who wants to be president is either an egomaniac or crazy."

. . . to indicate irony (use sparingly). 838

▶ After an unsuccessful stint as president of Columbia University, Eisenhower let himself be "persuaded" to run for the US presidency.

. . . to refer to words as words. 837

▶ "Popular" is an adjective often attached to Eisenhower's presidency.

(Italics are also widely used for this purpose.)

Do *not* use quotation marks . . .

. . . to set off indirect quotations (paraphrases). 836

▶ Eisenhower once said that ~~"~~lunatics or narcissists are the only people who would desire the presidency.~~"~~

. . . for emphasis. 838

▶ Eisenhower was a five-star general and ~~"~~Supreme~~"~~ Commander of Allied forces in Europe during World War II.

. . . with slang or clichés. 838

▶ ~~"~~Snafus~~"~~ occur regularly in the army, but Eisenhower generally avoided them through careful planning.

In formal contexts, consider recasting to avoid slang. Clichés are rarely appropriate; rewrite to avoid them.

Quotation Marks in American English Use of quotation marks varies from place to place and culture to culture. In contemporary American English, double quotation marks signal a quotation, and single quotation marks signal a quotation within a quotation:

▶ Janelle complained, "For the third time this month, Mary said, 'I need a few bucks to tide me over till payday.' And it's only June 15!"

British usage is the opposite:

▶ Janelle complained, 'For the third time this month, Mary said, "I need a few bucks to tide me over till payday." And it's only June 15!'

Writing Responsibly: Using Quotations Fairly

You have a responsibility to your reader and other writers to supply quotation marks whenever you borrow language from a source. Omitting quotation marks when needed can undermine your reputation as a writer to be trusted.

to OTHER WRITERS

More about
Plagiarism, 279–301
Patchwriting, 292–94

Indirect quotations, which paraphrase someone's words, do *not* use quotation marks:

- Albert Einstein said that "the unknown inspires scientists as well as artists."
- Barbara Jordan felt that "she was excluded by the founding fathers when they drafted the US Constitution."

1. In dialog

When quoting dialog, start a new paragraph each time the speaker changes, and put all spoken words in quotation marks:

- "Have you brought women here before?" He smiled and kept chewing, so I said, "Do you always use the same tricks?"
- "What tricks?" He looked at me like he didn't understand.

—Leslie Marmon Silko, "Yellow Woman"

If one speaker continues for more than a paragraph, use quotation marks at the beginning of each paragraph, but omit closing quotation marks until the end of the speech.

2. With long quotations

> Generally, introduce block quotations with a complete sentence plus a colon.

For lengthy quotations, omit quotation marks, and indent quotations in a block from the left margin:

- Lucio Guerrero examines how local Goths feel about their lifestyle's mass-market appeal:

> In block quotations, use double quotation marks for quotations within a quotation.

> For some, that suburbanization of Goth may be what saves the sub-culture. "If someone who identifies as Goth doesn't have easy access to the fashion or accouterments that they feel drawn to, but they do have access to a store like Hot Topic, then it's a positive thing," said Scary Lady Sarah, a local DJ and supporter of Chicago's Goth community.
>
> —Lucio Guerrero, "Like a GOTH," *Chicago Sun-Times*

> **More about**
> Formatting block quotations, 339, 346, 380–81 (MLA style), 426 (APA style)

3. With quotations from poetry

When quoting one to three lines of poetry, use quotation marks and run the lines into your text. Indicate the end of each line by inserting a slash, with a space on each side:

- Shelley sets the tone right away. The violence in lines 3–4 ("Millions to fight compell'd, to fight or die / In mangled heaps on War's red altar lie") is a clear criticism of the ruling class into which he was born.

> **Student Model**
> "My View on a Long-Lost but Timeless Poem: Shelley's 'Poetical Essay on the Existing State of Things,'" 488, 503–5

When quoting four or more lines, omit quotation marks, set the poetry as a block, and retain the original line breaks:

- Shakespeare's "Sonnet 147" begins with evocative imagery:

  > My love is as a fever, longing still
  > For that which longer nurseth the disease,
  > Feeding on that which doth preserve the ill,
  > Th' uncertain sickly appetite to please. (lines 1–4)

51b Indicating Titles of Short Works

Most American style guides suggest placing titles of short works in quotation marks and titles of long works in italics:

> **More about**
> Italicizing titles of longer works, 865–66

- Lahiri's short story "Year's End" appeared in the collection *Unaccustomed Earth*.
- "Front Lines," a poem by Gary Snyder, is from his book *No Nature*.
- Ben Brantley's review of *Romeo and Juliet*, "Rash and Unadvis'd Seeks Same," ran in *The New York Times*.
- *Outlander* is my guilty pleasure; "The Wedding" is my favorite episode.
- The podcast "Of Two Minds, One Consciousness" from the *Scientific American* website uses results from split-brain studies to explore thought.
- "Good for You," from Selena Gomez's album *Revival*, reached the top of the *Billboard* charts.

> **More about**
> Citing and documenting sources (MLA style, ch. 18), 334–96 (APA style, ch. 19), 397–438 (*Chicago* style, ch. 20), 439–69 (CSE style, ch. 21), 470–84

In APA, CSE, and *The Chicago Manual of Style* parenthetical style, omit quotation marks from the titles of short works in bibliographic entries.

51c Indicating Words Used in a Special Sense

Quotation marks can call attention to words used in a special sense. When talking *about* a word, enclose it in quotation marks to avoid confusion:

- Many people confuse "lay" and "lie."

Italics can also be used for this purpose.

To signal that you are using a word ironically or sarcastically, place it in quotation marks:

▶ I didn't know that the Indian "problem" on the plains began in the 1860s. . . .

—James Welch, *Killing Custer*

Use quotation marks sparingly for indicating irony. Overuse can annoy readers. Your words should usually be able to convey irony on their own.

Set a term to be defined in italics and the definition in quotation marks:

▶ Many writers don't realize that *e.g.* stands for "for example" in Latin.

51d Misusing Quotation Marks

It is important to use quotation marks where needed; it is also important to omit them where they are not needed.

> *More about*
> Using italics for emphasis, 867

1. Not for emphasis

▶ Beyoncé's debut album was "amazing," hitting no. 1 on *Billboard* in its first week.

Let your words and the rhythms of your sentences create emphasis. On the rare occasion when something more is needed, use *italics,* not quotation marks.

2. Not with slang

If slang is acceptable in the context, use it without the apology that quotation marks represent; if it is not (as in business or academic writing), choose a more appropriate word or phrase:

▶ "Writing's on the Wall" won the Academy Award for best original song, "~~beating out~~ besting" several strong contenders.

Detail Matters • Punctuating Quotations   51e   839

3. *Not* with clichés

Clichés are rarely appropriate; instead of attempting to justify them with quotation marks, revise the sentence to avoid them altogether:

▶ I left the party before ~~the "sun was over the yardarm."~~ *drinks were served.*

51e Punctuating Quotations

Whether punctuation appears before or after the closing quotation mark depends on the punctuation mark.

1. With periods and commas

In American English, commas and periods go *inside* the closing quotation mark, except when a citation follows the quotation:

▶ "Sacred cows," said the sixties radical Abbie Hoffman, "make the tastiest hamburger."

▶ According to sixties radical Abbie Hoffman, "sacred cows make the tastiest hamburger" (qtd. in Albert 43).

Commas and Periods with Quotation Marks In Britain, as well as in many other countries that use the roman alphabet, commas and periods follow the closing quotation mark. Since American punctuation rules require that commas and periods come before the closing quotation mark, be sure to adjust your usage to meet US readers' expectations.

2. With question marks, exclamation points, and dashes

Question marks, exclamation points, and dashes go *inside* the closing quotation mark when they are part of the quotation:

▶ In Megan Mayhew Bergman's short story "The Seige at Whale Cay," Marlene asks, "You like girls with guns, don't you, Joe?"

They go *outside* the closing quotation mark when they are not:

▶ Why does Robert Duvall's character in *Apocalypse Now* say "I love the smell of napalm in the morning"? He explains that "it smells like victory"!

> **More about**
> Periods, 843–44
> Commas (ch. 48), 802–19
> Question marks, 844–45
> Exclamation points, 845
> Dashes, 847–49

> **More about**
> Citing indirect sources, 300–1, 347–48 (MLA), 406 (APA)

3. With colons and semicolons

Colons and semicolons go outside the closing quotation mark:

- "I was not going to ask for mercy"; so wrote Cheryl Strayed in *Wild*.

- "Lions and tigers and bears": These are the only problems Dorothy doesn't encounter on her yellow-brick road to self-knowledge.

51f Altering Quotations with Ellipses and Square Brackets

> **Original passage from Gary Snyder interview:** "Sometimes driven behind the origin is the rhythm, and the rhythm, as it comes out, causes the rest of the poem to follow. Rhythm is, in a very real sense, primary."

To fit a quotation into your own sentence, you may alter the wording (but not the meaning) by adding, changing, or deleting words. You have a responsibility, though, to alert your readers to your changes: Enclose additions or changes in brackets, and replace deleted words with ellipses:

- In an interview, the poet Gary Snyder explained that "[s]ometimes driven behind the origin is the rhythm. . . . Rhythm is, in a very real sense, primary." *(changed letter in brackets; deletion marked by ellipses)*

> **More about** Altering quotations fairly, 851, 854

Remember, too, it is unethical to distort the meaning of the original text by altering a quotation or taking a quotation out of context.

NOTE In MLA style, if you must change a capital to a lowercase letter (or vice versa), place brackets around the letter to alert readers to the change.

51g Introducing and Identifying Quotations

> **More about** Clauses, 654–56

Use a colon to introduce a quotation if the clause preceding the quotation could stand on its own as a sentence and could make sense without the quotation:

- Darwin's own words clarify the issue: "It is not the strongest of the species that survive . . . but the ones most responsive to change."

> **More about** Using signal phrases, 314, 315, 335–36, 399–400

Use a comma with signal phrases such as "Darwin said" or "she wrote":

- Charles Darwin said, "It is not the strongest of the species that survive . . . but the ones most responsive to change." *(signal phrase)*

Use no punctuation if the quotation is needed to complete the sentence (as when the word *that* precedes it), and do not capitalize the first word in the quotation:

▶ Darwin asserts [that] "[i]t is not the strongest of species that survive . . . but the ones most responsive to change."

If a signal phrase interrupts the quotation, insert a comma before the closing quotation mark and after the signal phrase:

signal phrase

▶ "It is not the strongest of species that survive(,)" [Darwin asserts](,) ". . . but the ones most responsive to change."

EXERCISE 51.1 Correcting problems with quotation marks and other punctuation

Edit the sentences below as needed to correct problems with quotation marks and other punctuation.

EXAMPLE

Ashley said that "~~Our~~ ^{our} research would go a lot faster if we did it ~~together"~~^{together,"} and I said ^{,"Why not?"} ~~why not.~~

1. On our way to the library, I said You're right. Some sources may not be available online.

2. In fact, didn't Professor Iron Cloud say "It may be useful to ask a research librarian about your topic?" asked Ashley. And that's something that's best to do in person.

3. "Yes," I said, but that depends on whether the library is staffed at this hour; "I pointed to the clock above the front desk."

4. Opening a copy of *The New York Post* to an article titled Resisting the Rush to a World of No Cash, I said that "wouldn't this be a good place to start"?

5. Ashley smiled and said What you call "a good place to start" is not what I would call an authoritative source.

6. In any case, she added, "I haven't been able to find a particular Michael Chabon story online, and said she wanted to find the print magazine in which it originally appeared."

7. "Okay, you do that," I said, because I needed to look through the "Oxford English Dictionary" for the derivation of the word turncoat.

8. Then I noted that "in our paper, I'd like to go beyond the standard definition of turncoat: One who traitorously switches allegiance".

9. Kiddada asked Can you work in the quote from the *Godfather* trilogy, "Keep your friends close, but your enemies closer?"

Make It **Your Own**

Review your use of quotation marks in a recent writing project of two or more pages. Add quotation marks where needed and cross through unnecessary ones. Then analyze the impact these changes would have on your reader. (Refer to the sections in this chapter as needed.)

Work **Together**

Exchange Exercise 51.1 with a partner. Check your classmate's use of quotation marks. Do you see any errors? If so, refer to sections in this chapter to help you explain the effect these errors had on you as a reader. (Be specific.)

Text Credits

Pg. 836: Silko, Leslie Marmon, "Yellow Woman" from *Storyteller*, copyright © 1981 by Leslie Marmon Silko (New York: Seaver Books, 1981). **Pg. 836:** Guerrero, Lucio, "Like a GOTH," *The Chicago Sun-Times*, September 16, 2005. **Pg. 837:** Percy Bysshe Shelley, *Poetical Essay on the Existing State of Things* (1811). **Pg. 837:** William Shakespeare, "Sonnet 147: My Love Is as a Fever Longing Still." **Pg. 838:** Welch, James, with Paul Stekler, *Killing Custer: The Battle of Little Bighorn and the Fate of the Plains Indians*, copyright © 1994 by James Welch and Paul Stekler (New York: W. W. Norton, 1994). **Pg. 839:** Hoffman, Abbie, quoted in *The New York Times*, April 20, 1989. **Pg. 839:** Bergman, Megan Mayhew, "The Seige at Whale Cay," *The Kenyon Review* Fall 2014, Volume XXXVI, Number 4. **Pg. 840:** Strayed, Cheryl, *Wild: From Lost to Found on the Pacific Crest Trail* (New York: Alfred A. Knopf, 2013). **Pg. 840:** My View from the Sidelines: Gary Snyder's 'Front Lines'. **Pg. 840, 841:** Darwin, Charles, *On the Origin of the Species* (London: John Murray, 1859).

52 Using End Punctuation
Periods, Question Marks, and Exclamation Points

IN THIS CHAPTER

a. Using periods, 843

b. Using question marks, 844

c. Using exclamation points, 845

Luliia Kanivets/Getty Images

In face-to-face encounters, sight and sound play a huge role in how we interpret tone and meaning, but in a written text, we depend on words and punctuation—especially the punctuation ending the sentence—to signal mood. Think of the question mark as a raised eyebrow, the exclamation point as wide eyes and an open mouth, and the period as the neutral expression we usually wear.

52a Using Periods to End Statements and Mild Commands

Periods mark the end of most sentences, including statements (or *declarative sentences*), *indirect* (or reported) *questions,* and mild commands:

843

! Detail Matters • Using End Punctuation

STATEMENT	Our library has survived a flood and two fires.
MILD COMMAND/ INSTRUCTION	Please urge the council to situate the new library building on higher ground.
INDIRECT QUESTION	She wondered whether the water had ever risen so fast before.

> **More about**
> Using periods with abbreviations, 869

Periods are also used with some, but not all, abbreviations.

52b Using Question Marks to End Direct (Not Indirect) Questions

Most writers do not need a handbook to tell them to use a question mark to end a *direct question:*

- When did Uzbekistan declare its independence?
- Did you know that the median age in Uzbekistan is only 27.8 years?

Use a period, not a question mark, to punctuate *indirect* questions, that is, questions that are reported, not asked directly:

- Dr. Wilson asked why the median age in Uzbekistan is so low.

Use a period, not a question mark, in requests phrased as questions:

- Would you please find out the life expectancy in Uzbekistan.

Writing Responsibly / Question Marks and Exclamation Points

In an email to a friend, you might use a series of question marks or exclamation points to convey surprise or lend emphasis:

- Isn't it about time Jason got rid of the soul patch???!

But such techniques are not appropriate in more formal contexts, such as an email to an instructor:

- I look forward to studying American history with you next term.!!!!

Overusing exclamation points or other punctuation may undermine your credibility with readers. Your responsibility to yourself as an authoritative writer is to use restraint.

to SELF

A question mark in parentheses can also suggest doubt about a date, number, or word.

- Life expectancy at birth in Uzbekistan is 71.73 (?).

You may also punctuate a series of questions with question marks, even when they are part of the same sentence:

- Do you know what Uzbekistan's primary crop is? what language the majority speaks? what countries surround this landlocked nation?

> Note that capital letters are optional if each question is not a complete sentence.

52c Using Exclamation Points with Strong Commands or to Express Excitement or Surprise

When giving an emphatic command or expressing sudden excitement or surprise, use an exclamation point to end the sentence:

- Don't go there!
- "Mom is coming!"

The same sentence, when ended with a period, conveys much less urgency:

- Don't go there.
- "Mom is coming."

> **Tech — Using Exclamation Points in Email Messages**
>
> Because warmth can be difficult to convey in email, writers sometimes use an exclamation point to soften the tone. Compare:
>
> - We look forward to seeing you next week.
> - We look forward to seeing you next week!
>
> Use exclamation points sparingly; otherwise they lose their effectiveness.

EXERCISE 52.1 Editing end punctuation

Insert end punctuation—periods, question marks, and exclamation points—as needed. If multiple end punctuation is appropriate, explain why you chose the punctuation mark you did.

EXAMPLE

"Could you repeat the question?" That's the most common response law professor David Cole gets when he calls on disengaged students during class at Georgetown University.

The laptop—the favorite in-class tool for college and university students across the country—is coming unplugged When used responsibly—for taking notes or quickly accessing research—a laptop provides valuable educational

52c ! Detail Matters • Using End Punctuation

> support But when used irresponsibly—for watching YouTube, . . . playing games, checking sports scores, and shopping for shoes instead of engaging in class—laptops become the scourge of professors, some of whom are now banning them, especially in law schools
>
> . . . Herzog banned all laptops from his classes for a day, and was so "stunned by how much better the class was," that he has vowed to make the embargo permanent in the fall
>
> —Kathy McManus, "Class Action: Laptops Not Allowed,"
> *Responsibility Project*

Make It **Your Own**

Review your use of end punctuation in a recent writing project of two or more pages. Add end punctuation where needed and cross through unnecessary marks. Then analyze the impact these changes would have on your reader. (Refer to the sections in this chapter as needed.)

Work **Together**

Exchange Exercise 52.1 with a classmate. Check your partner's use of end punctuation. Do you see any errors? If so, refer to sections in this chapter to help you explain the effect these errors had on you as a reader. (Be specific.)

Text Credit

Pg. 846: Mcmanus, Kathy, "Class Action: Laptops Not Allowed." Responsibility Project by Liberty Mutual.

53 Using Other Punctuation
Dashes, Parentheses, Brackets, Colons, Ellipses, and Slashes

IN THIS CHAPTER
a. Using dashes, 847
b. Using parentheses, 849
c. Using brackets, 851
d. Using colons, 852
e. Using ellipses, 854
f. Using slashes, 856

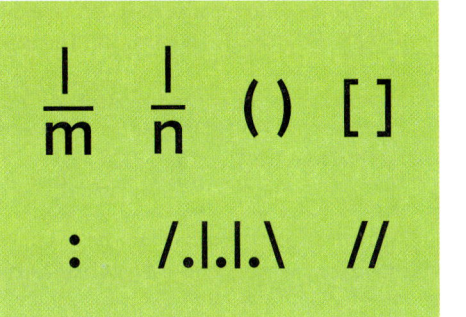

Writers thinking about punctuation typically focus on the comma, the semicolon, the period, and maybe the quotation mark—the punctuation used most commonly. But accurate use of dashes, parentheses, brackets, colons, ellipses, and slashes is also essential to writing that the audience can readily process and understand. The Quick Reference box on the next page summarizes how these punctuation marks are used.

53a Using Dashes

Em dashes There are two kinds of dashes. One is the em dash, which is approximately the same width as the capital letter "M." It can be used singly, when the information to be set off falls at the end of the sentence, or in pairs, when it falls in the middle. Dashes are used to lend emphasis and to mark examples, explanations, and appositives:

▸ In almost every era of Western culture, women's clothing has been decidedly restrictive and uncomfortable—and the garments of the nineteenth century are a prime example. *[example]*

▸ To be fashionable, women had to wear clothing that hampered their mobility—cumbersome petticoats and long dresses dragged in puddles and snagged on stairways, turning even a short walk into a navigational challenge. *[explanation]*

847

Quick Reference: What These Punctuation Marks Do

Em dashes lend emphasis and set off examples, explanations, appositives, contrasts, definitions, series items, interruptions, and shifts.

En dashes indicate the range between two things.

Parentheses set off information of lesser importance.

Brackets set off a writer's insertions in a quoted passage or replace parentheses within parentheses.

Colons link introductory independent clauses to examples, explanations, appositives; they introduce lists (when the introductory clause does *not* include the words *including, like,* or *such as*); and they introduce quotations (when the introductory clause can stand on its own and make sense without the quotation).

Ellipses indicate an omission or a delay for dramatic effect.

Slashes divide lines of poetry, fractions, and URLs. In formal writing, slashes are not used to separate alternatives (*and/or, he/she*) or parts of dates (*10/23/09*).

Tech: Typing Dashes

The built-in keyboards on many phones do not have a single key for dashes. To type en dashes and em dashes, do the following.

- On an iPhone, hold down the hyphen key. Three choices will appear: the hyphen, en dash, and em dash.
- On the Android or other smartphone, hold down the dash key. The same above choices will appear.

> **More about**
> Apostrophes
> (ch. 50), 827–33

▶ In the 1870s another torture device—the bustle—was introduced. *[appositive]*

Em dashes also emphasize contrasts, definitions, and items in a list:

▶ The bustle, which emphasized a woman's backside, was considered erotic in its day—but from a modern perspective, it is quite modest. *[contrast]*

▶ For both daytime and evening wear, women were strapped into corsets—close-fitting undergarments that laced tightly around the torso. *[definition]*

▶ The trappings of mid-nineteenth-century dress—six petticoats, a long hem, a bulky bustle, and a tight corset—guaranteed women's discomfort. *[list]*

Em dashes can also be used to indicate a break in thought, speech, or tone:

▸ Women's dress today ranges from the prim to the uninhibited—*break (in tone)* anything goes!

CAUTION If you use dashes more than once or twice over several pages, consider replacing one or more with commas: As with antibiotics, overuse of dashes undermines their effectiveness.

En dashes The second type of dash is the en dash, which is smaller than the em dash and approximately the same width as the capital letter "N." The en dash is used to represent the words "to" or "through," indicating the distance or range between things, such between dates or pages.

▸ During the Edwardian Era (1904–1911) *en dash represents "to" or "through"* corsets were designed to create a new type of silhouette and lessen the stress on the wearer's internal organs.

53b Using Parentheses

Use parentheses to set off supplementary information (such as examples, dates, abbreviations, or citations) to avoid distracting readers from the main point. Parentheses also enclose letters or numbers delineating items in a list.

▸ The English word for a trifling flaw or offense (*peccadillo*) *example* comes from the Spanish word for a small sin, but many other borrowings from Spanish (*barbecue, chocolate, hammock, potato, tomato*) *examples* actually originated in languages of the peoples whom the Spanish conquered in what is now the Caribbean, Mexico, and South America.

▸ In 1991, the Spanish government founded the Instituto Cervantes (IC), *abbrev.* named for Miguel de Cervantes (1547–1616), *dates* the author of *Don Quixote* (1605, 1615). *dates*

> Unless a complete sentence is enclosed, punctuation goes outside closing parenthesis.

Writing Responsibly: Em Dashes, Parentheses, or Commas?

Responsible writers remain alert to the tone their punctuation conveys. Compare these three versions of the same sentence and consider the effect the punctuation has on you as a reader:

- Zinc is reputed—despite many scientists' skepticism—to prevent and relieve colds.
- Zinc is reputed (despite many scientists' skepticism) to prevent and relieve colds.
- Zinc is reputed, despite many scientists' skepticism, to prevent and relieve colds.

Em dashes lend emphasis—sometimes even a touch of drama—to the material they enclose, while the parentheses downplay that material. The comma is the most neutral mark. Select the punctuation mark best suited to the effect you want your words to have on your readers.

to AUDIENCE

▸ The goals of the IC are (1) [*parentheses enclose numbers in a list*] to promote the study of Spanish worldwide, (2) [*list item 2*] to improve the methods of teaching Spanish as a second language, and (3) [*list item 3*] to advance understanding of Spanish and Latin American cultures.

▸ The proverb "Make hay while the sun shines" first appeared in *Don Quixote* (vol. 1, ch. 11). [*parentheses enclose an in-text citation*]

EXERCISE 53.1 Choosing between em dashes and parentheses

Edit the sentences below to add em dashes or parentheses as needed. If either is possible, explain why you chose one over the other.

EXAMPLE

Getting old does not necessarily mean getting frail — spending decades in pain, being stooped over, and having to use a walker — for many people are now in good mental and physical health well into their nineties.

I used dashes here to emphasize the description of "getting frail."

1. People over 85 constitute the fastest-growing segment of our population, and by 2050 researchers project that a substantial number of Americans 800,000 will be over 100 years old.
2. Many studies predicting the length of people's lives indicate that about 35 percent of the factors are determined by genes that we cannot control which leaves about 65 percent that we may be able to influence.
3. One particular long-term study it tracked elderly men for 25 years pointed out that the men who lived to at least age 90 were primarily the ones who did not smoke; prevented diabetes, obesity, and high blood pressure; and exercised regularly.
4. A key indicator for many of the "young-elderly" 70-year-olds is eating healthily limiting calories, saturated fat, and sugar as well as getting high-quality protein and whole grains with plenty of fiber.
5. In addition, several long-term studies have shown that exercise for both women and men is the strongest predictor of healthy longevity.

53c Using Brackets

> **More about**
> Altering quotations with ellipses and brackets, 840

Square brackets have two primary uses—to indicate additions or changes to a quotation and to replace parentheses within parentheses:

▸ Ramo and Burke explain that "[i]n 1456, when the first Bible rolled off [Gutenberg's] press, there were fewer than 30,000 books in Europe."

Capital replaced to fit quotation into writer's sentence.

▸ Only four years after Gutenberg printed his first book, the Spanish explorer Vincente Yanez Pinzón reached the mouth of the Amazon, which he called Río Santa María de la Mar Dulce ("River St. Mary of the Sweet [Freshwater] Sea").

Gutenberg's replaces his in source for clarity.

Freshwater added to explain an antiquated meaning of "sweet."

Square brackets are also used to enclose the Latin word *sic,* which means *thus* or *so*. It is inserted into a quotation following an error to make clear that it was the original writer, not the person using the quotation, who made the mistake:

▸ The most compelling review noted that "each of these blockbusters are [sic] flawed in a different, and interesting, way."

Writer uses [sic] to point out subject-verb agreement error (are should be is).

NOTE The Modern Language Association (MLA) and the Council of Science Editors (CSE) do not recommend underlining or italicizing *sic; The Chicago Manual of Style* and the American Psychological Association (APA), on the other hand, do recommend setting this Latin word in italics.

Writing Responsibly — Using [sic]

Use *[sic]* cautiously: Calling attention to an error simply to point out the writer's mistake can make you look condescending and undermine your reputation (or ethos). When you come across a simple error in a passage you want to quote (*teh* instead of *the*, for example), either paraphrase or simply correct the error.

to SELF

53d Using Colons

> **More about**
> Independent clauses, 654–56, 671–73

A colon is usually used after an independent (or main) clause to introduce and call attention to what follows. Colons are also used to separate titles from subtitles and in other conventional ways.

1. To introduce an example, an explanation, an appositive, or a list

Use a colon following an independent (or main) clause to introduce an example, an explanation, an appositive, or a list:

- [colon introduces examples] Cervantes was unlucky: At the battle of Lepanto, he lost the use of his left hand; on the return journey, he was captured by pirates.

- Writing *Don Quixote* gave its impoverished author something more than just satisfaction: [colon introduces appositive] the opportunity to make some money.

- A number of important writers died on April 23: [colon introduces list] Rupert Brooke, William Wordsworth, Miguel de Cervantes, and William Shakespeare.

A dash can substitute for a colon in these cases, but a colon is more appropriate in formal writing.

NOTE The MLA recommends beginning an independent clause following a colon with a lowercase letter unless the first word is usually capitalized or the colon introduces a series of sentences, a question, or a rule.

Colons are also used to introduce a list that is preceded by the phrases *as follows* or *the following*:

> **More about**
> Punctuating complicated lists, 823

- The following writers all died on April 23: [colon introduces list] Rupert Brooke, William Wordsworth, Miguel de Cervantes, and William Shakespeare.

Do not use a colon when the clause concludes with *like*, *such as*, or *including*:

> **More about**
> Using commas in quotations, 813–14

- A number of important writers all died on April 23, including: Rupert Brooke, William Wordsworth, Miguel de Cervantes, and William Shakespeare.

2. To introduce a quotation

Use a colon to introduce a quotation only when it is preceded by an independent clause that would make sense without it, but not when the quotation is introduced by a signal phrase such as *she said* or *Hughes asks*.

COLON
independent clause makes sense without quotation
In 1918, William Strunk Jr. gave writers a piece of timeless advice: "Omit needless words."

COMMA
signal phrase needs quotation to make sense
In 1918, William Strunk, Jr., said, "Omit needless words."

3. Other conventional uses

- Between title and subtitle and between publication date and page numbers (for periodicals) and location and publisher (for books) in bibliographic citations for some documentation styles:

  title *subtitle*
  DelRosso, Jeana. "De-tangling Motherhood: Adoption Narratives in Disney's *Tangled*." *The Journal of Popular Culture*.

  title *subtitle* *location* *publisher*
  Satrapi, Marjane. *Persepolis 2: The Story of a Return*. New York: Pantheon, 2004.

> **More about**
> MLA style (ch. 18), 334–96
> APA style (ch. 19), 397–438
> *Chicago* style (ch. 20), 439–69
> CSE style (ch. 21), 470–84

- Following the salutation and following *cc* in formal business correspondence:
  - Dear Professor Howard:
  - cc: Caroline Richardson

- Between chapter and verse in scripture; between hours, minutes, and seconds; in ratios:
  - Song of Solomon 3:1–11
  - 4:30 p.m.
  - Women outnumber men in college 2:1.

> **More about**
> Business letter formats, 537–42

4. Common mistakes with colons

- Do not insert a colon between a verb and its complement or object.

  verb *object*
  - Young readers awaited: the next volume in Stephenie Meyer's vampire love saga.

- Do not insert a colon between a preposition and its object.

  ▶ *Vogue* announced a return to: hippie-style clothing.
  (preposition: to; object: hippie-style clothing)

> **EXERCISE 53.2 Using colons in a sentence**
>
> Write two sentences using colons, one to introduce an example or explanation and the other to introduce an appositive, list, or quotation. (See the section above for examples.)

53e Using Ellipses

Ellipses are sets of three periods, or *ellipsis points,* with a space between each. They are most often used to replace words removed from quotations, but they are also sometimes used to create a dramatic pause or to suggest that the writer is unable or unwilling to say something.

1. To indicate deletions from quotations

Although it is not acceptable to alter the meaning of a quotation, writers can and do omit words from quotations as needed to delete irrelevant information or to make a quotation fit into their own sentence. The ellipses alert readers that a change has been made:

> Use four dots—a period plus the ellipses—if a deletion occurs at the end of the sentence.

▶ *Don Quixote* begins like a fable: "In a village of La Mancha, . . . there lived not long since one of those gentlemen that keep a lance, . . . a lean hack, . . . and an old greyhound for coursing. . . ."
(comma + ellipses; comma + ellipses; comma + ellipses; period + ellipses)

With a parenthetical citation, insert the ellipses before the closing quotation marks and the period after the citation.

▶ "They will have it his surname was Quixada . . ." (1).
(ellipses + close quote; citation + period)

When only a few words are quoted or when the quotation begins with a lowercase letter, it is obvious that words have been omitted from the quotation, so no ellipses are needed:

▶ That Don Quixote keeps "a lean hack" suggests that he is no romantic hero, but instead minor, rather poor, country gentry.

NOTE If you are quoting a complete sentence, no ellipses are needed to indicate that the sentence comes from within a longer passage.

> **More about**
> Altering quotations, 322–23, 840, 851

Writing Responsibly | Altering Quotations

Exercise care when changing quotations: Never make a change that might distort the original or that might mislead readers, and always use ellipses and brackets to indicate an alteration.

to OTHER WRITERS

2. To indicate the omission of a line (or lines) of poetry

Use not a single ellipsis mark (three dots) but a whole line of dots to replace one or more missing lines of poetry:

▶ One of the most famous lines in Robert Frost's poem "Mending Wall" is "Good fences make good neighbors," but the speaker's meaning is lost when this line is taken out of context:

> There where it is we do not need the wall:
>
> ....
>
> My apple trees will never get across
> And eat the cones under his pines, I tell him.
> He only says, "Good fences make good neighbors." (lines 23–27)

3. To indicate a dramatic pause or interruption in dialog

An ellipsis can indicate an incomplete thought, a dramatic pause, or an interruption in speech:

▶ The disgruntled writer muttered, "The only word to describe my editor is ... unprintable."

➔ EXERCISE 53.3 Using brackets and ellipses with quotations

Write a paragraph in which you quote a passage from another text, marking deletions with ellipses and enclosing additions in brackets. Your paragraph must include at least one addition and two deletions. Be sure to identify the quoted passage by using a signal phrase and parenthetical page number.

> **More about**
> Signal phrases, 314, 315, 335–36, 399–400

53f Using Slashes

The slash (or *virgule*) marks the ends of lines in poetry when the poetry is run into a sentence:

- *Don Quixote* opens with some "commendatory verses" that warn the writer "Whoso indites frivolities, / Will but by simpletons be sought" (lines 62–63).

Slashes are also used in fractions and URLs:

- 1/2   1/3   3/4
- www.unh.edu/writing/cwc/handouts/

In informal contexts, the slash is sometimes used to indicate that either term is applicable:

- I've got so many courses this semester that I decided to take Spanish pass/fail.

In more formal contexts (such as academic or business writing), replace the slash with the word *or,* or rewrite the sentence:

DRAFT	An effective writer revises his/her work.
BETTER	An effective writer revises his or her work.
BEST	Effective writers revise their work.

Slashes are also used in dates, but only in informal or technical contexts or in tables where space is at a premium.

TECHNICAL OR INFORMAL	6/26/21
FORMAL	June 26, 2021 or 26 June 2021

EXERCISE 53.4 Editing dashes, parentheses, brackets, colons, ellipses, and slashes

In the following paragraph, add or delete en and em dashes, parentheses, brackets, colons, ellipses, and slashes as necessary.

American poet Anne Bradstreet 1612-1672 wrote many poems (expressing her religious devotion). She was a friend of Anne Hutchinson, who also wrote and spoke [on religious matters]. The American Puritans—of Bradstreet and Hutchinson's time—were unforgiving on religious matters [and banished Hutchinson for her beliefs]. It is not surprising, then, that Bradstreet's religious poetry expresses simple piety, as in the closing lines to the poem "Here Follow Several

Occasional Meditations" "I'll serve Him here whilst I shall live And love Him to eternity." It is unsurprising, too, given the censorship exercised upon writers of the time, that she was reluctant to publish her poems. Today's readers may consider her excessively modest or timid about announcing herself as an author, but we must take her historical context into account . . . if we are to read her work—fairly.

Make It **Your Own**

Review your use of dashes, parentheses, brackets, colons, ellipses, and slashes in a recent writing project of two or more pages. Add punctuation marks where needed and cross through unnecessary ones. Then analyze the impact these changes would have on your reader. (Refer to the sections in this chapter as needed.)

Work **Together**

Exchange Exercise 53.4 with a classmate. Check your partner's use of punctuation. Do you see any errors? If so, refer to sections in this chapter to help you explain the effect these errors had on you as a reader. (Be specific.)

Text Credits

Pg 854: de Cervantes Saavedra, Miguel, *The Ingenious Gentleman Don Quixote of La Mancha*, Volume 1, Chapter 11, translated by John Ormsby (Smith, Elder & Co., 1885). **Pg 855:** Frost, Robert, "Mending Wall." from *North of Boston* (1914).

54 Capitalizing

IN THIS CHAPTER

a. First word of a sentence, 858
b. Proper nouns and proper adjectives, 860
c. Titles and subtitles, 861
d. Pronoun *I* and interjection *O*, 862
e. Abbreviations and acronyms, 863

> **More about**
> Nouns, 635–37
> Adjectives, 640, 724–31
> Titles and subtitles, 837, 861–62, 865–66
> Pronouns, 637–38

Capital letters call attention to words. Although the rules of capitalization vary from language to language, the Quick Reference box on page 860 outlines the most important rules of capitalization in English. For cases not covered here, or when you are not sure, consult a dictionary.

Polygraphus/Shutterstock

Capitalization English capitalization can be confusing to people for whom English is a foreign language. In Spanish, French, and German, the first-person singular pronoun is lowercase (*yo, je, ich*), but in English it is capitalized (*I*), although the other personal pronouns (*she, he, it, they*) are not. In Spanish and French, the names of months and days of the week are lowercased, but not in English. In German, all nouns are capitalized, but in English only proper nouns are. Languages such as Arabic and Korean have no capital letters at all. Proofread your work carefully to adhere to the conventions of capitalization in the language in which you are writing, referring to this chapter and a good college dictionary as needed.

54a Capitalizing the First Word of a Sentence

Capitalize the first letter of the first word of every sentence:

- In response to Franklin Roosevelt's long tenure, the US Congress passed an amendment limiting a president to two terms.

This rule applies even to sentences in parentheses, unless they are incorporated into another sentence:

- His vice president, Harry S. Truman, decided not to run for reelection, although the amendment did not apply to him. (The sitting president was exempted.)

> **More about**
> Parentheses, 849–50

- Although the amendment did not apply to him (the sitting president was exempted), Truman decided not to run for reelection.

Capitalize the first word of a sentence you are quoting, even when it is incorporated into your own sentence:

- In response to a question about the amendment, President Eisenhower said, "By and large, the United States ought to be able to choose for its president anybody that it wants, regardless of the number of terms he has served."

Do not capitalize the first word when you are quoting only a phrase:

phrase
- President Eisenhower's "faith in the long-term common sense of the American people" made him feel the amendment was unnecessary.

When interrupting a quoted sentence, do not capitalize the first word of the second part:

- "By and large," Eisenhower said, "the United States ought to be able to choose for its president anybody that it wants, regardless of the number of terms he has served."

> **More about**
> Brackets, 851
> Altering quotations, 840, 851, 854–55

NOTE In MLA style, if you must change a capital to a lowercase letter (or vice versa) to incorporate a quotation into your sentence, place brackets around the letter to alert readers to the change.

If a colon links two *independent clauses,* capitalizing the first word following the colon is optional, but be consistent:

- Before Franklin Roosevelt, no US president had held office for more than two terms: That precedent was broken with Roosevelt's third inauguration.

> **independent (or main) clause** A word group that contains a subject and a main verb and that does not begin with a subordinating conjunction, relative pronoun, or relative adverb

cap   Detail Matters • Capitalizing

> **Quick Reference** — Common Capitalization Do's and Don'ts
>
> **Do capitalize . . .**
>
> . . . **the first word of a sentence. (858)**
> - The day broke gray and dull. —Somerset Maugham, *Of Human Bondage*
>
> . . . **proper nouns and proper adjectives. (860)**
> - Aunt Julia, Beijing, Dad (used as a name), Band-Aid, Shakespearean, Texan
>
> . . . **the first, last, and important words in titles and subtitles. (861)**
> - *Avengers: Age of Ultron*
>
> . . . **the first-person pronoun *I*. (862)**
> - I think; therefore, I am. —René Descartes
>
> . . . **abbreviations and acronyms. (863)**
> - Eng. Dept., UCLA, NYPD
>
> **Do *not* capitalize . . .**
>
> . . . **common nouns. (860)**
> - dog, cat, aunt, city, my dad, bandage
>
> . . . **compass directions. (861)**
> - north, south, northwest, southeast
>
> . . . **seasons or academic years and terms. (861)**
> - spring, sophomore, intersession

or

- Before Franklin Roosevelt, no US president had held office for more than two terms: that precedent was broken with Roosevelt's third inauguration.

NOTE The MLA recommends beginning with a lowercase letter unless the clause starts with a word that is usually capitalized, such as a proper noun, or the colon introduces a series of sentences, a question, or a rule.

54b Capitalizing Proper Nouns and Proper Adjectives

Capitalize the first letter of ***proper nouns*** (names of specific people, places, and things) and adjectives derived from them. Do not capitalize common nouns (names for general groups of people, places, and things). The Quick Reference guide on page 861 provides examples of words in each group.

> **Quick Reference** — Capitalize Proper Nouns and Proper Adjectives, but Not Common Nouns
>
> | Proper Nouns and Proper Adjectives | Common Nouns |
> |---|---|
> | **ACADEMIC DEPARTMENTS AND DISCIPLINES** | |
> | Political Science Department, Linguistics 101 | political science, linguistics |
> | **PEOPLE** | |
> | Senator Amy Klobuchar, Mom (used as a name), Dickensian | the senator, my mother, novelistic |
> | **PLACES, COMPASS DIRECTIONS** | |
> | Yosemite National Park, Neptune, the Northwest | the park, that planet, northwest, midwestern |
> | **TIME PERIODS AND HOLIDAYS** | |
> | Tuesday, June, Memorial Day | a weekday, this summer, spring break |
> | **HISTORICAL EVENTS, PERIODS, AND DOCUMENTS** | |
> | Korean War, Roaring Twenties, the Emancipation Proclamation | the war, the twenties, the proclamation |
> | **ORGANIZATIONS, OFFICES, COMPANIES** | |
> | National Wildlife Federation, General Accounting Office, National Broadcasting Corporation | a conservation group, the legislative branch, the network, the corporation |
> | **TRADE NAMES** | |
> | Coke, Kleenex, Google | a soda, a tissue, a search engine |
> | **NATIONS, ETHNIC GROUPS, RACES, AND LANGUAGES** | |
> | Pakistan, Pakistani, African American, Black, Caucasian, Swahili | her country, his nationality, her ethnicity, their language |
> | **RELIGIONS, RELIGIOUS DOCUMENTS, AND RELIGIOUS TERMS** | |
> | Buddhism, Jewish, Vedas, Bible, Allah, God | your religion, a religious group, a sacred text, biblical, the deity |
> | **TRANSPORTATION** | |
> | Greyhound, Amtrak, U.S.S. *Constitution* | a bus, the train, this battleship |

54c Capitalizing Titles and Subtitles

In general, capitalize the first and last words of titles and subtitles, as well as any other important words: nouns (*Pride, Persuasion*), verbs (*Is, Ran*), pronouns (*It, Their*), adjectives (*Green, Starry*), and adverbs (*Slow, Extremely*). Do not capitalize prepositions (*in, at, to, by*), coordinating conjunctions (*and, but, for, nor, or, so, yet*), *to* in infinitive verbs, or articles (*a, an, the*) unless they begin or end the title or subtitle or are part of the title of a periodical (*The New Yorker, The New York Times*).

Go Set a Watchman: A Novel

"In the Basement of the Ivory Tower" (article)

Pokémon XD: Gale of Darkness (game)

"Dákiti" (song)

Nomadland (movie)

Flying Popcorn (software)

> **More about**
> MLA style (ch. 18), 334–96
> APA style (ch. 19), 397–438
> *Chicago* style (ch. 20), 439–69
> CSE style (ch. 21), 470–84

NOTE Style guides may recommend different capitalization for titles and subtitles in reference lists and bibliographies. Check the style guide you are using and follow the rules described there.

54d Capitalizing the First-Person Pronoun *I* and the Interjection *O*

In all formal contexts, capitalize the first-person singular pronoun *I*:

▸ I wish I could meet myself in twenty years.

Although rarely used in contemporary prose, the interjection *O* should always be capitalized:

▸ Awake, O north wind, and come, O south wind! —Song of Solomon 4.16

However, the word *oh* should be capitalized only when it begins a sentence:

▸ "Oh literature, oh the glorious art, how it preys upon the marrow in our bones." —D. H. Lawrence

Writing Responsibly
Capitalizing in Email, Social Media, and Text Messages

In general, the rules of capitalization are the same online as they are in print. But while in print a writer may sometimes type a word in all capital letters for emphasis, in email or other online contexts, words typed in all capital letters are interpreted as shouting. When formatting is available, use italics (or boldface type) for emphasis in online writing; when such formatting is unavailable, place an asterisk before and after the word you want to emphasize. Also, although omitting capital letters in email, social media, and text messages may be acceptable in informal contexts, follow the formal rules of capitalization described in this chapter when you want to maintain a professional tone.

to SELF

54e Capitalizing Abbreviations and Acronyms

Abbreviations of proper nouns should be capitalized, and acronyms should be typed in all capital letters:

ABBREVIATIONS   U. of Mich., Anthro. Dept.

ACRONYMS   RADAR, NASA, OPEC

> **More about**
> Abbreviations
> (ch. 56), 869–73

> **acronym** Word formed from the first letter of each major word in a name

EXERCISE 54.1 Correcting capitalization

The following sentences have been typed entirely in lowercase letters. Supply correct capitalization.

EXAMPLE

When I ~~when i~~ moved into my first apartment this ~~september,~~ *September, I* quickly realized that ~~i~~ *I* had to watch my pennies at ~~stop~~ *Stop* and ~~shop~~ *Shop*.

1. when i went shopping with my friend jason, he called me an overspender.

2. my cart was filled with products with names like kellogg's, starbucks, and tide, but his cart had mostly store brands.

3. i told him that my mom would ask me, "why do you always have to have levi's? aren't the walmart jeans just as good?" now that it was my own money, i understood.

4. on monday, i saw jason in the english class we have together, and as we opened up our books to a short story titled "king of the bingo game," i whispered to him, "thanks to you i saved twenty dollars at the supermarket yesterday."

5. as we walked out of tyler hall and headed west to our history class, he said, "you'll have more money to spend on fashion if you spend less on detergent and ketchup."

Make It **Your Own**

Review your use of capitalization, abbreviations, and acronyms in a recent writing project of two or more pages. Revise capitalization as necessary, add abbreviations and acronyms where needed, and cross through unnecessary ones. Then analyze the impact these changes would have on your reader. (Refer to the sections in this chapter as needed.)

Work **Together**

The rules of English capitalization have not always been firmly fixed. In groups of two or three, revise the passage below to follow today's rules of capitalization in English. Refer to this chapter or to a good dictionary to settle any disputes.

> I do here in the Name of all the Learned and Polite Persons of the Nation, complain to your Lordship, as First Minister, that our Language is extremely imperfect; that its daily Improvements are by no means in proportion to its daily Corruptions; and the Pretenders to polish and refine it, have chiefly multiplied Abuses and Absurdities; and, that in many Instances, it offends against every Part of Grammar.
>
> —Jonathan Swift, *Proposal for Correcting, Improving, and Ascertaining the English Tongue* (1712)

Text Credits

Pg. 860: Dwight D. Eisenhower, News Conference, Washington, D.C., October 5, 1956. *Public Papers of the United States Presidents: Dwight D. Eisenhower* **Pg. 862:** Song of Solomon 4.16, NET Bible®, copyright © 1996–2006 by Biblical Studies Press, LLC. **Pg. 862:** Lawrence, D. H., letter of June 10, 1912 to Walter De La Mare, *The Letters of D. H. Lawrence, Volume 1*, edited by James T. Boulton (Cambridge University Press, 1979). **Pg. 864:** Swift, Jonathan, *A Proposal for Correcting, Improving, and Ascertaining the English Tongue* (1712).

55 Italics and Underlining

IN THIS CHAPTER

a. Titles of longer works, 865

b. Emphasis, 867

c. Names of vehicles, 867

d. Words, letters, and numbers used as words, 867

e. Unfamiliar non-English words, 868

Before the computer, writers typed on typewriters and used underlining to emphasize words; set off the titles of longer works; distinguish words, letters, and numbers used as words; set off unfamiliar non-English words; and call out the names of ships, airplanes, spacecraft, and other vehicles. Now that writers type on computers and use italics for these purposes, underlining is used to indicate hyperlinks. The Quick Reference box on the next page outlines the most important rules for using italics and underlining.

> **More about**
> Using quotation marks with titles of shorter works, 837

55a Italicizing Titles of Longer Works

Use italics for titles of longer works, such as books, periodicals (magazines, journals, and newspapers), films, television series, and websites; use quotation marks for shorter works, such as stories, articles, songs, television episodes, and web pages:

▸ Annie Proulx's collection *Close Range: Wyoming Stories* includes the story "Brokeback Mountain," which originally appeared in *The New Yorker* magazine. Kenneth Turan, critic for *The Los Angeles Times,* called the 2005 film *Brokeback Mountain* groundbreaking, and Roger Ebert of *The Chicago Sun-Times* gave it four stars. The *Brokeback Mountain* soundtrack includes songs like "He Was a Friend of Mine" by Willie Nelson and "The Devil's Right Hand" by Steve Earle.

865

> **Quick Reference** — **Common Italics Do's and Don'ts**
>
> *Do use italics . . .*
>
> **. . . with titles of longer works. (865)**
>
> ▶ We will be discussing the novel *Wuthering Heights* for the next two weeks. By the way, the novel's main character has nothing to do with the comic strip *Heathcliff.*
>
> **. . . for emphasis. (867)**
>
> ▶ I ask you *not* to read beyond the first chapter until we have discussed it in class.
>
> (Use italics for emphasis sparingly in academic prose.)
>
> **. . . for names of vehicles. (867)**
>
> ▶ On May 20, 1927, Charles Lindbergh took off from Long Island, New York, in the *Spirit of St. Louis.*
>
> **. . . with words, letters, and numbers used as words. (867)**
>
> ▶ You will notice that several of the characters' names begin with the letter *h;* this can be confusing.
>
> **Do *not* use italics . . .**
>
> **. . . with titles of short works. (865)**
>
> ▶ Jamaica Kincaid's story ~~*Girl*~~ "Girl" is only one page long.
>
> **. . . with historical documents and religious works. (866)**
>
> ▶ The ~~*Declaration of Independence*~~ Declaration of Independence and the ~~*Bible*~~ Bible take pride of place on my grandmother's bookshelf.

In addition, stand-alone items like court cases and works of art (paintings and sculptures) are italicized:

▶ *Bowers v. Hardwick*

▶ *Mona Lisa*

▶ *The Bronco Buster*

In contrast, the titles of major historical documents and religious works are not italicized:

▶ Magna Carta, Mayflower Compact, Kyoto Protocol

▶ Bible, Qur'an, Vedas

Writing Responsibly — Using Italics for Emphasis

When using italics for emphasis, consider your reader. Sometimes italics can help convey the writer's feelings, but will readers be interested? In a personal context, the use of italics in the sentence below might be acceptable:

▶ Should *I* call *him*, or should I wait for *him* to call *me*?

But such emphasis on the writer's emotions is usually inappropriate in a business or academic context.

to AUDIENCE

55b Italicizing for Emphasis

Italics are sometimes used for emphasis:

▶ George Eliot wants readers to *identify* with Dorothea, not merely to *sympathize* with her.

In the sentence above, the italics heighten attention to the contrast. To be effective, use italics sparingly for emphasis. Using italics haphazardly or overusing them can annoy or even confuse readers:

▶ She wanted *readers* to know *her* characters, not *merely* to observe them.

55c Italicizing Names of Vehicles

The names of individual trains, ships, aircraft, and spacecraft are all italicized:

Titanic, Spirit of St. Louis, Challenger

However, vehicles referred to by company, brand, or model names are not:

Corvette, Boeing 747

55d Italicizing Words, Letters, or Numbers Used as Words

When referring to words, letters, or numbers used as words, set them off from the rest of the sentence with italics:

▶ My chemistry instructor used the word *interesting* to describe the results I got on my last lab. She told me to be more careful next time, to dot all my *i*'s and cross all my *t*'s.

> **More about**
> Plurals of letters, 831–32

55e Italicizing Unfamiliar Non-English Words and Latin Genus and Species

English is an opportunistic language; when encountering new things or ideas, English speakers often adopt words already used in other languages. The word *raccoon,* for example, comes from Algonquian and the word *sushi* from Japanese. Once they are fully absorbed, they are typed with no special formatting. Until then, borrowings should be italicized:

- The review provides a good example of *diegesis* in that it describes the film without making a judgment about it.

To determine whether a non-English word warrants italics, check your dictionary: Words familiar enough to be found in a college dictionary should not be set in italics.

Latin genus and species names are also set in italics:

- *Acer saccharum* are the Latin genus and species for the sugar maple.

Make It Your Own

Review your use of italics and underlining in a recent writing project of two or more pages. Add italics and underlining where needed and revise unnecessary uses. Then analyze the impact these changes would have on your reader. (Refer to the sections in this chapter as needed.)

Work Together

Exchange a piece of writing with a partner. Check your classmate's use of italics and underlining. Did your partner make any errors? If so, explain the effect these errors had on you as a reader. (Be specific.)

56 Using Abbreviations

IN THIS CHAPTER

a. Abbreviating titles, 871
b. Using familiar abbreviations, 871
c. Abbreviating years, hours, numbers, dollars, 872
d. Avoiding certain abbreviations, 872
e. Replacing Latin abbreviations, 873

> **More about**
> MLA style (ch. 18), 334–96
> APA style (ch. 19), 397–438
> *Chicago* style (ch. 20), 439–69
> CSE style (ch. 21), 470–84

Abbreviations convey information rapidly, but they work only when readers know what they stand for.

While they are used frequently in business, scientific, and technical contexts, abbreviations are used sparingly in writing in the humanities and for a general audience, except in tables (where space is at a premium) and in bibliographic citations.

When you do abbreviate, use a period with a person's initials and with most abbreviations that end in lowercase letters:

▶ S. E. Hinton   Perry Mason, Esq.   St. John

▶ St.   Blvd.   Ave.

Use a period after each letter with abbreviations of more than one word:

▶ i.e.   e.g.   a.m.   p.m.

Most abbreviations made up of all capital letters no longer use periods:

▶ BS   MA   DVD   UN

The Quick Reference box on the next page outlines the most important rules for using abbreviations.

Quick Reference: Common Abbreviation Do's and Don'ts

***Do* use abbreviations . . .**

. . . of titles before or after names. (871)

▶ Dr. Neil deGrasse Tyson *or* Neil deGrasse Tyson, PhD

. . . when they are familiar to readers. (871)

▶ The role of the CIA has changed dramatically since 2001.

. . . with specific numerals and dates. (872)

▶ My class on ancient Rome meets at 8:30 a.m. to study the period from 509 BCE to 476 CE. The book for that class costs $87.50.

. . . in names of businesses when they are part of the official name. (873)

▶ Warner Bros. Entertainment, Inc.   Spindletop Oil & Gas Co.

***Do not* use abbreviations . . .**

. . . of titles not used with a proper name. (871)

      doctor   colonel
▶ My ~~dr.~~ is married to a ~~col.~~ in the Marines.

. . . of popular online terms in formal prose. (872)

Too much information
▶ ~~TMI~~ with very little focus makes this work a data parade without a point.

. . . of names, words, courses, parts of books, states and countries, days and months, holidays, and units of measurement in formal prose. (872)

     brothers   William Joseph
▶ My ~~bros.~~ ~~Wm.~~ and ~~Jos.~~, even though they are both now over

     feet   morning Christmas
six ~~ft.~~ tall, still love waking up early in the ~~a.m.~~ on ~~Xmas~~.

. . . of Latin terms. (873)
(Replace with English equivalents in prose.)

                         for example
▶ Leafy green vegetables, ~~e.g.~~, arugula, kale, and spinach, can reduce the risk of heart disease.

56a Abbreviating Titles before and after Names

- Mr. Mike Moore
- Ms. Aoife Shaughnessy
- Dr. Jonnelle Price
- Rev. Jane Genung

Margaret Aviles, PhD
Namazi Hamid, DDS
Robert Min, MD
Frederick C. Copelston, SJ

In most cases, avoid abbreviating titles when they are not used with a proper name:

- I'm hoping my English ~~prof.~~ *professor* will write me a letter of recommendation.

Academic degrees are an exception:

- My auto mechanic comes from a highly educated family: His father has an MS, his mother has an MLS, and his sister has a PhD.

Never use a title both before and after a name: Change *Dr. Hazel L. Cunningham, PhD* to either *Dr. Hazel L. Cunningham* or *Hazel L. Cunningham, PhD*.

56b Using Familiar Abbreviations: Acronyms and Initialisms

Acronyms and *initialisms* are abbreviations made of all capital letters formed from the first letters of a series of words. Acronyms are pronounced as words (*AIDS, CARE, NASA, NATO, OPEC*), while initialisms are pronounced as a series of letters (*DNA, HBO, JFK, USA*). Familiar acronyms and initialisms are acceptable in any context:

- The Swedish environmental activist Greta Thunberg met with a number of UN dignitaries during her trip to New York.

However, if the abbreviation is likely to be unfamiliar to readers, spell out the term on first use and follow it with the abbreviation in parentheses. Subsequently, just use the abbreviation:

- The International Olympic Committee (IOC) failed to take action following the arrest of two elderly Chinese women who had applied for permission to protest in the designated protest areas during the Beijing Olympics. A spokesperson claimed that the IOC has no control over the protest areas.

> ## Writing Responsibly
> ### Using Online Abbreviations Appropriately
>
> A new breed of initialism has emerged in online discourse. Here are some examples:
>
> | | |
> |---|---|
> | BFN (bye for now) | OIC (oh, I see!) |
> | IDK (I don't know) | OTOH (on the other hand) |
> | IMO (in my opinion) | ROTFL (rolling on the floor laughing) |
> | LOL (laughing out loud) | TMI (too much information!) |
> | FWIW (for what it's worth) | TBH (to be honest) |
>
> The irreverence of some of these initialisms fits with the casual tone of online discourse. Use them in text messages or on social media, but avoid them in college and professional writing, including emails. While they might establish your online savvy or serve as a handy shorthand, they might also annoy readers in more formal contexts, undermining your ethos (credibility).
>
> *to SELF*

> **More about**
> Ethos, 153–54

56c Using Abbreviations with Specific Years (BC, BCE, AD, CE), Hours (a.m., p.m.), Numbers (no.), Dollars ($)

> AD precedes the number; BC, BCE, and CE follow the number.

- The emperor Augustus ruled Rome from 27 BCE until his death in 14 CE.
- The Roman historian Livy lived from 59 BC until AD 17.
- I didn't get home until 11:45 p.m. because the no. 27 bus was so late.
- I owe my sister $27.32, and she won't let me forget it.

NOTE The abbreviations BCE (for *before the common era*) and CE (for *common era*) are now generally preferred over BC (*before Christ*) and AD (*anno domini,* "the year of the Lord" in Latin).

56d Avoiding Abbreviations of Names, Words, Courses, Parts of Books, States and Countries, Days and Months, Holidays, and Units of Measurement in Prose

- In ~~Fr.,~~ *France,* people receive gifts not on ~~Xmas~~ *Christmas* but on ~~Jan.~~ *January* 6.

- On ~~Mon.~~ *Monday* mornings, ~~Psych.~~ *Psychology* 121 meets in a tiny classroom: It is only 10 ~~ft.~~ *feet* wide.

> ▸ My ~~Eng.~~ teacher, ~~Eliz.~~ Santos, recommends that we always read the ~~intro.~~ first.
> (English) (Elizabeth) (introduction)

An exception is the names of businesses, when the abbreviation is part of the official name:

> ▸ Dun & Bradstreet, Inc., was ~~inc.~~ in New York ~~&~~ is still located there.
> (incorporated) (and)

56e Replacing Latin Abbreviations with English Equivalents in Formal Prose

Latin abbreviations, like those below, are generally avoided in formal writing (except in bibliographies).

- ▸ e.g.   for example
- ▸ i.e.   in other words
- ▸ etc.   and so forth
- ▸ cf.   compare
- ▸ et al.   and others
- ▸ N.B.   note especially

NOTE Both *etc.* and *and so forth* are best avoided in formal prose. Instead, include all the items or precede a partial list with *such as* or *for example*. Follow *e.g.* and *i.e.* with a comma if you use them in tables or parenthetical material. Common Latin abbreviations are not italicized or underlined.

Make It **Your Own**

Rewrite a recent text message to avoid abbreviations. Then write a paragraph explaining how this change affects the tone of the message. (If you do not have such a text message, write one using at least two of the abbreviations in the Writing Responsibly box on p. 872.)

Work **Together**

In groups of two or three, craft a text message using as many abbreviations and initialisms as you can. Then trade messages with another group and translate.

57 Using Numbers

IN THIS CHAPTER

a. Spelling numbers of one or two words, 874

b. Using numbers for dates, times, other quantitative information, and parts of literary works, 875

Rules for deciding whether to use numerals or to spell out numbers vary widely according to context. In business and the news, single-digit numbers are usually spelled out, while numerals are used for numbers over nine. In the humanities, numbers that can be written in one or two words are usually spelled out, while numerals are used for larger numbers. In the sciences, numerals are customarily used for all numbers. The best practice is to choose a style that will make sense to your audience, and then be consistent in its use. The rules that follow are appropriate to an academic audience in the humanities.

> **More about**
> Appropriate language (ch. 30), 596–603
> Ethos, 153–54

Writing Responsibly — Ethos and Convention

Using numbers and symbols in conventional ways does not normally affect meaning. Yet conventional usage is important, especially in formal contexts like school or the workplace, because it lends support to your ethos, or credibility. As a marker of appropriateness, it can subtly affect the way your audience perceives you and how seriously they take what you have to say.

to SELF

57a Spelling Out Numbers When They Can Be Expressed in One or Two Words

Spell out numbers under a hundred and round numbers—numbers that can be expressed in one or two words:

▶ Satchel Paige pitched sixty-four scoreless innings and won twenty-one games in a row.

If your text uses a combination of numbers—some that can be expressed in one or two words and others that cannot—use numerals throughout for consistency's sake:

▶ Satchel Paige pitched an estimated ~~two thousand~~ *2,000* baseball games during his career. At his first game, 78,383 fans were in attendance, and at his first game as a starter, 72,434 spectators looked on.

Avoid beginning a sentence with numerals. Instead, spell out the number or revise your sentence:

Seventy-eight thousand
▶ ~~78,000~~ people attended Satchel Paige's first game as a pitcher.

▶ Satchel Paige's first game as a pitcher drew 78,000 fans.

Numbers over a million are often best expressed as a combination of words and numerals:

▶ Over 10 million fans attended Negro League baseball games in 1930.

57b Following Conventions for Dates, Times, Addresses, Specific Amounts of Money and Other Quantitative Information, and Divisions of Literary Works

- **Dates:** May 4, 2017   the fourth of May   429 BCE   1066 CE   AD 1066
- **Times, years:** 4:15 p.m.   seven o'clock   1990s   the nineties   1999–2021   from 1999 to 2021
- **Phone numbers, addresses:** (800) 555-5789
  26 Peachtree Lane   221 W. 34th Street
  Atlanta, GA 30303   New York, NY 10001
- **Exact sums of money:** $10.95 $579.89 $24 million
- **Decimals and fractions:** half   ½   three-quarters   ¾   4⅝   3.95

NOTE MLA style generally recommends spelling out percentages expressed in one to three words in contexts with few numbers (*ten percent, fifty-five percent*). For percentages requiring more than three words or in texts with many numbers, use numerals (55.3%). The *Chicago Manual* recommends using the word *percent* with numerals in writing for the humanities and the symbol % with numerals in writing for the sciences.

- **Scores, statistics, and percentages:** 5 to 4   42–28   13.3 percent (or 13.3%)   3 out of 10
- **Measurements:** 55 mph   90–100 rpm   135 pounds   5 feet   9 liters   41°F
- **Divisions of books, plays, poems:** part 3   book 7   chapter 15   page 419 or p. 419   act 1   scene 3   lines 4–19

Punctuating Numbers in American English Conventions for punctuating numbers differ across cultures. In many European countries, for instance, commas separate whole numbers from decimal fractions, where periods mark divisions of thousands. In the United States, the convention is reversed:

▸ 2,541   94.7

Make It **Your Own**

Review your use of numerals in a recent writing project of two or more pages. Add numerals where needed and cross through unnecessary ones. Then analyze the impact these changes would have on your reader. (Refer to the sections in this chapter as needed.)

Work **Together**

Read the student project in chapter 19 (pp. 430–38). In groups of two or three, discuss whether the writer has followed the rules for using numbers laid out in this chapter. What effect does context have on following the rules? What effect would changing her treatment of numbers have on her intended audience?

58 Using Hyphens

IN THIS CHAPTER
a. Forming compounds, 877

b. Breaking words at ends of lines, 879

> *More about*
> Using a dictionary, 615–17

Skovalsky/Shutterstock

Hyphens connect pieces of words into a new whole. They join parts of a compound adjective or number, link some prefixes and suffixes to the root word, connect numbers in a fraction, and link word parts that split at the end of a line.

Keep in mind, though, that while some words, like *cross-purposes* or *cross-examination,* use a hyphen, not all compounds need that glue: Some are so closely bound by usage that they have become a single unit (*crosscurrent*), while others are linked merely by placement (*crosshairs*). Consult a dictionary to determine how the parts of a compound should be connected, and if a compound word is not in the dictionary, follow the rules below.

58a Using Hyphens to Form Compounds

1. Hyphenate compound adjectives before the noun but not after.

Hyphenate compound modifiers when they precede the noun but not when they follow it:

▶ The well-intentioned efforts [noun] by the International Olympic Committee (IOC) to allow peaceful protests were blocked by the Chinese government.

877

hyph Detail Matters • Using Hyphens

Writing Responsibly
Hyphenating with Readers in Mind

Correct hyphenation can make reading easier for your audience, but over-hyphenating may drive readers crazy. When editing your paper, check a dictionary to make sure not only that all compounds are hyphenated correctly but also that you have not added hyphens where they are not needed. Keep a particularly close eye on phrasal (or multiword) verbs and subject complements, which do not need hyphens:

- The neighbor knocked on our door after Leia *turned up* [phrasal verb] the volume on the stereo.
- Leia's new jacket is *black and white* [subject complement].

to AUDIENCE

> **More about**
> Phrasal verbs, 776–78
> Subject complements, 649

- The *efforts* [noun] of the IOC to allow peaceful protests were well-intentioned but ill-conceived.

When an adverb ending in *-ly* is part of a compound adjective, no hyphen is necessary:

- In China, politically-sensitive websites were blocked by the government.

When two or more parallel compound adjectives share the same base word, avoid repetition by putting a space after the first hyphen and stating the base word only once:

- Class- and race-based analyses of *To Kill a Mockingbird* show that Harper Lee was not completely able to rise above her social background.

When a word begins with an *e* that stands for the word *electronic* (as in *ebook*, *email*, and *ecommerce*), no hyphen is needed to set it off from the main word:

- I don't think *eBay* accepts ecurrency.

2. Use a hyphen to link certain prefixes and suffixes to the root word.

In general, hyphens are not needed to attach prefixes and suffixes to the root word:

*de*compress   *pre*test   *re*define   *sub*category

But the prefixes *all-*, *ex-*, and *self-* and the suffix *-elect* are always attached to the root word with a hyphen:

- *all*-star   *ex*-boyfriend   *self*-absorbed   president-*elect*

When *all, elect, self,* and even *ex* (a word in Latin, meaning *from*) are freestanding words, they do not need a hyphen:

- *all* the participants in the game
- her sense of *self*
- to *elect* the candidates
- an *ex* officio member

In most cases, to avoid double or triple letter combinations, add a hyphen:

- *anti*-inflationary   *multi*-institutional   *re*-education   ball-*like*
- Exceptions: override   cooperate

If the prefix will be attached to a numeral or to a root that begins with a capital letter, insert a hyphen:

- post-1914   pre-1945   anti-Muslim   un-American

Finally, if the prefix-plus-root combination could be misread as another word, add a hyphen to avoid confusion:

- He finally recovered from a bout of the flu.
- We re-covered the sofa with a floral fabric.

3. Use a hyphen in compound numbers under one hundred.

Numbers over twenty and under one hundred are hyphenated when written out:

- Workaholics would work twenty-four hours a day, seven days a week, fifty-two weeks a year if their bodies would cooperate.

58b Using Hyphens to Break Words at the Ends of Lines

Word processing programs generally "wrap" text (that is, they move a too-long word at the end of a line to the beginning of the next line). Still, you may occasionally need to break words manually. If you do, follow these rules:

syllable breaks

re•spon•si•bil•i•ty (ri spon'sə bil'i tē), *n., pl.* **-ties.** 1. the state, fact, or quality of being responsible. 2. an instance of being responsible: *The responsibility for this mess is yours!* 3. a particular burden of obligation upon one who is responsible: *the responsibilities of authority.* 4. a person or thing for which one is responsible.

FIGURE 58.1 Syllable breaks in the dictionary Dictionaries indicate syllabification by placing dots between syllables.

- Break words between syllables. (Check your dictionary for syllable breaks, such as those shown in Figure 58.1.)

► CIA operatives in the Middle East have found it impossible to ~~infiltr-~~ ^infil-^ ~~ate~~ ^trate^ al Qaeda.

- Break compound words between parts or after hyphens.

    ► Washington, DC's long-standing handgun ban was ~~overturn-~~ ^over-^ ~~ed~~ ^turned^ by the Supreme Court.

- Do not break one-syllable words or contractions.

    ► To determine surface area, multiply the ~~wid-~~ ^width^ ~~th~~ of a room by its length.

- Break words so that at least two letters remain at the end of a line and at least three letters move down to the beginning of the next line.

    ► Increases in the cost of gas and food have ~~reduc-~~ ^re-^ ~~ed~~ ^duced^ discretionary spending.

Tech | **Breaking URLs and Email Addresses**

Most word processing software automatically hyphenates words. However, you must break URLs or email addresses manually. MLA style guidelines caution against introducing hyphens or spaces in URLs and recommend disabling features that automatically hyphenate words, but otherwise MLA prioritizes the accuracy of the URL over its appearance on the page. If you are following CSE style guidelines, break URLs only after a slash. If you are following *Chicago Manual* guidelines, break a URL or an email address before a period or other punctuation, or after the @ symbol, a single or double slash, or a colon. Do *not* insert a hyphen.

Detail Matters • Using Hyphens to Break Words at the Ends of Lines   hyph   **58b**   **881**

➤ EXERCISE 58.1 Adding and deleting hyphens

Add and delete hyphens as needed in the following sentences. (You may consult a dictionary.)

EXAMPLE

The Deadhead phenomenon began in the mid-1960s, when the Grateful Dead became active in the Haight–Ashbury music scene.

1. In 1971, a long time friend of the Grateful Dead took on a self assigned project to put together a mailing list to keep fans informed of upcoming shows.
2. Clearly, there were more than just fifty or seventy five people on this list, because city to city caravans of tie dye wearing Deadheads soon sprang up.
3. Their long distance travel was motivated by changes night to night in the songs the musicians played.
4. Shows sold out for the long lived and well loved band, and a true blue community of Deadheads was created.
5. Although the band is now defunct, well and long proven loyalty is still highly-visible in thruway rest stops, where large groups of slack jawed fans, exhausted from concerts by Grateful Dead spinoff bands like RatDog and Phil Lesh and Friends, still congregate.

Make It **Your Own**

Review your use of hyphens in a recent writing project of two or more pages. Add hyphens where needed and cross through unnecessary ones. Then analyze the impact these changes would have on your reader. (Refer to the sections in this chapter as needed.)

Work **Together**

Exchange Exercise 58.1 with a classmate. Check your partner's use of hyphens. Do you see any errors? If so, explain the effect these errors had on you as a reader. (Be specific.)

Glossary of Key Terms

A

ableism (209, 219)   The practice of treating disabled people as inferior to non-disabled people.

absolute phrase (588, 654)   A phrase consisting of a noun or pronoun followed by a participle (the *-ing* or *-ed* form of a verb) that modifies an entire clause or sentence: <u>Our spirits rising</u>, *we began our vacation.*

abstract (113, 246, 428)   Overview of a text, including a summary of its main claims and most important supporting points.

abstract noun (636)   See *noun.*

acronym (385, 840, 850)   An abbreviation formed from the first letters of a series of words and pronounced as a word (*AIDS, NASA*). Compare *initialism.*

active voice (593, 649, 709)   See *voice.*

adjective (553, 608, 697, 762)   A word that modifies a noun or pronoun with descriptive or limiting information, answering questions such as *what kind, which one,* or *how many: a happy camper, the tall building.*

adjective clause (655)   A subordinate clause, usually beginning with a relative pronoun (such as *who, whom, which,* or *that*), that modifies a noun or pronoun: *Sam baked the pie <u>that won first prize</u>.* Adjective clauses can also begin with the subordinating conjunctions *when* and *where.*

adverb (587, 641-42, 724, 786)   A word that modifies a verb, adjective, other adverb, or entire phrase or clause, answering questions such as *how? where? when?* and *to what extent or degree? The door opened <u>abruptly</u>.*

adverb clause (656, 812)   A subordinate clause, usually introduced by a subordinating conjunction such as *although, because,* or *until,* that functions as an adverb within a sentence: *I walk to work <u>because I need the exercise.</u>*

agreement (680–93)   The matching of form between one word and another. Verbs must agree with, or match, their subjects in person and number (subject-verb agreement), and pronouns must agree in person, number, and gender with their antecedents (pronoun-antecedent agreement). See also *antecedent, gender, number, person.*

alignment (154)   Arrangement in a straight line (vertical, horizontal, or diagonal) of elements on a page or screen to create connections among parts and ideas.

alternating pattern of organization (65)   A method of organizing a comparison-contrast paragraph or essay by discussing each common or divergent trait of both items before moving on to the next trait. See also *block pattern of organization.*

analogy (609)   An extended comparison of something familiar with something unfamiliar. (See also *figurative language, simile, metaphor.*) An analogy becomes a false analogy (150) when the items being compared have no significant shared traits.

analysis (64, 143-46, 223)   The process of dividing an entity, concept, or text into its component parts to study its meaning and function. Analysis is central to critical reading and is a common strategy for developing paragraphs and essays in academic writing. Also called *classification, division.*

annotated bibliography (235, 236)   A bibliography that includes not only retrieval information for each source but also information about the source, such as its content, its relevance to the writer's project, or the writer's evaluation of it.

annotation (126)   The process of taking notes on a text, including writing down definitions, identifying key concepts, highlighting unfamiliar vocabulary and words that reveal tone, and making connections or noting personal responses.

antecedent (637, 688, 689)   The noun or noun phrase to which a pronoun refers. In the sentence *The pitcher caught the ball and threw it to first base,* the noun *ball* is the antecedent to the pronoun *it.*

antonyms (614)   Words with opposite meanings—for example, *good* and *bad.* Compare *synonyms.*

APA style (397–438)   The citation and documentation style of the American Psychological Association, used frequently in the social sciences.

appeals (156)   Efforts to engage the reader. Emotional appeals (**pathos**) engage the reader's feelings; intellectual appeals (**logos**) engage the reader's rational faculties; ethical appeals (**ethos**) engage the reader's sense of fairness and respect for good character.

appositive (572, 588, 651, 665)   A noun or noun phrase that renames a preceding noun or noun phrase and is grammatically equivalent to it: *Miguel, <u>my roommate,</u> avoids early morning classes.*

arguable claim (77)   A claim on which reasonable people might hold differing opinions and that can be supported by evidence.

argument (16, 144)   An attempt to persuade others to accept your opinion by providing logical supporting evidence. See also *persuasive argument, purpose.*

article (768–71)   The words *a, an,* and *the.* *A* and *an* are **indefinite articles**; *the* is a **definite article.** The **zero article** refers to nouns that appear with no article.

asynchronous media (211)   Communication media such as email and discussion lists that allow users to participate at their own convenience. Compare *synchronous media;* see also *discussion list.*

audience (18–22, 88, 213)   The intended readers for a written text or listeners for a presentation.

authority (135, 178)   An expert on a topic. An authority becomes a false authority when the person from

G1

whom the writer draws evidence is not truly an expert on the topic.

B

bar graph (78)   An information graphic that compares data in two or more categories using bars of different heights or lengths.

belief (145–46)   A conviction based on values.

biased or hurtful language (120, 600–03)   Language that unfairly or offensively characterizes a group and, by extension, the individual members of that group.

bibliographic notes (378)   Notes that add information or point readers to other sources on the topic.

bibliography (214–17)   A list of works cited in a text, with full retrieval information (usually including author, title, publisher, date of publication, and type of publication) for each entry. Bibliographies are usually constructed following a style sheet such as MLA or APA. In *Chicago* style, the word bibliography is used for the end-of-project source list; in APA, it is called a reference list; and in MLA, it is called list of works cited.

block pattern of organization (64)   A method of organizing a paragraph or text by discussing all the significant traits of one item (such as a source, event, or theory) before moving on to discuss all the traits of another item. See also *alternating method*.

block quotations (339)   Exact quotations of longer than four lines (MLA style) or forty words (APA style) in which quotation marks are omitted and the quotation is indented as a block from the left margin of the text.

block-style letter (201)   A format for business letters in which all text is flush with the left margin and a line space is inserted before paragraphs. In **modified block style**, all text begins flush left except for the return address, date, closing, and signature.

blog (or **weblog**) (210, 320, 367)   An online journal that chronicles thoughts, opinions, and information often on a single topic. See also *asynchronous media*.

body (40, 214–215)   The portion of a text or presentation that develops and supports the thesis.

Boolean operator (248)   The terms *and*, *not*, and *or* used in databases and search engines for refining keyword searches.

brainstorming or listing (27)   A technique for generating ideas by listing all the ideas that come to you during a fixed amount of time; brainstorming can also take place in groups.

breadcrumb trail (or **click trail**) (205)   The sequence of links followed while navigating pages on a website.

C

case (712–19)   The form of a noun or pronoun that corresponds to its grammatical role in a sentence. Many pronouns have three cases: **subjective** (for example, *I, we, he, she, they, who*), **objective** (for example, *me, us, him, her, them, whom*), and **possessive** (for example, *mine, ours, his, hers, theirs, whose*). Nouns change form only to indicate possession.

cause and effect (64)   A method of paragraph or essay development that explains why something happened or what its consequences were or will be.

***Chicago* style** (491)   The citation and documentation style recommended in the *Chicago Manual of Style*, used frequently in the humanities.

chronological organization (41)   A pattern of organization in which events are discussed in the order in which they occurred; chronological organization is used when telling a story (narrative) or explaining a process (process analysis).

citation (303, 334, 363)   The acknowledgment of sources in the body of a research project, usually tagged to a bibliography, works-cited list, or reference list. See also *in-text citation, parenthetical citation, signal phrase.*

citation index (129)   System or program that tracks the links established when one source cites another, which enables users to track the development of the ideas and information being referenced.

citation-name system (436–37)   In CSE style, a system of acknowledgment for research projects that provides a superscript number in the text and a list of references, numbered in alphabetical order (usually by author's surname) at the end of the project.

citation-sequence system (436–37)   In CSE style, a system of acknowledgment for research projects that provides a superscript number in the text and a list of references, numbered in order of appearance, at the end of the project.

claim (37, 140, 144, 151)   An assertion that is supported by evidence. A *claim of fact* asserts a verifiable piece of information; it can be a central claim in an informative text but not in an argumentative text. A *claim of causation* asserts the causes or effects of a problem; a *claim of policy* asserts how best to resolve a problem or what is the best course of action to take; a *claim of judgment or value* asserts that one's personal beliefs or convictions should be embraced. Claims of causation, policy, and value are all appropriate central claims in argumentative texts.

classical model (174)   A model for organizing an argument composed of five parts: introduction, background, evidence, counterclaims and counterevidence, and conclusion. Compare *Rogerian* and *Toulmin models.*

classification   See *analysis.*

clause (535–38, 563–64, 643, 654–55, 740, 754, 804)   A word group with a subject and a predicate. An **independent clause** can stand on its own as a sentence. A **subordinate** (or **dependent**) **clause** functions within a sentence as a noun, adjective, or adverb but cannot stand as a sentence on its own. See also *sentence.*

cliché (610–12)   A figure of speech, idiom, or other expression that has grown stale from overuse. See also *figurative language, idiom.*

click trail   see *Breadcrumb Trail.*

climactic organization (41)   A pattern of organization that orders supporting paragraphs from least to most engaging or compelling.

clustering or mapping (28)   An idea-generating technique for organizing, developing, or discovering connections among ideas by writing a topic in the center of the page, adding related topics and subtopics around the central topic, and connecting them to show relationships.

coauthorship (51)   Two or more writers working together to research, brainstorm, compose, revise, or edit a text.

Glossary of Key Terms **G3**

coherence, coherent (44, 62) The quality of a text in which sentences and paragraphs are organized logically and clearly so that readers can move from idea to idea without having to puzzle out the relationships among parts.

collaborative learning (32, 51) A process by which classmates or colleagues enhance understanding by studying together and reviewing one another's writing.

collective noun (685) See *noun*.

colloquialism (597) An informal expression common in speech but usually out of place in formal writing.

comma splice (671, 804, 823) The incorrect joining of two independent clauses with a comma alone—without a coordinating conjunction.

common knowledge (289) General information that is available from a number of different sources and that is considered factual and incontestable. Common knowledge does not require documentation.

common noun (767) See *noun*.

commonplace book (26) A written record (quotations, summaries, paraphrases) of the ideas of others and your own reactions to those ideas, preserved in a notebook or online document.

comparative form (729) See *comparison of adjectives and adverbs*.

comparison and contrast (64) A pattern of paragraph or essay development in which the writer points out the similarities and differences among items. See also *alternating method, block method*.

comparison of adjectives and adverbs (724–25) The form of an adjective or adverb that indicates the relative degree of the quality or manner it specifies. The **positive form** is the base form of the adjective (for example, *brave*) or adverb (for example, *bravely*). The **comparative form** indicates a relatively greater or lesser degree (*braver, more bravely*). The **superlative form** indicates the greatest or least degree (*bravest, most bravely*).

complement (689) See *subject complement, object complement*.

complete predicate (647) See *predicate*.

complete subject (645) See *subject*.

complete verb (660) A main verb together with any helping verbs needed to express tense, mood, and voice.

complex sentence (552, 658, 824) See *sentence*.

compound-complex sentence (587, 658) See *sentence*.

compound predicate (665–66) See *predicate*.

compound sentence (552, 674, 804) See *sentence*.

compound subject (645, 683) See *subject*.

conciseness (545) The statement of something in the fewest and most effective words needed for clarity and full understanding.

conclusion (40, 113, 215) The closing paragraph or section in a text. An effective conclusion provides readers with a sense of closure.

concrete noun (791) See *noun*.

conditional clause (708) A subordinate clause that begins with *if* and describes a set of circumstances (*conditions*) and that modifies an independent clause that describes what follows from those circumstances.

confirmation bias (157) Recognizing only the information that supports what one already believes; ignoring or dismissing information that contradicts what one already believes; misinterpreting new information as if it supports what one already believes, regardless of whether it actually does.

conjunction (636, 683) A word that joins a word, phrase, or clause to other words, phrases, or clauses and specifies the way the joined elements relate to one another. **Coordinating conjunctions** (*and, but, or, for, nor, yet,* and *so*) join grammatically equivalent elements, giving them each equal significance: *Jack and Jill went up the hill*. **Correlative conjunctions** are pairs of terms (such as *either ... or, neither ... nor,* and *both ... and*) that join grammatically equivalent elements: *Both Jack and Jill fell down*. **Subordinating conjunctions** link subordinate clauses to the clauses they modify. *After Jack and Jill went up the hill, they both fell down*.

conjunctive adverb (641, 807) A transitional expression (such as *for example, however,* and *therefore*) that can relate one independent clause to a preceding independent clause.

connected (52) See *transition*.

connotation (20, 91, 606) The emotional resonance of a word. Compare *denotation*.

container (357, 362, 372, 795) When documenting a source, if it is part of a larger whole, in MLA style that whole—that host–is called a *container*, and it is part of the entry in the list of works cited.

content notes (378) Footnotes or endnotes that clarify or justify a point in your text or that acknowledge the contributions of others in the preparation of your project.

context (14, 22, 32, 188, 204) The social, rhetorical, and historical setting in which a text is produced or read. The context in which Lincoln's Gettysburg Address was produced is different from the context in which it may be read today, but both are important for fully understanding the text.

contrast (184) In design, differences that call attention to and highlight one element among others.

coordinate adjectives (809) Two or more adjectives that separately and equally modify the noun they precede. Coordinate adjectives should be separated by a comma: *an innovative, exciting vocal group*.

coordinating conjunction (804) See *conjunction*.

coordination (563–64) The joining of elements of equal weight or importance in a sentence. See also *subordination*.

correlative conjunction (545) See *conjunction*.

counterevidence (145, 156) Evidence that undermines or contradicts your claim.

count noun (or **countable noun**) (767) See *noun*.

critical reading and thinking (106–08) A careful, systematic approach to a text or idea, going below the surface to uncover meaning and draw conclusions. Critical reading and thinking begins with reading actively; it requires analysis, interpretation, synthesis, and critique.

critique (133–35, 453, 460) An evaluation based on evidence accumulated through careful reading, analysis, interpretation, and synthesis. It may be positive, negative, or a bit of both.

CSE style (511) The citation and documentation style recommended in *Scientific Style and Format: The CSE Manual for Authors, Editors, and Publishers,* used frequently in the sciences.

cumulative adjectives (809) Two or more adjectives that modify not only the noun or pronoun they precede but also the next adjective in the series. Cumulative adjectives should not be separated by commas: *A great American rock band.*

cumulative sentence (555) A sentence that begins with the subject and verb of an independent clause and accumulates additional information in subsequent modifying phrases and clauses: *The mountaineers set off, anticipating the view from the peak but wary of the dangers they faced to get there.*

D

dangling modifier (745–46) A word, phrase, or clause that erroneously does not actually modify the subject or anything else in a sentence, leaving it to the reader to infer the intended meaning. In the sentence *As your parent, you should put on a sweater when it is cold,* the phrase *as your parent* dangles; it appears illogically to modify the subject, *you,* but actually refers to the speaker, as in *As your parent, I recommend that you put on a sweater when it is cold.*

database (232, 362) A collection of data, now usually available in digital form. In research, databases provide citations to articles in academic journals, magazines, and newspapers.

declarative sentence (645) See *sentence.*

deductive reasoning (152) A form of reasoning that moves from a general principle to a specific case to draw a conclusion; if the premises are true, the conclusion must be true. Compare *inductive reasoning;* see also *syllogism.*

definite article (768) See *article.*

definition (67–68, 119, 348) An explanation of the meaning of a word or concept made by including it in a larger class and then providing the characteristics that distinguish

it from other members of that class: In the definition *People are reasoning animals, people* is the term to be defined, *animals* is the larger class to which people belong, and *reasoning* is the trait that distinguishes people from other animals. Also, a pattern of paragraph or essay development in which the writer explains the special meaning of a term by explaining what the term includes and excludes.

degree (729) See *comparison of adjectives and adverbs.*

demonstrative pronouns (772) The pronouns *this, that, these,* and *those* used as nouns or adjectives to rename and point to nouns or noun phrases: *These are interesting times we live in.*

denotation (91, 604) The literal meaning of a word; its dictionary definition. Compare *connotation.*

dependent clause (655) A subordinate clause. See *clause.*

description (64) A pattern of paragraph or essay development that draws on specific, concrete details to depict a scene or object in terms of the senses: seeing, hearing, smelling, touching, tasting.

determiner (640, 743) An article (*a, an,* or *the*) or a possessive, demonstrative, or indefinite pronoun that functions as an adjective to specify or quantify the noun it modifies: *a cat, some cats, that cat, her cat.*

development (40, 46, 68, 222–23) The depth at which a topic or idea is explored.

dialect (597) A language variety with its own distinctive pronunciation, vocabulary, and grammar.

diction (604–06) The choice of words that will best convey an idea.

direct object (587, 701) See *object.*

direct question (844–45) A sentence that asks a question and ends with a question mark. Compare *indirect question.*

direct quotation (737–38, 813) A copy of the exact words that someone has written or spoken, enclosed in quotation marks or, for longer quotations, indented as a block. Compare *indirect quotation.*

direct source (839) A text that you are reading (as contrasted to a source *quoted in* a text you are reading).

discussion (409, 429, 447) In APA and CSE style, the last section of a research project; the Discussion section provides the writer's opinion of the implications of the research.

discussion list (211) An electronic mailing list that enables a group of people to participate in email conversations on a specific topic. See also *asynchronous media.*

disinformation (270) Deliberate lies or distortions of the facts.

diversity Variety in demographic features such as nationality, gender, and race; or variety in perspectives and beliefs.

division (357, 358, 665) See *analysis.*

documentation (303, 363) Information in a bibliography, reference list, or list of works cited that allows readers to locate a source cited in the text. See also *citation.*

document design (184–98) The arranging and formatting of text elements on a page or screen using proximity (nearness), alignment, repetition, and contrast to indicate their relative importance and their relation to each other.

DOI (362, 450, 477) Digital object identifier, a permanent identifier assigned to electronic publications.

domain (271) The ending of the main portion of a URL; the most common domains are *.com* (commercial), *.edu* (educational), *.gov* (governmental), and *.net* (network).

double-entry reading journal (125) An online or printed journal with one column for passages from sources (quotations, summaries, or paraphrases) and another column for the writer's response to the passage.

doublespeak (600) Euphemisms that are deliberately deceptive, used to obscure bad news or sanitize an ugly truth.

drafting (44–47, 303–04) The stage of the writing process in which the writer puts ideas on paper in complete sentences and paragraphs.

E

editing (91–93) The stage of the writing process in which the writer fine-tunes the draft by correcting words and sentences and revises them to enhance clarity and power.

Glossary of Key Terms **G5**

ellipses (840) A set of three periods, or *ellipsis points,* with a space between each. Ellipses are used to replace words deleted from quotations; they are also sometimes used to create a dramatic pause or to suggest that the writer is unable or unwilling to say something.

elliptical construction (561, 753) A construction in which grammatically necessary words can be omitted as understood because their meaning and function are otherwise clear from the context: *The movie [that] we saw last night is excellent.*

endnote (440) A note that appears in a list at the end of the project.

entertaining text (15) See *purpose.*

essential (or **restrictive**) **element** (660, 813) A word, phrase, or clause that provides essential information about the word or words it modifies. Essential elements are not set off by commas: *The train that she is on has been delayed.* See also *nonessential element.*

et al. (341, 373) Abbreviation of the Latin phrase *et alia,* "and others."

ethos (150) See *appeals.*

euphemism (600) An inoffensive word or expression used in place of one that might be offensive or emotionally painful.

evaluation (269) In research, assessment of sources to determine their relevance and reliability.

evidence (81) The facts, examples, statistics, expert opinions, and other information writers use to support their claims.

excessive coordination (533–34) The joining of tediously long strings of independent clauses with *and* and other conjunctions.

excessive subordination (538–39) The stringing together of too many subordinate structures.

exclamatory sentence (645) See *sentence.*

exemplification (64) A pattern of paragraph or essay development that explains by example or illustration.

expletive construction (562, 646) A kind of inverted construction in which *there* or *it* precedes a form of the verb *to be* and the subject follows the verb: *There are seven days in a week.*

explicate (460) To read a text closely, analyzing it line by line or even word by word; explications of a text are common in literary analysis.

exploratory argument (143) An argument in which the author considers a wide range of evidence before arriving at the most plausible position; in exploratory arguments, the thesis is often offered at the conclusion of the text. See also *argument, persuasive argument, purpose.*

expository report (146) See *informative report.*

expressive text (15) See *purpose.*

F

fact (146) A piece of information that can be verified.

fallacy (177) A mistake in reasoning.

familiar to unfamiliar (41) A method of organization that begins with material that is known by the audience and moves toward material that the audience will not know.

faulty predication (751) A logical or grammatical mismatch between subject and predicate.

field research (338) The gathering of research data in person rather than from sources. Field research includes interviews, observational studies, and surveys. See also *primary source.*

figurative language or figures of speech (609) The imaginative use of language to convey meaning in ways that reach beyond the literal meaning of the words involved. See *analogy, hyperbole, irony, metaphor, personification, simile, understatement.*

flaming (210) Writing a scathing, often ad hominem, response to someone with whom the writer disagrees, usually in email or on Internet forums.

focused freewriting (27) See *freewriting.*

font (192–94) Typeface; fonts may be serif (such as Times Roman) or sans serif (such as Arial), may be set in boldface, italics, or underlining, and may be in a larger or smaller size (the most common sizes are 10 point and 12 point).

footer (428) Material (most often a page number, sometimes accompanied by title or author's name) appearing at the bottom of every page of a text.

footnote (440) A note that appears at the bottom of the page.

formal outline (42) See *outline.*

formalist approach (453) An approach to literature and art that focuses on the work itself rather than on the author's life or other theoretical approaches.

format (98–99) The look of a document created by choice of font and color and use of white space, lists, headings, and visuals. See also *layout.*

fragment (628, 660) An incomplete sentence punctuated as if it were complete, beginning with a capital letter and ending with a period, question mark, or exclamation point.

freewriting (27) An idea-generating technique that requires writing nonstop for a fixed period of time (often ten to fifteen minutes); in *focused freewriting,* the writer writes nonstop about a specific topic or idea.

function word (546) A word that indicates the relationship among other words in a sentence. Examples include **articles, conjunctions,** and **prepositions.**

funnel introduction (68) An essay introduction that begins with broad statements and narrows in focus to conclude with the thesis statement. See also *introduction.*

fused sentence or **run-on sentence** (671–79) A sentence in which one independent clause improperly follows another with no punctuation or joining words between them.

future perfect progressive tense (705) See *tense.*

future perfect tense (703) See *tense.*

future progressive tense (704) See *tense.*

future tense (703) See *tense.*

G

gender (690) The classification of nouns and pronouns as feminine (*woman, mother, she*), masculine (*man, father, he*), or neuter (*table, book, it, they*).

gender bias (628) Stereotyping people according to their gender.

general to specific (39) A method of organization that begins with a general statement (the **thesis statement** or **topic sentence**) and proceeds to provide specific supporting evidence.

generalization (177) A broad statement. If not supported by specific details, a generalization becomes a hasty generalization (jumping to conclusions) or a sweeping generalization (application of a claim to all cases when it applies only to a few).

generic noun (690) A noun used to designate a whole class of people or things rather than a specific individual or individuals: *the average child*.

genre (14, 22, 189, 204) A category or type of writing; in literature, genres include poetry, fiction, and drama; in college writing, genres may include analytical essays, case studies, or observational reports.

gerund (583, 653, 687, 717) The present participle of a verb (the *-ing* form) used as a noun: *Walking is good exercise*.

grammar (726) The rules of a language that structure words so they can convey meaning.

grounds (150) In an argument, the evidence that supports the claim. See *Toulmin model*.

H

hate speech (158) Generalizations about entire demographics (such as gender, race, or nationality) that use rhetorical tactics such as ad hominem attacks and verbal cruelty to relegate the targeted demographic to second-class citizenship or even non-human status. Hate speech promotes fear, contempt, or hatred of its targeted demographic, often for the purpose of harassing or intimidating an individual.

header (380) Material (most often a page number, sometimes accompanied by title or author's name) appearing at the top of every page of a text.

heading (193–94) A brief caption describing or labeling a section of text.

helping verb or auxiliary verb (639, 697, 782) A verb that combines with a main verb to provide information about tense, voice, mood, and manner. Helping verbs include forms of *be*, *have*, and *do* and the modal verbs *can*, *could*, *may*, *might*, *must*, *shall*, *should*, *will*, *would*, and *ought to*.

home page (106, 203, 204) On a website, the page designed to introduce visitors to the site.

homonyms (618) Words that sound exactly alike but have different spellings and meanings: *their*, *there*, *they're*.

HTML (246, 450) Hypertext Markup Language, a coding system used to format texts for the web.

hyperbole (609) Deliberate exaggeration for emphasis: *That restaurant makes the best pizza in the universe.* See *figurative language*.

hyperlink (868) A navigation tool that allows users to jump from place to place on a web page or from web page to web page; hyperlinks (or links) appear as highlighted words or images on a web page.

hypertext (450) An online text that provides links to other online files, texts, images, audio files, and video files, allowing readers to jump to other related sites rather than reading *linearly*.

hypothesis (261, 303) A proposed answer to a research question that is subject to testing and modification during the research process.

I

idea journal (26) An online or printed record of your thoughts that you can draw on to develop or explore a topic.

idiom (610) A customary expression whose meaning cannot be determined from the literal meaning of the words that compose it: *They struggled to make ends meet*.

imperative (700, 733) See *mood*, *sentence*.

indefinite article (768) See *article*.

indefinite pronoun (685, 690, 828) A pronoun such as *anybody*, *anyone*, *somebody*, *some*, or *several* that does not refer to a specific person or thing.

independent clause (655, 660, 664, 802, 804, 820) See *clause*.

indicative (707) See *mood*.

indirect object (650, 761-61) See *object*.

indirect question (738) A sentence that reports a question and ends with a period: *My teacher asked us if we texted each other even when we're in the same room.* Compare *direct question*.

indirect quotation (814, 836) A sentence that uses paraphrase or summary to report what someone has said rather than quoting word-for-word. Indirect quotations need to be cited but should not be marked with quotation marks or block indenting. Compare *direct quotation*.

indirect source (347–48, 372, 457) If you read a text that quotes or uses ideas from another source, that other source is for you an "indirect source": You are not reading that other source yourself but are reading about its ideas. If you want to use that material from the indirect source, you should acknowledge the indirect source as well as the source that was talking about it.

inductive reasoning (151) A form of reasoning that draws conclusions based on specific examples or facts. Compare *deductive reasoning*.

infinitive (652, 706, 740, 780) A verbal formed by combining *to* with the base form of the verb (*to decide*, *to eat*, *to study*). Infinitives can function as adjectives and adverbs as well as nouns. See *verbal*.

informal (scratch) outline (41) See *outline*.

information graphics (78–80) Graphics that convey and depict relationships among data; information graphics include tables, bar graphs, line graphs, and pie charts.

informational note (378, 391–92) In APA style, a note that occurs on the first page of a text to identify the author, provide contact information, and acknowledge support and conflicts of interest; student projects usually omit informational, or author, notes.

informative (or **expository**) **report** (16, 23, 146) A text in which the main purpose is to explain a concept or report information. See also *purpose*.

initialism (871) Abbreviation formed from the first letters of a series of words and pronounced as letters (*DNA*, *HBO*). Compare *acronym*.

inseparable (777) A transitive phrasal verb whose direct object can fall only after the particle, not before it.

intensive pronoun (638) A pronoun that renames and emphasizes its antecedent: *Dr. Collins herself performed the operation*.

Glossary of Key Terms G7

interesting (52) Paragraphs and essays that make the audience want to continue reading.

interjection (612) Words like *alas* and *ugh* that express strong feeling but otherwise serve no grammatical function.

interpret, interpretation (127, 453) Explain the meaning or significance of a text, artwork, or event.

interpretive analysis (459–61) An in-depth interpretation of the meaning or significance of literary texts, cultural works, political events, and so on.

interrogative pronoun (638, 717) A pronoun such as *who, whom, whose, what,* or *which* used to introduce a question: *What did she say?*

interrogative sentence (645) See *sentence*.

intertextual analysis (129) Considering the source in the context of the conversations it engages in, including analyzing the author's attitude toward their sources; evaluating the author's expertise and trustworthiness; and learning how many other sources cite this source, and how they treat it.

in-text citation (288, 313, 334, 335) A citation that appears in the body of the research project. See also *parenthetical citation, signal phrase*.

intransitive verb (648, 701) A verb that does not require a direct object: *The child smiled.*

introduction (40, 68, 70, 87, 89, 113) The opening paragraph or section of a text. An effective introduction should identify your topic and your stance toward the topic, establish your purpose, and engage your readers. See also *funnel introduction*.

invention techniques (25s) Prewriting strategies that help you generate and explore ideas. See *brainstorming, freewriting*.

inversion (591) An inversion is a sentence in which, contrary to normal English word order, the verb precedes the subject, usually to emphasize the point being made.

inverted-funnel conclusion (70) A conclusion that begins with a restatement of the thesis (in different words) and broadens out to discuss implications, next steps, or possible solutions. See also *conclusion*.

irony (609) The use of language to suggest the opposite of its literal meaning or to express an incongruity between what is expected and what occurs. See *figurative language*.

irregular verb (696) A verb that does not form the past tense or past participle by adding *-ed* to the base form.

J

jargon (597) The specialized vocabulary of a particular profession or discipline; inappropriately technical language.

journal (124–25) A place to record observations and ideas in writing. Also, a periodical that publishes scholarly articles. See also *periodical*.

journalists' questions (plus two) (29–30) Questions that ask *who, what, where, when, why,* and *how* to help you explore a topic. In college writing, also ask yourself about the significance of your topic (*Is it important?*) and its consequences (*What are its effects?*).

K

keyword (298) (a) A term entered into an Internet search engine, online database, or library catalog to find sources of information. (b) A word or phrase in a text that highlights or is essential to the message of the text.

L

labeling (601) Applying a word or phrase to describe an entire group, such as *autistic, Cub Scout,* or *Asian American*. When the label does not apply to all group members, or when it unfairly characterizes the group, it contributes to **stereotyping**.

layout (192) The visual arrangement of text and images using proximity (nearness), alignment, repetition, and contrast. See also *format*.

level of diction (20) The choice of words to convey a tone (formal or informal) appropriate to the audience. See *tone, connotation*.

linear text (204) A document, such as a novel or magazine article, that is arranged so that readers begin at page 1 and read through to the end. Compare *hypertext*.

line graphs (80, 85) A type of information graphic that uses lines and points on a graph to show changes over time.

link (242, 333, 878) See *hyperlink*.

linking verb (640, 648, 689) A verb that expresses a state of being rather than an action and connects the subject to its subject complement. The verb *be,* when used as a main verb, is always a linking verb. *They are excited.* See also *subject complement*.

logical fallacy (176–79) See *fallacy*.

logical organization (41) The arrangement of a sentence, paragraph, or entire text in a way that will seem sensible to readers, that will not confuse or puzzle them.

logos (150, 153) See *appeals*.

M

main verb (697, 782) The part of a verb phrase that carries its principal meaning. See *verb phrase*.

mechanics (871) Conventions controlling capitalization, italics, abbreviation, numbers, and hyphenation.

menu (107, 205) A list of the main sections of a website.

metaphor (609) An implied comparison between unlike things stated without *like, as,* or other comparative expressions: *Her mind buzzed with original ideas.* See *figurative language, simile*.

metasearch engine (242–43) Internet search engines that return the top search results from several search engines at once, with duplicate entries deleted.

methods (261, 427, 447) In APA and CSE style, the section of a research project that explains the research methods and describes any research participants (such as people interviewed) or data collected.

misinformation (270) Inaccuracies circulated by well-meaning people who mistakenly believe they are correct.

misplaced modifier (740) An ambiguously, confusingly, or disruptively placed modifying word, phrase, or clause.

mixed construction (749) A sentence with parts that do not fit together grammatically or logically.

Glossary of Key Terms

mixed metaphor (608) A combination of multiple conflicting figures of speech for the same concept. See *figurative language*.

MLA style (284–85) The citation and documentation style of the Modern Language Association, used frequently in literature and languages.

modal verb (639, 699) See *helping verb*.

modified block-style letter (538) See *block-style letter*.

modifier (553–55) A word, phrase, or clause that functions as an adjective or adverb to qualify or describe another word, phrase, or clause.

mood (695, 707–09) The form of a verb that indicates how the writer or speaker views what is written or said. The **indicative mood** states facts or opinions and asks questions: *I finished my paper.* The **imperative mood** issues commands, gives instructions, or makes requests: *Hand in your papers by Friday.* The **subjunctive mood** expresses possibility, as in hypothetical situations or wishes: *If I were finished, I could go to bed.*

N

name-year system (436–37) In CSE style, a system of acknowledgment for research projects that includes the last name of the author and the year of publication in parentheses in the text; is accompanied by an alphabetical list of references at the end of the project.

narration (64–65) A pattern of paragraph or essay development that tells a story, usually in chronological (time) order. See also *chronological organization*.

near-homonyms (618) Words that are close but not the same in pronunciation (*moral, morale*) or are different forms of the same word (*breath, breathe*).

neologism (597) A newly coined word or expression.

netiquette (544) A word composed of parts of the words *Internet* and *etiquette* that refers to conventions of politeness in online contexts.

noncount noun (or **uncountable** or **mass noun**) (767) See *noun*.

nonessential (or **nonrestrictive**) **element** (811) A modifying word, phrase, or clause that adds information to the element it modifies but does not identify it. Commas should set off nonessential elements from the rest of the sentence. *My grandfather, who recently retired, worked for the same company for forty-five years.*

noun (635–37) A word that names an idea (*justice*), thing (*chair*), quality (*neatness*), action (*judgment*), person (*Albert Einstein*), or place (*Tokyo*). Proper nouns name specific places, people, or things and are usually capitalized: *Nairobi, Hillary Rodham Clinton.* Common nouns name members of a class or group: *turtle, skyscraper.* Collective nouns name a collection that can function as a single unit: *committee, family.* Concrete nouns name things that can be seen, touched, heard, smelled, or tasted: *planet, symphony, skunk.* Abstract nouns name qualities or ideas that cannot be perceived by the senses: *mercy, fear.* Count (or countable) nouns name countable things and can be either singular or plural: *cat/cats, idea/ideas.* **Noncount** (or **uncountable** or **mass**) **nouns** name ideas or things that cannot be counted and do not have a plural form: *knowledge, pollution.*

noun clause (656) A subordinate clause that functions as a noun. See *clause*.

noun phrase (637, 750, 811) A noun and its modifiers.

number (652, 695, 734) The form of a word that indicates whether it is singular, referring to one thing (*a student*), or plural, referring to more than one (*two students*).

O

object (713, 737–39) A noun or pronoun (or a noun phrase or noun clause) that receives or benefits from the action of a transitive verb or that follows a preposition. A **direct object** receives the action of the verb: *My friend wrote a letter.* An **indirect object** benefits from the action of the verb: *My friend wrote me a letter.* The **object of a preposition** usually follows a preposition to form a prepositional phrase. *She sent the letter by mail.*

object complement (650, 762–63) An adjective or noun phrase that follows the direct object and describes the condition of the object or a change that the subject has caused it to undergo: *The candidate declared his opponent incompetent.*

objective case (714) See *case*.

objectivity (156, 265) A text is objective when it makes reasonable claims supported by logical evidence; recognizes alternative perspectives; and treats those alternatives respectfully.

object of a preposition (781) See *object*.

opinion (146) The most plausible answer for now, based on an evaluation of the available facts. Opinions are subject to revision in light of new evidence and are often the basis of argumentation.

organization (88, 213) Arranging the parts of a sentence, paragraph, or essay so that readers can most readily understand and appreciate it.

outline (41) A method of classifying information into main points, supporting points, and specific details. An **informal** (or **scratch**) **outline** arranges ideas in order of presentation; a **formal outline** uses roman and arabic numerals, upper- and lowercase letters, and indentions to classify information into main points, supporting points, and specific details; a **sentence outline** writes out main points, supporting points, and specific details in complete sentences; a **topic outline** uses words and phrases to indicate the ideas to be discussed.

P

paragraph (53–61) A group of sentences that focus on a single topic or example, often organized around a *topic sentence*.

parallelism (542–48) In writing, the expression of equivalent ideas in equivalent grammatical structures. In an outline, the use of the same pattern or form for headings at each level.

paraphrase (114, 290, 292–95) The statement of the ideas of others in one's own words and sentence structures.

Glossary of Key Terms **G9**

parenthetical citation (287, 288, 301, 335, 365)   A citation to a source that appears in parentheses in the body of a research paper. Compare *signal phrase;* see also *in-text citation.*

participial phrase (553, 652)   A phrase in which the present or past participle of a verb acts as an adjective: *the writing assignment, the written word.*

participles (653, 696)   Forms of a verb that combine with helping verbs to form certain tenses and that, as verbals, can function as adjectives. The **present participle** is the *-ing* form of the verb. The **past participle** is the *-ed* form in regular verbs (the same as the past tense) but takes various forms in irregular verbs. See *participial phrase, tense, verbal.*

particle (776)   A preposition or adverb that combines with a verb to create a new verb with a meaning that differs from the verb's meaning on its own—for example, *throw away* versus *throw.*

parts of speech (635)   The categories in which words can be classified according to the role they play in a sentence. English has eight parts of speech: *noun, pronoun, verb, adjective, adverb, preposition, conjunction,* and *interjection.*

passive voice (562, 710)   See *voice.*

past participle (781)   See *participle.*

past perfect progressive tense (703)   See *tense.*

past perfect tense (703)   See *tense.*

past progressive tense (703)   See *tense.*

past tense (703)   See *tense.*

patchwriting (114, 285)   A faulty paraphrase that relies too heavily on the language or sentence structure of the source text. Patchwritten texts may replace some terms from the source passage with synonyms, add or delete a few words, or alter the sentence structure slightly, but they do not put the passage fully into fresh words and sentences. At some colleges and universities, *patchwriting* is considered plagiarism.

pathos (154)   See *appeals.*

patterns of development (68)   See *analysis, cause and effect, comparison and contrast, definition, description,* *exemplification, narration,* and *process analysis.*

PDF (portable document format) (208, 349, 450)   A file format developed by Adobe that allows documents to be opened in different systems without altering their formatting.

peer review   Evaluation by the writer's peers. Students provide feedback to each other's work in progress; before publishing an article, scholarly journals ask one or more experts in the field (the author's *peers*) to evaluate the article.

peer revising (93–95)   A revising strategy in which the writer solicits feedback on a text from classmates, colleagues, or friends. See also *revising.*

perfect progressive tense (704)   See *tense.*

perfect tenses (704)   See *tense.*

periodical (246)   A publication, such as a magazine, newspaper, or scholarly journal, that is issued at regular intervals—daily, weekly, monthly, quarterly. See also *journal.*

periodic sentence (555–57)   A sentence that reserves the independent clause for the end, building suspense that highlights key information when it finally arrives.

person (664, 695, 735)   The form of a word that indicates whether it corresponds to the speaker or writer (*I, we*), the person addressed (*you*), or the people or things spoken or written about (*he, she, it, they, Marta, milkshakes*).

persona (12, 107)   The personality of the writer as reflected in tone and style.

personal pronoun (762, 828)   The pronouns *I, me, you, he, him, she, her, it, we, us, they, them,* which take the place of specific nouns or noun phrases.

personal statement (107)   In a portfolio, the writer's description of the contents and explanation for the choice and arrangement of selections. See also *portfolio.*

personification (609)   The attribution of human qualities to nonhuman creatures, objects, ideas, or phenomena: *The tornado swallowed the house.* See *figurative language.*

persuasive argument (16, 38, 128)   An argument that advocates for a claim. The writer's purpose is to convince readers to agree with or at least to respect a position on a debatable issue. See also *argument, exploratory argument, purpose.*

phrasal verb (700, 776–79)   A verb combined with one or two particles that together create a new verb with a meaning different from that of the original verb alone. See *particle.*

phrase (563–64, 639, 689, 804)   A group of related words that lacks a subject, predicate, or both. A phrase cannot stand alone as a sentence, but it can function *in* a sentence as a noun, a verb, or a modifier.

pie chart (78)   An information graphic that depicts the relationship of the parts to the whole; its sections must add up to 100 percent.

plagiarism (285, 447)   Presenting a work or a portion of a work of any kind—a paper, a photograph, a speech, a web page—by someone else as if it were one's own.

plain text (201)   A computer text format that does not allow for styling such as boldface and italics.

plural (681)   Referring to more than one thing. See *number.*

point of view (489)   The perspective of the narrator in a work of literature.

polluted information (270)   Information that is inaccurate because of misunderstanding, misrepresentation, or deliberate disinformation.

portfolio (106–08)   A printed or online collection of a writer's work. A portfolio may contain the writer's best work, a range of types of writing (a proposal, a report, a set of instructions), or a collection of texts from a single project (prewriting, outline, first draft, revised draft). A portfolio usually also includes a table of contents and a personal statement. See also *personal statement.*

positive form (729)   See *comparison of adjectives and adverbs.*

possessive case (713)   See *case.*

possessive pronoun (829)   The pronouns *my, mine, your, yours, his, hers, its, our, ours, your, yours, their,* and *theirs,* which indicate possession.

predicate (665)   The part of a sentence or clause that states (*predicates*) something about the subject. The **simple predicate** consists of a main

Glossary of Key Terms

verb together with any helping verbs: *Marta is writing her parents a long email.* The **complete predicate** consists of the simple predicate together with any objects, complements, and modifiers: *Marta is writing her parents a long email.* A **compound predicate** is a complete predicate with two or more simple predicates joined with a conjunction: *Marta wrote the email but decided not to send it.*

prefix (621)   A group of letters that attaches to the beginning of a root word to modify its meaning: *act*, *react*.

prejudice (146, 148)   Ascribing qualities to an individual based on generalities about a group, generalities that are often inaccurate. See also *stereotype*.

premise (152)   A claim or assumption on which the conclusion of an argument is based. See *syllogism*.

preposition (643, 854)   A word or term that relates nouns or pronouns to other words in a sentence in terms of time, space, cause, and other attributes.

prepositional phrase (762, 793)   A preposition followed by its object—a noun or pronoun and its modifiers. Prepositional phrases function as adjectives and adverbs: *the cat with gray fur*.

present participle (781)   See *participle*.

present perfect progressive tense (704)   See *tense*.

present perfect tense (703)   See *tense*.

present progressive tense (703)   See *tense*.

present tense (705)   See *tense*.

press, or media, releases (554)   Brief articles that announce events to newspapers, magazines, and online media outlets.

previewing (113)   Scanning the title, subtitle, abstract, introduction, conclusion, sidebars, key terms, headings, subheadings, figures, and illustrations of a text to get a sense of its content, organization, and emphases before reading it in full.

primary source (297, 476, 487, 489)   Firsthand information, such as an eyewitness account, a research report, a recorded interview, or a work of literature or art. See also *field research*.

process analysis (64–65)   A pattern of paragraph or essay development that explains a process step by step.

progressive tenses (705)   See *tense*.

pronoun (62, 618, 685)   A word that renames or takes the place of a noun or noun phrase.

pronoun reference (719–720)   The relationship between a pronoun and its antecedent (the word it replaces). Pronoun reference is clear when readers can tell effortlessly what a pronoun's antecedent is.

proofreading (96–98)   Reading a text to identify and correct spelling and typographical mistakes as well as punctuation and mechanical errors.

proper noun (767)   See *noun*.

proximity (184)   In design, the arrangement of content to show relationships. Material that is related should be placed close together; material that is unrelated should be placed at a distance.

purpose (14, 15–17, 189, 204)   Your main reason for writing: to express your feelings or impressions or to entertain, inform, or persuade your audience.

Q

quantifier (775)   An adjective such as *some, many, much, less,* or *few* that indicates the amount of a noun.

quotation (285, 297)   A restatement of what someone else has said or written, either in a *direct quotation* (word for word) or an *indirect quotation* (a report of what was said or written). See *direct quotation, indirect quotation*.

R

reading journal (124–125)   An online or printed record of a reader's reactions to, analysis of, or critique of a text.

reciprocal pronoun (638)   A pronoun that refers to the individual parts of a plural antecedent: *The candidates debated one another.*

redundancy (561)   Unnecessary repetition: *It was a cloudy, overcast day.*

reference list (374, 397, 435, 447–48)   In APA and CSE style, a section at the end of a writing project in which the writer provides full bibliographic information for all sources cited in the text.

reference work (268)   Sources, such as dictionaries, encyclopedias, bibliographies, almanacs, and atlases, that provide overview and background information on a word or topic. Specialized reference works may be appropriate sources for college projects, but general reference works are not.

reflection (119–23)   The process of thinking about, annotating, and writing about a text in a reading journal; reflection is a necessary step for coming fully to terms with the text. See also *annotation, reading journal*.

reflexive pronoun (638)   A pronoun that refers back to the subject of a sentence: *She helped herself to the buffet.*

regionalism (597)   Nonstandard usage characteristic of people in a particular locality.

regular verbs (696)   Verbs whose past-tense and past-participle forms end in *-d* or *-ed*.

relative clause (655)   An adjective clause introduced by a relative pronoun such as *who, whom,* or *that.* See *adjective clause*.

relative pronouns (638)   Pronouns such as *who, whom, whose, that,* and *which* used to introduce a subordinate clause that describes the pronoun's antecedent: *The apartment that I rented is small.*

relevance (52, 242)   The extent to which supporting evidence not only addresses the general topic of a text but also contributes to the reader's understanding of or belief in the text's main idea (the *thesis*). A relevant source offers information that will enrich understanding, provide background information or evidence to support claims, or suggest alternative perspectives.

reliability (248)   The extent to which a source is accurate and trustworthy.

research hypothesis (303)   A tentative assertion of what the writer expects the research to prove.

research log (304)   A journal in which a researcher records research questions and hypotheses; a working thesis; information gathered from sources; interpretation, analysis, synthesis, and critique of sources; and ideas for next steps.

Glossary of Key Terms

research questions (303) Questions about a topic that research might answer.

response (120, 452–56) Your own reactions to and insights about a text. Response occurs while a reader reads, and it often changes and develops as a result of rereading and studying the text.

restrictive element (811) See *essential element*.

résumé (545) A brief summary of an applicant's qualifications and experience.

revising (82, 106, 202) The stage of the writing process in which the writer assesses global issues such as whether the text fulfills its purpose, addresses its intended audience, is fully developed, and is organized clearly and logically; also the stage in which the writer assesses local issues such as word choice, sentence variety and emphasis, and wordiness. See also *conciseness, peer revising*.

rhetorical appeal (150) See *appeal*.

rhetorical citation (319) Identifying the source of information, words, or ideas while providing information about the source and your evaluation of it.

rhetorical question (558) A question that is meant to call attention to an issue, not to elicit an answer.

rhetorical situation (15–22) The fluid interplay of purpose, audience, culture, occasion, and topic as a writer devises, develops, and presents a project. See also *writing situation*.

Rogerian model (175–76) A model for organizing an exploratory argument that discusses evidence and counterevidence before drawing a conclusion. Compare *classical* and *Toulmin models*.

roundabout expression (560) A wordy expression that should be more concise.

S

scholarly sources (266) Peer-reviewed journal articles and books by experts, often published by university presses.

scratch (informal) outline (41) See *outline*.

search engine (242) Computer software that retrieves information from the internet, online databases, and library catalogs.

secondary sources (491) Sources that describe, evaluate, or interpret primary sources or other secondary sources. A textbook is a secondary source.

sentence (562–64) A word group with a subject and predicate that does not begin with a subordinating expression. A **declarative sentence** makes a statement: *The phone rang.* An **imperative sentence** gives a command: *Answer the phone.* An **interrogative sentence** asks a question: *Did the phone ring?* An **exclamatory sentence** expresses strong or sudden emotion: *How I hate annoying ring tones!* A **simple sentence** has only one independent clause and no subordinate clauses: *The phone rang.* A **compound sentence** has two or more independent clauses but no subordinate clauses: *The phone rang, and I answered it.* A **complex sentence** consists of a single independent clause with at least one subordinate clause: *My cell phone rang while I was in the elevator.* A **compound-complex sentence** has two or more independent clauses with one or more subordinate clauses: *My cell phone rang, but I didn't answer it because I was in a crowded elevator.*

sentence fragment (660–70) A word group punctuated like a sentence but lacking one or more of the essential parts of a sentence: an independent clause, a complete verb, and a subject.

sentence outline (42) See *outline*.

separable (777) A transitive phrasal verb is *separable* if its direct object can fall either between the verb and the particle (separating them) or after the particle.

sequence of tenses (706) The choice of tenses that best reflect the time relationship among the events described in the clauses of a sentence.

server (202) A computer that links other computers into a network.

setting (455) In works of literature, where and when the action occurs.

signal phrase (288, 308, 335, 364–65, 436, 813) A phrase that identifies, discusses, or describes the author or source being cited: *"How do I know what I think,"* E. M. Forster asked, *"until I see what I say?"*

simile (609) An explicit comparison between two unlike things, usually expressed with *like* or *as*: *run like the wind* (see also *figurative language, metaphor*).

simple future tense (703) See *tense*.

simple past tense (703) See *tense*.

simple predicate (647) See *predicate*.

simple present tense (702) See *tense*.

simple sentence (552, 657) See *sentence*.

simple subject (645) See *subject*.

simple tenses (672–73) See *tense*.

singular (638) Referring to one thing.

site map (204) A list of a website's contents.

slang (597) The informal, inventive, often colorful (and off-color) vocabulary of a particular group. Slang is usually inappropriate in formal writing.

slash (848) Punctuation used to mark the ends of lines in poetry when the poetry is run into a sentence.

spam (544) Unsolicited advertising sent to email or social software accounts such as Twitter.

spatial organization (41) An organizational strategy that structures a description visually, from left to right, from inside to outside, from top to bottom, and so on.

sponsors (273) Corporations, agencies, and organizations that are responsible for creating and making available a website's content.

squinting modifier (742) A modifier that appears confusingly to modify both what precedes it and what follows it.

Standard American English (728) The dialect of English that prevails in academic and business settings in the United States.

stereotype (602) A simplified, uncritical, and often negative generalization about an entire group of people. See also *prejudice*.

styles of documentation (335, 363, 397, 435) A set of specifications for citing and documenting sources. Most of the well-known style sheets, such as MLA, APA, *Chicago*, and CSE, are sponsored and updated by professional organizations or publishers.

subject (645, 660) The part of a sentence that identifies what the predicate is making a statement about. The **simple subject** is a noun or pronoun: *The cat hissed at the dog.* The **complete subject** is the simple subject with any modifying words or phrases: *The excitable gray cat chased the dog.* A **compound subject** is a complete subject with two or more simple subjects joined with a conjunction: *The cat and the dog usually get along.*

subject complement (554, 640, 689, 714, 750) An adjective, pronoun, or noun phrase that follows a linking verb and describes or refers to the sentence subject: *This food is delicious.*

subject directory (31) A collection of websites organized into groups by topic and arranged hierarchically from most general to most specific.

subjective case (714) See *case.*

subjunctive mood (708–09) See *mood.*

subordinate clause, or dependent clause (571, 587, 588, 654, 717) See *clause.*

subordinating conjunction (634) See *conjunction.*

subordination (565–77) The incorporation of secondary or modifying elements into a sentence or clause: *Although he got a late start, he arrived on time.*

suffix (724) A group of letters that attaches to the end of a root word to change its meaning and grammatical form: *act, action.*

summary (115, 291, 295–96) A passage restating the main idea and major supporting points of a source text in the reader's own words and sentence structures. A summary should be at least 50 percent shorter than the text it restates.

superlative form (729) See *comparison of adjectives and adverbs.*

superstition (146) A belief with no basis in fact: *A wish made on a falling star will come true.*

s.v. (447) Abbreviation of the Latin phrase *sub verbo,* "under the word."

symbolism (455) The use of a character, event, or object to represent something more than its literal meaning.

synchronous media (211) Communication media such as instant messaging and online chat in which participants discuss topics in real time. Compare *asynchronous media.*

synonyms (61) Words with similar meanings—for example, *wrong* and *incorrect.* Compare *antonyms.*

synthesis (116, 134) The process of making connections among ideas in a text, ideas in other texts, and the writer's own ideas and experiences. Synthesis is an important component in critical thinking and reading and is central to much successful college writing.

T

table (78) An information graphic that organizes data into rows and columns.

tense (695, 706) The form of a verb that indicates the time in which an action or event occurs, when it occurred relative to other events, and whether it is ongoing or completed. The three **simple tenses** are the simple present (*I practice*), the simple past (*I practiced*), and the simple future (*I will practice*). The **perfect tenses** generally indicate the completion of an action before a particular time. They include the present perfect (*I have practiced*), the past perfect (*I had practiced*), and the future perfect (*I will have practiced*). The **progressive tenses** indicate ongoing action. They include the present progressive (*I am practicing*), the past progressive (*I was practicing*), the future progressive (*I will be practicing*), the present perfect progressive (*I have been practicing*), the past perfect progressive (*I had been practicing*), and the future perfect progressive (*I will have been practicing*).

tense sequence (706) See *sequence of tenses.*

theme (487) The main point of a work of literature.

thesis statement (36–39, 81, 89, 534) A brief statement (one or two sentences) of a text's main idea.

title page (106) A cover sheet for a printed portfolio, with identifying information, including the work's title, author's name, course number, and date of submission.

tone (14, 20–22, 120) The attitude of the writer toward the audience, the topic, and the writer her- or himself as conveyed through word choice, style, and content.

topic (14, 25, 31, 36, 188) The subject of a text.

topic outline (42) See *outline.*

topic sentence (55–58) A sentence (sometimes two) that states a paragraph's main idea.

Toulmin model (176–177) A model for organizing an argument based on *claims* (or assertions), *grounds* (or evidence), and *warrants* (or assumptions linking claims to grounds). Compare *classical* and *Rogerian* models.

transitional expressions (61, 554, 807) Words and phrases, such as *in addition, however,* and *since,* that show the relationship between sentences or paragraphs.

transitive verb (709, 761) A verb that takes a direct object.

tree diagram (39) A way to depict the relationships among topics and subtopics visually by placing the main idea at the top of the page and letting topics and subtopics branch off below it.

U

understatement (609) The deliberate use of less forceful language than a subject warrants: *An A average is pretty good.* See *figurative language.*

unfamiliar to familiar (41) An organization pattern that presents surprising ideas, examples, or information first, before moving on to familiar ground.

unified, unity (44, 52) A quality of a text in which all the examples and evidence support the paragraph's topic sentence and in which each of the supporting paragraphs supports the text's thesis statement.

unmarked infinitive (780) The base verb alone, without *to.*

URL (271) Universal resource locator, a website's Internet address.

V

verb (639, 696) A word that expresses action (*The quarterback throws a pass*), occurrence (*The play happened in the second half*), or state of being

Glossary of Key Terms **G13**

(*The fans are happy*). Verbs also carry information about time (tense), as well as person, number, voice, and mood.

verbal (639, 681, 697, 804)   A verb form that functions as a noun, adjective, or adverb. Verbals may have objects and complements, but they lack the information about tense required of a complete verb.

verb phrase (639, 696, 746)   A main verb with any helping (or auxiliary) verbs.

verbal phrase (652)   A verbal and any modifiers, objects, or complements.

vested interest (265)   A participant or stakeholder who might personally benefit from the results of a decision, event, or process has a vested (not objective) interest in that decision, event, or process and thus might influence it not for the welfare of others but for personal gain.

voice (562, 695, 710–11)   In grammar, the form of a transitive verb that indicates whether the subject is acting or acted upon. In the **active voice**, the subject performs the action of the verb: *The dog chased the cat.* In the **passive voice**, the subject receives the action of the verb: *The cat was chased by the dog.* Also, in writing, the sense of the writer's personality as conveyed through the writer's word, style, and content choices. See also *persona, tone.*

W

warrant (159)   An unstated assumption that underlies an argument's main claim. See *Toulmin model.*

web browser (201)   The software program that interprets HTML code, making it possible for users to view websites and web pages.

weblog (or **blog**) (245, 271)   See *blog.*

web pages (203)   Files on a website in addition to the home page; web pages may include text, audio, video, still images, and database files.

website (203)   A collection of files located at a single address (URL) on the World Wide Web.

well developed (52)   Paragraphs or essays that supply the information readers need to be persuaded of the writer's point.

white space (194)   The portion of a page or screen with no text, graphics, or images.

wiki (204)   A website designed for collaborative writing and editing.

working bibliography (230–31)   A list of sources a researcher compiles before and during the research process.

working thesis (495)   The first version of a thesis that a writer can imagine for the text he or she is writing. Typically the working thesis goes through several revisions as the writer drafts and revises the text.

works-cited list (491)   In MLA style, a section at the end of a research project in which the writer provides full bibliographic information for all sources cited in the text.

writing process (14–110)   The process a writer engages in to produce a writing project. The writing process includes analyzing the assignment, planning the project, generating ideas, drafting, revising, editing, designing, proofreading, and publishing.

writing situation (15–22)   The characteristics of a text, including its purpose, audience, context, and genre, as well as its length, due date, and format.

Z

zero article (768)   See *article.*

Glossary of Usage

This usage glossary includes words that writers often confuse (*infer, imply*) or misuse (*disinterested, uninterested*) and expressions that are nonstandard and sometimes even pretentious. As a responsible writer, strive to avoid words and expressions that will confuse or distract your readers or that will undermine their confidence in you. Of course, not all words and expressions that cause writers problems are listed here; if a word or expression with which you have trouble is *not* included here, check the index, review chapters 30 and 31 ("Choosing Appropriate Language" and "Choosing Effective Words"), review the list of homonyms and near-homonyms on p. 565, consult the usage notes in a dictionary, or consult another usage guide, such as Fowler's *Modern English Usage*, *The New York Times Manual of Style and Usage*, *100 Words Almost Everyone Confuses and Misuses*, or *The American Heritage Book of English Usage*.

A

a, an   *A* and *an* are indefinite articles. Use *a* before a word that begins with a consonant sound: *a car, a hill, a one-way street*. Use *an* before a word that begins with a vowel sound: *an appointment, an hour, an X-ray*.

accept, except   *Accept* is a verb meaning "agree to receive": *I accept the nomination. Except* is a preposition that means "but": *Everyone voted for me except Paul.*

adapt, adopt   *Adapt* means "to adjust": *Instead of migrating, the park's ducks adapt to the changing climate. Adopt* means "to take as one's own": *I adopted a cat from the shelter.*

adverse, averse   *Adverse* means "unfavorable" or "hostile"; *averse* means "opposed": *She was averse to buying a ticket to a play that had received such adverse criticism.*

advice, advise   The noun *advice* means "guidance"; the verb *advise* means "to suggest": *I advised her to get some sleep. She took my advice and went to bed early.*

affect, effect   As a verb, *affect* means "to influence" or "to cause a change": *Study habits affect one's grades.* As a noun, *affect* means "feeling or emotion": *The defendant responded without affect to the guilty verdict.* As a noun, *effect* means "result": *The decreased financial aid budget is an effect of the recession.* As a verb, *effect* means "to bring about or accomplish": *Submitting the petition effected a change in the school's policy.*

aggravate, irritate   *Aggravate* means "to intensify" or "worsen": *Dancing until dawn aggravated Giorgio's bad back. Irritate* means "to annoy": *He was irritated that his chiropractor could not see him until Tuesday.* Colloquially, *aggravate* is often used to mean *annoy*, but this colloquial usage is inappropriate in formal contexts.

agree to, agree with   *Agree to* means "to consent to": *Chris agreed to host the party. Agree with* means "be in accord with": *Anne agreed with Chris that a party was just what everyone needed.*

ain't   *Ain't* is a nonstandard contraction for *am not, are not,* or *is not* and should not be used in formal writing.

all ready, already   *All ready* means "completely prepared"; *already* means "previously": *They were all ready to catch the bus, but it had already left.*

all right, alright   *All right* is the standard spelling; *alright* is nonstandard.

all together, altogether   *All together* means "as a group": *When Noah's family gathered for his graduation, it was the first time they had been all together in years. Altogether* means "completely": *Noah was altogether overwhelmed by the attention.*

allude, elude, refer to   *Allude* means "to refer to indirectly"; *elude* means "to avoid" or "to escape": *He eluded further questioning by alluding to his troubled past.* Do not use *allude* to mean "refer directly"; use *refer to* instead: *The speaker referred to* [not *alluded to*] *slide six of her PowerPoint presentation.*

allusion, illusion   An *allusion* is an indirect reference: *I almost missed the author's allusion to Macbeth.* An *illusion* is a false appearance or belief: *The many literary quotations he drops into his speeches give the illusion that he is well read.*

almost, most   *Almost* means "nearly"; *most* means "the majority of": *My roommate will tell me almost* [not *most*] *anything, but I talk to my sister about most of my own problems.*

a lot, alot   *Alot* is nonstandard; always spell *a lot* as two words.

among, amongst   *Amongst* is a British alternative to *among;* in American English, *among* is preferred.

among, between   Use *among* with three or more nouns or with words that stand for a group composed of three or more members; use *between* with two or more nouns: *I'm double majoring because I could not decide between biology and English. Italian, art history, and calculus are among my other favorites.*

amoral, immoral   *Amoral* means "neither moral nor immoral" or "indifferent to moral standards"; *immoral* means "violating moral standards": *While secularists believe that nature is amoral, religionists often view natural disasters as punishments for immoral behavior.*

amount, number   Use *amount* with items that cannot be counted (noncount or mass nouns); use *number* with items that can be counted (count nouns): *The dining hall prepares the right amount of food based on the number of people who eat there.*

an   See *a, an.*

G15

Glossary of Usage

and/or *And/or* is shorthand for "one or the other or both." It is acceptable in technical and business writing, but it should be avoided in most academic writing.

ante-, anti- The prefix *ante-* means "before," as in *antebellum,* or "before the war"; the prefix *anti-* means "against," as in *antibiotic* ("against bacteria").

anxious, eager *Anxious* means "uneasy": *Dan was anxious about writing his first twenty-page paper.* *Eager* indicates strong interest or enthusiasm: *He was eager to finish his first draft before spring break.*

anybody, any body; anyone, any one *Anybody* and *anyone* are singular indefinite pronouns: *Does anybody [or anyone] have an extra pen?* *Any body* and *any one* are a noun and pronoun (respectively) modified by the adjective *any*: *She was not fired for making any one mistake but, rather, for making many mistakes over a number of years.*

anymore, any more *Anymore* means "from now on": *She does not write letters anymore.* *Any more* means "additional": *I do not need any more stamps.* Both are used only in negative contexts, for example, with *not* or other negative terms such as *hardly* or *scarcely.*

anyplace *Anyplace* is an informal way of saying *anywhere. Anywhere* is preferable in formal writing.

anyways, anywheres *Anyways* and *anywheres* are nonstandard; use *anyway* and *anywhere* instead.

as *As* should not be used in place of *because, since,* or *when* if ambiguity will result: *As people were lining up to use the elliptical machine, the management posted a waiting list.* Does this sentence mean that management posted the sign *while* people were lining up, or does it mean that the management posted the sign *because* there was such demand for the machine?

as, as if, like Use *as,* or *as if,* not *like,* as a conjunction in formal writing: *The president spoke as if [not like] he were possessed by the spirit of Abraham Lincoln. Like* is acceptable, however, as a preposition that introduces a comparison: *The president spoke like a true leader.*

at *At* is not necessary to complete *where* questions: *Where is Waldo?* not *Where is Waldo at?*

averse, adverse See *adverse, averse.*

awful, awfully In formal writing, use *awful* and *awfully* to suggest the emotion of fear or wonder, not as a synonym for *bad* or to mean *very*. *The high priest gave forth an awful cry before casting the captive from the top of the pyramid toward the crowd below.*

awhile, a while *Awhile* is an adverb: *They talked awhile before going to dinner. A while* is an article and a noun, and should always follow a preposition: *Rest for a while between eating and exercising.*

B

bad, badly In formal writing, use the adjective *bad* to modify nouns and pronouns and after linking verbs (as a subject complement): *Because I had a bad day, my husband feels bad.* Use the adverb *badly* to modify verbs, adjectives, and adverbs: *Todd's day went badly from start to finish.*

being as, being that *Being as* and *being that* are nonstandard substitutes for *because*: *Because* [not *being as*] *Marcus did well as a teaching assistant, he was asked to teach a class of his own the next year.* Avoid them.

beside, besides *Beside* is a preposition that means "next to" or "along side of": *You will always find my glasses beside the bed. Besides* is an adverb meaning "furthermore" or a preposition meaning "in addition to": *Besides, it will soon be finals. Besides chemistry, I have exams in art history and statistics.*

between, among See *among, between.*

bring, take Use *bring* when something is coming toward the speaker and *take* when it is moving away: *When the waiter brought our entrees, he took our bread.*

burst, bursted; bust, busted *Burst* is a verb meaning to break apart violently; the past tense of *burst* is also *burst,* not *bursted. Bust* is slang for *to burst* or *to break* and should be avoided in formal writing: *The boiler burst* [not *bursted* or *busted*] *in a deadly explosion.*

C

can, may Use *can* when discussing ability: *I know she can quit smoking.* Use *may* when discussing permission: *The server told her that she may not smoke anywhere in the restaurant.*

capital, capitol *Capital,* a noun, can mean "funds," or it can mean "the city that is the seat of government": *The student council did not have enough capital to travel to Harrisburg, Pennsylvania's capital.* The word *capitol* means "the building where lawmakers meet": *The state's capitol is adorned with a golden dome.* When capitalized, *Capitol* refers to the building in Washington, DC, where the US Congress meets.

censor, censure *Censor* means both "to delete objectionable material" (a verb) and "one who deletes objectionable material" (a noun): *The bedroom scenes, but not the battle scenes, were heavily censored. Clearly, the censors object more to sex than to violence. Censure* means both "to reprimand officially" (verb) and "an official reprimand" (noun): *The ethics committee censured the governor for lying under oath. Members of his party were relieved that a censure was all he suffered.*

cite, sight, site *Cite,* a verb, means "to quote" or "mention": *Cite your sources according to MLA format. Sight,* a noun, means "view" or "scene": *The sight of a field of daffodils makes me think of Wordsworth. Site,* a noun, means "location" or "place" (even online): *That site has the best recipes on the internet.*

climactic, climatic *Climactic* is an adjective derived from the noun *climax* and means "culminating" or "most intense"; *climatic* is an adjective derived from the noun *climate*: *The climactic moment of a thunderstorm occurs when the center of the storm is overhead. Tornados are violent climatic phenomena associated with thunderstorms.*

complement, compliment *Complement* is a noun meaning "that which completes or perfects something else"; it can also be used as a verb meaning "the process of completing or making perfect." *Compliment* means either "a flattering comment"

Glossary of Usage

or "the act of giving a compliment": *My husband complements me and makes me whole; still, it annoys me that he rarely compliments me on my appearance.*

conscience, conscious *Conscience* is a noun meaning "sense of right and wrong": *Skipping class weighed heavily on Sunil's conscience. Conscious* is an adjective that means "aware" or "awake": *Maria made a conscious decision to skip class.*

continual(ly), continuous(ly) *Continual* means "repeated frequently": *The continual request for contributions undermined her resolve to be more charitable. Continuous* means "uninterrupted": *The continuous stream of bad news forced her to shut off the television.*

could care less *Could care less* is an illogical, and nonstandard, substitute for *could not care less*: If one *could care less*, then one must care, at least a little, and yet this is not the intended meaning.

could of, must of, should of, would of These are misspellings of *could have, must have, should have,* and *would have.*

criteria, criterion *Criteria* is the plural form of the noun *criterion,* Latin for "standard": *His criteria for grading may be vague, but I know I fulfilled at least one criterion by submitting my paper on time.*

D

data, media, phenomena *Data, media,* and *phenomena* are plural nouns (*datum, medium,* and *phenomenon* are their singular forms): *The data suggest that the economy will rebound by the time you graduate. The news media raise the alarm about public corruption, but it is the voters who must take action. The Aurora Borealis is one of many amazing natural phenomena.* (*Data* is increasingly used as a singular noun, but continuing to use it as a plural is never wrong.)

differ from, differ with *Differ from* means "to lack similarity": *Renaissance art differs greatly from art of the Middle Ages. Differ with* means to disagree: *Martin Luther's forty-nine articles spelled out the ways in which he differed with the Catholic Church.*

discreet, discrete *Discreet,* an adjective, means "tactful" or "judicious": *Please be discreet—don't announce that you saw Ada crying in the bathroom. Discrete* means "distinct" or "separate": *The study revealed two discrete groups, those who can keep a secret and those who cannot.*

disinterested, uninterested *Disinterested* means "impartial": *A judge who cannot be disinterested should recuse him- or herself from the case. Uninterested* means "indifferent": *The book seems well-written, but I am uninterested in the topic.*

don't, doesn't *Don't* is a contraction of *do not;* it is used with *I, you, we, they,* and plural nouns: *I don't want to drive, but the trains don't run very often. Doesn't* is a contraction of *does not;* it is used with *he, she, it,* and singular nouns: *It doesn't matter whether you're a little late; Fred doesn't mind waiting.*

E

each and every *Each and every* is a wordy substitute for *each* or *every;* use one or the other but not both.

eager, anxious See *anxious, eager.*

effect, affect See *affect, effect.*

e.g., i.e. *E.g.* is an abbreviation of a Latin phrase meaning "for example" or "for instance"; *i.e.* is an abbreviation of a Latin phrase meaning "that is." In formal writing, use the English equivalents rather than the Latin abbreviations; the Latin abbreviations are acceptable in tables, footnotes, and other places where space is at a premium.

elicit, illicit *Elicit,* a verb, means "to draw out": *Every week, American Idol contestants try to elicit enough support to avoid elimination. Illicit,* an adjective, means "illegal" or "impermissible": *In 2003, American Idol contestant Frenchie Davis was disqualified for posing in illicit photos.*

elude, allude, refer to See *allude, elude, refer to.*

emigrate from, immigrate to *Emigrate from* means "to leave one's country and settle in another": *Jake's grandmother emigrated from Poland in 1919. Immigrate to* means "to move to and settle in a new country": *Jake's grandmother immigrated to the United States in 1919.*

eminent, imminent, immanent *Eminent* means "renowned": *The university hosts lectures by many eminent scientists. Imminent* means "about to happen" or "looming": *In the last year of the Bush administration, many felt that a recession was imminent. Immanent* means "inherent" or "pervasive throughout the world": *Many religions teach that God's presence is immanent.*

enthused *Enthused* is a colloquial adjective meaning "enthusiastic." In formal writing, use *enthusiastic*: *Because of the team's excellent record, Eric was enthusiastic* [not *enthused*] *about joining.*

etc. *Etc.* is an abbreviation of the Latin phrase *et cetera,* meaning "and others." Because *et* means "and," adding the word *and* before *etc.* is redundant. In a series, include a comma before *etc.*: *A great deal of online media are used in classes today: blogs, wikis, Blackboard, Facebook, etc.* In most formal writing, concluding with a final example or *and so on* (the English equivalent of *etc.*) is preferable.

everybody, everyone; every body, every one *Everybody* and *everyone* are interchangeable singular indefinite pronouns: *Everybody* [or *everyone*] *who went to the concert got a free T-shirt. Every body* and *every one* are a noun and a pronoun (respectively) modified by the adjective *every*: *Coroners must treat every body they examine with respect.*

except, accept See *accept, except.*

expect, suppose *Expect* means "to anticipate": *I expect to be home when she arrives. Suppose* means "to presume": *I suppose she should have a key just in case.*

explicit, implicit *Explicit,* an adjective, means "overt" or "stated outright": *The rules are explicit : "No running." Implicit* is an adjective that means "implied": *Implicit in the rules is a prohibition against skipping.*

F

farther, further Use *farther* with distances: *I'd like to drive a hundred miles farther before we pull over for dinner.* Use *further* to mean "more" or "in addition": *I have nothing further to add.*

Glossary of Usage

fewer, less Use *fewer* with items that can be counted (count nouns). Use *less* with items that cannot be counted (noncount or mass nouns): *This semester, I am taking three fewer classes than I took in the fall, but because I have a job now, I have less time to study.*

first, firstly *Firstly* is used in Britain, but it sounds overly formal in the United States. *First* (and *second* and *third*) is the standard form in the United States.

flaunt, flout *Flaunt* means "to parade" or "show off": *Ivan flaunted his muscular torso on the quad.* *Flout* means "to disobey" or "ignore": *He flouted school policy by parading about without his shirt on.*

further, farther See *farther, further.*

G

get Many colloquial expressions with *get* should not be used in formal writing. Avoid expressions such as *get with the program, get your act together, get lost,* and so on.

good, well *Good* is an adjective; *well* is an adverb: *Playing well in the tournament made Lee feel good.* In references to health, however, *well* is an adjective: *She had a cold, but now she is well and back at work.*

H

hanged, hung Use the past-tense verb *hanged* only to describe a person executed by hanging. Use the past-tense verb *hung* to describe anything else (pictures, clothing) that can be suspended.

hardly Use *can hardly* instead of *can't hardly,* a double negative: *I can hardly keep my eyes open.*

he, she; he/she; s/he Historically, the pronoun *he* was used generically to mean *he or she;* in informal contexts, writers avoid bias by writing *he/she* or *s/he.* In formal writing, however, revise your sentence to avoid a gendered pronoun: *Sensible students are careful what they post on social networking sites* [not *The sensible student is careful what he posts about himself on social networking sites*].

hisself *Hisself* is a nonstandard substitute for *himself.* Avoid it.

I

i.e., e.g. See *e.g., i.e.*

if, whether Use *whether* not *if* when alternatives are offered: *If I must go out, I insist that we go to a decent restaurant. I do not care whether we eat Chinese food or Italian, but I refuse to eat at Joe's.*

illicit, elicit See *elicit, illicit.*

illusion, allusion See *allusion, illusion.*

immigrate to, emigrate from See *emigrate from, immigrate to.*

imminent, eminent, immanent See *eminent, imminent, immanent.*

immoral, amoral See *amoral, immoral.*

implicit, explicit See *explicit, implicit.*

imply, infer *Imply* means "to suggest indirectly": *The circles under Phillip's eyes implied that he had not slept much. Infer* means "to conclude": *From the way he devoured his dinner, I inferred that Raymond was famished.*

incredible, incredulous *Incredible* means "unbelievable": *Debbie told an incredible story about meeting the Dalai Lama. Incredulous* means "unbelieving": *I am incredulous of everything that the tabloids print.*

infer, imply See *imply, infer.*

in regards to *In regards to* is nonstandard. Use *in regard to, as regards,* or *regarding* instead.

irregardless *Irregardless* is nonstandard; use *regardless* instead.

irritate, aggravate See *aggravate, irritate.*

is when, is where Avoid these phrases in definitions: *An oligarchy is a system of government in which the many are ruled by a few,* or *Oligarchy is government of the many by the few* [not *An oligarchy is when the many are ruled by a few*].

it's, its *It's* is a contraction of "it is" or "it has," and *its* is a possessive pronoun: *It's been a long time since the ailing pigeon flapped its wings in flight.* One trick for distinguishing the two is to recall that contractions such as *it's* are often avoided in formal writing, while possessive pronouns like *its* are perfectly acceptable.

K

kind, kinds *Kind* is a singular noun: *This kind of weather is bad for asthmatics. Kinds* (a plural noun) is used only to denote more than one kind: *Many kinds of pollen can adversely affect breathing.*

kind of, sort of *Kind of* and *sort of* are colloquial; in formal writing, use "somewhat" or "a little" instead: *Julia was somewhat* [not *kind of*] *pleased to be going back to school.* Use *kind of* and *sort of* in formal writing only to mean "type of": *E. E. Cummings's poetry creates a new kind of grammar.*

L

lay, lie *Lay* means "to place"; it requires a direct object. Its main forms are *lay, laid,* and *laid: She laid her paper on the professor's desk. Lie* means "to recline"; it does not take a direct object. Its main forms are *lie, lay,* and *lain: She fell asleep as soon as she lay down.*

leave, let *Leave* means "to go away"; *let* means "to allow." *If I leave early, will you let me know what happens?*

less, fewer See *fewer, less.*

like, as, as if See *as, as if, like.*

loose, lose The adjective *loose* means "baggy" or "not securely attached": *I have to be careful with my glasses because one of the screws is loose.* The verb *lose* means "to misplace": *I am afraid I will lose the screw and have to attach the earpiece with duct tape.*

lots, lots of *Lots* and *lots of* are colloquial and should be avoided in academic writing; use terms like *much, many,* and *very* instead.

M

may, can See *can, may.*

maybe, may be The adverb *maybe* means "possibly" or "perhaps": *The verb phrase may be means "have the possibility to be": Maybe I'll apply for an internship next semester, but if I wait too long all of the positions may be filled.*

may of, might of *May of* and *might of* are misspellings of *may have* and *might have.*

media See *data, media, phenomena.*

moral, morale *Moral* means "ethical lesson": *Aesop's fables each have a moral, such as "don't judge others by their appearance." Morale* means "attitude" or "spirits": *April's warm weather significantly raised student morale.*

most, almost See *almost, most.*

Glossary of Usage

must of See *could of, must of, should of, would of.*

myself, himself, herself, etc. Use pronouns that end with *-self* to refer to or intensify other words: *Obama himself made an appearance.* Do not use them when you are unsure whether to use a pronoun in the nominative case (*I, she, he, we, they*) or the objective case (*me, her, him, us, them*): *This conversation is between him and me* [not *himself and myself*].

N

nohow, nowheres *Nohow* and *nowheres* are nonstandard forms of *anyway, in any way, in any place, in no place,* and *nowhere.* Avoid them.

number, amount See *amount, number.*

O

off of Omit *of*: *Sarah took the pin off* [not *off of*] *her coat.*

OK, O.K., okay These are all acceptable spellings, but the term is inappropriate in formal writing. Choose a more specific word instead: *Food served in the dining hall is mediocre* [not *okay*].

P

phenomena See *data, media, phenomena.*

plus Avoid using *plus* as a substitute for the coordinating conjunction *and* or the transition *moreover.*

precede, proceed *Precede* means "come before"; *proceed* means "continue": *Despite warnings from those who preceded me, I proceeded to take six classes in one semester.*

principal, principle *Principal,* a noun, refers to the leader of an organization. *Principal,* used as an adjective, means "main." *Principle,* used as a noun, means "belief" or "standard": *The school principal's principal concern is the well-being of her students. She runs the school on the principle that fairness is essential.*

proceed, precede See *precede, proceed.*

R

raise, rise The verb *raise* means "lift up" or "move up" and takes a direct object: *Joseph raised the blinds.* The verb *rise* means "to go upward" and does not take a direct object: *We could see the steam rise as the solution started to boil.*

real, really Do not use *real* or *really* as a synonym for *very*: *Spring break went very* [not *real* or *really*] *fast.*

reason is because, reason why To avoid redundancy and faulty predication, choose either *the reason is that* or *because*: *The reason Chris fell is that he is uncoordinated. It is not because his shoe was untied.*

refer to, allude, elude See *allude, elude, refer to.*

relation, relationship Use *relation* to refer to a connection between things: *There is a relation between the amount one sleeps and one's overall health.* Use *relationship* to refer to a connection between people: *Tony has always had a close relationship with his grandfather.*

respectfully, respectively *Respectfully* means "with respect": *Ben treats his parents respectfully. Respectively* means "in the given order": *My mother and father are 54 and 56, respectively.*

rise, raise See *raise, rise.*

S

set, sit The verb *set* means "to place" or "to establish," and it takes a direct object. *The professor set the book on the desk.* The verb *sit* means "to assume a sitting position," and it does not take a direct object: *You can sit in the waiting room until the doctor is ready.*

shall, will In the past, *shall* was used as a helping verb with *I* and *we,* and *will* was used with *he, she, it,* and *they*: *I shall go on dancing, and they will go home.* Now *will* is generally used with all persons: *I will go on singing, and they will all cover their ears. Shall* is used mainly with polite questions (*Shall we invite your mother?*) and in rules and regulations (*No person shall enter these premises after dusk.*).

should of See *could of, must of, should of, would of.*

since *Since* can mean "because" or "from that time," so use it only when there is no chance that readers will infer the wrong meaning. In the sentence that follows, either meaning makes sense: *Since I moved to the country, I have had no trouble sleeping.* Revise to make your meaning clear: *Since January, when I moved to the country ...* or *Because I moved to the country, ...*

sit, set See *set, sit.*

site, sight, cite See *cite, sight, site.*

somebody, someone *Somebody* and *someone* are interchangeable singular indefinite pronouns: *Someone* [or *somebody*] *is at the door.*

sometime, sometimes *Sometime* is an adverb meaning "at an indefinite time"; *sometimes* is an adverb meaning "on occasion," "now and then": *Sometimes I wish my future would come sometime soon.*

somewheres *Somewheres* is nonstandard; use *somewhere* instead.

stationary, stationery *Stationary* means "not moving"; *stationery* means "writing paper." (Thinking of the *e* in "stationery" as standing for *envelope* may help.)

supposed to, used to *Supposed to* means *should; used to* means "did regularly in the past." In speech, the final *-d* is often dropped, but in writing, it is required: *I was supposed* [not *suppose*] *to practice piano daily; instead, I used* [not *use*] *to play hockey.*

sure and, sure to; try and, try to *Sure to* and *try to* are standard; *sure and* and *try and* are not.

T

take, bring See *bring, take.*

than, then *Than* is a conjunction used in comparisons; *then* is an adverb of time. *If Betsy is already taller than I, then I will be impressed.*

that, which In formal writing, *that* is generally used with essential (or restrictive) clauses and *which* with nonessential (nonrestrictive) clauses: *The project that I am working on now is due on Monday, which is why I really have to finish it this weekend.*

that, who In formal writing, use *who* or *whom,* not *that,* to refer to people: *I. M. Pei is the architect who* [not *that*] *designed this building.*

their, there, they're *Their* is a possessive pronoun, *there* is an adverb of place, and *they're* is a contraction of "they are": *They're always leaving their dishes in the sink. Why must they*

G20 Glossary of Usage

leave them *there* instead of putting them in the dishwasher?

theirself, theirselves, themself   *Theirself, theirselves,* and *themself* are nonstandard. Use *themselves* instead.

them   In colloquial speech, the pronoun *them* is sometimes used in place of the demonstrative adjective *those;* avoid this nonstandard usage: *Those* [not *them*] *are the books I need for class.*

then, than   See *than, then.*

this here, these here, that there, them there   *This here, these here, that there,* and *them there* are nonstandard for *this, these, that,* and *them.*

to, too, two   *To* is a preposition, *too* is an adverb, and *two* is a number: *To send two dozen roses to your girlfriend for Valentine's Day is too expensive.*

try and, try to   See *sure and, sure to; try and, try to.*

U

uninterested, disinterested   See *disinterested, uninterested.*

unique   *Unique* means "the one and only thing of its kind," so it is illogical to modify it with words like *somewhat* or *very* that suggest degrees: *Your approach to the issue is unique* [not *somewhat unique*].

usage, use   The noun *usage,* which means a "customary manner, approach," should not be used in place of the noun *use: The use* [not *usage*] *of cell phones in this restaurant will not be tolerated.*

use, utilize   The verb *utilize,* which means "to use purposefully," should not be used in place of *use: Students must use* [not *utilize*] *parking lots D, E, and F, not those parking lots reserved for faculty and staff.*

W

wait for, wait on   Although *wait on* is sometimes used colloquially as a substitute for "wait for," it is nonstandard. Use *wait on* to mean "serve" and *wait for* to mean "await": *I am waiting for* [not *waiting on*] *my mother, who is always late.*

ways   *Ways* is sometimes used colloquially as a substitute for "distance." Avoid this usage in formal writing: *We still have quite a distance* [not *ways*] *to go before we get to a rest area.*

weather, whether   *Weather,* a noun, means "the state of the atmosphere"; *whether,* a conjunction, indicates a choice between alternatives: *It does not matter whether you prefer rain or snow; the weather will be what it will be.*

well, good   See *good, well.*

whether, if   See *if, whether.*

which, that   See *that, which.*

who, that   See *that, who.*

who, whom   Use *who* for the subject of clauses; use *whom* for the object of clauses: *Who will be coming to the party? Whom did you ask to bring the cake?*

who's, whose   *Who's* is a contraction of "who is" or "who has"; *whose* is a possessive pronoun: *Who's at the door? Whose coat is this?*

will, shall   See *shall, will.*

would of   See *could of, must of, should of, would of.*

Y

you   *You* (the second-person singular pronoun) should be used only to refer to the reader, not to refer to people in an indefinite sense (to replace *one*): *In medieval society, subjects* [not *you*] *had to swear an oath of allegiance to the king.*

your, you're   *Your* is a possessive pronoun; *you're* is a contraction of "you are": *You're as stubborn as your brother.*

Index

A

a, an. See Articles (*a, an, the*)
Abbreviated file, MLA style in-text citations and, 337
Abbreviated vs. complete notes, in *Chicago*-style, 441
Abbreviations
   acronyms, 859, 863, 871
   apostrophes in plurals of, 831–832
   to avoid, 873
   of business names, 873
   capitalizing, 859, 863, 869
   common do's and don'ts, 870
   of group authors, 341–342, 354, 403, 873
   initialisms, 871, 872
   Latin, 870, 873
   online, 598, 872
   parentheses around, 849
   periods in, 869
   of specific years, hours, numbers, and dollars, 872, 875
   of titles in citations, 342, 345, 349, 364
   unfamiliar, 871
about, 796
Abridged dictionaries, 613–614
Absolute phrases, 589, 654, 730–731, 806
absolutely, 559
Abstract words, 91, 216, 606–607, 635–636
Abstracts
   in APA-style papers, 415, 419, 427
   in business reports and proposals, 552
   in critical reading, 113
   in database searching, 241, 246, 415
   in previewing, 225
   relevance and, 264
   in research and laboratory reports, 514
Academic context, 14, 22, 487, 490
Academic degrees, abbreviating, 871
Academic honesty/integrity.
   See Plagiarism
Academic Onefile database, 246
Academic Search Premier database, 227, 246, 248, 251

Academic writing. *See also* Literature and humanities, writing in; Sciences and social sciences, writing in; Student Model
   analysis of assignments, 23–24
   audience, 14–15, 18–19, 23
   collaboration, 32–34
   discipline-specific vocabulary in, 512, 598
   evidence in, 46–50
   example, 4–6
   format of, 98–106
   genre and context for, 22
   idea generation in, 26–31
   illustrations decision, 77–78
   in literature and humanities, 485–509
   organization of, 35–51
   portfolios in, 106–110
   purpose of writing, 14–17, 20–21
   responsibilities to readers, 8
   style guide selection, 489, 491
   subjunctive in, 708
   thesis statement in, 35–39
   tone in, 14, 20–21
   topic selection in, 14, 23, 25, 31–32
Academic years and terms, 859, 861
accede, 622
accept, except, 619
Accessibility
   of design, 189, 208–209
   of website, 186, 187–188, 190, 208–209
Accuracy
   of citations, 287–290
   in science writing, 511
   in synonyms, 615
   in visuals, 82–83
Acknowledging sources. *See also* Citations
   common knowledge and, 283–284, 288
   for counterevidence, 305
   reasons for, 334, 398, 439, 470
   responsibilities for, 9–10
Acronyms, 872
   as abbreviations, 859, 863, 871
   brackets around, 403
   capitalizing, 859, 863

   definition of, 863, 871
   in online communication, 598
   pronunciation of, 871
Action verbs, 725
Active listening, 219
Active voice, 594–595
   concise writing and, 562
   definition of, 695
   for emphasis, 586
   in literature and humanities, 493
   passive voice confusing shifts from, 632
   passive voice vs., 695, 710–711
   reasons for using, 709–710
   in résumés, 549
   shifting voice, 733–734
   transitive verbs and, 649
Actors performance, in drama writing, 507
actually, 559
AD, BC, CE, BCE, 872
Ad hominem fallacy, 11, 180, 210
add up to, 777
Addition, conjunctions and, 568
Addresses
   for business correspondence, 539
   commas in, 815
   email, 880
   numbers in, 875
Adjective clauses, 655
Adjective phrases, 588–589, 652, 653, 696, 781
Adjectives, 724–731
   absolute, 730–731
   adverbs vs., 724
   bad and *good*, 726
   commas separating, 803, 810
   comparative form, 640, 729
   compound, 877–878
   coordinate, 803, 809–810
   cumulative, 809, 810
   definition of, 588, 640
   functions of, 636, 725
   grammar checkers on, 726
   -ly endings on, 727
   nouns used as, 728
   as object complements, 727
   ordering of, 640, 728, 786, 809, 810
   overuse of, 786

I1

12 Index

Adjectives (*continued*)
  participles and participial phrases as, 588, 653, 696, 781
  placement of, 588, 640
  plurals not used for, 724
  positive form, 728
  prepositional phrases as, 652
  prepositions with, 787
  pronouns as, 640
  proper, 859, 860–861
  as subject complements after linking verbs, 725
  superlative form, 729
admit, 780
Adverb clauses, 580
  commas setting off nonessential, 812
  function of, 636, 656
  placement of, 587
Adverbial phrases, 588, 642, 652
Adverbial prepositional phrase, 588, 652
Adverbial subordinate clause, 588
Adverbs, 724–731, 776
  adjectives vs., 724
  badly and *well*, 726
  beginning a sentence, 764–765
  clauses, 812
  comparative form, 641, 729
  in compound adjectives, 878
  conjunctive, 807
  definition of, 587
  functions of, 641, 725
  grammar checkers and, 726
  hard and *hardly*, 791
  hyphens and, 878
  negative, 789
  not and *no*, 791
  not used with direct objects, 727
  as phrases, 588, 642
  placement of, 587–588, 788–790
  positive form, 728
  prepositional phrases as, 588, 652
  sentence variety and, 588
  such and *so*, 791
  superlative form, 729
  too and *either*, 790
  too and *so*, 790
  word order and, 764–765, 788–790
Advertisements, 146, 185
  comma splices in, 674
  MLA style documenting for, 376
  scholarly source and, 266
  as visual evidence, 85, 177
advice, advise, 618, 619
advise, 780
affect, effect, 619
after, 571
  to indicate time, 573
  as subordinating conjunction, 663

Afterword, citing
  APA-style of, 413
  Chicago-style, 447
  MLA style of, 358
agree, 780
Alignment, in design, 184, 185
all-, 878–879
all
  count and noncount nouns with, 773
  placement of, 640
  pronoun-antecedent agreement, 692
  subject-verb agreement, 685
all ready, already, 619
Alliteration, in poetry, 502
allow, 780
allude, elude, refer to, 619
Allusion, as literature element, 489
allusion, illusion, 619
-ally and *-ly* suffixes, 622, 878
Almanac of American Politics, 240
Almanacs, 240
almost, 742
already, 61
already, all ready, 619
altar, alter, 619
Alternating method, in comparison and contrast, 65–66
Alternative viewpoints
  assumptions and common ground, 158–159
  evaluation of, 157–158
  hate speech, misinformation, disinformation, trolls, 158
although
  in sentence fragments, 660
  in subordination, 571, 573, 663
am, 697
a.m., 872
Amara, 197
Amazon Prime, MLA style documenting for, 371
Ambiguity
  comma use to avoid, 817
  in comparisons, 754
  in limiting modifiers, 741–743
  in pronoun reference, 720
  in sentence fragments, 664
American Heritage Book of English Usage, 614
American Heritage College Dictionary, 613
American Heritage Dictionary of Idioms, 610
American National Biography, 241
American Psychological Association style. *See* APA-style
Amounts, subject-verb agreement in, 686
Ampersand, 398
an, a, 768
Analogous colors, 195

Analogy, 177, 608
Analysis
  of assignments, 23–24, 222–223
  of design, 185
  of document, 189
  of emails, 203
  of essay exam questions, 533
  of evidence, 47–50, 128–129
  of genres, 14, 22
  intertextual, 129
  literature and humanities textual, 487, 488, 490, 495
  in note making, 286
  in paragraph development, 67
  patterns of development, 67
  process analysis, 64–65
  of purpose, 17
  in research projects, 222–223
  in revising, 86–90
  of texts, 487
  of thesis statement, 35–36
  of writing situation, 14–17
analyze, 23, 222, 315, 533
and
  in compound subjects, 645, 683
  in coordinating independent clauses, 657, 804
  in coordination, 566, 643
  in correcting comma splices and fused sentences, 676
  indicating addition, 568
  in parallel structures, 579
  in sequences, 568
  subject-verb agreement, 692
AND, as Boolean operator, 250
and others, 873. *See also et al.*
and so forth, 873
Andrews, Jewel
  "A Close Reading of Shelley's 'Poetical Essay on the Existing State of Things'" (Andrews) explication, 501–506
  "A Close Reading of Shelley's 'Poetical Essay on the Existing State of Things'" text evidence, 495
  "A Close Reading of Shelley's 'Poetical Essay on the Existing State of Things'" textual analysis, 488, 490
Anecdotes, 46
Annotated bibliographies, 224, 234–235
Annotation
  in critical reading, 119–120
  of images, 120, 127
  note making vs., 287
  of online text, 120
  of working bibliography, 224, 234–235

Index

Anonymous (unsigned) sources
　APA-style for in-text citations, 398, 404
　APA-style for reference list, 411
　Chicago-style works cited list, 444
　MLA style for in-text citations, 342
　MLA style for works cited list, 354–355
another
　count and noncount nouns with, 768, 773
　subject-verb agreement, 685
answer, 762
Antecedents of pronouns. *See also* Pronoun-antecedent agreement
　agreement of, 689–693
　clarity of pronoun reference to, 721
　collective nouns as, 692
　compound, 692–693
　definition of, 637, 689
　generic noun as, 736
　singular vs. plural, 692
Anthologies, documenting
　APA-style for, 413
　Chicago-style for, 446
　MLA style for, 344, 356, 357
Antonyms, 614–615
Anxiety, in presentations, 217
any
　in comparisons, 755
　count and noncount nouns with, 773
　pronoun-antecedent agreement, 692
　subject-verb agreement, 685
any other, 755
anybody, 685
anyone
　pronoun-antecedent agreement, 736
　subject-verb agreement, 685
anything, 685
APA-style (American Psychological Association style), 230, 232, 439. *See also* Format, of APA-style papers; In-text citations, APA-style; *Publication Manual of the American Psychological Association*; Reference list, APA-style
　abstracts in, 415, 419, 427
　audio and visual sources, 422–424
　for bibliographic notes, 420
　block quotation, 289
　for books, 330, 408–415
　disciplines using, 491, 511–512
　for endnotes, 428
　for informational notes, 425–426
　in-text quotation, 288
　miscellaneous sources, 424–425

"Nature versus Nurture" (Worthington) research paper, 430–438
　for online databases, 332, 362
　parenthetical notes, 398, 399–407
　for periodicals, 331, 415–422
　printing, paper, and binding, 430
　reasons for citing sources, 398
　sciences and social sciences writing and, 511–512
　[sic] in, 851
　for websites and web pages, 333
APA-style paper, "Nature versus Nurture" (Worthington) research paper, 430–438
Apology, letters of, 540, 542
　sample, 541
Apostrophes, 827–833
　common do's and don'ts, 828
　in compound nouns, 830–831
　in contractions and abbreviated years, 827, 831
　grammar checkers and, 829
　misuse of, 828
　plurals and, 828, 829–832
　possession indicated by, 713, 827–833
　possessives and, 637
App (e-device), MLA style documenting for, 370
Appeals
　analyzing, 129
　bandwagon appeal fallacy, 178
　to credibility (ethos), 129, 130, 131, 153–154, 155, 175, 874
　to emotions (pathos), 129, 131, 154–155, 175
　to intellect (logos), 129, 150–153, 155, 175
　visual, 156
appear
　infinitive after, 780
　as linking verb, 649, 725
Appendix
　in research and laboratory reports, 515
　in research paper/project, 438
Apple Keynote, 216
Appositives/appositive phrases
　colons and, 848, 852
　commas and, 811–813
　dashes and, 847–848
　definition of, 572, 588, 651, 716, 811
　as fragments, 665
　placement of, 588
　pronoun case in, 716
　to subordinate information, 572
appreciate, 705

Appropriate language, 596–603
are, 562, 697
are, our, 619
Arguable claim, 77
argue, 23, 222
Argumentative writing. *See* Persuasive arguments
Arguments, 153, 225. *See also* Exploratory arguments; Persuasive arguments
　appeals in, 150–156
　assumptions in, 158–159
　audience for, 143–145, 150, 158–159
　circular, 178
　claims in, 77
　classical model, 175, 179
　common ground for, 158–159
　concessions in, 157
　confirmation bias and, 157–158
　counterevidence in, 175–176
　debates and, 143–144
　evidence in, 148–149
　for group beliefs affirmation, 145–146
　to learn, 144–145
　logical fallacies in, 176–181
　logical reasoning in, 151
　oral, 156
　organizational models, 174–176
　purpose of, 16
　revising, 179
　Rogerian model, 175–176, 179
　thesis-driven, 149
　tone in, 181–182
　topic selection in, 148
　Toulmin model, 179
　visuals as, 151
around, 796
Art history, primary sources for, 490
Art works, documenting, 374–375, 456–457, 710, 866
Articles (*a, an, the*)
　a or *an* usage, 640, 768, 769
　in alphabetizing titles, 482
　capitalizing, in titles and subtitles, 859
　with common nouns, 768–770
　definite and indefinite, 640, 768, 769–771
　as determiners, 637
　with proper nouns, 771
　the usage, 768, 769–771
　zero, 768
Articles in periodicals (online and printed)
　APA-style documentation for, 331, 415–422
　Chicago-style documentation for, 449–454

Articles in periodicals (*continued*)
copying from databases, 246, 251
CSE-style documentation for, 477–480
finding, 246–251
general databases of, 251
magazine, 363, 417, 451–452, 478–479
microform, 365
MLA style documentation for, 331, 361–366
newspaper, 364, 417–418, 452–453, 479–480
online articles documentation, 332, 363–365, 416–419, 451–453, 478, 480
from online databases, 362, 363, 416, 417, 418, 450, 451, 452, 453, 477–478
in PDFs, 246, 350, 361
printed articles documentation, 362, 364, 416, 417, 418, 419, 451, 452, 477, 479
quotation marks around titles of, 837
scholarly journal, 362–363, 416, 449–450, 477–478
"Time Blindness" (Brooks), 121–125
URLs of, 362, 363, 364, 420
Arts and Humanities Citation Index, 491
as
ambiguity of, 573
in comparisons, 581, 717, 755
contrast indicated, 573
to indicate time, 573
pronoun case with, 717
in similes, 609
in subordination, 573, 663
as cited in, 406
as follows, 852
as if
subjunctive with, 708
in subordination, 573, 663
as though, 708
as well as, 682
ascent, assent, 619
ask
indirect object with, 650, 761
infinitive after, 780
ask out, 777
Ask search engine, 246
aspect, 559
assent, ascent, 619
assess, 23
Assignment calculators, 224
Assignments
analyzing, 23–24
calculators, 224
due dates for, 24

in literature and humanities, 494
for research projects, 222–223
scheduling, 24, 34
in sciences and social sciences, 513–515
time management in, 24, 281
Assistive Technology Resource Center, 209
Assonance, in poetry, 502
Assumptions, 120, 127, 132, 134
Asterisk, 201, 250, 862
Asynchronous media, 211. *See also* Blogs and blog postings; Discussion list postings; Emails
at
to indicate location, 795
to indicate time, 795
at all times, 560
at no time, 560
at that point in time, 560
At the Opera (Cassatt), 586
at the present time, 560
Atlases. *See* Maps
Attachments, emails, 202
audience, 692
Audience
academic, 14–15, 18–19, 23
analyzing, 14–15, 18–19, 23
appealing to, 143–145, 150, 158–159
for business reports and proposals, 553
design and, 188–189
for emails, 200
expectations of, 18
general vs. specialist, 18
identifying and addressing, 18–20
information provided to, 18
instructor as, 19–20, 23, 223
language and, 18–19
multilingual, 19
for multimedia presentations, 213–214
for portfolio, 106
for research paper/project, 222–223
responsibilities to, 8
revising and, 88, 89
specialist, 18
tone and, 14, 20–21
topics interest for, 14
for websites, 204
Audio aids, in multimedia presentations, 216
Audio sources, documenting
APA-style for, 422–424
Chicago-style for, 455–457
MLA style for, 370–371
Audiobooks, documenting, 373, 423
Auditory disabilities, 188

Author-date system, 439. *See also* APA-style (American Psychological Association style); CSE-style (Council of Science Editors style)
Authority. *See* Credibility
Authors. *See also* Single authors
anonymous, 342, 354–355, 398, 404, 411, 444
in anthologies, 344, 356, 357, 413, 446
APA-style in-text citations, 398, 400–405
APA-style reference list, 400, 405, 409–412
of audio and video sources, 370–371
avatars, 422
Chicago-style, 442, 444–446
CSE-style, 473–474
editors and, 357, 412, 445–446
ghostwriting, 281–282
group or corporate, 341–342, 356, 403–404, 445, 474
MLA style in-text citations, 337, 340–343
MLA style works cited list, 342, 352–357
multiple pseudonyms of, 356
with same surname, 343, 400, 405, 412
Auxiliary verbs. *See* Helping verbs
Avatar, 422, 716
avoid, 780
avoided, 790
Awkward shifts. *See* Shifts

B

Background information, 20, 69, 132, 134
in arguments classical model, 175
for interviews, 260
in Rogerian model, 175
Backing, in Toulmin model, 176
Backup of data files, 229
bad, badly, 726
Ball, Phelicia, "Website Usability Report," 190–191
Balzer, Ashley, "Website Usability Report," 190–191
Bandwagon appeal fallacy, 178
Bar graphs, 78–79, 84, 85, 140
bare, bear, 619
barely, 728
barge in on, 777
Bartleby.com, 614
Base form, of verbs, 694, 695, 698, 708
BCC. *See* Blind carbon copy
BCE, CE, BC, AD, 872

Index I5

be
    in expletive constructions, 759
    faulty predication and, 752
    forms of, 697
    as helping verb, 639, 681, 697, 782
    as linking verb, 725
    omitted from absolute phrases, 654
    questions beginning with, 764
    subject-verb agreement with, 681
bear, bare, 619
because
    in sentence fragments, 669
    in subordinating term, 571, 573, 663
because of, 796
Beck, Isabel
    "Fast Fashion" MLA style in-text parenthetical citation for paraphrase, 287
    "Fast Fashion" MLA style paper, 383–396
    "Fast Fashion" MLA style paraphrase citation, 289
    "Fast Fashion" MLA style summary citation, 289
    "Fast Fashion" outline, 306–307
    "Fast Fashion" source material integration and identification, 321–322
    "Fast Fashion" supporting claims, 309–310
    "Fast Fashion" thesis statement, 303–304
become, 725
been, 697
before, as subordinating term, 571, 573, 663
beg, 780
Begging the question fallacy, 178
begin, 780
being, 697
Beliefs, claims of value and, 38, 147
belong, 705
Bhagavad-Gita, citation of, 346–347
Bias
    in field research, 260
    gender, 603
    in interviews, 260
    keeping an open mind, 267
    in observational studies, 260
Biased language, 88, 90, 91, 120, 600–603
Bible, citation of. *See also* Sacred texts
    APA-style for, 406, 414
    MLA style for, 346–347, 360
Bibliographic notes
    APA-style for, 420
    Chicago-style for, 440, 441, 458
    MLA style for, 367, 375, 378

Bibliographies. *See also* Reference list, APA-style; Reference list, CSE-style; Works cited list, *Chicago*-style; Works cited list, MLA style
    annotated, 224, 234–235
    as sources, 241, 292
    working, 241
Bilingual dictionaries, 618
Bing search engine, 242, 248
Biographical approach to literature, 490
Black's Law Dictionary, 614
Blackwell Dictionary of Political Science, 239
Blind carbon copy (BCC), 201
Block method, in comparison-contrast, 65–66
Block quotations
    APA-style, 289
    MLA style for, 285, 339
    punctuation of, 836
Block-style business letters, 538, 545
Blog search engines, 245
Blogarama, 245
Blogs and blog postings
    APA-style documenting, 421–422
    Chicago-style documenting, 455
    CSE-style documenting, 481
    language shortcuts in, 598, 872
    locating, 245
    MLA style documenting, 367
blue in color, 560
board, bored, 619
Body
    of business letter, 539
    of multimedia presentations, 214–215
    paragraph development in, 68–70, 89
    planning, 40
    revising globally, 86–90
Boldface type, 192, 193, 862
Book Review Digest, 491
Book series, documenting
    Chicago-style for, 448
    MLA style for, 359–360
Bookmarking, 245
Books
    APA-style for documenting, 330, 408–415
    avoiding abbreviating parts of, 870, 872–873
    Chicago-style for documenting, 441–449
    commonplace, 26
    CSE-style citation-sequence for documenting, 473–475
    CSE-style for documenting, 473–476
    CSE-style name-year documenting for, 473–474

ebooks, 231, 353, 409, 440, 443
editions other than first, 358, 413, 446–447
introductions, prefaces, forewords, or afterwords by different author, 358, 413, 447
library catalogs and finding, 251–254
MLA style for documenting, 330, 352–360
numerals used with divisions of, 875
popular vs. scholarly, 246, 267
reprinted or republished, 360, 414
titles of, 235, 360, 865
Boolean logic, 250
bored, board, 619
borrow from, 798
both
    count and noncount nouns with, 773
    placement of, 640
    pronoun-antecedent agreement, 691
    subject-verb agreement, 685, 691
both . . . and
    as correlative conjunction, 566, 580, 643
    indicating addition, 568
    subject-verb agreement and, 683
Brackets
    for acronyms in in-text citations, 403
    functions of, 848
    in quotations, 840, 848, 851
    to replace parentheses within parentheses, 851
    with *sic*, 851
Brainstorming, 27–28, 32, 224, 532
Brainstorming list, of Wedd, 28, 32
brake, break, 619
Breadcrumb (click) trails, 205, 233
break, brake, 619
breath, breathe, 618
bring, 650
British English
    commas and periods with quotation marks, 839
    serial commas in, 808
    single and double quotation marks in, 835
    spelling, 619–620
Broadening, of topic, 31–32, 92
Brochures, documenting
    APA-style for, 424–425
    MLA style for, 361
Brooks, René, "Time Blindness" article, 121–125
Browsers, 82, 209
Business and public writing, standard letter format, 853
Business context, 22

Index

Business letters
  colons in, 853
  envelopes and addresses for, 539
  format for, 537–540
  guidelines for, 538–539
  on plain paper, 539
  sample, 541
  standard elements in, 539–540
Business memos
  sample memo (emailed), 543
  standard format of, 542–543
Business names
  abbreviations in, 873
  capitalizing, 861
  as singular, 687
Business reports and proposals, 552–553
but
  in contrast, 568
  in coordination, 566, 643, 804
  in correcting comma splices and fused sentences, 676
  in parallelism, 579
buy, 650
buy from, 798
by, 795, 796

C

Cached results, 420
Calder, Alexander, 565
Calendars, 24, 224
call, 650
Call numbers, searching by, 231
call on, 777
calm down, 777
can
  meanings of, 783
  as modal verb, 639, 699, 782, 783
  subject-verb agreement, 681
can, could, 783
capital, capitol, 619
Capitalization, 864
  of abbreviations and acronyms, 859, 863, 869
  altering with brackets, 840, 851
  common do's and don'ts, 859
  in emails, 544
  of first word of sentence, 858–860
  of first-person pronouns, 858
  of independent clauses linked by colons, 860
  of interjection O, 862
  omitting, 862
  prefixes before, 879
  of proper nouns and adjectives vs. common nouns, 859, 860–861
  of questions that are incomplete sentences, 845
  of quoted sentences, 860
  spelling checkers and, 623
  in titles and subtitles, 859, 861–862
Captions of figures, 351, 374, 381–382, 428
Carbon copy (Cc) line, in communication, 201, 543, 853
Caricatures, 78
carry, 762
Cartoons, MLA style for, 375
Case studies, as evidence, 46
Cassat, Mary, 586
Causation, claim of, 148
cause, 780
Cause, prepositions indicating, 796
Cause and effect, 66
  for in, 796
  conjunctions and, 568
  patterns of development, 223
  prepositions, 796
  subordinating terms and, 668
  transitional expressions indicating, 61
Cc. *See* Carbon copy
CD-ROMs, documenting
  Chicago-style for, 455
  MLA style for, 359, 373
CDs, 321, 359, 373
CE, AD, with dates, 872
-cede, -ceed, -sede suffixes, 622
cf., 873
-ch, plurals of words that end in, 624
change, 762
character, 559
Character, as literature element, 489
Characters, literary, 733
Charts. *See also* Visuals
  MLA style for, 350–351
  pie, 78–80, 85
Chicago Manual of Style (17th ed.), 439, 440, 442, 458, 491
Chicago-style, 439–469. *See also* Works cited list, *Chicago*-style
  abbreviated vs. complete notes, 441
  audio and visual sources in, 455–457
  author-date system, 439
  author-notes, citations in footnote, 288
  basic bibliographic entry format in, 441
  for bibliographic notes, 440, 441, 458
  bibliography models, 467–469
  bibliography page format in, 459
  books in, 441–449
  directory to models, 439, 440, 442, 458
  endnotes in, 441
  examples of, 440
  footnotes in, 441
  formatting a paper in, 458–459
  indirect sources in, 457–458
  interviews in, 457
  miscellaneous sources, 457–458
  other electronic sources in, 454–455
  percent symbols in, 875
  periodicals in, 449–454
  personal communications in, 457
  reasons for citing sources, 439, 441
  "Rise and Fall of Bound Feet in China" (Sweetwood) research paper, 459–469
  sources citing and documenting, 441
  tables and figures in, 458
Chicago-style paper, "Rise and Fall of Bound Feet in China" (Sweetwood) research paper, 459–469
child, children, 681
Choice, expressions of, 568
chorus, 692
Chronological organization, 41
Chronology, transitional expressions of, 61
CIA World Factbook, 240
Circular reasoning, 178
Circulation, design and, 189
Citation indexes, 269
Citation management software, 223, 247
Citations, 20. *See also* APA-style; *Chicago*-style; CSE-style; MLA style; Parenthetical citations
  accuracy of, 287–290
  APA-style in-text citations, 397–407, 412
  author voice vs., 316–318
  Chicago-style author-notes in footnote, 288
  common knowledge and, 283–284, 288
  CSE-style in-text, 470–472
  cultural knowledge and, 283, 284
  examples, 316–318
  in first draft, 308
  framing of, 288
  for ideas and information, 283
  MLA style in-text, 313, 335–352
  in paraphrases, 283
  plagiarism and, 282–284, 312
  quotations and, 283, 288–289, 312, 322–324
  reasons for, 334, 398, 439, 440, 470
  reliability and, 265
  rhetorical use of, 312
  source boundaries in, 312, 314–316
  in summaries, 283, 337
  voice emphasis, 316–318

Index

Citation-sequence and citation-name systems, CSE
　books with group or corporate authors, 474
　books with one author, 473–474
　books with two or more authors, 474
　conference paper, 475–476
　discussion lists, blog postings, social media posting, 481
　dissertations, 476
　edited book selections or conference proceedings, 475
　edited books, 475
　emails, 481
　information in, 482–483
　magazine articles, 478–479
　newspaper articles, 479–480
　numbering, 482–483
　scholarly journal articles, 477–478
　technical reports or government documents, 482
　web pages and websites, 480–481
cite, site, sight, 618
"The City Upon a Hill" speech (Kennedy), 74–76
Civic writing. *See* Professional and civic writing
claim, 780
Claims
　analysis, interpretation, synthesis to evaluate and support, 308–310
　analysis of, 129–130
　arguable, 77
　assessment of, 149, 179
　of causation, 148
　with evidence from text, 495
　with evidence outside text, 496
　of fact, 37, 146–147
　"Fast Fashion" (Beck) supporting, 309–310
　of judgment, 38, 147, 148
　linked to grounds by warrants, 176
　of policy, 148
　reasons and evidence support of, 37, 38
　supporting with appeals to readers, 148, 150–153
　in Toulmin model, 176
　of value, 38, 147
　visual, 85, 146, 177
　weak, 147
Claims and evidence analysis, of René Brooks' "Time Blindness" (Fernandez), 129–130
Clarity
　commas and, 802
　pronoun reference to antecedents, 721
　rhetorical citations and, 312
　of visuals, 82, 84
Class discussion, 201
Classical model of arguments
　evidence and counterevidence in, 175
　introduction, background, conclusion in, 175
　persuasive, 175
Classics, 344, 406, 414, 490
Classification. *See* Analysis
Clauses. *See also* Independent clauses; Subordinate clauses
　adjective, 655
　adverb, 580, 587, 636, 656, 812
　capitalization of, 860
　colons and, 673, 676
　commas and, 566, 673, 676, 804, 812–813
　conditional, 708
　consolidating, 563
　definition of, 563, 566, 654, 758
　incomplete constructions of, 632
　introductory, 848
　noun, 656
　as sentence fragments, 655, 662–663, 667–668
　stated subject in, 758
Clichés
　avoiding, 610–612
　conclusions not use of, 72
　quotation marks not used for, 835, 839
Click (breadcrumbs) trails, 205, 233
Clickbait, 271
Climactic organization, 41
close, 762
Close reading, 23. *See also* Critical reading and thinking
"A Close Reading of Mohsin Hamid's *The Reluctant Fundamentalist*" (Williams), 496–501
"A Close Reading of Shelley's 'Poetical Essay on the Existing State of Things'" (Andrews)
　explication, 501–506
　text evidence, 495
　textual analysis, 488, 490
Closings
　in emails, 202
　in letters, 540
Clustering, 28–29
CMS. *See* Content Management System
Coauthored projects, 51. *See also* Collaboration
"Code of Best Practices in Fair Use for Media Literacy Education," 11
Cognitive disabilities, 188
Coherence
　analyzing of, 62–63
　in outlines, 44
　in paragraphs, 44, 52, 58–64
　revising for, 90
Collaboration, 32–34
　cohesive group formation, 33
　pitfalls anticipation, 33
　schedule and task assignments, 34
Collective nouns
　antecedents matching pronouns with, 692
　definition of, 635, 685
　as pronoun antecedents, 692
　as subjects, 685–686
　subject-verb agreement, 685–686
College English, 266
Colloquialisms, 597–598
Colons
　in bibliographic citations, 853
　in business letters, 853
　in correcting fragments, 666, 675
　emphasis and, 591
　in formal business correspondence, 853
　functions of, 848
　introducing examples, explanations, appositives, or lists, 848, 852
　joining independent clauses, 673, 676, 853, 860
　not between preposition and object, 854
　not between verb and object, 853
　quotation marks and, 840
　quotations and, 814, 848, 853
　in ratios, 853
　in scripture, 853
　before subtitles, 853
　in time notations, 853
Color wheel, 195
Colors, in document design, 185, 195–196
The Columbia Dictionary of Modern Literary and Cultural Criticism, 492
.com (commercial) domain, 271
come across, 777
Comic books, MLA style documenting for, 375
Comma splices, 629, 804
　in advertising, 674
　boundaries obscured by, 672
　causes of, 673–675
　correcting, 675–678
　definition of, 671, 823
　identifying, 673
　semicolons and, 676, 821, 823
command, 780

Index

Commands
  for describing processes, 592
  end punctuation of, 843–844, 845
  imperative mood in, 707
  subject in, 662
  unstated subjects in, 592, 645, 662, 758
Commas, 566, 802–819
  absolute phrases and, 806
  appositive phrases and, 811
  with appositives, 811–813
  to avoid ambiguity, 817
  British use of, 808, 839
  clarity and, 802
  common do's and don'ts, 803
  in compound sentences, 657, 802–805
  with conjunctive adverbs and transitional phrases, 807
  with contrasting information, 807–808
  in coordinate adjectives, 803, 809–810
  coordinating conjunctions and, 657, 803
  in dates, 815–816
  in expression of direct address, 807–808
  in interjections, 807–808
  after introductory elements, 803, 805–807
  with nonessential clauses, 812–813
  nonessential elements and, 668, 803, 811–813
  with nonessential phrases, 668, 812
  in numbers, 814
  in parenthetical and conversational expressions, 807–808
  in personal names and titles, 815
  in place names and addresses, 815
  with quotations, 813–814, 839, 841
  to replace omitted words, 817
  to separate ideas, 817
  to separate independent clauses, 673, 676, 804
  to separate items in series, 566, 803, 808–809
  with signal phrases, 813, 841
  subordinate structures and, 572
  with tag questions, 807–808
Commas, common misuses
  common do's and don'ts, 803
  after coordinating conjunctions, 803
  between cumulative adjectives, 803
  with indirect quotations, 814
  between paired elements, 803
  before or after a series, 803
  to set off essential elements, 811

between subjects and verbs, verbs and objects, 803, 817
  after subordinating conjunctions, 803
comment, 315
committee, 692
Common knowledge, 283–284, 288
Common nouns
  articles with, 768–769
  count vs. noncount, 769, 770
  definition of, 635, 767
  not capitalized, 859, 860
Commonplace books, 26
Communication, Cc line in, 201, 543
Company names
  abbreviations in, 873
  capitalizing, 861
  as singular, 687
Comparative adjectives and adverbs, 640, 641, 729–730
compare, 315, 533
Comparison and contrast
  block vs. alternating method, 65–66
  paragraph development through, 65–66, 223
  transitional expressions in, 61
Comparisons
  of adjectives and adverbs, 729–730
  as in, 717
  incomplete or ambiguous, 754
  parallelism in, 581
  redundant, 729
  than in, 717
Compass directions, 859, 861
Compelling words, 606–611
Complaint letters, 540
complement, compliment, 619
Complementary colors, 195
Complements, object, 650, 727, 762–763
complete, 762
Complete predicates, 647, 657
Complete subjects, 645
Complete verbs, 661, 697–700
Complete verbs vs. verbals, 639
Complex sentences, 587, 658, 824
Compound adjectives, 877–878
Compound antecedents, 692–693
Compound nouns, 625, 830–831
Compound numbers, hyphenation of, 879
Compound objects, pronoun case in, 714
Compound possessives, 714
Compound predicates, 647, 665–666
Compound sentences
  comma splices in, 674
  commas in, 657, 802–805
  conjunctive adverbs and, 657
  coordinating conjunctions and, 657, 802

definition of, 587, 657, 802
  elliptical conjunction and, 753–754
Compound subjects
  agreement of pronouns with, 692–693
  definition of, 645
  pronoun case in, 714–715
  subject-verb agreement with, 683–684
Compound words
  hyphens in, 880
  possessives of, 714, 715
Compound-complex sentences, 587, 658
Comprehension, in reading, 112
  gist in, 114
  text enjoyment, 116–119
  text preview, 113–114
  text summarization, 114–115
Computer software. *See also specific software*
  APA-style documenting of, 422
  citation management, 223, 247
  for header creation, 380
  MLA style and, 380
  presentation, 216, 218
Computerized databases. *See* Databases
Computerized library catalogs. *See* Library catalogs
Computerized sources. *See* Electronic sources; Online sources
Computers. *See also* Internet; Websites and web pages
  assignment calculators, 224
  backing up, 229
  calendars, 24
  citation management software, 223, 247
  electronic calendars, 24, 224
  in essay exams, 531, 535
  peer revising on, 95
  for research log, 229
  spelling checkers, 97, 623, 626, 829
concede, 622
Concede, transitional expressions of, 61
Concentration, 112
Concessions, in arguments, 157
Concise Columbia Electronic Encyclopedia, 239
Conciseness, 545
  brevity vs., 558
  in business memos, 543
  editing for, 563
  elliptical constructions and, 561, 753
  empty phrases and, 559
  expletive constructions and, 562
  indirect constructions avoidance, 562
  nouns derived from verbs and, 562
  passive voice and, 562
  phrases, clauses, sentences consolidating, 563
  repetition, redundancy and, 561

Index **I9**

roundabout expressions and, 560
strategies to increase, 92–93
style checkers and, 561
wordy expressions and, 559–561
conclude, 315
Conclusions
   in arguments classical model, 175
   assessing strength of, 157
   in business reports and proposals, 552
   five don'ts for, 72
   inverted-funnel, 70
   in multimedia presentations, 215
   planning, 40
   relevance and, 264
   revising, 71–72, 89
   in Rogerian model, 176
   thesis restatement, 72–73
   transitional expressions in, 61
   writing, 72–73
Concrete vs. abstract words
   choosing between, 606–607
   definitions of, 635–636
   in multimedia presentations, 216
   in revising, 91
Conditional clauses, subjunctive verbs in, 708
Conference paper, CSE-style for, 475–476
Conference presentations, APA-style for, 423
Conference proceedings, documenting
   APA-style for, 425
   CSE-style for, 475
   MLA style for, 361
Confidentiality, in emails, 201
Confirmation bias, 157–158
Confusing shifts. *See* Shifts
Congressional documents, MLA style for, 376
Conjunctions. *See also* Coordinating conjunctions
   addition and, 568
   in compound subjects, 645, 683
   correlative, 566, 567, 580, 643, 764
   definition of, 683
   functions of, 636, 643
   inverted word order and, 764
   meaning of, 568
   in parallelism, 581
   subordinating, 643, 655, 663
Conjunctive adverbs
   comma splices and, 673, 676
   in compound sentences, 657
   in coordinating independent clauses, 566, 568
   definition of, 641, 807
   list of, 641
   semicolons and, 641, 821, 822
   as transitional expression, 641

Connotation, 20–21
   credibility and, 603
   emotional associations, 91
   in poetry, 502
   of synonyms, 603, 606
   tone and, 91
conscience, conscious, 618, 619
Consequence, discussing, 822
consider, 23, 780
Consonance, in poetry, 502
Consonants, suffixes for words that end with, 622
Consumer network posts and reviews, MLA style documenting of, 370
Contact information
   in emails, 202
   in résumés, 549
contain, 705
Container, for MLA style citations, 362, 372
Content Management System (CMS), 197
Content notes
   Chicago-style for, 449
   MLA style for, 378
Context
   analyzing, 14
   audience, 14, 22
   design, 189
   in emails, 200, 202–203
   genre and, 22
   for images, 198
   of multimedia presentations, 213–214
   references to, 320, 321
   sentence fragments and, 664
   in websites, 204
continue, 780
Contract cheating, 281–282
Contractions
   apostrophes in, 827, 831
   double negatives in, 728
   at ends of lines, 880
   in formal writing, 827
   with *have not of*, 782
   with *have* rather than *of*, 700
   in helping verbs, 699
contrast, 315, 533
Contrast
   commas, 807–808
   conjunctions indicating, 568
   in design, 184, 185
   paragraph development and, 65–66
   semicolons and, 821
   subordinating terms and, 573
   transitional expressions and, 61
Contrast, repetition, alignment, proximity (CRAP) design principles, 184, 185, 190

Controlling idea. *See* Thesis/thesis statement
Convention, credibility and, 874
Conversational expressions, commas after, 807
convince, 780
Coordinate adjectives, 803, 809–810
Coordinating conjunctions
   commas and, 657, 803
   in compound predicates, 666
   in compound sentences, 657, 802
   in correcting comma splices and fused sentences, 675
   function of, 566, 643
   list of, 804
   meanings of, 568
   in parallelism, 579–580, 582
   semicolons and, 674, 821
   in titles and subtitles, 861
Coordination
   definition of, 565
   excessive, 569, 570
   inappropriate, 568–569, 570
   of independent clauses, 566–567, 657, 804
   in parallelism, 582
   punctuation in, 566, 567, 802, 804, 821
   style checkers and, 565
   subordination used with, 575–577
   of terms and phrases, 566
Copyright clearance
   for academic work, 10–11
   for borrowed images, 82
   websites and, 207
Corporate authors. *See* Group or corporate authors
Correlative conjunctions
   examples of, 566, 643
   function of, 643
   in parallelism, 580
   word order and, 764
Costumes, in drama writing, 507
could
   for ability, possibility, and willingness, 783
   in *if* clauses, 700
   meanings of, 783
   as modal verb, 639, 699, 782, 783
   subject-verb agreement with, 681
could, can, 783
could've, could have, 782
council, counsel, 619
Council of Science Editors style. *See* CSE-style
Count (countable) nouns
   articles with, 769
   determiners with, 772
   examples of, 768

Count (countable) nouns (*continued*)
  grammar importance from, 636, 637
  noncount vs., 636, 637, 767–769, 770, 772, 773
Counterevidence, 20, 38
  acknowledgment of, 305
  alternative viewpoints as, 156–157
  in arguments classical model, 175
  assessment of, 179
  inductive reasoning and, 128
  in multimedia presentations, 219
  reliability and, 265
  in revising, 88, 89, 92
  in Rogerian model, 176
  thesis statement and, 305
  in Toulmin model, 176
Countries
  abbreviations of, 870, 872–873
  names, 861
a couple of, 773
Courses, avoiding abbreviations of, 870, 872–873
Court cases, italics for, 866
Cover letters, in job applications, 544–546
COVID-19 pandemic, memes and, 275
CRAP. See Contrast, repetition, alignment, proximity
Creative Commons License, 207
Credibility
  convention and, 874
  ethos, 129, 130, 131, 153–154, 155, 175, 874
  evaluating, 129, 262, 265–269
  evidence and, 265
  exclamation points and, 844
  fair use of quotations and, 298
  introductions and, 70
  online abbreviations and, 872
  peer review and, 265–267
  plagiarism, 298
  typographical errors and, 538
  of websites, 239, 265
  of Wikipedia, 239
  word choice and, 607
Credo Reference, 240
Critical analysis, "A Critical Analysis of René Brooks' Article 'Time Blindness'" (Fernandez), 135–139
"A Critical Analysis of René Brooks' Article 'Time Blindness'" (Fernandez) article, 53, 115
  claims and evidence analysis, 129–130
Critical framework, in literature and humanities
  biographical approach, 490
  critique in, 487

deconstructionist approach, 490
feminist approach, 490
interpretation in, 487
Marxist approach, 490
new historical approach, 490
postcolonial approach, 490
queer approach, 490
reader response approach, 490
synthesis in, 487
Critical reading and thinking
  abstracts in, 113
  alternative viewpoints, 128, 156–157
  analysis of, 127, 128–131
  annotating, 119–120
  assumptions and, 120, 127, 132, 134, 159
  comprehension in, 112–119
  critiques, 127, 133–135
  drawing inferences, 133
  engaging, 116–119
  enjoying, 116–119
  evaluation of sources, 134, 141–142
  interpreting, 127, 132
  journal keeping, 125–126, 531
  in literature and humanities, 487
  logical fallacies and, 129, 176–181
  logical reasoning and, 128
  note taking, 120, 285–286
  omissions, 127, 132, 134
  paraphrasing, 114
  preparing to write, 127–140
  previewing, 113–114
  reflecting, 119–126
  steps in developing, 119–120, 127
  summarizing, 114–115
  synthesizing, 127, 132
  visuals and, 113–114
Critical response, 135, 140
Critical thinking. See Critical reading
Critical understanding, 127
criticism, 133
Critiques
  in critical reading, 487
  definition of, 133
  issues for, 133–134
  of sources, 126
  understanding criticism, 133
  writing, 140
CSE-style (Council of Science Editors style), 230, 232. See also Citation-sequence and citation-name systems, CSE; Reference list, CSE-style; Scientific Style and Format
  books in, 473–476
  citation-name system in, 471–472
  citation-sequence or citation-name, in footnotes, 288

citation-sequence system in, 471–472
directory to models, 470
formatting papers in, 482–483
in-text citations, 470–472
miscellaneous sources, 480–482
name-year system in, 471–482
periodicals in, 477–480
reasons for citing sources, 470
reference list in, 472–482
sample reference section, 483–484
sciences and social sciences writing and, 511–512
sections of paper in, 482
[*sic*] in, 851
sources citing and documenting, 470
superscript numbers in, 471
Cultural knowledge, 283, 284
Cultural labels, 603
Cumulative adjectives, 809, 810
Cumulative sentences, 590
Cunning projection fallacy, 180
Cyberstalking, 207

D

-d, -ed endings, 700–701
DAI. See Dissertation Abstracts International database
Dangling modifiers, 633, 745–748
Dashes
  avoiding overuse of, 849
  in correcting fragments, 666, 675
  creating emphasis with, 591, 847, 848, 850
  functions of, 848
  to indicate break in thought, 849
  to join independent clauses, 591, 673, 676
  parentheses and commas vs., 850
  quotation marks and, 839
  to set off information in sentence, 847
  typing, 848
Data sets, 424
Databases. See also Online databases; *specific database*
  abstracts on, 241, 246, 415
  bibliographic entry in, 232
  Boolean searches of, 250
  citation index of, 269
  copying articles from, 246, 251
  discipline-specific, 246
  documentation information location, 224–225, 234
  general, 251
  hidden benefits of library, 248
  HTML vs. PDF in, 362
  PsycARTICLES, 224–225

Index I11

reliability of, 265
searching, 248–250
selection of, 246–248
in topic selection, 224
Data-Planet Statistical Datasets, 240
Date of publication, 263–264, 359, 360, 472
Dates
　abbreviations in, 870, 872
　apostrophes in, 828, 831–832
　in business letters, 539
　commas in, 815–816
　formats for, 875
　hyphens in, 879
　in parentheses, 849
　question marks in parentheses after, 845
　slashes in, 856
Davids, Brianna
　"Inmate Access to Technology" exploratory argument, 156, 159–174
　"Inmate Access to Technology" works cited list, 172–174
Days of week, 870
Debates, MLA style documenting for, 374
decide, 780
Decimals, 875
Declarative sentences
　definition of, 592, 645
　periods at end of, 843–844
　sentence variety and, 592
　word order in, 758
Deconstructionist approach to literature, 490
Deductive order of paragraphs, 58
Deductive reasoning, 128, 151–152
define, 533
Definite article (*the*), 768, 769–771
definitely, 559
Definitions
　dashes and, 848
　in dictionary entries, 616
　extended, 67
　in paragraph development, 67–68
Deliberate (intentional) fragments, 669–670
deliver, 762
Delivery, of multimedia presentations, 219
Demands, verbs in, 709
Demonstrative pronouns, 318, 638, 772
Denotation, 91, 604–606
deny, 780
Dependent clauses. *See* Subordinate clauses
descent, dissent, 619

describe, 315
　in assignments, 23, 222
　in expressive writing, 15
　indirect objects not taken by, 762
Description, as pattern of development, 64
desert, dessert, 619
Design principles. *See also* Document design; Electronic document design
　accessibility and, 189, 208–209
　audience and, 188
　circulation and, 189
　context and, 189
　of CRAP, 184, 185, 190
　genre and, 189
　of POUR, 187–188, 190
　POUR accessible, 187–188, 190
　purpose and, 188
　topic and, 188
　in web design, 184, 185, 187–188
Desk dictionaries, 613–614
dessert, desert, 619
Determiners
　articles as, 637
　few, a few, 772
　little, a little, 772
　nouns with, 640
　possessive nouns or pronouns, 638, 640, 772, 829
　preceding adjectives, 771
　pronouns, 640
　quantifying words or phrases as, 773
　this, that, these, and *those*, 772
　word order of, 771, 787
Development
　patterns of, 52, 64–68
　in research projects, 223
device, devise, 619
Diagrams, 85
Dialects
　appropriate use of, 597, 599
　definition of, 597
　double negatives in, 728
　helping verbs in, 699
　nonstandard, 597
　omission of verb endings in, 700
　subject-verb agreement in, 682
Dialog
　ellipses in, 855
　quotation marks in, 836
Diary, MLA style documenting of, 377
Diction. *See also* Words
　connotation and, 606
　definition of, 604–605
　denotation in, 91, 604–606
　formal, 20–21
　grammar, style checkers, and, 605

informal, 20–21, 200
tone and, 20–21
Dictionaries. *See also specific dictionary*
　abridged, 613–614
　bilingual, 618
　Chicago-style documentation for, 447
　definitions in, 616
　discipline-specific, 239, 491–492, 512
　for ESL, 614
　grammatical functions and, 615
　information in, 615–617, 787, 879
　MLA style documentation for, 348–349
　online, 239–240, 613–614
　plurals in, 623–625
　sample entry, 616, 617
　specialized, 239, 240, 614–615
　subject-specific, 614–615
　synonym, 614
　thesauruses, 614
　unabridged, 239, 614
　of usage, 614
　using, 615–617
Dictionary of Anthropology, 614
Dictionary of Business and Management, 614
Dictionary of the English Language (1755), 613
Digital media, documenting
　CD-ROMs, 359, 373, 455
　CDs, 321, 359, 373
　DVDs, 359, 371, 455–456
Digital object identifiers (DOI)
　APA-style for, 410, 414, 417, 420
　checking, 420
　Chicago-style for, 443, 450–451
　MLA style for, 362–365
　in working bibliography, 230
Digital portfolios, 107–108
Digital sources. *See* Online sources
Direct address, commas after, 807–808
Direct objects
　in adjective clauses, 655
　adverbs not used to modify, 727
　nouns as, 656
　of phrasal verbs, 777
　pronouns as, 778
　sentence structure and, 761–762
　of transitive verbs, 649, 650, 761
Direct questions, 738, 844–845
Direct quotations, 737–738, 813, 834, 835
Direction, in drama writing, 507
Directions, compass, 859, 861
Disabilities
　biased language and, 603
　website accessibility for, 186–187, 188

Disciplines
  databases for, 246
  dictionaries for, 239, 491–492, 512
  noncount nouns for, 769
  plagiarism and, 279
  style guide selection, 98
  tone and, 21
Discovery services, 249
discreet, discrete, 619
discuss, 315
  in assignments, 23, 222
  infinitive after, 780
Discussion list postings
  APA-style documenting, 421
  Chicago-style documenting, 455
  CSE-style documenting, 481
  evaluating, 321
  location of, 245
  MLA style documenting, 367
Discussion section, reports in sciences and social sciences, 515
Diseases, noncount nouns for, 769
Disinformation, 158, 270–271
Disruptive modifiers, 743–745
dissent, descent, 619
Dissertation Abstracts International (DAI) database, 415
Dissertations, documenting
  APA-style for, 414–415
  Chicago-style for, 449
  CSE-style for, 476
  MLA style for, 361
Distortion, in visuals, 83
Diversity evaluation, 269–270
  evidence and, 270
  points of view in, 270
do
  forms of, 699
  as helping verb, 639, 681, 699, 764, 782
  in questions, 764
Document design. *See also* Electronic document design; Format; Web design
  for academic texts, 98, 189, 195
  analysis of, 189
  APA-style figures and, 428–429
  APA-style reference list, 400, 408–425
  Chicago-style figures and, 458
  Chicago-style works cited list, 439–469
  color in, 185, 195–196
  CSE-style reference list, 470–484
  design principles, 184, 185, 187–188, 190, 208–209
  in emails, 201
  figure captions, 351, 374, 381–382, 428
  fonts, 98, 192–194, 201
  format for, 192–196

  headers, 98, 201, 380, 428
  headings in, 98, 194–195
  indentations, 98, 381, 427
  layout, 192, 198
  for letters, 539–540
  for lists, 195
  margins, 98, 379, 426
  MLA style figures and, 350–351, 381
  MLA style works cited list, 352–377
  overall impression in, 192
  page numbers, 349–350, 426–427
  portfolio, 106–107
  résumés, 547
  spacing, 539
  table numbers, 98, 382, 428
  visuals in, 196–197
  white space, 185, 194, 547
  for writing in sciences and social sciences, 514–515
  writing situation and, 196
Document size, visuals and, 82
Documentation, 280
Documentation styles. *See* APA-style (American Psychological Association style); *Chicago*-style; CSE-style (Council of Science Editors style); MLA style (Modern Language Association style)
DOI. *See* Digital object identifiers
Domains, 271, 272
Double (redundant) comparisons, 729
Double (redundant) expressions, 730
Double negatives, 728
Double quotation marks. *See* Quotation marks
Double-entry reading journals, 125
  "How Accurate Is the Myers-Briggs Personality Test?" (Gholipour), 126
Double-spacing, 379, 426
Doublespeak, 600
Drafting. *See also* First draft; Organizing a project
  acknowledging sources in first draft, 310
  analysis, interpretation, and synthesis in, 303, 308–309
  of body paragraphs, 40, 68
  in collaborative projects, 51
  of conclusions, 71–73
  evidence and counterevidence in, 20, 38, 46–50, 303
  ideas explanation and support, 45–47
  integrating quotations in, 308
  of introductions, 68–72
  organization of ideas in, 39–44, 303–307
  outline in, 41–44
  preparation for, 44–45

  prewriting in, 39
  signal phrases in, 308
  summaries, paraphrases, and quotations in, 310
  thesis statement, 29, 36–37, 302–303
  visuals as evidence in, 78–81, 308
  work protection, 47
  writer's block and, 45
Drama writing
  actors performances in, 507
  costumes in, 507
  direction in, 507
  lighting and sound design, 507
  numbers in divisions of plays, 875
  props in, 507
  stage set in, 507
  Uncle Vanya play review (Lower), 507–509
Drawings. *See* Visuals
drop in, 777
Dropbox, 202
due to the fact that, 560
Durand, Emily, "Field Research Report on the Mental Health of College Students," 516–529
DVDs, documenting
  Chicago-style for, 455–456
  MLA style for, 359, 371

E

each
  count and noncount nouns with, 773
  as determiner, 772
  subject-verb agreement, 683, 685, 690
each and every, 560
EasyBib, 223
eBay, MLA style documenting for, 370
ebooks, 231
  APA-style for documenting, 409
  Chicago-style for documenting, 440, 443
  MLA style for documenting, 353
ed., eds., 358, 412, 413, 445, 446
E-device. *See* App
Edited books, documenting
  APA-style for, 413
  Chicago-style for, 446
  CSE-style for, 475
  MLA style for, 356, 357
Editing. *See* Revising
Editorial board, 266
Editorials, 16
  Chicago-style documenting, 453
  MLA style documenting, 365
Editors, in documentation
  APA-style for, 412
  Chicago-style for, 445–446
  MLA style for, 357

Index I13

.edu (educational) domain, reliability and, 271
Education Source database, 246
effect, affect, 619
-efy and *-ify* suffixes, 622
e.g., 873
ei / ie spelling rule, 620–621
either
    count and noncount nouns with, 773
    subject-verb agreement, 685
either, too, 790
either . . . or
    choice indicated by, 568
    compounds joined by, 692
    in coordination, 566, 643
    as correlative conjunction, 643
    parallelism with, 580
    pronoun-antecedent agreement, 692
    subject-verb agreement, 684
Either-or-fallacy, 179
-elect, 878–879
Electronic document design. *See also* Web design
    breadcrumb (click) trails, 205, 233
    color in, 185, 195–196
    design principles in, 184, 185, 187–188, 190
    emails, 201, 862
    fonts in, 185, 201
    genre, 204
    headings in, 193–195
    home page, 204–206, 208
    layout in, 192
    links in, 106, 232, 866, 868
    lists in, 195
    navigation tools for, 205, 206, 208
    overall impression in, 192
    visuals in, 206, 207
    website content in, 203–204
    website structure, 204–205
    white spaces in, 185, 194, 547
Electronic documents
    APA-style documenting, 406–407, 419–422
    backing up, 229
    Chicago-style documenting, 454–455
    CSE-style documenting, 473–482
    MLA style documenting, 349–350
    research logs, 228–230
    résumés, 551
Electronic peer review, 95
Electronic portfolio, 107–108
Electronic résumés, 551
Electronic source numbers, 349–350
Electronic sources, documenting. *See also* Online sources
    APA-style for, 406–407, 419–422
    Chicago-style for, 454–455

CSE-style for, 480–482
MLA style for, 349–350
elicit, illicit, 619
Ellipses
    in APA-style, 398
    in dialog, 855
    functions of, 848, 854
    omitted lines of poetry and, 855
    in quotations, 285, 298, 840, 854
Elliptical construction, 561, 753–754
elude, allude, refer to, 619
Em dashes. *See* Dashes
Emails
    addresses, line breaks in, 880
    analysis of, 203
    answering, 199, 202–203, 544
    APA-style documenting for, 407, 425
    archiving, 202, 544
    attachments to, 202
    business memos and, 542–543
    capitalization in, 544, 862
    closings in, 202
    confidentiality, 201
    contact information in, 202, 544
    design conventions, 201
    emoticons in, 200, 598
    emphasis in, 201
    etiquette for, 544
    exclamation points in, 844, 845
    MLA style for documenting, 350, 377
    online abbreviations in, 598, 872
    organization and length of, 201
    paragraph format in, 201
    personal, at work, 545
    privacy and, 203
    recipients for, 200, 203
    revising, 202, 544
    salutations in, 200
    spam in, 544
    style of, 201
    subject line in, 200
    task-oriented, 200
    tone in, 199, 543, 544
    writing, 199–202
eminent, imminent, immanent, 619
Emoticons, 200, 598
Emotional appeals, 129, 131, 154–155, 175
Emotional associations. *See* Connotation
Empathy-driven design, 186–187, 188
Emphasis
    active voice for, 586
    asterisks for, 862
    colons for, 676
    dashes for, 676, 847, 848, 850
    in emails, 201, 862
    emphatic verbs, 583, 593–594
    inverted word order for, 646

italics in, 837, 866, 867
multiple question marks or exclamation points, 844
from parallelism, 578, 584–585
punctuation and, 586, 591
quotation marks and, 835, 838
repetition for, 593
rhythm and, 586, 590–591
transitional expression for, 61
Emphatic verbs, 586, 593–594
Empirical research, 510
Empty phrases, 559
En dashes. *See* Dashes
encourage, 780
Encyclopedia
    APA-style documenting, 413–414
    appropriate use of, 239
    Chicago-style documenting, 447
    discipline-specific, 239–240, 491–492, 512
    MLA style documenting, 348–349
    Wikipedia, 239
End punctuation. *See* Exclamation points; Period; Periods; Question marks
end result, 560
Endnotes
    APA-style for, 428
    Chicago-style for, 441
    MLA style for, 378, 379
engaged to, 798
English as second language (ESL)
    connotation, 91
    dictionaries for, 614
    paraphrases and summaries, 294
    Writing Responsibly around the World, 10
English language
    British, 618, 808, 835, 839
    colloquialisms, 597–598
    dialects, 597, 599, 682, 699, 700
    et al. equivalent in, 354
    idioms, 610, 611, 614
    regionalisms, 597
    slang, 598, 614, 835, 838
    Standard American, 634
enjoy, 780
enough, 773
Envelopes, for business letters, 539
envy, 705
equal, 730
-er, in comparisons, 729
escape, 780
Essay
    freewriting, of Wedd, 27
    "How Accurate Is the Myers-Briggs Personality Test?" (Gholipour), 116–119

Essay (*continued*)
scratch outline, of Wedd, 41–42
topic and sentence outline, of Wedd, 42–43
Essay exams
analyzing questions on, 533
common verbs in, 533
computer use in, 531, 535
effective answers for, 534
effective exam response (Okada), 535–536
note making for, 530–531
parameters of exam, 532
practice questions, 531–532
previewing exam, 532–533
reviewing notes for, 530–531
strategy reading and developing, 532
study groups for, 531
writing effective answers in, 533–534
essential, 730
Essential elements, 572, 668, 811
-est, in comparisons, 729
et al.
APA-style for, 403
avoiding, in formal writing, 873
English equivalent for, 354
MLA style for, 341–342
etc., 873
Ethical issues. *See also* Bias; Plagiarism
biased language, 88, 90, 91
blind copies in emails, 201
in field research, 260
in interviews, 260
keeping an open mind, 267
in observations and surveys, 260
patchwriting and, 285
scholarly sources and, 266
Ethnic group names, 861
Ethnic labels and bias, 603
Ethnic Notions, 491
Ethos, 129, 130, 131, 153–154, 175, 874
assessment of, 155
in U.S., 153
Etsy, MLA style documenting for, 370
Euphemisms, 600
evaluate, 23, 533
Evaluation. *See* Credibility; Sources, evaluating
even, 742
even if, 573
as subordinating conjunction, 663
even though, 573
as subordinating conjunction, 663
Evernote, 26, 229, 531
every, 683, 773
everybody, 685, 690

everyone
pronoun-antecedent agreement, 736
subject-verb agreement, 685, 690
everything, 685
Evidence. *See also* Counterevidence
analysis of, 47–50, 128–129
in arguments classical model, 175
assessment of, 179, 305
credibility and, 265
diversity evaluation, 270
made-up, 46
in multimedia presentations, 215, 219
revising, 88, 89, 92
in Rogerian model, 176
in Toulmin model, 176
types of, 46, 150–156
in writing about literature and humanities, 495–496
ex-, 878–879
exactly, 742
Examinations. *See* Essay exams
Examples
colons to introduce, 852
dashes to set off, 847, 848
in dictionary entries, 616
as fragments, 666
ideas support by, 46
paragraph development through, 56
transitional expressions and, 61
exceed, 622
except, 780
except, accept, 619
Excessive subordination, 574–575
Exclamation points
in emails, 844, 845
in exclamations, 592, 669
quotation marks and, 839
series of, 844
strong commands and excitement and, 845
Exclamations, 592, 669
Exclamatory sentences, 645
Executive summaries, in reports and proposals, 552, 553
Exemplification, 64
Experimental research, 510
Expert opinion, as evidence, 46
explain, 23, 315, 533, 762
Explanations
colons before, 852
in Rogerian model, 176
Expletive constructions, 562, 646, 759–760
Expletives, 759–760
Explication of literature, "A Close Reading of Shelley's 'Poetical Essay on the Existing State of Things'" (Andrews), 501–506

Exploitative images, 81
Exploratory arguments, 128, 144–145, 153, 225
inductive logic use in, 151
"Inmate Access to Technology" (Davids), 156, 159–174
Expository writing. *See* Informative writing
Expressive writing, 15, 17–18
Extended definitions, 67
Eye contact, in multimedia presentations, 215, 217, 219

F

-f, -fe, -ff, -ffe, plurals of words that end in, 624
Facebook, 245
MLA style documenting for, 367–369
status update, 14
Fact check, 271
Facts
claims of, 37, 146–147
as common knowledge, 283–284, 288
as evidence, 46, 47
in letters to editor, 542
the fact is, 559
the fact that, 750
faculty, 692
fair, fare, 619
Fair use, in copyright law, 10–11
fall, 649
Fallacies, 11, 120, 176–181, 210. *See also specific fallacy*
False analogy fallacy, 177
False authority fallacy, 178
False cause fallacy, 179
False dilemma fallacy, 179
Familiar-to-unfamiliar order, 41
family, 692
FAQs. *See* Frequently asked questions
far, farther, farthest, 641
fare, fair, 619
"Fast Fashion" (Beck)
MLA style in-text parenthetical citation for paraphrase, 287
MLA style paraphrase citation, 289
MLA style research paper, 383–396
MLA style summary citation, 289
outline for, 306–307
source material integration and identification, 321–322
supporting claims of, 309–310
thesis statement, 303–304
Faulty predication, 751–753
fear, 705
Federated searching, 249
Feedly, 245

feel
  as linking verb, 649, 725
  unmarked infinitives after, 780
Feminist approach to literature, 490
Fernandez, Joe
  claims and evidence analysis of René Brooks' "Time Blindness," 129–130
  "A Critical Analysis of René Brooks' Article 'Time Blindness'" (Fernandez) critical analysis essay, 135–139
  "A Critical Analysis of René Brooks' 'Time Blindness' article," 53, 115
few
  count and noncount nouns with, 772, 773
  pronoun-antecedent agreement, 691
  subject-verb agreement, 685, 691
few in number, 560
a few, 773
fewer, 773
fewest, 773
Fiction writing, 494–501
Field research
  fair reporting in, 262
  interviews, 259–260
  observational studies, 260–261
  surveys, 261–262
"Field Research Report on the Mental Health of College Students" (Durand), 516–529
Figurative language (figures of speech), 216, 502, 608–609
Figure captions, 351, 374, 381–382, 428
Figures, 113
  APA-style, 428–429
  Chicago-style, 458
  MLA style for, 350–351, 381
  relevance and, 264
  in research and laboratory reports, 515
Figures of speech. *See* Figurative language
fill with, 798
Films
  APA-style documenting for, 422
  Chicago-style documenting for, 455
  MLA style documenting for, 371
  movie stills, 85
  primary sources for studies in, 490
final, 730
Final draft, "Rethinking Alternative Energy" (Wedd), 105
final outcome, 560
find, 650, 761
finish, 780
First draft, 37
  acknowledging sources in, 310
  of research paper/project, 308

Student Model sentence problems, 630–631
  time allocation for, 44
  writing methods for, 44–45
First person
  in academic writing, 21, 318, 735
  capitalization of *I*, 858, 859, 862
  in literature and humanities, 492–493
Fitzpatrick-Woodson, David, "Website Usability Report," 190–191
Five-paragraph theme, 40
fix, 762
Flaming, 210, 544
focus on, 315
Focused freewriting, 27
the following, 852
Fonts (typeface)
  APA-style for, 426–427
  font size, 98, 185, 188, 192, 193
  MLA style for, 380
  for résumés, 547
  selecting, 98, 192, 193–194, 201
  in web design, 185, 201
foot, feet, 681
Footnotes. *See also* Endnotes
  Chicago-style citations in, 288, 441
  in critical reading, 120
  CSE-style citations in, 288
  MLA style for, 378, 379
  superscript numbers for, 378
for
  in coordination, 566, 568, 643, 804
  in correcting comma splices, 676
  to indicate cause, 796
  in indirect-object phrase, 650
  in parallel constructions, 579
for example
  in comma splices and fused sentences, 673
  in coordination, 566–567
  semicolons and, 822
  in transitions, 666
force, 780
Forewords, documenting
  APA-style, 413
  Chicago-style for, 447
  MLA style, 358
forget, 780
Formal diction, 20–21
Formal outlines, 42–43. *See also* Outlines
Formalist approach, for literature and humanities writing, 487
Formality, appropriate, 599–600
Format
  of academic texts, 98, 99–105
  of block quotations, 836
  of block-style letters, 538
  of *Chicago*-style papers, 458–459

  of CSE-style papers, 482–483
  of dates, 875
  for document design, 192–196
  of fractions, 875
  of letters, 537–540
  PDF, 208, 230
  of portfolios, 106–110
  of scientific reports, 514–515
  of URLs, 856
Format, of APA-style papers
  abstract, 427
  deadlines and paperclips, 430
  headers, 428
  indentation, 427
  margins and spacing, 426
  printing, paper, and binding, 430
  reference list, 429–430
  tables and figures, 428–429
  title page, 427
  typeface and page number, 426–427
Format, of MLA style papers
  deadlines and paperclips, 382
  headers, 380
  identifying information, 380
  indentation, 381
  margins and spacing, 379
  portfolios, 382
  printing and binding, 382
  of tables and figures, 350–351, 381
  title, 380
  typeface or font, 380
Forster, E. M., 16
forth, fourth, 619
Forums, online. *See* Discussion list postings
Fractions
  formats for, 875
  slashes in, 856
  subject-verb agreement and, 686
Fragments. *See* Sentence fragments
Framing, of citations, 288
Freedom of Information Act, 545
Freewriting, 224
  Wedd essay of, 27
frequently, 788
frequently, more / less frequently, most / least frequently, 641
Frequently asked questions (FAQs), 242
friendly, 580
from, 796, 797
full, 730
Full block-style business letters, 538, 541
"Full text"/"full text PDF," 246, 248
Function words, parallelism and, 581–582
fungus, fungi, funguses, 625
Funnel introductions, 68
furthermore, 822

Fused (run-on) sentences
　boundaries obscured by, 672
　causes of, 673–675
　correcting, 675–678
　definition of, 629, 671
　grammar checker and, 629
　identifying, 673
Future perfect progressive tense, 704, 705
Future perfect tense, 703, 704
Future progressive tense, 704
Future tenses, 703, 704

G

Gaslighting, 181
Gender agreements, 689
Gender bias, avoiding, 601–603
General vs. abstract words, 607
Generalizations, 770
Generic noun antecedents, 690–691
Generic nouns
　articles with, 770
　in pronoun-antecedent agreement, 736
Genre
　analyzing before writing, 14, 22
　context and, 22
　design and, 189
　images and, 198
　of literature, 22
　as literature element, 489
　in multimedia presentations, 213–214
　of websites, 204
Genus and species names, italicizing, 868
Geographic names, 687, 771, 861
Gerund phrases
　functions of, 653
　parallelism of, 583
　subject-verb agreement, 687
Gerunds
　definition of, 583, 653, 687, 779
　functions of, 653
　after prepositions, 781
　pronoun case with, 717
　subject-verb agreement, 687
　after verbs, 653, 779–780
Gestures, in multimedia presentations, 217
get, 650
get out of, 777
Gholipour, Bahar
　"How Accurate Is the Myers-Briggs Personality Test?" double-entry reading journal, 126
　"How Accurate Is the Myers-Briggs Personality Test?" essay, 116–119
Ghostwriting, 281–282
Ginsie, Megan, "Plagiarism an Issue on Campus, Faculty Says," 12–13

Gist, in thesis statement, 114
give, 650, 761
give in, 700, 777
give to, 798
give up, 777
Global business, in U.S., 545
good, well, 726
Google
　advanced search on, 244
　blog searching, 245
　Boolean search on, 250
　keyword searching in, 242–244
　links number to sites, 242
　reliability of, 265
　Web searching, 248
Google Docs, 26, 261, 441, 531
Google Drive, 202
Google Groups, 245
Google Scholar, 129, 247, 269
Google Slides, 216
gorilla, guerrilla, 619
.gov (governmental) domain, 271
government, 692
Government publications
　APA-style documenting, 424
　Chicago-style documenting, 457
　CSE documenting, 482
　finding, 255
　MLA style documenting, 376
　online access to, 255
Grammar, 605, 634. *See also specific grammatical elements*
　dictionaries and, 615
Grammar checkers
　adjective-adverb problems and, 632, 725
　apostrophes, 829
　comma splices and fused sentences, 629, 675
　confusing shifts and, 733
　irregular verb forms, 629
　misplaced modifiers and, 740
　mixed constructions avoidance, 632
　modifiers and, 633
　pronoun case, 633
　pronoun reference avoidance, 629
　pronoun-antecedent agreement and, 628, 690
　sentence fragments and, 665
　subject-verb agreement, 628, 680
　verb problems and, 639, 696
　verb tense and voice confusing shifts, 632
Grammatically mixed constructions, 749–753
Graphic novel, MLA style documenting, 375
Graphics. *See* Visuals

Graphs, 78–80, 84, 85, 278
grate, great, 619
a great deal of, 773
Grounds, 150
　in Toulmin model, 176
Group or corporate authors, documenting. *See also et al.*
　APA-style for, 403–404
　Chicago-style for, 445
　CSE-style for, 474
　MLA style for, 342, 356
GroupMe, 51
grow up, 777
guerrilla, gorilla, 619
Guilt by association fallacy, 180

H

hand, 650
hand in, hand out, 777
hanged, hung, 698
Hanging indent
　in APA-style documenting, 426
　in *Chicago*-style documenting, 459
　in MLA style documenting, 379
hard, hardly, 791
hardly, 728, 742, 791
has the ability to, 560
Hasty generalization fallacy, 177
hate, 780
Hate speech, 158
have
　forms of, 700
　as helping verb, 639, 681, 699, 782
　infinitive after, 780
　not used with modal, 700
　in perfect tenses, 703
　unmarked infinitives after, 780
he (generic), 601–602
he or *she*, 602, 633, 689, 736
Headers
　in academic texts, 98
　in APA-style, 428
　in emails, 201
　in MLA style, 380
Headings, 113
　in document design, 98, 194–195
　in electronic document design, 193–195
　levels of, 98
　online and library catalogs subject, 252–253
　parallelism in, 195, 583
　relevance and, 264
hear, 780
hear, here, 619
Helping (auxiliary) verbs
　in complete verbs, 697–700
　contraction and omission of, 699

Index

in dialects and informal speech, 699
functions of, 639, 647
kinds of, 782
modal verbs, 639, 699, 782, 783–784
placement of, 639, 646, 788
in questions, 764
simple, 782
subject-verb agreement and, 681
her or *him*, 689
Highlighting, 287, 530, 531
Hightail, 202
him or *her*, 689
hint at, 777
his or *her*, 689
Historical Abstracts, 491
Historical documents, not italicized, 866
Historical events, capitalization of, 861
Historical Statistics of the United States, 240
History, primary sources for, 491
hole, whole, 619
Holiday names
abbreviating, 872–873
capitalizing, 861
Home pages
construction of, 205–206
electronic document design and, 204–206, 208
MLA style documenting, 366–367
planning, 204
titles of, 205
Homonyms, 618, 619
hope, 780
Hours, abbreviating, 872
how, 656
"How Accurate Is the Myers-Briggs Personality Test?" (Gholipour), 116–119, 126
however
in comma splices and fused sentences, 673
in coordination, 566–567
semicolons and, 822
as transitional expression, 589
HTML. *See* HyperText Markup Language
Hulu, 255
humanity, humankind, humans, 602
Hurtful (biased) language, 88, 90, 91, 600–603
Hyperbole, 608
Hyperlinks. *See* Links
HyperText Markup Language (HTML)
Chicago-style for files in, 450
in databases, 362
PDF compared to, 246, 248, 249, 350, 361, 362, 450
in source copies, 230

Hyphens, 877–882
in APA-style, 410
automatic hyphenation, 880
to avoid confusion, 878, 879
before capital letters, 879
in compound adjectives, 877–878
in compound numbers, 879
between dates, 879
at ends of lines, 615, 879–880
overuse of, 878
after prefixes and suffixes, 618, 878–879
in URLs and email addresses, 880
Hypotheses
drafting, 225–226
in field research, 260
from research questions, 226–227, 303

I

in academic writing, 21
capitalization of, 858, 859, 862
in writing in humanities, 492–493
I or *me,* 714
ICTs. *See* information and communication technologies
Idea generation
brainstorming, 27–28, 29, 224
clustering, 28–29
freewriting, 27, 224
idea journals and commonplace books, 26
Internet, library, and classroom tools for, 26, 31
journalists questions, 29–30
in thesis drafting, 29, 36
topics discussion with others, 30–31
Idea journals, 26
Ideas
citations for, 283
explanation and support, 45–47
organization of, 39–44, 305
transitional expressions to add to, 61
Identifying information, in MLA style, 380
Idioms, 610, 611, 614, 700, 787
i.e., 873
ie / ei spelling rule, 620–621
if
in noun clauses, 656
in subjunctive clauses, 708
as subordinating conjunction, 573, 663
-ify and *-efy* suffixes, 622
illicit, elicit, 619
Illogical subordination, 574–575
illusion, allusion, 619
illustrate, 315, 533

Illustrations, 113
plagiarism and, 284
relevance and, 264
Imagery, in poetry, 502
Images
annotating, 120, 127
audience for, 198
context and genre for, 198
as evidence, 78–81
manipulated, 46
manipulative, 46, 83–85
power of, 277
purpose of, 198
web design and, 208–209
writing about, 126
imagine, 780
imminent, eminent, immanent, 619
Imperative mood, 695, 707, 733
Imperative sentences, 645, 662
impossible, 730
Imprints. MLA style for documenting, 330
in, indicating location or time, 795
in addition, in addition to, 566–567, 666, 682
in close proximity, 560
in contrast, 507, 568, 666
in fact, 559
in order that, 573
in spite of the fact that, 560
in the event that, 560
in the neighborhood of, 560
in the process of, 559
in this day and age, 560
incidence, incidents, 619
including, 852
Incomplete constructions, 753–756
indeed, 61
Indefinite articles (*a, an*). *See* Articles (*a, an, the*)
Indefinite pronouns, 640
definition of, 828
forms of, 638
possessive, 828
pronoun-antecedent agreement, 690–692
subject-verb agreement, 685, 690–691
Indentation
in academic texts, 98
in APA-style format, 427
in *Chicago* format, 459
in MLA style format, 381
Independent clauses, 805–806
capitalization of, 860
colons and, 673, 676, 853, 860
comma splices of, 672–673
commas to separate, 673, 676, 804
coordinating, 566–567, 657, 804
in correcting fragments, 664, 675–678

Independent clauses (*continued*)
dashes to join, 591, 673, 676
definition of, 566, 654, 758, 802, 820, 860
punctuation between two, 566, 591, 671–672, 675–676, 821
semicolons linking, 567, 673, 676, 805–806, 820–822
index, indexes, indices, 625
Index cards
for essay exam, 531
for research log, 229, 305
Indexes
citation, 269
searching, 246–251, 264
indicate, 315
Indicative mood, 695, 707, 733
indices, indexes, 625
Indirect objects, 650, 761–762
Indirect questions, 738, 843–844
Indirect quotations
in awkward shifts, 737–738
definition of, 814
punctuation and, 835, 836
Indirect sources, documenting
APA-style for, 406
Chicago-style for, 457–458
description of, 300–301
MLA style for, 347–348
Individual ownership, apostrophes and, 830
Inductive order of paragraphs, 59
Inductive reasoning, 128
Inferences, drawing, 133
infinite, 730
Infinitive phrases, 579, 652, 653, 746
Infinitives
dangling, 746
definition of, 653, 716, 779
in fragments, 661
gerunds vs., 653, 779–780
objective case pronouns and, 716
split, 740, 744
unmarked, 780
verb tenses used with, 706–707
Informal diction, 20–21, 200
Informal outlines, 41–42
Information, citations for, 283
information and communication technologies (ICTs), 158
Information graphics, 78–80, 275
Informational notes, documenting
APA-style for, 425–426
MLA style for, 378–379
Informative reports
approach to, 23
claims of fact in, 146
purpose of, 18

research assignments and, 225
thesis statements in, 37–38
Informative writing, 16, 17–18
-ing words, 653
Initialisms, 871, 872. See also Acronyms
Initials, periods with, 869
"Inmate Access to Technology" (Davids), 156, 159–174
Inoreader, 245
Inquiry-based arguments. See Exploratory arguments
Inseparable phrasal verbs, 777
Inside address, in business letters, 539
Inspiration porn, 212
Instagram, 245, 367–369, 531
Instant messaging (IM)
acronyms in, 872
capitalizing, 862
language shortcuts in, 598, 872
instead, 61
instruct, 780
Instructors
as audience, 19–21, 23
revising with, 92, 95–96
vocabulary used by, 512
Intellectual periodicals, 266
Intensifiers, 726
Intensive pronouns, 638
Intentional fragments. See Deliberate fragments
Interactive media. See also Emails; Instant messaging
discussion lists, 245, 321, 367, 421, 455, 481
flaming in, 210, 544
searching, 245
social networking sites, 245, 598, 602
synchronous vs. asynchronous media, 211
wikis, 367, 421, 454–455
Interesting paragraphs, 52
Interjections
capitalization of O, 862
commas after, 807–808
definition of, 644
examples of, 644
functions of, 636, 644
Internet
citations and, 283
collaborating on, 51
evaluating sources on, 263–278
flaming on, 210, 544
idea generation and, 26, 31
peer revising on, 95
plagiarism and, 269
subject directories on, 31, 33
website and web page creation on, 204–209

Interpretation
in critical reading, 127, 132, 487
of literature, 496–501
of sources, 286–287
of texts, 132
thesis example, 114
of visuals, 140
Interpretive analysis, 494
"A Close Reading of Mohsin Hamid's *The Reluctant Fundamentalist*" (Williams), 496–501
Interpretive analytical thesis, 495
Interrogative pronouns
case in, 713
definition of, 713
examples of, 638
relative pronouns vs., 662–663
who, whom, whoever, and *whomever*, 717–719
Interrogative sentences, 645, 646
Interrupted periodic sentences, 590
Intertextual analysis, 129
Interviews, 260
APA-style documenting for, 407, 425
Chicago-style documenting for, 457
conducting fairly, 259
job, 547
MLA style documenting for, 350
In-text citations, 97
CSE-style, 470–472
general principles for, 337, 398
In-text citations, APA-style, 397–407
authors with two or more works published in same year, 405, 411
directory to model, 397
examples of, 400
general principles of, 398
group or corporate authors, 403–404
indirect sources, 406
multiple authors, 403
one author, paraphrase or summary, 401
one author, quotation, 401–402
parenthetical citations, 398, 399–400, 401, 402
personal communication, letters, interviews, or emails, 407
placement of, 399–400
reprinted or republished works, 405–406
sacred texts, 406
signal phrases in, 399, 401, 402
source match with, 401–407
two authors, 398, 402–403
two or more authors with same surname, 400, 405, 412
two or more sources by same author, 404–405

Index

two or more sources by same author in same year, 405
two or more sources in one citation, 404
unnamed or anonymous authors, 398, 404
websites or other electronic sources, 406–407
In-text citations, CSE-style, 470–472
In-text citations, MLA style, 313, 335–352
  abbreviated file and, 337
  anthology selections, 344
  block quotations, 339
  after clause, 338
  dictionary or encyclopedia entries, 348–349
  directory to model, 330
  of entire source, 343
  examples of, 341
  general principles of, 337
  government documents, 351
  group or corporate authors, 341–342
  indirect sources, 347–348
  legal sources, 351
  literary sources, 344–345
  to match source, 339
  motion picture, television, or radio broadcast, 347
  multiple sources in one citation, 336, 352
  multiple sources in one sentence, 351–352
  multivolume sources, 344
  one author, 340
  parenthetical citation, for paraphrase, 287
  in parenthetical citations, 336, 338
  parenthetical note format, 336
  personal communications, 350
  after phrase, 339
  placement of, 337–339
  reasons for, 334, 398
  sacred texts, 346–347
  after sentence, 338
  signal phrases in, 335, 337, 338, 340
  tables, charts, or figures, 350–351
  three or more authors, 341–342
  two authors, 340
  two authors with same surname, 343
  two or more sources by same author, 337, 343
  unnamed or anonymous authors, 342
  of unpaginated sources, 337, 338, 339
  web pages, 337
  websites or other electronic sources, 333, 349–350, 366
  works cited list information, 336

Intransitive verbs, 648, 700–701
introduce, 315
Introductions
  APA-style for, 413
  in arguments classical model, 175
  in business reports and proposals, 552
  funnel, 68
  length of, 69, 92
  MLA style for, 358
  in multimedia presentations, 214
  planning, 40
  relevance and, 264
  in research or laboratory reports, 514
  revising, 70–71, 87–89
  in Rogerian model, 175
  seven don'ts for, 70
  thesis restatements, 72
  of Wedd, 70–71
  writing, 72
Introductory clauses, 848
Introductory elements, commas after, 803, 805
Introductory phrases, comma after, 806
Invention techniques, for topic, 25
Inverted word order
  conjunctions or adverbs beginning clauses and, 764–765
  for emphasis, 591, 646
  subject-verb agreement in, 688
Inverted-funnel conclusion, 70
Irony
  definition of, 608
  as literature element, 489
  quotation marks indicating, 835, 837
Irregular plurals, 624–625
Irregular verbs, 615, 694, 696–698
  list of common, 698
  use of, 629
Irrelevant argument, 178
is, 562, 697
is where, is when, 752
Issue numbers, in publications, 233
it
  confusingly broad use of, 720
  as expletive, 759–760
  indefinite use of, 721
  as stated subject, 752
it is . . ., sentences beginning with, 562
Italics
  in art works, 866
  common do's and don'ts, 866
  in court cases, 866
  in emails, 862
  for emphasis, 837, 866, 867
  in genus and species names, 868
  in long works titles, 865–866
  not used for links, 866, 868
  not used for short works, 866
  sacred text titles and, 866
  in talking about word, 868
  in unfamiliar non-English words, 868
  in vehicle names, 867
  in words, letters, or numbers used as words, 835, 866, 867
Italics type, 192
it's, its, 619, 828

J

Jargon, 598–599
Job application
  cover letter format, 544–546
  photographs in, 78, 545
  references in, 549
  résumés in, 547–550
  Student Model sample, 546
  writing in, 545, 547
Job interviews, 547
Joint ownership, apostrophes and, 830
Journal articles. *See* Periodicals
The Journal of American History, 266
Journal or diary entries, MLA style documentation for, 377
Journalists questions, 29–30
  of Wedd, 30
Journals, keeping
  double-entry reading, 125–126
  essay exams and, 531
Judgment, claims of, 147, 148
Jumping on bandwagon fallacy, 178
Jumping to conclusions fallacy, 177
just, 742

K

Keefe, Alicia, CSE-style reference list, 483–484
keep, 762
Kelley, Aidan, "A Rhetorical Analysis of Konstantin Ivanov's 'The Road Is Open to Humans'" poster, 130–131
Kennedy, John F., "The City Upon a Hill" speech, 74–76
Key terms
  in paraphrases, 292, 294
  in résumés, 551
Keyword searches, 224, 238, 242–244, 253
Killer quotes, 286
kind, 559
know, 705
Knowledge, common, 283–284, 288
Kumar, Adithya, 186
Ky, Rachana, personal statement of, 108–110

Index

L

Labeling people, 601, 602
Laboratory notebooks, 513
Laboratory reports
   "Field Research Report on the Mental Health of College Students" (Durand), 517–529
   format, 514–515
The Lancet, 266
Language. *See also* Words
   abstract vs. concrete, 91, 216, 606–607, 635–636
   active vs. passive case, 695, 710–711
   appropriate formality in, 596–603
   audience and, 18–19
   biased or hurtful, 88, 90, 91, 120, 600–603
   British vs. American English, 618, 835, 839
   capitalizations in, 858, 861
   colloquialisms, 597–598
   dialects, 699, 700
   diction, 20–21, 200, 604–606
   doublespeak, 600
   editing for, 599–600
   euphemisms, 600
   figurative, 216, 608–609
   first and third person, 21, 318
   first person, 858
   formal, 91
   idioms, 610, 611, 614, 700
   jargon, 598–599
   as literature element, 489, 491–494
   in multimedia presentation, 216
   nonstandard dialects, 597
   online shortcuts, 598
   regionalisms, 597
   in sciences and social sciences, 512–513
   slang, 598, 614, 835, 838
   Standard American English, 634, 699
a large number of, 773
Latin abbreviations, 870, 873
lay, lie, 698, 701–702
lead, led, 619
Learn, arguments to, 144–145
least
   count and noncount nouns with, 773
   as superlative, 729
leave, 650
Lectures, documenting
   APA-style for, 423
   MLA style for, 374
Legal cases, documenting
   APA-style for, 425
   MLA style for, 351, 376
lend, 650

lend to, 798
less
   in comparisons, 729
   count and noncount nouns with, 773
   as determiner, 772
let, 780
Letters
   APA-style documenting, 407, 425
   of apology, 540–542
   business, 537–541
   of complaint, 540
   to editor, 542
   envelopes for, 539
   formats in, 538–540
   job application, 543–547
   letterhead, 538, 555
   MLA style documenting, 350
   rejection, 542
Letters to editor
   APA-style documenting for, 419
   Chicago-style documenting, 453
   MLA style documenting, 365
   writing, 542
Letters used as words, apostrophes and, 828
Level of diction, 21–22
LexisNexis Academic. *See* Nexus Uni database
LexisNexis Congressional, 258
Library catalogs, 251
   browsing, 253–254
   media in, 258
   reliability of sources in, 265
   searching, 252
   subject headings in, 252–253
Library databases. *See* Databases
Library of Congress, 255, 272
Library stacks, 253–254
Library websites, 26, 31, 252
lie, lay, 698, 701–702
Lighting and sound design, in drama writing, 507
like
   colons not used after, 852
   gerund or infinitive after, 780
   not used in progressive tense, 705
   in similes, 609
Limiting modifiers, 742–743
Line graphs, 80, 85
Lines, of poetry, 345, 380, 502
Linking verbs
   adjectives after, 725, 786
   definition of, 640, 751, 786
   faulty predication and, 751
   sentence pattern with, 649
   subject-verb agreement, 689
   verbs that function as, 649

Links (hyperlinks)
   in document design, 106, 232, 866, 868
   italicizing, 866, 868
   in portfolios, 106
   underlining, 868
   in web design, 185, 205, 207, 866, 868
   in websites, 106, 205, 272, 866
   working bibliographies and, 232
list, 533
List of works cited. *See* Reference list, APA-style; Reference list, CSE-style; Works cited list, *Chicago*-style; Works cited list, MLA style
List of works consulted, 352
Listening, active, 219
Lists
   colons before, 852
   dashes in, 848
   in document design, 195
   as fragments, 666
   parallelism in, 195, 582–583
   parentheses around numbers in, 849
Literacies types, abbreviations in, 873
Literary analyses. *See* Literature and humanities, writing in
Literary Criticism Index, 491
Literary sources, MLA style for, 344–345
Literature and humanities, writing in.
   See also Poetry
   abbreviations in, 869
   active voice in, 493
   approach of, 486–489
   assignment types, 494
   author name in, 493
   "A Close Reading of Mohsin Hamid's The Reluctant Fundamentalist" (Williams) interpretive analysis, 496–501
   "A Close Reading of Shelley's 'Poetical Essay on the Existing State of Things'" (Andrews) textual analysis, 488, 490, 495
   critical framework in, 487, 490
   drama, 507–509
   elements of, 489
   evidence in, 495–496
   fiction, 494–501
   first and third person in, 492–493
   formalist approach in, 487
   genres in, 21
   interpretive analysis of fiction, 496–501
   language of literature in, 491–494
   numbers in, 875
   past and present tense in, 492, 705
   primary sources for, 489–491
   reading actively and reflectively, 486–487

secondary sources for, 491
shifts in person in, 735–736
textual analysis, 487, 488, 490, 495
thesis statements, 494–495
title in, 493–494
verb tenses, 492
vocabulary, specialized, 491–492, 598
Literature genre, 22
Literature reviews, in sciences, 513–514
little, 772
Location, prepositions for, 795
Logical fallacies
in critical reading, 129, 176–181
in political websites, 181
Logical organization, 41
Logical reasoning, 151
Logos, 129, 150–153, 175
assessment of, 155
in U.S., 153
visuals for, 151
Long quotations, MLA style format and, 380–381
Longman Dictionary of American English, 614
look, 649, 725
look at, 780
look down on, 777
look up, 776, 777
look up to, 777
a lot of, 773
lots of, 773
love, 780
Lower, Jenny, *Uncle Vanya* play review, 507–509
LP, MLA style documenting for, 373
-ly and *-ally* suffixes, 622, 878

M

Made-up evidence, 46
Magazine articles
APA-style documentation, 417
Chicago-style documentation, 451–452
CSE-style documentation, 478–479
MLA style documentation, 363
Main clauses. *See* Independent clauses
Main idea. *See also* Topic sentences
implied, 57
statement, 35
Main verbs, 639, 697–700, 710
make, 649
man, mankind (generic, sexist use), 602
-man words, gender bias and, 602
manage, 780
Manipulative images, 46, 83–85
manner, 559
Manuscript formatting. *See* Document design

many
count and noncount nouns with, 768, 773
pronoun-antecedent agreement, 691
subject-verb agreement, 685, 691
many in number, 560
Mapping, 28–29
Maps
MLA style for, 375
as visual evidence, 85
Margins
of APA-style papers, 426
in document design, 98, 379, 426
of MLA style papers, 379
married to, 798
Marxist approach to literature, 490
Mass (noncount) nouns, 767
may
meanings of, 783
as modal verb, 639, 699, 782, 783
subject-verb agreement with, 681
may, might, 784
McGraw-Hill's Dictionary of American Slang and Colloquial Expressions, 614
mean, 780
Meanings
of coordinating conjunctions, 568
modals and, 783
of phrasal verbs, 777
meat, meet, 619
Media releases, 361, 554–556
Memes, 275
Memoranda (memos)
business, 542–543
MLA style documenting, 377
men (generic), 602
mention, 762
Menu with hyperlinks, for portfolio, 106
Menus, in websites, 205
merely, 742
Merriam-Webster Online Dictionary, 614, 615
Merriam-Webster's Collegiate Dictionary, 613, 614, 615
Merriam-Webster's Dictionary of Synonyms, 615
Metaphors, 608, 609
Metasearch engines, 242–243, 249
Methods section
in business reports and proposals, 552
in research and laboratory reports, 514–515
Microform articles, MLA style documenting, 365
Microsoft PowerPoint, 216
Microsoft Word
footnote and endnotes creation, 441
header creation in, 380

might
meaning of, 783
as modal verb, 639, 699, 782, 783
subject-verb agreement with, 681
might, may, 783
Milner, Ryan, 270
mind, 780
Misinformation, 158, 270–271
Misplaced modifiers, 633
ambiguous limiting modifiers, 741–743
importance of avoiding, 741–743
separation from modified words, 741
separation of subject from verb, 743–744
separation of verb from object, 743–744
split infinitives, 740, 744
squinting modifiers, 742
miss, 780
Mixed constructions, 632
faulty predication, 751–753
grammatically mixed, 749–753
Mixed metaphors, 609–610
MLA Handbook for Writers of Research Papers (8th ed.), 334
MLA Handbook for Writers of Research Papers (9th ed.), 339, 491
MLA International Bibliography, 491
MLA style (Modern Language Association style), 230, 232. *See also* Format, of MLA style papers; In-text citations, MLA style; Works cited list, MLA style
apostrophes in plurals of letters, 832
for audio and visual sources, 370–371
block quotations in, 285
for books, 330
brackets for changed capitals in quotations, 840
brief quotations in, 284
changing capitalization in quotations, 860
citations in figures and tables, 350–351, 381
content and bibliographic notes in, 367, 375, 378
for endnotes, 378
format of paper in, 379–382
indentation, 381
for informational notes, 378–379
in-text citations in, 313, 335–352
for online databases, 332, 416, 417, 418
paraphrase citation, 289
parenthetical notes in, 336
percent symbols in, 875
for periodicals, 331, 361–366

Index **I21**

MLA style *(continued)*
  reasons for citing sources, 334, 398
  summary citation, 289
  URLs and email addresses, 880
  for websites and web pages, 333, 349–350, 366
MLA style paper, 47
  "Fast Fashion" (Beck), 383–396
Modal auxiliaries, 639, 708, 782, 783–784
Modal verbs, 639, 699, 782, 783–784
Modern Language Association style. *See* MLA style
Modified block-style business letters, 538, 545
Modifiers, 632. *See also* Adjectives; Adverbs
  absolute phrases as, 589, 654, 730
  appositives as, 588
  dangling, 633, 745–748
  grammar checkers and, 740
  misplaced, 633, 741
  repeated in elliptical construction, 754
  in subordination, 572
Money, 872, 875
Months, 870, 872–873
Mood, in verbs
  awkward shifts in, 733
  imperative, 695, 707, 733
  indicative, 695, 707, 733
  information from, 695
  subjunctive, 695, 707–709, 733
more
  in comparatives and superlatives, 729
  pronoun-antecedent agreement, 692
  as quantifier, 773
  subject-verb agreement, 685
more unique, 730
most
  in comparatives and superlatives, 729
  pronoun-antecedent agreement, 692
  as quantifier, 773
  subject-verb agreement, 685
most of the time, 560
most perfect, 730
Motion picture, MLA style documentation of, 347
Motor disabilities, 188
Movie stills, 85
MP3/MP4 files, MLA style for, 373
much, 685
Multilingual audience, 19
Multilingual students, peer review with, 94
Multimedia presentations, 265
  delivery of, 219
  eye contact in, 215, 217, 219
  gestures in, 217
  listening actively in, 219
  organizing, 214–215
  preparing and rehearsing, 215–217
  presentation anxiety in, 217
  presentation software in, 216, 218
  purpose, audience, context, and genre in, 213–214
  repetition in, 216
  speaking responsibly, 219–220
  topic and thesis selection in, 214
  visuals in, 216
Multimedia resources. *See also* Audio sources, documenting; Visuals
  borrowing vs. creating, 256–257
  illustrations, 255, 284
Multiple authors
  ampersand in, 398
  APA-style documenting for, 403
  et al. in, 341–342, 354, 403, 873
  MLA style documenting for, 336, 351–352
Multivolume works, documenting
  APA-style for, 414
  Chicago-style for, 448
  MLA style for, 344, 359
Musical compositions, MLA style documenting for, 374
Musicals and other audio recordings, documenting
  APA-style for, 423
  MLA style for, 373
must
  meanings of, 783
  as modal verb, 639, 699, 782, 783
  subject-verb agreement with, 681
my, 772

N

Names
  abbreviations of, 870, 872–873
  commas with, 815
  of companies, 687, 861, 873
  of countries, 861
  of genus and species, 868
  geographic, 687, 771, 861
  of holidays, 861, 872–873
  of occupations, 602
  of organizations, 687, 861
  personal, 815, 861, 869
  of places, 687, 771, 815, 861
  of races, 861
  of religions, 861
  subject-verb agreement and, 687
  of vehicles, 867
Name-year system, CSE
  books with group or corporate authors, 474
  books with one author, 473–474
  books with two or more authors, 474
  conference paper, 475–476
  discussion lists, blog postings, social media posting, 481
  dissertations, 476
  edited book selections or conference proceedings, 475
  edited books, 475
  emails, 481
  information in, 482
  magazine articles, 478–479
  newspaper articles, 479–480
  numbering, 482
  scholarly journal articles, 477–478
  technical reports or government documents, 482
  web pages and websites, 480–481
Narration, 64–65
Narrowing topic, 31–32, 92, 223
National Commission on Writing, 7
Natural sciences. *See* Sciences and social sciences, writing in
Nature, 266
"Nature versus Nurture" (Worthington)
  APA-style in-text parenthetical citation for paraphrase, 287
  APA-style in-text quotation, 288
  APA-style research paper, 430–438
Navigation links, 185
Navigation tools, 205, 206, 208
N.B., 873
Nearest antecedent rule, 693
Near-homonyms, 618, 619
Necessity, modals expressing, 783
need
  infinitive after, 780
  not used in progressive tense, 705
Negatives
  double, 728
  placement of, 789
  too and *either* and, 790
neither
  count and noncount nouns with, 773
  subject-verb agreement, 685
neither . . . nor
  compounds joined by, 692
  in coordination, 566, 643
  as correlative conjunction, 643
  indicating choice, 568
  inverted word order and, 764–765
  parallelism with, 580
  pronoun-antecedent agreement and, 692
  subject-verb agreement, 684
Neologisms, 598
.net (network) domain, 272
Netflix, MLA style documenting for, 371
Netiquette, 544
NetTutor, 95

Index

Networking, of websites, 204
The New American Roget's College Thesaurus, 615
The New Encyclopedia Britannica, 239
The New Fowler's Modern English Usage, 614
New historicist approach to literature, 490
News alerts, 245
Newspaper articles, documenting
    APA-style for, 417–418
    Chicago-style for, 452–453
    CSE-style for, 479–480
    MLA style for, 364
Nexus Uni database, 246
no, not, 791
no longer, 765
no one, 685
no sooner, 765
nobody, 685
Non sequitur fallacy, 178
Noncount (uncountable) nouns
    articles with, 769
    count vs., 636, 637, 767–769, 770, 772, 773
    determiners with, 772
    examples of, 768, 769
    grammar importance from, 636, 637
A Non-Designer's Design Book (Williams), 184
Non-English words, italicizing, 868
Nonessential elements
    commas and, 668, 803, 811–813
    dashes and, 591
    omission of, 753
    subordination of, 572, 668
nor
    choice indicated by, 568
    compounds joined by, 684, 692
    in coordination, 566, 643, 804
    in correcting comma splices and fused sentences, 676
    inverted word order and, 764
    in parallelism, 579
    pronoun-antecedent agreement and, 692
NOT, as Boolean operator, 250
not, no, 791
not just . . . but, 568
not only . . . but also
    in contrast, 568
    as correlative conjunctions, 580, 643
    inverted word order with, 764
note, 315
Note making
    analyzing, interpreting, synthesizing and critiquing sources, 286–287
    annotating vs., 287
    for essay exams, 530–531
    highlighting vs., 287

organization of, 305
paraphrasing in, 135, 285, 286
plagiarism and, 26, 285
quotations in, 285, 286
research notes, 303
rhetorical, 286
summarizing in, 286
in writing about literature, 487
Notebooks, for research log, 229
Notes. *See also* Endnotes; Footnotes
    APA-style documenting, 425–426
    bibliographic, 367, 375, 378, 440, 441, 458
    Chicago-style for, 288, 441
    content, 378, 449
    for figures and tables, 351, 374, 381–382, 428
    MLA style documenting, 378–379
    for speaking, 229
    superscript numbers for, 378
Note-taking technologies, 531
nothing, 685
Noun clauses, 656
Noun phrases, 637, 651, 665
Nouns, 767–776
    a, an, the with, 637, 769
    abstract vs. concrete, 91, 216, 606–607, 635–636
    as adjectives, 728
    collective, 635, 685–686, 692
    common vs. proper, 635, 767
    compound, 625, 830–831
    count vs. noncount, 636, 637, 767–769, 770, 772
    definition of, 828
    determiners and, 640
    as direct objects, 656
    functions of, 636
    generic, 736, 770
    gerund phrases as, 583, 653, 687
    gerunds, 583, 653, 687, 717, 779–781
    as object complements, 727
    personal, 635
    plurals of, 624, 625, 637, 681, 767, 828
    possessive, 637, 772
    present participles as, 696
    quantifying words or phrases with, 773
    singular, that end in *s*, 687
Novels, MLA style for documenting, 345
number, no., 872
a number of, 773
Numbers
    apostrophes in, 828, 831–832
    at beginning of sentence, 875
    commas in, 814, 876
    definition of, 735
    hyphens in, 879
    italicizing, 866, 867

numerals vs. spelled out, 875–876
page, 349–350, 426–427
periods in, 876
prefixes in, 878–879
shifts in, 736
specific formats in, 875–876
subject-verb agreement in, 686
superscript, 378

O

O (interjection), 862
-o, plurals of words that end in, 624
Object complements
    adjectives or nouns as, 727
    definition of, 650, 727
    sentence structure and, 650, 762–763
Object of preposition, 652
Objective case, in pronouns, 713, 714, 716, 717
Objects
    complements, 650, 727, 762–763
    compound, 714
    direct, 649, 650, 727
    indirect, 650, 761–762
    of prepositions, 652, 762
Obligatory words, 752
Observational studies, 261
    empirical research, 510
    manipulation and bias in, 260
Observations, as evidence, 46
observe, 315
Occupation names, avoiding gender-specific, 602
OED. *See Oxford English Dictionary*
of
    with fractions or portions, 796
    to indicate cause or condition, 796
    to indicate possession, attribute, or origin, 797
    not used with modal, 700
    to show reason, 796
offer, 650, 780
often, 788
oh, 862
Okada, Taiji, effective exam response, 535–536
Omissions, 127, 132, 134
on, 795
on the other hand, 822
once, 663
one, 685, 773
one of, 688
OneNote, 26, 229, 531
Online articles, documenting
    in APA-style, 332, 416–419
    in *Chicago*-style, 451–453
    in CSE-style, 478, 480
    in MLA style, 332, 363–365

Online assignment calendars, 224
Online communication. *See also* Blogs and blog postings; Emails; Instant messaging; Social media
   asynchronous media, 211
   discussion list postings, 245, 321
   open vs. moderated forums, 273
   social networking, 245, 598, 602
   synchronous media, 211
Online databases
   APA-style and, 332, 362
   Chicago-style and, 450, 451, 452, 453
   CSE-style and, 477–478
   MLA style and, 332, 416, 417, 418
Online dictionaries, 239–240, 613–614
Online forums. *See* Discussion list postings
Online journals, documenting
   APA-style for, 416
   Chicago-style for, 451
   MLA style for, 363
Online magazines, documenting
   APA-style for, 417
   Chicago-style for, 451–452
   CSE-style for, 478
   MLA style for, 363
Online media. *See* Interactive media
Online newspapers, documenting
   APA-style for, 418
   Chicago-style for, 453
   CSE-style for, 479
   MLA style for, 365
Online plagiarism, 269
Online postings. *See* Blogs and blog postings; Discussion list postings
Online sources. *See also* Internet
   almanacs and yearbooks, 240
   annotating, 120
   asynchronous media, 211
   dictionaries and encyclopedias, 613–614
   discussion list postings, 245, 321, 367, 421, 455, 481
   evaluating, 263–278
   HTML vs. PDF, 246, 248, 249, 350, 361, 362, 450
   multimedia, 255–257
   plagiarism in, 269
   social networking sites, 245, 598, 602
   subject directories, 31
   synchronous vs. asynchronous media, 211
   in working bibliographies, 232, 241
Online sources, finding. *See also* Databases
   advanced search options, 242
   almanacs and yearbooks, 240
   bibliographies, 241

   biographical reference works, 241
   Boolean searches, 250
   copying database articles, 246, 251
   on databases, 248–250
   dictionaries and encyclopedias, 239–240
   Google Scholar, 129, 247
   government publications, 255
   interactive media, 245
   keyword searches, 242–244
   library catalogs, 251–254
   metasearch engines in, 242–243, 249
   multimedia, 255
   RSS feeds and news alerts, 245
   search engines, 242–245
   subject directories, 31, 33
   subject headings, 252–253
   Wikipedia, 239
Online surveys, 261
only, 742
only one of, 688
open, 762
Open or moderated URLs, 273
Opposing arguments. *See* Counterevidence
or
   compounds joined by, 684, 692
   in coordination, 566, 643, 804
   in correcting comma splices and fused sentences, 676
   indicating choice, 568
   in parallelism, 579
   pronouns matched with compound antecedents, 692
   slashes instead of, 856
OR, as Boolean operator, 250
Oral arguments, 156
Oral presentations. *See* Multimedia presentations
order
   indirect object with, 761
   infinitive after, 780
.org (organization) domain, 272
Organizing a project. *See also* Planning a project
   arguments, 179
   assessment of, 179
   checking for unity and coherence, 44
   draft preparation, 44–45
   ideas explanation and support, 45–47
   ideas organization, 39–44
   of multimedia presentations, 214–215
   organizational strategies selection, 41
   outlining, 41–44
   résumés, 548–549
   revising, 88–90
   thesis crafting, 35–38, 304
Orientals, Asians, 603
Origin, prepositions indicating, 797

Orphaned phrases. *See* Sentence fragments
other, 773
others
   pronoun-antecedent agreement, 691
   subject-verb agreement, 685, 691
the other, 773
ought to
   meanings of, 783
   as modal verb, 639, 699, 782, 783
   subject-verb agreement with, 681
ought to, shall, should, 783
our, are, 619
Outlines
   for essay exam answers, 531
   of "Fast Fashion" (Beck), 306–307
   formal sentence or topic, 42–43
   informal or scratch, 41–42
   in organizing ideas, 534
   outlining techniques, 41–44
   parallelism in, 583–584
   for research paper/project, 305–307
   in revising, 87
   sentence, 42–43
   unity and coherence in, 44
Overgeneralization, 177
owe, 705
own, 705
Oxford Dictionary of American English, 614
Oxford Dictionary of National Biography, 241
The Oxford Encyclopedia of British Literature, 492
Oxford English Dictionary (OED), 239, 614

P

Page numbers
   in APA-style, 426–427
   in electronic documents, 349–350, 426–427
   in MLA style, 349–350
Pamphlets, documenting
   APA-style for, 424–425
   MLA style for, 361
Paper clips on papers, 382, 480
Paragraphs. *See also* Patterns of development
   coherence in, 44, 52, 58–64
   concluding, 70–74
   connecting, 52, 73–76
   interesting, 52
   introductory, 68–70, 72
   main idea implied in, 57
   organization of, 58–59
   pronouns and synonyms in, 61

Index **I25**

relevance in, 52, 53
repetition in, 60–61
revising body, 89
techniques combination in, 62–63
topic sentences in, 55–58
transitions within and between, 59–60
unity in, 52, 53–55
well developed, 52
Parallelism, 578–586
   to clarify relationship ideas, 582
   comparisons and, 581
   coordinating conjunctions and, 579–580, 582
   correlative conjunctions and, 580
   deceptive, 580
   definition of, 578
   emphasis from, 578, 584–585
   example of, 579
   function words and, 581–582
   in headings, 195
   items in list, 582–583
   items in outlines, 583–584
   items in series, 580–581
   in multimedia presentations, 216
   phrases and, 579, 583
   in repetition, 581, 592
   in résumés, 549
   subordinate clauses and, 582
Paraphrases
   APA-style in-text parenthetical citation for, 287
   citations in, 283, 287, 289
   in critical reading, 114, 126
   effective use of, 292–294
   elements of, 292
   examples of patchwriting and, 292–294
   first draft and, 308
   MLA style citation, 289
   MLA style in-text parenthetical citation for, 287
   patchwriting in, 114, 115, 141, 285, 290–291
   source boundaries in, 314–316
   to support claims, 310
Parentheses
   in Boolean searches, 250
   capitalization of sentences in, 859
   commas and dashes vs., 850
   around dates, 849
   downplaying material in, 849
   functions of, 848
   around numbers in list, 849
   within parentheses, 851
   punctuation and, 850
   around question marks, 845
   for supplementary information, 848

Parenthetical citations, 283, 301, 313–314, 321, 324
   APA-style in-text, for paraphrase, 287
   APA-style in-text, for source quoting, 288
   in-text, APA-style, 398, 399–400, 401, 402
   in-text, MLA style for paraphrase, 287
   in-text MLA style, 336, 338
   signal phrase use, 317
Parenthetical expressions, commas after, 807–808
Parenthetical notes
   APA-style, 398, 399–407
   MLA style, 336
Participial phrases, 696, 781
   as dangling modifiers, 746
   definition of, 588, 653
   placement of, 588
Participles. *See also* Past participles; Present participles
   as adjectives, 781
   infinitives and, 706–707
   participial phrases, 588, 653, 696, 746, 781
   placement of, 589
   tense sequence and, 707
Parts of speech, 635, 636. *See also specific parts of speech*
pass, 650
passed, past, 619
Passive voice
   active voice confusing shifts to, 632
   active voice vs., 695, 710–711
   concise writing and, 562
   definition of, 695
   in literature and humanities, 493
   past participles in, 710
   reasons for using, 709–710
   in science and social science writing, 513, 594, 705
   shifting voice, 710, 733–734
   transitive verbs in, 649, 709
past history, 560
Past participles
   as adjectives, 696, 781
   forms of, 698
   with infinitives, 706–707
   of irregular verbs, 694, 695, 698
   in participial phrases, 653
   in passive voice, 710
   tense sequences and, 707
   as verbals, 661, 696
Past perfect subjunctive, 708
Past perfect tense, 703, 704
   APA reference list and, 706
Past progressive tense, 703, 704, 705
Past subjunctive mood, 708

Past tenses
   APA reference list and, 706
   of irregular verbs, 694, 695, 698
   in literature and humanities writing, 492, 705
   of regular verbs, 694, 695, 696–697
   in science and social science writing, 513, 705
   simple, 703, 704
   in verb phrases, 699
Patchwriting
   definition of, 285
   in paraphrasing, 114, 115, 141, 285, 290–291
   paraphrasing examples and, 292–294
   in summarizing, 290
Pathos, 129, 131, 175
   assessment of, 155
   visuals for, 154, 155
patience, patients, 619
Patterns of development
   analysis, 67
   cause and effect, 66–67, 223
   comparison-contrast, 65–66, 223
   for connecting paragraphs, 52
   definition, 67–68
   description, 64
   exemplification, 64
   narration, 64–65
pay, 650
PDF. *See* Portable Document Format
peace, piece, 619
Peer review, 93–95
   credibility and, 265–267
   electronic, 95
   with multilingual students, 94
Pen names or pseudonym, MLA style documenting of, 356
The Penguin Dictionary of Literary Terms and Literary Theory, 491–492
Perceivable, operable, understandable, robust (POUR) principles of accessible design, 187–188, 190
Percents, 874, 875
perfect, 730
Perfect infinitive, 707
Perfect progressive tenses, 704, 705
Perfect tenses, 703, 704
Performances, documenting
   Chicago-style for, 456
   MLA style for, 374
Periodic sentences, 590
Periodicals. *See also* Magazine articles
   APA-style for documenting, 331, 415–422
   Chicago-style for documenting, 449–454
   CSE-style for documenting, 477–480

Periodicals (*continued*)
  finding articles in, 246–251
  issue numbers, 233
  MLA style for documenting, 331, 361–366
  scholarly vs. popular, 246, 267
Periods
  in abbreviations, 869
  conjunctive adverbs and, 641
  in correcting comma splices, 675
  with initials, 869
  in questions, to soften tone, 843–844
  quotation marks and, 839
  in requests phrased as questions, 844
  in sentences and mild commands, 843–844
Permission for borrowed images. *See* Copyright clearance
Perry Castaneda Library Map Collection, 258
Person, 695
  definition of, 735
  first, 21, 318, 858, 859, 862
  plurals and, 689
  second, 592, 721, 735
  shifts in, 735–736
  third, 735
  use of, 735
personal, personnel, 618
Personal beliefs, 38, 145–147
Personal communications, documenting
  APA-style for, 407
  Chicago-style for, 457
  MLA style for, 350
Personal context, 22
Personal correspondence, documenting, MLA style for, 377
Personal experiences, writing about, 15
Personal names
  abbreviations in, 869
  capitalization of, 861
  commas and, 815
Personal pronouns, 638, 713, 829
Personal statement, in portfolio, 107
  of Ky, 108–110
Personal websites, 272
Personification, 608
Persons with disabilities
  empathy-based design for, 186–187, 188
  Ramp Up on, 212
  visual, auditory, cognitive, motor, 188
Perspective, gaining, 86–87
persuade, 780
Persuasive arguments, 17–18, 144, 175, 176
  approach in, 23
  deductive logic in, 128, 152
  editorials as, 16

  in research assignments, 222, 225
  thesis statements in, 38
phenomenon, phenomena, 681
Phillips, Whitney, 270
Philosopher's Index, 491
Philosophy, primary sources for, 491
Phone numbers, 875
Photographs
  in emotional appeals, 154
  as evidence, 81, 85
  in job applications, 78, 545
Phrasal verbs, 776, 778
  as idioms, 610, 700
  list of, 777
  separable vs inseparable in, 777
Phrases
  absolute, 589, 654, 730–731, 806
  as adjectives, 588–589, 652, 653, 696, 781
  as adverbs, 588, 642, 652
  appositive, 572, 588, 651, 661, 665, 716, 811–813, 847–848, 852
  commas to set off nonessential, 668, 812
  in concise writing, 563
  coordinating, 566
  definition of, 563, 566, 651, 806
  as disruptive, 743–745
  empty, 559
  as fragments, 651, 661, 665–667, 749–750
  gerund, 583, 653, 687
  incomplete constructions in, 632
  infinitive, 579, 652, 653, 746
  introductory, 806
  noun, 637, 651, 665
  in parallelism, 579, 583
  participial, 588, 653, 696, 746, 781
  quantifying, 772, 773
  transitional, 59–60, 589, 807
  verb, 639, 652, 682, 697, 699, 779–780
  verbal, 652–654, 661, 665, 681
Pie charts, 78–80, 85
piece, peace, 619
Pinterest, 245
Place names
  articles with, 771
  capitalization of, 861
  commas with, 815
  as singular, 687
Plagiarism
  college policy on, 11
  common knowledge and, 283–284, 288
  contract cheating, 281–282
  culture and, 283, 284
  definition of, 279

  electronic research logs and, 230
  ghostwriting, 281–282
  illustrations and, 284
  lack of citation, 282–284, 312
  note making and, 26, 285
  online, 269
  patchwriting, 285, 290–291
  prevalence of, 281–282
  quotations and, 283, 284–285
  self-plagiarism, 282
  source materials requiring citation, 283
  student essay on, 12–13
  unintentional, 230, 312
  of visuals, videos, and sound files, 284
  works cited list and, 310
"Plagiarism an Issue on Campus, Faculty Says" (Ginsie), 12–13
plain, plane, 619
Plain form (unmarked) infinitives, 780
plan, 780
plane, plain, 619
Planning a project
  assignment analyzing, 23–24
  assignment calendar setting, 24, 224
  collaborative projects, 32–34
  idea generation, 26–31
  identifying and addressing audience, 18–20
  purpose of writing determined, 17–18
  tone and genre setting, 20–21
  topic narrowing or broadening, 31–32, 92
  writing situation analyzing, 14–17
plans for the future, 560
Plays
  MLA style documenting, 345
  numbers in divisions of, 875
  Uncle Vanya review (Lower), 507–509
Plot, as literature element, 489
Plurals
  apostrophes and, 828, 829–832
  articles and, 768
  awkward shifts and, 736
  of compound nouns, 625
  of count nouns, 767
  in dictionary entries, 623–625
  indefinite pronouns and, 691–692
  irregular, 624–625, 637
  possession in plural nouns, 637, 828
  of pronouns, 638
  of proper nouns, 624
  quantifying words with, 773
  regular, 624, 637, 681
  of verbs, 695
p.m., 872
Pocket, 245

Podcasts, documenting
    APA-style for, 423
    Chicago-style for, 456
    MLA style for, 373
Poetry
    "A Close Reading of Shelley's
        'Poetical Essay on the Existing
        State of Things'" (Andrews)
        explication, 501–506
    divisions of, 875
    elements of, 502
    ellipses in, 855
    lines of, 345, 380, 502
    MLA style for documenting, 345–346
    quotations from, 836–837
    slashes to mark ends of lines in,
        836, 856
    writing about, 501–506
Points of view
    in diversity evaluation, 270
    as literature element, 489
Policy, claims of, 148
Polluted information, 270–271
Popular press, 266, 267
Portable Document Format (PDF)
    APA-style for files in, 407
    Chicago-style for files in, 450
    CSE-style for files in, 477
    database articles in, 246
    definition of, 208
    HTML vs., 246, 248, 249, 350, 361,
        362, 450
    MLA style for files in, 350
    in posting documents online, 208,
        246, 249, 350, 361, 362, 450
    for source copies, 246
    in working bibliography, 230
Portfolio
    electronic, 107–108
    MLA style format for, 382
    personal statement in, 107, 108–110
    submission of, 107
    table of contents for, 107
    title page for, 106–107
Positive form of adjectives and adverbs, 728
positively, 580
Possession, prepositions indicating, 797
Possessive case
    apostrophes in, 713, 827–833
    determiners in, 638, 640, 772
    with gerunds, 717
    its in, 828
    nouns and, 637, 772
    of to indicate possession, 797
    prepositions and, 797
    pronoun forms in, 638, 640, 713,
        714, 717
    pronoun-antecedent agreement, 690

Possessive pronouns, 638, 640, 772, 829
Possibility
    modals expressing, 782, 783
    verb mood and, 707
Post hoc, ergo propter hoc fallacy, 179
Postal abbreviations, 538
Postcolonial approach to literature, 490
Poster session, APA-style documenting
    for, 423
Postings. *See* Blogs and blog postings;
    Discussion list postings
postpone, 780
POUR. *See* Perceivable, operable,
    understandable, robust
practice, 780
Predicates
    complete, 647
    compound, 647, 665–666
    faulty predication, 751–752
    in mixed construction, 750
    simple, 647
Prefaces, documenting
    APA-style for, 413
    Chicago-style for, 447
    MLA style for, 358
prefer, 780
Prefixes, 621, 878–879
Prejudices, 148–149. *See also* Bias
Preliminary thesis, 36–37
Preparing to write, 44–45, 127–140
Prepositional phrases
    as adjectives and adverbs, 652
    as dangling modifiers, 746
    definition of, 652
    direct object recipients in, 762
    as fragments, 665, 749–750
    functions, 652
    as indirect objects, 650
    list of, 650, 798
    time and, 795
Prepositions, 793–800
    adjectives with, 787
    for cause or reason, 796
    for condition or degree, 796
    definition of, 642, 793
    functions of, 636, 794–797
    gerunds after, 781
    lists of common, 643, 794
    multiword, 794
    necessary and unnecessary, 799–800
    objects of, 652
    in phrasal verbs, 610
    for possession/attribute/origin, 797
    recognizing, 793–794
    specified for certain verbs or nouns,
        798
    in titles and subtitles, 861
presence, presents, 619

Present infinitive tense, 706
Present participles
    as adjectives, 696, 780
    forms of, 698, 699
    as nouns, 696
    tense sequences and, 707
    as verbals, 661, 696
Present perfect participles, 707
Present perfect progressive tense, 704
Present perfect tense, 703, 704
Present progressive tense, 703, 704
Present subjunctive mood, 708
Present tenses, 492, 705–706
Presentation anxiety, 217
Presentations. *See* Multimedia
    presentations
Press release, 361, 554–556
pretend, 780
Previewing, in reading critically,
    113–114
Primary sources, 511
    for literature and humanities,
        489–491
principal, principle, 619
Printed sources, 227
Printing and binding
    APA-style format for, 430
    MLA style format for, 382
Privacy, emails and, 203
Probability, modals expressing, 783
Problem-solution organization, 71
Process analysis, 64–65
Professional and civic writing, 537–557
    email etiquette, 544
    job application letters, 543–547
    letters of complaint, apology, and
        rejection, 540–542
    memos, 542–543
    press releases, 361, 554–556
    reports and proposals, 552–553
    résumés, 547–540
    standard letter format, 542–544
Professional Models
    apology business letter, 541
    "The City Upon a Hill" speech
        (Kennedy), 74–76
    "How Accurate Is the Myers-Briggs
        Personality Test?" (Gholipour),
        116–119
    press release, 554–556
    "Time Blindness" (Brooks) article,
        121–125
    Uncle Vanya play review (Lower),
        507–509
Professional titles, 550, 551
Progressive tenses, 703–705
Projection fallacy, 180
promise, 650, 780

Pronoun case
  in appositives, 716
  in comparisons with *than* or *as*, 717
  in compounds, 714–715
  errors in, 713–714
  forms of, 713
  grammar checker and, 633
  with infinitives, 716
  with *ing* form of verb, 717
  interrogative, 713
  objective, 713, 714, 716, 717
  personal pronouns, 713
  possessive, 638, 640, 713, 714, 717
  relative pronouns in, 713, 717–719
  subjective, 713, 714, 715, 716,
    717–719
  tone and, 718
  we or *us* before noun, 716
  with *who, whom, whoever,* and
    whomever, 717–719
Pronoun reference, 629, 719–722
Pronoun-antecedent agreement,
    689–693
  collective noun antecedents and, 692
  compound antecedents and,
    692–693
  definition of, 628
  gender bias and, 602
  generic noun antecedents, 736
  grammar checker and, 628, 690
  nearest antecedent rule in, 693
  pitfalls, 691
  plural or variable indefinite, 691–692
  possessive pronouns and, 690
  in subordinate clauses, 688
Pronouns. *See also* Relative pronouns
  as adjectives, 640
  for coherence, 61
  in comma splices, 673
  definition, 689
  demonstrative, 318, 638, 640
  as determiners, 640, 772
  as direct objects, 778
  functions of, 636, 637, 638
  gender bias and, 601–603
  implied references for, 721
  indefinite, 638, 640, 685, 690–692,
    828
  intensive, 638
  interrogative, 638, 662, 713, 717–719
  objective case, 713, 714, 716, 717
  in paragraphs, 61
  personal, 638, 713, 829
  possessive, 638, 640, 772, 829
  pronoun reference, 719–722
  reciprocal, 638
  redundant subject and object
    pronouns, 760–761

  reflexive, 638
  as subject complements, 714
  subjective case, 713, 714, 715, 716,
    717–719
  subject-verb agreement, 689–693
  types of, 638
  who, whom, whoever, and *whomever*
    as, 717–719
  you, to address reader directly,
    721
Pronunciation
  in dictionaries, 615
  spelling and, 618
Proofreading, 96–98, 209, 547
Proper adjectives, 859, 860–861
Proper nouns
  articles with, 771
  capitalizing, 859, 860–861
  function of, 635, 767
  plurals of, 624
Proposals, 552–553
propose, 762
Props, in drama writing, 507
ProQuest database, 232–233, 240, 246,
    251, 269
prove, 649, 725
provided that, 573
Provisional course of action, 224
Proximity, in design, 184, 185, 190
Pseudonyms. *See* Pen names or
    pseudonym
PsycARTICLES database, 224–225, 246
Public context, 22
*Publication Manual of the American
    Psychological Association* (7th ed.),
    397, 401, 413
Publications
  date identification, 320
  name locations, 234
  relevance and date of, 263–264
  sponsors of, 233–234
  volume and issue numbers in, 233
Publisher, in working bibliography,
    231–234
Punctuation
  in compound sentences, 657
  conjunctive adverbs, 641
  in coordination, 566, 802, 804
  emphasis and, 586, 591
  end, 843–846
  of nonessential subordinate clauses,
    572, 591, 668, 805, 812, 822
  in proofreading, 97
  in quotations, 835, 836, 848, 851
  in subordination, 572
  between two independent clauses,
    566, 591, 671–672, 675–676, 821
  in URLs, 856

Purpose of writing
  analysis of, 17
  in assignments, 23
  in business letters, 538
  design and, 188
  to entertain, 15
  examples, 17–18
  to express, 15
  to inform, 16, 37–38
  to learn, 16–17
  to persuade or argue, 16, 37–38
  research paper/project, 222–223
  statement of, 538
  tone and, 14, 20–21
put, 762
put back, 777
put down, 777
put up with, 777

Q

Qualitative data, 511
Quantifiers, 768, 772, 773
Quantitative data, 511
Quarterly Journal of Medicine, 511
Queer approach to literature, 490
Question marks
  in direct questions, 844–845
  multiple, 844
  in parentheses, 845
  quotation marks and, 839
  in series of questions, 845
  in wildcard searches, 250
Questionnaires (surveys), 261
Questions
  answers to, 669
  direct, 738, 844–845
  incomplete sentences as, 845
  indirect, 738, 844
  periods used to soften tone, 843–844
  relative pronouns beginning,
    662–663
  research, 225–227, 303
  rhetorical, 592
  series of, 845
  shifts between direct and indirect,
    737–738
  tag, 807–808
  verb mood in, 707
  word order in, 646, 764
quit, 780
Quotation marks, 310, 828–842
  in American vs. British usage, 835, 839
  in Boolean searches, 250
  common do's and don'ts, 835
  in definitions, 838
  in dialog, 836
  for direct copying, 303, 316
  in direct quotations, 834, 835

Index

double changed to single, 834
in irony, 835, 837
lack of, 284–285
not for emphasis, 835, 838
not in long quotations, 836
not with clichés, 835, 839
not with indirect quotations, 835
not with slang, 835, 838
in quotations from poetry, 836–837
single, 834
around titles, 865
in titles or short works, 837
for words used as words, 835, 837
Quotations, 26, 126
APA-style block, 289
APA-style in-text, 288
brackets in, 848, 851
brief, MLA style, 284
capitalizing first words in, 860
circumstances for use of, 283, 297
citing, 283
colons and, 814, 848, 853
commas between signal phrases and, 813
copying into notes, 297–298
direct, 737–738, 813, 834, 835
ellipses in, 285, 298, 840, 854
first draft and, 308
indirect, 737–738, 814, 835, 836
integration in citations, 322–324
interrupted by signal phrases, 840, 860
introducing and identifying, 840–841
MLA style block, 285, 339
MLA style format and long, 380–381
overusing in notes, 298
from poetry, 836–837
within quotations, 834
shifts between direct and indirect, 737–738
source authority established with, 290
strategic use of, 297–300
to support claims, 310
using fairly, 298
quoted in, qtd. in, 348
Qur'an, documenting
APA-style for, 406, 414
MLA style for, 346–347, 360

R

Races, names of, 861
Racial labels, 603
Radio broadcasts, documenting
APA-style for, 423
MLA style for, 347, 372
rain, reign, rein, 619
raise, raze, 619

raise, rise, 701–702
Random House Webster's College Dictionary, 613
Random House Webster's Unabridged Dictionary, 614
rarely, 765
Ratios, colons in, 853
raze, raise, 619
read, 650
Reader response approach to literature, 490
Reading. *See also* Critical reading and thinking
for comprehension, 112–119
engagement in, 112
of essay exams, 532
proofreading, 87–88
with study guides, 487
Reading journals, 125–126, 531
Reading note, Student Model for, 299
real, really, 726
really, 559, 726
Reason, prepositions indicating, 796
reason is because, reason why, 752
Reasoning, logical, 151
Reasons for writing. *See* Purpose of writing
Rebuttal, in Toulman model, 176
recall, 780
Recipients, in emails, 200
Reciprocal pronouns, 638
recommend, 762
Recommendations, verbs in, 709
record, 315
Red herring fallacy, 180
Reddit, 245
MLA style documenting for, 367–369
Redundant comparisons, 729
Redundant expressions, 560–561, 730
Reference list, APA-style, 408–425
abstracts, 419, 427
audio and visual sources, 422–424
authors with two or more works published in same year, 411
blogs and blog postings, 421–422
book editions other than first, 413
books with author and editor or translator, 412
books with authors of same surname and first initial, 400, 405, 412
books with group or corporate authors, 412
books with multiple authors, 410–411
books with one author, 409
books with two authors, 410
books with unnamed or anonymous authors, 411

computer software, 422
conference proceedings, 425
data set, 424
discussion list postings, 421
dissertations, 414–415
DOIs, 410, 414, 417, 420
DOIs and URLs in, 409–410, 415, 420
edited books or anthologies, 413
electronic sources, 419–422
entry in encyclopedia or other reference work, 413–414
examples of, 408–409
fact sheets, brochures, and pamphlets, 424–425
government publications, 424
interview, 425
introduction, preface, foreword, or afterword, 413
journal special issue, 417
lectures, speeches, conference presentations, or poster session, 423
legal sources, 425
letters to editor, 419
magazine articles, 417
map, 424
motion pictures, 422
multivolume works, 414
musicals and other audio recordings, 423
newspaper articles, 417–418
nongovernmental report, 424
past tense or past perfect tense for, 706
periodicals, 415–419
personal communications, 425
podcast, 423
presentation slides, 422
reference work entries, 413–414
republished books, 414
reviews, 418
sacred or classical sources, 414
scholarly journal articles, 416
selection from edited book or anthology, 413
short work from website, 420–421
in Student Model sample paper, 437
television or radio broadcasts, 423
thesis, 414–415
two or more books by same author, 411
vlogs, 423
websites and web pages, 420
wiki articles, 421
Reference list, CSE-style
books with groups or corporate authors, 474
books with one author, 473–474

Index

Reference list, CSE-style (*continued*)
   books with two or more authors, 474
   conference paper (published), 475–476
   conference paper (unpublished), 476
   directory to models, 470
   discussion lists or blog postings, 481
   dissertations, 476
   edited book selections or conference proceedings, 475
   edited books, 475
   electronic documents, 473–482
   electronic sources, 480–482
   emails, 481
   examples of, 472
   format of, 482–483
   Keefe laboratory report sample reference list, 483–484
   magazine articles, 478–479
   newspaper articles, 479–480
   scholarly journal articles, 477–478
   short work from website, 481
   social media posting, 481
   technical reports or government documents, 482
   websites, 480
Reference Universe, 240
Reference works
   almanacs and yearbooks, 240
   bibliographies, 241
   biographical, 241
   citation indexes, 246–251
   databases, 248–250
   dictionaries, 239–240, 348–349, 447, 491–492, 613–625, 787, 879
   encyclopedias, 239–240
   idea generation and, 26, 31
   library catalogs as, 238, 251–254
   locating, 238–241
   subject-specific, 238
References, in job applications, 549
Reflection
   reading journal, 125–126
   text annotation, 119–120
Reflexive pronouns, 638
refuse, 780
refused, 790
RefWorks, 231
Regionalisms, 597
Regular plurals, 624
Regular verbs, 629, 694, 696–697
Rehearsing presentations, 215–217
reign, rain, rein, 619
Rejection, letters of, 542
Relative (adjective) clauses, 655
Relative pronouns, 638
   in adjective clauses, 655
   case in, 713, 717–719

   definition of, 713
   forms of, 656
   interrogative pronouns vs., 662–663, 718
   list of, 663
   in noun clauses, 656
   omitting, 655
   in questions, 662–663
   subject-verb agreement and, 688
   in subordinate clauses, 571, 655
   who, whom, whoever, and *whomever* as, 717–719
Relevance
   abstract, introduction and, 264
   conclusion and, 264
   evaluating for, 263–264
   figures, illustration and, 264
   headings and subheadings for, 264
   index search and, 264
   of paragraphs, 52, 53
   publication date and, 263–264
Reliability. *See* Credibility
Religion names, 861
Religious works. *See* Sacred texts
remark, 315
remember, 705, 780
remind, 780
repair, 762
repeat again, 560
Repetition
   in design, 184, 185
   emphasis and, 593
   in multimedia presentations, 216
   in paragraphs, 60–61
   in poetry, 502
   strategic, 586
   unacceptable, 752
   unnecessary, 561
   using commas to replace omitted words, 817
reply all, 544
reports, 315
Reports. *See also* Sciences and social sciences, writing in
   business, 552–553
   "Field Research Report on the Mental Health of College Students" (Durand), 517–529
   laboratory, 514–515
   standard form for, 514–515
   writing, 513–515
Republished or reprinted works, documenting
   APA-style for, 405–406, 414
   MLA style for, 360
Requests, verbs in, 709
require, 780
Research data accuracy, 511

Research hypothesis, 226–227
Research logs, 228–229, 230, 304
   back up of electronic, 229
   components of, 229
   index cards, notebooks, computers for, 229, 305
Research notebooks, 510, 514
Research notes, 303
Research paper/project, 16
   analysis, interpretation, and synthesis in, 303
   assignment analysis, 222–223
   citations, 303
   CSE-style reference list (Keefe), 483–484
   documentation, 303
   drafting, 307–310
   evidence and counterevidence, 303
   factors in planning, 223
   "Fast Fashion" (Beck) MLA style, 383–396
   field research, 259–262
   first draft of, 308
   formatting, 311
   informative vs. persuasive, 222, 225
   "Nature versus Nurture" (Worthington) APA-style, 430–438
   organizing ideas, 303, 304–307
   plagiarism avoidance, 230
   proofreading, 311
   publishing, 311
   purpose and audience for, 222–223
   questions and hypotheses in, 225–226
   research logs in, 228–229
   revising, 311
   "Rise and Fall of Bound Feet in China" (Sweetwood) *Chicago*-style, 459–469
   schedule in, 223–224
   source selection strategies in, 227–228
   thesis statement in, 302–304
   topic selection in, 224–225
   Wedd final draft of, 99–105
   Wedd first draft of, 47–50
   working bibliographies in, 224, 230–235
Research questions
   hypotheses from, 226–227
   inquiry importance and, 226
   of quantity and degree, 225
   reframing of, 226
Research report, 4–6
   context for, 14
   "Field Research Report on the Mental Health of College Students" (Durand), 516–529

Index

Research topics, 224–225
resemble, 705
resist, 780
respectfully, respectively, 619
Response. *See* Critical response
Responsibilities to readers, 8
Restrictive (essential) elements, 572, 668, 811
Results section, in research and laboratory reports, 515
Résumés
 context for, 14
 designing, 547
 sample, 548
 scannable or electronic, 550
 traditional print, 548–549
"Rethinking Alternative Energy" (Wedd), 105
Return address, for business letters, 539
Review of play, *Uncle Vanya* play review (Lower), 507–509
Reviews
 APA-style documenting of, 418
 Chicago-style documenting of, 453
 of drama, 507–509
 MLA style documenting of, 365, 370
Revising
 analysis in, 86–90
 arguments, 179
 audience and, 88, 89
 big picture in, 89, 94
 for coherence and unity, 90
 emails, 202
 evidence and counterevidence, 88, 89, 92
 globally and locally, 86–90
 with instructors or tutors, 92, 95–96
 introductions, 87–89
 organization and, 88–90
 peer, 93–95
 perspective gained in, 86–87
 proofreading in, 96–98
 sentences, 91–93
 sources use and, 324
 thesis statements, 37–39, 87–89
 titles, 90
 visuals, 82–85
 websites, 92, 106, 108, 209
 words, 91
Rhetorical analysis
 of image, 130–131
 memes and, 275
"A Rhetorical Analysis of Konstantin Ivanov's 'The Road Is Open to Humans'" poster (Kelley), 130–131

Rhetorical appeals, 150–156
 Ethos, 129, 130, 131, 153–154, 155, 175, 874
 Logos, 129, 150–153, 155, 175
 Pathos, 129, 131, 154–155, 175
Rhetorical citations, 312–327
Rhetorical ecologies, 210
Rhetorical questions, 592
Rhetorical search, 237–238, 280
Rhetorical situation, 8, 14–15, 210
Rhyme, in poetry, 502
Rhythm, 502, 586, 590–591
right, rite, wright, write, 619
Right, Wrong, and Risky dictionary, 614
Rippington, Maya, "Website Usability Report," 190–191
rise, raise, 701–702
risk, 780
rite, right, wright, write, 619
road, rode, 619
Rogerian argument, 17, 129
 background in introduction of, 175
 conclusion in, 176
 evidence and counterevidence in, 176
Rogers, Carl, 175
round in shape, 560
Roundabout expressions, 560
RSS feeds, 245
run into, 777

S

-s, -es
 as plural noun ending, 624, 637
 subject-verb agreement and, 687
 as verb ending, 700–701, 828, 830
-s form, of verbs, 694, 695
Sacred texts, 360, 407, 414, 448
 capitalization of, 861
 chapter and verse notations, 853
 MLA style for documenting, 346–347
 not italicized, 866
Salutations
 in business letters, 539
 in emails, 200, 544
Sample papers. *See* Student Model
Sarcasm, 159, 837
say, 762
Scannable résumés, 550–551
scarcely, 728, 742
Scheduling
 assignment calculators, 224
 assignments, 24, 34
 in collaborative projects, 34
 first draft, 44
Scholarly journals, documenting
 APA-style for, 416
 Chicago-style for, 449–450

CSE-style, 477–478
 MLA style for, 362–363
Scholarly sources
 characteristics of, 267
 expert author, 268
 peer review of, 266
 tone of, 268
Science Direct database, 246
Sciences and social sciences, writing in
 approaches to, 510
 discipline-specific vocabulary in, 512, 598
 "Field Research Report on the Mental Health of College Students" (Durand), 516–529
 language of, 512–513
 passive voice in, 513, 594, 710
 past and present tense in, 705
 qualitative and quantitative data in, 511
 reference list in, 515
 research methods, 511
 standard format for, 514–515
 style guide selection in, 511–512
 third person in, 513
 types of, 513–515
Scientific Style and Format (8th ed.), 470
Scopus database, 269
Scores, in sports, 875
Scratch outline, of Wedd, 41–42
Screenshots, 85
Search engines
 blog, 245
 database, 242–245
 federated searching on, 249
 metasearch, 242–243, 249
 using, 242–244
Second person, 735
 addressing reader, 721
 in commands, 592
Secondary sources, 491
see, 780
seem, 649, 705
seldom, 765
self-, 878–879
Self-plagiarism, 282
sell to, 798
Semicolons, 820–826
 in compound sentences, 657
 conjunctive adverbs and, 641, 821, 822
 coordinating conjunctions and, 674, 821
 do's and don'ts, 821
 linking independent clauses with, 567, 673, 676, 805–806, 820–822
 between long items in series, 808, 823
 not before lists, 821

Semicolons (*continued*)
  overuse of, 824
  quotation marks and, 840
  in repairing comma splices, 676, 821, 823
  sending signal with, 820
  in series, 808, 821, 823
  stressing equal importance with, 824
  in transitional expressions, 821, 822
send, 650, 761
Sentence fragments
  ambiguities from, 664
  context and, 664
  correcting, 664–669
  definition of, 628, 651, 749
  grammar checkers and, 665
  identification of, 661
  imperatives vs., 662
  intentional, 669–670
  lists and examples as, 666
  mixed construction and, 749–751
  with no subject, 661–662
  with no verb, 661
  phrases as, 651, 661, 665–667, 749–750
  prepositional phrases as subjects in, 665, 749–750
  recognizing, 660–664
  subordinate clauses as, 655, 662–663, 667–668
  verbals as, 661, 665
Sentence outline, of Wedd, 42–43
Sentence structure. *See also* Word order
  certain conjunctions or adverbs beginning a clause, 764–765
  direct and indirect objects in, 648–650
  elliptical constructions, 561, 753–754
  faulty predication, 751–753
  grammatically mixed, 749–753
  incomplete constructions, 753–756
  inverted word order in, 591, 646, 688, 764–765
  normal word order in, 758
  object complements in, 650
  in questions, 646
  redundant subject and object pronouns in, 760–761
  sentence patterns, 648–650
  stated subject, 752, 758, 759
  subject and predicate in, 645
  there and *it* constructions, 646
  variety in, 587
  verb types and, 648–650
Sentence variety, 586–596
Sentences
  capitalization of first word in, 858–860
  commands, 592

common problems in, 216
complete, 660
complex, 587, 658, 824
compound, 587, 657
compound-complex, 587, 658
cumulative, 590
declarative, 592, 645, 758, 843–844
exclamations, 592
exclamatory, 645
imperative, 645
interrogative, 645, 646
inverted word order in, 591, 646, 688, 764–765
length of, 586, 587
openings, 589
paraphrases and, 292
periodic, 590
revising, 91–93
simple, 587, 657
stated subject requirement in, 752, 758, 759
Student Model first draft with problems in, 630–631
topic, 42–43, 55–58
variety and emphasis in, 586–596
Separable phrasal verbs, 777, 778
Sequence, conjunctions and, 568
Sequence of tenses, 695, 706–707
Serial commas, 566, 808
Series
  of books, 359–360, 448
  commas separating items in, 566, 803, 808–809
  dashes setting off, 848
  parallelism and, 580–581
  semicolons in, 808, 821, 823
Servers, 229
set, sit, 700–701
Setting, as literature element, 489
several
  count and noncount nouns with, 768
  as determiner, 773
  pronoun-antecedent agreement, 691
  subject-verb agreement, 685, 691
Sexual orientation, 603
-sh, plurals of words that end in, 624
shall
  meanings of, 783
  as modal verb, 639, 699, 782, 783
  subject-verb agreement with, 681
shall, should, ought to, 783
she, or he, 602, 736
she or *her*, 714
Shifts
  grammar checker and, 733
  in number, 736
  in person, 735–736
  in questions, 738

in quotations, 737–738
in verb mood, 733
in verb tense, 732–733
in voice, 733–734
should
  advisability and expectation and, 783
  with *if* clauses, 708
  as modal verb, 639, 699, 782
  subject-verb agreement with, 681
  subjunctive used with, 699
should, shall, ought to, 783
should've, should have, 782
shout at, 798
shout to, 798
show, 650, 761
shows, 315
sic, 851, 852
sight, cite, site, 618
Signal phrases, 288, 301, 317, 321, 324
  APA-style for, 399, 401, 402
  citations and, 283, 312, 314
  commas with, 813, 841
  definition of, 813
  interrupting quotations, 840, 860
  introducing quotations, 840, 853
  MLA style for, 335, 337, 338, 340
  in multimedia presentations, 219
  paraphrases and, 292
  signal verb list, 315, 324
  in summaries, 291
Signal verbs, 315, 324
Signatures, in letters, 540
Silent *-e*, word that end in, 621
Similes, 608, 609
Simple future tense, 703, 704
Simple helping verbs, 782
Simple past tense, 703, 704
Simple predicates, 647
Simple present tense, 702, 704
Simple sentences, 587, 657
Simple subjects, 645
Simple tenses, 702–703, 704
simply, 742
since
  meanings of, 573
  as subordinating conjunction, 573, 663
Single authors
  APA-style for documenting, 401–402, 409
  Chicago-style for documenting, 442
  CSE-style for documenting, 473–474
  MLA style for documenting, 340, 352–353
  with same surname, 343, 400, 405, 412

two or more sources by same, 337, 343, 404–405
with two or more works published in same year, 405, 411
sit, set, 701–702
site, sight, cite, 618
Slack, 51
Slang, 598, 614, 835, 838
Slashes
functions of, 848
in poetry quotations, 836, 856
Slippery slope fallacy, 181
smell, 649
Snapchat, 531
so
in coordination, 566, 643, 804
in correcting comma splices and fused sentences, 676
indicating cause and effect, 568
in parallelism, 579
so, such, 791
so, too, 790
so that, 573, 663
Social media, 210–211, 273–274
asynchronous media, 211
memes and, 275
misinformation, disinformation on, 270
synchronous media, 211
Social networking sites, 245, 598, 602
Social sciences. *See* Sciences and social sciences, writing in
Software. *See* Computer software
some
count and noncount nouns with, 768
pronoun-antecedent agreement, 692
as quantifying word, 772
subject-verb agreement, 685
somebody, 685
someone, 685
something, 685
sound, 649, 725
Source boundaries, 314–316
Sources
acknowledgment of, 310–311
common knowledge, 283–284, 288
copying, 246, 251
establishing authority of, in papers, 290
explaining choice of, 326–327
in field research, 259–262
key terms for search of, 224
multimedia, 255
popular vs. scholarly, 246, 267
primary, 489–491
printed, 227, 230, 231
relevance of, 265
secondary, 491

selection strategies, 246
working bibliographies, 232, 241
for writing about literature, 489–491
Sources, citing, 20, 335. *See also* Citations
Chicago-style, 441
claims support and, 313
credibility of, 10, 267–268
CSE-style, 470
Sources, documenting, 335
Chicago-style, 441
CSE-style, 470
explain sources choice, 319
"Fast Fashion" (Beck) source material integration and identification, 321–322
larger discussion identification, 321
publication date identification, 320
source type identification, 320
Sources, evaluating, 263–278. *See also* Credibility
in critical reading and thinking, 134, 141–142
critiquing, 126
diversity, 269–270
graphs, 278
interactive media, 245
popular v. scholarly sources, 246, 267
for relevance, 263–264
visual sources, 274–278
web pages, 277
Sources, finding. *See also* Online sources, finding
abstracts, 241, 264
blogs and blog postings, 245
databases and indexes, 246–251
government publications, 255
interactive media and, 245
library catalogs and, 251–254
multimedia sources, 255
reference works, 238–254
on Web, 277
Spacing
in APA-style, 426
in business letters, 539
in MLA style, 379
in résumés, 547
Spam/spamming, 544
SparkNotes, 487
Spatial organization, 41
Speaking off-the-cuff, in multimedia presentation, 215
Speaking outline, for multimedia presentation, 215–216
Special pleading fallacy, 178
Special relationships, transitional expressions for, 61
Specialist audience, 18
Specialized dictionaries, 239, 240, 614–615

Specific words, 603
Speech
APA-style documenting for, 423
"The City Upon a Hill" (Kennedy), 74–76
MLA style documenting for, 374
Spelling
American vs. British, 619–620
bilingual dictionaries and, 618
dictionaries and, 615
of homonyms and near-homonyms, 618, 619
ie / ei rule, 620–621
impact of errors in, 617–620
improvement of, 625–626
plurals, 623–625
prefixes, 621
pronunciation and, 615
proofreading, 97
rules for, 620–623
spelling checkers, 97, 623, 626, 829
suffixes, 621–623
Spelling checkers, 623, 626, 829
Split infinitives, 740, 744
Sponsors
of publications, 233–234
of URLs, 273
SquareSpace, 197
Squinting modifiers, 742
Stacking the deck fallacy, 178
Stage fright, 217
Stage set, in drama writing, 507
stand in for, 777
Standard American English, 634, 699
Standard word order, 758
Stanzas, in poetry, 502
Staples on papers, 382
start, 780
states, 315
stationary, stationery, 619
Statistics, 47, 875
Stereotypes, 600–601, 602
stop, 780
Strategic repetition, 586, 592–593
Student Models
brainstorming list (Wedd), 28, 32
"A Close Reading of Mohsin Hamid's The Reluctant Fundamentalist" (Williams) interpretive analysis, 496–501
"A Close Reading of Shelley's 'Poetical Essay on the Existing State of Things'" (Andrews) explication, 501–506
"A Close Reading of Shelley's 'Poetical Essay on the Existing State of Things'" (Andrews) text evidence, 495

Student Models (*continued*)
"A Close Reading of Shelley's 'Poetical Essay on the Existing State of Things'" (Andrews) textual analysis, 488, 490
"A Critical Analysis of René Brooks' Article 'Time Blindness'" (Fernandez) critical analysis essay, 135–139
"A Critical Analysis of René Brooks' 'Time Blindness' article" (Fernandez), 53, 115
CSE-style reference list (Keefe), 483–484
effective exam response (Okada), 535–536
"Fast Fashion" (Beck) MLA style in-text parenthetical citation for paraphrase, 287
"Fast Fashion" (Beck) MLA style paraphrase citation, 289
"Fast Fashion" (Beck) MLA style research paper, 383–396
"Fast Fashion" (Beck) MLA style summary citation, 289
"Fast Fashion" (Beck) outline, 306–307
"Fast Fashion" (Beck) supporting claims, 309–310
"Fast Fashion" (Beck) thesis statement, 303–304
"Field Research Report on the Mental Health of College Students" (Durand), 516–529
first draft of research paper (Wedd), 47–50
first draft with sentence problems, 630–631
freewriting essay (Wedd), 27
"How Accurate Is the Myers-Briggs Personality Test?" (Gholipour) double-entry reading journal, 126
"Inmate Access to Technology" (Davids), 156, 159–174
job application, 546
journalists' question (Wedd), 30
"Nature versus Nurture" (Worthington) APA-style in-text parenthetical citation for paraphrase, 287
"Nature versus Nurture" (Worthington) APA-style in-text quotation, 288
"Nature versus Nurture" (Worthington) APA-style research paper, 430–438
personal statement (Ky), 108–110

"Plagiarism an Issue on Campus, Faculty Says" (Ginsie), 12–13
reading note, 299
"Rethinking Alternative Energy" (Wedd) final draft of research paper, 99–105
"A Rhetorical Analysis of Konstantin Ivanov's 'The Road Is Open to Humans'" poster (Kelley), 130–131
"Rise and Fall of Bound Feet in China" (Sweetwood) *Chicago*-style research paper, 459–469
scannable, optimized résumé, 550–551
scratch outline (Wedd), 41–42
summary of source, 296
topic or sentence outline (Wedd), 42–43
traditional résumé, 548
"Website Usability Report" (Ball, Balzer, Fitzpatrick-Woodson, Rippington), 190–191
Study groups, 531
Study guides, 487
Style, as literature element, 489
Style checkers
confusing shifts and, 733
coordination, subordination and, 565
misplaced modifiers, 740
parallelism and, 581
word choice and, 605
wordiness and, 561
Style guide selection, 98
Styles of documentation. *See also specific documentation style*
APA, 339–438
Chicago, 439–469
CSE, 470–484
MLA, 329–396
Subheadings, relevance and, 264
Subject complements
adjective phrases as, 588
adjectives as, 640, 725
compound, 714–715
definition of, 588, 640, 714, 750
mixed constructions with, 750–751
placement of, 588
pronouns as, 714
sentence pattern with, 640, 649
subject-verb agreement and, 689
Subject directory, 31, 33
Subject headings, 252–253
Subject line, in emails, 200
Subjects
complete, 645
compound, 645, 683–684

dangling modifiers and, 745, 746
definition, 660
in expletive constructions, 646
explicit, 662
finding, 646
fragments and, 661–662, 667
in imperatives, 662
in interrogative sentences, 646
question words as, 758
redundant subject and object pronouns, 760–761
shifting voice to maintain, 710
simple, 645
singular nouns ending in -s, 687
there as, 646
titles, names, and words treated as words, 687
unstated, 592, 645, 662, 759
word order and, 646, 647
Subject-specific dictionaries, 614
Subject-verb agreement
with *be*, 681
collective nouns and, 685–686
compound subjects and, 683–684
definition of, 628
dialects and, 682
faulty predication and, 751–752
grammar checker and, 628, 680
helping verbs and, 681
indefinite pronouns and, 685
intervening words and, 682
linking verbs and, 689
measurement or number subjects and, 686
person and number definitions, 680
pitfalls in, 682, 683
relative pronouns and, 688
singular nouns ending in -s, 687
subject following the verb and, 682
with *there*, 688
titles, names, and words treated as words, 687
Subject-verb order. *See* Word order
Subject-verb-object (S-V-O) order, 758
Subjunctive mood, 707–709, 733
Subordinate clauses
adverbial, 588
comma splices and, 675
commas and, 805, 812
definition of, 566, 571, 655, 717, 758, 805
as fragments, 655, 662–663, 667–668
functions of, 570–571
fused sentences and, 675
introducing an independent clause, 805–806
in mixed construction, 750
parallelism and, 582

Index

punctuation and, 572, 591, 668, 805, 812, 822
relative pronouns in, 655
semicolons and, 822
in sentence structure, 570–571
stated subject required in, 759
as subjects, 750
subjunctive in, 708
subordinating conjunctions in, 643
techniques of, 571–572
types of, 573
who or *whoever* as subject of, 718
whom or *whomever* as object of, 718
Subordinating conjunctions
in adjective clauses, 655
in adverb clauses, 656
functions of, 643
list of, 644, 663
meanings of, 571
in noun clauses, 656
in sentence fragments, 667–668
in subordinate clauses, 573, 643
Subordination
coordination used with, 575–577
in correcting comma splices, 675
definition of, 566, 571–572
essential vs. nonessential information and, 572, 666
excessive, 574–575
functions of, 571
illogical, 574–575
punctuation and, 572
style checkers and, 565
techniques of, 571–572
term selection in, 572–573
Subtitles
capitalization of, 859, 861–862
colons before, 853
Subtweeting fallacy, 180–181
succeed, 622
such, so, 791
such as, 852, 873
Suffixes, 621–623, 878–879
suggest, 780
sum total, 560
Summaries, 141
in assignments, 17
citations in, 283, 289
in critical reading, 114–115, 126
effective use of, 295–297
elements of, 297
executive, 552, 553
first draft and, 308
length of, 295
MLA style citation, 289
signal phrase in, 291
of sources, 295–297

to support claims, 310
writing, 295–296
summarize, 533
Summary, "A Critical Analysis of René Brooks 'Time Blindness' article" (Fernandez), 53, 115
Summary thesis, 495
Superlative adjectives and adverbs, 729–730
Superscript, 378
supersede, 622
Superstitions, 147
Support. *See* Evidence
Supporting claims, 313
of "Fast Fashion" (Beck), 309–310
summary, paraphrase, and quotations for, 310
SurveyGizmo, 261
SurveyMonkey, 261
Surveys, 261–262
S-V-O order. *See* subject-verb-object order
Sweeping generalization fallacy, 177
Sweetwood, Sara, "Rise and Fall of Bound Feet in China" Chicago-style research paper, 459–469
Syllables, in dictionary entries, 622, 879
Symbol, as literature element, 489
Synchronous media, 211
Synonym dictionaries, 614, 617
Synonyms
accurate, 615
for coherence, 61
in dictionary entries, 614, 617
in paragraphs, 61
paraphrases and, 292
in thesauruses, 614–615
Synthesis
in critical reading, 116, 487
of literature texts, 487

T

Tables, 78, 85
APA-style for, 428–429
document design table numbers, 98, 382, 428
MLA style for, 350–351, 374, 381
notes for, 351, 374, 381–382, 428
in research and laboratory reports, 515
Tag questions, commas after, 807–808
take back, 777, 778
take from, 777, 798
take off, 777
take on, 777, 778
take up, 777
Talmud, documenting
APA-style for, 406, 414
MLA style for, 346–347

Task-oriented emails, 200
taste, 649, 725
teach, 650, 761
TED talk, 212
Television broadcasts, documenting
APA-style for, 423
MLA style for, 347, 372
tell
indirect object with, 650, 761
infinitive after, 670
Tense sequences, 695, 706–707
Tenses. *See* Verb tenses
Test-taking. *See* Essay exams
Text passages, as evidence, 46
Textbooks, as sources, 512
Text-messaging, 22, 211, 545, 598, 872
Texts
analysis of, 487
claims with evidence from, 495
claims with evidence outside text, 496
Textual analysis of literature, "A Close Reading of Shelley's 'Poetical Essay on the Existing State of Things'" (Andrews), 487, 488, 490, 495
than
in comparisons, 581, 717
pronoun case and, 717
as subordinating conjunction, 663
than, then, 619
Thank-you notes, 260
that
antecedents of, 688
confusingly broad use of, 720
count and noncount nouns with, 772
as determiner, 772
identification indicated by, 573
omitted from elliptical constructions, 754
in parallel clauses, 580
people not designated by, 722
preceding quotations, 841
purpose indicated by, 573
redundant object pronouns with, 760
as relative pronoun, 663
in sentence fragments, 660, 666
subject-verb agreement and, 688
subordinate clauses beginning with, 571
as subordinating conjunction, 571, 663
that clauses, commas not used with, 812–813
the. *See* Articles (*a, an, the*)
their, there, they're, 619
Theme, in literature and humanities, 487, 488

Index

then, 61, 560
then, than, 619
there, as expletive, 646, 759
there, their, they're, 619
there are, 562, 688
there is, 688
there was, 688
there were, 688
therefore
  in comma splices, 673
  in coordination, 566–567
  semicolons and, 822
Thesauruses, 614–615
these, 772
Thesis/thesis statement, 35–39
  arguable theses, 149–150
  in conclusion, 71–72
  counterevidence and, 305
  devising, 534
  drafting, 29, 36–37
  in effective exam response (Okada), 536
  in essay exam answers, 534
  evidence assessment for, 305
  in "Fast Fashion" (Beck), 303–304
  gist in, 114
  interpretive analytical thesis, 495
  in introduction, 70–71
  literary, 494–495
  in multimedia presentations, 214
  placement of, 68
  preliminary, 36–37
  revising, 37–39, 87–89
  summary thesis, 495
they, 602, 633, 721
they're, their, there, 619
thinks, 315
Third person, 513, 735
  in literature and humanities, 492–493
this, 772
  confusingly broad use of, 720
those, 772
though, 573
  as subordinating conjunction, 663
throw, 650
throw out, 777
TikTok, MLA style documenting for, 367–369
Time, formats for, 875
"Time Blindness" (Brooks), 121–125
Time management
  in assignments, 24, 281
  in collaborative projects, 34
  in drafting, 44
  for first draft, 44
Time relationships
  adverbs and, 788
  colons and, 853

prepositions, 795–796
sequence of tenses and, 706–707
Time sequences, 706–707
Timing, in emails, 202
Title page
  in academic texts, 113
  in APA-style format, 427
  in MLA style format, 380
  for portfolio, 106–107
  in research or laboratory reports, 514
Titles
  abbreviating, 342, 345, 349, 364
  capitalizing, 861
  of home pages, 205
  italics in, 865–866
  of long works, 837, 865–866
  of people, 550, 551, 815, 861, 870, 871
  quotation marks around, 837, 865
  revising, 90
  of sacred texts, 346–347, 360, 414, 448
  of short works, 837, 866
  subject-verb agreement, 687
  subtitles, 853, 861–862
  within titles, 493–494
to
  direct objects and, 762
  indirect objects and, 650, 798
  in infinitives, 653, 744
  in titles and subtitles, 861
to, too, two, 618
to all intents and purposes, 559
together with, 682
tolerate, 780
Tone
  audience and, 14, 20–21
  in business letters, 538
  diction and, 20–21
  in emails, 199, 543, 544
  in memos, 543
  planning a project genre setting and, 20–21
  pronoun case and, 718
  of scholarly source, 268
  use of, 181–182
  in visuals, 78
  well-tempered, 159
too, either, 790
too, so, 790
too, to, two, 618
Topic. *See also* Idea generation
  assignment and, 23
  audience interest in, 14
  broadening, 31–32, 92
  design and, 188
  expert author of, 268
  fresh, 148
  invention techniques for, 25
  in multimedia presentations, 214

narrowing, 31–32, 92, 223
in research assignments, 237
responsibilities to, 9
selection, 36–37, 223
Topic outline, of Wedd, 42–43
Topic sentences, 42–43, 55–56
  identification of, 57–58
totally, 559
Toulmin, Stephen, 129, 176
Toulmin model of arguments, 129
  backing and rebuttal in, 176
  claim, grounds, warrants in, 176
Trade names, 861
Transgender Studies Quarterly, 266
Transitional expressions
  comma splices and fused sentences, 673
  commas and, 807
  conjunctive adverb as, 641
  definition of, 807
  examples of, 62
  within and between paragraphs, 59–60
  placement of, 589
  semicolons and, 821, 822
  transitional words and phrases, 59–60
Transitional paragraphs, 59–60
Transitive verbs
  active voice and, 649
  direct objects with, 649, 650, 761
  examples of, 700–701
  indirect objects with, 650
  passive voice and, 649, 709
  phrasal, 777
Translation dictionaries, 618
Translators, documenting
  APA-style for, 412
  Chicago-style for, 445–446
  MLA style for, 357
Transportation names, 861
TripAdvisor, MLA style documenting for, 370
Trolls, 158
try, 780
turn up, 777
Twitter, 245
  MLA style documenting for, 367–369
two, to, too, 618
type, 559
Typeface. *See* Fonts
Typographical errors, 538

U

Unabridged dictionaries, 239, 614
unanimous, 730
Uncountable nouns. *See* Noncount nouns
Uncle Vanya play review (Lower), 507–509
Underlining type, 192, 868

understand, 780
Understatement, 608
Unfamiliar-to-familiar order, 4
Unintentional plagiarism, 230
unique, 730
United States (U.S.), global business in, 545
Units of measure, 686, 870, 872–873
Unity
　in outlines, 44
　in paragraphs, 44, 52, 53–55
Universal design principles, 186–187
Universal resource locator (URLs)
　APA-style documenting, 409–410, 415, 420
　Chicago-style documenting, 443, 447, 450–451
　.com (commercial) domain, 271
　CSE-style documenting, 477, 480
　.edu (educational) domain, 271
　in emails, 203, 210
　.gov (governmental) domain, 271
　line breaks, 443, 880
　misinformation check, 271
　MLA style documenting, 353, 359, 362–365, 369
　.net (network) domain, 272
　open or moderated, 273
　.org (organization) domain, 272
　slashes in, 856
　social media and, 273–274, 369
　sponsor of, 273
University of Chicago Press, 439
unless, 573
　as subordinating conjunction, 663
Unmarked infinitives, 780
Unnamed authors, documenting
　APA-style for, 398, 404, 411
　Chicago-style for, 444
　MLA style for, 342, 354–355
Unpaginated source material, 316
Unpublished dissertations, documenting
　APA-style for, 414–415
　Chicago-style for, 449
　CSE-style for, 476
　MLA style for, 361
until, 573
　as subordinating conjunction, 663
until such time as, 560
urge, 780
URLs. *See* Universal resource locator
us
　before a noun, 716
　as personal pronoun, 638, 829
Usage, dictionaries of, 614

V

Value, claims of, 146
Variety, 586–596

Vehicle names, 867
Verb phrases, 669, 779
　definition of, 639
　forming, 697
　functions of, 639, 652
　subject-verb agreement with, 682
　types of verbs in, 780
Verb tenses
　awkward shifts in, 732–733
　choosing, 702–705
　confusing shifts in, 632
　definition of, 702
　future tenses, 703, 704
　infinitives, 706–707
　in literature and humanities writing, 492, 705
　past, 694, 695–697, 699, 704, 705
　past perfect subjunctive, 708
　past subjunctive, 708
　perfect, 703, 704, 706
　perfect infinitive, 707
　perfect progressive, 704, 705
　present, 705–706
　present infinitive, 706
　present subjunctive, 708
　progressive, 703, 704, 705
　in science writing, 705
　sequences, 706–707
　simple, 702–703, 704
　subjunctive, 708
Verbal phrases
　as fragments, 661, 665
　functions of, 652
　subject-verb agreement and, 681
　types of, 652–654
Verbals
　complete verbs vs., 639
　dangling modifiers and, 746
　definition of, 696, 746
　examples of, 696
　past and present participles as, 661, 696
Verbs. *See also* Helping verbs; Subject-verb agreement
　as adjectives, 781
　basic forms of, 694–696
　complete, 661, 697–700
　in dictionary entries, 615
　emphatic, 586, 593
　on essay exams, 533
　functions of, 636, 639, 694
　gerunds and infinitives after, 653, 779–780
　grammar checkers and, 696
　imperative mood, 695, 707, 733
　indicative mood, 695, 707, 733
　indirect objects taken by, 650, 762
　information revealed in, 694

-ing form, pronoun case with, 717
　intransitive, 648, 700–701
　in inverted sentences, 591, 646, 688
　irregular, 615, 629, 694, 696–698
　lie, lay, 698, 701–702
　main, 639, 697–700, 710
　modal, 639, 699, 782, 783–784
　phrasal, 610, 700, 776–778
　regular, 694, 695, 696–697
　rise, raise, 701–702
　-s form of, 694, 695
　-s or *-es* and *-d* or *-ed* endings on, 700–701, 828, 830
　sentence fragments and, 661, 665
　sentence patterns and, 648–650
　signal, 315, 324
　sit, set, 701–702
　transitive, 649, 650, 700–701, 709, 761, 777
　verb phrases, 639, 652, 682, 697, 699, 779–780
　verbal phrases, 652–654, 661, 665, 681
　verbals, 639, 652, 661, 696, 746
Verse form, in poetry, 502
Video blogs (vlogs), APA-style documenting, 423
Video games, MLA style documenting for, 370
Video sources
　APA-style documenting, 423
　Chicago-style documenting, 455
　MLA style documenting, 370–371, 372
Virgules. *See* Slashes
Visual aids, in multimedia presentations, 216
Visual claims, 85, 146, 177
Visual fallacies, 177
Visual impairments, 188
Visual literacy, 28–29
Visual sources
　evaluating, 274–278
　information graphics, 78–80, 275
　memes, 275
Visuals. *See also* Images
　accuracy in, 82–83
　annotating, 120, 127
　as arguments, 151
　bar graphs, 78–79, 84, 85, 140
　clarity of, 82, 84
　copyright clearance for, 82
　decision to include, 77–78
　distortion of, 83
　document design and, 196–197
　document size and, 82
　in emotional appeals, 154
　evaluating, 274–278

Index

Visuals (*continued*)
 as evidence, 78–81
 exploitative, 81
 false dilemmas in, 179
 first draft and, 308
 illustrations, 113, 264, 284
 information graphics, 78–80, 275
 interpretation of, 140
 manipulative, 46, 83–85
 maps, 85
 in multimedia presentations, 216
 original vs. borrowed, 82
 photographs in job applications, 78, 545
 preparing to write about, 134
 reading critically, 113–114
 revising, 82–85
 tone in, 78
 in websites, 206, 207
Vlogs. *See* Video blogs
Vocabulary, specialized, 598
Vocabulary logs, 625
Voice. *See also* Active voice; Passive voice; Tone
 blending of, 290–292
 emphasis and, 312, 316–318, 493
 in-text citations and, 292
 shifts in, 733–734
 of writer, 297–299, 318
Volume numbers, 247
Volumes, in publications, 233

W

W3C. *See* World Wide Web Consortium
waist, waste, 619
wait, 780
want, 705, 780
warn, 780
Warrants, 159, 176
was, 562, 697
waste, waist, 619
we
 before a noun, 716
 as personal pronoun, 713, 829
weak, week, 619
Weak claims, 147
wear, where, were, 619
weather, whether, 619
Web design. *See also* Electronic document design
 accessibility and, 189, 208–209
 alignment in, 185
 breadcrumb (click) trails, 205, 233
 color in, 185, 195–196
 content in, 187–188
 design principles in, 184, 185, 187–188
 dynamic templates for, 208

fonts in, 185, 201
headings in, 193–195
home page, 204–206, 208
image, sound and video files in, 208, 209
layout in, 192
links in, 185, 205, 207, 866, 868
lists in, 195
maintaining, 210
navigation tools in, 205, 206, 208
overall impression in, 192
revising, 209
visuals in, 206, 207
white space in, 185, 194, 547
writing situation in, 196
Web of Science database, 227, 269
"Website Usability Report" (Ball, Balzer, Fitzpatrick-Woodson, Rippington), 190–191
Websites and web pages. *See also* Internet; Universal resource locator
 accessibility of, 186, 187–188, 190, 208–209
 APA-style documenting, 333, 406–407, 420–421
 college library, 31, 255
 content creation in, 187–188
 context and audience for, 204
 copyright protection, 207
 creating, 197
 CSE-style documenting, 480, 481
 editing and revising, 295
 evaluating sources on, 277
 evaluation of, 277
 for fact checks, 271
 FAQs on, 242
 finding source titles and publishers, 231–235
 home pages, 204–206, 208
 identification of personal, 272
 links to, 106, 205, 272, 866
 locating, as sources, 197
 metasearch engines and, 242–243, 249
 MLA style documenting, 333, 349–350, 366
 networking of, 204
 planning, 203–204
 revising and, 92, 106, 108, 209
 search function for, 207
 site structure, 204
 subject directories in, 31, 33
 updates for, 205
 visuals in, 206, 207
Webster's New World College Dictionary, 613
Webster's Third New International Dictionary, Unabridged, 614

Wedd, Michael
 brainstorming list, 28, 32
 first draft of researched essay, 47–50
 freewriting essay, 27
 introduction of, 70–71
 journalists' questions, 30
 "Rethinking Alternative Energy" final draft, 99–105
 scratch outline of, 41
 works cited list, 104
well, good, 726
Well-designed document, "Website Usability Report" (Ball, Balzer, Fitzpatrick-Woodson, Rippington), 190–191
Well-developed paragraphs, 52
Well-tempered tone, 159
were, 562, 697
were, where, wear, 619
what
 as relative pronoun, 663
 in subordinate clauses, 571
 word order in questions with, 764
whatever, as relative pronoun, 663
when
 in adjective clauses, 655
 in adverb clauses, 752
 to indicate time, 573
 in noun clauses, 656
 in sentence fragments, 661
 to show identification, 573
 in subordinate clauses, 571
 as subordinating conjunction, 663
whenever
 in noun clauses, 656
 as subordinating conjunction, 573, 663
where
 in adjective clauses, 655
 in adverb clauses, 752
 to indicate place, 573
 in noun clauses, 656
 to show identification, 573
 as subordinating conjunction, 663
where, wear, were, 619
whereas, 573
 as subordinating conjunction, 663
wherever, 573, 656
whether, 656
whether, weather, 619
whether . . . or, 568
 as correlative conjunction, 643
which
 antecedents of, 683
 commas and, 812, 813
 confusingly broad use of, 720
 identification shown by, 573
 people not designated by, 722
 redundant object pronouns with, 760

Index

as relative pronoun, 663
subject-verb agreement, 688
in subordinate clauses, 571
as subordinating conjunction, 663
which, witch, 619
whichever
as relative pronoun, 663
as subordinating conjunction, 663
while, 573
as subordinating conjunction, 663
White space, 185, 194, 547
who
antecedents of, 683
designating people with, 722
identification shown by, 573
as interrogative pronoun, 717–718
pronoun case and, 633
as relative pronoun, 663, 717–719
in sentence fragments, 660
subject-verb agreement, 688
in subordinate clauses, 571
word order in questions with, 764
who, whom, 717–719
whoever, 718
as relative pronoun, 663
whole, hole, 619
whom
designating people with, 722
as interrogative pronoun, 717–719
as relative pronoun, 663, 717–719
whomever, 717–719
as relative pronoun, 663
who's, whose, 619
whose
designating people with, 722
as relative pronoun, 663
in subordinate clauses, 571
why
as subordinating conjunction, 663
word order in questions with, 764
Wii, MLA style documenting for, 370
Wikipedia, 239
Wikis, 367, 421, 454–455
Wildcard characters, 250
will
meanings of, 783
as modal verb, 639, 699, 782, 783
subject-verb agreement with, 681
will, would, 783
Williams, Jordan, "A Close Reading of Mohsin Hamid's *The Reluctant Fundamentalist*" interpretive analysis, 496–501
Williams, Robin, 184
Windows OneDrive, 202
wish, 780
Wishes, verbs in, 708, 709
witch, which, 619

with, 797
Wix, 197
woman, women, 681
womankind, 601
Word clouds, 29
Word division, in dictionaries, 615
Word order
in adjective clauses, 655
adjectives in, 640, 728, 787, 809, 810
adverbs in, 764–765, 788–790
conjunctions or adverbs beginning a clause, 764–765
inverted, 591, 646, 688, 764–765
of multiple adjectives, 728
in questions, 646, 764
S-V-O, 758
variety in, 581
in verb phrases, 779, 780
with *whom* or *whomever*, 718
Wordiness, 92, 216. *See also* Conciseness
WordPress, 197, 204
Words. *See also* Spelling
abbreviating, 870, 872–873
abstract vs. concrete, 91, 216, 635–636
breaking at ends of lines, 879–880
choice of, 91
clichés, 72, 610–612
compelling, 606–611
compound, 625, 714, 715, 880
connotation of, 91, 606
credibility and, 607
denotation of, 91, 604–605
division of, 615
empty, 559
figures of speech, 216, 502, 608–609
general vs. specific, 606–607
homonyms and near-homonyms, 618, 619
idioms, 610, 611, 614
mixed metaphors, 609–610
non-English, 896
numbers spelled out, 874–875
referred to as words, 687, 831–832, 835, 837, 866, 867
revising and, 91
Words, used as words
apostrophes in plurals of, 831–832
italicizing, 835, 866, 867
quotation marks for, 835, 837
subject-verb agreement, 687
Wordy expressions, eliminating, 559–561
Working bibliography
annotation of, 224, 234–235
components of, 230–231
DOI in, 230
links and, 232
source title and publisher name, 231–235

Workplace writing. *See* Business and public writing
Works cited list, 10, 20, 97, 175
"Inmate Access to Technology" (Davids), 172–174
paraphrase and, 292
plagiarism and, 310
for research paper/project, 303
"Rethinking Alternative Energy" (Wedd), 105
Works cited list, APA-style. *See* Reference list, APA-style
Works cited list, *Chicago*-style, 439–469
anthology or edited book selections, 446
art works, 456–457
book editions other than first, 446–447
books in series, 448
books with authors and editors or translators, 445–446
books with editors (no author), 445
books with group or corporate authors, 445
books with more than three authors, 444
books with one author, 442
books with two or more works by same author, 444–445
books with two or three authors, 443–444
books with unnamed (anonymous) author, 444
CD-ROMs, 455
discussion list or blog postings, 455
dissertations or thesis, 449
DOIs, 443, 450–451
ebook, 443
encyclopedia or dictionary, 447
format of, 458–459
government publications, 457
indirect sources, 457–458
interviews, 457
introductions, prefaces, forewords, or afterwords, 447
letters to editor, 453
magazine articles, 451–452
motion pictures, 455
multivolume works, 448
music or other audio recordings, 456
newspaper articles, 452–453
newspaper editorial, 453
performances, 456
personal communications, 457
podcasts, 456
reviews, 453
sacred texts, 448
scholarly journal articles, 449–450

Works cited list, *Chicago*-style *(continued)*
  URLs and email addresses, 880
  videos, 455
  web pages or wiki articles, 454–455
  website, 454
Works cited list, CSE-style. *See* Reference list, CSE-style
Works cited list, MLA style, 352–377
  advertisements, 376
  for App (e-device), 370
  art works, 374–375
  audio and visual sources, 370–371
  author using pen name or pseudonym, 356
  basic entry for printed books, 330
  blogs and blog postings, 367
  book editions other than first, 358
  books from imprint of larger publishing company, 358
  books in series, 359–360
  books with author and editor or translator, 357
  books with group or corporate authors, 356
  books with one author, 352–353
  books with three or more authors, 342, 353
  books with two authors, 353
  books with unnamed or anonymous authors, 354–355
  CD-ROMs, 359, 373
  comics or cartoons, 375
  computer software, 380
  conference proceedings, 361
  congressional documents, 376
  consumer network posts and reviews, 370
  diary or journal entries, 377
  directory to model, 330
  discussion list postings, 367
  dissertations, 361
  DOIs, 362–365
  DVD extras, 359, 371
  edited books or anthologies, 356, 357
  editorials, 365
  email, 377
  examples, 354–355
  film, 371
  government publications, 376
  home page (academic), 366–367
  interviews, 377
  introductions, prefaces, forewords, or afterwords, 358
  lectures, speeches, or debates, 374
  legal sources, 376
  letters, 376–377
  letters to editor, 365
  live performances, 374
  magazine articles, 363
  maps or charts, 375
  memoranda, 377
  microform articles, 365
  missing publication information, 360
  motion pictures, 371–372
  multivolume works, 359
  musical compositions, 374
  musicals or other audio recordings, 373
  newspaper articles, 364
  pamphlets, brochures, or press releases, 361
  for parenthetical citation, 336, 338
  periodicals, 331, 361–366
  personal correspondence, 377
  podcasts, 373
  reference work entries, 358–359
  republished books, 360
  reviews, 365
  sacred texts, 360
  scholarly journal articles, 362–363
  for signal phrase, 336, 337, 338, 340
  social media posts, 367–369
  in Student Model, 394–395
  television or radio broadcasts, 372
  titles within titles, 360
  two or more works by same author, 356
  video games, 370
  videos, 370–371, 372
  web pages, 366
  websites, 333, 349–350, 366
  wiki articles, 367
Works of art. *See* Art works
World Almanac and Book of Facts, 240
World Wide Web. *See* Websites and web pages
World Wide Web Consortium (W3C), 187–188
Worthington, Robyn
  "Nature versus Nurture" APA-style in-text parenthetical citation for paraphrase, 287
  "Nature versus Nurture" APA-style in-text quotation, 288
  "Nature versus Nurture" APA-style research paper, 430–438
would
  with *if* clauses, 708
  intention or willingness indicated by, 783
  meanings of, 783
  as modal verb, 639, 699, 782, 783
  subject-verb agreement with, 681
would, will, 783
wright, write, rite, right, 619
write, 650, 761
Writer's block, 45
Writer's voice. *See* Voice
writes, 315
Writing. *See also* Academic writing; Drafting; Literature and humanities, writing in; Sciences and social sciences, writing in
  for accessibility, 187–188, 190
  centers, 281–282
  first draft methods, 44–45
Writing situation, 14–17, 200. *See also* Audience; Context; Genre; Purpose of writing; Tone

X

-x, plurals of words that end in, 624
Xbox, MLA style documenting for, 370

Y

-y
  plurals of words that end in, 624
  suffixes for words that end with, 622
Yahoo! Education, 613
Yearbook of Immigration Statistics, 240
Yearbooks, 240
Years, 831, 872, 875
Yelp, MLA style documenting for, 370
yet
  in contrast, 568
  in coordination, 566, 643, 804
  in correcting comma splices, 676
  in parallelism, 579
you
  to address reader directly, 721
  unstated, 592, 645, 662, 759
Young, Stella, 212
your, you're, 619
YouTube, 197, 208, 245, 255
  MLA style documenting for, 372

Z

-z, plurals of words that end in, 624
Zero article, 768
Zip codes, 815
Zoomerang, 261
Zotero, 223, 231

EFL Index

A

a, an, 768–75
Adjectives
    nouns used as, 728
    past participles, 781
    placement of, 640
    present participles, 781
Adverb(s)
    hard and *hardly*, 791
    not and *no*, 791
    not used with direct objects, 727
    placement of, 788–90
    too and *either*, 790
    word order and, 788–89
Agreement, pronoun-antecedent, 689–690
Arguments, exploratory *vs.* persuasive, 153
Articles (*a, an, the*)
    with common nouns, 768–70
    definite and indefinite, 768–70
    as determiners, 640
    with proper nouns, 771
    zero, 768

B

Bilingual dictionaries, 618
British *vs.* American English, 620, 808, 835, 839
Business, conducting in the US, 545

C

can, could, 783
Capitalization, 858
Class discussions, contributing to, 214
Clichés, 611
Common nouns, 767, 768–70
Conciseness, 559
Conjunctions, word order and, 764–65
Connotation, 21
could, can, 783
Count (countable) nouns
    articles with, 768–70
    determiners with, 771–74

D

Declarative sentences, 758
Definite article (*the*), 768–70
Demonstrative pronouns, 772
Determiners, 771–74
Dictionaries, 614
    bilingual, 618
Direct objects, 761–62

E

emails, 200
Ethos, 153–54
Expletives, 759–60
Explicit subjects, 662

F

few, a few, 772

G

Gerunds, 653, 779–80
Gestures, in presentations, 217

H

h-, articles for words beginning with, 769
hard and *hardly*, 791
Helping (auxiliary) verbs
    modal verbs, 782–84
    simple, 782

I

Idea generation, 26
Idioms, 610, 611
Indefinite articles (*a, an*), 768–71
Indirect objects, 650, 761–62
Infinitives, 653, 779–80
Inseparable phrasal verbs, 777–78
Introductions, 68
Inverted word order, 764–65
it, as expletive, 759–60

J

Job applications, 78, 545

L

little, a little, 772
Location, prepositions for, 795
Logos and ethos, 153–54

M

Main idea, stating the, 35
may, might, 783
Modal verbs, 782–84
must, 783

N

Noncount nouns, 767–70, 771–74
not and *no*, 791
Note taking in English, 294
Noun(s), 767–50
    articles with, 768–74
    common, 767
    count and noncount, 767–68, 772–74
    quantifying words with, 772–74
Numbers, 876

O

Object complements, 762–63
Objects
    direct, 761–62
    indirect, 650, 761–62
Obligatory words, 752–53
ought to, should, shall, 783

P

Parallelism, deceptive, 580
Participles, as adjectives, 781
Peer revising, 93
Personal experiences, writing about, 15
Phrasal verbs
    as idioms, 610
    list of, 777
    separable *vs.* inseparable, 777–78
Plagiarism, 10, 279–80
Praise for the reader, avoiding, 68
Preposition(s)
    adjectives with, 787
    of cause or reason, 796
    of condition or degree, 796
    definition of, 636, 642
    functions of, 794–97
    gerunds after, 781
    necessary and unnecessary, 799–800
    in phrasal verbs, 610
    recognizing, 793–94
Prepositions, 793–800
Present participles, 781

EFL1

Progressive tenses, 705
Pronouns
    antecedent agreement with, 689–90
    demonstrative, 318, 772
    redundant, 760
Proofreading, 97
Proper nouns, 767, 771
Punctuation, 835, 839, 876
    quotation marks, 835, 839

Q

Quantifying words or phrases, 772–73
Questions, word order in, 763–64
Quotation marks, 835, 839

R

Reading for comprehension, 113
Reason, prepositions indicating, 796
Redundant pronouns, 760
Repetitions, 752–53

S

sell to, 798
Sentences
    commands, 592
    declarative, 758
    questions, 592
Sentence structure, 758–60
    stated subjects, 758–59
Separable phrasal verbs, 777–78
Serial comma, 808
shall, should, ought to, 783
should've, should have, 782
Sources, conversations with, 313
Spelling
    American *vs.* British, 620
    bilingual dictionaries and, 618
Study groups, 531
Subjects
    redundant pronouns, 760
    stated, 662, 752–53, 758–59
Subordination, 576
such and *so*, 791

T

that, 760
the, 769–70
there and *it* constructions, 759–60
these, 772
Thesis statements, 35
this, 772
those, 772
Time, prepositions of, 795–96
Transitive verbs, 761–62, 777

U

Unmarked infinitives, 780

V

Verbs
    gerund after, 779–80
    have as, 782
    modal, 782–84
    phrasal, 777–78
    progressive tenses, 705
    transitive, 761–62, 777

W

which, 760
will, would, 783
Word order
    adjectives in, 786–87
    adverbs in, 788–89
    inverted, 764–65
    in questions, 763–64
    subject-verb-object, 758
would, will, 783
Writing Responsibly around the World, 10

Z

Zero article, 768

Quick Reference *EFL Tips*

Argumentation
Exploratory versus Persuasive Approaches to Argument 153
Logos and Ethos in the United States 153

Grammar
Countable and Noncountable Nouns 637
Do Not Use the Progressive Tenses with All Verbs 705
English Adjectives Do Not Have Plural Forms 724
English Word Order 647
Including a Stated Subject 662
Indirect Objects 650
Infinitive versus Gerund after the Verb 653
Modal Auxiliaries 639
Modal Verbs 699
Obligatory Words and Unacceptable Repetitions in English 752
Order of Adjectives in a Series 728
Ordering of Adjectives, The 640
Phrasal Verbs 700
Possessive Pronoun Agrees with Its Antecedent, Not the Word It Modifies, A 690

Learning
Contributing to Class Discussion 214
Study Groups 531

Paragraphs
Avoid Praising the Reader in Your Introduction 68

Paraphrasing
Taking Notes in English 294

Peer Review
Peer Review with Multilingual Students 94

Plagiarism
Writing Responsibly around the World 10

Presentations
Adjusting Your Gestures to Appeal to a Multicultural Audience 217

Proofreading
Proofreading When English Is Not Your First Language 98

Punctuation
Capitalization 858
Commas and Periods with Quotation Marks 839
Punctuating Numbers in American English 876
Quotation Marks in American English 835
To Use or Not to Use the Serial Comma 808

Reading
Reading for Comprehension 113

Sentences and words
Conciseness 559
Coordination and Subordination 576
Deceptive Parallelism 580
Developing an Ear for Sentence Variety 591
Idioms, Prepositions, and Phrasal Verbs 610
Recognizing Differences in Connotation 21
What Is the Difference between an Idiom and a Cliché? 611

Sources, citing and integrating
Having a Conversation with Sources 313
Writing Responsibly around the World 10

Spelling
Dictionaries for Second-Language Learners 614
Use American Rather Than British Spelling 620

Using a Bilingual Dictionary as an Aid to English Spelling 618

Thesis statements
Stating the Main Idea 35

Topics for writing
Generating Ideas in English or Your First Language 26

Writing about Personal Experiences 15

Workplace, business writing
Conducting Global Business in the United States 545
Photographs in Job Applications 78
Task-Oriented Emails Get Right to the Point 200

Quick Reference *Tech Tips*

File saving, sharing
Back Up Your Electronic Research Log 229
Consider the Size of Your Document 82
Protecting Your Work 47
Use a Lower Resolution to Avoid Memory-Hogging Image Files 209

File types
HTML versus PDF 249

Formatting
Creating Footnotes and Endnotes 441
Creating a Header 380, 428
Creating Superscript Numbers 471
Guidelines for Formatting URLs 443
Indention 427

Research
Hidden Benefits of Library Databases 248
HTML versus PDF 249
Identifying Personal Websites 272
Note-Taking Technologies 531
Online Surveys 261
Using Google Scholar 247

Scheduling
Using an Assignment Calculator 224

Sources, annotating, citing, documenting
Annotating Online Texts 120
Checking URLs and DOIs 420
Citation Management Software 231
Citing Sources: Digital Object Identifiers (DOIs) and URLs 410
Creating Footnotes and Endnotes 441
Creating Superscript Numbers 471
Guidelines for Formatting URLs 443
Page References and Web Pages 337

Grammar and style checkers
Apostrophes and Spelling or Grammar Checkers 829
Breaking URLs and Email Addresses 880
Catching Confusing Shifts 733
Comma Splices, Fused Sentences, and Grammar Checkers 673
Grammar Checkers and Adjective-Adverb Problems 726
Grammar Checkers and Pronoun-Antecedent Agreement 690
Grammar Checkers and Sentence Fragments 665
Grammar Checkers and Subject-Verb Agreement 680
Grammar Checkers and Verb Problems 696
Misplaced Modifiers and Grammar and Style Checkers 740
Parallelism and Computer Style Checkers 581
Style Checkers and Coordination and Subordination 565
Style Checkers and Wordiness 561
Typing Dashes 848
Use Spelling Checkers Cautiously 623
Using Exclamation Points in Email Messages 845
Word Choice and Grammar and Style Checkers 605

Quick Reference *Writing and Citation Guidance, Checklists, and Tutorials*

Writing and Citation Guidance

APA
APA-Style In-Text Citations, Examples of 400
APA-Style Reference List Entries, Examples of 408

Argumentation
Devising an Arguable Thesis 147
Matching Visual Evidence to Claims 85

Assignments
Analyzing the Purpose of an Assignment 23

Drafting
Drafting the Research Project 303
Overcoming Writer's Block 45
Seven Ways to Gain Objectivity about Your Work 87
Strategies for Writing Concisely 559
Writing the First Draft 308

Email
Consider Your Writing Situation when Composing Email 200
Email Etiquette 544

Essay exams
Common Verbs on Essay Exams 533
What an Effective Answer Does—and Does Not Do 534

Formatting
Common Italics Do's and Don'ts 866
Designing a Print Résumé 547
Formatting Academic Texts 98
Including Visuals (Images and Graphics) 198

Grammar and clarity
Agreement
   Avoiding Pronoun-Antecedent Agreement Pitfalls 691
   Avoiding Subject-Verb Agreement Pitfalls 683
Conjunctions
   Common Subordinating Conjunctions 644
   Conjunctions and Their Meaning 568
   Seven Coordinating Conjunctions, The 804
Figures of Speech 609
Parts of Speech, The 636
Pronouns
   Avoiding Pronoun-Antecedent Agreement Pitfalls 691
   Common Indefinite Pronouns 685
   Editing for Case in Compounds 715
   Pronouns and Their Functions 638

Language
Adjectives
   Capitalize Proper Nouns and Proper Adjectives, but Not Common Nouns 861
   Forming Comparatives and Superlatives 730
   Functions of Adjectives and Adverbs, The 725
   Putting Cumulative Adjectives in Standard Order 787
   Testing for Coordinate and Cumulative Adjectives 810
Adverbs
   Common Conjunctive Adverbs 641
   Forming Comparatives and Superlatives 730
   Functions of Adjectives and Adverbs, The 725
Nouns
   Capitalize Proper Nouns and Proper Adjectives, but Not Common Nouns 861
   Matching Nouns with Quantifying Words and Phrases 773
   Some Common Noncount Nouns 769
Prepositions
   Common Prepositions 643
   Common Single-Word and Multiword Prepositions 794
   Identifying Functions of Prepositions 795

Verbs
- *Common Irregular Verbs* 698
- *Common Verbs on Essay Exams* 533
- *Gerund or Infinitive after Selected Verbs* 780
- *Modals and Meaning* 783
- *Overview of Verb Tenses and Their Forms, An* 704
- *Signal Verbs* 315
- *Some Common Phrasal Verbs and Their Meanings* 777
- *What Information Do Verbs Reveal?* 695

Literature, writing about
Critical Approaches to Literature 490
Drama, Writing about 507
Elements of Literature 489
Poetry, Writing about 502

MLA
MLA-Style In-Text Citations, Examples of 341
MLA-Style Works-Cited Entries, Examples of 354

Paragraphs
Five Don'ts for Conclusions 72
Sample Transitional Expressions 61
Seven Don'ts for Introductions 70

Plagiarism
Your College's Plagiarism Policy 11

Presentations
Overcoming Presentation Anxiety 217

Punctuation and Mechanics
Apostrophes
- *Common Apostrophe Do's and Don'ts* 828

Capitalization
- *Common Capitalization Do's and Don'ts* 859
- *Capitalize Proper Nouns and Proper Adjectives, but Not Common Nouns* 861

Commas
- *Common Comma Do's and Don'ts* 803
- *Identifying Comma Splices and Fused Sentences* 673
- *Ways to Correct Comma Splices and Fused Sentences* 675

Punctuation Marks
- *What These Punctuation Marks Do* 848

Quotation Marks
- *Common Quotation Mark Do's and Don'ts* 835

Semicolons
- *Common Semicolon Do's and Don'ts* 821

Subordination and Punctuation 572

Reference works
Almanacs and Yearbooks 240
Biographical Reference Resources 241
Dictionaries and Encyclopedias 240

Research
Boolean Search, Conducting a 250
Government Information Online, Accessing 255
Research Projects
- *Research Project, Drafting the* 303
- *Research Project, Factors in Planning* 223

Resources, Multimedia 258
Search Engines and Metasearch Engines 243
Working Bibliography, Components of 231

Résumés
Print Résumé, Designing a 547

Revision
Objectivity about Your Work, Seven Ways to Gain 87

Rhetorical situations
Consider Your Writing Situation when Composing Email 200
Consider Your Writing Situation when Creating a Website 204

Sentences
Fragments, Identifying 661
Sentences, Fused
- *Comma Splices and Fused Sentences, Identifying* 673
- *Comma Splices and Fused Sentences, Ways to Correct* 675

Sentence Patterns, Five 648
Subject, Finding the 646
Subordination
- *Subordinating Terms* 663
- *Subordinating Terms and Their Meaning* 573
- *Subordination and Punctuation* 572

Variety and Emphasis, Achieving 586

Sources, citing and documenting
APA-Style In-Text Citations, Examples of 400
APA-Style Reference List Entries, Examples of 408

Chicago-Style Note and Bibliography Entries,
    Examples of 440
CSE-Style Reference List Entries, Examples of 472
In-Text Citations, General Principles of 337, 398
MLA-Style In-Text Citations, Examples of 341
MLA-Style Works-Cited Entries, Examples of 354
Working Bibliography, Components of 231

Sources, evaluating

Judging Reliability 265
Scholarly versus Popular Periodicals 267

Thesis

Devising an Arguable Thesis 147

Thinking, critical

Steps in Developing Critical Understanding 127

Visuals

Including Visuals (Images and Graphics) 198
Matching Visual Evidence to Claims 85

Websites

Consider Your Writing Situation when Creating a
    Website 200

Words

Common Abbreviation Do's and Don'ts 870
Distinguishing *Rise* from *Raise*, *Sit* from *Set*, and
    Lie from *Lay* 701
Dodging Deadly Clichés 611
Figures of Speech 609
Homonyms and Near-Homonyms, Some 619
Parts of Speech, The 636

Checklists for Self-Assessment

Drafting

Checking Your Draft 89

Group work

Ensuring Your Group Is Effective 34

Presentations

*Ten Steps to Using Presentation Software
    Effectively 218*

Proofreading 97

Revision

As You Revise Projects 324
Revising a Thesis 37
Revising Your Argument 179

Sources

*Reviewing Your Work with Each Source 142, 257,
    291, 327*
Summarizing 258

Visuals

Annotating an Image 120
Preparing to Write about a Visual 134

Writing

Writer's Responsibilities 2, 3

Tutorials

Documentation Matters

*Documenting a Source in MLA and
    APA Style 330*

Grammar Matters

Identifying Common Sentence Problems 628

Writing Matters

Writer's Responsibilities Checklist 2, 3

Writing Responsibly

Integrating Sources
    Blending Voices in Your Text 290
Sources
    Acknowledging Indirect Sources 300
    Choosing and Unpacking Complex Sources 256
    Explaining Your Choice of Sources 326
    Understanding and Representing the
        Entire Source 141

Quick Reference *Writing Responsibly Notes*

Accessibility
Checking Accessibility 209
Establishing a Consistent Font 193
Selecting Fonts with Readers in Mind 192

Argumentation
Acknowledging Counterevidence 305
Choosing an Engaging Topic 148
Drawing Inferences 133
Keeping an Open, Inquiring Mind
 (avoiding bias) 267
Letters to the Editor 542
Made-up Evidence 46
Preparing Oral Arguments 156
Understanding Criticism 133
Visual Claims and Visual Fallacies 177
Well-Tempered Tone, The 159

Audience / readers
Avoiding Online Shortcuts (acronyms,
 abbreviations) 598
Big Picture, The 89
Blending Voices in Your Text 290
Checking Accessibility 209
Deadlines and Paperclips, Of 382, 430, 459, 483
Establishing a Consistent Font 193
Establishing Yourself as a Responsible Writer 154
Euphemisms and Doublespeak 600
Exploitative Images 81
Flaming 210
Guiding the Reader 62
Making Considerate Attachments 202
Selecting Fonts with Readers in Mind 192
Using Parallelism to Clarify Relationships
 among Ideas 582
Voice and Responsibility 594
Well-Tempered Tone, The 159
Word Choice and Credibility 607

Design and formatting
Checking Accessibility 209
Citing and Documenting Sources (styles,
 formats) 335, 398, 441, 470
Deadlines and Paperclips, Of 382, 430, 459, 483
Establishing a Consistent Font 193
Making Considerate Attachments 202
Selecting Fonts with Readers in Mind 192
Using Italics for Emphasis 867
Using Quotations Fairly (ellipses and brackets) 298

Ethics
Acknowledging Counterevidence 305
Altering Quotations 855
Avoiding Manipulation and Bias in
 Observations 260
Checking Accessibility 209
Choosing and Unpacking Complex
 Sources 256
Citing and Documenting Sources 335, 398,
 441, 470
Conducting Interviews Fairly 259
Drawing Inferences 133
Euphemisms and Doublespeak 600
Exploitative Images 81
Guiding the Reader 62
Keeping an Open, Inquiring Mind
 (about sources) 267
Listening Actively 219
Made-up Evidence 46
Maintaining Confidentiality in Email 201
Note Taking and Plagiarism 26
Personal Emails and Texts at Work 545
Preparing Oral Arguments 156
Presenting Data Accurately 511
Reporting Results Fairly (field research) 262
Understanding Email and Privacy 203

Using Quotations Fairly 298
Visual Claims and Visual Fallacies 177
Voice and Responsibility 594

Grammar, style

Case and Tone 718
Clarifying Boundaries (comma splices, fused sentences) 672
Contractions in Formal Writing 827
Dialect Variation in Subject-Verb Agreement 682
Is a Comma Splice Ever Acceptable? 674
Misplaced Modifiers in the Real World 744
Using the Subjunctive in Formal Writing 708
Using [sic] (to point out errors) 852
Why Grammar Matters 635

Language

Altering Quotations 855
Avoiding Online Shortcuts (acronyms, abbreviations) 598
Blending Voices in Your Text 290
Choose Accurate Synonyms 615
Euphemisms and Doublespeak 600
Using Online Abbreviations Appropriately (e.g., "TBH") 872
Spelling
  Beware the Spelling Checker! 97
  Spelling Errors 620
  Using [sic] (to point out errors) 852
Word Choice and Credibility 607

Learning

Reading with Study Guides 487

Note taking

Acknowledging Counterevidence 305
Note Taking and Plagiarism 26
Using Illustrations and Avoiding Plagiarism 284

Paragraphs

Blending Voices in Your Text 290
Conciseness versus the Too-Short Paper 558
Guiding the Reader 62
Sentence Fragments and Context 664

Using Parallelism to Clarify Relationships among Ideas 582
Voice and Responsibility 594

Plagiarism

Avoiding Accidental Plagiarism 230
Citing and Documenting Sources 335, 398, 441, 470
Highlighting versus Making Notes 287
Made-up Evidence 46
Note Taking and Plagiarism 26
Using Illustrations and Avoiding Plagiarism 284
Using Signal Phrases to Demonstrate Your Relationships with Sources 340

Presentations

Listening Actively 219
Preparing Oral Arguments 156

Punctuation

Is a Comma Splice Ever Acceptable? 674
Commas and Clarity 802
Dashes, Parentheses, or Commas? 850
Hyphenating with Readers in Mind 878
Question Marks and Exclamation Points 844
Sending a Signal with Semicolons 820
Using Quotations Fairly (ellipses and brackets) 298
Using Quotation Marks Fairly 835

Research (see also Sources)

Choosing and Unpacking Complex Sources 256
Citing and Documenting Sources 335, 398, 441, 470
Field research
  Avoiding Manipulation and Bias in Observations 260
  Conducting Interviews Fairly 259
  Reporting Results Fairly 262

Revision

Big Picture, The 89
Blending Voices in Your Text 290
Conciseness versus the Too-Short Paper 558
Making Your Text Long Enough without Wordiness 92
Using Parallelism to Clarify Relationships among Ideas 582

Rhetorical situations

Establishing Yourself as a Responsible Writer 154
Ethos and Convention (using numbers, symbols) 874
Flaming 210
Letters to the Editor 542
Preparing Oral Arguments 156
Well-Tempered Tone, The 159

Sources

Annotating sources
  Highlighting versus Making Notes 287
Avoiding Accidental Plagiarism 230
Choosing and Unpacking Complex Sources 256
Citing and Documenting Sources 335, 398, 441, 470
Conducting Interviews Fairly 259
Engaging with What You Read 112
Explaining Your Choice of Sources 326
Going beyond Reference Sources 241
Integrating Sources
  Acknowledging Indirect Sources 300
  Altering Quotations 855
  Blending Voices in Your Text 290
  Using Quotations Fairly 298
  Using Quotation Marks Fairly 835
  Using Signal Phrases to Demonstrate Your Relationships with Sources 340
Keeping an Open, Inquiring Mind (avoiding biased sources) 267
Made-up Evidence 46
Note Taking and Plagiarism 26
Presenting Data Accurately 511
Really Reading Real Sources 246
Understanding and Representing the Entire Source 141
Using Printed Sources 227
Using Wikipedia Responsibly 239

Thinking and reading, critical

Choosing an Engaging Topic 148
Choosing and Unpacking Complex Sources 256
Drawing Inferences 133
Keeping an Open, Inquiring Mind (avoiding bias) 267
Listening Actively 219
Reading, Critically
  Engaging with What You Read 112
  Keeping an Open, Inquiring Mind (about sources) 267
  Reading with Study Guides 487
  Really Reading Real Sources 246
Seeing and Showing the Whole Picture 20
Understanding Criticism 133

Topics, ideas

Big Picture, The 89
Choosing an Engaging Topic 148
Using Parallelism to Clarify Relationships among Ideas 582

You, as a writer

Establishing Yourself as a Responsible Writer 154
Taking Yourself Seriously as a Writer 12
Voice and Responsibility 594
Your Responsibilities as a Writer 9

Visuals

Checking Accessibility 209
Exploitative Images 81
Using Illustrations and Avoiding Plagiarism 284
Visual Claims and Visual Fallacies 177

Writing, types of

Academic writing (college writing)
  Conciseness versus the Too-Short Paper 558
  Contractions in Formal Writing 827
  Using the Subjunctive in Formal Writing 708
  Word Choice and Credibility 607
Civic Writing
  Letters to the Editor 542
Email
  Avoiding Online Shortcuts (acronyms, abbreviations) 598
  Capitalizing in Email and Text Messages 862
  Flaming 210
  Maintaining Confidentiality in Email 201
  Making Considerate Attachments 202
  Personal Emails and Texts at Work 545
  Understanding Email and Privacy 203
Essay Exams
  Using Your Computer during an Essay Exam 534